DATA STRUCTURES

An Algorithmic Approach with C++
FOR
(All Indian Universities, Engineering and Technical Colleges and Institutions, IIT's and IT Organizations)

DATA STRUCTURES

An Algorithmic Approach with C++
FOR
(All Indian Universities, Engineering and Technical Colleges and Institutions, IIT's and IT Organizations)

R Singh • I Singh

Khanna Book Publishing Co. (P) Ltd.
Delhi

ISBN: 978-93-80016-85-6

First Edition 2010

Published by:
Khanna Book Publishing Co. (P) Ltd.
4C/4344, Ansari Road, Darya Ganj, New Delhi-110 002
Phone: 011-23244447, 23244448
E-mail: contact@khannabooks.com
Website: www.khannabooks.com

Regd. Off: 1694-95, 1st Floor, Nai Sarak, Delhi-110006 (India)
Phone: 011-23283211, 23256658
Fax: 011-23256658

Cover Design & Layout by
Limited Colors, Delhi-92

Printed in India

Dedicated to God
And
Our Parents

PREFACE

The study of data structure is both exiting and challenging. It is exiting because it presents a wide range of programming techniques that make it possible to solve more complex problems. It is challenging because the complex nature of the data structures brings with it many concepts that change the way we approach to design of program. The chapters are mainly organized in increasing degree of complexity.

Chapter 1 introduces the reader to the fundamental of C++ language: features, data types, operators, flow control statements, array, structure, union and classes etc.

Chapter 2 deals with introduction to data structures and string processing. It includes various types of data structures array, linked list, stack, queues, trees, graphs, etc. and pattern matching algorithms brute-force, boyer-moore etc.

Chapter 3 describes the concept of algorithm design and complexity; it also covers the features of abstract data type, big O notation, and asymptotic notations, primitive and non-primitive data types with examples.

Chapter 4 deals with arrays. It covers one, two and multidimensional arrays and contains numerous examples. It also covers row major and column major arrays. Pointers and Records are also described at the end of the chapter.

Chapter 5 discusses linked list, another significant type of data structures. It covers various operations such as traversing a list, searching and retrieving an element from a list. Types of linked lists, single, double and circular linked list are also described in detail.

Chapter 6 describes another building block of data structures in stack. Terminologies of stack, pictorial representation of stack, push and pop operations and applications are discussed in the chapter. Evaluation of postfix expression and infix to postfix expression, Recursion, balancing symbols and parenthesis matching are also given at the end of the chapter. Direct and indirect recursive are explained through programs, and popular examples such as the Tower of Hanoi and factorial are also covered in the chapter.

Chapter 7 presents Queue data structure, Representation of queue, insertion and deletion of an element in a queue, its static and dynamic implementation, and its applications are covered in the chapter. In addition, circular queue, deque and priority queues are explained in detail.

Chapter 8 and 9 explain one of the non-linear data structures, Tree. Basic terms used in binary tree are described at the beginning of this chapter. Topics such as binary tree, complete binary tree, extended binary tree, traversal of tree, threshold binary tree, binary search tree, AVL tree, B+-tree and red black trees are all covered in this chapter.

Chapter 10 covers heaps with its insertion and deletion procedures. It also covers the building block of heap tree using various operations and applications.

Chapter 11 implements the concept of graph. It deals with the basic terminologies of graph, representation of graph, traversals in graph, spanning tree algorithms, Connected component of graph and shortest path algorithms etc.

Chapter 12 is devoted to sorting methods. Various sorting techniques such as selection insertion, bubble, tree, merge, heap sot methods have been elaborated with simple algorithms, their explanation and implementation in C++ language. Partition exchange and radix sort methods have been discussed and supported with programming examples. It also covers various searching techniques such as linear and binary search with the help of examples. Attention has also been paid on establishing the efficiency of some searching methods.

Chapters 13 elaborate the latest concept hashing by using mid-division, mid-square and folding methods etc. It also contains the solution of collision problem using various techniques like open addressing, separate chaining, linked list etc.

Chapter 14 is covered the most important topic presented on storage of data in memory. Here we will discuss all the fundamental concepts of memory like garbage collection and compaction techniques.

Algorithms are presented in a form which is machine and language independent. Moreover, they are written using mainly flow control statements like IF-THEN-ELSE and REPEAT-WHILE, and using an indentation pattern for easier reading and understating. Accordingly, each of our algorithms may be readily translated into C++ programming language.

Adopting an elementary approach to the subject matter with many examples and diagrams, this book should appeal to a wide audience, and is particularly suited as an effective self-study guide.

Each and Every chapter contains clear statements of definitions and principles together with illustrative and other descriptive material. Suggestions for improvement of the book will be gratefully accepted for future editions.

R Singh
I Singh

ACKNOWLEDGEMENT

First we would like to thanks almighty for giving us courage to bring up this book. We duly acknowledge the contribution of our collegues Prof. Harbhajan Singh, Prof. Mani Arora, Mr. Baljinder Singh, Mr. Jagbir Singh, Mr. Sukhwant Singh, Mr. Avtar Singh Sandhu, Mr. Lovedeep Singh, Mr. Avtar Singh Riar, Mr. Navjeet Singh and Mr. Kawaljeet Singh for their valuable co-operation and guidance. We are grateful to the entire team of M/s Khanna Book Publishing Co. (P) Ltd., Delhi for their encouragement and motivation during this project.

R Singh
I Singh

CONTENTS

1 CHAPTER

Introduction to C++ Language

1.1 INTRODUCTION

A programming language is a set of instructions and a series of lexical conventions specifically designed to order computers what to do. When choosing a programming language to make a project, many different considerations can be taken. First, one must decide what is known as the *level* of the programming language. The level determines how near to the hardware the programming language is. In the lower level languages, instructions are written thinking directly on interfacing with hardware, while in "high level" ones a more abstract or conceptual code is written.

Generally, high level code is more portable, that means it can work in more different machines with a smaller number of modifications, whereas a low level language is limited by the peculiarides of the hardware which it was written for. Nevertheless, the advantage of low level code is that it is usually faster due to the fact that it is indeed written taking advantage of the possibilities of a specific machine.

A higher or lower level of programming is to be chosen for a specific project depending on the type of program that is being developed. For example, when a hardware driver is developed for an operating system obviously a very low level is used for programming. While when big applications are developed usually a higher level is chosen, or a combination of critic parts written in low level languages and others in higher ones.

Although there are languages that are clearly thought to be low level, like Assembly, whose instruction sets are adapted to each machine the code is made for, and other languages are inherently high level, like the Java, that is designed to be totally independent of the platform where is going to run. The C++ language is in a middle position, since it can interact directly with the hardware almost with no limitations, and can as well abstract lower layers and work like one of the most powerful high level languages.

Based on the C programming language, C++ was designed to be used in a C programming environment on a UNIX system. C++ retains most of C's efficiency and flexibility, incorporates all the features of C, and also supports features that are unavailable in the C language. Many of the added features were designed to support object-oriented programming.

1.2 C++ IS BORN

C++ was invented by Bjarne Stroustrup in 1979, at Bell Laboratories in Murray Hill, New Jersey. He initially called the new language "C with Classes." However, in 1983 the name was changed to C++. Stroustrup built C++ on the foundation of C, including all of C's features, attributes, and benefits. He also adhered to C's underlying philosophy that the programmer, not the language, is in charge. At this point, it is critical to understand that Stroustrup did not create an entirely new programming language.

Bjarne Stroustrup

Instead, he enhanced an already highly successful language. Most of the features that Stroustrup added to C were designed to support object-oriented programming. In essence, C++ is the object-oriented version of C. By building upon the foundation of C, Stroustrup provided a smooth migration path to OOP. Instead of having to learn an entirely new language, a C programmer needed to learn only a few new features before reaping the benefits of the object-oriented methodology.

When creating C++, Stroustrup knew that it was important to maintain the original spirit of C, including its efficiency, flexibility, and philosophy, while at the same time adding support for object-oriented programming. Happily, his goal was accomplished. C++ still provides the programmer with the freedom and control of C, coupled with the power of objects.

Although C++ was initially designed to aid in the management of very large programs, it is in no way limited to this use. In fact, the object-oriented attributes of C++ can be effectively applied to virtually any programming task. It is not uncommon to see C++ used for projects such as editors, databases, personal file systems, networking utilities, and communication programs. Because C++ shares C's efficiency, much high-performance systems software is constructed using C++. Also, C++ is frequently the language of choice for Windows programming.

1.2.1 Characteristics of C++

C++ has certain characteristics over other programming languages. The most remarkable are:

1. Object-oriented programming

The possibility to orientate programming to objects allows the programmer to design applications from a point of view more like a communication between objects rather than on a structured sequence of code. In addition it allows a greater reusability of code in a more logical and productive way.

2. Portability

You can practically compile the same C++ code in almost any type of computer and operating system without making any changes. C++ is the most used and ported programming language in the world.

3. Brevity

Code written in C++ is very short in comparison with other languages, since the use of special characters is preferred to key words, saving some effort to the programmer (and prolonging the life of our keyboards!).

4. Modular programming

An application's body in C++ can be made up of several source code files that are compiled separately and then linked together. Saving time since it is not necessary to recompile the complete application when making a single change but only the file that contains it. In addition, this characteristic allows to link C++ code with code produced in other languages, such as Assembler or C.

5. C Compatibility

C++ is backwards compatible with the C language. Any code written in C can easily be included in a C++ program without making any change.

6. *Speed*

The resulting code from a C++ compilation is very efficient, due indeed to its duality as high-level and low-level language and to the reduced size of the language itself.

1.2.2 Features or Characteristics of Object Oriented Programming

One of the most important characteristics of OOP (Object Oriented Programming) is the data encapsulation concept, which means that there is a very close attachment between data items and procedures. The procedures (methods) are responsible for manipulating the data in order to reflect its behavior. The public interface, formed by the collections of messages understood by an object, completely defines how to use this object.

Programs that want to manipulate an object only have to be concerned about which messages this object understands, and do not have to worry about how these tasks are achieved or the internal structure of the object. The hiding of internal details makes an object abstract, and the technique is normally known as data abstraction. Normally, objects of a given type are instances of a class, whose definition specifies the private (internal) working of these objects as well as their public interface. Basically the creation of an object is referred to as instantiation, and it consists of a class definition with appropriate initial values.

Another powerful feature of OOP, is the concept of inheritance (derived classes in C++), meaning the derivation of a similar or related object (the derived object) from a more general based object. The derived class can inherit the properties of its base class and also adds its own data and routines. The concept above is known

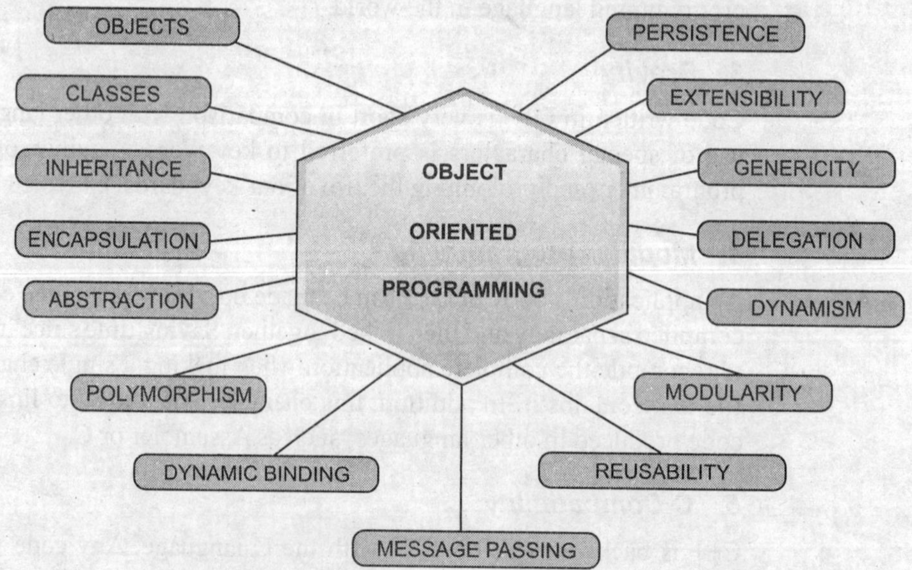

Figure 1.1: Features of Object Oriented Programming

as single inheritance, but it is also possible to derive a class from several base classes, which is known as multiple inheritances. Overloading, in OOP, means the ability to assign multiple meanings to the names of operators and functions.

For example, the operator +, normally associated with arithmetic addition can be overloaded to add one list to another in a certain context. Polymorphism means the sending of a message to an object without concern about how the software is going to accomplish the task, and furthermore it means that the task can be executed in completely different ways depending on the object that receives the message (in C++, polymorphism is implemented through the use of virtual functions). When the decision as to which actions are going to be executed is made at run-time, the polymorphism is referred to as late binding (as in the case of virtual functions). If they are made at compile time then it is known as early binding.

1. OBJECTS

In object-oriented programming language C++, the data and functions (procedures to manipulate the data) are bundled together as a self-contained unit called an ***object.*** An object is a component of a program that knows how to perform certain actions and to interact with other pieces of the program. An object is a region of storage with associated semantics.

An object is a software bundle of related state and behaviour. Software objects are often used to model the real-world objects that you find in everyday life.

Definition: *"An object is a bundle of variables and related methods."*

The term "Object" that gives OOP it's name, refers to a *conceptual* object that represents an item in our program or system. This could be anything from an online form or a computer file, to a real world object such as a car.

This representation consists of ***attributes***—the characteristics of our object; and ***methods***—a set of functions and calculations that are either performed to modify the object itself, or are involved in some external effect.

Objects are further subdivided into physical objects and logical objects. For example a person, a place, a bank account, a table, a chair etc. are physical objects.

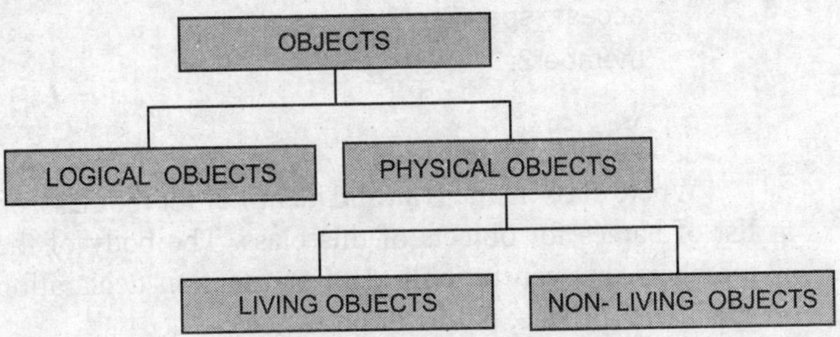

Figure 1.2: Different types of objects

2. CLASSES

A class is a blueprint for an object. Classes are data types based on which objects are created. Objects with similar properties and methods are grouped together to form a Class. Thus a Class represent a set of individual objects. Characteristics of an object are represented in a class as **Properties**. The actions that can be performed by objects become functions of the class and are referred to as **Methods**.

A class is an actual representation of an Abstract Data Type (ADT). A class is the implementation of an abstract data type (ADT). It defines attributes and methods which implement the data structure and operations of the ADT, respectively. Instances of classes are called objects. Consequently, classes define properties and behaviour of sets of objects.

Actually the concept of class should come first rather than the concept object. Once a class has been defined, we can create any number of objects belonging to that class. For example, mango, apple and orange are members of the class **fruit**. If fruit has been defined as a class than the statement *fruit mango* will create an object mango belonging to the class fruit. All the objects in a class will share some common property. Some will less, some will more. This depends on inheritance.

Definition: "A class is a collection of objects of similar type. Once a class is defined, any number of objects can be created which belong to that class."

A class is a mechanism for creating user-defined data types. It is similar to the C language structure data type. In C, a structure is composed of a set of data members. In C++, a class type is like a C structure, except that a class is composed of a set of data members and a set of operations that can be performed on the class.

Classes are generally declared using the keyword class, with the following format:

```
class class_name
{
access_specifer_1:
member1;
access_specifier_2:
member2;
...
} object_name;
```

Where class_name is a valid identifier for the class, object_names is an optional list of names for objects of this class. The body of the declaration can contain members that can be both data or function declarations, and optionally access specifiers (private, public or protected).

In the object-oriented world, these categories are represented by classes, where a class is a description of the common properties of a category of objects.

For example consider we have a Class of *Cars* under which *Santro, Xing*, *Alto* and *WaganR* represents individual Objects. In this context each *Car* Object will have its own, Model, Year of Manufacture, Colour, Top Speed, Engine Power etc., which form **Properties** of the *Car* class and the associated actions i.e., object functions like Start, Move, and Stop form the **Methods** of *Car* Class.

No memory is allocated when a class is created. Memory is allocated only when an object is created, i.e., when an instance of a class is created. A class in C++ is an encapsulation of data members and functions that manipulate the data. The class can also have some other important members which are architecturally important.

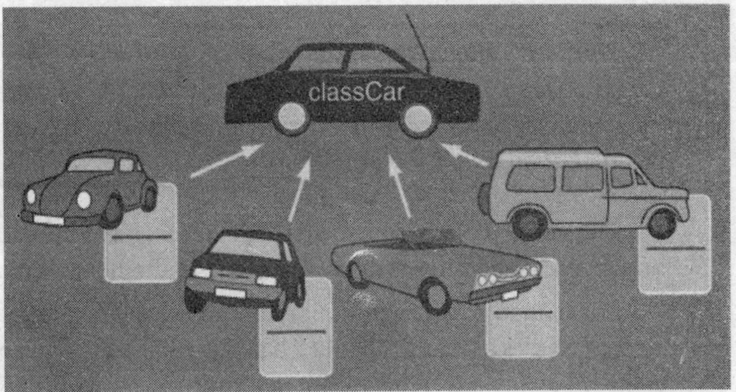

Figure 1.3: Class car having different types of cars having different

Given below are some examples of class data type:

	class car **Properties:** company, model and colour **Behaviour:** speed and average
	class laptop **Properties:** company, hard disk, RAM size and price **Behaviour:** processing and resolution
	class CD **Properties:** company, size and copacity **Behaviour:** storing and retrieving

3. *INHERITANCE*

Inheritance is the process by which objects can acquire the properties of objects of other class. In OOP, *inheritance* provides reusability, like, adding additional features to an existing class without modifying it. This is achieved by deriving a new class from the existing one. The new class will have combined features of both the classes.

In object-oriented methodology, inheritance enables you to extend the functionality of an existing class. You create a class that inherits the attributes and behaviour of another class. In addition, the new class can consist of a few new attributes and behaviours that are specific to the class. In terms of classes and objects, attributes refer to the data and behaviour refers to the methods.

For example, you might have the Student class that consists of the basic characteristics of students, such as name, date of birth, and gender. You can extend the functions of the student class to a day scholar, who in addition to characteristics of the Student class contains its own features, such as locker number and residential address.

***Definition:** "Inheritance is the process of forming a new class from an existing class or base class. The base class is also known as parent class or super class, the new class that is formed is called derived class. Derived class is also known as a child class or sub class."*

The derived classes have all the features of the base class and the programmer can choose to add new features specific to the newly created derived class.

For example, a programmer can create a *base* class named fruit and define *derived* classes as mango, orange, banana, etc. Each of these derived classes, (mango, orange, banana, etc.) has all the features of the *base* class (fruit) with additional attributes or features specific to these newly created derived classes. Mango would have its own defined features, orange would have its own defined features, banana would have its own defined features, etc.

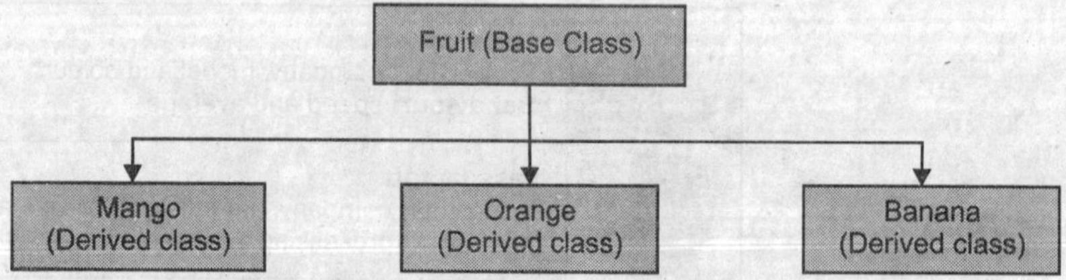

Figure 1.4: Base class defined three derived classes

This concept of *Inheritance* leads to the concept of *polymorphism.*

Types of Inheritance

There are five different inheritances supported in C++:

1. Single Inheritance
2. Multiple Inheritance

3. Multilevel Inheritance
4. Hierarchical Inheritance
5. Hybrid Inheritance

1. **Single inheritance:** If a class is derived from a single base class, it is called as single inheritance.

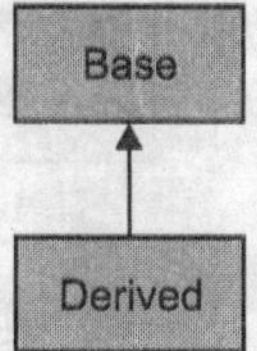

2. **Multiple Inheritance:** If a class is derived from more than one base class, it is known as multiple inheritance.

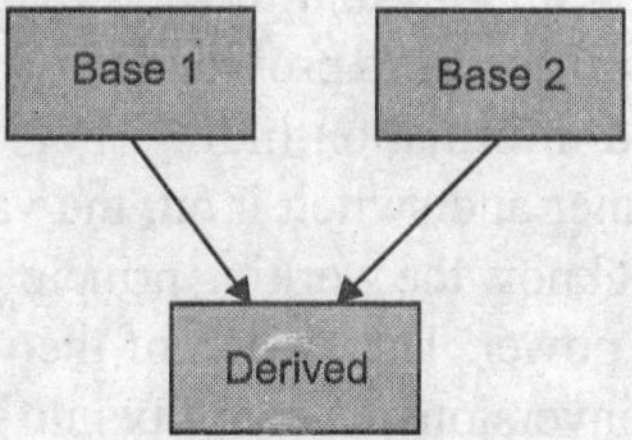

3. **Multilevel inheritance:** The classes can also be derived from the classes that are already derived. This type of inheritance is called multilevel inheritance.

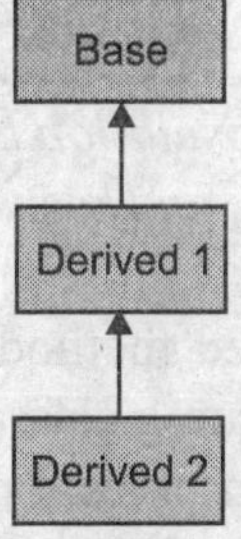

4. **Hierarchical inheritance:** If a number of classes are derived from a single base class, it is called as hierarchical inheritance.

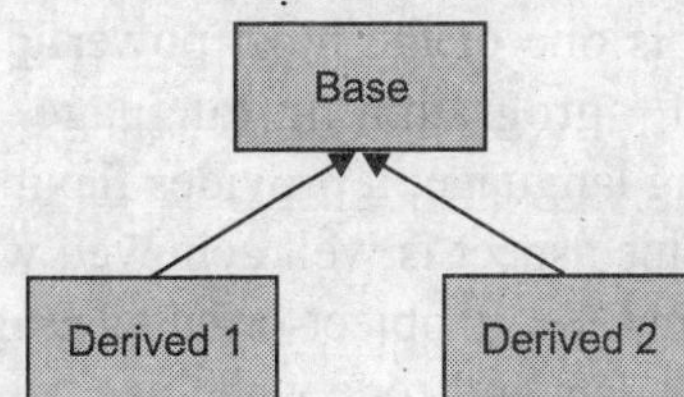

5. **Hybrid inheritance:** The combination of one or more types of inheritance is called hybrid inheritance.

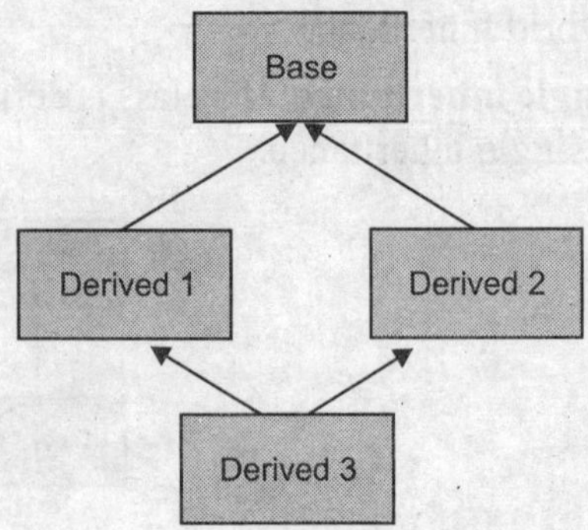

4. *ENCAPSULATION*

Encapsulation implies that the non-essential details of an object are hidden from the user and an access is provided to its essential details. Therefore, encapsulation is also called information hiding. For example, when you plug in the cord of a vacuum cleaner and switch it on, the vacuum cleaner starts functioning. An end-user need not know the working principle of a vacuum cleaner to convert electricity into suction power. The switch of the vacuum cleaner encapsulates the complex process of conversion of electricity into suction power. The complexity of an object is hidden as a result of encapsulation.

Computer games also use the feature of encapsulation. The user only needs to know how to play the game. However, the complex working of game is hidden from the user.

Definition: *"Encapsulation is the mechanism that binds together code and the data it manipulates, and keeps both safe from outside interference and misuse."*

In object-oriented methodology, need of encapsulation arises because the emphasis is on designing classes in such a manner that the classes share data and methods among themselves. Encapsulation is the feature that provides security to the data and the methods of a class.

5. *ABSTRACTION*

Abstraction is one of the most powerful and vital features provided by object-oriented C++ programming language. Modularity is very important in any programming language; it provides flexibility to users for using the programming language. This aspect is well achieved with high performance by the concept of abstraction in C++. In object-oriented programming language the programmer can abstract both data and code when needed.

The concept of abstraction relates to the idea of hiding data that are not needed for presentation. The main idea behind data abstraction is to give a clear separation between properties of data type and the associated implementation details. This separation is achieved in order that the properties of the abstract data type are visible to the user interface and the implementation details are hidden. Thus, abstraction forms the basic platform for the creation of user-defined data types called objects. Data abstraction is the process of refining data to its essential form. An Abstract Data Type is defined as a data type that is defined in terms of the operations that it supports and not in terms of its structure or implementation. Classes use the concept of abstraction and are defined as a list of abstract attributes.

In object-oriented programming language C++, it is possible to create and provide an interface that accesses only certain elements of data types. The programmer can decide which user to give or grant access to and hide the other details. This concept is called data hiding which is similar in concept to data abstraction.

Definition: *"Abstraction refers to the act of representing essential without including the background details or explanations."*

Abstraction is a process of identifying the relevant qualities and behaviors an object should possess. Let's take an example to understand abstraction. A Laptop consists of many things such as processor, motherboard, RAM, keyboard, LCD screen, wireless antenna, web camera, USB ports, battery, speakers etc. To use it, you don't need to know how internally LCD screens, keyboard, web camera, battery, wireless antenna, speaker's works.

Figure 1.5: Abstract machine

6. POLYMORPHISM

Object-oriented programming languages support *polymorphism*, which is characterized by the phrase "one interface, multiple methods."

Polymorphism is derived from two Latin words-Poly, which means many, and morph, which means forms. Anything that exists in more than one form is known as a polymorph. You might have noticed that a person assumes different roles in different scenarios. For example, a person assumes various roles when he interacts with the members of his family. He is a father to his children, child to his parents, and husband to his wife. Although, the person is same, he behaves differently with the family members as per his relation with the member.

Definition: *"Polymorphism is defined as one interface to control access to a general class of actions."*

Polymorphism allows routines to use variables of different types at different times. An operator or function can be given different meanings or functions. Polymorphism refers to a single function or multi-functioning operator performing in different ways.

Types of Polymorphism: There are mainly two types of polymorphism one is **compile time polymorphism (static polymorphism)** and the other is **run time polymorphism (dynamic polymorphism)**. Compile time polymorphism is functions and operators overloading. Runtime time polymorphism is done using inheritance and virtual functions.

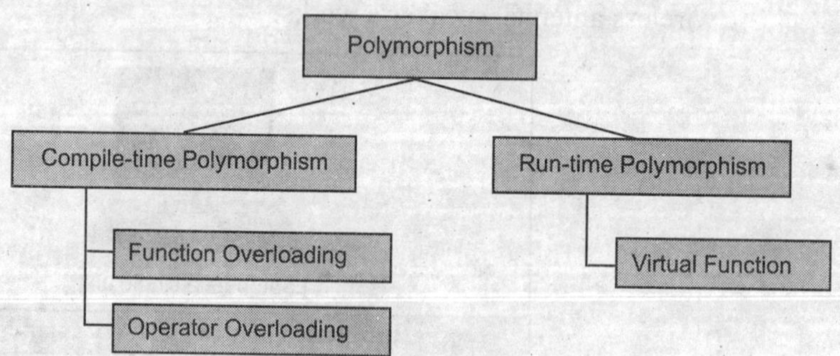

Figure 1.6: Types of polymorphism

7. DYNAMIC BINDING

Dynamic binding means that the code associated with a given procedure call is not known until the time of the call at run-time. Think as an object which has a certain function and that was inherited from its respective class. Thus every object of that class will inherit the function but won't have any effect unless or until it is called.

Definition: *"The concept of dynamic binding allows a variable to take different types dependent on the content at a particular time. This ability of a variable is called polymorphism."*

One important reason for having dynamic binding is that it provides a mechanism for selecting between alternatives which is arguably more robust than explicit selection by conditionals or pattern matching. When a new subclass is added, or an existing subclass changes, the necessary modifications are localized: you don't have incomplete conditionals and broken patterns scattered all over the program.

8. MESSAGE PASSING

Object Oriented Programming (OOP) restructures the programming problem to allow for a higher level of abstraction. It groups operations and data into modular units called objects. These objects can be combined into structured networks to form a complete program, similar to how the pieces in a puzzle fit together to create a picture. In contrast to procedural programming, it focus on the interaction between data and functions, the design of objects and the interactions between those objects become the primary elements of object oriented program design.

By breaking down complex software projects into small, self-contained, and modular units, object orientation ensures that changes to one part of a software project will not adversely affect other portions of the software. Object orientation also aids software reuse. Once functionality is created in one program, it can easily be reused in other programs.

An object oriented program consists of a set of objects that communicate with each other. Object communicates with one another by sending data receiving information much same way as people passes messages to one another. A message for an object is a request for the execution of a procedure and therefore will invoke function in the receiving object that generates desire results.

Definition: *"It is the process of invoking an operation on an object. In response to a message the corresponding method is executed in the object."*

When a program is executed, the objects interact by **sending message** to one another. For example let us assume there is another object called 'Marks' which include the data Name (two objects can have same entity and function), Marks, Course etc. and associated functions are Total, Average, Display, Grade etc. Here the first object 'student' can communicate with the second object 'Marks' through the common data or functions. Any data can be called only and only by its respective functions. This is also known as data abstraction. The Figure 1.7 given below represents communication between different objects.

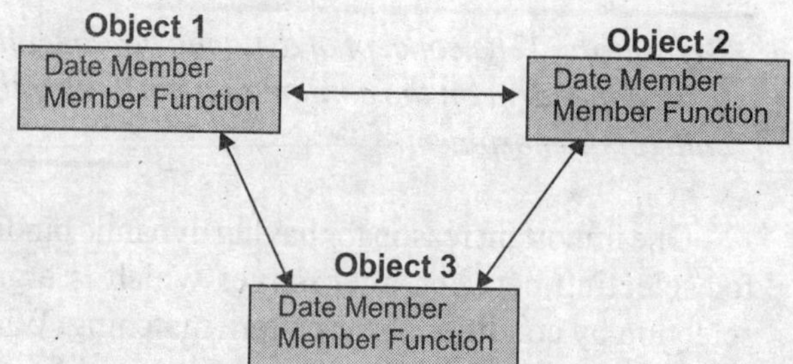

Figure 1.7: Message passing between objects

9. REUSABILITY

A main platform of object-oriented programming is code reusability. Rather than starting from scratch with each new application, a programmer will consult libraries of existing components to see if any are appropriate as starting points for the design of a new application.

This usage is achieved by the above explained terminology called as inheritance. Reusability is nothing but re-usage of structure without changing the existing one but adding new features or characteristics to it. It is very much needed for any programmers in different situations. Reusability gives the following advantages to users.

It helps in reducing the code size since classes can be just derived from existing one and one need to add only the new features and it helps users to save their time.

Definition: *"Reusability is the ability of software elements to serve for the construction of many different applications."*

This term refers to the ability for multiple programmers to use the same written and debugged existing class of data. This is a time saving device and adds code efficiency to the language. Additionally, the programmer can incorporate new features to the existing class, further developing the application and allowing users to achieve increased performance. This time saving feature optimizes code, helps in gaining secured applications and facilitates easier maintenance on the application.

10. MODULARITY

Modularity is closely tied with encapsulation; think of modularity as a way of mapping encapsulated abstractions into real, physical modules.

Modularity is the property of computer programs that measures the extent to which they have been composed out of separate parts called modules. **In computing,** a module is a software entity that groups a set of (typically cohesive) **subprograms** and data structures.

Modular programming techniques are those which increase modularity. Structured programming can be seen as a subset or subdiscipline of procedural programming, one of the major programming paradigms. Procedural programming is a programming paradigm based upon the concept of the procedure call. In computer science, object-oriented programming, OOP for short, is a computer programming paradigm.

One of the advantages of object oriented programming is that the process makes good use of modularity. That is, objects and tasks are grouped in a way that each module is capable of independent consideration. This can be a great help when making enhancements to a program, as modularity makes it possible to address the task of making alternations to the setup of one portion of the programming without impacting the structure and function of the other modules.

11. DYNAMISM

At one time in programming history, the question of how much memory a program would use was settled when the source code was compiled and linked. All the memory the program would ever need was set aside for it as it was launched. This memory was fixed; it could neither grow nor shrink.

In hindsight, it's evident what a serious constraint this was. It limited not only how programs were constructed, but what you could imagine a program doing. It constrained design, not just programming technique. Functions (like **malloc()**) that dynamically allocate memory as a program runs opened possibilities that didn't exist before.

Compile-time and link-time constraints are limiting because they force issues to be decided from information found in the programmer's source code, rather than from information obtained from the user as the program runs.

Although dynamic allocation removes one such constraint, many others, equally as limiting as static memory allocation, remain. For example, the elements that make up an application must be matched to data types at compile time. And the boundaries of an application are typically set at link time. Every part of the application must be united in a single executable file. New modules and new types can't be introduced as the program runs.

Object-oriented programming seeks to overcome these limitations and to make programs as dynamic and fluid as possible. It shifts much of the burden of decision making from compile time and link time to run time. The goal is to let program users decide what will happen, rather than constrain their actions artificially by the demands of the language and the needs of the compiler and linker.

Three kinds of dynamism are especially important for object-oriented design:

1. Dynamic typing, waiting until run time to determine the class of an object
2. Dynamic binding, determining at run time what method to invoke
3. Dynamic loading, adding new components to a program as it runs

12. DELEGATION

Delegation is a way of making object composition as powerful as inheritance. In delegation two objects are involved in handling a request receiving object delegates operations to its delegate. This is analogous to child class sending requests to the parent class. Delegation allows the behaviour of an object to be defined in terms of the behaviour of another object.

13. GENERICITY

It is technique for defining software components that have more than one interpretation depending on the data type of parameters. Thus it allows the declaration of data items without specifying their exact data type. The compiler identifies the data type at run time. The programmer can create a function that can be used for any type of data. The template function in C++ allows generic programming.

14. EXTENSIBILITY

C++ allows the extension of the functionality of the existing software components. In C++ this is achieved through abstract classes and inheritance. It is a feature which allows the extension of the functionality of the existing software components.

15. PERSISTENCE

The phenomenon where the object (data) outlives the program execution time and exists between executions of a program is known as persistence. All data base systems support persistence. In C++ it is not supported. However the user can build it explicitly using file streams in a program.

1.3 CHARACTER SET

There are mainly four categories of the character set as shown in the figure 1.8 below:

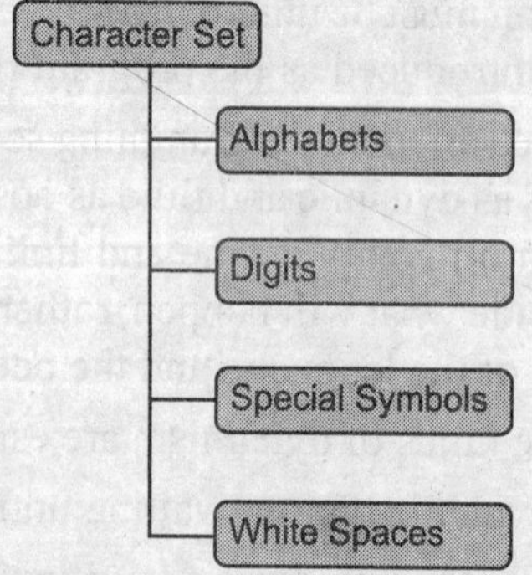

Figure 1.8: Categories of character set

1. Letter or Alphabet

In the character set, character or alphabet are represented by A-Z or a-z. C++ Language is case sensitive so it takes different meaning for small and upper case letters. There are total 26 letters used in C++ programming.

2. Digit

In the character set digit are represented by 0-9 or by combination of these digits. There are total 10 digits used in the C++ programming.

3. Special Characters

All the keyboard keys except alphabet, digits and white spaces are the special character. These are some punctuation marks and some special symbols used for special purpose.

Special characters are used for C++ statements like to create an arithmetic statement +, -, * etc. , to create relational statement <, >, <=, >=, == etc. , to create assignment statement =, to create logical statement &&, || etc. are required.

4. Empty Space Character or White Spaces

White spaces has blank space, new line return, Horizontal tab space, carriage ctrl, Form feed etc. are all used for special purpose.

1.4 KEYWORDS AND IDENTIFIERS

Every word in C++ language is a keyword or an identifier. Keywords in C++ language cannot be used as a variable name. They are specifically used by the compiler for its own purpose and they serve as building blocks of a C++ program. C++ language has some reserve words which are called keywords of C++ language. These are the part of the C++ Tokens.

There are 63 keywords currently defined for Standard C++. Together with the formal C++ syntax, they form the C++ programming language. Also, early versions of C++ defined the overload keyword, but it is obsolete. Keep in mind that C++ is a case-sensitive language and it requires that all keywords be in lowercase.

Identifier

The name of a variable, function, class, or other entity in C++ is called an **identifier**. C++ gives you a lot of flexibility to name identifiers as you wish. However, there are a few rules that must be followed when naming identifiers:

- The identifier can not be a keyword. Keywords are reserved.
- The identifier can only be composed of letters, numbers, and the underscore character. That means the name can not contains symbols (except the underscore) nor whitespace.

- The identifier must begin with a letter or an underscore. It can not start with a number.
- C++ distinguishes between lower and upper case letters. nvalue is different than nValue is different than NVALUE.

1.5 CONSTANT

Constants refer to fixed values that the program may not alter. Constants can be of any of the basic data types. The way each constant is represented depends upon its type. Constants are also called literals.

***Definition:** "A constant value is the one which does not change during the execution of a program."*

Constant uses the secondary storage area. Constants are those quantities whose value does not vary during the execution of the program i.e. constant has fixed value. Constants in every language are the same. For example, in the C++ language some valid constant are: 52.7 , -43.4, +83.65, "Sukhwant", 'M', "2010" , "\n" etc.

In C++ language constants are of two types:

1. Numeric Constant
2. Non-Numeric Constant (Character Constant)

These are further sub-divided into more categories as shown in the Figure 2.2 below:

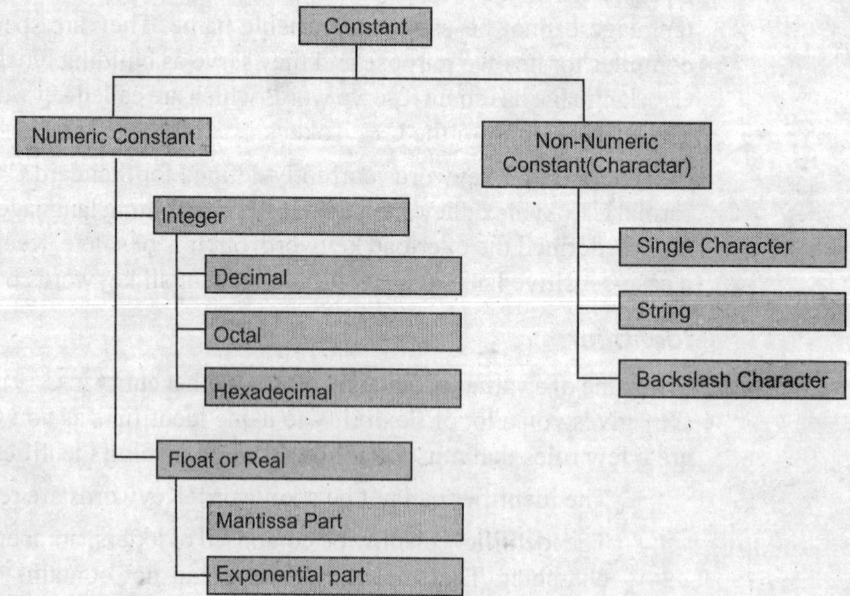

Figure 1.9: Different types of constants

1.6 VARIABLES

A variable is a value that can change any time. It is a memory location used to store a data value. A variable name should be carefully chosen by the programmer so that its use is reflected in a useful way in the entire program. Variable names are case sensitive.

Example of variable names are: Sun, number, Salary, Emp_name, average1 etc.

Any variable declared in a program should confirm to the following points:

1. They must always begin with a letter, although some systems permit underscore as the first character.
2. The length of a variable must not be more than 8 characters.
3. White space is not allowed and
4. A variable should not be a Keyword
5. It should not contain any special characters.

Examples of Invalid Variable names are: 123, (area), 6th, %abc etc.

A variable must be declared before it can be used. Variables can be declared at the start of any block of code, but most are found at the start of each function. Most local variables are created when the function is called, and are destroyed on return from that function. Variables uses the primary storage area.

Definition: *"Variables are those quantities whose value can vary during the execution of the program."*

Variables are basically memory locations which are given names and these locations are refereed in the program by variable names to read and write data in it. Variables are used for identification for entering the information or data. In variable you can enter integer value or real or character value (string value) according to the requirement. So we can say that variable are either of integer or float type or string type according to the data type used in C++ programming. Variables are used in C++ programs for reading data from the keyboard or from the file, process some formula and printing the information. In C++ language variables have no length for declaration, but some compilers allows either 31 character or 8 character long variables. It contains the name of a valid identifier.

For example:

area, simple, roll_no, name, student1 etc. are some valid variables.

A declaration begins with the type, followed by the name of one or more variables. For example,

```
int roll_no, marks;
```

Declarations can be spread out, allowing space for an explanatory comment. Variables can also be initialised when they are declared, this is done by adding an equals sign and the required value after the declaration.

```
int roll_no = 12;    // Variable roll_no stores value 12
int marks = 40;      // Variable marks stores value 40
```

Note that each variable in the C++ program has some features or properties associated with it called its **storage class** like auto, extern, static and register which are described in later section.

1.7 BASIC STRUCTURE OF A COMPLETE C++ PROGRAM

There are mainly two ways to design C++ program as shown below:

1. Basic structure of a complete C++ program without classes
2. Basic structure of a complete C++ program with classes

1.7.1 Basic Structure of A Complete C++ Program without Classes

A C++ program can be developed from a general structure. The general structure of C++ program without classes is as shown below (which is also called overview of a C++ program):

1. Documentation Section
2. Preprocessor Directives or Compiler Directives Section
   (i) Link Section
   (ii) Definition Section
3. Global Declaration Section
4. Main C-program function called main ( )
5. Beginning of the program: Left brace {
   (i) Local declaration or local variable declaration;
   (ii) Executable Part or C-executable statements;
6. End of the main program: Right brace }
7. Sub-program Section or User-defined functions.
   Function 1( )
      { User Defined Program }
   Function 2( )
      { Sub Program }

1.7.2 Basic Structure of A Complete C++ Program with Classes

A C++ program can be developed from a basic structure. The general structure of C++ program **with classes** is as shown below (which is also called overview of a C++ program):

1. Documentation Section
2. Preprocessor Directives or Compiler Directives Section
   (i) Link Section
   (ii) Definition Section
3. Global Declaration Section
4. Class declaration or definition
5. Main C++ program function called main ( )
6. Beginning of the program: Left brace {
   (i) Object declaration part;
   (ii) Accessing member functions(using dot operator);
7. End of the main program: Right brace }

***Note:** A class declaration or definition is further has its own relevant structure with its access specifiers.*

1.8 DATA TYPES

A programming language is proposed to help programmer to process certain kinds of data and to provide useful output. The task of data processing is accomplished by executing series of commands called program. A program usually contains different types of data types (integer, float, character etc.) and need to store the values being used in the program. C++ language is rich of data types. A C++ programmer has to employ proper data type as per his requirement. C++ has different data types for different types of data and can be broadly classified as:

1. Primary data types
2. Secondary data types

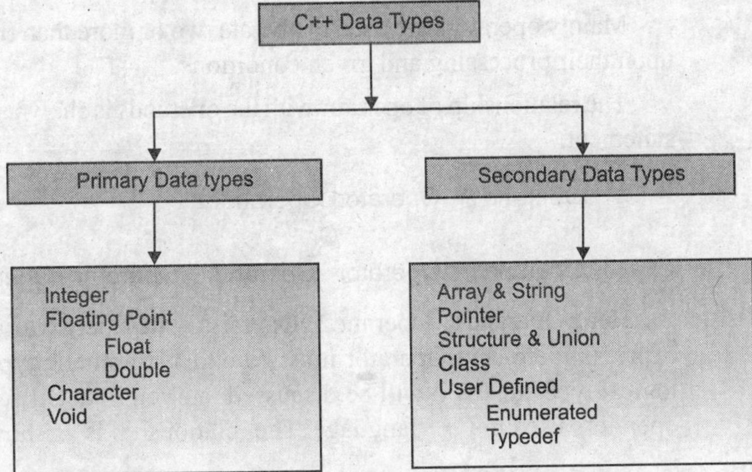

Figure 1.10: Different types of data types used in C++

Table 1.1 below shows all valid data type combinations supported by C++, along with their minimal ranges and typical bit widths. Remember, the table shows the range that these types will have.

Table 1.1: Data Types in C++, Size & Range of Data Types

Variable type	Keyword	Bytes required	Range
Character	char	1	–128 to 127
Unsigned character	unsigned char	1	0 to 255
Integer	int	2	–32768 to 32767
Short integer	short int	2	–32768 to 32767
Long integer	long int	4	–2,147,483,648 to 2,147,483,647
Unsigned integer	unsigned int	2	0 to 65535
Unsigned short integer	unsigned short int	2	0 to 65535
Unsigned long integer	unsigned long int	4	0 to 4,294,967,295
Float	float	4	1.2E-308 to
Double	double	8	2.2E-308 to
Long double	long double	10	3.4E-4932 to 1.1E+4932
Boolean value	bool	1	true or false
Wide character	wchar_t	2 or 4	1 wide character (65535)

1.9 OPERATORS

An operator is a symbol that tells the compiler to perform specific mathematical or logical manipulations.

Mainly operators are used to operate two or more than two operands depending upon their processing and given conditions.

The relationship of operator with the operands is shown as in the below common statement:

Operand1 Operator Operand2

Or

Operand1 Operator Operand2 Operator Operand3

Here Operand1, Operand2, Operand3 may be a variable, a constant or an expression etc. and Operator must be either arithmetic type or relational type or logical type etc. (as it will be discussed later on in detail). There are mainly eight operators used in C++ language. The relationship is as shown below:

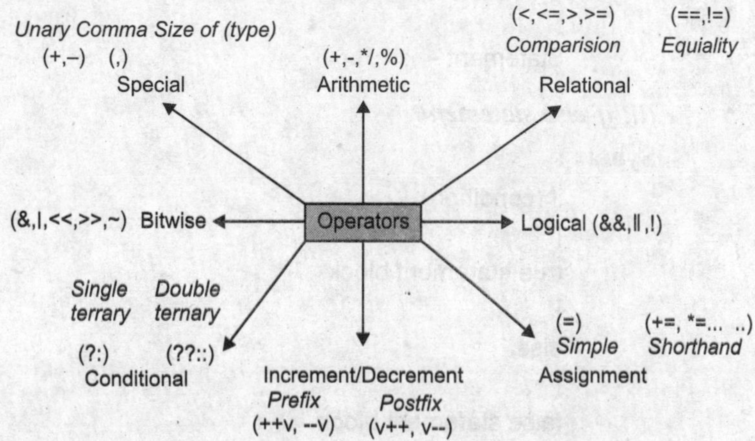

Figure 1.11: Types of Operators used in C Language

1.10 DECISION-MAKING STATEMENT

C++ supports many branching statements depending upon their flow of control and according their decision making policy. So it is also called decision-making statement. The various branching statements used are as:

1. if statements
2. switch statement
3. conditional operator statement

1. if statements

The if statement is a powerful decision making statement which can handle a single condition or group of statements. These have either true or false action.

There are four types of if statements:

(i) Simple if statement
(ii) if-else statement
(iii) nested if statement
(iv) else-if or ladder if or multi-condition if statement

(i) Simple if statement

The general syntax is:

```
if (condition)
{
/*True-statement block is executed.*/
```

```
}
Statement – x;
```

(ii) if-else statement

Syntax :

```
if (condition)
{
true statement block;
}
else
{
false statement block;
}
statement-x;
```

(iii) Nested if Statement

When an if statement occurs within another if statement, then such type of is called nested if statement.

Syntax :

```
if (condition-1)
{
if (condition-2)
{
st-1;
}
else
{
sf-1;
}
}
else
{
if (condition-3)
{
st-2;
}
else
{
sf-2;
}
```

```
}
statement-x;
```

(iv) Ladder if or else if statement

When in a complex problem number of conditions arise in a sequence, then we can use Ladder-if or else if statement to solve the problem in a simple manner.

Syntax :

```
if (condition-1)
{
st-1;
}
else if (condition-2)
{
st-2;
}
else if (condition-3)
{
st-3;
}
...
...
...
else if (condition-n)
{
st-n;
}
else
{
default-statement;
}
statement-x;
```

2. Switch Statement

It is also called Case statement because it has different cases and different blocks. It is also called multi-decision statement having multiple blocks.

Syntax :

```
switch (e or v)
{
case value1 :
```

```
block1;
break;
case value2 :
block2;
break;
case value3 :
block3;
break;
...
...
case value n :
block n;
break;
default :
block n+1;
}
statement-x;
```

3. Conditional Control Statement

This statement is based on conditional operator. This statement solves the problem's condition in a single line and is a fast executable operation. For this purpose, we can take combination of ? and :.

Syntax :

```
exp1 ? exp2 : exp3;
```

1.11 LOOPING STATEMENTS

When a single statement or a group of statements will be executed again and again in a program (in an iterative way), then such type processing is called loop.

There are four types of looping statements:

1. while statement
2. do-while statement
3. for statement
4. nested for statement

1. While statement

In this, first of all condition is checked and if it is true, then group of statements or body of loop is executed. It will execute again and again till condition becomes false.

Syntax:

```
while (test condition)
{
block of statements;
}
statement-x;
```

2. Do-while statement

In this statement, first body of the loop is executed and then the condition is checked. If condition is true, then the body of the loop is executed. When condition becomes false, then it will exit from the loop.

Syntax:

```
do
{
block of statements;
}
while (condition);
statement-x;
```

3. For statement

It is one step loop, which initialize, check the condition and increment / decrement the step in the loop in a single statement.

Syntax:

```
for (initial value; test condition; increment/ decrement)
{
body of the loop;
}
statement-x;
```

4. Nested for statement

When a for statement is executed within another for statement, then it is called nested for statement. We can apply number of nested for statements in C++ language.

Syntax:

```
for (initial value1; test condition1; increment1 / decrement1)
{
for (initial value2; test condition2; increment2 / decrement2)
{
inner- body of the loop;
}
```

```
outer-body of the loop;
}
statement-x;
```

1.12 ARRAY

Array is similar type of data collection name i.e. it is a collection of same data type elements. An array is a group of related data items, which share common name.

"It is the set of homogeneous data (same type)".

Suppose salary of the 50 employees named by salary variables name and we write it sal1,sal2,sal3……sal50. We repeat the variable name of employees by using the subscript. Because of use of single subscript or more than one subscript, it is also called subscripted variable. So Array's representation for the 10th employee is:

```
Salary [50];
```

Syntax:

```
Common name variable [size];
     or
array-name [subscript1] [subscript2];
```

Array representation can be done as:

```
storage-type data-type  array-name[size];
     Or
storage-type  data-type  array-name[row size][column size];
```

1.13 STRINGS

Combination of characters (group of character) is called string. "I am a good boy" is a string. We can print or display the string by using the cout function as:

```
cout<<"\n I am a good boy \n";
```

Syntax:

```
char city [20];
cout<<city;                    or
char city[10][20];
for (i=0; i <10; i++)
{
cout<<city[i];
}
```

1.13.1 Initializing String Variable

Syntax:

```
static data-type array-name[size] ={list of values};
```

For example, suppose you want to enter the string "BOMBAY" to the city variable, then the procedure is as:

```
static char city[10] = {'B', 'O', 'M', 'B', 'A', 'Y'};
```

For example, suppose if you want to assign three different cities data values to the city string variable, then this can be done as:

```
static char city[2][20] = { {'B', 'A', 'T', 'A', 'L', 'A'}
                            {'A', 'M', 'R', 'I', ' T','S','R'} }
```

character data-type must be used in strings.

1.14 POINTERS

Pointers are memory addresses variable. A Pointer contains a memory address. Further we can say pointers are directly linked to the memory address. Actually pointer is a variable having address of another variable. If one variable contains the address of another variable, the first variable is said to point to the second. For example, suppose q is an integer variable and this variable have value 412 stored in the memory.

Represented as:

Variable name	Memory value	Memory address		Pointer variable
q	412	4000	←	p (pointer)

Here the value 412 is stored at address 4000. We give name to memory address as p. The p is a memory variable, which gives the address of the q variable having value 412. Then p is called pointer.

Syntax:

```
data-type *pointer-variable ;
```

1.15 STRUCTURE

A structure is heterogeneous collection of related fields. Here fields are called structure member or structure element.

For example, suppose if you want to store a book in library using C++ program, then you give information about the title of the book, name of the author, number of pages in the book and the price of the book. Then before coding the problem you will examine it according to following table

Title of the Book	Name of Author	Pages of the Book	Price of the Book
Solved programming in C	Rachhpal Singh	450	300
Fundamental of C	Rachhpal Singh	500	200
Let Us C	Yashvant K.	700	300

```
struct library
{
char   title [40] ;
char   author [40] ;
int    pages ;
float  price ;
} ;
void main()
{ }
```

1.16 UNION

A union is a variable that declares a set of multiple variables (called members or elements having different data-types) sharing the same memory area.

The compiler allocates sufficient memory to hold the largest variable of the union. All the members of union occupy the same memory locations called addresses. The old value of the already declared member will be destroyed and new value to the new member will be assigned in the memory by using the union concept.

Syntax:

```
union union-tag
{
        datatype-1  member-element-1;
        ......................................;
        dartatype-n  member-element-n;
}v1,v2,...vn;
```

1.17 CLASS

A class is the implementation of an abstract data type (ADT). It defines attributes and methods which implement the data structure and operations of the ADT, respectively.

A class is an expanded concept of a data structure: instead of holding only data, it can hold both data and functions.

Definition (Class): *"A class is an organization of data and functions which operate on them. Data structures are called data members and the functions are called member functions. The combination of data members and member functions constitute a data object or simply an object."*

Definition (object): *"An object is an instantiation of a class. In terms of variables, a class would be the type, and an object would be the variable."*

The above said two definitions are impressive to explain the concept of classes and objects and its related tasks.

A class is a data type whose variables are objects. Object as a variable has member functions as well as the ability to hold data values. A class is specified just like a structure with a name. The class is specified by keyword "class".

Classes are generally declared using the keyword class, with the following format:

```
class class_name
{
access_specifier_1:
member1;
access_specifier_2:
member2;
...
} object_names;
```

Where class_name is a valid identifier for the class, object_names is an optional list of names for objects of this class. The body of the declaration can contain members, which can be both data or function declarations, and optionally access specifiers.

All is very similar to the declaration on data structures, except that we can now include also functions and members, but also this new thing called access specifier. An access specifier is one of the following three keywords: private, public or protected. These specifiers modify the access rights that the members following them acquire:

- private members of a class are accessible only from within other members of the same class or from their friends.
- protected members are accessible from members of their same class and from their friends, but also from members of their derived classes.
- Finally, public members are accessible from anywhere where the object is visible.

Program 1: Write a C++ program to declare class instance(create object).

```
#include <iostream.h>
#include<conio.h>
class myclass
{
private:
int a;
public:
myclass(int x)
{
a = x;
}
int geta()
{
return a;
}
};
void main()
{
myclass ob(4);
cout << ob.geta();
getch();
}
```

Output:

4

SOLVED PROGRAMMING

Program 1: Write a C++ program to find the area and circumference of the circle.

```
#include<iostream.h>
#include<conio.h>
#define PI 3.1427
void main()
{
int r;
float cir, area;
clrscr();
cout<<"\n ENTER THE RADIUS OF THE CIRCLE: ";
```

```
cin>>r;
cir = 2*PI*r;
area=PI*r*r;
cout<<"\n THE CIRCUMFERENCE OF CIRCLE IS= "<<cir;
cout<<"\n THE AREA OF CIRCLE IS= "<<area;
getch();
}
```

Output:

```
ENTER THE RADIUS OF THE CIRCLE: 5
THE CIRCUMFERENCE OF CIRCLE IS= 31.427
THE AREA OF CIRCLE IS= 78.5675
```

Program 2: Write a C++ Program to compute the circumference and volume of a sphere.

```
#include<iostream.h>
#include<conio.h>
#define PI 3.1427
void main()
{
int r;
float cir, vol;
clrscr();
cout<<"\n ENTER THE RADIUS OF THE SPHERE: ";
cin>>r;
cir=4*PI*r*r;
vol=4/3*PI*r*r*r;
cout<<"\n CIRCUMFERENCE OF SPHERE IS= "<<cir;
cout<<"\n THE VOLUME OF SPHERE IS=  "<<vol;
getch();
}
```

Output:

```
ENTER THE RADIUS OF THE SPHERE: 5
CIRCUMFERENCE OF SPHERE IS=314.27
THE VOLUME OF SPHERE IS= 523.78331
```

Program 3: Write a C++ Program to compute simple interest and compound interest.

```
#include<iostream.h>
#include<math.h>
#include<dos.h>
```

```
void main()
{
float p, r, t, si, ci;
cout<<"\n Enter the value of Principle, Rate, Time: ";
cin>>p>>r>>t;
si=(p*r*t)/100;
ci=p*pow((1+r/100),t)-p;
cout<<"\n Simple interest is = "<<si;
cout<<"\n Compound interest is = "<<ci;
getch();
}
```

Output:

Enter the value of Principle, Rate, Time: 1200 10 2

Simple interest is 240

Compound interest is 252

Program 4: Write a C++ Program to find the greatest number between two numbers.

```
#include<iostream.h>
#include<conio.h>
void main ( )
{
int a,b,g;
clrscr();
cout<<"\n Enter the value of two numbers: ";
cin>>a>>b;
if (a > b)
{
g = a;
}
else
{
g = b;
}
cout<<"\n Greatest Number is: "<< g;
getch( );
}
```

Output:

Enter the value of two numbers: 40 36

Greatest Number is: 40

Program 5: Write a C++ Program to find greatest number among three integer numbers.

```
#include<iostream.h>
#include<conio.h>
#include<dos.h>
void main()
{
int a,b,c,g;
cout<<"\n Enter the three numbers:";
cin>>a>>b>>c;
if(a>b)
{
if(a>c)
{
g=a;
}
else
{
g=c;
}
}
else
{
if(b>c)
{
g=b;
}
else
{
g=c;
}
}
cout<<"\n Greatest number is: "<<g;
getch();
}
```

Output:

Enter the three numbers: 20 30 10

Greatest number is:30

Program 6: Write a C++ Program to print the color according to the code.

```
#include<iostream.h>
#include<conio.h>
void main()
{
int code;
cout<<" \n  MAIN MENU  ";
cout<<" \n1. For color Red ";
cout<<" \n2. For color Green ";
cout<<" \n3. For color White ";
cout<<" \n4. For color Yellow ";
cout<<"\n Enter the color code: ";
cin>>code;
switch(code)
{
case 1:
cout<<"\n color is  RED ";
break;
case 2:
cout<<"\n color is GREEN";
break;
case 3:
cout<<"\n color is WHITE ";
break;
case  4:
cout<<"\n color is YELLOW ";
break;
default :
cout<<"\n Color does not found";
}
getch();
}
```

Output:

```
MAIN MENU
1. For color Red
2. For color Green
3. For color White
4. For color Yellow
Enter the color code: 2
color is GREEN
```

Program 7: Write a C++ Program to find factorial of a number.

```
#include<iostream.h>
#include<dos.h>
#include<conio.h>
void main()
{
int n,i,m;
clrscr();
cout<<"\n Enter the number : ";
cin>>n;
m=1;
for(i=1;i<=n;i++)
{
m=m*i;
}
cout<<" \n Factorial of "<<n<<" is = "<<m;
getch();
}
```

Output:

Enter the number: 5

Factorial of 5 is = 120

Program 8: Write a C++ Program to print

```
*
**
***
****
```

```
#include<conio.h>
#include<iostream.h>
void main()
{
int a;
clrscr( );
cout<<"\n Enter any number :";
cin>>a;
for(int i=1;i<=a;i++)
{
for(int j=1;j<=i;j++)
cout<<"*";
cout<<"\n";
```

```
}
getch();
}
```

Program 9: Write a C++ Program to print

```
    *
   * *
  * * *
```

```
#include<conio.h>
#include<iostream.h>
void main()
{
int a,j,i,space;
clrscr( );
cout<<"\nEnter any number :";
cin>>a;
for(space=a-1,i=1;i<=a;i++,space--)
{
for(j=1;j<=space;j++)
cout<<" ";
for(j=1;j<=i;j++)
cout<<"* ";
cout<<"\n";
}
getch();
}
```

Program 10: Write a C++ Program to find average of N numbers.

```
#include<iostream.h>
#include<conio.h>
void main ( )
{
int n, a[50], i, s;
float av;
clrscr();
cout<<"\n Enter the value of n:";
cin>>n;
cout<<"\n Enter the different"<<n<<" values:";
for (i = 0; i < n; i++)
{
```

```
cin>>a[i];
}
s=0;
for(i=0; i<n; i++)
{
s=s+a[i];
}
cout<<"\n Sum is "<<s;
av=(float)s/n;
cout<<"\n Average is <<av;
getch();
}
```

Output:

```
Enter the value of n: 5
Enter the different 5 values:
20
30
40
10
50
Sum is 150
Average is 30.0
```

Program 11: Write a C++ Program to search a number by using LINEAR SEARCH of Numeric data (NUMBERS).

```
# include <iostream.h>
# include <conio.h>
# include <dos.h>
void main()
{
int c,i,n,b,s[30],s1;
clrscr();
cout<<"\n ENTER HOW MANY NUMBERS YOU WANT TO ENTER: ";
cin>>n;
cout<<"\n ENTER THE NUMBERS: ";
for(i=1;i<=n;i++)
{
cin>>s[i];
}
clrscr();
```

```
cout<<"\n ENTER THE NUMBER YOU WANT  TO SEARCH: ";
cin>>s1;
i=1;
while(i<=n)
{
b=s[i]-s1;
if(b==0)
{
c=i;
break;}
else
{
c=0;
}
i++;
}
if(c==0)
{
cout<<"\n SEARCH UNSUCCESSFUL";
}
else
{
cout<<"\n SEARCH SUCCESSFUL AND LOCATION IS "<<c;
}
getch();
}
```

Output:

```
ENTER HOW MANY NUMBERS YOU WANT TO ENTER: 6
ENTER THE NUMBERS
88
66
44
22
55
11
ENTER THE NUMBER YOU WANT  TO SEARCH:
44
SEARCH SUCCESSFUL AND LOCATION IS 3
```

Program 12: Write a C++ Program to illustrate the concept of displaying the address of a Pointer variable.

```
#include<conio.h>
#include<iostream.h>
void main ( )
{
int x, *q ;
x = 220 ;
q = &x ;
cout<<"/n "<<x<<" is stored at address "<<&x;
cout<<"/n "<<x<<" is stored at address "<< q;
cout<<"/n "<<*q<<" is stored at address "<<q;
cout<<"/n "<<*&x<<" is stored at address" <<&x;
getch( ) ;
}
```

Output:

```
220 is stored at address 5010
220 is stored at address 5010
220 is stored at address 5010
220 is stored at address 5010
```

Program 13: Write a C++ Program to reverse the string using pointer.

```
#include <iostream.h>
#include <conio.h>
#include<string.h>
void main()
{
char a[20];
void f(char [20]);
void (*p)(char [20]);
clrscr();
cout<<"\n Enter the string :";
cin>>a;
p=&f;
(*p)(a);
getch();
}
void f(char *s)
{
int i,n;
```

```
char t;
n=strlen(s);
for(i=0;i<n/2;i++)
{
t=*(s+i);
*(s+i)=*(s+n-i-1);
*(s+n-i-1)=t;
}
cout<<"\n Reversed string is  :";
for(i=0;*(s+i)!=0;i++)
cout<<*(s+i);
}
```

Output:

Enter the string : rama

Reversed string is : amar

Program 14: Write a C++ Program to read and write the student data (illustrate the concept of accessing the value of structure variable).

```
#include<iostream.h>
#include<conio.h>
void main ( )
{
Struct student
{
int rn ;
char name [20] ;
char   add [30] ;
float   fees ;
} ;
struct   student   st1;
cout<<" \ n Enter the data of any student : ";
cin>>st1.rn>> st1.name>> st1.add>>st1.fees;
cout<<"\ n Roll No. of the student is "<<st1.rn;
cout<<"\ n Name of  the student is  "<<st1.name;
cout<<"\ n Address of the  student  is "<<st1.add;
cout<<"\ n Fees submitted by the student is "<<st1.fees;
getch( ) ;
}
```

Output:

Enter the data of any student :

```
12
dany
Abc nagar, Asr
155.20
Roll No. of the student is 12
Name of  the student is dany
Address of the  student  is Abc nagar, Asr
Fees submitted by the student is 155.20
```

Program 15: Write a C++ Program to read and display student data using Union.

```
#include<iostream.h>
#include<conio.h>
void main()
{
union student
{
char grade;
int rollno;
float marks;
double fees;
}
union student s;
cout<<"\n Enter the garde, rollno, marks and fees of the student :";
cin>>s.grade>>s.rollno>>s.marks>>s.fees;
cout<<"\n Grade is: "<<s.garde;
cout<<"\n Rollno is: "<<s.rollno;
cout<<"\n Marks are : "<<s.marks;
cout<<"\n Fees paid  is: "<<s.fees;
getch ();
}
```

Output:

```
Enter the garde, rollno, marks and fees of the student :
B
12
190.50
22346.8888787
Grade is: B
Rollno is: 12
Marks are :1 90.50
```

```
Fees paid  is: 22346.8888787
```

Program 16: Write a C++ program to illustrate the concept of class having one object.

```
#include<iostream.h>
#include<conio.h>
class student
{
private:
int rn;
float fees;
public:
void readdata()
{
cout<<"Enter the rollno. and fees of the student:";
cin>>rn>>fees;
}
void writedata()
{
cout<<"The rollno. is "<<rn<<endl;
cout<<" The fees is "<<fees<<endl;
}
};
void main()
{
student st;
st.readdata();
st.writedata();
getch();
}
```

Output:

```
Enter the rollno. and fees of the student: 4 12.25
The rollno. is 4
The fees is 12.25
```

Program 17: Write a C++ program to illustrate the concept of class having two objects.

```
#include<iostream.h>
#include<conio.h>
class student
```

```
{
private:
int rn;
float fees;
public:
void readdata()
{
cout<<"Enter the rollno. and fees of the student:";
cin>>rn>>fees;
}
void writedata()
{
cout<<"The rollno. is "<<rn<<endl;
cout<<" The fees is "<<fees<<endl;
}
};
void main()
{
student st1, st2;
st.readdata();
st.writedata();
st2.readdata();
st2.writedata();
getch();
}
```

Output:

```
Enter the rollno. and fees of the student: 4 12.25
The rollno. is 4
The fees is 12.25
Enter the rollno. and fees of the student: 5 12.55
The rollno. is 5
The fees is 12.55
```

PROGRAMMING PROBLEMS

1. Program to find average of three numbers.
2. Program to find volume of a box.
3. Program to convert time in seconds to time hours, minutes and seconds.
4. Write a program to print the following outputs using for loops.

(a)
```
1
2 2
3 3 3
4 4 4 4
```
(b)
```
* * * *
* * *
* *
*
```

5. Write a C++ program to draw Reverse Pascal Triangle.
6. Write a C++ Program to find the leap year.
7. Write a program to print a Fibonacci series 1 2 3 5 8 …..upto 100.
8. Program to find the biggest number among N numbers.
9. Program to Sort an array (list) having N elements using Bubble Sort method.
10. Program to Calculate Matrix Multiplication, Matrix Addition and Matrix Transpose by using SWITCH statements (A menu driven program).
11. Program to count the negative elements from the list.
12. Program to transpose a matrix.
13. Program to find the sum of Diagonal Elements of a matrix (Trace a Matrix).
14. Write a C++ Program to reverse numbers in an array.
15. Write a C++ Program to remove duplicate numbers from an array.
16. Write a C++ Program to convert a square matrix into a unit matrix.
17. Program to find whether a sub string is present in the string or not, if it is present then find location of sub string in the string.
18. Program to search a string using Binary Search.
19. Program to find whether the string is PALINDROMEM or not.
20. Write a C++ Program to find all combination of characters of a word.
21. Write a C++ Program to find sum of row and columns in a matrix-using pointer.
22. Write a C++ Program to find the roots of quadratic equation using pointer.
23. Write a C++ Program to find max. & min. value from array using pointer.
24. Write a C++ Program to determine the area and perimeter of triangle using pointer.
25. Write a C++ Program to construct a pay bill structure of an employee in an organization.
26. Write a C++ Program to access one-dimensional array structure.

27. Write a C++ Program to compute the size of union.
28. Write a C++ program to design and print the DMC (Detail Marks card) of every student in a class of n students in a college.

EXERCISES

1. What do you mean by C++ language? Explain various features of C++.
2. Explain character set of C++ language.
3. What are Keywords and Identifiers?
4. Explain different types of constant.
5. What are variables?
6. Explain basic structure of a complete C++ program.
7. Explain various data types used in C++ language.
8. Explain different types of operators used in C++ language.
9. Why we use decision-making statement? Explain all.
10. Explain all looping statements in detail.
11. What do you mean by array?
12. What do you mean by strings?
13. What is pointer?
14. What do you mean by structure? Explain with the help of program.
15. What do you mean by union? Explain with the help of program.
16. What do you mean by class? Explain with the help of program.

2 CHAPTER

Introduction to Data Structures and String Processing

2.1 INTRODUCTION

A data structure is considered as a way of storing data in a computer so that it can be used efficiently. A well-designed data structure uses few resources, both execution time and memory space to perform a variety of critical operations. Data structures are implemented using the data types, references and operations on them provided by a programming language.

This view has given rise to many formalized design methods and programming languages in which data structures, rather than algorithms, they are the key organizing factor. The Procedure-oriented programming languages like C++ allow data structures to be safely reused in different applications by hiding their verified implementation details. Different kinds of data structures are suited to different kinds of applications, and some are highly specialized to certain tasks.

In the design of many types of programs, the choice of data structures is a primary design consideration, as experience in building large systems has shown that the difficulty of implementation and the quality and performance of the final result depends heavily on choosing the best data structure. After the data structures are chosen, the algorithms to be used often become relatively obvious. Sometimes things work in the opposite direction—data structures are chosen because certain key tasks have algorithms that work best with particular data structures. In either case, the choice of appropriate data structures is crucial.

2.2 ELEMENTARY DATA ORGANIZATION

2.2.1 Introduction to Computer

Computer is an information processing system, which is used to process raw data to produce information (meaningful data).

Computer data processing is any process that uses a computer program to enter data and summarize, analyze or otherwise convert data into usable information. The process may be automated and run on a computer. It involves recording, analyzing, sorting, summarizing, calculating, disseminating and storing data.

To be more precise, let us consider a simple example explaining raw data. Take the case of student roll no (5). When it is unprocessed i.e. it is only number when we process on it like Roll no. is 5.Then it is use to identify the student uniquely.

The processed data is called as information. So inputting of raw data and getting the information after processing is shown in the Figure.

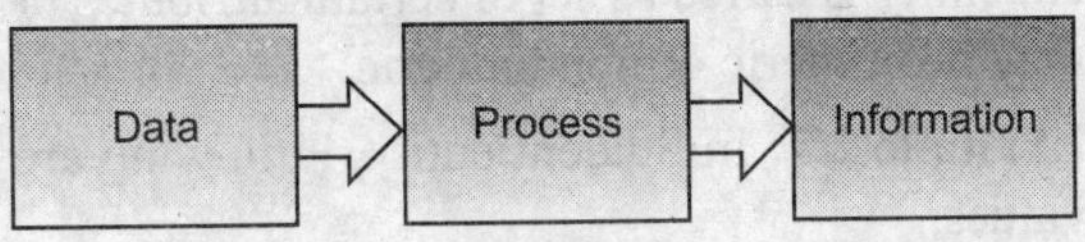

Figure 2.1: Processing of Data

2.2.2 Data and Data Item

Data are simply values or sets of values. Data is raw hand information collected by us. Data may be collected in the form of characters, words, and text and code numbers. Data are facts from which a conclusion can be drawn. Let us take an example of integers data is:

{23, 65, 87, 43}

Data of character type:

{A, B, ..., Z}

Data item is refers as single unit of values. Data items are divided into two sub items.

1. Group item
2. Elementary item

1. **Group item:** Data items, which are divided into sub items, are called as group items. For example, the name of student can be divided into subitems– first name, middle name and last name.
2. **Elementary item:** Data items, which are not divided into sub items, are called elementary items. For example, the Roll number of student cannot be divided into subitems.

2.2.3 Storage of Data

Now comes the idea of Data Storage. There are some guidelines for a data management system as:

1. Data must be represented and stored, for later accessing and processing.

2. Data must be organized for their selective and effective use.
3. Data must be processed for the effective support of user environment.
4. Data must be protected for retaining their value.

2.2.4 Data Organization

Data is organized in the form of fields, records and files.

Entity

An entity is called as set of certain attributes or properties with values. The values may be numeric or non numeric.

Example 2.1: In Student entity, Following are attributes and their corresponding values.

Attributes:	Roll no.	Name	Class	Address
Values:	1204	Avtar Singh	BCA	76 Aazad nagar, U.P

Field

A field refers to single elementary unit of information used to representing an attribute of an entity. The elements of a record are called as fields. A field is a specified area of record used for a particular kind of information.

Record

A record is defined as a finite, ordered collection of possibly heterogeneous elements of given entity. It is sometimes also called as simply a structure. In this structure, logically related data items of different types are grouped together under one name.

File

A file is the collection of records of the entities in a given entity set.

Key

Each record in a file may contain many of field items, but in each record there exists field that uniquely determines the record in the file. The uniquely field of a record is called as key field. The key of a record may be either an elementary item or a group item.

Primary key

The key, which is uniquely, self sufficient enough to determine the record in a file, is called as primary key. The example of primary key in above Student Entity is Roll no.

A file stores two types of records.

1. Fixed length records
2. Variable length records.

1. **Fixed length records:** All the records can have the same data items with the same amount of space assigned to each data item. There are fixed number of characters in each memory location.
2. **Variable length records:** All the records may contain different lengths. For example student records have variable length format.

2.2.5 Comparison of Fixed Length Storage and Variable Length Storage

Fixed Length Storage	Variable Length Storage
It gives more speed of processing records	Speed of processing is less as compared to fixed word-length storage
Memory space is not properly utilized	Memory space is properly utilized

2.3 DATA STRUCTURES

A data structure is a particular way of storing and organizing data in a computer so that it can be used efficiently. The term data structure refers to a scheme for organizing related pieces of information.

"The organized collection of data in mathematical or logical way is called data structure"

The study of different data structures includes:

1. Logical description of data.
2. Implementation detail of the data structure.
3. Quantitative analysis of the data structures, includes amount of memory required to store the data structure and the time required to process

The choice of particular data structure is depends mainly on two factors:

1. It must be rich in structure to represents real world relationship between data.
2. Structure should be simple and easy to use that the data can be access and process effectively when required.

Different kinds of data structures are suited to different kinds of applications, and some are highly specialized to certain tasks.

2.4 VARIOUS TYPES OF DATA STRUCTURES

Data structures are sometimes also called as data types. The complete hierarchical structure of data structure is represented as:

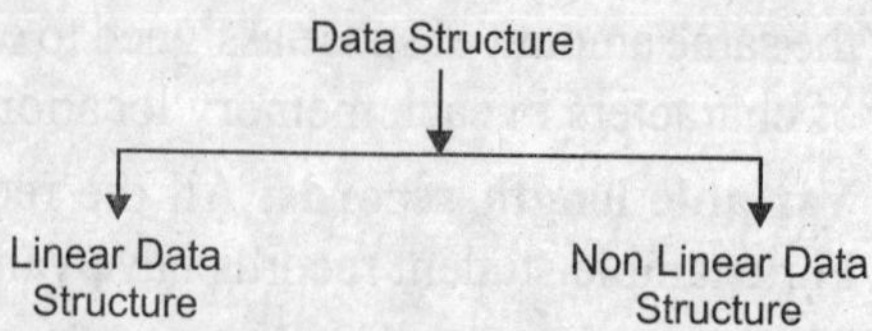

Figure 2.2: Types of Data structure

There are mainly two types of data structure:

1. **Linear Data Structures:** A data structure whose elements forms a proper sequence, or a having sequential structure, every element in the structure has a unique predecessor and unique successor. For examples: arrays, linked lists, stacks and queues.
2. **Non-linear Data Structure:** A data structure whose elements do not forms a sequence, or a having complex structure, there is no unique predecessor or unique successor. For examples: trees and graphs.

Other types are:

1. **Homogenous:** In this, data values of same types of data are stored as in an array.
2. **Non-homogenous:** In this, data values of different types are grouped as in structures and classes.
3. **Dynamic:** In dynamic data structures such as references and pointers, size and memory locations can be changed during program execution.
4. **Static:** Static keyword in C++ is used to initialize the variable to 0. The value of static variable remains in the memory throughout the program.

2.4.1 Linear Data Structure

Linear Data Structure is comprised of an ordered set of data elements. Let us consider linear list A having n data elements as

$$A = [A_0, A_1, A_2, A_3 \ldots A_{n-1}]$$

If n is zero, it is called as empty list.

1. Array

An array is a group of homogeneous collection of data of same data type and array data can be stored in contiguous memory locations.

Here, homogeneous data means, the data with same data type. Each data entry stored in an array is accessed with an array index or subscript. Either the subscript or index value keeps track of the serial location number or occurrence of each data entry that is stored.

Arrays are divided into two categories:

(i) Linear array

(ii) Non-linear array

For example, the array A[N] is a finite set of integer numbers as shown in Figure 2.3:

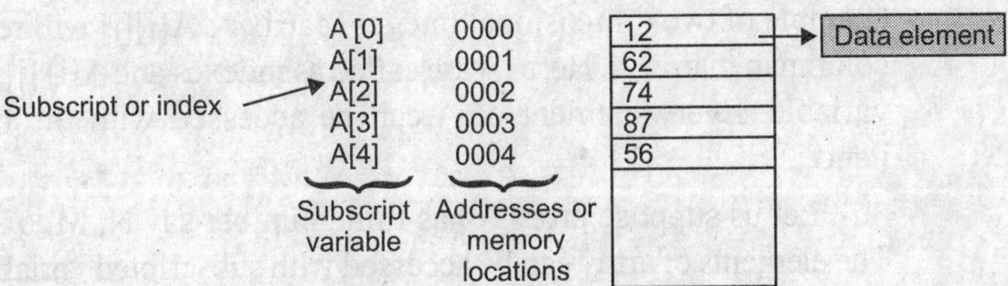

Figure 2.3: Array Addressing

Let us suppose array A[N] has finite no of data elements, say N, it means total number of elements in array A are N. Then A [N] will be called as subscript variable and N will be called as an index or subscript value. The index value of array starts from zero. The elements of array A will be accessed as A[0], A[1], A[2].... A[N–1], giving a total as N elements.

(i) Linear array or one-dimensional array

This is also called list array. Another name of linear array is single-dimensional array. These types are of ladder type. In the linear array only one subscript is used. It is written either in row or in column form.

Let us suppose array A[N] has finite no of data elements, say N, it means total number of elements in array A are N. Then its elements can be denoted as

$A_1, A_2, \ldots\ldots, A_N$ (Mathematical notation)

A(1), A(2),........, A(N) (parenthesis notation)

A[0], A[1], A[2]......, A[N–1] (bracket notation or in C++ language)

A[N] will be called as subscript variable and N will be called as an index or subscript value. The elements of array A will be accessed as A[0], A[1], A[2].... A[N-1], giving a total as N elements. So when we assign different values to the declared array, then it can be written (in the computer memory) as:

A[0] = 55

A[1] = 35

A[2] = 40

A[3] = 47

A[4] = 33

(ii) Non-linear array or two dimensional array

These arrays are also called double dimensional arrays or two subscripted arrays. Another name of two-dimensional array is Tabular or Rectangular Array. These arrays are in both row and column form. These arrays have two subscripts. The example is two-dimensional array, which is set of finite no of homogeneous data elements and each element is accessed by two subscripts. For example, take the example of two dimensional integer Matrix A. A[i][j] will represent ith row and jth column in matrix A. Here i, j are called as indexes and A[i] [j] is called as subscripted variable. Every element of A can be accessed with the help of two subscripts i and j.

Let us suppose array A has finite number say N, M, of integer data elements. The elements of array can be accessed with subscripted variables. A two dimensional array is an array in which each element is itself an array.

Also an array having N number of rows and M number of columns as shown in the below Figure 1.8 can be called as N X M array.

In other words such types of array can store different values in those cells which is the intersection of rows and columns. We can say that values can be easily stored at particular space in the table.

As shown in the Figure 2.4, we can store the value either at A[0][0] or at a A[0][1] or A[0][2] or so on at the space A[i][j], where i is the number of rows varying from 0 to N and j is the number of columns varying from 0 to M.

	columns i=0	j=1 ----------------		j=M-1 upper limit of column
Rows i=0	A[0][0]	A[0][1]		
i=1	A[1][0]	A[1][1]		
-				
-				
i=N-1		A[i][j]		
Upper limit of row				

Example NxM array

Figure 2.4: Intersection of Rows and Columns (NXM array)

Now take simple example of matrix having 2 or more rows. In memory the array elements will be stored as shown in the Figure 2.5. Here we can see the

A[0][0] is the array element number having value 5 stored at the address 0000, similarly the element A[0][1] has the vale 6 stored at the address 0001.

This procedure continues till we store the values according to either our requirement or according to the given set of values.

Here we can see that finally we have stored 9 value at the address 0003 in the address A[1][3] or a subscripted array.

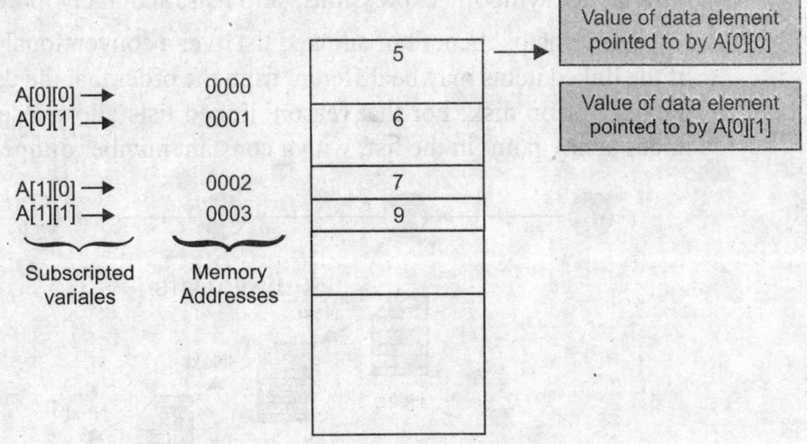

Figure 2.5: Storage of Array Elements

2. *String*

String is defined as an array of characters. Example of string is "AMRITSAR", where the double quotes (" ") are not part of string. The length of this string is 8. A string with length 0 is called as Null string or empty string, which is typically denoted as Null.

In memory Array representation of string named as str is shown in the Figure 2.6

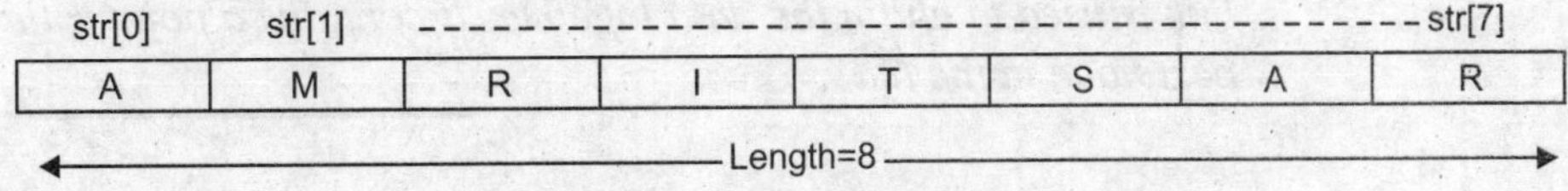

Figure 2.6: Array representation of String

An extra character is appended to the end of every string, called as NULL character '\0'. This null character denotes an end of string. Always remember that the total number of characters in the array is always 1 more than string length as shown in the Figure 2.7.

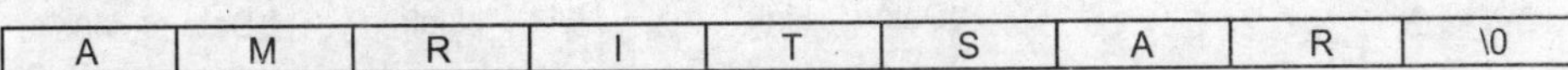

Figure 2.7: Array representation of string with NULL as last character

3. *Linked List*

A linked list is a data structure that consists of a sequence of data records such that in each record there is a field that contains a reference (i.e., a link) to the next record in the sequence.

Linked lists are among the simplest and most common data structures, and are used to implement many important abstract data structures, such as stacks, queues, hash tables, symbolic expressions, skip lists, and many more.

The principal benefit of a linked list over a conventional array is that the order of the linked items may be different from the order that the data items are stored in memory or on disk. For that reason, linked lists allow insertion and removal of nodes at any point in the list, with a constant number of operations.

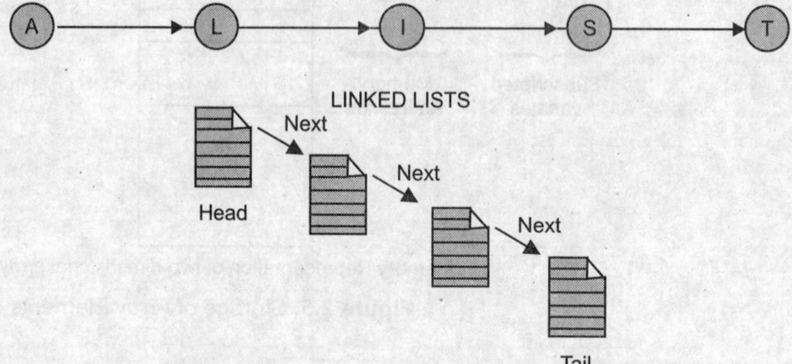

Figure 2.8: Different Views of Linked Lists

Definition: *"A linked list is an ordered collection of data in which each element contains the location of the next element, that is, each element has 2 parts: data and link. The data part holds the useful information, the data to be processed. The link is used to chain the data together. It contains a pointer that identifies the next node in the list".*

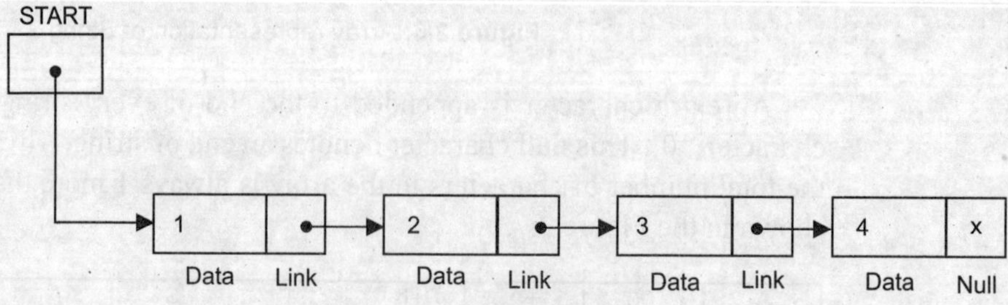

Figure 2.9: Simple Linked List

Linked lists are files or arrays with a pointer field included within each record or entry.

Disadvantages to Linked List

1. More primary memory is required to store size of the pointer field.
2. Processing time is more for accessing a unique data entry.

Difference between Array and Linked List

Array	Linked List
It uses contiguous memory space i.e. continuous memory.	Data in linked list can be stored at discontinues locations.
We can access data randomly.	Data access is sequential in this approach.
It is less flexible as compare to linked list.	It is more flexible as compare to an array.
Only first element address is stored and the addresses of further elements can be fetched from this base address.	Every node has two parts the data part and address part.
Every data fragment is known as element.	Every data fragment is known as node.
The complexity for insertion and deletion of an element is O(1).	The complexity for insertion and deletion of a node is O(n), where n denotes the location where insertion or deletion takes place.
It's locality is good.	It has bad locality.

There are some problems occurs with the stack and queue which create a problem for the organization of data by the data structures.

These problems are discussed as written below:

1. **Storage problem:** The storage space to stack, queue or in general to arrays, is allocated, when the program is written, and can not be changed while the program is running. The programmer has to decide on the maximum amount of memory that would be required for these arrays at the time of declarations. If the program is run with less amount of data, the reasonable space allocated, is wasted. On the other side, if the program is run with larger amount of data, then problem of overflow arises i.e. space is not available for the new data.
2. **Data movement problem:** Insertion and deletion from the middle of arrays is very difficult.

Take the example of 100 elements in an array. Let us suppose a new element is to be added at 50th location. Hey, you've to move 51st location element to 52nd, 52nd location element to 53rd, ... 100th location element to 101st. Likewise we've to shift the elements when deletion is to be performed. Here comes the idea of linked lists. Linked lists are data structures that enable us to keep records in a file or entries in an array in logical order even though they may not be in physical order.

(i) Doubly linked list

In a doubly-linked list, each node contains, besides the next-node link, a second link field pointing to the previous node in the sequence. The two links may be called forward(s) and backwards.

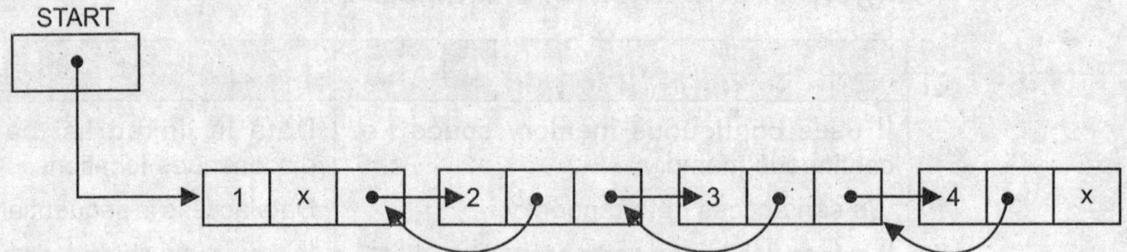

Figure 2.10: Doubly Linked List

(ii) Circular linked list

In a circularly linked list, all nodes are linked in a continuous circle, without using null. For lists with a front and a back (such as a queue), one stores a reference to the last node in the list. The next node after the last node is the first node. Elements can be added to the back of the list and removed from the front in constant time.

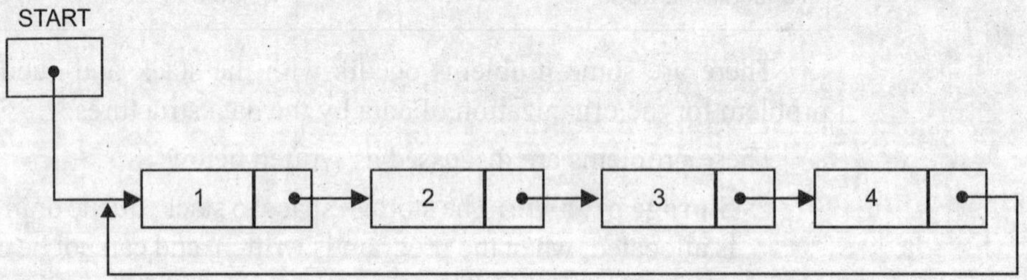

Figure 2.11: Circular Linked List

4. Stack

A stack is a last in, first out (LIFO) abstract data type and data structure. A stack can have any abstract data type as an element, but is characterized by only two fundamental operations, the push and the pop.

The two main operations applicable to a stack are:

1. **Push:** an item is put on top of the stack, increasing the stack size by one. As stack size is usually limited, this may provoke a stack overflow if the maximum size is exceeded.
2. **Pop:** the top item is taken from the stack, decreasing stack size by one. In

the case where there was no top item (i.e. the stack was empty), a stack underflow occurs.

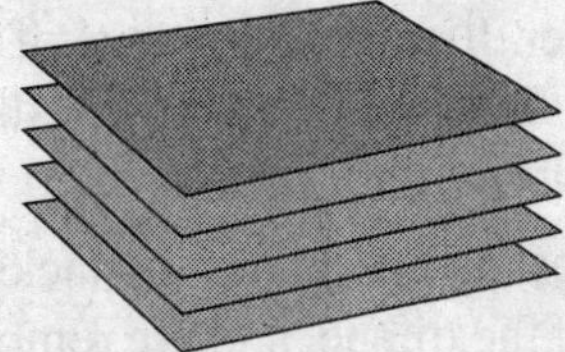

Figure 2.12: A Physical Stack of Plates

Stacks are the special data structure in which, entries are added to it or are removed from it, at one end or location. This location is called as Top of the stack. Stacks exhibit a type of behavior known as LIFO i.e. Last In, First Out. When any entry is added to stack, you push on to the Top of stack. When last entry is removed from stack you POP it off the top of stack. Remember that Top of stack is referred to in both instances. Let us take an example of stack with five items.

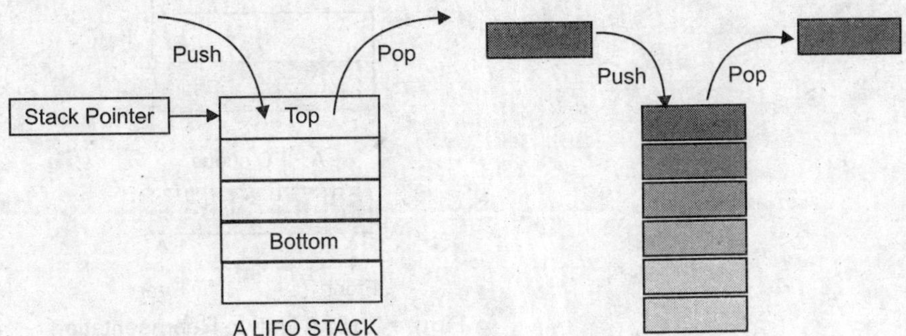

Figure 2.13: A Stack Representation

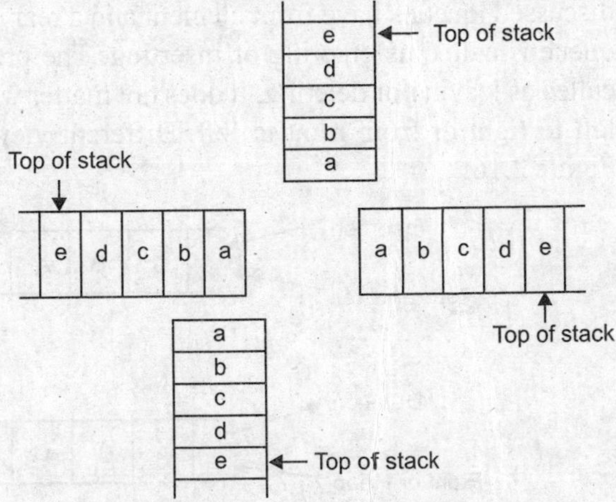

Figure 2.14: Different Views of Stacks

5. *Queue*

Queue is a linear data structure in which data can be added to one end and retrieved from the other. Just like the queue of the real world, the data that goes first into the queue is the first one to be retrieved. That is why queues are sometimes called as First-In-First-Out data structure.

In queues, as compared to stacks, entries are added to it at one end called as rear or tail of the queue, and are removed at other end called as front or head of the queue. The information in such list is processed in the same order as it was received i.e. on a First –In, First- Out (FIFO) or First-Come, First-Served (FCFS) basis. When a group forms a line it becomes a queue.

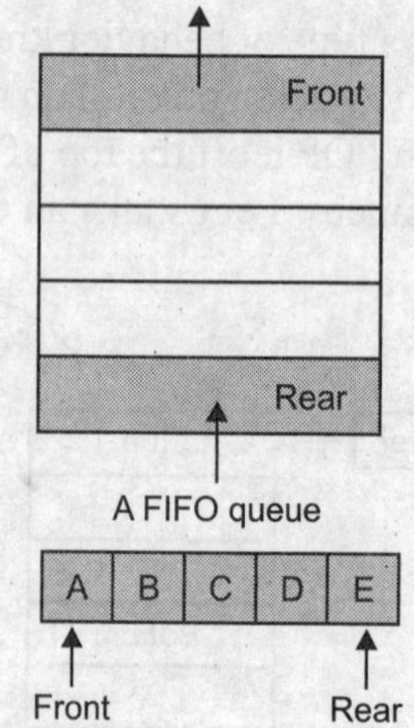

Figure 2.15: A Queue Representation

Student registration procedures in colleges and universities form the queue. As discussed, queues have front element and a rear element. The process of adding to queue is called as entering or inserting. The process of removing from queue is called as leaving or deleting. It does not matter when we draw queue growing from left to right or from right to left. Different views of Queue are as shown in the Figure 2.16:

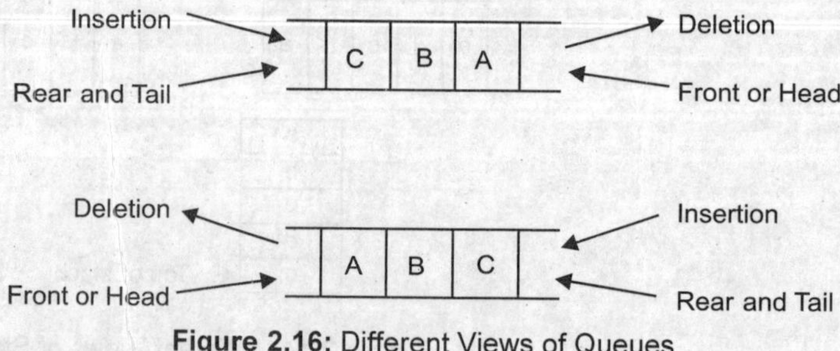

Figure 2.16: Different Views of Queues

(i) Circular queue

As the name suggests, this queue is not straight but circular, it looks like this

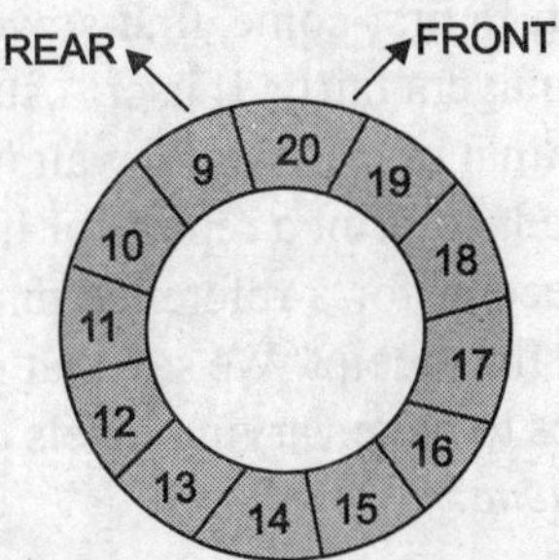

Figure 2.17: Circular Queue

In this Circular queue, once the queue is full, the "first" element of the queue becomes the "rear" most element of the queue. Initially when the queue is empty "front" and "rear" values are 0 and –1. Queue has got null values to all its elements. Every time when we add an element to the queue, the "rear" value increments by one till the time it reaches the upper limit of the queue after which it starts all over again from 0. Here the condition front>rear wont work

(ii) Double-ended queue

A double-ended queue (often abbreviated to deque, pronounced deck) is an abstract data structure that implements a queue for which elements can only be added to or removed from the front (head) or back (tail). It is also often called a head-tail linked list.

Definition: *A* deque *is a sequence where elements can be added and removed at both ends (front and rear) of the sequence, but not in the middle.*

In the preceding section we saw that a Queue comprises a pile of objects into which we insert items at one end and from which we remove items at the other end. In this section we examine an extension of the Queue, which provides a means to insert and remove items at both ends of the pile. This data structure is a *Deque*. A Deque is as shown in the Figure 2.18

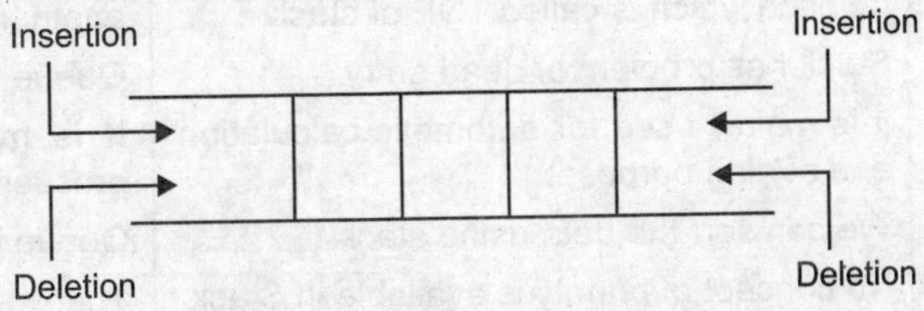

Figure 2.18: Double-Ended Queue

(iii) Priority queue

Previously, we've looked at the Queue data structure, which allowed accessing the data elements in first-come, first-serve fashion. Queues are useful for implementing resource managers fairly. If user A submits his print job to a printer before user B, it's only fair that user B should wait until user A is done to get his output. But what if user B needs to print a report for his meeting with the boss, while user A is just printing a receipt for a reference manual he just ordered. Obviously, user A can wait to print the receipt. We say that user B's job has higher *priority* than user A's. To allow jobs to have varying levels of priority, we replace our regular queue with a *priority queue*.

Definition: *"A data structure that supports efficient insertions of new element and deletion of elements with the highest priority is known as Priority Queue".*

In case the two or more elements have the same priority then these elements are processed in the order they were added to the Queue. The Queues are called "priority" Queues because they enable you to retrieve elements not by the insertion time (as in a stack or queue), nor by a key match (as in a dictionary), but by which element has the highest priority of retrieval.

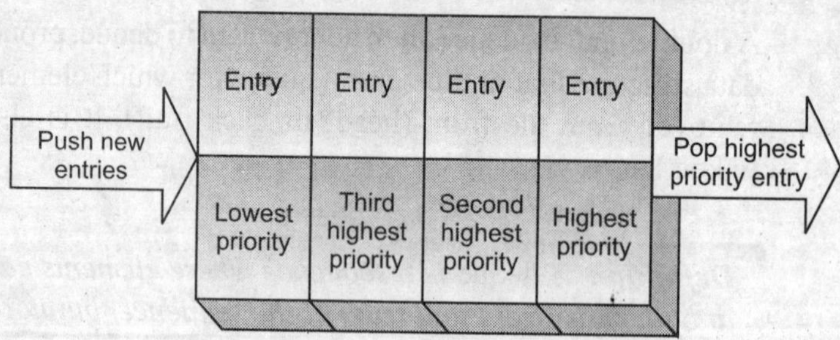

Figure 2.19: Priority Queue

Stack	Queue
It is based on the concept of LIFO stand for last in first out.	It is based on the concept of FIFO stand for first in first out.
It has only one end for insertion as well as deletion which is called TOP of stack.	It has two ends one Rear for insertion and another Front for deletion.
Stack has problem of dead entry.	Queue is free from dead entry problem.
it is mainly used for arithmetic calculation and sorting purpose.	It is mainly in operating system job processing and in simulation.
We can sort the data using stack.	Queue is not used in sorting purpose.
No concept of priority is available in Stack.	There are some queue which are based on priority concept

2.4.2 Non-Linear Data Structure

A data structure whose elements do not forms a sequence, or a having complex structure, there is no unique predecessor or unique successor. For example tree, graph, hash tables etc.

1. *Tree*

Tree is one of the most important nonlinear data structure. It is extremely useful whenever data naturally fit together in a hierarchical structure. It is an acyclic connected graph where each node has a set of zero or more children nodes, and at most one parent node.

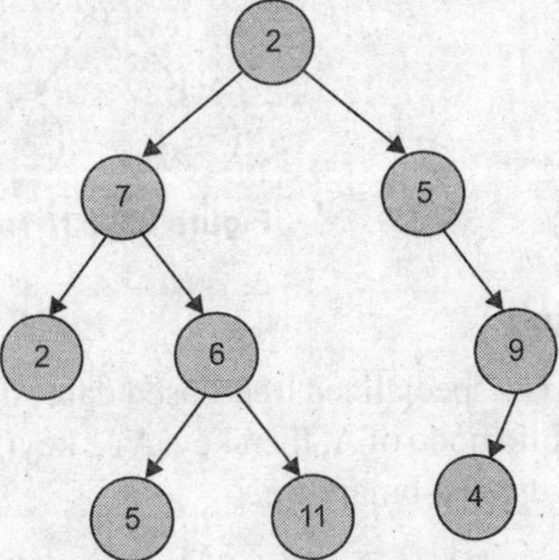

Figure 2.20: Simple Tree Structure

A node is a structure which may contain a value, a condition, or represent a separate data structure (which could be a tree of its own). Each node in a tree has zero or more child nodes, which are below it in the tree (by convention, trees grow down, not up as they do in nature). A node that has a child is called the child's parent node (or ancestor node, or superior). A node has at most one parent.

Nodes that do not have any children are called leaf nodes. They are also referred to as terminal nodes.

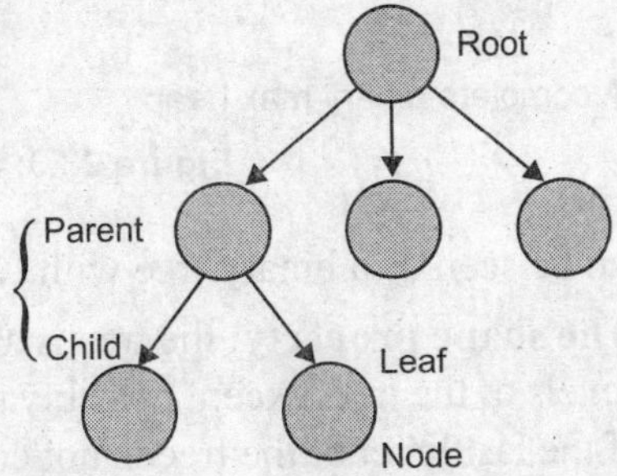

Figure 2.21: Representation of Tree Data Structure

Data contained in the tree exist in a logical relationship i.e. like that of parents to children. Each node, or child, in the tree may have one, many or no children.

A tree is defined as finite set 'T' having one or more nodes, such that there is specially designated node called the Root of the Tree, the remaining nodes are partitioned into disjoint sets T1, T2 … Tn and each of these sets is a tree, in turn.

The portioned trees are called as children or sub- trees of the Root.

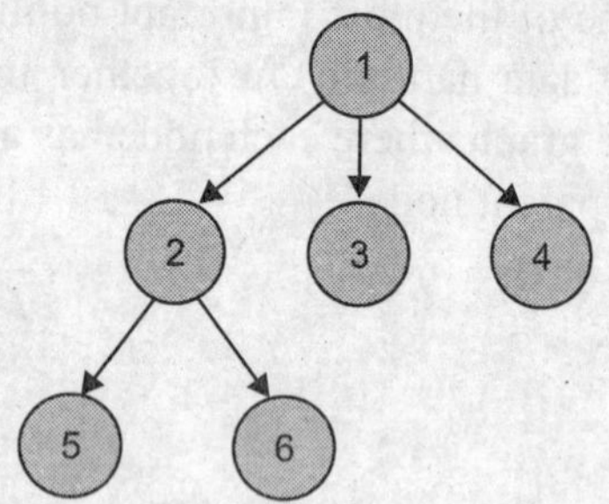

Figure 2.22: N-Tree Data Structure

2. Heaps

A heap is a specialized tree-based data structure that satisfies the heap property: if B is a child node of A, then key(A) ≥ key(B). A binary heap is a heap data structure created using a binary tree.

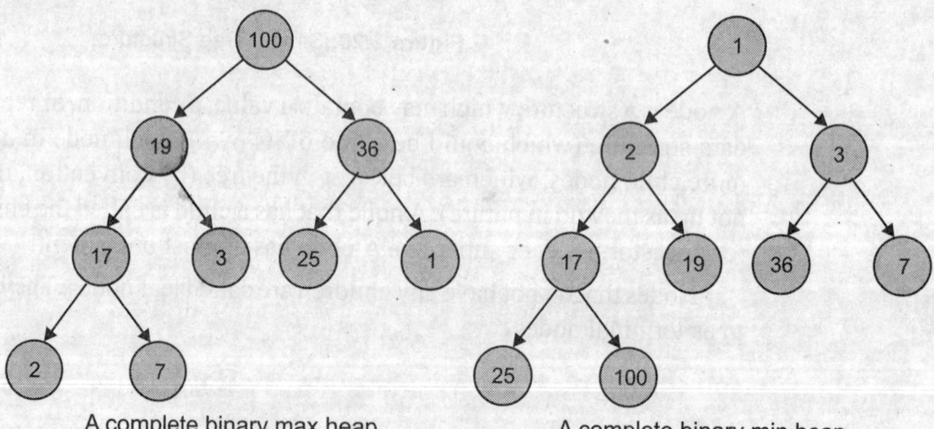

Figure 2.23: Binary Heaps

It can be seen as a binary tree with two additional constraints:

1. **The shape property:** the tree is an almost complete binary tree; that is, all levels of the tree, except possibly the last one (deepest) are fully filled, and, if the last level of the tree is not complete, the nodes of that level are filled from left to right.

2. **The heap property:** each node is greater than or equal to each of its children according to some comparison predicate which is fixed for the entire data structure.

"Greater than" means according to whatever comparison function is chosen to sort the heap, not necessarily "greater than" in the mathematical sense (since the quantities are not always numerical). Heaps where the comparison function is mathematical "greater than" are called max-heaps; those where the comparison function is mathematical "less than" are called "min-heaps."

The several variants of heaps are the prototypical most efficient implementations of the abstract data type priority queues. Priority queues are useful in many applications. In particular, heaps are crucial in several efficient graph algorithms.

3. Graph

The tree structure is a special kind of graph in which the relationship between parent and child is hierarchical. A general graph is a structure that represents a less restrictive relationship between data elements.

Definition: *"A graph data structure consists mainly of a finite (and possibly mutable) set of ordered pairs, called edges or arcs, of certain entities called nodes or vertices. As in mathematics, an edge (x,y) is said to point or go from x to y."*

A graph is a set of points and a set of lines, with each line joining one point to another. The points are called the nodes of the graph and the lines are called the edges. A graph is a set of node and edges. Node is a data element of the graph; an edge is a path between two nodes.

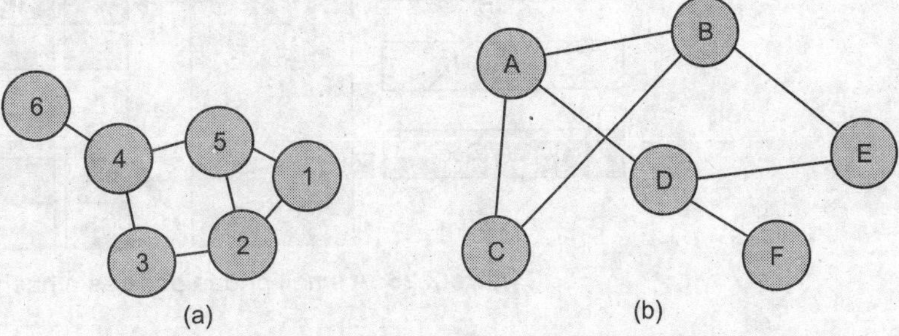

Figure 2.24: Graphs having 6 vertices and 7 edges

Figure 2.25 shows three examples of graphs. Notice that graphs, unlike trees, can have sets of nodes that are disconnected from other sets of nodes. For example, graph (a) has two distinct, unconnected sets of nodes. Graphs can also contain cycles. Graph (b) has several cycles. One cycle is the path from v_1 to v_2 to v_4 and back to v_1. Another one is from v_1 to v_2 to v_3 to v_5 to v_4 and back to v_1. (There are also cycles in graph (a)). Graph (c) does not have any cycles, as it has one less edge than it does number of nodes, and all nodes are reachable. Therefore, it is a tree.

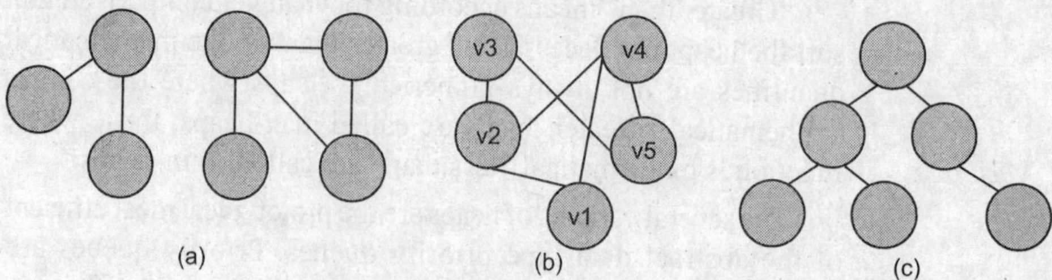

Figure 2.25: Three Examples of Graphs

Many real-world problems can be modeled using graphs. For example, search engines like Google model the Internet as a graph, where Web pages are the nodes in the graph and the links among Web pages are the edges. Programs like Microsoft MapPoint that can generate driving directions from one city to another use graphs, modeling cities as nodes in a graph and the roads connecting the cities as edges.

4. *Hash Tables*

The simplest data structure is the hash table. The basis of a hash table is a hash function. A hash function is a function that takes an element of whatever data type you are storing (integer, string, etc) and outputs an integer in a certain range. This integer is used to determine the location in the table for that element.

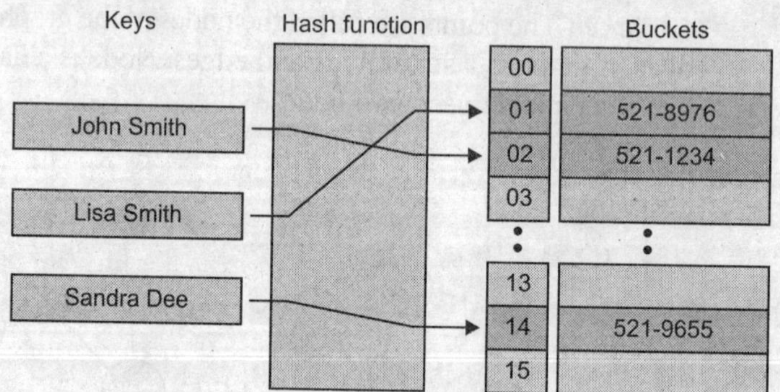

Figure 2.26: A small phone book as a hash table

The hash table itself consists of an array whose indices are the range of the hash function. A hash table or hash map is a data structure that uses a hash function to efficiently map certain identifiers or keys (e.g., person names) to associated values (e.g., their telephone numbers). The hash function is used to transform the key into the index (the hash) of an array element (the slot or bucket) where the corresponding value is to be sought.

Hash function

At the heart of the hash table algorithm is a simple array of items; this is often simply called the hash table. Hash table algorithms calculate an index from the data item's key and use this index to place the data into the array. The implementation of this calculation is the hash function, *f*:

$$\text{Index} = f(\text{key, Array Length})$$

The hash function calculates an index within the array from the data key. Array Length is the size of the array.

2.5 COMPARISON OF DATA STRUCTURES

Different characteristics having some advantages and disadvantages are as shown in a tabular form:

Data structure	Advantages	Disadvantages
Array	Quick inserts Fast access if index known	Slow search Slow deletes Fixed size
Ordered array	Faster search than unsorted array	Slow inserts Slow deletes Fixed size
Stack	Last-in, first-out access	Slow access to other items
Queue	First-in, first-out access	Slow access to other items
Linked List	Quick inserts Quick deletes	Slow search
Tree	Quick search Quick inserts Quick deletes *(Tree always remains balanced)* *(Similar trees good for disk storage)*	Complex to implement
Binary Tree	Quick search Quick inserts Quick deletes *(If the tree remains balanced)*	Deletion algorithm is complex
Graph	Best models real-world situations	Some algorithms are slow and very complex
Heap	Quick inserts Quick deletes Access to largest item	Slow access to other items

2.6 COMMON OPERATIONS ON DATA STRUCTURES

Data structure as we know that is a collection of data element arranged in either mathematical or logical form. Following are the operations, which are frequently used with data structures.

1. **Creation:** It is used to create data structure.

   For example:

   (i) In C++ programming language, you often have used declaration statement.

   int a;

   That creates space for variable a, which store integer type of value or data.

   (ii) In C++ programming language malloc (size) function also dynamically allocates a portion of memory of size, size and returns a pointer to an item of type char.

   Syntax: pointer-variable = (data type *) malloc (size);

2. **Selection:** It accesses data within data structure. The form of the selection depends to a significant degree on the type of data structure being accessed.
3. **Updating:** It changes the data in structure. An assignment operator is an example of an update operation. The cost of performing an update operation is an important property, which must be considered in data structure.
4. **Deletion or Destroy:** It destroys the data structure, which was created with the help of creation operation. Destroy operation is not a necessary operation; it helps in the efficient use of memory. For example:

   (i) In C++ programming language, you have used free ( ) function to free the storage of a dynamically allocated variable using malloc ( ) Function.

   Syntax: free (pointer_variable)

   Calling free (p) makes the storage occupied by pointer p available for reuse, if necessary.

5. **Sorting:** This operation is used to arrange data in some logical order that is either in Ascending or Descending order. There are various type of sorting algorithm available with different space and time complexities. The commonly used algorithm for sorting are: Bubble sort, Quick Sort, Heap Sort, Insertion sort etc.
6. **Searching:** Computer systems are often used to store large amounts of data from which individually records must be retired according to some search criterion. Thus the efficient facilitate fast searching is an important issue

this operation is used to search some particular item from list of items. There are two major method used for searching, known as Linear search and Binary Search.

7. **Traversing:** Traversing is one of the most common operations that mean to see each and every element at least once. The algorithm used to traverse an array is:

```
For I=1 to 10
Process A [I]
I=I+1
End for
```

8. **Copying:** This data structure operation is used to copy the contents of one object to another object.
9. **Concatenation:** This data structure is used to join two or more object into single object; this operation is normally used with string data structures.
10. **Merging:** It is similar to concatenation but the basic difference is that is can be applied on integers, floating pointer number as well.
11. **Splitting:** In this operation, records in a very large file are split into smaller files for processing.

2.7 APPLICATION OF DATA STRUCTURE

Thorough knowledge of a programming language is not a sufficient base upon which to make these decisions. The study of data structure will expose you to a vast collection of tried and proves methods used in designing efficient programs. Thus as you develop awareness of data structures you will begin to realize the considerations involved in large scale software projects. There are some applications of various data structure in such diverse area as:

1. It gives considerable help in Compiler design
2. It provides the methods of representing the data elements in the memory of computer efficiently.
3. It describe the physical and logical relationship between the data item
4. It provides considerable help in managing the Operating Systems
5. Data base management system
6. Statistical analysis packages
7. We can solve several numerical problems with the help of data structure.
8. It helps lot in Graphics applications.
9. Data structure find its major applications in Artificial intelligence

10. Data structure is also useful in Simulation
11. Data structures are used to find the shortest between two nodes in a network and to analyze the network completely.

The greatest difficulties of writing large computer program are not in deciding what the goals of the program should be, not even in finding methods that can be used to reach these goals. The president of a bassinet might say, "Let's get a computer to keep track of all our inventory information, accounting records and personnel file, and let it tell us when inventories need to be recorded and budget lines are overspent and let it handle the payroll," with enough time and effort, a staff of system analysts and programmers might be able to determine how various staff members are now doing these tasks and write program to do the work in the same way. The essence of programming and contemporary data processing requires efficient algorithms for accessing the data both in main memory and so secondary storage devices. The efficiency is fiercely linked to the structure of the data being preceded.

2.8 STRINGS

Combination of characters (group of character) is called string. "I am a good boy" is a string. We can print or display the string by using the cout function as:

```
cout<<"\n I am a good boy \n";
```

But if the string is stored in variable, then such type of variable should be of character type. Also character variable should be declared in the array form (single dimensional form if you read or write a single string, but if you want to read / write more than one string, then use two-dimensional array).

The use of string is as follows:

```
char city [20];
cout<< city;                    /* to print a single dimensional string */
      or
char city[5][20];
for (i=0; i <5; i++)            /* to print multi-dimensional strings */
{
cout<<city[i];
}
```

2.9 VARIOUS OPERATIONS ON STRING

String has number of operations in the C++ language, but some commonly used are as follow:

(i) Initialization of string variable
(ii) Reading and writing of string

(iii) Combining strings together
(iv) Copy one string to another
(v) Comparing two strings
(vi) Extracting a portion of string
(vii) To reverse a string
(viii) To find whether a string is palindrome or not

2.9.1 Initialization of String Variable

We can initialize or declare string variable by using the character data-type. For example, below is a valid string declaration statement:

```
char city[10];            (if it is a single string – one dimensional string array )
```

Here in such type of declaration only one string you can read / write having maximum length 9 characters. Last character always be a null character.

```
char city[10] [20];  (if it has multiple strings – two dimensional string array)
```

Similarly in this declaration you can read / write number of strings, but not more than 10 strings and every string has length not more than 19 characters. Last character always be a null character.

The general syntax is as follows:

```
static data-type array-name[size] = {list of values};
```

For example, suppose you want to enter the string "BOMBAY" to the city variable, then the procedure is as:

```
static char city[10] = {'B', 'O', 'M', 'B', 'A', 'Y','\0'};
```

The data type always should be character type in the string handling.

Also more than one string can be handled by using the double dimensional string array.

The general syntax is as:

```
static data-type array-name[row size][col. size] =  { {list of row 1};
                                                       {list of row 2};
                                                       ... ... ...
                                                       {list of row n} };
```

For example, suppose if you want to assign three different cities data values to the city string variable, then this can be done as:

```
static char city[2][20] = { {'A', 'M', 'R', 'I', 'T', 'S', 'A', 'R', '\0'}
                            {'M', 'O', 'G', 'A', '\0'}}
```

Note that data-type always should be of character type.

2.9.2 Reading and Writing A String

We can read the string by using the cin function. The function cin is used to read the character string from the terminal.

For example, if you want to read only single city data, then the procedure is as:

```
char city [10];
cin>>city;
```

Also if you want to read more than one strings (10 strings and every string have maximum 19 number of character, 20th is the null character), then the procedure is as follows:

```
char city [10][20];
for (i=0; i < 10; i++)
{
cin>>city[i];
}
```

Similarly the procedure to write or print the above said string(s) on monitor screen or to print on printer is as:

```
char city[10];
cout<<city;
```

The procedure for more than one string is as:

```
char city[10][20];
for (i=0; i < 10; i++)
{
cout<<city[i];
}
```

If you want to read two strings, then this can be done as:

```
char city1[10], city2[10];
cin>>city1>>city2;
```

2.10 STRING HANDLING FUNCTIONS

C++ language is rich in library functions, but to handle or operate some operations with string, we use some powerful string-handling functions. All these function are linked with the "string.h" header file stored in the include sub-directory in the Turbo-C++ compiler. So note that all the string handling function requires to declare "string.h" header file in the link section before declaration and use.

Here we explain the five commonly used string handling function as:

(i) strcat ( )

(ii) strcmp ( )

(iii) strcpy ( )
(iv) strlen ( )
(v) strrev ( )
(vi) strlwr ( )
(vii) strupr ( )

(i) strcat ( )

The purpose of this string handling function strcat ( ) is to concatenate or combine two different strings together.

The general syntax used for this is as:

```
strcat(string1, string2);
```

Here string1 is combined with string2 and result will be stored {combined string} in string1.

Also we can concatenate more than one string by using nested concatenation:

```
strcat (strcat (string1, string2), string3);
```

Program 1: Write a C++ program to append string: how to use strcat.

```
#include<conio.h>
#include<iostream.h>
#include<string.h>
void main()
{
char str[80];
clrscr();
strcpy (str,"part I,  ");
strcat (str,"part II, ");
strcat (str,"part III.");
cout<<str;
getch();
}
```

Output:

part I, part II, part III.

(ii) strcmp( )

The purpose of this function is to compare two strings. It will check which string is alphabetically above the others. For comparison ASCII (American Standard Code for Information Interchange) values are used.

The general syntax is as:

```
strcmp (string1, string2);
```

If the ASCII difference of each character in the two different strings from the first alphabet (till null character of any string occurs first) is zero, then both the strings are equal. If difference is -ve, then string2 is larger than the string1, but if the difference is +ve, then string1 is larger than the string2.

```
char string1[20] , string2[20];
```

Program 2: Write a C++ program to compare strings: strcmp.

```
#include<conio.h>
#include<iostream.h>
#include<string.h>
void main()
{
char word1[20];
char word2[20];
cout<<" first word:\n1: ";
cin>>word1;
cout<<" second word:\n 2: ";
cin>>word2;
if(strcmp(word1,word2) == 0)
cout<<"identical words";
else
cout<<" (strcmp(word1, word2) > 0) ? word2 : word1<< "comes before"<<(strcmp(word1, word2) < 0) ? word2 : word1;
getch();
}
```

Output:

```
first word:
1: 2009
second word:
2: 2008
2008 comes before 2009
```

(iii) strcpy ( )

The purpose of this function is to copy one string into another string. Target or destination field should be larger than the source field. In other words size of the string1 should be larger to receive the contents of the string2.

The general syntax is as follows:

```
strcpy (string1, string2);
```

It will copy the data from the string2 to the string1 variable. Also note that the length of the string1 should be larger than string2.

Program 3: Write a C++ program to show how to use strcpy (string copy).

```
#include<conio.h>
#include<string.h>
#include<iostream.h>
char name[30]; // First name of someone
void main()
{
strcpy(name, "Sam"); // Initialize the name
cout<<"The name is "<< name<<"\n";
getch();
}
```

Output:

The name is sam

(iv) strlen ( )

The purpose of this function is to count the number of character in a string i.e. to find the length of the string.

The general syntax is as:

```
n = strlen (string);
```

where n should be of integer type and string variable should be of character type.

Program 4: Write a C++ program to computes the length of a line.

```
#include<conio.h>
#include<string.h>
#include<iostream.h>
void main()
{
char line[100];
cout<<"Enter a line: ";
cin.get(line,100)
cout<<"The length of the line is: "<<strlen(line)<<"\n";
getch();
}
```

Output:

Enter a line:good boy

Length (including newline) is: 9

(v) strrev ( )

The purpose of this function is to reverse a string. This function takes string variable as its single (only one) argument. Here the first character becomes last and last character becomes first in a string.

The general syntax used for this function is as follows:

```
strrev(st);
```

Here st is a string (character type) variable.

Program 5: Write a C++ program to reverse a string.

```
#include<iostream.h>
#include<string.h>
#include<conio.h>
void main()
{
char b[70];
cout<<"\nSpecify the string:";
cin.get(b,70);
cout<<"\nString before reversing:"<<b;
cout<<"\nString after reversing:"<<strrev(b);
getch();
}
```

Output:

String before reversing: world
String after reversing: dlrow

(vi) strlwr ( )

This function converts all characters in a string from uppercase to lowercase.

The general syntax is:

```
strlwr(string);
```

For example: strlwr("BABY") converts to baby.

Program 6: Write a C++ program to covert uppercase string to lowercase. How to use strlwr.

```
#include<conio.h>
#include<iostream.h>
#include<string.h>
void main()
{
char str[80];
clrscr();
cout<<"Enter the string in uppercase:";
cin>>str;
strlwr(str);
cout<<"The string in lowercase is "<< str;
```

```
getch();
}
Output:
Enter the string in uppercase: BABY
The string in lowercase is baby
```

(vii) strupr( )

This function converts all characters in a string from lower case to uppercase.

The general syntax is:

```
strupr(string);
```

For example: strupr("baby") will convert the string to BABY.

Program 7: Write a C++ program to covert lowercase string to uppercase. How to use strupr.

```
#include<conio.h>
#include<iostream.h>
#include<string.h>
void main()
{
char str[80];
clrscr();
cout<<"Enter the string in lowercase:";
cin>>str;
strupr(str);
cout<<"The string in uppercase is "<< str;
getch();
}
```

Output:

```
Enter the string in lowercase: baby
The string in uppercase is BABY
```

2.11 STRING SEARCHING ALGORITHM

String searching algorithms, sometimes called **string matching algorithms**, are an important class of string algorithms that try to find a place where one or several strings (also called patterns) are found within a larger string or text.

Let Σ be an alphabet (finite set). Formally, both the pattern and searched text are concatenations of elements of Σ. The Σ may be a usual human alphabet (for example, the letters A through Z in English). Other applications may use binary alphabet (Σ = {0,1}) or DNA alphabet (Σ = {A,C,G,T}) in bioinformatics.

In practice, how the string is encoded can affect the feasible string search algorithms. In particular if a variable width encoding is in use then it is slow (time proportional to N) to find the Nth character. This will significantly slow down many of the more advanced search algorithms. A possible solution is to search for the sequence of code units instead, but doing so may produce false matches unless the encoding is specifically designed to avoid it.

2.12 BASIC CLASSIFICATION

The various algorithms can be classified by the number of patterns each uses.

2.12.1 Single Pattern Algorithms

Let m be the length of the pattern and let n be the length of the searchable text.

Algorithm	Preprocessing time	Matching time
Naïve string search algorithm	0 (no preprocessing)	Θ((n–m+1) m)
Rabin-Karp string search algorithm	Σ(m)	average Θ(n+m), worst Θ((n–m+1) m)
Finite state automaton based search	Θ(m |Σ|)	Θ(n)
Knuth-Morris-Pratt algorithm	Θ(m)	Θ(n)
Boyer–Moore string search algorithm	Θ(m + |Σ|)	Ω(n/m), O(n)
Bitap algorithm (shift-or, shift-and, Baeza-Yates-Gonnet)	Θ(m + |Σ|)	O(mn)

Asymptotic times are expressed using O, Ω, and Σ notation

The **Boyer–Moore string search algorithm** has been the standard benchmark for the practical string search literature.

Algorithms using finite set of patterns

- Aho-Corasick algorithm
- Commentz-Walter algorithm
- Rabin-Karp string search algorithm

Algorithms using infinite number of patterns

Naturally, the patterns can not be enumerated in this case. They are represented usually by a regular grammar or regular expression.

2.12.2 Other Classification

Other classification approaches are possible. One of the most common uses preprocessing as main criteria.

Classes of string searching algorithms

	Text not preprocessed	Text preprocessed
Patterns not preprocessed	Elementary algorithms	Index methods
Patterns preprocessed	Constructed search engines	Signature methods

1. *NAÏVE String Search*

The simplest and least efficient way to see where one string occurs inside another is to check each place it could be, one by one, to see if it's there. So first we see if there's a copy of the needle in the first character of the haystack; if not, we look to see if there's a copy of the needle starting at the second character of the haystack; if not, we look starting at the third character, and so forth.

In the normal case, we only have to look at one or two characters for each wrong position to see that it is a wrong position, so in the average case, this takes O(n + m) steps, where n is the length of the haystack and m is the length of the needle; but in the worst case, searching for a string like "aaaab" in a string like "aaaaaaaaab", it takes O(nm) steps.

2. *Finite State Automaton Based Search*

In this approach, we avoid backtracking by constructing a deterministic finite automaton (DFA) that recognizes strings containing the desired search string. These are expensive to construct—they are usually created using the powerset construction—but very quick to use.

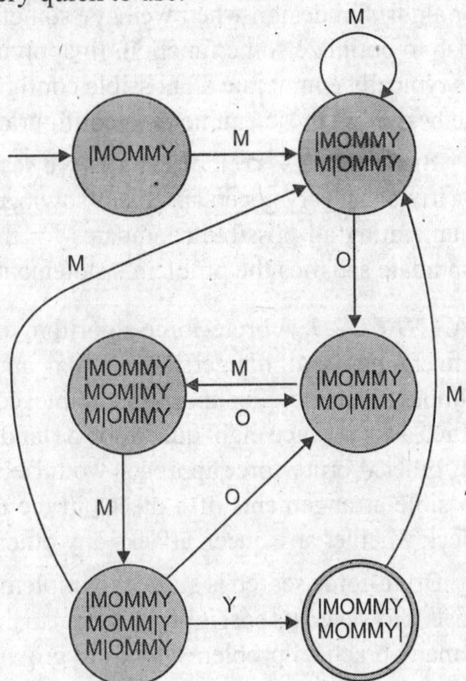

For example, the DFA shown to the right recognizes the word "MOMMY". This approach is frequently generalized in practice to search for arbitrary regular expressions.

3. Stubs

Knuth–Morris–Pratt computes a DFA that recognizes inputs with the string to search for as a suffix, Boyer–Moore starts searching from the end of the needle, so it can usually jump ahead a whole needle-length at each step. Baeza–Yates keeps track of whether the previous j characters were a prefix of the search string, and is therefore adaptable to fuzzy string searching. The bitap algorithm is an application of Baeza-Yates' approach.

4. Index Methods

Faster search algorithms are based on preprocessing of the text. After building a substring index, for example a suffix tree or suffix array, the occurrences of a pattern can be found quickly. As an example, a suffix tree can be built in $\Theta(m)$ time, and all z occurrences of a pattern can be found in $O(m + z)$ time (if the alphabet size is viewed as a constant).

2.13 BRUTE FORCE ALGORITHM

In computer science, the brute force algorithm design pattern is a powerful technique for algorithm design when we have something we wish to search for or when we wish to optimize some function. In applying this technique in a general solution, we typically enumerate all possible configurations of the inputs involved and pick the best of all these enumerated configurations.

Brute-force search or **exhaustive search**, also known as **generate and test,** is a trivial but very general problem-solving technique that consists of systematically enumerating all possible candidates for the solution and checking whether each candidate satisfies the problem's statement.

EXAMPLE 2.2: A brute-force algorithm to find the divisors of a natural number n is to enumerate all integers from 1 to n, and check whether each of them divides n without remainder. For another example, consider the popular eight queens puzzle, which asks to place eight queens on a standard chessboard so that no queen attacks any other. A brute-force approach would examine all the 64!/56!8! = 4,426,165,368 possible arrangements of 8 pieces in the 64 squares, and, for each arrangement, check whether any queen attacks any other.

Brute-force search is simple to implement, and will always find a solution if it exists. However, its cost is proportional to the number of candidate solutions, which, in many practical problems, tends to grow very quickly as the size of the problem increases. Therefore, brute-force search is typically used when the problem size is limited, or when there are problem-specific heuristics that can be used to reduce the set of candidate solutions to a manageable size.

2.13.1 Main Features of Brute Force Algorithm

- no preprocessing phase;
- constant extra space needed;
- always shifts the window by exactly 1 position to the right;
- comparisons can be done in any order;
- searching phase in **O**(mn) time complexity;
- 2n expected text characters comparisons.

2.13.2 Description

The brute force algorithm consists in checking, at all positions in the text between 0 and n-m, whether an occurrence of the pattern starts there or not. Then, after each attempt, it shifts the pattern by exactly one position to the right.

The brute force algorithm requires no preprocessing phase, and a constant extra space in addition to the pattern and the text. During the searching phase the text character comparisons can be done in any order. The time complexity of this searching phase is **O**(mn) (when searching for $a^{m-1}b$ in a^n for instance). The expected number of text character comparisons is 2n.

The C++ code

```
void BF(char *x, int m, char *y, int n) {
int i, j;
/* Searching */
for (j = 0; j <= n - m; ++j) {
for (i = 0; i < m && x[i] == y[i + j]; ++i);
if (i >= m)
OUTPUT(j);
}}
```

This algorithm can be rewriting to give a more efficient algorithm in practice as follows:

```
#define EOS '\0'
void BF(char *x, int m, char *y, int n) {
char *yb;
/* Searching */
for (yb = y; *y != EOS; ++y)
if (memcmp(x, y, m) == 0)
```

```
OUTPUT(y - yb);
}
```

The brute-force pattern matching algorithm compares the pattern **P** with the text **T** for each possible shift of **P** relative to **T**, until either

- a match is found, or
- all placements of the pattern have been tried

Brute-force pattern matching runs in time **O(nm)**

EXAMPLE 2.3: Worst Case

- **T = aaa … ah**
- **P = aaah**
- may occur in images and DNA sequences
- unlikely in English text

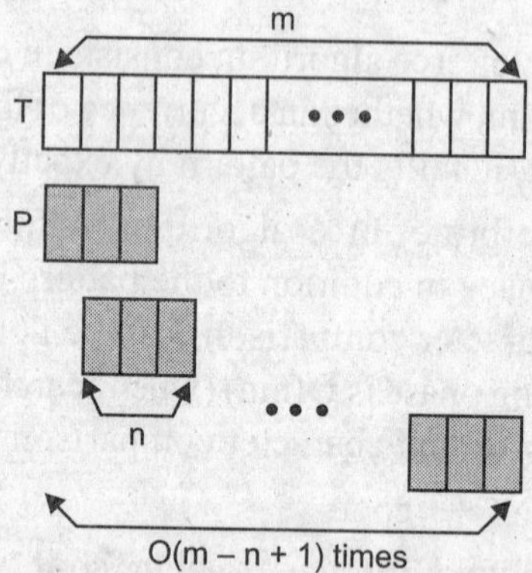

ALGORITHM 2.1: BruteForceMatch(T, P)

Step 1: Input text T of size n and pattern P of size m

Step 2: Output starting index of a substring of T equal to P or –1 if no such substring exists

Step 3: for i ← 0 to n – m

{ test shift i of the pattern }

Step 4: j ← 0

Step 5: while j < m – T[i + j] = P[j]

Step 6: j ← j + 1

Step 7: if j = m

return i {match at i}

else break while loop {mismatch}

return -1 {no match anywhere}

Step 8: End.

The brute-force pattern matching algorithm could not be simpler. It consists of two nested loops, with the outer loop indexing through all possible starting indices of the pattern in the text, and the inner loop indexing through each character of the pattern, comparing it to its potentially corresponding character in the text. Thus, the correctness of the brute-force pattern matching algorithm follows immediately.

The running time of brute-force pattern matching in the worst case is not good, however, because, for each candidate indeed in T, we can perform up to m character comparisons to discover that P does not match T at the current index. Referring to Algorithm, we see that the outer for-loop is executed at most n – m + 1 times, and the inner loop is executed at most m times. Thus, the running time of the brute-force method is O((n – m + 1), which is O(nm). Note that, when m = n/2, this algorithm has quadratic running time $O(n^2)$.

EXAMPLE 2.4:

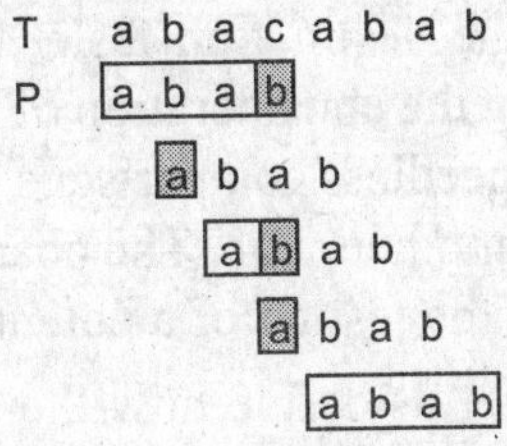

```
T  a b a c a b a b
P  a b a b
     a b a b
       a b a b
         a b a b
             a b a b
```

Simple, but not efficient because it cannot avoid rescanning **T**.

2.14 BOYER-MOORE HEURISTICS

The Boyer-Moore string search algorithm is a particularly efficient string searching algorithm, and it has been the standard benchmark for the practical string search literature. It was developed by Bob Boyer and J Strother Moore in 1977. The algorithm preprocesses the target string (key) that is being searched for, but not the string being searched in (unlike some algorithms that preprocess the string to be searched and can then amortize the expense of the preprocessing by searching repeatedly). The execution time of the Boyer-Moore algorithm can be sub-linear: it doesn't need to check every character of the string to be searched, but rather skips over some of them. Generally the algorithm gets faster as the key being searched for becomes longer. Its efficiency derives from the fact that with each unsuccessful attempt to find a match between the search string and the text it's searching, it uses the information gained from that attempt to rule out as many positions of the text as possible where the string cannot match.

At first, we might feel that it is always necessary to examine every character in T in order to locate a pattern P as a substring. But this is not always the case, for the Boyer-Moore (BM) pattern matching algorithm, which we study in this section, can sometimes avoid comparisons between P and a sizeable fraction of the characters in T. The only caveat is that, whereas the brute-force algorithm can work even with a potentially unbounded alphabet, the BM algorithm assumes the alphabet is of fixed, finite size. It works the fastest when the alphabet is moderately sized and the pattern is relatively long. It works on following two heuristics:

Looking-Glass Heuristic: When testing a possible placement of P against T, begin the comparisons from the end of P and move backward to the front of P.

Character-Jump Heuristic: During the testing of a possible placement of P against T, mismatch of test character T[i] = c with the corresponding pattern character P[j] is handled as follows. If c is not contained anywhere in P, then shift P completely past T[i] (for it cannot match nay character in P). Otherwise, shift P until an occurrence of character c in P gets aligned with T[i].

The looking-glass heuristic sets up the other heuristic to allow us to avoid comparisons between P and whole groups of characters in T. In this case at least, we can get to the destination faster by going backwards, for if we encounter a mismatch during the consideration of P at a certain location in T, then we are likely to avoid lots of needless comparisons by significantly shifting P relative to T using the character-jump heuristic. The character-jump heuristic pays off bit if it can be applied early in the testing of a potential placement of P against T.

Therefore, let us define how the character-jump heuristics can be integrated into a string pattern matching algorithm. To implement this heuristic, we define a function last (c) that takes a character c from the alphabet and specifies how far we shift the pattern P if a character equal to c is found in the text that does not match the pattern. In particular, we define last (c) as follows:

If c is in P, last (c) is the index of the last (right-most) occurrence of c in P. Otherwise, we conventionally define last (c) = –1.

If characters can be used as indices in arrays, then the last function can be easily implemented as a looking table. We leave the method for computing this table efficiently as a simple exercise. The last function will give us all the information we need to perform the character-jump heuristic. In Algorithm below, we show the BM pattern matching method. The ump step is illustrated in Figure 2.27.

Algorithm 2.2: BoyerMooreMatch(T, P, Σ)

```
Step 1: L ← lastOccurenceFunction(P, Σ )
Step 2: i ← m – 1
Step 3: j ← m – 1
Step 4: repeat if T[i] = P[j]
Step 5: if j = 0
return i { match at i }
else
```

```
i ← i – 1
j ← j – 1
else
{ character-jump }
l ← L[T[i]]
i ← i + m – min(j, 1 + l)
j ← m – 1
until i > n – 1
return – 1 { no match }
Step 6: End.
```

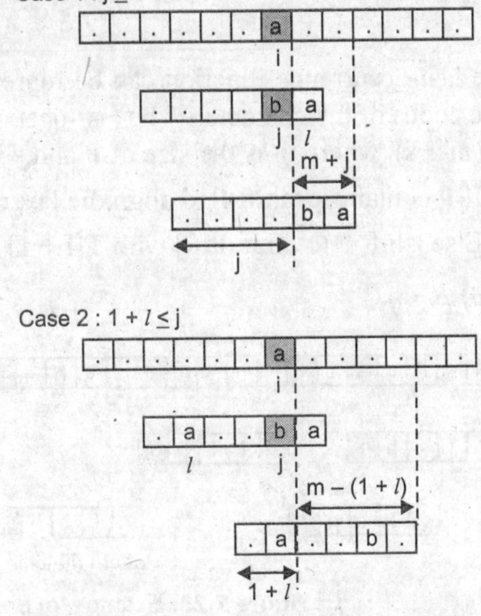

Figure 2.27: BM pattern matching method.

In Figure 2.28, we illustrate the execution of the Boyer-Moore matching algorithm.

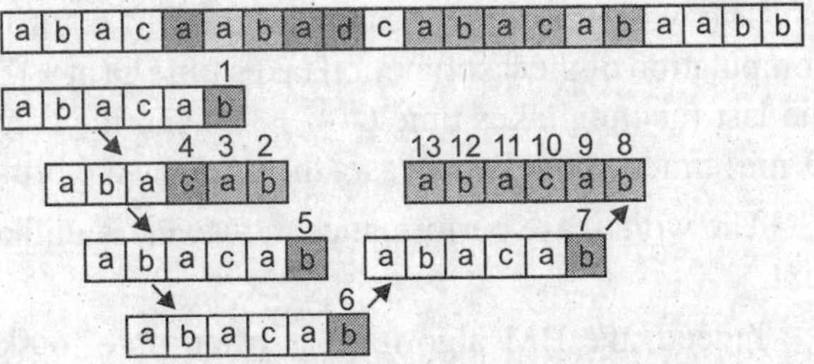

Figure 2.28: Execution of BM algorithm

2.14.1 Last-occurrence Function

Boyer-Moore's algorithm preprocesses the pattern **P** and the alphabet **Σ** to build the last-occurrence function **L** mapping **Σ** to integers, where **L(c)** is defined as

- the largest index **i** such that **P[i]** = **c** or
- –1 if no such index exists

Example 2.5

Σ = {**a, b, c, d**}

P = **abacab**

c	a	b	c	d
L(c)	4	5	3	–1

The last-occurrence function can be represented by an array indexed by the numeric codes of the characters The last-occurrence function can be computed in time **O**(**m** + **s**), where **m** is the size of **P** and **s** is the size of Σ.

- If **P** contains **c**, shift **P** to align the last occurrence of **c** in **P** with **T[i]**
- Else, shift **P** to align **P**[0] with **T**[**i** + 1]

EXAMPLE 2.6

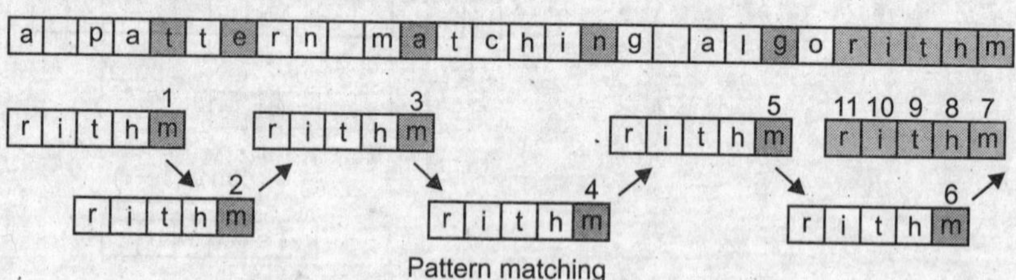

Pattern matching

Figure 2.29: Example of pattern matching

The correctness of the BM pattern matching algorithm follows from the fact that each time the method makes a shift, it is guaranteed not to 'skip' over any possible matches. For last (c) is the location of the last occurrence of c in P.

The worst-case running time of the BM algorithm is O(nm + |Σ|. Namely, the computation of the last function takes time O(m + |Σ|). Namely, the computation of the last function takes time O(m + |Σ|) and the actual search for the pattern takes O(nm) times in the worst case, the same as the brute-force algorithm.

The worst-case performance, however, is unlikely to be achieved for English text.

Indeed, the BM algorithm is often able to skip over large portions of the text. (Figure 2.29) There is experimental evidence that on English text, the average number of comparisons done per text character is approximately 0.24 for a five-character pattern string. The payoff is not as great for binary strings or for very short patterns, however, in which case the KMP algorithm, discussed or, for very short patterns, the brute-force algorithm, may be better.

EXAMPLE 2.7: Boyer-Moore's algorithm runs in time O(nm + s)

Example of worst case:

- **T = aaa … a**
- **P = baaa**

The worst case may occur in images and DNA sequences but is unlikely in English text

Boyer-Moore's algorithm is significantly faster than the brute-force algorithm on English text

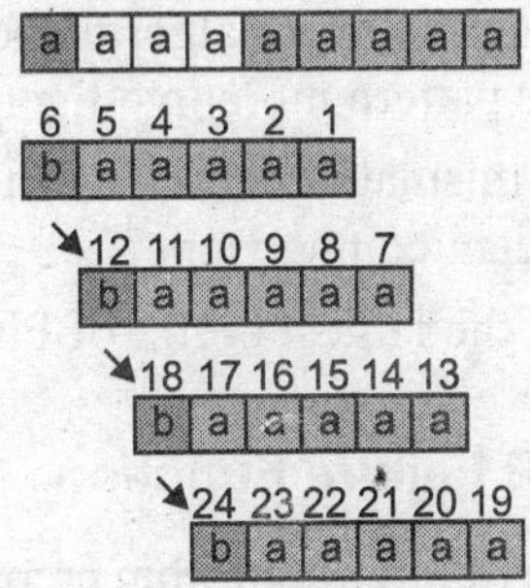

Figure 2.30: Example of boyer-moore's

We have actually presented a simplified version of the Boyer-Moore (BM) algorithm. The original BM algorithm achieves running time O(n + m + |Σ|) by using an alternative shift neuristic to the partially matches text string, whenever it shifts the pattern more than the character-jump heuristic. This alternative shift heuristic is based on applying the main idea from the Knuth-Morris-Pratt pattern matching algorithm, which we discuss next.

2.15 KNUTH–MORRIS–PRATT ALGORITHM

The **Knuth–Morris–Pratt string searching algorithm** (or **KMP algorithm**) searches for occurrences of a "word" W within a main "text string" S by employing the observation that when a mismatch occurs, the word itself embodies sufficient information to determine where the next match could begin, thus bypassing re-examination of previously matched characters.

The algorithm was conceived by Donald Knuth and Vaughan Pratt and independently by J. H. Morris in 1977, but the three published it jointly.

In this article, we will be using zero-based arrays for our strings; thus the 'C' in W (shown below) will be denoted W.

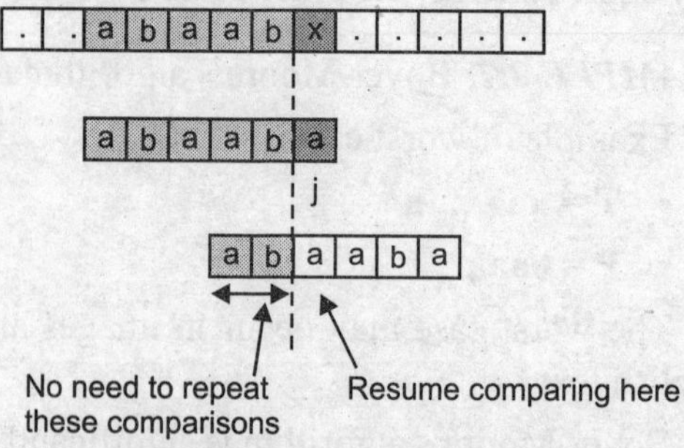

Figure 2.31: Knuth-Morris-Pratt

Knuth-Morris-Pratt's algorithm compares the pattern to the text in **left-to-right**, but shifts the pattern more intelligently than the brute-force algorithm.

When a mismatch occurs, what is the **most** we can shift the pattern so as to avoid redundant comparisons?

Answer: the largest prefix of **P**[0..**j**] that is a suffix of **P**[1..**j**]

2.15.1 KMP Failure Function

Knuth-Morris-Pratt's algorithm preprocesses the pattern to find matches of prefixes of the pattern with the pattern itself.

The **failure function F(j)** is defined as the size of the largest prefix of **P**[0..**j**] that is also a suffix of **P**[1..**j**]

Knuth-Morris-Pratt's algorithm modifies the bruteforce algorithm so that if a mismatch occurs at **P**[**j**] ≠ **T**[**i**] we set **j** ← **F**(**j** – 1)

j	0	1	2	3	4	5
P[j]	a	b	a	a	b	a
F(j)	0	0	1	1	2	3

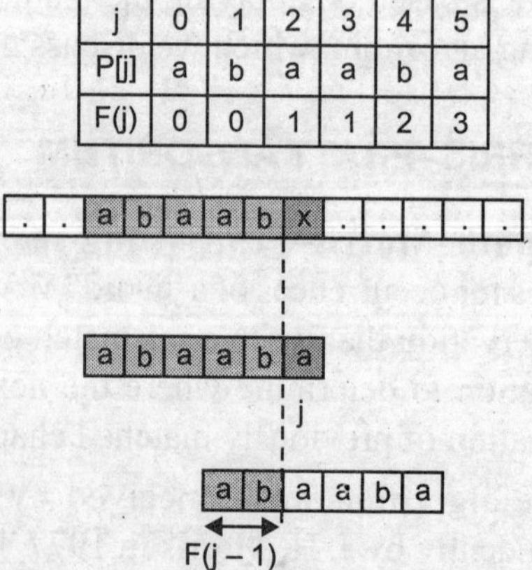

Figure 2.32: KMP failure function

2.15.2 The KMP Algorithm

The failure function can be represented by an array and can be computed in **O(m)** time At each iteration of the whileloop, either

- **i** increases by one, or
- the shift amount **i – j**

increases by at least one (observe that **F(j – 1) < j**). Hence, there are no more than 2**n** iterations of the while-loop. Thus, KMP's algorithm runs in optimal time **O(m + n)**.

Algorithm 2.3: KMPMatch(T, P)

```
Step 1: F ← failureFunction(P)
Step 2: i ← 0
Step 3: j ← 0
Step 4: while i < n
Step 5: if T[i] = P[j]
Step 6: if j = m – 1
return i – j { match }
else i ← i + 1
j ← j + 1
else if j > 0
j ← F[j – 1]
else i ← i + 1
return – 1 { no match }
Step 7: End.
```

2.15.3 Computing the Failure Function

The failure function can be represented by an array and can be computed in **O(m)** time The construction is similar to the KMP algorithm itself At each iteration of the whileloop, either

- **i** increases by one, or
- the shift amount **i – j**

increases by at least one (observe that **F(j – 1) < j**). Hence, there are no more than 2**m** iterations of the while-loop.

EXAMPLE 2.8

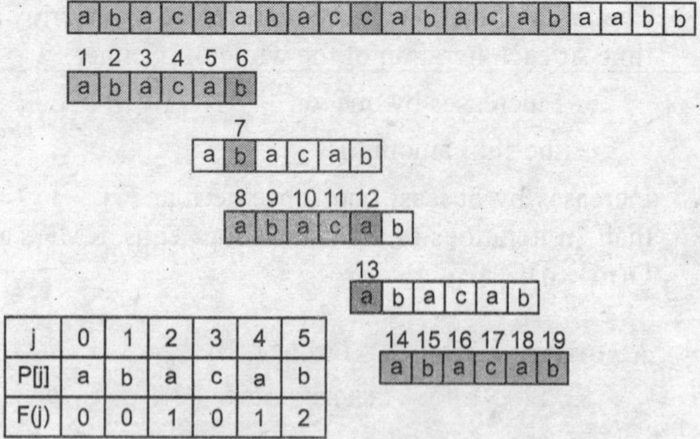

j	0	1	2	3	4	5
P[j]	a	b	a	c	a	b
F(j)	0	0	1	0	1	2

Figure 2.33: Compute failure function

Algorithm 2.4: failureFunction(P)

```
Step 1: F[0] ← 0
Step 2: i ← 1
Step 3: j ← 0
Step 4: while i < m
if P[i] = P[j]
{we have matched j + 1 chars}
F[i] ← j + 1
i ← i + 1
j ← j + 1
else if j > 0 then
{use failure function to shift P}
j ← F[j – 1]
else
F[i] ← 0 { no match }
i ← i + 1
Step 5: End.
```

2.15.4 Efficiency of the Search Algorithm

Assuming the prior existence of the table T, the search portion of the Knuth–Morris–Pratt algorithm has complexity O(k), where k is the length of S and the O is big-O notation. As except for the fixed overhead incurred in entering and exiting the function, all the computations are performed in the **while** loop, we will calculate a bound on the number of iterations of this loop; in order to do this we first make a key observation about the nature of T. By definition it is constructed so that if a match which had begun at S[m] fails while comparing S[m + i] to W[i], then the next possible match must begin at S[m + (i - T[i])]. In particular the next possible match must occur at a higher index than m, so that T[i] < i.

Using this fact, we will show that the loop can execute at most 2k times. For in each iteration, it executes one of the two branches in the loop. The first branch invariably increases i and does not change m, so that the index m + i of the currently scrutinized character of S is increased. The second branch adds i - T[i] to m, and as we have seen, this is always a positive number. Thus the location m of the beginning of the current potential match is increased. Now, the loop ends if m + i = k; therefore each branch of the loop can be reached at most k times, since they respectively increase either m + i or m, and m ≤ m + i: if m = k, then certainly m + i ≥ k, so that since it increases by unit increments at most, we must have had m + i = k at some point in the past, and therefore either way we would be done.

Thus the loop executes at most 2k times, showing that the time complexity of the search algorithm is O(k).

EXERCISES

1. What do you mean by computer?
2. Explain the concept of data and data item.
3. Explain the concept of data organization.
4. Comparison between fixed length storage and variable length storage?
5. What do you understand by data structures? Explain different types of data structure in detail.
6. Difference between Array and Linked List.
7. Difference between stack and queue.
8. Explain comparison of various data structures.
9. What are the various applications of data structure?
10. Differentiate between linear and non-linear data structure?
11. Explain common operations on data structures.
12. What do you mean by strings? Explain various operations on string.
13. Explain various string handling functions.
14. Explain various string searching algorithms in detail.
15. Explain brute force algorithm in detail.
16. Explain boyer-moore heuristics in detail.
17. Explain knuth-morris-pratt algorithm with the help of example.
18. What do you mean by efficiency of the search algorithm?

3 CHAPTER

Algorithm Design and Complexity

3.1 INTRODUCTION

The word algorithm comes from the name of the famous Persian mathematician Mohammed al-Khowarizmi who is credited for inventing the rules for adding, subtracting, multiplying and dividing decimal numbers. An informal definition of an algorithm would state that it is 'a step by step procedure for solving a problem or accomplishing some end'. Harel defines it as 'an abstract recipe, prescribing a process which may be carried out by a human, a computer or by other means'. Although this can mean that algorithms may be applied in any context, our main interest is in how algorithms are implemented on a computer.

An algorithm is only useful if it can be translated into instructions that are executable. In other words, algorithms need to be implemented using a computer language. Several language paradigms, such as imperative, functional, and logic paradigms, are available to the algorithm implementor. The best-known one is the imperative (or procedural) paradigm which forms the basis for most common languages such as Pascal and C. Translating an algorithm into an imperative language involves building the solution using data structures such as variables and arrays and joining them with control structures such as conditional and loop statements. The main advantage of using imperative languages is that they have been designed with the computer architecture in mind, so the way the algorithm is executed by the computer is fairly straightforward. If another language paradigm is used, then the algorithm must be formulated using the constructs offered by this new paradigm. These constructs are then turned into machine code by the compiler for this language. For example, the functional language paradigm offers recursion as the main control structure, and non-updatable lists as one of the main data structures. The use of these higher level constructs eases the implementation of an algorithm but can make it harder to reason about the efficiency of the program.

The main motivation for using computers to implement algorithms is that of speed. As millions of instructions can be executed in only a few seconds, some problems that are too large to be solved by hand can be easily tackled. Then, an important question arises: given several algorithms for solving the same problem, which one should be selected for implementation? The answer is that the most efficient one should be used, that is, the one that takes less time to execute. Given that algorithms would have to work on large problems, the payoff for designing a 'good' algorithm can be significant at execution time.

At this stage, we must decide on the criteria that should be used to measure the efficiency of an algorithm. The exact execution time could constitute one possible measure but this approach suffers from several serious defects. First, this time varies according to the computer being used. Secondly, it depends on how various language constructs are translated into machine code by the compiler. In addition, it is often desirable to compare different algorithms before implementing them so as to avoid developing code unnecessarily. The usual technique used in analyzing an algorithm is to isolate an operation fundamental to the problem under study. This is called the complexity measure. Then, a walk through the algorithm reveals how many times the operation that corresponds to our measure is invoked. The result of the analysis is often expressed as a function of the size of the input. The size of the input is often related to the size of the data structure used in the algorithm.

This chapter describes concept of the algorithms, efficiency of an algorithm, Time and Space Complexity, it also describes various control structure that are building blocks for structured programming. Asymptotic notations: Big-Oh, Time-Space trade-off., Abstract Data Types (ADT).

3.2 PROBLEM ANALYSIS

A computer can be used to solve a problem by following set of stored instructions called a program. The problem solving process needs initial data, the operations that are to be performed and results in the form of output. The following steps are required for problem solving:

(i) Define the Problem

The first step is to give a clear, concise problem statement. The problem definition should clearly specify the desired input and output. This step demands that user should have full knowledge of the background of the problem. A stated goal will help in the organization of the remaining steps.

For Example

- To compute the average of a set of data values.
- Given a quadratic equation, to compute its real and complex roots.
- To print a table of weight and height values for a normal human being.

(ii) Formulate a Mathematical Model

Most technical problems can be modeled mathematically. An existing model must be chosen or a new one if no standard mathematical model exists. This step also requires full knowledge of the problem and its underlying mathematical concepts.

For Example

- Average = (Value1+ Value2 +Value3) / 3
- Root = (–b + sqrt(b*b – 4*a*c))/ (2*a)

(iii) Develop an Algorithm

The next step is to devise and describe a precise plan of what you want the computer to do. This plan, expressed as a sequence of operations, is called an **algorithm**.

(iv) Coding the Program

The above algorithm cannot be as such understandable by the computer. It first must be written in a programming language as a program. A compiler or translator will then convert program into machine code that the computer can understand and act upon. Learning a computer language is required first to be a programmer so as to translate the algorithm derived in step 3 into a program.

(v) Testing the Program

If the program compiles correctly, use a simple set of test values to verify that the result is what you expected. If the results seem valid, test the program with a variety of "real" data sets. The mistakes if encountered in a program are called **bugs** and "debugging" code can take longer than writing the code.

To solve a problem some tools are used to simplify it and make it in the readable form. Following are the commonly used tools to solve the problem.

3.3 INTRODUCTION TO ALGORITHMS

3.3.1 Algorithm

An algorithm is a finite sequence of instructions, logic, an explicit, step-by-step procedure for solving a problem. An algorithm may be expressed as a pseudo code that is shorthand notation of English sentences.

Definition: *"An algorithm is a finite set of instructions which, if followed, accomplish a particular task".*

In addition every algorithm must satisfy the following criteria:

Step 1: Input: There are zero or more quantities which are externally supplied.

Step 2: Output: At least one quantity is produced.

Step 3: Definiteness: Each instruction must be clear and unambiguous.

Step 4: Finiteness: If we trace out the instructions of an algorithm, then for all cases the algorithm will terminate after a finite number of steps.

Step 5: Effectiveness: Every instruction must be sufficiently basic that it can in principle be carried out by a person using only pencil and paper. It is not enough that each operation be definite, but it must also be feasible.

A problem can be solved by using a computer only if an algorithm can be written for it. In addition, the use of algorithm provides many other benefits:

1. While writing an algorithm, you identify the step-by-step procedure, the major decision points, and the variables necessary to solve the problem. This helps you in the development of the corresponding program.
2. Identification of the procedure and the decision points reduces the problem into a series of smaller problems of more manageable size. Therefore, problems that would be difficult or impossible to solve as a whole can be approached as a series of small solvable sub problems.
3. With the use of an algorithm, decision making becomes a more rational process. This is because algorithms comprise of sub tasks, where each sub task is atomic in nature and is supported by facts.
4. With the use of an algorithm, the same specified steps are used for performing the tasks. This makes the process more consistent and reliable.

Algorithm 3.1: Add Two Numbers

Step 1: Start
Step 2: Enter the value of A and B.
Step 3: A=10, B=5.
Step 4: Perform operation C = A + B.
Step 5: Store the result in C.
Step 6: End

Let us take one more example, to find biggest number between two given numbers. Think the logic, and you'll feel it's very easy to write the steps of an algorithm.

Algorithm 3.2: Find the Greater number among two numbers.

Step 1: Start
Step 2: Read two positive integer numbers 'A' and 'B'
Step 3: If A is greater than B, then go to step 4 else goto step 5.

Step 4: Print "A is greater than B" goto step 6.

Step 5: Print "B is greater than A"

Step 6: End.

Once these steps are performed on data specified in the problem, the desired result or output is obtained. Whenever an algorithm can be specified it makes sense to wonder about its behaviour.

This was realized by Charles Babbage, the father of Computers in 1830. An algorithm is a finite set of instructions, which when followed, perform a particular task.

3.3.2 Types of Algorithm

An algorithm is defined as "Step by step approach to solve any problem". There are mainly three types of algorithm exist, which are given as below:

1. Sequential Algorithm
2. Conditional Algorithm
3. Iterative Algorithm

1. **Sequential Algorithm:** an algorithm whose steps are executed sequentially i.e. execution of algorithm takes place in the same order in which an algorithm is developed. For example consider following algorithm to add two numbers

    Read A

    Read B

    C=A+B

    Print "Sum is"

    Print C

2. **Conditional Algorithm:** An algorithm whose execution depends upon certain conditions are called conditional algorithms. For example consider the following algorithm to check whether a given number is positive or negative.

    Read A

    If A>0 then

    Print "A is positive"

    Else

    Print "A is negative"

    End IF

3. **Iterative Algorithm:** an algorithm that repeat a statement of group of statement for number of times such an algorithm is called iterative algorithm. For example consider the following algorithm that will find the sum of first 100 Natural numbers:

```
Set S=0
For I=1 to 100
S=S+I
I=I+1
End For
Print "Sum of First 100 Natural numbers is"
Print S
```

Describing algorithms requires a notation for expressing a sequence of steps to be performed. The three most common options are (1) English, (2) pseudocode, or (3) a real programming language. Pseudocode is perhaps the most mysterious of the bunch, but it is best defined as a programming language that never complains about syntax errors. All three methods can be useful in certain circumstances, since there is a natural tradeoff between greater ease of expression and precision. English is the most natural but least precise language, while C and Pascal are precise but difficult to write and understand. Pseudocode is useful because it is a happy medium. The correct choice of which notation is best depends upon which of the three methods you are most comfortable with. I prefer to describe the *ideas* of an algorithm in English, moving onto a more formal, programming-language-like pseudocode to clarify sufficiently tricky details of the algorithm. A common mistake among my students is to use pseudocode to take an ill-defined idea and dress it up so that it looks more formal. In the real world, you only fool yourself when you pull this kind of stunt.

An algorithm can be described in several ways. One way is to give it a graphical form of notation which is known as Flow Chart. This form places each processing step in a "box" and uses arrows to indicate the next step. Different shaped boxes stand for different kinds of operations.

3.3.3 Flow-chart

A diagram that uses graphic symbols to depict the nature and flow of the steps in a process. To solve a problem in a sequence or stepwise diagrammatically or pictorially is called Flow Chart.

"A flowchart is a common type of chart, which represents an algorithm or process, showing the steps as boxes of various kinds, and their order by connecting these with arrows. Flowcharts are used in analyzing, designing, documenting or managing a process or program in various fields."

Flowcharts are tools used by programmers because they facilitate breaking down a problem into its simplest steps, each symbol in a flowchart can represent only one step in the algorithm. Flowcharts use easy-to-understand symbols to represent actions on data and the flow of data. The following are the basic flowchart symbols:

(i) Terminator or Start/Stop Box

The Terminator symbol is used to begin and end of each flowchart. It also has egg like shape called oval. It is used to indicates start/stop of a program.

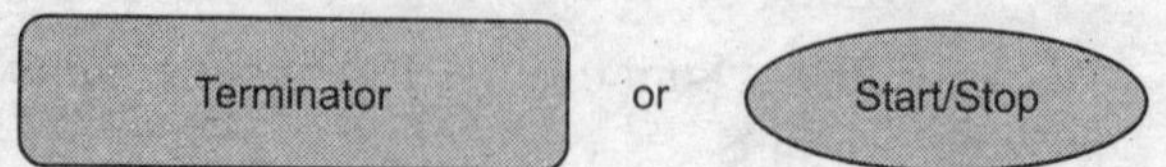

(ii) Input/Output Box

Input boxes are used for input value to program and Output boxes are used for output value to outside world. This is also called read/write box and it has parallelogram shape.

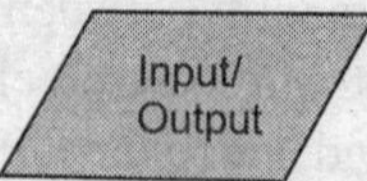

(iii) Process or Computation Or Assignment Box

It has square shape or rectangular shape. It indicates information processing e.g., addition, subtraction, or movement of data to computer memory.

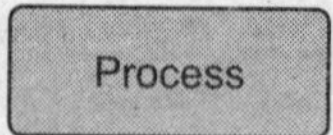

(iv) Decision or Condition Box

Decision diamonds create two data flows from one. A Decision diamond always has True/False or Yes/No written on the left and right sides. It is also called decision making box.

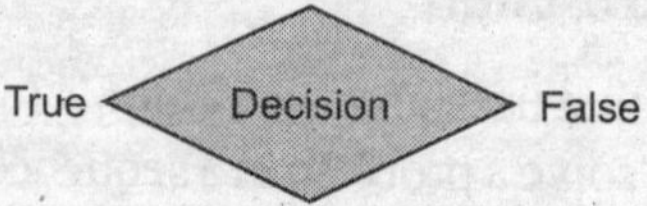

(v) Flow Line or Data Flow

Data Flows connect the different symbols, showing the order that is followed in the algorithm. Data Flows can only go in one direction, hence the arrow. When two or more data flows meet, they always meet at a connector. It has arrow shape.

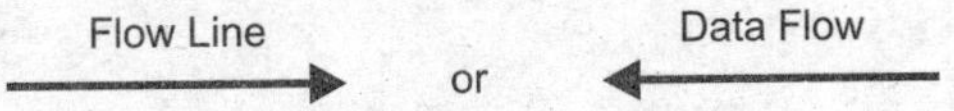

(vi) Loop or Iterative Box

This box has hexagon shape. It is used when a problem has repetitive steps or iterative steps i.e. a problem has solution with steps repeating again and again till a condition ends or definite number of times.

(vii) Connector or Flow Linker

This has circular shape. A small circle with any number or letter in it is used as a connector symbol. It connects various parts of a flow-chart which are far apart or spread over pages. This makes the flow chart simple and in short. It means it removes complexity of the flowchart.

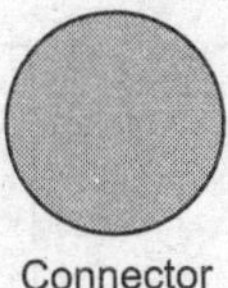
Connector

(viii) Function or Procedure or Sub-program Box

This symbol has a rectangle shape with two cuts or lines inside. It is used to denote a subprocess which is given elsewhere as indicated by connector symbol.

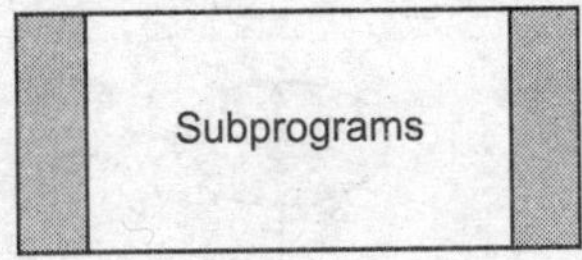

There are mainly three types of construct used in the programming which are useful in drawing the flow chart. The three programming constructs are known as:

Sequence construct that is used to carry out one step at a time, then next step and so on.

Selection construct performs an action based on the condition if it is true.

Iteration construct or looping construct performs an action as long as condition is true by carrying out the looping. When a problem has repetitive steps or iterative steps i.e. a problem has solution with steps repeating again and again till a condition ends or definite number of times.

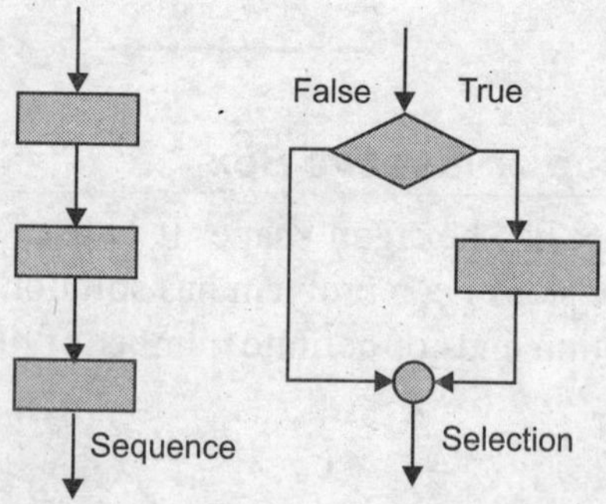

The third construct known as Iteration is derived from the selection construct by transferring the control to the start position as along as the condition remains true. Once the condition becomes false, the control will be transferred to the next level after decision making.

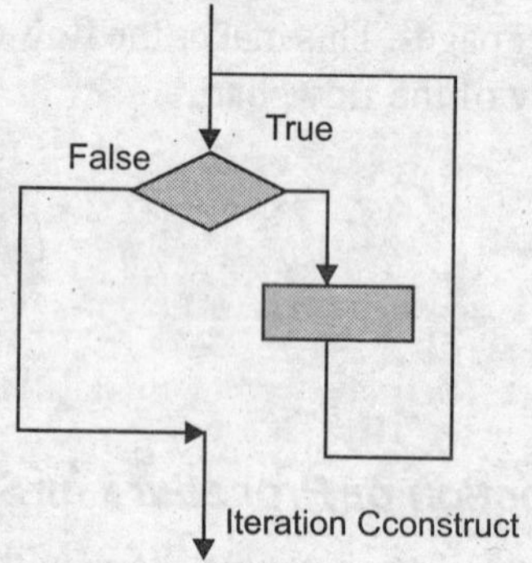

EXAMPLE 3.1: Flowchart to calculate the Average of set of values (Sequence Construct).

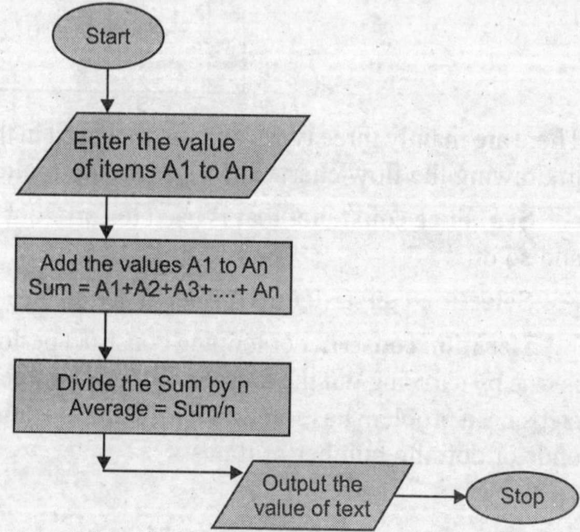

EXAMPLE 3.2: Flowchart to find the largest number from two numbers (Selection Construct).

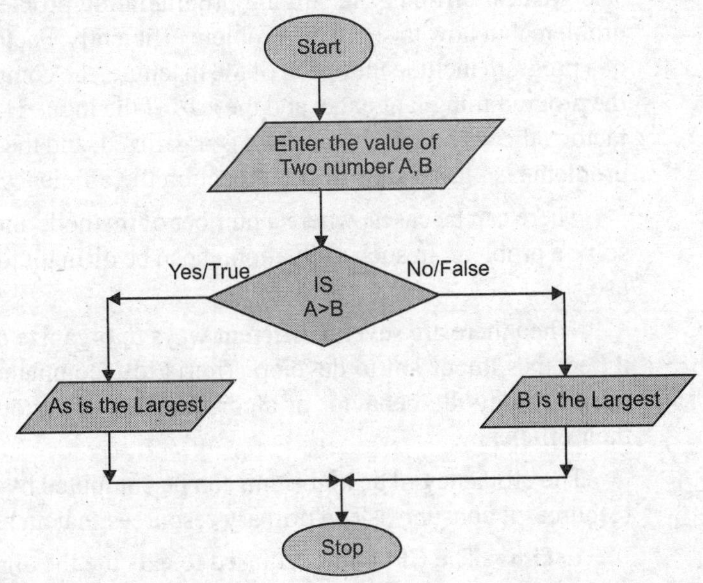

EXAMPLE 3.3: Flowchart to Compute or Calculate the Average of N number i.e. From 1 to N (Iteration Construct or Looping Construct):

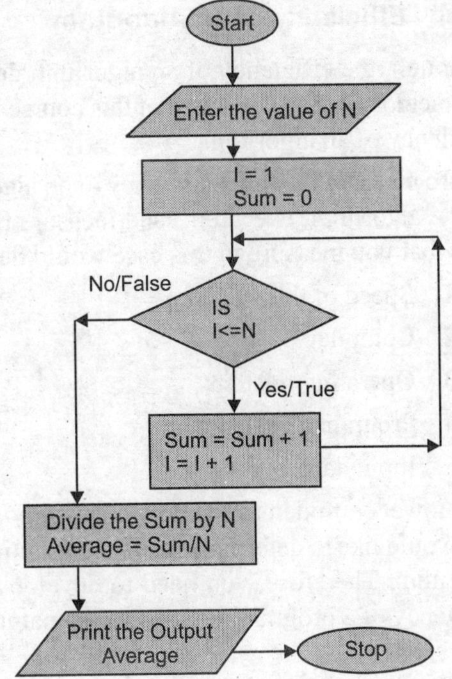

3.4 DETERMINING THE EFFICIENCY OF AN ALGORITHM

The greatest difficulty in solving programming problems is not how to solve the problem, but how to solve the problem efficiently. Factors that affect the efficiency of a program include the speed of the machine, the compiler. The operating system, the programming language, and the size of the input. However, in addition to these factors, the way data of a program is organized, and the algorithm used to solve the problem also has a significant impact on the efficiency of a program.

There can be cases, where a number of methods and algorithms can be used to solve a problem. In such a situation, it can be difficult to decide which algorithm to use.

When there are several different ways to organize data and devise algorithms, it becomes important to develop criteria to recommend a choice. Therefore, you need to study the behavior of algorithms under various conditions and compare their efficiency.

The efficiency of an algorithm can be computed by determining the amount of resources it consumes. The primary resources that an algorithm consumes are:

1. **Time:** The CPU time required to execute the algorithm
2. **Space:** The amount of memory used by the algorithm for execution.

The lesser resources that an algorithm uses, the more efficient it is.

3.4.1 Efficiency of an Algorithm

Although, the efficiency of an algorithm depends on how efficiently it uses time and memory space, the scope of this course is limited to determining only the time efficiency of an algorithm.

To measure the time efficiency of an algorithm, you can write a program based on the algorithm, execute it, and measure the time it takes to run. The execution time that you measure in this case would depend on a number of factors such as:

1. Speed of the machine
2. Compiler
3. Operating System
4. Programming language
5. Input data

However, to determine how efficiently an algorithm solves a given problem, you would like to determine how the execution time is affected by the nature of the algorithm. Therefore, you need to develop fundamental laws that determine the efficiency of a program in terms of the nature of the underlying algorithm.

To understand how the nature of an algorithm affects the execution, consider a simple example. Suppose assignment, comparison, write, and increment statements take a, b, c, and d time units to execute respectively. Now, consider the following code used to display the elements stored in an array:

1. Set I = 0 // 1 assignment
2. While(I < n): // n comparisons
    (a) Display a[I] // n writes
    (b) Increment I by 1 // n increments

The execution time required for the preceding algorithm is given by:

$$T = a + b \text{ X } n + c \text{ X } n + d \text{ X } n$$
$$T = a + n(b + c + d)$$

Here, T is the total running time of the algorithm expressed as a linear function of the number of elements (n) in the array. From the preceding expression, it is clear that T is directly proportional to n.

In fact, the total running time T is directly proportional to the number of iterations involved in the algorithm. The number of iterations can be determined by counting the number of comparisons involved in the algorithm.

In the preceding code segment, a total of n comparisons are being made. Therefore, the total running time of the algorithm, T is directly proportional to n.

As T is directly proportional to n, an increase in the value of n will result in a proportional increase in the value of T, as shown in the following figure.

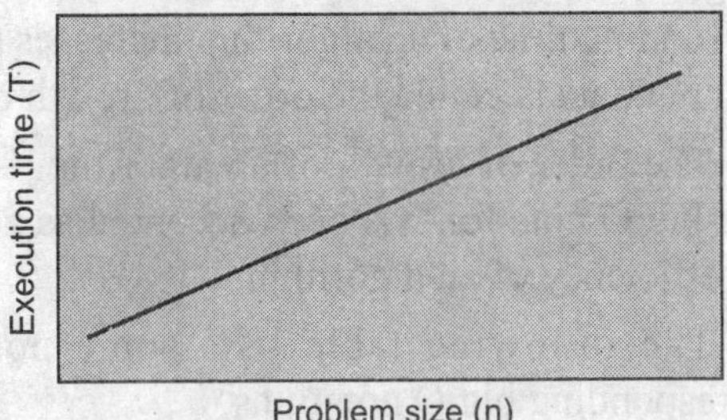

Now, consider the following algorithm:

Algorithm 3.3: Count number of comparisons.

Step 1: Set I = 0 // 1 assignment
Step 2: While (I < n): // n comparisons
    a. Set J = 0 // n assignments
    b. While (J < n): // n x n comparisons
        i. Display (a[I][J]) // n x n writes
        ii. Increment J by 1 // n x n increments
    c. Increment I by 1 // n increments

If you count the number of comparisons in the preceding code segment, they come out to be $(n^2 + n)$, which is a quadratic function of n. Therefore, the total running time is directly proportional to n^2.

Note: *Although the number of comparisons is $n^2 + n$, the value of n is very small as compared to the value of n^2 (especially when n is very large). Therefore, the value of n can be ignored for finding the approximate running time.*

As the running time is directly proportional to n^2, an increase in the value of n will result in a quadratic increase in the running time. This means that if the value of n is doubled, the running time will increase four times. The rate of change of T with an increase in the value of n is depicted in the following figure:

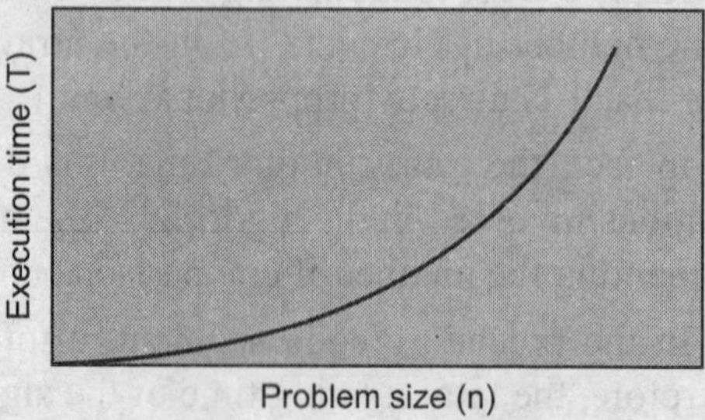

From the preceding discussion, you can conclude that the running time of a program is a function of n, where n is the size of the input data. The rate at which the running time of an algorithm increases as a result of an increase in the volume of input data is called the order of growth of the algorithm.

The order of growth of an algorithm is defined by using the big O notation. The big O notation has been accepted as a fundamental technique for describing the efficiency of an algorithm.

The following table lists some possible orders of growth, and their corresponding big O notations.

Order of Growth	Big O notation
Constant	O(1)
Logarithmic	O(log n)
Linear	O(n)
Log linear	O(n log n)
Quadratic	$O(n^2)$
Cubic	$O(n^3)$
Exponential	$O(2^n)$, O(10n)

3.4.2 Big O Notations

If an algorithm has a linear order of growth, the algorithm is said to be of the order O(n). Similarly, if an algorithm has a quadratic order of growth, the algorithm is said to be of the order $O(n^2)$.

3.4.3 Selecting an Efficient Algorithm

Now that you know how the efficiency of a particular algorithm is determined, let us see how this knowledge can be used to select an efficient algorithm.

According to their orders of growth, the big O notations can be arranged in an increasing order as:

$O(1) < O(\log n) < O(n) < O(n \log n) < O(n^2) < O(n^3) < O(2^n) < O(10^n)$

Therefore, if a problem can be solved by using algorithms each of the preceding orders of growth, an algorithm of the order of O(1) will be considered best, and an algorithm of the order $O(10^n)$ will be considered the worst. The goal of algorithm development should be to make algorithms of the smallest possible orders.

The following table depicts the orders of growth for the preceding big O notations.

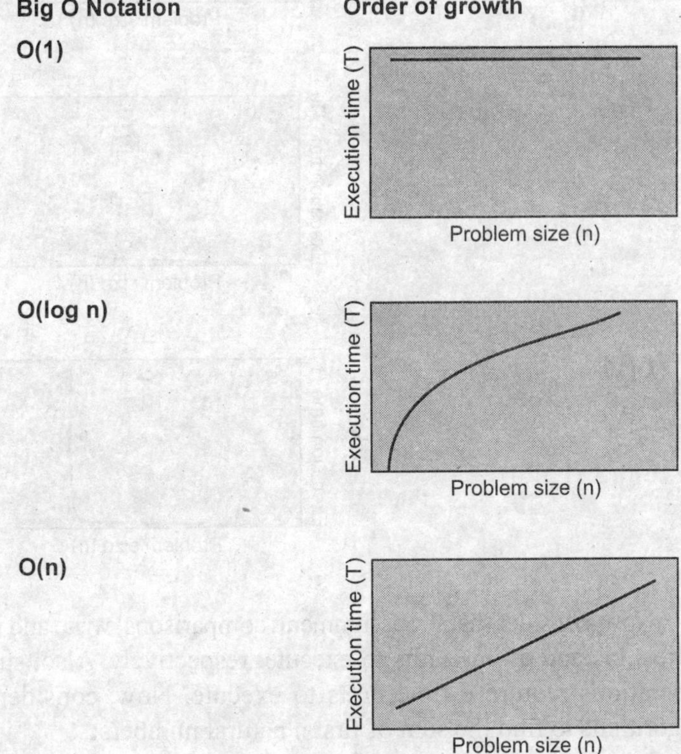

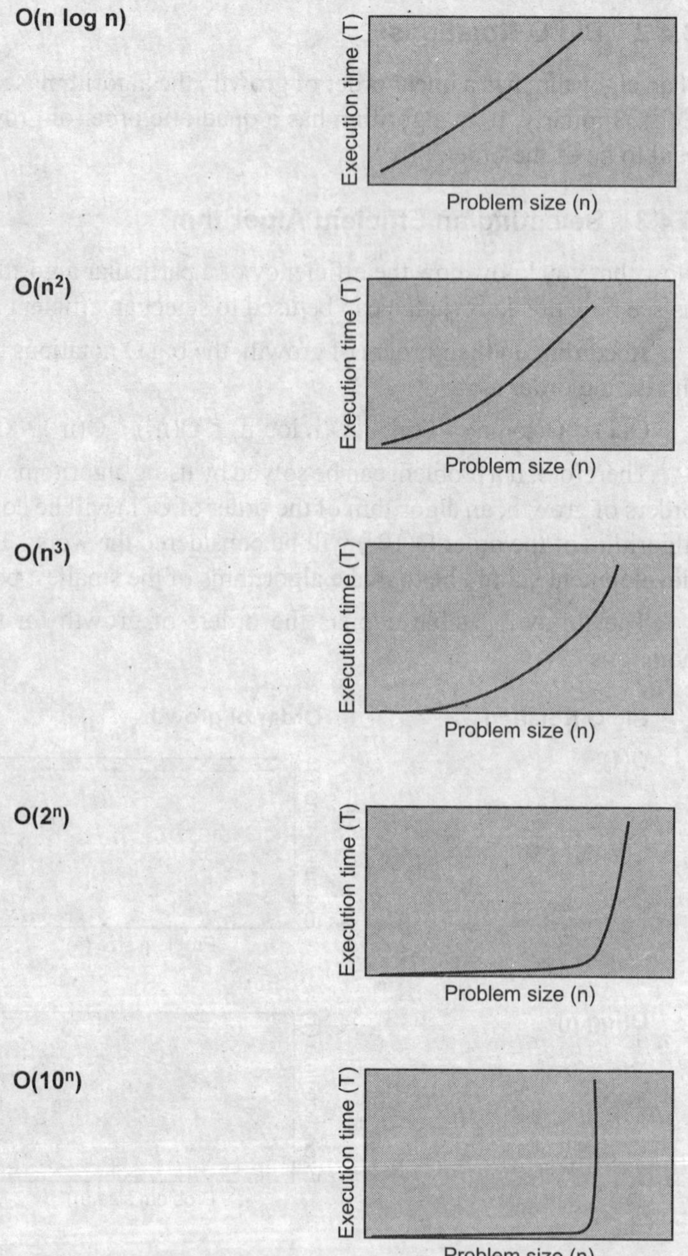

Now, consider that the assignment, comparisons, write and increment statements take a,b,c and d time units to execute, respectively. Also, suppose all arithmetic operations require e time units to execute. Now, consider the following two algorithms to find the sum of first n natural numbers:

Algorithm 3.4: Find sum of first n natural numbers.

Step 1: Set sum = 0 // 1 assignment
Step 2: Set i = 0 // 1 assignment
Step 3: While (i <= n) // n comparisons
a. Set sum = sum + i // n arithmetic operations, n assignments
b. Increment i by 1 // n increments
Step 4: Display (sum) // 1 write

Algorithm 3.5: Find sum of first n natural numbers.

Step 1: Set sum = (n x (n + 1))/2 // 3 arithmetic operations, 1 assignment
Step 2: Display (sum) // 1 write

Both Algorithm 3.4 and Algorithm 3.5 perform the same task, that is, both determine the sum of the first n natural numbers. Algorithm 3.4 adds each number iteratively to a variable sum. However, Algorithm 3.5 uses a formula to calculate the sum of the first n natural numbers.

The execution time requires for Algorithm 3.4 is given by:

$$T = (n + 2) \times a + (n \times b) + (1 \times c) + (n \times d) + (n \times e)$$

$$T = an + 2n + bn + c + dn + en$$

$$T = c + n(a + b + d + e + 2)$$

As T is a linear function of n.

Therefore, the algorithm is of the order O(n).

Now determine the time required to execute algorithm 3.5:

$$T = (1 \times a) + (1 \times c) + (3 \times e)$$

$$T = a + c + 3e$$

Unlike Algorithm 3.4, the time taken by Algorithm 3.5 is a constant, and does not depend on the value of n. Therefore, the algorithm is of the order O(1).

Because Algorithm 3.4 is of the order O(n), the execution time of Algorithm 3.4 increases linearly with the value of n. However, Algorithm 3.5 is of the order O(1). Therefore, the execution time of Algorithm 3.5 is constant. This means that an increase in the value of n does not have any impact on the execution time of the algorithm. Therefore, however large the problem be, Algorithm A solves it in the same amount of time.

Suppose for n = 10, both Algorithm 3.4 and 3.5 take 10 nanoseconds (ns) to execute. However when n is increased to 100, Algorithm 3.4 will take 100 ns to execute, but Algorithm 3.5 will take only 10 ns to execute, Similarly, when n is increased to 1000, Algorithm 3.4 will take 1000 ns to execute, but Algorithm 3.5 will take only 10 ns.

This means that when the problem is very large in size, Algorithm 3.5 would prove to be much more efficient than Algorithm 3.4.

3.4.4 Best, Worst, and Average Case Efficiency

Suppose you have a list of names in which you have to search for a particular name. You have designed an algorithm that searches the name in the list of n elements, by comparing the name to be searched with each element in the list sequentially.

The best case in this scenario would be if the first element in the list matches the name to be searched. The efficiency in that case would be expressed as O(1) because only one comparison was made.

Similarly, the worst case in this scenario would be if the complete list is traversed and the element is found at the end of the list or is not found in the list. The efficiency in that case would be expressed as O(n) because n comparisons were made.

Continuing with the same example, the average case efficiency can be obtained by finding the average number of comparisons. Here,

Minimum number of comparisons = 1

Maximum number of comparisons = n

Therefore, average number of comparisons = (n + 1)/2

(n + 1)/2 is a linear function of n. Therefore, the average case efficiency will be expressed as O(n).

The worst case efficiency of the preceding search program can be improved by using an alternate search algorithm that provides a better worst case efficiency.

3.5 ROLE OF DATA STRUCTURES

Multiple algorithms can be designed to solve a particular problem. However, the algorithm may differ in how efficiently they can solve the problem. In such a situation, an algorithm that provides the maximum efficiency should be used for solving the problem. Efficiency here means that the algorithm should work in minimal time and use minimal memory.

One of the basic techniques for improving the efficiency of algorithms is to structure the data that they operate on in such a way that the resulting operations can be efficiently performed. The way in which the various data elements are organized in memory with respect to each other is called a data structure.

Data can be organized in many different ways; therefore, you can create as many data structures as you want. However, there are some standard data structures that have proved useful over the years. These include arrays, linked lists, stacks, queues, trees and graphs. We will learn more about these data structures in the subsequent tutorials.

All these data structures are designed to hold a collection of data items. However, the difference lies in the way the data items are arranged with respect to each other and the operations that they allow. Because of the different ways in which the data items are arranged with respect to each other, some data structures prove to be more efficient that others to solve a given problem.

Suppose you have to write an algorithm that enables printer to service the requests of multiple users on a first-come-first-served (FCFS) basis. In this case, using a data structure that stores and retrieves the requests in the order of their arrival would be much more efficient than a data structure that stores and retrieves the requests in a random order.

In addition to improving the efficiency of an algorithm, the use of appropriate data structures also allows you to overcome some other programming challenges, such as:

- Simplifying complex problems
- Creating standard, reusable code components
- Creating programs that are easy to understand and maintain

Consider an example where you have to find the maximum value in a set of 50 numbers, In this scenario, you can either use 50 variables or a data structure, such as an array of size 50, to store the numbers. When 50 different variables are used to store the numbers, the algorithm to determine the maximum value among the numbers can be written as:

1. Accept 50 numbers and store them in num1, num2, num3, .. num50
2. Set max = num1
3. If num2 > max then: max = num2
4. If num3 > max then: max = num3:

   ....

   ....
5. If num50 > max then max = num50
6. Display max

On the other hand, when an array of size 50 is used, the algorithm can be written as:

1. Set max = num[0]
2. Repeat step3 varying i from 1 to 49
3. If num[i] > max then: max = num[i]
4. Display max

From the preceding two algorithms, it can be seen that the algorithm using an array manipulates memory much more efficiently than the algorithm using 50 variables. Also, the algorithm using an array involves few steps and is therefore, easier to understand and implement as compared to the algorithm that uses 50 variables.

Data structures also enable the creation of reusable code components. Suppose you have created a class to implement a data structure that stores and retrieves requests in the order of their arrival. Once the class is created, the same class can be used in several different applications that need to service the requests of multiple users on a FCFS basis.

This means that a data structure once implemented can be used as a standard component to provide a standard solution to a specific set of problems. The use of standard components helps simplify the maintenance process. This is because the standard components are time tested and therefore, do not need much maintenance.

3.6 COMPLEXITY OF ALGORITHMS

An algorithm is a sequence of statements, each of which has a clear meaning and can be performed with a finite amount of effort is a finite length of time. An algorithm is supposed to do two things.

1. Compute the correct answer given valid Input data.
2. Perform the computation in a reasonable time.

The second point is of course essential. A correct algorithm is useless if it is too slow. In such cases, we must find another algorithm or any be we will have to accept some approximation which allow us to use another algorithm, which runs in reasonable time but only generates an approximately correct results. Computer science is the science that deals with the issues of provide that an algorithm is correct and what its properties are such as how long time it can be expected to need in the average case or how much time it will use in the worst case.

These analyses are done without reference to any specific computer or programming language, the issüe is how, many calculation steps (such as additions and multiplications or exchanges of items is an array) are needed to obtain the result and how this depends on the size of the problem. One of the most important properties of an algorithm is how its execution time increases as the problem is made large. By a larger problem, we mean sequences to align or longer sequences to align. This is so called algorithmic (or computational) complexity of the algorithm. As an algorithm is a sequence of steps to solve a problem, there may be more than one algorithm to solve a problem.

The choice of particular algorithm depends on following considerations:

1. **Performance requirements:** Time Complexity (how much time algorithm required to run to completion?)

2. **Memory requirements:** Space complexity (how much memory algorithm required to run to completion?)

3. **Programming requirements**

Since programming requirement one difficult to analyze, precisely, complexity theory concentrate on performance and memory requirements. Specifically it is used to help in determining how the resource requirements of an algorithm grow in relation to the size of the data being manipulated.

Performance requirements one usually more critical than memory requirements, hence in general, it is not necessary to worry about memory unless they grow faster than performance requirements. Therefore in general the algorithms one analyzed only on the basic of performance requirements, i.e. running time.

3.6.1 Space Complexity

This is essentially the number of memory cells which an algorithm needs. A good algorithm keeps this number as small as possible, too. If the program is to run on multi user system it may be required to specify the amount of memory to be allocated to the program. A programme with sometime seek a trade off between space and time complexity. For example, a programme might choose a data structure that requires a lot of Storage in order to reduce the computation time. There is an element of art in making such tradeoffs but the programmer must make the choice from an informed point of view.

1. The programmer must have some verified basic on which to make the selection of a data structure or algorithm.
2. We may be interested to know in advance that whether deficient memory is available to run the program.
3. There may be several possible solutions with different space requirements.
4. Can be used to estimate the size of the largest problem that a program can solve.

In other words complexity refers to the rate at which the storage or time grows as a function of the problem size. The absolute growth depends on the machine used to execute program, the compiler used to construct the program and, many other factors we would like to have a way of describing the inherent complexity of a program, independent of machine/ compiler considerations. This means that we must not try to describe the absolute time or storage need. Space complexity is the measure of how much memory is used by a program relative to some measure of the size of the problems.

1. Most Primitives use constant space
2. Tail recursive calls also use constant space
3. General Recursive calls use linear space.

The amount of space needed by recursive functions is called the recursive stack space. For each recursive function, this space depends on the space needed by the local variables and the formal parameters. In addition, this space depends on the maximum depth of the recursion. In general the total space need by a program can be divided into parts.

1. A fixed part that is independent of particular problem and includes instruction space, space for constants, simple variables and fixed structured variables.
2. A variable part that includes structured variables whose size depends on the particular problem being solved, dynamically allocated space and the recursion stack space.

3.6.2 Time Complexity

The time complexity of an algorithm is the amount of time it needs to run to completion. To measure the time complexity accurately we can count the all sort of operations performed in an algorithm. If we know the time for each one of the primitive operations performed on given computer, we can easily computer the time taken by an algorithm to complete its execution. A key operation in our algorithm is an operation that takes maximum time among all possible operations in the algorithm. The time complexity can be expressed as a function of number of key operations performed.

3.6.3 Computational Complexity

Computational complexity is the study of how of a given resource a program uses. The resource in question is usually either space (how much memory) or time (how many basic operations). Complexity can be looked at from many angles:

1. **Worst-case** complexity is the most commonly discussed it give a guaranteed upper bound for how much of a resource a program will use.
2. **Average-case** complexity is often useful, but more difficult to compute.
3. **Best-case** complexity is rarely useful, except as a contrast with the average and worst cases. It given a guaranteed lower bound for how much of a resource a program will use.

3.7 ASYMPTOTIC NOTATION

A problem may have numerous algorithmic solutions. In order to choose the best algorithm for a particular task, you need to be able to judge how long a particular solution will take to run. Or, more accurately, you need to be able to judge how long two solutions will take to run, and choose the better of the two. You don't need to know how many minutes and seconds they will take, but you do need some way to compare algorithms against one another.

Asymptotic complexity is a way of expressing the main component of the cost of an algorithm, using idealized units of computational work. Consider, for example, the algorithm for sorting a deck of cards, which proceeds by repeatedly searching through the deck for the lowest card. The asymptotic complexity of this algorithm is the square of the number of cards in the deck. This quadratic behavior is the main term in the complexity formula, it says, e.g., if you double the size of the deck, then the work is roughly quadrupled.

The exact formula for the cost is more complex, and contains more details than are needed to understand the essential complexity of the algorithm. With our deck of cards, in the worst case, the deck would start out reverse-sorted, so our scans would have to go all the way to the end. The first scan would involve scanning 52 cards, the next would take 51, etc. So the cost formula is 52 + 51 + ... + 1. Generally, letting N be the number of cards, the formula is 1 + 2 + ... + N, which equals $(N + 1) * (N / 2) = (N^2 + N) / 2 = (1 / 2) N^2 + N / 2$. But the N^2 term dominates the expression, and this is what is key for comparing algorithm costs. (This is in fact an expensive algorithm; the best sorting algorithms run in sub-quadratic time.)

Asymptotically speaking, in the limit as N tends towards infinity, 1 + 2 + ... + N gets closer and closer to the pure quadratic function (1/2) N^2. And what difference does the constant factor of 1/2 make, at this level of abstraction. So the behavior is said to be $O(n^2)$.

Now let us consider how we would go about comparing the complexity of two algorithms. Let f(n) be the cost, in the worst case, of one algorithm, expressed as a function of the input size n, and g(n) be the cost function for the other algorithm. E.g., for sorting algorithms, f(10) and g(10) would be the maximum number of steps that the algorithms would take on a list of 10 items. If, for all values of n >= 0, f(n) is less than or equal to g(n), then the algorithm with complexity function f is strictly faster. But, generally speaking, our concern for computational cost is for the cases with large inputs; so the comparison of f(n) and g(n) for small values of n is less significant than the "long term" comparison of f(n) and g(n), for n larger than some threshold.

Note that we have been speaking about bounds on the performance of algorithms, rather than giving exact speeds. The actual number of steps required to sort our deck of cards (with our naive quadratic algorithm) will depend upon the order in which the cards begin. The actual time to perform each of our steps will depend upon our processor speed, the condition of our processor cache, etc., etc. It's all very complicated in the concrete details, and moreover not relevant to the essence of the algorithm.

3.8 BIG-O NOTATION

Big-O is the formal method of expressing the upper bound of an algorithm's running time. It's a measure of the longest amount of time it could possibly take for the algorithm to complete.

More formally, for non-negative functions, f(n) and g(n), if there exists an integer n0 and a constant c > 0 such that for all integers n > n0, f(n) ≤ cg(n), then f(n) is Big O of g(n). This is denoted as "f(n) = O(g(n))". If graphed, g(n) serves as an upper bound to the curve you are analyzing, f(n).

It is generally not possible to perform a simple analysis of an algorithm to determine the exact time required to execute it.

Following are the reasons for this:

(i) Exact time depends on the implementation of the algorithm and on the machine we are executing on.

(ii) Time requirement to be found in time analysis, depends on amount of input.

Since the data structure used by an algorithm can greatly affect the algorithm's performance, it is important that there exists a rigorous method by which to compare the efficiency of various data structures. What we, as developers utilizing a data structure, are primarily interested in is how the data structures performance changes as the amount of data stored increases. That is, for each new element stored by the data structure, how are the running times of the data structure's operations effected?

Methodical way of computing the running time of a block of code is to do follow these simple steps:

1. Determine the steps that constitute the algorithm's running time. Typically, you want to concern yourself with steps that involve the data structure itself, and not simple, atomic operations performed by the computer. In Figure 3.23, with the block of code we analyze its running time by only counting how many times the data structure needs to be accessed, and do not bother worrying about the time for creating and initializing variables.
2. Find the line(s) of code that perform the steps you are interested in counting. Put a 1 next to each of those lines.
3. For each line with a 1 next to it, see if it is in a loop. If so, change the 1 to 1 times the maximum number of repetitions the loop may perform. If you have two or more nested loops, continue the multiplication for each loop.
4. Find the largest single term you have written down. This is the running time.

Let's apply these steps to the blocks of code in Figure 3.23.

Referring to Figure 3.23, for example, Let us take simple example considering the statement x = x + 1. We would determine two numbers for this statement. The first is the amount of time a single execution will take and the second is the number of times. i is executed. The multiplication of these numbers will give total time taken by this statement. The second statistics is the frequency count and it varies from data set to data set.

Now let us consider three different situations of the same statement in three different algorithms, considering these, we will calculate frequency count for all three types as shown in the Figure 3.23 as in the below table:

Algorithm (a)	Algorithm (b)	Algorithm (c)

x = x+1	for (i=1; i<=n; i++)
	x= x+1
		for (I=1; i<=n; i++)
		for (j=1; j<=n; j++)
		x= x+1

Figure 3.23

In the case of (a), let us suppose that the statement x= x+1 is not contained within any loop. Then its frequency count is 1.

In the case of (b) the statement is executed n times (time taken to execute single statement i.e. 1) * (No. of times it is executed i.e. n). So frequency count is n.

In the case of (c), Time taken to execute single statement =1

No. of times it is executed = $n*n = n^2$

So frequency count is $1 * n^2 = n^2$

1, n , n^2 are said to be different and increasing order of magnitude.

An order notation has been developed to facilitate the handling of order of magnitude functions. It will be clear from definition.

Mathematical description of Big-oh notation

Assume f(n) and g(n) be two arbitrary functions, such that

f(n) = O (g (n)), read as f(n) is "big-oh" of g(n) or f(n) is of order g(n), if there exists positive constants n_0 and c , such that f(n) <= c * g(n) for all n> n_o.

Examples are:

(i) $100 n^3 \Rightarrow 100 * n^3$ is $o(n^3)$

(ii) 1000 is 0(1)

(iii) n +log n is o (n) because log n < n

(iv) $2n^2 + 3 n + 4$ is o (n^2)

Points to be kept in mind, while reading Big-oh definition are as:

- Complexity expressed in o-notation is only an upper bound and the actual complexity may be much lower.
- So this complexity can be treated as worst-case, complexity.
- The constants c and n_o are unknown and are not necessarily small.

The different effects of constants on f(n) are as shown in the Figure 3.24:

N	log n	$\sqrt{n}$	n log n	n^2
10	3	3	30	100
100	6	10	600	10000
1000	9	31	9000	1000000
10000	13	100	130000	100000000

Figure 3.24: Effect of constants on f(n)

Some of common computing times of algorithms you'll study are:

n: When the time complexity of an algorithm is n, then the algorithm is said to be linear. This is the case, where processing has to be carried out on each individual element of the input. In this case time required by an algorithm is linearly proportional to 'n'.

n^2: When the time complexity of an algorithm is n^2 , then the algorithm is said to be Quadratic. As n^2 increases very rapidly with an increase in 'n', quadratic algorithms are practically useful only for relatively small problems

n^3: When the time complexity of an algorithm is n^3, then algorithm is said to be cubic. These types of algorithms are never practically useful.

logn: When the time complexity of an algorithm is log n, then the algorithm is said to be logarithmic. When a program is logarithmic, the program becomes slightly slower as 'n' increases. This time complexity usually occurs in algorithms, which solve big-problems by transforming it into smaller ones.

n log n: This type of time complexity occurs in those algorithms which solve a problem by breaking it up into smaller sub-problems and solve these sub-problems independently.

2^n : When the time complexity of an algorithm is 2^n, the algorithm is called as an exponential. These are not suitable for practical use.

So in general, the most common computing times of algorithms, as discussed will be written as:

$$O(1) < 0(\log n) < 0(n) < 0(n \log n) < o(n^2) < 0(n^3) < 0(2^n)$$

3.8.1 How to Calculate Overall Time Complexity of an Algorithm?

The most common metric for calculating time complexity is Big Oh notation. This removes all constant factors so that the running time can be estimated in relation to N as N approaches infinity. In general you can think of it like this:

Code:

```
statement;
```

is constant. The running time of the statement will not change in relation to N.

Code:

```
for (i = 0; i < N; i++)
 statement;
```

is linear. The running time of the loop is directly proportional to N. When N doubles, so does the running time.

Code:

```
for (i = 0; i < N; i++)
{
 for (j = 0; j < N; j++)
 statement;
}
```

is quadratic. The running time of the two loops is proportional to the square of N. When N doubles, the running time increases by N * N.

Code:

```
while ( low <= high )
{
 mid = ( low + high ) / 2;
        if ( target < list[mid] )
 high = mid - 1;
        else if (target > list[mid])
 low = mid + 1;
        else break;
}
```

is logarithmic. The running time of the algorithm is proportional to the number of times N can be divided by 2. This is because the algorithm divides the working area in half with each iteration.

Code:

```
void quicksort (int list[], int left, int right)
{
 int pivot = partition (list, left, right);
 quicksort (list, left, pivot - 1);
 quicksort (list, pivot + 1, right);
}
```

is N * log (N). The running time consists of N loops (iterative or recursive) that are logarithmic, thus the algorithm is a combination of linear and logarithmic.

In general, doing something with every item in one dimension is linear, doing something with every item in two dimensions is quadratic, and dividing the working area in half is logarithmic.

There are other Big Oh measures such as cubic, exponential, and square root, but they're not nearly as common. Big Oh notation is described as O (<type>) where <type> is the measure.

The quicksort algorithm would be described as O (N * log (N)).

Note that none of this has taken into account best, average, and worst case measures. Each would have its own Big Oh notation. Also note that this is a VERY simplistic explanation. Big Oh is the most common. There are also other notations such as big omega, little o, and big theta.

3.8.2 Theory Examples

So, let's take an example of Big-O. Say that f(n) = 2n + 8, and g(n) = n2. Can we find a constant c, so that 2n + 8 <= n2? The number 4 works here, giving us 16 <= 16. For any number c greater than 4, this will still work. Since we're trying to generalize this for large values of n, and small values (1, 2, 3) aren't that important, we can say that f(n) is generally faster than g(n); that is, f(n) is bound by g(n), and will always be less than it.

It could then be said that f(n) runs in O(n2) time: "f-of-n runs in Big-O of n-squared time".

To find the upper bound — the Big-O time — assuming we know that f(n) is equal to (exactly) 2n + 8, we can take a few shortcuts. For example, we can remove all constants from the runtime; eventually, at some value of c, they become irrelevant. This makes f(n) = 2n. Also, for convenience of comparison, we remove constant multipliers; in this case, the 2. This makes f(n) = n. It could also be said that f(n) runs in O(n) time; that lets us put a tighter (closer) upper bound onto the estimate.

3.8.3 Practical Examples

O(n): printing a list of n items to the screen, looking at each item once.

O(log n): also "log n", taking a list of items, cutting it in half repeatedly until there's only one item left.

O(n^2): taking a list of n items, and comparing every item to every other item.

3.8.4 Big-omega Notation

For non-negative functions, f(n) and g(n), if there exists an integer n0 and a constant c > 0 such that for all integers n > n0, f(n) e" cg(n), then f(n) is omega of g(n). This is denoted as "f(n) = Ω(g(n))".

This is almost the same definition as Big Oh, except that "f(n) e" cg(n)", this makes g(n) a lower bound function, instead of an upper bound function. It describes the best that can happen for a given data size.

1. **Theta Notation:** For non-negative functions, f(n) and g(n), f(n) is theta of g(n) if and only if f(n) = O(g(n)) and f(n) = Ω(g(n)). This is denoted as "f(n) = Θ(g(n))".

   This is basically saying that the function, f(n) is bounded both from the top and bottom by the same function, g(n).
2. **Little-O Notation:** For non-negative functions, f(n) and g(n), f(n) is little o of g(n) if and only if f(n) = O(g(n)), but f(n) ≠ Θ(g(n)). This is denoted as "f(n) = o(g(n))".

   This represents a loose bounding version of Big O. g(n) bounds from the top, but it does not bound the bottom.
3. **Little Omega Notation:** For non-negative functions, f(n) and g(n), f(n) is little omega of g(n) if and only if f(n) = Ω(g(n)), but f(n) ≠ Θ(g(n)). This is denoted as "f(n) = ω(g(n))". Much like Little Oh, this is the equivalent for Big Omega. g(n) is a loose lower boundary of the function f(n); it bounds from the bottom, but not from the top.

3.8.5 How Asymptotic Notation Relates to Analyzing Complexity

Temporal comparison is not the only issue in algorithms. There are space issues as well. Generally, a trade off between time and space is noticed in algorithms. Asymptotic notation empowers you to make that trade off. If you think of the amount of time and space your algorithm uses as a function of your data over time or space (time and space are usually analyzed separately), you can analyze how the time and space is handled when you introduce more data to your program.

This is important in data structures because you want a structure that behaves efficiently as you increase the amount of data it handles. Keep in mind though those algorithms that are efficient with large amounts data are not always simple and efficient for small amounts of data. So if you know you are working with only a small amount of data and you have concerns for speed and code space, a trade off can be made for a function that does not behave well for large amounts of data.

3.8.6 A Few Examples of Asymptotic Notation

Generally, we use asymptotic notation as a convenient way to examine what can happen in a function in the worst case or in the best case. For example, if you want to write a function that searches through an array of numbers and returns the smallest one:

```
Function find-min(array a[1..n])
Let j = ∞
For i = 1 to n:
j = min(j, a[i])
Repeat
Return j
End
```

Regardless of how big or small the array is, every time we run find-min, we have to initialize the i and j integer variables and return j at the end. Therefore, we can just think of those parts of the function as constant and ignore them.

So, how can we use asymptotic notation to discuss the find-min function? If we search through an array with 87 elements, then the for loop iterates 87 times, even if the very first element we hit turns out to be the minimum. Likewise, for n elements, the for loop iterates n times. Therefore we say the function runs in time O(n).

What about this function:

```
Function find-min-plus-max(array a[1..n])
// First, find the smallest element in the array
Let j = ∞;
For i = 1 to n:
j = min(j, a[i])
Repeat
Let min = j
// Now, find the biggest element, add it to the smallest and
j = −∞;
For i = 1 to n:
j = max(j, a[i])
Repeat
Let max = j
// return the sum of the two
Return min + max;
End
```

What's the running time for find-min-plus-max? There are two for loops, that each iterate n times, so the running time is clearly O(2n). Because 2 is a constant, we throw it away and write the running time as O(n). Why can you do this? If you recall the definition of Big-O notation, the function whose bound you're testing can be multiplied by some constant. If f(x) = 2x, we can see that if g(x) = x, then the Big-O condition holds. Thus O(2n) = O(n). This rule is general for the various asymptotic notations.

3.9 SPACE VS TIME COMPLEXITY

In general, the amount of space used is less than the amount of time used because space cab be reused and time cannot. For most applications, we focus on time complexity, since memory tends to be cheap compared to time (three days). Some times, space is still and issue-particularly if the problem size is very large and the solution requires relatively low time complexity. (An example would be sorting very large (on the order of one billion element) data sets.). A simple space example – adding two arrays of integers. Assume our array size is N and A.B are input arrays.

1. The following code requires N+N+N= 3N space:
2. int C [N}
3. for (int i=o; < N; i++)
4. C (i) = A (i) + B (i);
5. Suppose we no larger need B- we can reuse it. The following code requires only N+N = 2N space:
6. For (int i = o; i < N; i ++)
7. B (i) = A (i) + B (i);

Running –Time Analysis

How much time does each function require?

Actual time (i.e. seconds) hard to measure – varies from machine to machine and system to system

Consider time as number of basic operations:

1. One arithmetic op, e/g. + -*
2. One assignment
3. One read
4. One writes etc.

3.10 TIME SPACE TRADE OFF

To solve a given programming problem, many different algorithms may be used. Some of these algorithms may be extremely time-efficient and others extremely space-efficient. A space-time or time-memory tradeoff is a situation where the memory use can be reduced at the cost of slower program execution, or vice versa, the computation time can be reduced at the cost of increased memory use. As the relative costs of CPU cycles, RAM space, and hard drive space change — hard drive space has for some time been getting cheaper at a much faster rate than other components of computers— the appropriate choices for space-time tradeoffs have changed radically. Often, by exploiting a space-time tradeoff, a program can be made to run much faster.

The most common situation is an algorithm involving a lookup table: an implementation can include the entire table, which reduces computing time, but increases the amount of memory needed, or it can compute table entries as needed, increasing computing time, but reducing memory requirements.

A space-time tradeoff can be applied to the problem of data storage. If data is stored uncompressed, it takes more space but less time than if the data were stored compressed (since compressing the data reduces the amount of space it takes, but it takes time to run the compression algorithm). Depending on the particular instance of the problem, either way is practical.

In most of the cases, the space and time required by an algorithm are inversely related as:

i.e. $S \propto 1/T$ (Here $\propto$ is inversely proportional)

Where S is space required by an algorithm and T is time required by an algorithm.

We can reduce the space requirements by increasing running time or vice-versa.

This situation is referred to as time-space tradeoff. Let us take a simple example of computing the exponential function x^n, where n is positive integer. The function x^n is defined as:

$$x * x * x * x \text{———} n \text{ times.}$$

We will solve this problem with two different approaches as:

Approach 1

Algorithm 3.6: Let's discuss the algorithm of time-space tradeoff

Step 1: Start

Step 2: Read the variables n, x

Step 3: Assign the value of x to y

Step 4: Execute step 5 for n–1 times.
Step 5: Multiply the values of y & x and assign the calculated value to y
Step 6: Print the value of y
Step 7: End

This approach executes n-1 multiples, so **f1(n) = 0(n).**

Approach 2

This approach uses recursion. Let us consider the following function Exp(x,n), to find an exponent using recursion.

```
Exp (x, n)
{
if (n==1)
return x;
y = exp (x, n/2);
if (n%2==0)
return (y *y);
else
return (y * y* x);
}
```

This is a segment of a program to find exponent using recursion. Let us define it in an algorithm.

Algorithm 3.7: Let's discuss the algorithm of time-space tradeoff using recursion.

Step 1: Start
Step 2: Read the variables n, x
Step 3: if the value of n is 1 then print the value of x else goto step 4.
Step 4: Call the same function algorithm with value of x, value of n as n/2 and goto step 5
Step 5: If value of n is odd then assign the value of y *y *x to y and Print the same value else goto step 6.
Step 6: assign the value of y * y to y and print the same value
Step 7: End

Running times of two approaches discussed, are related to the number of multiplications they perform.

Thus for large exponents, the running time of approach 2 is much less than that of approach 1, however, memory space required by approach2 is much greater than approach 1, as it makes large number of recursive function calls.

3.11 INTRODUCTION TO PRIMITIVE DATA STRUCTURE AND NON PRIMITIVE DATA STRUCTURE

3.11.1 Primitive Data Structure

A new, primitive type is definable by enumerating the distinct values belonging to it. Such a type is called an *enumeration type*. Its definition has the form

TYPE T = (c_1, c_2, ... , c_n)

T is the new type identifier, and the ci are the new constant identifiers.

Examples

TYPE shape = (rectangle, square, ellipse, circle)

TYPE color = (red, yellow, green)

TYPE sex = (male, female)

TYPE weekday = (Monday, Tuesday, Wednesday, Thursday, Friday, Saturday, Sunday)

TYPE currency = (franc, mark, pound, dollar, shilling, lira, guilder, krone, ruble, cruzeiro, yen)

TYPE destination = (hell, purgatory, heaven)

TYPE vehicle = (train, bus, automobile, boat, airplane)

TYPE rank = (private, corporal, sergeant, lieutenant, captain, major, colonel, general)

TYPE object = (constant, type, variable, procedure, module)

TYPE structure = (array, record, set, sequence)

TYPE condition = (manual, unloaded, parity, skew)

The definition of such types introduces not only a new type identifier, but at the same times the set of identifiers denoting the values of the new type. These identifiers may then be used as constants throughout the program, and they enhance its understandability considerably. If, as an example, we introduce variables

s, d, r, and b.

VAR s: sex

VAR d: weekday

VAR r: rank

then the following assignment statements are possible:

s := male

d := Sunday

r := major

b := TRUE

Evidently, they are considerably more informative than their counterparts

s := 1 d := 7 r := 6 b := 2

which are based on the assumption that c, d, r, and b are defined as integers and that the constants are mapped onto the natural numbers in the order of their enumeration. Furthermore, a compiler can check against the inconsistent use of operators. For example, given the declaration of s above, the statement

s :=s+1 would be meaningless.

If, however, we recall that enumerations are ordered, then it is sensible to introduce operators that generate the successor and predecessor of their argument. We therefore postulate the following standard operators, which assign to their argument its successor and predecessor respectively:

INC(x) DEC(x)

3.11.2 Standard Primitive Types

Standard primitive types are those types that are available on most computers as built-in features. They include the whole numbers, the logical truth values, and a set of printable characters. On many computers fractional numbers are also incorporated, together with the standard arithmetic operations. We denote these types by the identifiers

1. Integer
2. Real
3. Boolean
4. Char
5. Set

1. INTEGERS

The type INTEGER comprises a subset of the whole numbers whose size may vary among individual computer systems. If a computer uses *n* bits to represent an integer in two's complement notation, then the admissible values x must satisfy $-2^{n-1} \leq x < 2^{n-1}$. It is assumed that all operations on data of this type are exact and correspond to the ordinary laws of arithmetic, and that the computation will be interrupted in the case of a result lying outside the representable subset. This event is called *overflow*. The standard operators are the four basic arithmetic operations of addition (+), subtraction (–), multiplication (*), and division (/).

Whereas the slash denotes ordinary division resulting in a value of type REAL, the operator DIV denotes integer division resulting in a value of type INTEGER. If we define the quotient q = m DIV n and the remainder r = m MOD n, the following relations hold, assuming n > 0:

q*n + r = m and 0 d" r < n

Examples:

31 DIV 10 = 3 31 MOD 10 = 1

–31 DIV 10 = –4 –31 MOD 10 = 9

We know that dividing by 10^n can be achieved by merely shifting the decimal digits n places to the right and thereby ignoring the lost digits. The same method applies, if numbers are represented in binary instead of decimal form. If two's complement representation is used (as in practically all modern computers), then the shifts implement a division as defined by the above DIV operaton. Moderately sophisticated compilers will therefore represent an operation of the form m DIV 2^n or m MOD 2^n by a fast shift (or mask) operation.

2. REAL

The type REAL denotes a subset of the real numbers. Whereas arithmetic with operands of the types INTEGER is assumed to yield exact results, arithmetic on values of type REAL is permitted to be inaccurate within the limits of round-off errors caused by computation on a finite number of digits. This is the principal reason for the explicit distinction between the types INTEGER and REAL, as it is made in most programming languages.

The standard operators are the four basic arithmetic operations of addition (+), subtraction (–), multiplication (*), and division (/). It is an essence of data typing that different types are incompatible under assignment. An exception to this rule is made for assignment of integer values to real variables, because here the semantics are unambiguous. After all, integers form a subset of real numbers. However, the inverse direction is not permissible: Assignment of a real value to an integer variable requires an operation such as truncation or rounding.

3. BOOLEANS

The two values of the standard type BOOLEAN are denoted by the identifiers TRUE and FALSE. The Boolean operators are the logical conjunction, disjunction, and negation. The logical conjunction is denoted by the symbol &, the logical disjunction by OR, and negation by "~". Note that comparisons are operations yielding a result of type BOOLEAN. Thus, the result of a comparison may be assigned to a variable, or it may be used as an operand of a logical operator in a Boolean expression.

```
p := x = y
q := (xd"y) & (y < z)
yield p = FALSE and q = TRUE.
```

Table 3.1 Boolean Operators.

p	q	p & q	p OR q	~p
True	True	True	True	False
True	False	True	False	False
False	True	True	False	True
False	False	False	False	True

The Boolean operators & (AND) and OR have an additional property in most programming languages, which distinguishes them from other dyadic operators. Whereas, for example, the sum $x+y$ is not defined, if either x or y is undefined, the conjunction p&q is defined even if q is undefined, provided that p is FALSE.

This conditionality is an important and useful property. The exact definition of & and OR is therefore given by the following equations:

p & q = if p then q else FALSE

p OR q = if p then TRUE else q

4. CHARACTERS

The standard type CHAR comprises a set of printable characters. Unfortunately, there is no generally accepted standard character set used on all computer systems. Therefore, the use of the predicate "standard" may in this case be almost misleading; it is to be understood in the sense of "standard on the computer system on which a certain program is to be executed."

The character set defined by the International Standards Organization (ISO), and particularly its American version ASCII (American Standard Code for Information Interchange) is the most widely accepted set. The ASCII set is therefore tabulated in Appendix A. It consists of 95 printable (graphic) characters and 33 control characters, the latter mainly being used in data transmission and for the control of printing equipment.

In order to be able to design algorithms involving characters (i.e., values of type CHAR) that are system independent, we should like to be able to assume certain minimal properties of character sets, namely:

1. The type CHAR contains the 26 capital Latin letters, the 26 lower-case letters, the 10 decimal digits, and a number of other graphic characters, such as punctuation marks.
2. The subsets of letters and digits are ordered and contiguous, i.e.,
3. The type CHAR contains a non-printing, blank character and a line-end character that may be used as separators.

5. SET

The type SET denotes sets whose elements are integers in the range 0 to a small number, typically 31 or 63. Given, for example, variables

VAR r, s, t: SET

possible assignments are

r := {5}; s := {x, y .. z}; t := {}

Here, the value assigned to r is the singleton set consisting of the single element 5; to t is assigned the empty set, and to s the elements x, y, y+1, … , z–1, z.

The following elementary operators are defined on variables of type SET:

* set intersection

\+ set union

– set difference

/ symmetric set difference

IN set membership

Constructing the intersection or the union of two sets is often called set multiplication or set addition, respectively; the priorities of the set operators are defined accordingly, with the intersection operator having priority over the union and difference operators, which in turn have priority over the membership operator, which is classified as a relational operator. Following are examples of set expressions and their fully parenthesized equivalents:

r * s + t = (r*s) + t

r – s * t = r – (s*t)

r – s + t = (r–s) + t

r + s / t = r + (s/t)

x IN s + t = x IN (s+t)

3.11.3 Non Primitive Data Structure

The data structures which are developed by programmer/User for his or her convenience are known as non primitive data structures. For example Array, Linked List, Stack etc.

1. FILE

A file is a collection of number of related records that may have the same or varying length. For example collection of all employee records for one company would be an employee file. Similarly collection of all inventory records for a company forms an inventory file. It is customary to set up a *master file* of permanent data and to use *transaction file* containing data of temporary nature. A file is a collection of related data stored in a particular area on the disk. There are two types of access on the files (two ways to access the files). These are sequential access files and random access file. In the sequential access files, the data or text can be store or read back sequentially. In the random access files, data can be accessed and processed randomly. Also files can be divided into two types. One is data file and second one is program file. There are two types of operations can be done on data i.e. data can be transferred between the console and the program and further can be transferred between program and a disk file.

3.11.4 Applications of Primitive Data Structures

1. *Polynomial ADT*

A polynomial can be represented with primitive data structures. For example, a polynomial represented as $a_k x^k a_{k-1} x^{k-1} + ... + a_0$ can be represented as a linked list. Each node is a structure with two values: a_i and i. Thus, the length of the list will be k. The first node will have (a_k, k), the second node will have (a_{k-1}, k–1) etc. The last node will be (a_0, 0).

The polynomial $3x^9 + 7x^3 + 5$ can be represented in a list as follows: $(3,9) \rightarrow (7,3) \rightarrow (5,0)$ where each pair of integers represent a node, and the arrow represents a link to its neighbouring node. Derivatives of polynomials can be easily computed by proceeding node by node. In our previous example the list after computing the derivative would represented as follows: $(27,8) \rightarrow (21,2)$. The specific polynomial ADT will define various operations, such as multiplication, addition, subtraction, derivative, integration etc. A polynomial ADT can be useful for symbolic computation as well.

2. *Large Integers ADT*

Large integers can also be implemented with primitive data structures. To conform to our previous example, consider a large integer represented as a linked list. If we represent the integer as successive powers of 10, where the power of 10 increments by 3 and the coefficient is a three digit number, we can make computations on such numbers easier. For example, we can represent a very large number as follows:

$$513(10^6) + 899(10^3) + 722(10^0).$$

Using this notation, the number can be represented as follows:

$$(513) \rightarrow (899) \rightarrow (722).$$

The first number represents the coefficient of the 10^6 term, the next number represents the coefficient of the 10^3 term and so on. The arrows represent links to adjacent nodes.

The specific ADT will define operations on this representation, such as addition, subtraction, multiplication, division, comparison, copy etc.

3. *Window Manager ADT*

A window interface can be represented by lists. Consider an environment with many windows. The first node in the list could represent the current active window. Subsequent windows are further along the list. In other words, the nth window corresponds to the nth node in the list.

The ADT can define several functions, such as Find_first_window which would bring a window clicked upon to the front of the list (make it active). Other functions could perform window deletion or creation.

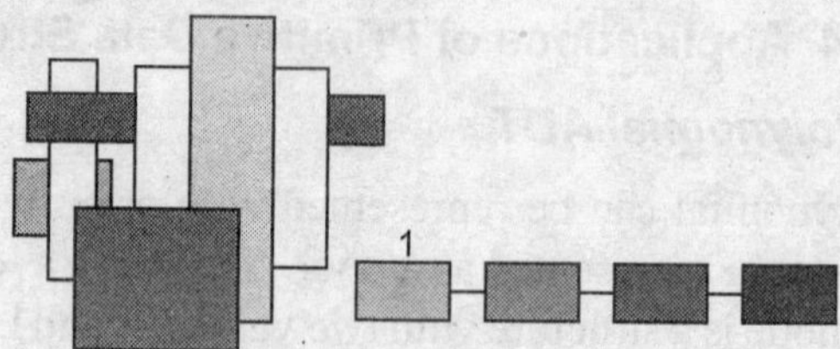

4. *Management of Free Space*

When memory is requested, a list of available blocks of memory might be useful. Again, a list could represent blocks in memory available to the user, with nodes containing pointers to these available blocks. The list can be used like a stack (LIFO). The last freed memory becomes the next available to the user. Such lists are called 'free space lists' or 'available space lists'. Since addition and deletion of nodes is at one end, these lists behave like stacks. All operations on free space lists can be done in O(1) time.

3.12 ABSTRACT DATA TYPE

An abstract data type or abstract data structure is a mathematical model for a certain class of data structures that have similar behavior; or for certain data types of one or more programming languages that have similar semantics. An abstract data type is defined indirectly, only by the operations that may be performed on it and by mathematical constraints on the effects (and possibly cost) of those operations.

For example, an abstract stack data structure could be defined by two operations: push, that inserts some data item into the structure, and pop, that extracts an item from it; with the constraint that each pop always returns the most recently pushed item that has not been popped yet. When analyzing the efficiency of algorithms that use stacks, one may also specify that both operations take the same time no matter how many items have been pushed into the stack, and that the stack uses a constant amount of storage for each element.

Abstract data types are purely theoretical entities, used (among other things) to simplify the description of abstract algorithms, to classify and evaluate data structures, and to formally describe the type systems of programming languages. However, an ADT may be implemented by specific data types or data structures, in many ways and in many programming languages; or described in a formal specification language. ADTs are often implemented as modules: the module's interface declares procedures that correspond to the ADT operations, sometimes with comments that describe the constraints. This information hiding strategy allows the implementation of the module to be changed without disturbing the client programs. Abstract data types are also an important conceptual tool in object-oriented programming and design by contract methodologies for software development.

In computing, an abstract data type (ADT) is a specification of a set of data and the set of operations that can be performed on the data. Such a data type is abstract in the sense that it is independent of various concrete implementations. The definition can be mathematical, or it can be programmed as an interface. The interface provides a constructor, which returns an abstract handle to new data, and several operations, which are functions accepting the abstract handle as an argument.

3.12.1 Examples

ADTs typically seen in textbooks and implemented in programming languages (or their libraries) include:

*String

*List

*Linked List

*Stack

*Queue

*Binary search tree

*Priority queue

*Complex number

*Associative array

*Multimap

The name "abstract data type" apparently was coined by researchers in software engineering and programming language design; while "abstract data structure" was coined by researchers in data structures and algorithms.

3.12.2 Defining an Abstract Data Type

Since ADTs are theoretical concepts, there are no standard conventions for defining them. A broad division may be drawn between "imperative" and "functional" definition styles.

3.12.3 Imperative Abstract Data Type

In the "imperative" view, which is closer to the philosophy of imperative programming languages, an abstract data structure is conceived as an entity that is mutable — meaning that it may be in different states at different times. Some operations may change the state of the ADT; therefore, the order in which operations are evaluated is important, and the same operation on the same entities may have different effects if executed at different times — just like the instructions of a computer, or the commands and procedures of an imperative language. To underscore this view, it is customary to say that the operations are executed or applied, rather than evaluated. The imperative style is often used when describing abstract algorithms.

3.12.4 Functional ADT

Another way to define an ADT, closer to the spirit of functional programming, is to consider each state of the structure as a separate entity. In this view, any operation that modifies the ADT is modeled as a mathematical function that takes the old state as an argument, and returns the new state as part of the result. Unlike the "imperative" operations, these functions have no side effects. Therefore, the order in which they are evaluated is immaterial, and the same operation applied to the same arguments (including the same input states) will always return the same results (and output states). In the functional view, in particular, there is no way (or need) to define an "abstract variable" with the semantics of imperative variables (namely, with fetch and store operations). Instead of storing values into variables, one passes them as arguments to functions.

3.12.5 Example: Abstract Stack (Functional)

For example, a complete functional-style definition of a stack ADT could use the three operations:

- push: takes a stack state and an arbitrary value, returns a stack state;
- top: takes a stack state, returns a value;
- pop: takes a stack state, returns a stack state;

with the following axioms:

- top(push(s,x)) = x (pushing an item onto a stack leaves it at the top)
- pop(push(s,x)) = s (pop undoes the effect of push)

In a functional-style definition there is no need for a create operation. Indeed, there is no notion of "stack instance". The stack states can be thought of as being potential states of a single stack structure, and two stack states that contain the same values in the same order are considered to be identical states. This view actually mirrors the behavior of some concrete implementations, such as linked lists with hash cons.

Instead of create(), a functional definition of a stack ADT may assume the existence of a special stack state, the empty stack, designted by a special symbol like Λ or "()"; or define a bottom() operation that takes no aguments and returns this special stack state. Note that the axioms imply that

- push(Λ, x) ≠ Λ

In a functional definition of a stack one does not need an empty predicate: instead, one can test whether a stack is empty by testing whether it is equal to Λ.

Note that these axioms do not define the effect of top(s) or pop(s), unless s is a stack state returned by a push. Since push leaves the stack non-empty, those two operations are undefined (hence invalid) when s = Λ. On the other hand, the axioms (and the lack of side effects) imply that push(s,x) = push(t,y) if and only if x = y and s = t.

As in some other branches of mathematics, it is customary to assume also that the stack states are only those whose existence can be proved from the axioms in a finite number of steps. In the stack ADT example above, this rule means that every stack is a finite sequence of values, that becomes the empty stack (Λ) after a finite number of pops. By themselves, the axioms above do not exclude the existence of infinite stacks (that can be poped forever, each time yielding a different state) or circular stacks (that return to the same state after a finite number of pops). In particular, they do not exclude states s such that pop(s) = s or push(s,x) = s for some x. However, since one cannot obtain such stack states with the given operations, they are assumed "not to exist".

3.12.6 Use of Abstract Data Type

Abstract Data Types can minimize dependencies in your code, which is important when your code needs to be changed. Because you are abstracted away from lower-level details, some of the higher-level commonalities one data structure shares with a different data structure can be used to replace one with the other.

3.12.7 Why ADT?

Although most programming languages support some standard data types, they are not enough for most of applications. So programming languages usually support creating new data types in terms of "structured types". This can be done in "C" language by defining a "struct".

However just by defining a structured type, the operations applicable to objects of that type cannot be specified. This is why the concept of an Abstract Data Type is required.

3.12.8 Need and Importance of Structure

The most significant way that structured documents differ from unstructured ones is that structured documents include "rules." These rules proscribe the order in which text, graphics, and tables may be entered. For example, in an unstructured document, a paragraph has specific formatting—font, size, and spacing. In a structured document, this same paragraph adds to this formatting an exterior "wrapper" or "element" that governs the elements that appear before and after it. The elements rules come from a **Document Type Definition** (DTD).

Basically, you move away from working with formatting and instead work with information rules for how things fit together and when things can occur. In most tools, the formatting is automated so that you can concentrate on your content while authoring rather than on formatting and layout.

3.12.9 Benefits of Structure

Structure brings to your documents a level of control that formatting alone cannot provide. Using structure has long-term and short-term benefits. These benefits include:

- re-use of information
- standardization of documents
- guided authoring
- improved information management

1. *Information Control*

Another consideration is information control. If data retrieval from documents is a goal, then structured documents are the obvious choice. Structured documents can interact with, or in some cases act as a database, with information sorted, extracted, and reused.

Another part of information control deserving of its own mention is translation. When sending documents for translation, regular word processing files would be sent for translation in full. With structure, however, additional data (part of a structured document's metadata) can include information on translation status. This means that each paragraph within a document can be marked as needing translation, translated already, modified since prior translation, and so forth. Companies doing the translation can then selectively translate new and modified content without retranslating content that has already been translated and has not changed.

2. *Consistency*

Documentation consistency issues also figure into the structured/unstructured debate. Structured data adds rules to prompt programmers, providing extra control. Consider simple example of workgroups in which many authors are working on same book. Each author holds biases and preferences, any of which can be good or bad. Multiple authors working the same document may each organize their chapter in a different way. Structure adds rules to prompt authors. So, structure is a very good direction to enforce consistency.

3.12.10 Separation of Interface and Implementation

When realized in a computer program, the ADT is represented by an interface, which shields a corresponding implementation. Users of an ADT are concerned with the interface, but not the implementation, as the implementation can change in the future. (This supports the principle of information hiding, or protecting the program from design decisions that are subject to change.)

The strength of an ADT is that the implementation is hidden from the user. Only the interface is published. This means that the ADT can be implemented in various ways, but as long as it adheres to the interface, user programs are unaffected.

There is a distinction, although sometimes subtle, between the abstract data type and the data structure used in its implementation. For example, a List ADT can be represented using an array-based implementation or a linked-list implementation. A List is an abstract data type with well-defined operations (add element, remove element, etc.) while a linked-list is a pointer-based data structure that can be used to create a representation of a List. The linked-list implementation is so commonly used to represent a List ADT that the terms are interchanged in common use.

Similarly, a Binary Search Tree ADT can be represented in several ways: binary tree, AVL tree, red-black tree, array, etc. Regardless of the implementation, the Binary Search Tree always has the same operations (insert, remove, find, etc.)

3.12.11 Abstract Data Structure

An abstract data structure is an abstract storage for data defined in terms of the set of operations to be performed on data and computational complexity for performing these operations, regardless of the implementation in a concrete data structure.

Selection of an abstract data structure is crucial in the design of efficient algorithms and in estimating their computational complexity, while selection of concrete data structures is important for efficient implementation of algorithms.

This notion is very close to that of an abstract data type, used in the theory of programming languages. The names of many abstract data structures (and abstract data types) match the names of concrete data structures.

3.12.12 Built-in Abstract Data Types

Because some ADTs are so common and useful in computer programs, some programming languages build implementations of ADTs into the language as native types or add them into their standard libraries. For instance, Perl arrays can be thought of as an implementation of the List or Deque ADTs and Perl hashes can be thought of in terms of Map or Table ADTs. The C++ Standard Library and Java libraries provide classes that implement the List, Stack, Queue, Map, Priority Queue, and String ADTs.

3.12.13 Rational Numbers as an Abstract Data Type

Rational numbers (numbers that can be written in the form a/b where a and b are integers) cannot be represented natively in a computer. A Rational ADT could be defined as shown below.

Construction: Create an instance of a rational number ADT using two integers, a and b, where a represents the numerator and b represents the denominator.

Operations: addition, subtraction, multiplication, division, exponentiation, comparison, simplify, conversion to a real (floating point) number.

To be a complete specification, each operation should be defined in terms of the data. For example, when multiplying two rational numbers a/b and c/d, the result is defined as ac/bd. Typically, inputs, outputs, preconditions, postconditions, and assumptions for the ADT are specified as well.

Stack Interface

The interface for a Stack ADT, written in C-style notation, might be:

```
long stack_create(); /* create new instance of a stack */
void stack_push(long stack, void *item); /* push an item on the stack */
void *stack_pop(long stack); /* get item from top of stack */
void stack_delete(long stack); /* delete the stack */
```

Usage

This ADT could be used in the following manner:

```
long stack;
struct foo *f;
stack = stack_create(); /* create a stack */
stack_push(stack, f); /* add foo structure to stack */
f = stack_pop(stack); /* get top structure from stack */
```

Implementation variants

The above stack ADT could be initially implemented using an array, and then later changed to a linked list, without affecting any user code.

The number of ways a given ADT can be implemented depends on the programming language. For example, the above example could be written in C++

using a struct and an accompanying set of data structures using arrays or linked lists to store the entries; however, since the constructor function returns an abstract handle, the actual implementation is hidden from the user. In object-oriented languages such as C++ and Java, ADTs are typically represented using the class construct where the data is represented by data members (attributes) and the operations are represented by member functions (methods). In addition, some languages such as C++ and Java provide a mechanism of enforcement (the private or protected keywords) to only allow the defined functions to operate on the data. When using object-oriented ADTs, the user can often expand the ADT by creating a subclass of the ADT.

3.12.14 Implementation

Implementing an ADT means providing one procedure or function for each abstract operation. The ADT instances are represented by some concrete data structure that is manipulated by those procedures, according to the ADT's specifications.

Usually there are many ways to implement the same ADT, using several different concrete data structures. Thus, for example, an abstract stack can be implemented by a linked list or by an array.

An ADT implementation is often packaged as one or more modules, whose interface contains only the signature (number and types of the parameters and results) of the operations. The implementation of the module — namely, the bodies of the procedures and the concrete data structure used — can then be hidden from most clients of the module. This makes it possible to change the implementation without affecting the clients.

When implementing an ADT, each instance (in imperative-style definitions) or each state (in functional-style definitions) is usually represented by a handle of some sort.

In object-oriented programming languages, such as C++ and Java, an ADT is typically implemented as class, and each instance of the ADT is an object of that class. The module's interface typically declares the constructors as ordinary procedures, and most of the other ADT operations as methods of that class.

EXAMPLE: Implementation of the Stack ADT

As an example, here is an implementation of the stack ADT above in the C++ programming language.

Imperative-style interface

An imperative-style interface might be:

```
typedef struct stack_Rep stack_Rep;
/* Type: instance representation (an opaque record). */
```

```
typedef stack_Rep *stack_T;
/* Type: handle to a stack instance (an opaque pointer). */
typedef void *stack_Item;
/* Type: value that can be stored in stack (arbitrary address). */
stack_T stack_create(void);
/* Create new stack instance, initially empty. */
void stack_push(stack_T s, stack_Item e);
/* Add an item at the top of the stack. */
stack_Item stack_pop(stack_T s);
/* Remove the top item from the stack and return it . */
int stack_empty(stack_T ts);
/* Check whether stack is empty. */
```

This implementation could be used in the following manner:

```
#include <stack.h> /* Include the stack interface. */ stack_T t =
stack_create(); /* Create a stack instance. */ int foo = 17; /* An arbitrary
datum. */ t = stack_push(t, &f); /* Push the address of 'foo' onto the stack.
*/ … void *e = stack_pop(t); /* Get the top item and delete it from the stack.
*/ if (stack_empty(t)) { … } /* Do something if stack is empty. */ …
```

This interface can be implemented in many ways. The implementation may be arbitrarily inefficient, since the formal definition of the ADT, above, does not specify how much space the stack may use, nor how long each operation should take. It also does not specify whether the stack state t continues to exist after a call s ← pop(t).

In practice the formal definition should specify that the space is proportional to the number of items pushed and not yet popped; and that every one of the operations above must finish in a constant amount of time, independently of that number. To comply with these additional specifications, the implementation could use a linked list, or an array (with dynamic resizing) together with two integers (an item count and the array size).

OBJECTIVE TYPE QUESTIONS

1. Data structure is
   (a) Physical and logical model of organization
   (b) Logical and mathematical model of organization
   (c) Physical and mathematical model of organization
   (d) All of the above
   (e) None

2. Which of the following data items lead to variable length record when included as item in the record?

(a) Name of spouse (b) Name of children

(c) Education (d) Pervious employee

(e) All of the above

3. LIFO is related with

(a) Stack (b) Queue

(c) Both (d) None

4. The complexity of binary search is

(a) Log n^2 (b) O log n^2

(c) n/2 (d) None of the above

5. Before traversing data should be

(a) Indexed (b) non-indexed

(c) Either a or b (d) None

6. For ascending purpose, bubble sort has one major operation before interchanging as:

(a) a[i]–a[i+1] (b) a[i]+a[i+1]

(c) a[i]=a[i+1] (d) None

7. Complexity of Bubble sort is

(a) O log n (b) O(n)

(c) log n (d) None

8. Binary search comparison to linear search is

(a) Fast (b) Slow

(c) Both (d) None

9. Before applying binary search data should be:

(a) Sorted (b) Unsorted

(c) Both (d) None

10. The mid point in binary search should be of type:

(a) integer (b) Real

(c) Both (d) None

11. Information is represented by ....

(a) data (b) characters

(c) numeral (d) bits

12. In this method a positive integer is converted to negative by changing each bit to its opposite value.
    (a) one's complement (b) two's complement
    (c) both (a) and (b) (d) none of the above
13. The data type defined by the user is known as ....
    (a) abstract data type (b) built-in data type
    (c) classic data type (d) none of the above
14. The keyword class or struct can be used to create ....
    (a) abstract data type (b) built-in data type
    (c) logical data type (d) all of the above
15. An integer data type is ....
    (a) primitive (b) non-linear
    (c) (a) and (b) (d) non-primitive

EXERCISES

1. What do you understand by algorithms? Explain various types of algorithm in detail.
2. What is flow-chart?
3. How we can determine the efficiency of an algorithm?
4. Explain concept of Big O notations.
5. Explain in detail complexity of algorithms.
6. What do you mean by asymptotic notation?
7. What do you understand by time space trade off?
8. Difference between primitive data structure and non primitive data structure?
9. What are various applications of primitive data structures?
10. What is abstract data type? Explain various uses of ADT.
11. Explain the need and importance of structure.

Arrays, Pointers and Records

4.1 INTRODUCTION

In computer science, Data structure is said to be linear if its element store in proper sequence or in form of simple linear list or linear relationship between the elements represented by means of sequential memory locations. An **Array** is a data structure that consists of a group of elements having a common name and these elements are accessed by using indexing. In most programming languages each element has the same data type and the elements of the array are stored in successive memory locations.

These are the various operations perform on array:

1. **Traversing:** Accessing and processing of each element exactly once.
2. **Searching:** Find the location of the element from the given array.
3. **Insertion:** Adding a new element in the array.
4. **Deletion:** Removing an element from the array.
5. **Sorting:** Arranging the elements in some type of order.
6. **Merging:** Combining two arrays into a single array.

Array elements are usually numbered (as opposed to an associative array) and individual elements are accessed by their numeric position in the array. Some arrays are multi-dimensional, meaning that more than one index is needed to access an element. For instance, a two-dimensional array might be thought of as the elements in a plane that are indexed by x and y coordinates, while a three-dimensional array might be thought of as a volume that is indexed by x, y, and z coordinates and so on.

An array is simply a number of memory locations, each of which can store an item of data of the same data type and which are all referenced through the same variable name. An array data structure or simply array is a data structure consisting of a collection of elements (values or variables), each identified by one or more integer indices, stored so that the address of each element can be computed from its index tuple by a simple mathematical formula. For example, an array of 10 integer variables, with indices 0 through 9, may be stored as 10 words at memory addresses 2000, 2004, 2008, … 2036; so that the element with index i has address $2000 + 4 \times i$.

Array is same type of data collection i.e. it is a collection of same data type elements. An array is a group of related data items, which can share common name. It is the set of homogeneous data.

Now question arises, why we need array. This can be explained by taking an example for preparing the grade of 100 students in an examination. So to solve this problem, we declare 100 different variables. But if in the next session, 50 more students sit in the examination, then it will require number of changes in the program and also program becomes more complex. So to solve such type of problem, we need to define and declare array. Also processing speed becomes fast with the declaration and use of an array.

The simplest of composite data structures is the *array*. It's just a group of data items stored in successive locations in computer memory. The data items can be any of the aforementioned basic types.

But arrays are a poor data structure when you must frequently change the data. The *linked lists*, often called just *lists*, are better. Linked lists store sequences of data items like arrays do, but the items do not have to be in successive locations in computer memory; each is paired with a pointer giving the memory location of the next data item in sequence, with the last data item in the list having a special pointer called *NULL*. So a list can be scattered around in computer memory, provided you keep item-pointer pairs together and store the location of the first data item. Linked lists need more space to store data items than an array would, but allow more flexibility in the use of computer memory. Lists are more common in artificial-intelligence programming than arrays, and in fact the programming language Lisp is built entirely around lists: lists even represent programs in Lisp.

Arrays and lists order their items. An unordered set can be stored as an array or list in some random order, but there is an alternative. If data items can take on one of N data values—as for instance, data items for ages of employees in years, which must be positive integers less than 100—then we can represent sets as an N-element *bit array* (an array whose data items are bits) where a "true" in location K of the array means that the Kth possible is present in the set. Bit arrays can make set operations like intersection run very fast, and many computers have bit-handling instructions to speed things even more.

4.2 ARRAY

An array is a data structure used to process multiple elements with the same data type when a number of such elements are known. An array is a fixed-sized, homogeneous, and widely-used data structure. By homogeneous, we mean that it consists of components which are all of the same type, called element type or base type. And by fixed sized, we mean that the number of components is constant, and so does not change during the lifetime of the structure. An array is also called a random-access data structure, because all components can be selected at random and are equally accessible.

An array can be used to structure several data objects in the programming languages. A component of an array is selected by giving its subscript, which is an integer indicating the position of the component in the sequence. Therefore, an array is made of the pairs (value, index); it means that with every index, a value is associated. If every index is one single value then it is called a one-dimensional array, whereas if every index is a n-tuple $\{i_1, i_2, i_3, \ldots, i_n\}$, the array is called a n-dimensional array.

An array is a particular method of storing elements of indexed data. Elements of data are stored sequentially in blocks within the array. Each element is referenced by an index, or subscript.

Think of a notebook with pages numbered 1 through 12. Each page may or may not contain information on it. The notebook is an array of pages. Each page is an element of the array 'notebook'. Programmatically, you would retrieve information from a page by referring to its number or subscript, i.e., notebook(4) would refer to the contents of page 4 of the array notebook.

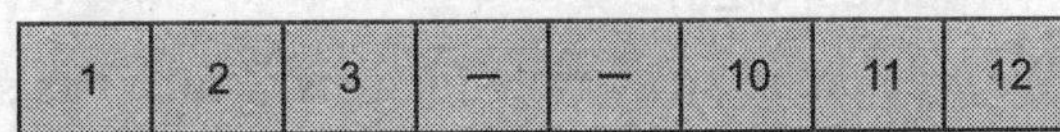

Figure 4.1: The notebook (array) contains 12 pages (elements).

The index is usually a number used to address an element in the array.

An array is a systematic arrangement of objects, usually in rows and columns. Array is similar type of data collection name i.e. it is a collection of same data type elements. An array is a group of related data items, which share common name.

"It is the set of homogeneous data (same type)".

Now question arises, why we need array. This can be explained by taking an example for preparing the grade of 50 students in an examination. So to solve this problem, we declare 50 different variables. But if in the next session, 10 more students sit in the examination, then there will be require number of changes in the program and also program becomes more complex. So to solve such type of problem, we need to define and declare array. Also processing speed becomes fast with the declaration and use of an array.

Also the concept of array can be explained by taking a problem with the C++ program. Let us suppose, there are four variables declared in a program having different type of data, but if we add more variable (50 variable), then it will create a problem for the declaration and use of variable. Also program becomes lengthy and complex.

Arrays are a data structure which hold multiple variables of the same data type. Consider the case where a programmer needs to keep track of a number of people within an organisation. So far, our initial attempt will be to create a specific variable for each user. This might look like,

```
int name1 = 101;
int name2 = 232;
int name3 = 231;
```

It becomes increasingly more difficult to keep track of this as the number of variables increase. Arrays offer a solution to this problem.

An array is a multi-element box, a bit like a filing cabinet, and uses an indexing system to find each variable stored within it. In C++, indexing starts at zero.

Arrays, like other variables in C++, must be declared before they can be used. The replacement of the above example using arrays looks like,

```
int names[4];
names[0] = 101;
names[1] = 232;
names[2] = 231;
names[3] = 0;
```

We created an array called names, which has space for four integer variables. You may also see that we stored 0 in the last space of the array. This is a common technique used by C++ programmers to signify the end of an array.

Arrays have the following syntax, using square brackets to access each indexed value (called an element).

Syntax: x[i]

So that x[5] refers to the sixth element in an array called x. In C++, array elements start with 0. Assigning values to array elements is done by,

```
x[10] = g;
```

and assigning array elements to a variable is done by,

```
g = x[10];
```

In the following example, a character based array named word is declared, and each element is assigned a character. The last element is filled with a zero value, to signify the end of the character string (in C++, there is no string type, so character based arrays are used to hold strings). A printf statement is then used to print out all elements of the array.

Suppose salary of the 10 employees named by salary variables name and we write it sal1, sal2, sal3......sal10. We repeat the variable name of employees by using the subscript. Because of use of single subscript or more than one subscript, it is also called subscripted variable.

So Array's representation for the 10th employee is:

Salary [10];

Array has syntax:

Common name variable [size];

or

array-name [subscript1] [subscript2];

We can represent number of elements as a1, a2, ... an . Where a is an array name and 1, 2, 3, ... n are subscript. We can write the above array statement as:

a[i] , where i = 1, 2, 3, ... n

Here i work as subscript and array-name a works as subscripted variable.

Array representation can be done as:

storage-type data-type array-name[size];

or

storage-type data-type array-name[row size][column size];

4.3 TYPES OF ARRAY

The types of the array depend upon the given problem. Arrays are mainly of two types:

(i) Linear Array

(ii) Non-Linear Array

4.4 LINEAR ARRAY

A data structure is said to be linear if its elements form a sequence or a linear list. This type of array is also called one Dimensional Array. This is also called list array. Another name of linear array is called **single-dimensional array**. In the linear array only one subscript is used. It is written either in row or in column form.

Syntax to define or declare linear array is:

data-type array-name [size];

where data types are integer (int), real(float), double and character(char) .

For example, some of the valid one dimensional array declaration statements are written as below:

```
int a[50];
float salary[30];
char name[20];
```

Suppose if you want to store the data "TEMPLE" in the array name city, then the representation for declaration be as:

```
char name[7];
```

We can declare that data type char for city variable and you can store maximum 8 character in the different cells of the city variable. So we see that when we declare character type array, size should be one cell more than the given data length, because last cell should be empty or null cell i.e. the end of the string has null character. It is denoted by "\0".

```
char name[7];
name
T     0
E     1
M     2
P     3
L     4
E     5
'\0'  6
```

Suppose if we want to assign values 5, 15, 30, 27, 53 is an array integer variable, then it can be written (in the computer memory) as:

```
number[0] = 55
number[1] = 35
number[2] = 40
number[3] = 47
number[4] = 33
```

We can declare these numbers in the array form as:

```
int number[5];
```

4.4.1 Storage Structure of One Dimensional Array

The general form to use one dimensional array is given below:

```
int Age[10];
```

Here array_type declares base type of array which is the type of each element in array. In our example array_type is int and its name is Age. Size of the array is defined by array_size i.e. 10. We can access array elements by index, and first item in array is at index 0. First element of array is called lower bound and its always 0. Highest element in array is called upper bound.

1. Storage of an array in one statement

```
int Age [5] = {30, 22, 33, 44, 25};
```

2. Storage of an array separately

Look at the following C code which demonstrates the declaration and initialization of an array.

```
int Age [5];
Age [0]=30;
Age [1]=22;
Age [2]=33;
Age [3]=44;
Age [4]=25;
```

Array can also be initialized in a ways that array size is omitted, in such case compiler automatically allocates memory to array.

```
int Age [] = {30, 22, 33, 44, 25};
```

4.4.2 Representation of One-dimensional Array

An array is represented in memory by using a sequential mapping. The basic characteristic of the sequential mapping is that every element is at a fixed distance apart. Therefore, if the ith element is mapped into a location having an address a, then the $(i + 1)^{th}$ element is mapped into the memory location having an address (a + 1), as shown in Figure 4.2.

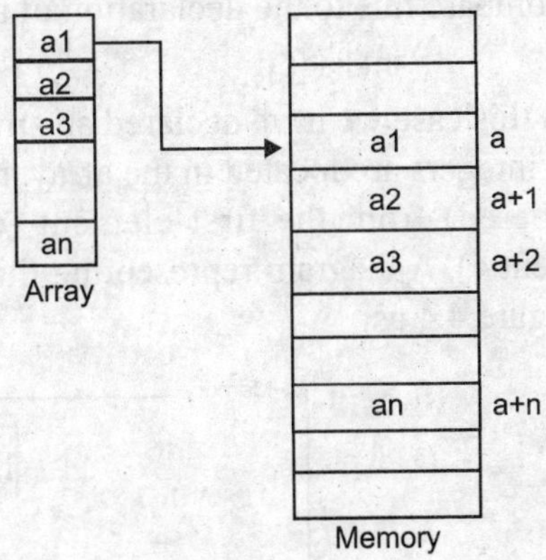

Figure 4.2: Representation of an array.

The address of the first element of an array is called the base address, so the address of the the ith element is

Base address + offset of the ith element from base address

Where the offset is computed as:

Offset of the ith element = number of elements before the ith * size of each element.

If LB is the lower bound, then the offset computation becomes:

offset = (i – LB) * size.

The fundamental concept of an array in any language is that of a sequential collection of values, all of the same type, all accessed by the same variable name. Individual values in an array are individually accessed by using the array name and an index (a number) to specify which value is being accessed.

For a starting example, consider this declaration:

```
int number;
```

This declares one variable of type integer capable of holding a single whole number. A diagram as shown in the figure 4.3, this variable's memory allocation would look like this:

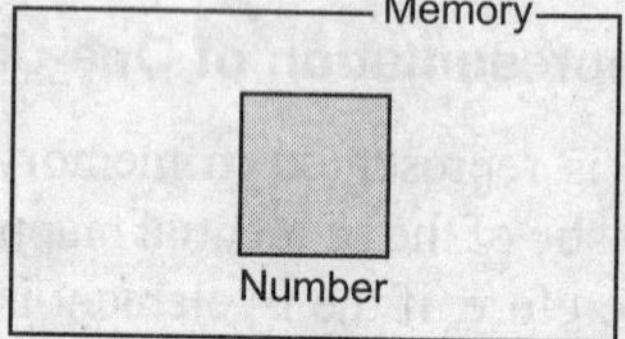

Figure 4.3: Representation of number in memory.

Compare this to the declaration of an array of integers:

```
int list[5];
```

In this case we have declared an array, which is capable of holding 5 integers. The 5 integers are located in the array, next to each other in memory, and indexed (numbered) from the first element (element 0) through to the last element (element 4). A diagram representing this array in memory would be as shown in the Figure 4.4 as:

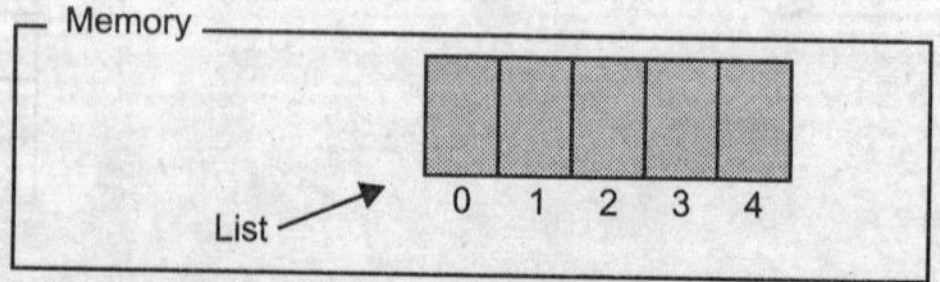

Figure 4.4: Representation of list in memory.

In C++ all arrays are indexed from 0 to n-1 where n is the size of the array. Arrays can be of any type, so for example, we can have:

```
int list[67];       // an array of 67 integers indexed from 0 to 66
char string[20];    // an array of 20 characters indexed from 0 to 19
float price[30];    // an array of floating point numbers indexed from 0 to 29
```

The elements in an array can be accessed and used by specifying the array name and, in square brackets, the index of the element you want to use. For example, to store 78.54 into the first element of the array price, we would write:

```
price[0] = 78.54;            // Note, first element is index 0
```

To store 100.25 into element 5 of the array price, we would write:

```
price[5] = 100.25;           // Note, this is the 6th element
```

To print the last element of the array price having value 220.32, we would write:

```
price[29]= 220.32;
```

When this index notation is used to access elements of an array, the individual elements can be treated as individual variables.

Array Memory Diagrams

Here is an array declaration and code to initialize it.

```
int a[5];                    // Allocates memory for 5 integers.
. . .
a[0] = 1;
for (int i=1; i<5; i++)
{
a[i] = a[i–1] * 2;
}
```

Arrays are often represented with diagrams that represent their memory use. The diagram below as shown in the Figure 4.5 is one typical way to represent the memory used by an array. Each box represents the amount of memory needed to hold one array element. For integer this is usually 4 bytes.

We can write the value of an element inside the box. Pointers hold the memory address of other data and are represented by a black disk with an arrow pointing to the data it references. The actual array variable, a in this example, is a pointer to the memory for all of its elements. A common shortcut is to omit writing the array variable, and write only the elements that hold the data because these are usually the focus of attention. Sometimes the cells are written horizontally, especially when showing arrays of characters.

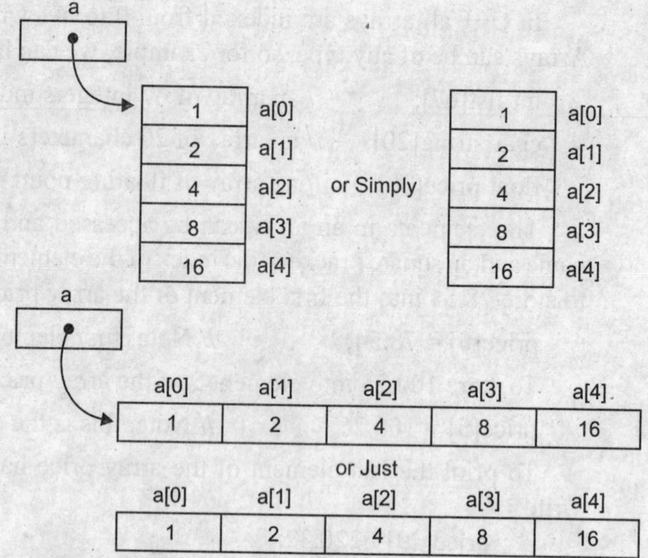

Figure 4.5: Various memory diagrams.

4.4.3 Various Operations on Linear Array

Array can be used for handling same type of numbers or text data. Mainly there are various operations can be applied with the linear array.

These different operations are discussed as below:

1. Traversing or Visiting
2. Inserting
3. Deleting
4. Searching
5. Sorting
6. Merging
7. Reversing
8. Copying
9. Swapping

Here we will discuss Traversing, Inserting and deleting in this chapter in detail. The next three operations with their different methods will be discussed in the chapter 6 naming Sorting and Searching.

1. Traversing A Linear Array

Traversing means visiting and accessing each element of the array exactly once. Values are stored and retrieved from the array-type variable by indicating its position in an array. Because the array is an ordered collection, the position of an element is its index.

Figure 4.6 shows an array, seven elements long, containing numeric values. To traverse the array sequentially, we may use the algorithm in Figure 4.6 using the C++ syntax. The maximum number of comparisons is 7, and occurs when the key we are searching for as in A[6].

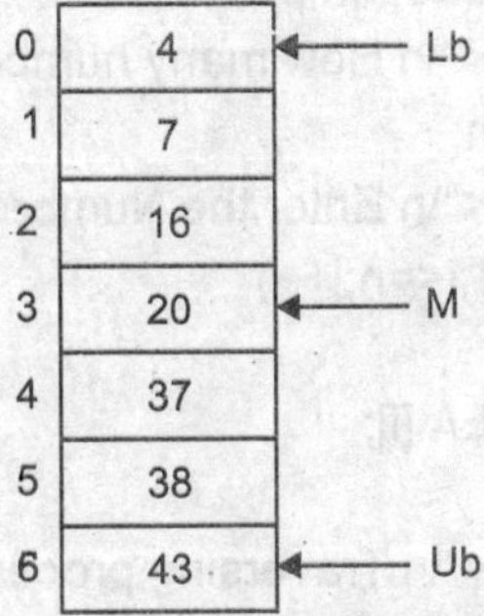

Figure 4.6: Traversing of linear array.

Algorithm 4.1: Traversing or Visiting a Linear Array

TRAVERSE (I, LB, UB)

Taking LA is a linear array having lower bound LB and upper bound UB. This algorithm is used to traverses linear array (LA) by applying an operation visiting to each element of LA.

Step 1: [Initialize Value of I.] Set I = LB.

Step 2: Repeat Steps 3 and 4 while I ≤UB.

Step 3: [Visit each element exactly once.] Apply VISTING to LA [I].

Step 4: [Increment the value of I.] Set I= I + 1.

[End of while loop.]

Step 5: End.

Algorithm 4.2: Simple approach for traversing a Linear Array

TRAVERSE (I, LB, UB)

This algorithm traverses a linear array LA with lower bound LB and upper bound UB.

Step 1: Repeat Steps for I = LB to UB.

Apply PROCESS to LA [I].

[End of loop.]

Step 2: End.

Program 1: Write a C++ program to traversing or visiting a list (One dimensional array).

```
#include<iostream.h>
#include<conio.h>
void main()
{
int LA [50],i,n,p;
cout<<"\n How many numbers  you want to insert: ";
cin>>n;
cout<<"\n Enter the Numbers:";
for(i=1;i<=n;i++)
{
cin>>LA [i];
}
cout<<"\n Traversing process is: ";
for(i=1;i<=n;i++)
{
p= LA [i];
cout<<p;
}
getch();
}
```

Output:

```
How many numbers you want to insert: 5
Enter the Numbers:
44
22
33
11
55
Traversing process is:
44
22
33
11
55
```

Here the array LA is traversed starting from first element to last element. Each element is printed on the screen.

Note: To access the elements in the array the index is varied from lower bound to upper bound. Time to access every element is same. For array of size say, n, for loop executes n times. The traversal operation on linear arrays is of O(n).

2. *Inserting in Linear Array*

Inserting in array means, the operation of adding new element in the array is to be performed. Inserting an element at the end of the linear array can be easily done.

But, inserting an element at given position is little-bit complex.

Algorithm 4.3: Inserting into a Linear Array

INSERT (LA, N, J, ITEM).

Taking LA is a linear array with N elements and J is a positive in LA such that J ≤ N. This algorithm inserts an element ITEM into the Jth position in linear array (LA).

Step 1: [Initialize Value of I.] Set I = N.

Step 2: Repeat Steps 3 and 4 while I ≥ J.

Step 3: [Move Ith element downward position.] Set LA [I + 1] = LA [I].

Step 4: [Decrement the value of I.] Set I = I – 1.

[End of while loop.]

Step 5: [Insert new element in linear array.] Set LA [J] = ITEM.

Step 6: [Reset the value of N in LA.] Set N = N + 1.

Step 7: End.

Explanation

Let us take an example of an array of size 8 as in figure 4.7. Here N is 5 i.e. there are total 5 elements in the array.

LA[0]	1
LA[1]	5
LA[2]	4
LA[3]	8
LA[4]	9

Figure 4.7: Linear array having 5 elements. (Before insertion)

Let us suppose an element 3 is to be inserted at position 2 i.e. at LA[1].

Step 1: I=N=5

Step 2: Repeat Steps 3 and 4 while I ≥ J.

Step 3: [Move Ith element downward position.]

Set LA [I + 1] = LA [I].

A[5+1]=A[5] i.e. the element stored at position 5 is moved downward by one position.

Step 4: [Decrement the value of I.]

Set I = I – 1.

So, after complete executions of step 3 and 4. Following statements have been executed:

LA[4+1]=LA[4]

LA[3+1]=LA[3]

LA[2+1]=LA[2]

LA[1+1]=LA[1]

Now position LA[1] is vacant so that new element can be inserted

Step 5: Insert new element in linear array.

Set LA [J] = ITEM=3

The element 3 has been inserted at required position

Step 6: [Reset the value of N in LA.] Set N = N + 1.

As now there are total 6 elements in array LA. So, now array LA will look like:

LA[0]	1
LA[1]	3
LA[2]	5
LA[3]	4
LA[4]	8
LA[5]	9

Figure 4.8: Linear array having 6 elements. (After insertion)

Step 7: End.

Note : *The worst case occurs when the element is to be inserted at the first position, as all elements (n) are to be moved down.*

The best case occurs when the element is inserted at the last position, as no element is moved down. Hence the complexity of insertion operation is O(n).

Program 2: Write a C++ program to insert an element in array at a specific position.

```
# include<iostream.h>
# include<conio.h>
# define size 21
class array
{
private:
int i, a[size];
public:
void read (int);
void insert (int, int, int); // for insertion of element
void display (int);
};
void array : : read (int n)
{
for(i=0;i<n;i++)
cin>>a[i];
}
void array : : display (int n)
{
for (i=0;i<n;i++)
cout<<a[i]<<" ";
}
void array : : insert (int n, int position, int info)
{
// back shifting
for (i=n-1;i>=(position-1);i--)
a[i+1]=a[i];
// insertion
a [position-1] = info;
}
void main ( )
{
array obj;
int n, pos, info;
clrscr ( );
cout <<"Read no of elements<=<<size-1<<"\n";
cin>>n;
```

```
cout<<"\n Read "<<n<<"elements\n";
obj.read (n);
cout<<"\nRead the element to be inserted: ";
cin>>info;
cout<<"\n\nRead the position of insertion<="<<n+1<<end1;
cin>>pos;
cout<<"\nGiven array is \n\n";
obj.display (n);
cout<<"\n\nElement to be inserted is "<<info;
cout<<"\n\nPosition of insertion is "<<pos<<"\n\n;
obj.insert (n, pos, info);
cout<<"\nArray after insertion is \n\n";
obj.display (n+1);
getch ( );
}
```

Output:

```
Read no of elements <=20
6
Read 6 elements
12    30    36    70    37    84
Read the element to be inserted: 50
Read the position of insertion <=7
4
Given array is
12    30    36    70    37    84
Element to be inserted is 50
Position of insertion is 4
Array after insertion is
12    30    36    50    70    37    84
```

Program 3: Write a C++ program for Insertion in a sorted array.

```
# include<iostream.h>
# include<conio.h>
# define size 21
class array
{
private:
int i, position,a[size];
public:
void read (int);
```

```
void insert (int, int, int); // for insertion of element
void display (int);
};
void array : : read (int n)
{
for(i=0;i<n;i++)
cin>>a[i];
}
void array : : display (int n)
{
for (i=0;i<n;i++)
cout<<a[i]<<" ";
}
void array : : insert (int n, int info)
{
if(info>=a[n-1])
a[n] = info;
else
{
position=0;
while(a[position]<=info)
position++;
for (i=n-1;i>=(position-1);i--)
a[i+1]=a[i];
a [position] = info;
}
}
void main ( )
{
array obj;
int n, info;
clrscr ( );
cout <<"Read no of elements<=<<size-1<<"\n";
cin>>n;
cout<<"\n Read "<<n<<"elements\n";
obj.read (n);
cout<<"\nRead the element to be inserted: ";
cin>>info;
cout<<"\nGiven array is \n\n";
```

```
obj.display (n);
cout<<"\n\nElement to be inserted is "<<info;
obj.insert (n, info);
cout<<"\nArray after insertion is \n\n";
obj.display (n+1);
getch ( );
}
```

Output:

```
Read no of elements <=20
6
Read 6 elements
12    30    36    39    50    84
Read the element to be inserted: 45
Given array is
12    30    36    39    50    84
Element to be inserted is 50
Array after insertion is
12    30    36    39    45    50    84
```

3. Deleting From Linear Array

Deleting from array means, the operation of deleting an element from array is to be performed. Deleting last element from array is simple. But deleting an element from given position is to be performed carefully.

Algorithm 4.4: Deleting from a Linear Array

DELETE (LA, N, J, ITEM)

Taking LA is a linear array with N elements and J is a positive in LA such that J ≤ N. This algorithm deletes the Jth element from linear array (LA).

Step 1: Set ITEM = LA [J].

Step 2: Repeat for I = J to N – 1

[Move (I + 1)st element upward position.] Set LA [I] = LA [I + 1].

[End of loop.]

Step 3: [Reset the value of N in LA.] Set N = N – 1.

Step 4: End.

Explanation:

Let us take an example of an array of size 8 as in figure 4.9. Here N is 5 i.e. there are total 5 elements in the array.

LA[0]	1
LA[1]	5
LA[2]	4
LA[3]	8
LA[4]	9

Figure 4.9: Linear array having 5 elements. (Before deletion)

Let us suppose an element 5 is to be deleted from the array and this element is stored at position J=1.

Step 1: Set ITEM = LA [J] = 5

Step 2: Repeat for I = J to N – 1

[Move (I + 1)st element upward position.]

Set LA [I] = LA [I + 1].

Step 3: [Reset the value of N in LA.] Set N = N – 1.

Step 4: End.

Now, there will be 4 total elements in the array as one element has been deleted. The array will look like:

LA[0]	1
LA[1]	4
LA[2]	8
LA[3]	9

Figure 4.10: Linear array having 4 elements. (After deletion)

Note: *The worst case occurs when the element is deleted from the first position, as all the elements (n-1) are to be moved upward.*

The best case occurs when the element is deleted from the last position. In this case, no element is to be moved up.

Hence the complexity of deletion operation is O(n).

Program 4: Write a C++ program for deletion from a specific position.

```
# include<iostream.h>
# include<conio.h>
# define size 21
class array
{
private:
int i, a[size];
public:
void read (int);
void del (int, int);
void display (int);
};
void array : : read (int n)
{
for(i=0;i<n;i++)
cin>>a[i];
}
void array : : display (int n)
{
for (i=0;i<n;i++)
cout<<a[i]<<" ";
}
void array : : del (int pos, int n)
{
for (i=pos;i<=n-1;i++)
a[i-1]=a[i];
a [n-1] = 0.0; //for last element
}
void main ( )
{
array obj;
int n, pos;
clrscr ( );
cout <<"Read no of elements<=<<size-1<<"\n";
cin>>n;
cout<<"\n Read "<<n<<"elements\n";
obj.read (n);
cout<<"\nGiven array is \n\n";
```

```
obj.display (n);
cout<<"\n\nRead the position of deletion<="<<n<<end1;
cin>>pos;
cout<<"\n\nPosition of deletion is "<<pos<<"\n\n;
obj.del (pos,n);
cout<<"\nArray after deletion is \n\n";
obj.display (n-1);
getch ( );
}
```

Output:

```
Read no of elements <=20
6
Read 6 elements
32      30      36      10      37      84
Given array is
32      30      36      10      37      84
Read the position of deletion <=37
4
Position of deletion is 4
Array after deletion is
32      30      36      10      84
```

Program 5: Write a C++ program for deletion from an unsorted array.

```
# include<iostream.h>
# include<conio.h>
# define size 21
class array
{
private:
int i, position,a[size];
public:
void read (int);
void del (int, int, int);
void display (int);
};
void array : : read (int n)
{
for(i=0;i<n;i++)
cin>>a[i];
}
```

```
void array : : display (int n)
{
for (i=0;i<n;i++)
cout<<a[i]<<" ";
}
void array : : del (int info, int n)
{
for(i=0;i<n;i++)
{
if(a[i]= = info)
{
for (int pos =i+1;pos<n;pos++)
a[pos-1]=a[pos];
a [n-1] = 0.0;
retun(i);
}
}
return(-1);
}
void main ( )
{
array obj;
int n, info,flag;
clrscr ( );
cout <<"Read no of elements<=<<size<<"\n";
cin>>n;
cout<<"\n Read "<<n<<"elements\n";
obj.read (n);
cout<<"\nGiven array is \n\n";
obj.display (n);
cout<<"\nRead the element to be deleted: ";
cin>>info;
cout<<"\n\nElement to be deleted is "<<info;
flag=obj.del (info,n);
if(flag!= -1)
{
cout<<"\nArray after deletion is \n\n";
obj.display (n-1);
}
```

```
else
cout<<info<<"Not found in array\n";
getch ( );
}
```

Output:

```
Read no of elements <=20
6
Read 6 elements
32    30    36    39    10    84
Given array is
32    30    36    39    10    84

Read the element to be deleted: 36

Element to be deleted is 36
Array after deletion is
32    30    39    45    10    84
```

Program 6: Write a C++ program for deletion from a sorted array.

```
# include<iostream.h>
# include<conio.h>
# define size 21
class array
{
private:
int i, position,a[size];
public:
void read (int);
int del (int, int, int);
void display (int);
};
void array : : read (int n)
{
for(i=0;i<n;i++)
cin>>a[i];
}
void array : : display (int n)
{
for (i=0;i<n;i++)
cout<<a[i]<<" ";
```

```
}
int array : : del (int info, int n)
{
if((info<a[0]) || (info>a[n-1]))
return (-1);
else
{
int position =0;
while(a[position]<info)
position++;
if(a[position]= = info)
{
for(i=position+1;i<n;i++)
a[i-1]=a[i];
a [n-1] = 0.0;
retun(position);
}
else
return(-1);
}
void main ( )
{
array obj;
int n, info,flag;
clrscr ( );
cout <<"Read no of elements<=<<size<<"\n";
cin>>n;
cout<<"\n Read "<<n<<"elements in ascending order\n";
obj.read (n);
cout<<"\nGiven array is \n\n";
obj.display (n);
cout<<"\nRead the element to be deleted: ";
cin>>info;
cout<<"\n\nElement to be deleted is "<<info;
flag=obj.del (info,n);
if(flag!= -1)
{
cout<<"\nArray after deletion is \n\n";
obj.display (n-1);
```

```
}
else
cout<<info<<"Not found in array\n";
getch ( );
}
```

Output:

```
Read no of elements <=20
6
Read 6 elements in ascending order
12    30    36    39    50    84
Given array is
12    30    36    39    50    84

Read the element to be deleted: 50

Element to be deleted is 50
Array after deletion is
12    30    36    39    84
```

4. Searhing in Linear Array

The process of finding specified element in an array. Computer systems are often used to store large amounts of data from which individual records must be retrieved according to some search criterion. Thus the efficient storage of data to facilitate fast searching is an important issue. We are using two searching algorithm to find the element from a given array. Detailed description of searching and sorting is given in Chapter 12.

Algorithm 4.5: Linear Search

LINEAR (LA, N, ITEM, LOC)

Taking LA is a linear array with N elements, and ITEM is a given item of information. This algorithm find the location LOC of ITEM in LA, or set LOC = 0 if the search is unsuccessful.

Step 1: [Insert ITEM at the end of LA.] Set LA [N + 1] = ITEM.

Step 2: [Initialize the value of LOC.] Set LOC = 1.

Step 3: [Search for ITEM.]

  Repeat steps while LA [LOC] ≠ ITEM

    Set LOC = LOC + 1

  [End of while loop.]

Step 4: [Successful or Unsuccessful?] if LOC = N + 1, then Set LOC = 0.

Step 5: End.

Algorithm 4.6: Binary Search

BINARY (LA, LB, UB, ITEM, LOC)

Taking LA is a sorted array with lower bound LB and upper bound UB, and ITEM is a given item of information. The variables BEGIN, END and MIDLOC denote as beginning, ending and middle locations of elements of LA. This algorithm find the location LOC of ITEM in LA or if LOC not found set LOC = NULL.

Step 1: [Initialize starting variables.]

Set BEGIN = LB, END = UB and MIDLOC = INT ((BEGIN + END)/2).

Step 2: Repeat steps 3 and 4 while BEGIN ≤ END and LA [MIDLOC] ≠ ITEM.

Step 3: If ITEM < LA [MID], then

Set END = MIDLOC - 1.

Else

Set BEGIN = MIDLOC + 1.

[End of If statement.]

Step 4: Set MIDLOC = INT ((BEGIN + END)/2).

[End of Step 2 loop.]

Step 5: If LA [MIDLOC] = ITEM, then: Set LOC = MIDLOC else

Set LOC = NULL.

[End of If statement.]

Step 6: End.

Algorithm 4.7: Binary Search and Insertion

LA is a sorted array with N elements, and ITEM is a given item of information. This algorithm finds the location LOC of ITEM in LA or inserts ITEM in its proper place in LA.

SEARCH AND INSERTION (LA, LB, UB, ITEM, LOC, N, J)

Step 1: [Initialize starting variables.]

Set BEGIN = LB, END = UB and MIDLOC = INT ((BEGIN + END)/2).

Step 2: Repeat steps 3 and 4 while BEGIN ≤ END and LA [MIDLOC] ≠ ITEM.

Step 3: If ITEM < LA [MID], then

Set END = MIDLOC - 1.

Else

Set BEGIN = MIDLOC + 1.

[End of If statement.]

Step 4: Set MIDLOC = INT ((BEGIN + END)/2).

[End of Step 2 loop.]

Step 5: If ITEM < LA [MIDLOC], then:

Set LOC = MIDLOC.

```
Else:
    Set LOC = MIDLOC + 1.
  [End of If statment.]
Step 6: Insert ITEM into LA [LOC]
Step 7: [Initialize Value of I.] Set LOC = N.
Step 8: Repeat Steps 9and 10 while LOC ≥ J.
Step 9: [Move Ith element downward position.] Set LA [LOC + 1] = LA [LOC].
Step 10: [Decrement the value of I.] Set LOC = LOC – 1.
  [End of while loop.]
Step 11: [Insert new element in linear array.] Set LA [J] = ITEM.
Step 12: [Reset the value of N in LA.] Set N = N + 1.
Step 13: End.
```

5. Sorting A Linear Array

Arranging elements in a specific order, either ascending or descending, is known as sorting. Many types of sorting techniques are available in data structures.

Algorithm 4.8: Bubble Sort

```
BUBBLE (LA, N, TEMP)
Taking LA is an array with N elements. TEMP is used as temporary variable
for interchanging values. This algorithm sorts the elements in LA.
Step 1: Repeat Steps 2 and 3 for J = 1 to N – 1.
Step 2: Set P = 1. [Initializes starting pointer P.]
Step 3: Repeat steps while P ≤ N – J [This loop executes for passes.]
(a) If LA [P] > LA [P + 1] then
Interchange LA [P] and LA [P + 1].
TEMP= LA [P].
LA [P] = LA [P + 1].
LA [P + 1] =TEMP.
[End of If statement.]
(b) Set P = P+1.
[End of Step 3 inner loop.]
[End of Step 1 outer loop.]
Step 4: End.
```

6. Merging Arrays

The merging means to concatenate or merge two arrays into a single one.

Suppose we have two sorted arrays A[] of m elements and B[] of n elements. Write a function merge which would merge this two arrays into new sorted array C[] in O(n) time as shown on the picture".

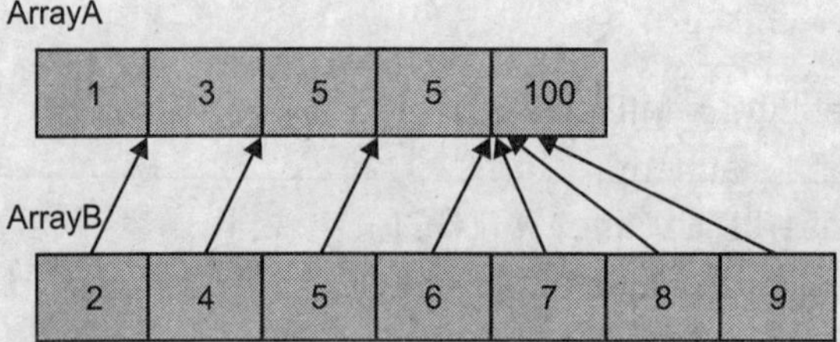

Resulting Array: Merge (A,B)

1	2	3	4	5	5	5	6	7	8	9	100

C++ code:

```
#include<iostream.h>
#include<conio.h>
void main()
{
int A[10],B[10],C[30],i,j,t,m,n,temp;
clrscr();
cout<<"\n Enter the number of elements of Array-A: ";
cin>>m;
cout<<"\n Enter the elements :\n";
for(i=1;i<=m;i++)
cin>>A[i];
cout<<"\n  Enter the number of elements of Array-B: ";
cin>>n;
cout<<"\n Enter the elements:  ";
for(i=1;i<=n;i++)
cin>>B[i];
t=m+n;
for(i=1;i<=m;i++)
C[i]=A[i];
for(i=1;i<=n;i++)
C[i+m]=B[i];
cout<<"\n  Merged array-C is:";
for(i=1;i<=t;i++)
cout<<C[i];
cout<<"\n  Sorted array -C is: ";
for(i=1;i<=m-1;i++)
{
for(j=1;j<=m-i;j++)
```

```
{
if(C[j]>C[j+1])
{
temp=C[j+1];
C[j+1]=C[j];
C[j]=temp;
}
else
continue;
}
}
for(i=1;i<=t;i++)
cout<<C[i];
getch();
}
```

7. Reversing the Array

Reverses the order of the elements of a given array. For example, if the given array contains five elements:

3 5 7 2 4

After reversing the order of elements, the result is

4 2 7 5 3

C++ code:

```
#include<iostream.h>
#include<conio.h>
void main()
{
int a[10],n,i,j,temp;
clrscr();
cout<<"Enter the size of array:";
cin>>n;
cout<<"\n Enter the elements of array:";
for(i=0;i<n;i++)
{
cin>>a[i];
}
for(i=0,j=n-1;i<n/2;i++,j--)
{
temp=a[i];
```

```
a[i]=a[j];
a[j]=temp;
}
cout<<"\n Elements of array after reversing are:";
for(i=0;i<n;i++)
{
cout<<a[i];
}
getch();
}
```

Output:

Enter the size of array: 2
Enter the elements of array: 40 50 60
Elements of array after reversing are: 60 50 40

8. Copying the Elements of One Array into Another in Reverse Order

C++ code:

```
#include <iostream.h>
#include <conio.h>
void main()
{
int arr1[5], arr2[5], i, j ;
clrscr( ) ;
cout<<"\nEnter 5 elements of array:";
for ( i = 0 ; i <= 4 ; i++ )
cin>>arr1[i] ;
for ( i = 0, j = 4 ; i <= 4 ; i++, j-- )
arr2[j] = arr1[i];
cout<<"\nElements in reverse order:";
for ( i = 0 ; i <= 4 ; i++ )
cout<<arr2[i];
cout<<"\nPress any key to exit.";
getch( ) ;
}
```

Output:

Enter 5 elements of array: 7 4 8 1 3
Elements in reverse order:
3
1
8

4
7
Press any key to exit.

9. Swapping Two Arrays

The swapping means to interchange two arrays.

C++ code:

The C++ code for this is actually simpler than the description:

```
int nTemp;
nTemp = nArray[1];
nArray[1] = nArray[2];
nArray[2] = nTemp;
```

Of course, the above makes more sense when placed into a function:

```
void SwapElements( int * nArray, int nFirst, int nSecond)
{
int nTemp = nArray[nFirst];
nArray[nFirst] = nArray[nSecond];
nArray[nSecond] = nTemp;
}
```

Please feel free to clip the code sample, and use it in your own projects. Of course, if you need to swap different data types, then the code will need to be adjusted.

4.5 NON-LINEAR ARRAY

Non-linear array are further subdivided into n categories as:

1. Two Dimensional Array
2. Three Dimensional Array
3. N Dimensional Array

We will discuss here two and three-dimensional array only.

4.5.1 Two Dimensional Array

These arrays are also called double dimensional array or two subscripted array. Another name of two-dimensional array is Tabular or Rectangular Array. These arrays are in row and column form. So these are also called as Row-Column or square Array. These arrays have two subscripts. We can write the double dimensional array in tabular form as:

```
a11   a12   a13   ...   ...   ...   a1n
a21   a22   a23   ...   ...   ...   a2n
...   ...   ...   ...   ...   ...   ...
an1   an2   an3   ...   ...   ...   ann
```

The general syntax used for declaration of two dimensional array is as:

data type array-name [row size] [column size];

For example, some valid use of two-dimensional array are:

```
int a[10][10];
float b[50][50];
char name[10][20];
```

Also you can declare two dimensional array in static form i.e. these types of array declarations have fixed or constant values during declaration.

4.5.1.1 Storage Structure of Two Dimensional Array

The general form to use two dimensional array is given below:

int matrix [2][3];

Here array_type declares base type of array which is the type of each element in array. In our example array_type is int and its name is matrix. Size of the array is defined by array_name[row size][column size]; i.e. [2][3]. We can access array elements by index, and first item in array is at index [0][0]. First element of array is called lower bound and its always [0][0]. Highest element in array is called upper bound.

1. Storage of an array in one statement

```
int matrix [2][3] = {15, 70, 12, 22, 20, 18};
```

2. Storage of an array separately

Look at the following C++ code which demonstrates the declaration and initialization of an array.

```
int matrix [2][3];
```

Here the values assigned to the tabular array-name are as:

```
matrix [0][0] = 15
matrix [0][1] = 70
matrix [0][2] = 12
matrix [1][0] = 22
matrix [1][1] = 20
matrix [1][2] = 18
```

Also we can write the above statement as:

```
int matrix [ ][ ] = {15, 70, 12, 22, 20, 18};
```

Above statement fails in some cases. Another way to write the above statement is as follows:

```
int matrix [ ][ ] = {{15, 70, 12}, {22, 20, 18}};
        or
int matrix [ ][ ] = {{15,70}, {12, 22}, {20, 18}};
```

Two-dimensioned arrays have two or more index values which specify the element in the array.

Two [i][j]

In the above example, the first index value i specifies a row index, while j specifies a column index.

4.5.1.2 Representation of Two-dimensional Array

1. Row-major Representation

A two-dimensional array can be considered as a one-dimensional array whose elements are also one-dimensional arrays. So, we can view a two dimensional array as one single column of rows and map it sequentially as shown in Figure 4.11. Such a representation is called a **row-major representation.**

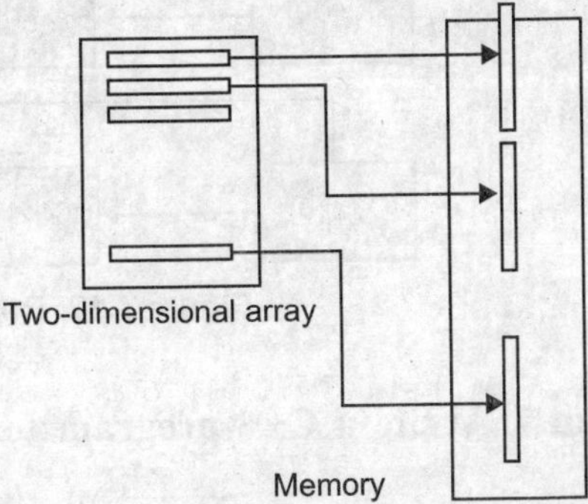

Figure 4.11: Row-major representation of a two-dimensional array.

The address of the element of the ith row and the jth column therefore is:

addr(a[i, j]) = (number of rows placed before i^{th} row * size of a row) + (number of elements placed before the jth element in the ith row * size of element)

where Number of rows placed before i^{th} row = (i – LB1), and LB1 is the lower bound of the first dimension.

Size of a row = number of elements in a row * a size of element.

Number of elements in a row = (UB2 – LB2+1), where UB2 and LB2 are the upper and lower bounds of the second dimension, respectively.

Therefore:

addr(a[i, j]) = ((i – LB1) * (UB2 – LB2+1) * size) + ((j – LB2)*size)

Row-major Arrays

A Row-major array is a technique in which elements in an array are arranged row-wise. We can store elements row by row shown in Figure 4.12.

COLUMN-0	COLUMN-1	COLUMN-2	
X[0][0]	X[0][1]	X[0][2]	ROW-0
X[1][0]	X[1][1]	X[1][2]	ROW-1
X[2][0]	X[2][1]	X[2][2]	ROW-2

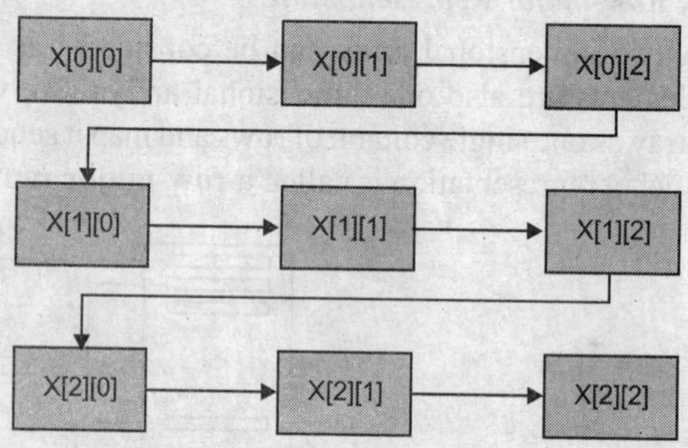

Figure 4.12: Row-major array

Program 7: Write a C++ program to implement an array by row-major method.

```
#include<iostream.h>
#include<conio.h>
void main()
{
int mat[3][3];
int i,j;
clrscr();
cout<<"Enter Elements of Matrix\n";
for(i=0;i<3;i++)
{
for(j=0;j<3;j++)
{
cin>>mat[i][j];
}
}
cout<<"\n Row major array: \n";
for(i=0;i<3;i++)
{
```

```
for(j=0;j<3;j++)
{
cout<<mat[i][j];
cout<<"row-["<<i+1<<"]\n";
}
}
getch();
}
Output:
Enter Elements of Matrix: 5 8 9 2 5 4 7 5 2
Row major array:
5 8 9 row-[1]
2 5 4 row-[2]
7 5 2 row-[3]
```

2. Column-major Representation

It is also possible to view a two-dimensional array as one single row of columns and map it sequentially as shown in Figure 4.13. Such a representation is called a **column-major representation.**

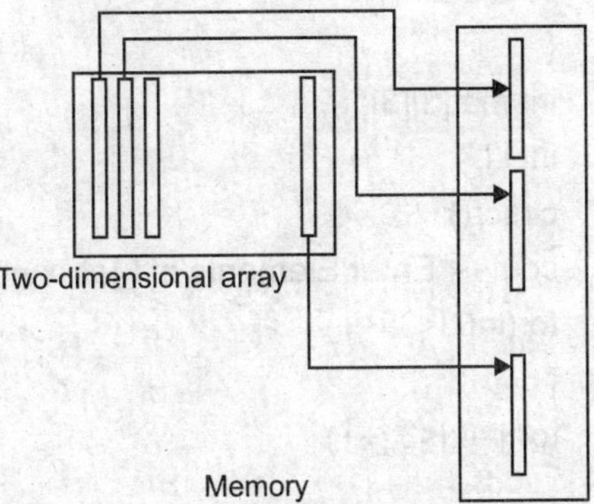

Figure 4.13: Column major representation of a two-dimensional array.

The address of the element of the ith row and the jth column therefore is:

addr(a[i, j]) = (number of columns placed before j^{th} column * size of a column) + (number of elements placed before the ith element in the jth column * size of each element)

Number of columns placed before j^{th} column = (j – LB2) where LB2 is the lower bound of the second dimension.

Size of a column = number of elements in a column * size of element Number of elements in a column = (UB1 – LB1 + 1), where UB1 and LB1 are the upper and lower bounds of the first dimension, respectively.

Therefore:

addr(a[i, j]) = ((j – LB2) * (UB1 – LB1+1) * size) + ((i – LB1)*size)

Column-major Arrays

In column major array elements are stored column-by-column as shown in figure.

COLUMN-0	COLUMN-1	COLUMN-2	
X[0][0]	X[0][1]	X[0][2]	ROW-0
X[1][0]	X[1][1]	X[1][2]	ROW-1
X[2][0]	X[2][1]	X[2][2]	ROW-2

X[0][0]	X[1][0]	X[2][0]	X[0][1]	X[1][1]	X[2][1]	X[0][2]	X[1][2]	X[2][2]
COLUMN-0			COLUMN-1			COLUMN-2		

Program 8: Write a C++ program to implement an array by column-major method.

```
#include<iostream.h>
#include<conio.h>
void main()
{
int mat[3][3];
int i,j;
clrscr();
cout<<"Enter Elements of Matrix\n";
for(i=0;i<3;i++)
{
for(j=0;j<3;j++)
{
cin>>mat[i][j];
}
}
cout<<"\n Column major array: \n";
for(i=0;i<3;i++)
{
for(j=0;j<3;j++)
{
cout<<mat[i][j];
cout<<"\n";
```

```
}
}
getch();
}
```

Output:

Enter Elements of Matrix: 5 8 9 2 5 4 7 5 2

Column major array:

5 2 7

8 5 5

9 4 2

Program 9: Write a C++ program for addition of two matrices.

```
# include<iostream.h>
# include<conio.h>
# define s 5
class array
{
private:
int i, j, x[s] [s], y[s] [s], z[s] [s];
public;
void enter (int x[s] [s], int, int);
void display (int x[s] [s], int, int);
void mat_add (int x[s] [s], int y[s] [s], int z[s] [s], int, int);
};
void array : : enter (int x[s] [s], int row, int column)
{
for (i=0; i<row; i++)
cin>>x[i] [j];
}
}
void array : :display (int x[s] [s], int row, int column)
{
for (i=0; i<row; i++)
{
for (j=0; j<column;j++)
cout<<x[i] [j]<<'\t';
cout<<endl;
```

```
}
}
void array : : mat_add (int x[s] [s], int y[s] [s], int z[s] [s], int row, int column)
{
// Matrix addition
for (i=0; i<<row; i++)
{
for (j=0;j<column;j++)
z[i] [j] =x [i] [j] +y [i] [j];
}
}
void main ( )
{
array obj;
int a[s] [s], b[s] [s], c[s] [s], rowl, columnl, row2, column2;
clrscr ( );
cout<<\nEnter the order of first matrix <="<<s<<" * "<<s<<"\n";
cin>>row1>>column1;
cout<<\nEnter the order of second matrix <="<<s<<" * <<<s<<"\n};
cin>>row2<<column2;
if((row1= =row2) && (column1= =column2))
{
cout<<"\nEnter the first matrix of order "<<row1<<" * "<<column1<<end1;
obj.enter (a, row1, column1);
cout<<"\nEnter the second matrix of ordre "<<row2<<" * "<<column1<<end1;
obj.enter(b, row2, column2);
clrscr ( );
cout<<"\nFirst matrix is \n\n";
obj.display (a, row1, column1);
cout<<"\nSecond matrix is \n\n";
obj.display(b, row2, column2);
obj.mat_add (a, b, c, row1, column1);
cout<<"\nAddition of two matrices is \n\n";
obj.display (c, row1, column1);
}
else
```

```
cout<<"\nMatrix addition is not possible";
getch ( );
}
```

Output:

```
Enter the order  of first matrix <=5 * 5
2     2
Enter the order of second matrix <=5 * 5
2     2
Enter the first matrix of order 2 * 2
1     4
3     6
Enter the second matrix of order 2 * 2
2     5
1     2
First matrix is
1     4
3     6
Second matrix is
2     5
1     2
Addition of two matrices is
3     9
4     8
```

Program 10: Write a C++ program for subtraction of two matrices.

```
# include<iostream.h>
# include<conio.h>
# define s 5
class array
{
private:
int i, j, x[s] [s], y[s] [s], z[s] [s];
public;
void enter (int x[s] [s], int, int);
void display (int x[s] [s], int, int);
void mat_add (int x[s] [s], int y[s] [s], int z[s] [s], int, int);
};
void array : : enter (int x[s] [s], int row, int column)
```

```
{
for (i=0; i<row; i++)
cin>>x[i] [j];
}
}
void array : :display (int x[s] [s], int row, int column)
{
for (i=0; i<row; i++)
{
for (j=0; j<column;j++)
cout<<x[i] [j]<<'\t';
cout<<endl;
}
}
void array: : mat_subtract (int x[s] [s], int y[s] [s], int z[s] [s], int row, int
column)
{
//Matrix subtraction
for (i=0;i<row;i++)
{
for (j=0;j<column;j++)
z[i] [j] =x [i] [j] -y [i] [j];
}
}
void main ( )
{
array obj;
int a[s] [s], b[s] [s], c[s] [s], rowl, columnl, row2, column2;
clrscr ( );
cout<<\nEnter the order of first matrix <="<<s<<" * "<<s<<"\n";
cin>>row1>>column1;
cout<<\nEnter the order of second matrix <="<<s<<" * <<<s<<"\n};
cin>>row2<<column2;
if((row1= =row2) && (column1= =column2))
{
cout<<"\nEnter the first matrix of order "<<row1<<" * "<<column1<<end1;
obj.enter (a, row1, column1);
cout<<"\nEnter the second matrix of ordre "<<row2<<" *
"<<column1<<end1;
obj.enter(b, row2, column2);
```

```
clrscr ( );
cout<<"\nFirst matrix is \n\n";
obj.display (a, row1, column1);
cout<<"\nSecond matrix is \n\n";
obj.display(b, row2, column2);
obj.mat_add (a, b, c, row1, column1);
cout<<"\nAddition of two matrices is \n\n";
obj.display (c, row1, column1);
}
else
cout<<"\nMatrix addition is not possible";
getch ( );
}
```

Output:

```
Enter the order  of first matrix <=5 * 5
2   2
Enter the order of second matrix <=5 * 5
2   2
Enter the first matrix of order 2 * 2
5   4
8   2
Enter the second matrix of order 2 * 2
1   2
7   3
First matrix is
5   4
8   2
Second matrix is
1   2
7   3
Subtraction of two matrices is
4   2
1   -1
```

Program 11: Write a C++ program for multiplication of two matrices

```
# include<iostream.h>
# include<conio.h>
# define s 5
class array
```

```
{
private:
int i, j, x[s] [s], y[s] [s], z[s] [s];
public;
void enter (int x[s] [s], int, int);
void display (int x[s] [s], int, int);
void mat_add (int x[s] [s], int y[s] [s], int z[s] [s], int, int);
};
void array : : enter (int x[s] [s], int row, int column)
{
for (i=0; i<row; i++)
cin>>x[i] [j];
}
}
void array : :display (int x[s] [s], int row, int column)
{
for (i=0; i<row; i++)
{
for (j=0; j<column;j++)
cout<<x[i] [j]<<'\t';
cout<<endl;
}
}
void array : : mat_multiply (int x[s] [s], int y[s] [s], int z[s] [s], int row1, int
column1, int column2)
{
// Matrix multiplication
for (i=o; i<row1; i++)
{
for (j=0; jcolumn2;j++)
{
z[i] [j] =0;
for (k=0; k<column1; k++)
z[i] [j] +=x [i] [k] *y[k] [j];
}
}
}
```

```
void main ( )
{
array obj;
int a[s] [s], b[s] [s], c[s] [s], rowl, columnl, row2, column2;
clrscr ( );
cout<<\nEnter the order of first matrix <="<<s<<" * "<<s<<"\n";
cin>>row1>>column1;
cout<<\nEnter the order of second matrix <="<<s<<" * <<<s<<"\n};
cin>>row2<<column2;
if((row1= =row2) && (column1= =column2))
{
cout<<"\nEnter the first matrix of order "<<row1<<" * "<<column1<<end1;
obj.enter (a, row1, column1);
cout<<"\nEnter the second matrix of ordre "<<row2<<" * "<<column1<<end1;
obj.enter(b, row2, column2);
clrscr ( );
cout<<"\nFirst matrix is \n\n";
obj.display (a, row1, column1);
cout<<"\nSecond matrix is \n\n";
obj.display(b, row2, column2);
obj.mat_add (a, b, c, row1, column1);
cout<<"\nAddition of two matrices is \n\n";
obj.display (c, row1, column1);
}
else
cout<<"\nMatrix addition is not possible";
getch ( );
}
```

Output:

```
Enter the order  of first matrix <=5 * 5
2    2
Enter the order of second matrix <=5 * 5
2    2
Enter the first matrix of order 2 * 2
1    3
4    5
```

```
Enter the second matrix of order 2 * 2
6    7
1    8
First matrix is
1    3
4    5
Second matrix is
6    7
1    8
Multiplication of two matrices is
9    31
29   68
```

4.5.2 Three Dimensional Array

Three Dimensional Array is also called space array or xyz array. As it has three subscripts, so these are also called triple dimensional array.

The syntax used for three dimensional array is as:

data-type array-name [space size] [row size] [column size];

For example, it can be declared as:

int st[5] [2] [3];

Suppose there are five students in a class and get different marks in three subjects in two house tests, then their marks be displayed by using three dimensional-array as:

st[1][1][1] = 55 , st[1][1][2] = 33, st[1][1][3] = 10, st[1][2][1] = 5
st[1][2][2] = 35, st[1][2][3] = 34, st[2][1][1] = 50, ..., st[5][2][3] = 75

4.5.3 N-dimensional or Multi-dimensional Array

This type of array has n size of rows, columns and spaces and so on.

The syntax used for declaration of this type of array is as follows:

Data-type array-name [s1][s2] ... ... [sn];

In this sn is the nth size of the array. This type of array is less used in C language.

4.6 MULTI DIMENSIONAL ARRAY

Up to now we have been talking about one-dimensional arrays (or alternatively, single-dimensional arrays. These arrays are by far the most common type of array, and so often we just say "array" when we mean this kind of array. However, it is possible to have arrays of multiple dimensions as well. For example, if you would find it useful to have an array with both rows and columns (i.e. with two dimensions) and more than that is called Multidimensional.

Ordinary arrays are indexed by a single integer. Also useful, particularly in numerical and graphics applications, is the concept of a multi-dimensional array, in which we index into the array using an ordered list of integers, such as in a[3,1,5]. The number of integers in the list used to index into the multi-dimensional array is always the same and is referred to as the array's dimensionality, and the bounds on each of these are called the array's dimensions. An array with dimensionality k is often called k-dimensional. One-dimensional arrays correspond to the simple arrays discussed thus far; two-dimensional arrays are a particularly common representation for matrices. In practice, the dimensionality of an array rarely exceeds three. Mapping a one-dimensional array into memory is obvious, since memory is logically itself a (very large) one-dimensional array. When we reach higher-dimensional arrays, however, the problem is no longer obvious.

Suppose we want to represent this simple two-dimensional array:

$$A = \begin{bmatrix} 1 & 2 & 3 \\ 4 & 5 & 6 \\ 7 & 8 & 9 \end{bmatrix}$$

It is most common to index this array using the RC-convention, where elements are referred in row, column fashion or $A_{row, col}$, such as:

$$A_{1,1} = 1, A_{1,2} = 2, ..., A_{3,2} = 8, A_{3,3} = 9$$

In computer science, a few common array indexing includes:

1. **Row-major order:** Used most notably by statically-declared arrays in C. The elements of each row are stored in order.

1	2	3	4	5	6	7	8	9

2. **Column-major order:** Used most notably in C. The elements of each column are stored in order.

1	4	7	2	5	8	3	6	9

Arrays of Arrays

A multidimensional array is an 'array of arrays'. A multidimensional array is the one in which each element of the array is an array itself. It is similar to tables in a database where each primary element (row) is a collection of secondary elements (columns). If the secondary elements do not contain a collection of other elements, it is called a 2-dimensional array (the most common type of multidimensional array), otherwise it is called an n-dimensional array where n is the depth of the chain of arrays. There are two types of multidimensional arrays in C++: 1. Rectangular array (one in which each row contains an equal number of columns) 2. Jagged array (one in which each row does not necessarily contain an equal number of columns)

The images below show what the different kinds of arrays look like. The figure also shows the indexes of different elements of the arrays. Remember, the first element of an array is always zero (0).

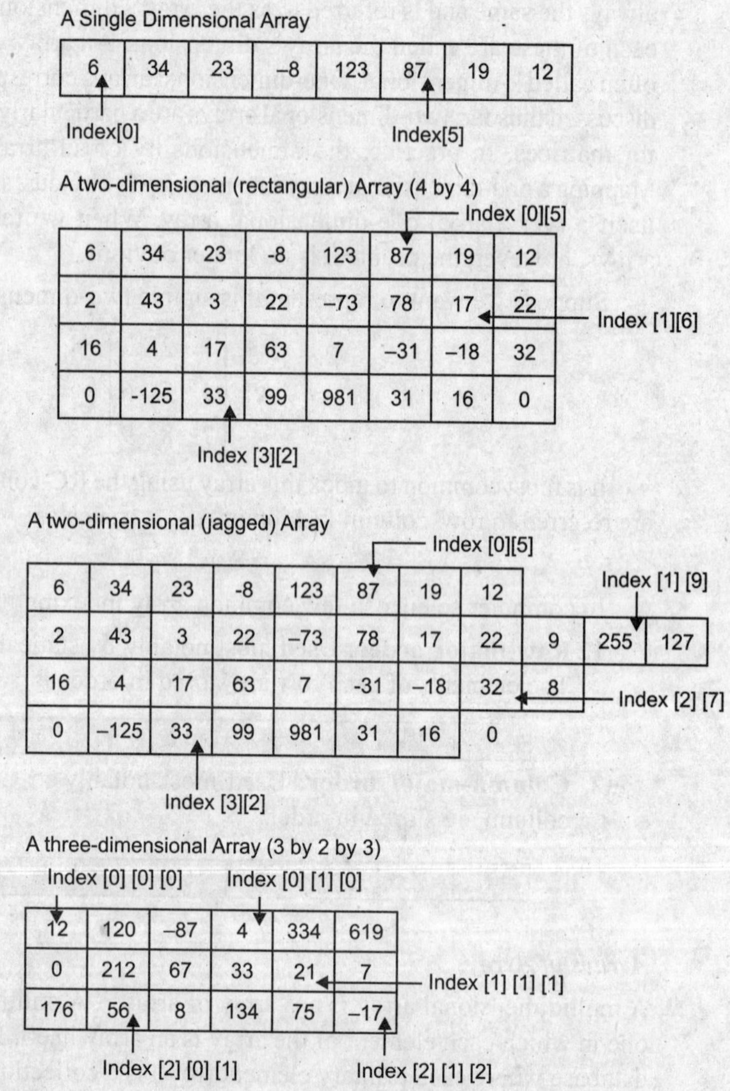

Figure 4.14: Various types of array

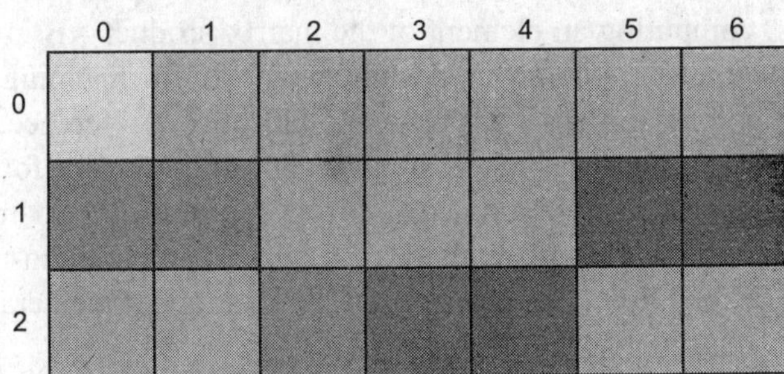

Figure 4.15: 2D jagged array

Multi-dimensional arrays are typically represented by one-dimensional arrays of references (Iliffe vectors) to other one-dimensional arrays. The subarrays can be either the rows or columns.

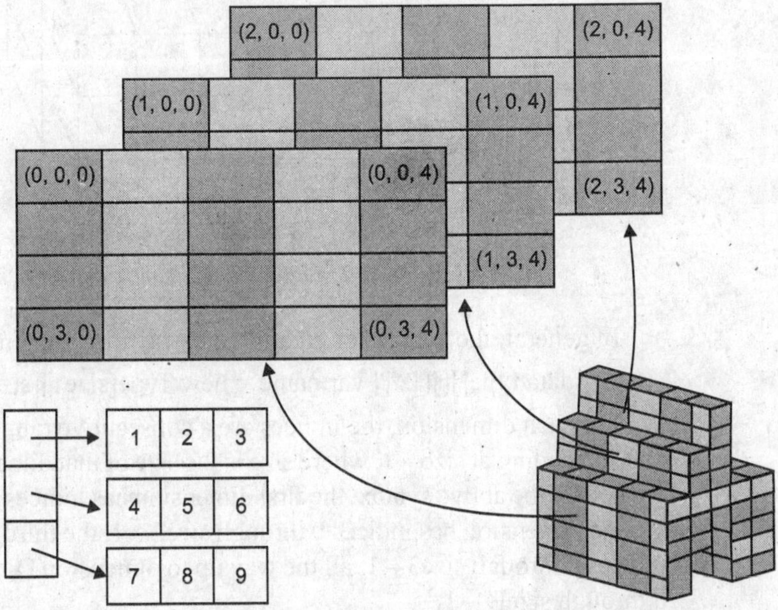

Figure 4.16: Representation of multidimensional arrays

The first two forms are more compact and have potentially better locality of reference, but are also more limiting; the arrays must be **rectangular,** meaning that no row can contain more elements than any other. Arrays of arrays, on the other hand, allow the creation of **ragged arrays**, also called **jagged arrays**, in which the valid range of one index depends on the value of another, or in this case, simply that different rows can be different sizes. Arrays of arrays are also of value in programming languages that only supply one-dimensional arrays as primitives.

In many applications, such as numerical applications working with matrices, we iterate over rectangular two-dimensional arrays in predictable ways. For example, computing an element of the matrix product **AB** involves iterating over a row of **A** and a column of **B** simultaneously. In mapping the individual array indexes into memory, we wish to exploit locality of reference as much as we can. A compiler can sometimes automatically choose the layout for an array so that sequentially accessed elements are stored sequentially in memory; in our example, it might choose row-major order for **A**, and column-major order for **B**. Even more exotic orderings can be used, for example if we iterate over the main diagonal of a matrix.

It is represented in a structural form as shown in the Figure 4.17 below:

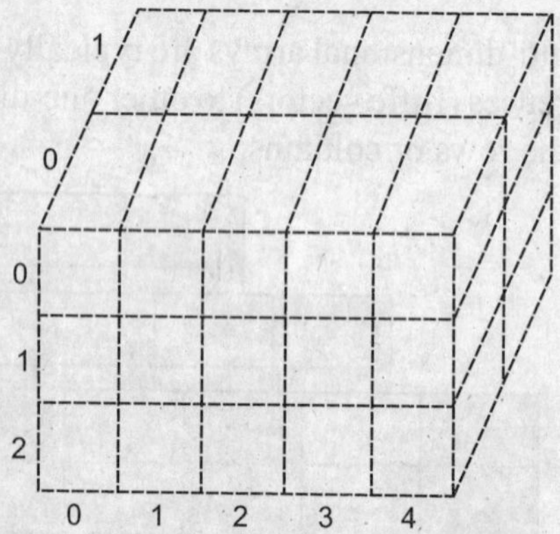

Figure 4.17: Structure of multidimensional arrays

In general, the syntax for creating an array of D dimensions is as follows:

data type[][][]...[] var name = new Type[size1][size2][size3]...[sizeD];

For each dimension, the indices are a consecutive range of integers beginning at 0 and ending at size – 1, where size is the size of that dimension. So, for the array created by the above syntax, the first dimension has indices 0 through size1 – 1, the second dimension has indices 0 through size2 – 1, the third dimension would have indices 0 through size3 – 1, all the way up to dimension D, which has indices from 0 through sizeD – 1.

For multi-dimensional arrays, such as the picture you have seen earlier, you decide which will be the first dimension, and which will the second dimension, and so on (if there are more than two dimensions), and then use the general syntax above. For example, for a two-dimensional array, we simplify the general syntax to two sets of brackets:

data type[][] varname = new Type[sizeOfFirstDimension][sizeOfSecondDimension];

In the two-dimensional array , if we wanted the number of rows in our picture to be the first dimension in our array (note there are four rows) and we wanted the number of columns in our picture to be the second dimension in our array (note there are five columns), and we wanted to hold values of type int, then we would write a statement such as the following one, in order to create that array:

```
int[][] theMatrix = new int[4][5];
```

and we have now created a two-dimensional array, with a variable name theMatrix, which has space for twenty integers. If we wanted to create an array to match the three-dimensional example from above, and we wanted the dimension with three cells (indexed with 0, 1, and 2) to be the first dimension, and we wanted the dimension with five cells (indexed with 0, 1, 2, 3, and 4) to be the second dimension, and we wanted the dimension with two cells (indexed with 0 and 1) to be the third dimension, and wanted the array to hold values of type char, then in order to create such an array, we would use the following statement:

```
char[][][] threeDarray = new char[3][5][2];
```

Note that the syntax for one-dimensional arrays – is just the above syntax, with D being equal to 1, since there is only one dimension. So, you would have exactly one pair of square brackets before the variable name, and one pair of square brackets with a size in it after the assignment operator – exactly as you saw in the previous notes packet:

```
Type[] varname = new Type[size1];
```

4.7 ACCESSING CELLS OF MULTI-DIMENSIONAL ARRAYS

Just as the syntax for creating a one-dimensional array was a special case of the more general syntax for creating a D-dimensional array, the syntax for accessing a one-dimensional array is a special case of the more general syntax for accessing a D-dimensional array.

Accessing a D-dimensional array is done with the following expression:

varname[index1][index2]...[indexD]

In the case of a two-dimensional array, you would have two sets of brackets:

varname[index1][index2]

In the case of a three-dimensional array, you would have three sets of brackets:

varname[index1][index2][index3]

and so on.

4.8 ADVANTAGES (PROS) AND DISADVANTAGES (CONS)

Arrays permit efficient (constant-time, O(1)) random access, but not efficient insertion and deletion of elements (which are O(n), where n is the size of the array). Linked lists have the opposite trade-off. Consequently, arrays are most appropriate for storing a fixed amount of data which will be accessed in an unpredictable fashion, and linked lists are best for a list of data which will be accessed sequentially and updated often with insertions or deletions.

Another advantage of arrays that has become very important on modern architectures is that iterating through an array has good locality of reference, and so is much faster than iterating through (say) a linked list of the same size, which tends to jump around in memory. However, an array can also be accessed in a random way, as is done with large hash tables, and in this case this is not a benefit.

Arrays also are among the most compact data structures; storing 100 integers in an array takes only 100 times the space required to store an integer, plus perhaps a few bytes of overhead for the pointer to the array (4 on a 32-bit system). Any pointer-based data structure, on the other hand, must keep its pointers somewhere, and these occupy additional space. This extra space becomes more significant as the data elements become smaller. For example, an array of ASCII characters takes up one byte per character, while on a 32-bit platform, which has 4-byte pointers, a linked list requires at least five bytes per character. Conversely, for very large elements, the space difference becomes a negligible fraction of the total space.

Because arrays have a fixed size, there are some indexes which refer to invalid elements — for example, the index 17 in an array of size 5. What happens when a program attempts to refer to these varies from language to language and platform to platform.

A drawback of the simplicity of arrays is the possibility of referencing a non-existent element by using an index outside the range of valid indices. This is known as exceeding the array bounds. The result is, at best, a program working with incorrect data. At worst, the whole system can crash (it is important to note that in cases where data integrity is critical, such as online banking, a crash may be preferable to working with incorrect data). This problem is particularly felt in the C++ programming language, the powerful syntax of which is unfortunately prone to this kind of error. Some other languages as Java have built-in bounds checking, and will refuse to index an array outside of its permitted range - although there may be alternative access functions which bypass the checks. Other languages, such as C++, offer facilities to create a data type that functions like a standard array with bounds checking, or offer such a data structure in their standard library. The advantage of providing both checked and unchecked versions, whichever way round the problem is approached, is that you can choose the unchecked version in the rare applications where bounds checking would impose an unreasonable performance penalty, without sacrificing safety in cases where performance is less critical.

4.9 APPLICATION OF ARRAYS

Whenever we require a collection of data objects of the same type and want to process them as a single unit, an array can be used, provided the number of data items is constant or fixed. Arrays have a wide range of applications ranging from business data processing to scientific calculations to industrial projects.

4.9.1 Implementation of A Static Contiguous List

A list is a structure in which insertions, deletions, and retrieval may occur at any position in the list. Therefore, when the list is static, it can be implemented by using an array. When a list is implemented or realized by using an array, it is a contiguous list. By contiguous, we mean that the elements are placed consecutively one after another starting from some address, called the base address. The advantage of a list implemented using an array is that it is randomly accessible. The disadvantage of such a list is that insertions and deletions require moving of the entries, and so it is costlier. A static list can be implemented using an array by mapping the ith element of the list into the ith entry of the array, as shown in Figure 4.18.

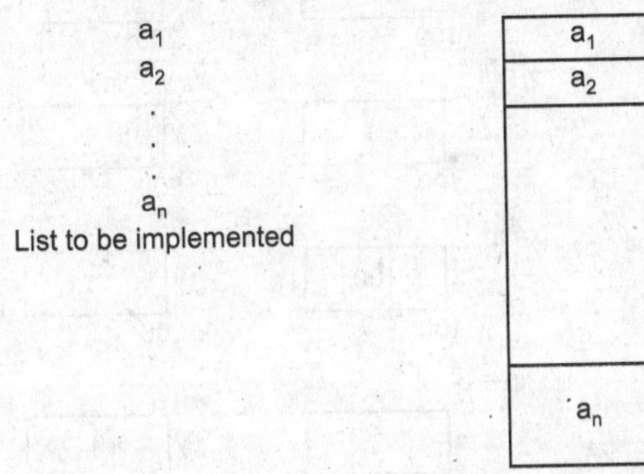

Figure 4.18: Implementation of a static contiguous list.

4.10 POINTER

A pointer is a variable which contains the address in memory of another variable. We can have a pointer to any variable type.

The unary or monadic operator **&** gives the "address of a variable".

The indirection or dereference operator * gives the "contents of an object pointed to by a pointer".

To declare a pointer to a variable do:

```
int *pointer;
```

Consider the effect of the following code:

```
int x = 1, y = 2;
int *ip;
ip = &x;
y = *ip;
x = ip;
*ip = 3;
```

It is worth considering what is going on at the *machine level* in memory to fully understand how pointer work. Consider Figure 4.19. Assume for the sake of this discussion that variable x resides at memory location 100, y at 200 and ip at 1000.

***Note:** A pointer is a variable and thus its values need to be stored somewhere. It is the nature of the pointers value that is* new.

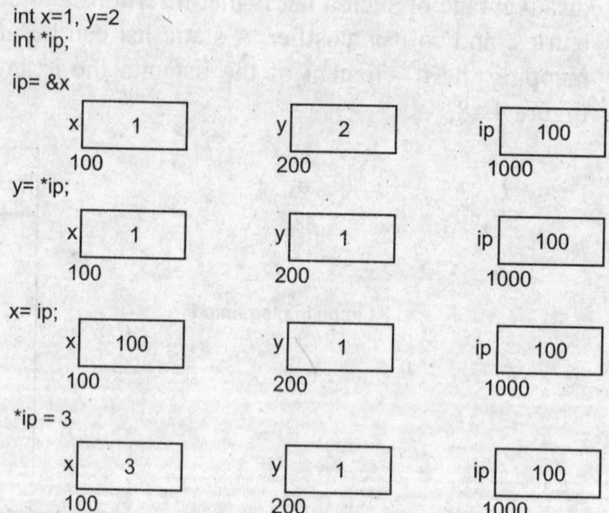

Figure 4.19: Pointer, Variables and Memory

Now the assignments x = 1 and y = 2 obviously load these values into the variables. ip is declared to be a *pointer to an integer* and is assigned to the address of x (&x). So ip gets loaded with the value 100.

Next y gets assigned to the contents of ip. In this example ip currently *points* to memory location 100 — the location of x. So y gets assigned to the values of x — which is 1.

We have already seen that C is not too fussy about assigning values of different type. Thus it is perfectly **legal** (although not all that common) to assign the current value of ip to x. The value of ip at this instant is 100.

Finally we can assign a value to the contents of a pointer (*ip).

***Important**: When a pointer is declared it does not point anywhere. You must set it to point somewhere before you use it.*

So ...

```
int *ip;
*ip = 100;
```

will generate an error (program crash!!).

The correct use is:

```
int *ip;
int x;
ip = &x;
*ip = 100;
```

We can do integer arithmetic on a pointer:

```
float *flp, *flq;
*flp = *flp + 10;
++*flp;
(*flp)++;
flq = flp;
```

***Note**: A pointer to any variable type is an address in memory — which is an integer address. A pointer is definitely NOT an integer.*

The reason we associate a pointer to a data type is so that it knows how many bytes the data is stored in. When we increment a pointer we increase the pointer by one "block" memory.

So for a character pointer ++ch_ptr adds 1 byte to the address.

For an integer or float ++ip or ++flp adds 4 bytes to the address.

Consider a float variable (fl) and a pointer to a float (flp) as shown in Figure 4.20.

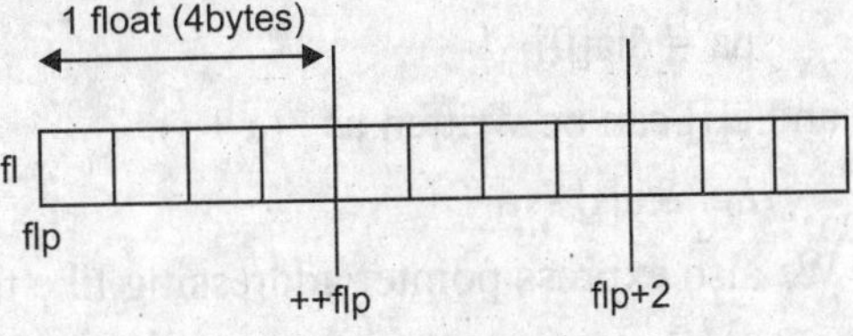

Figure 4.20: Pointer Arithmetic

Assume that flp points to fl then if we increment the pointer (++flp) it moves to the position shown 4 bytes on. If on the other hand we added 2 to the pointer then it moves 2 **float positions** i.e 8 bytes as shown in the Figure.

4.11 POINTERS AND ARRAYS

Pointers and arrays are very closely linked in C++.

***Hint:** think of array elements arranged in consecutive memory locations.*

Consider the following:

```
int a[10], x;
int *pa;
pa = &a[0];        /* pa pointer to address of a[0] */
x = *pa;           /* x = contents of pa (a[0] in this case) */
```

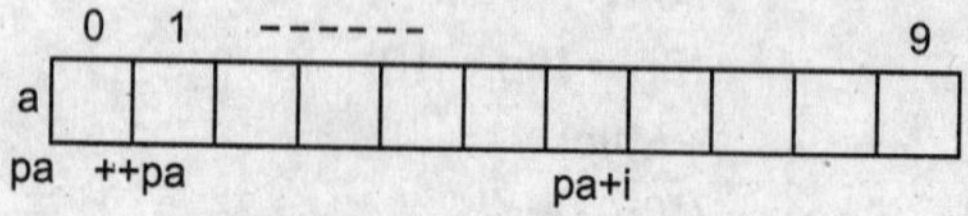

0 1 ------ 9
a
pa ++pa pa+i

Figure 4.21: Arrays and Pointers

To get somewhere in the array (Figure 4.21) using a pointer we could do:

pa + i = a[i]

***Warning:** There is no bound checking of arrays and pointers so you can easily go beyond array memory and overwrite other things.*

C++ however is much more subtle in its link between arrays and pointers. For example we can just type

pa = a;

instead of

pa = &a[0]

and a[i] can be written as *(a + i).

i.e. &a[i] = a + i.

We also express pointer addressing like this:

pa[i] = *(pa + i).

However pointers and arrays are different:

1. A pointer is a variable. We can do pa = a and pa++.
2. An Array is not a variable. a = pa and a++ ARE ILLEGAL.

This stuff is very important. Make sure you understand it. We will see a lot more of this.

4.11.1 Arrays of Pointers

We can have arrays of pointers since pointers are variables.

Example use: *Sort lines of text of different length*

Note: *Text can't be moved or compared in a single operation.*

Arrays of Pointers are a data representation that will cope efficiently and conveniently with variable length text lines.

How can we do this?

1. Store lines end-to-end in one big char array (Figure 4.22). \n will delimit lines.
2. Store pointers in a different array where each pointer points to 1st char of each new line.
3. Compare two lines using strcmp() standard library function.
4. If 2 lines are out of order — swap pointer in pointer array (not text).

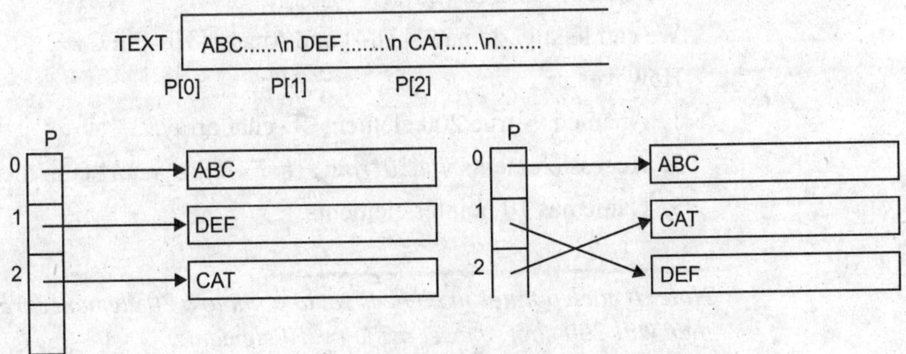

Figure 4.22: Arrays of Pointers (String Sorting Example)

This eliminates:

1. Complicated storage management.
2. High overheads of moving lines.

4.11.2 Multidimensional Arrays and Pointers

We should think of multidimensional arrays in a different way in C++:

A 2D array is really a 1D array, each of whose elements is itself an array Hence a[n][m] notation.

Array elements are stored row by row. When we pass a 2D array to a function we must specify the number of columns — the number of rows is irrelevant. The reason for this is pointers again. C++ needs to know how many columns in order that it can jump from row to row in memory.

Consider int a[5][35] to be passed in a function:

We can do:

```
f(int a[][35]) {.....}
```

or even:

```
f(int (*a)[35]) {.....}
```

We need parenthesis (*a) since [] have a higher precedence than * So:

int (*a)[35]; declares a pointer to an array of 35 ints.

int *a[35]; declares an array of 35 pointers to ints.

Now lets look at the (subtle) difference between pointers and arrays. Strings are a common application of this.

Consider:

```
char *name[10];
char Aname[10][20];
```

We can legally do name[3][4] and Aname[3][4] in C++.

However

1. Aname is a true 200 element 2D char array.
2. Access elements via *20*row + col + base_address* in memory.
3. Name has 10 pointer elements.

Note: *If each pointer in name is set to point to a 20 element array then and only then will 200 chars be set aside (+ 10 elements).*

The advantage of the latter is that each pointer can point to arrays be of different length.

Consider:

```
char *name[] = { "no month", "jan", "feb" ... };
char Aname[][15] = { "no month", "jan", "feb", ... };
```

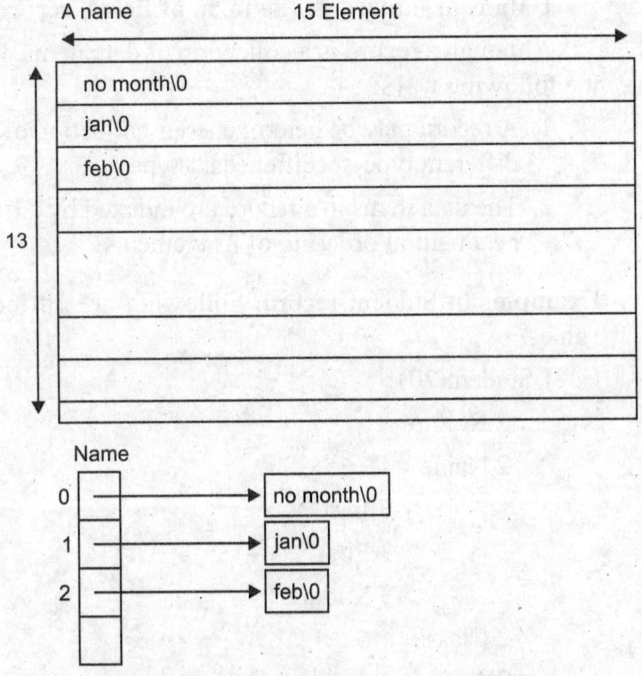

Figure 4.23: 2D Arrays and Arrays of Pointers

4.12 RECORDS

A record is a special type of data structure that, unlike arrays, collects different data types that define a particular structure such a book, product, person and many others. Collections of data are frequently organized into a hierarchy of field, records and files.

"A record is defined as a finite, ordered collection of possibly heterogeneous elements of given entity. It is sometimes also called as simply a structure. In this structure, logically related data items of different types are grouped together under one name."

A record is a collection of related data items, each of which is called a field or attribute, A field refers to single elementary unit of information used to representing an attribute of an entity. The elements of a record are called as fields. A field is a specified area of record used for a particular kind of information and a file is a collection of similar records. Data items, which are divided into sub items, are called as **group items**. For example, the name of student can be divided into subitems – first name, middle name and last name.

Data items, which are not divided into sub items, are called **elementary items**. For example, the Roll number of student cannot be divided into subitems.

Data is organized in the form of fields, records and files.

Although a record is a collection of data items, it differs from a linear array in the following ways:

1. A record may be heterogeneous collection of related fields. Every field has different type-specifier (data-type).
2. The data items in a record are indexed by attribute names, so there may not be a natural ordering of its elements.

Example: In Student record, Following are attributes and their corresponding values.

1 Student(20)

  2 Rollno

  2 Name

    3 Last

    3 First

    3 Middle

  2 Class

  2 Address

Table 4.1: Representation of Student record.

Attributes:	Student#	Rollno.	Name			Class	Address
			Last	First	Middle		
Values:	1	1201	Rair	Avtar	Singh	BCA	76A azad nagar, U.P
	2	1202	Sandhu	Avtar	Singh	BCA	34B galli nagar,U.P
	...	......	.....	...	......	.....	...
	...	......	.....	...	......	.....	...
	20	1220	Brar	Manbir	Singh	.....	67A Moga, Punjab

For example, suppose if you want to store a book in library using C++ program, then you give information about the title of the book, name of the author, number of pages in the book and the price of the book. Then before coding the problem you will examine it according to following table

Title of the Book	Name of Author	Pages of the Book	Price of the Book
C programming	Ikvinderpal Singh	450	300
Fundamental of C	Rachhpal Singh	500	200
Let Us C	Yashvant K.	700	300

To elaborate this problem, we set some data-types and width (size) as shown below:

Field name	Type	Width
Title	Character	20
Author	Character	20
Pages	Integer	8
Price	Real (Float)	7.2

In C++ language, to maintain such type of records we use structure data type, which is heterogeneous collection of related fields. Every field has different type-specifier (data-type).

```
struct    library
{
char      title [20] ;
char      author [20] ;
int       pages ;
float     price ;
};
```

4.13 RECORD STRUCTURES

A **record structure** is an aggregate entity containing one or more elements. (Record elements are also called fields or components.) You can use records when you need to declare and operate on multi-field data structures in your programs.

Creating a record is a two-step process:

1. You must define the form of the record with a multistatement **structure declaration.**
2. You must use a RECORD statement to declare the record as an entity with a name. (More than one RECORD statement can refer to a given structure.)

In computer science, a **record** (also called **tuple** or **struct**) is one of the simplest data structures, consisting of two or more values or variables stored in consecutive memory positions; so that each component (called a **field** or **member** of the record) can be accessed by applying different offsets to the starting address.

For example, a date may be stored as a record containing a 16-bit numeric field for the year, a three-letter field for the month, and an 8-bit numeric field for the day-of-month. As this example shows, the fields of a record need not all have the same size and encoding; therefore, in general one cannot easily obtain the field which has a run-time computed index in the field sequence, as one can do in an array.

A **record type** is a data type that describes such values and variables. Most modern computer languages allow the programmer to define new record types. The definition includes specifying the data type of each field, its position in the record, and an identifier (name or label) by which it can be accessed. In type theory, product types are generally preferred due to their simplicity, but proper record types are studied in languages such as System F-sub. Since type-theoretical records may contain first-class function-typed fields in addition to data, they can express many features of object-oriented programming.

Records can exist in any storage medium, including main memory and mass storage devices such as magnetic tapes or hard disks. Records are a fundamental component of most data structures, especially linked data structures. Many computer files are organized as arrays of logical records, often grouped into larger physical records or blocks for efficiency.

The parameters of a function or procedure can often be viewed as the fields of a record variable; and the arguments passed to that function can be viewed as a record value that gets assigned to that variable at the time of the call. Also, in the call stack that is often used to implement procedure calls, each entry is an **activation record** or **call frame,** containing the procedure parameters and local variables, the return address, and other internal fields.

4.14 REPRESENTATION OF RECORDS IN MEMORY; PARALLEL ARRAYS

A **parallel array** is a data structure for representing arrays of records. It keeps a separate, homogeneous array for each field of the record, each having the same number of elements. Then, objects located at the same index in each array are implicitly the fields of a single record. Pointers from one object to another are replaced by array indices. This contrasts with the normal approach of storing all fields of each record together in memory. For example, one might declare an array of 100 names, each a string, and 100 ages, each an integer, associating each name with the age that has the same index.

An example in C using parallel arrays:

```
int ages[]  = {0,        17,        2,        52,       25};
char *names[] = {"None",    "Mike",    "Billy",   "Tom",     "Stan"};
int parent[] = {0 /*None*/, 3 /*Tom*/, 1 /*Mike*/, 0 /*None*/, 3 /*Tom*/};
for(i = 1; i <= 4; i++) {
printf("Name: %s, Age: %d, Parent: %s \n",
names[i], ages[i], names[parent[i]]);
}
```

Since records may contain homogeneous data, the elements of a record cannot be store in an array. Assuming the records contain nonhomogeneous data, the records may have to be stored in individual variables, one for each of its elementary data items. On the other hand, suppose one wants to store an entire file of records. Note that all data elements belonging to the same identifier do have the same type. Such a file may be stored in memory as a collection of **parallel arrays**, where elements in different arrays with same subscript belong to the same record. This is illustrated in example below.

Example: Suppose a student list contains the name, roll no, class, mobile number of each student. We can store the file in four parallel arrays NAME, ROLLNO, CLASS, and MOBILE NO. as shown in figure for given subscript K, the elements NAME[K], ROLLNO[K], CLASS[K] and MOBILE NO.[K] belong to the same record.

Table 4.2: Representation of Student record.

Name	Roll no.	Class	Mobile no.
Sukhwant Singh	1	MCA	9889876519
Jagbir Singh	2	MCA	9871543298
Jagminder Singh	3	MCA	9845639856
Sukhminder Singh	4	MCA	9254378651
Prabhjeet Singh	5	MCA	9834276598

Parallel arrays have a number of practical advantages over the normal approach:

1. They can be used in languages which support only arrays of primitive types and not of records (or perhaps don't support records at all).
2. Parallel arrays are simple to understand and use, and are often used where declaring a record is more trouble than it's worth.
3. They can save a substantial amount of space in some cases by avoiding alignment issues. For example, one of the fields of the record can be a single bit, and its array would only need to reserve one bit for each record, whereas in the normal approach many more bits would "pad" the field so that it consumes an entire byte or a word.
4. If the number of items is small, array indices can occupy significantly less space than full pointers, particularly on architectures with large words.
5. Sequentially examining a single field of each record in the array is very fast on modern machines, since this amount to a linear traversal of a single array, exhibiting ideal locality of reference and cache behavior.

However, parallel arrays also have several strong disadvantages, which serves to explain why they are not generally preferred:

1. They have significantly worse locality of reference when visiting the records sequentially and examining multiple fields of each record, which is the norm.
2. They obscure the relationship between fields of a single record.
3. They have little direct language support (the language and its syntax typically express no relationship between the arrays in the parallel array.)
4. They are expensive to grow or shrink, since each of several arrays must be reallocated.

The bad locality of reference is the worst issue. However, a compromise can be made in some cases: if a structure can be divided into groups of fields that are generally accessed together, an array can be constructed for each group, and its elements are records containing only these subsets of the larger structure's fields. This is a valuable way of speeding up access to very large structures with many members, while keeping the portions of the structure tied together. An alternative to tying them together using array indexes is to use references to tie the portions together, but this can be less efficient in time and space. Some compiler optimizations, particularly for vector processors, are able to perform this transformation automatically when arrays of structures are created in the program.

4.15 FIXED LENGTH RECORDS

A file where all the records are of the same length is said to have **fixed length records**.

Some **fields** are always the same length (eg **Postcode** is always 7 characters). Some **fields** may need to be 'padded out' so they are the correct length

(eg Surname - If 15 characters are stored then Jenkins would be stored as 'JENKINS' - 7 characters followed by 8 spaces).

Advantage

Access is **fast** because the computer knows where each record starts.

E.g. If each record is 120 bytes long then

- The 1st record starts at [Start of File] + 0 bytes
- The 2nd record starts at [Start of File] + 120 bytes
- The 3rd record starts at [Start of File] + 240 bytes etc.....

Disadvantage

Using Fixed length records, the records are usually **larger** and therefore need **more storage space** and are **slower** to transfer (load or save).

In the Example

Table 4.3: Representation of fixed length record.

Number	Surname	Forename	Year	Form	DOB
92013	JONES	Sidney	12	B	23/04/78
92107	LAIDLAW	Lorraine	12	Y	12/11/79
92114	MERRITT	Mandy	12	G	08/03/79
92167	NASH	Natasha	12	B	19/08/78

...the field lengths may be..

Number : 5

Surname: 15

Forename: 15

Year: 2

Form: 1

DOB: 8

Each record would be **46 bytes** long.The first record of the example file would be stored as ...(each box represents one byte of storage)..

9	2	0	1	3	J	O	N	E	S									
S	i	d	n	e	y									1	2	B	2	3
/	0	4	/	7	8													

4.16 VARIABLE LENGTH RECORDS

A record that has at least one variable-length field. The length of the entire record, therefore, varies according to what data is placed in the variable-length field.

One or more of the fields can be of **differing** lengths in each record.

Advantages

- the records will be **smaller** and will need less storage space
- the records will **load faster**

Disadvantages

- The computer will be unable to determine where each record starts so **processing** the records will be **slower**.

In the Example

Table 4.4: Representation of variable length record.

Number	Surname	Forename	Year	Form	DOB
92013	JONES	Sidney	12	B	23/04/78
92107	LAIDLAW	Lorraine	12	Y	12/11/79
92114	MERRITT	Mandy	12	G	08/03/79
92167	NASH	Natasha	12	B	19/08/78

Storage Method 1

When the record is stored, each field has a **field terminator** byte stored at the end of it, and there is often a **record terminator** at the end of the whole record.

9	2	0	1	3	*	J	O	N	E	S	*	S	i	d	n	e	y	*	1
2	*	B	*	2	3	/	0	4	/	7	8	%							

* is a field terminator   % is a record terminator

This record requires **33** bytes of storage.....but each record will be a different size.

Storage Method 2

Each field starts with a **byte** showing the **length** of the field. The whole record starts with a byte giving the size of the record. The first record of the example would be stored as....

34	**5**	9	2	0	1	3	**5**	J	O	N	E	S	**6**	S	i	d	n	e	y
2	1	2	**1**	B	**8**	2	3	/	0	4	/	7	8						

This record requires **34** bytes of storage....but again, each record would be a different size.

4.17 MATRIX

A **matrix** is a rectangular array of numbers, such as

$$\begin{bmatrix} 1 & 9 & 13 \\ 20 & 55 & 4 \end{bmatrix}.$$

An item in a matrix is called an entry or an element. The example has entries 1, 9, 13, 20, 55, and 4. Entries are often denoted by a variable with two subscripts, as shown on the right.

A matrix is an ordered set of numbers listed rectangular form A matrix is a two dimensional array of numbers or expressions arranged in a set of rows and columns. An m × n matrix **A** has m rows and n columns and is written

m-by-n matrix

$a_{i,j}$ n columns — j changes →

m rows, i changes ↓

$$\begin{bmatrix} a_{1,1} & a_{1,2} & a_{1,3} & \cdots \\ a_{2,1} & a_{2,2} & a_{2,3} & \cdots \\ a_{3,1} & a_{3,2} & a_{3,3} & \cdots \\ \vdots & \vdots & \vdots & \ddots \end{bmatrix} \qquad A = \begin{bmatrix} a_{11} & a_{12} & \cdots & a_{1n} \\ a_{2,1} & a_{2,2} & \cdots & a_{2n} \\ \vdots & \vdots & \ddots & \vdots \\ a_{m1} & a_{m2} & \cdots & a_{mn} \end{bmatrix}$$

Figure 4.24: Specific entries of a matrix are often referenced by using pairs of subscripts.

where the element aij, located in the ith row and the jth column, is a scalar quantity; a numerical constant, or a single valued expression. If m = n, that is there are the same number of rows as columns, the matrix is square, otherwise it is a rectangular matrix.

A matrix having either a single row (m = 1) or a single column (n = 1) is defined to be a vector because it is often used to define the coordinates of a point in a multi-dimensional space. (In this note the convention has been adopted of representing a vector by a lower case "bold-face" letter such as **x**, and a general matrix by a "bold-face" upper case letter such as **A**.) A vector having a single row, for example

$$x = [x_{11} \ \ x_{12} \ \ \cdots \ \ x_{1n}]$$

is defined to be a row vector, while a vector having a single column is defined to be a column vector

$$y = \begin{bmatrix} y_{11} \\ y_{21} \\ \vdots \\ y_{m1} \end{bmatrix}$$

Two special matrices are the square identity matrix, **I**, which is defined to have all of its elements equal to zero except those on the main diagonal (where i = j) which have a value of one:

$$I = \begin{bmatrix} 1 & 0 & \cdots & 0 \\ 0 & 1 & \cdots & 0 \\ \vdots & \vdots & \ddots & \vdots \\ 0 & 0 & \cdots & 1 \end{bmatrix}$$

and the null matrix **0**, which has the value of zero for all of its elements:

$$0 = \begin{bmatrix} 0 & 0 & \cdots & 0 \\ 0 & 0 & \cdots & 0 \\ \vdots & \vdots & \ddots & \vdots \\ 0 & 0 & \cdots & 0 \end{bmatrix}$$

A matrix is a rectangular arrangement of numbers. For example,

$$A = \begin{bmatrix} 9 & 8 & 6 \\ 1 & 2 & 7 \\ 4 & 9 & 2 \\ 6 & 0 & 5 \end{bmatrix}$$

An alternative notation uses large parentheses instead of box brackets:

$$A = \begin{pmatrix} 9 & 8 & 6 \\ 1 & 2 & 7 \\ 4 & 9 & 2 \\ 6 & 0 & 5 \end{pmatrix}$$

The horizontal and vertical lines in a matrix are called **rows** and **columns**, respectively. The numbers in the matrix are called its **entries** or its **elements**. To specify a matrix's size, a matrix with **m** rows and **n** columns is called an **m-by-n** matrix or **m × n** matrix, while **m** and **n** are called its **dimensions**. The above is a 4- by-3 matrix.

A matrix where one of the dimensions equals one is also called a **vector,** and may be interpreted as an element of real coordinate space. An m × 1 matrix (one column and m rows) is called a column vector and a 1 × n matrix (one row and n columns) is called a row vector. For example, the third row vector of the above matrix **A** is [4 9 2].

Most of this article focuses on **real and complex matrices,** i.e., matrices whose entries are real or complex numbers. More general types of entries are discussed below.

Square Matrix: If a matrix A has n rows and n columns then we say it's a square matrix.

In a square matrix the elements $a_{i,i}$, with i = 1,2,3,..., are called diagonal elements.

Remark. *There is no difference between a 1 x 1 matrix and an ordenary number.*

Diagonal Matrix: A diagonal matrix is a square matrix with all de non-diagonal elements 0.

The diagonal matrix is completely denoted by the diagonal elements.

Example [7 0 0]
[0 5 0]
[0 0 6]

The matrix is denoted by diagonal (7 , 5 , 6).

Row Matrix: A matrix with one row is called a row matrix

Column Matrix: A matrix with one column is called a column matrix

Matrices of the Same Kind: Matrix A and B are of the same kind if and only if A has as many rows as B and A has as many columns as B

The Tranpose of a Matrix: The n x m matrix A' is the transpose of the m x n matrix A if and only if

The ith row of A = the ith column of A' for (i = 1,2,3,..n)

So $a_{i,j} = a_{j,i}'$. The transpose of A is denoted T(A) or A^T

Zero-matrix: When all the elements of a matrix A are 0, we call A a 0-matrix.

We write shortly 0 for a 0-matrix.

An identity matrix I: An identity matrix I is a diagonal matrix with all diagonal element = 1.

A scalar matrix S: A scalar matrix S is a diagonal matrix with all diagonal elements alike.

$a_{1,1} = a_{i,i}$ for (i = 1,2,3,..n)

The opposite matrix of a matrix: If we change the sign of all the elements of a matrix A, we have the opposite matrix -A. If A' is the opposite of A then $a_{i,j}' = -a_{i,j}$, for all i and j.

A symmetric matrix: A square matrix is called symmetric if it is equal to its transpose.

Then $a_{i,j} = a_{j,i}$, for all i and j.

A skew-symmetric matrix: A square matrix is called skew-symmetric if it is equal to the opposite of its transpose. Then $a_{i,j} = -a_{j,i}$, for all i and j.

Elementary matrix arithmetic—Matrix addition: The operation of addition of two matrices is only defined when both matrices have the same dimensions. If **A** and **B** are both (m × n), then the sum

$$\mathbf{C} = \mathbf{A} + \mathbf{B}$$

is also (m × n) and is defined to have each element the sum of the corresponding elements of **A** and **B**, thus

$$cij = aij + bij\ .$$

Matrix addition is both associative, that is

$$\mathbf{A} + (\mathbf{B} + \mathbf{C}) = (\mathbf{A} + \mathbf{B}) + \mathbf{C},$$

and commutative

$$\mathbf{A} + \mathbf{B} = \mathbf{B} + \mathbf{A}.$$

The subtraction of two matrices is similarly defined; if **A** and **B** have the same dimensions, then the difference

$$\mathbf{C} = \mathbf{A} - \mathbf{B}$$

implies that the elements of **C** are

$$cij = aij - bij.$$

Multiplication of a matrix by a scalar quantity: If **A** is a matrix and k is a scalar quantity, the product **B** = k**A** is defined to be the matrix of the same dimensions as **A** whose elements are simply all scaled by the constant k, bij = k × aij.

Matrix multiplication: Two matrices may be multiplied together only if they meet conditions on their dimensions that allow them to conform. Let **A** have dimensions m × n, and **B** be n × p, that is **A** has the same number as columns as the number of rows in **B**, then the product

$$\mathbf{C} = \mathbf{AB}$$

is defined to be an m × p matrix with elements

$$c_{ij} = \sum_{k=1}^{n} a_{ik} b_{kj}$$

The element in position ij is the sum of the products of elements in the ith row of the first matrix (**A**) and the corresponding elements in the jth column of the second matrix (**B**).

Notice that the product **AB** is not defined unless the above condition is satisfied, that is the number of columns of the first matrix must equal the number of rows in the second.

Matrix multiplication is associative, that is

$$\mathbf{A}(\mathbf{BC}) = (\mathbf{AB})\mathbf{C}$$

but is not commutative in general

$$\mathbf{AB} \neq \mathbf{BA}$$

In fact unless the two matrices are square, reversing the order in the product will cause the matrices to be nonconformal. The order of the terms in the product is therefore very important. In the product **C** = **AB**, **A** is said to pre-multiply **B**, while **B** is said to post-multiply **A**. It is interesting to note in passing that unlike the scalar case, the fact that **AB** = **0** does not imply that either **A** = **0** or that **B** = **0**.

Multiplication of a row matrix by a column matrix: This multiplication is only possible if the row matrix and the column matrix have the same number of elements. The result is a ordinary number (1 x 1 matrix).

To multiply the row by the column, one multiplies corresponding elements, and then adds the results. Example:

[1]
[2 1 3]. [2] = [19]
[5]

Multiplication of two matrices a.b: This product is defined only if A is a (l x m) matrix and B is a (m x n) matrix.

So the number of columns of A has to be equal to the number of rows of B.

The product C = A.B then is a (l × n) matrix.

The element of the ith row and the jth column of the product is found by multiplying the ith row of A by the jth column of B.

$$c_{i,j} = \text{sum}_k (a_{i,k}.b_{k,j})$$

EXAMPLE

[1 2][1 3] = [5 7]

[2 1][2 2] [4 8]

[1 3][1 2] = [7 5]

[2 2][2 1] [6 6]

[1 1][2 2] = [0 0]

[1 1][-2 -2] [0 0]

From these examples we see that the product is not commutative and that there are zero divisors.

Algorithm 4.9: Matrix Multiplication

MATMUL(A, B, C, M, P, N)

Let A be an M X P matrix array, and let B be a P X N matrix array. This algorithm stores the product of A and B in an M x N matrix array C.

Step 1: Repeat Steps 2 to 4 for I = 1 to M:

Step 2: Repeat Steps 3 and 4 for I = 1 to N:

Step 3: Set C[I, J] := [Initializes C[I, J].]

Step 4: Repeat for J = 1 to P:

C[I, J] := C[I, J] + A[I, K] * B[K, J]

[End of Step 3 inner loop.]

[End of Step 2 middle loop.]

[End of Step 1 outer loop.]

Step 5: End.

Representing systems of equations in matrix form linear algebraic equations

The rules given above for matrix arithmetic allow a set of linear algebraic equations to be written compactly in matrix form. Consider a set of n independent linear equations in the variables xi for i = 1, 2. . . , n

$$\begin{array}{ccccccccc} a_{11}x_1 & + & a_{12}x_2 & + & \cdots & + & a_{1n}x_n & = & b_1 \\ a_{21}x_1 & + & a_{22}x_2 & + & \cdots & + & a_{2n}x_n & = & b_2 \\ \vdots & & \vdots & & \ddots & & \vdots & & \vdots \\ a_{n1}x_1 & + & a_{n2}x_2 & + & \cdots & + & a_{nn}x_n & = & b_n \end{array}$$

and write the coefficients aij in a square matrix **A** of dimension n

$$A = \begin{bmatrix} a_{11} & a_{12} & \cdots & a_{1n} \\ a_{21} & a_{22} & \cdots & a_{2n} \\ \vdots & \vdots & \ddots & \vdots \\ a_{n1} & a_{n2} & \cdots & a_{nn} \end{bmatrix}$$

the unknowns xij in a column vector **x** of length N

$$x = \begin{bmatrix} x_{11} \\ x_{21} \\ \vdots \\ x_{n1} \end{bmatrix}$$

and the constants on the right-hand side in a column vector

$$b = \begin{bmatrix} b_1 \\ b_2 \\ \vdots \\ b_n \end{bmatrix}$$

then equations may be written as the product

$$\begin{bmatrix} a_{11} & a_{12} & \cdots & a_{1n} \\ a_{21} & a_{22} & \cdots & a_{2n} \\ \vdots & \vdots & \ddots & \vdots \\ a_{n1} & a_{n2} & \cdots & a_{nn} \end{bmatrix} \begin{bmatrix} x_1 \\ x_2 \\ \vdots \\ x_n \end{bmatrix} = \begin{bmatrix} b_1 \\ b_2 \\ \vdots \\ b_n \end{bmatrix}$$

which may be written compactly as

$$\mathbf{Ax} = \mathbf{b}.$$

The transpose of a matrix

The transpose of an m×n matrix **A**, written $\mathbf{A}^T$, is the n×m matrix formed by interchanging the rows and columns of A. For example, if

$$A = \begin{bmatrix} a_{11} & a_{12} & a_{13} \\ a_{21} & a_{22} & a_{23} \end{bmatrix}$$

then in terms of the elements of the above matrix, the transpose is

$$A = \begin{bmatrix} a_{11} & a_{21} \\ a_{12} & a_{22} \\ a_{13} & a_{23} \end{bmatrix}$$

Notice that the transpose of a row vector produces a column vector, and similarly the transpose of a column vector produces a row vector. The transpose of the product of two matrices is the reversed product of the transpose of the two individual matrices,

$$(AB)^T = B^T A^T$$

The rules of matrix multiplication show that the product of a vector and its transpose is the sum of the squares of all of the elements

$$x(x^T) = \sum_{t=1}^{n} (x_i)^2$$

4.18 SPARSE MATRIX

A **sparse matrix also known as sparse array** in computing is an array where most of the elements have the same value (called the default value — usually 0 or null) and only a few elements have a non-default value. Arrays are data structures used in programming languages, databases, and other computer systems. They use a value, called a subscript or an index, that indicates a position to locate a particular value.

"It is special type of matrix in which majority of elements are zero or Null. It requires different type of representation than simple array"

A naive implementation may allocate space for the entire array, but this is inefficient since there are only a few non-default values. If the sparsity is known in advance, more space-efficient implementations can be used which allocate space only for the non-default values. Example: An array with length of one million, where only the indices 1, 3, 120 and 999999 have non-default values, is sparse. It would be inefficient to allocate any space for the 999996 array elements with default values. **Sparse array** is also called **Sparse Matrix**.

In the mathematical subfield of numerical analysis a **sparse matrix** is a matrix populated primarily with zeros. Conceptually, sparsity corresponds to systems which are loosely coupled. Consider a line of balls connected by springs from one to the next; this is a sparse system. By contrast, if the same line of balls had springs connecting every ball to every other ball, the system would be represented by a **dense matrix**. The concept of sparsity is useful in combinatorics and application areas such as network theory, of a low density of significant data or connections.

Huge sparse matrices often appear in science or engineering when solving partial differential equations. When storing and manipulating sparse matrices on a computer, it is beneficial and often necessary to used specialized algorithms and data structures that take advantage of the sparse structure of the matrix. Operations using standard matrix structures and algorithms are slow and consume large amounts of memory when applied to large sparse matrices. Sparse data is by nature easily compressed, and this compression almost always results in significantly less memory usage. Indeed, some very large sparse matrices are impossible to manipulate with the standard algorithms.

4.18.1 Difference Between Sparse Matrix and Dense Matrix

A sparse matrix is a two-dimensional array in which most of the elements are null. Figure 1(a) and (b) indicate sparse and dense matrices. The matrix, which is not a sparse matrix, is called dense matrix. One cannot exactly determine the boundary between sparse and dense matrix. The sparse matrices are very useful in various applications. In sparse matrices, memory is wasted because the NULL values stored and hence to overcome wastage of memory a mechanism must be followed.

3	0	32	0	11
1	5	4	9	23
0	3	0	2	0
7	14	13	17	8
1	0	1	0	1

Figure 4.25: Dense matrix

3	0	32	0	11
1	0	0	0	0
0	0	0	2	0
0	0	0	0	0
1	0	1	0	1

Figure 4.26: Sparse matrix

Sparse matrices are classified as shown below in the figure 4.27

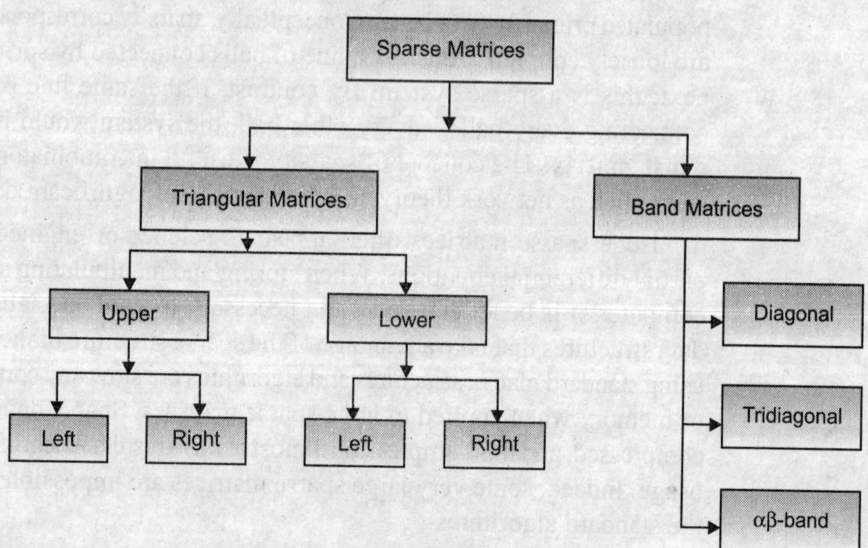

Figure 4.27: Different types of sparse matrices.

4.18.2 Upper Triangular Matrices

The upper matrix is a type of triangular matrix, which is also a type of sparse matrix. A sparse matrix is a matrix in which maximum of the elements are zero. The upper matrix is also of two types: Upper-left and Upper-right as shown in figure a and b.

0				
0	0			
0	0	0		
0	0	0	0	
0	0	0	0	0

(a) Upper right triangular

				0
			0	0
		0	0	0
	0	0	0	0
0	0	0	0	0

(b) Upper left triangular

Figure 4.28: Representation of upper triangular matrices.

4.18.3 Lower Triangular Matrices

The lower matrix is a type of triangular matrix, which is also a type of sparse matrix. A sparse matrix is a matrix in which maximum of the elements are zero. The lower matrix is also of two types: Lower -left and Lower -right as shown in figure a and b.

0	0	0	0	0
	0	0	0	0
		0	0	0
			0	0
				0

(a) Lower-left triangular

0	0	0	0	0
0	0	0	0	
0	0	0		
0	0			
0				

(b) Lower-right triangular

Figure 4.29: Representation of lower triangular matrices.

4.18.4 Diagonal Matrices

In diagonal matrices, only diagonal elements are non-zero and other values are NULL as shown in figures.

1	0	0	0	0
0	**2**	0	0	0
0	0	**3**	0	0
0	0	0	**4**	0
0	0	0	0	**5**

(a) Left to right

0	0	0	0	**5**
0	0	0	**4**	0
0	0	**3**	0	0
0	**2**	0	0	0
1	0	0	0	0

(b) Right to Left

Figure 4.30: Representation of diagonal matrices.

4.18.5 Tri-diagonal Matrices

These are two representations of the Tri-diagonal matrices.

1	**1**	0	0	0
1	**2**	**8**	0	0
0	4	**3**	**3**	0
0	0	**5**	**4**	**5**
0	0	0	**8**	**5**

(a) Left to Right

0	0	0	**2**	**5**
0	0	**4**	**4**	**1**
0	**7**	**3**	9	0
8	**2**	**7**	0	0
1	**4**	0	0	0

(b) Right to Left

Figure 4.31: Representation of Tri-diagonal matrices.

OBJECTIVE TYPE QUESTIONS

1. SPARSE Matrix is
   (a) Low proportion of zero (b) High proportion of zero
   (c) Both (d) None
2. Which of the following is the type of array?
   (a) Linear (b) Non-Linear
   (c) Both (d) None of the above
3. One Dimensional array is
   (a) Linear (b) Non-Linear
   (c) Both (d) None of the above
4. Linear search is
   (a) Fast Process (b) Slow Process
   (c) Both (d) None
5. Which of the following is the operation of array.
   (a) Sorting (b) Searching
   (c) Inserting (d) Deleting
   (e) All of the above (f) None of the above
6. Traversing is also called:
   (a) Sorting (b) Searching
   (c) Inserting (d) Deleting
   (e) Visiting (f) None of the above
7. An array is a .... type of data structure.
   (a) linear (b) non-linear
   (c) dynamic (d) (a) and (b)
8. Homogenous means ___________.
   (a) values of the same type (b) having all equal values
   (c) (a) and (b) (d) dissimilar values.
9. Array elements are stored in
   (a) successive memory locations (b) random memory locations
   (c) both (a) and (b) (d) none of the above
10. Accessing all elements of the array is known as
    (a) transverse (b) insertion
    (c) deletion (d) listing.

11. Merging of array elements means
    (a) combining two or more arrays
    (b) addition of elements of two arrays
    (c) interchanging elements of two arrays
    (d) none of the above.
12. Following one operation cannot be performed on arrays
    (a) merging (b) insertion
    (c) deletion (d) memory re-allocation.
13. Base address means
    (a) address of 0th element (b) address of array name
    (c) address of least element (d) none of the above.
14. Array elements are stored in
    (a) random memory locations (b) sequential memory locations
    (c) both of the above.
15. A character array always ends with
    (a) comma (,) (b) question mark (?)
    (c) null character (\0) (d) Full stop (.)
16. Arrays can not be initialized if they are
    (a) automatic (b) static
    (c) external (d) none of the above.
17. All the elements in the array must be
    (a) initialized (b) defined
    (c) none of the above.

EXERCISES

1. What do you mean by array? How we can declaration and initialization array.
2. How we can represent array in memory?
3. Explain different types of array in detail.
4. What are the various operations performed on linear array?
5. Write an algorithm for traversing a linear array.
6. Write an algorithm and C++ program for inserting element in linear array.
7. Write an algorithm and C++ program for deleting element from linear array

8. Write an algorithm for searching item from linear array.
9. Write an algorithm for sorting a linear array.
10. Write an algorithm and C++ program for merging two arrays.
11. Write an algorithm and C++ program for reversing the array.
12. Write an algorithm and C++ program for copying the elements of one array into another in reverse order.
13. What do you mean by multi dimensional array?
14. What is the various applications of arrays.
15. What is Pointer?
16. Explain concept of pointers and arrays.
17. What do you mean by Records?
18. What do you mean by Record structures?
19. Explain representation of records in memory using parallel arrays.
20. What do you mean by matrix? Write an algorithm for matrix multiplication.
21. What do you mean by sparse matrix?
22. Difference between sparse matrix and dense matrix.
23. What do you mean by diagonal matrices and tri-diagonal matrices?

5 CHAPTER

Linked Lists

5.1 INTRODUCTION

In computer science, a linked list is one of the fundamental INFO structures used in computer programming. It consists of a sequence of nodes, each containing arbitrary information fields and one or two references ("links") pointing to the next and/or previous nodes. The principle benefit of a linked list over a conventional list is that the order of the linked items may be different to the order that the INFO items are stored in memory or on disk, allowing the list of items to be traversed in a different order.

A linked list is a self-referential INFOtype because it contains a pointer or link to another INFO of the same type. Linked lists permit insertion and removal of nodes at any point in the list in constant time, but do not allow random access. Several different types of linked list exist: singly-linked lists, doubly-linked lists, and circularly-linked lists.

When dealing with many problems we need a dynamic list, dynamic in the sense that the size requirement need not be known at compile time. Thus, the list may grow or shrink during runtime. A linked list is a INFO structure that is used to model such a dynamic list of INFO items, so the study of the linked lists as one of the INFO structures is important.

Often in programming we are required to systematically store some type of information. A prime example of this is to use arrays but when you don't know the amount of information to be stored we need a dynamic INFO structure. One option for us is to use a linked list. A linked list works by creating a collection of objects (nodes) which both carry the INFO we want to store and a reference to the next node in the list.

So the first node in the list points to the next node and then the next points to the one after that until we reach the last node, which will point to null. This way all we really need to keep track of is the first node, as knowing it will enable us to access any node down the list (because they each point to each other, they are linked). And whenever you add a node it goes to the end of the list (as in the current last node begins to point to the new node and the new node, of course, to null [and it is the new last node now]). Linked lists allocate memory for an element when it's added. That's what makes them useful, because in practice though a lot of contexts may appear. Due to the allocation, you can't find every element one after another in memory.

That is why we must have a way to know where they are located: For the first allocated element that's easy, we put a pointer to it in the hash entry. For the second one we put a pointer in the first one to the second. For the third one we put a pointer in the second one and so on. In the last element the pointer to the next one equals 0. That's the way we know when we have reached the end of the linked list. In short words, an element in a linked list has the context information plus a pointer to the next element.

5.2 WHY WE USE LINKED LIST ?

Linked lists and arrays are similar since they both store collections of INFO. The terminology is that arrays and linked lists store "elements" on behalf of "client" code. The specific type of element is not important since essentially the same structure works to store elements of any type. One way to think about linked lists is to look at how arrays work and think about alternate approaches.

5.3 ARRAY REVIEW

Arrays are probably the most common INFO structure used to store collections of elements. An array is represented in memory using sequential mapping, which has the property that elements are fixed distance apart. But this has the following disadvantage: It makes insertion or deletion at any arbitrary position in an array a costly operation, because this involves the movement of some of the existing elements.

When we want to represent several lists by using arrays of varying size, either we have to represent each list using a separate array of maximum size or we have to represent each of the lists using one single array. The first one will lead to wastage of storage, and the second will involve a lot of INFO movement.

In most languages, arrays are convenient to declare and the provide the handy [ ] syntax to access any element by its index number. The following example shows some typical array code and a drawing of how the array might look in memory. The code allocates an array int scores[100], sets the first three elements set to contain the numbers 1, 2, 3 and leaves the rest of the array uninitialized...

```
void ArrayTest()
{
int scores[100];
// operate on the elements of the scores array...
scores[0] = 1;
scores[1] = 2;
scores[2] = 3;
}
```

Here is a drawing of how the scores array might look like in memory. The key point is that the entire array is allocated as one block of memory. Each element in the array gets its own space in the array. Any element can be accessed directly using the [ ] syntax.

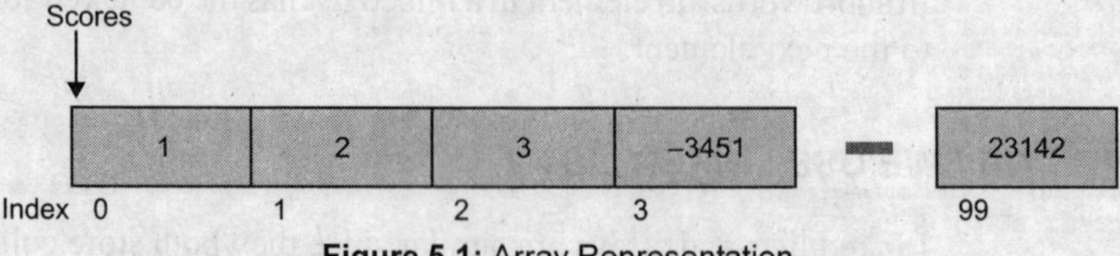

Figure 5.1: Array Representation

Once the array is set up, access to any element is convenient and fast with the [ ] operator. (Extra for experts) Array access with expressions such as scores[i] is almost always implemented using fast address arithmetic: the address of an element is computed as an offset from the start of the array which only requires one multiplication and one addition.

5.3.1 The Disadvantages of Arrays Are...

1. The size of the array is fixed — 100 elements in this case. Most often this size is specified at compile time with a simple declaration such as in the example above. With a little extra effort, the size of the array can be deferred until the array is created at runtime, but after that it remains fixed. (extra for experts) You can go to the trouble of dynamically allocating an array in the heap and then dynamically resizing it with realloc(), but that requires some real programmer effort.
2. Because of (1), the most convenient thing for programmers to do is to allocate arrays which seem "large enough" (e.g. the 100 in the scores example). Although convenient, this strategy has two disadvantages:
   (a) Most of the time there are just 20 or 30 elements in the array and 70% of the space in the array really is wasted.

(b) If the program ever needs to process more than 100 scores, the code breaks. A surprising amount of commercial code has this sort of naive array allocation which wastes space most of the time and crashes for special occasions (Extra for experts). For relatively large arrays (larger than 8k bytes), the virtual memory system may partially compensate for this problem, since the "wasted" elements are never touched.

3. (minor) Inserting new elements at the front is potentially expensive because existing elements need to be shifted over to make room. Linked lists have their own strengths and weaknesses, but they happen to be strong where arrays are weak. The array's features all follow from its strategy of allocating the memory for all its elements in one block of memory. Linked lists use an entirely different strategy.

As we will see, linked lists allocate memory for each element separately and only when necessary. So we have to use an alternative representation to overcome these disadvantages. One alternative is a linked representation. In a linked representation, it is not necessary that the elements be at a fixed distance apart. Instead, we can place elements anywhere in memory, but to make it a part of the same list, an element is required to be linked with a previous element of the list. This can be done by storing the address of the next element in the previous element itself. This requires that every element be capable of holding the INFO as well as the address of the next element. Thus every element must be a structure with a minimum of two fields, one for holding the INFO value, which we call a INFO field, and the other for holding the address of the next element, which we call link field.

Therefore, a linked list is a list of elements in which the elements of the list can be placed anywhere in memory, and these elements are linked with each other using an explicit link field, that is, by storing the address of the next element in the link field of the previous element.

5.4 LINKED LIST

A linked list is a *dynamic data structure*, which means that the memory to hold the INFO is created at run time (dynamic), and stored in a structured way (also called INFO structure). Also we can say Linked list is a linear INFO structure, i.e it is a linear collection of INFO elements called nodes, where the linear order is given by means of pointers. Each node consists of two fields, one containing the item and the other containing the address of the next item in the list. Each node contains two parts information part and link part. The last node of the linked list contains a special link part called Null Pointer (i.e. any invalid address).

***Defination:** "A linked list is an ordered collection of data elements called nodes in which linear order is given by means of pointers. Each node has 2 parts: information(INFO) and link. The information part holds the useful information of the element. The link part or nextpointer part is used identifies the next node in the list."*

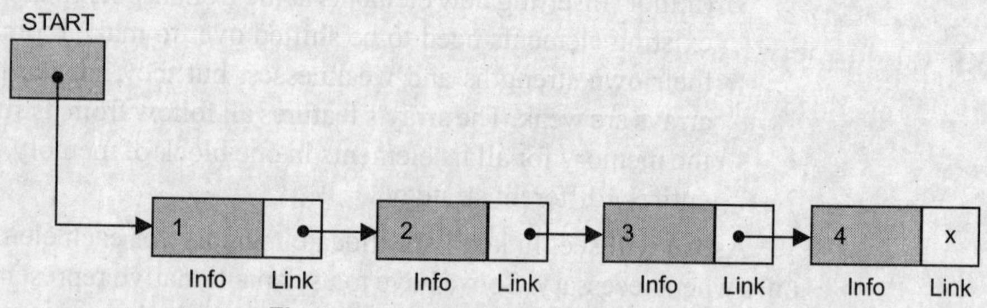

Figure 5.2: Linked list with four nodes.

A Linked List is generally an implementation structure. In other words, linked lists don't have an inherent ordering to them...making it difficult to insert/delete because no choice is made as to where things should be inserted or deleted. However, a linked list can be used to implement queues, stacks, and ordered linked lists (such as a sorted linked list). We may implement linked lists as an array, but it is much more common to implement them using a dynamic structure. The size of the list is only as big as the number of items in the list.

Example 5.1: A Linked list made up of a number of "date" records/structures.

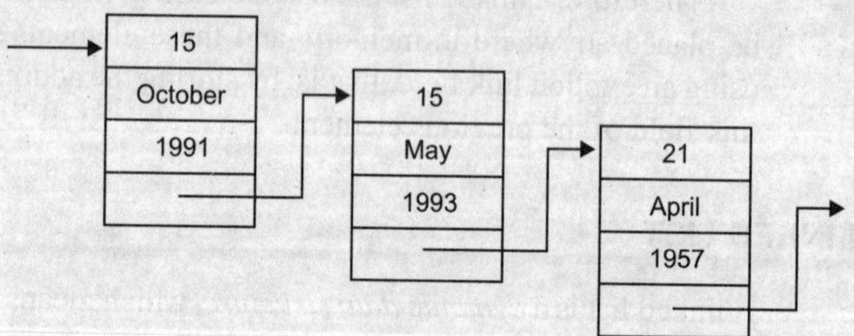

Figure 5.3: Linked list of "date" records.

5.4.1 Representation of Linked List

A linked list is a INFO structure which is built from structures and pointers. It forms a chain of "nodes" with pointers representing the links of the chain and holding the entire thing together. A linked list can be represented by a diagram like this one:

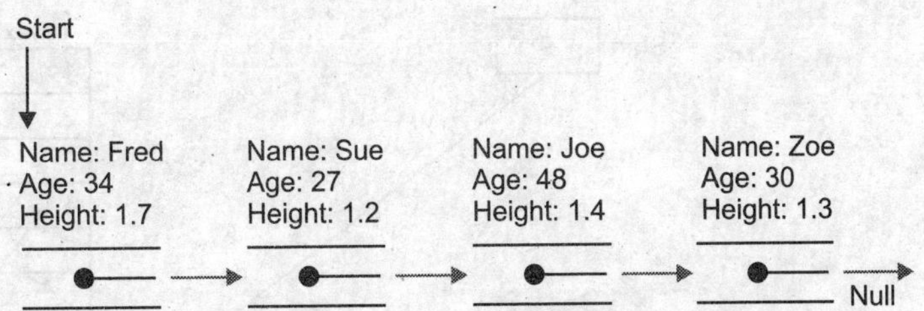

Figure 5.4: Linked list having student records.

This linked list has four nodes in it, each with a link to the next node in the series. The last node has a link to the special value NULL, which any pointer (whatever its type) can point to, to show that it is the last link in the chain. There is also another special pointer, called Start, which points to the first link in the chain so that we can keep track of it.

5.4.2 Array Implementation of Singly Linked List

The linked list requires two linear arrays. These are INFO and LINK.

INFO part contains the information

LINK Part contains the address of next node

Linked list also requires the pointer variable named START, which contains the address of the beginning of the list. We also need the NULL pointer, which is contained in the address part of the last node.

Let LIST be a linked list. Then LIST will be maintained in memory, unless otherwise specified or implied, as follows. First of all, LIST requires two linear arrays—we will call them here INFO and LINK—such that INFO[k] and LINK[k] contain, respectively, the information part and the next pointer field of a node of LIST. As noted above, LIST also requires a variable name—such as START — which contains the location of the beginning of the list, and a next pointer sentinel—denoted by NULL—which indicates the end of the list.

Since the subscripts of the arrays INFO and LINK will usually be positive, we will choose NULL = 0, unless otherwise stated.

The following example of linked lists indicates that the nodes of a list need not occupy adjacent elements in the arrays INFO and LINK, and that more than one list may be maintained in the same linear arrays INFO and LINK.

However, each list must have its own pointer variable giving the location of its first node.

Example 5.2: Figure 5.5 shows a linked list in memory where each node of the list contains a single character.

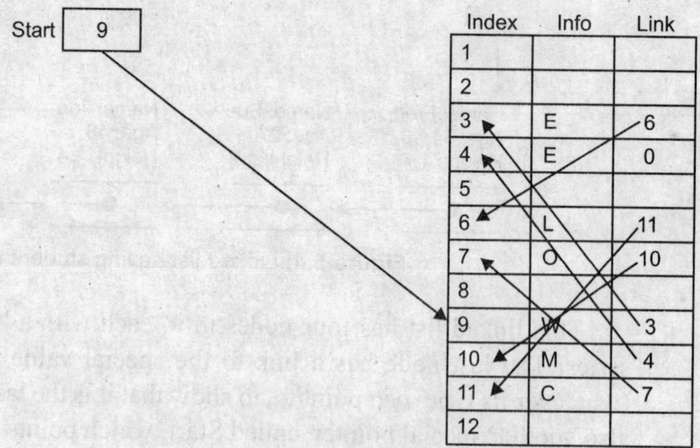

Figure 5.5: Memory representation of Linked List

We can obtain the actual list of character, or, in other words, the string, as follow:

START = 9, so INFO[9] = W is the first character.
LINK[9] = 3, so INFO[3] = E is the second character.
LINK[3] = 6, so INFO[6] = L is the third character.
LINK[6] = 11, so INFO[11] = C is the fourth character.
LINK[11] = 7, so INFO[7] = O is the fifth character.
LINK[7] = 10, so INFO[10] = M is the sixth character.
LINK[10] = 4, so INFO[4] = E is the seventh character.
LINK[4] = 0, the NULL value, so the list has ended.

In other words, WELCOME is the character string.

Example 5.3: Figure 5.6 pictures a linked list in memory where each node of the list contains a single character. We can obtain the actual list of characters, or, in other words, the string as follows:

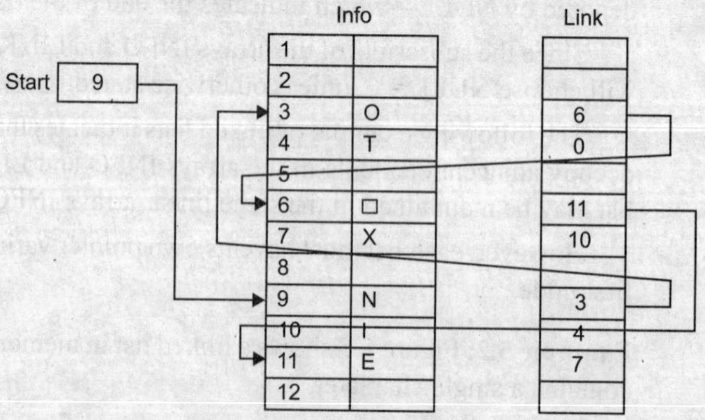

Figure 5.6: Memory representation of Linked List

START = 9, so INFO[9] = N is the first character.
LINK[9] = 3, so INFO[3] = O is the second character.
LINK[3] = 6, so INFO[6] = □ (blank) is the third character.
LINK[6] = 11, so INFO[11] = E is the fourth character.
LINK[11] = 7, so INFO[7] = X is the fifth character.
LINK[7] = 10, so INFO[10] = I is the sixth character.
LINK[10] = 4, so INFO[4] = T is the seventh character.
LINK[4] = 0, the NULL value, so the list has ended.

In other words, NO EXIT is the character string.

5.5 DYNAMIC DATA STRUCTURE: LINKED LISTS

The ADT known as a Linked List is the simplest example of a INFO structure providing the capability of 'dynamically adapting' to accommodate changes in the quantity of information stored. This structure also provides a basis for building more complex structures qualified by the precise regime in which applications wish to access individual records.

This is especially true when a very large collection (ca. 10^6+) of records is involved, and so in a typical modern INFObase setting, more sophisticated structures are needed. Linked lists and their basic variations do provide reasonable solutions in a number of systems' programming contexts, e.g. the management of processes in O/S environments; hardware modelling in simulation tools.

Definition: *A Linked List INFO structure,* ***L****, is recursively defined as:*

- L is the **empty** list, i.e. the list handle is the null reference.

  or
- L is of the form

  Head: L^*

where ***Head*** *contains a datum item and* L^* *is a list. The notation ':' indicates that part of the 'Head' cell is a handle indicating (pointing at/referencing) the linked list* L^**. The Figure below gives an informal depiction of linked list structure.*

In Figure 5.7, the box labelled 'List Handle' indicates the name of the list. This contains a reference (or pointer) to the start of the list. Each list cell comprises two parts: the first (labelled 'Datum' in the diagram) contains the information held in the list element: this could be anything from a simple value over a primitive type to an arbitrary Object (which could itself be a linked list, but we will defer consideration of more complex structures such as this until later). The second element of a list cell (labelled 'Link' in Figure 5.7) is a pointer to the remainder of the list. In the (currently) final list cell, this pointer is set to the null reference.

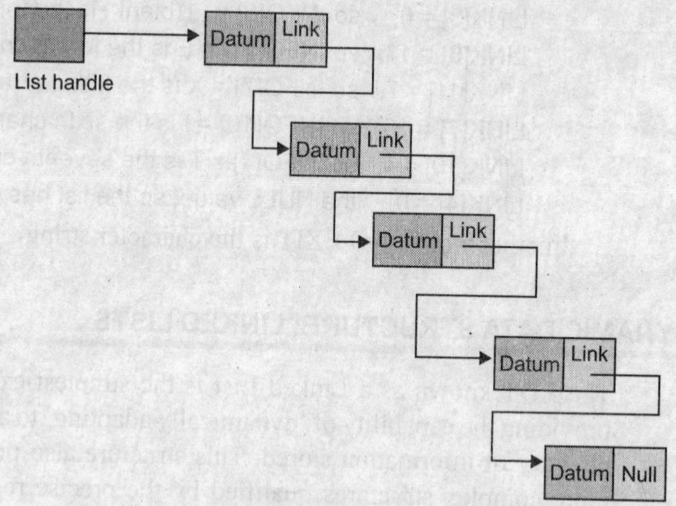

Figure 5.7: Linked List Structure

Most abstract INFO types are based on two "foundation INFO types". These are the array, and the linked list. Programming languages commonly provide the array as a part of the language, the linked list, though just as important is less likely to be provided in this way, it is however likely to be provided as a "library" item with a language.

Whereas an array provides a static collection of storage locations that may be accessed randomly using an index value, a linked list provides a dynamically allocated sequence of storage locations, each of which points to the next.

A good way to think of a linked list is as a chain, or string of beads. Each link not only contains the INFO, but also a pointer to the next link (Figure 5.8). As each INFO element is added, a link is created pointing from it to the next item in the list.

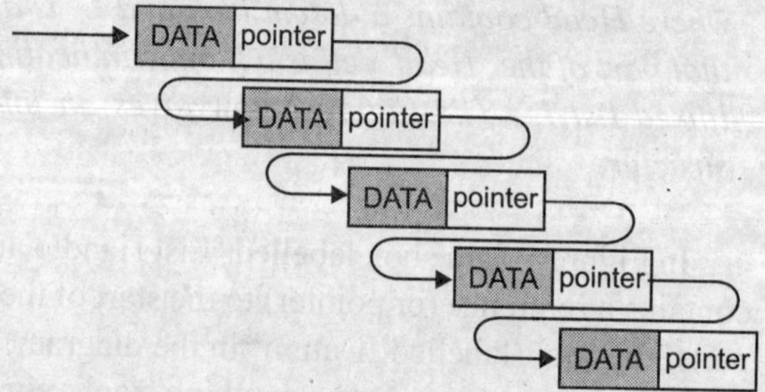

Figure 5.8: Structure of a linked list

Figure 5.8 shows a Singularly Linked List. This is the simplest of the linked INFO structures. At its most basic it is simply a sequence of dynamically allocated objects, each of which points to its successor in the list. There are however complications that lead to several implementations (Figure 5.9):

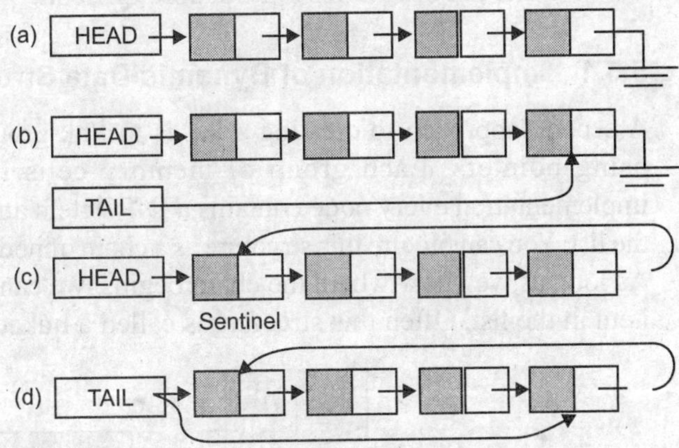

Figure 5.9: Singularly linked list varities

(a) Shows the simplest linked list. Each element refers to its successor; the last item in the list holds a null reference (doesn't point to anything). A single variable is used to point to the head of the list. The head pointer provides a mechanism for accessing the list from a programme. This pattern of list is easy to use for inserting and removing items from the head, but is inefficient when things are to be added to both ends of the list or in the middle. The tail of the list may only be found by traversing the whole list, making insertion and removal here quite a chore.

(b) Shows a list with two pointers, one each for the head and the tail. This alleviates the problem of finding the tail of a singularly linked list, but the increase in efficiency comes at the cost of the extra storage required for the tail pointer variable. Obviously this is a small overhead so is probably not a problem. It is still difficult however to remove items from the tail, or to access and add or remove items in the midst of the list.

(c) Shows two programming tricks that may be applied to singly linked lists. Firstly, c) is a circular list; the last element doesn't point to a null reference, but back to the head of the list. A circular list has identical operations for insertion at any point, be it the head, tail or at any arbitrary position within the list. The sentinel is used as it means that the head variable need never be changed. The sentinel is not used to hold any INFO, just point to (guard) the head of the list. The sentinel must be created when the list is initialised. The sentinel places extra storage requirements on the list. Insertion and removal of items of the list are still complex operations.

(d) The final implementation, shown is a circular list that does not use a sentinel [d)]. A single pointer variable is used to point at the tail of the list. As the head of the list follows the tail in a circular list, insertion at both the head and tail are easy. Unfortunately this type of implementation does makes some list operations a little more difficult.

5.5.1 Implementation of Dynamic Data Structure Using Pointer

A second approach to creating a list is to link groups of memory cells together using pointers. Each group of memory cells is called a node. With this implementation every node contains a INFO item and a pointer to the next item in the list. You can picture this structure as a chain of nodes linked together by pointers. As long as we know where the chain begins, we can follow the links to reach any item in the list. Often this structure is called a linked list.

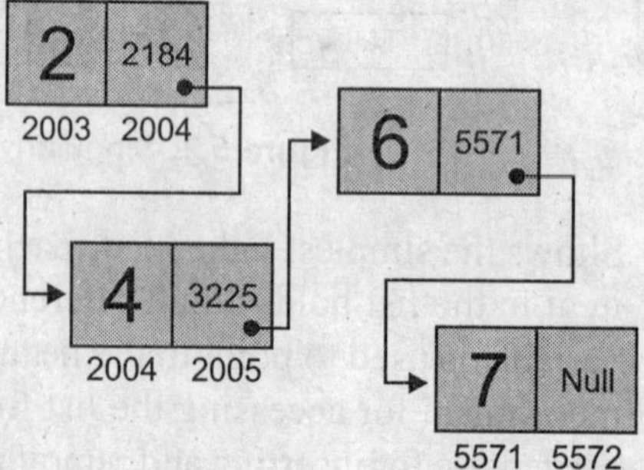

Figure 5.10: Dynamic Data Structure Using Pointer

Notice that the last memory cell in our chain contains a symbol called "Null". This symbol is a special value that tells us we have reached the end of our list. You can think of this symbol as a pointer that points to nothing.

5.5.2 Dynamic Implementation of Singly Linked List

A singly linked list is a sequence of INFO elements (of the same type) arranged one after another conceptually. Each element is stored in a node. Each node also contains a link that connects this node to the next node in the list. Here's a conceptual picture of a linked list containing N items, pointed to by a variable named L as shown in the Figure 5.11:

Here's a conceptual picture of a linked list containing N items, pointed to by a variable named L:

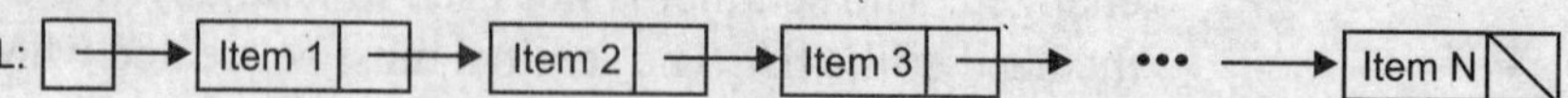

Figure 5.11: Dynamic implementation of single linked list.

Note that a linked list consists of one or more *nodes*. Each node contains some INFO (in this example, *item 1, item 2*, etc) and a pointer. For each node other than the last one, the pointer points to the next node in the list. For the last node, the pointer is null (indicated in the example using a diagonal line). The complete linked list structure as shown in the Figure 5.12 below shows this a lot better than the above-described explanation:

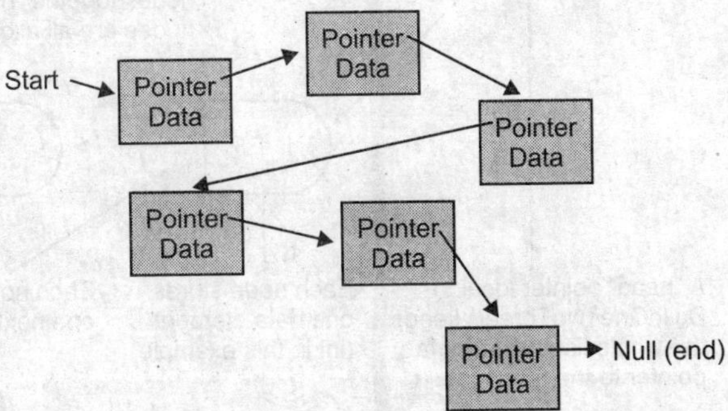

Figure 5.12: Structure of single linked list

In the diagram, each node is shown in the rectangles and contains a pointer to the next node in the list (shown by the arrows), and a INFO portion which holds the information for the node. The nodes are deliberately drawn in the diagram in a haphazard way to show that each node can exist in any portion of memory, not necessarily adjacent to or even close to the neighboring nodes in the list. The start of the list is also shown, which is just a pointer to the first node. From this start pointer any node can be referenced, for all but the first node though, other nodes will have to be "passed through" to get there. The end of the list is indicated by the final node pointing to NULL. Normally, when a linked list is initialized, the start pointer will hold NULL to indicate that the list is empty, but as soon as a node is added to the list, this changes.

5.5.3 Memory Allocation of Linked Lists Look Like

An array allocates memory for all its elements lumped together as one block of memory. In contrast, a linked list allocates space for each element separately in its own block of memory called a "linked list element" or "node". The list gets is overall structure by using pointers to connect all its nodes together like the links in a chain.

Each node contains two fields: a "INFO" field to store whatever element type the list holds for its client, and a "next" field which is a pointer used to link one node to the next node. Each node is allocated in the heap with a call to malloc(), so the node memory continues to exist until it is explicitly deallocated with a call to free(). The front of the list is a pointer to the first node. Here is what a list containing the numbers 1, 2, and 3 might look like...

The Drawing of List {1, 2, 3}

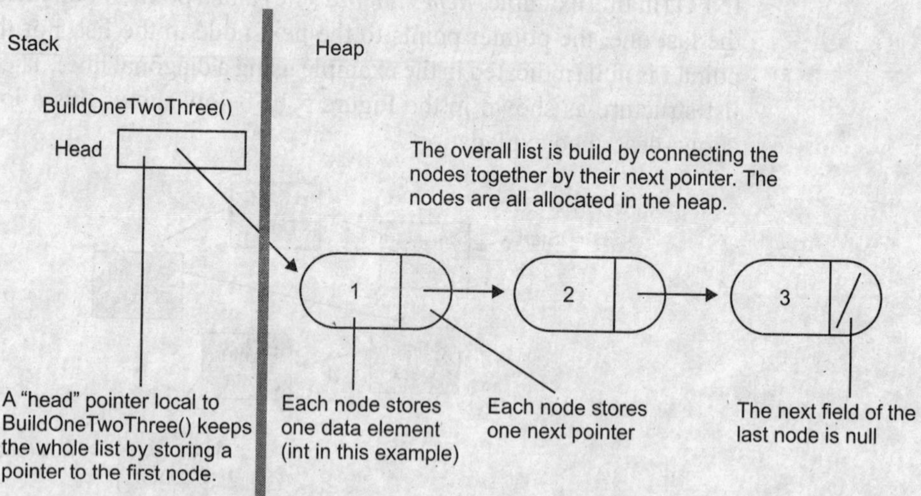

Figure 5.13: Memory Allocation of single Linked List.

The beginning of the linked list is stored in a "head" pointer which points to the first node. The first node contains a pointer to the second node. The second node contains a pointer to the third node, ... and so on. The last node in the list has its .next field set to NULL to mark the end of the list.

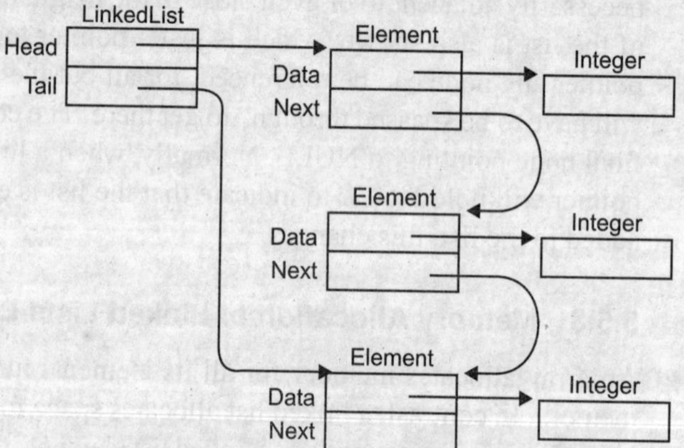

Figure 5.14: How a linked list resides in memory

Important Points:

- *Linked lists are used when the quantity of INFO is not known prior to execution.*
- *In linked lists, INFO is stored in the form of nodes and at runtime, memory is allocated for creating nodes.*

- *Due to overhead in memory allocation and deallocation, the speed of the program is lower.*
- *The INFO is accessed using the starting pointer of the list.*

5.5.4 Organization of Linked List

A linked list is a INFO structure used to maintain a dynamic series of INFO. Think of a linked list as a line of elephants in a circus where each elephant is holding on to the tail of the next elephant. If you know where the first elephant is, you can follow it's trunk to the next one. By following trunks, you can find any elephant in the chain. When you get to an elephant that isn't holding on to another elephant's tail, you know you are at the end.

Linked lists work in the same way, except programmers usually refer to nodes instead of elephants. A single node is defined the same way as any other user defined type or object, except that it also contains a pointer to a variable of the same type as itself.

C++ example node definition

```
typedef struct lnode
{
int INFO;
struct lnode *next;
}
listnode_t;
```

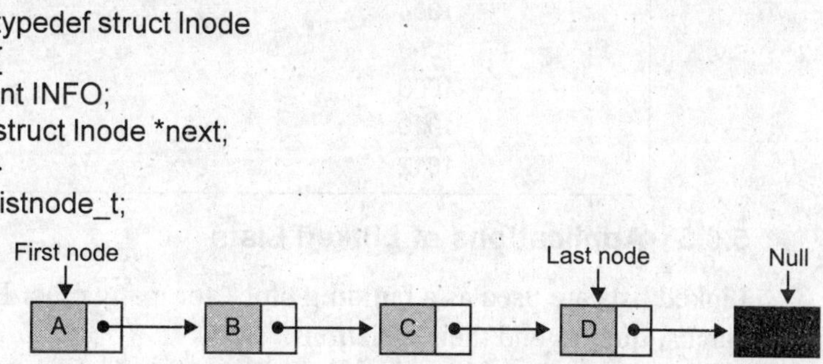

Figure 5.15: Linked list represents first node, last node and null pointer.

Note that a linked list consists of one or more *nodes*. Each node contains some INFO (in this example, *item 1, item 2*, etc) and a pointer. For each node other than the last one, the pointer points to the next node in the list. For the last node, the pointer is null (indicated in the example using a diagonal line).

How INFO can be assigned and link by using pointers can be created is organized in the Figure 5.16 as below:

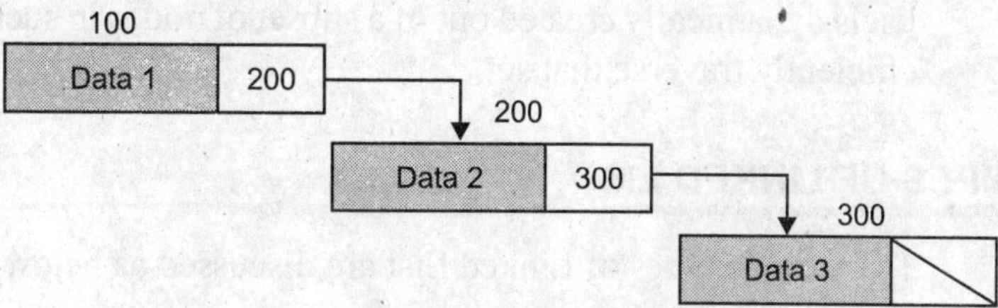

Figure 5.16: Linked list represents pointer addressess

Conceptual Picture: Representation of node conceptually having INFO and link part with a head value be as shown in the Figure 5.17 below:

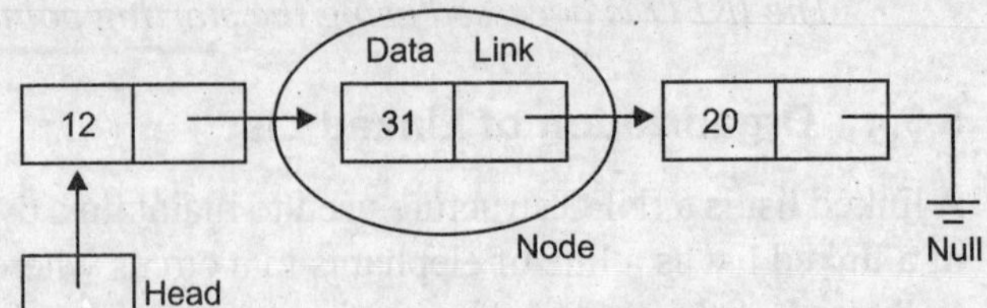

Figure 5.17: Head points to the first node.

Also the word addressing of every node shown in the Table 5.1 be shown in the table as:

Table 5.1: Defining a Node with word address and contents

Word Address	Contents
1000	31
1002	1008
1004	12
1006	1000
1008	20
1010	0
1012	1004

5.5.5 Applications of Linked Lists

Linked lists are used as a building block for many other INFO structures, such as **stacks, queues** and their variations.

The "INFO" field of a node can be another linked list. By this device, one can emulate arbitrary linked INFO structures with lists — a principle which is fundamental to the **Lisp programming language**, where linked lists are the primary (if not the only) INFO structuring mechanism.

Sometimes, linked lists are used to implement **associative arrays,** and are in this context called **association lists.** There is very little good to be said about this use of linked lists; they are easily outperformed by other INFO structures such as **self-balancing binary search trees** even on small INFO sets, sometimes a linked list is dynamically created out of a subset of nodes in such a tree, and used to more efficiently traverse that set.

5.6 TYPES OF LINKED LIST

The various types of Linked List are discussed as below:

1. Singular Linked List

2. Two Way Linked List or Doubly Linked List
3. Circular Linked List
4. Sorted Linked List
5. Endogenous/Exogenous Lists

5.7 SINGULAR LINKED LIST

Unless otherwise stated a particular type of linked list, the word "linked list" implies Singular linked list. A singly linked list is a sequence of INFO elements (of the same type) arranged one after another conceptually. Each element is stored in a node. Each node also contains a link that connects this node to the next node in the list.A singly linked list could be used to implement both stacks and queues, neither of which requires the ability to move backward through the list. A singly linked list could also be used for a sorted linked list.

5.7.1 Operations on A Linked List

Various Operations can be performed on this INFO structure, but we will be performing following list of operations stated below:

1. Traversing
2. Counting the items
3. Insertion
4. Deletion
5. Concatenating two lists
6. Searching
7. Reversing the direction of list
8. Copying linked list
9. Merging two lists
10. Erasing linked list
11. Spiliting linked list

5.7.1.1 Traversing A Linked List

Suppose we want to traverse a list in order to process each node exactly once. Suppose the list is sorted in memory as a linked list, our aim is to traverse the list starting from the first node to the end of the list.

In traversing algorithm we are using a pointer variable P which points to the node that is currently being processed. Therefore, LINK[P] points to the next node to be processed.

P = LINK[P]

This statement moves the pointer to the next node in the list, shown in Figure 5.18:

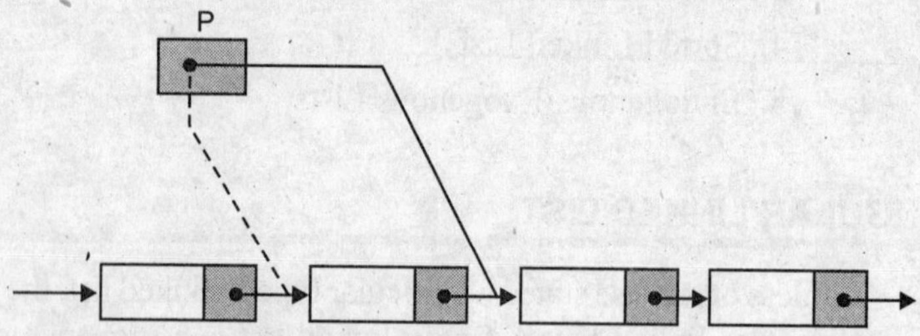

Figure 5.18: Pointer P performs traversing P = LINK[P].

First step, initialize P to START. Then process INFO [P], the information of the first node.Now, update PTR by assigning value to P = LINK [P], so that P points to next node. Then process INFO [P], the information of the next node.Again, update PTR by assigning value to P = LINK [P], and process INFO[P]. And so on. Continue until P ≠ NULL(tells the end of the list).

Algorithm 5.1: Traversing a Linked List

TRAVERSE (INFO, LINK, START, P)

Let LIST be a Linked list in memory. This algorithm traverses LIST, applying an operation PROCESS to each element of LIST. The variable P points to the node currently being processed.

Step 1: Set P = START. [Initializes pointer P.]

Step 2: Repeat Steps 3 and 4 while P ≠ NULL.

Step 3. Apply PROCESS to INFO [P].

Step 4: Set P = LINK [P]. [P now points to the next node.]

[End of Step 2 loop.]

Step 5: End.

This algorithm traverses the linked list applying an operation process to each element of the list.

This algorithm uses a pointer variable name P, which points to the node currently being processed. The step 4 P = Link [P], P now points to the next node.

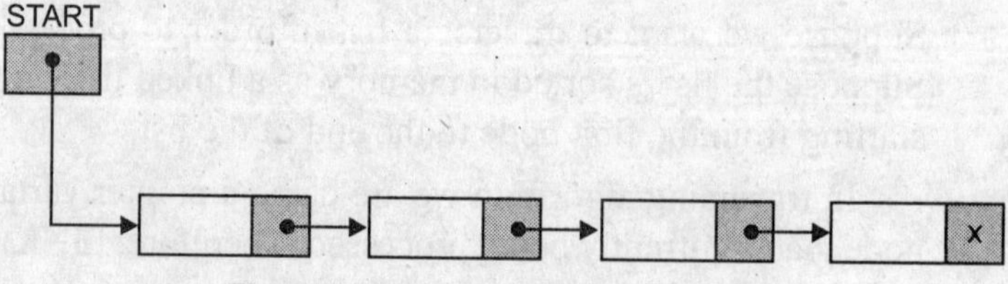

Figure 5.19 : Traversing a linked list

Program 1: Write a C++ program to create and display a linked list

```
#include <iostream.h>
# include <conio.h>
struct node
{
int info; // info field
node* link; //pointer to the link node
};
class link_list
{
private:
node* start;
public:
link_list ( ) //constructor
{
start=NULL; //initially the list has no node
}
void add_info (int i)
{
node* new_link= new node; //create a new node;
new_link->info=i;
new_link->=start; //make new node to point to the first node
start=new_link; // make new node as the first node in the list
}
void display ( ); //function prototype
}; //end of class
void link_list : : display ( )
{
node* move=start;
node* temp;
while (move)
{
cout<<move->info<<"->"; //display the info
temp= move;
move=move->link; //move to link node
delete temp; //delete the displayed node.
}
cout<<"NULL\n;
}
```

```
void main ( )
{
clrscr( );
link_list link;
for (int i=5; i<=10; i++)
link.add_info (i);
link.display( );
getch ( );
}
```

Output:

10->9->8->7->6->5->NULL

5.7.1.2 Counting the Number of Nodes of A Linked List

Counting is the next step after traversing the linked or during the traversing procedure. Counting means to find and display the number of node in a linked list till the Null part reaches.

Counting the number of nodes of a singly linked list requires maintaining a counter that is initialized to 0 and incremented by 1 each time a node is encountered in the process of traversing a list from the start.

Algorithm 5.2: Count the number num of nodes in a linked list.

COUNT (DATA, LINK, START, NUM)

Step 1: Set NUM = 0. [Initializes number NUM.]

Step 2: Set P = START. [Initializes pointer P.]

Step 3: Repeat Steps 4 and 5 while P ≠ NULL.

Step 4: Set NUM = NUM + 1. [Increment NUM by 1.]

Step 5: Set P = LINK [P]. [Updates pointer.]

[End of Step 3 loop.]

Step 6: End.

Figure 5.20: Count total number of nodes of linked list

5.7.1.3 Inserting Into A Linked List

Before inserting or deleting element it is necessary to understand the concept of AVAIL list and Overflow and underflow as discussed below:

Avail List

In the preceeding sections, linked lists are implemented by using parallel arrays (shown in Figure 5.21) and suppose insertions and deletions are performed on the linked list. Then the unused memory cells in the arrays will also be linked together to form a linked list using AVAIL as its pointer variable.

"A special list is maintained which consists of unused memory cells.This list, which has its own pointer, is called the list of free- storage or free-pool or Available free space list(AVAIL list)."

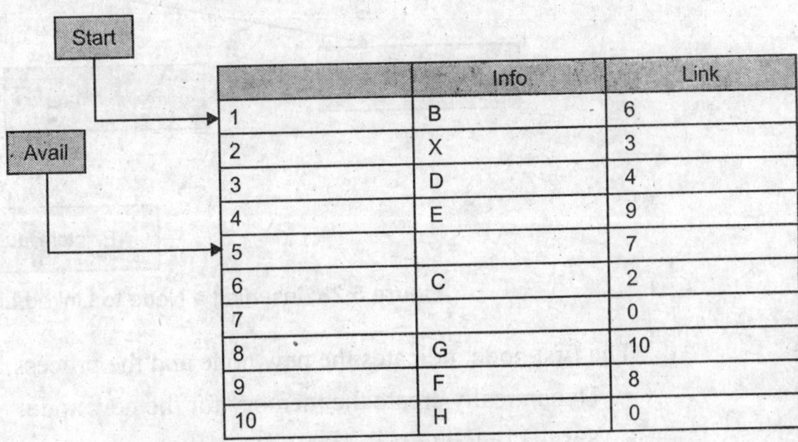

Figure 5.21: Linked list using AVAIL as its pointer variable.

Here location LOC=5 is unused space called free space which is pointed by pointer variable AVAIL.Next free space is ponted by LINK[5] is 7.

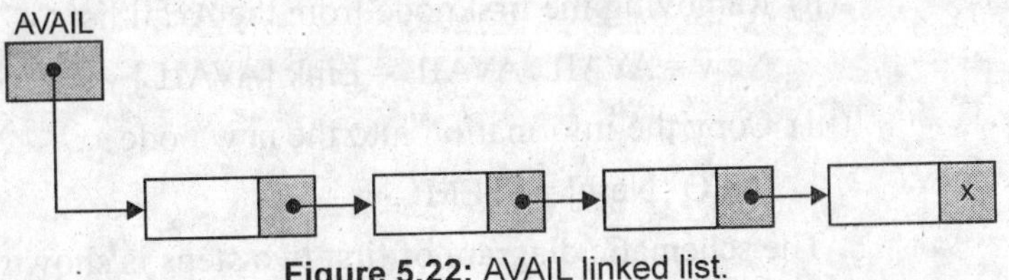

Figure 5.22: AVAIL linked list.

Overflow and Underflow

Overflow occurs when we want to insert a new INFO item, but there is no free space i.e. AVAIL=NULL.

Underflow occurs when we want to delete some node from the linked list, but the list is already empty i.e. START = NULL.

Inserting A Node to A Linked List

Inserting a node isn't to difficult, but can be depending on how you implement the list. With a simple single linked list, and not needing to worry about the position in the list the new node is added, it is a really easy task to add a node. This is done to the start of the list, as shown in the Figure 5.23 below:

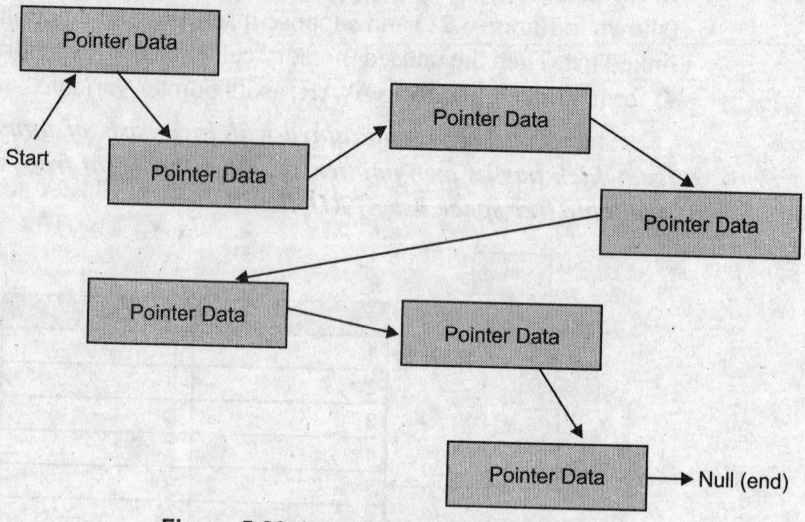

Figure 5.23: Inserting a Node to Linked List.

The first node indicates the new node and the process involves:

- Dynamically create the memory for the new node.
- Set the link pointer of the new node to equal the **start** pointer.

Set the start pointer to point to the new node. All the Insertion algorithms will include the following steps:

(i) Check for an overflow, if there is an overflow then exit

(ii) Removing the first node from the Avail list

New = AVAIL, AVAIL = Link [AVAIL]

(iii) Copy the information into the new node

INFO [New] = ITEM

The schematic diagram of first two steps is shown here:

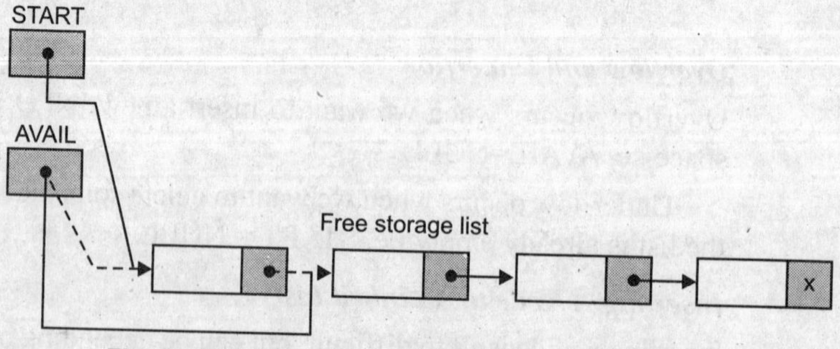

Figure 5.24: New = AVAIL and AVAIL = Link [AVAIL].

A. *Insertion at the Beginning of the Linked List*

Suppose our linked list is not sorted and then we have no reason that where we have to insert the new node.Then the easy way is to insert new node at the beginning of the list (shown in Figure 5.25).

Algorithm 5.3: To insert new node at the beginning of a list.

INSBEGNOD (INFO, LINK, START, AVAIL, ITEM)

This algorithm inserts ITEM as the first node in the list.

Step 1: [OVERFLOW?] If AVAIL = NULL, then: Write: OVERFLOW, and End.

Step 2: [Remove first node from AVAIL list.]
  Set NEW = AVAIL and AVAIL = LINK [AVAIL].

Step 3: Set INFO [NEW] = ITEM. [Copies new INFO into new node.]

Step 4: Set LINK [NEW] = START. [New node now points to original first node.]

Step 5: Set START = NEW. [Changes START so it points to the new node.]

Step 6: End.

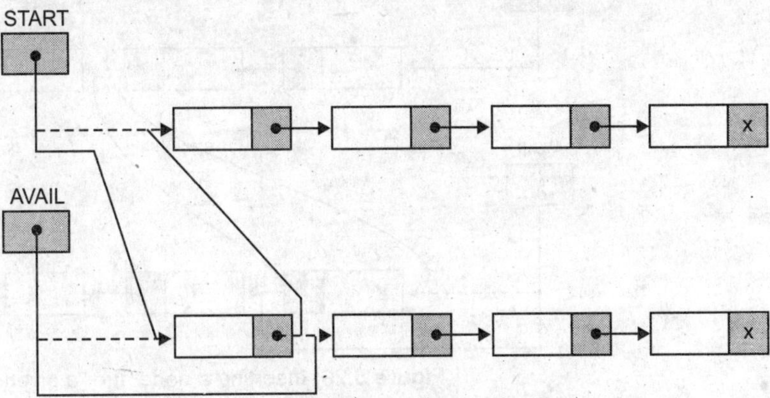

Figure 5.25: Insertion at the beginning of the Linked List.

B. *Inserting A Node After A Given Node*

The following algorithm which inserts ITEM into linked list so that ITEM follows Node N or, when LOC = NULL, so that ITEM is the first node.

Let the new node having location NEW. If LOC = NULL, then N is inserted as the first node described in previous algorithm. Otherwise, We insert the node after the given location by assigning

LINK [NEW] = LINK [LOC] and LINK [LOC] = NEW.

Algorithm 5.4: To insert new node after a given node into a linked list.

INSGVNNOD (INFO, LINK, START, AVAIL, LOC, ITEM)

This algorithm inserts ITEM so that ITEM follows the node with location LOC or insert ITEM at the first node when LOC = NULL.

Step 1: [OVERFLOW?] If AVAIL = NULL, then: Write: OVERFLOW, and End.

Step 2: [Remove first node from AVAIL list.]
  Set NEW = AVAIL and AVAIL = LINK [AVAIL].

Step 3: Set INFO [NEW] = ITEM. [Copies new INFO into new node.]

Step 4: If LOC = NULL, then [Insert as first node.]
    Set LINK [NEW] = START and START = NEW.
  Else: [Insert after node with location LOC.]
    Set LINK [NEW] = LINK [LOC] and LINK [LOC] = NEW.
  [End of if statement.]

Step 5: End.

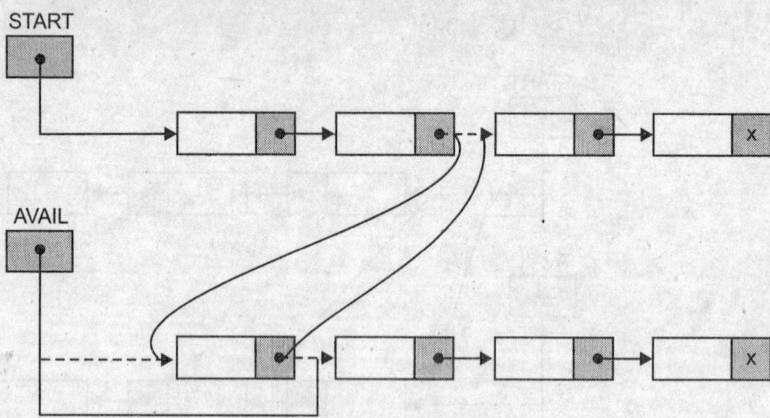

Figure 5.26: Inserting a node after a given node.

C. Insertion At The Last of the Linked List

Suppose the ITEM is to be inserted after the last node. First we have to reached at the last location and SAVE the last location then insert a new node at that point.

Algorithm 5.5: To find the location LOC of the last node in a sorted list.

FINDLOC (INFO, LINK, START, ITEM, LOC)

This algorithm finds the location LOC of the last node in a sorted list such that INFO [LOC] <ITEM, or sets LOC = NULL.

Step 1: [List empty?] If START = NULL, then: Set LOC = NULL, and Return.

Step 2: [Special case?] If ITEM < INFO [START], then: Set LOC = NULL, and Return.

Step 3: Set SAVE = START and P = LINK [START]. [Initializes pointers.]

Step 4: Repeat Steps 5 and 6 while P ≠ NULL.

Step 5: If ITEM < INFO [P], then

Set LOC = SAVE, and Return.

[End of If statement.]

Step 6: Set SAVE = P and P = LINK [P]. [Updates pointers.]

[End of Step 4 loop.]

Step 7: Set LOC = SAVE

Step 8: [Use Algorithm 5.4 to insert item after the last node with location LOC.]

Call INSGVNNOD (INFO, LINK, START, AVAIL, LOC, ITEM).

Step 9: End.

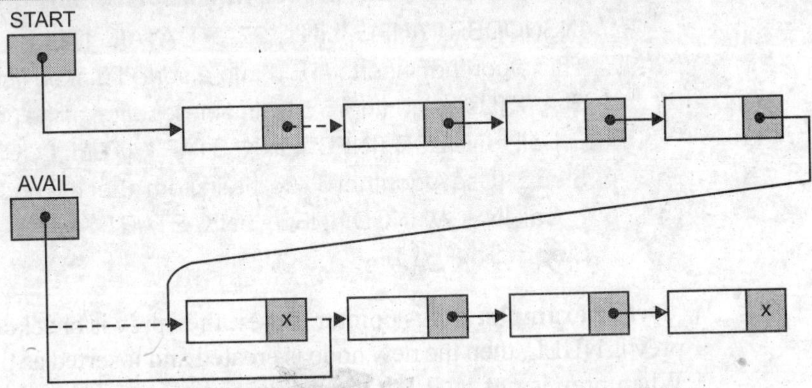

Figure 5.27: Insertion at the last Of The Linked List.

D. Inserting A New Node in A Sorted List

To insert a new node into an already sorted list, we compare the INFO value of the node to be inserted with the INFO values of the nodes in the list starting from the first node. This is continued until we get a pointer to the node that appears immediately before the node in the list whose INFO value is greater than the INFO value of the node to be inserted.

Suppose ITEM is to be inserted in a sorted linked list. Then ITEM must be inserted Between nodes X and Y.

$$INFO[X] < ITEM <= INFO[Y]$$

The given procedure first find the location LOC of node X , then insert the ITEM in between the node X and Y.

Traversing the list, using a pointer variable P and comparing ITEM with INFO [P] at each node. While traversing, keep track of the location of the proceeding node by using a pointer variable SAVE , as shown in Figure 5.28. Thus SAVE and P are updated by assigning values:

SAVE = P and P = LINK [P].

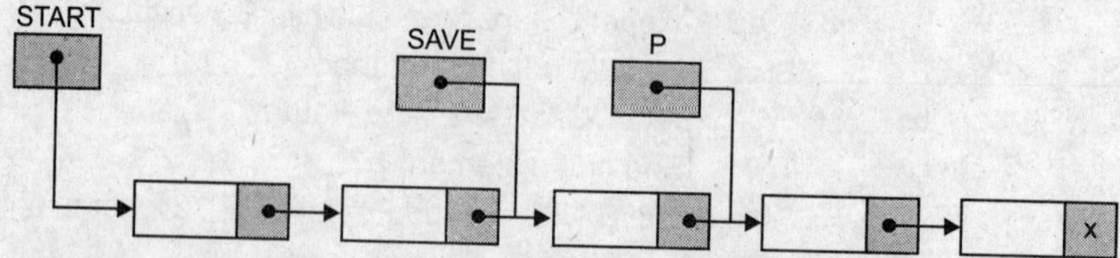

Figure 5.28: Save the proceeding node address and then P point towards next node.

The traversing continues as long as ITEM > INFO [P], or the traversing stopsITEM <= INFO [P]. Then P points to given node Y, so SAVE will contain the previous location X.

Algorithm 5.6: To insert new node into a sorted linked list.

INSNODSRT (INFO, LINK, START, AVAIL, ITEM)

This algorithm inserts ITEM into a sorted Linked list.

Step 1: [Use Algorithm 5.5 to find the location of the node preceding ITEM.]
  Call FINDLOC (INFO, LINK, START, ITEM, LOC).

Step 2: [Use Algorithm 5.4 to insert item after the node with location LOC.]
  Call INSGVNNOD (INFO, LINK, START, AVAIL, LOC, ITEM).

Step 3: End.

For example: If this pointer is prev, then prev is checked for a NULL value. If prev is NULL, then the new node is created and inserted as the first node in the list. When prev is not NULL, then a new node is created and inserted after the node pointed by prev, as shown in Figure 5.29.

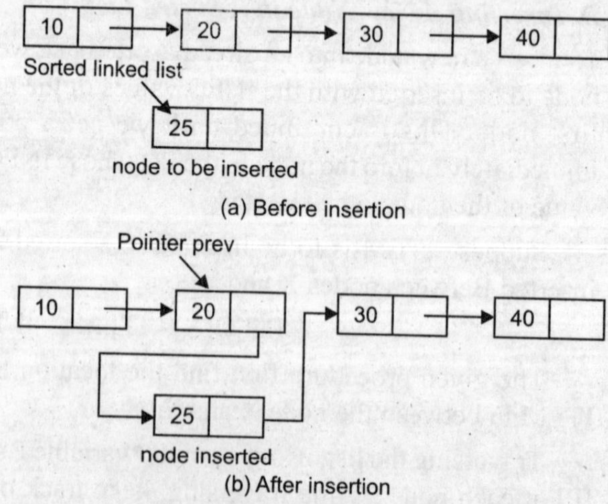

Figure 5.29: Insertion in a sorted list

Program 2: Write a C++ program to insert a node at the beginning or at the end of a linked list

```
#include <iostream.h>
# include <conio.h>
struct node
{
int info;                   // info field
node* link;                 //pointer to the link node
};
class link_list
{
private:
node* start;
public:
link_list ( )               //constructor
{
start=NULL;                 //initially the list has no node
}
void create (int i)
{
node* new_node= new node; //create a new node;
new_node->info=i;
new_node->=start;    //make new node to point to the first node
start=new_node;      // make new node as the first node in the list
}
void display (int);        //function prototype
void beginning (int info)
{
node* new_node = new node;     //create a new node;
new_node->link=start;          //make new node to point to the first node
start=new_node;
}
void end (int);                //function prototype
}; //end of class
//function definition display ( )
void link_list :: display (int delete_node)
{
node* move= start;
node* temp;
```

```
while (move)
{
cout<<move->info<<"->"; //display the info
temp=move;
move=move->link;                //move to link node
if (delete_node)
delete(temp);
}
cout<<"NULL";
}
//function definition end ( )
void link_list :: end (int info)
{
node* temp=start;
while (temp->link !=NULL)
temp=temp->link;
node* new_node= new node;                // create a new node
new_node->info=info;
temp->link=new_node;
new_node->link=NULL;
}
void main ( )
{
int info, choice;
clrscr ( );
link_list link;
for (int i=5; i<=10; i++)
link.create (i);
cout<<"\n\nThe list before any operation is performed :\n\n";
link.display (0);
cout<<"\n\nRead the info field value of the node to be inserted: "'
cin>>info;
cout<<"\n\nRead the option (1, 2): ";
cout<<\n1. At the beginning";
cout<<"\n2. At the end\n";
cin>>choice;
switch (choice)
{
case 1: link.beginning (info);
```

```
break;
case 2: link.end (info);
break;
default: cout<<"Invalid choice readed\n";
}
cout<<"\n\nThe list after insertion is: \n\n;
link.display(1);
getch ( ); //freeze the screen
}
```

Output:

```
The list before any operation is performed:
10->9->8->7->6->5->NULL
Read the info field value of the node to be inserted: 12
Read the option (1, 2):
1. At the beginning
2. At the end
1
The list after insertion is:
12->10->9->8->7->6->5->NULL

The list before any operation is performed
10->9->8->7->6->5->NULL

Read the info field value of the node to be inserted: 4
Read the option (1,2):
1. At the beginning
2. At the end
2
The list after insertion is:
10->9->8->7->6->5->4->NULL
```

Program 3: Write a C++ program to insert a node at the desired position in a linked list

```
#include <iostream.h>
# include <conio.h>
# include<process.h>
struct node
{
int info;                   // info field
node* link;                 //pointer to the link node
```

```
};
class link_list
{
private:
node* start;
public:
link_list ( )               //constructor
{
start=NULL;                 //initially the list has no node
}
void create (int i)
{
node* new_node= new node; //create a new node;
new_node->info=i;
new_node->link=start;          //make new node to point to the first node
start=new_node;                // make net node as the first node in the list
}
void display (int);            //function prototype
void insert(int, int);         //function prototype
}; //end of class
//function definition display ( )
void link_list :: display (int delete_node)
{
node* move= start;
node* temp;
while (move)
{
cout<<move->info<<"->"; //display the info
temp=move;
move=move->link; //move to link node
if (delete_node)
delete(temp);
}
cout<<"NULL";
}
//function definition insert ( )
void link_list :: insert (int position, int info)
{
node* move=start;
```

```
int steps=1;
while (steps<position-1)
{
move=move->link;
steps++;
}
node* new_node= new node;                    // create a new node;
new_node->info=info;
if (position= =1) //if node is to be inserted at the first place
{
new_node->link=start;
start=new_node;
}
else
{
new_node->link=move->link;
}
}
void main ( )
{
int value, info, choice, position, total=0;
clrscr( );
link_list link;
cout<<"Read the elements of the list terminated by negative number: \n";
cin>>value;
do
{
link.create(value);
total++; //increment with every node inserted
cin>>value;
}
while (value>=0);
cout<<"\n\nThe list before nay operation is performed (LIFO): \n\n;
link.display (0);
cout<<"\n\nTotal nodes: "<<total;
cout<<"\n\nRead the position where node is to be inserted: ";
cin>>position;
if(position<=0 || position >total+1) //check for valid position
{
```

```
cout<<\nWrong position inputted\n";
getch ( ); //freeze the screen
exit (1);
}
cout<<"\n\nRead the value of the node to be inserted: ";
cin>>info;
link.insert (position, info);
cout<<"\n\nThe list after insertion is: \n\n";
link.display(1);
getch ( );
}
```

Output:

```
Read the elements of the list terminated by negative number:
15      14      19      18      5       -99
The list before any operation is performed (LIFO):
5->18->19->14->15-> NULL
Total nodes: 5
Read the position where node is to be inserted: 3
Read the value of the node to be inserted: 17
The list after insertion is:
5->18->17->19->14->15-> NULL
```

Program 4: Write a C++ program to insert a node at the proper position in an arranged list

```
#include <iostream.h>
# include <conio.h>
struct node
{
int info;                // info field
node* link;              //pointer to the link node
};
class link_list
{
private:
node* start;
public:
link_list ( )            //constructor
{
start=NULL;              //initially the list has no node
}
```

```
void create (int i)
{
node* new_node= new node;          //create a new node;
new_node->info=i;
new_node->=start;                  //make new node to point to the first node
start=new_node;                    // make new node as the first node in the list
}
void reverse ( );                  //function prototype
void display(int) ;                //function prototype
void insert (int);                 //function prototype
};
void link_list :: reverse ( )
{
node* previous=start;
node* current=previous->link;
node* temp;
previous->link=NULL;
while(current !=NULL)
{
temp=current->link;
current->link=previous;
previous=current;
current=temp;
}
start=previous;
}
void link_list :: display (int delete_node)
{
node* move= start;
node* temp;
while (move)
{
cout<<move->info<<"->"; //display the info
temp=move;
move=move->link; //move to link node
if (delete_node)
delete (temp);
}
cout<<"NULL";
```

```
}
void link_list :: insert (int info)
{
node* move=start;
node* insert_after=move;
int is_first=0;
while (move->info<info && move != NULL)
{
is_first=1;
insert_after=move;
move=move->link;
}
node* new node= new node; //create a new node;
new_node->info=info;
if (is_first)
{
new_node->link=insert_after->link;
insert_after->link=new_node;
}
else
{
new_node->link=start;
start=new_node;
}
}
void main ( )
{
int value, info, choice;
clrscr ( );
link_list link;
cout<<"Read the elements of the list in ascending order terminated by"
<<"negative number: \n;
cin>>value;
do
{
link.create (value);
cin>>value;
}
while (value>=0);
```

```
cout<<"\n\nThe list before any operation is performed (LIFO) : \n\n;
link.display (0);
link.reverse ( );
cout<<"\n\nThe list after reversal is: \n\n";
link.display (0)l
cout<<"\n\nRead the value of the node to be inserted: ";
cin>>info;
link.insert (info);
cout<<"\n\nThe list after insertion is: \n\n";
link.display (1);
getch ( ); //freeze the screen
}
```

Output:

```
Read the elements of the list in ascending order terminated y negative
number:
2     15     37     48     59     85     96     -99
The list before any operation is performed (LIFO):
86->75->49->38->27->15->2->NULL
The list after reversal is:
2->15->27->38->49->75->86->NULL
Read the value of the node to be inserted: 17

The list after insertion is:
2->15->17->27->38->49->75->86->NULL
```

5.7.1.4 Deletion from a Linked List

Deleting a node from a linked list is a lot harder than adding one; this is especially true in the case of a single linked list as is being used here. The problem is that the link from the *parent node* has to be set up to point to the *child node* of the node being deleted.

In other words, the link from the node before the node that is being deleted has to be changed to point to the same link as the one being deleted points to. The nodes don't hold information on their parent nodes, just child nodes, which is why it requires more work.

The diagram below shows the state of the list after the node in separate form in the Figure 5.30 is removed.

The process of deleting a node involves:

- Find the node to be deleted, remembering the previous node as the list is traversed through

- If the previous node is the start, set the start to be the child of the node being deleted
- otherwise set the link from the previous node to point to the same link as the node being deleted points to.
- Free up the memory for the deleted node.

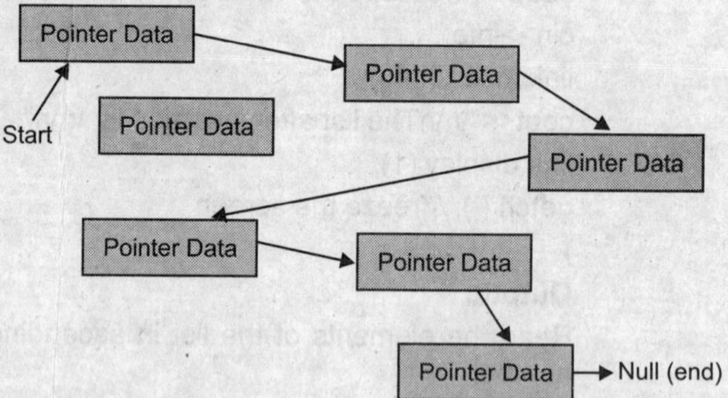

Figure 5.30: Deleting a Node from the Linked List.

All our deletions algorithms will return the memory space of the deleted node N to the beginning of the AVAIL list.Accordingly, all of our algorithms will include the following pair of assignments where LOC is the location of the deleted node N:

LINK [LOC] = AVAIL and AVAIL = LOC.

The operation is shown in Figure 5.31.

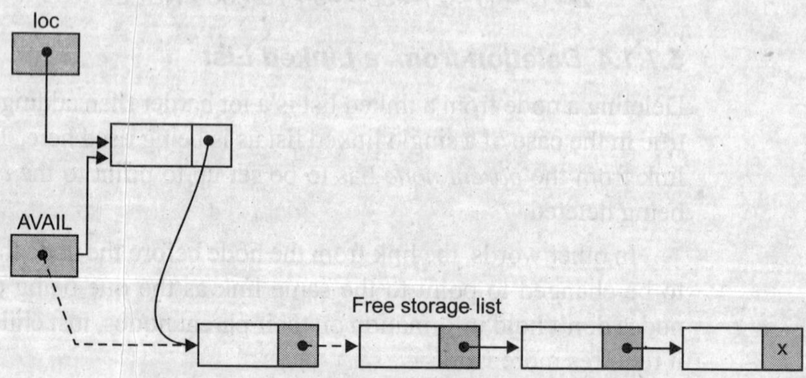

Figure 5.31: LINK [LOC] = AVAIL and AVAIL = LOC.

Garbage Collection

In many cases. we assumed that storage is allocated and freed one node at a time. There are two characteristics of nodes that make the above methods suitable. The first is that each node of a given type is of fixed size and the second is that the size clench node is fairly small. But in some cases a program might require a 'large amount of contiguous storage: which would be difficult to obtain uric block at a time, or a program may require storage blocks in a large variety of sizes. In such cases, memory management system must be able to process requests for variable length blocks. Thus processing certain types of data structures efficiently requires dynamic storage management capability.

Suppose some memory space becomes reusable because a node is deleted from a list or an entire list is deleted from a program then this space is available for future use. One way to bring this about is to immediately reinsert the space into free storage list, This is what we do when we implement linked lists through arrays. However, this method may be too time consuming for the operating system of a computer. Therefore, another method chosen by operating system of a computer is to periodically collect all the deleted space onto the free-storage list. The technique which does this collection is called garbage collection.

Under this method, nodes no longer in use remain allocated and undetected until all available storage has been allocated. A subsequent request for allocation cannot be satisfied until nodes that had been allocated but are no longer in use are recovered. When a request is made for additional nodes and there are none available a system routine called garbage collector is called. This routine searches through all the nodes in the system, identifies those that are no longer accessible from an external pointer and restores the inaccessible nodes to the available pool. The request for additional nodes is then fulfilled with some of the reclaimed nodes and the system continues processing the user request for more space. When available space is used up again, the garbage collector is called once again.

Garbage collection is usually done in two phases

The first phase called the marking phase involves marking of all nodes that are accessible from the external pointer.

The second phase called the collection phase which 'involves proceeding sequentially through memory and freeing all nodes that have not been marked.

Therefore, it can be said that first, the computer ruins through all lists, tagging those cells that are currently in use and then the computer runs through the mentor), collecting all untagged space on to the free-storage list. The garbage collection may take place when there is only some minimum amount of space left in the free storage list and when the CPU is idle and has time to do the collection.

Garbage collection is not an all-or-nothing proposition. It is possible to explicitly deallocate some common kinds of objects, and thus correspondingly decrease the frequency of garbage collections and garbage collection cost. It is possible to accommodate libraries that expect explicit deallocation calls. It is also possible to use the collector only as a debugging tool to locate leaks and remove it completely from the end product.

But for the sake of clarity, we'll look at the tradeoffs between exclusive use of explicit memory management (malloc/free or new/delete) and exclusive use of garbage collecting allocation.

A. Delete the Beginning Node from A Linked List

Suppose we are given location LOC of a node N in list. Furthermore, suppose we are given The location LOCP of the node Preceeding N or, when N is the first node, we are given LOCP = NULL.

Algorithm 5.7: To delete the node following a given node.

DELBEGNOD (INFO, LINK, START, AVAIL, LOC, LOCP)

This algorithm deletes the node N with location LOC. LOCP is the location of the node which precedes N or, when N is the first node, LOCP = NULL.

Step 1: If LOCP = NULL, then:
 Set START = LINK [START]. [Deletes first node.]
 Else:
 Set LINK [LOCP] = LINK [LOC]. [Deletes node N.]
 [End of If statement.]
Step 2: [Return deleted node to the AVAIL list.]
 Set LINK [LOC] = AVAIL and AVAIL = LOC.
Step 3: End.

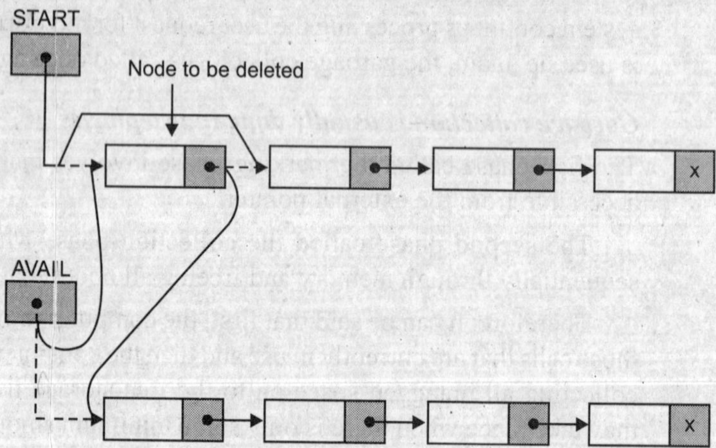

Figure 5.32: Delete the beginning node from a Linked List.

Set START = LINK [START].

This statement is used to delete the begining node from a list.

B. Deleting the Node with Given Item of Information

Algorithm 5.8: To find the location LOC of the node to be deleted.

FINDLOC (INFO, LINK, START, ITEM, LOC, LOCP)

This algorithm finds the location LOC of the first node N which contains ITEM and the location LOCP of the node preceding N. If ITEM does not appear in the list, then the procedure sets LOC = NULL; and if ITEM appears in the first node, then it sets LOCP = NULL.

Step 1: [List empty?] If START = NULL, then
    Set LOC = NULL and LOCP = NULL, and return.
  [End of If statement.]
Step 2: [ITEM in first node?] If INFO [START] = ITEM, then:
    Set LOC = START and LOCP = NULL, and Return.
  [End of If statement.]
Step 3: Set SAVE = START and P = LINK [START]. [Initializes pointers.]
Step 4: Repeat Steps 5 and 6 while P ≠ NULL.
Step 5: If INFO [P] = ITEM, then:
    Set LOC = P and LOCP = SAVE, and Return.
  [End of If statement.]
Step 6: Set SAVE = P and P = LINK [P]. [Updates pointers.]
  [End of Step 4 loop.]
Step 7: Set LOC = NULL. [Search unsuccessful.]
Step 8: Return.

Figure 5.33 is the schematic diagram of the assignment

Set LINK [LOCP] = LINK [LOC].

Which effectively deletes the node N when N is not the first node.

The simplicity of the algorithm comes from the fact that we are already given the location LOCP of the node which precedes node N.In many applications, we must first find LOCP.

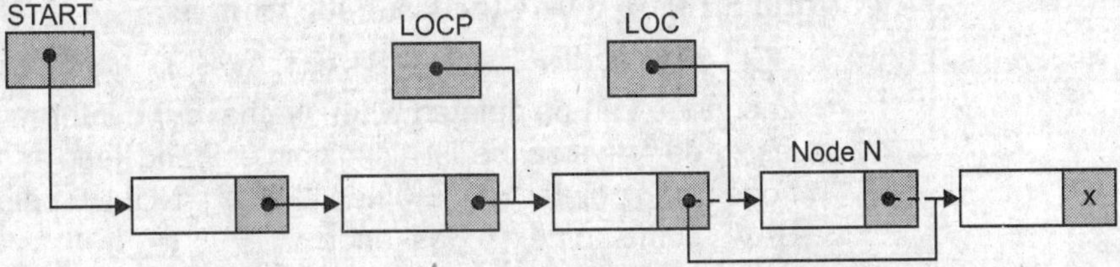

Figure 5.33: LINK [LOCP] = LINK [LOC]. [Deletes node N.]

This statement is used to delete the node N when N is not the first node.

Algorithm 5.9: To delete the node with a given item of information.

DELGVNNOD(INFO, LINK, START, AVAIL, ITEM)

This algorithm deletes from a Linked list the first node N which contains the given ITEM of information.

Step 1: [Use algorithm 10 to find the location of N and its preceding node.]
  Call FINDLOC(INFO, LINK, START, ITEM, LOC, LOCP)

Step 2: If LOC = NULL, then: Write: ITEM no in list, and End.

Step 3: [Delete node.]
  If LOCP = NULL, then
    Set LINK[LOCP] = LINK[LOC].
  [End of If statement.]

Step 4: [Return deleted node to the AVAIL list.]
  Set LINK[LOC] = AVAIL and AVAIL = LOC

Step 5: End.

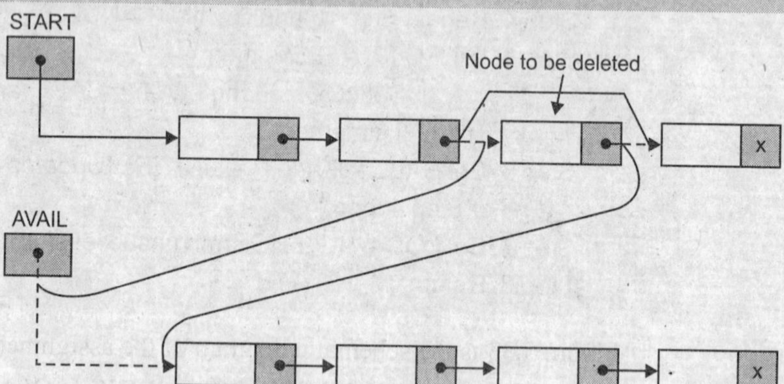

Figure 5.34: Deleting the node with given item of information.

C. Deleting the Last Node from List

In this operation, we have to delete the last node of the single linked list.

Algorithm 5.10: To delete the last node from list

DELLSTNOD(INFO, LINK, START, AVAIL)

Last node can be deleted when we have the information about next-to-last node.Traverse the list using pointer P and keep address of preceeding node using pointer SAVE.When LINK[P]=NULL P points to last node and SAVE points to next to last node.

Step 1: [List is empty?] If START = NULL, then Write: UNDERFLOW, and End.

Step 2: [List can contains only one element?]

If LINK[START] = NULL, then:

a. Set START = NULL. [Removes only node from list.]

b. Set LINK[START] = AVAIL and AVAIL = START.

[Returns node to AVAIL list.]

c. End.

[End of If structure]

Step 3: Set P = LINK[START] and SAVE = START. [Initialize pointers P.]

Step 4: Repeat Steps while LINK[P] ≠ NULL. [Traverses list, go for last node.]

Set SAVE = P and P = LINK[P]. [Updates SAVE and P.]

[End of If statement.]

Step 5: Set LINK[SAVE] = LINK[P]. [Removes last node From LIST.]

Step 6: Set LINK[P] = AVAIL and AVAIL = P. [Returns node to AVAIL list.]

Step 7: End.

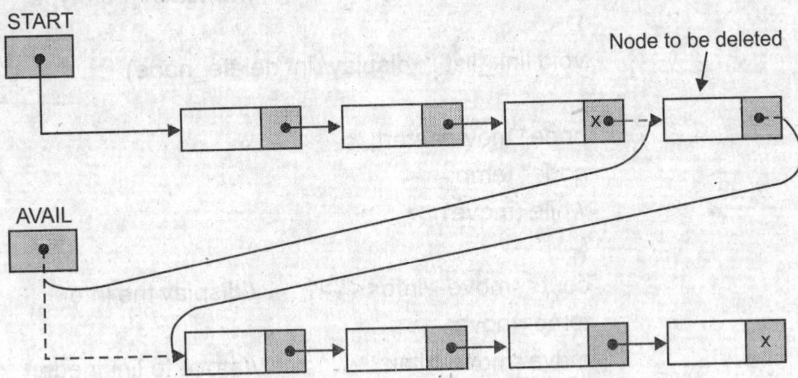

Figure 5.35: Deleting the last node from linked list.

Program 5: Write a C++ program to delete a node from a linked list

```
# include<iostream.h>
# include<conio.h>
# include<process.h> //for exit ( ) function
struct node
{
int info;                //info field
node* link;              //pointer to the link node
};
class link_list
{
private:
```

```
node* start;
public:
link_list ( )               //constructor
{
start=NULL;                 //initially the list has no node
}
void create (int i)
{
node* new_node= new node; //create a new node;
new_node->info=i;
new_node->link=start;             //make new node to point to the first node
start=new_node;                   // make new node as the first node in the list
}
void display ( );                 //function prototype
void remove (int);                //function prototype
};
void link_list : : display (int delete_node)
{
node* move= start;
node* temp;
while (move)
{
cout<<move->info<<"->";          //display the info
temp=move;
move=move->link;                 //move to link node
if (delete_node)
delete (temp);
}
cout<<"NULL";
}
void link_list : : remove (int position)
{
node* move=start;
int steps=1;
while (steps<position-1)
{
move=move->link;
steps++;
}
```

```
if (position= =1)                    // if to be inserted at the first place
{
node* temp= start;
start=start->link;
delete (temp);
}
else
{
node* temp= move->link;
move->link=move->link->link;
delete (temp);
}
}
void main ( )
{
int value, info, choice, number, total=0;
clrscr ( );
link_list link;
cout<<"Read the elements of the list terminated by negative number: \n;
cin>>value;
do
{
link.create(value);
total++; //increment with every node inserted
cin>>value;
} while (value>=0);
cout<<"\n\nThe list before any operation is performed (LIFO): \n\n";
link.display (0);
cout<<"\n\nTotal nodes: "<<total;
cout<<"\n\nRead the number of the node to be deleted: ";
cin>>number;
if(number<=0 | | number >total) //check for valid position
{
cout<<"\nWrong number inputted";
getch( ); //freeze the screen
exit (1);
}
total --;
link.remove (number);
```

```
cout<<"\n\nThe list after deletion is: \n\n";
link.display (1);
cout<<"\n\nTotal nodes: "<<total;
getch( );
}
```

Output:

Read the elements of the list terminated by negative number:

12 16 17 19 18 10 14 15 -99

The list before any operation is performed (LIFO):

15->14->10->18->19->17->16->12->NULL

Total nodes: 8

Read the number of the node to be deleted: 5

The list after deletion is:

15->14->10->18->17->16->12->NULL

Total nodes: 7

5.7.1.5 Concatenating Two Lists

Concatenating means to join or combine two different nodes into single node. Note that both the list should be ordered.

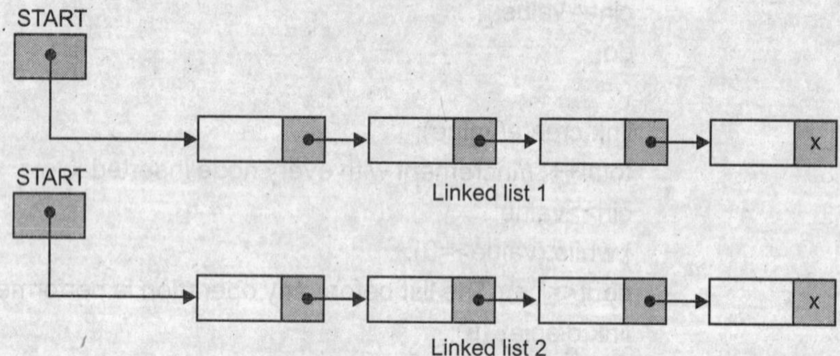

Figure 5.36: Two linked list

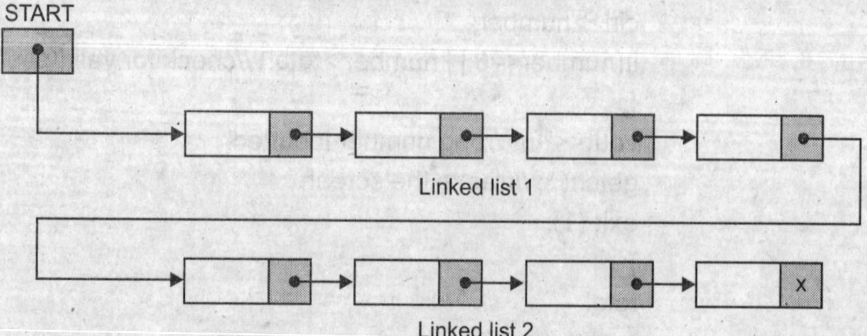

Figure 5.37: Concatenating two linked lists (linked list1 and linked list2)

Algorithm 5.11: To concatenate the two lists

This algorithm is used to concatenate two linked list into one.

CONCAT(START,LINK)

Step 1: Set P = START 1

Step 2: Repeat Step (3) while LINK [P] ≠ NULL

Step 3: P= LINK [P]

Step 4: Set LINK [P] = START 2

Step 5: End

Program 6: Write a C++ program to concatenate two linked lists

```
# include<iostream.h>
# include<conio.h>
# include<process.h>
struct node
{
int info;                  //info field
node* link;                //pointer to the link node
};
class link_list
{
private:
node* start;
public:
link_list ( )              //constructor
{
start=NULL;                //initially the list has no node
}
void create (int);                  //function prototype
void display (int);                 //function prototype
void concatenate (link_list);  //function prototype
};
void link_list : : create ( )
{
int value;
cin>>value;
do
{
node* new_node= new node;                  //create a new node;
new_node->info=value;
```

```
new_node->link=start;          //make new node to point to the first node
start=new_node;                //make new node as the first node in the list
cin>>value;
}
while (value>=0);
}
void link_list : : display (int delete_node)
{
node* move= start;
node* temp;
while (move)
{
cout<<move->info<<"->";               //display the info
temp=move;
move=move->link;                      //move to link node
if (delete_node)
delete (temp);
}
cout<<"NULL";
}
void link_list : : concatenate (link_list 11)
{
node* move=start;
while (move->link !=NULL)
move=move->link;
move->link=11.start;
}
void main ( )
{
clrscr ( );
link_list link1, link2;
cout<<"Read the elements of the first list terminated by"
<<"negative number: \n";
link1.create ( );
cout<<"Read the elements of the second list terminated by"
<<"negative number:\n;
link2.create ( );
cout<<"\n\nThe two lists before concatenation are: \n\n;
link1.display (0);
```

```
cout<<"\n\n";
link2.display (0);
link1.concatenate (1ink2);
cout<<"\n\nThe final list after concatenation is: \n\n;
link1.display (1);
getch ( );
}
```

Output:

```
Read the elements of the first terminated by negative number:
10    20    30    40    50    60    -99
Read the elements of the second list terminated by negative number:
15    25    35    45    55    65    -77
The two lists before concatenation are:
60->50->40->30->20->10->NULL
65->55->45->35->25->15->NULL
The final list after concatenation is:
60->50->40->30->20->10->65->55->45->35->25->15->NULL
```

5.7.1.6 Searching A Node in A Linked List

Searching a node in a Linked List is the same as finding the node before which or after another node is inserted. A pointer is defined and equated to pointer first. The pointer goes through the entire list. If the item is found, it displays the item found and name of the item on the screen otherwise it displays not found.

Algorithm 5.12: To search element from unsorted linked list

UNSORTSEARCH (INFO, LINK, START, ITEM, LOC)

LIST is a Linked list in memory. This algorithm find the location LOC of the node where ITEM first appears in LIST, or if item not exists in LIST set LOC = NULL.

Step 1: Set P = START. [Initializes pointer P.]

Step 2: Repeat Step 3 while P ≠ NULL.

Step 3:If ITEM = INFO [P], then;

    Set LOC = P, and End.

    Else:

    Set P = LINK[P]. [P now points to the next node.]

    [End of If statement.]

  [End of Step 2 loop.]

Step 4: [If search is unsuccessful.] Set LOC = NULL

Step 5: End.

Algorithm 5.13: To search element from sorted linked list.

SORTSEARCH (INFO, LINK, START, ITEM, LOC)

LIST is a sorted list in memory. This algorithm find the location LOC of the node where ITEM first appears in LIST, or if item not exists in LIST set LOC = NULL.

Step 1: Set P = START. [Initializes pointer P.]

Step 2: Repeat Step 3 while P ≠ NULL.

Step 3: If ITEM > INFO[P], then

Set P = LINK[P]. [P now points to next node.]

Else if ITEM = INFO[P], then:

Set LOC = P, and End. [Search is successful.]

Else:

Set LOC = NULL, and End. [ITEM now exceeds INFO[P].]

[End of If statement.]

[End of Step 2 loop.]

Step 4: Set LOC = NULL.

Step 5: End.

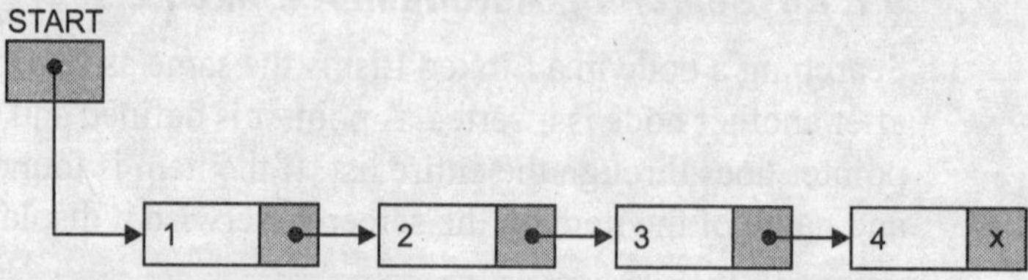

Figure 5.38: P = LINK[P] is used to search the given ITEM.

5.7.1.7 Reversing the Direction of Linked List

Reverse means to set the last node as first and first node as last and so on procedure continue.

Algorithm 5.14: To reverse the direction of linked list.

REVERSE(START, LINK, LOC)

This algorithm is used to reverse the given list.

Step 1: P = LINK [START]

Step 2: LINK [START] = NULL

Step 3: Repeat steps (4) & (5) while P ≠ NULL

Step 4: LOC= P, P = LINK [P]

Step 5: LINK [LOC] = START, START = LOC

Step 6: End

To reverse a list, we maintain a pointer each to the previous and the next node, then we make the link field of the current node point to the previous, make the previous equal to the current, and the current equal to the next, shown here.

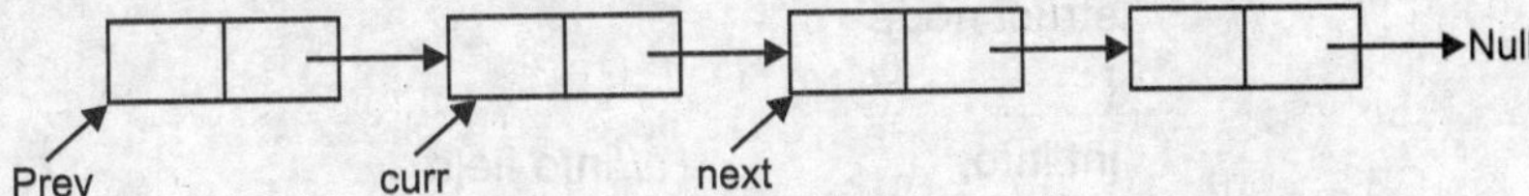

Figure 5.39: A linked list showing the previous, current, and next nodes at some point during reversal process.

Therefore, the code needed to reverse the list is

```
Prev = NULL;
while (curr !=NULL)
{
link =curr-> link;
curr-> link =prev;
prev=curr;
curr= link;
}
```

The working of a reverse function is shown here:

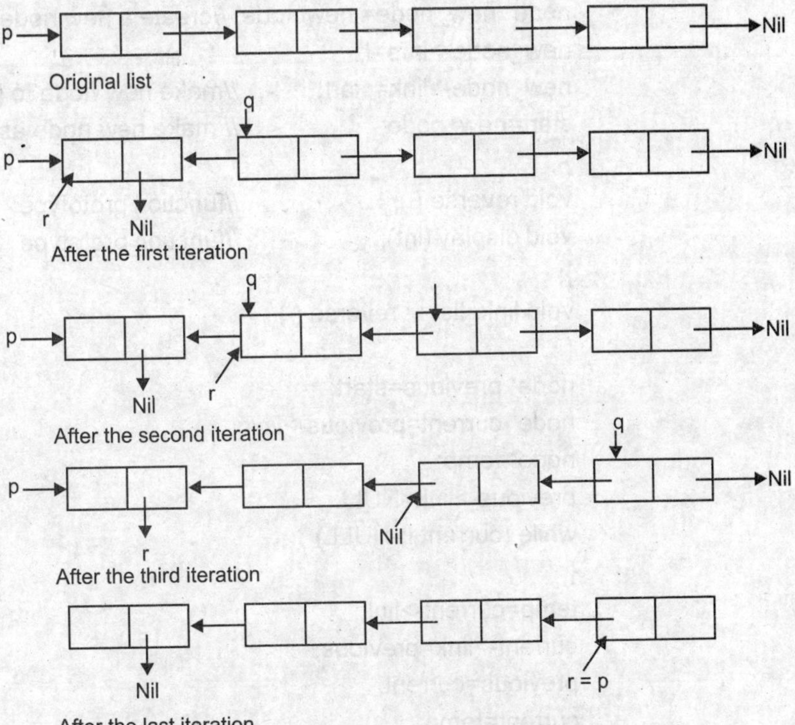

Figure 5.40: Reversal of a list.

Program 7: Write a C++ program to reverse a linked list

```
# include<iostream.h>
# include<conio.h>
struct node
{
int info;                   //info field
node* link;                 //pointer to the link node
};
class link_list
{
private:
node* start;
public:
link_list ( )               //constructor
{
start=NULL;                 //initially the list has no node
}
void create (int i)
{
node* new_node= new node; //create a new node;
new_node->info=i;
new_node->link=start;       //make new node to point to the first node
start=new_node;             // make new node as the first node in the list
}
void reverse ( );           //function prototype
void display (int);         //function prototype
};
void link_list : : reverse ( )
{
node* previous=start;
node* current=previous->link;
node* temp;
previous->link=NULL;
while (current !=NULL)
{
temp=current->link;
current->link=previous;
previous=current;
current=temp;
```

```
}
start=previous;
}
void link_list : : display (int delete_node)
{
node* move= start;
node* temp;
while (move)
{
cout<<move->info<<"->";      //display the info
temp=move;
move=move->link;             //move to link node
if (delete_node)
delete (temp);
}
cout<<"NULL";
}
void main ( )
{
int value, info, choice;
clrscr ( );
link_list link;
cout<<"Read the elements of the list terminated by negative number : \n";
cin>>value;
do
{
link.create (value);
cin>>value;
}
while (value>=0);
cout<<"\n\nThe list before any operation is performed (LIFO) : \n\n";
link.display (0);
link.reverse ( );
cout<<"\n\nThe list after reversal is: \n\n";
link.display (1);
getch ( ); //freeze the screen
}
```

Output:

Read the elements of the list terminated by negative number:

1 2 3 4 5 6 7 -99

The list before any operation is performed (LIFO):
7->6->5->4->3->2->1->NULL
The list after reversal is:
1->2->3->4->5->->6->7->NULL

5.7.1.8 Copying List1 into List2

Algorithm 5.15: To copy LIST1 list into LIST2 list

COPY(INFO, LINK, LIST1, LIST2, AVAIL)

This algorithm makes a copy of a list LIST1 using LIST2 as the list pointer variable of the new list.

Step 1: Set LIST2 = NULL.[Empty list.]

Step 2: [LIST1 is empty?] If LIST1 = NULL, then End.

Step 3: [Insert first node of LIST1 into LIST2.]

Call INSGVNLOC (INFO, LINK, LIST2, AVAIL, NULL, INFO [LIST1]) or:

(a) If AVAIL = NULL, then Write: OVERFLOW, and End.

(b) Set NEW = AVAIL and AVAIL = LINK[AVAIL]. [Removes first node from AVAIL list.]

(c) Set INFO [NEW] = INFO [LIST1]. [Copies INFO LIST1 into new node LIST2.]

[Insert new node as first node in LIST2.]

(d) Set LINK [NEW] = LIST2 and LIST2 = NEW.

Step 4: [Initializes pointers P and LOC.]

Set P = LINK [LIST1] and LOC = LIST2.

Step 5: Repeat Steps 6 and 7 while P ≠ NULL

Step 6: Call INSGVNLOC (INFO, LINK, LIST2, AVAIL, LOC, INFO [P]) or

(a) If AVAIL = NULL, then Write: OVERFLOW, and End.

(b) Set NEW = AVAIL and AVAIL = LINK [AVAIL].

(c) Set INFO [NEW] = INFO [P]. [Copies INFO into new node.]

(d) [Insert new node into LIST2 after the node with location LOC.]

Set LINK [NEW] = LINK [LOC], and LINK [LOC] = NEW.

Step 7:Set P = LINK [P] and LOC = LINK [LOC]. [Updates pointers P and LOC.]

[End of Step 5 loop.]

Step 8: End.

Check out this C program which creates an exact copy of a linked list:

```
copy_linked_lists(struct node *q, struct node **s)
{
if(q!=NULL)
{
```

```
*s=malloc(sizeof(struct node));
(*s)->data=q->data;
(*s)->link=NULL;
copy_linked_list(q->link, &((*s)->link));
}}
```

5.7.1.9 *Merging of Two Sorted Lists*

Merging of two sorted lists involves traversing the given lists and comparing the INFO values stored in the nodes in the process of traversing.

If p and q are the pointers to the sorted lists to be merged, then we compare the INFO value stored in the first node of the list pointed to by p with the INFO value stored in the first node of the list pointed to by q. And, if the INFO value in the first node of the list pointed to by p is less than the INFO value in the first node of the list pointed to by q, make the first node of the resultant/merged list to be the first node of the list pointed to by p, and advance the pointer p to make it point to the next node in the same list.

If the INFO value in the first node of the list pointed to by p is greater than the INFO value in the first node of the list pointed to by q, make the first node of the resultant/merged list to be the first node of the list pointed to by q, and advance the pointer q to make it point to the next node in the same list.

Repeat this procedure until either p or q becomes NULL. When one of the two lists becomes empty, append the remaining nodes in the non-empty list to the resultant list.

If the following lists are given as input, then what would be the output of the program after each pass? This is shown here:

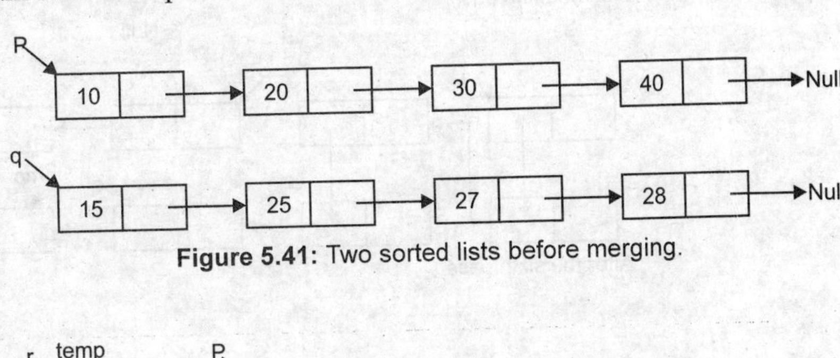

Figure 5.41: Two sorted lists before merging.

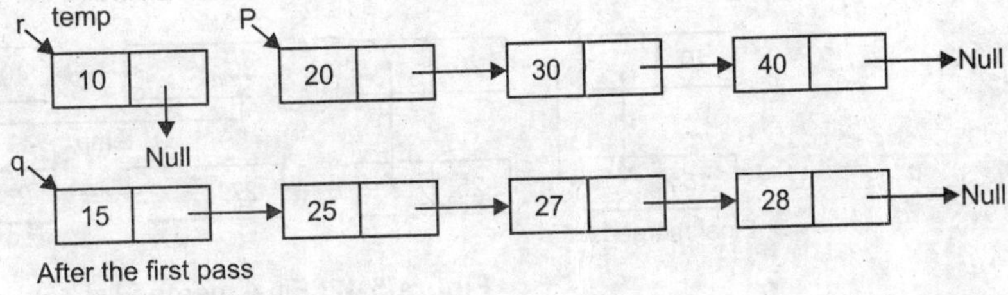

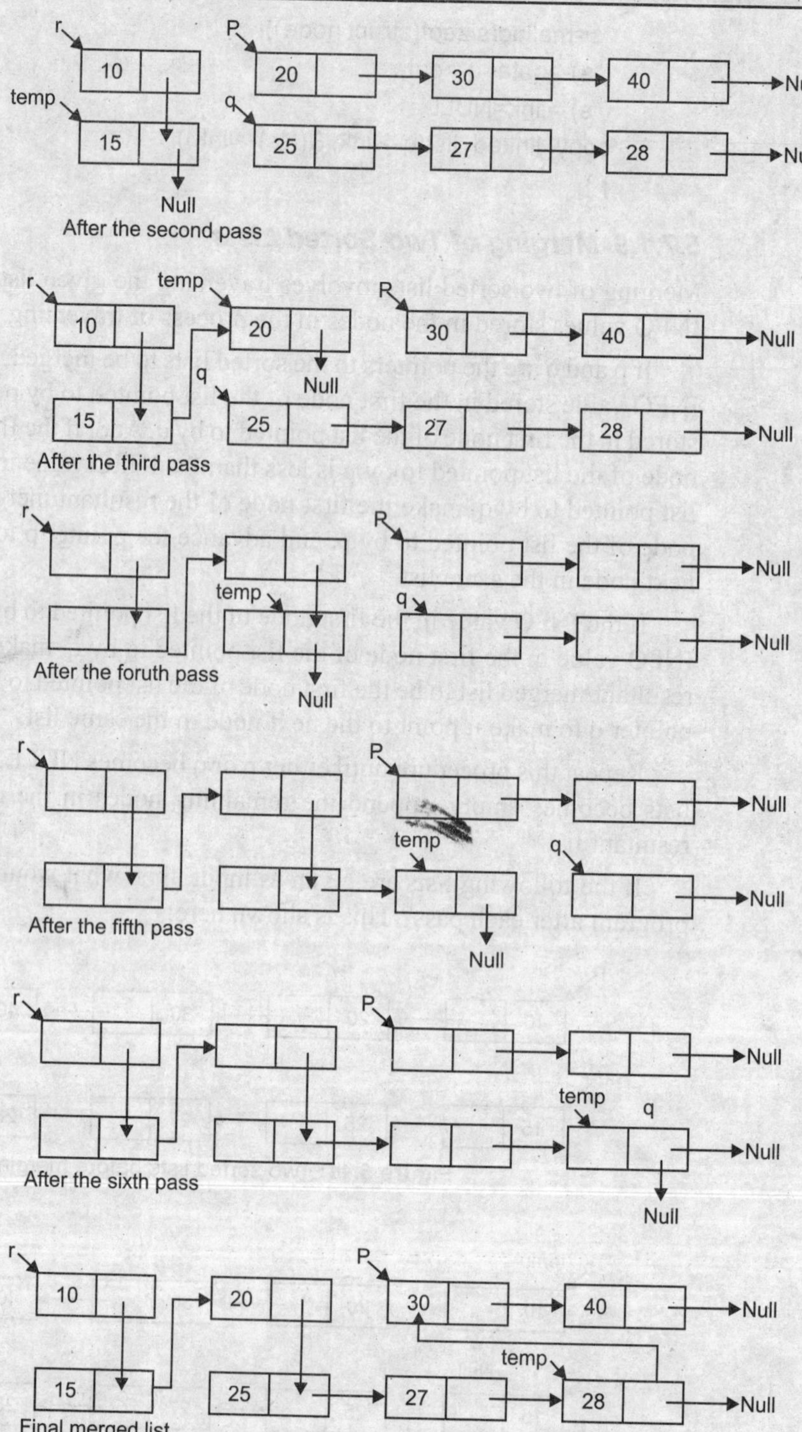

Figure 5.42: Final merged list.

Program 8: Write a C++ program to merge two linked lists by concatenating them first.

```
# include<iostream.h>
# include<conio.h>
struct node
{
int info;                   //info field
node* link;                 //pointer to the link node
};
class link_list
{
private:
node* start;
public:
link_list ( )               //constructor
{
start=NULL;                 //initially the list has no node
}
void add_info ( );                     //function prototype
void display (int);                    //function prototype
void concatenate (link_list);  //function prototype
void sort ( );                         //function prototype
};
void link_list : : add_info ( )
{
int value;
cin>>value;
while (value>0)
{
node* new_link= new node;  //create a new node;
new_link->info=value;
new_link->link=start;            //make new node to point to the first node
start=new_node;                  //make new node as the first node in the list
cin>.value;
}
}
while (value>=0);
}
void link_list : : display (int delete_node)
```

```
{
node* move= start;
node* temp;
while (move)
{
cout<<move->info<<"->"; //display the info
temp=move;
move=move->link; //move to link node
if (delete_node)
delete (temp);
}
cout<<"NULL";
}
void link_list : : concatenate (link_list 11)
{
node* move=start;
while (move->link !=NULL)
move=move->link;
move->link=11.start;
}
void link_list : : sort ( )
{
node* top=start;
while (top->link != NULL)
{
int min=top->info;
node* move=top->link;
node* min_node;
while (move != NULL)
{
if (move->info <min)
{
min=move->info;
min_node=move;
}
move=move->link;
}
if (min != top->info)
{
```

```
int temp=top->info;
top->info =min;
min_node->info=temp;
}
top=top->link;
}
}
void main ( )
{
clrscr ( );
link_list link1, link2;
cout<<"Read the info of the first list terminated by negative number: \n";
link1.add_info ( );
cout<<"Read the info of the second list terminated by negative number:
\n";
link2.add_info ( );
cout<<"\nInputted linked lists before sorting are: \n\n";
link1.display (0);
cout<<end1<<end1;
link2.display (0);
link1.concatenate(link2);
link1.sort ( );
cout<<"\n\nMerged linked list is: \n\n";
link1.display (1);
getch ( );
}
```

Output:

```
Read the info of the first link list terminated by negative number.
12    42    32    22    72    -99
Read the info of the second link list terminated by negative number:
26    36    16    56    46    -66
Inputted link lists before sorting are:
72->22->32->42->12->NULL
46->56->16->36->26-> NULL
Merged linked list is:
12->16->22->26->32->36->42->46->56->72->NULL
```

5.7.1.10 Erasing A Linked List

Erasing a linked list involves traversing the list starting from the first node, freeing the storage allocated to the nodes, and then setting the pointer to the list to NULL.

If p is a pointer to the start of the list, the actions specified through the following code will erase the list:

```
while(p != NULL)
{
temp = p;
p = p->link;
free(t);
}
```

But a better strategy of erasing a list is to mark all the nodes of the list to be erased as free nodes without actually freeing the storage of these nodes. That means to maintain this list, a list of free nodes, so that if a new node is required it can be obtained from this list of free nodes.

The method of erasing a list requires adding all the nodes of the list to be erased to the list of free nodes, as shown here.

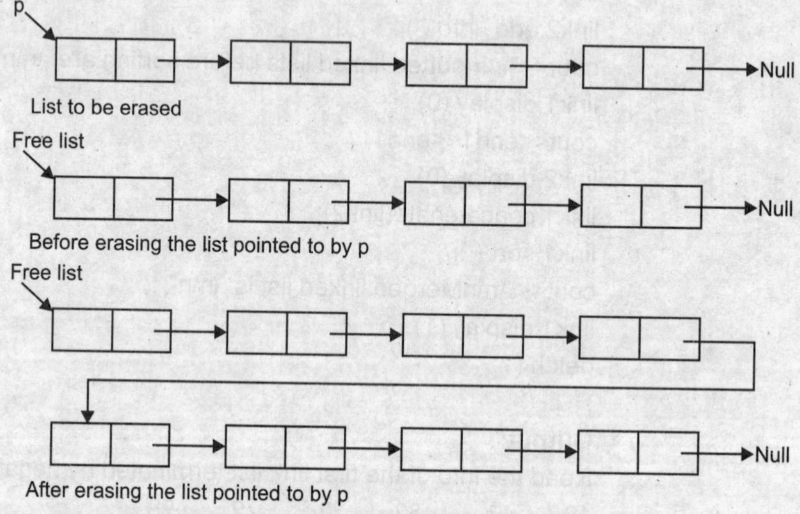

Figure 5.43: Final List After Erasing

5.7.1.11 Splitting A List

Once we build a linked list ,it can split int many sub-lists. The technique to splitting alist is very simple.

Consider a circular list containing 2n nodes, as shown in Figure 5.44.

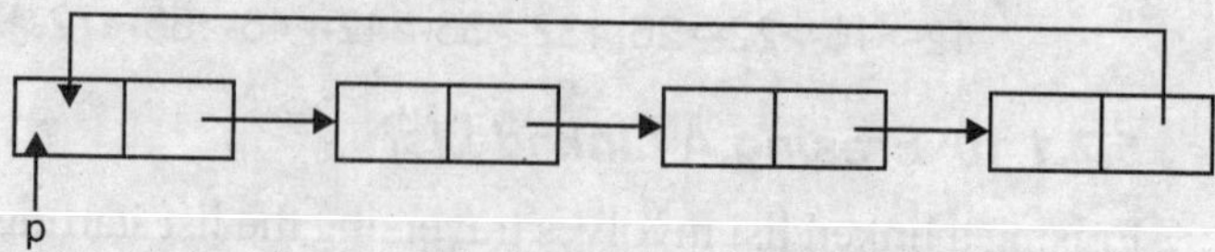

Figure 5.44: List containing 2n nodes

To split this list into two equal lists, it is required to traverse the list up to the nth node and store the link of the nth node, which is the address of $(n+1)^{th}$ node in the pointer, say q. After this, make the link field of the nth node point to the first node pointed to by p. Then traverse the list starting from the node pointed to by q up to the end. Then make the link field of the last node point to the node pointed to by q. The result of this is shown in Figure 5.45.

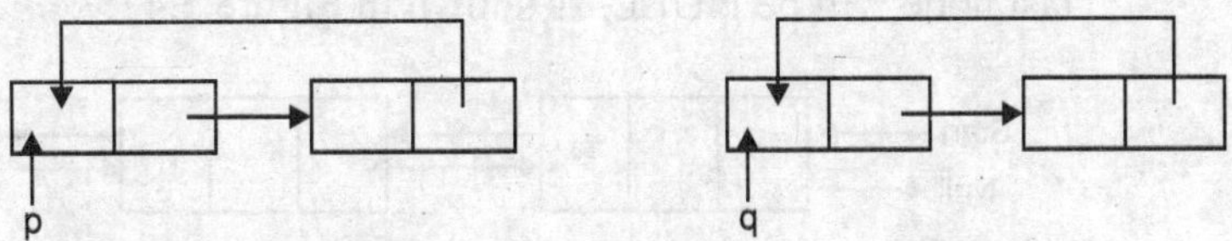

Figure 5.45: Splitting of a circular list

5.8 DOUBLY LINKED LIST

In a doubly linked list, also called a **two-way list**, each node is divided into three parts:

1. The first part, called the previous pointer field, contains the address of the preceding element in the list.
2. The second part contains the information of the list.
3. The third part, called the next pointer field, contains the address of the succeeding element in the list.

In addition, two pointer variables, named head and tail, are used that contain the address of first element and the address of last element of the list.

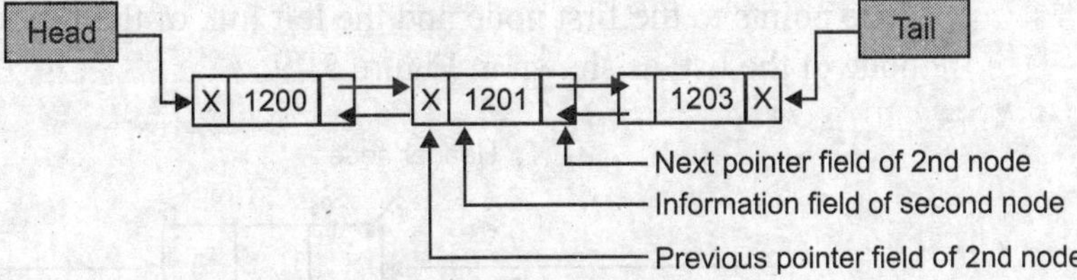

Figure 5.46: Two-way list.

The following are problems with singly linked lists:

1. A singly linked list allows traversal of the list in only one direction.
2. Deleting a node from a list requires keeping track of the previous node, that is, the node whose link points to the node to be deleted.
3. If the link in any node gets corrupted, the remaining nodes of the list become unusable.

These problems of singly linked lists can be overcome by adding one more link to each node, which points to the previous node. When such a link is added to every node of a list, the corresponding linked list is called a doubly linked list. Therefore, a doubly linked list is a linked list in which every node contains two links, called left link and right link, respectively. The left link of the node points to the previous node, whereas the right points to the next node. Like a singly linked list, a doubly linked list can also be a chain or it may be circular with or without a header node. If it is a chain, the left link of the first node and the right link of the last node will be NULL, as shown in Figure 5.47.

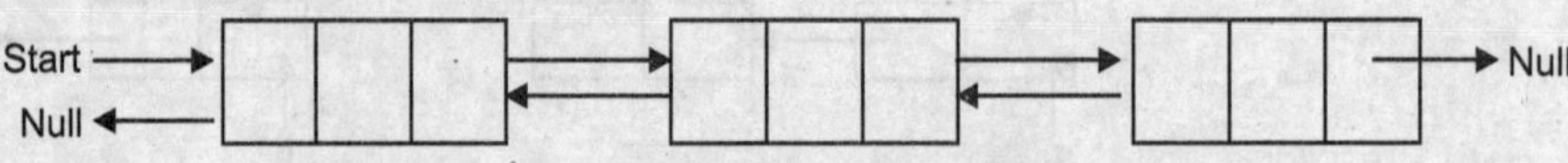

Figure 5.47: A doubly linked list maintained as chain

If it is a circular list without a header node, the right link of the last node points to the first node. The left link of the first node points to the last node, as shown in Figure 5.48.

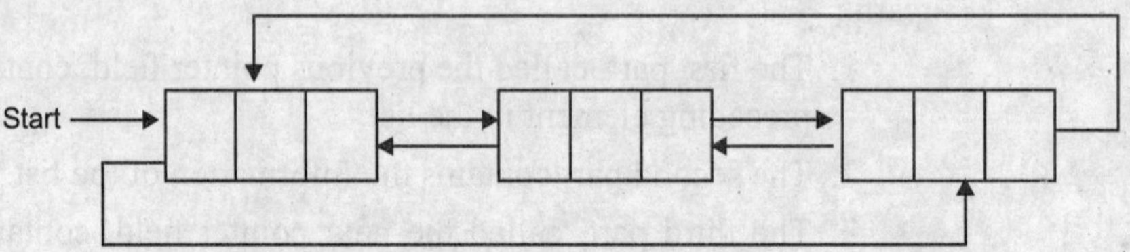

Figure 5.48: A doubly linked list maintained as a circular list

If it is a circular list with a header node, the left link of the first node and the right link of the last node point to the header node. The right link of the header node points to the first node and the left link of the header node points to the last node of the list, as shown in Figure 5.49.

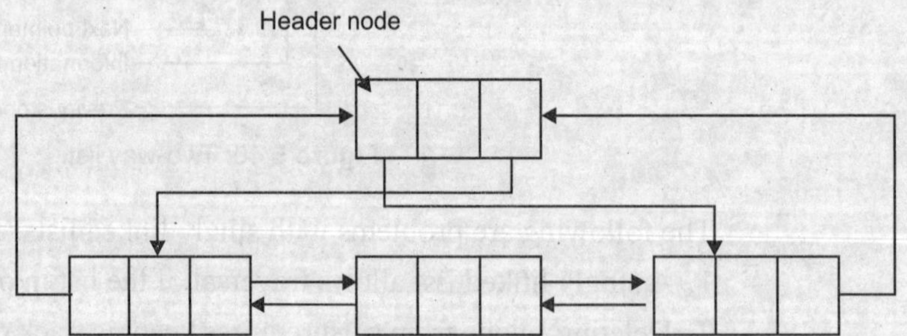

Figure 5.49: A doubly linked list maintained as a circular list with a header node

Therefore, the following representation is required to be used for the nodes of a doubly linked list.

```
struct dbnode
{
int INFO;
struct dnode *left,*right;
};
```

Recall that, given (only) a pointer to a node *n* in a linked list with N nodes, removing node *n* takes time O(N) in the worst case, because it is necessary to traverse the list looking for the node just before *n*. One way to fix this problem is to require **two** pointers: a pointer the node to be removed, and also a pointer to the node just before that one.

Another way to fix the problem is to use a **doubly linked** list. Here's the conceptual picture:

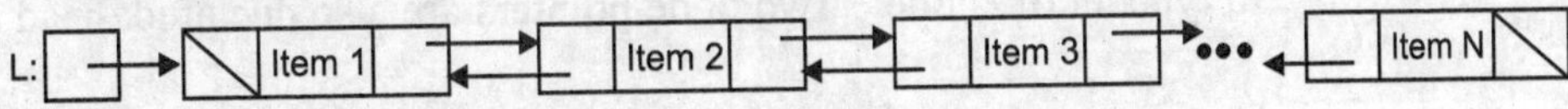

Figure 5.50: Representation of doubly linked list.

Each node in a doubly linked list contains **three** fields: the INFO, and two pointers. One pointer points to the previous node in the list, and the other pointer points to the next node in the list. The previous pointer of the first node, and the next pointer of the last node are both null.

To remove a given node *n* from a doubly linked list, we need to change the ***prev*** field of the node to its right, and we need to change the ***next*** field of the node to its left, as illustrated below.

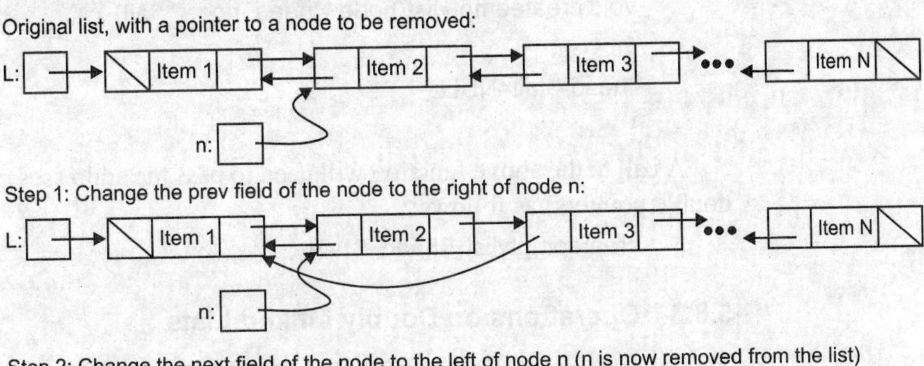

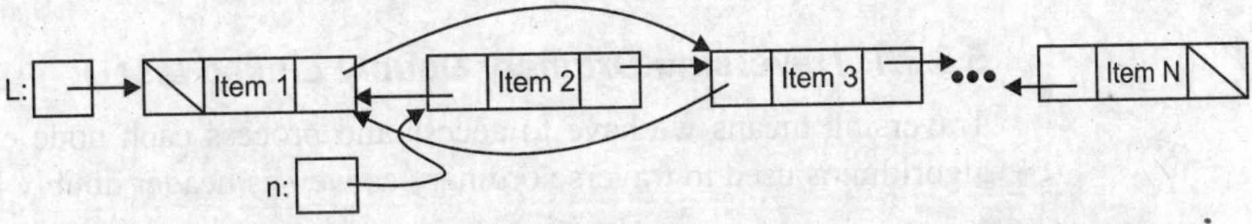

Figure 5.51: Conceptual diagram for removing node from doubly linked list.

5.8.1 Implementation of A Doubly Linked List

Suppose we want to store list of integers. Then, we define the following self-referential structure:

```
typedef struct nodetype
{
struct nodetype *prev;
int info;
struct nodetype *next;
}node;
node *head,*tail;
```

The above declaration defines a new INFO type called "struct nodetype" with a typedef of "node". Two node pointers are also declared: head and tail.

5.8.2 Creating an Empty List

- In the previous declaration, the variables head and tail are each declared as a pointer to a "node".
- These variables are not yet initialized.
- "head" is used to point to the first element of the list and "tail" is used to point to the last element of the list.
- Since the list will be empty in the beginning, the variables head and tail should be assigned a sentinel value to indicate the list is empty.

```
void createemptylist(node **head, node **tail)
{
*head=*tail=NULL;
}
```

A call to the above function will need to pass the addresses of head and tail (as double pointers) as follows:

```
createemptylist(&head, &tail);
```

5.8.3 Operations on Doubly Linked Lists

The following operations can be performed on doubly linked lists:

5.8.3.1 Traversing Ordinary Doubly Linked List

Traversing means we have to access and process each node exactly once. This algorithm is used to traverse ordinary as well as header doubly list.

Algorithm 5.16: To traverse the ordinary doubly linked list.

TRAVERSEDL(INFO, LINK, START, P)

Suppose we want to traverse LIST in order to process each element exactly once. If LIST is an ordinary doubly linked list Then use Algorithm 5.1:TRAVERSE(INFO, LINK, START, P).

Or

If LIST contains a header node. we can use algorithm 5.24 to traverse doubly header list.

Program 9: Write a C++ program to create and traverse a doubly linked list

```
# include<iostream.h>
# include<conio.h>
struct doubly
{
int info;
doubly* back;
doubly* front;
};
class doubly_class
{
private:
double* start;
public:
doubly_class ( )
{
start=new doubly;
start->front=NULL;
start->back=NULL;
start->info=-1;          // header node- can contain other information also
}
void create ( );         // function prototype
void display ( );        // function prototype
};
void doubly_class : : create ( )
{
int values;
doubly* new_node=new doubly;
new_node= start;
cout<<"\nRead the info terminated by negative number: \n;
cin>>value;
```

```
while (value>=0)
{
new_node->front=new doubly;
new_node->front->back=new_node;
new_node=new_node->front;
new_node->info=value;
new_node->front=NULL;
cin>>value;
}
}
void doubly_class : : display ( )
{
cout<<"\n\nTraversing in the forward direction: \n\n";
doubly* move=start;
do
{
move=move->info<<"<->";
}
while (move->front);
cout<<"NULL";
cout<<"\n\nTraversing in the back direction: \n\n;
do
{
cout<<move->info<<"<->";
move=move->back;
}
while (move->back);
cout<<'NULL";
}
void main( )
{
clrscr ( );
doubly_class d_list; // create an object
d_list.create ( );
d_list.display ( );
getch ( );
}
```

Output:

Read the info terminated by negative number:

12 13 11 14 16 15 -99

Traversing in the forward direction:

12<->13<->11<->14<->16<->15<->NULL

Traversing in the back direction:

15<->16<->14<->11<->13<->12<->NULL

5.8.3.2 Searching Ordinary Doubly Linked List

Searching means we have to find the given ITEM from the doubly linked list. This algorithm is used to find the ITEM from ordinary as well as header doubly list.

Algorithm 5.17: To search the ordinary doubly linked list.

SEARCHDL(INFO, LINK, START, ITEM, LOC)

Suppose we are given an ITEM of information. We have to find the location of ITEM in LIST. if LIST is an ordinary doubly linked list, Then we can use Algorithm 5.13

SORTSEARCH(INFO, LINK, START, ITEM, LOC).

Or

If LIST has a header node we can use algorithm 5.25 to search doubly header list. Advantage of two way list is that we can search the element from both directions(backward and forward).

5.8.3.3 Insertion into Doubly Linked List

Suppose we want to insert the node in the doubly linked list. We have three cases to insert the node.

One common operation for three cases is to insert the node in the doubly linked list. We remove the first node from the AVAIL list,then using the variable NEW to keep track of its location and then copy the new data ITEM into the NEW node that is;

NEW = AVAIL, AVAIL = FORW[AVAIL], INFO[NEW] = ITEM.

First case, is to insert the node at the beginning of the doubly linked list.

START = NEW, FORW[NEW] = LOCA.

BACK[NEW] = NULL, BACK[LOCA] = NEW.

Second case, is to insert the node after a given node in doubly linked list. Suppose we have the locations LOCA and LOCB in the doubly linked list.

We have to set the four pointers:

FORW[LOCA] = NEW, FORW[NEW] = LOCB,

BACK[LOCB] = NEW, BACK[NEW] = LOCA.

Third case, is to insert the node in the last of the doubly linked list. We have to set the three pointers:

FORW[LOCA] = NEW, FORW[NEW] = NULL,

BACK[NEW] = LOCA.

A. Insertion at the beginning of the doubly linked list

Algorithm 5.18: To insert new node at the beginning of the doubly linked list.

INSBEGNODDL(INFO, FORW, BACK, START, AVAIL, LOCA, LOCB, ITEM)

Step 1: [OVERFLOW?] If AVAIL = NULL, then: Write: OVERFLOW, and End.

Step 2: [Remove node from AVAIL list and copy new INFO into node.]
  Set NEW = AVAIL, AVAIL = FORW[AVAIL], INFO[NEW] = ITEM.

Step 3: [Insert node into the beginning of two way list.]
  Set START = NEW, FORW[NEW] = LOCA.
  BACK[NEW] = NULL, BACK[LOCA] = NEW.

Step 4: End.

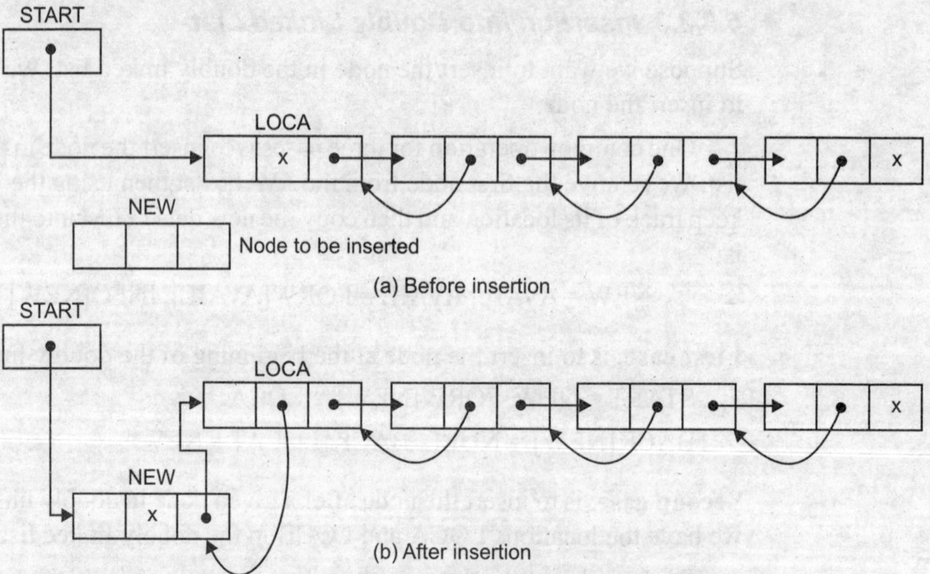

Figure 5.52: Insertion at the beginning of the doubly linked list.

B. Insertion of the node after a given node in the doubly linked list

Algorithm 5.19: To insert new node after a given node in the doubly linked list.

INSGVNNODDL(INFO, FORW, BACK, START, AVAIL, LOCA, LOCB, ITEM)

Step 1: [OVERFLOW?] If AVAIL = NULL, then: Write: OVERFLOW, and End.

Step 2: [Remove node from AVAIL list and copy new INFO into node.]
Set NEW = AVAIL, AVAIL = FORW[AVAIL], INFO[NEW] = ITEM.

Step 3: [Insert node into list.]
Set FORW[LOCA] = NEW, FORW[NEW] = LOCB,
BACK[LOCB] = NEW, BACK[NEW] = LOCA.

Step 4: End.

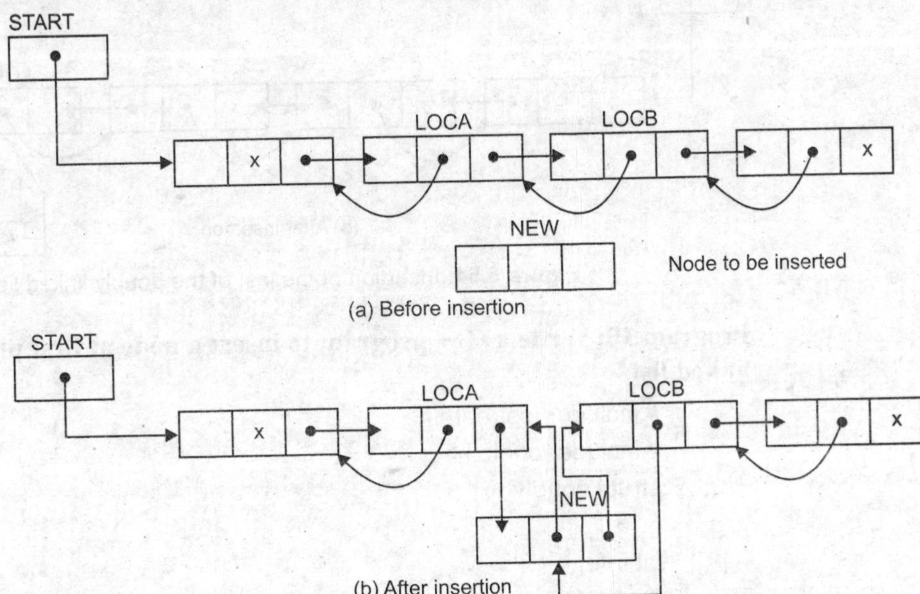

Figure 5.53: Insertion of the node after a given node in the doubly linked list.

C. Insertion at the Last of the Doubly Linked List

Algorithm 5.20: To insert new node in the last of the doubly linked list.

INSLSTNODDL(INFO, FORW, BACK, START, AVAIL, LOCA, LOCB, ITEM)

Step 1: [OVERFLOW?] If AVAIL = NULL, then: Write: OVERFLOW, and End.

Step 2: [Remove node from AVAIL list and copy new INFO into node.]
Set NEW = AVAIL, AVAIL = FORW[AVAIL], INFO[NEW] = ITEM.

Step 3: [Insert node into list.]
Set FORW[LOCA] = NEW, FORW[NEW] = NULL,
BACK[NEW] = LOCA.
Step 4: End.

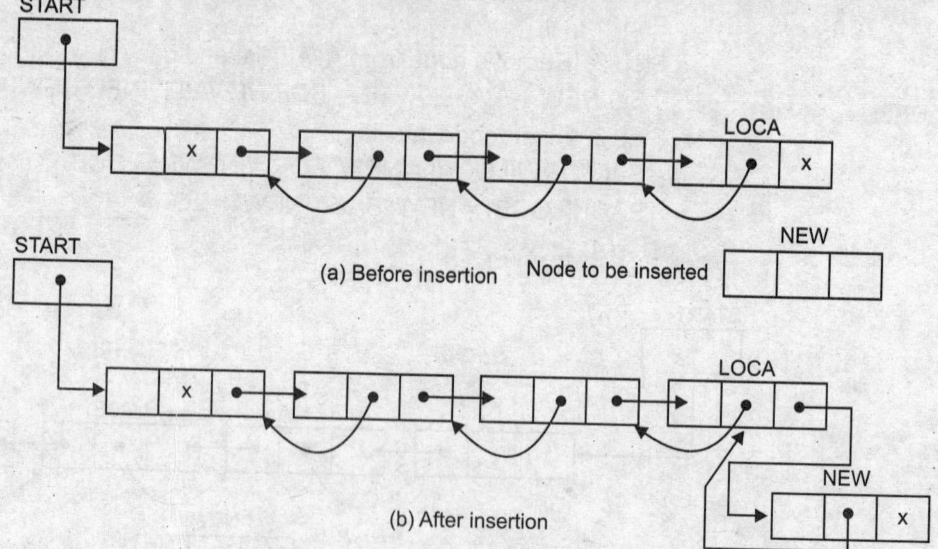

Figure 5.54: Insertion at the last of the doubly linked list.

Program 10: Write a C++ program to insert a node at first place in a doubly linked list

```
# include<iostream.h>
# include<conio.h>
struct doubly
{
int info;
doubly* back;
doubly* front;
};
class doubly_class
{
private:
double* start;
public:
doubly_class ( )
{
start=new doubly;
```

```
start->front=NULL;
start->back=NULL;
start->info=-1;         // header node- can contain other information also
}
void create ( );        // function prototype
void insert_first (int info)
{
doubly* temp=new doubly;
temp-info=info;
temp->front=start->front;
start->front=back=temp;
temp->back=start;
start->front=temp;
}
void display ( );                  //function prototype
};
function definition create ( )
void doubly_class : : create ( )
{
int values;
doubly* new_node=new doubly;
new_node= start;
cout<<"\nRead the info terminated by negative number: \n;
cin>>value;
while (value>=0)
{
new_node->front=new doubly;
new_node->front->back=new_node;
new_node=new_node->front;
new_node->info=value;
new_node->front=NULL;
cin>>value;
}
}
void doubly_class : : display ( )
{
cout<<"\n\nTraversing in the forward direction: \n\n";
doubly* move=start;
do
{
```

```
move=move->front<<"<->";
cout<<move=start;
do
{
move=move->front;
cout<<move->info<<"<->";
}
while (move->front);
cout<<"NULL";
cout<<"\n\nTraversing in the back direction: \n\n";
do
{
cout<<move->info<<"<->;
move=move->back;
}
while (move->back);
cout<<"NULL";
}
void main ( )
{
clrscr ( );
int value;
doubly_class list;
list.create ( );
cout<<"\nBefore any operation:";
list.display ( );
cout<<"\n\nRead the info value of the first node:";
cin>>value;
list.insert_first (value);
cout<<"\nAfter insertion operation:";
list.display ( );
getch ( );
}
```

Output:

Read the info terminated by negative number:

20 10 40 50 70 60 -99

Before any operation:

Traversing in the forward direction:

20<->10<->40<->50<->70<->60<->NULL

Traversing in the back direction:
60<->70<->50<->40<->10<->20<->NULL
Read the info value of the first node: 17
After insertion operation:
Traversing in the forward direction:
17<->20<->10<->40<->50<->70<->60<->NULL
Traversing in the back direction:
60<->70<->50<->40<->10<->20<->17<->NULL

Program 11: Write a C++ program to insert a node at end in a doubly linked list

```
# include<iostream.h>
# include<conio.h>
struct doubly
{
int info;
doubly* back;
doubly* front;
};
class doubly_class
{
private:
double* start;
public:
doubly_class ( )
{
start=new doubly;
start->front=NULL;
start->back=NULL;
start->info=-1;          // header node- can contain other information also
}
void create ( );                        // function prototype
void insert_end(int);
void display ( );                       //function prototype
};
function definition create ( )
void doubly_class : : create ( )
{
int values;
doubly* new_node=new doubly;
```

```
new_node= start;
cout<<"\nRead the info terminated by negative number: \n;
cin>>value;
while (value>=0)
{
new_node->front=new doubly;
new_node->front->back=new_node;
new_node=new_node->front;
new_node->info=value;
new_node->front=NULL;
cin>>value;
}
}
void doubly_class :: insert_end (int info)
{
doubly* temp=new doubly;
temp->info=info;
doubly* move=start;
while (move->front)
move=move->front;
temp->front=NULL;
temp->back=move;
move->front=temp;
}
void doubly_class : : display ( )
{
cout<<"\n\nTraversing in the forward direction: \n\n";
doubly* move=start;
do
{
move=move->front<<"<->";
cout<<move=start;
do
{
move=move->front;
cout<<move->info<<"<->";
}
while (move->front);
cout<<"NULL";
```

```
cout<<"\n\nTraversing in the back direction: \n\n";
do
{
cout<<move->info<<"<->;
move=move->back;
}
while (move->back);
cout<<"NULL";
}
void main ( )
{
clrscr ( );
int value;
doubly_class list;
list.create ( );
cout<<"\nBefore any operation:";
list.display ( );
cout<<"\n\nRead the info value of the last node:";
cin>>value;
list.insert_end (value);
cout<<"\nAfter insertion operation:";
list.display ( );
getch ( );
}
```

Output:

```
Read the info terminated by negative number:
20    50    30    10    70    60    -99
Before any operation:
Traversing in the forward direction:
20<->50<->30<->10<->70<->60<->NULL
Traversing in the back direction:
60<->70<->10<->30<->50<->20<->NULL
Read the info value of the last node: 14
After insertion operation:
Traversing in the forward direction:
20<->50<->30<->10<->70<->60<->14<->NULL
Traversing in the back direction:
14<->60<->70<->10<->30<->50<->20<->NULL
```

Program 12: Write a C++ program to insert a node at the desired position in a doubly linked list

```
# include<iostream.h>
# include<conio.h>
struct doubly
{
int info;
doubly* back;
doubly* front;
};
class doubly_class
{
private:
double* start;
public:
doubly_class ( )
{
start=new doubly;
start->front=NULL;
start->back=NULL;
start->info=-1; // header node- can contain other information also
}
void create ( ); // function prototype
void insert ();
void display ( ); //function prototype
};
function definition create ( )
void doubly_class : : create ( )
{
int values;
doubly* new_node=new doubly;
new_node= start;
cout<<"\nRead the info terminated by negative number: \n;
cin>>value;
while (value>=0)
{
new_node->front=new doubly;
new_node->front->back=new_node;
new_node=new_node->front;
```

```
new_node->info=value;
new_node->front=NULL;
cin>>value;
}
}
void doubly_class : : insert ( )
{
int info, position;
cout<<"\n\nRead the info value of the node to be inserted: ";
cin>>info;
cout<<"Read the position where node is to be inserted: ";
cin>>position;
if (position<=0 | | position>total+1)
{
cout<<"\nInvalid position inputted";
getch ( );
exit (1);
}
doubly* temp=new doubly;
temp->info=info;
if (position= =1)
{
temp->front=start->front;
temp->back=start;
if (temp->front)
start->front->back=temp;
start->front=temp;
}
else
{
int steps=1;
doubly* move=start->front;
while (steps<position-1)
{
move=move->front;
steps++;
}
temp->front=move->front;
temp->back=move;
```

```
if (temp->front)
move->front->back=temp;
move->front=temp;
}total ++;
}
void doubly_class : : display ( )
{
cout<<"\n Total number of nodes:"<<total;
cout<<"\n\nTraversing in the forward direction: \n\n";
doubly* move=start;
do
{
move=move->front<<"<->";
cout<<move=start;
do
{
move=move->front;
cout<<move->info<<"<->";
}
while (move->front);
cout<<"NULL";
cout<<"\n\nTraversing in the back direction: \n\n";
do
{
cout<<move->info<<"<->;
move=move->back;
}
while (move->back);
cout<<"NULL";
}
void main ( )
{
clrscr ( );
int value;
doubly_class list;
list.create ( );
cout<<"\nBefore any operation:";
list.display ( );
list.insert ();
```

```
cout<<"\nAfter insertion operation:";
list.display ( );
getch ( );
}
```

Output:

```
Read the info terminated by negative number:
20    10    50    70    30    -99
Before any operation:
Total number of nodes: 5
Traversing in the forward direction:
20<->10<->50<->70<->30<->NULL
Traversing in the back direction:
30<->70<->50<->10<->20<->NULL
Read the info value of the node to be inserted: 16
Read the position where node is to be inserted: 4
After insertion operation:
Total number of nodes: 6
Traversing in the forward direction:
20<->10<->50<->16<->70<->30<->NULL
Traversing in the back direction:
30<->70<->16<->50<->10<->20<->NULL
```

5.8.3.4 Deletion From Doubly Linked List

Suppose we want to delete a node from two-way list. We have three choices to delete the node.

One common operation for three cases is to delete the node in the doubly linked list. We remove the first node and first node is assign to the AVAIL list that is;

FORW[LOCA] = AVAIL and AVAIL = LOCA

First case, is to delete the beginning node in the doubly linked list.

START = FORW[LOCA], BACK[LOCB]= NULL, START= LOCB.

Second case, is to delete the middle node from the doubly linked list. Suppose we have the locations LOCA,LOCN and LOCB in the doubly linked list.LOCN is the middle location to be delete. We have to set the two pointers:

FORW[LOCA] = LOCB, BACK[LOCB]=LOCA.

Third case, is to delete the last node of the doubly linked list.

FORW[LOCA] = NULL.

A. Deletion at the beginning of the doubly linked list

Algorithm 5.21: To delete the beginning node from doubly linked list.

DELBEGNODDL(INFO, FORW, BACK, START, AVAIL, LOC)

Step 1: [Delete node from two-way list.]

Set START = FORW[LOCA], BACK[LOCB]= NULL, START= LOCB.

Step 2: [Return node to AVAIL list.]

Set FORW[LOCA] = AVAIL and AVAIL = LOCA

Step 3: End.

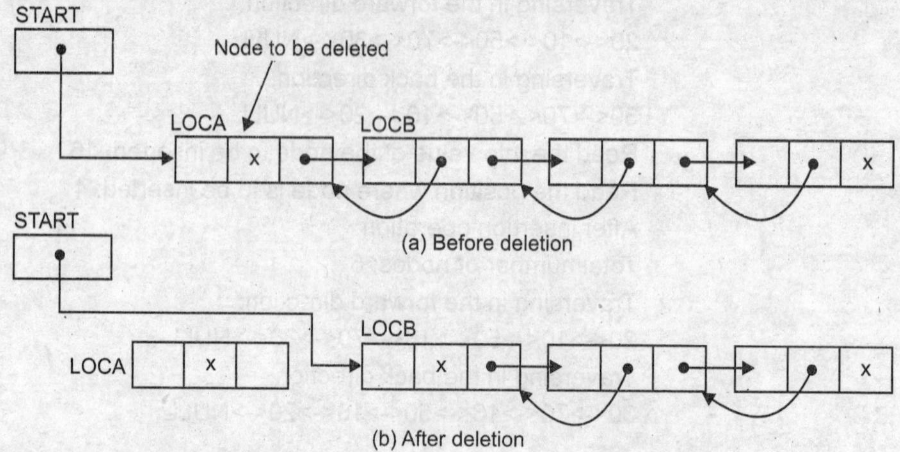

Figure 5.55: Deletion at the beginning of the doubly linked list.

B. Deletion the node after a given node of the doubly linked list

Algorithm 5.22: To delete the node with a given item of information from doubly linked list.

DELGVNNODDL(INFO, FORW, BACK, START, AVAIL, LOC)

Step 1: [Delete node from two-way list.]

Set FORW[LOCA] = LOCB, BACK[LOCB]=LOCA.

Step 2: [Return node to AVAIL list.]

Set FORW[LOCN] = AVAIL and AVAIL = LOCN

Step 3: End.

OR

Step 1: [Delete node from two-way list.]

Set FORW[BACK[LOC]] = BACK[LOC].

Step 2: [Return node to AVAIL list.]

Set FORW[LOC] = AVAIL and AVAIL = LOC

Step 3: End.

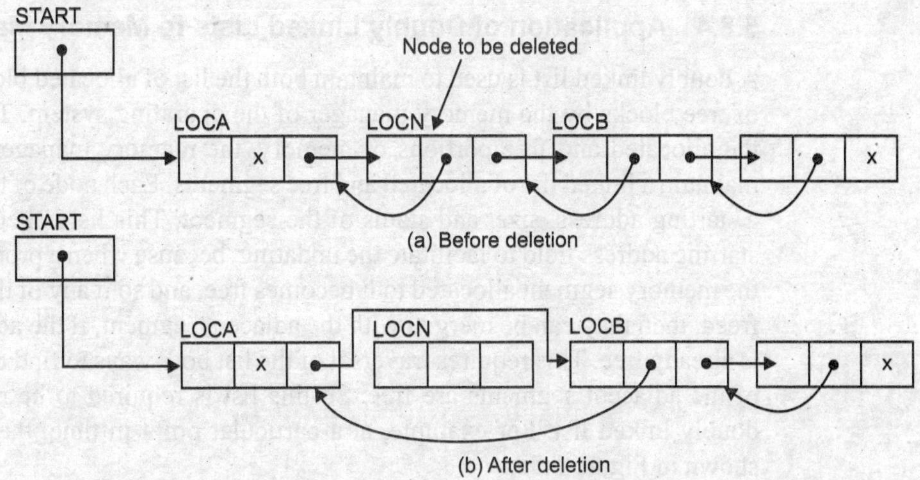

(a) Before deletion

(b) After deletion

Figure 5.56: Deletion the node after a given node of the doubly linked list

C. Deletion at the last of the doubly linked list

Algorithm 5.23: To delete the last node from doubly linked list.

DELLSTNODDL(INFO, FORW, BACK, START, AVAIL, LOC)

Step 1: [Delete node from two-way list.]
 Set FORW[LOCA] = NULL.

Step 2: [Return node to AVAIL list.]
 Set FORW[LOCN] = AVAIL, and AVAIL = LOCN

Step 3: End.

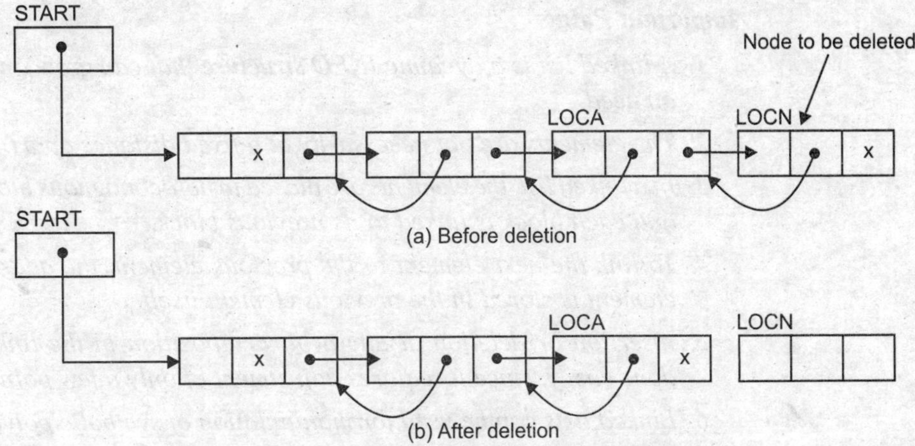

(a) Before deletion

(b) After deletion

Figure 5.57: Deletion at the last of the doubly linked list

5.8.4 Application of Doubly Linked Lists to Memory Management

A doubly linked list is used to maintain both the list of allocated blocks and the list of free blocks by the memory manager of the operating system. To keep track of the allocated and free portions of memory, the memory manager is required to maintain a linked list of allocated and free segments. Each node of this list contains a starting address, size, and status of the segment. This list is kept sorted by the starting address field to facilitate the updating, because when a process terminates, the memory segment allocated to it becomes free, and so if any of the segments are freed, then they can be merged with the adjacent segment, if the adjacent segment is already free. This requires traversal of the list both ways to find out whether any of the adjacent segments are free. So this list is required to be maintained as a doubly linked list. For example, at a particular point in time, the list may be as shown in Figure 5.58.

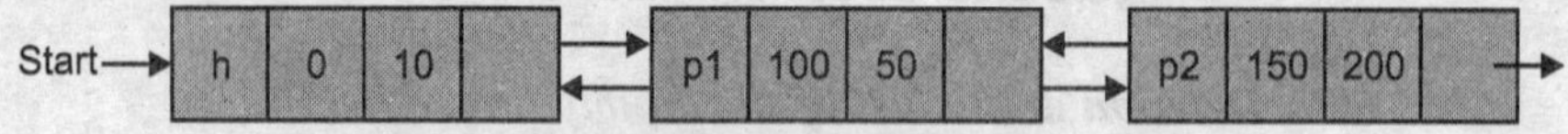

Figure 5.58: Before termination of process p1.

If the process p1 terminates, it is required to be modified as shown in Figure 5.59.

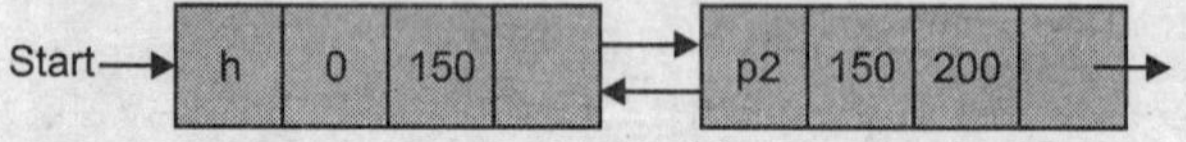

Figure 5.59: After termination of process p1.

Important Points

1. *A linked list is a dynamic INFO structure that can grow and shrink based on need.*
2. *The elements are not necessarily at a fixed distance apart.*
3. *In a linked list, the elements are placed in non-contiguous blocks of memory, and each block is linked to its previous block.*
4. *To link the next element to the previous element, the address of the next element is stored in the previous element itself.*
5. *Insertion or deletion at any arbitrary position in the linked list can be done easily, since it requires adjustment of only a few pointers.*
6. *Linked lists can be used for manipulation of symbolic polynomials.*
7. *A linked list is suitable for representation of sparse matrices.*
8. *A circular list is a list in which the link field of the last node is made to point to the start/first node of the list*

9. *A doubly linked list (DLL) is a linked list in which every node contains two links, called the left link and right link, respectively.*
10. *The left link of the node in a DLL is made to point to the previous node, whereas the right link is made to point to the next node.*
11. *A DLL can be traversed in both directions.*
12. *Having two pointers in a DLL provides safety, because even if one of the pointers get corrupted, the node still remains linked.*
13. *Deleting a particular node from a list, therefore, does not require keeping track of the previous node in a DLL.*

5.9 HEADER LINKED LISTS

A header linked list is a linked list which always contains a special node, called the header node, at the beginning of the list. The following are two kinds of widely used header lists:

1. A grounded header list is a header list where last node contains null pointer
2. Circular header list is a header list where the last node points back to the header node.

Figure 5.60 and 5.61 contains the diagram of these header lists.

The list pointer start always points to the header node. According to this, LINK[START]=NULL indicates that a grounded header list is empty, and LINK[START]= START indicates that a circular header list is empty.

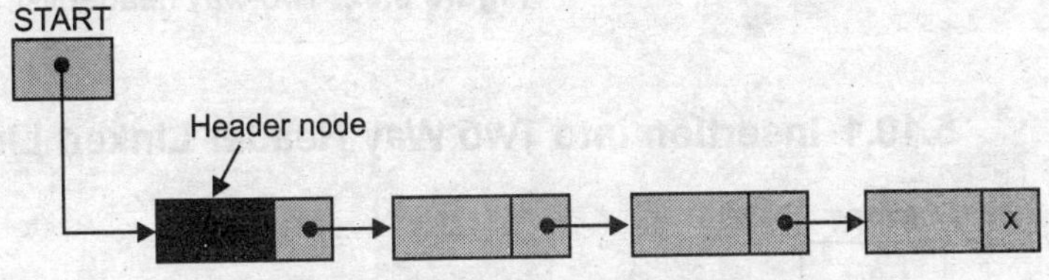

Figure 5.60: Grounded Header list

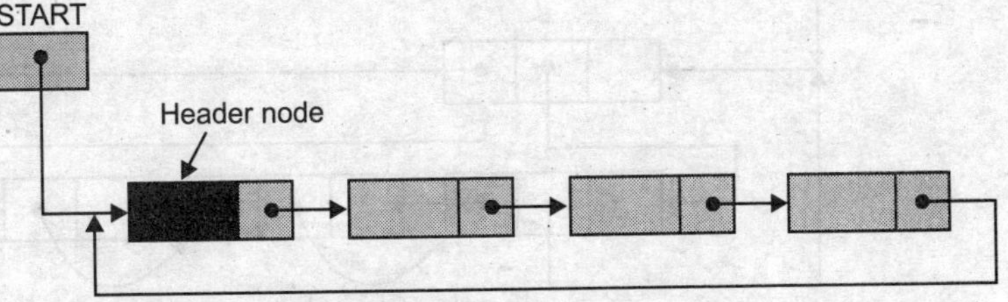

Figure 5.61: Circular Header list

Circular header list are frequently used instead of ordinary linked lists because many operations are much easier to state and implement using header list. This comes from two properties of circular header lists:

1. The null pointer is not used and hence all pointers contain valid addresses
2. Every ordinary node has predecessor, so the first node may not required a special case.

5.10 TWO-WAY HEADER LISTS

The advantages of a two-way list and a circular header list may be combined into a two-way circular header list as shown in Figure below. The list is circular because the two end nodes point back to the header node. Observe that such a two-way list requires only one list pointer variable START, which points to the header node. This is because the two pointers in the header node point to the two ends of the list.

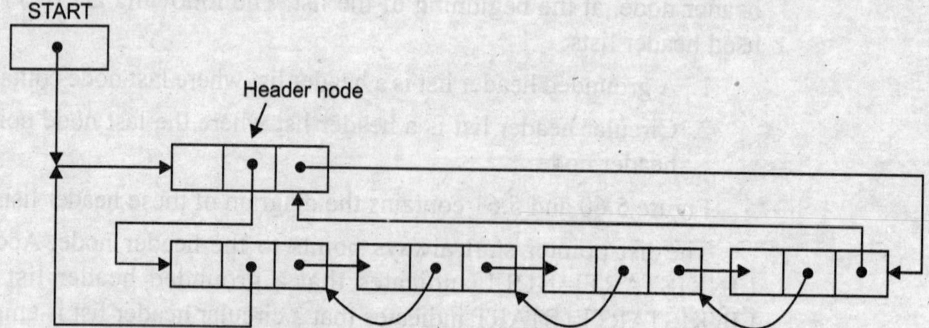

Figure 5.62: Two-way header list.

5.10.1 Insertion into Two Way Header Linked List

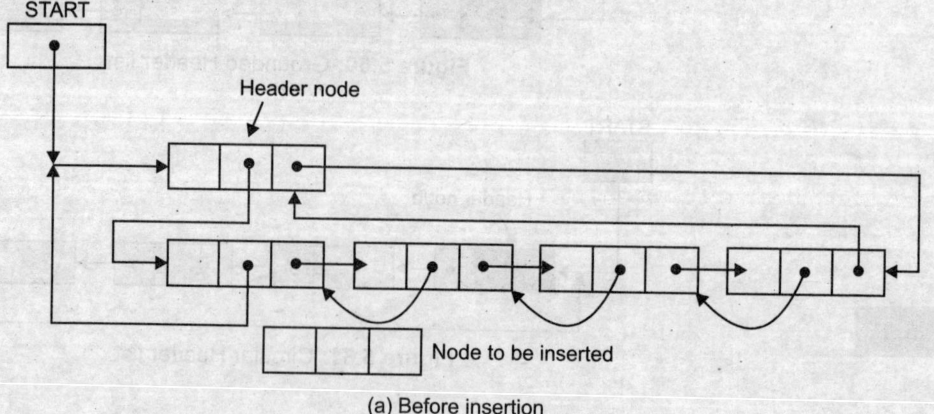

(a) Before insertion

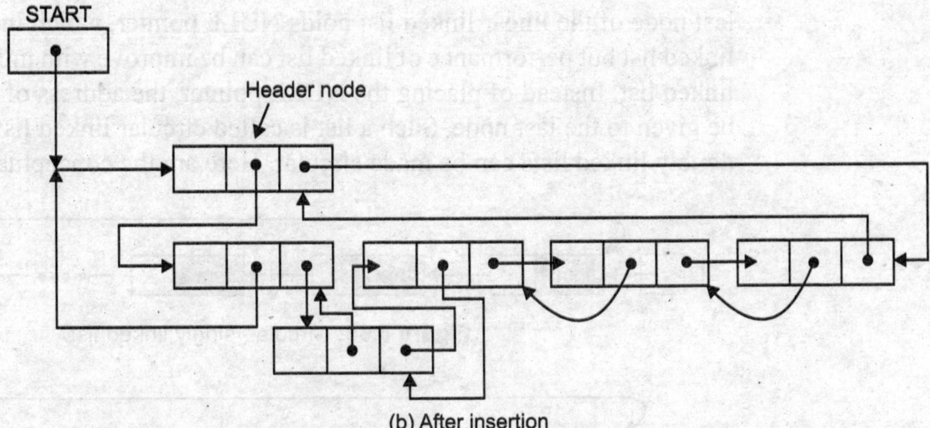

Figure 5.63: Insertion into two way header linked list

5.10.2 Deletion From Two Way Header Linked List

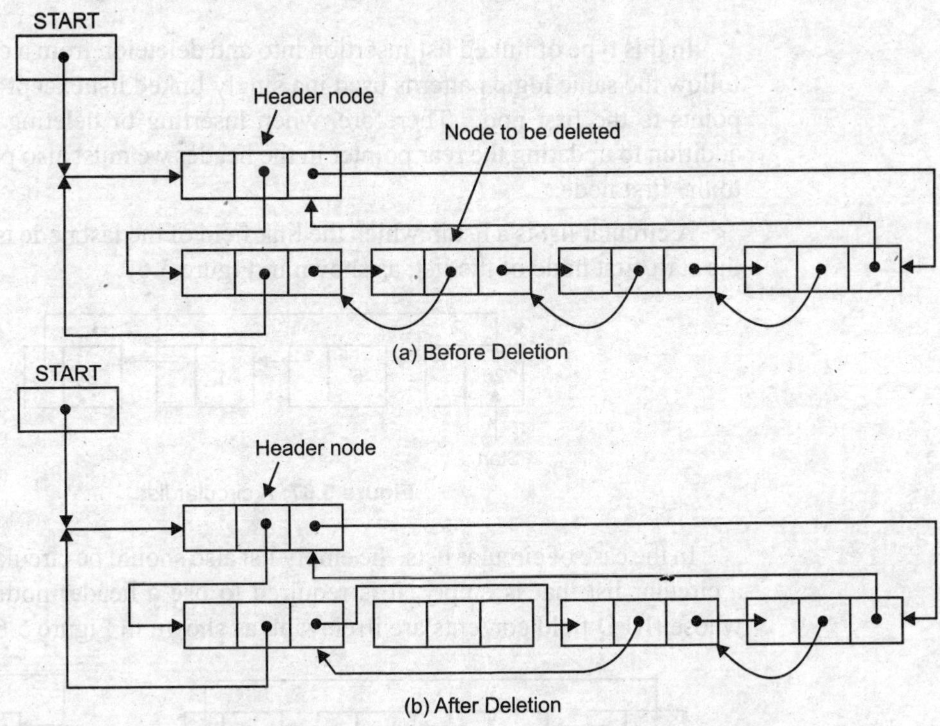

Figure 5.64: Deletion from two way header linked list

5.11 CIRCULAR LINKED LISTS

In circular linked list the last node points to header node. The linear linked list can be converted to circular linked list by linking the last node to the first node. The last node of the linear linked list holds NULL pointer, which indicates end of the linked list but performance of linked list can be improve with minor changes in the linked list. Instead of placing the NULL pointer, the address of the first node can be given to the last node, Such a list is called circular linked list. Both singly and doubly linked lists can be made circular. Here are the conceptual pictures:

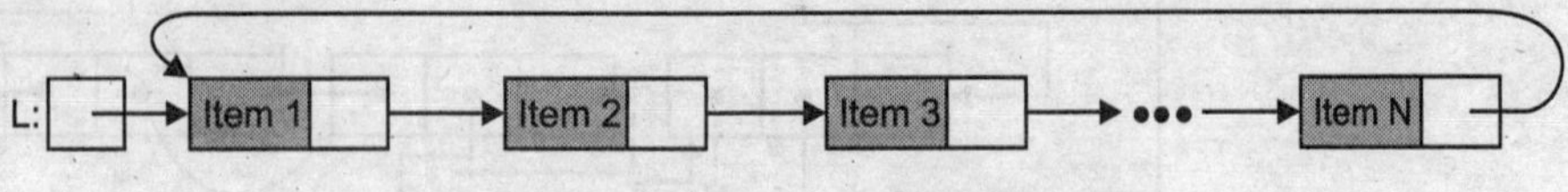

Figure 5.65: Circular, singly linked list.

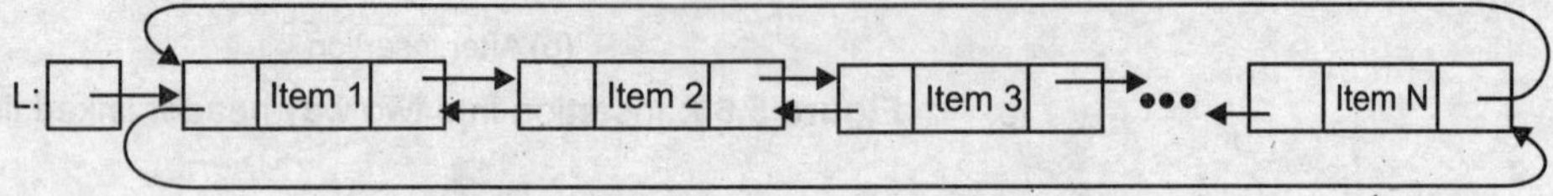

Figure 5.66: Circular, doubly linked list.

In this type of linked list,insertion into and deleteion from a circular linked list follow the same logic patterns used ina singly linked list except that the last node points to the first node. Therefore, when inserting or deleting the last node, in addition to updating the rear pointer in the header we must also point the link field to the first node.

A circular list is a list in which the link field of the last node is made to point to the start/first node of the list, as shown in Figure 5.67.

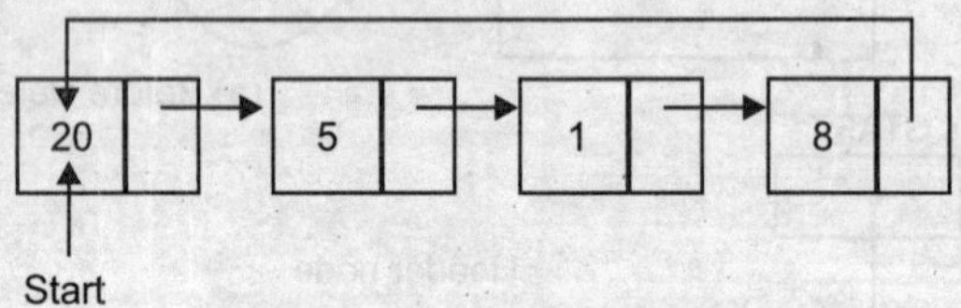

Figure 5.67: A circular list.

In the case of circular lists, the empty list also should be circular. So to represent a circular list that is empty, it is required to use a header node or a head-node whose INFO field contents are irrelevant, as shown in Figure 5.68.

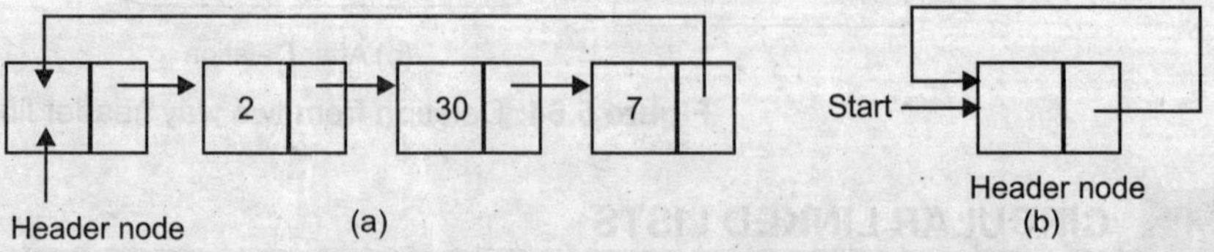

Figure 5.68: (a) A circular list with head node, (b) an empty circular list.

5.11.1 Operations on Circular Linked List

5.11.1.1 Traversing A Circular Linked List

This algorithm traverse the circular linked list.

Algorithm 5.24: Traversing a circular header list

TRAVERSECL (INFO, LINK, START, P)

Let LIST be a circular header list in memory. This algorithm traverses LIST, applying an operation PROCESS to each node of LIST.

Step 1: Set P = LINK[START]. [Initializes the pointer P.]

Step 2: Repeat Steps 3 and 4 while P ≠ START.

Step 3: Apply PROCESS to INFO[P].

Step 4: Set P = LINK[P]. [P now points to the next node.]

[End of Step 2 loop.]

Step 5: End.

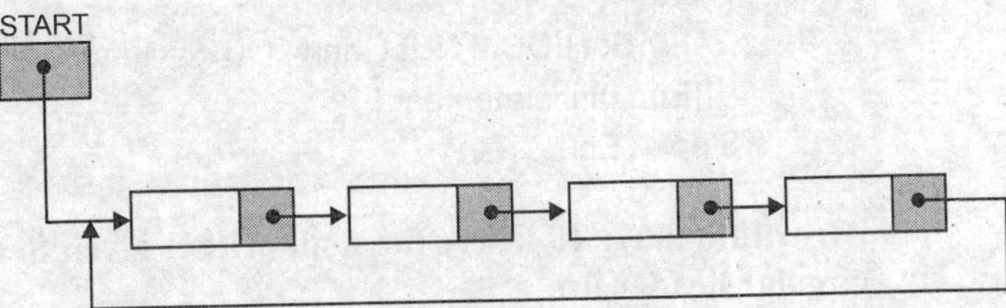

Figure 5.69: Traversing circular linked list.

5.11.1.2 Searching In Circular Linked List

Algorithm 5.25: To search element from circular header linked list

SRCHCL (INFO, LINK, START, ITEM, LOC)

LIST is a circular header list in memory. This algorithm finds the location LOC of the node where ITEM first appears in LIST or sets LOC = NULL.

Step 1: Set P = LINK[START].

Step 2: Repeat Steps while INFO[P] ≠ ITEM and P ≠ START

Set P = LINK[P]. [P now points to the next node.] [End of loop.]

Step 3: If INFO[P] = ITEM, then

Set LOC = P.

Else

Set LOC = NULL.

[End of If statement.]

Step 4: End.

5.11.1.3 Insertion in Circular Linked List

Algorithm 5.26: To find the location LOC of the specified node from a circular linked list.

FINDLOC (INFO, LINK, START, ITEM, LOC, LOCP)

This algorithm find the location LOC of the first node N which contains ITEM and also the location LOCP of the node preceding N when LIST is an ordinary linked list. The following is such an algorithm when LIST is a circular header list.

Step 1: Set SAVE = START and P = LINK [START]. [Initializes pointers.]

Step 2: Repeat Steps while INFO [P] ≠ ITEM and P ≠ START

Set SAVE = P and P = LINK [P]. [Updates pointers.]

[End of loop.]

Step 3: If INFO [P] = ITEM, then

Set LOC = P and LOCP = SAVE.

Else

Set LOC = NULL and LOCP = SAVE

[End of if statement.]

Step 4: End.

Algorithm 5.27: To insert the node with a given item of information from circular header list.

INSNODCHL(INFO, LINK, START, AVAIL, ITEM)

This algorithm insert the first node N which contains ITEM when LIST is an circular header list.

Step 1: [Use algorithm 5.26 to find the location of N and its preceding node.]

Call FINDLOC (INFO, LINK, START, ITEM, LOC, LOCP).

Step 2: [Use algorithm 5.4 to insert the node into a cicular linked list]

Call INSGVNNOD (INFO, LINK, START, AVAIL, LOC, ITEM)

Step 3: End.

A. Insertion of element at the beginning of the circular linked list

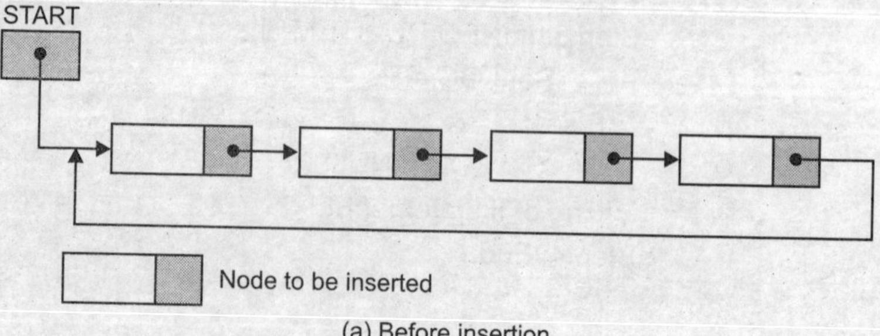

(a) Before insertion

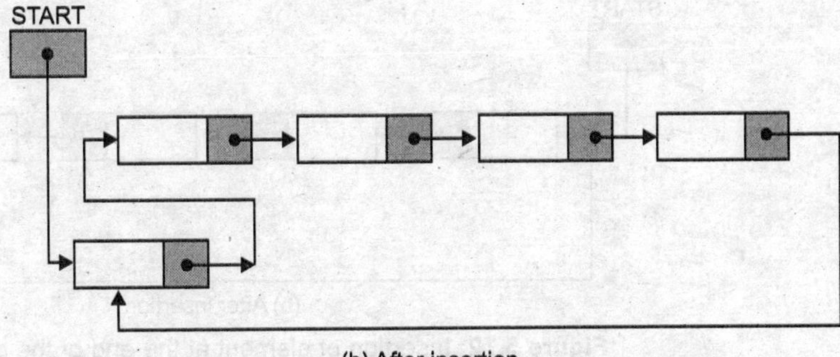

(b) After insertion

Figure 5.70: Insertion of element at the beginning of the circular linked list

B. Insertion of element at a given position in the circular linked list

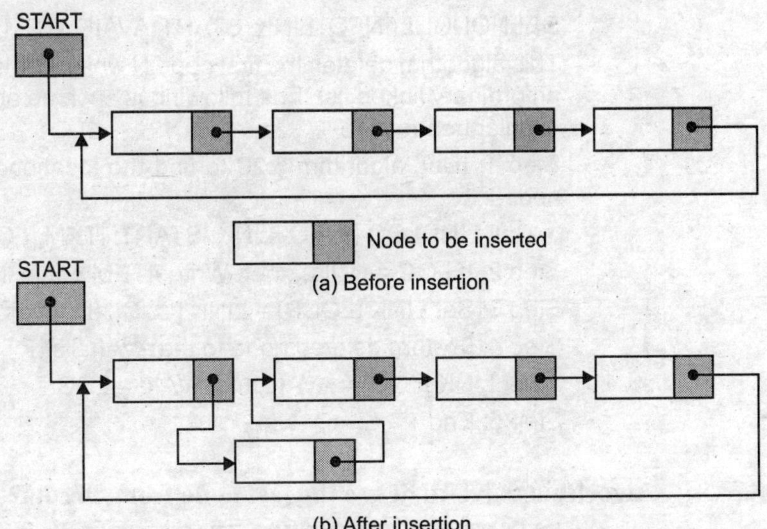

(a) Before insertion

(b) After insertion

Figure 5.71: Insertion of element at a given position in the circular linked list.

C. Insertion of element at the end of the circular linked list

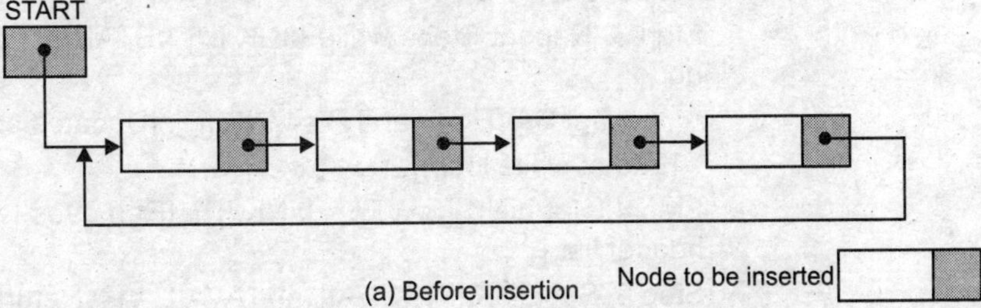

(a) Before insertion

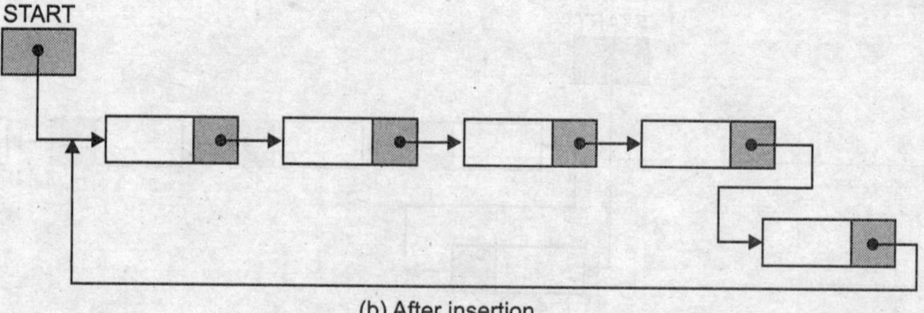

(b) After insertion

Figure 5.72: Insertion of element at the end of the circular linked list.

5.11.1.4 Deletion from Circular Linked List

Algorithm 5.28: To delete the node with a given item of information from circular header list.

DELNODCHL(INFO, LINK, START, AVAIL, ITEM)

This algorithm deletes the first node N which contains ITEM when LIST is an ordinary linked list. The following is such an algorithm when LIST is a circular header list.

Step 1: [Use algorithm 5.26 to find the location of N and its preceding node.]

Call FINDLOC (INFO, LINK, START, ITEM, LOC, LOCP).

Step 2: If LOC = NULL, then Write: ITEM not in list, and End.

Step 3: Set LINK [LOCP] = LINK [LOC]. [Deletes node.]

Step 4: [Return deleted node to the AVAIL list.]

Set LINK [LOC] = AVAIL and AVAIL = LOC.

Step 5: End.

Algorithm 5.29: To delete the last node from circular header list.

DELLSTNOD (INFO, LINK, START, AVAIL)

This algorithm deletes the last node from the header list.

Step 1: [List is empty?] If LINK [START] = NULL, then

Write: UNDERFLOW, and End.

Step 2: Set P = LINK [START] and SAVE = START. [Initializes pointers P.]

Step 3: Repeat Steps while LINK [P] ^{1} START [Traverses list go to last node.]

Set SAVE = P and P = LINK [P]. [Updates pointers SAVE and P.]

[End of while loop.]

Step 4: Set LINK [SAVE] = LINK [P]. [Removes last node from circular header list.]

Step 5: Set LINK [P] = AVAIL and AVAIL = P. [Returns node to AVAIL list.]

Step 6: End.

A. Deletion of beginning node from the circular linked list

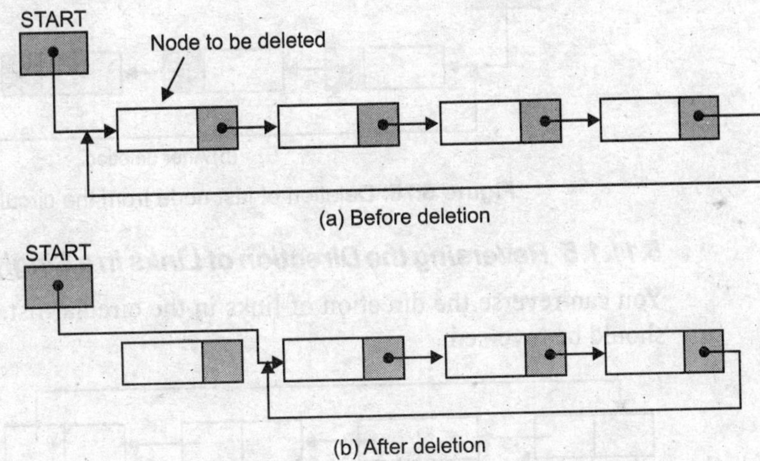

Figure 5.73: Deletion of beginning node from the circular linked list.

B. Deletion of node after a given node from the circular linked list

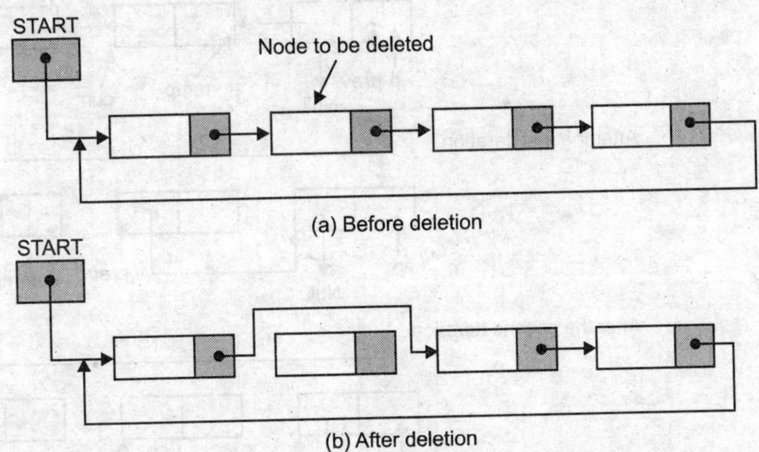

Figure 5.74: Deletion of node after a given node from the circular linked list.

C. Deletion of last node from the circular linked list

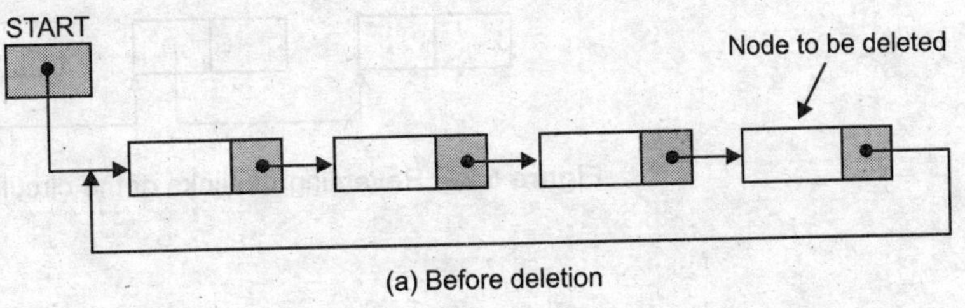

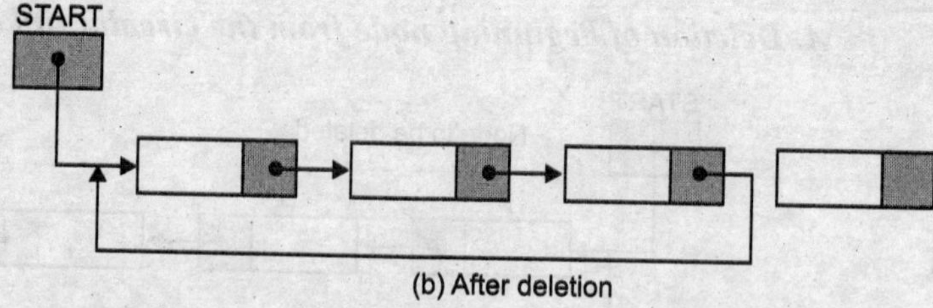

(b) After deletion

Figure 5.75: Deletion of last node from the circular linked list

5.11.1.5 Reversing the Direction of Links in a Singly Linked Circular List

You can reverse the direction of links in the circular list. If you do so, each link should be reversed.

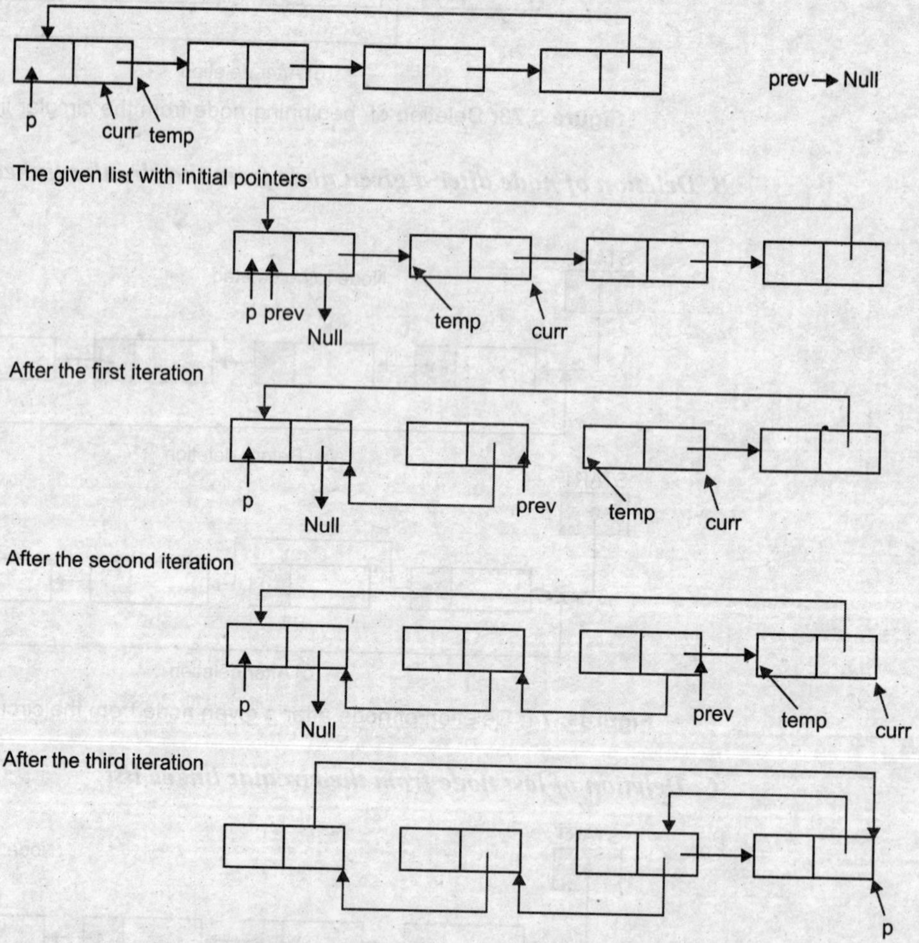

p curr temp prev → Null

The given list with initial pointers

p prev Null temp curr

After the first iteration

p Null prev temp curr

After the second iteration

p Null prev temp curr

After the third iteration

p

Figure 5.76: Reversing the links of the circular linked list

To reverse the links of a singly linked circular list, the list is required to be traversed from the start node until a node is encountered whose link points to the start node (that is, the last node in the list). For this, it is required to maintain the pointers to the current node and the previous node. An additional temporary pointer pointing to the current node is also required to be maintained. Initially, the current, temporary, and previous pointers are set as follows:

1. Set the current as well as the temporary pointer to the start pointer.
2. Set the previous pointer to NULL.
3. The pointers are manipulated in each iteration as follows:
   (i) Advance the current pointer to make it point to the next node.
   (ii) Set the link field of the node pointed to by the temporary pointer to the value of the previous pointer.
   (iii) Make the previous pointer point to the node pointed to by the temporary pointer.
   (iv) Make the temporary pointer point to the node pointed to by the current pointer.
   (v) When the last node is encountered, its link field is made to point to the previous node. After that, the link field of the node pointed to by the start pointer (first node) is made to point to this last node. And the start pointer is made to point to this last node. These manipulations are shown in the following diagrams.

5.11.1.6 Merging oif Two Circular Lists

You can merge two lists into one list. In order to merge or concatenate the two non-empty circular lists pointed to by p and q, it is required to make the start of the resultant list p. Then the list pointed to by p is required to be traversed until its end, and the link field of the last node must become the pointer q. After that, the list pointed to by q is required to be traversed until its end, and the link field of the last node is required to be made p.

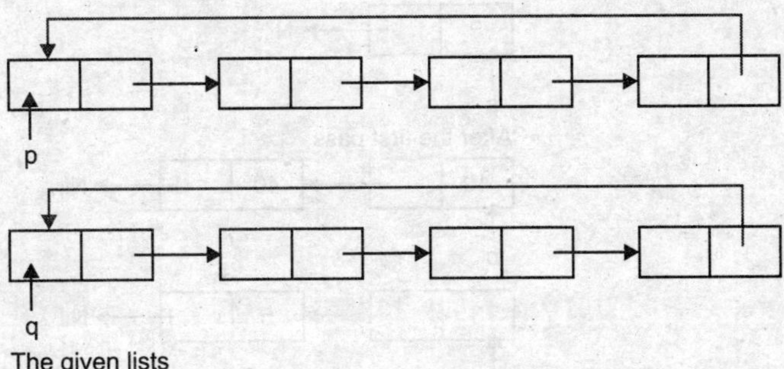

The given lists

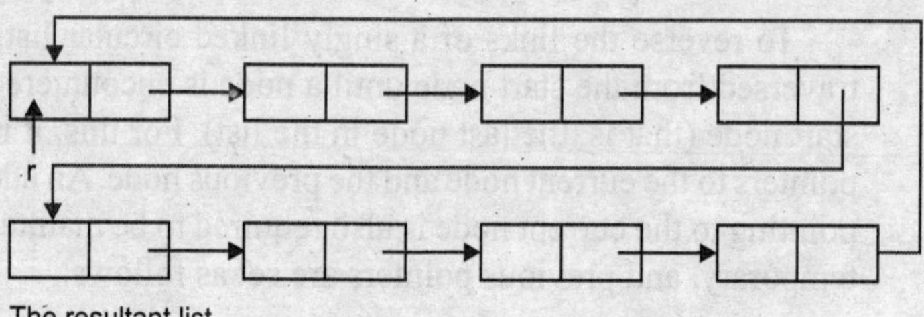

Figure 5.77: Merging of two circular lists

5.12 SORTED LINKED LISTS

To sort a linked list, first we traverse the list searching for the node with a minimum INFO value. Then we remove that node and append it to another list which is initially empty. We repeat this process with the remaining list until the list becomes empty, and at the end, we return a pointer to the beginning of the list to which all the nodes are moved.

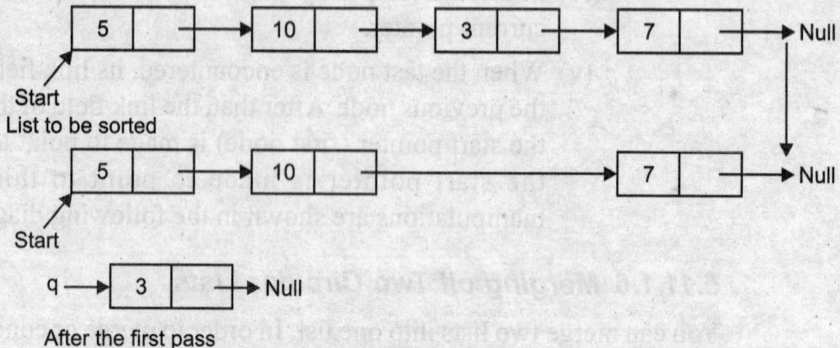

Figure 5.78: Sorting of a linked list.

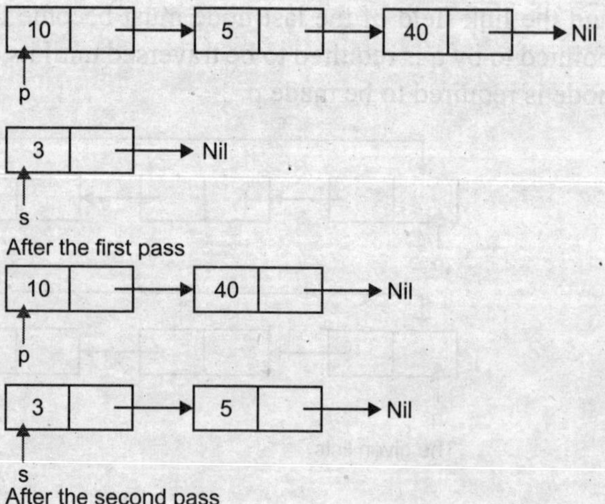

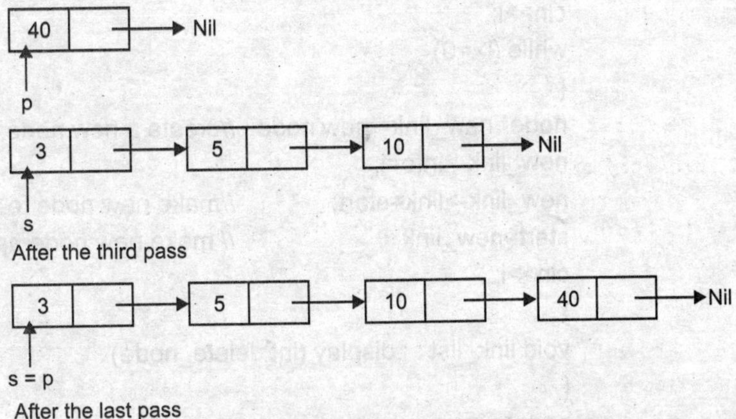

Figure 5.79: Sorting of a linked list.

Program 13: Write a C++ program to sort a linked list using selection sort method.

```
# include<iostream.h>
# include<conio.h>
struct node
{
int info;                    //info field
node* link;                  //pointer to the link node
};
class link_list
{
private:
node* start;
public:
link_list ( )                //constructor
{
start=NULL; //initially the list has no node
}
void add_info ( );                //function prototype
void display (int);               //function prototype
void sort( );                     //function prototype
}; //end of class
void link_list : : add_info ( )
{
int i;
cout<<"Read the info terminated by negative number\n;
```

```
cin>>i;
while (i>=0)
{
node* new_link= new node;  //create a new node;
new_link->info=i;
new_link->link=start;       //make new node to point to the first node
start=new_link;             // make new node as the first node in the list
cin>>i;
}
void link_list : : display (int delete_node)
{
node* move= start;
node* temp;
while (move)
{
cout<<move->info<<"->";          //display the info
temp=move;
move=move->link;                 //move to link node
if(delete_node)
delete (temp);
}
cout <<"NULL";
}
void link_list : : sort ( )              // employs selection sort method
{
node* top=start;
while (top->link !=NULL)
{
int min=top->info;
node* move=top->link;
node* min_node;
while (move ! =NULL)
{
if (move->info <min)
{
min=move->info;
min_node=move;
}
move=move->link;
```

```
}
if (min != top->info)          // checks if node with minimum info found
{
int temp=top->info;
top->info =min;
min_node->info=temp;
}
top=top->link;
}
}
void main ( )
{
clrscr ( );
link_list link;
link.add_info ( );
cout<<"\nInputted link list before sorting is: \n\n";
link.display (0);
link.sort ( );
cout<<"\n\nInputted link list after sorting is: \n\n";
link.display (1);
getch ( );
}
Output:
Read the info terminated by negative number
24    15    37    29    47    30    80    25    -99
Inputted link list before sorting is:
25->80->30->47->29->37->15->24->NULL
Inputted link list after sorting is:
15->24->25->29->30->37->47->80->NULL
```

5.13 ENDOGENOUS / EXOGENOUS LISTS

Endogenous lists have the INFO stored in the structure's KEY. The KEY is INFO stored **within** the structure.

Exogenous lists have the INFO stored **outside** the structure. Instead of a KEY, the structure has a pointer to the INFO in memory. Exogenous lists do not require INFO to be moved when individual cells are moved in a list; only the pointers to INFO must be changed. This can save considerable cost when dealing with large INFO in each cell. Another benefit of exogenous lists is many cells can point to the same INFO. Again, this may be useful depending on the application.

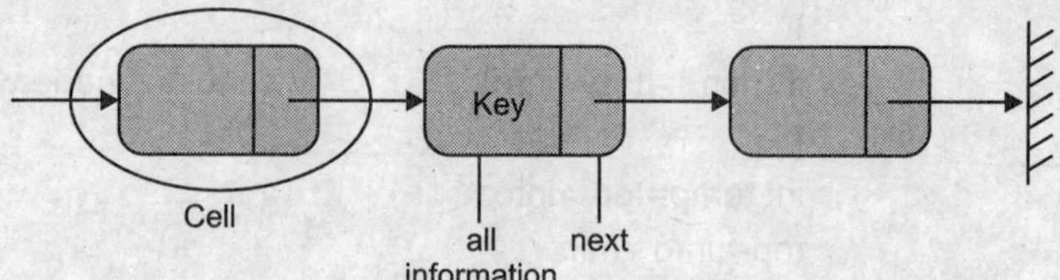

Figure 5.80: Exogenous lists

Here are example declarations of endogenous and exogenous structures:

```
struct endogenous
{
INFO_type key,
struct endogenous * next
};

struct exogenous
{
INFO_type * INFO,
struct exogenous * next
};
```

5.14 ADVANTAGES AND DISADVANTAGES OF USING LINKED LIST OVER ARRAY

Linked lists have several advantages over arrays. For one thing, a linked list allows a new element to be inserted or deleted in any position, with a constant number of operations (changing a couple of pointers). Linked lists can also save memory in applications that need one or more lists of unpredictable size, since the total space used will be proportional to the number of elements actually present in all lists (as opposed to the number of lists times the maximum size of each list).

Further memory savings can be achieved, in certain cases, by sharing the same tail elements among two or more lists. In this way, one can add new elements to the front of the list while keeping a reference to both the new and the old versions — which provides the simplest example of a persistent INFO structure.

On the other hand, compared to an array, the disadvantage of a linked list is that it only allows sequential access to elements, and only in one direction (from front to back). In particular, when removing or inserting an element in the middle of the list, one needs to know the address of the preceding element.

Another disadvantage of linked lists is the extra storage needed for the address fields, which often makes them impractical for lists of small INFO items such as characters or boolean values. Even more significant is the time cost of allocating memory separately for each new element (and, in some systems, of locating and recycling elements that cannot be reached; see garbage collection).

There are a number of techniques to reduce this overhead, such as using a free list or memory pool, storing the INFO itself inside the nodes, and CDR coding.The items in a linked list do not have to be stored in contiguous memory locations like an array.

5.14.1 Arrays vs Linked Lists

Arrays

1. Better for random access to any INFO value
2. Better if number of elements is known and doesn't vary much

Linked Lists

1. Better for additions and removals (other INFO elements do not need to be moved)
2. Better if number of elements varies greatly and is not known at runtime

5.14.2 Similarities between Linked List and Array

Both are used to store a sequence of similar INFO. Both are referred by the location of the first INFO/node.

5.14.3 Differences between Linked List and Array

Array INFO is ALWAYS continuous in memory, while link list nodes can be in anywhere and any order in the memory. Array's elements are accessed directly from the "distance" from the address to the first element. Linked list INFO is accessed indirectly. Each node will hold the location of the next node. To go to a particular element, we have to travel from node to node until we reach the node of interest.

When comparing the sequence implementations using linked lists and using arrays, we should consider:

- space requirements
- time requirements
- ease of implementation

In terms of space, each implementation has its advantages and disadvantages:

- In the linked-list implementation, one pointer must be stored for every item in the sequence, while the array stores only the items themselves.
- On the other hand, the space used for a linked list is always proportional to the number of items in the list. This is not necessarily true for the array

implementation as described: if a lot of items are added to a sequence and then removed, the size of the array can be arbitrarily greater than the number of items in the sequence. However, we could fix this problem by modifying the remove current operation to shrink the array when it becomes too empty.

In terms of time:

- The array implementation requires O(N) worst-case time to add or remove an item with N items, because existing items need to be moved.
- In contrast, adding and removing items in a linked list can be implemented to require only O(1) time (if we maintain pointers to the last node in the list, and the node before the current one, as well as a pointer to the current node).

In terms of ease of implementation:

Straightforward implementations of both the array and linked-list versions seem reasonably easy. However, the methods for the linked-list version seem to require more special cases, and achieving O(1) times for adding and removing items in the linked-list version requires maintaining extra pointers (to the last node and to the node before the current one).

Good Points

Adding elements early in a linked list is cheaper than in a Vector since we do not need to move anything to make room for the new element. If we search for a value, on average we need to search half the list to find the value or to determine that it is not in a list so this is better than an unsorted vector.

Bad Points

There is no direct access to elements given an index as there is with vectors. To find an element by position, we need to start at the beginning of the list and count nodes as we walk the list. Adding nodes towards the end of a linked list is expensive because we need to walk the list to get to the spot where the addition will occur.

Linked lists often require more memory than Vectors. Each value in a linked list requires additional memory to hold a pointer. In a Vector, there may be wasted space due to unused capacity. The closer our vector is to full, the less wasted space there is.

5.14.4 Comparison of Linked List Variations

The major disadvantage of doubly linked lists (over singly linked lists) is that they require more space (every node has two pointer fields instead of one). Also, the code to manipulate doubly linked lists needs to maintain the *prev* fields as well as the *next* fields; the more fields that have to be maintained, the more chance there is for errors.

The major advantage of doubly linked lists is that they make some operations (like the removal of a given node, or a right-to-left traversal of the list) more efficient.

The major advantage of circular lists (over non-circular lists) is that they eliminate some special-case code for some operations. Also, some applications lead naturally to circular list representations. For example, a computer network might best be modeled using a circular list.

5.15 UTILITY OF LINKED LIST IMPLEMENTATIONS

1. Stacks can easily be implemented as a linked list. One needs a pointer to the top of the stack (which is the front of the list).

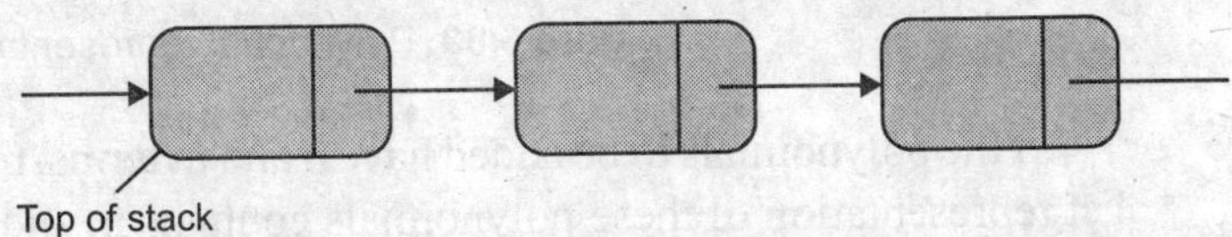

Figure 5.81: Stacks implemented using a linked list

2. Queues can easily be implemented as a linked list as well. One needs a pointer to the front of the queue (which is the front of the list); as well, one needs a pointer to the rear of the queue (which is the end of the list).

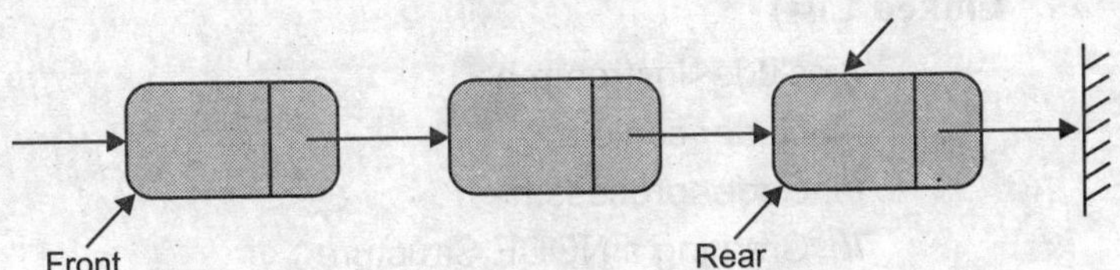

Figure 5.82: Queues implemented using a linked list

It is better, however, to implement a queue as a circular list. This circular list has a pointer to the list pointing at the **rear** rather than the front of the list.

3. Concatenating sublists can easily be done with a linked list. Conversely, concatenating sublists with an array implementation is expensive.
4. Referencing sublists with a linked list implementation is expensive. Conversely, sublists can be referenced easily with an array implementation.

5.16 POLYNOMIAL REPRESENTATION

One of the problems that a linked list can deal with is manipulation of symbolic polynomials. By symbolic, we mean that a polynomial is viewed as a list of coefficients and exponents. For example, the polynomial

$$3x^2 + 2x + 4$$

can be viewed as list of the following pairs

(3,2),(2,1),(4,0)

Therefore, we can use a linked list in which each node will have three fields, as shown in Figure 5.83.

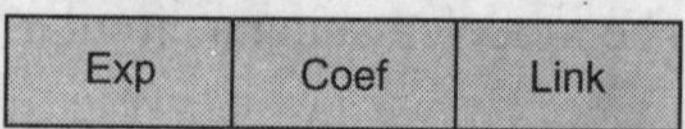

A polynomial $10x^4 + 5x^2 + 1$ can be represented as shown here:

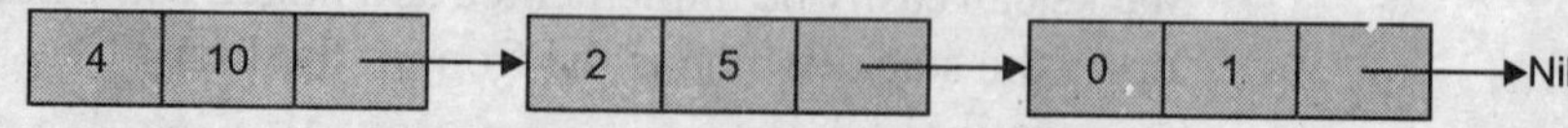

Figure 5.83: Polynomial representation

If the polynomials to be added have n and m terms, respectively, then the linked list representation of these polynomials contains m and n terms, respectively.

Since polyadd traverses each of these lists, sequentially, the maximum number of iterations that polyadd will make will not be more than m + n. So the computation time of polyadd is O(m + n).

Program 14: Write a C++ program to add and subtract two polynomials (Using Linked List)

```
#include<iostream.h>
#include<conio.h>
#include<process.h>
//  Creating a NODE Structure
struct node
{
int coe,exp;        // data
struct node *next; // link to next node and previous node
};
// Creating a class Polynomial
class polynomial
{
struct node *start,*ptrn,*ptrp;
public:
void get_poly(); // to get a polynomial
void show();       // show
void add(polynomial p1,polynomial p2); // Add two polynomials
void subtract(polynomial p1,polynomial p2); //Subtract2 polynomials
};
```

```
void polynomial::get_poly()    // Get Polynomial
{
char c='y';
ptrn=ptrp=start=NULL;
while(c=='y' || c=='Y')
{
ptrn=new node;
ptrp->next=ptrn;
if(start==NULL)
start=ptrn;
ptrp=ptrn;
cout<<"Enter the coefficient: ";
cin>>ptrn->coe;
cout<<"Enter the exponent: ";
cin>>ptrn->exp;
ptrn->next=NULL;
cout<<"Enter y to add more nodes: ";
cin>>c;
}
return;
}
void polynomial::show()  // Show Polynomial
{
struct node *ptr;
ptr=start;
while(ptr!=NULL)
{
cout<<ptr->coe<<"X^"<<ptr->exp<<" + ";
ptr=ptr->next;
}
cout<<"  ";
}
void polynomial::add(polynomial p1,polynomial p2)  // Add Polynomials
{
struct node *p1ptr,*p2ptr;
int coe,exp;
ptrn=ptrp=start=NULL;
p1ptr=p1.start;
p2ptr=p2.start;
```

```
while(p1ptr!=NULL && p2ptr!=NULL)
{
if(p1ptr->exp==p2ptr->exp) // If coefficients are equal
{
coe=p1ptr->coe+p2ptr->coe;
exp=p1ptr->exp;
p1ptr=p1ptr->next;
p2ptr=p2ptr->next;
}
else if(p1ptr->exp>p2ptr->exp)
{
coe=p1ptr->coe;
exp=p1ptr->exp;
p1ptr=p1ptr->next;
}
else if(p1ptr->exp<p2ptr->exp)
{
coe=p2ptr->coe;
exp=p2ptr->exp;
p2ptr=p2ptr->next;
}
ptrn=new node;
if(start==NULL)
start=ptrn;
ptrn->coe=coe;
ptrn->exp=exp;
ptrn->next=NULL;
ptrp->next=ptrn;
ptrp=ptrn;
} // End of While
if(p1ptr==NULL)
{
while(p2ptr!=NULL)
{
coe=p2ptr->coe;
exp=p2ptr->exp;
p2ptr=p2ptr->next;
ptrn=new node;
if(start==NULL)
```

```
start=ptrn;
ptrn->coe=coe;
ptrn->exp=exp;
ptrn->next=NULL;
ptrp->next=ptrn;
ptrp=ptrn;
}
}
else if(p2ptr==NULL)
{
while(p1ptr!=NULL)
{
coe=p1ptr->coe;
exp=p1ptr->exp;
p1ptr=p1ptr->next;
ptrn=new node;
if(start==NULL)
start=ptrn;
ptrn->coe=coe;
ptrn->exp=exp;
ptrn->next=NULL;
ptrp->next=ptrn;
ptrp=ptrn;
}
}
} // End of addition
// Subtract two polynomials
void polynomial::subtract(polynomial p1,polynomial p2) // Subtract
{
struct node *p1ptr,*p2ptr;
int coe,exp;
ptrn=ptrp=start=NULL;
p1ptr=p1.start;
p2ptr=p2.start;
while(p1ptr!=NULL && p2ptr!=NULL)
{
if(p1ptr->exp==p2ptr->exp) // If coefficients are equal
{
coe=p1ptr->coe-p2ptr->coe;
```

```
exp=p1ptr->exp;
p1ptr=p1ptr->next;
p2ptr=p2ptr->next;
}
else if(p1ptr->exp>p2ptr->exp)
{
coe=p1ptr->coe;
exp=p1ptr->exp;
p1ptr=p1ptr->next;
}
else if(p1ptr->exp<p2ptr->exp)
{
coe=0-p2ptr->coe;
exp=p2ptr->exp;
p2ptr=p2ptr->next;
}
ptrn=new node;
if(start==NULL)
start=ptrn;
ptrn->coe=coe;
ptrn->exp=exp;
ptrn->next=NULL;
ptrp->next=ptrn;
ptrp=ptrn;
} // End of While
if(p1ptr==NULL)
{
while(p2ptr!=NULL)
{
coe=0-p2ptr->coe;
exp=p2ptr->exp;
p2ptr=p2ptr->next;
ptrn=new node;
if(start==NULL)
start=ptrn;
ptrn->coe=coe;
ptrn->exp=exp;
ptrn->next=NULL;
ptrp->next=ptrn;
```

```
ptrp=ptrn;
}
}
else if(p2ptr==NULL)
{
while(p1ptr!=NULL)
{
coe=p1ptr->coe;
exp=p1ptr->exp;
p1ptr=p1ptr->next;
ptrn=new node;
if(start==NULL)
start=ptrn;
ptrn->coe=coe;
ptrn->exp=exp;
ptrn->next=NULL;
ptrp->next=ptrn;
ptrp=ptrn;
}
}
} // End of subtraction
void main()
{
clrscr();
polynomial p1,p2,sum,diff;
cout<<"First Polynomial.";
p1.get_poly();
cout<<"Second polynomial.";
p2.get_poly();
clrscr();
cout<<"The First polynomial is: ";
p1.show();
cout<<"The second polynomial is: ";
p2.show();
cout<<"The sum of two polynomials is: ";
sum.add(p1,p2);
sum.show();
cout<<"The difference of two polynomials is: ";
diff.subtract(p1,p2);
```

```
diff.show();
getch();
}
```

5.17 REPRESENTATION OF SPARSE MATRICES

A matrix is a two-dimensional INFO object made of m rows and n columns, therefore having m × n values. When m=n, we call it a square matrix.

The most natural representation is to use two-dimensional array A[m][n] and access the element of ith row and j^{th} column as A[i][j]. If a large number of elements of the matrix are zero elements, then it is called a sparse matrix.

Representing a sparse matrix by using a two-dimensional array leads to the wastage of a substantial amount of space. Therefore, an alternative representation must be used for sparse matrices. One such representation is to store only non- zero elements along with their row positions and column positions. That means representing every non-zero element by using triples (i, j, value), where i is a row position and j is a column position, and store these triples in a linear list. It is possible to arrange these triples in the increasing order of row indices, and for the same row index in the increasing order of column indices. Each triple (i,j,value) can be represented by using a node having four fields as shown in the following:

```
Struct snode{
int row,col,val;
Struct snode *next;
};
```

row	col	value	Link

So a sparse matrix can be represented using a list of such nodes, one per non–zero element of the matrix. For example, consider the sparse matrix shown in Figure 5.84.

0	2	0	0	2	0
0	0	0	1	0	5
0	0	4	0	0	0
0	0	0	0	0	0
0	0	0	0	0	0

Figure 5.84: A sparse matrix.

This matrix can be represented using the linked list shown in Figure 5.85.

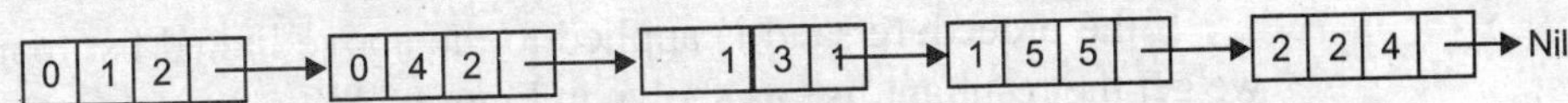

Figure 5.85: Linked list representation of sparse matrix of Figure 5.84.

In order to add two sparse matrices represented using the sorted linked lists as shown in the preceding program, the lists are traversed until the end of one of the lists is reached. In the process of traversal, the row indices stored in the nodes of these lists are compared.

If they don't match, a new node is created and inserted into the resultant list by copying the contents of a node with a lower value of row index. The pointer in the list containing a node with a lower value of row index is advanced to make it point to the next node. If the row indices match, column indices for the corresponding row positions are compared.

If they don't match, a new node is created and inserted into the resultant list by copying the contents of a node with a lower value of column index. The pointer in the list containing a node with a lower value of column index is advanced to make it point to the next node. If the column indices match, a new node is created and inserted into the resultant list by copying the row and column indices from any of the nodes and the value equal to the sum of the values in the two nodes. After this, the pointers in both the lists are advanced to make them point to the next nodes in the respective lists. This process is repeated in each iteration.

After reaching the end of any one of the lists, the iterations come to an end and the remaining nodes in the list whose end has not been reached are copied, as it is in the resultant list. Consider the following sparse matrices:

0	0	5	0
0	1	0	0
0	0	0	0
0	0	2	0

Sparse matrix a

0	0	0	0
0	3	0	1
0	0	0	0
0	0	5	0

Sparse matrix b

Figure 5.86: Given two sparse matrices.

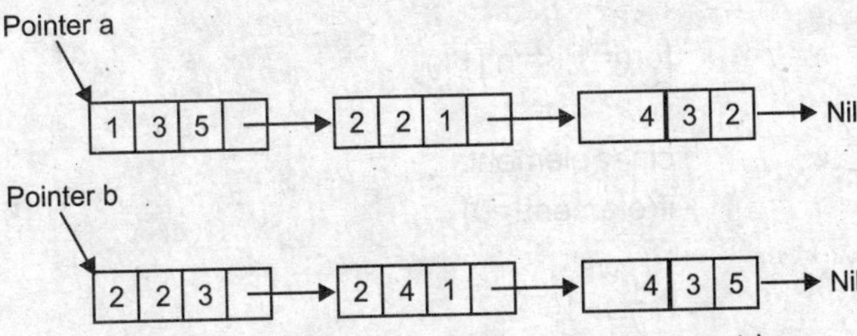

Figure 5.87: Linked representation of sparse matrices.

If the procedure sadd is applied to the above linked list representations then we get the resultant list, as shown in Figure 5.88.

Figure 5.88: Result of application of the procedure sadd.

This resultant list represents the matrix shown below:

0	0	5	0
0	4	0	1
0	0	0	0
0	0	7	0

Figure 5.89: Result of addition in matrix form.

This matrix is an addition of the matrices of a and b, respectively.

Program 15: Write a C++ program to add and subtract two sparse matrices.

```
#include<stdio.h>
#include<iostream.h>
#include<conio.h>
void main()
{
clrscr();
int sparse1[10][3],sparse2[10][3],sum[10][3],diff[10][3];
int m,n,p,q,t1,t2,s,d,element;
int i,j;
cout<<"Enter the number of rows and columns : ";
cin>>m>>n;
t1=t2=0;
cout<<"Enter the first matrix("<<m<<"*"<<n<<"):";
for(i=1;i<=m;i++)
{
for(j=1;j<=n;j++)
{
cin>>element;
if(element!=0)
{
t1=t1+1;
sparse1[t1][1]=i;
```

```
sparse1[t1][2]=j;
sparse1[t1][3]=element;
}
}
}
sparse1[0][1]=m;
sparse1[0][2]=n;
sparse1[0][3]=t1;
cout<<"Enter the second matrix("<<m<<"*"<<n<<"):";
for(i=1;i<=m;i++)
{
for(j=1;j<=n;j++)
{
cin>>element;
if(element!=0)
{
t2=t2+1;
sparse2[t2][1]=i;
sparse2[t2][2]=j;
sparse2[t2][3]=element;
}
}
}
sparse2[0][1]=m;
sparse2[0][2]=n;
sparse2[0][3]=t2;
// displaying the first sparse matrix
cout<<"The first sparse matrix is :Row      Column          Element";
cout<<"-----------------------";
for(i=0;i<=t1;i++)
{
cout<<sparse1[i][1]<<"        "<<sparse1[i][2]<<"    "<<sparse1[i][3]<<"";
}
// displaying the second sparse matrix
cout<<"The second sparse matrix is :Row  Column          Element";
cout<<"-----------------------";
for(i=0;i<=t2;i++)
{
cout<<sparse2[i][1]<<"        "<<sparse2[i][2]<<"    "<<sparse2[i][3]<<" ";
```

```
}
// Addition and subtraction
i=j=s=d=1;
while((i<=t1)&&(j<=t2))
{
if(sparse1[i][1]==sparse2[j][1])   // if rows are equal
{
if(sparse1[i][2]==sparse2[j][2]) // if columns are equal
{
sum[s][1]=diff[d][1]=sparse1[i][1];
sum[s][2]=diff[d][2]=sparse1[i][2];
sum[s][3]=sparse1[i][3]+sparse2[j][3];
diff[d][3]=sparse1[i][3]-sparse2[j][3];
i++;
j++;
if(sum[s][3]!=0)
s++;
if(diff[d][3]!=0)
d++;
}
else   // if columns are not equal
{
if(sparse1[i][2]<sparse2[j][2])
{
sum[s][1]=diff[d][1]=sparse1[i][1];
sum[s][2]=diff[d][2]=sparse1[i][2];
sum[s][3]=diff[d][3]=sparse1[i][3];
i++;
s++;
d++;
}
else
{
sum[s][1]=diff[d][1]=sparse2[j][1];
sum[s][2]=diff[d][2]=sparse2[j][2];
sum[s][3]=sparse2[j][3];
diff[d][3]=0-sparse2[j][3];
j++;
d++;
```

```
s++;
}
}
}
else  //  if rows are not equal
{
if(sparse1[i][1]<sparse2[j][1])
{
sum[s][1]=diff[d][1]=sparse1[i][1];
sum[s][2]=diff[d][2]=sparse1[i][2];
sum[s][3]=diff[d][3]=sparse1[i][3];
i++;
d++;
s++;
}
else
{
sum[s][1]=diff[d][1]=sparse2[j][1];
sum[s][2]=diff[d][2]=sparse2[j][2];
sum[s][3]=sparse2[j][3];
diff[d][3]=0-sparse2[j][3];
j++;
s++;
d++;
}
}
} // end of while
if(i<=t1)
{
for(p=i;p<=t1;p++)
{
sum[s][1]=diff[d][1]=sparse1[p][1];
sum[s][2]=diff[d][2]=sparse1[p][2];
sum[s][3]=diff[d][3]=sparse1[p][3];
s++;
d++;
}
}
else if(j<=t2)
```

```
{
for(p=j;p<=t2;p++)
{
sum[s][1]=diff[d][1]=sparse2[p][1];
sum[s][2]=diff[d][2]=sparse2[p][2];
sum[s][3]=sparse2[p][3];
diff[d][3]=0-sparse2[j][3];
s++;
d++;
}
}
// end of addition and subtraction
sum[0][1]=diff[0][1]=m;
sum[0][2]=diff[0][2]=n;
sum[0][3]=s-1;
diff[0][3]=d-1;
// displaying the sum matrix
cout<<"The sum is :Row      Column         Element";
cout<<"----------------------";
for(i=0;i<s;i++)
{
cout<<sum[i][1]<<"    "<<sum[i][2]<<"          "<<sum[i][3]<<"";
}
// displaying the difference matrix
cout<<"The difference is :Row       Column          Element";
cout<<"----------------------";
for(i=0;i<d;i++)
{
cout<<diff[i][1]<<"      "<<diff[i][2]<<""<<diff[i][3]<<"";
}
getch();
}
```

5.18 REVERSING LINKS IN THE CASE OF CIRCULAR LIST

Write a procedure for a singly linked circular list that reverses the direction of the links.

First we have to maintains three pointers, prev, curr, and next, while traversing the list. They point to consecutive nodes in the list.

If the list is non-empty, then prev points to the head node while curr and next are accordingly assigned to the next elements in the list. The circular list is traversed until curr = = head of the list. At every step, curr->next points to prev. At the end of the loop, all the nodes in the list except the head node point to their original previous nodes.

Thus at the end of the loop, head->next is assigned prev which is the last node in the list.

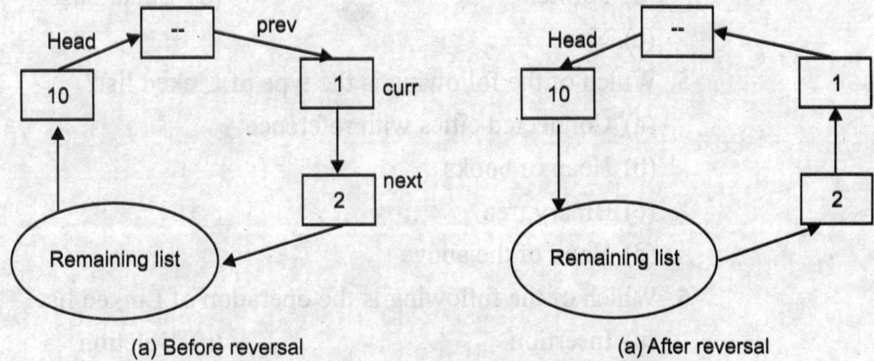

Figure 5.90: Reversing links in the case of circular list

Important Points :

1. *Note that the loop advances curr as curr=next rather than curr=curr->next, because curr->next gets changed in the loop.*
2. *The complexity of the reversal procedure is O(n).*
3. *If the head is maintained as a fixed node, that is, an empty list is denoted by a single node rather than NULL, then the functions operating on the list get simplified.*

OBJECTIVE TYPE QUESTIONS

1. Linked list is
   (a) Linear data structure (b) Non-linear data structure
   (c) Both (d) None
2. Which of the following operations can be performed on linked list?
   (a) Push (b) Pop
   (c) Insert a node (d) All of the above
   (e) None of the above

3. Linked list has how many nodes
   (a) One (b) Two
   (c) Three (d) Four
   (e) None of the above
4. Linked list can be implemented by using
   (a) Array (b) Queue
   (c) Pointer (d) Linked list
   (e) None
5. Which of the following is the type of Linked list?
   (a) Connected cities with reference
   (b) Heap of books
   (c) Binary tree
   (d) None of the above
6. Which of the following is the operation of Linked list
   (a) Insertion (b) Deletion
   (c) Create (d) Sorting
   (e) All of the above (f) None of the above
7. Which of the following is the linked list?
   (a) Singular Linked list (b) Two way linked list
   (c) Circular linked list (d) All of the above
   (e) None of the above
8. Which of the following is not the operation of Linked list:
   (a) Sorting (b) Merging
   (c) Inserting (d) All of the above
   (e) None of the above
9. Which of the following is the utility of linked list?
   (a) Stack (b) Queue
   (c) Concatenation (d) All of the above
   (e) None of the above
10. Traversing in Linked list means:
    (a) Sorting (b) Searching
    (c) Inserting (d) Deleting
    (e) Visiting (f) None of the above

11. The elements of static lists are stored in
    (a) successive memory locations (b) random memory locations
    (c) alternative memory locations (d) all of the above.
12. The elements of linked lists are stored in
    (a) successive memory locations (b) random memory locations
    (c) alternative memory locations (d) all of the above
13. Name the function that is used for memory allocation in implementation of linked list
    (a) malloc ( ) (b) realloc ( )
    (c) free ( ) (d) both (a) and (c).
14. If it is decided to create the linked list in C++, function that allocates memory is
    (a) malloc ( ) (b) new
    (c) delete (d) both (a) and (b)
15. The free () function is used to
    (a) release the memory (b) to unlink the node
    (c) to unlink the first and last node (d) None of the above
16. The pointer head points to the
    (a) first node (b) last node
    (c) either first or last node (d) None of the above
17. This type of linked list does not have null value in the last node
    (a) circular linked list (b) singly linked list
    (c) static list (d) None of the above
18. The first node of this type of linked list has NULL value
    (a) doubly linked list (b) doubly circular linked list
    (c) singly linked list (d) all of the above.
19. This type of linked list does not have first and last node
    (a) circular linked list (b) singly linked list
    (c) doubly linked list (d) static list.
20. When the malloc () function returns NULL value it means
    (a) memory is not allocated
    (b) memory is allocated but no data entered
    (c) memory is allocated
    (d) None of the above

21. If memory is not allocated, what further action will you suggest?
    (a) try again (b) exit from the program
    (c) both (a) & (b) (d) continue the program.

EXERCISES

1. Why we use linked list?
2. What is Linked list? Explain different types of linked list.
3. Explain various types of representation of linked list in memory.
4. What is Dynamic data structure.
5. Explain implementation of dynamic data structure using pointer.
6. Explain memory allocation of linked lists.
7. Write an algorithm and C++ program for different operations given below:
   (i) Traversing (ii) Insertion
   (iii) Deletion (iv) Concatenating two lists
   (v) Searching (vi) Reversing the direction of list
   (vii) Copying linked list (viii) Merging two lists
   (ix) Erasing linked list (x) Spiliting linked list
8. What do you mean by Garbage collection?
9. What do you mean by Doubly linked list? Explain various operations performed on doubly linked list.
10. Explain various application of doubly linked lists to memory management.
11. What is Header linked list. Also explain two-way header lists.
12. What do you mean by Circular linked lists? Explain various operations performed on circular linked list.

15. What do you mean by Endogenous / exogenous lists?
16. What are different advantages and disadvantages of using linked list over array?
17. What are the differences between linked list and array?
18. Write comparison of linked list variations.
20. Explain representation of sparse matrices in detail.

6 CHAPTER

Stacks

6.1 INTRODUCTION

In computer science, a stack is a special type of data structure (a temporary abstract data type and data structure) which is based on the principle of Last In First Out (LIFO). Stacks are used extensively at every level of a modern computer system. For example, a modern PC uses stacks at the architecture level, which are **used in** the basic design of an operating system for interrupt handling and operating **system** function calls.

A stack is a last-in first-out data structure (LIFO). Conceptually, the stack data structure behaves like a stack of books or a stack of plates. New data is placed on the top of the stack, and when data is removed it is taken from the top. Your browser's back button likely stores a set of URLs in a stack. A stack-based computer system is one that stores temporary information primarily in stacks, rather than hardware CPU registers (a register-based computer system). The *stack* is a very **common** data structure used in programs. Stacks are the data structures in which, **entries are** added to it and removed from, at one end or location. This end is called as **top of** stack. The stack maintains an order of LIFO (Last in First Out).

6.2 DESCRIPTION OF STACK STRUCTURE

A stack is simply a list of elements with insertions and deletions permitted at one end called the stack top or top of stack. That means that it is possible to remove elements from a stack in reverse order from the insertion of elements into the stack. Thus, a stack data structure exhibits the LIFO (last in first out) property. Push and pop are the operations that are provided for insertion of an element into the stack and the removal of an element from the stack, respectively. Shown in Figure 6.1 are the effects of push and pop operations on the stack.

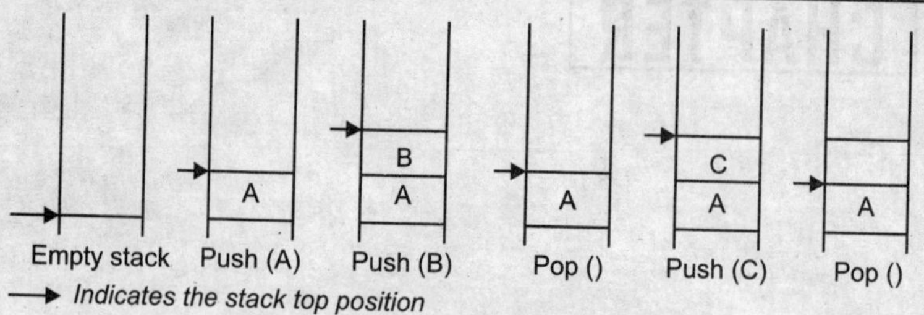

Figure 6.1: Stack operations.

The stack is a simple but important example of an abstract data type. It is used to store elements where the **L**ast element **in** is the **F**irst one **O**ut (LIFO). Anyone with a cluttered desk or an overfull sink of washing-up will be familiar with a stack. New elements are added or *pushed* onto the top of the stack. The first element to be removed or *popped* is taken from the top - the last one in. All recursive programming languages use an implicit system-stack to allocate space for local variables of routines as they are called. Some algorithms require the use of an explicit stack.

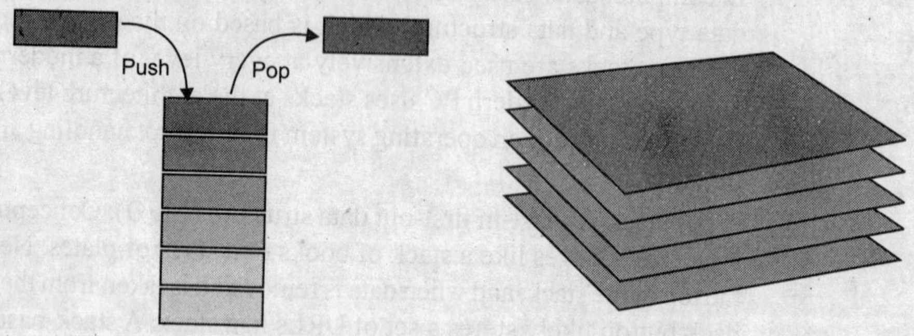

Figure 6.2: Diagrams of stacks.

Definition: *"Stack is a linear data structure that can be represented by using an array or linked list and is based on the methodology LIFO known as Last in First Out."*

Examples of Stack are:

- CD Rack
- Plates in cafeteria etc.

6.3 STACK

A stack is an ordered list in which all insertions and deletions are made at one end, called the top. Given a stack S= (a[1],a[2],.......a[n]) then we say that a1 is the bottommost element and element a[i]) is on top of element a[i-1], 1<i<=n.

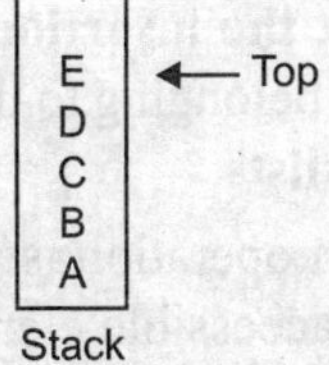

Figure 6.3: Stack Top.

The restrictions on a stack imply that if the elements A,B,C,D,E are added to the stack, n that order, then the first element to be removed/deleted must be E. Equivalently we say that the last element to be inserted into the stack will be the first to be removed. For this reason stacks are sometimes referred to as Last in First out (LIFO) lists.

6.3.1 Practical Approach: Stack

A **stack** is a temporary abstract data type and data structure based on the principle of Last in First out (LIFO). Stacks are used extensively at every level of a modern computer system. For example, a modern PC uses stacks at the architecture level, which are used in the basic design of an operating system for interrupt handling and operating system function calls. A common model of a stack is a plate or coin stacker. Plates are "pushed" onto to the top and "popped" off the top.

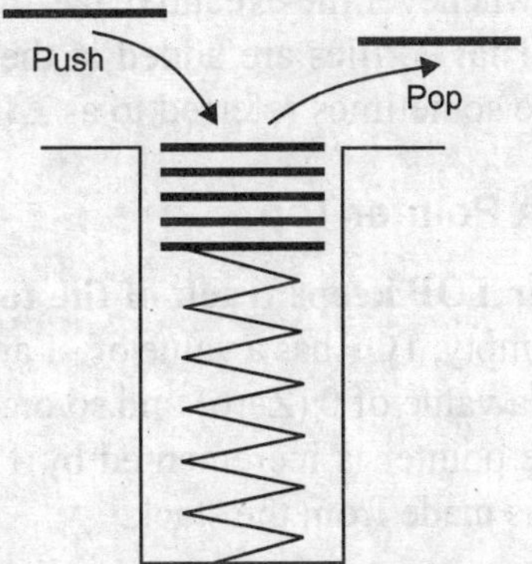

Figure 6.4: Stack operations push and pop.

There are two natural ways to implement a stack depending on the circumstances. A stack can be implemented by an array of elements. An integer "pointer" *top* indicates the element currently at the top of the stack. Initially top is zero for an empty stack. The array must be declared to have some fixed size. This is acceptable if an accurate estimate of the stack's maximum size can be made before the program runs. The other implementation uses a linked list. This is more suitable if an accurate estimate of the stack's maximum size cannot be made in advance.

Lists permit the insertion or deletion of an element to occur only at one end. A linear list belonging to this subclass is called a **stack**. They are also referred to as **pushdown lists.**

The insertion operation is referred to as **PUSH** and the deletion operation as **POP**. The most accessible element in a stack is known as the **TOP of the stack.** Since insertion and deletion operations are performed at one end of stack, the elements can only be removed in the opposite order from that in which they were added to the stack. Such a linear list is frequently referred to as a **LIFO** (Last-In First-Out) LIST.

Figure 6.5: Stack of files.

An example of stack is the "in" tray of a busy executive. The files pile up in the tray and whenever the executive has time to clear the files, he/she takes it off from the top. That is, files are added at the top and removed from the top. Therefore stacks are sometimes referred to as **LIFO structure.**

6.3.2 A Pointer Top

A pointer TOP keeps track of the top element in the stack. Initially when the stack is empty, TOP has a value of –1 and when the stack contains a single element, TOP has a value of 0 (Zero) and so on. Each time a new element is inserted in the stack, the pointer is incremented by 1. The pointer decrements by 1 each time a deletion is made from the stack.

Stack Structure

D = {d, F, A}

where,

d : Array or a node (structure)

d = { a , TOP }

Here, **a :** Simple array or structure

TOP: Index or Pointer

F: PUSH, POP, DISPLAY, MODIFY

A: EMPTY, OVERFLOW, UNDERFLOW

6.4 STACK MODEL

A stack is a list with the restriction that inserts and deletes can be performed in only one position, namely the end of the list called the top. The fundamental operations on a stack are push, which is equivalent to an insert, and pop, which deletes the most recently inserted element. The most recently inserted element can be examined prior to performing a pop by use of the top routine. A pop or top on an empty stack is generally considered an error in the stack ADT. On the other hand, running out of space when performing a push is an implementation error but not an ADT error. Stacks are sometimes known as LIFO (last in, first out) lists. The model depicted in Figure 6.6 signifies only that pushes are input operations and pops and tops are output. The usual operations to make empty stacks and test for emptiness are part of the repertoire, but essentially all that you can do to a stack is push and pop.

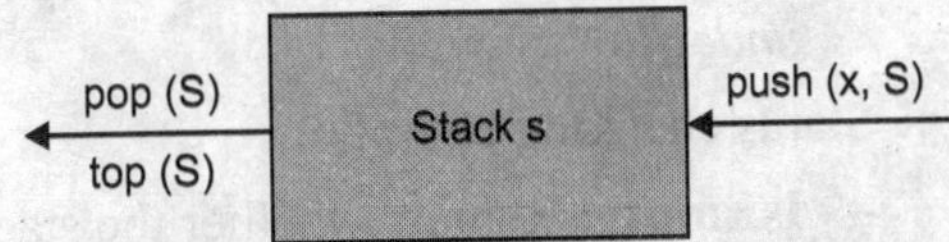

Figure 6.6: Stack model: input to a stack is by push, output is by pop.

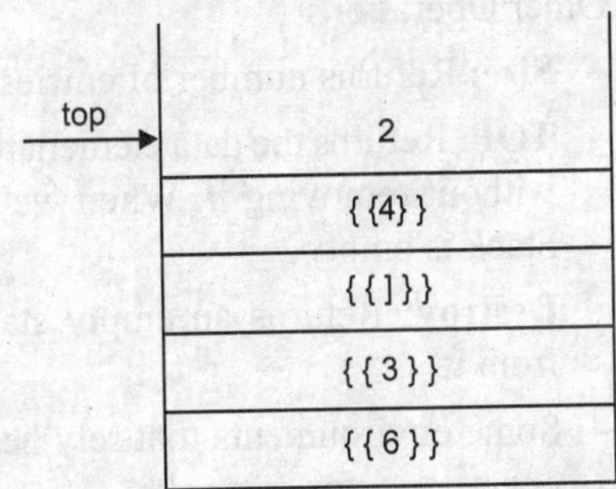

Figure 6.7: Stack model: only the top element is accessible.

Figure 6.7 shows an abstract stack after several operations. The general model is that there is some element that is at the top of the stack, and it is the only element that is visible.

6.5 COMMONLY USED STACK OPERATIONS

Now, let's think about a stack in an abstract way i.e., it doesn't hold any particular kind of thing (like books) and we aren't restricting ourselves to any particular programming language or any particular implementation of a stack.

Stacks hold objects, usually all of the same type. Most stacks support just the simple set of operations we introduced above; and thus, the main property of a stack is that objects go on and come off of the *top* of the stack (TOP).

Here are some operations, with their typical names, that are performed on stacks:

- Initialization operation
  - **Create:** Returns an empty stack.
- Basic Operations
  - **Push**: an item is put on top of the stack, increasing the stack size by one As stack size is usually limited, this may provoke a *stack overflow* if the maximum size is exceeded.
  - **Pop**: the top item is taken from the stack, decreasing stack size by one. In the case where there was no top item (i.e.the stack was empty), a *stack underflow* occurs.
- Status checking operations
  - **IsEmpty:** Reports whether the stack is empty or not?
  - **IsFull:** Reports whether the stack is full or not?
- Other Operations
  - **Size:** Returns number of entries in the stack.
  - **TOP:** Returns the data element that was most recently inserted into Stack without removing it. When we write TOP=0 or TOP=NULL, it means Stack is empty
  - **Destroy:** Returns an empty stack after deleting all the data elements from it
  - Some environments that rely heavily on stacks may provide additional operations, for example:
  - **Dup**: the top item is popped and pushed again twice, so that an additional copy of the former top item is now on top, with the original below it.
  - **Swap** or **exchange**: the two topmost items are exchanged.
  - **Rotate**: the three topmost items exchange places in a rotary fashion. Two variants of this operation are possible; most often called **left** and **right rotate**.

6.5.1 Algorithm for Stack Operations

1. Push Operation

This operation is used to insert element onto the stack.

Algorithm 6.1: To insert element onto stack.

Push(S, TOP, X): This algorithm inserts an element X to the top of the stack which is represented by a vector S consisting MAX elements with a pointer TOP denoting the top element in the stack.

Step 1: [Check for stack underflow]

If (TOP>=max-1)

then write(stack overflow)

Return

Step 2: [Increment TOP]

TOP <— TOP+1

Step 3: [Insert element]

S[TOP] <— X

Step 4: [Finished]

Return

Explanation: Consider the stack S

Step 1: The first step of this algorithm checks for an overflow condition. If such a condition exists, then the insertion can't be performed and an appropriate error message results.

Here the value of n is 9 and, say 12 is the value which is to be pushed on to stack i.e. X is 12. As TOP is 7 which is less than the value of MAX i.e. 9, step 2 will be executed.

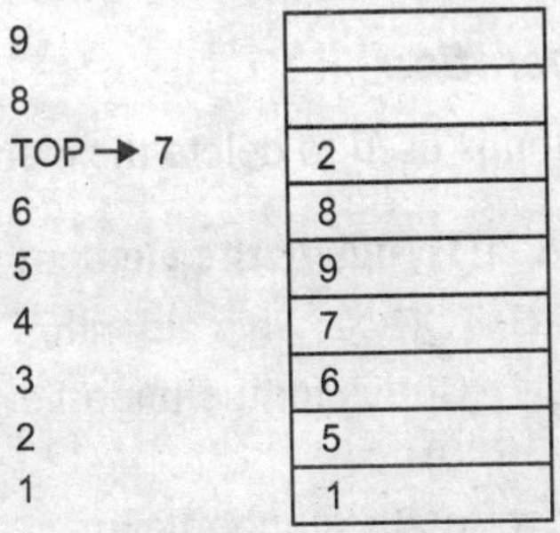

9	
8	
TOP → 7	2
6	8
5	9
4	7
3	6
2	5
1	1

Figure 6.8: Stack before push operation.

Step 2: Increment TOP by 1. Now TOP will be 8.

Step 3: Push the value of i i.e. 12 on to the stack at position pointed to by TOP use assignment

$$S[TOP] = S[8] = X = 12$$

Step 4: Return

The Stack after execution of push operation is:

9	
TOP → 8	12
7	2
6	8
5	9
4	7
3	6
2	5
1	1

Figure 6.9: Stack after push operation.

For example—Push (): This is the function which is used to insert and item in a Stack it should be noted that TOP will be incremented by 1 after every insertion. Suppose initially stack was empty now when we apply following operation we get:

push(1)
push(2)
push(3)

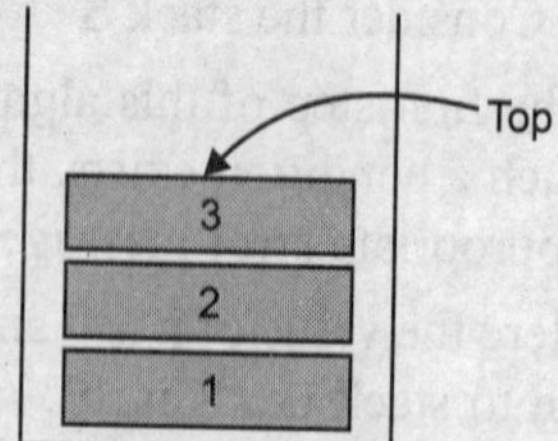

Figure 6.10: Stack perform push operations.

2. POP Operation

This operation is used to delete the element from the top of the stack.

Algorithm 6.2: To delete the element from top of stack.

Pop(S, TOP, X): This algorithm removes top element from the stack.
Step 1: [Check for the underflow on stack]
If (TOP<0)
then write(stack underflow)
Return
Step 2: [Hold the former top element of stack into X]
X <— S[TOP]
Step 3: [Decrement the TOP pointer or index by 1]
TOP <— TOP-1
Step 4: [finished-Return the popped item from the stack]
Return(X)

Explanation

Consider the stack S.

Step 1: As Underflow condition is checked for in the first step of the algorithm. If such a condition exists, then the deletion cannot be performed and an appropriate error message results. Here TOP is 7 which is greater than zero. So step 2 will be executed.

Step 2: Pop out the element stored on the top of the stack (data item stored on top of stack) X = S[7] = 2.

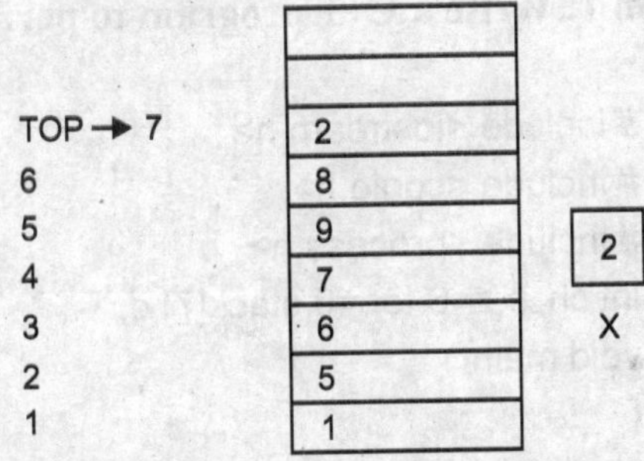

Figure 6.11: Stack before pop operation.

Step 3: The TOP is decremented by 1 and the value becomes TOP =6.

Step 4: Return

The stack after Pop Operation as:

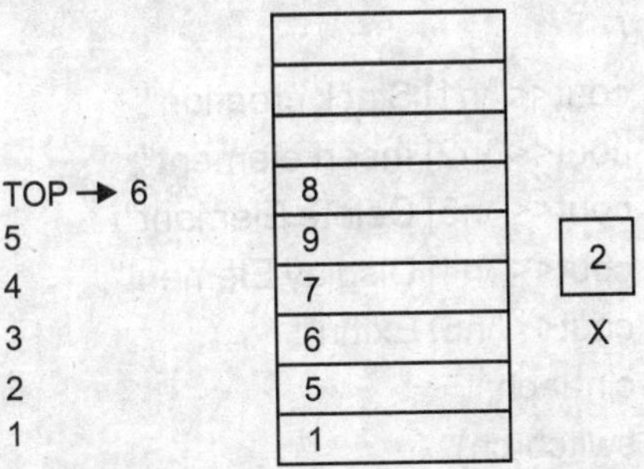

Figure 6.12: Stack after pop operation.

For example: Pop ()

This is the function which is for used for deletion (popping up) of an element from the stack It is similar to the deletion of an element at the end of a single linked list. This operation will decrement the value of TOP by 1. Now the following operation will do following changes in above stack.

Pop()

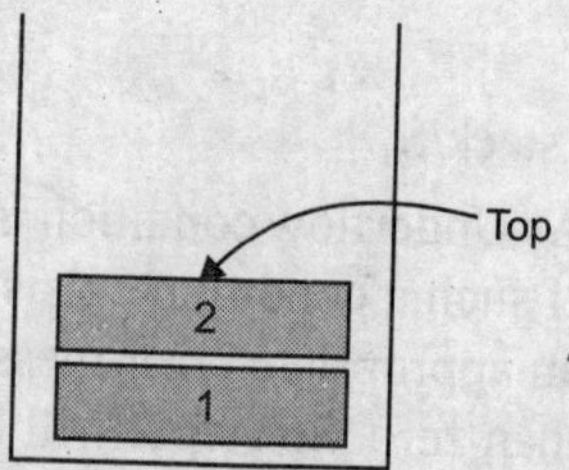

Figure 6.13: Stack perform pop operations.

Program 1: Write a C++ program to perform pop and push operation on the stack.

```
# include <iostream.h>
# include <conio.h>
# include <process.h>
int ch, p,z=6,top=0,stack[7],c;
void main()
{
void create ();
void push ();
void pop();
void show ();
clrscr ();
while(ch<5)
{
cout<<"\n1] Stack creation";
cout<<"\n2] Insert element";
cout<<"\n3] Delete Element";
cout<<"\n4] Display Element";
cout<<"\n5] Exit\n";
cin>>ch;
switch(ch)
{
case 1 : create();
continue;
case 2: push();
continue;
case 3: pop();
continue;
case 4: show ();
continue;
```

```
default: exit(0);
}
}
}
void create ()
{
cout<<"\n Enter number of elements in the stack (<7):";
cin>>c;
for (top=0;top<0;++top)
{
cout<<"Enter Element["<<top<<"]:-";
cin>>stack[top];
}
}
void push ()
{
if (top>=z)
{
cout<<"\n Stack is full";
getch();
}
else
{
cout<<"\n Enter number to be pushed:-";
cin>>stack[top];
top++;
}
}
void pop ()
{
if (top<=0)
{
cout<<"\nThe stack is empty";
getch();
}
else
top--;
}
void show()
```

```
{
for (p=top-1;p>=0;--p)
cout<<stack[p];
}
```

Output:

```
1] Stack creation
2] Insert element
3] Delete Element
4] Display Element
5] Exit
1

Enter number of elements in the stack (<7): 4
Enter Elements: 1 2 3 4
1] Stack Creation
2] Insert element
3] Delete Element
4] Display Element
5] Exit
4
0 4 3 2 1
1] Stack creation
2] Insert element
3] Delete Element
4] Display Element
5] Exit
```

3. Display Operation

This operation is used to display the element of the stack.

Algorithm 6.3: To display the element of the stack.

Display(S, TOP): This algorithm displays the contents of the stack i.e., vector S.

Step 1: [check for empty on stack]

if (TOP==-1)

then write('stack empty')

Return

Step 2: [Repeat through STEP 3 from i=TOP to 0]

Repeat through STEP 3 for i=TOP to 0 STEP-1]

Step 3: [Display the stack content]

write (S[i])

Step 4: [Finished]

Return

The first step of this algorithm checks for an empty condition. If such a condition exists, then the contents of the stack cannot be displayed and an appropriate error message results.

4. Peek Operation

This operation is used to print top most element of the stack.

Algorithm 6.4: To print top most element of the stack

Peek(S, TOP): This algorithm used to print top most element of the stack.

Step 1: [Check for the underflow on stack]

If (TOP<0)

then write(stack underflow)

Return

Step 2: [Print the value of Top most element]

write (S[TOP])

Step 3: [Finished]

Return

5. Dup Operation

This operation is used to first of all pop out the top item and then pushes the same item twice.

Algorithm 6.5: Dup operation first of all pops out the top item and then pushes the same item twice.

Dup(S, TOP, X): This algorithm will use both push and pop operations. Dup operation first of all pops out the top item and then pushes the same item twice.

An array stack, say stack S is declared with maximum size say, MAX, data item, say X and variable TOP points to the top of the stack.

Step 1: [Check for the underflow on stack]

If (TOP<0) then write (stack underflow)

Return Else go to step 9.

Step 2: [Pop out the data item into X using an assignment]. X = stack [TOP]

Step 3: [Decrement TOP by 1, as item has been popped out in step 2]. TOP <— TOP-1

Step 4: [Increment TOP]. TOP <— TOP+1

Step 5: [Push data item X onto stack using an assignment]. S [TOP] = X

Step 6: If (TOP>=max-1), then print that stack is full then Return else go to step 7.

Step 7: [Increment TOP]. TOP <— TOP+1

Step 8: [Push data item X onto stack using an assignment]

S[TOP] = X

Step 9: Return

Explanation

Consider the following stack with MAX =5, TOP=3 as shown in the Figure 6.14:

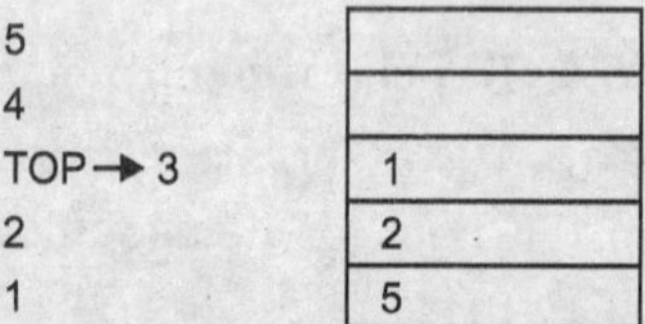

Figure 6.14: Stack with three elements

Step 1: Here TOP is 3 which is greater than 0, so step 2 will be executed.

Step 2: Pop the data item stored on top of the stack, and store it in variable X, using an assignment X = S[3] =1

Step 3: TOP = TOP-1 = 3-1=2

5	
4	
3	
TOP→ 2	2
1	5

Figure 6.15: Stack after step 3

Step 4: Increment TOP by 1. TOP = TOP +1 = 2+1 = 3.

Step 5: Push the value stored in X, i.e. 1 onto stack at position pointed to by TOP, using an assignment S [3] = X=1.

5	
4	
TOP→ 3	1
2	2
1	5

Figure 6.16: Stack after step 5

Step 6: As TOP now is 3 which is less than the value of MAX i.e. 5, so step 7 will be executed.

Step 7: Increment TOP by 1 and now TOP becomes TOP = TOP+1 = 3+1 =4

Step 8: Push the value stored in X, i.e. 1 onto stack at position pointed to by TOP using an assignment S[4] = X=1.

TOP → 4	1
3	1
2	2
1	5

Figure 6.17: Stack after step 8

Step 9: Return

6. Swap Operation

This operation is used to interchange variables or values.

Algorithm 6.6: To swap two elements.

Swap(S, TOP, X): In the algorithm, an array stack S, say stack is declared with maximum size say, MAX, data items, say X and Y and variable TOP pointing to the top of the stack.

Step 1: [Check for the underflow on stack]

If (TOP<0) then write(stack underflow)

go to step 12 else Return

Step 2: if (MAX < 2) goto step 12 else return.

Step 3: [Pop out data item into X using an assignment]. X = S [TOP]

Step 4: [Decrement TOP by 1]

TOP= TOP-1.

Step 5: [Pop out data item, pointed to by TOP, into Y using the an assignment].

Y = S[TOP]

Step 6: [Decrement TOP by 1]. TOP= TOP-1.

Step 7: If (TOP<0) then write(stack underflow)

Step 8: [Increment TOP by 1]

TOP = TOP+1

Step 9: [Push the data item stored in X onto stack using an assignment]

S[TOP]=X

Step 10: [Increment TOP by 1]

TOP = TOP+1

Step 11: [Push the data item stored in Y onto stack using an assignment]

S[TOP]=Y

Step 12: Return

Explanation

Consider the same stack S referring to Figure 6.14, as discussed in dup operation.

Step 1: Here TOP is 3 which is greater than 0, so step 2 will be executed. As there are more than 2 data items in stack so step 3 is executed.

Step 2: if (MAX < 2) goto step 12 else return.

Step 3: Pop out the data item stored on top of the stack and store it in variable i, i.e. X = S[3] =1 (the value of data item located at location 3 pointed to by TOP).

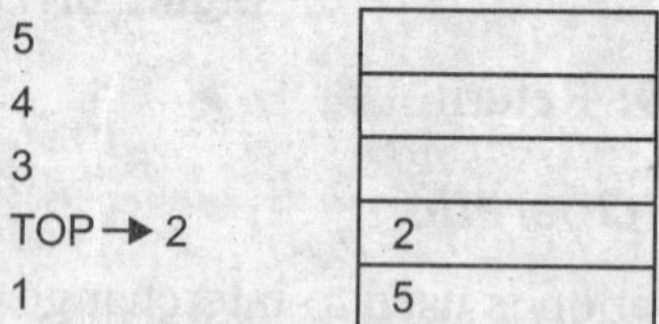

Figure 6.18: Stack after step 3

Step 4: TOP=TOP-1 =3-1=2. As TOP now is 2, which is greater than 0, so step 5 will be executed.

Step 5: Pop out the data item stored on Top of the stack and store it in variable Y, Y=S[TOP] = S[2] = 2 (the value of data item located at location 2 pointed to by TOP)

5	
4	
3	
2	
TOP → 1	5

Figure 6.19: Stack after step 5

Step 6: Decrement TOP by 1, i.e. TOP = TOP-1 = 2-1=1.

Step 7: If (TOP<0) then write(stack underflow)

Step 8: Increment TOP by 1, i.e. TOP = TOP+1 = 1+1=2

Step 9: Push onto, data item stored in X, at location now pointed by TOP, i.e. stack [TOP] = S[2] =X = 1 (the value stored in X)

5	
4	
3	
TOP → 2	1
1	5

Figure 6.20: Stack after step 9

Step 10: Increment TOP i.e. TOP = TOP+1 = 2+1=3

Step 11: Push onto, data item stored in Y, at location now pointed to by TOP, i.e. S[TOP] = S[3] = Y=2 (the value stored in Y). Final is Figure 6.21.

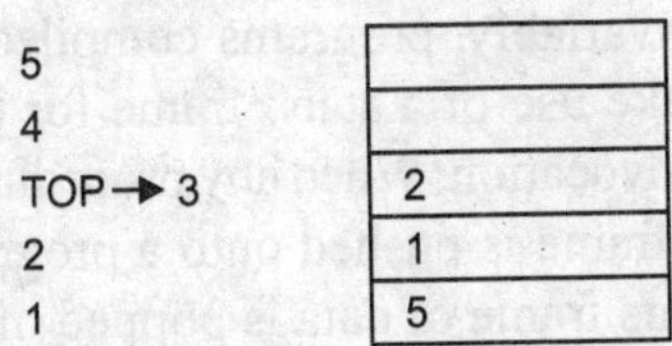

Figure 6.21: Stack after step 11

Step 12: Return

6.6 RIGHT ROTATE

Hint: *First of all check if n is greater than or equal to 3, because to perform rotation, we require at least three data items in the stack, then pop out the three uppermost data elements one by one adjusting pointer TOP accordingly. Store the popped out data elements in three different variables say X, Y, & Z.*

Then push the data item onto stack in the order X, Z, Y variables so that first element of stack, after right rotation, becomes the third, second becomes first and third becomes second.

All these operations, mentioned above, are performed in O (1) time. Stacks are either visualized growing from the bottom up, or growing from left to right, so that "topmost" becomes "rightmost". Let us take the same example of stack growing from left to right as shown in the Figure 6.22:

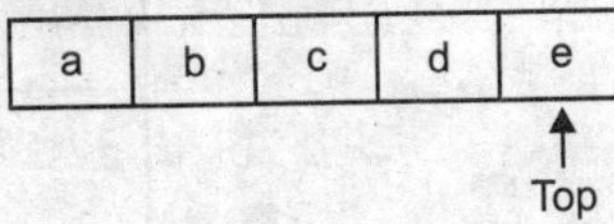

Figure 6.22: Stack growing from left to right

This means that a **right rotates** will move the first element to the third position, the second to the first and the third to the second. So the output for right rotate will be as shown in the Figure 6.23:

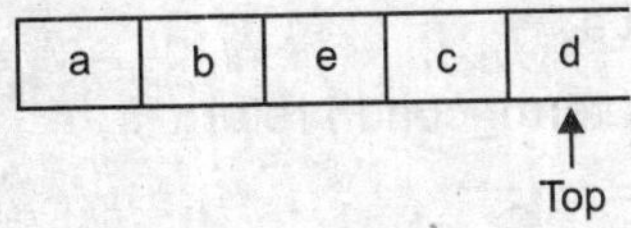

Figure 6.23: Stack after right rotate operation

6.7 STACK FRAMES

Almost invariably, programs compiled from modern high level languages (even C++!) make use of a stack frame for the working memory of each procedure or function invocation. When any procedure or function is called, a number of words—the stack frame is pushed onto a program stack. When the procedure or function returns, this frame of data is popped off the stack.

As a function calls another function, first its arguments, then the return address and finally space for local variables is pushed onto the stack. Since each function runs in its own "environment" or **context**, it becomes possible for a function to call itself — a technique known as recursion. This capability is extremely useful and extensively used - because many problems are elegantly specified or solved in a recursive way.

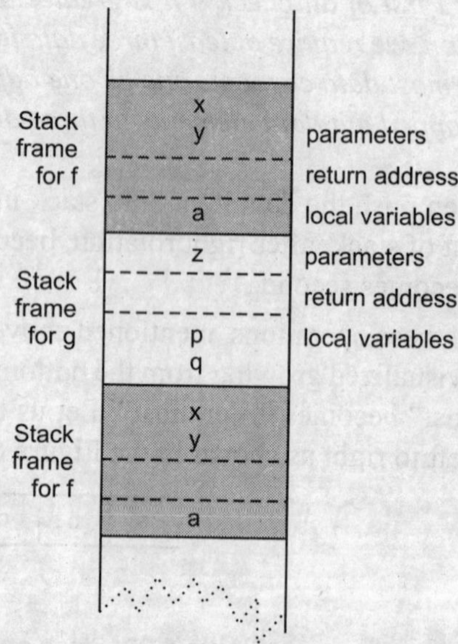

Figure 6.24: Stack frames.

Program stack after executing a pair of mutually recursive functions:

```
function f(int x, int y) {
int a;
if ( term_cond ) return ...;
a = .....;
return g(a);
}
function g(int z) {
```

```
int p,q;
p = ...; q = ...;
return f(p,q);
}
```

Note how all of function f and g's environment (their parameters and local variables) are found in the stack frame. When f is called a second time from g, a new frame for the second invocation of f is created.

6.8 MULTIPLE STACKS

Following pictures are two ways to do two stacks in array:

6.8.1 None Fixed Size of the Stacks

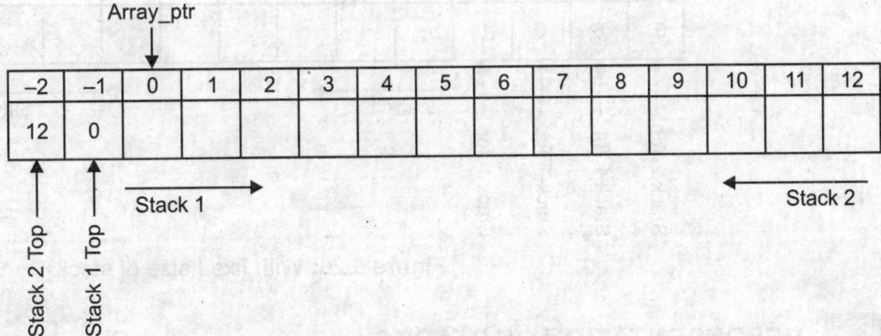

Figure 6.25: Without fixed size of stack.

- Stack 1 expands from the 0th element to the right
- Stack 2 expands from the 12th element to the left
- As long as the value of Top1 and Top2 are not next to each other, it has free elements for input the data in the array
- When both Stacks are full, Top1 and Top 2 will be next to each other
- There is no fixed boundary between Stack 1 and Stack 2
- Elements –1 and –2 are using to store the information needed to manipulate the stack (subscript for Top 1 and Top 2)

6.8.2 Fixed Size of the Stacks

- Stack 1 expands from the 0th element to the right
- Stack 2 expands from the 6th element to the left

- As long as the value of Top 1 is less than 6 and greater than 0, Stack 1 has free elements to input the data in the array
- As long as the value of Top 2 is less than 11 and greater than 5, Stack 2 has free elements to input the data in the array
- When the value of Top 1 is 5, Stack 1 is full
- When the value of Top 2 is 10, stack 2 is full
- Elements –1 and –2 are using to store the size of Stack 1 and the subscript of the array for Top 1 needed to manipulate Stack 1
- Elements –3 and –4 are using to store the size of Stack 2 and the subscript of the array for Top 2 needed to manipulate Stack 2

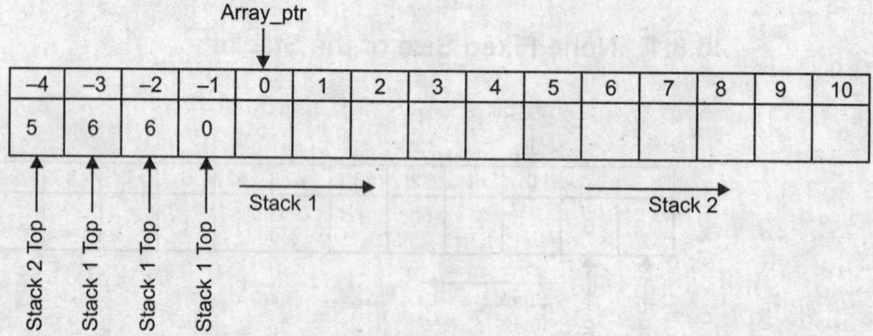

Figure 6.26: With fixed size of stack.

6.9 REPRESENTATION OF STACKS

A stack can be representation in memory using several data structures but usually it is representation using array or a linked list. The choice of representing stack has an array or a linked list depends upon whether the size of the stack is fixed or not. If the size of the stack is fixed then array representation of stack is more efficient as compared to linked list. We shall discuss both these representations in detail.

6.9.1 Array Representation of a Stack

For the sake of simplicity, we are using sequence array of Integer type items to explain the representation of stack. The top is represented by an integer denoting index of the location of top item of the stack. The stack items are placed from item[0] to item[top] continuously in that order with item[0] serving as bottom end. For instance to define a stack structure in C we can use the struct structure as shown below.

```
#define MAX 100
struct stack
```

```
{
int top ;
int item[MAX];
};
```

Once that have been done, an actual stack is s may be declared by

```
struct stack s;
```

A stack is represented as a normal array with the 0th element being the **top** of the stack. For example, the stack displayed to the left would become the following array:

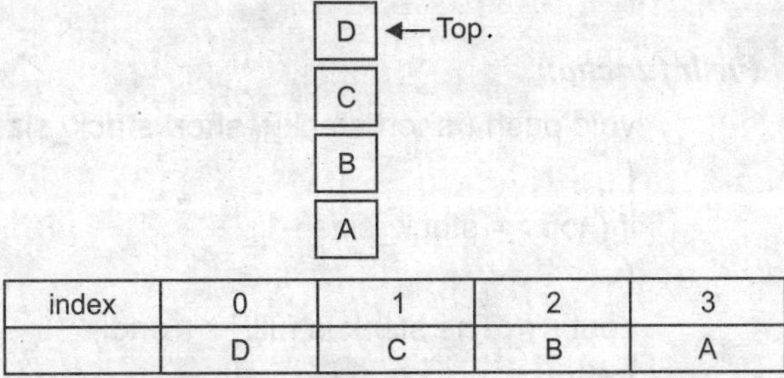

index	0	1	2	3
	D	C	B	A

Figure 6.27: Array representation of a stack.

Another way for Array Representation is as shown below:

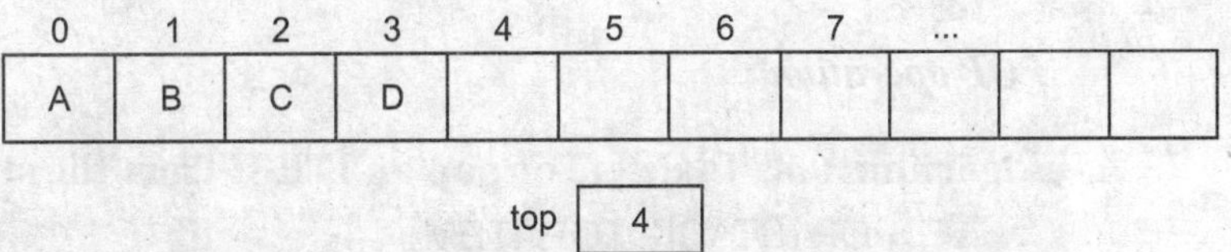

Figure 6.28: Array representation of a stack with pointer top.

Algorithm 6.7: To insert or push an ITEM in the stack.

PUSH (STACK, TOP, MAXSTK, ITEM)

This algorithm pushes an ITEM onto a stack

Step 1: [When stack is already filled?]

If TOP = MAXSTK, then print: OVERFLOW, and Return.

Step 2: Set TOP = TOP+ 1. [Increment TOP by 1.]

Step 3: Set STACK [TOP] = ITEM. [Inserts ITEM in new TOP position of the stack.]

Step 4: End.

Explanation

Add: a push( ) operation adds an item to the topmost location on the stack.

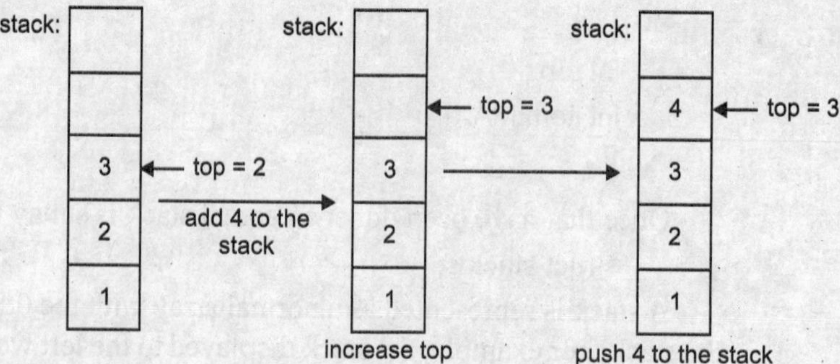

Figure 6.29: Push operation

Push function:

```
void push ( short stack[], short stack_size, short top, short item)
{
if ( top >= stack_size –1)
{
cout << "The stack is full!" << endl;
return;
}
stack[+ + top] = item;
}
```

POP operation

Algorithm 6.8: To delete or pop an ITEM from the stack.

POP (STACK, TOP, ITEM)

This algorithm deletes or pops the top element of STACK and assigns it to the variable name ITEM.

Step 1: [Stack has an item to be removed from it?]

If TOP = 0, then Print: UNDERFLOW, and Return.

Step 2: Set ITEM = STACK [TOP]. [Assign value of TOP element to ITEM.]

Step 3: Set TOP = TOP- 1. [Decrement TOP by 1.]

Step 4: End.

Explanation

Delete: a pop( ) operation removes an item from the topmost location on the stack

Pop function:

```
short pop (short stack[], short stack_size, short top)
{
if ( top = = –1)
```

```
{
cout << "The stack is empty!" << endl;
return 0;
}
return stack[top --] ;
}
```

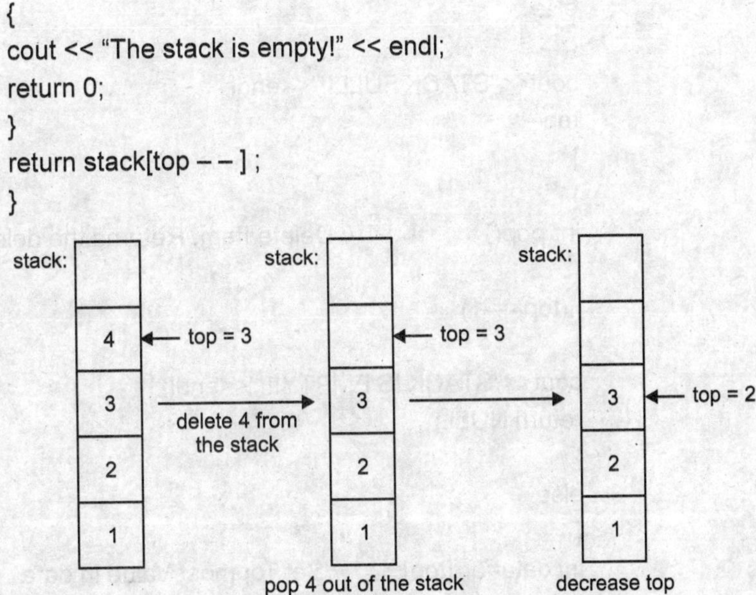

Figure 6.30: Pop operation

Program 2: Write a C++ program to implement stack using arrays.

```
#include <iostream>
#include<conio.h>
#define MAX 10        // MAXIMUM STACK CONTENT
class stack
{
private:
int arr[MAX];   // Contains all the Data
int top;        //Contains location of Topmost Data pushed onto Stack
public:
stack()         //Constructor
{
top=-1;         //Sets the Top Location to -1 indicating an empty stack
}
void push(int a)  // Push ie. Add Value Function
{
top++;       // increment to by 1
if(top<MAX)
{
arr[top]=a;  //If Stack is Vacant store Value in Array
}
```

```
else
{
cout<<"STACK FULL!!"<<endl;
top--;
}
}
int pop()            // Delete Item. Returns the deleted item
{
if(top==-1)
{
cout<<"STACK IS EMPTY!!!"<<endl;
return NULL;
}
else
{
int data=arr[top];     //Set Topmost Value in data
arr[top]=NULL;         //Set Original Location to NULL
top--;                 // Decrement top by 1
return data;           // Return deleted item
}
}
};
void main()
{
stack a;
a.push(3);
cout<<"3 is Pushed\n";
a.push(10);
cout<<"10 is Pushed\n";
a.push(1);
cout<<"1 is Pushed\n\n";
cout<<a.pop()<<" is Popped\n";
cout<<a.pop()<<" is Popped\n";
cout<<a.pop()<<" is Popped\n";
getch();
}
```

Output:

3 is Pushed

10 is Pushed

1 is Pushed

1 is Popped
10 is Popped
3 is Popped

Program 3: Write a C++ program for Stack implementation as a class.

```
# include<iostream.h>
# include<process.h>
# include<conio.h>
# define SIZE 20
class stack
{
int a[SIZE];
int tos; // Top of Stack
public:
stack();
void push(int);
int pop();
int isempty();
int isfull();
};
stack::stack()
{
tos=0; //Initialize Top of Stack
}
int stack::isempty()
{
return (tos==0?1:0);
}
int stack::isfull()
{
return (tos==SIZE?1:0);
}
void stack::push(int i)
{
if(!isfull())
{
a[tos]=i;
tos++;
```

```
}
else
{
cerr<<"A ! Possible Data Loss !";
}
}
int stack::pop()
{
if(!isempty())
{
return(a[--tos]);
}
else
{
cerr<<"Stack is empty! What to pop...!";
}
return 0;
}
void main()
{
stack s;
int ch=1,num;
while(ch!=0)
{
cout<<"Stack Operations Mani Menu
1.Push
2.Pop
3.IsEmpty
4.IsFull
0.Exit
";
cin>>ch;
switch(ch)
{
case 0:
exit(1); //Normal Termination of Program
case 1:
cout<<"Enter the number to push";
cin>>num;
s.push(num);
```

```
break;
case 2:
cout<<"Number popped from the stack is: "<<s.pop()<<endl;
break;
case 3:
(s.isempty())?(cout<<"Stack is empty."):(cout<<"Stack is not empty.");
break;
case 4:
(s.isfull())?(cout<<"Stack is full."):(cout<<"Stack is not full.");
break;
default:
cout<<"Illegal Option. Please try again ";
}
}//end of while
getch();
}
```

Program 4: Write a C++ program for Stack implementation and reversed its contents.

```
# include<iostream.h>
# include<conio.h>
# define SIZE 20
class stack
{
int a[SIZE];
int tos; // Top of Stack
public:
stack();
void push(int);
int pop();
int isempty();
int isfull();
};
stack::stack()
{
tos=0; //Initialize Top of Stack
}
int stack::isempty()
{
return (tos==0?1:0);
```

```
}
int stack::isfull()
{
return (tos==SIZE?1:0);
}
void stack::push(int i)
{
if(!isfull())
{
cout<<"Pushing "<<i<<endl;
a[tos]=i;
tos++;
}
else
{
cerr<<"Stack overflow error !
Possible Data Loss !";
}
}
int stack::pop()
{
if(!isempty())
{
cout<<"Popping "<<a[tos-1]<<endl;
return(a[--tos]);
}
else
{
cerr<<"Stack is empty! What to pop...!";
}
return 0;
}
void reverse(stack s)
{
stack s2;
while(!s.isempty())
{
s2.push(s.pop());
}
cout<<"Reversed contents of the stack..."<<endl;
```

```
while(!s2.isempty())
{
cout<<s2.pop()<<endl;
}
}//end of fn.
void main()
{
clrscr();
stack s;
s.push(1);
s.push(2);
s.push(3);
reverse(s);
getch();
}
```

Representation of two stacks using an array

Two stacks are represented in an array twostacks[0…N–1], such that one stack starts from start of the array and grows towards its end while the other one starts from the end of the array and grows towards the start. Thus at any time, the maximum number of elements that the two stacks together can accommodate is N. Write functions Push(stacki, data) and Delete(stacki) to add element data and to delete an element from stack number stacki, 1 <= stacki <= 2. The functions should be able to add elements to the stacks as long as there are fewer than N elements in both stacks together.

1. The two stacks are characterized by their indices (stack pointers). Index 1 starts from “1 and goes up to N “ 1 while index 2 starts from N and goes up to 0. When index 1 equals “1, it signifies that stack 1 is empty. When index 2 equals to N, that signifies that stack 2 is empty.
2. If the array is full, indices 1 and 2 point to consecutive elements. This situation is characterized as (index2 “ index1 == 1).

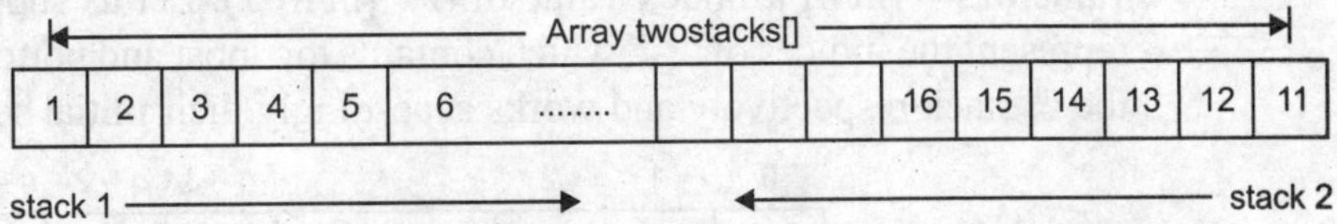

Figure 6.31: Representation of two stacks using an array

3. In Push(stacki,data), this condition is checked to signify overflow. If space is available, insertion of the element proceeds. If stacki == 1 then index 1 is

incremented and the data is inserted at the index. If stacki == 2, index 2 is decremented and the data is inserted at the index.

4. In Delete(stacki), the condition for underflow is checked. If stacki == 1 then index 1 == "1 signifies underflow of stack 1. If stacki == 2 then index 2 == N signifies underflow of stack 2. If an element exists, then deletion of the element at the stack top proceeds. If stacki == 1 then index 1 is decremented, whereas if stacki == 2 then index 2 is incremented.

The problem of underflow and overflow

Overflow problem is faced in push operation in a stack. If we push an item to the stack, which is already full, this called as overflow. Underflow problem is faced in pop operation in a stack. if we pop a data item from the stack, which is empty; this state is called as underflow. The problem of underflow is easily manageable, but the problem of overflow takes the shape of time-space trade-off. In this case, it is advisable to have two combined stacks, so that if required one stack can use the space of other.

Representing space of other multiple stacks in single array: Anchored lists are more appropriate for stacks, where the non-anchored end of the list represents the top of the stack.

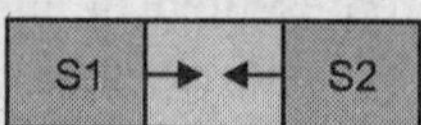

Figure 6.32: Concept of two stacks

Two stacks can be anchored at opposite ends of an array. As the stacks fill with data, they will "grow" towards each other. Figure 6.32 illustrates this concept. By filling the array with the two stacks anchored at opposite ends, the user can have the utility of two stacks while using the storage of one array.

In many applications, several stacks are required. Sometimes, we don't give memory space to different stacks; rather, we prefer to use single array to accommodate all stacks. Suppose "A" is an array of size "m" declared as, data type A [m].

Let us suppose n numbers of stacks are to be accommodated in single array "A" as shown in the Figure 6.33. We simply divide the array "A" in "n" approximately equal parts where the ith stack will be stored in "A" from index value of i * [m/n] to index value of (i * [m/n]-1). Let us suppose B [i] and C [i] represent the indices of "A" which contains top most and bottom most elements of the ith stack respectively and works accordingly their initial setting.

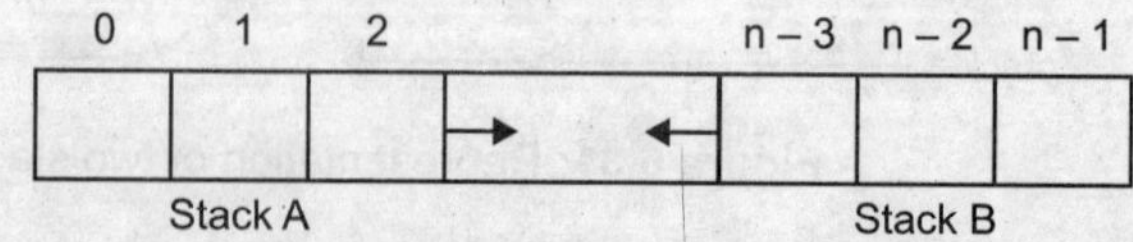

Figure 6.33: Representing two stacks in single array "A".

In this case, stack A, if required can use the space of stack B and vice-versa.

6.9.2 Representation of Stack using Linked-list

An alternative and efficient representation of stacks is possible by using linked lists for storing the data elements using dynamic memory. The advantages of linked list representation of stack over array representation are:

1. There is no need of knowing the stack size before implementing it, as dynamic memory allocation technique helps the programmer to declare the memory space at run time.
2. The stack is never full as long as the system has enough space for dynamic memory allocation.
3. Data movement, i.e. pushing or inserting and popping or deleting from stack is very easily handled with the concept of pointer in linked lists.

Remember that a stack implemented using linked list is called as linked stack.

***Definition of linked list:** A linked list is a set of nodes (a node can be a structure or a class) defined arbitrarily in memory; a node has a special variable (pointer) of the same type as the structure/class, which points to the next memory location, thus making the list values continuous. The following picture shows how a linked list looks like when it is created. The first node of a list is referred to as head/start most of the time and the last node is referred to as tail/end, the tail/end of the list always points to NULL or 0 (zero), which is also referred to as grounding as shown in the Figure 6.34.*

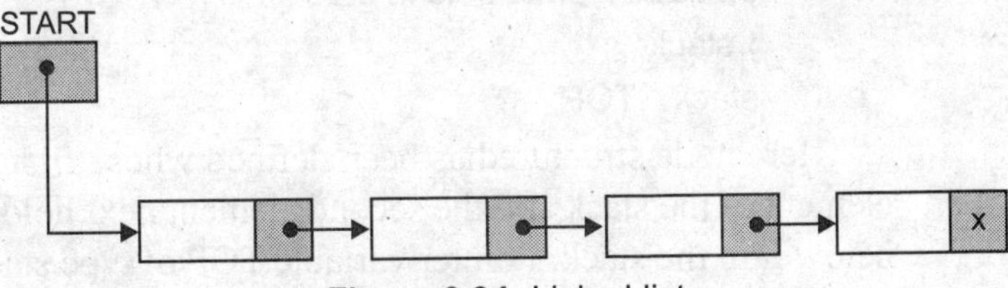

Figure 6.34: Linked list

Node organization

Basic element of a linked list is a "record" structure, of at least two fields (a class definition with these instance variables).

The object that holds the data and refers to the next element in the list, is called a **node**.

Data or Info next

data or Info component may actually be several fields or instance variables of any complexity. **next** is a pointer that points to the next element in the structure. There can be multiple reference fields but we won't consider that now.

Consider the stack of integers 10,20,30,40 (10 is the top, 40 the bottom). The logical order of the values in a stack is very clear; first comes the top element, next comes the element just below the top element, etc. In a linked implementation, the memory cell containing the top element will also contain a pointer to the second element, the memory cell containing the second element will contain a pointer to the third element, etc. What about the memory cell containing the bottom element?

There will be one memory cell for each element in the stack; in this memory cell we need to store *two* things: the value of the element, which is an integer in this example but could be anything, and a pointer to the memory cell of the next element. We can now draw the node-and-arc diagram representing Stack as shown in the Figure 6.35 as:

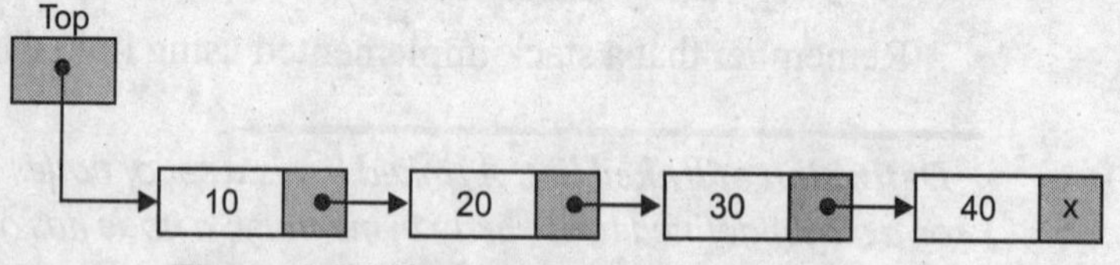

Figure 6.35: Node-and-arc representing stack

Formally a linked stack may be declared as:

```
typedef struct node
{
struct node * next ; /* pointer field in stack */
int data; /* data field in stack */
} stack;
stack * TOP;
```

Here node structure has been defined whose first element data holds the data element of the stack and the second element next holds the address of the element below it in the stack. Pointer variable TOP of type stack has also been declared.

Push operation

It's very similar to the addition in a dynamic linked list. The only difference is that here you'll add the new element only at the end of the list, which means addition can happen only from the TOP. Since a dynamic list is used for the stack, the Stack is also dynamic, means it has no prior size set. So, we don't have to check the Overflow condition in linked stack. This is as shown below:

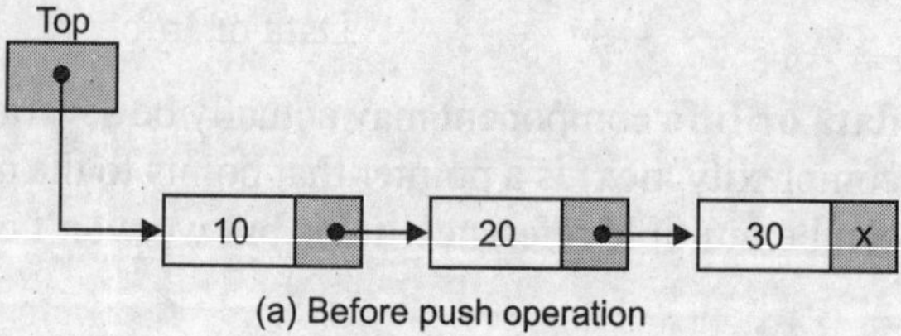

(a) Before push operation

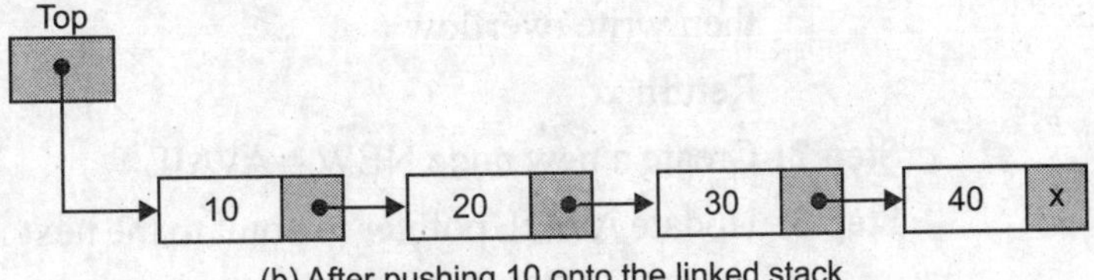

(b) After pushing 10 onto the linked stack

Figure 6.36: Push Operation

In Step [1] we create the new element to be pushed to the Stack.

In Step [2] the TOP most element is made to point to our newly created element.

In Step [3] the TOP is moved and made to point to the last element in the stack, which is our newly added element.

Algorithm 6.9: To insert node in the linked stack.

PUSH(AVAIL, TOP, LINK, NEW, INFO): Given a linked stack with pointer TOP pointing to the first node of the linked list. The AVAIL pointer points to the first node of the availability list. This algorithm pushes an ITEM onto the stack.

Step 1: [Check for AVAIL list]

If AVAIL = NULL

then write overflow

Return

Step 2: [Create a new node]

NEW = AVAIL

Step 3: [Update AVAIL, pointer]

AVAIL =LINK [AVAIL]

Step 4: [Copy ITEM into info part of new node]

INFO (NEW) = ITEM

Step 5: [Set link part of new node to top]

LINK (NEW) = TOP

Step 6: [TOP points to new node]

TOP =NEW

Step 7: Return

Explanation

In this procedure, first of all check stack.

Step 1: [Check for AVAIL list]

If AVAIL = NULL

then write overflow

Return

Step 2: Create a new node NEW = AVAIL

Step 3: Update AVAIL pointer to point to the next node of the availability list.

AVAIL =LINK [AVAIL]

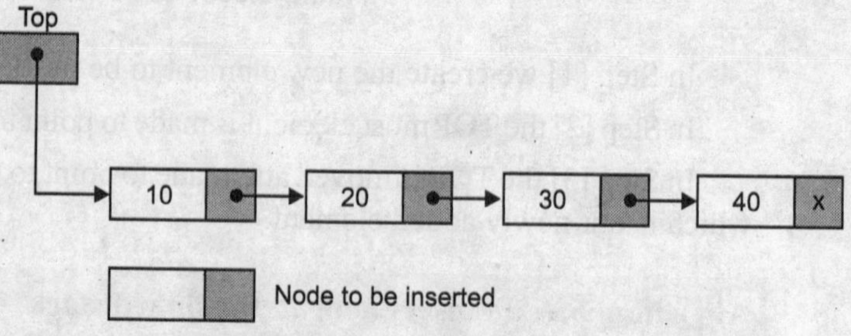

Figure 6.37: Before new node to be inserted.

Step 4: Now, Copy ITEM into INFO part of NEW node

INFO (NEW) = 5

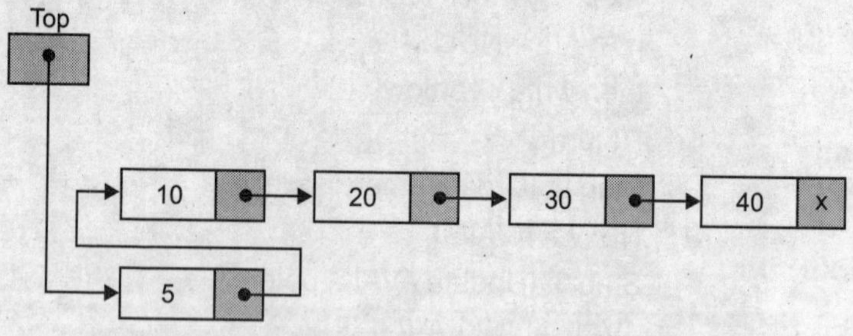

Figure 6.38: After insertion of new node having value 5.

Step 5: Set link part of NEW node to TOP

LINK (NEW) = TOP

Step 6: TOP points to new node

TOP =5

Step 7: Return

POP operation

This is again very similar to deletion in any Linked List, but you can only delete from the end of the list and that too, one at a time; and that makes it a stack. Here, we'll have a list pointer, "Next", which will be pointing to the last but one element in the List(stack). Every time we POP, the TOP most elements will be deleted and " Next " will be made as the TOP most element as shown below:

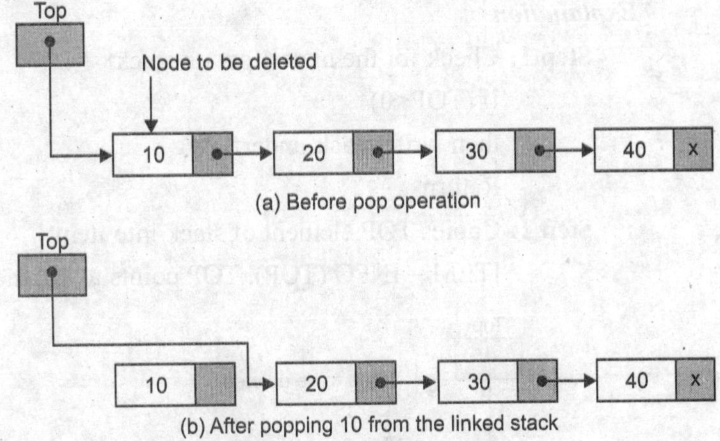

Figure 6.39: Pop operation.

In step [1] we delete topmost element 10 from linked stack

In step [2] we freed the TOP most element shown in Figure above

In step [3] we made the "Next" node as our TOP most element.

Algorithm 6.10: To delete node from linked stack.

POP(AVAIL, TOP, LINK, NEW, INFO, SAVE): Given a linked stack with pointer TOP pointing to the first node of the linked list. The AVAIL pointer points to the first node of the availability list. This algorithm pops the top element oh the linked stack and assign it to the local variable an ITEM. Here 'SAVE' is a local pointer variable ITEM and 'SAVE' is a local pointer variable which points to the deleted node.

Step 1: [Check for the underflow on stack]
If (TOP<0)
then write(stack underflow)
Return
Step 2: [Copies top element of stack into item]
ITEM = INFO (TOP)
Step 3: [Save TOP element]
SAVE =TOP
Step 4: [Reset TOP Element of stack into ITEM]
TOP = LINK [TOP]
Step 5: [Set link part to avail]
LINK (SAVE) = AVAIL
Step 6: [save pop node to avail list]
AVAIL = SAVE
Step 7: Return

Explanation

Step 1: Check for the underflow on stack

If (TOP<0)

then write(stack underflow)

Return

Step 2: Copies TOP element of stack into item

ITEM = INFO (TOP), TOP points to 10, then ITEM = 10

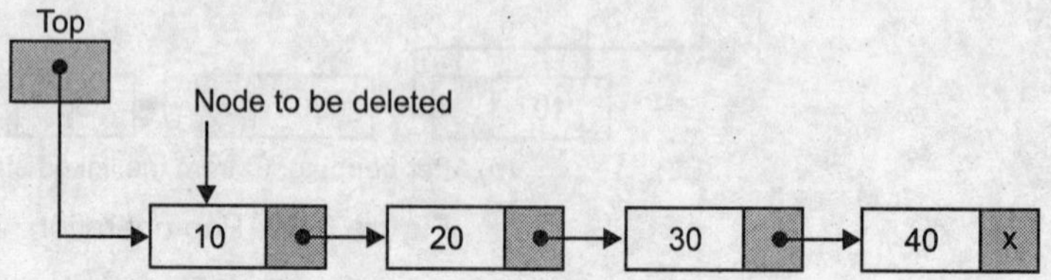

Figure 6.40: Before First node to be deleted.

Step 3: SAVE TOP element

SAVE =10

Step 4: Reset TOP Element of stack into ITEM, next ITEM is 20, now top points to 20.

TOP = 20

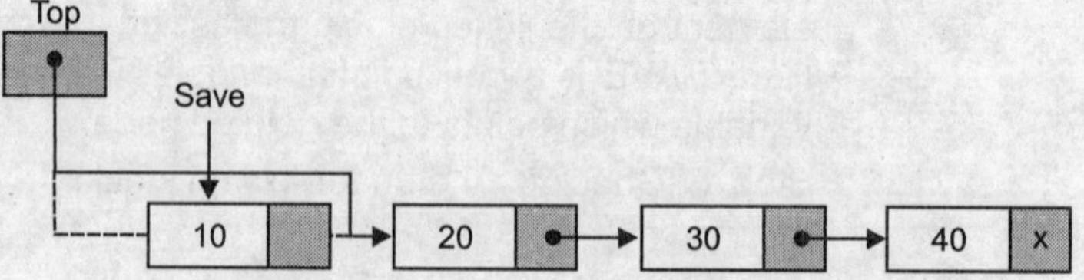

Figure 6.41: After deletion of first node having value 10.

Step 5: Set LINK part to AVAIL

LINK (SAVE) = AVAIL

Step 6: SAVE pop node to avail list

AVAIL = SAVE

Step 7: Return

Implementation of a stack using linked representation

In earlier section we had used arrays to store the elements that get added to the stack. But when implemented as an array it suffers basic limitation of an array that is its size cannot increased or decreased once it is declared. As a result, one ends up reserving too much space or too less space for an array and in turn for a stack. This problem can be solved by stack using linked list. For this type of implementation, let us use singly linked list for storing stack elements. In this type of implementation the top of the stack is given by a pointer top pointing to the first item of the list, ie. in the beginning of the list. So the stack elements ordered from top to bottom in linked list from left to right name of the list pointing to the top of the stack. The advantage of the this strategy is the push, pop operation takes constant time.

In C++ the stack node can be defined as

```
struct node
{
int data ;
node * link;
};
```

The operations are done using pointer manipulations, below **pseudo-code** explain the stack operations

```
push (item x,stack s)
{
temp =new node;
temp → data=x; //putting value into the node
temp → link=top; //Assigning temp's link to the top of the stack
top=temp //updating the top
}
int pop (s)
{ if (s=NULL)
"Stack is empty";
int item;
temp=top;
item=temp →data;
top=top→link;
return item;
}
```

Initially the list is empty, so the top pointer is NULL. The push function takes a pointer to an existing list as the first parameter and a data value to be pushed as the second parameter, creates a new node by using the data value, and adds it to the top of the existing list. A pop function takes a pointer to an existing list as the first parameter, and a pointer to a data object in which the popped value is to be returned as a second parameter. Thus it retrieves the value of the node pointed to by the top pointer, takes the top point to the next node, and destroys the node that was pointed to by the top.

If this strategy is used for creating a stack with the previously used four data values: 10, 20, 30, and 40, then the stack is created as shown in Figure 6.42.

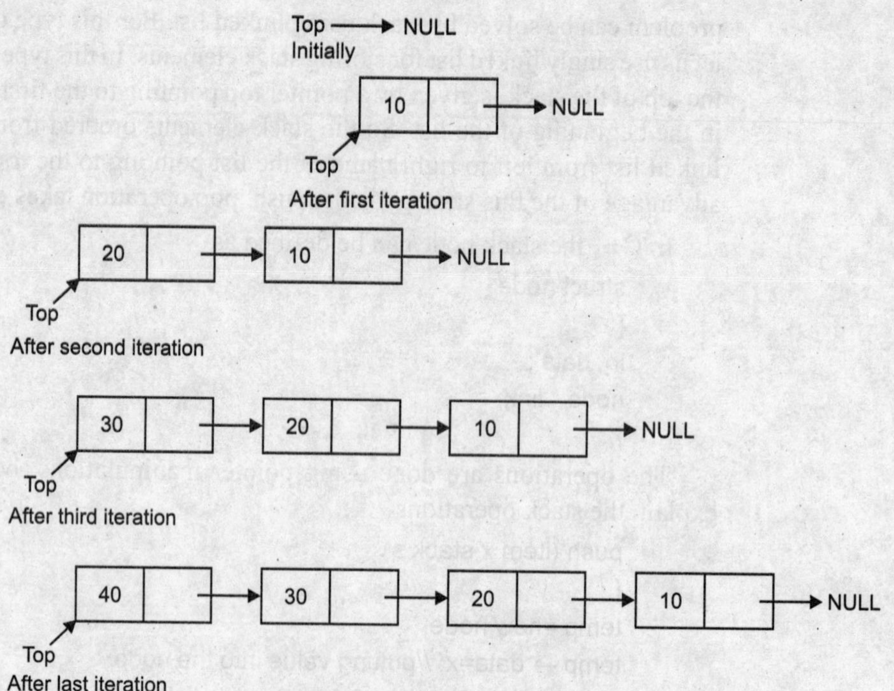

Figure 6.42: Linked stack.

Program 5: Write a C++ program to implement stack using linked list.

```
#include <iostream>
#include<conio.h>
struct node
{
int data;
node *link;
};
class lstack
{
private:
node* top;
public:
lstack()
{
top=NULL;
}
void push(int n)
```

```
{
node *tmp;
tmp=new node;
if(tmp==NULL)
cout<<"\nSTACK FULL";
tmp->data=n;
tmp->link=top;
top=tmp;
}
int pop()
{
if(top==NULL)
{
cout<<"\nSTACK EMPTY";
return NULL;
}
node *tmp;
int n;
tmp=top;
n=tmp->data;
top=top->link;
delete tmp;
return n;
}
~lstack()
{
if(top==NULL)
return;
node *tmp;
while(top!=NULL)
{
tmp=top;
top=top->link;
delete tmp;
}
}
};
void main()
{
```

```
Istack s;
s.push(11);
s.push(101);
s.push(99);
s.push(78);
cout<<"Item Popped = "<<s.pop()<<endl;
cout<<"Item Popped = "<<s.pop()<<endl;
cout<<"Item Popped = "<<s.pop()<<endl;
getch();
}
```

6.10 STACK APPLICATIONS

Five major applications of stacks are presented here. These examples are central to many activities that a computer must do and deserve time spent with them.

1. Expression evaluation
2. Backtracking (game playing, finding paths, exhaustive searching)
3. Memory management, run-time environment for nested language features.
4. Parenthesis matching
5. Balancing symbols

6.10.1 Expression Evaluation

In particular we will consider arithmetic expressions. Understand that there are boolean and logical expressions that can be evaluated in the same way. Control structures can also be treated similarly in a compiler.

This study of arithmetic expression evaluation is an example of problem solving where you solve a simpler problem and then **transform** the actual problem to the simpler one.

Aside: The NP-Complete problem. There are a set of apparently intractable problems: finding the shortest route in a graph (Travelling Salesman Problem), bin packing, linear programming, etc. that are similar enough that if a polynomial solution is ever found (exponential solutions abound) for one of these problems, then the solution can be applied to all problems.

Infix, Prefix and Postfix Notation

Infix Expression

In an expression if operator symbol is placed between two operands, it is called as infix expression and this way of writing an expression is called as Infix notation of an expression

Example is

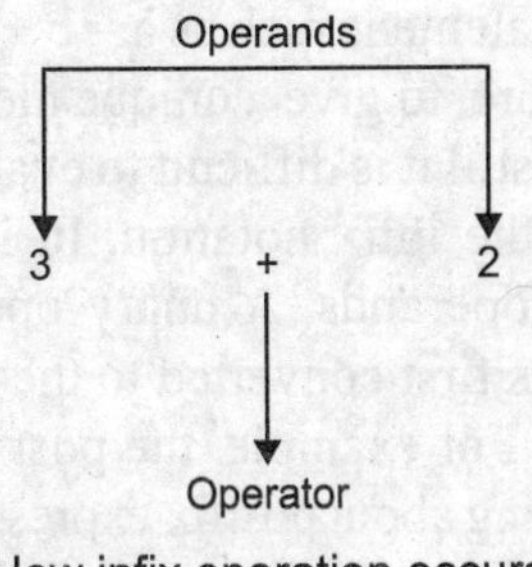

(How infix operation occurs)

Prefix Expression

In an expression if operator symbol is placed before its two operands, it is called as prefix expression or polish expression and this way of writing an expression is called as prefix or polish notation of an expression.

This notation was derived in 1920 by the polish mathematician Jan Lukasiewicz.

Example is:

The prefix or polish expression of infix expression 3+2 is +3 2 or +2 3.

Postfix expression

In an expression, if operator symbol is placed after its two operands, it is called as postfix expression or reverse polish expression and this way of writing an expression is called as postfix or reverse polish Notation (RPN) of an expression.

RPN was invented by Australian philosopher and computer scientist Charles Hamblin in the mid 1950s.

Example is:

The postfix or RPN of infix expression 3+2 is 3 2 + or 2 3 +

We are accustomed to write arithmetic expressions with the operation between the two operands: **a+b** or **c/d**. If we write **a+b*c**, however, we have to apply precedence rules to avoid the ambiguous evaluation (add first or multiply first?).

There's no real reason to put the operation between the variables or values. They can just as well precede or follow the operands. You should note the advantage of prefix and postfix: the need for precedence rules and parentheses are eliminated.

Infix	Prefix	Postfix
a + b	+ a b	a b +
a + b * c	+ a * b c	a b c * +
(a + b) * (c - d)	* + a b - c d	a b + c d - *

Postfix expressions are easily evaluated with the aid of a stack.

One of the applications of the stack is in expression evaluation. A complex assignment statement such as a = b + c*d/e–f may be interpreted in many different ways. Therefore, to give a unique meaning, the precedence and associativity rules are used. But still it is difficult to evaluate an expression by computer in its present form, called the infix notation. In infix notation, the binary operator comes in between the operands. A unary operator comes before the operand. To get it evaluated, it is first converted to the postfix form, where the operator comes after the operands. For example, the postfix form for the expression a*(b–c)/d is abc–*d/. A good thing about postfix expressions is that they do not require any precedence rules or parentheses for unique definition. So, evaluation of a postfix expression is possible using a stack-based algorithm.

Postfix expressions

Suppose we have a pocket calculator and would like to compute the cost of a shopping trip. To do so, we add a list of numbers and multiply the result by 1.06; this computes the purchase price of some items with local sales tax added. If the items are 4.99, 5.99, and 6.99, then a natural way to enter this would be the sequence

4.99 + 5.99 + 6.99 * 1.06 =

Depending on the calculator, this produces either the intended answer, 19.05, or the scientific answer, 18.39. Most simple four-function calculators will give the first answer, but better calculators know that multiplication has higher precedence than addition.

On the other hand, some items are taxable and some are not, so if only the first and last items were actually taxable, then the sequence

4.99 * 1.06 + 5.99 + 6.99 * 1.06 =

would give the correct answer (18.69) on a scientific calculator and the wrong answer (19.37) on a simple calculator. A scientific calculator generally comes with parentheses, so we can always get the right answer by parenthesizing, but with a simple calculator we need to remember intermediate results.

A typical evaluation sequence for this example might be to multiply 4.99 and 1.06, saving this answer as a_1. We then add 5.99 and a_1, saving the result in a_1. We multiply 6.99 and 1.06, saving the answer in a_2, and finish by adding a_1 and a_2, leaving the final answer in a_1. We can write this sequence of operations as follows:

4.99 1.06 * 5.99 + 6.99 1.06 * +

This notation is known as postfix or reverse Polish notation and is evaluated exactly as we have described above. The easiest way to do this is to use a stack. When a number is seen, it is pushed onto the stack; when an operator is seen, the operator is applied to the two numbers (symbols) that are popped from the stack and the result is pushed onto the stack. For instance, the postfix expression

6 5 2 3 + 8 * + 3 + *

is evaluated as follows: The first four symbols are placed on the stack. The resulting stack is

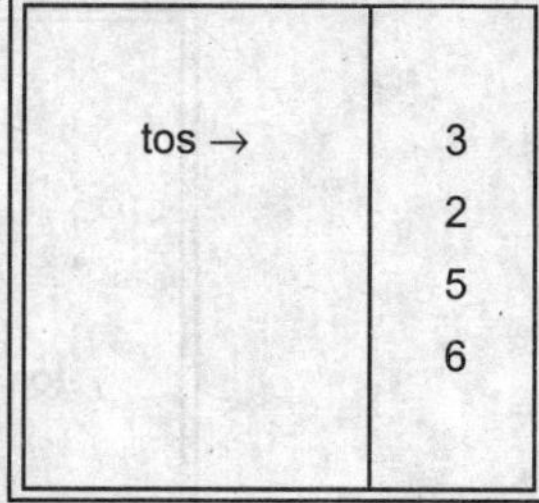

Next a '+' is read, so 3 and 2 are popped from the stack and their sum, 5, is pushed.

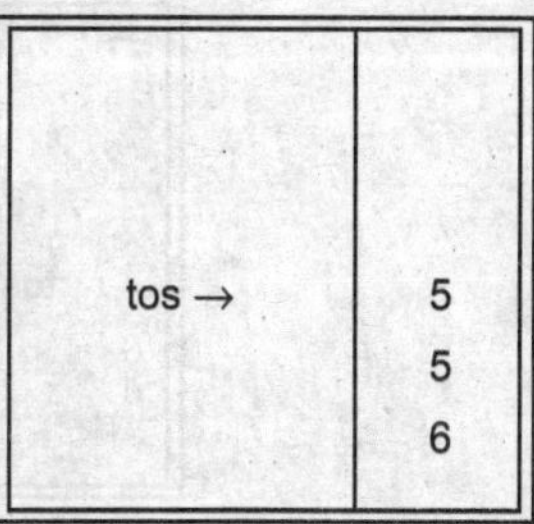

Next 8 is pushed.

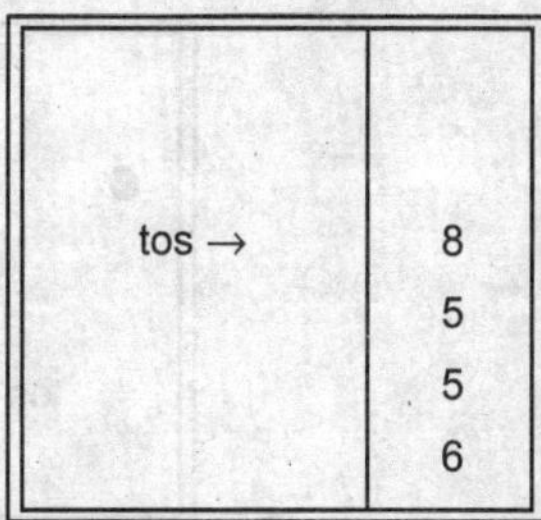

Now a '*' is seen, so 8 and 5 are popped as 8 * 5 = 40 is pushed.

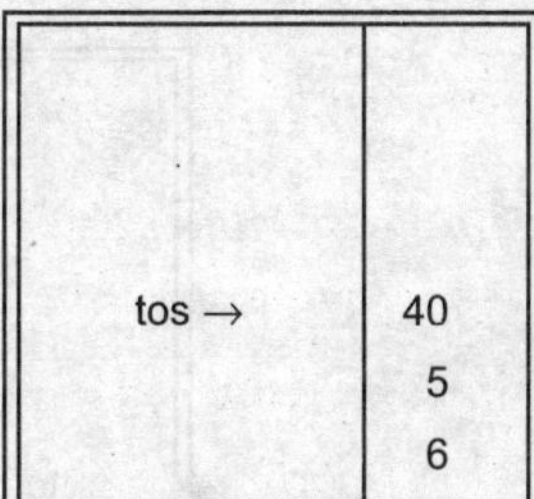

Next a '+' is seen, so 40 and 5 are popped and 40 + 5 = 45 is pushed.

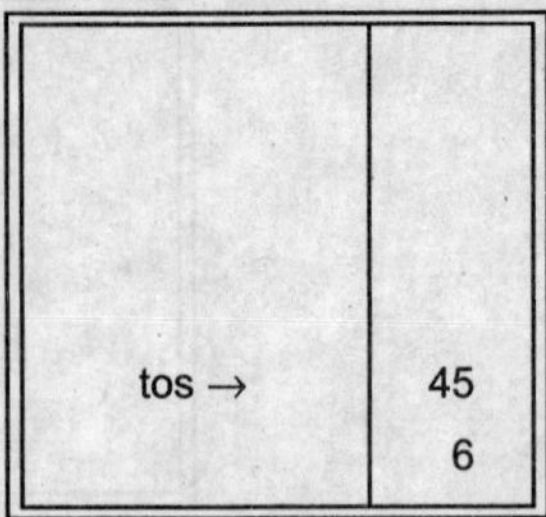

Now, 3 is pushed.

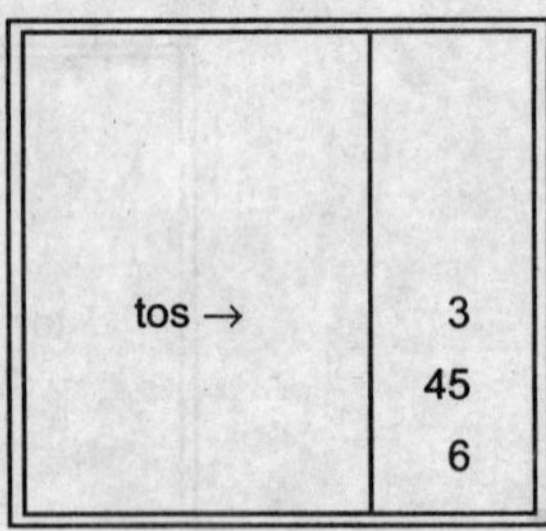

Next '+' pops 3 and 45 and pushes 45 + 3 = 48.

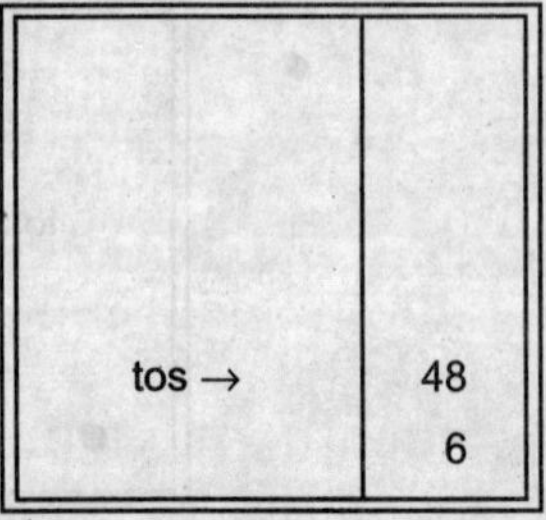

Finally, a '*' is seen and 48 and 6 are popped, the result 6 * 48 = 288 is pushed.

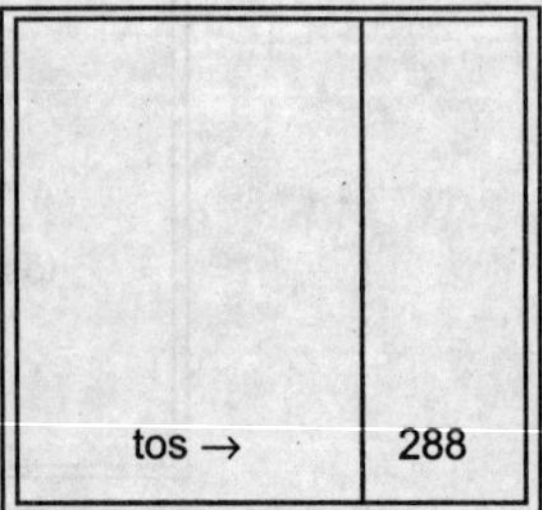

The time to evaluate a postfix expression is O(n), because processing each element in the input consists of stack operations and thus takes constant time. The algorithm to do so is very simple. Notice that when an expression is given in postfix notation, there is no need to know any precedence rules; this is an obvious advantage.

Algorithm 6.11: Postfix Evaluation

Assume we have a string of operands and operators, an informal, by hand process is

Scan the expression left to right

Skip values or variables (operands)

Step 1: When an operator is found, apply the operation to the preceding two operands

Step 2: Replace the two operands and operator with the calculated value (three symbols are replaced with one operand)

Step 3: Continue scanning until only a value remains—the result of the expression

The time complexity is O(n) because each operand is scanned once, and each operation is performed once.

Using stack it is very easy to evaluate postfix expression, the following pseudo code shows the procedure for evaluation.

A more formal algorithm:

```
create a new stack
while(input stream is not empty)
{
token = getNextToken();
if(token instanceof operand)
{
push(token);
} else if (token instance of operator)
op2 = pop();
op1 = pop();
result = calc(token, op1, op2);
push(result);
}
}
return pop();
Demonstration with 2 3 4 + * 5 -
```

EXAMPLE: Let us see how the above algorithm will be implemented using an example.

Postfix String: 123*+4-

Initially the Stack is empty. Now, the first three characters scanned are 1,2 and 3, which are operands. Thus they will be pushed into the stack in that order.

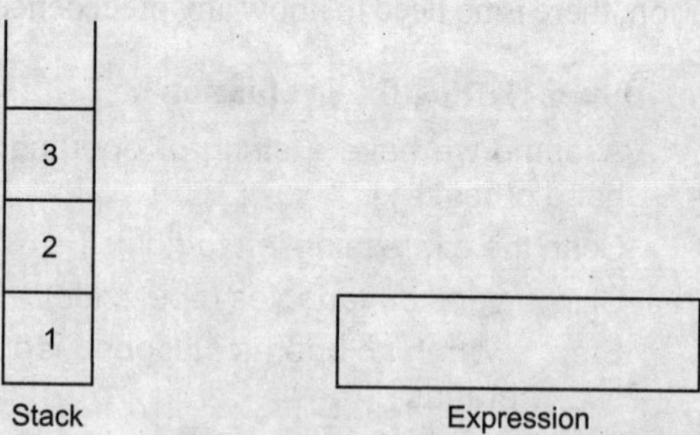

Next character scanned is "*", which is an operator. Thus, we pop the top two elements from the stack and perform the "*" operation with the two operands. The second operand will be the first element that is popped.

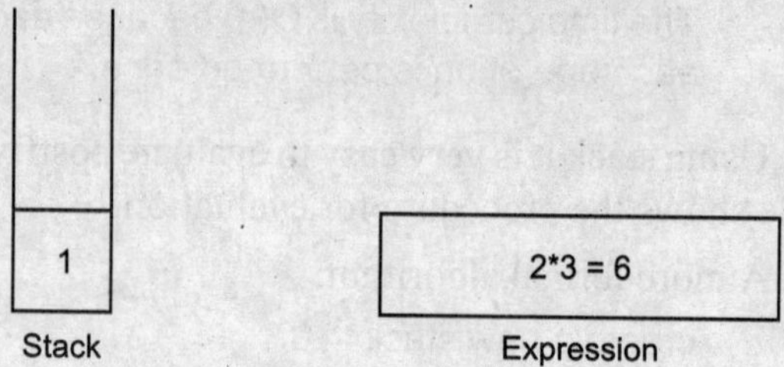

The value of the expression(2*3) that has been evaluated(6) is pushed into the stack.

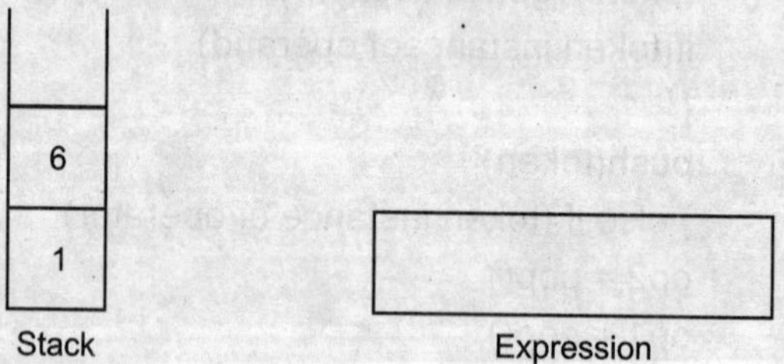

Next character scanned is "+", which is an operator. Thus, we pop the top two elements from the stack and perform the "+" operation with the two operands. The second operand will be the first element that is popped.

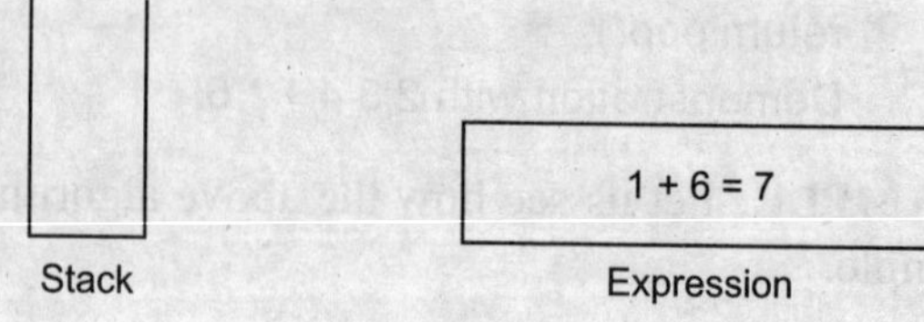

The value of the expression(1+6) that has been evaluated(7) is pushed into the stack.

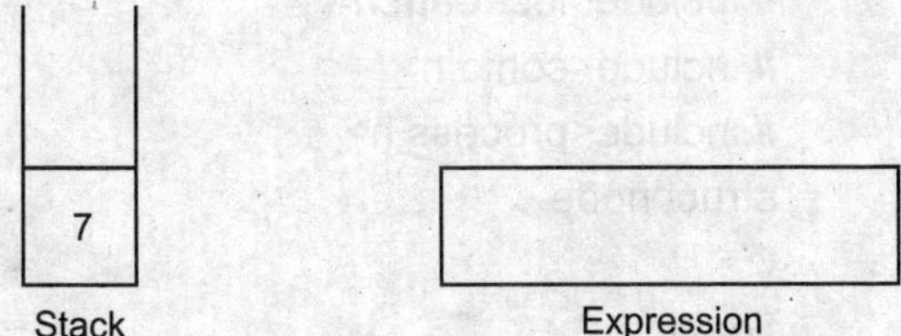

Next character scanned is "4", which is added to the stack.

Next character scanned is "-", which is an operator. Thus, we pop the top two elements from the stack and perform the "-" operation with the two operands. The second operand will be the first element that is popped.

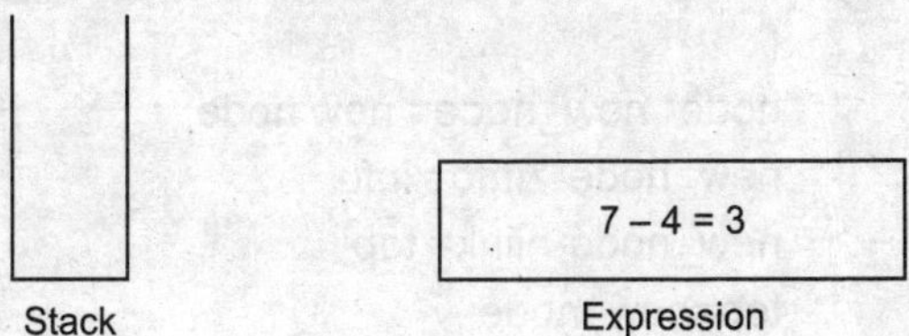

The value of the expression(7-4) that has been evaluated(3) is pushed into the stack.

Now, since all the characters are scanned, the remaining element in the stack (there will be only one element in the stack) will be returned.

End result:

Postfix String: 123*+4-

Result: 3

Program 6: Write a C++ program for postfix expression evaluation using stack.

```
# include<iostream.h>
# include<conio.h>
# include<process.h>
struct node
{
float info;
node* link;
};
class stack
{
private:
node* top;
public:
stack ( )
{
top=NULL;
}
void push(float info)
{
node* new_node= new node;
new_node->info= info;
new_node->link= top;
top=new_node;
}
float pop( )
{
if (!top)
{
cout<<"\nsome operand is missing";
getch ( );
exit (1);
}
node* temp=top;
top=top->link;
return (temp->info);
}
int total ( ); // function prototype
};
```

```
{
int count=0;
node* temp=top;
while (temp)
{
count++;
temp=temp->link;
}
return (count);
}
void main ( )
{
clrscr ( );
stack s;
char ch;
int digit, temp;
float d1, d2;
float result;
cout<<"Enter the expression (with spaces) terminated by carriage return:
\n);
do
{
ch=getche ( );
switch (ch)
{
case '+': s.push (s.pop ( )+s.pop ( ));
break;
case '-': d1=s.pop ( );
d2=s.pop ( );
s.push (d2-d1);
break;
case '*': s.push (s.pop ( ) *s.pop ( ));
break;
case '/': d1=s.pop ( ) *s.pop ( ));
d2=s.push(d2/d1);
break;
case '\r': if (s.total ( ) >1)
cout<<endl<<s.total ( ) -1<<" operator(s) is (are) missing";
else
{
```

```
result= s.pop ( );
cout<<"\n\nResult of the evaluation is: "<<result;
}
getch ( );
exit (0);
default: digit=int (ch) -int ('0');
temp=0;
if(digit >=0 && digit <=9)
{
ch=getche( );
while (ch!=' ')
{
temp=int (ch) -int ('0');
digit=digit*10+temp;
ch=getche ( );
}
s.push (digit);
}
}
}
while (1);
}
```

Output:

```
Enter the expression (with spaces) terminated by carriage return:
5    6     2     +     *     12     4     /     +
Result of the evaluation is: 37
```

Infix to Prefix Notation

Algorithm 6.12: Infix to Prefix Notation

Step 1: Read the given infix expression into string called infix.

Step 2: Reverse the infix string and read one character at a time and perform the following operations:

If the read character is an operand, then add the operand to the prefix string.

If the read character is not an operand, then check

If the stack is not empty and precedence of the top of the stack operator is higher than the read operator, then pop the operator from stack and add this operator to the prefix string.

Else push the operator onto the stack.

Step 3: Repeat STEP 2 till all characters are processed from the input string.

Step 4: If stack is not empty, then pop the operator from stack and add this operator to the prefix string.

Step 5: Repeat STEP 4 till all the operators are popped from the stack.

Step 6: Reverse the prefix string and display the result of the given infix expression or the resultant prefix expression stored in a string called prefix from this algorithm.

Infix to postfix conversion

Consider the sum of A and B. We think applying the operator "+" to the operands A and B write the sum as A+B. This particular representation is called infix. There are two alternate notations for expressing the sum of A and B using the symbols A, B, and + These are

+ AB **prefix**

AB + **postfix**

The 'pre-', 'post-', and 'in-' refer to the relative position of the operator with respect to the two operands. In prefix notation the operator preceded the two operands, in postfix notation the operator follows the two operands, and in in-fix notation the operator in between the two operands. The precedence of the operator allows us to evaluate the expression unambiguously.

- Exponentiation Highest priority
- Multiplication, Division Next highest priority
- Addition, Subtraction lowest priority

If we wish to override these priorities we can do so by using a pair of parenthesis as shown below.

(A + B) * C

A * (B " C)

(A + B)/(C – D)

The expression with in a pair of parenthesis is always evaluated earlier than the other operations.

The prefix and postfix expressions have three features:

1. The Operands maintain the same order as in the equivalent infix expression.
2. Parenthesis are not need to designate the expressions unambiguously.
3. While evaluating the expression the priority of the operators is irrelevant.

```
// pseudo code for converting infix to postfix expression
operandStack=the empty Stack;
```

```
while(not end of the input)
{
element=next input character;
if(element is an operand);
add element to the postfix string
else
{
while (!empty(operandStack) and precedence (Stacktop( operand-
Stack,element ) ) )
{
topelement=pop(operandStack);
add topelement to postfix string;
}
push(operandStack,element);
} }
//output of the remaining operator
while(!empty(operandStack))
{
topelement=pop(operandStack);
add topelment to postfix string;
} // end if while loop
return the post string ;
```

Not only can a stack be used to evaluate a postfix expression, but we can also use a stack to convert an expression in standard form (otherwise known as infix) into postfix. We will concentrate on a small version of the general problem by allowing only the operators +, *, and (,), and insisting on the usual precedence rules. We will further assume that the expression is legal. Suppose we want to convert the infix expression

a + b * c + (d * e + f) * g

into postfix. A correct answer is a b c * + d e * f + g * +.

When an operand is read, it is immediately placed onto the output. Operators are not immediately output, so they must be saved somewhere. The correct thing to do is to place operators that have been seen, but not placed on the output, onto the stack. We will also stack left parentheses when they are encountered. We start with an initially empty stack.

If we see a right parenthesis, then we pop the stack, writing symbols until we encounter a (corresponding) left parenthesis, which is popped but not output.

If we see any other symbol ('+','*', '('), then we pop entries from the stack until we find an entry of lower priority. One exception is that we never remove a '('

from the stack except when processing a ')'. For the purposes of this operation, '+' has lowest priority and '(' highest. When the popping is done, we push the operand onto the stack.

Finally, if we read the end of input, we pop the stack until it is empty, writing symbols onto the output.

To see how this algorithm performs, we will convert the infix expression above into its postfix form. First, the symbol a is read, so it is passed through to the output. Then '+' is read and pushed onto the stack. Next b is read and passed through to the output. The state of affairs at this juncture is as follows:

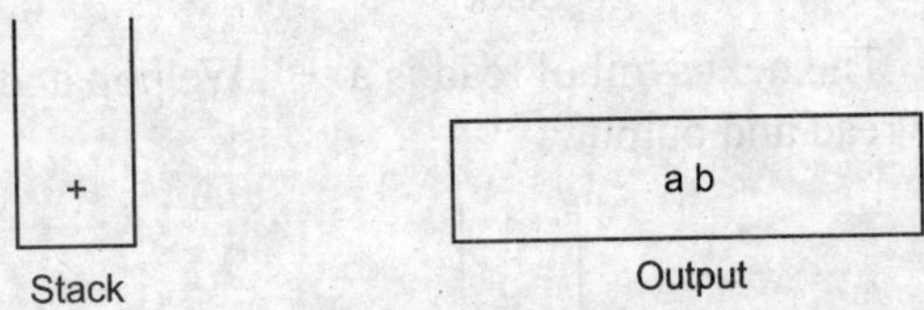

Next a '*' is read. The top entry on the operator stack has lower precedence than '*', so nothing is output and '*' is put on the stack. Next, c is read and output. Thus far, we have

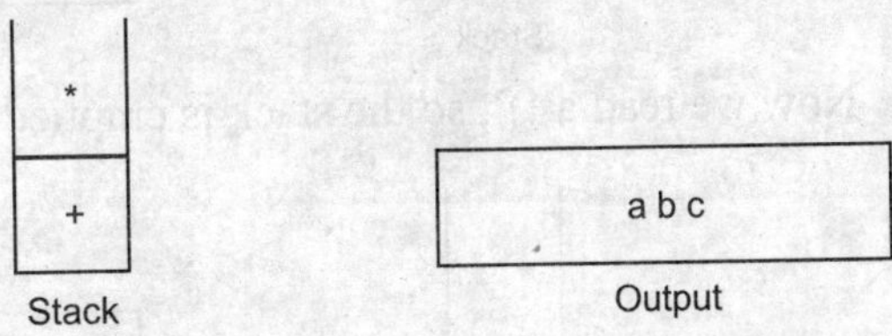

The next symbol is a '+'. Checking the stack, we find that we will pop a '*' and place it on the output, pop the other '+', which is not of lower but equal priority, on the stack, and then push the '+'.

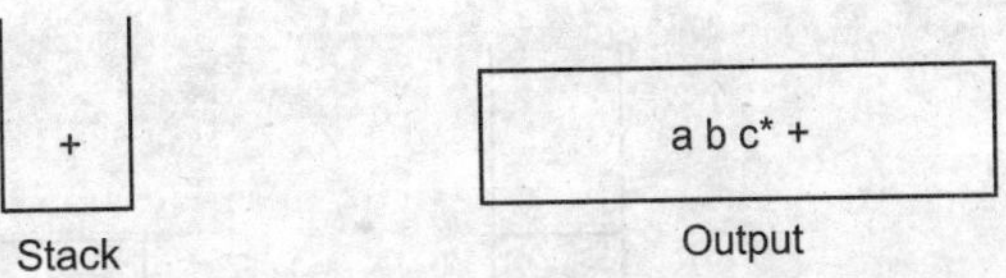

The next symbol read is an '(', which, being of highest precedence, is placed on the stack. Then d is read and output.

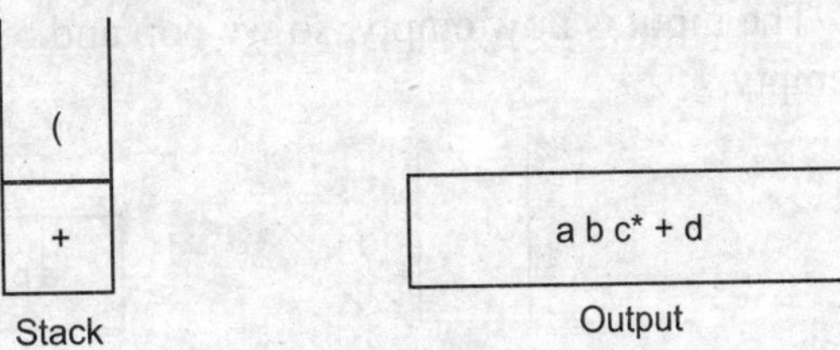

We continue by reading a '*'. Since open parentheses do not get removed except when a closed parenthesis is being processed, there is no output. Next, e is read and output.

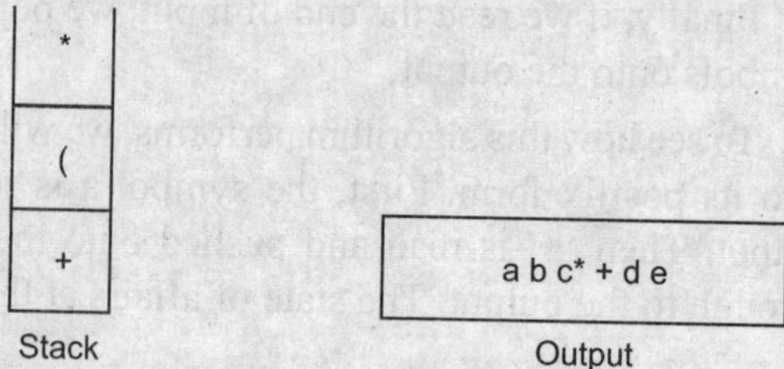

The next symbol read is a '+'. We pop and output '*' and then push '+'. Then we read and output.

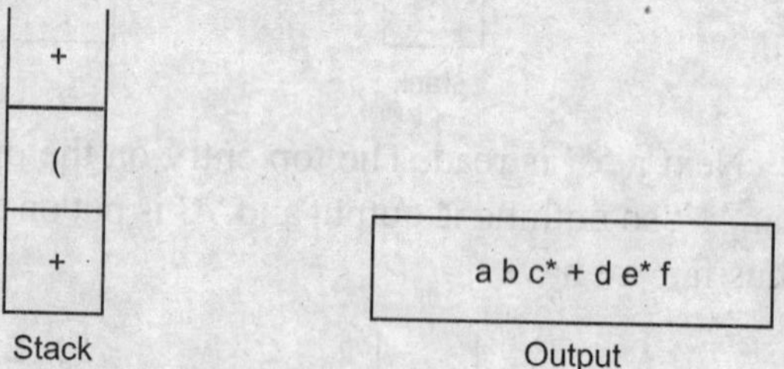

Now we read a ')', so the stack is emptied back to the '('. We output a '+'.

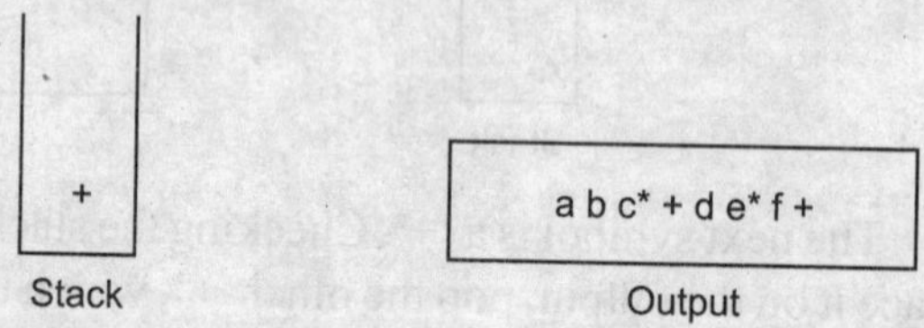

We read a '*' next; it is pushed onto the stack. Then g is read and output.

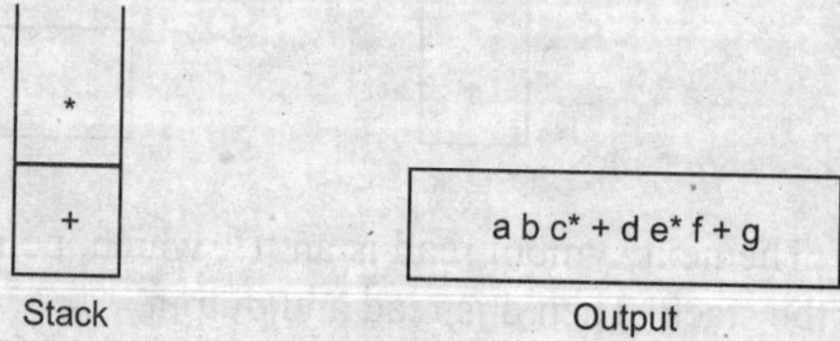

The input is now empty, so we pop and output symbols from the stack until it is empty.

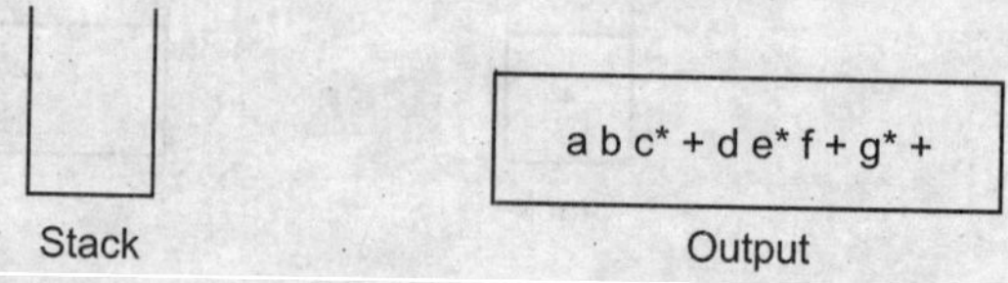

As before, this conversion requires only O(n) time and works in one pass through the input. We can add subtraction and division to this repertoire by assigning subtraction and addition equal priority and multiplication and division equal priority. A subtle point is that the expression a - b - c will be converted to ab - c- and not abc - -.

Our algorithm does the right thing, because these operators associate from left to right. This is not necessarily the case in general, since exponentiation associates right to left: 223 = 28 = 256 not 43 = 64. We leave as an exercise the problem of adding exponentiation to the repertoire of assignments.

Algorithm 6.13: Infix transformation to Postfix

This process uses a stack as well. We have to hold information that's expressed inside parentheses while scanning to find the closing ')'. We also have to hold information on operations that are of lower precedence on the stack. The algorithm is:

Step 1: Create an empty stack and an empty postfix output string/stream

Step 2: Scan the infix input string/stream left to right

Step 3: If the current input token is an operand, simply append it to the output string (note the examples above that the operands remain in the same order)

Step 4: If the current input token is an operator, pop off all operators that have equal or higher precedence and append them to the output string; push the operator onto the stack. The order of popping is the order in the output.

Step 5: If the current input token is '(', push it onto the stack

Step 6: If the current input token is ')', pop off all operators and append them to the output string until a '(' is popped; discard the '('.

Step 7: If the end of the input string is found, pop all operators and append them to the output string.

This algorithm doesn't handle errors in the input, although careful analysis of parenthesis or lack of parenthesis could point to such error determination.

For example consider the expression A+(B*C-(D/E)+F). To convert this infix to postfix expression we will perform the above mentioned steps i.e.We move from left to right in the infix expression. We keep on pushing elements onto the stack till we reach a operand.

Once we reach an operand, we add it to the output. If we reach a) symbol, we pop elements off the stack till we reach a corresponding (symbol. If we reach an operator, we pop off any operators on the stack which are of higher precedence than this one and push this operator onto the stack.

Symbol scanned	Stack	Expression	COMMENTS
A	(	A	
+	(+	A	
(	(+(	A	
B	(+(	AB	
*	(+(*	AB	
C	(+(*	ABC	
-	(+(-	ABC *	* has high priority
(	(+(-(	ABC*	
D	(+(-(	ABC*D	
/	(+(-(/	ABC*D	
E	(+(-(/	ABC*DE	
)	(+(-	ABC*DE/	) remove / and (from stack
+	(+(+	ABC*DE/-	
F	(+(+	ABC*DE/-F	
)	(+	ABC*DE/-F	
) SENTINEL		ABC*DE/-F+	

Program 7: Write a C++ program for infix to postfix conversion.

```
#include<iostream.h>
#include<string.h>
#include<stdlib.h>
#include<ctype.h>
#include<conio.h>
class expression
{
private:
char infix[100];
char stack[200];
int top;
int r;
char postfix[100];
public:
void convert();
int input_p(char);
int stack_p(char);
int rank(char);
};
int expression::input_p(char c)
```

```
{
if(c=='+' || c=='-')
return 1;
else if(c=='*' || c=='/')
return 3;
else if(c=='^')
return 6;
else if(isalpha(c)!=0)
return 7;
else if(c=='(')
return 9;
else if(c==')')
return 0;
else
{
cout<<"Invalid expression ::input error\n";
exit(0);
}
}
int expression::stack_p(char c)
{
if(c=='+' || c=='-')
return 2;
else if(c=='*' || c=='/')
return 4;
else if(c=='^')
return 5;
else if(isalpha(c)!=0)
return 8;
else if(c=='(')
return 0;
else
{
cout<<"Invalid expression  ::stack error\n";
exit(0);
}
}
int expression::rank(char c)
{
```

```
if(c=='+' || c=='-')
return -1;
else if(c=='*' || c=='/')
return -1;
else if(c=='^')
return -1;
else if(isalpha(c)!=0)
return 1;
else
{
cout<<"Invalid expression ::in rank\n";
exit(0);
}
}
void expression::convert()
{
cout<<"\n**************************************************\n"
<<"This program converts the given infix expression\n"
<<"in to postfix form"
<<"\n**************************************************\n";
cout<<"Enter an infix expression ::\n";
cin>>infix;
int l=strlen(infix);
infix[l]=')';
infix[l+1]='';
//Convertion starts
top=1;
stack[top]='(';
r=0;
int x=-1;
int i=0;
char next=infix[i];
while(next!='')
{
//Pop all the elements to outputin stack which have higher precedence
while( input_p(next) < stack_p(stack[top]) )
{
if(top<1)
{
```

```
cout<<"invalid expression ::stack error\n";
exit(0);
}
postfix[++x]=stack[top];
top-;
r=r+rank(postfix[x]);
if(r<1)
{
cout<<"Invalid expression  ::r<1\n";
exit(0);
}
}
if(input_p( next ) != stack_p( stack[top]))
stack[++top]=next;
else
top-;
i++;
next=infix[i];
}
postfix[++x]='';
if(r!=1 || top!=0)
{
cout<<"Invalid expression ::error in rank or stack\n";
exit(0);
}
cout<<"\n\nThe corresponding postfix expression is ::\n";
cout<<postfix<<endl;
}
void main()
{
expression obj;
obj.convert();
getch();
}
```

Output:

```
****************************************************
This program converts the given infix expression
in to postfix form
****************************************************
```

```
Enter an infix expression ::
(a+b^c^d)*(c+d)
The corresponding postfix expression is ::
abcd^^+cd+*
Press any key to continue
```

Let us take another example of an expression (10-6) * (9/3)

Add closing brace to an end of expression.

Input expression is (10-6) * (9/3))

Following is the explanation of steps involved in algorithm:

Token read	Process	Stack contents (growing from left to right)	Result expression
(	Push	(	-
10	Print	(	10
-	Push	(-	6
6	Print	(-	10 6
)	Pop symbols until '(' appers ,Pop (	Empty	10 6 -
*	Push	*	10 6 -
(	Push	* (	10 6 -
9	Print	*(	10 6 - 9
/	Push	*(/	10 6 - 9
3	Print	*(/	10 6-9 3
)	Pop all symbols	*as '(' appears, we stop popping out	10 6 –9 3 /
End of expression		Empty	10 6 –9 3 / *

So the converted postfix expression is: 10 6 –9 3 / *

6.10.2 Backtracking

Backtracking is used in algorithms in which there are steps along some path (state) from some starting point to some goal.

- Find your way through a maze.
- Find a path from one point in a graph (roadmap) to another point.
- Play a game in which there are moves to be made (checkers, chess).

In all of these cases, there are choices to be made among a number of options. We need some way to remember these decision points in case we want/need to come back and try the alternative

Consider the maze. At a point where a choice is made, we may discover that the choice leads to a dead-end. We want to retrace back to that decision point and then try the other (next) alternative.

Again, stacks can be used as part of the solution. Recursion is another, typically more favored, solution, which is actually implemented by a stack.

Recursion

Recursion, in mathematics and computer science, is a method of defining functions in which the function being defined is applied within its own definition. The term is also used more generally to describe a process of repeating objects in a self-similar way. For instance, when the surfaces of two mirrors are almost parallel with each other the nested images that occur are a form of recursion.When a called function in turn calls another function, then a process of 'chaining' occurs. Recursion is a special case of this process or chain. So when a function calls itself, then it is called **recursion.** This chain continues till a specific condition met. If it has not any stop condition, then it will create an indefinite loop. Recursion is also called self-reference loop. Recursion is used to solve for the problems, which cannot be solved by the iterative procedure for, while and do loops. It is useful to solve repetitive problems, where input of one sub-program can be used as starting value having the previous output. A recursion procedure is also called well-defined function, if it satisfies the following conditions:

(i) A recursive function should have specific condition.

(ii) A recursive function should have smaller argument each time than the previous argument value in the every recursive loop.

For example, below written program is a recursive (unconditional recursion) procedure:

```
main ( )
{
cout<< "\n I LOVE MY BABY \n";
main ( );
}
```

It will display the result infinite times (indefinite loop) as:

```
I LOVE MY BABY
I LOVE MY BABY
I LOVE MY BABY
........................
```

Another example, which will illustrate the recursion based on condition, is to write a C++ program to find the factorial of a number is written below as:

Program 8: Write a C++ program to find the factorial of a number by using the Recursion.

```
#include <iostream.h>
#include <conio.h>
void main ( )
{
int n, factorial( );
clrscr();
cout<<"\n Enter the value of N: ";
cin>>n;
cout<<"\n Factorial of number"<<n<<" is "<<factorial(n);
getch ( );
}
int factorial(n)
int n;
{
int m;
if (n = = 1)
{
return (n);
}
else
{
m = n * factorial(n-1);
return (m);
}
}
```

Output:

Enter the value of N: 5

Factorial of number 5 is 120

Working of Recursion

We hope you agree that it's difficult to visualize how the control flows from one function to another. Possibly given Figure on next page would make the things a bit clearer.Assume that the number entered through scanf() is 5 as above program. Using the Figure let's visualize what exactly happens when the recursive function factorial() gets called.

Go through the Figure carefully. The first time when factorial() function is called from main() function, n collects value 5. From here, since n is not equal to 1, the if block is skipped and factorial() function is called again with the argument (n-1), i.e 4. This is a recursive call. Since n is still not equal to 1, factorial() function is called yet another time , with argument(4-1), i.e 3.This is again recursive call. Since again n is still not equal to 1, factorial() function is called yet another time, with the argument(3-1), i.e 2. This process will carry on until the value of argument n is 1. When the value of n is 1, control goes back to previous factorial() function with the value 1, and m is evaluated as 2. And then control back to next previous factorial() function with the value 2 and m is again evaluated as 6.

Similarly, each factorial() function evaluates its m from the returned value, and finally 120 is return to main() function. The sequence would be grasped better by following the shown in the Figure:

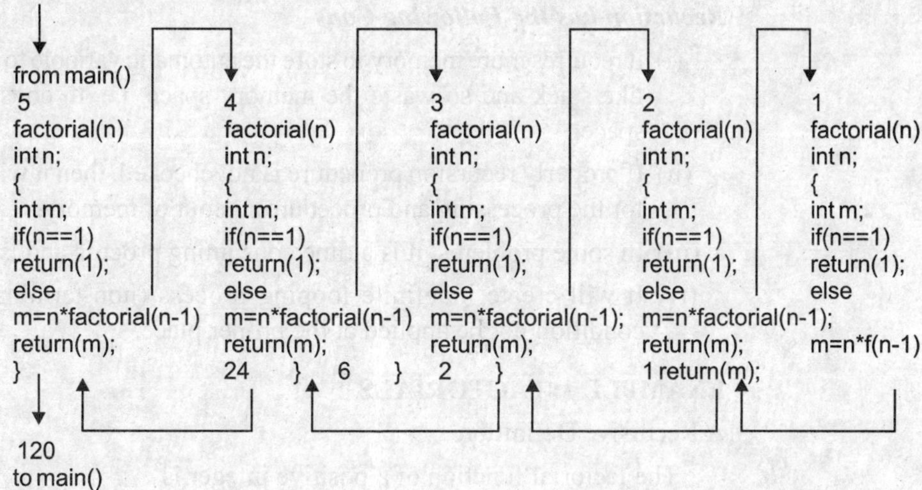

Note that while writing recursive function you have an if statement or a conditional statement somewhere in the recursive function to force the function to return without recursive calls being executed. If you don't do this and you call the function, you will fall in indefinite loop, and will never return from the called function.

Pros (Advantages) and Cons (Disadvantages) of Recursion

Recursion is a process in which a function calls itself that is function calling itself is known as Recursion. The various advantages of recursion are:

(i) It is simple, easily understandable, concise, compact and transparent to view a c program.

(ii) lesser number of programming statements (coding) required with the use of recursion.

(iii) It is very useful in solving mathematical (factorial, GCD, Fibonacci **series** etc.), trigonometric (compute hyperbolic trigonometric value), logical **games** (tower of Hanoi, generating random number in system simulation, puzzles) and algebraic problems (to solve Ackermann's function).

(iv) It is very useful where user-defined function or sub-program or procedure required.

(v) It is eminently useful if the solution to problem is in recursive terms.

(vi) It is more useful in the multiprocessing and multitasking environment.

(vii) It is very useful in solving the data structure problems like linked list, queues, stack, tree, Quick sort and merge sort etc.

(viii) Recursion saves the memory. In other words it utilizes the memory well.

Recursion has the Following Cons

(i) It requires more memory to store the automatic variable to solve the problems like stack and so waste the memory space. i.e. to consume more storage space.

(ii) If properly recursion procedure is not checked, then it will create a problem for the processing and procedure run out of memory.

(iii) In some problems, it is a time consuming process and is not efficient.

(iv) It will create indefinite looping process (non-terminating iteration), if condition not be applied at the proper place.

EXAMPLE 1: FACTORIALS

A Recursive Definition

The factorial function of a positive integer is

$$n! = n \times (n-1)\times \ldots \times 1$$

Formal Definition:

n! = 1 if n=0

= *n* (n-1)!* *If n>0*

Example:

3!= 3*2!

= 3*(2*1!)

= 3*(2*(1*0!))

= 3*(2*(1*1))

= 3*(2*1)

= 3*2 = 6

Factorials: A Recursive Definition:

Every recursive process or procedure consists of two parts:

- A smallest , base case that is processed without recursion
- A general method that reduces a particular case to one or more of the smaller cases, thereby making progress toward eventually reducing the problem all the way to the base case

EXAMPLE 2: TOWERS OF HANOI

Here we will explain how recursion can be used as a tool in developing an algorithm to solve a particular problem like Tower of Hanoi. Let us suppose there are three needles named 1, 2 and 3. Let a finite number say, n of disks with decreasing size, are placed on needle 1.We are to place disks from needle 1 to needle3 using needle 2 as temporary storage.

Rules are:

- Move only one disk at a time.
- No larger disk can be on top of a smaller disk.
- Move all disks from the 1st needle to the 3rd needle.

Notation: To move disks from one tower to another we will use notation

move(64, 1, 3, 2) which means Move 64 disks from tower 1 to tower 3 using tower 2 as temporary storage.

The Solution (Divide and Conquer)

In Divide and Conquer method, the problem to be solved is divided into two or more sub problems which are solved separately. The solutions are then combined together to find the solution of the given problem.

The examples of this technique are Quick sort and binary search algorithms, which are discussed in searching and sorting chapter. A Divide and Conquer algorithm can be called as a recursive procedure as the algorithm calls itself when it is implemented to smaller sets. The problem of Towers of Hanoi can also be solved with the help of Divide and Conquer method. Here we will reduce the solution for n disks to a solution for n-1 disks and a solution for n=1 disk.

To move the bottom disk from tower 1: - There is no way to reach the bottom disk until the top 63 disks have been moved- and they (the 63 disks) must all be on tower 2 so that we can move the bottom disk from tower 1 to tower 3.

Therefore, if we want: move (64,1,3,2), We need:

1. move(63,1,2,3)

   // Move 63 disks from tower 1 to 2 (tower 3 temporary).

2. " Move disk 64 from tower 1 to tower 3."

3. move(63,2,3,1)

// Move 63 disks from tower 2 to 3 (tower 1 temporary).

Now, move(63,2,3,1) is the same problem (and is a smaller problem) as move(64,1,3,2). Next: Repeat steps 1, 2 and 3 for move(63,2,3,1), and so on …

The solution of the **Tower of Hanoi** problem for n=3, is explained in the Figure 3.18.

Now we want: move(3,1,3,2)

We need:

1. move(2,1,2,3) // move 2 disks from tower1 to tower 2(tower3 temporary)
2. move disk 3 from tower 1 to tower 3.
3. move(2,2,3,1) // move 2 disks from tower 2 to tower 3 (tower1 temporary).

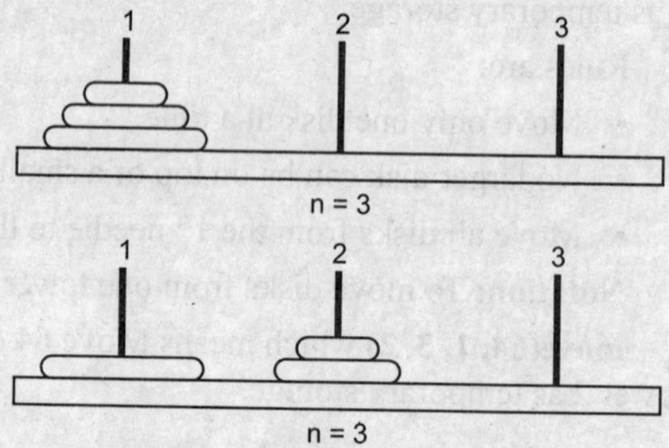

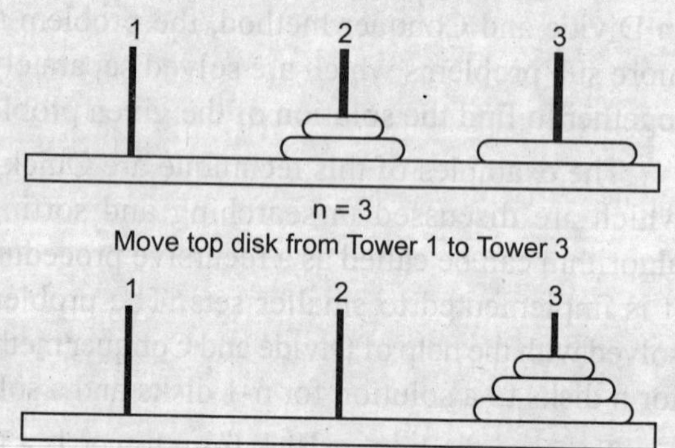

Figure 6.43: Towers of Hanoi problem solved with the help of Divide and Conquer algorithm in recursion

EXAMPLE 3: Ackermann Function

The Ackermann function is the simplest example of a well-defined total function, which is computable but not primitive recursive, providing a counterexample to the belief in the early 1900s that every computable function was also primitive recursive.

It grows faster than an exponential function, or even a multiple exponential function. The Ackermann function $A(x, y)$ is defined for integer x and y by:

$$A(x, y) = \begin{cases} y+1 & \text{if } x=0 \\ A(x-1,1) & \text{if } y=0 \\ A(x-1, A(x, y-1)) & \text{otherwise} \end{cases} \quad (1)$$

Special values for integer x include

$$A(0, y) = y+1 \quad (2)$$

$$A(1, y) = y+2 \quad (3)$$

$$A(2, y) = 2y+3 \quad (4)$$

$$A(3, y) = 2^{y+3} - 3 \quad (5)$$

$$A(4, y) = \underbrace{2^{2^{\cdot^{\cdot^{2}}}}}_{y=3} - 3 \quad (6)$$

Expressions of the latter form are sometimes called power towers. $A(0, y)$follows trivially from the definition. $A(1, y)$can be derived as follows,

$$\begin{aligned} A(1, y) &= A(0, A(1, y-1)) = A(1, y-1) + 1 \\ &= A(0, A(1, y-2)) + 1 = A(1, y-2) + 2 \\ &= \ldots = A(1, 0) + y = A(0, 1) + y = y + 2 \end{aligned} \quad (7)$$

$A(2, y)$ has a similar derivation,

$$\begin{aligned} A(2, y) &= A(1, A(2, y-1)) = A(2, y-1) + 2 \\ &= A(1, A(2, y-2)) + 2 = A(2, y-2) + 4 \\ &= A(2, 0) + 2y = A(1, 1) + 2y = 2y + 3 \end{aligned} \quad (8)$$

What do we mean by it is not primitive recursive?

The Ackermann function grows extremely fast; A(4,2) is already about $2.0035299*10^{19728}$. This extreme growth can be exploited to show that the computable function f(n) = A(n, n) grows faster than any primitive recursive function and is therefore not primitive recursive.

Table of values

Values of A(x,y)

x\y	0	1	2	3	4	y
0	1	2	3	4	5	y+1
1	2	3	4	5	6	y+2
2	3	5	7	9	11	2y+3
3	5	13	29	61	125	8*2^y-3
4	13	65533	2^{65536}-3	A(3,2^{65536}-3)	A(3,A(4,3))	$2^{2\ldots2}$-3 (y+3 terms)
5	65533	A(4,65533)	A(4,A(5,1))	A(4,A(5,2))	A(4,A(5,3))	
6	A(5,1)	A(5,A(5,1))	A(5,A(6,1))	A(5,A(6,2))	A(5,A(6,3))	

It might be noted that for each item, we need to compute its predecessor in the row just to find the position (index in programming terms) at which to look up the item in the previous row. A(4,2) is greater than the number of particles in the universe raised to the power 200. A(5,2) is the item at index A(5,1) in the x=4 row, and cannot be written as a decimal expansion in the physical universe.

It is also amusing to note that beyond row 4,the values can only be written by resorting to the definition of the Ackermann function - writing them as decimal expansions, or as references to rows with lower x, would not be possible. A(5,0) is an exception, as is A(5,1) = A(6,0), which can at least have their index in row 4 expressed as a decimal expansion.

Tail Recursion

Tail recursion (or tail-end recursion) is a special case of recursion in which the last operation of the function, the tail call, is a recursive call. Such recursions can be easily transformed to iterations. Replacing recursion with iteration, manually or automatically, can drastically decrease the amount of stack space used and improve efficiency. This technique is commonly used with functional programming languages, where the declarative approach and explicit handling of state promote the use of recursive functions that would otherwise rapidly fill the call stack.

Definition: *A special form of* recursion *where the last operation of a function is a recursive call. The recursion may be optimized away by executing the call in the current stack frame and returning its result rather than creating a new stack frame.*

A recursive function is said to be *tail recursive* if there are no pending operations to be performed on return from a recursive call.

Tail recursive functions are often said to "return the value of the last recursive call as the value of the function." Tail recursion is very desirable because the amount of information which must be stored during the computation is independent of the number of recursive calls. Some modern computing systems will actually compute tail-recursive functions using an iterative process.

The "infamous" factorial function fact is usually written in a non-tail-recursive manner:

```
int fact (int n)
{
if (n == 0) return 1;
return n * fact(n - 1);
}
```

Notice that there is a "pending operation," namely multiplication, to be performed on return from each recursive call. Whenever there is a pending operation, the function is non-tail-recursive. Information about each pending operation must be stored, so the amount of information is not independent of the number of calls.

The factorial function can be written in a tail-recursive way:

```
int fact_aux(int n, int result)
{
if (n == 1) return result;
return fact_aux(n - 1, n * result)
}
int fact(n)
{
return fact_aux(n, 1);
}
```

The "auxiliary" function fact_aux is used to keep the syntax of fact(n) the same as before. The recursive function is really fact_aux, not fact. Note that fact_aux has no pending operations on return from recursive calls. The value computed by the recursive call is simply returned with no modification. The amount of information which must be stored is constant (the value of n and the value of result), independent of the number of recursive calls.

6.10.3 Memory Management

Any modern computer environment uses a stack as the primary memory management model for a running program. Whether it's native code (x86, Sun, VAX) or JVM, a stack is at the center of the run-time environment for Java, C++, Ada, FORTRAN, etc.

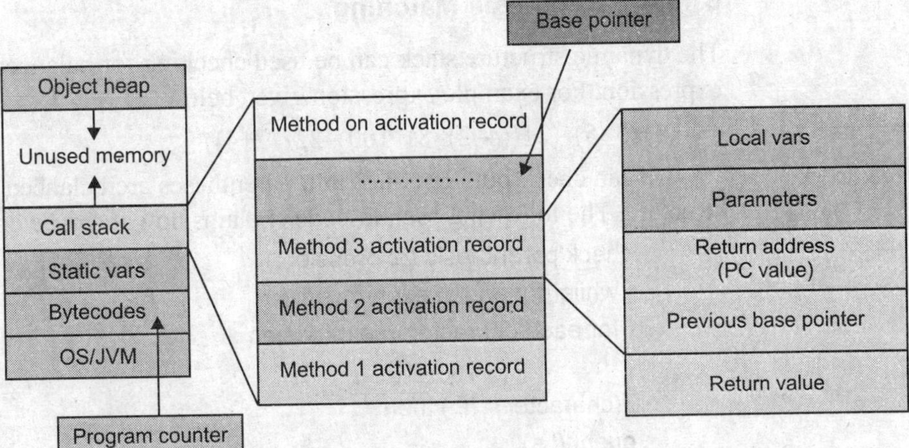

Figure 6.44: Memory management

The discussion of JVM in the text is consistent with NT, Solaris, VMS, Unix runtime environments.

Each program that is running in a computer system has its own memory allocation containing the typical layout as shown below.

Call and return process

When a method/function is called

1. An activation record is created; its size depends on the number and size of the local variables and parameters.
2. The Base Pointer value is saved in the special location reserved for it.
3. The Program Counter value is saved in the Return Address location.
4. The Base Pointer is now reset to the new base (top of the call stack prior to the creation of the AR).
5. The Program Counter is set to the location of the first bytecode of the method being called.
6. Copies the calling parameters into the Parameter region.
7. Initializes local variables in the local variable region.

While the method executes, the local variables and parameters are simply found by adding a constant associated with each variable/parameter to the Base Pointer.

When a method returns

1. Get the program counter from the activation record and replace what's in the PC.
2. Get the base pointer value from the AR and replace what's in the BP.
3. Pop the AR entirely from the stack.

6.10.4 Parenthesis Matching

The dynamic structure stack can be used checking for balanced parenthesis in an expression. For example expression given below

(1+(3×5)–(2+((4–2)×8)+100)–22×(2+4))

We can check both left and right parentheses are balanced or not using stack structure. The following pseudo-code explains how it can be done.

```
check parenthesis (expression )
{ while(not end of expression)
{ for each character in expression
{
if(character = '(' ) then
push('(',s)
if(character=')') then
```

```
pop(s)
}
} /* End of while loop */
if(isEmpty(s)) then
"The expression is valid "
else
" Invalid expression"
} /* End of function check parenthesis */
```

Algorithm above works as for every open parenthesis push them into the stack and closing parenthesis pop from the stack. Finally the empty stack shows the parenthesis balanced expression.

6.10.5 Balancing Symbols

Compilers check your programs for syntax errors, but frequently a lack of one symbol (such as a missing brace or comment starter) will cause the compiler to spill out a hundred lines of diagnostics without identifying the real error.

A useful tool in this situation is a program that checks whether everything is balanced. Thus, every right brace, bracket, and parenthesis must correspond to their left counterparts. The sequence [()] is legal, but [(]) is wrong. Obviously, it is not worthwhile writing a huge program for this, but it turns out that it is easy to check these things. For simplicity, we will just check for balancing of parentheses, brackets, and braces and ignore any other character that appears.

The simple algorithm uses a stack and is as follows:

Make an empty stack. Read characters until end of file. If the character is an open anything, push it onto the stack. If it is a close anything, then if the stack is empty report an error. Otherwise, pop the stack. If the symbol popped is not the corresponding opening symbol, then report an error. At end of file, if the stack is not empty report an error.

You should be able to convince yourself that this algorithm works. It is clearly linear and actually makes only one pass through the input. It is thus on-line and quite fast. Extra work can be done to attempt to decide what to do when an error is reported—such as identifying the likely cause.

Function Calls

The algorithm to check balanced symbols suggests a way to implement function calls. The problem here is that when a call is made to a new function, all the variables local to the calling routine need to be saved by the system, since otherwise the new function will overwrite the calling routine's variables. Furthermore, the current location in the routine must be saved so that the new function knows where to go after it is done. The variables have generally been assigned by the compiler to machine registers, and there are certain to be conflicts (usually all procedures get some variables assigned to register #1), especially if recursion is involved. The reason that this problem is similar to balancing symbols is that a function call and function return are essentially the same as an open parenthesis and closed parenthesis, so the same ideas should work.

When there is a function call, all the important information that needs to be saved, such as register values (corresponding to variable names) and the return address (which can be obtained from the program counter, which is typically in a register), is saved "on a piece of paper" in an abstract way and put at the top of a pile. Then the control is transferred to the new function, which is free to replace the registers with its values. If it makes other function calls, it follows the same procedure. When the function wants to return, it looks at the "paper" at the top of the pile and restores all the registers. It then makes the return jump.

Clearly, all of this work can be done using a stack, and that is exactly what happens in virtually every programming language that implements recursion. The information saved is called either an activation record or stack frame. The stack in a real computer frequently grows from the high end of your memory partition downwards, and on many systems there is no checking for overflow. There is always the possibility that you will run out of stack space by having too many simultaneously active functions. Needless to say, running out of stack space is always a fatal error.

In languages and systems that do not check for stack overflow, your program will crash without an explicit explanation. On these systems, strange things may happen when your stack gets too big, because your stack will run into part of your program. It could be the main program, or it could be part of your data, especially if you have a big array. If it runs into your program, your program will be corrupted; you will have nonsense instructions and will crash as soon as they are executed. If the stack runs into your data, what is likely to happen is that when you write something into your data, it will destroy stack information — probably the return address — and your program will attempt to return to some weird address and crash.

In normal events, you should not run out of stack space; doing so is usually an indication of runaway recursion (forgetting a base case). On the other hand, some perfectly legal and seemingly innocuous program can cause you to run out of stack space. The routine in Figure 3.45, which prints out a linked list, is perfectly legal and actually correct. It properly handles the base case of an empty list, and the recursion is fine. This program can be proven correct. Unfortunately, if the list contains 20,000 elements, there will be a stack of 20,000 activation records representing the nested calls of line 3. Activation records are typically large because of all the information they contain, so this program is likely to run out of stack space. (If 20,000 elements are not enough to make the program crash, replace the number with a larger one.)

This program is an example of an extremely bad use of recursion known as tail recursion. Tail recursion refers to a recursive call at the last line. Tail recursion can be mechanically eliminated by changing the recursive call to a goto preceded by one assignment per function argument. This simulates the recursive call because nothing needs to be saved — after the recursive call finishes, there is really no need to know the saved values. Because of this, we can just go to the top of the function with the values that would have been used in a recursive call. The program in Figure 3.46 shows the improved version. Keep in mind that you should use the more natural while loop construction. The goto is used here to show how a compiler might automatically remove the recursion.

Removal of tail recursion is so simple that some compilers do it automatically. Even so, it is best not to find out that yours does not.

```
void /* Not using a header */
print_list( LIST L )
{
/*1*/ if( L != NULL )
{
/*2*/ print_element( L->element );
/*3*/ print_list( L->next );
}
}
```

Figure 3.45: A bad use of recursion: printing a linked list

```
Void print_list( LIST L ) /* No header */
{
top:
if( L != NULL )
{
print_element( L->element );
L = L->next;
goto top;
}
}
```

Figure 3.46: Printing a list without recursion; a compiler might do this (you should not)

Recursion can always be completely removed (obviously, the compiler does so in converting to assembly language), but doing so can be quite tedious. The general strategy requires using a stack and is obviously worthwhile only if you can manage to put only the bare minimum on the stack. We will not dwell on this further, except to point out that although nonrecursive programs are certainly generally faster than recursive programs, the speed advantage rarely justifies the lack of clarity that results from removing the recursion.

Algorithm 6.14: Balance Symbol Checking

Step 1: Read expression.

Step 2: Create an empty stack.

Step 3: Read symbols from left to right, repeat steps 4 and 5, until end of expression

Step 4: If the symbol is an opening symbol then push it onto the stack else proceed.

Step 5: If it is a closing symbol do the following:

Step5 a: if the stack is empty report an error and goto step8 else proceed

Step5 b: pop the stack If the symbol popped does not match the closing symbol report an error and goto step8 else proceed .

Step 6: At the end of an expression if the stack is not empty report an error else proceed to next step

Step 7: Print Input expression is balanced

Step 8: Stop

Explanation

Step 1: Read an expression, say x = (( ))

Step 2: Write an empty stack.

Step 3: Start reading the symbols from left to right i.e. symbols will be read as in sequence as (( )). Scan the expression by repeating step 4 and 5 until

1 2 3 4

expression is completely read.

Step 4: The first symbol scanned is '('and it is opening symbol, so push it onto stack.

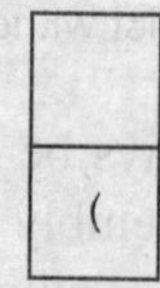

Next symbol scanned is again opening symbol '('. Push it on to stack

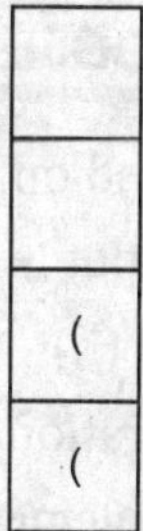

Step 5: Next symbol scanned is closing parenthesis ')',

(a) : so we will check whether stack is empty, which is not , so step 5b will be executed.

(b) Stack is to be popped, symbol popped is '('. It matches with the symbol scanned in step 5.

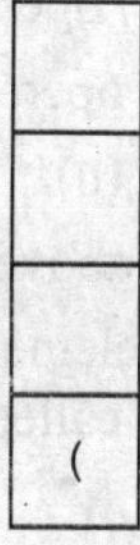

Read the last symbol ')', which is closing parenthesis, so step 5 will again be executed.

Step 5a: We will check if stack is empty, which is not, so step 5b will be executed.

Step 5b: Pop the stack i.e. pop '('. It matches with the symboll ')'

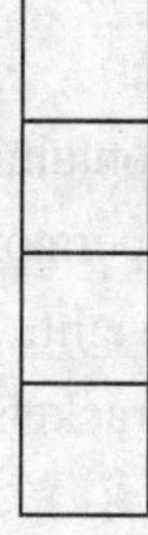

Step 6: Now expression is completely read, also stack is empty. So step 7 will be executed

Step 7: Print that input expression is balanced

OBJECTIVE TYPE QUESTIONS

1. The stack is based on the rule
   (a) first-in-last-out (b) last-in-first-out
   (c) both (a) and (b) (d) first-in-first-out
2. The push () operation is used
   (a) to insert an element (b) to remove an element
   (c) to move an element (d) all of the above.
3. The pop operation removes
   (a) the element lastly inserted (b) first element of the stack
   (c) any element randomly (d) None of the above
4. The top pointer is increased
   (a) when push () operation is done
   (b) when pop () operation is done
   (c) both (a) and (b)
   (d) None of the above
5. A stack holding elements equal to its capacity and if push is performed then such situation is called
   (a) stack overflow (b) stack underflow
   (c) illegal operation (d) None of the above
6. The prefix notation is also called as
   (a) polish notation (b) postfix notation
   (c) infix notation (d) None of the above
7. From the given options one is not a stack application
   (a) template (b) recursion
   (c) reverse string (d) conversion of number.
8. An expression containing more than one operation are solved according to
   (a) priority of operators (b) priority of operands
   (c) from left to right (d) right to left.
9. The following brackets changes the priority
   (a) ( ) (b) [ ]
   (c) { } (d) &
10. The postfix notation is also called as
    (a) reverse polish notation (b) polish notation
    (c) prefix notation (d) postfix notation.

11. Stack is
    (a) Linear data structure (b) Non-linear data structure
    (c) Both (d) None
12. Which of the following operations can be performed on stack?
    (a) Push (b) Pop
    (c, Insert (d) Both a and b
13. Overflow occurs if
    (a) Stack is full (b) Stack is empty
    (c) Stack is half (b) All of the above
14. Stack can be implemented by using
    (a) Array (b) Queue
    (c) Pointer (d) Linked list
    (e) None
15. Which of the following is the type of Stack?
    (a) Different cities (b) Heap of books
    (c) Binary tree (d) None of the above
16. Which of the following is the operation of stack
    (a) Tos (b) Peek
    (c) Create (d) Dup
    (e) All of the above (f) None of the above
17. Search is possible in stack
    (a) Yes (b) No
    (c) Fifty-fifty (b) None
18. Which of the following is the operation of Stack:
    (a) Sorting (b) Searching
    (c) Inserting (d) Deleting
    (e) All of the above
19. Which of the following is the application of stack
    (a) To set Infix expression
    (b) To set Prefix expression
    (c) To set postfix expression
    ( ) All of the above
    (e) None of the above

20. Traversing in stack means:
    (a) Sorting (b) Searching
    (c) Inserting (d) Deleting
    (e) Visiting (f) None of the above
21. When a function calls itself is called
    (a) Recursion (b) Iteration
    (c) Function (d) none of the above.
22. In indirect recursion a function calls
    (a) Another function (b) itself
    (c) Only main () function (d) none of the above.
23. In tower of Hanoi the following one condition is not applicable:
    (a) At a time only one disk may be moved
    (b) the disc may be moved from any needle to another needle
    (c) No larger disk may be placed on the smaller one
    (d) The disks can be placed in any order.
24. The function declarator is used to
    (a) declare formal arguments (b) declare function prototype
    (c) function call (d) all of the above.

EXERCISES

1. Write description of stack structure.
2. What do you mean by Stack?
3. Explain the stack model?
4. What are the various commonly used stack operations?
5. Write an algorithm and C++ program for stack operations:
    (i) Push (ii) Pop
    (iii) Display operation (iv) Peek operation
    (v) Dup operation (vi) Swap operation
    (vii) Right rotate
6. What do you mean by stack frames?
7. What do you mean by multiple stacks?
8. Explain various representations of stacks in detail.
9. Explain various applications of Stack.
10. Define prefix, Infix, and Postfix Expression.

11. What is the advantages of using postfix expressions as compared to Infix Expressions?
12. How an Arithmetic expression is evaluated?
13. Write an algorithm and C++ program to convert an Infix to Postfix expression.
14. Convert the following Infix expressions to Postfix and Prefix expressions.
    (i) (a+(b/d)) *(c/e) + f
    (ii) ((a+b*c) / (e+f)) / g
    (iii) a ! b ! c
    (iv) (a-b) * (c/d) + e
    (v) (a *(b-c) / d) + (e / (f*g-h))
15. Write an algorithm and C++ program to evaluate a Postfix expression.
16. Evaluate the following Postfix expressions:
    (i) 30 20 - 10 5 * 4 -
    (ii) 10 6 + 3 /3 10 + 6 +
    (iii) 10 6 4 + *
17. Explain the procedure to convert an infix arithmetic expression to prefix or polish expression.
18. Explain concept of Backtracking.
19. What do you mean by Recursion? Explain the various applications of recursion.
20. Explain concept of Parenthesis matching.
21. Write an algorithm for balanced symbol checking.
22. Write the entire valid symbol from inputs set of following symbol.
    [(( )], { [( )], ({ }]), ({ [ ] }), ((({ { }))) }

Queues

7.1 INTRODUCTION

A queue is a particular kind of collection in which the entities in the collection are kept in order and the principal (or only) operations on the collection are the addition of entities to the rear terminal position and removal of entities from the front terminal position. This makes the queue a First-In-First-Out (FIFO) data structure.

Figure 7.1: Waiting line for service called queue.

In a FIFO data structure, the first element added to the queue will be the first one to be removed. This is equivalent to the requirement that whenever an element is added, all elements that were added before have to be removed before the new element can be invoked. A queue is an example of a linear data structure.

A queue is an abstract data type in which insertion occurs at one end (the rear) and deletion occurs at the other end (the front). A queue is defined to hold one type of data element. Only the elements indicated by front and rear can be accessed.

7.2 CONCEPT OF QUEUE

A queue is defined as a data structure, which holds a series of items to be processed on a **first in first out** basis (though some queues can be sorted in priority).

A queue differs from a stack in the way its removal operation behaves—a removal removes and returns the element that has resided in the queue for the longest period of time. For this reason, a queue is called a "first in, first out" data structure. A queue is represented in Figure 7.2 and 7.3 as shown below:

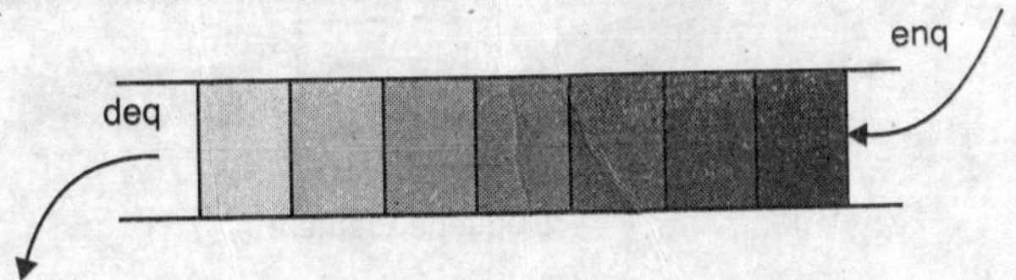

Figure 7.2: Representation of queue.

Figure 7.3: Explaining the concept of a Queue

A **queue** is an ordered list in which all insertions take place at one end, the **rear**, while all deletions take place at the other end, the **front**. When viewed as a queue with a[n] as the rear element one says that a[i+1] is behind a[i], 1<i<=n.

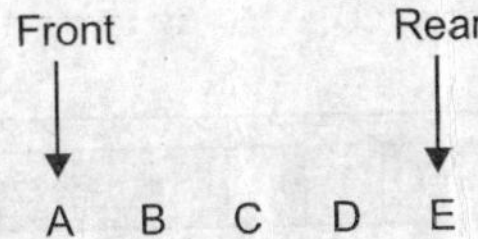

Figure 7.4: Queue having front and rear elements

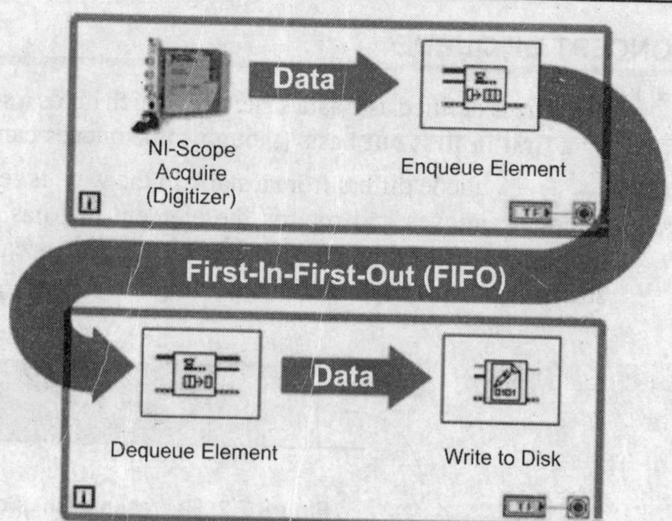

Figure 7.5: Various operations of queue. (Enqueue and Dequeue)

The restrictions on queue imply that the first element which is inserted into the queue will be the first one to be removed. Thus A is the first letter to be removed, and queues are known as First in First out (FIFO) lists. Note that the data object queue as defined here need not necessarily correspond to the mathematical concept of queue in which the insert/delete rules may be different.

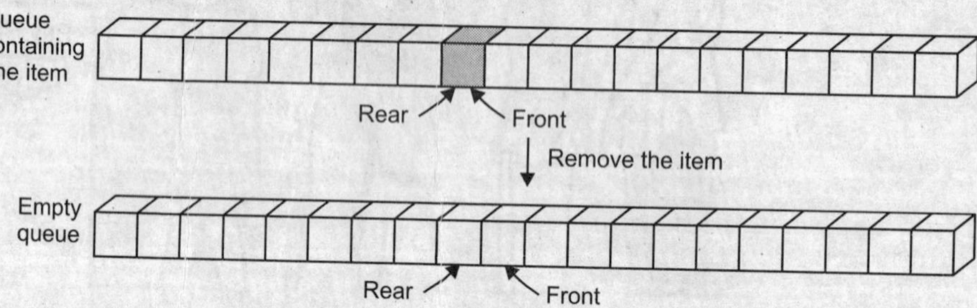

Figure 7.6: Remove the item from queue.

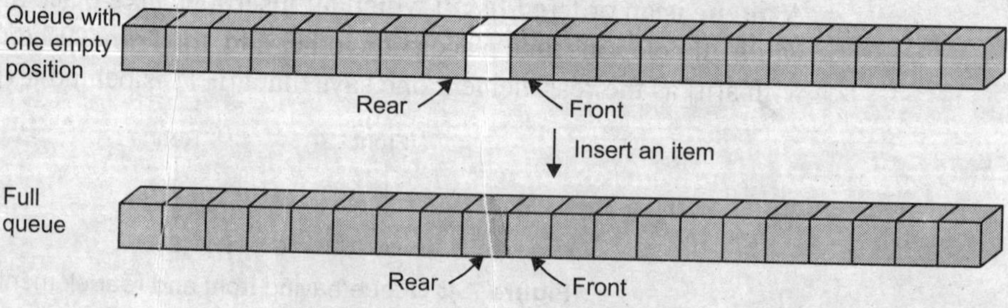

Figure 7.7: Insert an item in queue.

Definition: *A data structure which is based on first come first serve having two different ends one for insertion(Rear) and another for deletion(Front) is called Queue.*

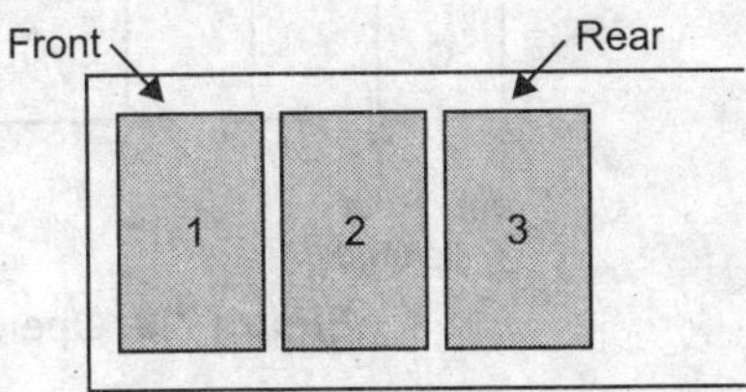

Figure 7.8: FIFO data structure

In a FIFO data structure, the first element added to the queue will be the first one to be removed. This is equivalent to the requirement that whenever an element is added, all elements that were added before have to be removed before the new element can be invoked. A queue is an example of a linear data structure. Queues provide services in computer science, transport and operations research where various entities such as data, objects, persons, or events are stored and held to be processed later. In these contexts, the queue performs the function of a buffer. Queues are common in computer programs, where they are implemented as data structures coupled with access routines, as an abstract data structure or in object-oriented languages as classes.

A queue is also a list of elements with insertions permitted at one end—called the rear, and deletions permitted from the other end—called the front. This means that the removal of elements from a queue is possible in the same order in which the insertion of elements is made into the queue. Thus, a queue data structure exhibits the FIFO (first in first out) property. Insert and delete are the operations that are provided for insertion of elements into the queue and the removal of elements from the queue, respectively. Shown in Figure 7.9 are the effects of insert and delete operations on the queue.

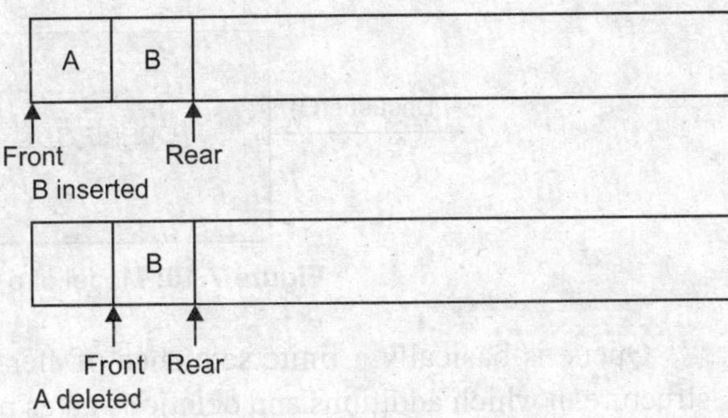

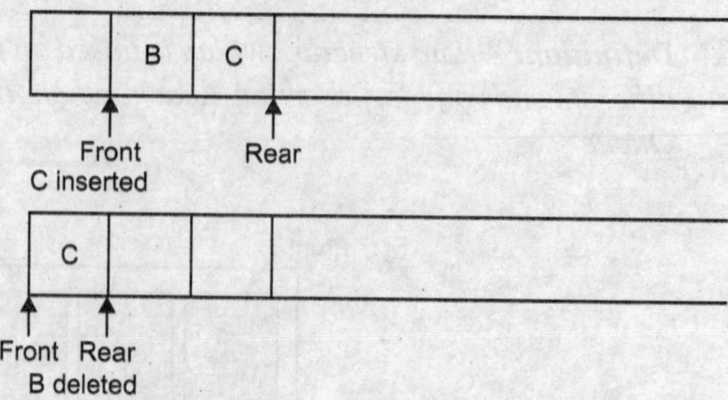

Figure 7.9: Operations on a queue.

The queue data structure is characterized by the fact that additions are made at the end, or tail, of the queue while removals are made from the front, or head, of the queue. For this reason, a stack is referred to as a FIFO structure (First-In First-Out). Queues occur naturally in situations where the rate at which clients' demand for services can exceed the rate at which these services can be supplied. For example, in a network where many computers share only a few printers, the print jobs may accumulate in a print queue. In an operating system with a GUI, applications and windows communicate using messages, which are placed in message queues until they can be handled.

7.3 QUEUE AS AN ABSTRACT DATA TYPE

Like stacks, queues are lists. With a queue, however, insertion is done at one end, whereas deletion is performed at the other end.

7.3.1 Queue Model

The basic operations on a queue are enqueue, which inserts an element at the end of the list (called the rear), and dequeue, which deletes (and returns) the element at the start of the list (known as the front). Figure 7.10 shows the abstract model of a queue.

Figure 7.10: Model of a queue

Queue is basically a finite sequence of elements of same type. It is a linear structure in which additions and deletions takes place at different ends. The end at which new elements are added is called the rear, and the end from which elements are deleted is called the front.

For Example:

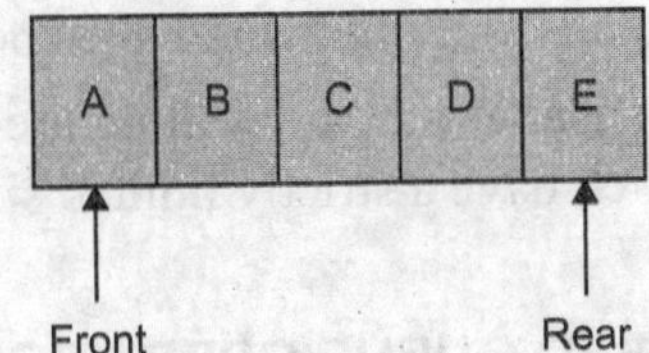

Figure 7.11: Queue having front and rear.

So a queue follows First-In-First-Out (FIFO) pattern of sequence. The FIFO property causes to operate like a line of people waiting to get their movie tickets for a show. We call the insert operation on a queue Enqueue, and we call the delete operation Dequeue. When an element is enqueued, it takes place at the rear end of the queue, the element dequeued is always the one at the front end of the queue.

7.4 APPLICATION OF QUEUES: SIMULATION OF AN AIRPORT

Simulation is the use of one system to imitate the behaviour of another system. A computer simulation is a program to imitate the behaviour of the system under study.

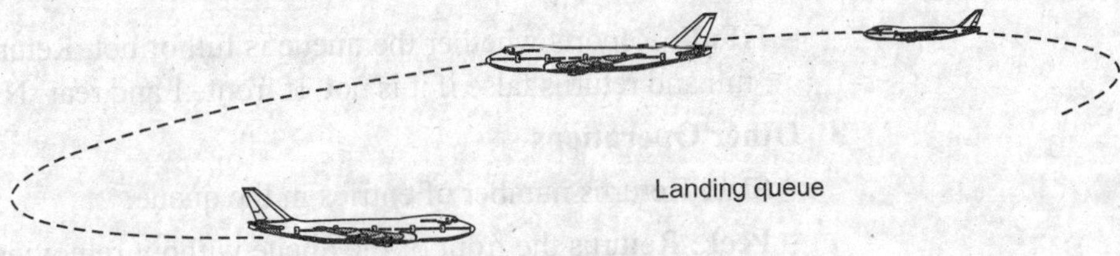

Figure 7.12: Landing queue.

Figure 7.13: Takeoff queue.

1. The same runway is used for both landings and takeoffs.
2. One plane can land or take off in a unit of time, but not both.
3. A random number of planes arrive in each time unit.
4. A plane waiting to land goes before one waiting to take off.
5. The planes that are waiting are kept in queues landing and takeoff, both of which have a strictly limited size.

7.5 COMMONLY USED QUEUE OPERATIONS

Here are some operations, with their typical names, that are performed on queues:

- **Initialization operation**
  – **Create:** Returns an empty queue.
- **Basic Operations**
  – **Enqueue:** Adds a new element at the rear of a queue.
  – **Dequeue:** Removes an element from the front of the queue and return it. (This operation cannot be performed if the queue is empty.)
- **Status checking operations**
  – **IsEmpty:** Reports whether the queue is empty or not. Returns true if queue is empty and returns false if it is not. If front=0 and rear=0 then queue is empty.
  – **IsFull:** Reports whether the queue is full or not. Returns true if queue is full and returns false if it is not. If front=1 and rear=N then queue is full.
- **Other Operations**
  – **Size:** Returns number of entries in the queue.
  – **Peek:** Returns the front of the queue without removing it.
  – **Rear:** Returns last element entered in queue.
  – **Equals:** checks if two queues are equal or not? Two queues are equal when their contents are equal (requires deep equality on each element of the queue).
  – **Destroy:** Returns an empty queue after deleting all the data elements from it.

All these operations, mentioned above, are performed in O(1) time.

7.6 ORDER PRODUCED BY A QUEUE

A static array can be used to implement the data structures. Consider, for example, a queue implemented as an array as shown in the Figure 7.14.

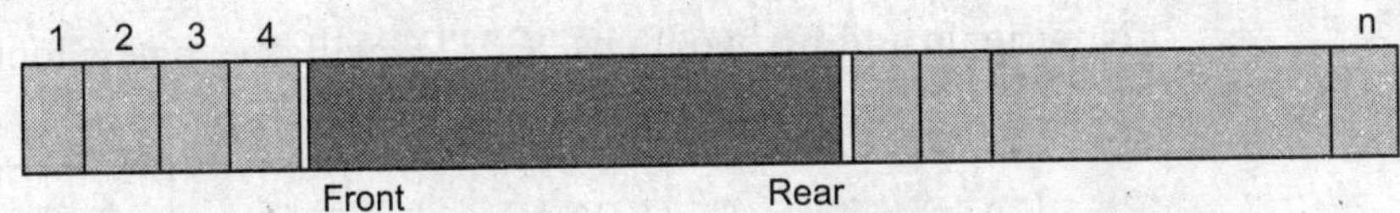

Figure 7.14: Queue with front and rear pointers.

As data is added to the rear of the queue, the cell labeled 'rear' (the cell containing the last enqueued data) is incremented to the right. If data is dequeued, the cell labeled 'front' (the cell containing the first enqueued data) is also incremented to the right. The following diagram shows an empty queue. It is identified as a series of ten locations, and two pointers named **front or head** and **rear or tail**. These two pointers keep track of where the front and rear of the queue is

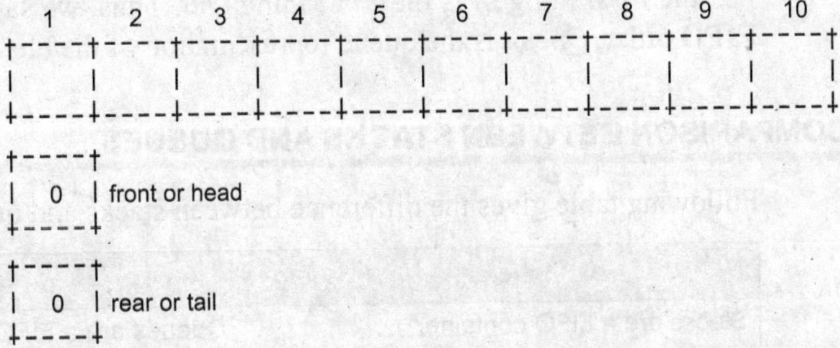

The front pointer is used to delete items, and the rear pointer insert items. Inserting two items called "A" and "B" will rearrange the queue to look like:

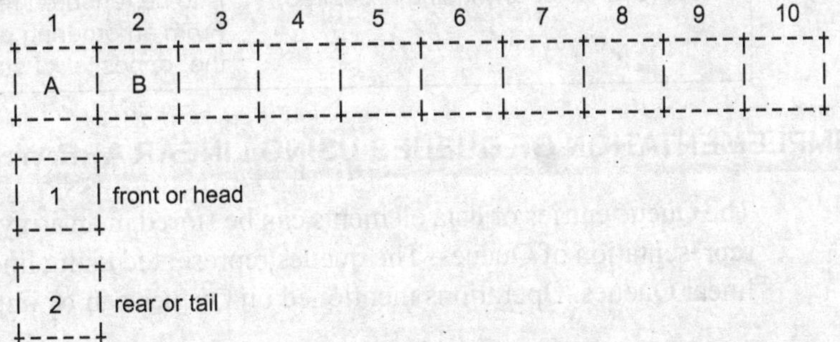

Now deleting one item "A", will rearrange the Queue to look like:

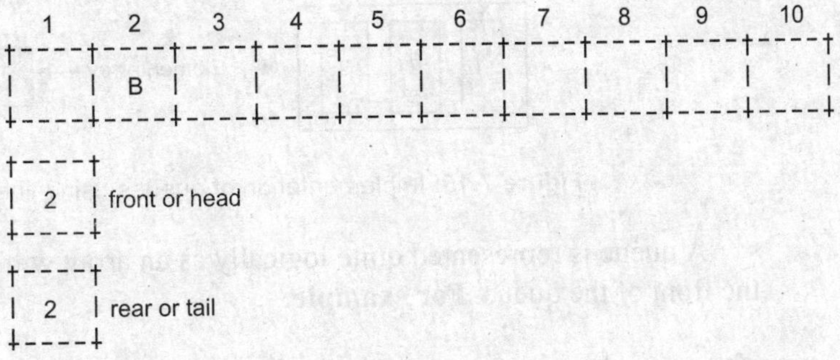

Now again adding two items "C","D" will give a new look to Queue:

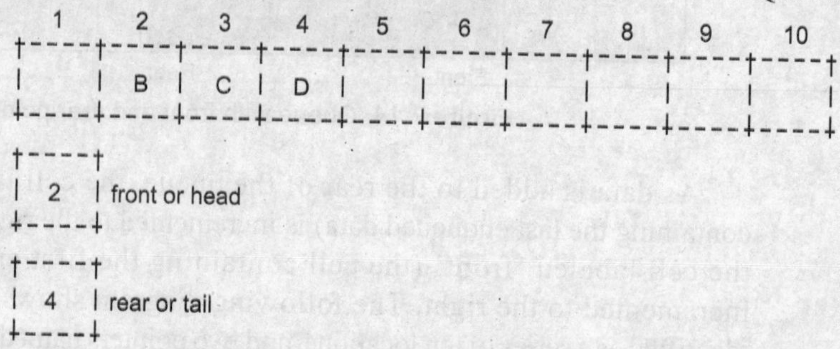

You'll notice that the queue enforces a certain *order* to the use of its contents, i.e., the *First* thing *In* is the *First* thing *Out*. Thus, we say that a queue enforces **FIFO** order. *Queue* is the queue representation of the elements in *List*.

7.7 COMPARISON BETWEEN STACKS AND QUEUES

Following table gives the difference between stacks and queues:

Stacks	Queues
Stacks are a LIFO container	Queues are a FIFO container
Store data in the reverse of order received	Store data in the order received
Stacks suggest applications where some sort of reversal or unwinding is desired.	Queues suggest applications where service is to be rendered relative to order received. From an ordering perspective, Queues are the "opposite" of stacks

7.8 IMPLEMENTATION OF QUEUES USING LINEAR ARRAYS

The Queue entries or data elements can be stored in an array. This is called as array representation of Queues. The queues represented using linear arrays are called as linear Queues. Operations mentioned on Queues can be implemented on an array.

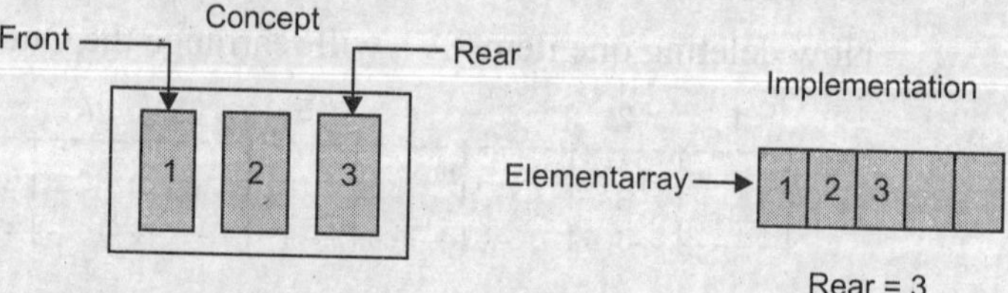

Figure 7.15: Implementation of queues using linear arrays.

A queue is represented quite logically as an array with the 0th element being the front of the queue. **For example:**

Figure 7.16: Front point to Todd.

The queue above would become the following array:

Index	0	1	2	3	4
	Todd	Bob	Phil	Kirt	Alice

Figure 7.17: Array index starting from zero.

Like a stack, a Queue usually holds things of the same type. We usually draw Queues horizontally. Here's a Queue of characters with 3 elements:

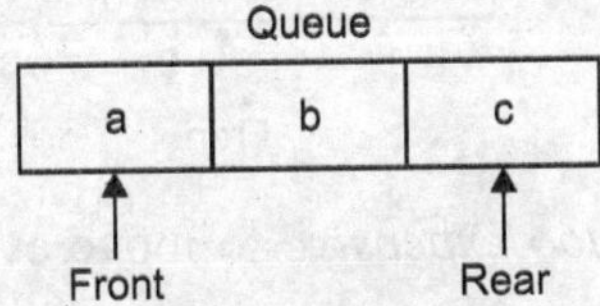

The main property of a queue is that objects go on the *rear* and come off of the front of the queue. One of the things we'll need to keep track of is the number of elements in the queue, i.e., not all the elements in the array may be holding elements of the queue at any given time. So far, the pieces of data we need for our array implementation of the queue are: an array and a count. So example mentioned above can be described as

Queue (made up of 'contents' and 'count')

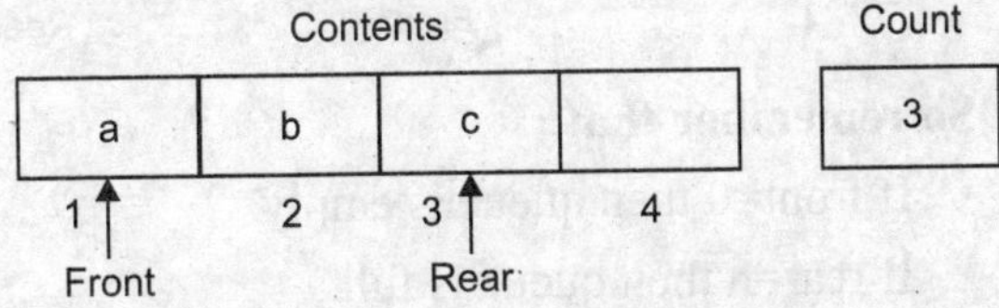

Where a is at the *front* and c is at the *rear*. Now, we *enter* a new element with Enqueue operation.

Queue (made up of 'contents' and 'count')

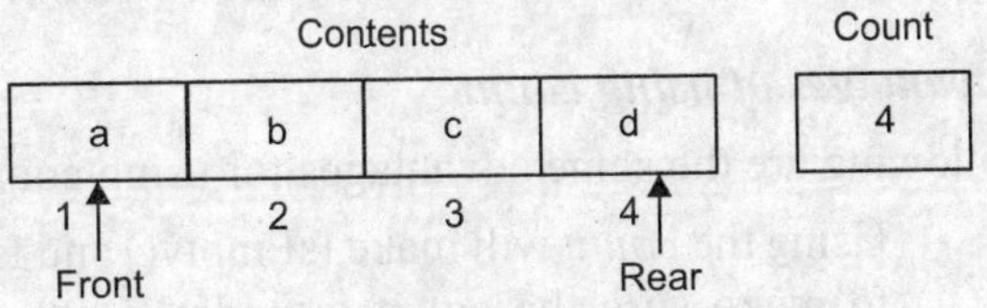

Now we remove an element with Dequeue operation and store it in variable ch

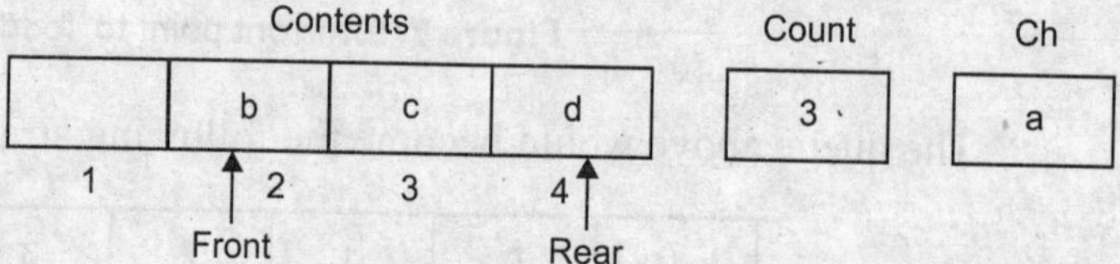

We have a problem because the *front* of the queue is no longer at array position 1. One solution would be to move all the elements down one, giving:

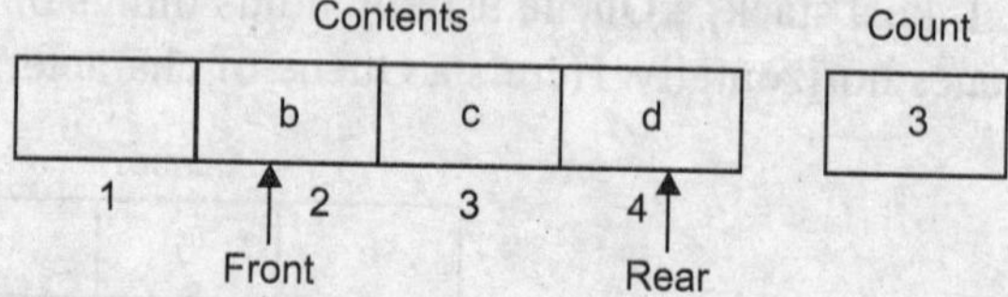

But it is *too expensive* to move everything down every time we remove an element.

Instead, we can use an additional piece of information to keep track of the front and rear, We can use the index of the elements at the front and rear, giving:

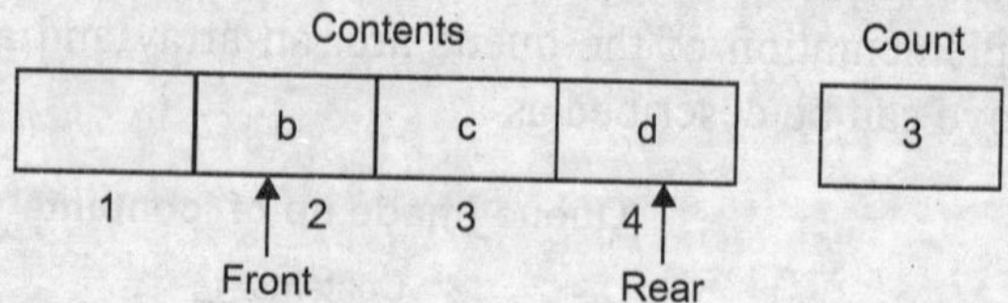

So remember that:

- If front=0 then queue is empty.
- If rear=n then queue is full.
- The value of rear is incremented by 1 when an element is entered in the queue, without affecting the value of front pointer.
- The value of the front is incremented by 1 when an element is deleted from the queue, without affecting the value of rear pointer.

Advantages of using count

Following are the some advantages for using count:

- Using the *count* will make IsEmpty() and IsFull() easy, although we'll have to make sure the count is updated properly in Enqueue and Dequeue operations. We haven't explored how to determine emptiness/fullness with *rear* or whether doing so presents any challenges.

- Using the *count* in Enqueue is similar to using *rear*. In both cases, the *front* won't move. With the count, we'll have to use *count* to calculate at which position to add new values.
- Using the *count* in Dequeue is not more difficult than using *rear*. In both cases, the *front* has to move.

7.8.1 Create Operation

Algorithm 7.1: To implement a queue using an array.

CREATEQ(N, FRONT, REAR, ITEM)

In the algorithm, an array Queue, say Queue is declared with maximum size as say, N and variables front and rear points to the first and last locations respectively of the Queue. The data item which is to be entered is stored in variable ITEM.

Step 1: Read the value of N i.e. total number of elements in Queue.

Step 2: Repeat steps 3 and 4 N times, starting from initial value of counter variable say] REAR = 1 to N.

Step 3: Read the value of element in ITEM.

Step 4: [Store the value entered of element in Queue current location using an assignment] QUEUE[REAR] = ITEM.

[Increment REAR by 1] REAR=REAR+1.

Step 5: [Decrement REAR by 1. So that it points to last element in Queue.]

REAR = REAR-1.

Step 6: End.

Explanation

Step 1: Let us create a QUEUE of size 4 i.e. the value of N is 4.

Step 2: Repeat steps 3 & step 4 for 4 times i.e. for REAR = 1 to 4

Step 3: Read the value of element, let us suppose user enters 10.

Step 4: Store this value into QUEUE in first location using an assignment

QUEUE [REAR] = QUEUE [1] = 10

Now if user enters the remaining elements as 20, 30, 40 using assignments

QUEUE [REAR+1] = QUEUE [1+1] = QUEUE [2] = 20

QUEUE [REAR+1] = QUEUE [2+1] = QUEUE [3] = 30

QUEUE [REAR+1] = QUEUE [3+1] = QUEUE [4] = 40

Queue will look like:

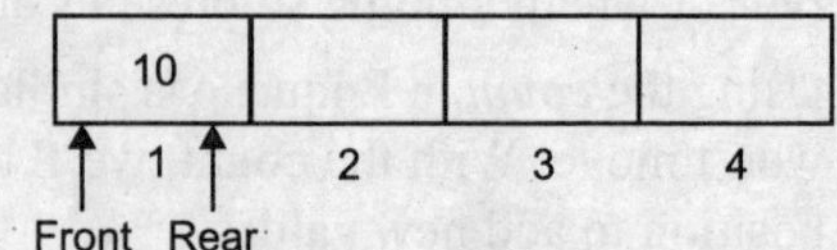

Figure 7.18: Queue Created for first element.

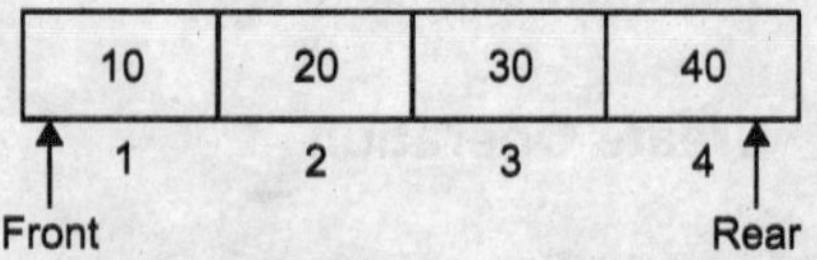

Figure 7.19: Final Queue Created.

After complete operation, FRONT pointer is 1 and REAR pointer is 4.

Step 5: After the step 3 & 4 have been executed for required no. of times i.e. 4 in this case, REAR will become 5 at step 5 so we should decrement it by 1 REAR=5-1= 4. So that it points to last element 4 in the QUEUE.

Step 6: End.

7.8.2 Enqueue Operation

Algorithm 7.2: To insert element in QUEUE structure.

INSRTQ(N, FRONT, REAR, ITEM)

This algorithm inserts an element ITEM into a queue. FRONT is used to delete the element from queue. REAR is used to insert element into queue.

Step1: [When the Queue is already filled?]

If FRONT = 1 and REAR = N, or if FRONT = REAR + 1, then

Write: OVERFLOW, and Return.

Step 2: [Find new value of REAR.]

If FRONT = NULL, then [Starting Queue initially empty.]

Set FRONT= 1 and REAR = 1.

Else if REAR = N, then

Set REAR = 1.

Else

Set REAR = REAR + 1.

[End of If statement.]

Step 3: Set QUEUE[REAR] = ITEM. [This inserts new element.]

Step 4: End.

Explanation

Consider the following Queue.

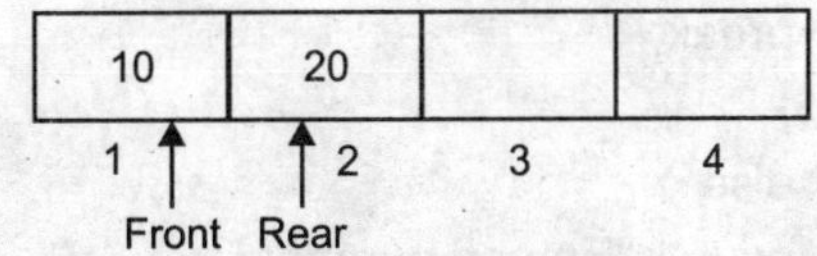

Figure 7.20: Before insertion. FRONT = 1 and REAR = 2.

Step 1: [When the Queue is already filled?]
If FRONT = 1 and REAR = 4, or if FRONT = 4 + 1, then
Write: OVERFLOW, and Return.

Step 2: [Find new value of REAR.]
If FRONT = NULL, then [Starting Queue initially empty.]
Set FRONT= 1 and REAR = 1.
Else if REAR = N, then
Set REAR = 1.
Else
Set REAR = REAR + 1. [SET REAR = 3]
[End of If statement.]

Step 3: Set QUEUE[3] = 30. [This inserts new element at position 3.]

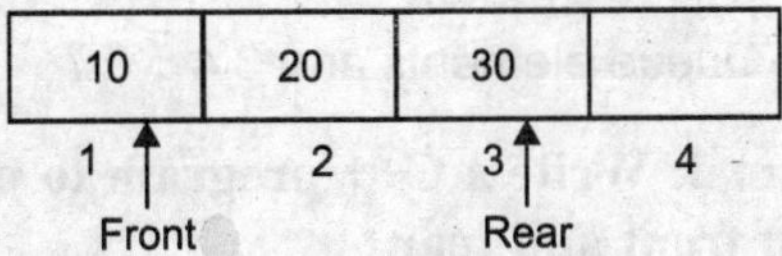

Figure 7.21: After insertion. FRONT = 1 and REAR = 3.

Step 4: End.

Program 1: Write a C++ program to insert elements in a queue.

```
# include <iostream.h>
# include <conio.h>
# include <process.h>
# define S 5
void main ()
{
int queue[S];
int r=0,n;
clrscr();
while (1) {
if (r>=S) {
cout<<"\n Queue overflow";
```

```
break;
}
else
cout<<"Enter a number:";
cin>>n;
queue[r]=n;
r++;
}
cout<<"\n Queue elements are:";
for (n=0;n<S;n++)
cout<<queue[n];
getch();
}
```

Output:

```
Enter a number: 3
Enter a number: 4
Enter a number: 5
Enter a number: 6
Enter a number: 7
Queue overflow
Queue elements are: 3 4 5 6 7
```

Program 2: Write a C++ program to perform insertion operation and show value of front and rear.

```
# include <iostream.h>
# include <conio.h>
void main ()
{
int queue[7];
int r=-1,f=-1,j;
clrscr();
while (r<6)
{
r++;
cout<<"rear="<<r<<"front="<<f<<" Enter element:";
cin>>queue[r];
if (r= =0) f=0;
}
cout<<"\n Queue elements are:";
for (j=0;<7;j++)
```

```
cout<<queue[j];
getch();
}
```

Output:

```
rear=-1 front=-1 Enter element:8
rear=0 front=0 Enter element:9
rear=1 front=0 Enter element:4
rear=2 front=0 Enter element:5
rear=3 front=0 Enter element:1
rear=4 front=0 Enter element:2
rear=5 front=0 Enter element:3
Queue elements are: 8 9 4 5 1 2 3
```

7.8.3 Dequeue Operation

Algorithm 7.3: To delete element from QUEUE structure.

DELQ(N, FRONT, REAR, ITEM)

This algorithm deletes an element from a queue and assigns it to the variable ITEM. FRONT is used to delete the element from queue. REAR is used to insert element into queue.

Step 1: [When the Queue is already empty?]

If FRONT = NULL, then Write: UNDERFLOW, and Return.

Step 2: Set ITEM =QUEUE[FRONT].

Step 3: [Find new value of front.]

If FRONT= REAR, then [Queue has only one element to start.]

Set FRONT = NULL and REAR = NULL

Else if FRONT = N, then

Set FRONT = 1

Else

Set FRONT = FRONT + 1.

[End of If statement.]

Step 4: End.

Explanation

Consider the following Queue:

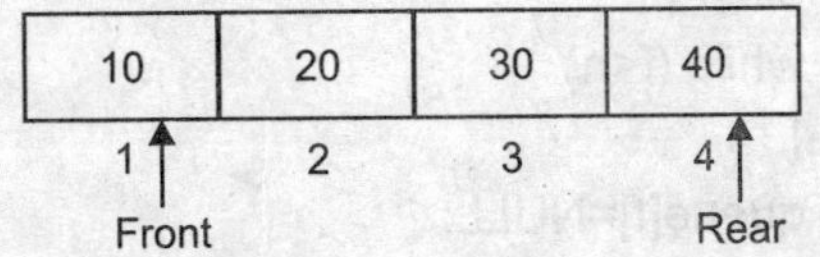

Figure 7.22: Before deletion. FRONT = 1 and REAR = 4.

Step 1: [When the Queue is already empty?]

If FRONT = NULL, then Write: UNDERFLOW, and Return.

Step 2: Set ITEM =QUEUE[1].[Element 10 is removed]

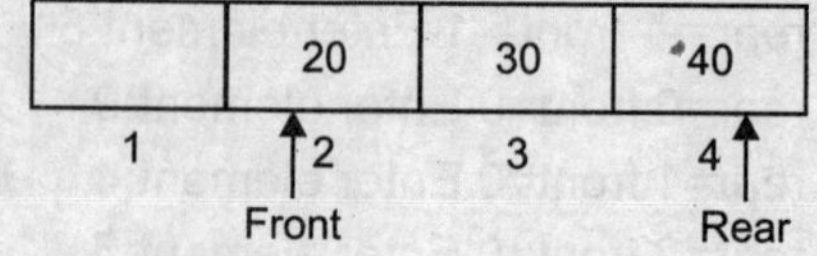

Figure 7.23: After deletion. FRONT = 2 and REAR = 4.

Step 3: [Find new value of front.]

If FRONT= REAR, then [Queue has only one element to start.]

Set FRONT = NULL and REAR = NULL

Else if FRONT = N, then

Set FRONT = 1

Else

Set FRONT = FRONT + 1. [SET FRONT =2]

[End of If statement.]

Step 4: End.

Program 3: Write a C++ program to perform deletion operation on queue and show value of front and rear.

```
# include <iostream.h>
# include <conio.h>
void main ()
{
int queue[7]={11,12,13,14,15,16,17};
int i,r=6,f=0,n;
clrscr();
cout<<"\nThe Elements of queue are as follows:-\n";
for(i=0;i<7;i++)
cout<<queue[i];
cout<<"\nInitial values rear="<<r<<"front="<<f;
cout<<"\nHow many elements u want to delete:";
cin>>n;
while (f<n)
{
queue[f]=NULL;
f++;
```

```
cout<<"\nrear="<<r<<" front="<<f;
}
cout<<"\n Queue elements are:";
for (n=0;n<7;n++)
cout<<queue[n];
getch();
}
Output:
The Elements of queue are as follows:-
11 12 13 14 15 16 17
Initial values rear=6 front=0
How many elements u want to delete: 3
rear=6 front=1
rear=6 front=2
rear=6 front=3
Queue elements are: 0 0 0 14 15 16 17
```

Program 4: Write a C++ program to perform different operations with queue such as insert, delete and display of elements.

```
# include <iostream.h>
# include <conio.h>
int queue[8];
int r;
void insert(void);
void del ();
void show (void);
void main ()
{
int c;
clrscr();
cout<<"\n1] Insert Element";
cout<<"\n2] Delete Element";
cout<< "\n3] Display element/s";
cout<<"\n4] Exit";
cout<<"\n Enter your choice:-";
cin>>c'
switch (c)
{
case 1: insert(); break;
case 2: del(); show();break;
```

```
case 3: show(); break;
default: exit(0);
}
main ();
getch();
}
void insert ()
{
Char ans='Y';
if (f>=7)
{
cout<<"\n Queue is full \n\n\n";
main ();
}
while (ans= ='Y'   ans= ='y')
{
cout<<"\n Enter element:-";
cin>>queue[r];
if (r= =7)
{
clrscr();
cout<<"\n Queue is Full";
getch();
break;
}
else
r++;
cout<<"\nContinue [Y/N]:-";
ans=getche();
}
}
void show()
{
int j;
for (j=0;j<r;j++)
cout<<queue[j];
getch();
}
void del ()
```

```
{
int j;
if (r= =0)
{
clrscr();
cout<<"\n Queue is empty \n\n\n";
main();
}
for (j=0;j<r;j++)
queue[j]= queue[j+1];
queue[r]=0;
r--;
}
Output:
1] Insert element
2] Delete element
3] Display element/s
4] Exit
Enter choice:- 1
Enter element:- 23
Continue [Y/N]:-y
Enter element:- 45
Continue [Y/N]:-
```

7.8.4 Peek Operation

Algorithm 7.4: To Print the front of the queue without removing it.

PEEKQ(N,FRONT, REAR)

In the algorithm, an array Queue, say Queue is declared with maximum size as say, n and variables front and rear points to the first and last locations respectively of the Queue.

Step 1: [When the Queue is already empty?]

If FRONT = NULL, then Write: UNDERFLOW, and Return.

Step 2: [Print the element stored at position]

If FRONT= REAR, then

FRONT=REAR=1 [Queue has only one element to print.]

Else Set FRONT = FRONT + 1. [Print elements one by one.]

[End of If statement.]

Step 3: End.

Explanation

Let us consider the following Queue

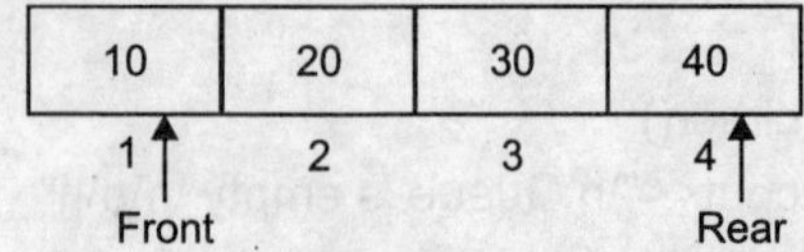

Figure 7.24: Print the FRONT = 10.

Step 1: [When the Queue is already empty?]

If FRONT = NULL, then Write: UNDERFLOW, and Return.

Step 2: [Print the element stored at position]

If FRONT= REAR, then [Queue has only one element to start.]

Set FRONT = NULL and REAR = NULL

Else if FRONT = N, then Set FRONT = 1

Else Set FRONT = FRONT + 1. [End of If statement.]

Step 3: End.

7.8.5 Rear Operation

Algorithm 7.5: To print last element entered in queue.

REARQ (N, FRONT, REAR,ITEM)

In the algorithm, an array Queue, say Queue is declared with maximum size as say, n and variables front and rear points to the first and last locations, respectively of the Queue.

Step 1: [When the Queue is already empty?]

If FRONT = NULL, then Write: UNDERFLOW, and Return.

Step 2: [Print the element stored at location pointed to by rear].

ITEM = QUEUE[REAR]

Step 3: End

Explanation

Let us consider the following Queue:

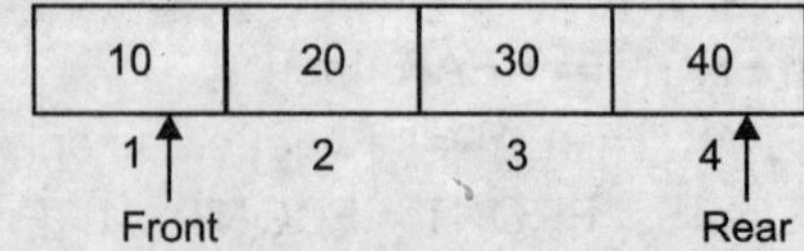

Figure 7.25: Print the REAR =40.

Step 1: [When the Queue is already empty?]

If FRONT = NULL, then Write: UNDERFLOW, and Return.

Step 2: [Print the element stored at location pointed to by rear].

Here it is 40. ITEM = QUEUE[4]. So 40 will printed.

Step 3: End

7.8.6 Equals Operation

Algorithm 7.6: To checks if two queues are equal or not? Two queues are equal when their contents are equal (requires deep equality on each element of the queue).

EQUALSQ (QUEUE1, QUEUE2, FRONT, N, M)

In the algorithm two array Queues say, Queue1 and Queue2 are declared with maximum size as say, n and m respectively and variables front and rear points to the first and last locations respectively of the Queues.

Step 1: IF QUEUE1[N] = QUEUE2[M] [if number of elements in QUEUE1 equal to number of elements in QUEUE2]

Then goto step 2. Else goto step 5.

Step 2: Repeat step 3 until FRONT > REAR.

Step 3: [Compare both queues]

IF QUEUE1[FRONT] = QUEUE2[FRONT] then

FRONT = FRONT +1

Else

goto step 5.

Step 4: Print the two Queues are equal.

Step 5: End.

Explanation

Consider the following two Queues:

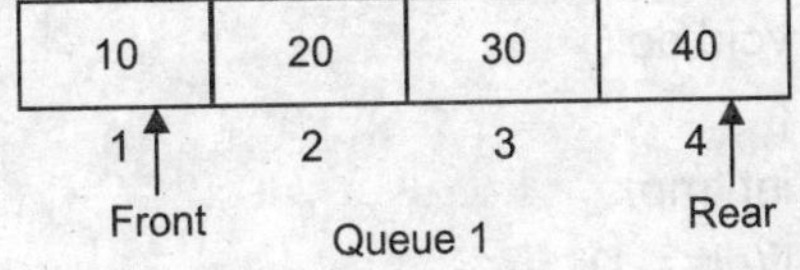

Figure 7.26: Queue1 having 4 elements.

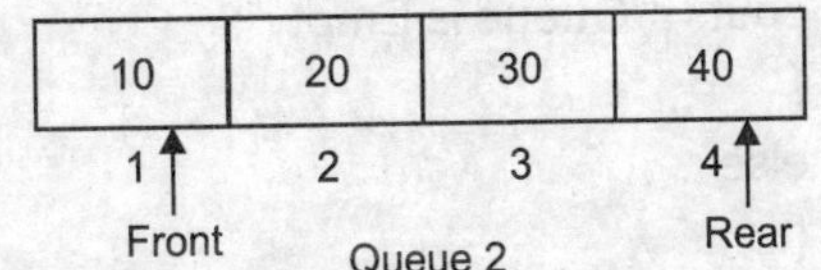

Figure 7.27: Queue2 having 4 elements.

Step 1: The total no of elements in QUEUE1 are 4 & total no of elements in QUEUE2 are 4, as these are equal so step 2 will be executed.

Step 2: Here front is 1 and rear is 4, as front is less than rear so steps 3 will be executed.

Step 3: Compare QUEUE1[FRONT] and QUEUE2[FRONT]. The value of these is 10, which is equal, so step 4 will be executed. FRONT = FRONT +1, So all the values of QUEUE1 will be compared with QUEUE2, till front is less than or equal to rear. As all these values are equal, so step 5 will be executed.

Step 4: Print that two Queues are equal

Step 5: End.

Program 5: Write a C++ program to implement queue using arrays.

```
#include <iostream>
#include<conio.h>
#define MAX 5            // MAXIMUM CONTENTS IN QUEUE
class queue
{
private:
int t[MAX];
int al;     // Addition End
int dl;     // Deletion End
public:
queue()
{
dl=-1;
al=-1;
}
void del()
{
int tmp;
if(dl==-1)
{
cout<<"Queue is Empty";
}
else
{
for(int j=0;j<=al;j++)
{
```

```
if((j+1)<=al)
{
tmp=t[j+1];
t[j]=tmp;
}
else
{
al--;
if(al==-1)
dl=-1;
else
dl=0;
} }
} }
void add(int item)
{
if(dl==-1 && al==-1)
{
dl++;
al++;
}
else
{
al++;
if(al==MAX)
{
cout<<"Queue is Full\n";
al--;
return;
}
}
t[al]=item;
}
void display()
{
if(dl!=-1)
{
for(int iter=0 ; iter<=al ; iter++)
cout<<t[iter]<<" ";
```

```
}
else
cout<<"EMPTY";
}
};
void main()
{
queue a;
int data[5]={32,23,45,99,24};

cout<<"Queue before adding Elements: ";
a.display();
cout<<endl<<endl;
for(int iter = 0 ; iter < 5 ; iter++)
{
a.add(data[iter]);
cout<<"Addition Number : "<<(iter+1)<<" : ";
a.display();
cout<<endl;
}
cout<<endl;
cout<<"Queue after adding Elements: ";
a.display();
cout<<endl<<endl;
for(iter=0 ; iter < 5 ; iter++)
{
a.del();
cout<<"Deletion Number : "<<(iter+1)<<" : ";
a.display();
cout<<endl;
}
getch();
}
```

Output:

```
Queue before adding Elements: EMPTY

Addition Number : 1 : 32
Addition Number : 2 : 32 23
Addition Number : 3 : 32 23 45
```

```
Addition Number : 4 : 32 23 45 99
Addition Number : 5 : 32 23 45 99 24

Queue after adding Elements: 32 23 45 99 24

Deletion Number : 1 : 23 45 99 24
Deletion Number : 2 : 45 99 24
Deletion Number : 3 : 99 24
Deletion Number : 4 : 24
Deletion Number : 5 : EMPTY
```

Program 6: Write a C++ program to implement Queue as a Class.

```
# include<iostream.h>
# include<conio.h>
# define SIZE 20
class queue
{
int a[SIZE];
int front;
int rear;
public:
queue();
~queue();
void insert(int i);
int remove();
int isempty();
int isfull();
};
queue::queue()
{
front=0;
rear=0;
}
queue::~queue()
{
delete []a;
}
void queue::insert(int i)
{
```

```
if(isfull())
{
cout<<" ******
Queue is FULL !!!
No insertion allowed further.
******";
return;
}
a[rear] = i;
rear++;
}
int queue::remove()
{
if(isempty())
{
cout<<" ******
Queue Empty !!!
Value returned will be garbage.
******";
return (-9999);
}
return(a[front++]);
}
int queue::isempty()
{
if(front == rear)
return 1;
else
return 0;
}
int queue::isfull()
{
if(rear == SIZE)
return 1;
else
return 0;
}
void main()
```

```
{
clrscr();
queue q;
q.insert(1);
q.insert(2);
cout<<" "<<q.remove();
cout<<" "<<q.remove();
cout<<" "<<q.remove();
getch();
}
```

7.9 MAJOR PROBLEM WITH SIMPLE QUEUE

Queue Migration is a problem commonly found in queues when implemented using arrays. As we remove the items from the queue, the queue migrates to one end and the other end remains empty. When we try to insert an element in the queue though there are empty spaces in the queue, it gives a message saying that the Queue is full.

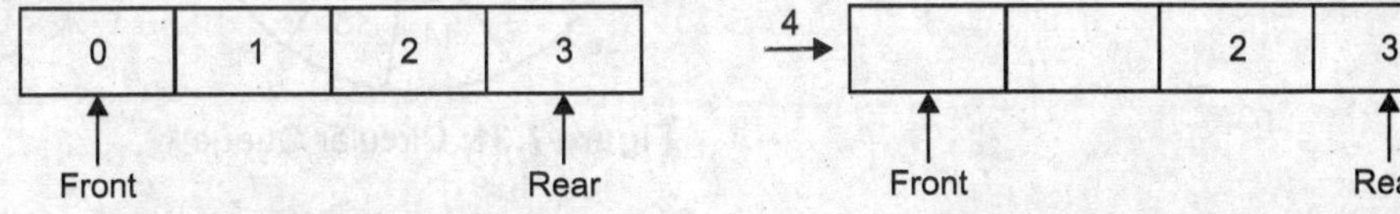

Figure 7.28: Queue Migration

Figure 7.29: Queue Migration

Here in this Figure 7.28 The maximum size of the array is 4 and four elements 0,1,2,3 are inserted in the queue. When i delete two elements from it, the queue changes like Fig 7.29. Now i insert a number 4 in the queue, it returns a message 'Queue is Full'.

This problem could be solved by implementing a circular queue in next sections.

7.10 CIRCULAR QUEUE

The problem with the previous implementation is that the insert function gives a queue-full signal even if a considerable portion is free. This happens because the queue has a tendency to move to the right unless the 'front' catches up with the 'rear' and both are reset to 0 again (in the delete procedure). To overcome this problem, the elements of the array are required to shift one position left whenever a deletion is made. But this will make the deletion process inefficient. Therefore, an efficient way of overcoming this problem is to consider the array to be circular, as shown in Figure 7.30.

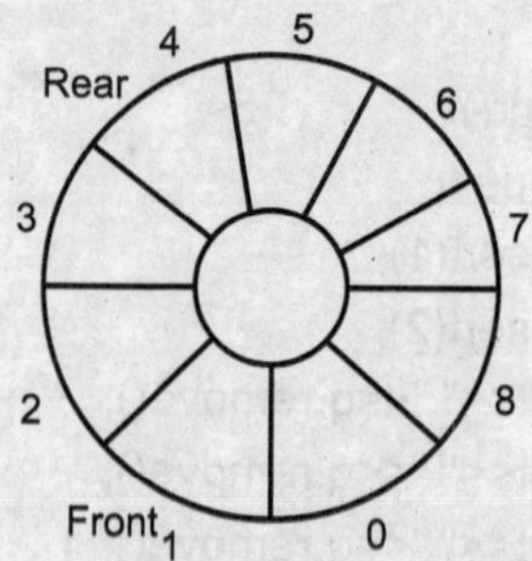

Figure 7.30: Circular queue.

Circular queue, as the name suggests, this queue is not straight but circular, it looks like this

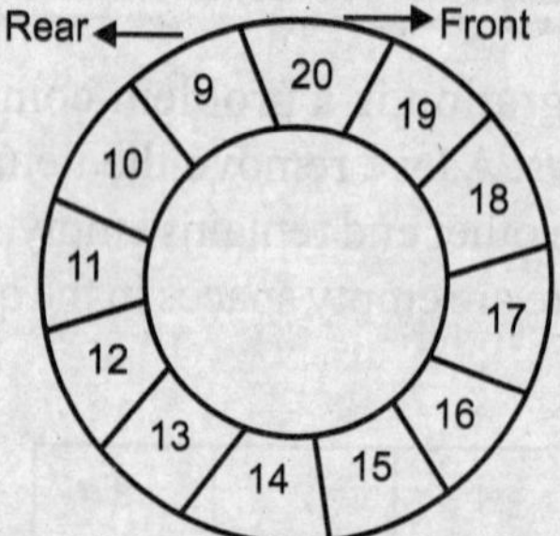

Figure 7.31: Circular Queue

In this Circular queue, once the queue is full, the "first" element of the queue becomes the "rear" most element of the queue. Initially when the queue is empty "front" and "rear" values are 0 and –1.

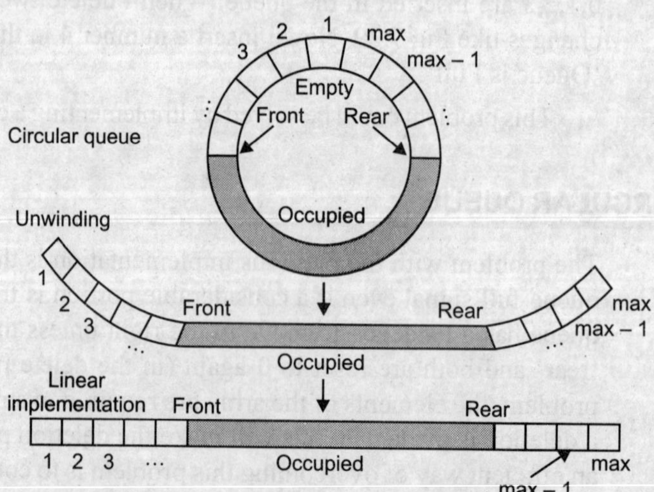

Figure 7.32: Circular queue, unwinding and linear implementation.

7.10.1 Storing a Queue In A Static Data Structure

This implementation stores the queue in an array. The array indices at which the head and tail of the queue are currently stored must be maintained. The head of the queue is not necessarily at index 0. The array can be a "circular array" – the queue "wraps round" if the last index of the array is reached.

EXAMPLE – **storing a queue in an array of length 5**

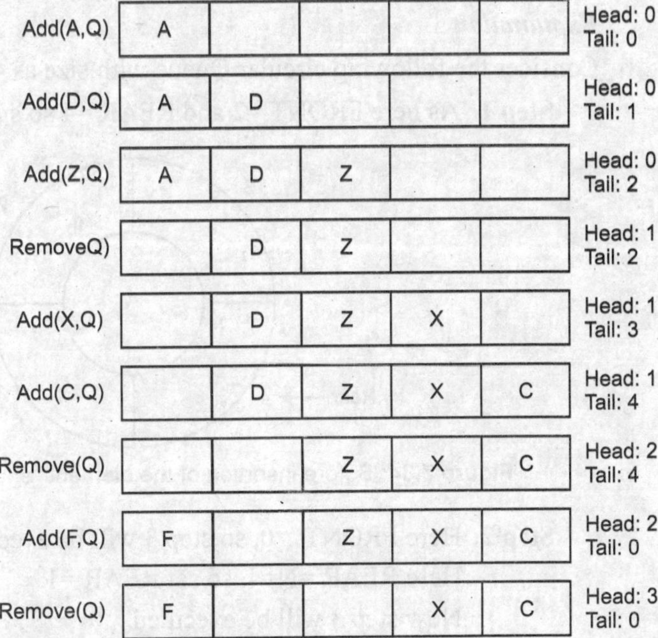

Figure 7.33: Storing a queue in a static data structure performing operation add and delete.

7.10.2 Enqueue Operation

Algorithm 7.7: To insert an element in a circular queue.

INSRTCQ(N, FRONT, REAR, ITEM)

In the algorithm, a circular Queue, say Queue is declared with maximum size as say, n and variables front and rear points to the first and last locations, respectively of the circular Queue. The data item which is to be entered is stored in variable i.

Step 1: [When the Queue is already filled?]

If FRONT = 1 and REAR = N, or if FRONT = REAR + 1, then

Write: OVERFLOW, and Return.

Step 2: [Find new value of **REAR.]**

If FRONT = NULL, then [**Starting Queue** initially empty.]

Set FRONT= 1 and REAR = 1.

Else if REAR = N, then
Set REAR = 1.
Else
Set REAR = REAR + 1.
[End of If statement.]
Step 3: Set QUEUE[REAR] = ITEM. [This inserts new element.]
Step 4: End.

Explanation

Consider the following circular Queue with size as 4 i.e. N=4.

Step 1: As here FRONT =2 and REAR =4 so step 2 will be executed.

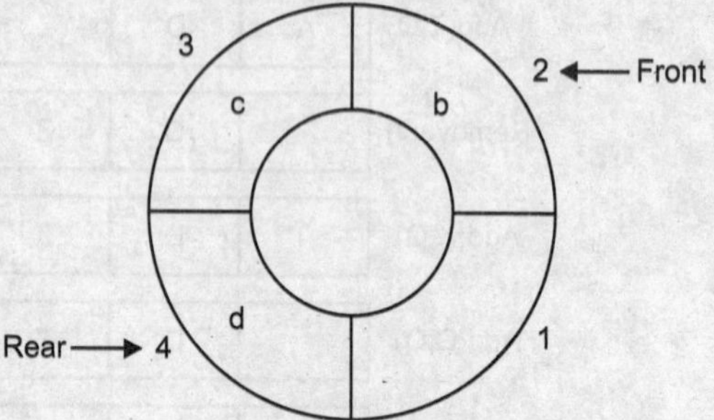

Figure 7.34: Before insertion of the element "e". FRONT = 2, REAR = 4.

Step 2: Here FRONT ""0, so step 3 will be executed.
Here REAR =N=4, so set REAR =1.
Now step 3 will be executed.

Step 3: Enter the element "e" stored in ITEM, in circular Queue, using an assignment QUEUE[REAR] = ITEM.
Queue will look like:

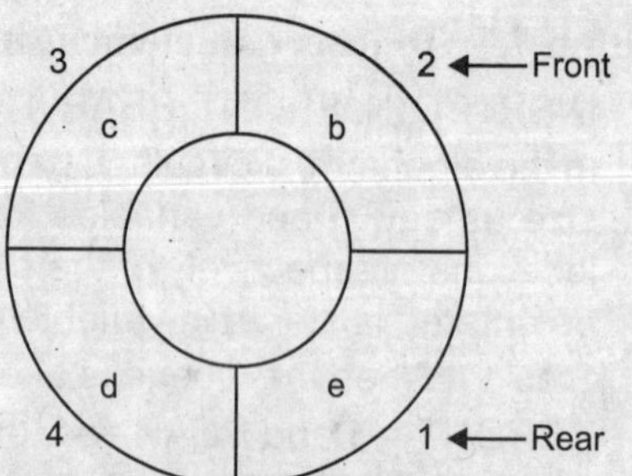

Figure 7.35: After insertion of the element 'e'. FRONT = 2, REAR = 1.

Step 4: End.

7.10.3 Dequeue Operation

Algorithm 7.8: To delete an element in a circular queue.

DELCQ(N, FRONT, REAR, ITEM)

In the algorithm, a circular Queue, say Queue is declared with maximum size as say, N and variables FRONT and REAR points to the first and last locations, respectively of the Queue.

Step 1: [When the Queue is already empty?]

If FRONT = NULL, then Write: UNDERFLOW, and Return.

Step 2: Set ITEM =QUEUE[FRONT].

Step 3: [Find new value of front.]

If FRONT= REAR, then [Queue has only one element to start.]

Set FRONT = NULL and REAR = NULL

Else if FRONT = N, then Set FRONT = 1

Else Set FRONT = FRONT + 1. [End of If statement.]

Step 4: End.

Explanation

Consider the following circular Queue with size as 4 i.e. n=4.

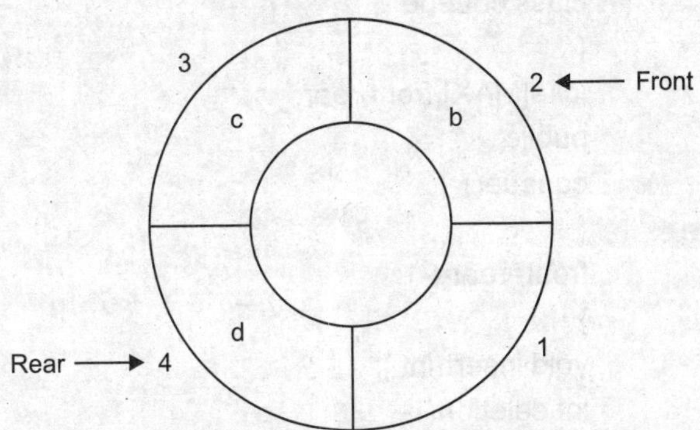

Figure 7.36: Before deletion of the element 'b'. FRONT = 2, REAR = 4.

Step 1: FRONT "" NULL. Goto step 2.

Step 2: Set ITEM =QUEUE[FRONT] , put value of FRONT=2

Set ITEM =QUEUE[2].

Step 3: [Increment front by 1 now front will become 3].

FRONT =FRONT + 1, last value of FRONT=2

After Increment, FRONT=2+1=3

Queue after deletion of an element will look like:

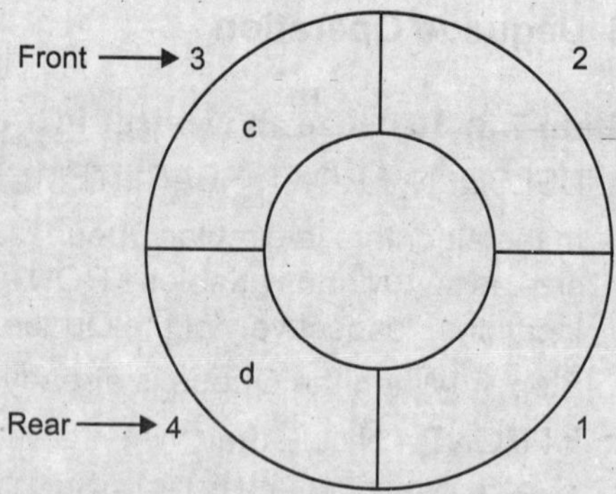

Figure 7.37: After deletion of the element 'b'. FRONT = 3, REAR = 4.

Step 4: End.

Program 7: Write a C++ program for Circular Queue Implementation using Arrays.

```
/* Circular Queues */
#include<iostream.h>
#include<conio.h>
const int MAX = 5;
class cqueue
{
int a[MAX],front,rear;
public :
cqueue()
{
front=rear=-1;
}
void insert(int );
int deletion();
void display();
};
void cqueue :: insert(int val)
{
if((front==0 && rear==MAX-1) || (rear+1==front))
cout<<" Circular Queue is Full";
else
{
if(rear==MAX-1)
rear=0;
```

```
else
rear++;
a[rear]=val;
}
if(front==-1)
front=0;
}
int cqueue :: deletion()
{
int k;
if(front==-1)
cout<<"Circular Queue is Empty";
else
{
k=a[front];
if(front==rear)
front=rear=-1;
else
{
if(front==MAX-1)
front=0;
else
front++;
}
}
return k;
}
void cqueue :: display()
{
int i;
if(front==-1)
cout<<"Circular Queue is Empty";
else
{
if(rear < front)
{
for(i=front;i<=MAX-1;i++)
cout<<a[i]<<"   ";
for(i=0;i<=rear;i++)
```

```
cout<<a[i]<<"  ";
}
else
{
for(i=front;i<=rear;i++)
cout<<a[i]<<"  ";
cout<<endl;
}
}
}
void main()
{
cqueue c1;
int ch,val;
char op;
do
{
clrscr();
cout<<"-----------Menu------------";
cout<<"1.Insertion
2.Deletion
3.Display
4.Exit
";
cout<<"Enter Your Choice <1..4> ?";
cin>>ch;
switch(ch)
{
case 1 : cout<<"Enter Element to Insert ?";
cin>>val;
c1.insert(val);
break;
case 2 : val=c1.deletion();
cout<<"Deleted Element :"<<val<<endl;
break;
case 3 : c1.display();
break;
}
cout<<"Do you want to continue<Y/N> ?";
```

```
cin>>op;
}while(op=='Y' || op=='y');
getch();
}
```

Program 8: Write a C++ program to perform insert, delete operations with circular queue and display elements.

```
# include <iostream.h>
# include <conio.h>
# include <process.h>
int queue[8];int r,f=0,x=0;
void insert(void);
void del ();
void show (void);
void main ()
{
int c;
clrscr();
cout<<"\n1] Insert Element";
cout<<"\n2] Delete Element";
cout<<"\n3] Display element/s";
cout<<"\n4] Exit";
cout<<"\n Enter your choice:-";
cin>>c;
switch (c)
{
case 1: insert(); break;
case 2: del(); show();break;
case 3: show(); break;
default: exit(0);
}
main ();
getch();
}
void insert () {
int n;
char ch,ans='Y';
if (r>=7) {
while (queue[x]= =0) {
cout<<"\n Enter a Number:";
```

```
cin>>n;
queue[x]=n;
x++;
cout<<"\n Continue Y/N;
ch=getch();
if (ch!='Y')break;
}
cout<<"\n Queue is full \n\n\n";
main();
}
cout<<"\n Enter elements:";
while (ans= ='Y')
{
cin>>queue[r];
if (r= =7)
{
clrscr();
cout<<"\n Queue is Full";
getch();
break;
}
else
r++;
cout<<"\n Continue Y/N:";
ans=getche();
}
}
void show()
{
int j;
for (j=0;j<8++)
cout<<queue[j];
getch();
}
void del ()
{
int j;
if (r= =0)
{
```

```
clrscr();
cout<<"\n Queue is empty \n\n\n";
main();
}
if (f= =8) f=0;
queue[f]=0;
f++;
}
```

Output:

```
1] Insert Element
2] Delete Element
3] Display element
4] Exit
Enter your choice: 2
0 2 0 0 0 0 0 0
```

7.11 IMPLEMENTATION OF QUEUES USING LINKED LIST

An alternative and efficient representation of Queues is possible by using linked lists for storing the data elements using dynamic memory. It is represented in the Figure 7.38 as shown below:

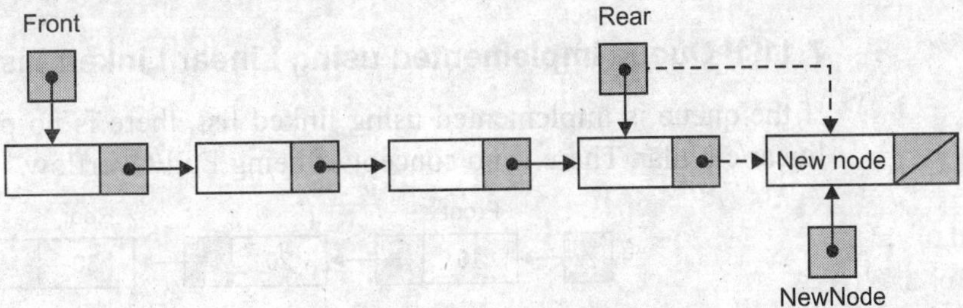

Figure 7.38: Queue using linked list

The advantages of linked list representation of Queues over array representation are:

1. There is no need of knowing the Queue size before implementing it, as dynamic memory allocation technique helps the programmer to declare the memory space at run time.
2. The Queue is never full as long as the system has enough space for dynamic memory allocation. So there is no need to check the IsFull or overflow condition of the Queue.
3. Data movement i.e. entering and deleting from Queue is very easily handled with the concept of pointer in linked lists

Remember that a Queue implemented using link list is called as linked Queue.

A linked list is a set of nodes (a node can be a struct or a class) defined arbitrarily in memory; a node has a special variable (pointer) of the same type as the structure/class, that points to the next memory location, thus making the list values continuous. The following picture shows how a linked list looks like when it is created. The first node of a list is referred to as head/start most of the time and the last node is referred to as tail/end, the tail/end of the list always points to NULL or 0 (zero), which is also referred to as grounding.

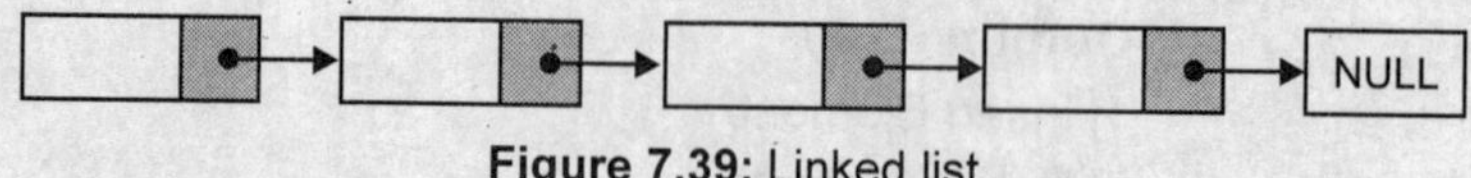

Figure 7.39: Linked list.

The following Figure 7.40 explains the same but with the concept of Queues:

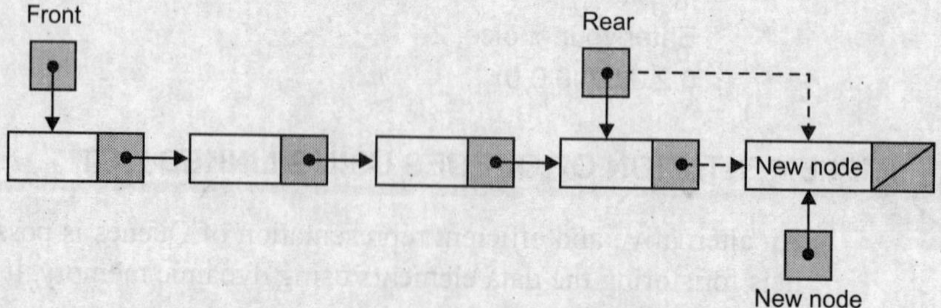

Figure 7.40: Linked Queue with front and rear pointers.

7.11.1 Queue Implemented using Linear Linked List

If the queue is implemented using linked list, there is no problem whether it is linear/circular. There is no concept of being Full/Overflow.

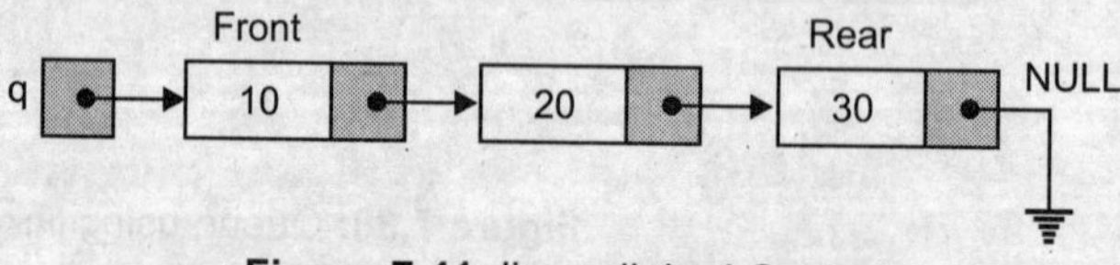

Figure 7.41: linear linked Queue

To check for Empty condition: Check whether q is NULL or not

For an element to be enqueued

//Create new(temp) or malloc(temp) temp.value = x

temp.next = NULL

rear.next = temp

For an element to be dequeued, it is just pointer jumping

front = front.next

q = q.next

Advantage

- No Queue Migration Problem
- Gives a natural way of handling queue

Disadvantage

- Pointer based Implementation is bit more complex and slower than array based implementation.

7.11.2 Queue Implemented using Circular Linked List

Instead of having a null pointer at the rear end, the pointer at the rear end points to the node at the front end of the list.

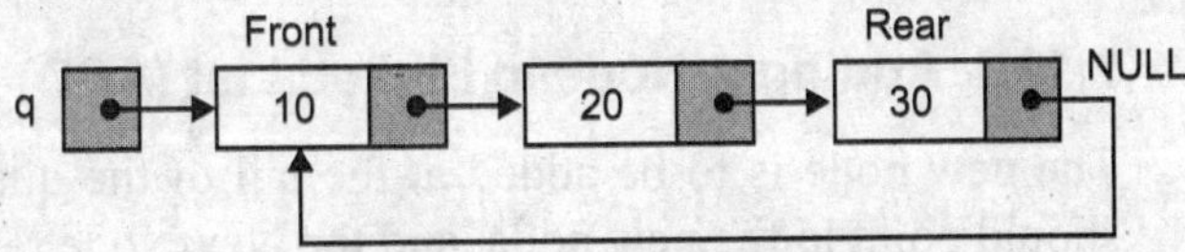

Figure 7.42: Circular linked queue

For an element to be enqueued

Pseudocode:

1. begin
2. Create newnode
3. if(front = null)
4. front = newnode
5. else
6. rear ! next = newnode
7. end //endif
8. rear = newnode
9. rear ! next = front
10 end

For an element to be dequeued

1. begin
2. if(front = rear)
3. delete front
4. else
5. q = front
6. front = q ! next
7. rear ! next = front
8. delete q
9. end //endif
10. end

7.12 STORING A QUEUE IN A DYNAMIC DATA STRUCTURE

As in the case of the stack, each node in a dynamic data structure contains data and a reference to the next node. A queue also needs a reference to the head node and a reference to the tail node. The following diagram describes the storage of a queue called Queue. Each node consists of data (DataItem) and a reference (NextNode).

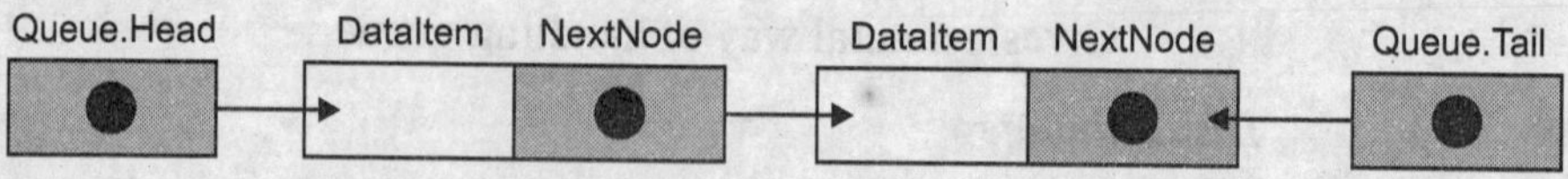

Figure 7.43: Representation of queue using linked list.

- The first node is accessed using the name **Queue.Head**.
- Its data is accessed using **Queue.Head.DataItem**
- The second node is accessed using **Queue.Head.NextNode**
- The last node is accessed using **Queue.Tail**

7.12.1 Adding A Node in Linked List (ADD)

The new node is to be added at the tail of the queue. The reference Queue.Tail should point to the new node, and the NextNode reference of the node previously at the tail of the queue should point to the DataItem of the new node.

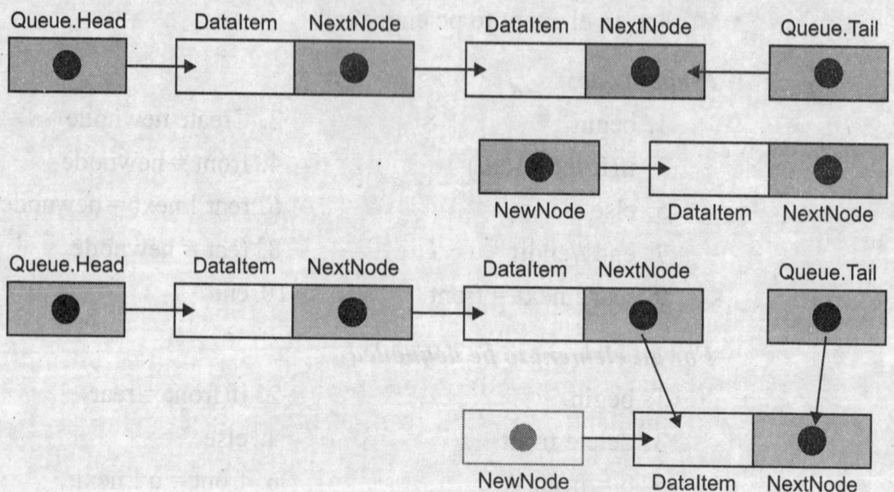

Figure 7.44: Adding a node in linked queue.

7.12.2 Removing A Node from the Linked List (REMOVE)

The value of Queue.Head.DataItem is returned. A temporary reference Temp is declared and set to point to head node in the queue (Temp = Queue.Head). Queue.Head is then set to point to the second node instead of the top node.The only reference to the original head node is now Temp and the memory used by this node can then be freed.

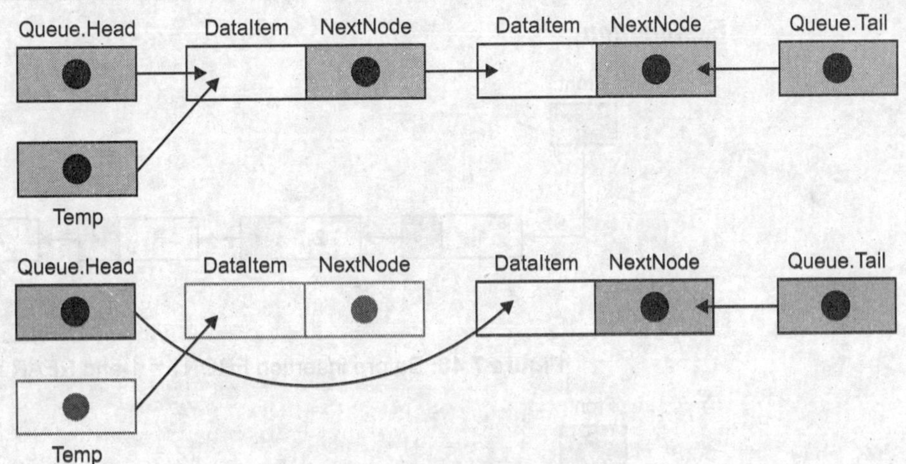

Figure 7.45: Removing a node from the linked queue.

7.12.3 Enqueue Operation

It's very similar to the addition in a dynamic linked list. The only difference is that here you'll add the new element only at the end of the list, since a dynamic list is used for the Queue, the queue is also dynamic, means it has no prior size set.

So, we don't have to check the Overflow condition in linked Queue.

Algorithm 7.9: To insert an element into linked queue.

(FRONT, REAR, AVAIL, ITEM)

The linked Queue say, Queue exists with two pointers front and rear pointing to first and last elements, respectively of the linked Queue.

Step 1: [Check for overflow, Avail list empty]

If AVAIL = NULL

Then write"overflow" return. [End of if structure]

Step 2: [Create a new node] NEW = AVAIL

Step 3: [Update AVAIL pointer] AVAIL = LINK[AVAIL]

Step 4: [save the ITEM into NEW node]INFO[NEW]=ITEM

Step 5: [Check queue is empty or not]

If FRONT = NULL then

a. FRONT =NEW

b. REAR = NEW

else[if queue is not empty]

a. [Update rear to point NEW node] LINK[REAR] = NEW

b. REAR = NEW

[End of if structure]

Step 6: [Set LINK part of NEW node to null]

LINK[NEW] = NULL

Step 7: End

Explanation

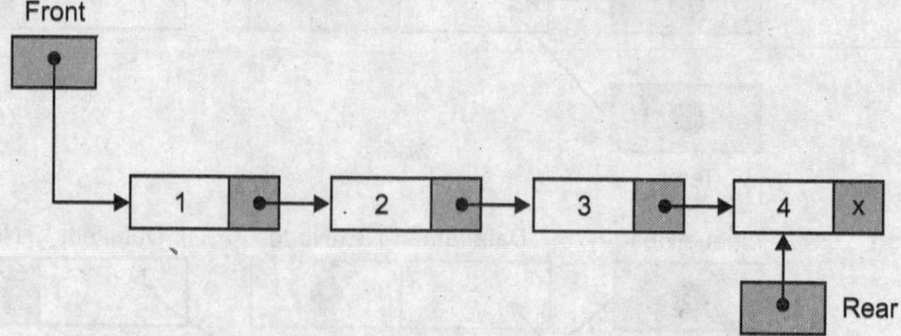

Figure 7.46: Before insertion FRONT = 1 and REAR = 4.

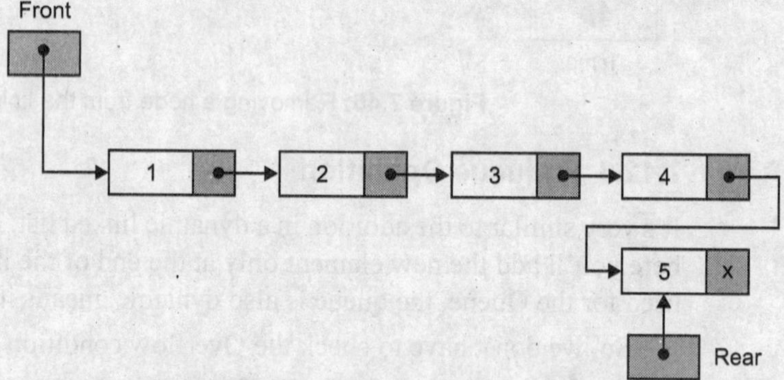

Figure 7.47: After insertion FRONT = 1 and REAR = 5.

7.12.4 Dequeue Operation

This is again very similar to deletion in any Linked List, but you can only delete from the head of the list, that makes it a Queue.

Algorithm 7.10: To delete an element from linked queue.

(FRONT, REAR, AVAIL, ITEM)

The linked Queue say, Queue exists with two pointers front and rear pointing to first and last elements, respectively of the linked Queue.

Step 1: [When the Queue is already empty?]

If FRONT = NULL, then Write: UNDERFLOW, and Return.

Step 2: Set ITEM =QUEUE[FRONT].

Step 3: [Assign Front to SAVE]

SAVE=FRONT

Step 4: [Reset FRONT to point to next node in LINK queue]

FRONT = LINK[SAVE]

Step 5: LINK[SAVE]= AVAIL

Step 6: [Save deleted node to AVAIL list] AVAIL = SAVE

Step 7: End.

Explanation

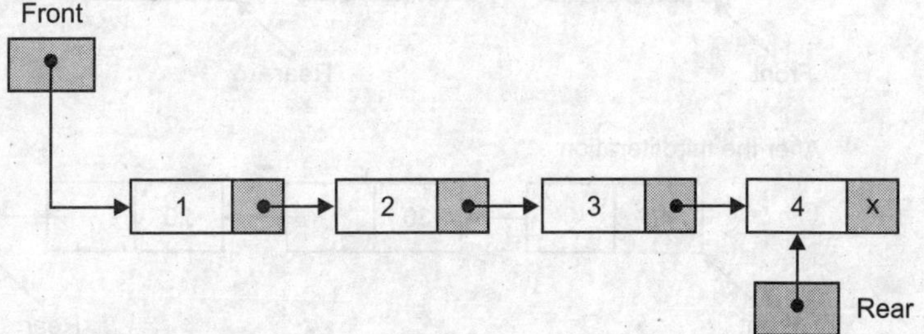

Figure 7.48: Before deletion FRONT = 1 and REAR = 4.

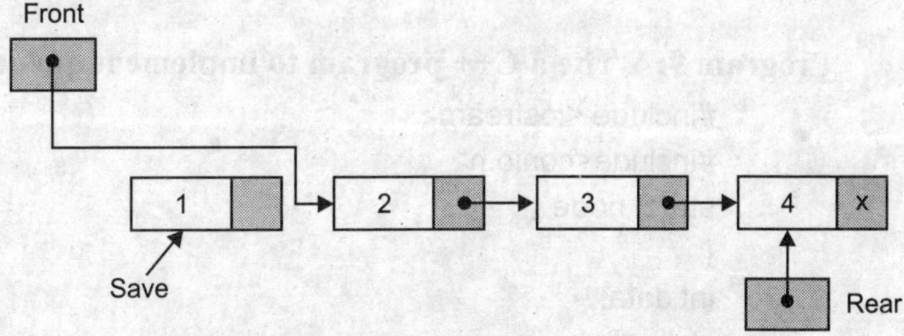

Figure 7.49: After deletion FRONT = 2 and REAR = 4.

For example: To create a linked queue. Initially, the list is empty, so both the front and rear pointers are NULL. The insert function creates a new node, puts the new data value in it, appends it to an existing list, and makes the rear pointer point to it. A delete function checks whether the queue is empty, and if not, retrieves the data value of the node pointed to by the front, advances the front, and frees the storage of the node whose data value has been retrieved.

If the above strategy is used for creating a queue with four data values —10, 20, 30, and 40, the queue gets created as shown in Figure 7.50.

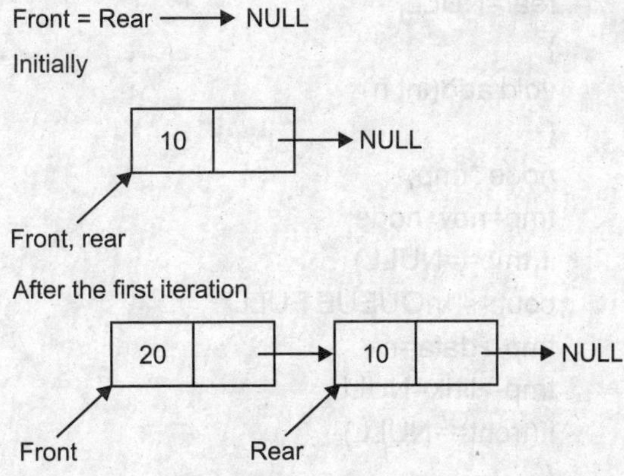

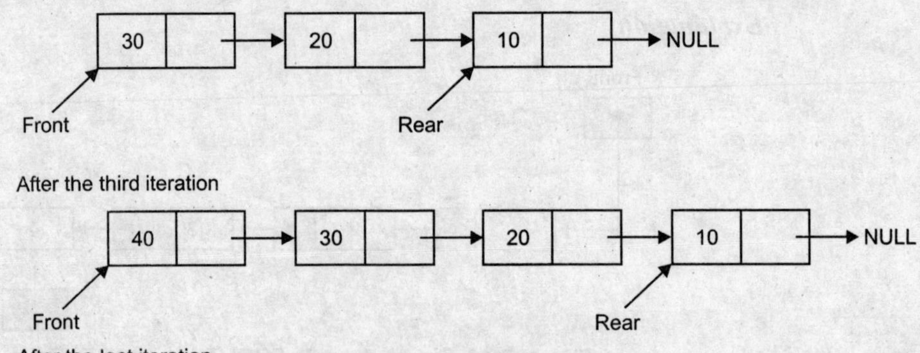

Figure 7.50: Linked queue.

Program 9: Write a C++ program to implement queue using liked list.

```
#include <iostream>
#include<conio.h>
struct node
{
int data;
node *link;
};
class lqueue
{
private:
node *front,*rear;
public:
lqueue()
{
front=NULL;
rear=NULL;
}
void add(int n)
{
node *tmp;
tmp=new node;
if(tmp==NULL)
cout<<"\nQUEUE FULL";
tmp->data=n;
tmp->link=NULL;
if(front==NULL)
{
```

```
rear=front=tmp;
return;
}
rear->link=tmp;
rear=rear->link;
}
int del()
{
if(front==NULL)
{
cout<<"\nQUEUE EMPTY";
return NULL;
}
node *tmp;
int n;
n=front->data;
tmp=front;
front=front->link;
delete tmp;
return n;
}
~lqueue()
{
if(front==NULL)
return;
node *tmp;
while(front!=NULL)
{
tmp=front;
front=front->link;
delete tmp;
}
}
};
void main()
{
lqueue q;
q.add(11);
q.add(22);
q.add(33);
q.add(44);
```

```
q.add(55);
cout<<"\nItem Deleted = "<<q.del();
cout<<"\nItem Deleted = "<<q.del();
cout<<"\nItem Deleted = "<<q.del();
getch();
}
```

7.13 DEQUE (DOUBLE ENDED QUEUES)

In computer science, a **deque** (short for double-ended queue) is an abstract data structure for which elements can be added to or removed from the front or back. This differs from a normal queue, where elements can only be added to one end and removed from the other. An input-restricted deque is one where deletion can be made from both ends, but input can only be made at one end. An output-restricted deque is one where input can be made at both ends, but output can be made from one end only. Both queues and stacks can be considered specializations of deques, and can be implemented using deques

Deque is usually pronounced deck, possibly due to the conceptual similarity to a deck of cards, where a card can be dealt from or returned to either the face or patterned side. In computer science, a **deque** (short for double-ended queue) is an abstract data structure for which elements can be added to or removed from the front or back. This differs from a normal queue, where elements can only be added to one end and removed from the other. Both queues and stacks can be considered specializations of deques, and can be implemented using deques.

Definition: *A deque is a sequence where elements can be added and removed at both ends (front and rear) of the sequence, but not in the middle.*

In the preceding section we saw that a Queue comprises a pile of objects into which we insert items at one end and from which we remove items at the other end. In this section we examine an extension of the Queue, which provides a means to insert and remove items at both ends of the pile. This data structure is a Deque. A Deque is as shown in the Figure 7.51:

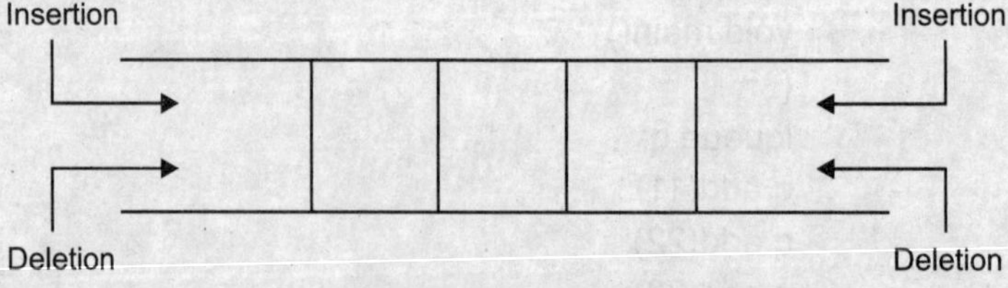

Figure 7.51: Deque

As an example let us suppose there is a deque with three elements as below:

Front = 4
Rear = 6

	1	4	1

Now performing Enque front (3) operation will make Deque to look like:

3	1	4	1

Performing Enque rear operation will make Deque to look like:

3	1	4	1	5

Performing Deque front will delete 3, leaving Deque to look like

1	4	1	5

Performing Deque rear will delete 5, leaving Deque to look like

1	4	1

The word *Deque* is an acronym derived from *double-ended queue*

The operations that are defined on deques are:

- Enquefront — inserts element at the front
- Enquerear — inserts element at the rear
- getfront — returns the item at the front
- getrear — returns the item at the rear
- Dequefront — returns and removes the item at the front
- Dequerear — returns and removes the item at the rear
- IsEmpty — returns true if the Deque is empty, false otherwise
- makeEmpty — makes an empty Deque

When Front=NULL, it means that Deque is empty. There are two variations of a Deque.

7.13.1 Input Restricted Deque

It allows insertions at only one end of the list structure but allows performing deletions at both ends.

Program 10: Write a C++ program to demonstrate input restricted deque.

```
# include <iostream.h>
# include <conio.h>
int ird[5];
void main ()
{
int r=0,c=1,op,f=-1;
int insert(int);
void deleter(int,int);
void deletef(int,int);
void show(void);
while(1)
{
clrscr();
cout<<"\n (1) Insert";
cout<<"\n (2) Delete from rear";
cout<<"\n (3) Delete from front";
cout<<"\n (4) Display";
cout<<"\n (0) Exit";
cout<<"\n Enter Your choice:-";
cin>>op;
switch(op)
{
case 1:        while (c && r<5)
{
c=insert(r);
r++;
}
if (c= =0)
{
c=1;
r-;
}
else
if (f<0)
cout<<"\n Deque is full";
getch();
break;
case 2: deleter(-r,f);break;
case 3: deletef(r,++f); break;
```

```
case 4: show (); break;
default: exit(0);
}
}
getch();
}
void show ()
{
int j;
cout<<"\n Elements of deque are:";
for (j=0;j<5;j++);
getch();
}
int insert (int h)
{
int k;
cout<<"\n Enter an element (enter 0 to exit):";
cin>>k;
ird[h]=k;
return (k);
}
void deleter(int m,int n)
{
if (m<=n)
cout<<"Deque is empty";
else
{
cout<<"\n "<<m<<" The element deleted: "<<ird[m];
ird[m]=0;
}
getch();
}
void deletef(int f,int j)
{
if(f<j)
cout<<"Deque is empty";
else
{
cout<<"\n "<<j<<" The element deleted:- "<<ird[j];
ird[f]=NULL;
```

```
}
getch();
}
```

Output:

```
(1) Insert
(2) Delete from rear
(3) Delete from front
(4) Display
(0) Exit
Enter Your choice:- 1
Enter an element (enter 0 to exit): 2
Enter an element (enter 0 to exit): 3
Enter an element (enter 0 to exit): 5
Enter an element (enter 0 to exit): 8
Enter an element (enter 0 to exit): 6
Deque if full
(1) Insert
(2) Delete from rear
(3) Delete from front
(4) Display
(0) Exit
Enter Your choice:- 4
Elements of deque are: 2 3 5 8 6
```

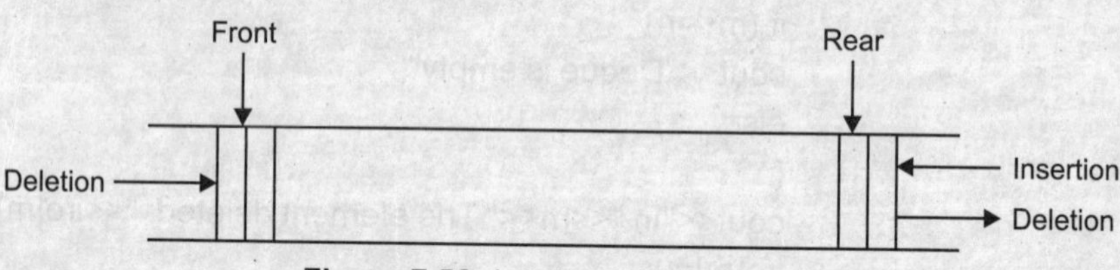

Figure 7.52: Input restricted deque.

7.13.2 Output-restricted Deque

It allows deletions at only one end of the list structure but allows performing insertions at both ends.

Program 11: Write a C++ program to demonstrate output restricted deque.

```
# include <iostream.h>
# include <conio.h>
# include <process.h>
int ird[5];
```

```
void main ()
{
int r=0,c=1,op,f=-1;
int insert(int);
int insertf(int);
void deletef(int);
void show(void);
clrscr();
while (1) {
cout<<"\n 1 Insert from rear:";
cout<<"\n 2 Insert from front";
cout<<"\n 3 Delete from front";
cout<<"\n 4 Display";
cout<<"\n 0 Exit";
cout<<"\n Enter Your choice:-";
cin>>op;
switch(op) {
case 1:
while (c && r<5)
{
c=insert(r);
r++;
}
if (c= =0)
{ c=1; r--; }
else if (f<0)
cout<<"\n Deque is full";
getch();
break;
case 2: f=insertf(f);break;
case 3: deletef(++f); break;
case 4: show (); break;
default: exit(0);
} }
getch();
}
void show () {
int j;
cout<<"\n Elements of deque are:";
```

```
for (j=0;j<5;j++);
getch();
}
int insertr (int h) {
int k;
cout<<"\n Enter an element (enter 0 to exit):";
cin>>k;
ird[h]=k;
return (k);
}
int insert(int m) {
int h;
if (ird[m]= =0 && m>=0) {
cout<<"\n Enter a element:";
cin>>h;
ird[m]=h;
} else
cout<<"\n no space available";
return -m;
}
void deletef(int f)
{ ird[f]=NULL;}
```

Output:

```
1 Insert from rear:
2 insert  from rear
3 Delete from front
4 Display
0 Exit
Enter Your choice:- 1
Enter a element (enter 0 to exit): 1
Enter a element (enter 0 to exit): 2
Enter a element (enter 0 to exit): 3
Enter a element (enter 0 to exit): 0
1 Insert from rear:
2 insert  from rear
3 Delete from front
4 Display
0 Exit
Enter Your choice: 4
Elements of deque are: 1 2 3 0 0
```

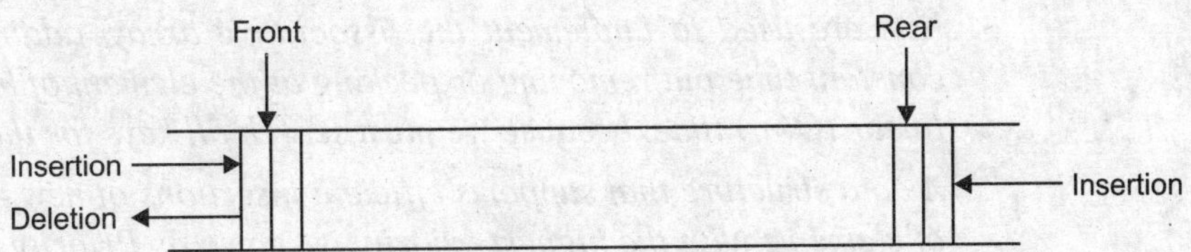

Figure 7.53: Ouput restricted deque.

7.13.3 Advantages of Deque

Deque provides random access in constant time

1. It provides Constant time i.e. of O (1), insert and delete operations at the front or the end.
2. A deque uses memory more effectively. if there isn't enough consecutive memory, the deque will use a series of smaller blocks.
3. The last or the first element can be obtained immediately

7.13.4 Disadvantages of Deque

1. Insert and delete operation in the middle take linear time.
2. There can be no splicing, no merges in comparison to lists.

7.14 PRIORITY QUEUE

Previously, we've looked at the Queue data structure, which allowed accessing the data elements in first-come, first-serve fashion. Queues are useful for implementing resource managers fairly. If user A submits his print job to a printer before user B, it's only fair that user B should wait until user A is done to get his output. But what if user B needs to print a report for his meeting with the boss, while user A is just printing a receipt for a reference manual he just ordered. Obviously, user A can wait to print the receipt. We say that user B's job has higher *priority* than user A's. To allow jobs to have varying levels of priority, we replace our regular queue with a *priority queue*.

Definition: *A priority queue is special type of queue that acts as an abstract data type in computer programming, supporting the following three operations:*

- *add an element to the queue with an associated priority*
- *remove the element from the queue that has the highest priority, and return it*
- *(optionally) peek at the element with highest priority without removing it*

The simplest way to implement a priority queue data type is to keep an associative array mapping each priority to a list of elements with that priority. If association lists are used to implement the associative array, adding an element takes constant time but removing or peeking at the element of highest priority takes linear (O(n)) time, because we must search all keys for the largest one.

A data structure that supports efficient insertions of new element and deletion of elements with the highest priority is known as Priority Queue.

In case the two or more elements have the same priority then these elements are processed in the order they were added to the Queue. The Queues are called "priority" Queues because they enable you to retrieve elements not by the insertion time (as in a stack or queue), nor by a key match (as in a dictionary), but by which element has the highest priority of retrieval.

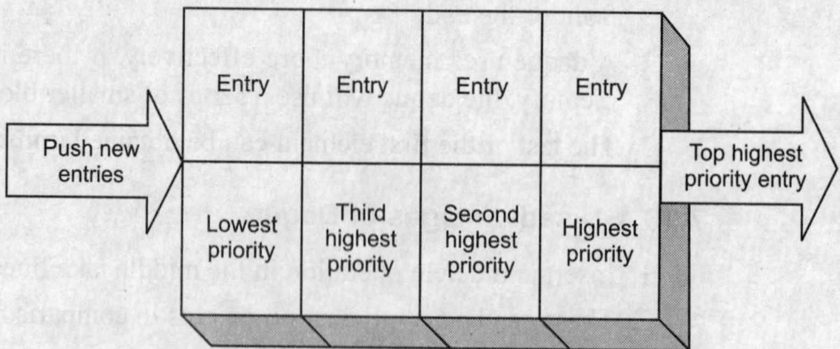

Figure 7.54: Shows a representation of a Priority Queue.

This type of Queue assigns a priority to every element that it stores. New elements are added to the Queue using the Insert operation, just as with a FIFO Queue. This Queue also has a delete operation, which differs from the FIFO Dequeue in one key area. When you call Delete for the priority queue, you don't get the oldest element in the queue. Instead, you get the element with the highest priority.

Applications of Priority Queues

Area	Examples
1. Operating systems.	task scheduling, interrupt handling
2. Event-driven simulation.	customers in a line
3. Numerical computation.	reducing round off error
4. Data compression.	Huffman codes
5. Graph searching.	shortest path
6. Computational number theory.	sum of powers
7. Artificial intelligence.	A* search

7.15 COMMONLY USED PRIORITY QUEUE OPERATIONS

Here are some operations, with their typical names, that are performed on Priority Queues:

- **Initialization operation**
  – **Create:** Returns an empty Priority Queue
- **Basic Operations**
  – **Insert:** Adds a new element in the Priority Queue.
  – **Delete:** returns and removes the element with the highest priority from the queue
- **Other Operations**
  – Replace the largest element with a new element in the Priority Queue.
  – Change the priority of an element in a Priority Queue
  – Join two Priority Queues into one
  – **FindMin:** Returns the element with highest Priority from the Queue, without removing it from the Queue.

Advantages

- operation FindMin is very efficient (of O (1))
- operations Insert and Delete are efficient (of O (logn))
- very useful in important application areas
- more efficient than Sorted Sequences
- more functionality than some related data types

Disadvantages

- Less functionality than Sorted Sequences.
- Less efficient than some related data types.

A priority queue is a collection of elements such that each element has been assigned a priority and such that the order in which elements are deleted and processed comes from the following rules:

1. An element of higher priority is processed before any element of lower priority.
2. Two element with same priority are processed according to the order in which they were added to the queue.

A simple example of a priority queue is a timesharing system: Programs of high priority are processed first, and programs with the same priority form a standard queue.

There are various ways of maintaining a priority queue in memory.

We discuss two of them here.

1. One way list and multiple queues
2. Array representation of a priority queue

7.16 ONE WAY LIST REPRESENTATION OF PRIORITY QUEUE

One way to maintain a priority queue in memory is by means of a one way list is, as follows:

1. Each node in the list will contain three items of information:
   - An information field calls INFO.
   - A priority number call PRT.
   - A next link number call LINK.
2. A node X precedes a node Y in the list.
   - When X has high priority than Y or
   - When both have same priority but X was added to the list before Y.

This means that the order in the one-way list corresponds to the order of the priority queue.

For example: A priority queue with seven elements show here:

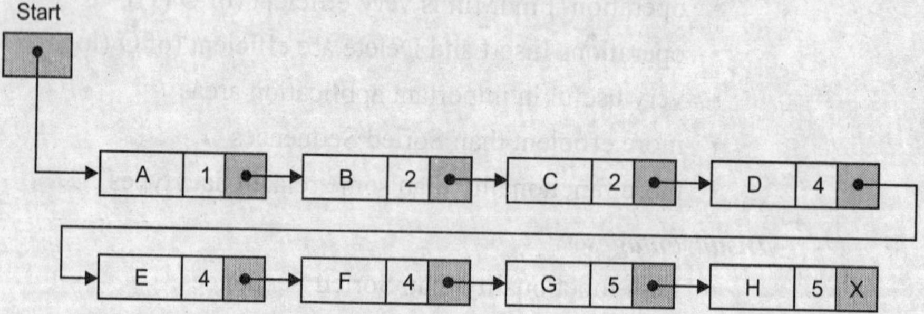

Figure 7.55: Schematic diagram of a priority queue using one way list.

Avail → 2

Start → 5

	INFO	PRT (priority)	LINK
1	B	2	6
2			7
3	D	4	4
4	E	4	8
5	A	1	1
6	C	2	3
7			0
8	G	5	10
9	F	4	8
10	H	5	0

Figure 7.56: Schematic diagram of a priority queue using linear arrays.

This Figure shows the way the priority queue may appear in memory using linear arrays INFO, PRT and LINK.

The main property of the one-way list representation of a priority queue is that the element in the queue that should be processed first always appears at the beginning of the one-way list. Accordingly, it is a very simple to delete and process an element from our priority queue.

7.16.1 Insert Operation in Linked List Representation of Priority Queue

The linked list of priority queue exists with the element to be processed at the beginning of the list. The element to be inserted say, item has priority number, say n.

Algorithm 7.11: This algorithm adds an ITEM with priority number N to a priority queue which is maintained in memory as a one-way list.

Step 1: Traverse the one-way list until finding a node X whose priority number exceeds N, Insert ITEM in front of node X.

Step 2: If no such node is found, insert ITEM as the last element of the list.

Step 3: End.

Traverse the list to find the first element whose priority number exceeds that of X. It is D, So insert X before D(after C) in the first empty cell, INFO[2]. This finally yields the structure in Figure shown below.

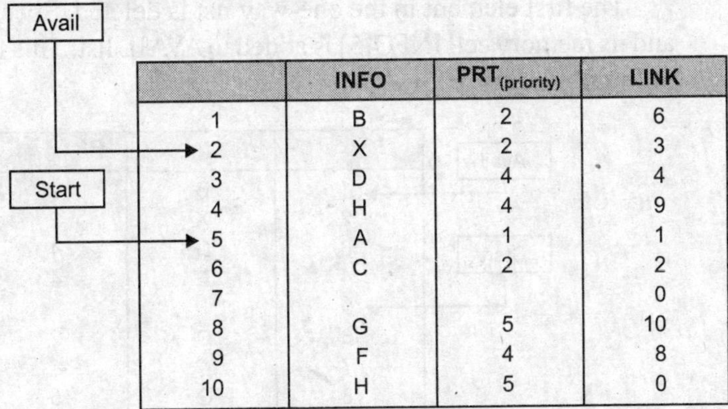

	INFO	$PRT_{(priority)}$	LINK
1	B	2	6
2	X	2	3
3	D	4	4
4	H	4	9
5	A	1	1
6	C	2	2
7			0
8	G	5	10
9	F	4	8
10	H	5	0

Figure 7.57: X is added as new element according to its priority number in parallel array.

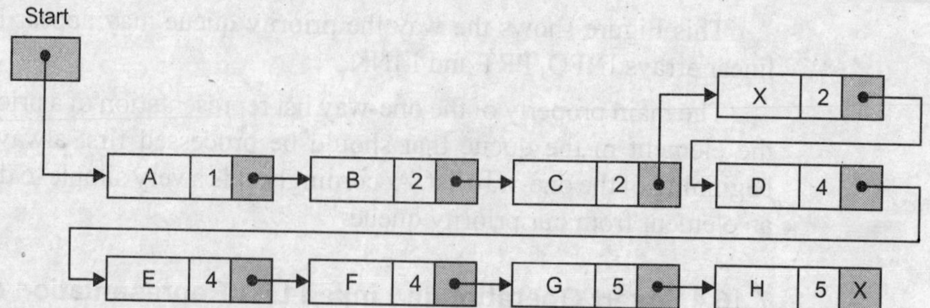

Figure 7.58: X is added as new element according to its priority number in linked list.

Important point: *Observe that START and AVAIL are changed accordingly.*

7.16.2 Delete Operation in Linked List Representation of Priority Queue

The linked list of Priority Queue exists. The element to be deleted (with the highest priority number) is the first element in the list i.e. it is a sorted list.

Algorithm 7.12: This algorithm deletes and processes the first element in a priority queue which appears in memory as a one-way list.

Step 1: Set ITEM = INFO[START]. [This saves the data in the starting or first node.]

Step 2: Delete first node from the list.

Step 3: Process ITEM.

Step 4: End.

The first element in the one-way list is deleted. Specifically, First A is deleted and its memory cell INFO[5] is added to AVAIL list. This finally yields the structure in Figure shown below.

Avail → 1, Start → 5

	INFO	PRT (priority)	LINK
1	B	2	6
2	X	2	3
3	D	4	4
4	E	4	9
5			
6	C	2	2
7			0
8	G	5	10
9	F	4	8
10	H	5	0

Figure 7.59: A is deleted from parallel arrays.

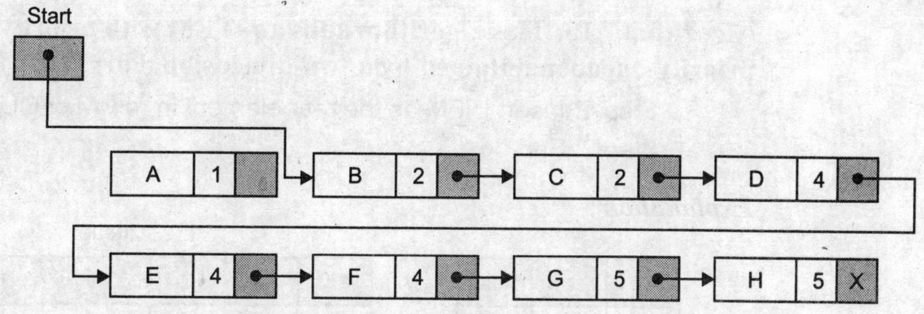

Figure 7.60: A is deleted from linked list.

Important point: *Observe that START and AVAIL are changed accordingly.*

7.17 IMPLEMENTATION OF PRIORITY QUEUE USING ARRAY

As the elements of the Priority Queue are assumed to contain only their priority values, hence, the type of elements is assumed to be integer only. The most used way to implement a Priority Queue of say, n elements, is to store these elements in an array of integers in a completely unordered manner.

Remember that the lower the priority value, the higher the priority.

One of the ways to maintain apriority queue in memory is to use a separate queue for each level of priority. Each such queue will appear in its own circular array and must have its own pair of pointers, FRONT and REAR. IN fact, if each queue is allocated the same amount of space, A Two-dimensional array queue can be used instead of the linear arrays. Figure shown below indicates this representation for the priority queue in fig above. Observe that FRONT[K] and REAR[K] contain , respectively, the front and rear elements of row K of queue, the row that maintains the queue of elements with priority number K.

	Front	Rear
1	2	2
2	1	3
3	0	0
4	5	1
5	4	5

(a)

Queue

R/C	1	2	3	4	5	6
1		A				
2	B	C	X			
3						
4	F				D	E
5				G	H	

(b)

Figure 7.61: Array representation of a priority queue.

7.17.1 Insert Operation

The priority queue, say PQ exists with n number of elements. The variable, value holds the value to be inserted in Queue.

Algorithm 7.13: This algorithm adds an ITEM with priority number M to a priority queue maintained by a two-dimensional array QUEUE.

Step 1: Insert ITEM as the rear element in row M of QUEUE.

Step 2: End.

Explanation

	Front	Rear
1	2	2
2	1	3
3	0	0
4	5	1
5	4	5

(a)

Queue

R/C	1	2	3	4	5	6
1		A				
2	B	C	X			
3						
4	F				D	E
5				G	H	

(b)

Figure 7.62: Before insertion priority queue look like.

Insert each element in its priority row. That is, add I as the rear element in row 3, add J as the rear element in row 4, add K as the rear element in row 1, add L as rear element in row 4, add M as rear element in row 2.This yields the structure in Figure given below. (Insertions with this array representation are usually simpler than insertions with the one-way list representation.)

	Front	Rear
1	2	3
2	1	4
3	1	1
4	5	3
5	4	5

(a)

Queue

R/C	1	2	3	4	5	6
1		A	K			
2	B	C	X	M		
3	I					
4	F	J	U		D	E
5				G	H	

(b)

Figure 7.63: After insertion priority queue look like.

Important point: *Observe that, In this case, FRONT and REAR are changed accordingly.*

7.17.2 Delete Operation

Algorithm 7.14: This algorithm deletes and processes the first element in a priority queue maintained by a two-dimensional array QUEUE.

Step 1: [Find first nonempty.]

Find the smallest K such that FRONT[K] '" NULL

Step 2: Delete and process the front element in row K of QUEUE.

Step 3: End.

Explanation

Queue

	Front	Rear
1	2	3
2	1	4
3	1	1
4	5	3
5	4	5

(a)

R/C	1	2	3	4	5	6
1		A	K			
2	B	C	X	M		
3	I					
4	F	J	U		D	E
5				G	H	

(b)

Figure 7.64: Before deletion priority queue look like.

First delete the elements with the highest priority in row 1. Since row 1 contains two elements, A and K, then the front element in row 2, B must also be deleted. This finally leaves the structure in Figure given below.

Queue

	Front	Rear
1	0	0
2	2	4
3	1	1
4	5	3
5	4	5

(a)

R/C	1	2	3	4	5	6
1						
2		C	X	M		
3	I					
4	F	J	U		D	E
5				G	H	

(b)

Figure 7.65: After deletion priority queue look like.

Important point: *Observe that, In this case, FRONT and REAR are changed accordingly.*

Program 12: Write a C++ program for Priority Queue.

```
#include<iostream.h>
#include<conio.h>
const int MAX=5;
class pqueue
{
int front,rear;
public:
struct data
{
int val,p,o;
}d[MAX];
pqueue()
{
```

```
front=rear=-1;
}
void insert(data d1);
data deletion();
void display();
};
void pqueue :: insert(data d1)
{
if(rear==MAX-1)
cout<<"Priority Queue is Full";
else
{
rear++;
d[rear]=d1;
if(front==-1)
front=0;
data temp;
for(int i=front;i<=rear;i++)
for(int j=i+1;j<=rear;j++)
{
if(d[i].p > d[j].p)
{
temp=d[i];
d[i]=d[j];
d[j]=temp;
}
else
{
if(d[i].p==d[j].p)
{
if(d[i].o > d[j].o)
{
temp=d[i];
d[i]=d[j];
d[j]=temp;
} }
} }
} }
data pqueue :: deletion()
{
data d1;
```

```
if(front==-1)
cout<<"Priority Queue is Empty";
else
{
d1=d[front];
if(front==rear)
front=rear=-1;
else
front++;
}
return d1;
}
void pqueue :: display()
{
if(front==-1)
cout<<"Priority Queue is Empty";
else
{
for(int i=front;i<=rear;i++)
{
cout<<"Object  :"<<i+1<<endl;
cout<<"Value ="<<d[i].val<<endl;
cout<<"Priority="<<d[i].p<<endl;
cout<<"Order =  "<<d[i].o<<endl;
}
}
}
void main()
{
pqueue p1;
data d1;
char op;
do
{
int ch;
clrscr();
cout<<"----------Menu-------------";
cout<<"1.Insertion
2.Deletion
3.Display
4.Exit
```

```
";
cout<<"Enter your Choice<1..4> ?";
cin>>ch;
switch(ch)
{
case 1 :  cout<<"Enter Value ?";
cin>>d1.val;
cout<<"Enter Priority?";
cin>>d1.p;
cout<<"Enter Order ?";
cin>>d1.o;
p1.insert(d1);
break;
case 2 :  d1=p1.deletion();
cout<<"Value = "<<d1.val<<endl;
cout<<"Priority = "<<d1.p<<endl;
cout<<"Order ="<<d1.o<<endl;
break;
case 3 :  p1.display();
break;
}
cout<<"Do You Want to Continue <Y/N> ?";
cin>>op;
}while(op=='Y' || op=='y');
getch();
}
```

7.18 IMPLEMENTATION OF PRIORITY QUEUE USING MULTIPLE QUEUES

Another way of representing a Priority Queue is to use a separate Queue for each priority number as shown in the Figure 7.66 below:

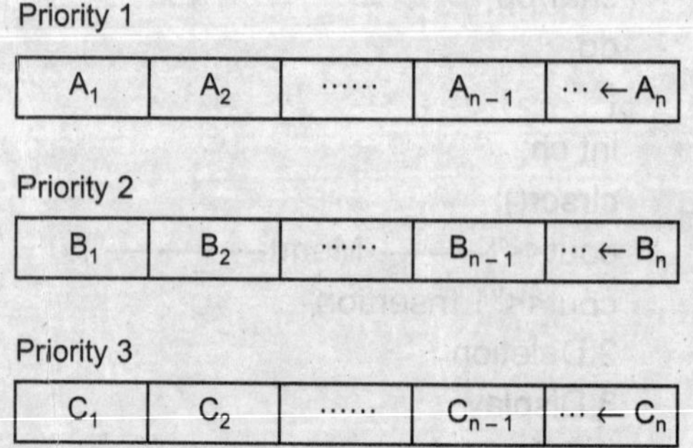

Figure 7.66: A Priority Queue as set of Queues

Each Queue has its own pair of front and rear pointers. Each Queue appears in circular array fashion. If each Queue is allocated the same amount of memory then these can be implemented using two-dimensional arrays. Remember that front[i] and rear[i] points to front and end of Queue with priority number i. See Figure 7.67.

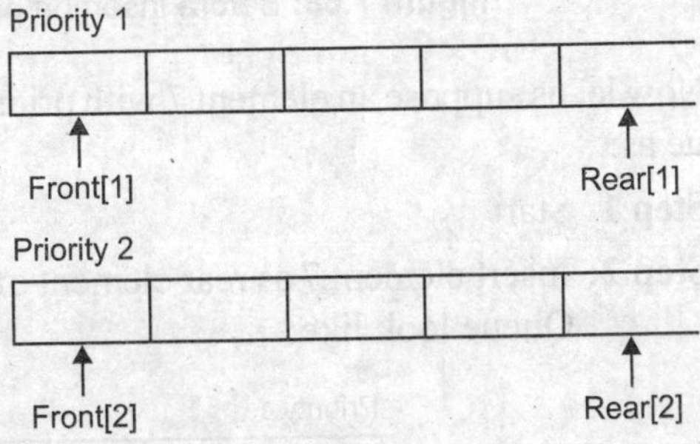

Figure 7.67: Priority Queue with pair of front and rear pointer

In order to process an element of the Priority Queue, element from the first non-empty highest priority number Queue is accessed. In case of Insert operation, a new element is inserted in the Priority Queue with given priority number.

7.18.1 Insert Operation in Priority Queue with Multiple Queue Representation

Algorithm 7.15: This algorithm inserts the element in priority queue using multiple queues. The Priority Queue with Multiple Queue representation exists. The element, say item with priority number, say n is to be inserted.

Step 1: Start

Step 2: Insert element, item as rear element in Queue with priority n

Step 3: End

Explanation

Consider the following Multiple Priority Queue:

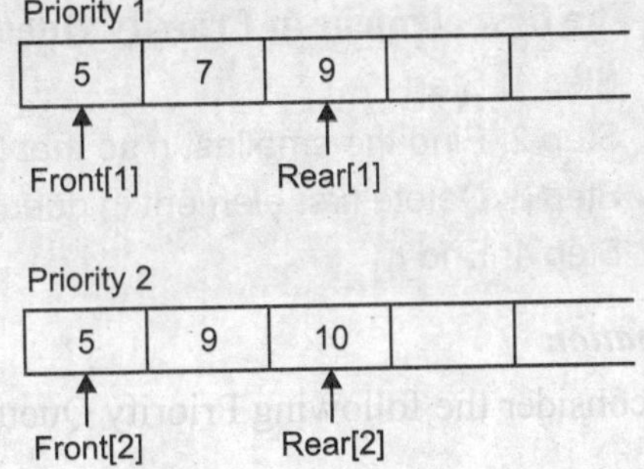

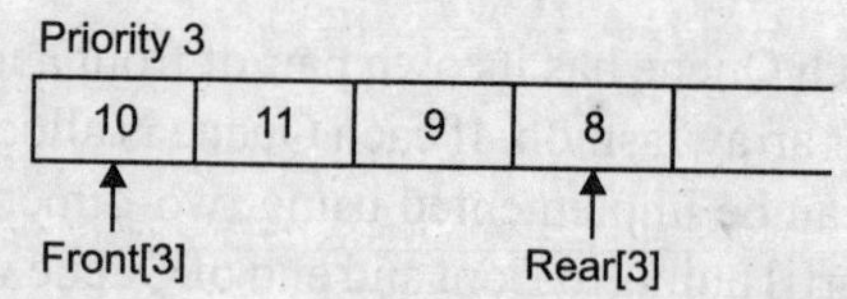

Figure 7.68: Before insertion priority queue look like

Now let us suppose an element 7 with priority 2, is to be added in above Priority Queue as:

Step 1: Start

Step 2: Insert element 7 as rear element of queue with priority 2. Now Priority Queue look like:

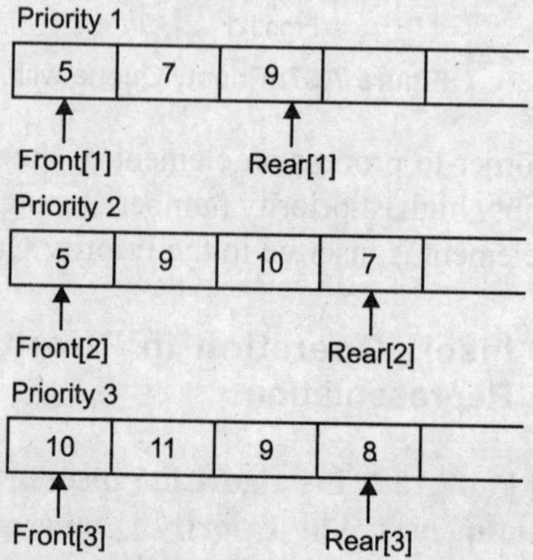

Figure 7.69: After insertion priority queue look like

Step 3: End.

7.18.2 Delete Operation in Priority Queue with Multiple Queue Representation

Algorithm 7.16: This algorithm inserts the element in priority queue using multiple queues. The Priority Queue with Multiple Queues representation exists. The first element in Priority Queue is to be deleted and processed.

Step 1: Start

Step 2: Find the smallest n so that front [n] '"NULL

Step 3: Delete first element in queue with priority number n

Step 4: End

Explanation

Let us consider the following Priority Queue:

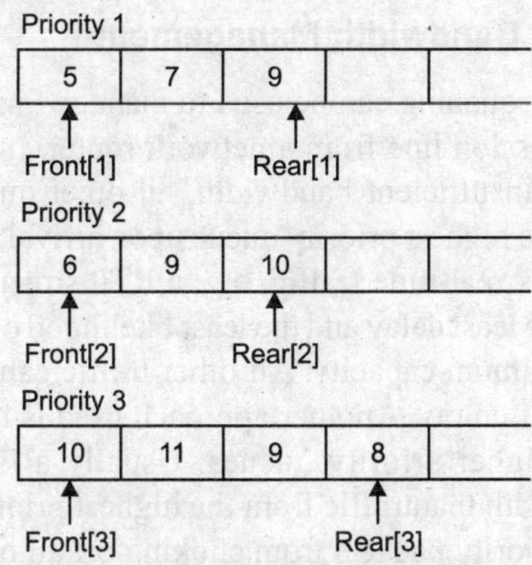

Figure 7.70: Before deletion priority queue look like

Step 1: Start

Step 2: Now find the smallest n so that front [n] '"NULL, In the above example Front [1] '"NULL

i.e. first element in Queue with priority 1 is not NULL and hence it is the element which will be deleted.

Step 3: Delete this first element. So Priority Queue will look like

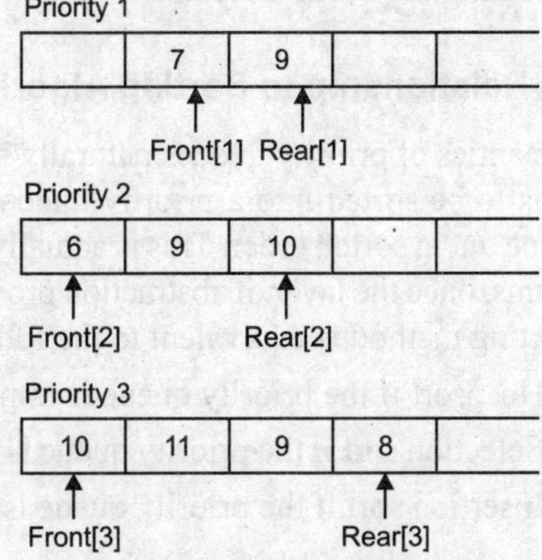

Figure 7.71: After deletion priority queue look like

Step 4: End.

7.19 APPLICATIONS OF PRIORITIY QUEUE

There are various applications areas where we apply priority queue some of them are:

7.19.1 Bandwidth Management

Priority queuing can be used to manage limited resources such as bandwidth on a transmission line from a network router. In the event of outgoing traffic queuing due to insufficient bandwidth, all other queues can be halted to send the traffic from the highest priority queue upon arrival. This ensures that the prioritized traffic (such as real-time traffic, e.g. a RTP stream of a VoIP connection) is forwarded with the least delay and the least likelihood of being rejected due to a queue reaching its maximum capacity. All other traffic can be handled when the highest priority queue is empty. Another approach used is to send disproportionately more traffic from higher priority queues. Usually a limitation (policer) is set to limit the bandwidth that traffic from the highest priority queue can take, in order to prevent high priority packets from choking off all other traffic. This limit is usually never reached due to higher lever control instances such as the Cisco Callmanager, which can be programmed to inhibit calls which would exceed the programmed bandwidth limit.

7.19.2 Discrete Event Simulation

Another use of a priority queue is to manage the events in a discrete event simulation. The events are added to the queue with their simulation time used as the priority. The execution of the simulation proceeds by repeatedly pulling the top of the queue and executing the event thereon.

7.19.3 Relationship to Sorting Algorithms

The semantics of priority queues naturally suggest a sorting method: insert all the elements to be sorted into a priority queue, and sequentially remove them; they will come out in sorted order. This is actually the procedure used by several sorting algorithms, once the layer of abstraction provided by the priority queue is removed. This sorting method is equivalent to the following sorting algorithms:

- Heapsort if the priority queue is implemented with a heap.
- Selection sort if the priority queue is implemented with an unordered array.
- Insertion sort if the priority queue is implemented with an ordered array.

7.20 APPLICATIONS OF QUEUES

There are various applications areas where we apply queue some of them are:

7.20.1 Scheduling and Buffering Queues

A queue is natural data structure for a system to serve the incoming requests. Most of the process scheduling or disk scheduling algorithms in operating systems use queues. Computer hardware like a processor or a network card also maintain buffers in the form of queues for incoming resource requests. A stack like data structure causes starvation of the first requests, and is not applicable in such cases. A mailbox or port to save messages to communicate between two users or processes in a system is essentially a queue like structure.

7.20.2 Search Space Exploration

Like stacks, queues can be used to remember the search space that needs to be explored at one point of time in traversing algorithms. Breadth first search of a graph uses a queue to remember the nodes yet to be visited.

7.20.3 Uses of Queues in Computer Systems

The purpose of a queue is to provide some form of buffering. Typical uses of queues in computer systems are:

- Process management
- Buffer between the fast computer and a slow printer

Everybody has experience with queues, as they are common place. Queues occur in cafeterias, petrol stations, shopping centers, any place where many people (customers) line up for few resources (cashier's, salespeople, petrol pumps etc).

7.20.4 Multiprogramming

One of the most important aspects of modern operating system is Multiprogramming. Multiprogramming is simply the ability for an operating system to execute many programs at once, and share different resources among them. These resources can vary from trying to writing to a disk, sharing memory, sharing CPU to managing ready and resource queues.

OBJECTIVE TYPE QUESTIONS

1. Queue is a
   (a) Linear data structure　　(b) Non-linear data structure
   (c) Both　　(d) None
2. Which of the following operations can be performed on Queue?
   (a) Push　　(b) Pop
   (c) Insertion　　(d) All of the above
   (e) None of the above

3. Queue has length
   (a) n (b) n-1
   (c) n+1 (d) All of the above
   (e) None of the above
4. Queue can be implemented by using
   (a) Array (b) Stack
   (c) Pointer (d) Linked list
   (e) None
5. Which of the following is the type of Queue?
   (a) Connected cities with reference
   (b) Heap of books
   (c) A Cinema Window
   (d) None of the above
6. Which of the following is the operation of Queue?
   (a) Insertion (b) Deletion
   (c) Create (d) Sorting
   (e) All of the above(f) None of the above
7. Which of the following is the Queue?
   (a) Singular queue (b) Deque
   (c) Priority queue (d) All of the above
   (e) None of the above
8. Which of the following is not the operation of Queue?
   (a) Sorting (b) Merging
   (c) Inserting (d) All of the above
   (e) None of the above
9. Which of the following is the utility of Queue?
   (a) Bus stop (b) Sorting
   (c) Concatenation (d) All of the above
   (e) None of the above
10. Traversing in Queue means:
   (a) Sorting (b) Searching
   (c) Inserting (d) Deleting
   (e) Visiting (f) None of the above

11. Queue follows the rule
    (a) FIFO (b) LIFO
    (c) LILO (d) FILO
12. The rear end of the queue is used
    (a) to insert an element (b) to remove an element
    (c) both (a) and (b) (d) None of the above
13. The front end of the queue is used
    (a) to insert an element (b) to remove an element
    (c) both (a) and (b) (d) None of the above
14. When an element is inserted in queue, the position of rear
    (a) increases (b) decreased
    (c) remains constant (d) None of the above
15. When an element is inserted in queue, the position of front
    (a) increments (b) decrements
    (c) unchanged (d) None of the above
16. Which one of the following is not a type of queue?
    (a) output restricted deque (b) circular queue
    (c) deque (d) priority queue.
17. In this queue elements can be inserted randomly
    (a) priority queue (b) simple queue
    (c) circular queue (d) None of the above
18. In the input restricted queue
    (a) deletion of element at both front and rear ends is done.
    (b) insertion of element at both front and rear ends is done.
    (c) deletion at only front end (d) all of the above
19. In this queue, smallest element of the queue is deleted first.
    (a) ascending priority queue (b) descending priority queue
    (c) circular queue (d) simple queue.
20. When the circular queue is full, and if one element is removed the next inserted element is stored at
    (a) first location (b) last location
    (c) intermediate location (d) None of the above

EXERCISES

1. Explain Concept of queue.
2. Why we call queue as an abstract data type.
3. Explain commonly used queue operations.
4. What is order produced by a queue.
5. Comparison between stacks and queues.
6. Explain implementation of queues using linear arrays.
7. Write an algorithm and C++ program for operations given below:
   (i) Enqueue operation (ii) Dequeue operation
   (iii) Peek operation (iv) Rear operation
   (v) Equals operation
8. Explain major problem with simple queue.
9. What do you understand by circular queue? Explain enqueue and dequeue operation with the help of an algorithm.
10. Explain implementation of queues using linked list.
11. What is Deque?
12. Explain input restricted deque and output-restricted deque with the help of program.
13. What do you mean by priority queue? Explain commonly used operations performed on priority queue.
14. Explain one way list representation of priority queue.
15. Explain implementation of priority queue using array.
16. Explain implementation of priority queue using multiple queues.
17. What are the various applications of priority queue?

8 CHAPTER

Trees

8.1 INTRODUCTION

Lists, stacks, and queues, are all linear structures: in all three data structures, one item follows another. Trees will be our first non-linear structure:

- More than one item can follow another.
- The number of items that follow can vary from one item to another.

A tree is a non-empty set, one element of which is designated the root of the tree while the remaining elements are partitioned into non-empty sets each of which is a subtree of the root.

A tree is a widely-used computer data structure that emulates a tree structure with a set of linked nodes. They are called that, because if you try to visualize the structure, it looks like a tree (root, branches, and leafs). See the following Figure 8.1.

See Figure 8.2. In this figure node representing 2 is root node and nodes representing 5, 11 and 4 are called leaf nodes.

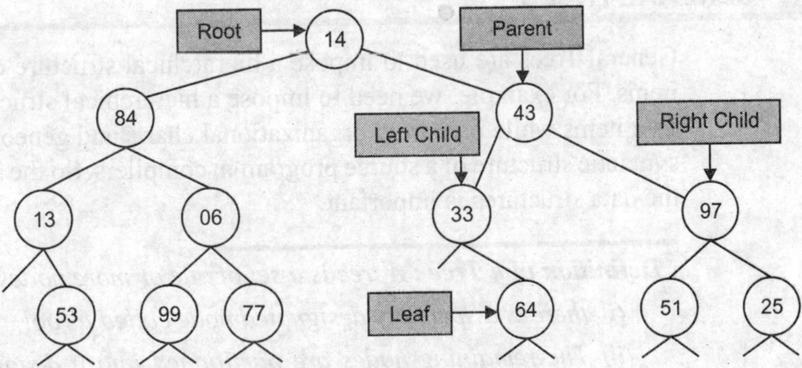

Figure 8.1: Tree structure.

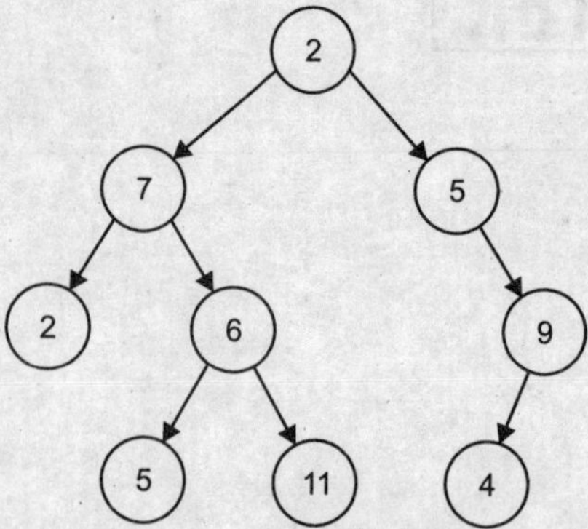

Figure 8.2: A simple tree structure

Trees are node based data structures, meaning that they're made out of small parts called nodes. You already know what a node is, and used one to build a linked list. Tree Nodes have two or more child nodes; unlike our list node, which only had one child. A node that has a child is called the child's parent node. In Figure 8.2 node representing 2 is the parent node of nodes representing 7 and 5. A child has at most one parent; The topmost node in a tree is called the root node e.g. node representing 2 in Figure 8.2 is root node. Being the topmost node, the root node will not have parents. Nodes at the bottom most level of the tree are called leaf nodes. Since they are at the bottom most level, they will not have any children.

Tree nodes have many useful properties:

- The **depth** of a node is the length of the path (or the number of edges) from the root to that node.
- The **height** of a node is the longest path from that node to its leaves. The height of a tree is the height of the root.
- A **leaf node** has no children — its only path is up to its parent.

8.2 GENERAL TREES

General Trees are used to impose a hierarchical structure on a collection of data items. For example, we need to impose a hierarchical structure on a collection of data items while preparing organizational charts and geneologies to represent the syntactic structure of a source program in compilers. So the study of trees as one of the data structures is important.

Definition of a Tree : *A tree is a set of one or more nodes T such that:*

(i) there is a specially designated node called a root

(ii) The remaining nodes are partitioned into n disjointed set of nodes T_1, T_2, ..., T_n, each of which is a tree.

A tree structure is shown in Figure 8.3.

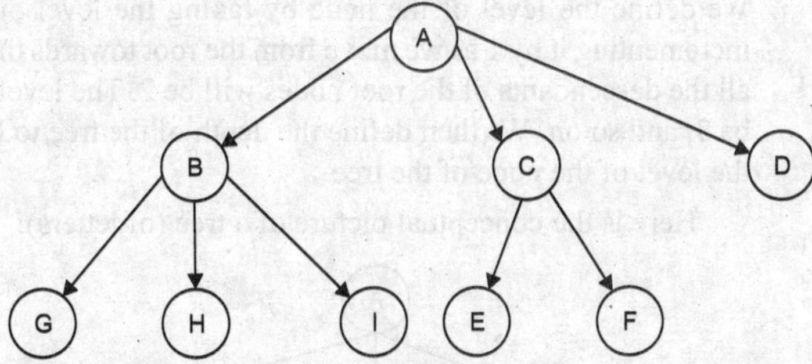

Figure 8.3: A tree structure.

This is a tree because it is a set of nodes {A,B,C,D,E,F,G,H,I}, with node A as a root node and the remaining nodes partitioned into three disjointed sets {B,G,H,I}, {C,E,F} and {D}, respectively. Each of these sets is a tree because each satisfies the aforementioned definition properly.

Shown in Figure 8.4 is a structure that is not a tree.

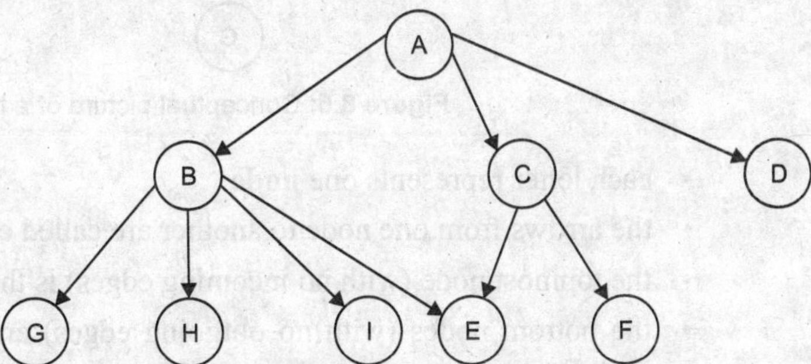

Figure 8.4: A non-tree structure.

Even though this is a set of nodes {A,B,C,D,E,F,G,H,I}, with node A as a root node, this is not a tree because the fact that node E is shared makes it impossible to partition nodes B through I into disjointed sets.

8.2.1 Degree of A Node of A Tree

The degree of a node of a tree is the number of subtrees having this node as a root. In other words, the degree is the number of descendants of a node. If the degree is zero, it is called a terminal or leaf node of a tree.

8.2.2 Degree of A Tree

The degree of a tree is defined as the maximum of degree of the nodes of the tree, that is, degree of tree = max (degree(node i) for I = 1 to n)

8.2.3 Level of A Node

We define the level of the node by taking the level of the root node as 1, and incrementing it by 1 as we move from the root towards the subtrees. So the level of all the descendants of the root nodes will be 2. The level of their descendants will be 3, and so on. We then define the depth of the tree to be the maximum value of the level of the node of the tree.

Here is the conceptual picture of a tree (of letters):

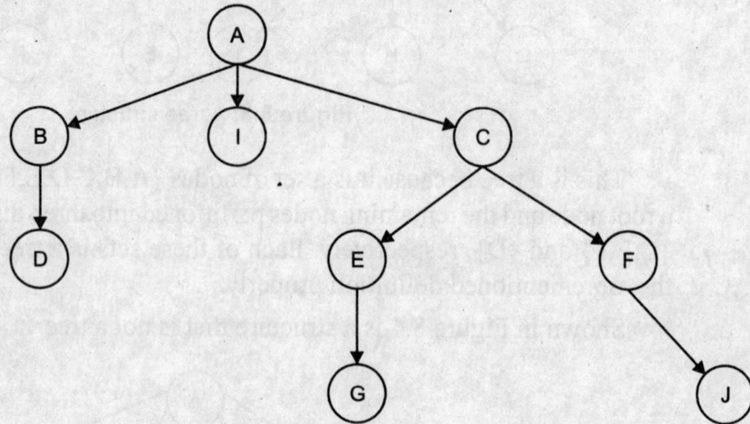

Figure 8.5: Conceptual picture of a tree.

- each letter represents one **node**
- the arrows from one node to another are called **edges**
- the topmost node (with no incoming edges) is the **root** (node A)
- the bottom nodes (with no outgoing edges) are the **leaves** (nodes D, I, G & J)

So a (computer science) tree is kind of like an upside-down real tree...

A **path** in a tree is a sequence of (zero or more) connected nodes; for example, here are 3 of the paths in the tree shown above:

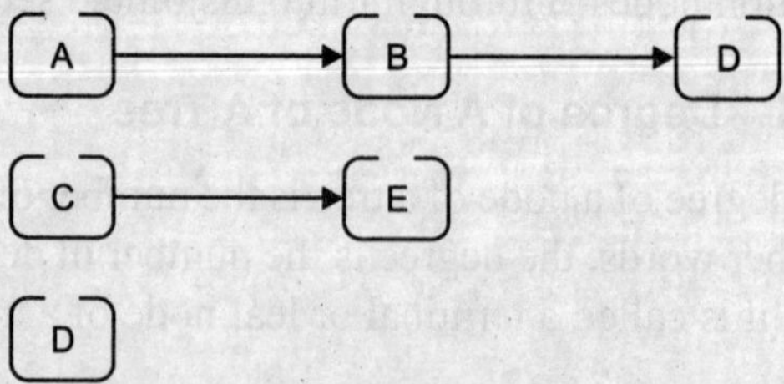

Figure 8.6: Describing tree Paths.

The **length** of a path is the number of nodes in the path, e.g:

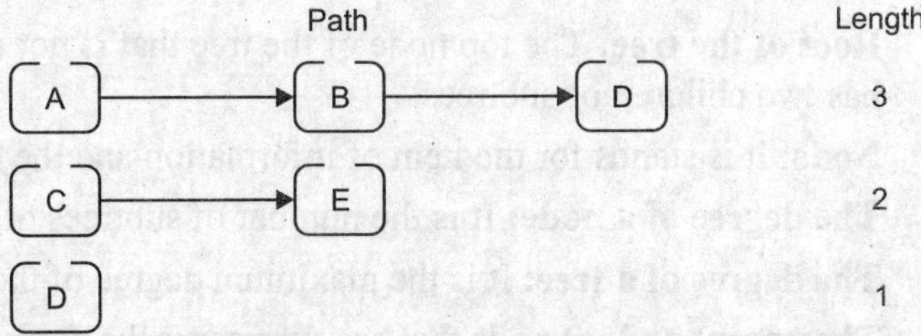

Figure 8.7: To find length of the path.

The **height** of a tree is the length of the longest path from the root to a leaf; for the above example, the height is 4 (because the longest path from the root to a leaf is A → C → E → G, or A → C → E → J). An empty tree has height = 0.

The **depth** of a node is the length of the path from the root to that node; for the above example:

- the depth of J is 4
- the depth of D is 3
- the depth of A is 1

Given two connected nodes like this:

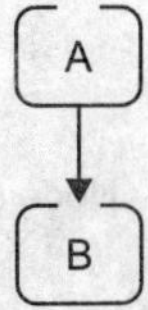

Figure 8.8: Parent and child relationship among nodes.

Node A is called the **parent,** and node B is called the **child**. A **subtree** of a given node includes one of its children and all of that child's **descendants**. The descen-dants of a node **n** are all nodes reachable from **n** (**n**'s children, its children's children, etc.). **In the original example, node A has three subtrees:**

1. B, D **2.** I **3.** C, E, F, G, J.

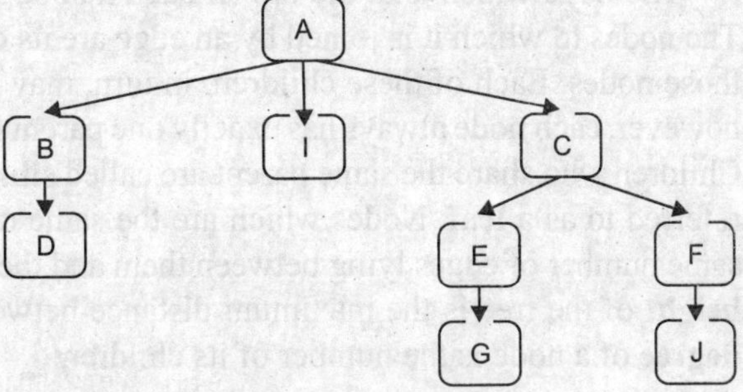

Figure 8.9: Node A having three subtrees.

8.2.4 Terminology

Root of the tree: The top node of the tree that is not a subtree to other node, and has two children of subtrees.

Node: It is stands for the item of information and the branches to other nodes.

The degree of a node: It is the number of subtrees of the node.

The degree of a tree: It is the maximum degree of the nodes in the tree

The parent node: a node that has subtrees is the parent of the roots of the subtrees

The child node: a node that is the roots of the subtrees are the children of the node

The Level of the tree: We define the level of a node by initially letting the root be at level one

The depth of a tree: It also called height of a tree. It is the maximum level of any node in the tree

GENERAL DESCRIPTION OF BINARY TREE

We can represent a tree as a construction consisting of nodes, and edges which represent a relationship between two nodes.

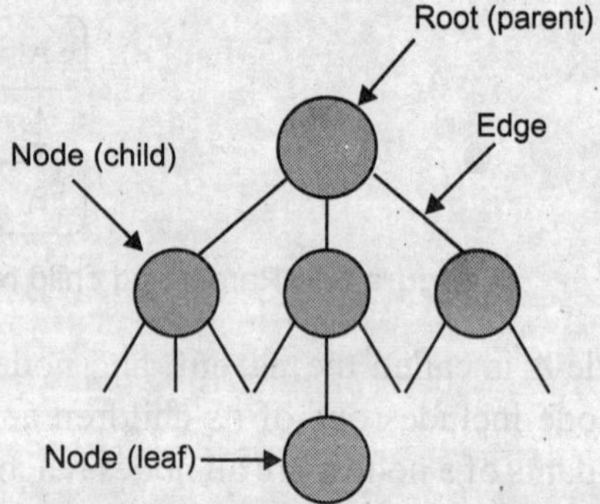

Figure 8.10: Representation of a tree.

The node which is at the top (if such a node exists) is termed the **root** node. The nodes to which it is joined by an edge are its **children**, and it is the **parent** of those nodes. Each of these children, in turn, may have one, many or no children, however, each node always has exactly one parent (except of course the root node). Children who share the same parent are called **siblings**. A node with no children is referred to as a **leaf**. Nodes which are the same distance from the root (have the same number of edges lying between them and the root) are at the same **level**. The **height** of the tree is the maximum distance between the root and any node. The **degree** of a node is the number of its children.

A **binary tree** is a tree, where every node has at most two children, one **drawn to the left**, called the **left child**, and one to the right, the **right child**. Every **node in a binary tree** is the root of at most two sub-trees, namely, its left sub-tree, **and the** right sub-tree.

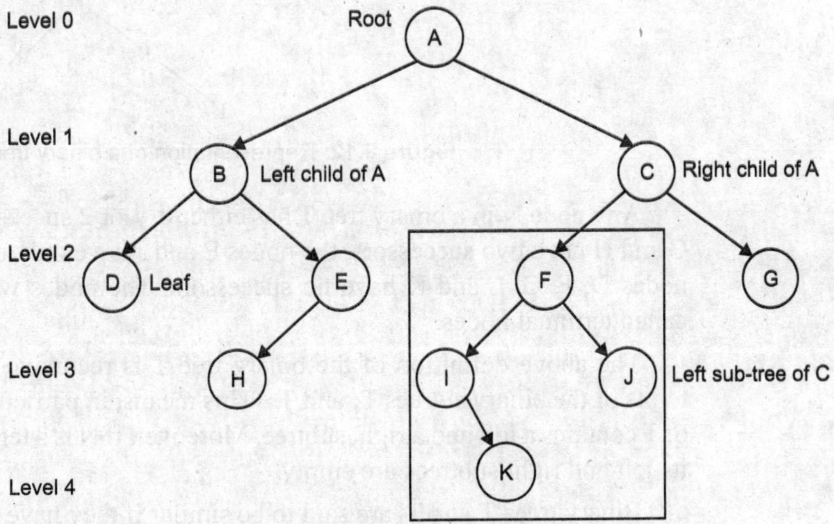

Figure 8.11: Height of the tree h =5.

If a binary tree contains n nodes, then its height is at least log2 (n+1), **and at** most n.

8.4 BINARY TREE

A binary tree T is defined as a finite set of nodes that T is either empty or consists of a root R and two disjoint binary trees called the left subtree T_1 and the right subtree T_2.If T_1 is nonempty, then its root is called the left successor of R; similarly, if T_2 is nonempty, then its root is called the right successor of R.

A binary tree T is frequently presented by means of a diagram. Specially, the diagram in Figure 8.11 represents a binary tree T as follows.

(i) T consists of 11 nodes, represented by the letters A through L, excluding I.

(ii) The root of T is the node A at the top of the diagram.

(iii) A left downward slanted line from a node N indicates a left successor of N, and a right-downward slanted line from N indicates a right successor of N. Observe that:

(a) B is a left successor and C is a right **successor** of the node A.

(b) The left subtree of the root A consists **of the nodes** B, D, E and F, and the right subtree of A consists **of the nodes** C, G, H, J, K and L.

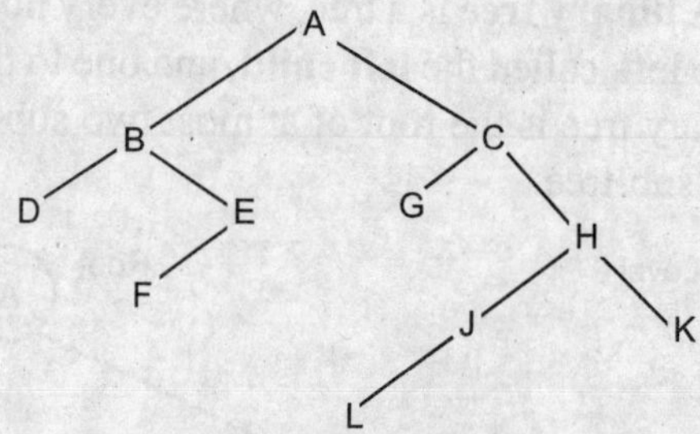

Figure 8.12: Representation of a binary tree.

Any node N in a binary tree T has either 0, 1 or 2 successors. The nodes A, B, C and H have two successors, the nodes E and J have only one successor, and the nodes D, F, G, L and K have no successors. The nodes with no successors are called terminal nodes.

The above definition of the binary tree T is recursive since T is defined in terms of the binary sutrees T_1 and T_2. This means, in particular, that every node N of T contains a left and a right subtree. Moreover, if N is a terminal node, then both its left and right subtrees are empty.

Binary trees T and T' are said to be similar if they have the same structure or, in other words, if they have the same shape. The trees are said to be copies if they are similar and if they have the same contents at corresponding nodes.

Example 8.1: Consider the four binary trees in Figure 8.13 The three trees (a), (c) and (d) are similar. In particular the trees (a) and (c) are copies since they also have the same data at corresponding nodes. The tree (b) is neither similar nor a copy of the tree (d) because, in a binary tree, we distinguish between a left successor and a right successor even when there is only one successor.

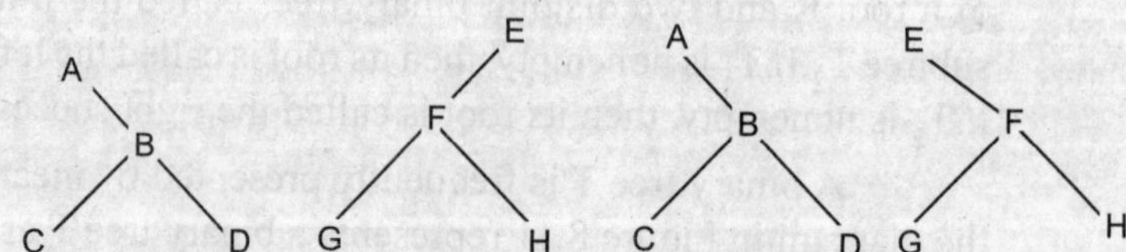

Figure 8.13: Comparison of four binary trees.

Program 1: Write a C++ program to find number of nodes and leaf nodes in the given tree.

```
#include<iostream.h>
#include<conio.h>
struct tree
{
```

```
long data;
struct tree *left;
struct tree *right;
};
int node=1,lev;
struct tree *bt=NULL;
struct tree *insert(struct tree*bt,long no);
void lev_count(struct tree*bt);
void node_count(struct tree*bt);
void main ()
{
long no;
clrscr();
cout<<"Enter the nodes of tree in preorder: and 0 to quit";
cin>>no;
while(no!=0)
{
bt=insert(bt,no);
cin>>no;
}
node_count(bt);
cout<<"The tree contains"<<node<<"nodes\n";
lev_count(bt);
cout<<"\nThe tree contains"<<lev<<"leaf nodes\n";
}
struct tree*insert(struct tree*bt,long no)
{
if(bt= =NULL)
{
else
{
if(struct tree*)malloc(sizeof(struct tree));
bt->left=bt->right=NULL;
bt->data=no;
}
else
}
if(no<bt->data)
bt->left=insert(bt->left,no);
```

```
else
if(no<bt->data)
bt->right=insert(bt->right,no);
else
if(no= =bt->data)
{
cout<<"Duplicates nodes: Program exited";
exit(0);
} }
return(bt);
}
void node_count(struct tree*bt)
{
If(bt!=NULL)
{
if(bt->left!=NULL)
{
node++;
node_count(bt->left);
}
if(bt->right!=NULL)
{
node++;
node_count(bt->right);
} } }
void dev_count(struct tree*bt)
{
if(bt!=NULL)
{
if((bt->left= =NULL)&&(bt->right= =NULL))
lev++;
else
lev_count(bt->left);
lev_count(bt->right);
} }
```

Output:

Enter the nodes of tree in preorder: and 0 to quit
5 3 11 0
The tree contains 3 nodes
The tree contains 2 leaf nodes

8.4.1 Binary Tree as Data Storage

Binary tree is one of the fundamental data storage structures used in programming. An important special kind of tree is the **binary** tree. In a binary tree:

- Each node has 0, 1, or 2 children.
- Each child is either a left child or a right child.

Here are two examples of binary trees that are different:

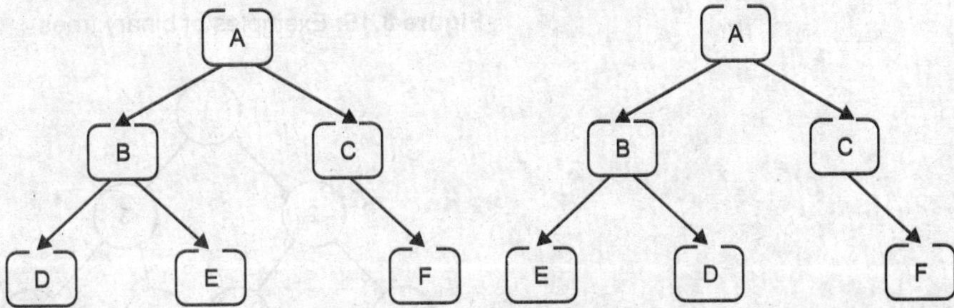

Figure 8.14: Binary tree as data storage

The two trees are different because the children of node B are different: in the first tree, B's left child is D and its right child is E; in the second tree, B's left child is E and its right child is D. Also note that lines are used instead of arrows. We sometimes do this because it is clear that the edge goes from the higher node to the lower node.

***Definition:** A binary tree is either **empty** or consists of a node called the **root** together with two binary trees called the **left subtree** and the **right subtree**.*

- If h = height of a binary tree,

  max # of leaves = 2^h

  max # of nodes = $2^{h+1} - 1$

- A binary tree with height h and $2^{h+1} - 1$ nodes (or 2^h leaves) is called a **full binary tree**

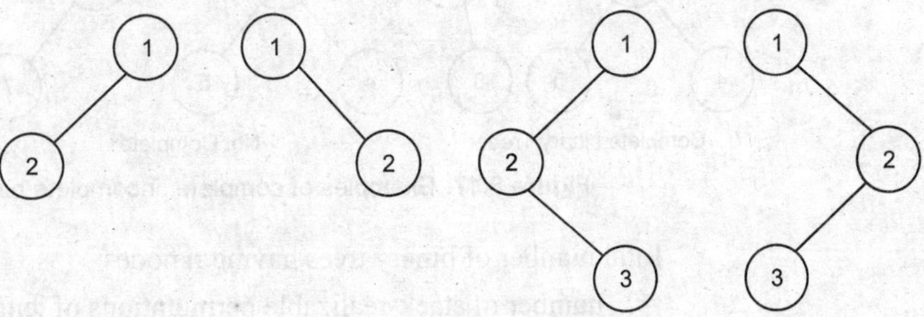

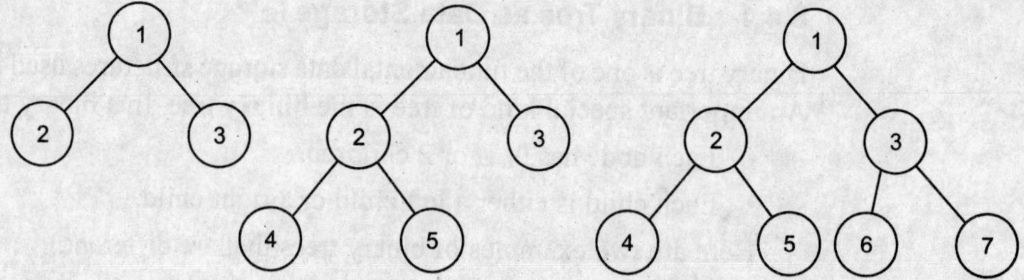

Figure 8.15: Examples of binary trees

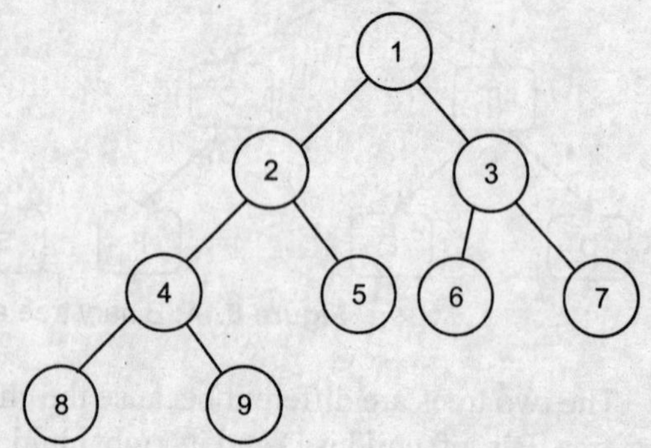

Figure 8.16: Level by level numbering of a binary tree

- Figure 8.15 shows several examples of binary trees.
- The nodes of a binary tree can be numbered in a natural way, level by level, left to right. For example, see Figure 8.16.
- A binary tree with n nodes is said to be **complete** if it contains all the first n nodes of the above numbering scheme. Figure 8.17 shows examples of complete and incomplete binary trees.

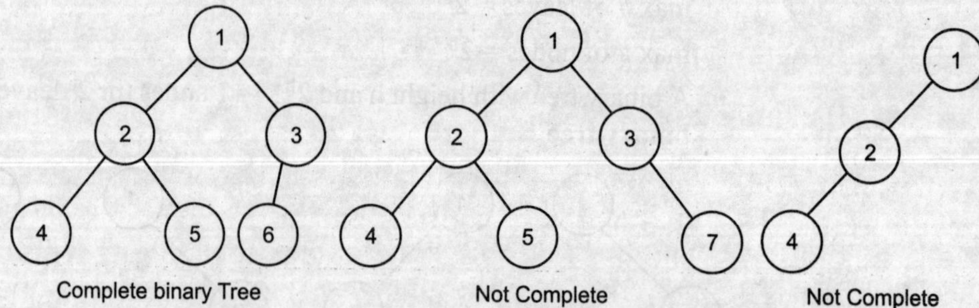

Figure 8.17: Examples of complete, incomplete binary trees

- Total number of binary trees having n nodes

  = number of stack-realizable permutations of length n

= number of well-formed parentheses (with n left parentheses and n right parentheses)

$$= \left(\frac{1}{n+1}\right)\binom{2n}{n} \text{ Catalan number}$$

8.4.2 Definitions for Rooted Trees

1. A **directed edge** refers to the link from the parent to the child (the arrows in the picture of the tree).
2. The root node of a tree is the node with no parents. There is at most one root node in a rooted tree.
3. A leaf node has no children.
4. The **depth** of a node n is the length of the path from the root to the node. The set of all nodes at a given depth is sometimes called a **level** of the tree. The root node is at depth zero.
5. The **height** of a tree is the length of the path from the root to the deepest node in the tree. A (rooted) tree with only a node (the root) has a height of zero.
6. **Siblings** are nodes that share the same parent node.
7. If a path exists from node p to node q, where node p is closer to the root node than q, then p is an **ancestor** of q and q is a **descendant** of p.
8. The **size** of a node is the number of descendants it has including itself.
9. **In-degree** of a node is the number of edges arriving at that node.
10. **Out-degree** of a node is the number of edges leaving that node.
11. Root is the only node in the tree with In-degree = 0.

8.4.3 Types of Binary Trees

1. A **rooted binary tree** is a **rooted** tree in which every node has at most two children.
2. A **full binary tree** (sometimes **proper binary tree** or **2-tree**) is a tree in which every node other than the leaves has two children.
3. A **perfect binary tree** is a full binary tree in which all leaves are at the same depth or same level. (This is ambiguously also called a complete binary tree.)
4. A **complete binary tree** is a binary tree in which every level, except possibly the last, is completely filled, and all nodes are as far left as possible.
5. An **infinite complete binary tree** is a tree with N_0 levels, where for each level d the number of existing nodes at level d is equal to 2^d. The cardinal

number of the set of all nodes is N_0. The cardinal number of the set of all paths is 2^{N_0}.

6. A **balanced binary tree** is where the depth of all the leaves differs by at most 1. Balanced trees have a predictable depth (how many nodes are traversed from the root to a leaf, root counting as node 0 and subsequent as 1, 2, ..., depth). This depth is equal to the integer part of $\log_2(n)$ where n is the number of nodes on the balanced tree. Example 1: balanced tree with 1 node, $\log_2(1) = 0$ (depth = 0). Example 2: balanced tree with 3 nodes, $\log_2(3) = 1.59$ (depth=1). Example 3: balanced tree with 5 nodes, $\log_2(5) = 2.32$ (depth of tree is 2 nodes).
7. A **rooted complete binary tree** can be identified with a free magma.
8. A **degenerate tree** is a tree where for each parent node, there is only one associated child node. This means that in a performance measurement, the tree will behave like a linked list data structure.

   A rooted tree has a top node as root.

8.4.4 Properties of Binary Trees

1. The number of nodes n in a perfect binary tree can be found using this formula: $n = 2^{h+1} - 1$ where h is the height of the tree.
2. The number of nodes n in a complete binary tree is minimum: $n = 2^h$ and maximum: $n = 2^{h+1} - 1$ where h is the height of the tree.
3. The number of nodes n in a perfect binary tree can also be found using this formula: $n = 2L - 1$ where L is the number of leaf nodes in the tree.
4. The number of leaf nodes n in a perfect binary tree can be found using this formula: $n = 2^h$ where h is the height of the tree.
5. The number of NULL links in a Complete Binary Tree of n-node is (n+1).
6. The number of leaf node in a Complete Binary Tree of n-node is UpperBound(n / 2).
7. For any non-empty binary tree with n_0 leaf nodes and n_2 nodes of degree 2, $n_0 = n_2 + 1$.

   Note that this terminology often varies in the literature, especially with respect to the meaning "complete" and "full".

8.5 BINARY SORT TREES

One of our examples using a list was a linked list of strings, in which the strings were kept in increasing order. While a linked list works well for a small number of strings, it becomes inefficient for a large number of items. When inserting an item into the list, searching for that item's position requires looking at, on average, half the items in the list. Finding an item in the list requires a similar amount of time. If the strings are stored in a sorted array instead of in a linked list, then searching becomes more efficient because binary search can be used. However, inserting a new item into the array is still inefficient since it means moving, on average, half of the items in the array to make a space for the new item. A binary tree can be used to store an ordered list of strings, or other items, in a way that makes both searching and insertion efficient. A binary tree used in this way is called a **binary sort tree.**

A binary sort tree is a binary tree with the following property: For every node in the tree, the item in that node is greater than every item in the left subtree of that node, and it is less than or equal to all the items in the right subtree of that node. Here for example is a binary sort tree containing items of type string. (In this picture, I haven't bothered to draw all the pointer variables. Non-NULL pointers are shown as arrows.)

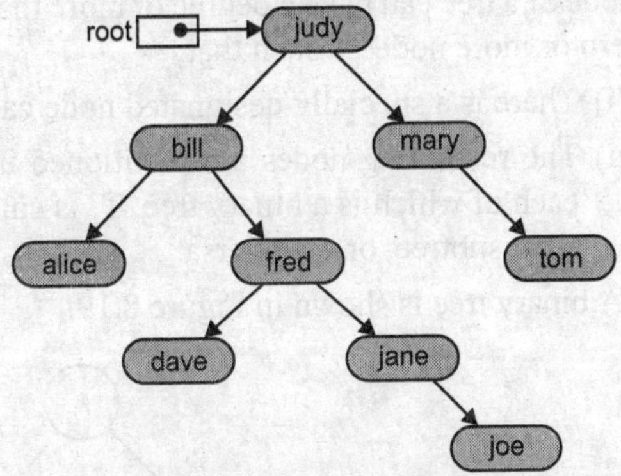

Figure 8.18: A binary sort tree.

Binary sort trees have this useful property: An inorder traversal of the tree will process the items in increasing order. In fact, this is really just another way of expressing the definition. For example, if an inorder traversal is used to print the items in the tree shown above, then the items will be in alphabetical order. The definition of an inorder traversal guarantees that all the items in the left subtree of "judy" are printed before "judy", and all the items in the right subtree of "judy" are printed after "judy". But the binary sort tree property guarantees that the items in the left subtree of "judy" are precisely those that precede "judy" in alphabetical order, and all the items in the right subtree follow "judy" in alphabetical order. So, we know that "judy" is output in its proper alphabetical position. But the same argument applies to the subtrees. "Bill" will be output after "alice" and before "fred" and its descendents. "Fred" will be output after "dave" and before "jane" and "joe". And so on.

Suppose that we want to search for a given item in a binary search tree. Compare that item to the root item of the tree. If they are equal, we're done. If the item we are looking for is less than the root item, then we need to search the left subtree of the root — the right subtree can be eliminated because it only contains items that are greater than or equal to the root.

Similarly, if the item we are looking for is greater than the item in the root, then we only need to look in the right subtree. In either case, the same procedure can then be applied to search the subtree. Inserting a new item is similar: Start by searching the tree for the position where the new item belongs. When that position is found, create a new node and attach it to the tree at that position.

8.6 BINARY TREE REPRESENTATION: ARRAY REPRESENTATION AND DYNAMIC REPRESENTATION

A binary tree is a special case of tree as defined in the preceding section, in which no node of a tree can have a degree of more than 2. Therefore, a binary tree is a set of zero or more nodes T such that:

(i) There is a specially designated node called the root of the tree

(ii) The remaining nodes are partitioned into two disjointed sets, T_1 and T_2, each of which is a binary tree. T_1 is called the left subtree and T_2 is called right subtree, or vice-versa.

A binary tree is shown in Figure 8.19.

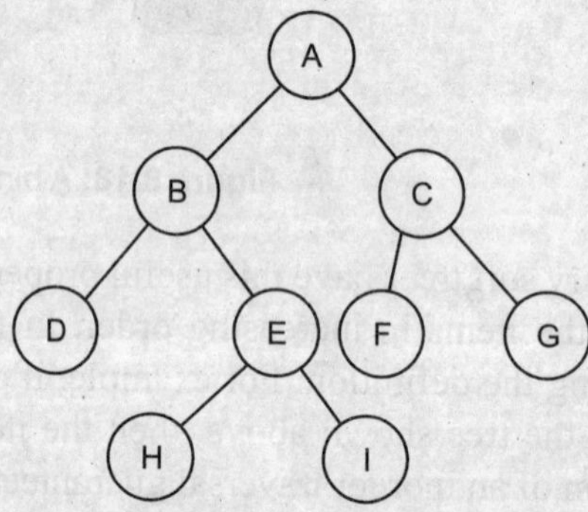

Figure 8.19: Binary tree structure.

So, for a binary tree we find that:

(i) The maximum number of nodes at level i will be 2^{kl}

(ii) If k is the depth of the tree then the maximum number of nodes that the tree can have is

$$2^k - 1 = 2^{k-1} + 2^{k-2} + \ldots + 2^0$$

Also, there are skewed binary trees, such as the one shown in Figure 8.20.

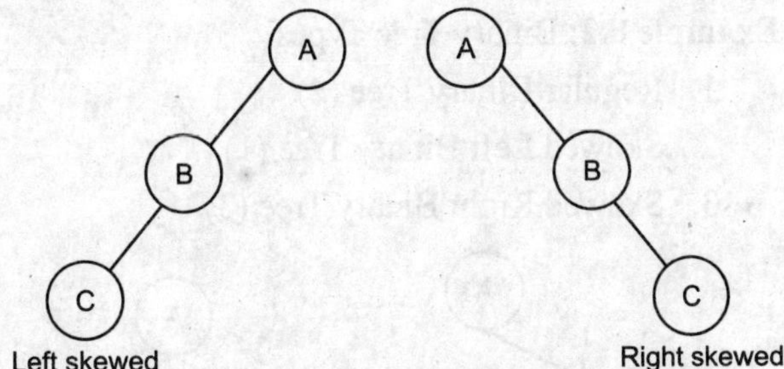

Figure 8.20: Skewed trees.

A full binary tree is a binary of depth k having $2^k - 1$ nodes. If it has $< 2^k - 1$, it is not a full binary tree. For example, for k = 3, the number of nodes = $2^k - 1 = 2^3 - 1 = 8 - 1 = 7$. A full binary tree with depth k = 3 is shown in Figure 8.21.

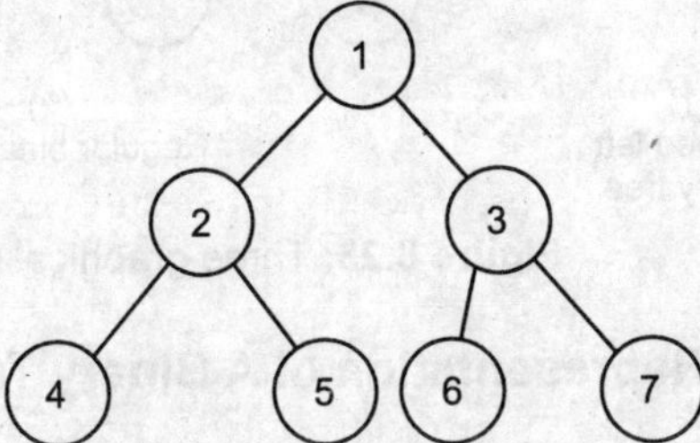

Figure 8.21: A full binary tree.

We use numbers from 1 to $2^k - 1$ as labels of the nodes of the tree. If a binary tree is full, then we can number its nodes sequentially from 1 to 2^{k-1}, starting from the root node, and at every level numbering the nodes from left to right.

A complete binary tree of depth k is a tree with n nodes in which these n nodes can be numbered sequentially from 1 to n, as if it would have been the first n nodes in a full binary tree of depth k.

A complete binary tree with depth k = 3 is shown in Figure 8.22.

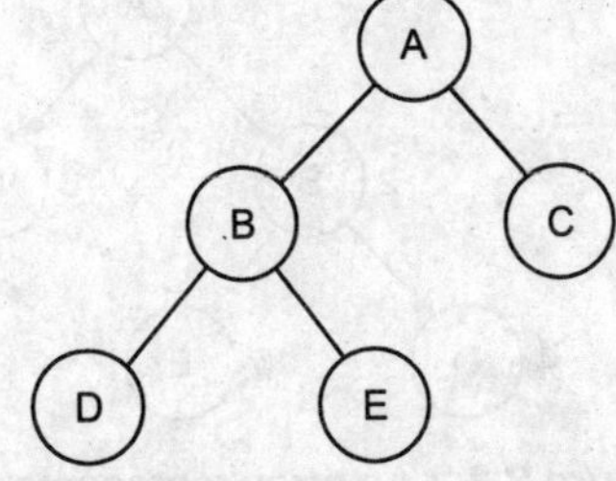

Figure 8.22: A complete binary tree.

Example 8.2: Binary Tree Types

1. Regular Binary Tree (2)
2. Skewed Left Binary Tree (1)
3. Skewed Right Binary Tree (3)

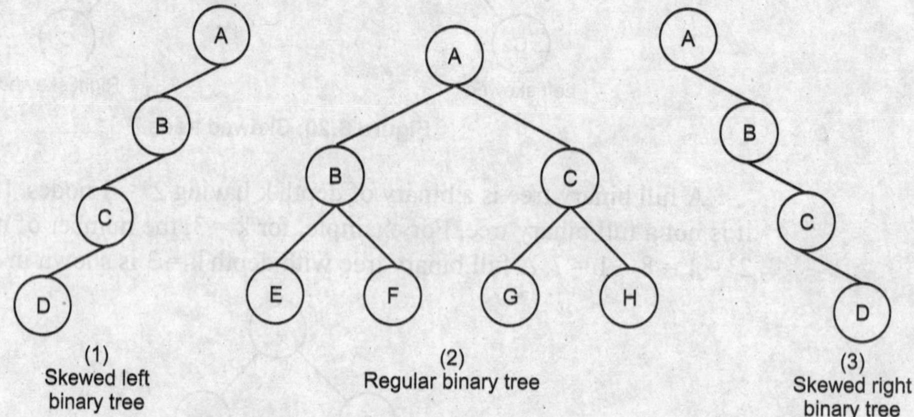

Figure 8.23: Three graphical pictures of the binary tree.

8.6.1 Representation of A Binary Tree

If a binary tree is a complete binary tree, it can be represented using an array capable of holding n elements where n is the number of nodes in a complete binary tree. If the tree is an array of n elements, we can store the data values of the ith node of a complete binary tree with n nodes at an index i in an array tree. That means we can map node i to the ith index in the array, and the parent of node i will get mapped at an index i/2, whereas the left child of node i gets mapped at an index 2i and the right child gets mapped at an index 2i + 1. For example, a complete binary tree with depth k = 3, having the number of nodes n = 5, can be represented using an array of 5 as shown in Figure 8.24.

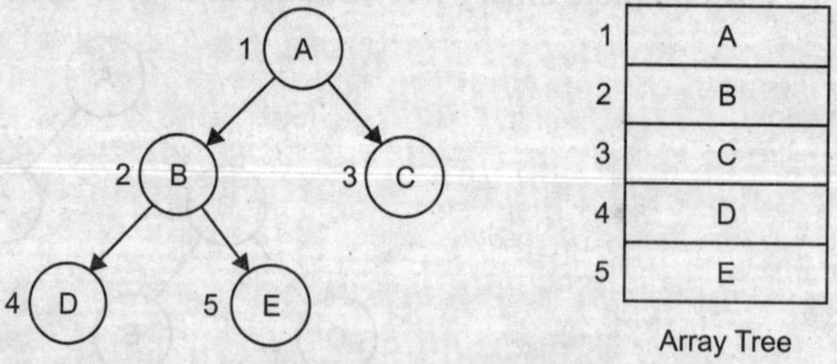

Figure 8.24: An array representation of a complete binary tree having 5 nodes and depth 3.

Shown in Figure 8.25 is another example of an array representation of a complete binary tree with depth k = 3, with the number of nodes n = 4.

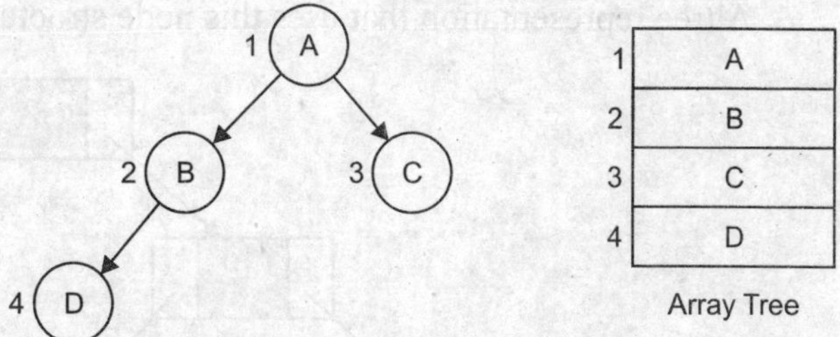

Figure 8.25: An array representation of a complete binary tree with 4 nodes and depth 3.

In general, any binary tree can be represented using an array. We see that an array representation of a complete binary tree does not lead to the waste of any storage. But if you want to represent a binary tree that is not a complete binary tree using an array representation, then it leads to the waste of storage as shown in Figure 8.26.

An array representation of a binary tree is not suitable for frequent insertions and deletions, even though no storage is wasted if the binary tree is a complete binary tree. It makes insertion and deletion in a tree costly.

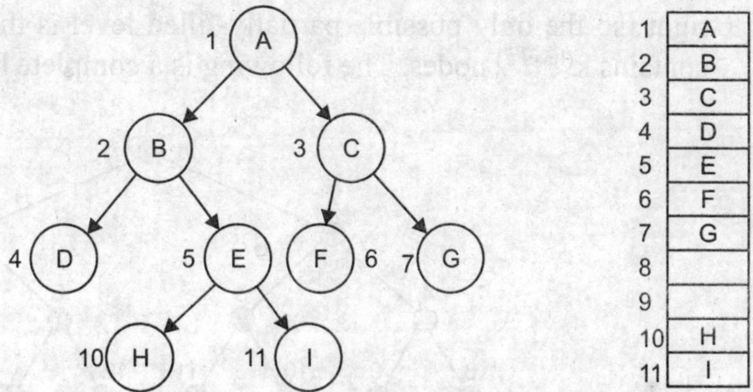

Figure 8.26: An array representation of a binary tree.

Therefore, instead of using an array representation, we can use a linked representation, in which every node is represented as a structure with three fields: one for holding data, one for linking it with the left subtree, and the third for linking it with right subtree as shown here:

leftchild	data	rightchild

We can create such a structure using the following C declaration:

```
struct tnode
{
int data
struct tnode *lchild,*rchild;
};
```

A tree representation that uses this node structure is shown in Figure 8.27.

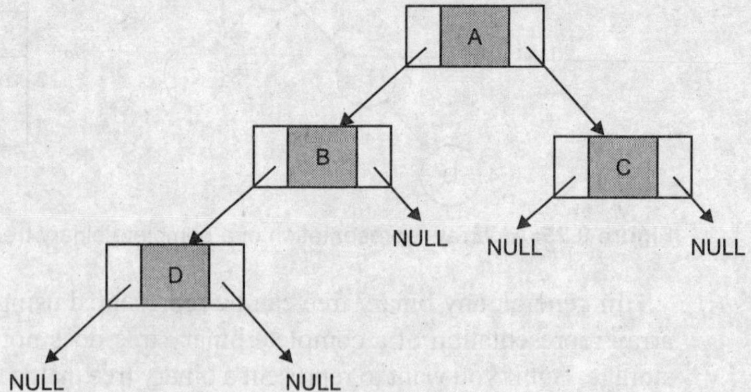

Figure 8.27: Linked representation of a binary tree.

8.7 COMPLETE TREES

A complete tree is a k-ary position tree in which all levels are filled from left to right (so the only possible partially-filled level is the last level). Each full level contains $k^{(\text{level \#})}$ nodes. The following is a complete binary (k=2) tree.

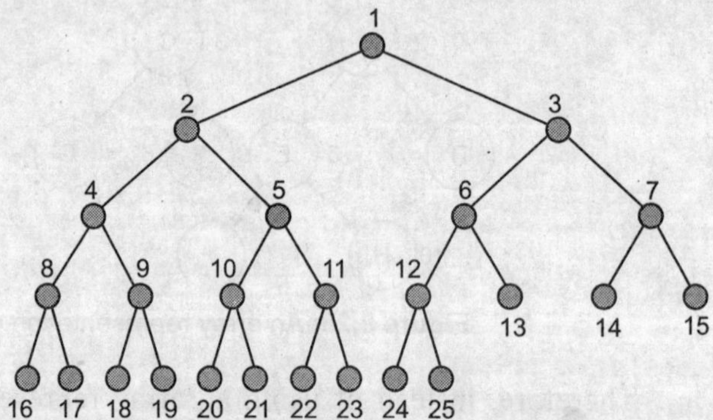

Figure 8.28: A labelled binary tree containing the labels 1 to with root 1, branches leading to nodes labelled 2 and 3, branches from these leading to 4, 5 and 6, 7, respectively, and so on.

Definition: *"A* complete binary tree *is a binary tree with the additional property that every node must have exactly two "children" if an internal node, and zero children if a leaf node."*

More precisely: For our base case, the complete binary tree of exactly one node is simply the tree consisting of that node by itself. The property of being "complete" is preserved if, at each step, we expand the tree by connecting exactly zero or two individual nodes (or complete binary trees) to any node in the tree (but both must be connected to the same node.)

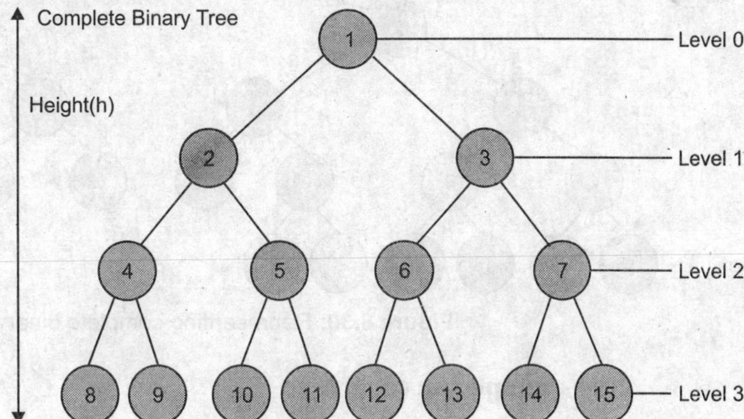

Figure 8.29: Complete binary tree.

The great advantage of a complete tree is that pointers are not required to implement its structure. The position of a node is implicit in the structure. They are, in addition, the "flattest" type of tree, i.e., they have the largest node to height ratio, where "height" is the maximum distance (number of edges traversed) between the root and any node in the tree. Height is a property of a tree, not of a node.

In a complete tree there is a connection between the height h and the number of nodes n. For k=2 (a complete binary tree) we have:

Noting that the total number of nodes is the sum of the number of nodes at each level:

$$1 + 2 + 2^2 + ... + 2^{(h-1)} < n <= 1 + 2 + 2^2 + ... + 2^h$$

$$2^h - 1 < n <= 2^{(h+1)} - 1$$

$$2^h < n+1 <= 2^{(h+1)}$$

take log of both sides:

$h < \log_2 (n+1) <= h + 1$

$h = \text{ceiling}(\log_2(n+1) - 1)$.

So for a complete binary tree of size n, h is:

n	**h**
1 000	10
1 000 000	20
1 000 000 000	30

We can access any element in a collection of one billion nodes in a maximum of 30 steps.

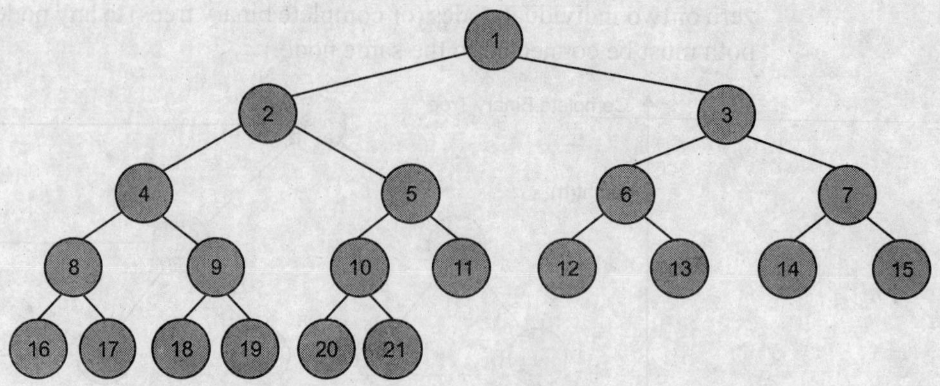

Figure 8.30: Representing complete binary tree.

For example, we could have

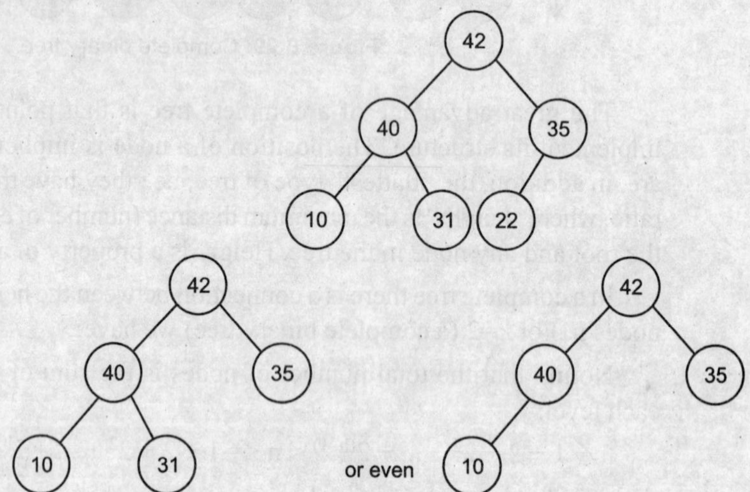

Figure 8.31: Various representation of complete binary tree.

But we don't want are trees like

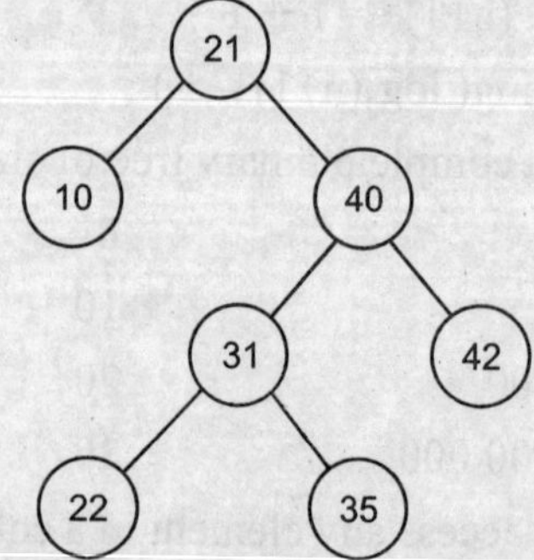

Figure 8.32: This is not a complete binary tree.

in which there are paths from some leaf to the root whose lengths differ by more than 1. We want trees in which every level is fully occupied except, possibly, for the bottom level.

It is also very convenient, as you will see, if the bottom level is filled from left to right. (It could alternatively be filled from right to left, but we need to agree on one or the other.) Binary trees of this type are called **complete**. They are defined as being completely filled, except possibly for the bottom level, which is filled from left to right. A **complete** binary tree which also satisfies the ordering property (H) is called a **binary heap**.

Example 8.3: Complete Binary Trees

Consider any binary tree T. Each node of T can have at most two children. Accordingly, one can show that level r or T can have at most 2^r nodes. The tree T is said to be complete if all its levels, except possibly the last, have the maximum number of possible nodes, and if all the nodes at the last level appear as far left as possible. Thus there is a unique complete tree T_n with exactly n nodes (we are, of course, ignoring the contents of the nodes). The complete tree T_{26} with 26 nodes appears in Figure 8.33.

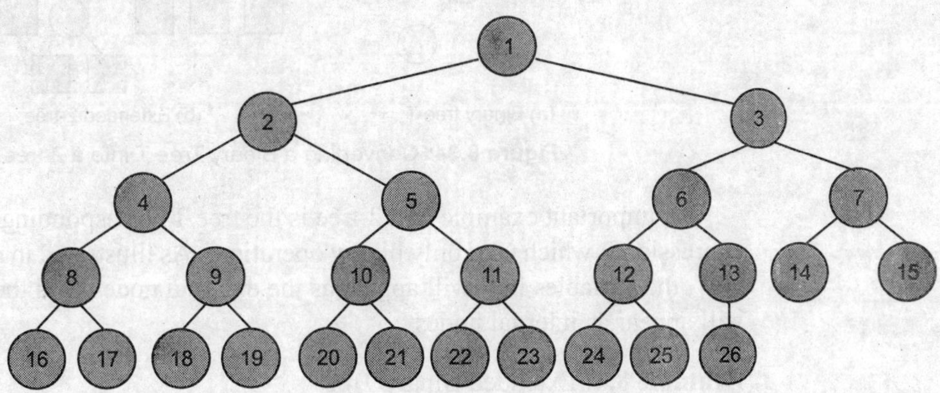

Figure 8.33: Complete Tree T_{26}

The nodes of the complete binary tree T_{26} in Figure 8.32 have been purposely labeled by the integers 1, 2, ..., 26, from left to right, generation by generation. With this labeling, one can easily determine the children and parent of any node K in any complete tree T_n. Specifically, the left and right children of the node K are, respectively, 2 * K and 2 * K + 1, and the parent of K is the node [K/2]. For example, the children or node 9 are the nodes 18 and 19 and its parent is the node [9/2] = 4. The depth d_n of the complete tree T_n with n nodes is given by $D_n = [\log_2 n + 1]$

This is a relatively small number. For example, if the complete tree T_n has n = 1 000 000 nodes, then its depth $D_n = 21$.

8.8 EXTENDED BINARY TREE

A binary tree tree T is said to be a 2-tree or an extended binary tree if each node N has either 0 or 2 children. In such a case, the node with 2 children are called internal nodes, and the nodes with 0 children are called external nodes. Sometimes the nodes are distinguished in diagrams by using circles for internal nodes and squares for external nodes. The term "extended binary tree" comes from the following operation. Consider any binary tree T, such as the tree in Figure 8.34(a). Then T may be "converted" into a 2-tree replacing each empty subtree by a new node, as pictured in Figure 8.34(b). Observe that the new tree is, indeed, a 2-tree. Furthermore, the nodes in the original tree T are now the internal nodes in the extended tree, and the new nodes are the external nodes in the extended tree.

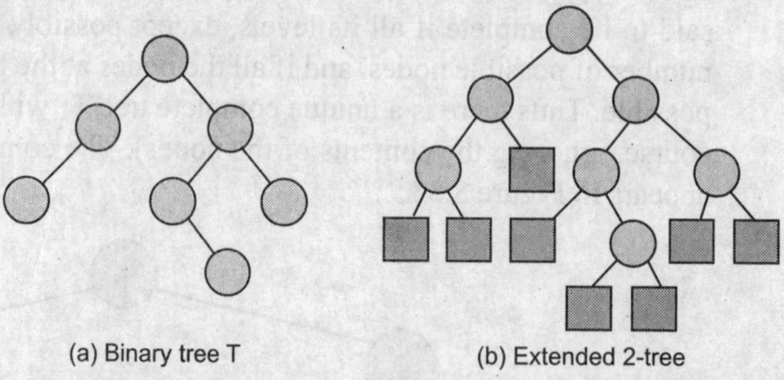

Figure 8.34: Converting a Binary Tree T into a 2-tree.

An important example of a 2-tree is the tree T corresponding to any algebraic expression E which uses only binary operations. As illustrated in next topic Figure 8.37, the variables in E will appear as the external nodes, and the operations in E will appear as internal nodes.

Example 8.4: Extended Binary Tree

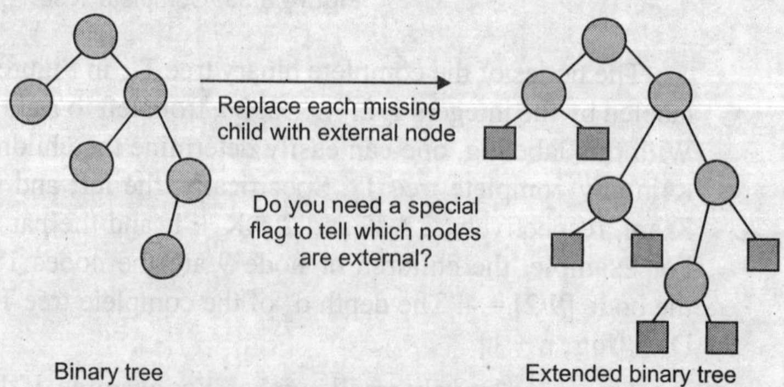

Figure 8.35: It shows the conversion of ordinary binary tree to extended binary tree.

8.8.1 Representation of Algebraic Expressions

A binary tree can be used to represent an algebraic expression that involves only binary arithmetic operators +, –, /, and *. The root node holds an operator, and each of its sub-trees represents either a variable (operand), or another expression. The following tree represents the expression A*(B+C)

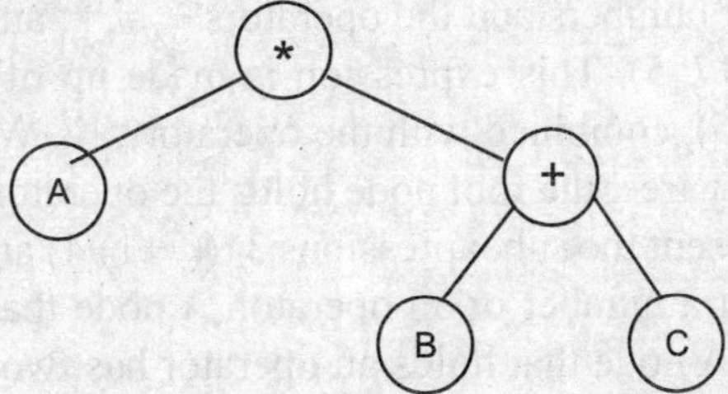

Figure 8.36: Representing algebraic expression A*(B+C).

1. **Inorder Expression:** Traversing the above tree **inorder** will generate the sequence A*B+C, and here we need to insert the parenthesis to get the correct expression.
2. **Preorder Expression:** Traversing the tree in preorder will generate the expression *A+BC, which is called the **prefix** notation.
3. **Postorder Expression:** Traversing the tree in postorder will generate the expression ABC+*, which is called the **postfix** notation.

Example 8.5: Consider any algebraic expression EXP involving only binary operations, such as EXP = (a – b) / (c * d) + e)

EXP can be represented by means of the binary tree T pictured in Figure 8.37. That is each variable, or constant in EXP appears as an "internal" node in T whose left and right subtrees correspond to the operands of the operation.

1. In the expression EXP, the operands of + are c * d and e.
2. In the tree T, the subtrees of the node + correspond to the sub expressions c * d and e.

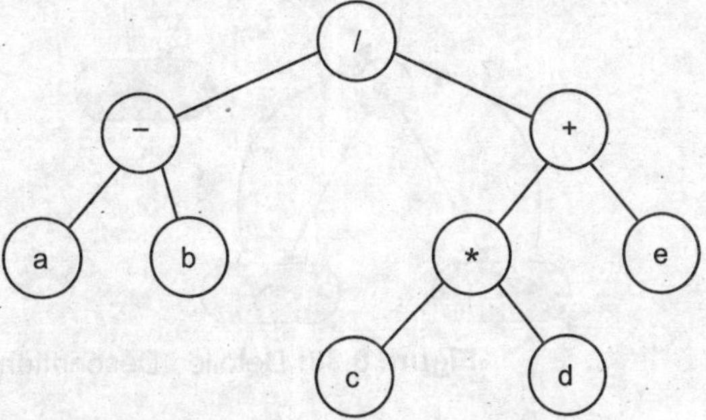

Figure 8.37: EXP = (a – b) / ((c * d) + e)

Clearly every algebraic expression will correspond to a unique tree, and vice versa.

Example 8.6: Detailed Description of Expression Trees

Another application of trees is to store mathematical expressions such as 15*(x+y) or sqrt(42)+7 in a convenient form. Let's stick for the moment to expressions made up of numbers and the operators +, –, *, and /. Consider the expression 3*((7+1)/4)+(17–5). This expression is made up of two subexpressions, 3*((7+1)/4) and (17–5), combined with the operator "+". When the expression is represented as a binary tree, the root node holds the operator +, while the subtrees of the root node represent the subexpressions 3*((7+1)/4) and (17–5). Every node in the tree holds either a number or an operator. A node that holds a number is a leaf node of the tree. A node that holds an operator has two subtrees representing the operands to which the operator applies. The tree is shown in the illustration below. I will refer to a tree of this type as an expression tree.

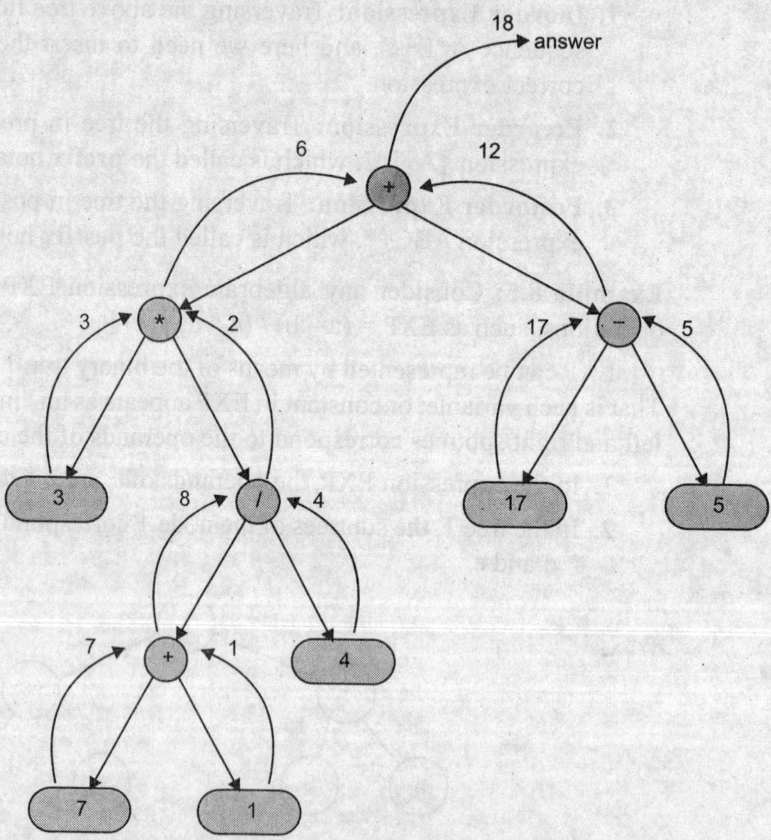

Figure 8.38: Detailed Description of Expression Trees

Given an expression tree, it's easy to find the value of the expression that it represents. Each node in the tree has an associated value. If the node is a leaf node, then its value is simply the number that the node contains. If the node contains an operator, then the associated value is computed by first finding the values of its child nodes and then applying the operator to those values.

The process is shown by the red arrows in the illustration. The value computed for the root node is the value of the expression as a whole. There are other uses for expression trees. For example, a postorder traversal of the tree will output the postfix form of the expression.

Example 8.7: Algebraic expressions such as

a/b + (c – d) e

have an inherent tree-like structure. For example, Figure shown below is a representation of the expression in Equation a/b + (c–d) e. This kind of tree is called an ***expression tree***.

The terminal nodes (leaves) of an expression tree are the variables or constants in the expression (a, b, c, d, and e). The non-terminal nodes of an expression tree are the operators (+, –, X, and /). Notice that the parentheses which appear in Equation a/b + (c-d) e. do not appear in the tree. Nevertheless, the tree representation has captured the intent of the parentheses since the subtraction is lower in the tree than the multiplication.

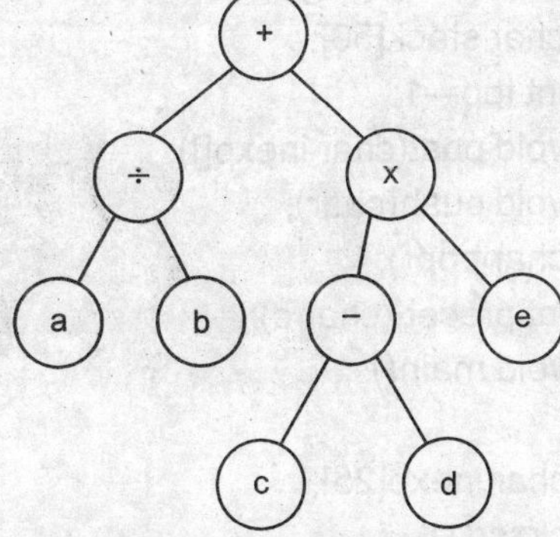

Figure 8.39: Tree representing the expression a/b+(c-d)*e

The common algebraic operators are either unary or binary. For example, addition, subtraction, multiplication, and division are all binary operations and negation is a unary operation. Therefore, the non-terminal nodes of the corresponding expression trees have either one or two non-empty subtrees. That is, expression trees are usually binary trees.

What can we do with an expression tree? Perhaps the simplest thing to do is to print the expression represented by the tree. Notice that an inorder traversal of the tree in Figure above, visits the nodes in the order

a, ÷, b, +, c, –, d, e

Except for the missing parentheses, this is precisely the order in which the symbols appear in Equation!

This suggests that an *inorder* traversal should be used to print the expression. Consider an inorder traversal which, when it encounters a terminal node simply prints it out; and when it encounters a non-terminal node, does the following:

1. Print a left parenthesis; and then
2. traverse the left subtree; and then
3. print the root; and then
4. traverse the right subtree; and then
5. print a right parenthesis.

Applying this procedure to the tree given in Figure above, we get

$$((a \div b) + ((c - d) \times e)),$$

which, despite the redundant parentheses, represents exactly the same expression as Equation.

Program 2: Write a C++ program to convert infix to postfix expression.

```
#include<iostream.h>
#include<conio.h>
#include<string.h>
char stack[50];
int top=-1;
void post(char inexp[]);
void push(char);
char pop();
int preced(char c);
void main()
{
char inexp[25];
clrscr();
cout<<"\nEnter the infix expression:-";
cin>>inexp;
post(inexp);
getch();
}
void push(char sy)
{ if(top>=49)
{
cout<<"\nstack overflow";
getch();
```

```
}
else {
top=top+1;
stack[top]=sy;
} }
char pop()
{ char item;
if(top= =-1)
{
cout<<"\nStack is empty";
getch();
}
else
{
item=stack[top];
top--;
}
return(item);
}
int preced(char ch)
{
if(ch= =47)
return(5);
if(ch= =42)
return(4);
if(ch= =43)
return(3);
return(2);
}
void post[char inexp[])
int len;
static int index=0,pt=0;
char oper,temp;
char postf[40];
len=strlen(inexp);
push('#');
while(index,len)
{
oper=inexp[index];
switch(oper)
{
```

```
case '(': push(oper);
break;
case '(': temp=pop();
while(temp!= '(')
{
post[pt]=temp;
pt++;
temp=pop();
}
break;
case '+':
case '-':
case '*':
case '/':
case '^':
while(preced(stack[top])>=preced(oper))
{
temp=pop();
postf[pt]=temp;
pt++;
}
push(oper);
break;
default:
postf[pt++]=oper;
break;
}
index++;
}
while(top>0)
{
temp=pop();
postf[pt++]=temp;
}
postf[pt++]= '\0';
cout<<"\nThe expression into postfix:-";
cout<<postf;
}
```

Output:

Enter the infix expression: (A+B)*(C/D)

The expression into postfix: AB+CD/*

8.9 REPRESENTING BINARY TREES IN MEMORY

Let T be a binary tree. This section discusses two ways of representing T in memory. The first and usual way is called the link representing of T and is analogous to the way linked lists are represented in memory. The second way, which uses a single array, called the sequential representation of T. The main requirement of any representation of T is that one should have direct access to the root R to T and, given any node N of T, one should have direct access to the children of N.

8.9.1 Array Representation of Binary Trees

Suppose T is a binary tree that is complete or nearly complete. Then there is an easy and efficient way of maintaining T in memory called the array representation of T. This representation uses only a single linear array TREE as follows:

1. The root R of T is stored in TREE[1].
2. If a node N occupies TREE[K], then its left child is stored in TREE[2 * k] and its right child is stored in TREE[2 * K + 1].

Again, NULL is used to indicate an empty subtree. In particular, TREE[1] = NULL indicates that the tree is empty.

Example 8.8: A complete binary tree has a simple array representation. Suppose we number the nodes from left to right, beginning at the top and ending at the bottom. Then we can store the various data items in the corresponding elements of an array. Like the way, shown below:

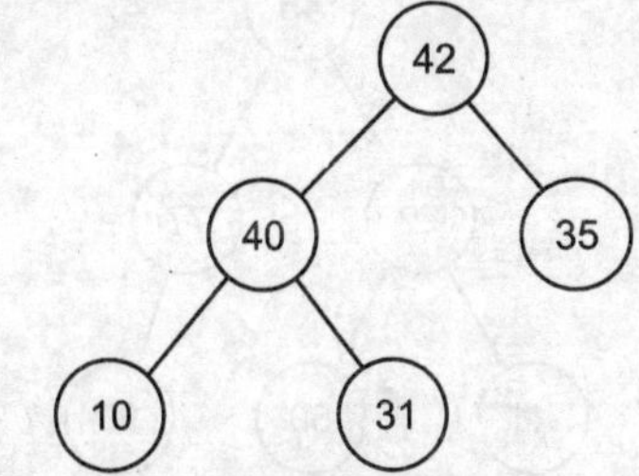

Figure 8.40: Complete binary tree.

It can be represented by the array form:

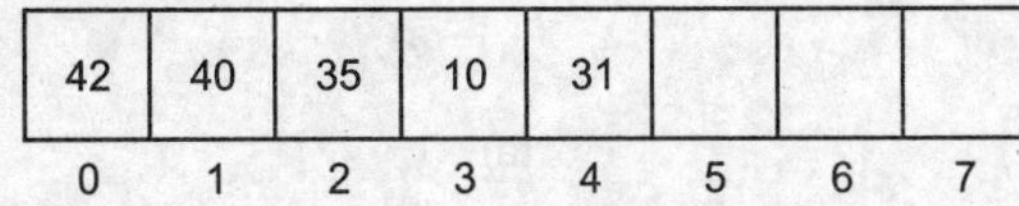

Figure 8.41: Representation of complete binary tree using array.

This in fact corresponds to the level order enumeration of the tree. Note that we only use an initial segment of the array. Provided the array is long enough, and we know the number of tree nodes, it doesn't matter how many unused components there are at the end.

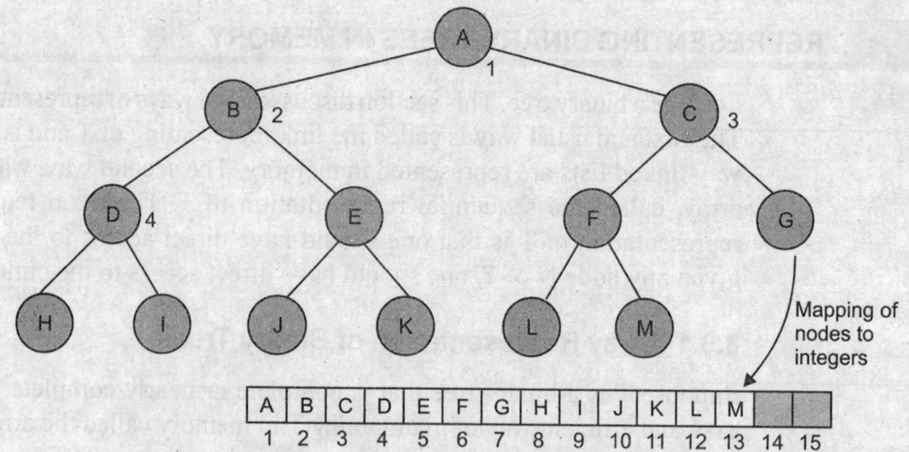

A	B	C	D	E	F	G	H	I	J	K	L	M		
1	2	3	4	5	6	7	8	9	10	11	12	13	14	15

Figure 8.42: Representation of complete binary tree using array.

Example 8.9: An array representation of the binary tree T in Figure 8.43(a) appears in Figure 8.43(b). Observe that we require 14 locations in the array TREE even though T has only 9 nodes. In fact, if we included null entries for the successors of the terminal nodes, then we would actually require TREE[29] for the right successor of TREE[14]. Generally speaking, the sequential representation of a tree with depth d will require an array with

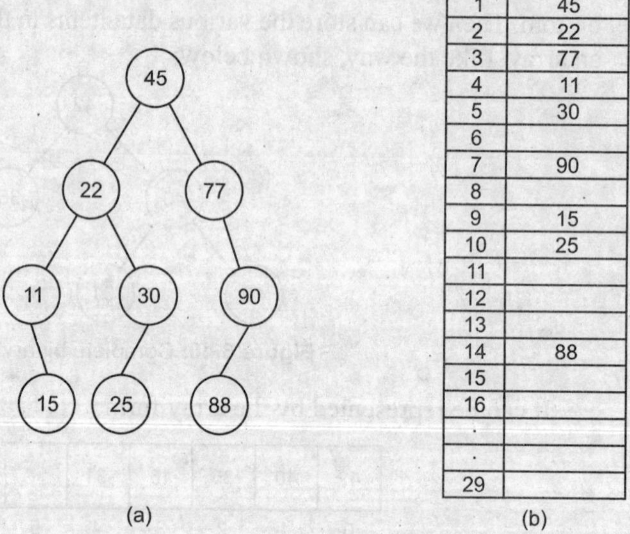

1	45
2	22
3	77
4	11
5	30
6	
7	90
8	
9	15
10	25
11	
12	
13	
14	88
15	
16	
.	
.	
29	

Figure 8.43: Array representation of the binary tree

approximately 2^{d+1} elements. Accordingly, this sequential representation is usually inefficient unless as stated above, the binary tree T is complete or nearly complete. For example, the tree T in Fig. 7.1 has 11 nodes and depth 5, which means it would require an array with approximately $2^6 = 64$ elements.

8.9.2 Linked Representation of Binary Trees

While the sequential representation is acceptable for complete binary trees, it wastes space for many other binary trees. In, addition, this representation suffers from the general inadequacies of other sequential representations. Thus, insertion or deletion of nodes from the middle of a tree requires the movement of potentially many nodes to reflect the change in the level of these nodes. We can easily overcome these problems by using a linked representation. Each node has three fields, left_child, data, and right_child as two pictures show the node representation of the binary tree below:

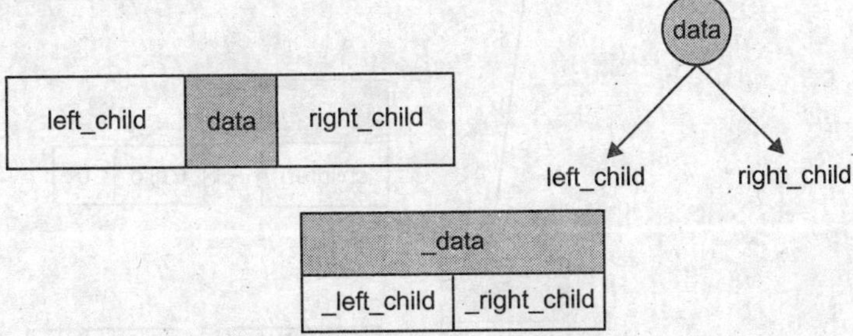

Figure 8.44: The representation of node in the tree structure

Define Structure Node for the tree

```
typedef struct node *ptr_node;
sturct node
{
int data;
ptr_node left_child;
ptr_node right_child;
}
```

Figure 8.45: Structure of Binary tree using linked list.

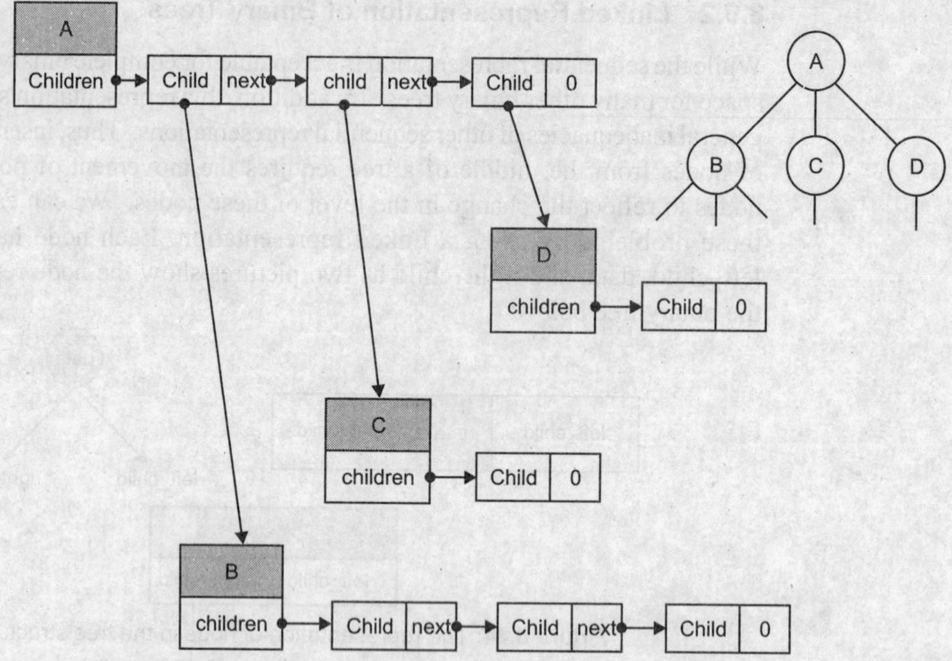

Figure 8.46: Representations of Binary tree using linked list.

Consider a binary tree T. Binary tree T will be maintained in memory by means of a linked representation which uses three parallel arrays, INFO, LEFT and RIGHT, and a pointer variable ROOT as follows. First of all, each node N of T will correspond to a location K such that:

1. INFO[K] contains the data at the node N.
2. LEFT[K] contains the location of the left child of node N.
3. RIGHT[K] contains the location of the right child of node N.

Furthermore, ROOT will contain the location of the root R of T. If any subtree is empty, then the corresponding pointer will contain the null value; if the tree T itself is empty, then ROOT will contain the null value.

Example 8.10: Consider the binary tree T in Figure 8.47. A schematic diagram of the linked representation of T appears in Figure 8.48. Each mode is represented with its three fields, and that the empty subtrees are pictured by using X for the null entries.

Table 8.1 shows how this linked representation may appear in memory. The choice of 20 elements for the arrays is arbitrary. Observe that the AVAIL list is maintained as a one-way list using the array LEFT.

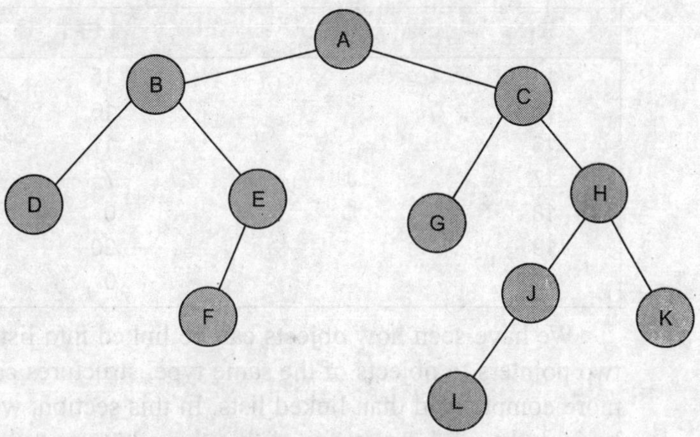

Figure 8.47: Binary tree T.

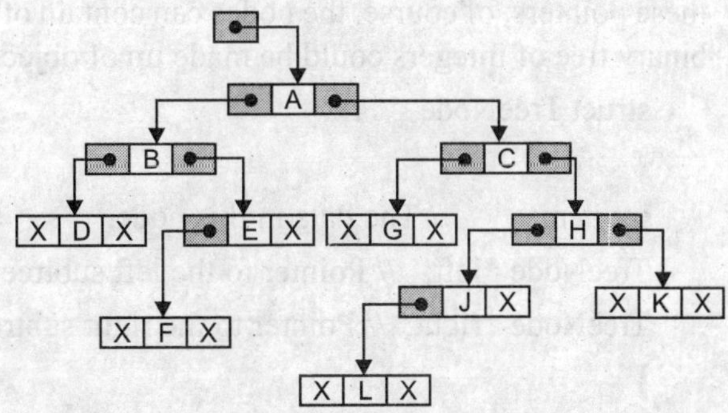

Figure 8.48: Linked representation of binary tree T.

Table 8.1: Linked representation of binary tree T may appear in memory.

S.No	INFO	LEFT	RIGHT
1	K	0	0
2	C	3	6
3	G	0	0
4		14	
5	A	10	2
6	H	17	1
7	L	0	0
8		9	
9		4	
10	B	18	13
11		19	
12	F	0	0
13	E	12	0

Contd...

S.No	INFO	LEFT	RIGHT
14		15	
15		16	
16		11	
17	J	7	0
18	D	0	0
19		20	
20		0	

We have seen how objects can be linked into lists. When an object contains two pointers to objects of the same type, structures can be created that are much more complicated than linked lists. In this section, we'll look at one of the most basic and useful structures of this type: **binary trees**. Each of the objects in a binary tree contains two pointers, typically called left and right. In addition to these pointers, of course, the nodes can contain other types of data. For example, a binary tree of integers could be made up of objects of the following type:

```
struct TreeNode
{
int item;         // The data in this node.
TreeNode *left;   // Pointer to the left subtree.
TreeNode *right;  // Pointer to the right subtree.
}
```

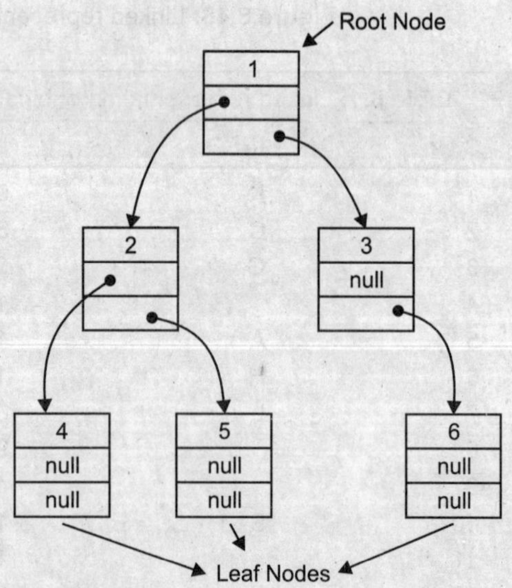

Figure 8.49: Linked representation of binary tree.

The left and right pointers in a TreeNode can be NULL or can point to other objects of type TreeNode. A node that points to another node is said to be the **parent** of that node, and the node it points to is called a **child**. In the figure above, for example, node 3 is the parent of node 6, and nodes 4 and 5 are children of node 2. Not every linked structure made up of tree nodes is a binary tree.

A binary tree must have the following properties:

- There is exactly one node in the tree which has no parent. This node is called the **root** of the tree. Every other node in the tree has exactly one parent. Finally, there can be no loops in a binary tree. That is, it is not possible to follow a chain of pointers starting at some node and arriving back at the same node.
- A node that has no children is called a **leaf**. A leaf node can be recognized by the fact that both the left and right pointers in the node are NULL. In the standard picture of a binary tree, the root node is shown at the top and the leaf nodes at the bottom — which doesn't show much respect with the analogy to real trees. But at least you can see the branching, tree-like structure that gives a binary tree its name.

Consider any node in a binary tree. Look at that node together with all its descendents (that is, its children, the children of its children, and so on). This set of nodes forms a binary tree, which is called a **subtree** of the original tree. For example, in the Figure, nodes 2, 4, and 5 form a subtree. This subtree is called the **left subtree** of the root. Similarly, nodes 3 and 6 make up the **right subtree** of the root. We can consider any non-empty binary tree to be made up of a root node, a left subtree, and a right subtree. Either or both of the subtrees can be empty.

Important points:

1. *Most of our examples will show a single item of information at each node N of a binary tree T. In actual practice, an entire record may be stored at the node N. In other words, INFO may actually be a linear array of records or a collection of parallel arrays.*
2. *Since nodes may be inserted into and deleted from our binary trees, we also implicitly assume that the empty locations in the arrays INFO, LEFT, and RIGHT form a linked list with pointer AVAIL. We will usually let the LEFT array contain the pointers for the AVAIL list.*
3. *Any invalid address may be chosen for the pointer denoted by NULL. In actual practice, 0 or a negative number is used for NULL.*

 TRAVERSING BINARY TREES

Binary tree is a non-linear data structures consist of a finite set of nodes which either empty, or consist of a root and two disjoint binary trees, called the left and right sub-trees. While a tree must have at least one node, a binary tree may be empty. Likewise, a tree may have any number of sub-trees; a binary tree can have at most two.

Many algorithms pertaining to tree structures usually involve a process in which each node of the tree is "visited", or processed, exactly once. Such a process is called a *traversal*. Three of such traversals are: ***preorder*** *traversal*, ***inorder*** *traversal* and ***postorder*** traversal. Binary tree traversals can be implemented recursively or non-recursively.

In this machine problem solution, the binary tree traversals were implemented using nonrecursive algorithm.

Problem Statement

Given a set of input representing the nodes of a binary tree, the program must be able to output the three traversal orders. The program must also capable of checking validity of the input, i.e., the program must know if the input is disjoint, duplicated and has a loop.

Problem Solution

8.10.1 Binary Tree Traversals

The procedure to obtain the preorder, inorder, and postorder traversals are given below:

Preorder traversal

1. Visit the root
2. Traverse the left sub-tree in preorder
3. Traverse the right sub-tree in preorder

Inorder traversal

1. Traverse the left sub-tree in inorder
2. Visit the root
3. Traverse the right subtree in inorder

Postorder traversal

1. Traverse the left subtree in postorder

2. Traverse the right subtree in postorder
3. Visit the oot

8.10.1.1 Tree Traversals

It is often useful to iterate through the nodes in a tree:

- to print all values
- to determine if there is a node with some property
- to make a copy

When we iterated through a List, we started with the first node and visited each node in turn. Since each node is visited, the best possible complexity is O(N) for a tree with N nodes. All of our traversal methods will achieve this complexity.

For trees, there are many different orders in which we might visit the nodes. There are three common traversal orders for general trees, and one more for binary trees: preorder, postorder, level order, and in-order, all described below. We will use the following tree to illustrate each traversal:

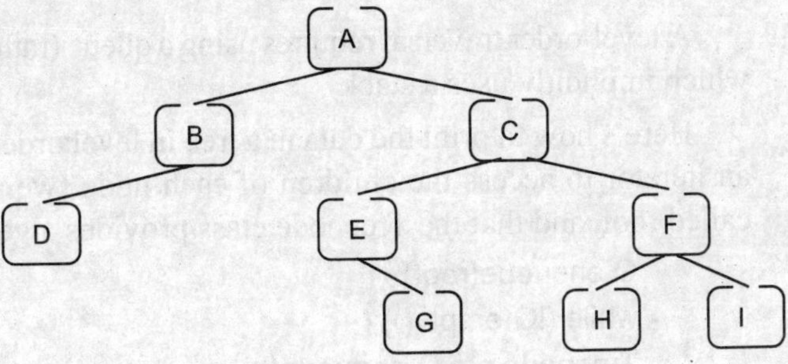

Figure 8.50: Binary tree.

8.10.1.2 Preorder

A preorder traversal can be defined (recursively) as follows:

1. visit the root
2. perform a preorder traversal of the first subtree of the root
3. perform a preorder traversal of the second subtree of the root
4. etc. for all the subtrees of the root

If we use a preorder traversal on the example tree given above, and we print the letter in each node when we visit that node, the following will be printed: A B D C E G F H I.

8.10.1.3 Postorder

A postorder traversal is similar to a preorder traversal, except that the root of each subtree is visited **last** rather than first:

1. perform a postorder traversal of the first subtree of the root
2. perform a postorder traversal of the second subtree of the root
3. etc. for all the subtrees of the root
4. visit the root

If we use a postorder traversal on the example tree given above, and we print the letter in each node when we visit that node, the following will be printed: D B G E H I F C A.

8.10.1.4 Level Order

The idea of a level-order traversal is to visit the root, then visit all nodes "1 level away" (depth 2) from the root (left to right), then all nodes "2 levels away" (depth 3) from the root, etc. For the example tree, the goal is to visit the nodes in the following order:

A	B C	D E F	G H I
root	1 level away	2 level away	3 level away

A level-order traversal requires using a queue (rather than a recursive algorithm, which implicitly uses a stack).

Here's how to print the data in a tree in level order, using a queue Q, and using an iterator to access the children of each node (we assume that the root node is called root, and that the Treenode class provides a getChildren method):

```
Q.enqueue(root)
while (!Q.empty()) {
Treenode n = Q.dequeue();
System.out.print(n.getData());
List L = n.getChildren();
Iterator it = L.iterator();
while (it.hasNext()) {
Q.enqueue(it.next());
} }
```

8.10.1.5 Inorder

An in-order traversal involves visiting the root "in between" visiting its left and right subtrees. Therefore, an in-order traversal only makes sense for binary trees. The (recursive) definition is:

1. perform an in-order traversal of the left subtree of the root
2. **visit the root**
3. perform an in-order traversal of the right subtree of the root

If we print the letters in the nodes of our example tree using an in-order traversal, the following will be printed: D B A E G C H F I

The primary difference between the preorder, postorder and in-order traversals is where the node is visited in relation to the recursive calls; i.e., before, after or in-between.

Example 8.11: Figure 8.51 shows several binary trees and the traversal sequences in preorder, inorder, and postorder. We can construct a binary tree uniquely from preorder **and inorder or postorder** and inorder but not preorder and postorder.

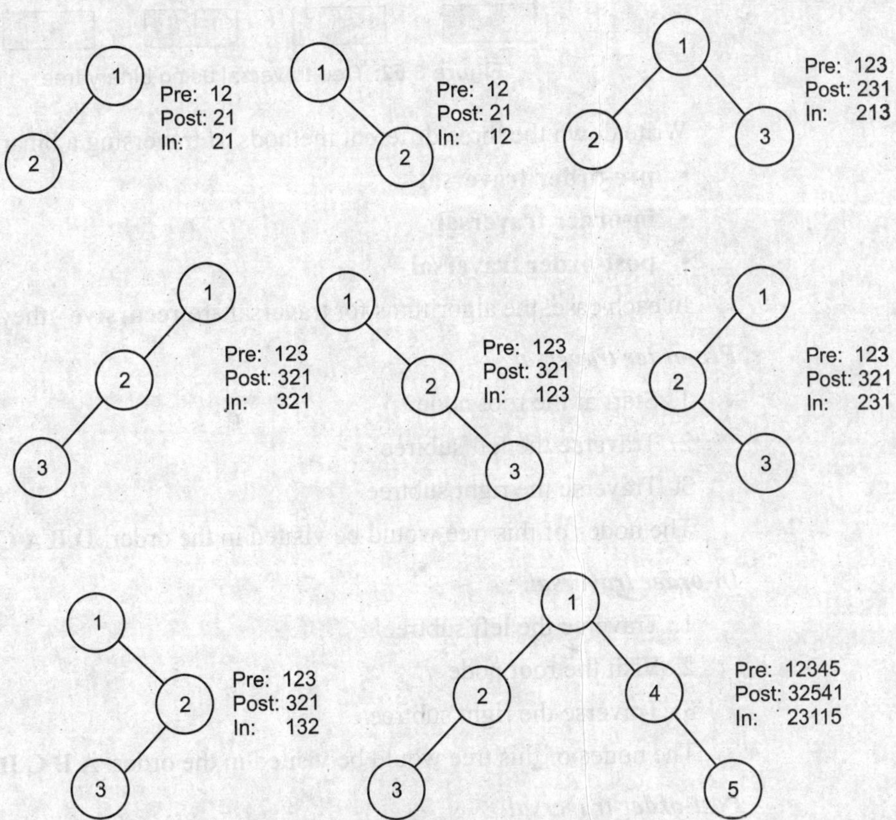

Figure 8.51: Binary tree traversals

8.10.1.6 Balancing

When entries that are already sorted are stored in a tree, all new records will go the same route, and the tree will look more like a list (such a tree is called a degenerate tree). Therefore the tree needs balancing routines, making sure that under all branches are an equal number of records. This will keep searching in the tree at optimal speed. Specifically, if a tree with n nodes is a degenerate tree, the longest path through the tree will be n nodes; if it is a balanced tree, the longest path will be log n nodes.

Example 8.12: Consider the binary tree T in figure below

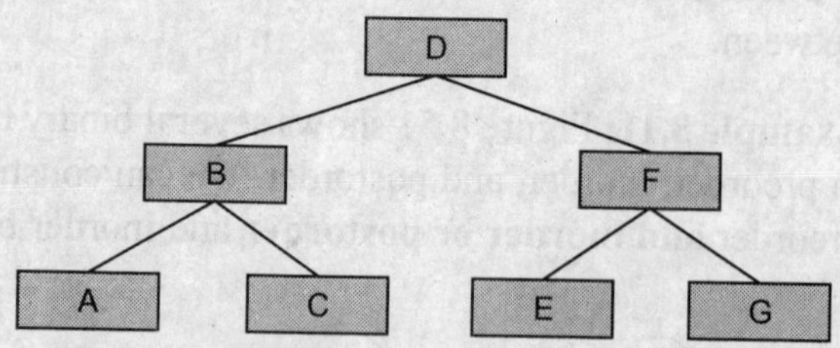

Figure 8.52: Tree traversal using binary tree.

Write down the three different methods of traversing a binary tree:

- **pre-order traversal**
- **in-order traversal**
- **post-order traversal**

In each case, the algorithms for traversal are **recursive** - they call themselves.

Pre-order traversal

1. Start at the root node
2. Traverse the left subtree
3. Traverse the right subtree

The nodes of this tree would be visited in the order: **D B A C F E G**

In-order traversal

1. Traverse the left subtree
2. Visit the root node
3. Traverse the right subtree

The nodes of this tree would be visited in the order: **A B C D E F G**

Post-order traversal

1. Traverse the left subtree
2. Traverse the right subtree
3. Visit the root node

The nodes of this tree would be visited in the order: **A C B E G F D**

8.10.2 Computer Implementation

The tree traversal was implemented using non-recursive method. The algorithm is as follows:

8.10.2.1 Preorder Traversal

1. Define a stack
2. Traverse the left sub-tree and output each visited node while pushing it in on the stack until the leftmost node has been visited.
3. If the right subtree is not null, pop the stack, then visit that sub-tree. Output that visited node while pushing it on the stack. If null, pop the stack.
4. Do 2 and 3 until the stack is empty.

Example 8.13: Preorder traversal

Consider the binary tree T in Figure 8.53 We simulate the above algorithm with T, showing the contents of STACK at each step.(P denotes as pointer)

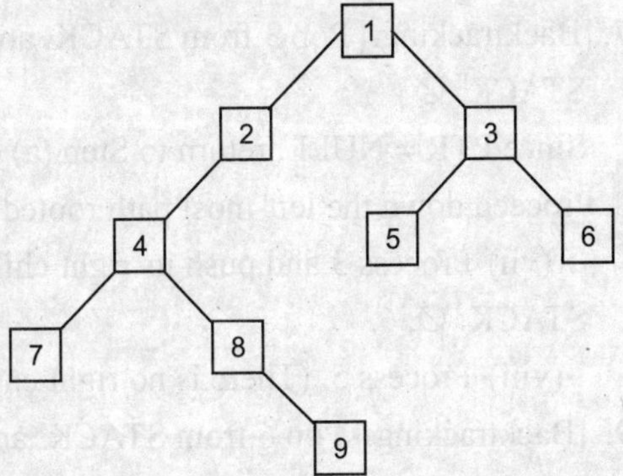

Figure 8.53: Binary tree T.

1. Initially push NULL onto STACK:
   STACK: ∅.
   Then set P = 1, the root of T.
2. Proceed down the left-most path rooted at P = 1 as follows:
   (i) Process 1 and push its right child 3 onto STACK:
   STACK: ∅, 3
   (ii) Process 2. (There is no right child.)
   (iii) Process 4 and push its right child 8 onto STACK:
   STACK: ∅, 3, 8.
   (iv) Process 7. (There is no right child.)
   No other node is processed, since 7 has no left child.
3. [Backtracking.] Pop the top element 8 from STACK, and set P = 8. This leaves:
   STACK: ∅, 3
   Since P ≠ NULL, return to Step (a) of the algorithm.

4. Proceed down the left-most path rooted at P = 8 as follows:

    (v) Process 8 and push its right child 9 onto STACK:

    STACK: ∅, 3, 9.

    No other node is processed, since 8 has no left child.

5. [Backtracking.] Pop 9 from STACK, and set P = 9. This leaves:

    STACK: ∅, 3.

    Since P ≠ NULL, return to Step (a) of the algorithm.

6. Proceed down the left-most path rooted at P = 9 as follows:

    (vi) Process 9. (There is no right child.)

    NO other id processed, since 9 has no left child.

7. [Backtracking.] Pop 3 from STACK, and set P = 9. This leaves:

    STACK: ∅

    Since PTR ≠ NULL, return to Step (a) of the algorithm.

8. Proceed down the left-most path rooted at P = 3 as follows:

    (vii) Process 3 and push its right child 6 onto STACK:

    STACK: ∅, 6.

    (viii) Process 5. (There is no right child.)

9. [Backtracking.] Pop 6 from STACK, and set P = 6. This leaves:

    STACK: ∅

    Since P ≠ NULL, return to Step (a) of the algorithm.

10. Proceed down the left-most path rooted at P = 6 as follows:

    (ix) Process 6. (There is no right child.)

    No other node is processed, since 6 has no left child.

11. [Backtracking.] Pop the top element NULL from STACK, and set P = NULL.

    Since P = NULL, the algorithm is completed.

    As in steps 2,4,6,8 and 10, the nodes are accessed and processed in order 1, 2, 4, 7, 8, 9, 3, 5, 6. This is the required preorder traversal of the binary tree T.

Algorithm 8.1: For Preorder Traversal

PREORDTRVSL (INFO, LEFTNOD, RIGHTNOD, ROOTNOD)

Suppose a binary tree T is in memory. This algorithm performs a preorder traversal of T, applying an operation PROCESS to each of its nodes. An array STACK is used to temporarily hold the addresses of nodes.

Step1: [Push NULL onto STACK, and initialize the value of pointer P by ROOT of tree T.]

Set TOP = 1, STACK[1] = NULL and P = ROOTNOD.

Step 2: Repeat Steps 3 to 5 while P ≠ NULL

Step 3: Apply operation PROCESS to INFO[P].

Step 4: [Check for RIGHTNOD child of a tree?]

If RIGHTNOD[P] ≠ NULL, then [Push onto STACK.]

Set TOP = TOP + 1, and STACK[TOP] = RIGHTNOD[P].

[End of If statement.]

Step 5: [Check for LEFTNOD child of a tree?]

If LEFTNOD[P] ≠ NULL, then

Set P = LEFTNOD[P].

Else [Pop nodes from STACK.]

Set P = STACK[TOP] and TOP = TOP – 1.

[End of If statement.] [End of while loop.]

Step 6: End.

Program 3: Write a C++ program for inserting the elements in the tree and display them in preorder.

```
#include<iostream.h>
#include<conio.h>
struct tree
{
long data;
struct tree *left;
struct tree *right;
};
struct tree *btree=NULL;
struct tree *insert(struct tree*btree,long digit);
void inorder(struct tree*btree);
void main()
{
long digit;
clrscr();
cout<<"Enter integers: and 0 to quit;
cin>>digit;
while(digit!=0) {
btree=insert(btree,digit);
cin>>digit;
}
cout<<"Preorder traversing of btree:\n;
```

```
preorder(btree);
}
struct tree*insert(struct tree*btree,long digit)
{
if(btree= =NULL) {
btree=(struct tree*)malloc(sizeof(struct tree));
btree->left=btree->right=NULL;
btree->data=digit;
}
else {
if(digit<btree->data)
btree->left=insert(btree->left,digit);
else
if(digit>btree->data)
btree->right=insert(btree->right,digit);
else
if(digit= =btree->data)
{ cout<<"Duplicates nodes: Program exited"; exit(0); } }
return(btree);
}
void preorder(struct tree*btree)
{ if (btree!=NULL) {
cout<<btree->data;
preorder(btree->left);
preorder(btree->right);}
}
```

Output:

Enter integers: and 0 to quit

50, 30, 20, 40, 90, 100 0

For Example

Enter integers: 50, 30, 20, 40, 90, 100

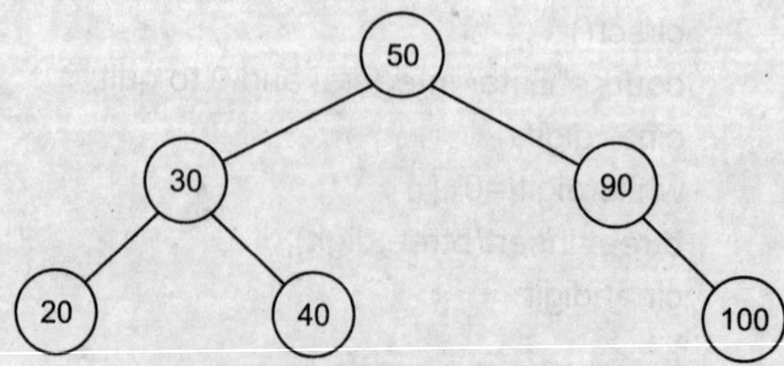

Figure 8.54: Traversing tree as preorder.

Preorder traversing binary tree:

50, 30, 20, 40, 90, 100

8.10.2.2 Inorder Traversal

1. Define a stack
2. Traverse the left sub-tree and push each visited node on the stack until the leftmost node has been visited.
3. If the right sub-tree in not null, pop the stack and output it, then visit the right sub-tree and push it on the stack. If null, pop the stack and output it.
4. Do 2 and 3 until the stack is empty.

Example 8.14: Inorder Traversal

Consider the binary tree T in Figure 8.55. We simulate the above algorithm with T, showing the contents of stack.

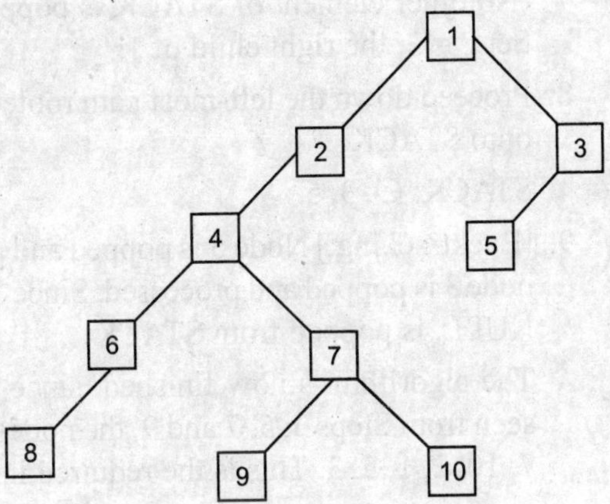

Figure 8.55: Binary tree T.

1. Initially push NULL onto STACK:

   STACK: ∅.

   Then set P = 1, the root of T.
2. Proceed down the left-most path rooted at P = 1, pushing the nodes 1, 2, 4, 6 and 8 onto STACK:

   STACK: ∅, 1, 2, 4, 6, 8.
3. [Backtracking.] The nodes 8, 6 and 4 are popped and processed, leaving:

   STACK: ∅, 1, 2.

   (We stop the processing at 4, since 4 has a right child.) Then set P = 7, the right child of 4.
4. Proceed down the left-most path rooted at P = 7, pushing the nodes 7 and 9 onto STACK:

STACK: ∅, 1, 2, 7, 9.

(No other node is pushed onto STACK, since 9 has no left child.)

5. [Backtracking.] The nodes 9 and 7 popped and processed, leaving:

   STACK: ∅, 1, 2.

   (We stop the processing at 7, since 7 has a right child.) Then set P = 10, the right child of 7.

6. Proceed down the left-most path rooted at P = 10, pushing node 10 onto STACK:

   STACK: ∅, 1, 2, 10.

   (No other node is pushed onto STACK, since 10 has no left child.)

7. [Backtracking.] The nodes 10, 2 and 1 are popped and processed, leaving:

   STACK: ∅.

   (No other element of STACK is popped, since 1 does have a right child.) Set P = 3, the right child of 1.

8. Proceed down the left-most path rooted at P = 3, pushing the nodes 3 and 5 onto STACK:

   STACK: ∅, 3, 5.

9. [Backtracking.] Node 5 is popped and processed. Since 5 has no right child, node 3 is popped and processed. Since 3 has no right child, the next element, NULL, is popped from STACK.

   The algorithm is now finished, since NULL is popped from STACK. As seen from Steps 3, 5, 7 and 9, the nodes are processed in the order 8, 6, 4, 9, 7, 10, 2, 1, 5, 3. This is the required inorder traversal of the binary tree T.

   As in steps 3, 5, 7 and 9, the nodes are accessed and processed in order 8, 6, 4, 9, 7, 10, 2, 1, 5, 3. This is the required inorder traversal of the binary tree T

Algorithm 8.2: For inorder Traversal

INORDTRVSL (INFO, LEFTNOD, RIGHTNOD, ROOTNOD)

Suppose a binary tree is in memory. This algorithm performs a inorder traversal of T, applying an operation PROCESS to each of its nodes. An array STACK is used to temporarily hold the addresses of nodes.

Step 1: [Push NULL onto STACK, and initialize the value of pointer P by ROOT of tree T.] Set TOP = 1, STACK[1] = NULL and P = ROOTNOD.

Step 2: Repeat steps while P ≠ NULL [Pushes LEFTNOD-most path onto STACK.]

(a) Set TOP = TOP + 1 and STACK[TOP] = P. [Saves node.]

(b) Set P = LEFTNOD[P]. [Updates pointer P.]

[End of while loop.]

Step 3: Set P = STACK[TOP] and TOP = TOP -1. [POPS node from the STACK.]

Step 4: Repeat Steps 5 to 7 while P ≠ NULL [Backtracking the process.]

Step 5: Apply operation PROCESS to INFO[P].

Step 6: [Check for RIGHTNOD child?] If RIGHTNOD [P] ≠ NULL, then

(a) Set P = RIGHTNOD[P].

(b) Go to Step 3.

[End of If statement.]

Step 7: Set P = STACK[TOP] and TOP = TOP -1. [Pops node.]

[End of Step 4 while loop.]

Step 8: End.

Program 4: Write a C++ program for inserting the elements into the tree and traverse the tree by the inorder.

```
#include<iostream.h>
#include<conio.h>
struct tree
{
long data;
struct tree *left;
struct tree *right;
};
struct tree *btree=NULL;
struct tree *insert(struct tree*btree,long digit);
void inorder(struct tree*btree);
void main()
{
long digit;
clrscr();
cout<<"Enter integers: and 0 to quit;
cin>>digit;
while(digit!=0) {
btree=insert(btree,digit);
cin>>digit;
}
cout<<"Inorder traversing of btree:\n;
```

```
inorder(btree);
}
struct tree*insert(struct tree*btree,long digit)
{
if(btree= =NULL)
{
btree=(struct tree*)malloc(sizeof(struct tree));
btree->left=btree->right=NULL;
btree->data=digit;
}
else
{
if(digit<btree->data)
btree->left=insert(btree->left,digit);
else
if(digit>btree->data)
btree->right=insert(btree->right,digit);
else
if(digit= =btree->data)
{
cout<<"Duplicates nodes: Program exited";
exit(0);
}
}
return(btree);
void inorder(struct tree*btree)
{
if(btree!=NULL)
{
inorder(btree->left);
cout<<btree->data;
inorder(btree->right);
}
}
```

Output:

Enter integers: and 0 to quit

50, 30, 20, 40, 90, 100 0

For Example

Enter integers: 50, 30, 20, 40, 90, 100

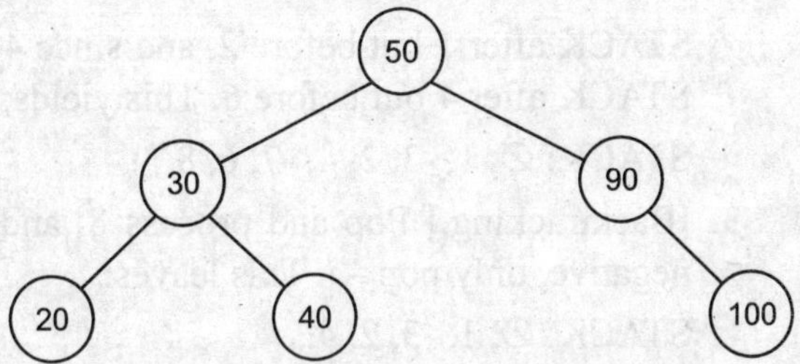

Figure 8.56: Traversing tree as inorder.

Inorder traversing binary tree:
20, 30, 40, 50, 90, 100

8.10.2.3 Postorder Traversal

1. Define a stack
2. Traverse the left sub-tree and push each visited node on the stack until the leftmost node has been visited.
3. If the right sub-tree in not null, visit the right sub-tree and push it on the stack. If null, pop the stack and output it.
4. Do 2 and 3 until the stack is empty.

Example 8.15: Postorder Traversal

Consider again the binary tree T in Figure 8.58. We simulate the above algorithm with T, showing the contents of STACK.

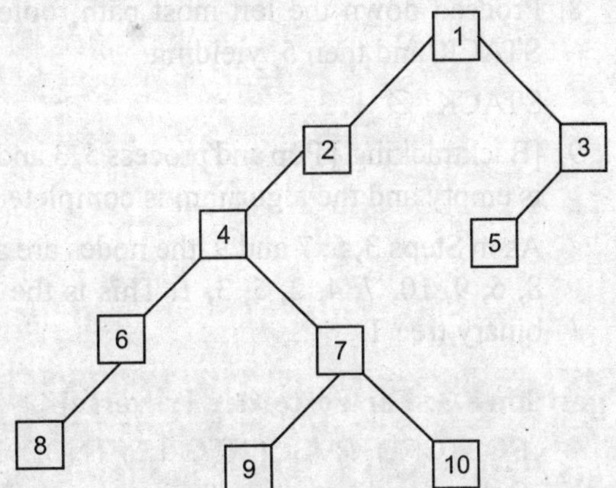

Figure 8.57: Binary tree T.

1. Initially, push NULL onto STACK and set P = 1, the root of T:

   STACK: ∅.
2. Proceed down the left-most path rooted at P = 1, pushing the nodes 1, 2, 4, 6 and 8 onto STACK. Furthermore, since 1 has a right child 3, push –3 onto

STACK after 1 but before 2, and since 4 has a right child 7, push –7 onto STACK after 4 but before 6. This yields:

STACK: ∅, 1, -3, 2, 4, -7, 6, 8.

3. [Backtracking.] Pop and process 8, and pop and process 6. Since –7 is negative, only pop –7. This leaves:

   STACK: ∅, 1, -3, 2, 4.

   Now P = -7. Reset P = 7 and return to Step (a).

4. Proceed down the left-most path rooted at P = 7. First push 7 onto STACK. Since 7 has a right child 10, push –10 onto STACK after 7. Last, push 9 onto STACK. This gives:

   STACK: ∅, 1, -3, 2, 4, 7, -10, 9.

5. [Backtracking.] Pop and process 9, but only pop –10. This leaves:

   STACK: ∅, 1, -3, 2, 4, 7.

   Not P = -10. Reset P = 10 and return to Step (a).

6. Proceed down the left-most path rooted at P = 10. Now, only 10 is pushed onto STACK. This yields:

   STACK: ∅, 1, -3, 2, 4, 7, 10.

7. [Backtracking.] Pop and process 10, 7, 4 and 2, but only pop –3. This leaves:

   STACK: ∅, 1

   Now P = -3. Reset P = 3, and return to Step (a).

8. Proceed down the left-most path rooted at P = 3. First 3 is pushed onto STACK and then 5, yielding:

   STACK: ∅, 1, 3, 5.

9. [Backtracking.] Pop and process 5, 3 and 1. When NULL is popped, STACK is empty and the algorithm is completed.

   As in Steps 3, 5, 7 and 9, the nodes are accessed and processed in the order 8, 6, 9, 10, 7, 4, 2, 5, 3, 1. This is the required postorder traversal of the binary tree T.

Algorithm 8.3: For Postorder Traversal

POSTORDTRVSL (INFO, LEFTNOD, RIGHTNOD, ROOTNOD)

Suppose a binary tree T is in memory. The algorithm performs a preorder traversal of T, applying an operation PROCESS to each of its nodes. An array STACK is used to temporarily hold the addresses of nodes.

Step 1: [Initially push NULL onto STACK, and initialize pointer P.]
 Set TOP = 1, STACK[1] = NULL and P = ROOTNOD.

Step 2: [Push LEFTNOD-most path onto STACK.]
 Repeat Steps 3 to 5 while P ≠ NULL:

Step 3: Set TOP = TOP + 1 and STACK[TOP] = P.
[Pushes P on STACK.]
Step4: If RIGHTNOD[P] ≠ NULL, then: [Push on STACK.]
Set TOP = TOP + 1 and STACK[TOP] = –RIGHTNOD[P].
[End of If statement.]
Step 5: Set P = LEFTNOD[P]. [Updates pointer P.]
[End of Step-2 loop.]
Step 6: Set P = STACK[TOP] and TOP = TOP –1.
[Pops node from STACK.]
Step 7: Repeat while P > 0
(a) Apply PROCESS to INFO[P].
(b) Set P = STACK[TOP] and TOP = TOP – 1.
[Pops node from STACK.]
[End of loop.]
Step 8: If P <0, then
(a) Set P = –P.
(b) Go to Step 2.
[End of If statement.]
Step 9: End.

Program 5: Write a C++ program for inserting the nodes in tree and traversing these nodes by using the postorder method.

```
#include<iostream.h>
#include<conio.h>
struct tree
{
long data;
struct tree *left;
struct tree *right;
};
struct tree *btree=NULL;
struct tree *insert(struct tree*btree,long digit);
void postorder(struct tree*btree);
void main()
{
long digit;
clrscr();
cout<<"Enter integers: and 0 to quit;
cin>>digit;
while(digit!=0)
{
```

```
btree=insert(btree,digit);
cin>>digit;
}
cout<<"Postorder traversing of btree:\n;
postorder(btree);
}
struct tree*insert(struct tree*btree,long digit)
{
if(btree= =NULL)
{
btree=(struct tree*)malloc(sizeof(struct tree));
btree->left=btree->right=NULL;
btree->data=digit;
}
else
}
if(digit<btree->data)
btree->left=insert(btree->left,digit);
else
if(digit>btree->data)
btree->right=insert(btree->right,digit);
else
if(digit= =btree->data)
{
cout<<"Duplicates nodes: Program exited";
exit(0);
}
}
return(btree);
}
void postorder(struct tree*btree)
{
if (btree!=NULL)
{
postorder(btree->left);
postorder(btree->right);
cout<<btree->data;
}
}
```

Output:

Enter integers: and 0 to quit

50, 30, 20, 40, 90, 100 0

For Example

Enter integers: 50, 30, 20, 40, 90, 100

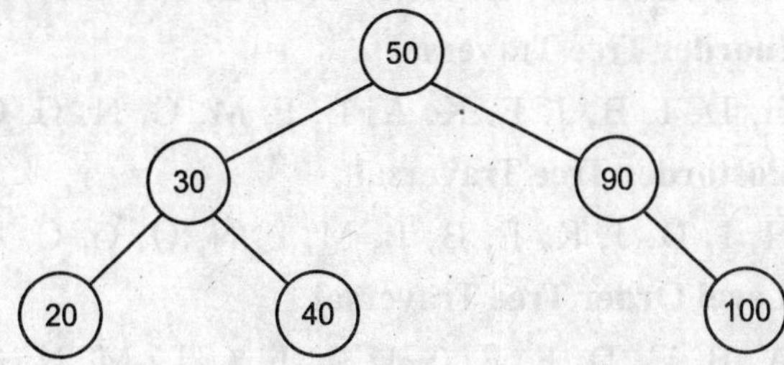

Figure 8.58: Traversing tree as postorder.

Postorder traversing binary tree:

20, 40, 30, 100, 90, 50

8.10.3 Error Checking

1. The tree has a loop. The tree has a loop if;
   - The input left subtree or right subtree duplicates,
   - The input left subtree appear on the right subtree.
2. The tree is not a binary tree. The tree is not a binary tree if;
   - The input root duplicates.
3. The tree has a loop and it has no root. The tree has no root if;
   - The input has no leaf and does not terminate.
4. The tree is disjoint. The tree is disjoint if;
   - The total number of input nodes is not equal to the nodes traversed.

Example 8.16: Consider a binary tree T. Write output for each traversal.

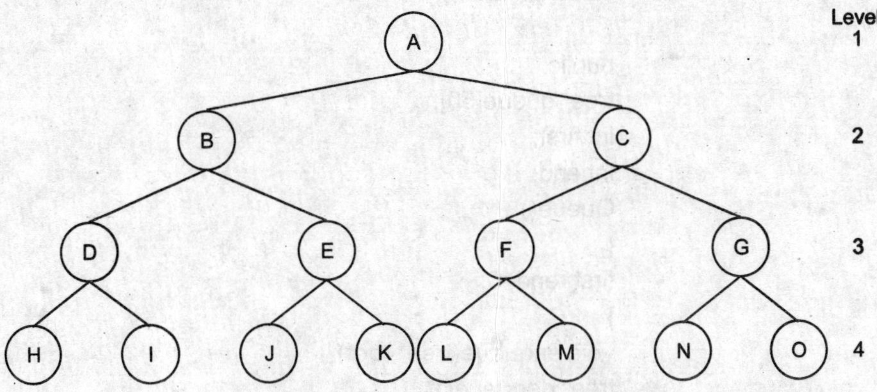

Figure 8.59: Binary tree traversing.

Preorder Tree Traversal

A, B, D, H, I, E, J, K, C, F, L, M, G, N, O

Inorder Tree Traversal

H, D, I, B, J, E, K, A, L, F, M, C, N, G, O

Postorder Tree Traversal

H, I, D, J, K, E, B, L, M, F, N, O, G, C, A

Level Order Tree Traversal

A, B, C, D, E, F, G, H, I, J, K, L, M, N, O

Program 6: Write a C++ program for Binary Tree Traversals(using classes).

```
#include<iostream.h>
#include<conio.h>
class tree
{
int data;
tree* lptr;
tree* rptr;
public:
tree* build_root(tree* root,int key);
tree* build_tree(tree* root);
void display(tree*);
void inorder(tree*);
void preorder(tree*);
void postorder(tree*);
void levelorder(tree*);
}*root;
class Queue
{
public:
tree* queue[50];
int first;
int end;
Queue()
{
first=end=0;
}
void enqueue(tree* root);
tree* dequeue();
bool isempty();
};
```

```
void Queue::enqueue(tree* root)
{
if(first==0)
queue[first]=root;
else
queue[end]=root;
end++;
}
tree* Queue::dequeue()
{
if(end==first)
return NULL;
else
return queue[first++];
}
bool Queue::isempty()
{
if(first==end)
return true;
else
return false;
}
tree* tree::build_root(tree* root,int key)
{
tree* temp;
temp=new tree;
temp->data=key;
temp->lptr=temp->rptr=NULL;
if(key!=-1)
root=temp;
return root;
}
tree* tree::build_tree(tree* root)
{
cout<<"\n------------------------\n";
tree* temp;
temp=root;
int key;
char ch;
root->lptr=NULL;
```

```
root->rptr=NULL;
cout<<"\nis there any left subtree for "<<root->data<<" ,if yes enter 's' else
enter 'n'\n";
cin>>ch;
if(ch=='s'||ch=='S')
{
root->lptr=new tree;
cout<<"\nenter the data for the left subtree of "<<root->data<<endl;
cin>>key;
root->lptr->data=key;
root->lptr=build_tree(root->lptr);
}
else
root->lptr=NULL;
cout<<"\nis there any right subtree for "<<root->data<<" ,if yes enter 's'
else enter 'n'\n";
cin>>ch;
if(ch=='s'||ch=='S')
{
root->rptr=new tree;
cout<<"\nenter the data for the right subtree of "<<root->data<<endl;
cin>>key;
root->rptr->data=key;
root->rptr=build_tree(root->rptr);
}
else
root->rptr=NULL;
cout<<"\n------------------------\n";
root=temp;
return root;
}
void tree::display(tree* root)
{
if(root!=NULL)
inorder(root);
else
cout<<"\nthe tree is empty\n";
}
void tree::inorder(tree* root)
{
if(root!=NULL)
```

```
{
inorder(root->lptr);
cout<<root->data<<"->";
inorder(root->rptr);
}
}
void tree::preorder(tree* root)
{
if(root!=NULL)
{
cout<<root->data<<"->";
preorder(root->lptr);
preorder(root->rptr);
}
}
void tree::postorder(tree* root)
{
if(root!=NULL)
{
postorder(root->lptr);
postorder(root->rptr);
cout<<root->data<<"->";
}
}
void tree::levelorder(tree* root)
{
Queue q;
q.enqueue(root);
while(q.isempty()!=true)
{
root=q.dequeue();
if(root!=NULL)
{
cout<<root->data<<"->";
if(root->lptr!=NULL)
q.enqueue(root->lptr);
if(root->rptr!=NULL)
q.enqueue(root->rptr);
}
}
```

```
}
void choice(tree* root)
{
tree object;
int ch;
cout<<"\nchoose the operation to be performed\n";
cout<<"\n1.PREORDER TRAVERSAL\t2.INORDER TRAVERSAL\t3.POSTORDER TRAVERSAL\n";
cout<<"\n4.LEVEL ORDER TRAVERSAL\t5.EXIT\n";
cin>>ch;
while(ch!=5)
{
switch(ch)
{
case 1:
cout<<"\npreorder traversal of the tree is \n\n";
object.preorder(root);
cout<<"\n\n";
break;
case 2:
cout<<"\ninorder traversal of the tree is \n\n";
object.inorder(root);
cout<<"\n\n";
break;
case 3:
cout<<"\npostorder traversal of the tree is \n\n";
object.postorder(root);
cout<<"\n\n";
break;
case 4:
cout<<"\nlevel order traversal of the tree is \n\n";
object.levelorder(root);
cout<<"\n\n";
break;
case 5:
break;
default:
cout<<"\nenter correct choice\n";
break;
}
cout<<"\nchoose the operation to be performed\n";
```

```
cout<<"\n1.PREORDER TRAVERSAL\t2.INORDER
TRAVERSAL\t3.POSTORDER TRAVERSAL\n";
cout<<"\n4.LEVEL ORDER TRAVERSAL\t5.EXIT\n";
cin>>ch;
}
}
void main()
{
tree object;
int key;
cout<<"\nenter the data for the root,if the tree is empty enter -1\n";
cin>>key;
root=object.build_root(root,key);
if(root!=NULL)
root=object.build_tree(root);
if(root!=NULL)
{
choice(root);
}
else
cout<<"\nthe tree is empty,hence we can't perform any type of traversal\n";
getch();
}
```

Program 7: Write a C++ program to create binary tree, find mirror image of it, find height, print original tree and mirror image tree level wise, display leaf nodes.

```
#include<iostream.h>
#include<conio.h>
#include<stdlib.h>    //header for standard library function  exit();
typedef class bin_tree
{
public:
int data,status;
class bin_tree *lchild,*rchild; //pointers to class bin_tree
bin_tree():data(0),lchild(NULL),rchild(NULL),status(0){}//constructor
class bin_tree* createbt(class bin_tree*,int data); //create
function
void leafnodes(class bin_tree*);
void display(class bin_tree*);
class bin_tree* mirrorimage(class bin_tree*,class bin_tree*);
```

```
void levelprint(class bin_tree*,int&);
}nodebt;//typedef for simplicity
typedef class queue
{
public:
nodebt *data;
class queue *next;
queue():data(NULL),next(NULL){}
nodebt* deletefront(queue **front,queue **rear);
queue *insertrear(queue **front,queue **rear,nodebt *data);
}que;
void nodebt::levelprint(class bin_tree* r,int &height)
{
que q1;
nodebt *check=NULL,*pt=r;
que *front=NULL,*rear=NULL;
q1.insertrear(&front,&rear,r);
q1.insertrear(&front,&rear,check);
while(front!=NULL)//q not empty
{
while(pt!=NULL)
{
pt=q1.deletefront(&front,&rear);
if(pt==NULL)
{
cout<<endl;
height++;
q1.insertrear(&front,&rear,check);
pt=q1.deletefront(&front,&rear);
}
if(front==NULL)
return;
cout<<pt->data<<" ";
if(pt->lchild!=NULL)
q1.insertrear(&front,&rear,pt->lchild);
if(pt->rchild!=NULL)
q1.insertrear(&front,&rear,pt->rchild);
}
}
}
nodebt* que::deletefront(que **front,que **rear)
{
```

```
nodebt *temp=NULL;
if(*front==NULL)
{
cout<<" queue is empty";
}
else
{      temp=(*front)->data;
(*front)=(*front)->next;
if((*front)==NULL)
{
*rear=NULL;
}
}
return temp;
}
que *que::insertrear(que **front,que **rear,nodebt *data)
{
que *temp=NULL;
temp=new queue;
temp->data=data;
temp->next=NULL;
if(*front==NULL)
{
*front=temp;
*rear=temp;
}
else
{
(*rear)->next=temp;
*rear=(*rear)->next;
}
return *front;
}
nodebt* nodebt::mirrorimage(class bin_tree *r,class bin_tree* m)
{
nodebt *ret=NULL;
if(r==NULL)
return r;
if(r->status==2)
{
nodebt *temp=new nodebt;
temp->data=r->data;
```

```
temp->status=2;
m=temp;
ret=temp;
}
if(r->status==0)
{
nodebt *temp=new nodebt;
temp->data=r->data;
temp->status=1;
m->rchild=temp;
m=m->rchild;
}
if(r->status==1)
{
nodebt *temp=new nodebt;
temp->data=r->data;
temp->status=0;
m->lchild=temp;
m=m->lchild;
}
mirrorimage(r->lchild,m);
mirrorimage(r->rchild,m);
return ret;
}
void nodebt::leafnodes(class bin_tree* r)
{
if(r==NULL)
return;
if(r->lchild==NULL && r->lchild==NULL)
cout<<r->data<<" ";
leafnodes(r->lchild);
leafnodes(r->rchild);
}
void nodebt::display(class bin_tree* r)
{
if(r==NULL)
return;
cout<<" "<<r->data<<" ";
display(r->lchild);
display(r->rchild);
}
nodebt* nodebt::createbt(nodebt *r,int data)
```

```
{
int ch=0;
if(r==NULL)
{
nodebt *temp=new nodebt;
temp->data=data;
temp->status=2;
r=temp;
}
else
{
cout<<" 1.INSERT AT LEFT OF"<<" "<<r->data;
cout<<" 2.INSERT AT RIGHT OF"<<" "<<r->data;
cout<<" ENTER YOUR CHOICE=";
cin>>ch;
switch(ch)
{
case 1:if(r->lchild==NULL)
{
nodebt *temp=new nodebt;
temp->data=data;
temp->status=0;
r->lchild=temp;
}
else
createbt(r->lchild,data);
break;
case 2:if(r->rchild==NULL)
{
nodebt *temp=new nodebt;
temp->data=data;
temp->status=1;
r->rchild=temp;
}
else
createbt(r->rchild,data);
break;
}
}
return r;
}
int main()
```

```
{	int ch=0,data=0,height=0;
nodebt *head=NULL,*m=NULL;
nodebt t2;
do
{	clrscr();
cout<<" MENU";
cout<<" 1.CREATE OR INSERT BINARY TREE";
cout<<" 2.PRINT LEAF NODES";
cout<<" 3.FIND MIRROR IMAGE OF THE TREE";
cout<<" 4.PRINT ORIGINAL AND MIRROR IMAGE LEVELWISE";
cout<<" 5.HEIGHT OF TREE";
cout<<" 6.EXIT";
cout<<" ENTER YOUR CHOICE=";
cin>>ch;
switch(ch)
{
case 1:
nodebt t1;
do
{
cout<<" ENTER THE DATA=";cin>>data;
head=t1.createbt(head,data);
cout<<" DO U WANT TO ADD MORE NODES(1.YES/2.NO)";
cout<<" ENTER YOUR CHOICE";
cin>>ch;
}while(ch!=2);
t1.display(head);
break;
case 2:
t1.leafnodes(head);
break;
case 3:
m=t2.mirrorimage(head,m);
cout<<" MIRRORIMAGE TREE LEVELWISE";
height=0;
t2.levelprint(m,height);
break;
case 4:
cout<<" ORIGINAL TREE LEVELWISE ";
t1.levelprint(head,height);
m=t2.mirrorimage(head,m);
cout<<" MIRRORIMAGE TREE LEVELWISE";
```

```
height=0;
t2.levelprint(m,height);
cout<<" HEIGHT OF BINARY TREE="<<height-1;
break;
case 5:cout<<" HEIGHT OF BINARY TREE="<<height-1;
break;
case 6:exit(1);
}
getch();
}while(ch!=6);
return 1;
}
```

8.11 THREADED BINARY TREE

Traversing the binary tree is the most important operation and used in almost every application. The iterative implementation of traversing the binary tree is implemented using either stack (simulation of recursion) or using the threaded binary trees, later being the more efficient. The idea is to maintain extra information of a particular traversal which saves a lot of pushing and popping in stack implementation. This is done by maintaining extra pointer to the leaf nodes (right child in case of right-in threaded binary tree, named on the basis of same) known as thread.

Defination: *"A binary tree is threaded by making all right child pointers that would normally be null point to the inorder successor of the node, and all left child pointers that would normally be null point to the inorder predecessor of the node."*

A threaded binary tree makes it possible to traverse the values in the binary tree via a linear traversal that is more rapid than a recursive in-order traversal.

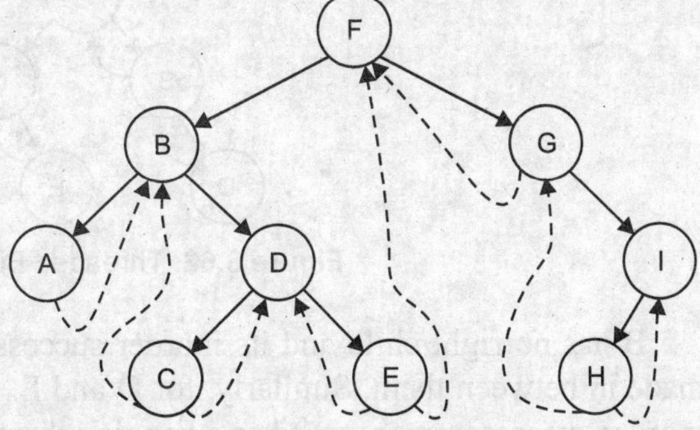

Figure 8.60: A threaded tree, with the special threading links shown by dashed arrows.

It is also possible to discover the parent of a node from a threaded binary tree, without explicit use of parent pointers or a stack, albeit slowly. This can be useful where stack space is limited, or where a stack of parent pointers is unavailable (for finding the parent pointer via DFS).

A Threaded Binary Tree is a binary tree in which every node that does not have a right child has a THREAD (in actual sense, a link) to its INORDER successor. By doing this threading we avoid the recursive method of traversing a Tree, which makes use of stacks and consumes a lot of memory and time.

The node structure for a threaded binary tree varies a bit and its like this —

```
struct NODE
{
 struct NODE *leftchild;
 int node_value;
 struct NODE *rightchild;
 struct NODE *thread;
}
```

Let's make the Threaded Binary tree out of a normal binary tree...

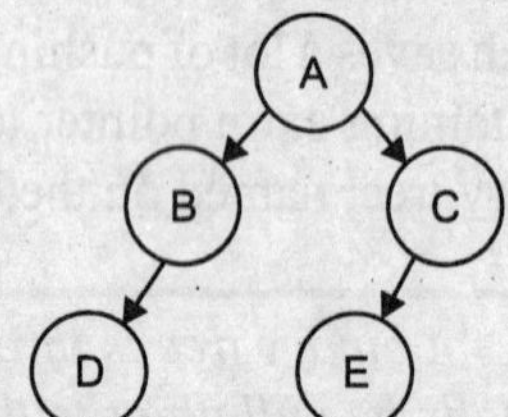

Figure 8.61: Normal binary tree.

The INORDER traversal for the above tree is — **D B A E C**. So, the respective Threaded Binary tree will be —

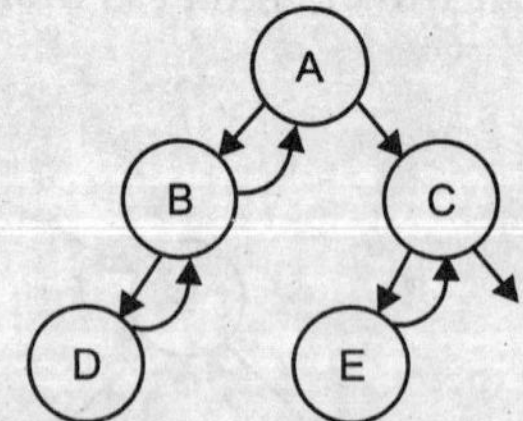

Figure 8.62: Threaded Binary tree.

B has no right child and its inorder successor is A and so a thread has been made in between them. Similarly, for D and E. C has no right child but it has no inorder successor even, so it has a hanging thread. Clear!

Now consider a **Threaded Binary Tree**. This is a tree constructed in such a way that no parent pointers are required. Both child pointers of leaf nodes are set to the node's successor in a pre-order traversal. This greatly simplifies the algorithm and allows us to drop the parent pointers altogether, while not increasing the storage!

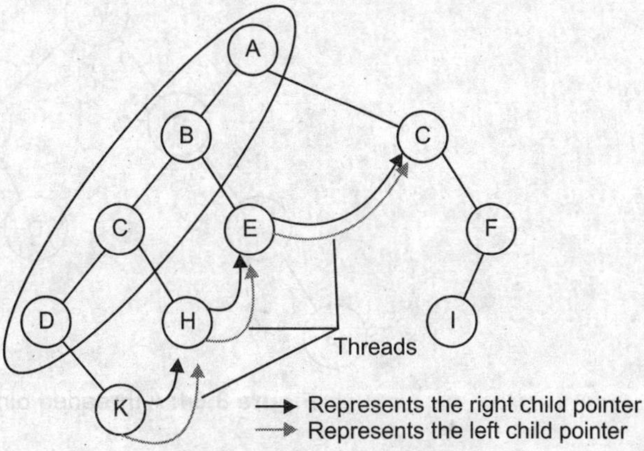

Figure 8.63: Threaded Binary tree.

For a threaded binary tree, then, the algorithm for stackless pre-order traversal given above can be rewritten as follows:

```
p<-root
repeat
while( (left[p] != right[p]) AND (left[p] != null) )
p<-left[p]
visit(p)
if( (left[p] != right[p]) AND (right[p] != null) )
p<-right[p]
visit(p)   //end of 1 phase
if (p=root) exit
else p=left[p]
visit(p)
```

The linked representation of the binary tree discussed in Section 8,5 showed that for a binary tree with n nodes, 2n pointers are required of which (n+1) are null pointers. A.J. Perlis and C. Thornton devised a prudent method to utilize these (n+l) empty pointers, introducing what are called threads. Threads are also links or pointers but replace null pointers by pointing to some useful information in the binary tree, Thus, for a node NODE if RCHILD(NODE) is NIL then the null pointer is replaced by a thread which points to the node which would occur after NODE when the binary tree is traversed in inorder. Again if LCHILD (NODE) is NIL then the null pointer is replaced by a thread to the node which would immediately precede NODE when the binary tree is traversed in inorder.

Inorder Traversal: G F B A D C E

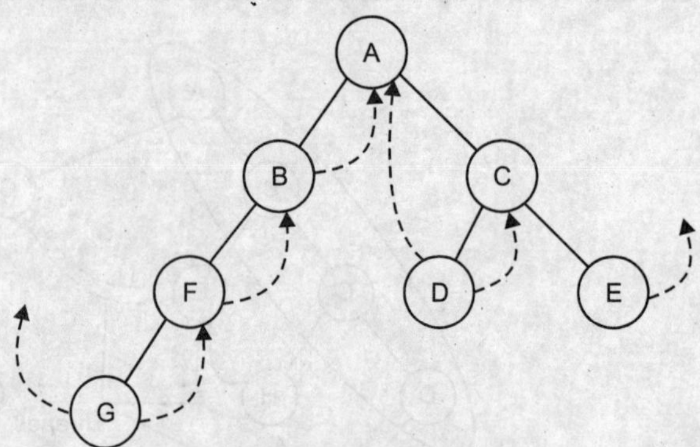

Figure 8.64: A threaded binary tree

Figure 8.64. Illustrates a threaded binary tree. The threads are indicated using broken lines to distinguish them from the normal links indicated with solid lines. The inorder traversal of the binary tree is also shown in the figure.

Note that the Left child of G and the right child of E have threads which are left dangling due to the absence of an inorder predecessor and successor respectively.

There are many ways to thread a binary tree T, corresponding to the specific traversal chosen. In this work, we have the threading correspond to an inorder traversal. Also the threading can be of WA-) representations viz.., one-way threading and two-way threading. One-way threading is where a thread appears only on the RCHILD field of a node, when it is null, pointing to the inorder successor of the node. On the other hand, in two-way threading, which had been introduced above, a thread appears in the LCHILD field also, if it is null, which points to the inorder predecessor of the node. However, the first and the last of the nodes in the inorder traversal will carry dangling threads.

8.11.1 Linked Representation of A Threaded Binary Tree

A linked representation of the threaded binary tree (two-way threading) has a node structure as shown in Figure 8.65.

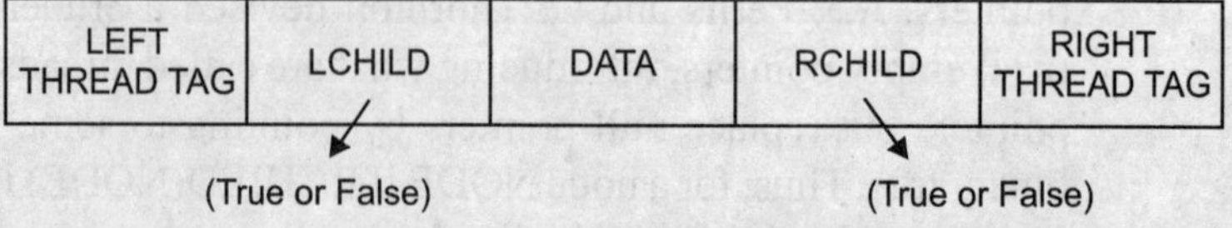

Figure 8.65: Node Structure of a linked representation of a threaded binary free.

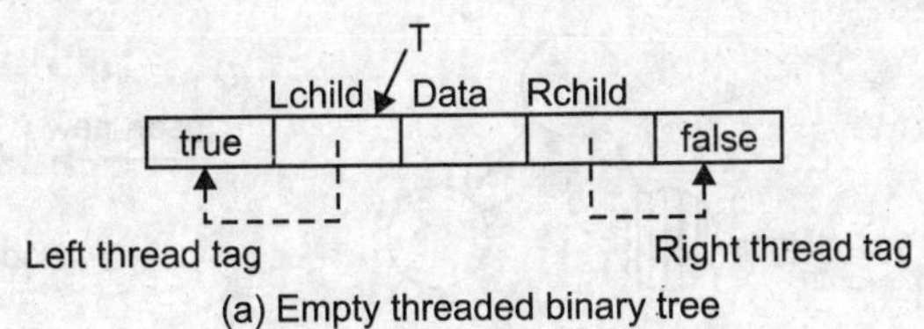

(a) Empty threaded binary tree

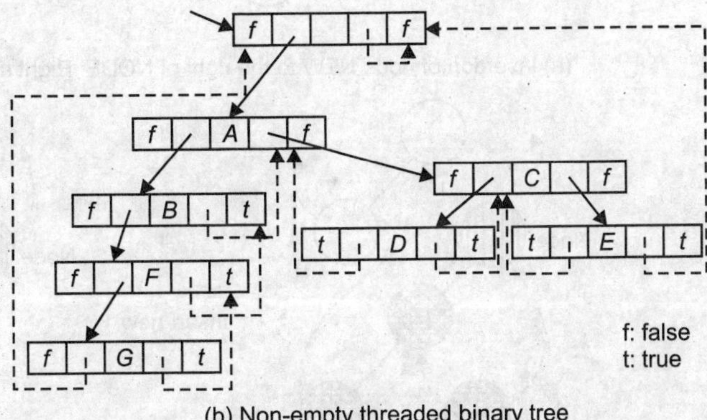

(b) Non-empty threaded binary tree

Figure 8.66: Linked representation of threaded binary trees.

Since the LCHILD and RCHILD fields are utilized to represent both links and threads it becomes essential for the node structure to clearly distinguish between them to avoid confusion while processing the threaded binary tree. Hence it is necessary that the node structure includes two more fields which act as flags to indicate if the LCHILD and RCHILD fields represent a thread or a link.

If the LEFT THREAD TAG or RIGHT THREAD TAG is marked trice then LCHILD and RCHILD fields represent threads otherwise they represent links Also, to tuck in the dangling threads which are bound to arise, the linked representation of a threaded binary tree includes a head node. The dangling threads point to the head node. The head node by convention has its LCHILD pointing to the root node of the threaded binary tree and therefore has its LEFT THREAD TAG set to false. THE RIGHT THREAD TAG field is also set to false but the RCHILD link points to the head node itself. Figure 8.66(a) shows the linked representation of an empty threaded binary tree and Fig. 8.66(b) that of a non-empty threaded binary tree.

8.11.2 Growing Threaded Binary Trees

Here we discuss the insertion of nodes contributing to the growth of threaded binary trees. The insertion of a node calls not only for the realignment of links but also of the threads involved.

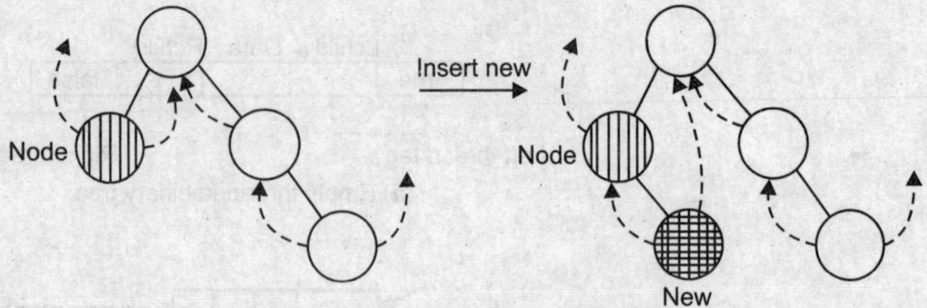

(a) Insertion of node NEW to the right of NODE: Right subtree of NODE is empty

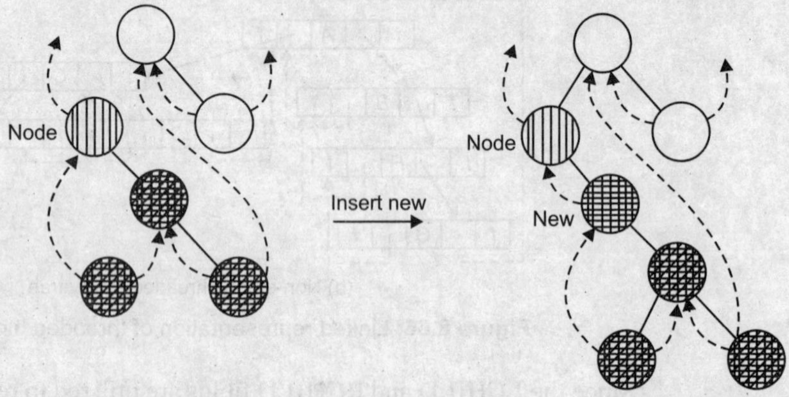

(b) Insertion of node NEW to the right of NODE: Right subtree of NODE is non-empty

Figure 8.67: Insertion of a node in the right subtree of a threaded binary tree.

Consider the case of inserting a node NEW to the right of a node NODE in the threaded binary tree. If the node NODE had no right subtree then the case is trivial, Attach NEW as right child of NODE and appropriately reset the threads (LCHILD and RCHILD) of NEW to point to its inorder predecessor and successor respectively. Figure 8.67(a) illustrates this insertion.

In the next case, if NODE already had a right subtree then attach NEW as the right child of the node NODE and link the previous right subtree of NODE to the right of node NEW When this is done, the threads of the appropriate nodes are reset as shown in Figure 8.67(b).

A similar procedure is followed to insert a node in the left subtree of a threaded binary tree.

8.12 PATH LENGTHS; HUFFMAN'S ALGORITHM

An extended binary tree or 2-tree is a binary tree T in which each node has either 0 or 2 children. The nodes with 0 children are called **external nodes**, and the nodes with 2 children are called **internal nodes**. Figure 8.69 shows a 2-tree where the internal nodes are denoted by circles and the external nodes are denoted by squares.

In any 2-tree, the number $\mathbf{N_E}$ of external nodes is 1 more than the number $\mathbf{N_I}$ of internal nodes; that is,

No. of external nodes (N_E) = No. of internal nodes (N_I) + 1

$$N_E = N_I + 1 = 7.$$

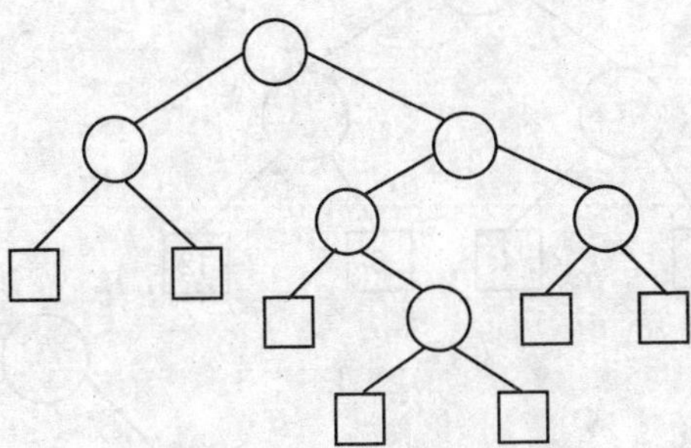

Figure 8.68: Huffman tree.

Frequently, an algorithm can be represented by a 2-tree T where the internal nodes represent tests and the external nodes represent actions. Accordingly, the running time of the algorithm may depend on the lengths of the paths in the tree. With this in mind, we define the external path length L_E of a 2-tree T to be the sum of all path lengths summed over each path from the root R of T to external nodes. For the tree in Figure 8.68.

$$L_E = 2 = 2 + 3 + 4 + 4 + 3 + 3 = 21 \quad \text{and} \quad L_I = 0 + 1 + 1 + 2 + 3 + 2 = 9$$

Observe that

$$L_I + 2n = 9 + 2.\ 6 = 9 + 12 = 21 = L_E$$

Where n = 6 is the number of internal nodes. In fact, the formula

$L_E = L_I + 2n$ is true for any 2-tree with n internal nodes.

Suppose T is a 2-tree with n external nodes, and suppose each of the external nodes is assigned a (nonnegative) weight. The (external) weighted **path length P** of the tree T is defined to be the sum of the weighted path lengths; i.e.

$$P = W_1L_1 + W_2L_2 + \ldots + W_nL_n$$

Where $\mathbf{W_i}$ and $\mathbf{L_i}$ denote, respectively, the weight and path length of an external node N_i.

Consider now the collection of all 2-trees with n external nodes. Clearly, the complete tree among them will have a minimal external path length $\mathbf{L_E}$. On the other hand, suppose each tree is given the same n weights for its external nodes. Then it is not clear which tree will give a minimal weighted path length P.

Example 8.17: Figure 8.69 shows three 2-trees, T_1, T_2 and T_3, each having external nodes with weights 2, 4, 6 and 12. The weighted path lengths of the three trees are as follows:

$$P_1 = 2.\,2 + 4.\,2 + 6.\,2 + 12.\,2 = 48$$
$$P_2 = 2.\,1 + 4.\,3 + 6.\,3 + 12.\,2 = 56$$
$$P_3 = 2.\,3 + 4.\,3 + 6.\,2 + 12.\,1 = 42$$

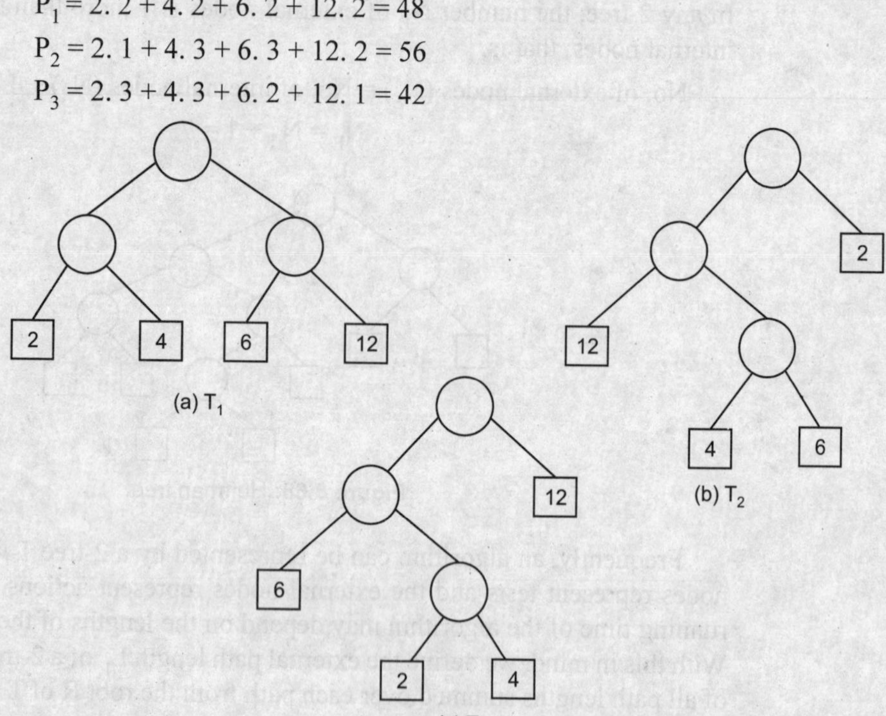

Figure 8.69: 2 trees having weighted nodes.

The quantities P_1 and P_3 indicate that the complete tree need not give a minimum length P, and quantities P_2 and P_3 indicate that similar trees need not give the same lengths. The general problem that we want to solve is as follows. Suppose a list of n weights is given:

$$w_1, w_2, \ldots, w_n$$

Among all the 2-trees with n external nodes and with the given n weights, find a tree T with a minimum-weighted path length. (Such a tree T is seldom unique). Huffman gave an algorithm, which we now state, to find such a tree T.

Observe that the Huffman algorithm is recursively defined in terms of the number of weights and the solution for one weight is simply the tree with one node. On the other hand, in practice, we use an equivalent iterated form of the Huffman algorithm constructing the tree from the bottom up rather that from the top down.

8.12.1 Huffman Algorithm

Suppose w_1 and w_2 are two minimum weights among the n given weights w_1, w_2, …, w_n. Find a tree T' which gives a solution for the n – 1 weights

$$w_{1-} + w_2, w_3, w_4, \ldots, w_n$$

Then, in the tree T', replace the external node

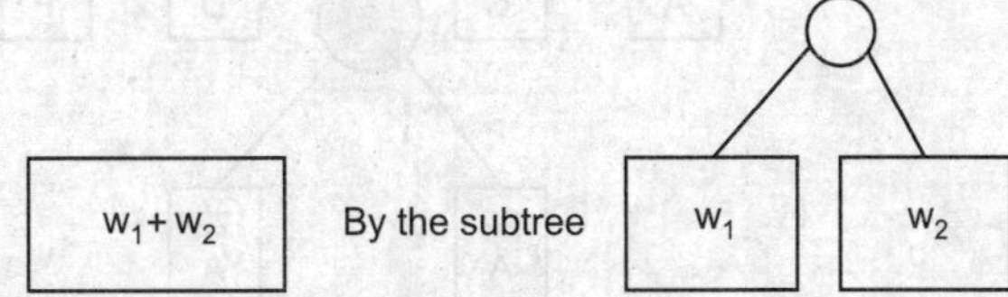

Figure 8.70

The new 2-tree T is the desired solution.

Example 8.18: Suppose A, B, C, D, E, F, G and H are 8 data items, and suppose there are assigned weights as follows:

Data item:	A	B	C	D	E	F	G	H
Weight:	22	5	11	19	2	11	25	5

Figure 8.70(a) through (h) shows how to construct the tree T with minimum-weighted path length using the above data and Huffman's algorithm. We explain each step separately.

(a) Here each data item belongs to its own subtree. Two subtrees with the smallest possible combination of weights, the one weighted 2 and one of those weighted 5, are shaded.

(b) Here to subtrees that were shaded in Figure 8.71(a) are joined together to form a subtree with weight 7. Again, the current two subtrees of lowest weight are shaded.

(c) to (g) Each step joins together two subtrees having the lowest existing weights (always the ones that were shaded in the preceding diagram), and again, the two resulting subtree of lowest weight are shaded.

(h) This is the final desired tree T, formed when the only two remaining subtrees are joined together.

8.12.2 Computer Implementation of Huffman's Algorithm

Consider again the data in Example 8.18. Suppose we want to implement the Huffman algorithm using the computer. First of all, we require an extra array WT to hold the weights of the nodes; i.e., our tree will be maintained by four parallel arrays, INFO, WT, LEFT and RIGHT. Figure 8.71(a) shows how the given data may be stored in the computer initially. Observe that there is sufficient room for the additional nodes. Observe that NULL appears in the left and right pointers for the initial nodes, since these nodes will terminal in the final tree.

22	5	11	19	2	11	25	5
A	B	C	D	E	F	G	H

(a)

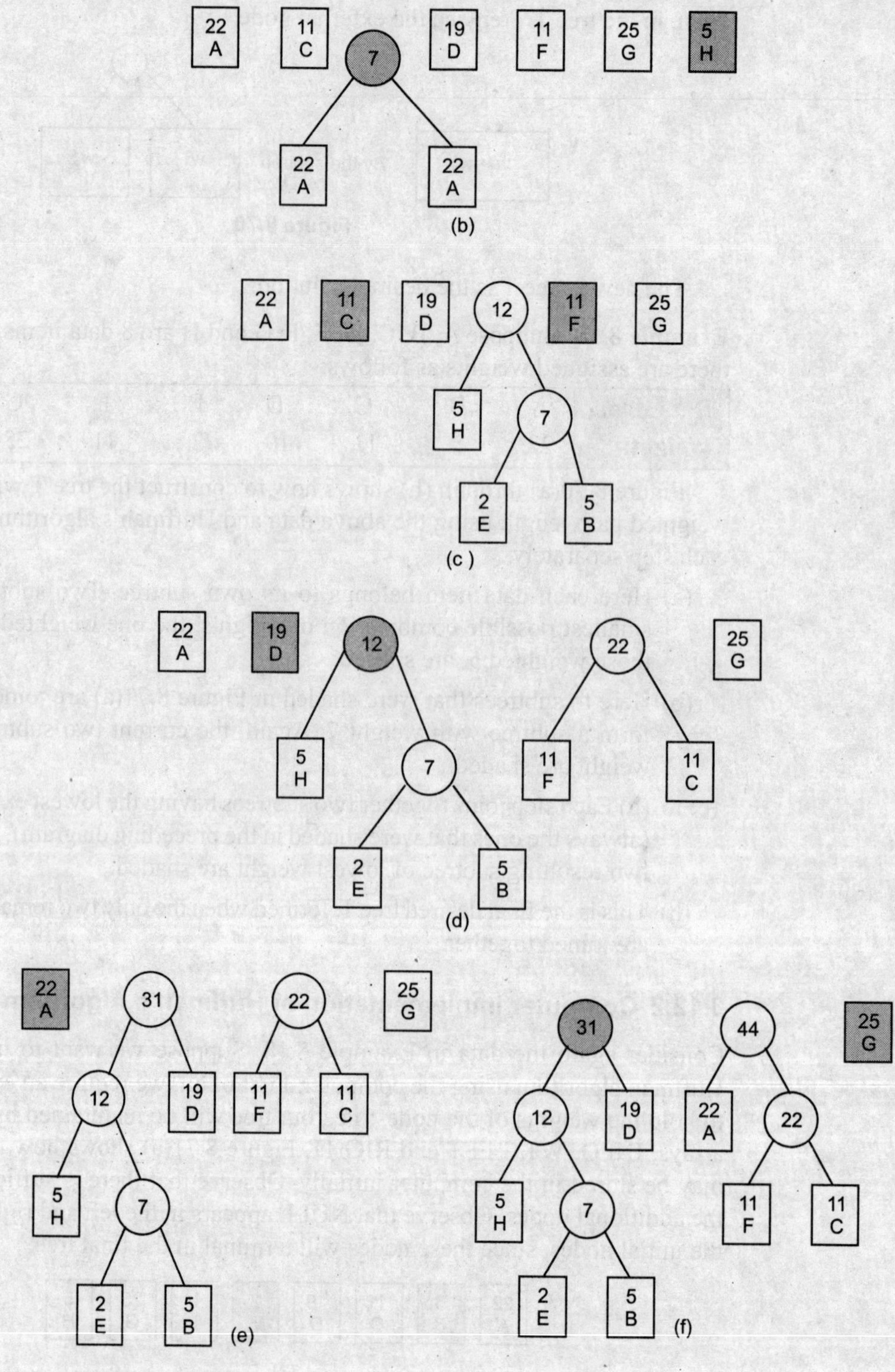
22
A
11
C
7
19
D
11
F
25
G
5
H
22
A
22
A
(b)
22
A
11
C
19
D
12
11
F
25
G
5
H
7
2
E
5
B
(c)
22
A
19
D
12
22
25
G
5
H
7
11
F
11
C
2
E
5
B
(d)
22
A
31
22
25
G
12
19
D
11
F
11
C
5
H
7
2
E
5
B
(e)
31
44
25
G
12
19
D
22
A
22
5
H
7
11
F
11
C
2
E
5
B
(f)

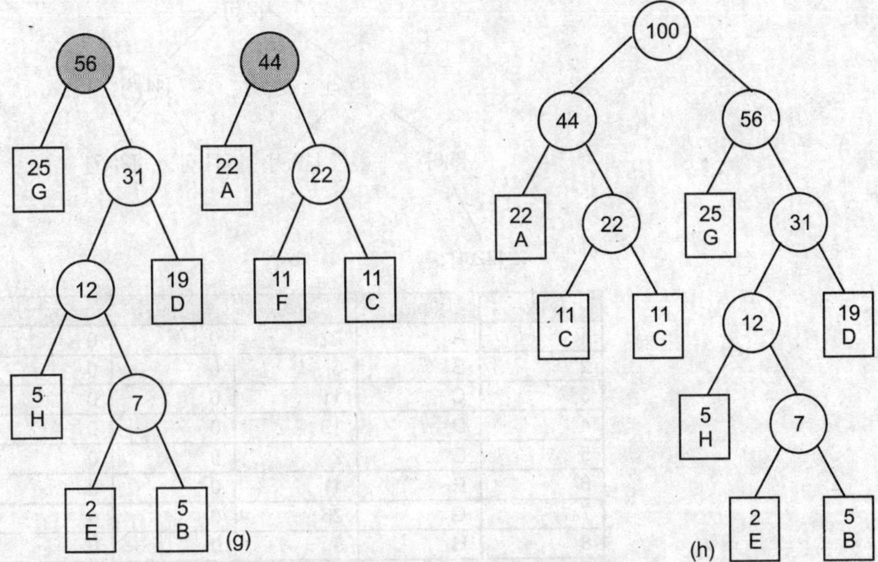

Figure 8.71: Building a Huffman Tree

During the execution of the algorithm, one must be able to keep track of all the different subtrees and one must also be able to find the subtrees with minimum weights. This may be accomplished by maintaining an auxiliary minheap, where each node contains the weight and the location of the root of a current subtree. The initial minheap appears in Figure 8.72(b). (The minheap is used rather than a maxheap since we want the node with the lowest weight to be on the top of the heap.)

S.No.	Info	Wt	Left	Right
1	A	22	0	0
2	B	5	0	0
3	C	11	0	0
4	D	19	0	0
5	E	2	0	0
6	F	11	0	0
7	G	25	0	0
8	H	5	0	0
9			10	
10			11	
11			12	
12			13	
13			14	
14			15	
15			16	
16			0	

AVAIL = 9

(a)

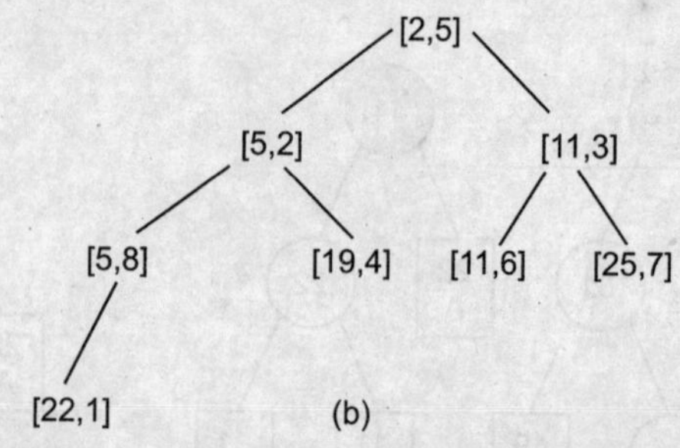

(b)

S.No.	Info	Wt	Left	Right
1	A	22	0	0
2	B	5	0	0
3	C	11	0	0
4	D	19	0	0
5	E	2	0	0
6	F	11	0	0
7	G	25	0	0
8	H	5	0	0
9		7	5	2
10		12	8	9
11		22	6	3
12		31	10	4
13		44	1	11
14		56	7	12
15		100	13	14
16				

ROOT = 15, AVAIL = 16

(c)

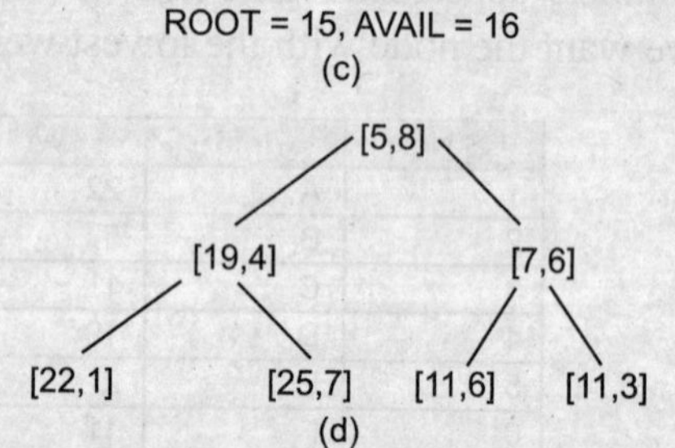

(d)

Figure 8.72: Implementation of Huffman's Algorithm

The first step in building the required Huffman tree T involves the following substeps:

(i) Remove the node N_1 = [2, 5] and the node N_2 = [5, 2] from the heap. (Each time a node is deleted, one must reheap.)

(ii) Use the data in N_1 and N_2 and the first available space AVAIL = 9 to add a new node as follows:

WT[9] = 2 + 5 = 7 LEFT[9] = 5 RIGHT[9] = 2

Thus N_1 is the left child of the new node and N_2 is the right child of the new node.

(iii) Adjoin the weight and location of the new node, that is, [7, 9], to the heap.

The shaded area in Figure 8.72(c) shows the new node, and Figure 8.72(d) shows the new heap, which has one less element than the heap in Figure 8.72(b).

Repeating the above step until the heap is empty, we obtain the required tree T in Figure 8.72(c). We must set ROOT = 15, since this is the location of the last node added to the tree.

OBJECTIVE TYPE QUESTIONS

1. Traversing means
   (a) visiting all the nodes of the list (b) shifting all the nodes at forward
   (c) randomly accessing the elements (d) None of the above
2. Every tree structure must contain
   (a) root node
   (b) either left right branch with root node
   (c) both left and right branches with root
   (d) all of the above
3. When ever no-leaf node in binary tree has filled left and right sub-trees, the tree is called
   (a) strictly binary tree (b) complete binary tree
   (c) binary search tree (d) none of the above
4. The last node of this binary tree contains two branches. Such a tree is called
   (a) strictly binary tree (b) complete binary tree
   (c) extended binary tree (d) None of the above
5. The following sequence of the traversing is called
   Go to the root
   Traverse the left sub-tree
   Traverse the right sub-trees
   (a) inroder (b) postorder
   (c) preorder (d) pre-postorder.
6. The following sequence of the traversing is called
   Traverse the left sub tree in inorder.
   Visit root node.

Traverse the right sub tree in inorder.

(a) inroder (b) postorder

(c) preorder (d) pre-postorder.

7. The following sequence of the traversing is called

Traversing the left sub-tree in postorder style.

Traverse the right sub tree in postorder.

Visit the root node (N).

(a) inroder (b) postorder

(c) preorder (d) pre-postorder.

8. The tree given below is called as

(a) complete tree (b) left-skewed binary tree

(c) right-skewed binary tree (d) None of the above

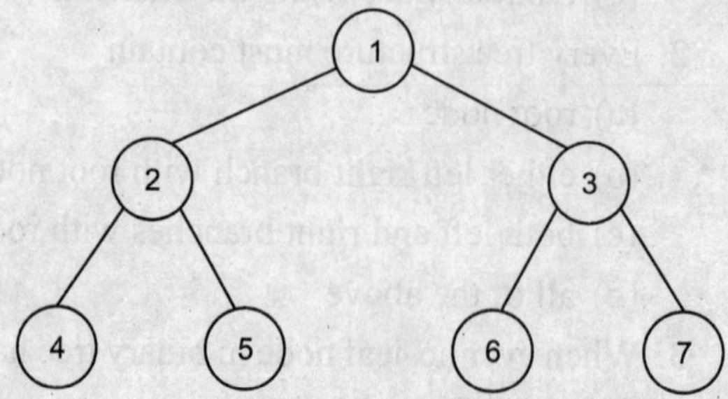

Consider the above figure for the following questions:

9. The tree contains .... level(s).

(a) one (b) zero

(c) two (d) None of the above

10. Degree of the B node is

(a) one (b) two

(c) three (d) None of the above

11. Height of the tree is

(a) two (b) three

(c) four (d) None of the above

12. Siblings of B are

(a) F and G (b) D and E

(c) A and C (d) None of the above

13. If root node 'A' is deleted then the left sub tree contains the elements
    (a) C, F, and G
    (b) B, D, and E
    (c) A, B, and C
    (d) None of the above

EXERCISES

1. What do you mean by general trees?
2. Explain the basic terminology of trees.
3. What is binary tree? Explain binary tree as data storage.
4. Explain different types of binary trees.
5. What do you mean by binary sort trees?
6. Explain binary tree representation: array representation and dynamic representation.
7. Explain the concept of complete trees.
8. What do you understand by extended binary tree?
9. Explain representation of algebraic expressions.
10. Explain how we can represent binary trees in memory.
11. Explain traversing of binary trees: preorder, inorder and postorder.
12. Write an algorithm and C++ for preorder, inoder and postorder traversing.
13. What do you mean by threaded binary tree.
14. Explain linked representation of a threaded binary tree.
15. What do you understand by path lengths?
16. Explain computer implementation of huffman's algorithm.

9 CHAPTER

Search Trees

9.1 GENERAL CONCEPT OF BINARY SEARCH TREE

In computer science, one of the most important data structures is a binary search tree. a binary search tree (BST) is a node based binary tree data structure which has the following properties:

- The left subtree of a node contains only nodes with keys less than the node's key.
- The right subtree of a node contains only nodes with keys greater than the node's key.

Both the left and right subtrees must also be binary search trees. This structure enables one to search for and find an element with an average running time f(n) = $O(\log_2 n)$. It also enables one to easily insert and delete elements. This structure contrasts with the following structures:

(a) Sorted linear array: Here one can search for and find an element with a running time f(n) = $O(\log_2 n)$, but it is expensive to insert and delete elements.

(b) Linked list: Here one can easily insert and delete elements, but it is expensive to search for and find an element, since one must use a linear search with running time f(n) O(n).

Although each node in a binary search tree may contain an entire record of data, the definition of the binary tree depends on a given field whose values are distinct and may be ordered.

Suppose T is a binary tree. Then T is called a binary search tree (or binary sorted tree) if each node N of T has the following property:

- The value at N is greater than every value in the left subtree of N and is less than every value in the right subtree of N. (it is not difficult to see that this property guarantees that the inorder traversal of T will yield a sorted listing of the elements of T.)

Example 9.1

(a) Consider the binary tree T in Figure 9.1. T is a binary search tree; that is, every node N in T exceeds every number in its left subtree and is less than every number in its right subtree. Suppose the 22 were replaced by 33. Then T would still be a binary search tree. On the other hand, suppose the 22 were replaced by 42. Then T would not be a binary search tree, since the 36 would not be greater than the 42 in its left subtree:

(b) Consider the binary search tree T in Figure 9.1(b). A binary search tree of size 9 and depth 3, with root 8 and leaves 1, 4, 7 and 13.

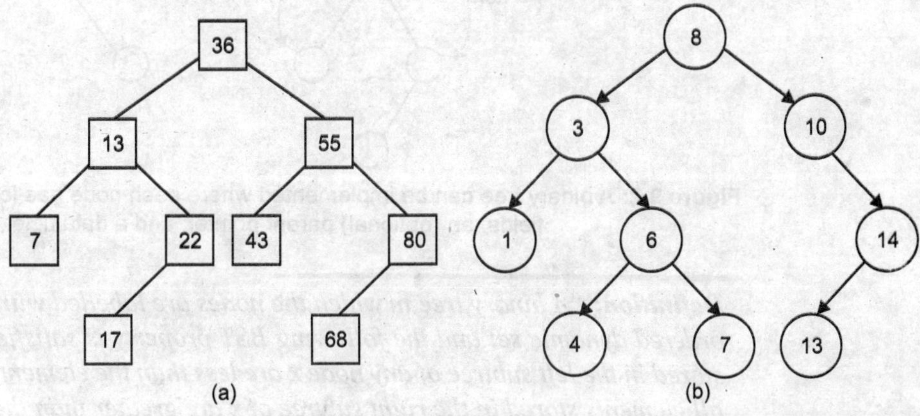

Figure 9.1

The definition of a binary search tree given in this section assumes that all the node values are distinct.

Generally, the information represented by each node is a record rather than a single data element. However, for sequencing purposes, nodes are compared according to their keys rather than any part of their their associated records.

The major advantage of binary search trees over other data structures is that the related sorting algorithms and search algorithms such as in-order traversal can be very efficient. Binary search trees are a fundamental data structure used to construct more abstract data structures such as sets, multisets, and associative arrays.

9.2 BINARY SEARCH TREE

A binary search tree is a data structure whose data elements are organized as a binary tree, with the additional condition that if a node contains a value k, then every node in its left sub-tree contains a value less than k, and every node in its right sub-tree contains a value greater than or equal to k. The above condition implies that every left child must have a key less than its parent, and every right child must have a key greater than or equal to its parent.

A binary tree is a rooted tree where each node contains at most two children. Each child can be identified as either a left or right Child.

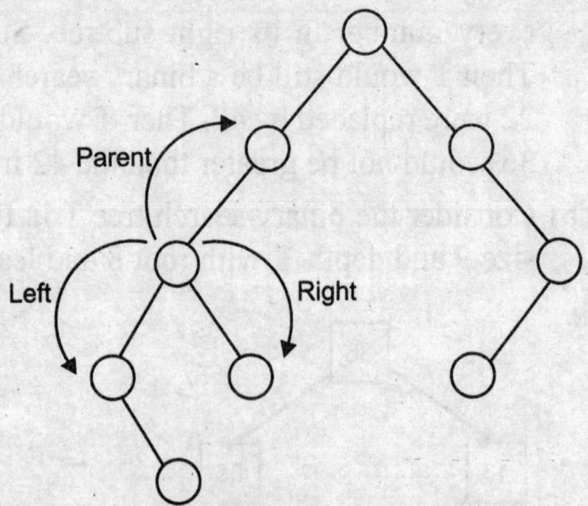

Figure 9.2: A binary tree can be implemented where each node has left and right pointer fields, an (optional) parent pointer, and a data field.

Definition: *"A binary tree in which the nodes are labelled with elements of an ordered dynamic set and the following BST property is satisfied: all elements stored in the left subtree of any node x are less than the element stored at x and all elements stored in the right subtree of x are greater than the element at x."*

Example 9.2: Figure 9.3 shows a binary search tree. Notice that this tree is obtained by inserting the values 13, 3, 4, 12, 14, 10, 5, 1, 8, 2, 7, 9, 11, 6, 18 in that order, starting from an empty tree.

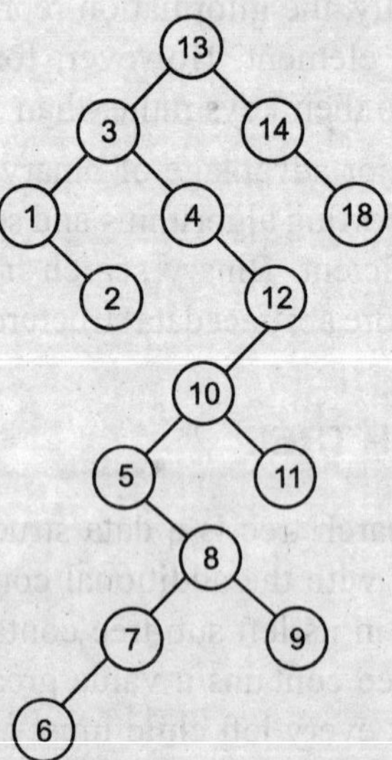

Figure 9.3: An example of a binary search tree

An important consequence of the above property is that an inorder traversal on a binary tree will always visit the vertices of the tree in ascending order.

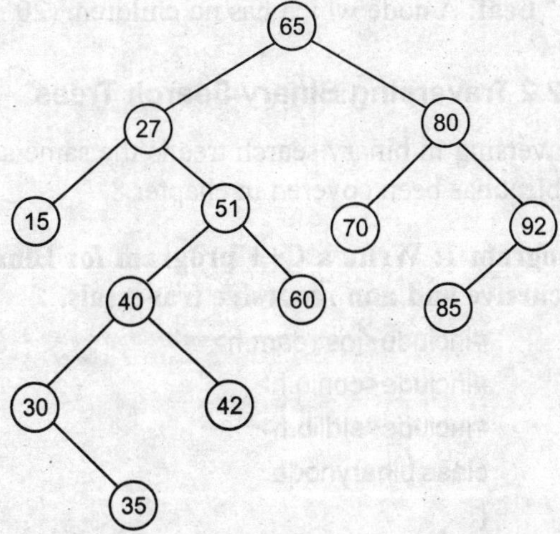

Figure 9.4: Binary search tree

The inorder traversal of the above tree gives the sequence:

15, 27, 30, 35, 40, 42, 51, 60, 65, 70, 80, 85, 92

With reference to the above sequence, the node containing the value 30 is called the inorder successor of the node containing the value 27. If a node has a right sub-tree, its inorder successor is the last left node on this right sub-tree.

9.2.1 Terminology of Binary Search Trees

A typical binary search tree looks like this:

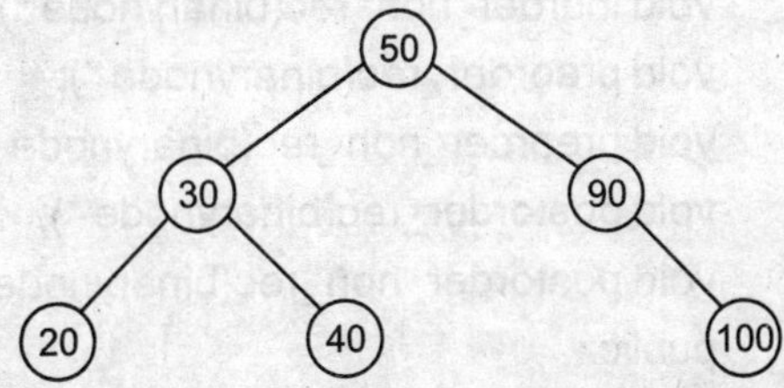

Figure 9.5: Terminology of binary search trees.

Node: Any item that is stored in the tree.

Root: The top item in the tree. (50 in the tree above)

Child: Node(s) under the current node. (20 and 40 are children of 30 in the tree above)

Parent: The node directly above the current node. (90 is the parent of 100 in the tree above)

Leaf: A node which has no children. (20 is a leaf in the tree above)

9.2.2 Traversing Binary Search Trees

Traversing in binary search tree is the same as traversing in any binary tree; this subject has been covered in chapter 8.

Program 1: Write a C++ program for Binary search tree with all the three recursive and non recursive traversals.

```
#include<iostream.h>
#include<conio.h>
#include<stdlib.h>
class binarynode
{
public:
int data;
binarynode *left;
binarynode *right;
};
class binsrctree
{
 private:
binarynode *root;
void inorder_rec(binarynode *);
void inorder_non_rec(binarynode *);
void preorder_rec(binarynode *);
void preorder_non_rec(binarynode *);
void postorder_rec(binarynode *);
void postorder_non_rec(binarynode *);
public:
binsrctree()
{
root=NULL;
}
void insert(int );
void print_inorder_rec();
void print_inorder_non_rec();
```

```
void print_preorder_rec();
void print_preorder_non_rec();
void print_postorder_rec();
void print_postorder_non_rec();
};
class stack
{
int top;
binarynode *stackel[20];
public:
stack()
{
top=-1;
}
void push(binarynode *);
binarynode* pop();
int empty()
{
if(top==-1)
return(1);
return(0);
}
};
void stack::push(binarynode *node)
{
stackel[++top]=node;
}
binarynode *stack::pop()
{
return(stackel[top--]);
}
class stack_int
{
int top;
int stack_int[20];
public:
stack_int()
{
```

```
top=-1;
}
void push(int flag);
int pop();
int empty_int()
{
if(top==-1)
return(1);
return(0);
}
};
void stack_int::push(int flag)
{
stack_int[++top]=flag;
}
int stack_int::pop()
{
return(stack_int[top--]);
}
/*------------------------------------------------------------------*/
/* FUNCTION TO INSERT A NODE IN THE TREE */
/*------------------------------------------------------------------*/
void binsrctree::insert(int val)
{
binarynode *temp,*prev,*curr;
temp=new binarynode;
temp->data=val;
temp->left=temp->right=NULL;
if(root==NULL)
{
root=temp;
}
else
{
curr=root;
while(curr!=NULL)
{
```

```
prev=curr;
if(temp->data<curr->data)
curr=curr->left;
else
curr=curr->right;
}
if(temp->data<prev->data)
prev->left=temp;
else
prev->right=temp;
}
}
/* ----------------------------------------------*/
/*INORDER RECURSIVE TRAVERSAL*/
/*----------------------------------------------*/
void binsrctree::inorder_rec(binarynode *root)
{
if(root!=NULL)
{
inorder_rec(root->left);
cout<<root->data<<" ";
inorder_rec(root->right);
}
}
/*----------------------------------------------*/
/*INORDER NON RECURSIVE TRAVERSAL*/
/*----------------------------------------------*/
void binsrctree::inorder_non_rec(binarynode *root)
{
stack stk;
binarynode *temp;
if(root!=NULL)
{
temp=root;
do
{
while(temp!=NULL)
{
```

```
stk.push(temp);
temp=temp->left;
}/*end while*/
if(!stk.empty())
{
temp=stk.pop();
cout<<temp->data<<"   ";
temp=temp->right;
}/*end if*/
else
break;
}while(1); /*end do while*/
}/* end if */
else
cout<<"
Empty tree";
} /*end function */
/*-------------------------------------------------*/
/*PREORDER RECURSIVE TRAVERSAL */
/*-------------------------------------------------*/
void binsrctree::preorder_rec(binarynode *root)
{
if(root!=NULL)
{
cout<<root->data<<" ";
preorder_rec(root->left);
preorder_rec(root->right);
}
}
/*-------------------------------------------------*/
/*PREORDER NON RECURSIVE TRAVERSAL */
/*-------------------------------------------------*/
void binsrctree::preorder_non_rec(binarynode *root)
{
stack stk;
binarynode *temp=root;
stk.push(temp);
while(!stk.empty())
```

```
{
temp=stk.pop();
if(temp!=NULL)
{
cout<<temp->data<<"            ";
stk.push(temp->right);
stk.push(temp->left);
}
}
}
/*-------------------------------------------------*/
/*POSTRDER RECURSIVE TRAVERSAL */
/*-------------------------------------------------*/
void binsrctree::postorder_rec(binarynode *root)
{
if(root!=NULL)
{
postorder_rec(root->left);
postorder_rec(root->right);
cout<<root->data<<" ";
}
}
/*-------------------------------------------------*/
/*POSTORDER NON RECURSIVE TRAVERSAL */
/*-------------------------------------------------*/
void binsrctree::postorder_non_rec(binarynode *root)
{
stack stk;
stack_int stk1;
int flag;
binarynode *temp=root;
do
{
if(temp!=NULL)
{
stk.push(temp);
stk1.push(1);
temp=temp->left;
```

```
}
else
{
if(stk.empty())
break;
temp=stk.pop();
flag=stk1.pop();
if(flag==2)
{
cout<<temp->data;
temp=NULL;
} /*end if */
else
{
stk.push(temp);
stk1.push(2);
temp=temp->right;
} /* end else */
} /* end if */
}while(1);/*end do while*/
}/*end function*/
/*-----------------------------------------------*/
/*FUNCTION TO PRINT INORDER RECURSIVE TRAVERSAL */
/*-----------------------------------------------*/
void binsrctree::print_inorder_rec()
{
cout<<" ";
inorder_rec(root);
cout<<" ";
}
/*-----------------------------------------------*/
/*FUNCTION TO PRINT INORDER NON RECURSIVE TRAVERSAL */
/*-----------------------------------------------*/
void binsrctree::print_inorder_non_rec()
{
cout<<" ";
inorder_non_rec(root);
cout<<" ";
```

```
}
/*----------------------------------------------*/
/*FUNCTION TO PRINT PREORDER RECURSIVE TRAVERSAL */
/*----------------------------------------------*/
void binsrctree::print_preorder_rec()
{
cout<<" ";
preorder_rec(root);
cout<<" ";
}
/*----------------------------------------------*/
/*FUNCTION TO PRINT PREORDER NON RECURSIVE TRAVERSAL */
/*----------------------------------------------*/
void binsrctree::print_preorder_non_rec()
{
cout<<" ";
preorder_non_rec(root);
cout<<" ";
}
/*----------------------------------------------*/
/*FUNCTION TO PRINT POSTORDER RECURSIVE TRAVERSAL */
/*----------------------------------------------*/
void binsrctree::print_postorder_rec()
{
cout<<" ";
postorder_rec(root);
cout<<" ";
}
/*----------------------------------------------*/
/*FUNCTION TO PRINT POSTORDER NON RECURSIVE TRAVERSAL
*/
/*----------------------------------------------*/
void binsrctree::print_postorder_non_rec()
{
cout<<" ";
postorder_non_rec(root);
cout<<" ";
}
```

```
/*-----------------------------------------------*/
/* MAIN FUNCTION */
/*-----------------------------------------------*/
void main()
{
binsrctree BST;
int ch,element;
clrscr();
do
{
cout<<"1.Insert a node in binary tree";
cout<<"2.Recursive Inorder traversal";
cout<<"3.Non Recursive Inorder traversal";
cout<<"4.Recursive preorder traversal";
cout<<"5.Non recursive preorder traversal";
cout<<"6.Recursive postorder traversal";
cout<<"7.Non recursive postorder traversal";
cout<<"8.Exit";
cout<<"Enter your choice";
cin>>ch;
switch(ch)
{
case 1:
cout<<" Enter the element you wnat to insert";
cin>>element;
BST.insert(element);
break;
case 2:
cout<<" Recursive Inorder traversal";
BST.print_inorder_rec();
break;
case 3:
cout<<"NonRecursive Inorder traversal";
BST.print_inorder_non_rec();
break;
case 4:
cout<<"Recursive preorder traversal";
```

```
BST.print_preorder_rec();
break;
case 5:
cout<<"Non recursive preorder traversal ";
BST.print_preorder_non_rec();
break;
case 6:
cout<<" Recursive postorder traversal";
BST.print_postorder_rec();
break;
case 7:
cout<<"Non recursive postorder traversal";
BST.print_postorder_non_rec();
break;
case 8:
exit(1);
}
}while(ch<8);
}
```

For example

Enter the tree t1 elements: 3 2 4

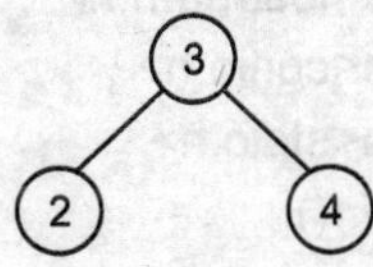

The preorder of the t1 is

3 2 4

The inorder of the t1 is

2 3 4

The post order of the t1 is 2 4 3

9.3 OPERATIONS PERFORMED ON BINARY SEARCH TREE

The important operations on a binary search tree are:

1. Searching and Inserting an item to a binary search tree
2. Deleting an item from a binary search tree
3. Computing the minimum and maximum values in a binary search tree

9.3.1 Searching and Inserting an Item to A Binary Search Tree

To search for an item in a binary tree:

1. Start at the root node
2. If the item that you are searching for is less than the root node, move to the left child of the root node, if the item that you are searching for is more than the root node, move to the right child of the root node and if it is equal to the root node, then you have found the item that you are looking for.
3. Now check to see if the item that you are searching for is equal to, less than or more than the new node that you are on. Again if the item that you are searching for is less than the current node, move to the left child, and if the item that you are searching for is greater than the current node, move to the right child.
4. Repeat this process until you find the item that you are looking for or until the node doesn't have a child on the correct branch, in which case the tree doesn't contain the item which you are looking for.

Program 2: Write a C++ program to search an element from the binary search tree.

Binary Search is a good searching algorithm and also Fast in processing. Here you have to input sorted number in an array first then find out the number

```
//Binary Searching
#include<iostream.h>
#include<conio.h>
#include<stdio.h>
void main()
{
clrscr();
int l_v=1;
int h_v;
int a[51];
int middle;
int num,i=0;
cout<<"Input your sorted num : ";
while((cin>>a[i])!=EOF)
i++;
h_v=i;
cout<<"The input numbers are :";
i=0;
```

```
while(i<h_v)
{
cout<<a[i]<<endl;
i++;
}
getch();
cout<<"Input your searching number : ";
cin>>num;
for(int n=0;a[middle]!=num;n++)
{
middle = (l_v + h_v)/2;
if(a[middle]>num)
h_v = middle - 1;
else if(a[middle]<num)
l_v = middle + 1;
else if(a[middle]==num)
cout<<"Found your number in "<<middle+1<<" position.";
}
cout<<"This program's loop is executed "<<n<<" times to find out the number.";
getch();
}
```

Example 9.3

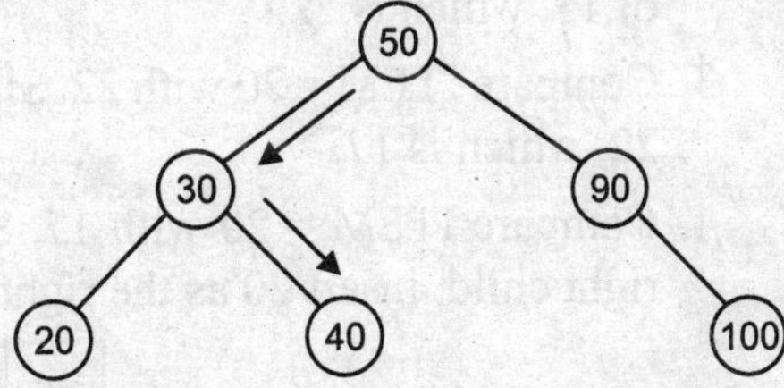

Figure 9.6: Searching the node 40.

For example, to find the node 40...

1. The root node is 50, which is greater than 40, so you go to 50's left child.
2. 50's left child is 30, which is less than 40, so you next go to 30's right child.
3. 30's right child is 40, so you have found the item that you are looking for.

9.3.2 Algorithm for Searching and Inserting in Binary Search Trees

Suppose T is a binary search tree. This section discusses the basic operations of searching and inserting with respect to T. In fact, the searching and inserting will be given by a single search and insertion algorithm. The operation of deleting is treated in the next section.

Suppose an ITEM of information is given. The following algorithm finds the location of ITEM in the binary search tree T, or inserts ITEM as a new node in its appropriate place in the tree.

(a) Compare ITEM with the root node N of the tree.
  (i) If ITEM < N, proceed to the left child of N.
  (ii) If ITEM > N, proceed to the right child of N.

(b) Repeat Step (a) until one of the following occurs:
  (i) We meet a node N such that ITEM = N. In this case the search is successful.
  (ii) We meet an empty subtree, which indicates that the search is unsuccessful, and we insert ITEM in place of the empty subtree.

In other words, proceed from the root R down through the tree T until finding ITEM in T or inserting ITEM as a terminal node in T.

Example 9.4

(a) Consider the binary search tree T in Figure 9.7. Suppose ITEM = 20 is given. Simulating the above algorithm, we obtain the following steps:

1. Compare ITEM = 20 with the root, 36, of the tree T. Since 20 < 36, proceed to the left child of 36, which is 13.
2. Compare ITEM = 20 with 13. Since 20 > 13, proceed to the right child of 13, which is 22.
3. Compare ITEM = 20 with 22. Since 20 < 22, proceed to the left child of 22, which is 17.
4. Compare ITEM = 20 with 17. Since 20 > 17 and 17 does not have a right child, insert 20 as the right child of 17.

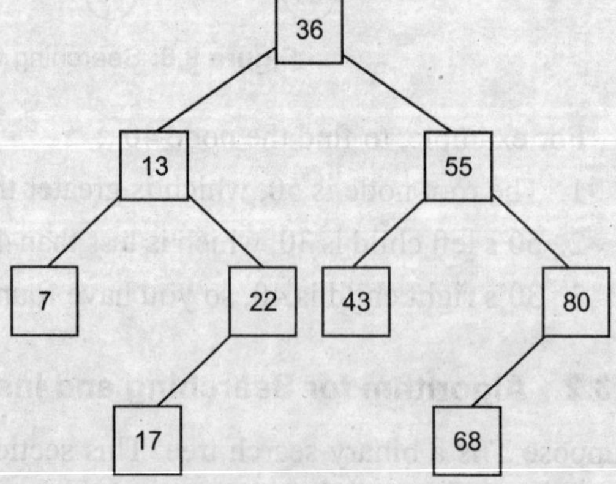

Figure 9.7: Before Inserting the new node 20.

Figure 9.8 shows the new tree with ITEM = 20 inserted. The shaded edges indicate the path down through the tree during the algorithm.

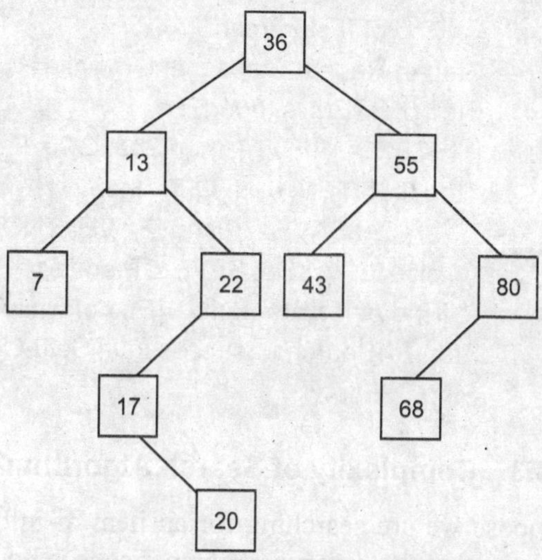

Figure 9.8: After insertion of new node 20.

Algorithm 9.1: To find the location LOC of ITEM in tree T and also find the PARENT location of the ITEM.

FINDLOC(INFO, LEFTNOD, RIGHTNOD, ROOTNOD, ITEM, LOC, PARENT)

Suppose a binary search tree T is in memory and an ITEM of information is given. This algorithm finds the location LOC of ITEM in tree T and also the PARENT location of the ITEM.

There are three special cases:

(i) LOC = NULL and PARENT = NULL will tell that the tree is empty.

(ii) LOC ≠ NULL and PARENT = NULL will tell that ITEM is the ROOTNOD of T.

(iii) LOC = NULL and PARENT ≠ NULL will tell that ITEM is not in T and can be added to T as a child of the node N with location PARENT.

Step 1: [Tree is empty?]
If ROOTNOD = NULL, then Set LOC = NULL and PARENT = NULL, and Return.

Step 2: [ITEM is at ROOTNOD?]
If ITEM = INFO[ROOTNOD], then Set LOC = ROOTNOD and PARENT = NULL, and return.

Step 3: [Initialize pointers P and SAVE.]
If ITEM < INFO[ROOTNOD], then

```
        Set P = LEFTNOD[ROOTNOD] and SAVE = ROOTNOD.
    else     Set P = RIGHTNOD[ROOTNOD] and SAVE = ROOTNOD.
    [End of If statement.]
Step 4: Repeat Steps 5 and 6 while P ≠ NULL.
Step 5: [ITEM is found?]
    If ITEM = INFO[P], then Set LOC = P and PARENT = SAVE and Return.
Step 6: If ITEM < INFO[P], then
        Set SAVE = P and P = LEFTNOD[P].
    else        Set SAVE = P and P = RIGHTNOD[P].
    [End of If statement.]  [End of while loop.]
Step 7: [Search unsuccessful.] Set LOC = NULL and PARENT = SAVE.
Step 8: End.
```

9.3.3 Complexity of Search Algorithm

Suppose we are searching for an item of information in a binary search tree T. observe that the number of comparisons is bounded by the depth of the tree. This comes from the fact that we proceed down a single path of the tree. Accordingly, the running time of the search will be proportional to the depth of the tree.

Suppose we are given n data items, $A_1, A_2, ... A_N,$ and suppose the items are inserted in order into a binary search tree T. Recall that there are n! permutation of the n items. Each such permutation will give rise to corresponding tree. It can be shown that the average depth of the n! trees is approximately $c \log_2 n$, where c = 1.4.

Accordingly, the average running time f(n) to search for an item in a binary tree T with n elements is proportional to $\log_2 n$, that is, $f(n) = O(\log_2 n)$.

Example 9.5: Suppose the following six numbers are inserted in order into an empty binary search tree:

40, 60, 50, 33, 55, 11

Figure 9.9 shows the six stages of the tree. We emphasize that if the six numbers were given in a different order, then the tree might be different and we might have a different depth.

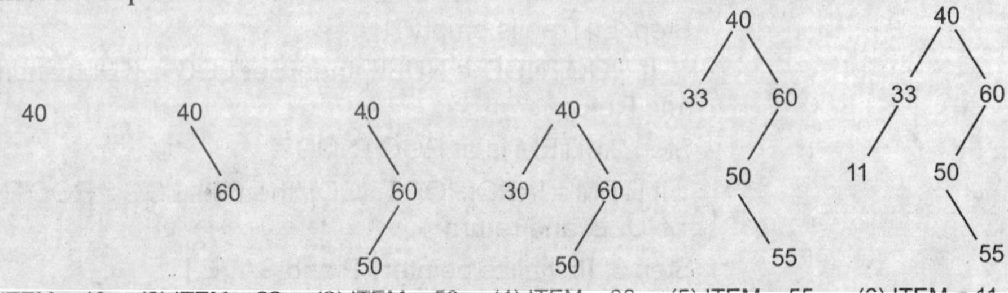

Figure 9.9: Creation of Binary search tree.

The formal presentation of our search and insertion algorithm will use the following procedure, which finds the locations of a given ITEM and its parent. The procedure traverses down the tree using the pointer P and the pointer SAVE for the parent node. This procedure will also be used in the next section, on deletion.

Observe that, in Step 6, we move to the left child or the right child according to whether

ITEM < INFO[P] or ITEM > INFO[P].

The formal statement of our search and insertion algorithm follows.

Example: Inserting an Item to a Binary Search Tree

1. To add an item, you first must search through the tree to find the position that you should put it in. You do this following the steps above.
2. When you reach a node which doesn't contain a child on the correct branch, add the new node there.

Example 9.6

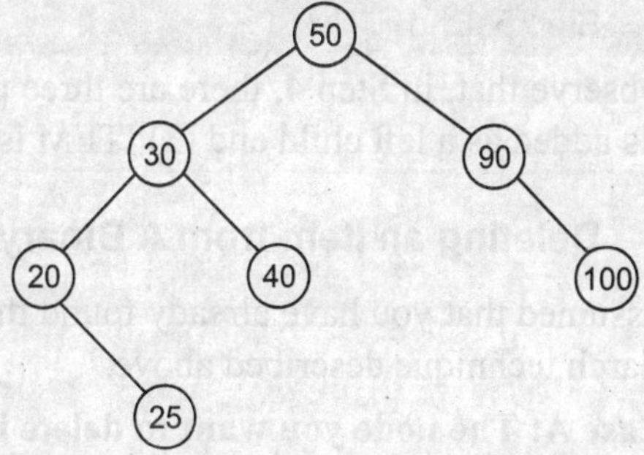

Figure 9.10: Addition of new node 25 in a binary search tree.

For example, to add the node 25...

1. The root node is 50, which is greater than 25, so you go to 50's left child.
2. 50's left child is 30, which is greater than 25, so you go to 30's left child.
3. 30's left child is 20, which is less than 25, so you go to 20's right child.
4. 20's right child doesn't exist, so you add 25 there.

Algorithm 9.2: INSBST(INFO, LEFTNOD, RIGHTNOD, ROOTNOD, AVAIL, ITEM, LOC)

Suppose a binary search tree T is in memory and an ITEM of information is given. This algorithm finds the location LOC of ITEM in T and inserts an ITEM as a new node in tree T at location LOC.

```
Step 1: Call FINDLOC(INFO, LEFTNOD, RIGHTNOD, ROOTNOD, ITEM,
LOC, PARENT).
Step 2: If LOC ≠ NULL, then End.
Step 3: [Copy ITEM into new node in AVAIL list.]
   (a) If AVAIL = NULL, then Write: OVERFLOW, and End.
   (b) Set NEW = AVAIL, AVAIL = LEFTNOD[AVAIL] and
    INFO[NEW] = NULL.
Step 4: [Add ITEM to tree.]
   If PARENT = NULL, then:
   Set ROOTNOD = NEW
   Else if ITEM < INFO[PARENT], then:
   Set LEFTNOD[PARENT] = NEW.
   Else
   Set RIGHTNOD[PARENT] = NEW.
[End of If statement.]
Step 5: End.
```

Observe that, in Step 4, there are three possibilities: (a) the tree is empty, (2) Item is added as a left child and (3) ITEM is added as a right child.

9.3.4 Deleting an Item from A Binary Search Tree

It is assumed that you have already found the node that you want to delete, using the search technique described above.

Case A: The node you want to delete is a leaf

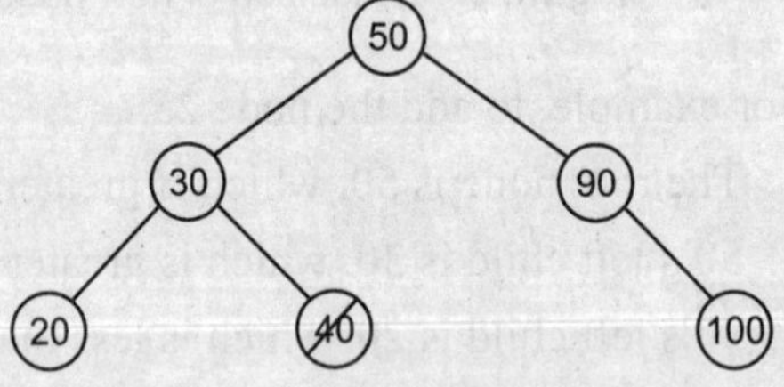

Figure 9.11: Delete the leaf node 40.

For example, do delete 40...

- Simply delete the node!

Example 9.7: Consider the binary search tree in Figure 9.12(a). Suppose T appears in memory as in Figure 9.12(b).

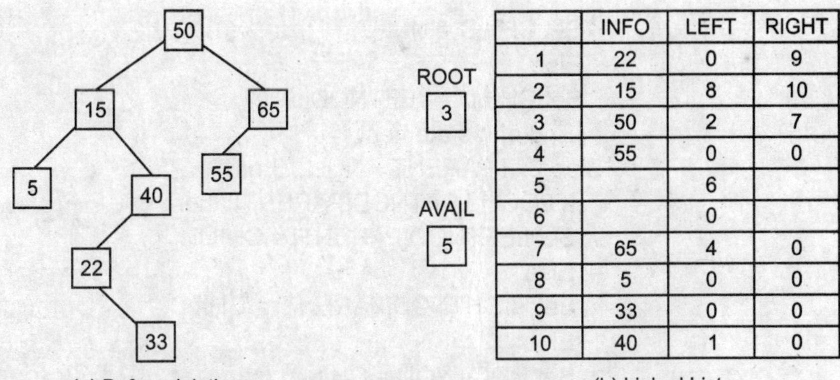

	INFO	LEFT	RIGHT
1	22	0	9
2	15	8	10
3	50	2	7
4	55	0	0
5		6	
6		0	
7	65	4	0
8	5	0	0
9	33	0	0
10	40	1	0

(a) Before deletions (b) Linked List

Figure 9.12: Binary search tree T.

(a) Suppose we delete node 33 from the tree T in Figure 9.12. Note that node 33 has no children. Figure 9.13(a) pictures the tree after 33 is deleted, and Figure 9.13(b) shows the linked representation in memory. The deletion is accomplished by simply assigning NULL to the parent node, 22. (The shading indicates the changes.)

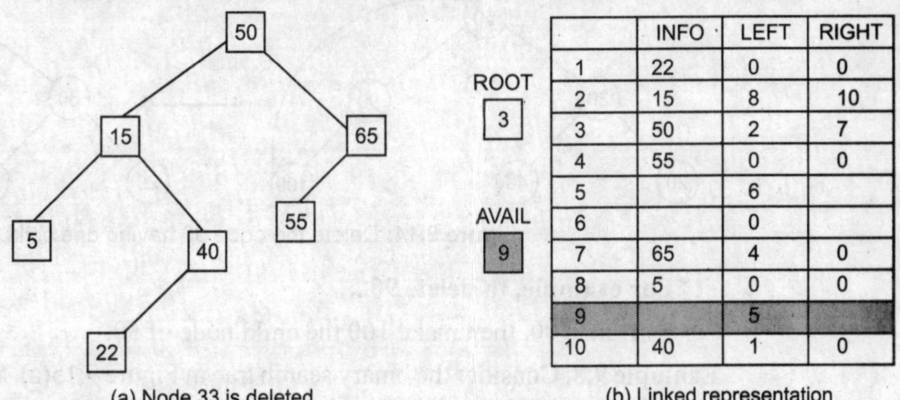

	INFO	LEFT	RIGHT
1	22	0	0
2	15	8	10
3	50	2	7
4	55	0	0
5		6	
6		0	
7	65	4	0
8	5	0	0
9		5	
10	40	1	0

(a) Node 33 is deleted (b) Linked representation

Figure 9.13: After deletion of node 33.

Algorithm 9.3: CASEA (INFO, LEFTNOD, RIGHTNOD, ROOTNOD, LOC, PARENT)

This algorithm deletes the node N at location LOC, where N does not have two children.

Two pointers are used to delete the node N.

First, pointer PARENT gives the location of the PARENT of N, or else PARENT = NULL indicates that N is the ROOTNOD node.

Second, pointer CHILD gives the location of the only child of N, or else CHILD = NULL indicates N has no children.

Step 1: [Initializes CHILD.]

If LEFTNOD[LOC] = NULL and RIGHTNOD[LOC] = NULL, then

```
Set CHILD = NULL.
Else
Set CHILD = LEFTNOD[LOC].
[End of If statement.]
Step 2: If PARENT ≠ NULL, then:
  If LOC = LEFTNOD[PARENT], then:
  Set LEFTNOD[PARENT] = CHILD.
  Else
  Set RIGHTNOD[PARENT] = CHILD.
  Else
  Set ROOTNOD = CHILD.
  [End of If statement.]
Step 3: End.
```

Case B: The node you want to delete has one child

1. Directly connect the child of the node that you want to delete, to the parent of the node that you want to delete.

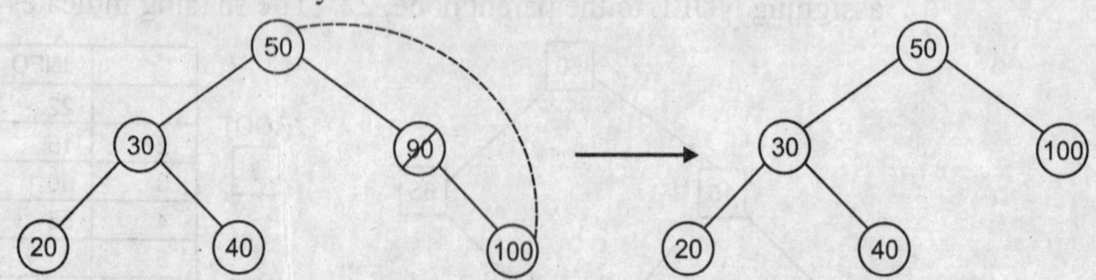

Figure 9.14: Delete the node 90 having one child.

For example, to delete 90...

- Delete 90, then make 100 the child node of 50.

Example 9.8: Consider the binary search tree in Figure 9.15(a). Suppose T appears in memory as in Figure 9.15(b).

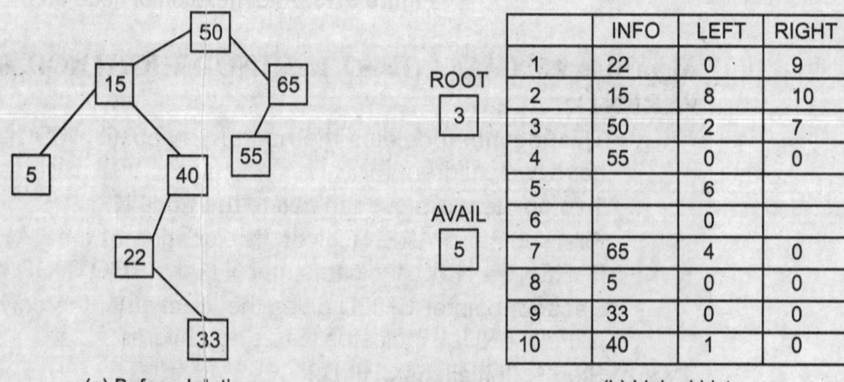

	INFO	LEFT	RIGHT
1	22	0	9
2	15	8	10
3	50	2	7
4	55	0	0
5		6	
6		0	
7	65	4	0
8	5	0	0
9	33	0	0
10	40	1	0

(a) Before deletions (b) Linked List

Figure 9.15: Binary search tree T.

(b) Suppose we delete node 65 from the tree T in Figure 9.15 instead of node 33. Note that node 65 has only one child. Figure 9.16(a) pictures the tree after 65 is deleted, and Figure 9.16(b) shows the linked representation. The deletion is accomplished by changing the right pointer of the parent node 50, which originally pointed to 65, so that it now points to node 55, the only child of 65. (The shading indicates the changes.)

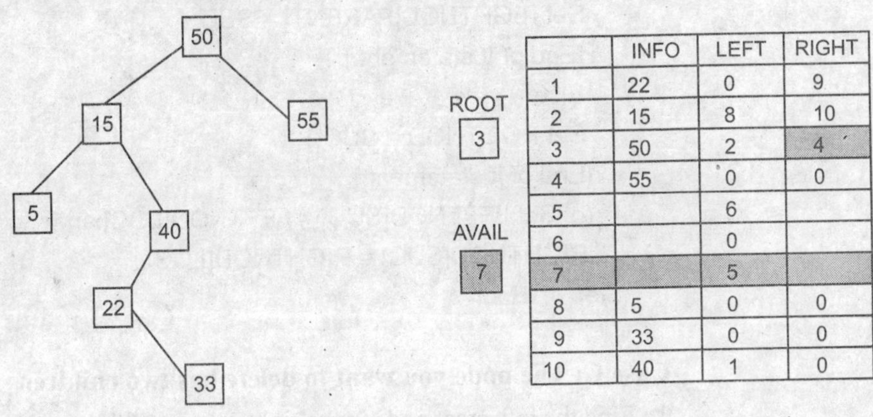

	INFO	LEFT	RIGHT
1	22	0	9
2	15	8	10
3	50	2	4
4	55	0	0
5		6	
6		0	
7		5	
8	5	0	0
9	33	0	0
10	40	1	0

(a) Node 65 is deleted (b) Linked representation

Figure 9.16: After deletion of node 65.

Algorithm 9.4: CASEB(INFO, LEFTNOD, RIGHTNOD, ROOTNOD, LOC, PARENT)

This procedure will delete the node N at location LOC, where N has two children.

Two pointers are used to delete the node N.

First, pointer PARENT gives the location of the PARENT of N, or else PARENT = NULL indicates that N is the ROOTNOD node.

Second, pointer SUC gives the location of the inorder successor of N, and PARENTSUC gives the location of the PARENT of the inorder successor.

Step 1: [Find SUC and PARENTSUC.]

(a) Set P = RIGHTNOD[LOC] and SAVE = LOC.

(b) Repeat while LEFTNOD[P] ≠ NULL.

Set SAVE = P and P = LEFTNOD[P].

[End of loop.]

(c) Set SUC = P and PARENTSUC = SAVE.

Step 2: [Delete inorder successor, using Procedure 7.6.]

Call CASEA(INFO, LEFTNOD, RIGHTNOD, ROOTNOD, SUC, PARENTSUC).

```
Step 3: [Replace node N by its inorder successor.]
    (a) If PARENT ≠ NULL, then
    If LOC = LEFTNOD[PARENT], then
    Set LEFTNOD[PARENT]= SUC.
    Else
    Set RIGHTNOD[PARENT] = SUC.
    [End of If statement.]
    Else
    Set ROOTNOD = SUC.
   [End of If statement.]
   (b) Set LEFTNOD[SUC] = LEFTNOD[LOC] and
   RIGHTNOD[SUC] = RIGHTNOD[LOC].
Step 4: End.
```

Case C: The node you want to delete has two children

1. Find the left-most node in the right subtree of the node being deleted. (After you have found the node you want to delete, go to its right node, then for every node under that, go to its left node until the node has no left node) From now on, this node will be known as the successor.

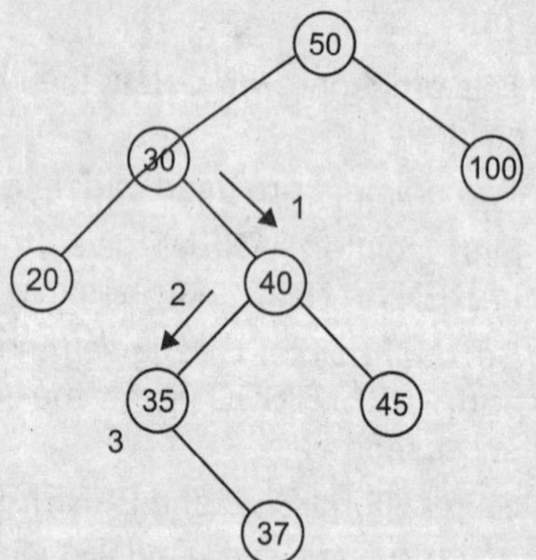

Figure 9.17: Delete the node 30 having two children.

For example, to delete 30

1. The right node of the node which is being deleted is 40.
2. (From now on, we continually go to the left node until there isn't another one...) The first left node of 40, is 35.
3. 35 has no left node, therefore 35 is the successor!

Case 1: The successor is the right child of the node being deleted

1. Directly move the child to the right of the node being deleted into the position of the node being deleted.
2. As the new node has no left children, you can connect the deleted node's left subtree's root as it's left child.

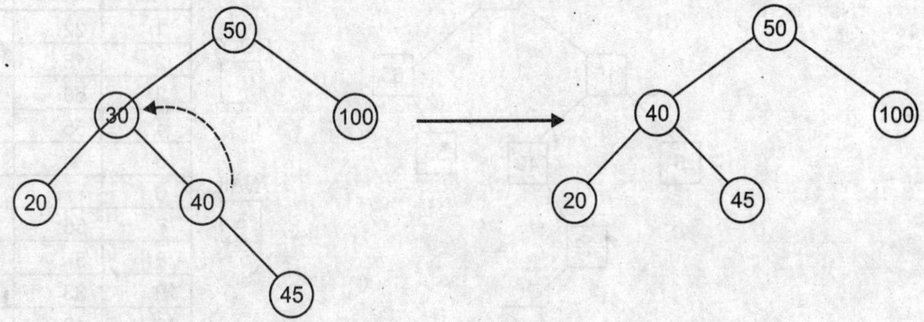

Figure 9.18: Successor is the right child of the node being deleted.

For example, to delete 30

1. Move 40 up to where 30 was.
2. 20 now becomes 40's left child.

Case 2: The successor isn't the right child of the node being deleted

This is best shown with an example

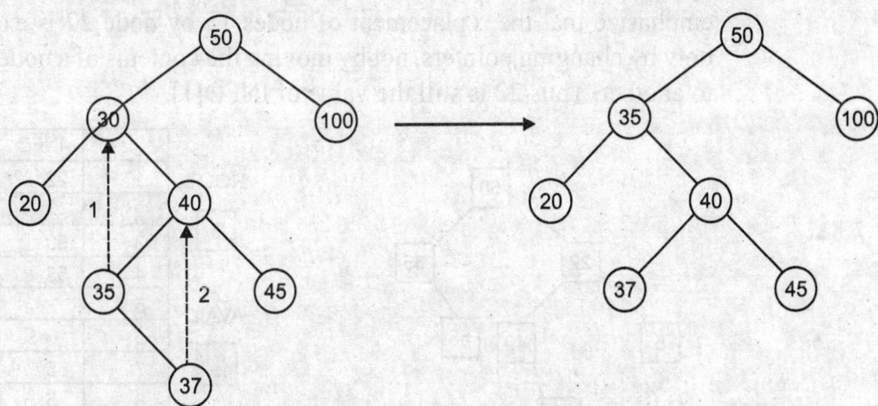

Figure 9.19: Successor isn't the right child of the node being deleted.

To delete 30...

1. Move the successor into the place where the deleted node was and make it inherit both of its children. So 35 moves to where 30 was and 20 and 40 become its children.

2. Move the successor's (35s) right subtree to where the successor was. So 37 becomes a child of 40.

Example 9.9: Consider the binary search tree in Figure 9.20(a). Suppose T appears in memory as in Figure 9.20(b).

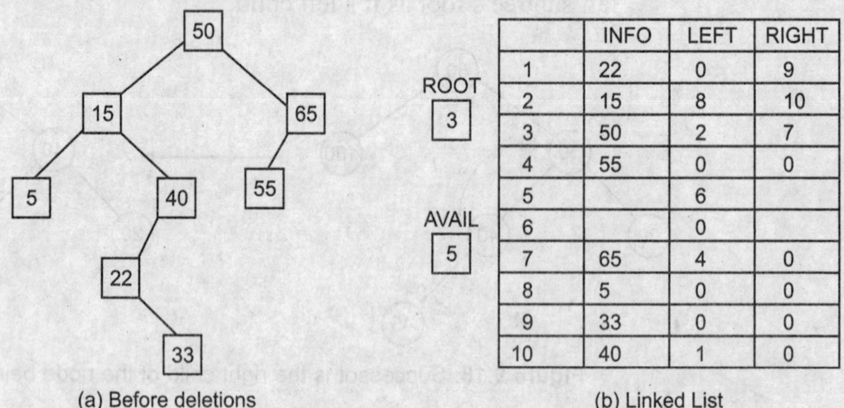

	INFO	LEFT	RIGHT
1	22	0	9
2	15	8	10
3	50	2	7
4	55	0	0
5		6	
6		0	
7	65	4	0
8	5	0	0
9	33	0	0
10	40	1	0

(a) Before deletions (b) Linked List

Figure 9.20: Binary search tree T.

(c) Suppose we delete node 15 from the tree T in Figure 9.20 instead of node 33 or node 65. Note that node 15 has two children. Also observe that node 22 is the inorder successor of node 15. Figure 9.21(a) pictures the tree after 15 is deleted, and Figure 9.21(b) shows the linked representation. The deletion is accomplished by first deleting 22 from the tree and then replacing node 15 by node 22. We emphasize that the replacement of nodes 15 by node 22 is executed in memory only by changing pointers, not by moving the contents of a node from one location to another. Thus 22 is still the value of INFO[1].

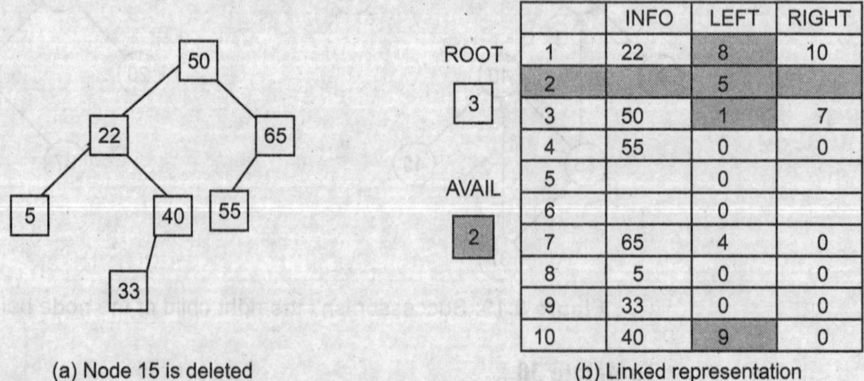

	INFO	LEFT	RIGHT
1	22	8	10
2		5	
3	50	1	7
4	55	0	0
5		0	
6		0	
7	65	4	0
8	5	0	0
9	33	0	0
10	40	9	0

(a) Node 15 is deleted (b) Linked representation

Figure 9.21: After deletion of node 15.

Algorithm 9.5: DEL(INFO, LEFTNOD, RIGHTNOD, ROOTNOD, AVAIL, ITEM)

Suppose a binary search tree T is in memory, and an ITEM information is given. This algorithm deletes ITEM from the tree.

Step 1: [Find the locations of ITEM and its PARENT, using Procedure 7.4.]

Call FINDLOC(INFO, LEFTNOD, RIGHTNOD, ROOTNOD, ITEM, LOC, PARENT).

Step 2: [ITEM in tree?]

If LOC = NULL, then: Write: ITEM not in tree, and End.

Step 3: [Delete node containing ITEM.]

If RIGHTNOD[LOC] ≠ NULL and LEFTNOD[LOC] ≠ NULL, then:

Call CASEA(INFO, LEFTNOD, RIGHTNOD, ROOTNOD, LOC, PARENT).

Else

CASEB(INFO, LEFTNOD, RIGHTNOD, ROOTNOD, LOC, PARENT).

[End of If statement.]

Step 4: [Return deleted node to the AVAIL list.]

Set LEFTNOD[LOC] = AVAIL and AVAIL = LOC.

Step 5: End.

Our deletion algorithm will be stated in terms of Procedures 7.6 and 7.7, which follow. The first procedure refers to Cases A and B, where the deleted node N does not have two children: and the second procedure refers to Case C, where N does have two children. There are many subcases which reflect the fact that N may be left child, a right child or the root. Also, in Case B, N may have a left child or a right child.

Procedure 7.7 treats the case that the deleted node N has two children. We note that the inorder successor of N can be found by moving to the right child of N and then moving repeatedly to the left until meeting a node with an empty left subtree.

9.3.5 Deletion of A Node from Binary Search Tree

To delete a node from a binary search tree, the method to be used depends on whether a node to be deleted has one child, two children, or no children.

Deletion of a node with two children

Consider the binary search tree shown in Figure 9.22.

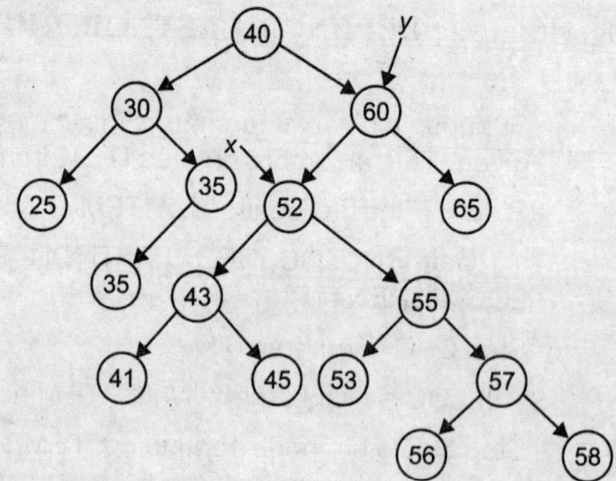

Figure 9.22: A binary tree before deletion of a node pointed to by x.

To delete a node printed to by *x*, we start by letting *y* be a pointer to the node that is the root of the node pointed to by *x*. We store the pointer to the left child of the node pointed to by *x* in a temporary pointer temp. We then make the left child of the node pointed to by *y* the left child of the node pointed to by *x*. We then traverse the tree with the root as the node pointed to by temp to get its right leaf, and make the right child of this right leaf the right child of the node pointed to by *x*, as shown in Figure 9.23.

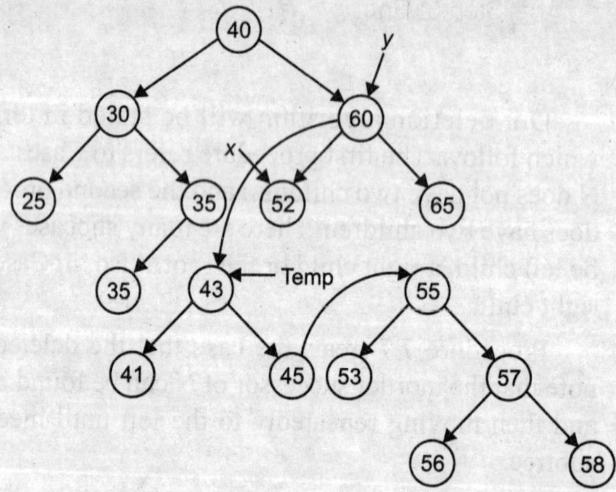

Figure 9.23: A binary tree after deletion of a node pointed to by x.

Another method is to store the pointer to the right child of the node pointed to by *x* in a temporary pointer temp. We then make the left child of the node pointed by *y* to be the right child of the node pointed to by *x*. We then traverse the tree with the root as the node pointed to by temp to get its left leaf, and make the left child of this left leaf the left child of the node pointed to by *x*, as shown in Figure 9.24.

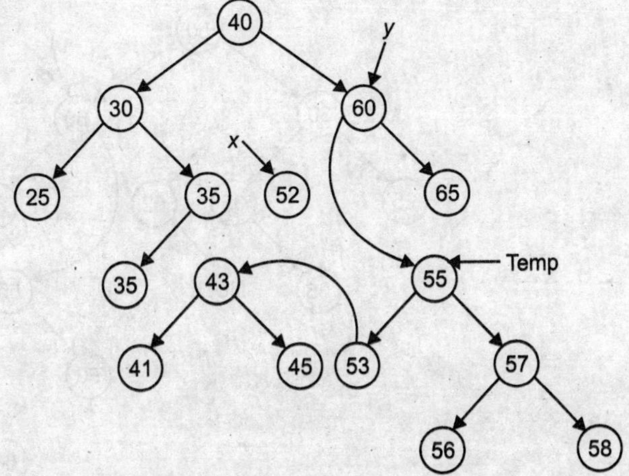

Figure 9.24: A binary tree after deletion of a node pointed to by x.

Deletion of a Node with One Child

Consider the binary search tree shown in Figure 9.25.

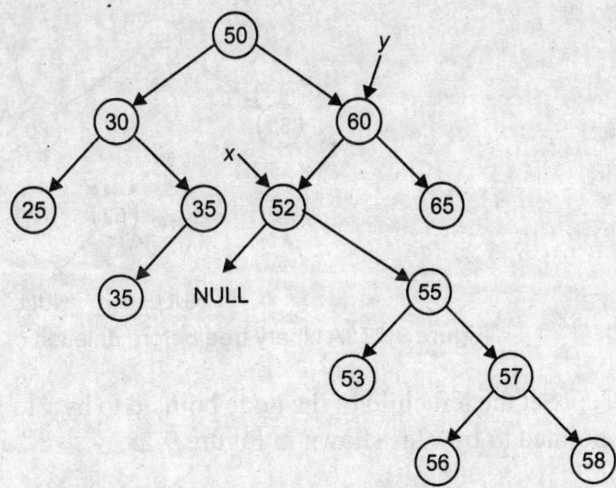

Figure 9.25: A binary tree before deletion of a node pointed to by x.

If we want to delete a node pointed to by *x*, we can do that by letting *y* be a pointer to the node that is the root of the node pointed to by *x*. Make the left child of the node pointed to by *y* the right child of the node pointed to by *x*, and dispose of the node pointed to by *x*, as shown in Figure 9.26.

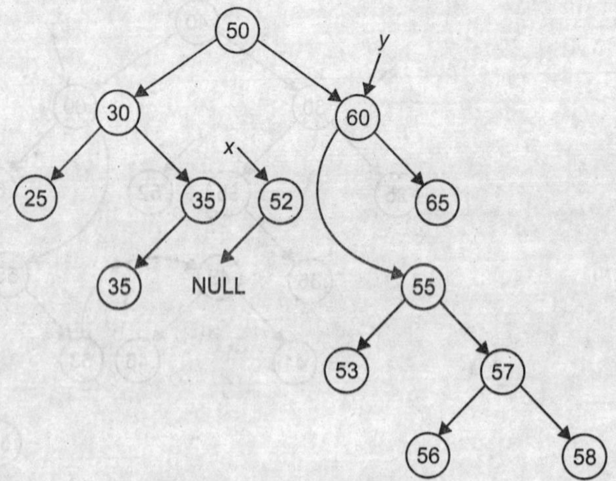

Figure 9.26: A binary tree after deletion of a node pointed to by x.

Deletion of a Node with No Child

Consider the binary search tree shown in Figure 9.27.

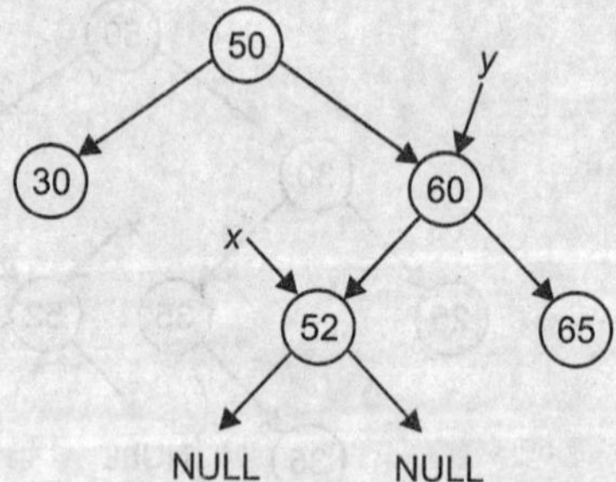

Figure 9.27: A binary tree before deletion of a node pointed to by x.

Set the left child of the node pointed to by *y* to NULL, and dispose of the node pointed to by *x*, as shown in Figure 9.28.

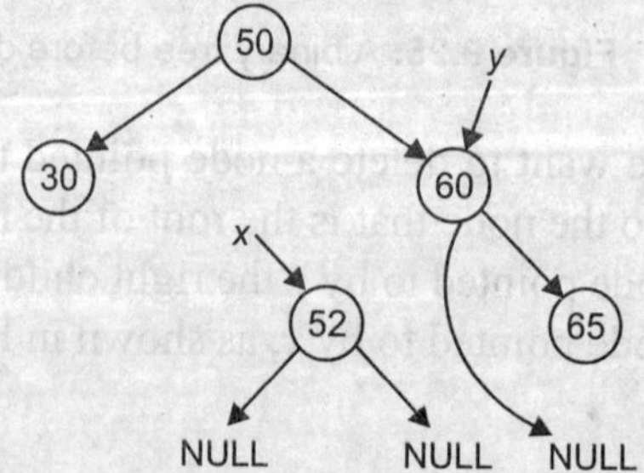

Figure 9.28: A binary tree after deletion of a node pointed to by x.

9.4 COMPUTING THE MINIMUM AND MAXIMUM VALUES IN A BINARY SEARCH TREE

To find the minimum in a binary search tree, we go the left child of the root; then go to the left child of that child and so on, until we get a node that has no left child. In other words, the minimum value is contained in the last left node in the left sub-tree of the root.The maximum can be similarly obtained by traversing the right sub-tree, and visiting the last right child in this tree.

Example 9.10: Explain the different operations performed on binary search tree using graphical representation.

Solution: There are mainly three operations are performed on binary search tree as follows:

1. Searching a binary search tree
2. Inserting a new node in a binary search tree
3. Deleting a node from a binary search tree

9.4.1 Searching a Binary Search Tree

Starting at the root node, the search algorithm compares the search key with the data stored in the current node.

(a) If the search key is equal to the data of the current node, the value has been found, and the search is terminated.

(b) If the search key is greater than the data of the current node, the search proceeds with the right child as the new current node.

(c) If the search key is less than the data of the current node, the search proceeds with the left child as the new current node.

(d) If the current node is null, the search is terminated as unsuccessful.

Since the above search algorithm visits at most one node in each level of the binary tree, the algorithm runs in Θ(h) time, where h is the height of the tree.

Graphical Representation

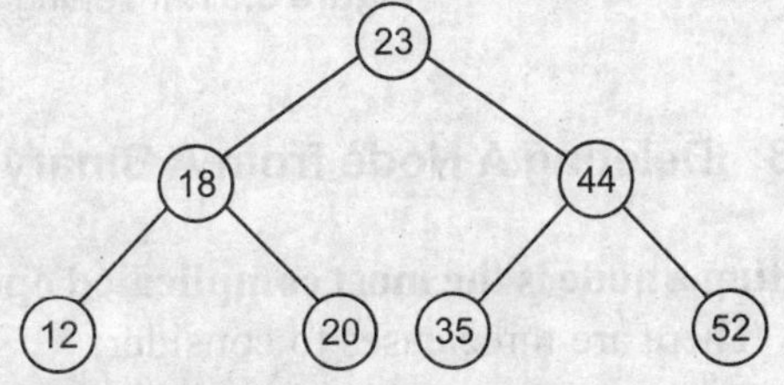

Figure 9.29: Searching in a binary search tree.

Starting with 23, the binary search examines either 18 or 44, depending on the search key. From 18 it examines either 12 or 20; from 44 it examines either 35 or 52. Let assumed that we are searching for 20. Therefore, by comparing 20 is less than the rood value 23, and because we know that all values less than the root lie in its left subtree, we go left. We now compare the search argument with the value in the subtree, 18. Because we know that values greater than the tree root must lie in its right subtree, we go right and find our desired value.

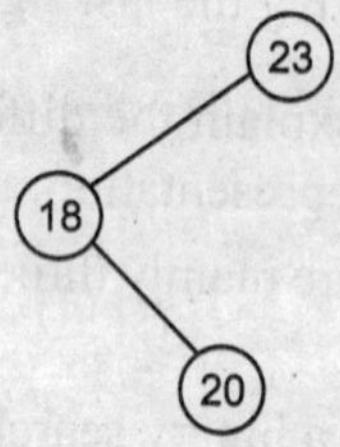

Figure 9.30: Search completes node find is 20.

9.4.2 Inserting A New Node in A Binary Search Tree

The operation of inserting a new node proceeds in the same sequence as the search operation, until it encounters a "null", where the new node is inserted and connected to the previous node as its parent.

Graphical Representation

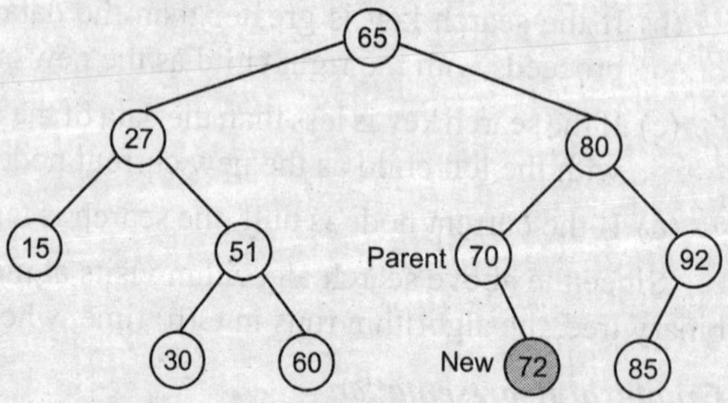

Figure 9.31: Inserting a new node 72.

9.4.3 Deleting A Node from A Binary Search Tree

Deleting a node is the most complicated operation required for binary search tree. There are three cases to consider:

(a) The node to be deleted is a leaf (has no children).

(b) The node to be deleted has one child.

(c) The node to be deleted has two children.

To delete a leaf node, we appropriately change the child field in the node's parent to point to null, instead of the node (see figure below).

Graphical Representation

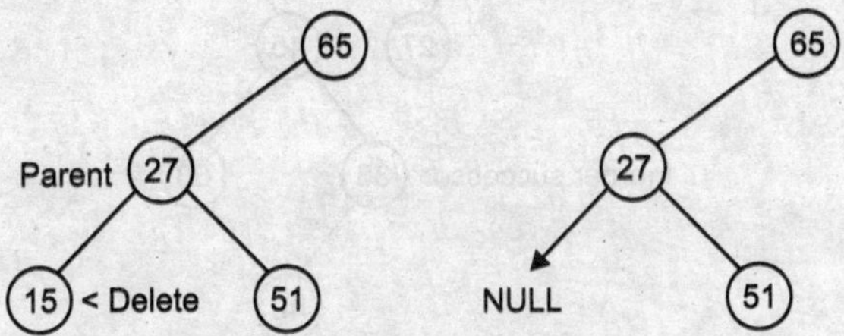

Figure 9.32: Deleting leaf node 15.

To delete a node with one child, we change the appropriate reference in the node's parent to point to the child of the deleted node. The child along with its sub-trees, now takes the place of the deleted node.

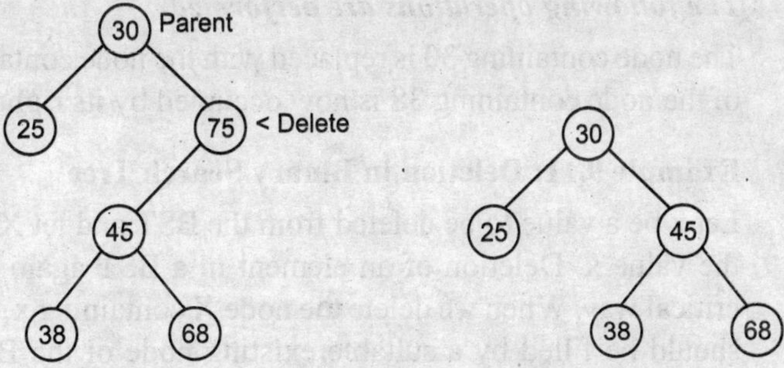

Figure 9.33: Delete node 75 having one child.

To delete a node with two children, we adopt the following procedure.

Step 1: Replace the node with its inorder successor. Since the node to be deleted has two children, it has a right sub-tree, and its inorder successor is the last left node in this sub-tree. This operation, however, involves the deletion of the inorder successor, and this has to be appropriately taken care of.

Step 2: Since the inorder successor is the last left node in a sub-tree, it cannot have a left child. Therefore it can have at most one child. If it has a right child, the deletion of the node causes the right child to occupy its position.

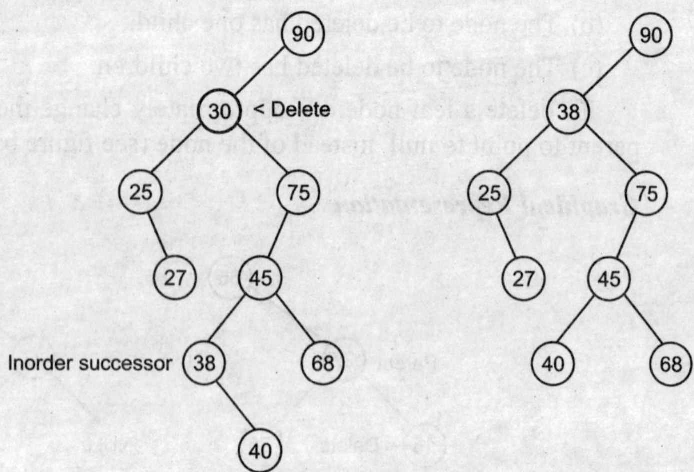

Figure 9.34: Delete the node 30 having two children.

In the above example, the node marked for deletion has a value 30, and its inorder successor is the node with value 38 (the last left node in the right sub-tree of the deleted node).

The following operations are performed

The node containing 30 is replaced with the node containing 38. The initial position of the node containing 38 is now occupied by its right child (node containing 40).

Example 9.11: Deletion in Binary Search Tree

Let x be a value to be deleted from the BST and let X denote the node containing the value x. Deletion of an element in a BST again uses the BST property in a critical way. When we delete the node X containing x, it would create a "void" that should be filled by a suitable existing node of the BST. There are two possible candidate nodes that can fill this void, in a way that the BST property is not violated:

1. Node containing highest valued element among all descendants of left child of X.
2. Node containing the lowest valued element among all the descendants of the right child of X.

In case (1), the selected node will necessarily have a null right link which can be conveniently used in patching up the tree.

In case (2), the selected node will necessarily have a null left link which can be used in patching up the tree. Figure 9.35 illustrates several scenarios for deletion in BSTs.

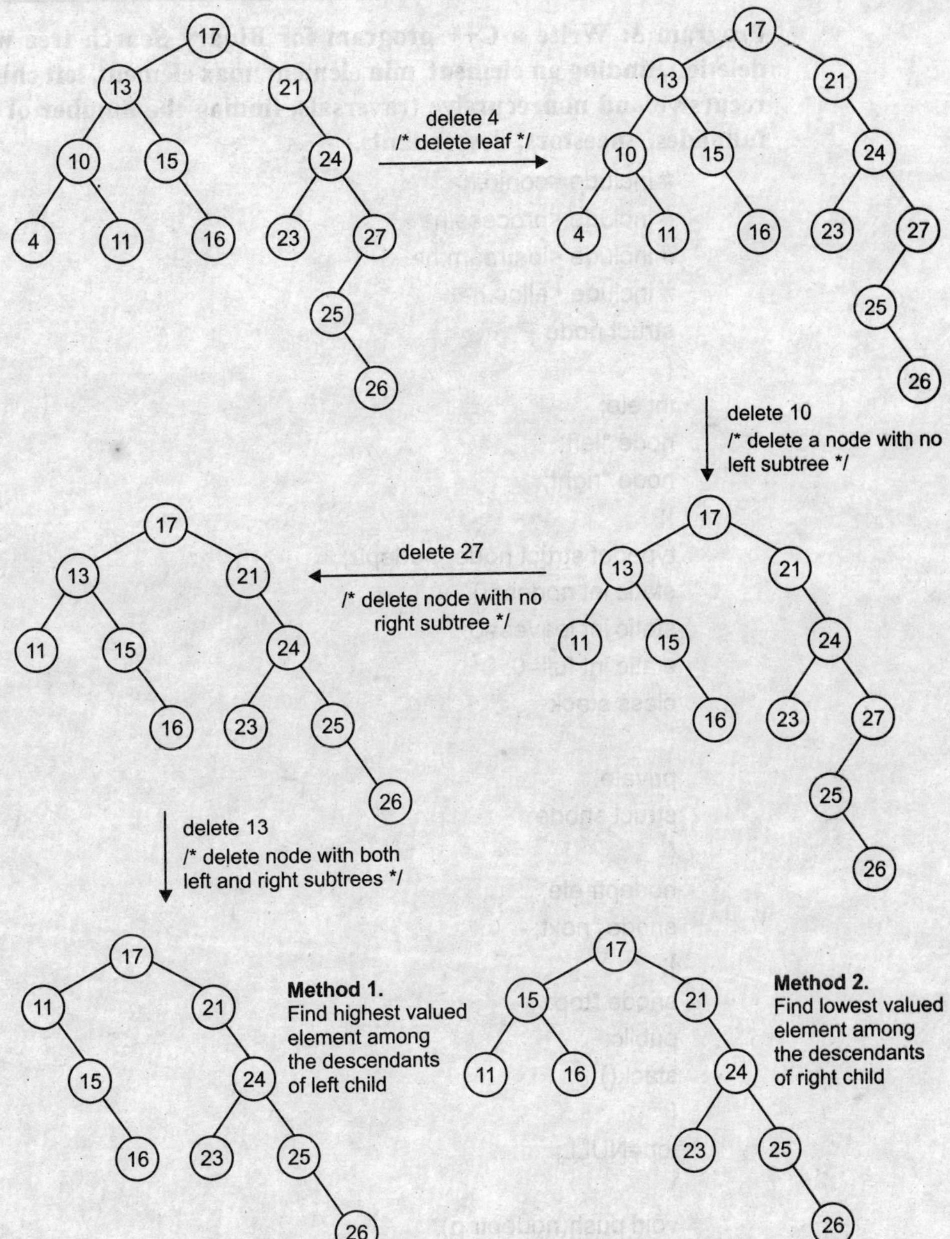

Figure 9.35: Deletion in binary search trees: An example

Program 3: Write a C++ program for Binary Search tree with insertion, deletion, finding an element, min element, max element, left child, right child, recursive and nonrecursive traversals, finding the number of nodes, leaves, fullnodes, ancestors, descendants.

```
# include <conio.h>
# include <process.h>
# include <iostream.h>
# include <alloc.h>
struct node
{
int ele;
node *left;
node *right;
};
typedef struct node *nodeptr;
static int nodes=0;
static int leaves=0;
static int full=0;
class stack
{
private:
struct snode
{
nodeptr ele;
snode *next;
};
snode *top;
public:
stack()
{
top=NULL;
}
void push(nodeptr p)
{
snode *temp;
temp = new snode;
temp->ele = p;
temp->next = top;
top=temp;
```

```
}
void pop()
{
if (top != NULL)
{
nodeptr t;
snode *temp;
temp = top;
top=temp->next;
delete temp;
}
}
nodeptr topele()
{
if (top !=NULL)
return top->ele;
else
return NULL;
}
int isempty()
{
return ((top == NULL) ? 1 : 0);
}
};
class bstree
{
public:
void insert(int,nodeptr &);
void del(int,nodeptr &);
int deletemin(nodeptr &);
void find(int,nodeptr &);
nodeptr findmin(nodeptr);
nodeptr findmax(nodeptr);
void copy(nodeptr &,nodeptr &);
void makeempty(nodeptr &);
nodeptr nodecopy(nodeptr &);
void nonodes(nodeptr);
void fullnodes(nodeptr);
void ances(int,nodeptr &);
```

```
void desc(int,nodeptr &);
void allleaves(nodeptr);
void noleaves(nodeptr);
void preorder(nodeptr);
void inorder(nodeptr);
void postorder(nodeptr);
void preordernr(nodeptr);
void inordernr(nodeptr);
void postordernr(nodeptr);
void leftchild(int,nodeptr &);
void rightchild(int,nodeptr &);
};

void bstree::insert(int x,nodeptr &p)
{
if (p==NULL)
{
p = new node;
p->ele=x;
p->left=NULL;
p->right=NULL;
}
else
{
if (x < p->ele)
insert(x,p->left);
else if (x>p->ele)
insert(x,p->right);
else
cout<<"Element already Exits !";
}
}
void bstree:: del(int x,nodeptr &p)
{
nodeptr d;
if (p==NULL)
cout<<"Element not found ";
else if (x < p->ele)
del(x,p->left);
```

```
else if (x > p->ele)
del(x,p->right);
else if ((p->left == NULL) && (p->right ==NULL))
{
d=p;
free(d);
p=NULL;
}
else if (p->left == NULL)
{
d=p;
free(d);
p=p->right;
}
else if (p->right ==NULL)
{
d=p;
p=p->left;
free(d);
}
else
p->ele=deletemin(p->right);
}
int bstree::deletemin(nodeptr &p)
{
int c;
if (p->left == NULL)
{
c=p->ele;
p=p->right;
return c;
}
else
c=deletemin(p->left);
return c;
}
void bstree::copy(nodeptr &p,nodeptr &p1)
{
makeempty(p1);
```

```
p1=nodecopy(p);
}
void bstree::makeempty(nodeptr &p)
{
nodeptr d;
if (p!=NULL)
{
makeempty(p->left);
makeempty(p->right);
d=p;
free(d);
p=NULL;
}
}
nodeptr bstree::nodecopy(nodeptr &p)
{
nodeptr temp;
if (p == NULL)
return p;
else
{
temp = new node;
temp->ele=p->ele;
temp->left = nodecopy(p->left);
temp->right = nodecopy(p->right);
return temp;
}
}
nodeptr bstree::findmin(nodeptr p)
{
if (p==NULL)
{
cout<<"Tree is empty !";
return p;
}
else
{
while (p->left !=NULL)
p=p->left;
```

```
return p;
}
}
nodeptr bstree::findmax(nodeptr p)
{
if (p==NULL)
{
cout<<"Tree is empty !";
return p;
}
else
{
while (p->right !=NULL)
p=p->right;
return p;
}
}
void bstree::find(int x,nodeptr &p)
{
if (p==NULL)
cout<<"Element not found  !";
else
{
if (x <p->ele)
find(x,p->left);
else if ( x> p->ele)
find(x,p->right);
else
cout<<"Element Found !";
}
}
void bstree::desc(int x,nodeptr &p)
{
if (p==NULL)
cout<<"Element not found  !";
else
{
if (x <p->ele)
desc(x,p->left);
```

```
else if ( x> p->ele)
desc(x,p->right);
else
{
if (p->left !=NULL)
preorder(p->left);
else
preorder(p->right);
}
//cout<<"Element Found !";
}
}
void bstree::ances(int x,nodeptr &p)
{
if (p==NULL)
cout<<"Element not found  !";
else
{
if (x <p->ele)
{
cout<<p->ele<<"-->";
ances(x,p->left);
}
else if ( x> p->ele)
{
cout<<p->ele<<"-->";
ances(x,p->right);
}
else
cout<<"Element Found !";
}
}
void bstree::nonodes(nodeptr p)
{
if (p!=NULL)
{
nodes++;
nonodes(p->left);
nonodes(p->right);
```

```
}
}
void bstree::noleaves(nodeptr p)
{
if (p!=NULL)
{
noleaves(p->left);
if ((p->left == NULL) && (p->right == NULL))
leaves++;
noleaves(p->right);
}
}
void bstree::allleaves(nodeptr p)
{
if (p!=NULL)
{
allleaves(p->left);
if ((p->left == NULL) && (p->right == NULL))
cout<<p->ele<<"-->";
allleaves(p->right);
}
}
void bstree::fullnodes(nodeptr p)
{
if (p!=NULL)
{
fullnodes(p->left);
if ((p->left != NULL) && (p->right != NULL))
full++;
fullnodes(p->right);
}
}
void bstree::preorder(nodeptr p)
{
if (p!=NULL)
{
cout<<p->ele<<"-->";
preorder(p->left);
preorder(p->right);
```

```
}
}
void bstree::inorder(nodeptr p)
{
if (p!=NULL)
{
inorder(p->left);
cout<<p->ele<<"-->";
inorder(p->right);
}
}
void bstree::postorder(nodeptr p)
{
if (p!=NULL)
{
postorder(p->left);
postorder(p->right);
cout<<p->ele<<"-->";
}
}
void bstree::preordernr(nodeptr p)
{
stack s;
while (1)
{
if  (p != NULL)
{
cout<<p->ele<<"-->";
s.push(p);
p=p->left;
}
else
if (s.isempty())
{
cout<<"Stack is empty";
return;
}
else
{
```

```
nodeptr t;
t=s.topele();
p=t->right;
s.pop();
}
}
}
void bstree::inordernr(nodeptr p)
{
stack s;
while (1)
{
if  (p != NULL)
{
s.push(p);
p=p->left;
}
else
{
if (s.isempty())
{
cout<<"Stack is empty";
return;
}
else
{
p=s.topele();
cout<<p->ele<<"-->";
}
s.pop();
p=p->right;
}
}
}
void bstree::postordernr(nodeptr p)
{
stack s;
while (1)
{
```

```
if  (p != NULL)
{
s.push(p);
p=p->left;
}
else
{
if (s.isempty())
{
cout<<"Stack is empty";
return;
}
else
if (s.topele()->right == NULL)
{
p=s.topele();
s.pop();
cout<<p->ele<<"-->";
if (p==s.topele()->right)
{
cout<<s.topele()->ele<<"-->";
s.pop();
}
if (!s.isempty())
p=s.topele()->right;
else
p=NULL;
}
}
}
}
void bstree::leftchild(int q,nodeptr &p)
{
if (p==NULL)
cout<<"The node does not exists ";
else
if (q < p->ele )
leftchild(q,p->left);
else
```

```
if (q > p->ele)
leftchild(q,p->right);
else
if (q == p->ele)
{
if (p->left != NULL)
cout<<"Left child of "<<q<<"is "<<p->left->ele;
else
cout<<"No Left child !";
}
}
void bstree::rightchild(int q,nodeptr &p)
{
if (p==NULL)
cout<<"The node does not exists ";
else
if (q < p->ele )
rightchild(q,p->left);
else
if (q > p->ele)
rightchild(q,p->right);
else
if (q == p->ele)
{
if (p->right != NULL)
cout<<"Right child of "<<q<<"is "<<p->right->ele;
else
cout<<"No Right Child !";
}
}
int main()
{
int ch,x,leftele,rightele;
bstree bst;
char c='y';
nodeptr root,root1,min,max;
root=NULL;
root1=NULL;
do
```

```
{
//      system("clear");
clrscr();
cout<<"                    Binary Search Tree";
cout<<"                     -------------------";
cout<<"         1.Insertion
                2.Deletion
                3.NodeCopy ";
cout<<"         4.Find
                5.Findmax
                6.Findmin";
cout<<"              7.Preorder
                8.Inorder
                9.Postorder";
cout<<"
                10.Leftchild
                11.Rightchild
                12.Counting
";
cout<<" Enter your choice :";
cin>>ch;
switch(ch)
{
case 1:
cout<<"                 1.Insertion";
cout<<"Node Element ?";
cin>>x;
bst.insert(x,root);
cout<<"Inorder traversal is :";
bst.inorder(root);
break;
case 2:
cout<<"                 2.Deletion";
cout<<"Delete Element ?";
cin>>x;
bst.del(x,root);
bst.inorder(root);
break;
case 3:
```

```
cout<<"                    3.Nodecopy";
bst.copy(root,root1);
cout<<"The new tree is :";
bst.inorder(root1);
break;
case 4:
cout<<"                    4.Find";
cout<<"Search Element ?";
cin>>x;
bst.find(x,root);
cout<<" The ancestors are :";
bst.ances(x,root);
cout<<" The descendants are :";
bst.desc(x,root);
break;
case 5:
cout<<"                    5.Findmax";
if (root == NULL)
cout<<"Tree is empty";
else
{
max=bst.findmax(root);
cout<<"Largest element is :  "<<max->ele<<endl;
}
break;
case 6:
cout<<"                    6.Findmin";
if (root == NULL)
cout<<" Tree is empty";
else
{
min=bst.findmin(root);
cout<<"Smallest element is : "<<min->ele<<endl;
}
break;
case 7:
cout<<"                    7.Preorder";
if (root==NULL)
cout<<"Tree is empty";
```

```
else
{
cout<<"Preorder traversal (Non-Recursive) is :";
bst.preordernr(root);
cout<<" Preorder traversal (Recursive) is :";
bst.preorder(root);
}
break;
case 8:
cout<<"                    8.Inorder";
if (root==NULL)
cout<<" Tree is empty";
else
{
cout<<" Inorder traversal (Non-Recursive) is :";
bst.inordernr(root);
cout<<"Inorder traversal (Recursive) is :";
bst.inorder(root);
}
break;
case 9:
cout<<"                    9.Postorder";
if (root==NULL)
cout<<"Tree is empty";
else
{
cout<<"Postorder traversal (Non-Recursive) is :";
bst.postordernr(root);
cout<<"
Postorder traversal (Recursive) is :";
bst.postorder(root);
}
break;
case 10:
cout<<"                    10.Finding the left Child";
if (root==NULL)
cout<<"Tree is empty";
else
{
```

```
cout<<"Parent of the left child ?";
cin>>leftele;
bst.leftchild(leftele,root);
}
break;
case 11:
cout<<"          11.Finding the Right Child ";
if (root==NULL)
cout<<" Tree is empty";
else
{
cout<<"Parent of the right child ?";
cin>>rightele;
bst.rightchild(rightele,root);
}
break;
case 12:
bst.nonodes(root);
cout<<"Number of nodes : "<<nodes<<endl;
nodes=0;
bst.noleaves(root);
cout<<"Number of leaves :"<<leaves<<endl;
leaves=0;
bst.fullnodes(root);
cout<<"Number of fullnodes :"<<full<<endl;
full=0;
cout<<"All leaf nodes are :";
bst.allleaves(root);
break;
}
cout<<"Continue (y/n) ?";
cin>>c;
}while (c=='y' || c == 'Y');
return 0;
}
```

9.5 AVL TREES

An AVL tree is a self-balancing binary search tree, and it is the first such data structure to be invented. In an AVL tree, the heights of the two child subtrees of any node differ by at most one; therefore, it is also said to be height-balanced. Lookup, insertion, and deletion all take O(log n) time in both the average and worst cases, where n is the number of nodes in the tree prior to the operation. Insertions and deletions may require the tree to be rebalanced by one or more tree rotations.

***Defination:** Named after Adelson, Velskii, and Landis.*

Trees of height O*(log* n*) are said to be **balanced**. AVL trees consist of a special case in which the subtrees of each node differ by at most 1 in their height.*

Balanced trees can be used to search, insert, and delete arbitrary keys in O*(log* n*) time. In contrast, height-biased leftist trees rely on non-balanced trees to speed-up insertions and deletions in priority queues.*

9.5.1 Height

To prove: AVL trees are balanced.

Proof: Let N_h denote the number of nodes in an AVL tree of depth h

$$\begin{aligned} N_h &\geq N_{h-1} + N_{h-2} + 1 \\ &\geq 2N_{h-2} + 1 \\ &\geq 1 + 2(1 + 2N_{h-4}) \\ &= 1 + 2 + 2^2 N_{h-4} \\ &\geq 1 + 2 + 2^2 + 2^3 N_{h-6} \\ &\ldots \\ &\geq 1 + 2 + 2^2 + 2^3 + \ldots + 2^{h/2} \\ &= 2^{h/2} - 1 \end{aligned}$$

Hence,

$$\begin{aligned} 2^{h/2} - 1 &\leq n \\ h/2 &\leq \log_2(n+1) \\ h &\leq 2 \log_2(n+1) \end{aligned}$$

A more careful analysis, based on Fibonacci numbers theory, implies the tighter bound of $1.44 \log_2(n+2)$.

An AVL tree (named after its inventors, G. M. Adel'son-Vel'skii and and E. M. Landis) is a binary search tree in which no node has subtrees that differ in height by more than one level. In other words, every node is balanced (its left and right subtrees are the same height), left-tall (its left subtree is one level higher than its right subtree), or right-tall (its right subtree is one level higher than its left subtree). First we show that an AVL tree is a "balanced enough" to guarantee that it won't be too deep (so lookups, insertions and deletions will be fast). Then we show how an insertion or deletion that violates the AVL balance requirement can be quickly repaired.

In the worst-case (least bushy) AVL tree, the only balanced nodes are leaves; all the other nodes are left-tall or right-tall. For example, here is a worst-case tree of height 5, in which all internal nodes are left-tall:

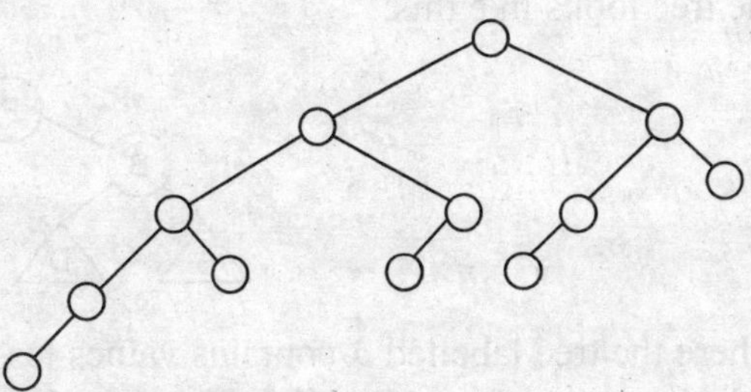

Figure 9.36: AVL tree.

Note that the left subtree is a worst-case tree of height 4 and the right subtree is a worst-case tree of height 3. In general, a worst-case AVL tree of height h consists of a root and two subtrees, one a worst case AVL tree of height h-1 and the other a worst-case AVL tree of height h-2. It can be proved that in the height of a worst case AVL tree is approximately 1.44*log(n), where n is the number of nodes in the tree. Since this is the worst possible case, searching an AVL tree with n nodes is guaranteed to require no more than O(log(n)) operations.

The best (bushiest) tree of height h is the complete binary tree, which has 2^h-1 nodes, so h is approximately log(n) in the best case. Thus the worst AVL tree is only about 1.44 times as bad as the best possible one.

To put this in perspective, suppose we insert one million records into a binary search tree. If we are really lucky and the tree comes out completely balanced, its height will be 20, meaning that no lookup (or insertion or deletion) will require more than 20 operations. However, if we are unlucky and the records arrive in nearly sorted order, we will end up with a spindly tree like the one shown above and a random lookup will require 500,000 comparisons on the average. On the other hand, the worst-case AVL tree of height 29 has 1,346,268 nodes, so an AVL tree with one million records is guaranteed to have height no greater than 29, and lookups will never need more than 29 comparisons.

9.5.2 Keeping an AVL Tree Balanced

Suppose the root of the tree is left-tall and we insert a new value that is less than the value stored in the root. The BST member function insert will add a new node to the left subtree, which might make it taller. If so, the AVL balance condition will be violated: Before the insertion, the left tree was taller than the right tree. When the left tree gets still taller, it becomes two levels higher than the right tree. We will fix this by inserting some new "rebalancing" code just after calling the original BST insert. The rebalancing code checks whether the heights of the two subtrees differ by two levels, and if so, adjusts a few links in the vicinity of the root to make the tree "balanced enough" again.

After the performing the normal BST insert, but before rebalancing the root, the tree looks like this:

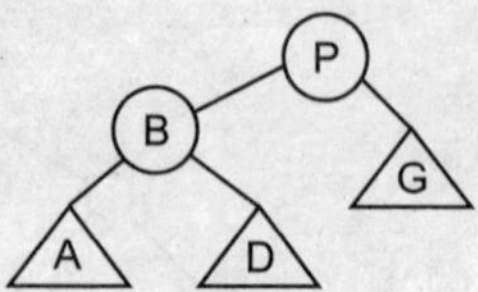

where the tree labelled A contains values less than B, the tree labelled D contains values between B and F, and the tree labelled G contains values greater than F. Let h be the height of the tree G. We are assuming that the root got out of balance because a node was added to its left subtree. Thus the left subtree must have height h+2. The main trick is to restore the AVL balance condition by rotating the tree to the right. A single right rotation makes B the root rather than F, thus raising B and lowering F:

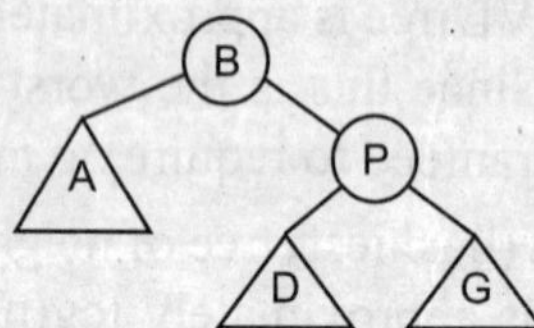

Note that the left-to-right ordering condition required of binary search trees still holds.

Does the rotation always restore the balance condition? Unfortunately not.

There Are Three Cases to Consider: The subtree rooted at node B is **left-tall, right-tall, or balanced.**

First suppose B is left-tall before the rotation. Then tree A has height h+1, tree D has height h, and the rotation has this effect:

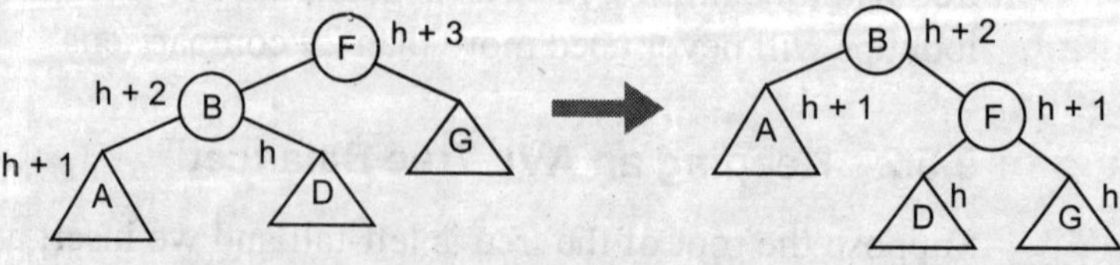

After the rotation, F and B are both balanced, and the whole tree is AVL. The case in which B is balanced before the rotation is similar, although in this case, F becomes left-tall and B becomes right-tall (try it yourself!). But the case in which B is right-tall before the rotation has a problem:

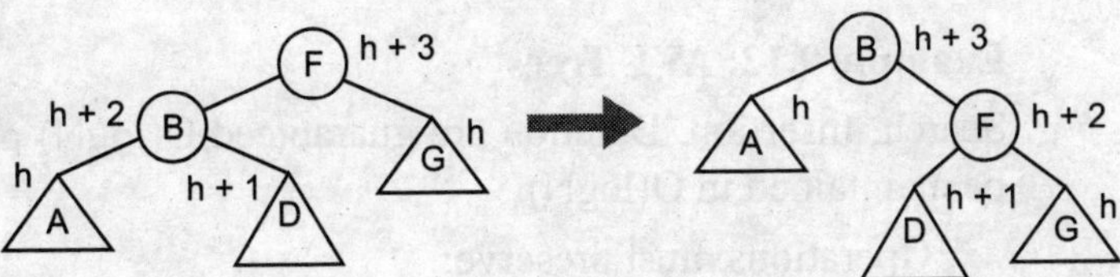

In this case, the rotation over-does it. Instead of a left tree that is two levels higher than the right tree, we end up with a right tree that is two levels higher than the left tree.

In this case (and only in this case), we have to do something a little more complicated. Since tree D has height h+1, we know it is not empty. In other words, before the rotation, the tree looks like this:

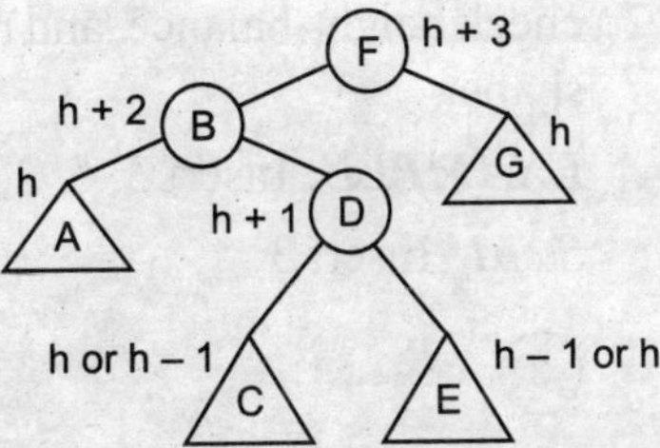

where each of C and E has height h or h - 1. In this case, we can do a double rotation to get a tree that satisfies the AVL balance condition:

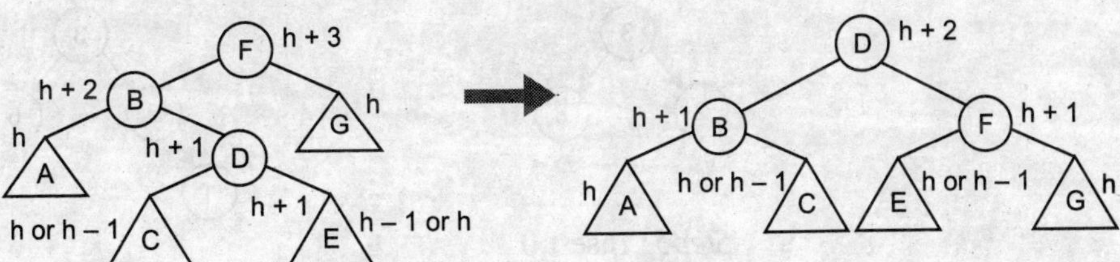

The same technique can be used for deletions. After performing a basic binary search tree remove to remove a node from one of the children, AVL's remove must check to see if one of the resulting subtrees is two levels higher than the other (it cannot be worse than that), and if so, do a single or double rotation to restore the AVL condition.

By the way, it is interesting to note that in all but one of the cases where we needed to do a rotation (single or double), the final tree ends up having the same height as the original tree before the insertion: h+2. The only exception is the case where B is balanced, and it can be shown that this case cannot arise for a single insertion. Thus each insertion will cause at most one rotation anywhere in the tree. (But deletion may cause more than one rotation.)

Example 9.12: AVL Trees

Search, Insertion, Deletion are guaranteed O(logN) provided height balance can be maintained in O(logN).

Operations must preserve:

1. Heights of left and right subtrees are within 1.
2. Values in left subtree are smaller than root value.
3. Values in right subtree are bigger than root value.

9.5.3 Insertion

Step 1: BST insertion

Step 2: check height-balance, and rebalance if necessary by changing the tree's shape.

***EXAMPLE*:** Insert 3, 6, 2, 1, 0 to the tree

Step1: Insert 3

Step2: Insert 6

Step3: Insert 2

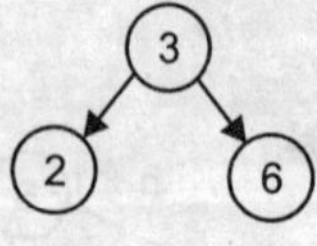

Step4: Insert 1

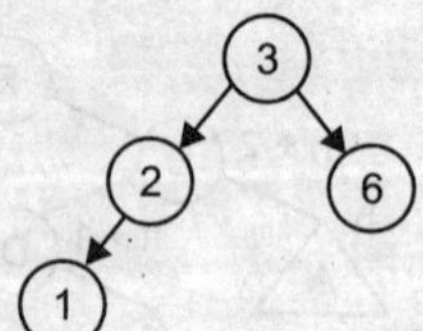

Step5: Insert 0

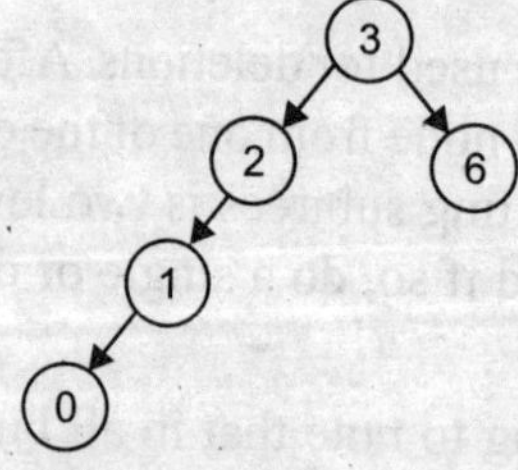

Imbalance, one tree is tall and the other tree is short.

9.5.4 Rotation Algorithm

Pivot: deepest imbalanced node.

Rotator: root of pivot's taller subtree.

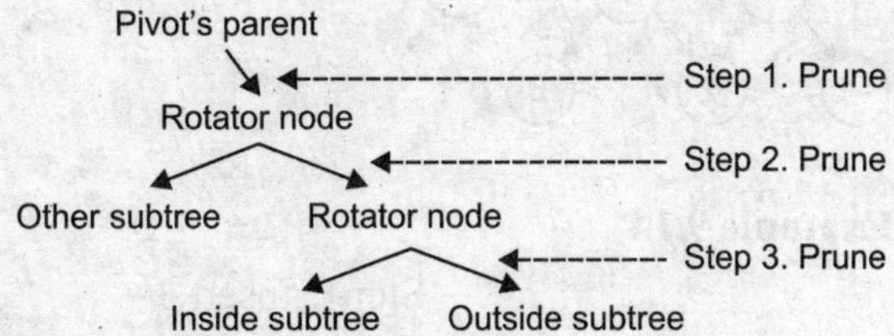

Step 4: Join inside subtree to pivot in place of rotator.

Step 5: Join pivot to rotator in place of inside subtree.

Step 6: Join rotator to pivot's original parent in place of pivot.

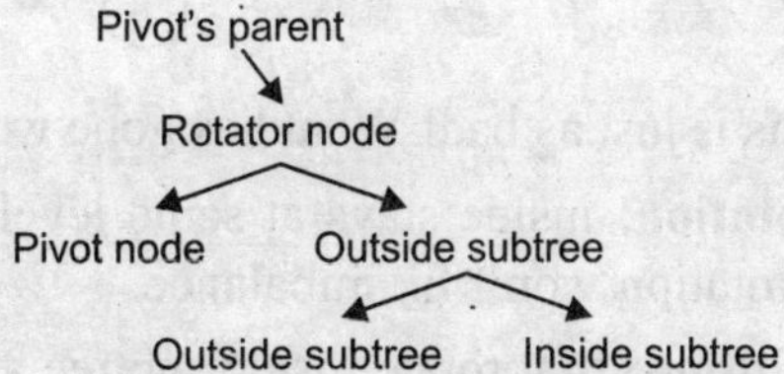

Example 9.13

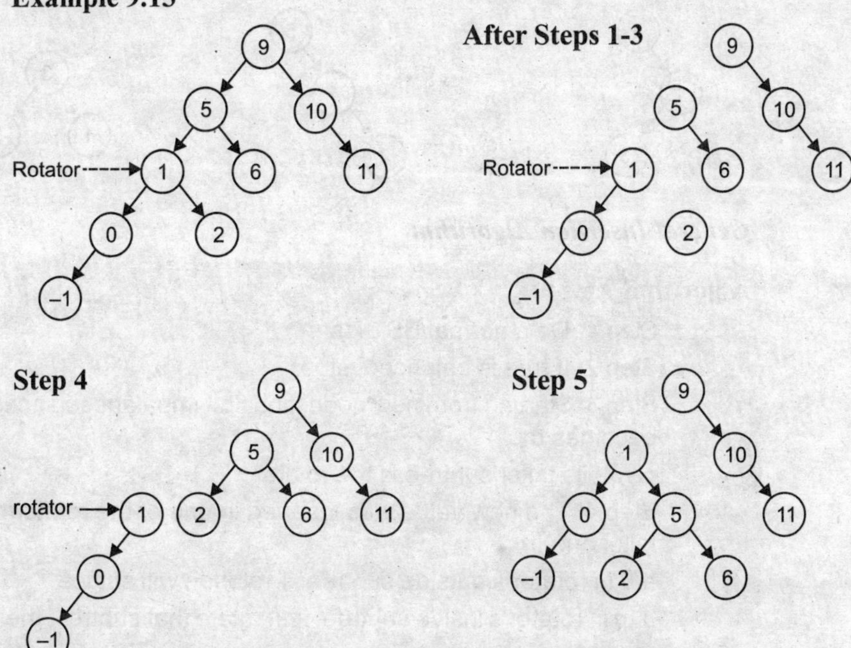

Step 6

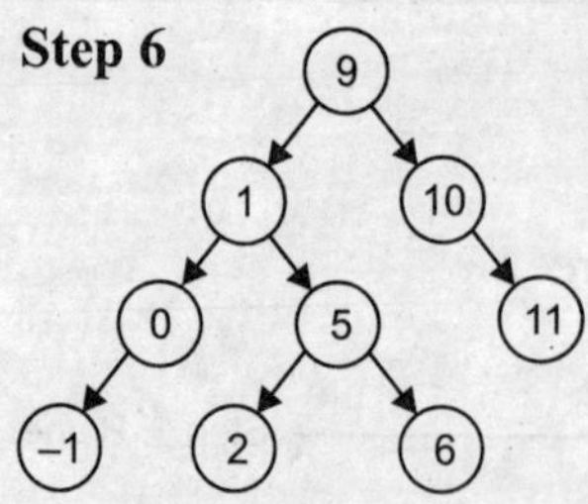

Example 9.14

Step1: Insert 3 Step2: Rotate

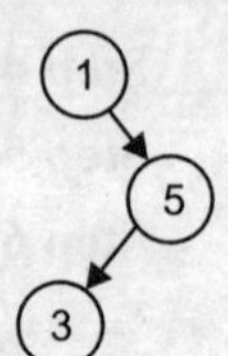

This is just as bad! What has gone wrong?

Rotation: inside stays at same level, outside moves up 1 level. If inside is taller, rotation won't fix imbalance.

Solution: first rotate inside subtree to the outside.

After Insert 3 Rotate Inside Main Rotation

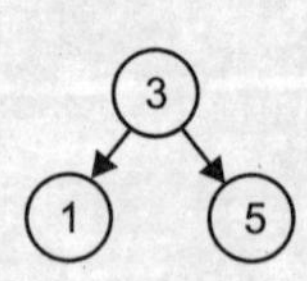

General Insertion Algorithm

Algorithm 9.6

Step 1: Do a normal BST insert.

Step 2: If tree is balanced, stop.

Step 3: Starting from new node, find first imbalanced ancestor. This node becomes the

pivot; its taller subtree is the rotator.

Step 4: The new value was inserted in one of the rotator's subtrees (the taller one).

a.If in rotator's outside subtree: 1 rotation will suffice.

b.In in rotator's inside subtree: first rotate that subtree, then perform main rotation.

Example 9.15

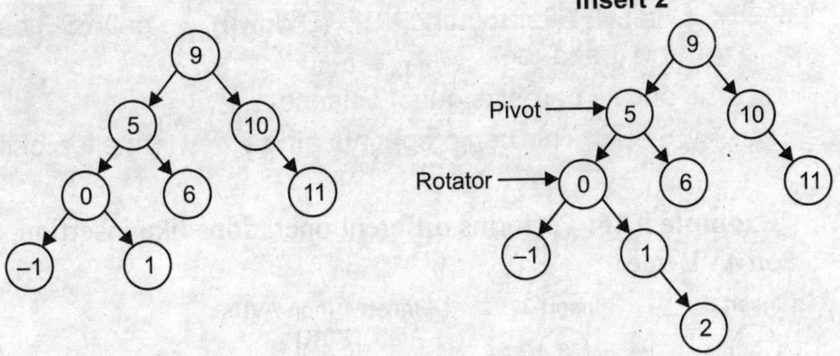

The new value is in the rotator's inside subtree.

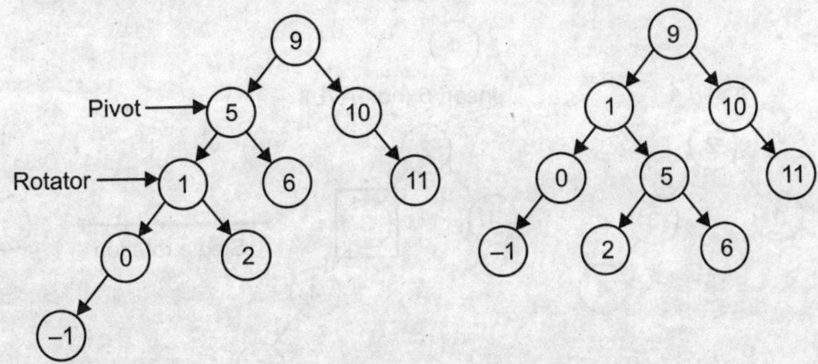

Deletion

Given a value X and an AVL tree T, delete the node containing X and rebalance the result.

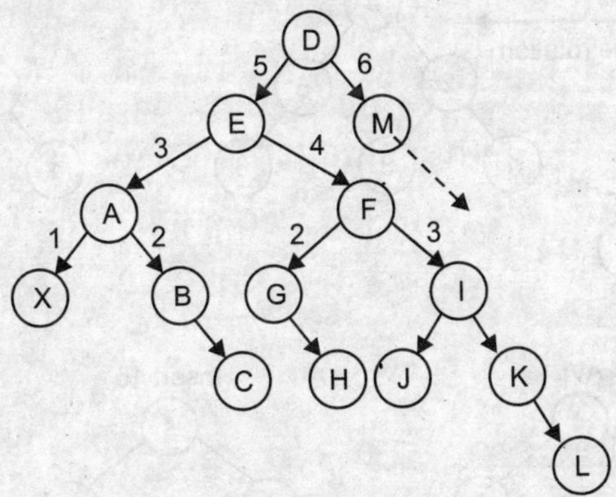

General DeletionAlgorithm

Algorithm 9.7

Step 1: Deleting X upsets A.

Step 2: After rotating B up, E is upset.

Step 3: After rotating F up, D's left subtree is shorter. D is upset.
Step 4: After rotating M up (D down), we get a 5-5 balance at D. So now it is 1 shorter
and its parent is out of balance.
Step 5: This can propagate all the way to the top of the tree.

Example 9.16: Performs different operations like insertion, rotation and deletion on AVL tree.

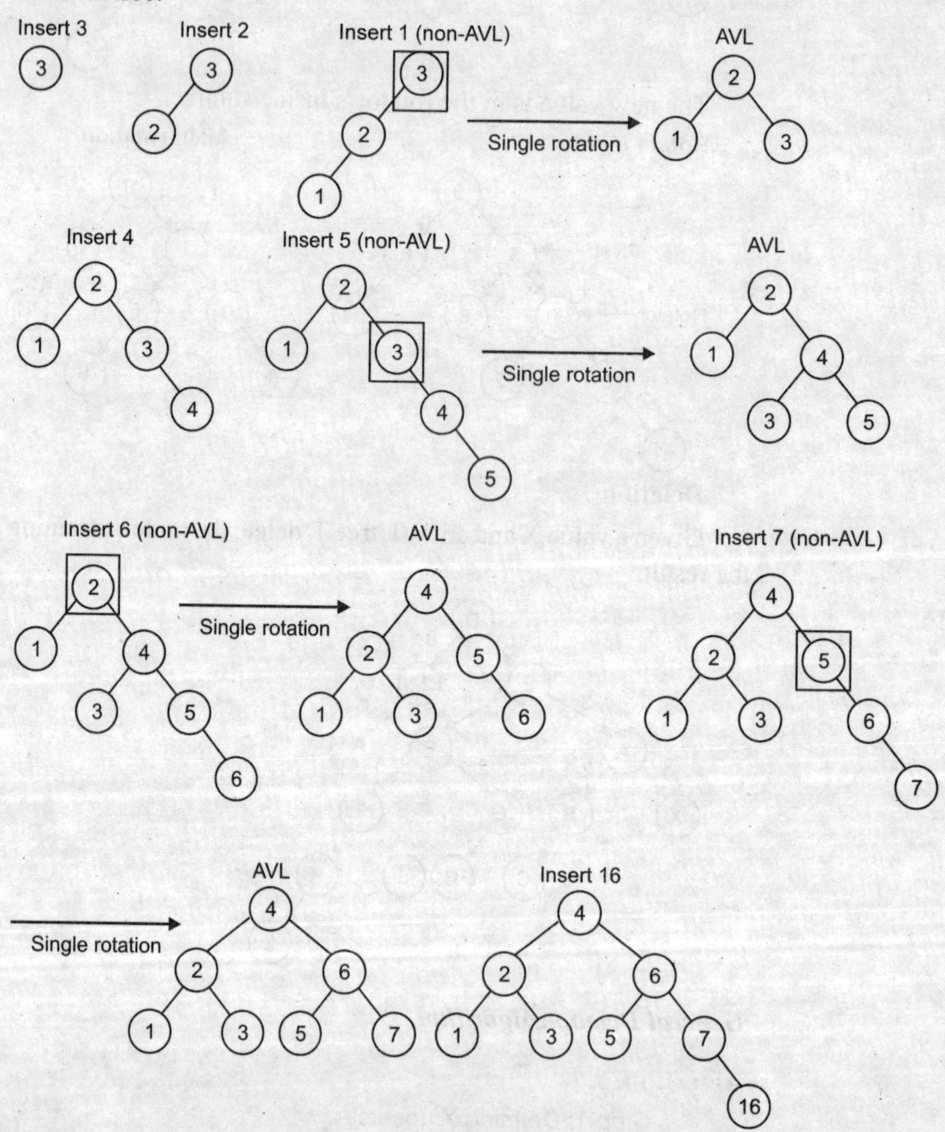

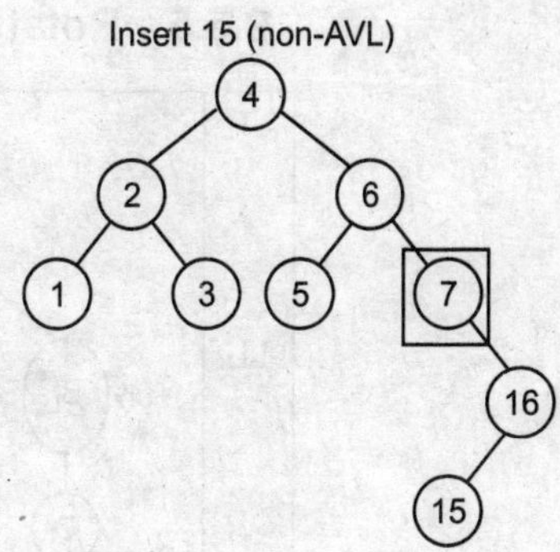

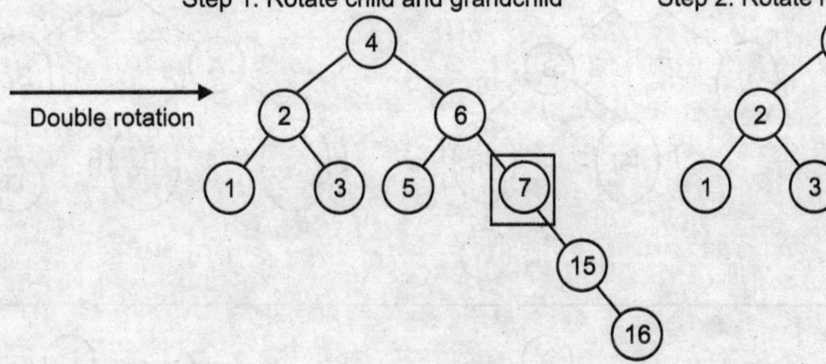

Step 2: Rotate node and new child (AVL)

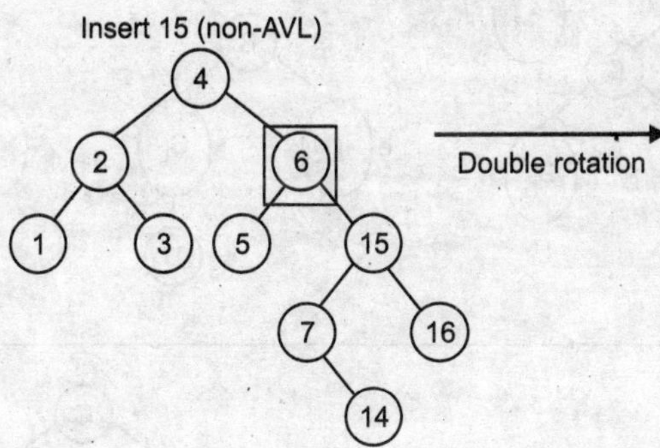

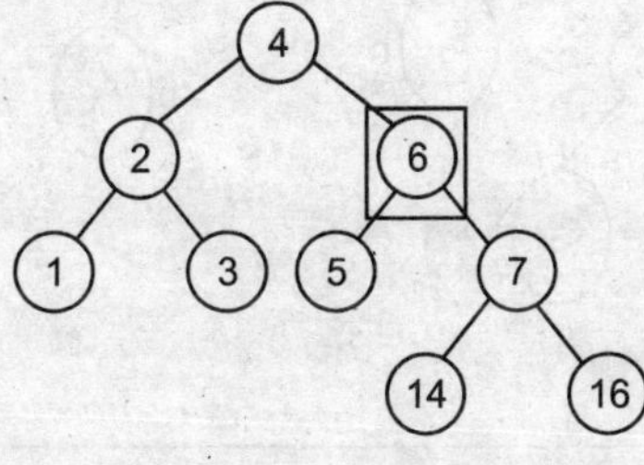

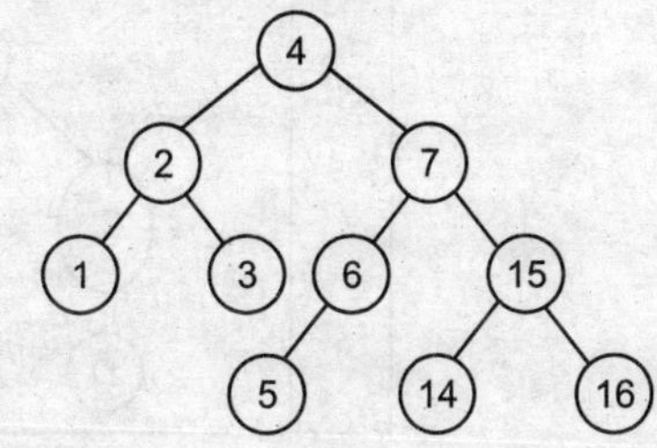

9.5.5 Rotations

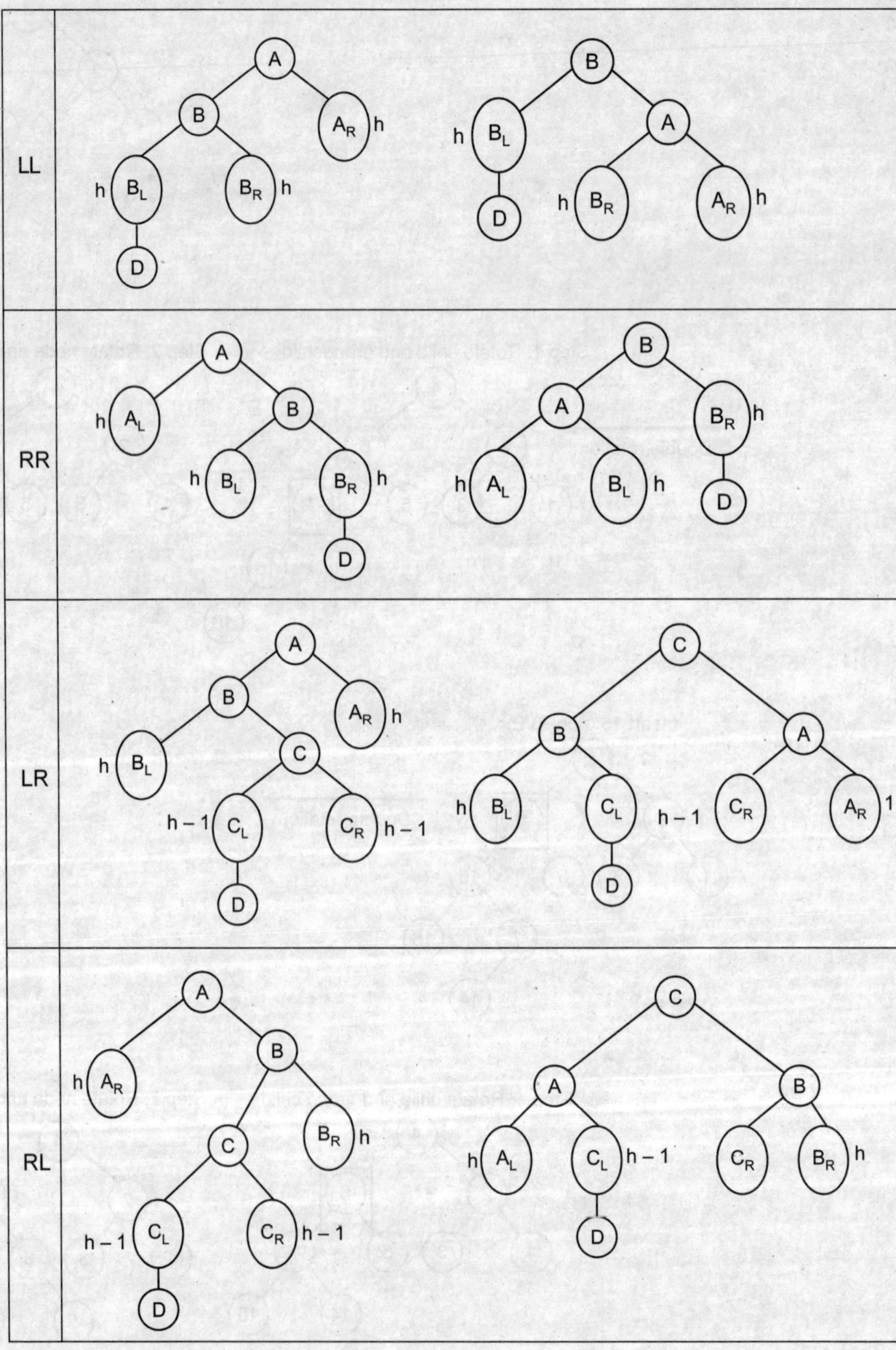

LL & LR ⇒ LL	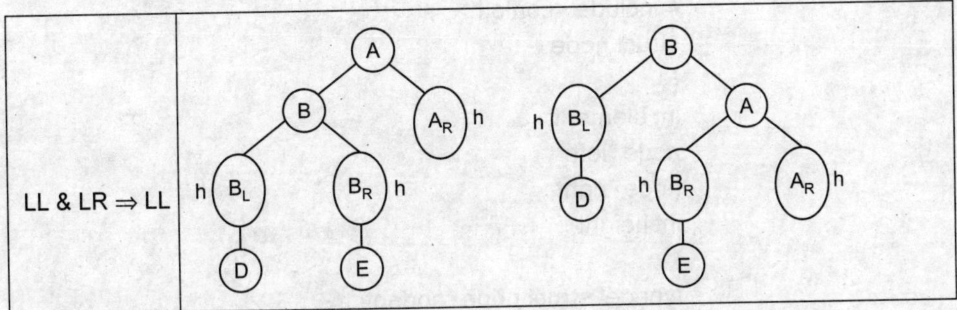

9.5.6 Insertions and Deletions

Insertions and deletions are performed as in binary search trees, and followed by rotations to correct imbalances in the outcome trees. In the case of insertions, one rotation is sufficient. In the case of deletions, O(log n) rotations at most are needed from the first point of discrepancy going up toward the root.

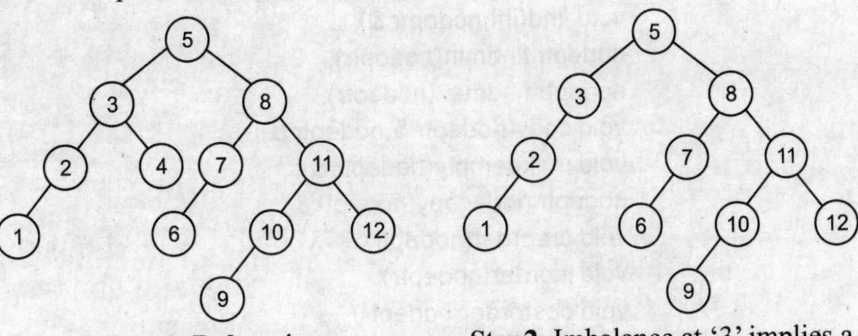

Step 1. Delete 4

Step2. Imbalance at '3' implies a LL rotation with '2'

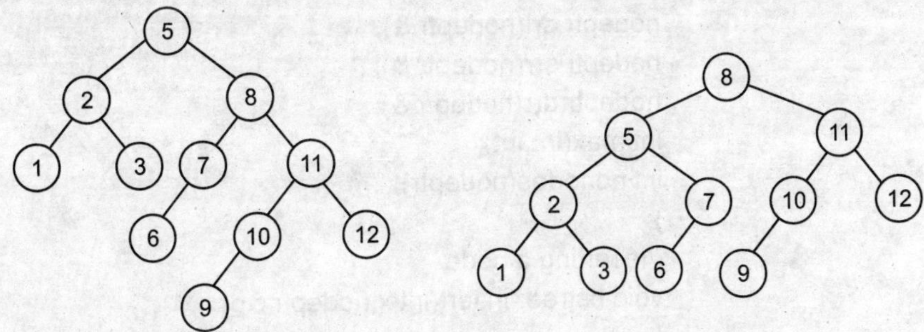

Step3. Imbalance at '5' implies a RR rotation with '8'.

Program 4: Write a C++ program for AVL tree with insertion, deletion and balancing height.

```
# include <iostream.h>
# include <stdlib.h>
```

```
# include <conio.h>
struct node
{
int element;
node *left;
node *right;
int height;
};
typedef struct node *nodeptr;
class bstree
{
public:
void insert(int,nodeptr &);
void del(int, nodeptr &);
int deletemin(nodeptr &);
void find(int,nodeptr &);
nodeptr findmin(nodeptr);
nodeptr findmax(nodeptr);
void copy(nodeptr &,nodeptr &);
void makeempty(nodeptr &);
nodeptr nodecopy(nodeptr &);
void preorder(nodeptr);
void inorder(nodeptr);
void postorder(nodeptr);
int bsheight(nodeptr);
nodeptr srl(nodeptr &);
nodeptr drl(nodeptr &);
nodeptr srr(nodeptr &);
nodeptr drr(nodeptr &);
int max(int,int);
int nonodes(nodeptr);
};
//Inserting a node
void bstree::insert(int x,nodeptr &p)
{
if (p == NULL)
{
p = new node;
p->element = x;
p->left=NULL;
p->right = NULL;
```

```
p->height=0;
if (p==NULL)
cout<<"Out of Space";
}
else
{
if (x<p->element)
{
insert(x,p->left);
if ((bsheight(p->left) - bsheight(p->right))==2)
{
if (x < p->left->element)
p=srl(p);
else
p = drl(p);
}
}
else if (x>p->element)
{
insert(x,p->right);
if ((bsheight(p->right) - bsheight(p->left))==2)
{
if (x > p->right->element)
p=srr(p);
else
p = drr(p);
}
}
else
cout<<"Element Exists";
}
int m,n,d;
m=bsheight(p->left);
n=bsheight(p->right);
d=max(m,n);
p->height = d + 1;
}
//Finding the Smallest
nodeptr bstree::findmin(nodeptr p)
{
if (p==NULL)
```

```
{
cout<<" Empty Tree";
return p;
}
else
{
while(p->left !=NULL)
p=p->left;
return p;
}
}
//Finding the Largest
nodeptr bstree::findmax(nodeptr p)
{
if (p==NULL)
{
cout<<" Empty Tree";
return p;
}
else
{
while(p->right !=NULL)
p=p->right;
return p;
}
}
//Finding an element
void bstree::find(int x,nodeptr &p)
{
if (p==NULL)
cout<<"Element not found";
else
if (x < p->element)
find(x,p->left);
else
if (x>p->element)
find(x,p->right);
else
cout<<" Element found !";
}
//Copy a tree
```

```
void bstree::copy(nodeptr &p,nodeptr &p1)
{
makeempty(p1);
p1 = nodecopy(p);
}
//                  Make a tree empty
void bstree::makeempty(nodeptr &p)
{
nodeptr d;
if (p != NULL)
{
makeempty(p->left);
makeempty(p->right);
d=p;
free(d);
p=NULL;
}
}
//Copy the nodes
nodeptr bstree::nodecopy(nodeptr &p)
{
nodeptr temp;
if (p==NULL)
return p;
else
{
temp = new node;
temp->element = p->element;
temp->left = nodecopy(p->left);
temp->right = nodecopy(p->right);
return temp;
}
}
//Deleting a node
void bstree::del(int x,nodeptr &p)
{
nodeptr d;
if (p==NULL)
cout<<"Element not found ";
else if ( x < p->element)
del(x,p->left);
```

```
else if (x > p->element)
del(x,p->right);
else if ((p->left == NULL) && (p->right == NULL))
{
d=p;
free(d);
p=NULL;
cout<<" Element deleted !";
}
else if (p->left == NULL)
{
d=p;
free(d);
p=p->right;
cout<<" Element deleted !";
}
else if (p->right == NULL)
{
d=p;
p=p->left;
free(d);
cout<<" Element deleted !";
}
else
p->element = deletemin(p->right);
}
int bstree::deletemin(nodeptr &p)
{
int c;
cout<<"inside deltemin ";
if (p->left == NULL)
{
c=p->element;
p=p->right;
return c;
}
else
{
c=deletemin(p->left);
return c;
}
```

```
}
void bstree::preorder(nodeptr p)
{
if (p!=NULL)
{
cout<<p->element<<"-->";
preorder(p->left);
preorder(p->right);
}
}
//Inorder Printing
void bstree::inorder(nodeptr p)
{
if (p!=NULL)
{
inorder(p->left);
cout<<p->element<<"-->";
inorder(p->right);
}
}
//PostOrder Printing
void bstree::postorder(nodeptr p)
{
if (p!=NULL)
{
postorder(p->left);
postorder(p->right);
cout<<p->element<<"-->";
}
}
int bstree::max(int value1, int value2)
{
return ((value1 > value2) ? value1 : value2);
}
int bstree::bsheight(nodeptr p)
{
int t;
if (p == NULL)
return -1;
else
{
```

```
t = p->height;
return t;
}
}
nodeptr bstree:: srl(nodeptr &p1)
{
nodeptr p2;
p2 = p1->left;
p1->left = p2->right;
p2->right = p1;
p1->height = max(bsheight(p1->left),bsheight(p1->right)) + 1;
p2->height = max(bsheight(p2->left),p1->height) + 1;
return p2;
}
nodeptr bstree:: srr(nodeptr &p1)
{
nodeptr p2;
p2 = p1->right;
p1->right = p2->left;
p2->left = p1;
p1->height = max(bsheight(p1->left),bsheight(p1->right)) + 1;
p2->height = max(p1->height,bsheight(p2->right)) + 1;
return p2;
}

nodeptr bstree:: drl(nodeptr &p1)
{
p1->left=srr(p1->left);
return srl(p1);
}
nodeptr bstree::drr(nodeptr &p1)
{
p1->right = srl(p1->right);
return srr(p1);
}
int bstree::nonodes(nodeptr p)
{
int count=0;
if (p!=NULL)
{
nonodes(p->left);
```

```
nonodes(p->right);
count++;
}
return count;
}
int main()
{
clrscr();
nodeptr root,root1,min,max,flag;
int  a,choice,findele;
int delele,leftele,rightele,flag;
char ch='y';
bstree bst;
//system("clear");
root = NULL;
root1=NULL;
cout<<"          AVL Tree";
cout<<"          ========";
do
{
cout<<"          1.Insertion
                 2.FindMin";
cout<<"          3.FindMax
                 4.Find
                 5.Copy ";
cout<<"          6.Delete
                 7.Preorder
                 8.Inorder";
cout<<"                  9.Postorder
                 10.height";
cout<<"Enter the choice:";
cin>>choice;
switch(choice)
{
case 1:
cout<<"New node's value ?";
cin>>a;
bst.insert(a,root);
break;
case 2:
if (root !=NULL)
```

```
{
min=bst.findmin(root);
cout<<"Min element :"<<min->element;
}
break;
case 3:
if (root !=NULL)
{
max=bst.findmax(root);
cout<<"Max element :            "<<max->element;
}
break;
case 4:
cout<<"Search node : ";
cin>>findele;
if (root != NULL)
bst.find(findele,root);
break;
case 5:
bst.copy(root,root1);
bst.inorder(root1);
break;
case 6:
cout<<"Delete Node ?";
cin>>delele;
bst.del(delele,root);
bst.inorder(root);
break;
case 7:
cout<<" Preorder Printing... :";
bst.preorder(root);
break;
case 8:
cout<<" Inorder Printing.... :";
bst.inorder(root);
break;
case 9:
cout<<" Postorder Printing... :";
bst.postorder(root);
break;
case 10:
```

```
cout<<" Height and Depth is ";
cout<<bst.bsheight(root);
cout<<"No. of nodes:- "<<bst.nonodes(root);
break;
}
cout<<" Do u want to continue (y/n) ?";
cin>>ch;
}while(ch=='y');
return 0;
}
```

9.6 GENERAL CONCEPT OF MULTI-WAY TREES

A multiway tree of order m is an ordered tree where each node has at most m children. For each node, if k is the actual number of children in the node, then k - 1 is the number of keys in the node. If the keys and subtrees are arranged in the fashion of a search tree, then this is called a multiway search tree of order m.

For example, the following is a multiway search tree of order 4. Note that the first row in each node shows the keys, while the second row shows the pointers to the child nodes. Of course, in any useful application there would be a record of data associated with each key, so that the first row in each node might be an array of records where each record contains a key and its associated data. Another approach would be to have the first row of each node contain an array of records where each record contains a key and a record number for the associated data record, which is found in another file. This last method is often used when the data records are large. The example software will use the first method.

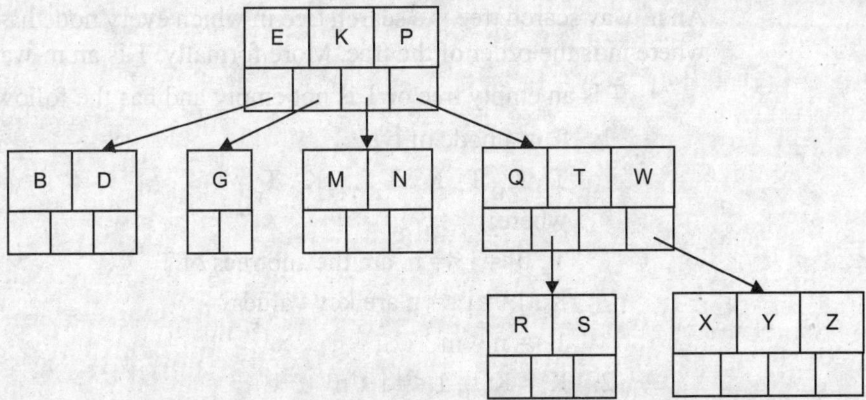

Figure 9.37: Multi-way trees.

What does it mean to say that the keys and subtrees are "arranged in the fashion of a search tree"? Suppose that we define our nodes as follows:

```
typedef struct
{ int Count;        // number of keys stored in the current node
ItemType Key[3];  // array to hold the 3 keys
long Branch[4];   // array of fake pointers (record numbers)
} NodeType;
```

Then a multiway search tree of order 4 has to fulfill the following conditions related to the ordering of the keys:

- The keys in each node are in ascending order.
- At every given node (call it Node) the following is true:
  - The subtree starting at record Node.Branch[0] has only keys that are less than Node.Key[0].
  - The subtree starting at record Node.Branch[1] has only keys that are greater than Node.Key[0] and at the same time less than Node.Key[1].
  - The subtree starting at record Node.Branch[2] has only keys that are greater than Node.Key[1] and at the same time less than Node.Key[2].
  - The subtree starting at record Node.Branch[3] has only keys that are greater than Node.Key[2].

Note that if less than the full number of keys are in the Node, these 4 conditions are truncated so that they speak of the appropriate number of keys and branches.

This generalizes in the obvious way to multiway search trees with other orders.

9.6.1 Multi-way Trees

An m-way search tree is a search tree in which every node has at most m children, where m is the order of the tree. More formally, T is an m-way search tree if

- T is an empty tree or T is not empty and has the following properties:
  1. T is a node of type:

     $T_0, K_1, T_1, K_2, T_2, \ldots, K_n, T_n$

     where:

     T_i, $0 <= i <= n$, are the subtrees of T

     K_i, $1 <= i <= n$ are key values,

     $1 <= n < m$
  2. $K_i < K_{i+1}$, $1 <= i < n$
  3. For every key value V in subtree T_i , $K_i < V < K_{i+1}$
  4. Subtrees T_i, $0 <= i <= n$ are also m-way search trees.

With this definition, one can see that if a node has k children, it must have k-1 keys.

Example 9.17: The following is a 5-way search tree.

To search an m-way search tree for a key x, first we find an i for which $K_i <= x < K_{i+1}$. If our key x is equal to K_i, then we have found our key. Else, if we find that subtree T_i is empty, we can stop since we know that our key x is not in the tree. Otherwise, we recursively search subtree T_i for key x.

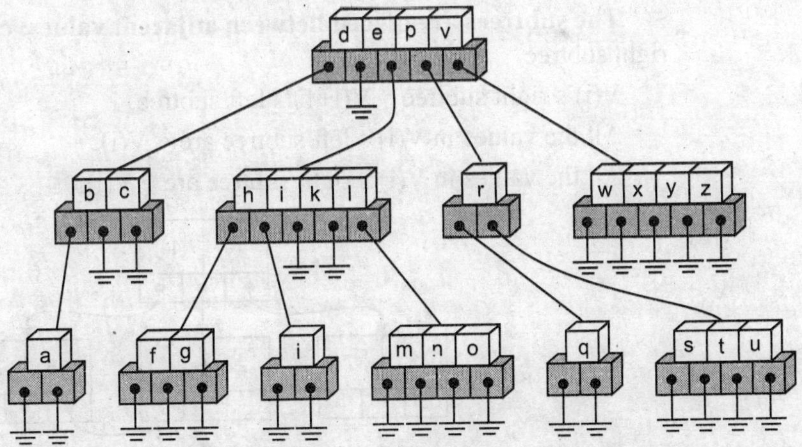

Figure 9.38: 5-way search tree.

To minimize disk accesses, we want our m-way tree to have the following properties:

- All leaves are on the same level.
- Every node (except the root) has at least a minimum number of children.

Defination: *A m-way search tree is a tree in which*

(a) The nodes hold between 1 to m-1 distinct keys

(b) The keys in each node are sorted

(c) A node with k values has k+1 subtrees, where the subtrees may be empty.

(d) The i'th subtree of a node $[v_1, ..., v_k]$, $0 \leq i \leq k$, *may hold only values v in the range* $v_i \leq v \leq v_{i+1}$ (v_0 *is assumed to equal* $-\infty$, *and* v_{k+1} *is assumed to equal* infty).

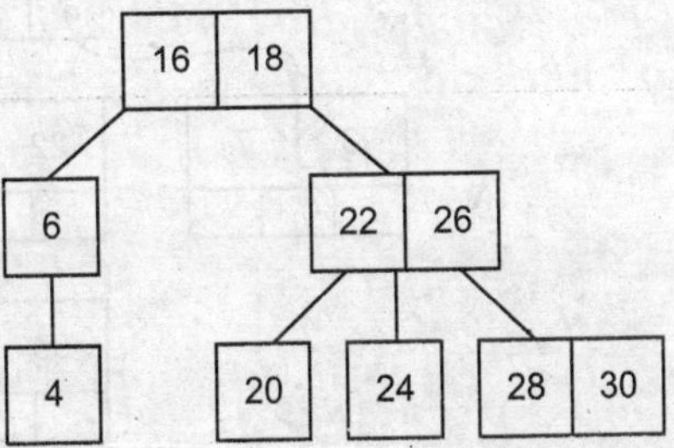

Figure 9.39: A m-way tree of height h has between h and $m^h - 1$ keys.

Binary search tree: 1 value and 2 subtrees per node.

M-way search tree: m - 1 values and m subtrees per node. m is the degree of the tree. In fact, each may contain up to m - 1 values. A node with k values must have k + 1 subtrees.

In a node, values are stored in ascending order: V1 < V2 < ... < Vk

The subtrees are placed between adjacent values: each value has a left and right subtree.

V(i)'s right subtree = V(i+1)'s left subtree.

All the values in V(i)'s left subtree are < V(i).

All the values in V(i)'s right subtree are > V(i).

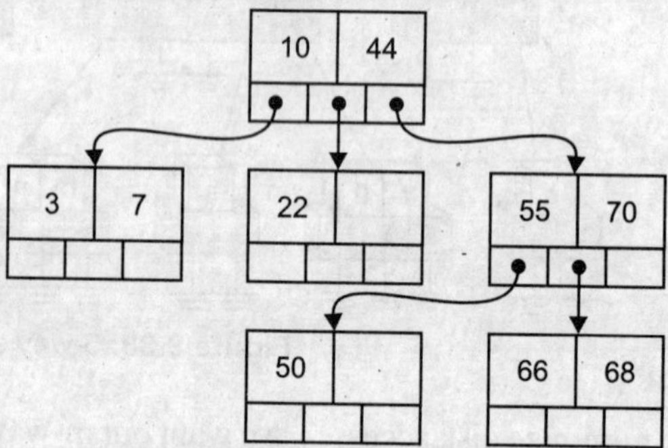

Figure 9.40: M- way trees.

9.6.2 Search in M-way Trees

Searching for X:

1. If X < V(1), recursively search in V(1)'s left subtree.
2. If X > V(k), recursively search in V(k)'s right subtree.
3. If X = V(i), for some i, X is found!
4. Else, for some i, V(i) < X < V(i+1); recursively search in subtree between V(i) and V(i+1). Search for 68 in:

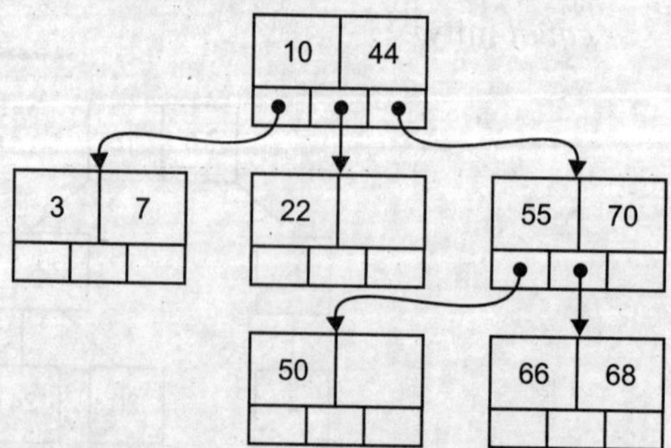

Figure 9.41: Search in m-way trees.

9.6.3 Insertions in Multi-way Trees

- Search the key going down the tree until reaching an empty subtree
- Insert the key to the parent of the empty subtree, if there is room in the node.

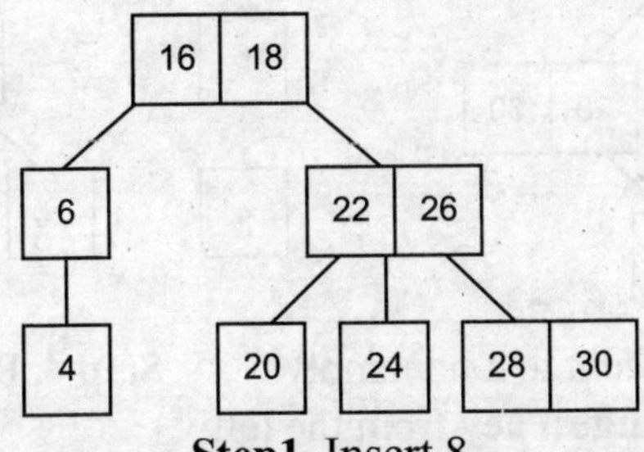

Step1. Insert 8

Step2. Insert the key to the subtree, if there is no room in its parent.

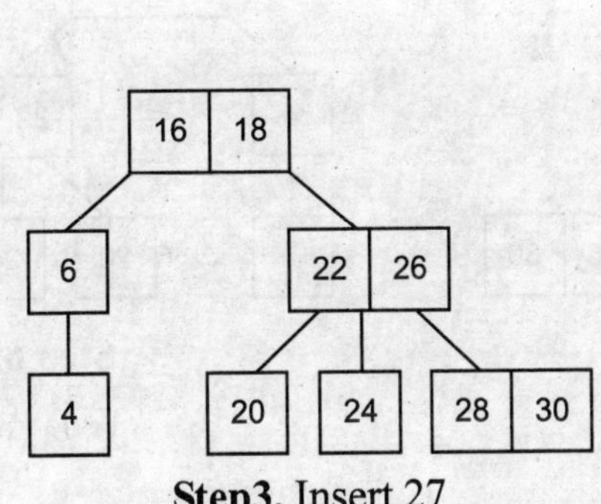

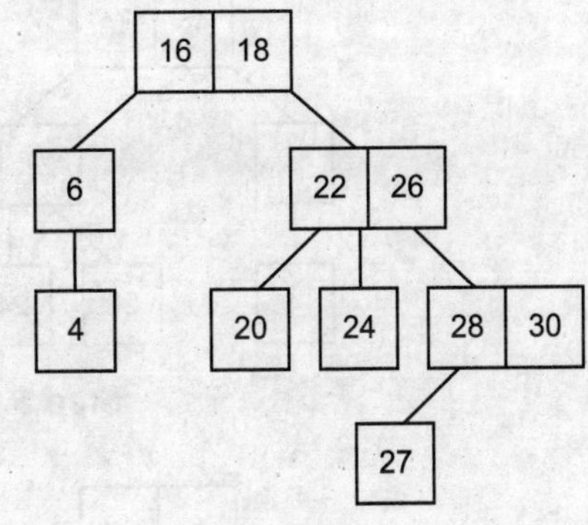

Step3. Insert 27

9.6.4 Deletions from Multi-way Trees

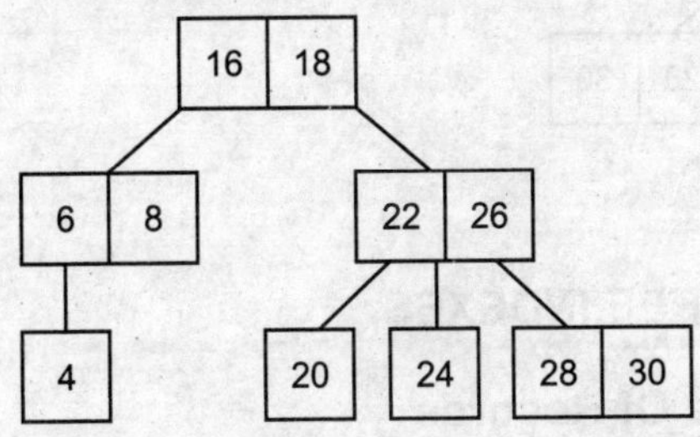

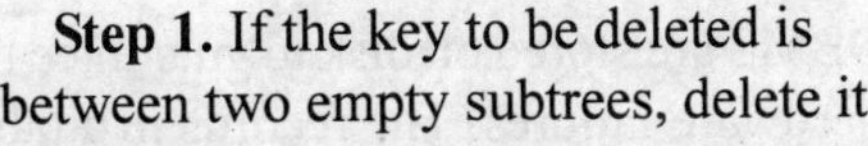

Step 1. If the key to be deleted is between two empty subtrees, delete it

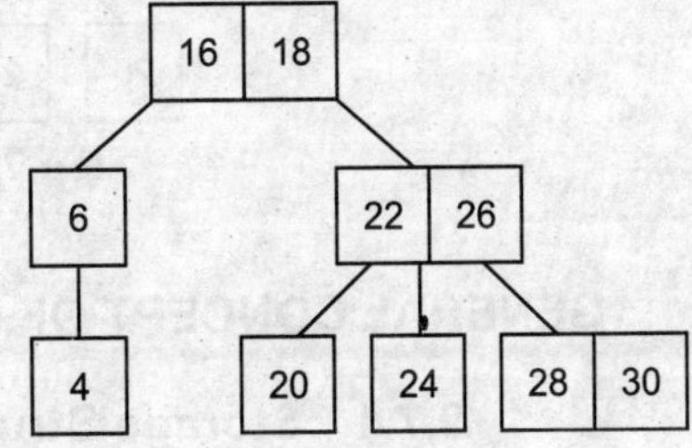

Step 2. Delete 8

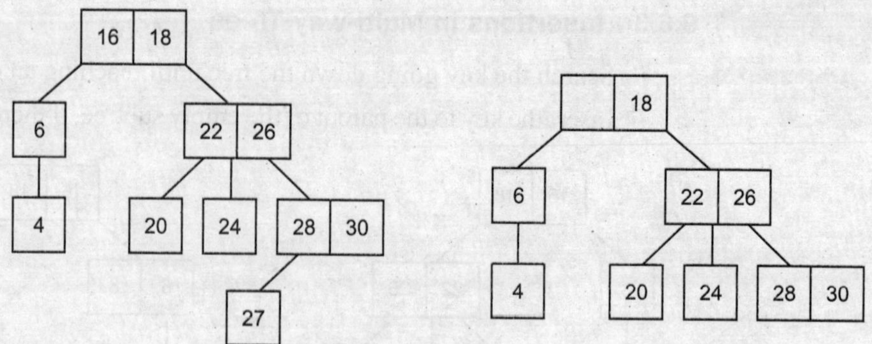

Step 3. If the key is adjacent to a nonempty subtree, replace it with the largest key from the left subtree or the smallest key from the right subtree

Step 4. Remove 16

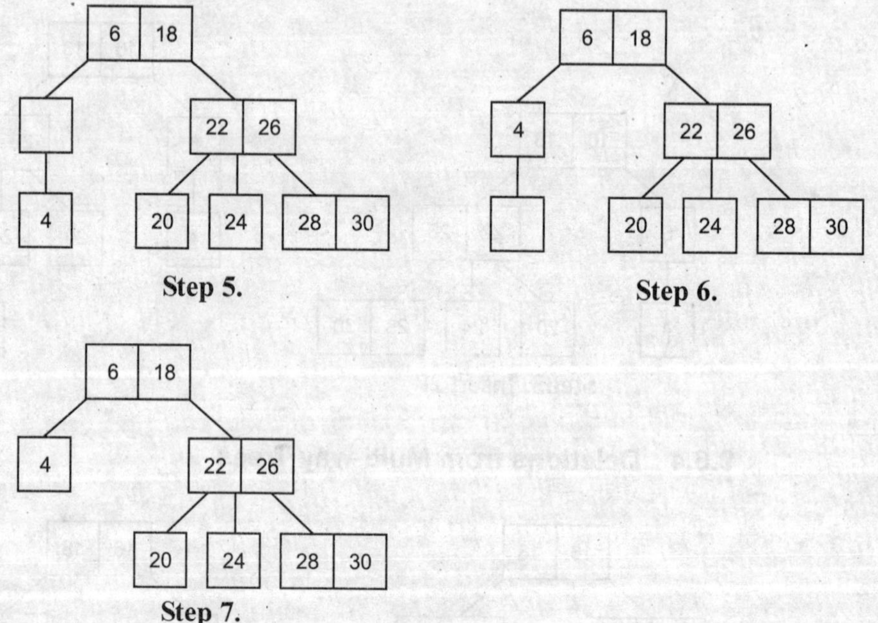

Step 5.

Step 6.

Step 7.

9.7 GENERAL CONCEPT OF B+-TREE INDEXES

9.7.1 Storage Structure Of Records

All records of a table in a RDBMS are stored on disk to guarantee their permanence in case of software and/or hardware failures. The records in a table are organized in files that are managed by the DBMS — not by the OS. Whenever a query is submitted to the RDBMS, the query is processed and the records in the relational database table(s) that satisfy the query are returned by the DBMS. The way in which the query is processed depends on the particular storage structure of the records in the file. If the records are organized in no particular order then the storage structure is referred to as a heap. Whereas when the records are ordered according to some of its attributes' values, then the storage structure of the file is said to be sorted. To retrieve records in a heap organized file, all that the RDBMS can do is a sequential scan of the disk pages where the records are stored. Typically the pages that make up the file are contiguous on disk.

If, on the other hand, the records are in a sorted file, then a binary search on the disk pages of the file can be used to retrieve records as long as the query's criteria uses the same attributes as the ones used to maintain sorted order of the records in the file. For example, if a file that stores the records for the Students table is sorted on last name and first name (in that order), then binary search can be used to process queries that search for students by last name only or queries that search for students by their full name. A query that searches for students by their date of birth must be processed using a sequential scan of the sorted file; similarly if the query searches for students by their first name.

A table index is a data structure and its associated algorithms that provide a mechanism by which records of the table can be searched for more efficiently than either sequential scan or binary search. The most common index structures used by RDBMS are B+-trees — another index structure is the Hash table. The rest of this webpage describes the B+-tree index structure.

9.7.2 Balanced Multiway Search Trees

Retrieval time from external memory (e.g. disk) is thousands of times greater than high-speed memory. The goal in external searching is to minimize the number of disk accesses, since disk access takes longer than computations. This is different than the goal of minimizing the number of computations (i.e. comparisons) in searching data that is in the faster main memory. For this reason, typical access of a record from external memory reads an entire page or block of data at once. By fetching a disk page that contains many records, we take advantage of the locality of reference — if a record is being retrieved and we have organized the records based on how they are accessed, then it is likely that the records that are in the fetched block will be retrieved next.

9.8 B+-TREE

A B+-tree is one in a family of multiway search trees (others are: B-tree, 2-3-4 Tree, B*-Trees). These trees were first proposed by Bayer and McCreight in 1972 and in just a few years had replaced almost all large file access methods other than hashing. These multiway balanced search trees are now the standard file organization for applications requiring insertion, deletion, and key range searches.

They have the following advantages:

- B-trees are always height balanced, with all leaf nodes at the same level
- Update and search operations affect only a few disk pages, so performance is good.
- B-trees keep related records on the same disk page, which takes advantage of locality of reference.
- B-trees guarantee that every node in the tree will be full at least to a certain minimum percentage. This improves space efficiency while reducing the typical number of disk fetches necessary during a search or update operation over many thousands of records.

9.8.1 B+-tree Structure

A B+-tree in certain aspects is a generalization of a binary search tree (BST). The main difference is that nodes of a B+-tree will point to many children nodes rather than being limited to only two. Since our goal is to minimize disk accesses whenever we are trying to locate records, we want to make the height of the multiway search tree as small as possible. This goal is achieved by having the tree branch in large amounts at each node.

A B+-tree of order m is a tree where each internal node contains up to m branches (children nodes) and thus store up to m-1 search key values — in a BST, only one key value is needed since there are just two children nodes that an internal node can have. m is also known as the branching factor or the fanout of the tree.

- The B+-tree stores records (or pointers to actual records) only at the leaf nodes, which are all found at the same level in the tree, so the tree is always height balanced.
- All internal nodes, except the root, have between Ceiling(m/2) and m children
- The root is either a leaf or has at least two children.
- Internal nodes store search key values, and are used only as placeholders to guide the search. The number of search key values in each internal node is one less than the number of its non-empty children, and these keys partition the keys in the children in the fashion of a search tree. The keys are stored in non-decreasing order (i.e. sorted in lexicographical order).
- Depending on the size of a record as compared to the size of a key, a leaf node in a B+-tree of order m may store more or less than m records. Typically this is based on the size of a disk block, the size of a record pointer, etcetera. The leaf pages must store enough records to remain at least half full.
- The leaf nodes of a B+-tree are linked together to form a linked list. This is done so that the records can be retrieved sequentially without accessing the

B+-tree index. This also supports fast processing of range-search queries as will be described later.

9.8.2 B+-tree Operations

To understand the B+-tree operations more clearly, assume, without loss of generality, that there is a table whose primary is a single attribute and that it has a B+-tree index organized on the PK attribute of the table.

9.8.2.1 Searching for Records that Satisfy A Simple Condition

To retrieve records, queries are written with conditions that describe the values that the desired records are to have. The most basic search on a table to retrieve a single record given its PK value K.

Search in a B+-tree is an alternating two-step process, beginning with the root node of the B+-tree. Say that the search is for the record with key value K — there can only be one record because we assume that the index is built on the PK attribute of the table.

Algorithm 9.8: Search element from B+- tree.

Step 1: Perform a binary search on the search key values in the current node — recall that the search key values in a node are sorted and that the search starts with the root of the tree. We want to find the key Ki such that Ki ≤ K < Ki+1.

Step 2: If the current node is an internal node, follow the proper branch associated with the key Ki by loading the disk page corresponding to the node and repeat the search process at that node.

Step 3: If the current node is a leaf, then:

a. If K=Ki, then the record exists in the table and we can return the record associated with Ki

b. Otherwise, K is not found among the search key values at the leaf, we report that there is no record in the table with the value K.

9.8.2.2 Inserting into a B+-tree

Insertion in a B+-tree is similar to inserting into other search trees, a new record is always inserted at one of the leaf nodes. The complexity added is that insertion could overflow a leaf node that is already full. When such overflow situations occur a brand new leaf node is added to the B+-tree at the same level as the other leaf nodes. The steps to insert into a B+-tree are:

Algorithm 9.9: Insert element into B+-tree.

Step 1: Follow the path that is traversed as if a Search is being performed on the key of the new record to be inserted.

Step 2: The leaf page L that is reached is the node where the new record is to be indexed.

Step 3: If L is not full then an index entry is created that includes the seach key value of the new row and a reference to where new row is in the data file. We are done; this is the easy case!

Step 4: If L is full, then a new leaf node Lnew is introduced to the B+-tree as a right sibling of L. The keys in L along with the an index entry for the new record are distributed evenly among L and Lnew. Lnew is inserted in the linked list of leaf nodes just to the right of L. We must now link Lnew to the tree and since Lnew is to be a sibling of L, it will then be pointed to by the partent of L. The smallest key value of Lnew is copied and inserted into the parent of L — which will also be the parent of Lnew. This entire step is known as commonly referred to as a split of a leaf node.

a.If the parent P of L is full, then it is split in turn. However, this split of an internal node is a bit different. The search key values of P and the new inserted key must still be distributed evenly among P and the new page introduced as a sibling of P. In this split, however, the middle key is moved to the node above — note, that unlike splitting a leaf node where the middle key is copied and inserted into the parent, when you split an internal node the middle key is removed from the node being split and inserted into the parent node. This splitting of nodes may continue upwards on the tree.

b.When a key is added to a full root, then the root splits into two and the middle key is promoted to become the new root. This is the only way for a B+-tree to increase in height — when split cascades the entire height of the tree from the leaf to the root.

9.8.2.3 Deletion From a B+-tree

Deletion from a B+-tree again needs to be sure to maintain the property that all nodes must be at least half full. The complexity added is that deletion could underflow a leaf node that has only the minimum number of entries allowed. When such underflow situations take place, adjacent sibling nodes are examined; if one of them has more than the minimum entries required then some of its entries are taken from it to prevent a node from underflowing. Otherwise, if both adjacent sibling nodes are also at their minimum, then two of these nodes are merged into a single node. The steps to delete from a B+-tree are:

Algorithm 9.10: Delete element from B+- tree.

Step 1: Perform the search process on the key of the record to be deleted. This search will end at a leaf L.

Step 2: If the leaf L contains more than the minimum number of elements (more than m/2 - 1), then the index entry for the record to be removed can be safely deleted from the leaf with no further action.

Step 3: If the leaf contains the minimum number of entries, then the deleted entry is replaced with another entry that can take its place while maintaining the correct order. To find such entries, we inspect the two sibling leaf nodes Lleft and Lright adjacent to L — at most one of these may not exist.

a. If one of these leaf nodes has more than the minimum number of entries, then enough records are transferred from this sibling so that both nodes have the same number of records. This is a heuristic and is done to delay a future underflow as long as possible; otherwise, only one entry need be transferred. The placeholder key value of the parent node may need to be revised.

b. If both Lleft and Lright have only the minimum number of entries, then L gives its records to one of its siblings and it is removed from the tree. The new leaf will contain no more than the maximum number of entries allowed. This merge process combines two subtrees of the parent, so the separating entry at the parent needs to be removed — this may in turn cause the parent node to underflow; such an underflow is handled the same way that an underflow of a leaf node.

c. If the last two children of the root merge together into one node, then this merged node becomes the new root and the tree loses a level.

9.8.2.4 Determining the Size of A B+-tree

Consider a relation of 2,000,000 tuples (that's 2million tuples) stored in a heap file structure. How large (in number of disk pages) would a B+-tree index on this relation be? We will assume that we are building a B+-tree that is filled up as much as possible. To determine this, we need to know the following:

- The size of one disk page. While pages are usually 4KBytes or 8KBytes, to make our calculations easier we will use a page size of 1,000 bytes
- The size of the search key value. Say that we index the relation by using an attribute that is a 40-byte string and which is a candidate key of the relation.
- The size of physical page addresses. This is needed in our calculations since every node in our B+-tree will store search key values as well as references to disk pages — i.e. the address of the disk page being referenced. Again, for ease of calculations, we use a 10-byte page address.

Now that we have the information above, we can proceed with determining the size of our B+-tree index. We will determine this by working from bottom to the top of the tree:

1. Since a page is 1,000bytes, it can only store a limited number of index entries. Also, we are building a B+-tree that is filled up as much as possible so we will store as many index entries as can fit in a disk page. An index entry is a pair of values: [search key value, reference to tuple], and in our case, size(search key value)=40 and size(reference to tuple)=10. So, to

determine the number of index entries that can fit in a leaf page we can use this calculation:

- Number of index entries per leaf page = Floor(Page_size / (size(search key value) + size(reference to tuple)))
- Number of index entries per leaf page = Floor(1000 / (40 + 10)) = 20

2. Now we must determine the number of leaf pages that are necessary. Since the table we are indexing is stored as a heap, the tuples are not ordered in the data file. So, our B+-tree index must contain one index enter per tuple in the table; this is known as a dense index. So, there will be 2million index entries collectively stored in the leaf pages. The number of leaf pages necessary is given by:
   - Number of leaf pages = Ceiling ((Number of index entries to be stored) / (Number of index entries per leaf page))
   - Number of leaf pages = Ceiling (2,000,000 / 20) = 100,000
3. Next, we must determine the branching factor, m, of our B+-tree. This can be done by repeating step 1 above with some slight modifications. In a B+-tree of order m, each internal node must be able to store up to m branches (i.e. pointers to nodes in the level below) and thus, up to m-1 search key values (usually called separator values when they appear in the internal nodes).
   - Page_size >= (m-1) * size(search key value) + m * size(pointer)
   - In our case, we have:

     1,000 >= (m-1) * 40 + m * 10
   - Solving for m, which must be a whole number, we get:

     m = Floor((1,000 + 40) / 50) = 20
   - So, each internal node will store 20 pointers to nodes in the level below and a corresponding 19 search key values. Note the slight but important difference between internal nodes and leaf nodes.
4. Now that we have m, we can determine the number of pages at each level in the B+-tree. Since every leaf in our tree needs to be referenced from the level above, collectively we will need 100,000 pointers (i.e. branches), one per leaf page. Therefore the number of internal pages in the level above the leaves is:
   - Number of pages in level above leaves = Ceiling (Number of leaf pages / branching factor)
   - Number of pages in level above leaves = Ceiling (100,000/20) = 5,000
   - We need to continue doing this computation until we reach the point where we have just one internal node that will be the root of our tree

- Number of pages in the next level above = Ceiling(5000 / 20) = 250
- Number of pages in the next level above = Ceiling(250 / 20) = 13
- Number of pages in the next level above = Ceiling(13 / 20) = 1
- Notice that we have repeated this process 5 times, and that in fact:

  Height of B+-tree = Ceiling(logmNumberOfLeafPages)

  And in our case, Height of B+-tree = Ceiling(log20100000) = 4.

5. We can finally answer the question as to the size of our B+-tree:
   - Total number of pages = 100,000 + 5,000 + 250 + 13 + 1 = 105,264 pages
   - We have a 5-level B+-tree indexing 2million tuples, so by accessing 5 disk pages of the B+-tree followed by 1 page of the file, we can find any one of these tuples.
6. Note that database systems use caching and it is common for the top two levels of a B+-tree to be in the cache, thus saving two disk accesses in this example.
7. It is finally worth noting that this example used a small page size of 1,000 bytes for easier calculations. Common page sizes are 4Kbytes, 8Kbytes, or even 16Kbytes. Larger page sizes lead to larger branching factors and thus shallower trees. There is of course a trade-off between the page size and page utilization. Occupying only half of a 4Kbyte page is not as significant as occupying only half of a 16Kbyte page. B*-trees can address this issue, see next section.

Finally, if we were asked to find the size of a B+-tree whose pages are filled to their minimum capacity we can follow the process above with one additional consideration. Pages of a B+-tree must have a minimum of Ceiling(m/2) children nodes (i.e. half of the page must be full). So, the computations above would need to take this into account to find the size of such a tree.

9.9 GENERAL CONCEPT OF B-TREES

A B-tree is a specialized multiway tree designed especially for use on disk. In a B-tree each node may contain a large number of keys. The number of subtrees of each node, then, may also be large. A B-tree is designed to branch out in this large number of directions and to contain a lot of keys in each node so that the height of the tree is relatively small. This means that only a small number of nodes must be read from disk to retrieve an item. The goal is to get fast access to the data, and with disk drives this means reading a very small number of records. Note that a large node size (with lots of keys in the node) also fits with the fact that with a disk drive one can usually read a fair amount of data at once.

Definition: *A m-way tree in which*

- *The root has at least one key*
- *Non-root nodes have at least* $\lceil m/2 \rceil$ *subtrees (i.e., at least* $\lfloor (m-1)/2 \rfloor$ *keys)*
- *All the empty subtrees (i.e., external nodes) are at the same level*

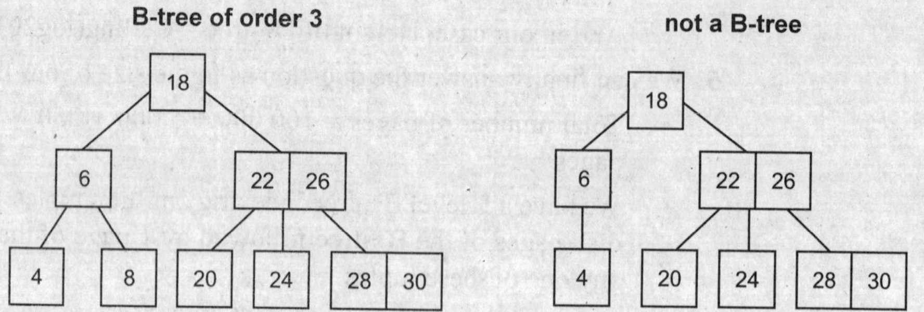

B-trees are especially useful for trees stored on disks, since their height, and hence also the number of disk accesses, can be kept small.

The growth and contraction of m-way search trees occur at the leaves. On the other hand, B-trees grow and contract at the root.

9.9.1 Insertions

- Insert the key to a leaf
- Overfilled nodes should send the middle key to their parent, and split into two at the location of the submitted key.

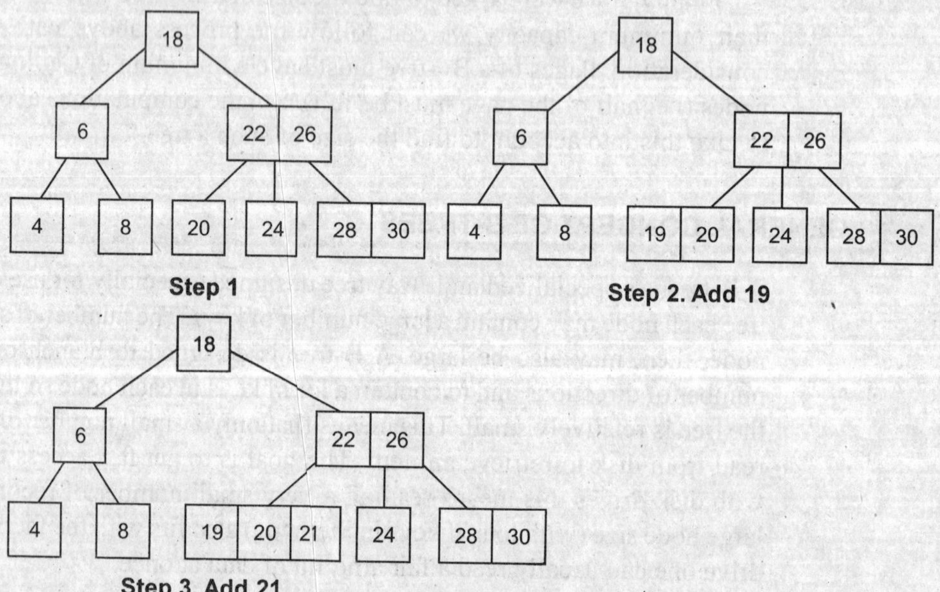

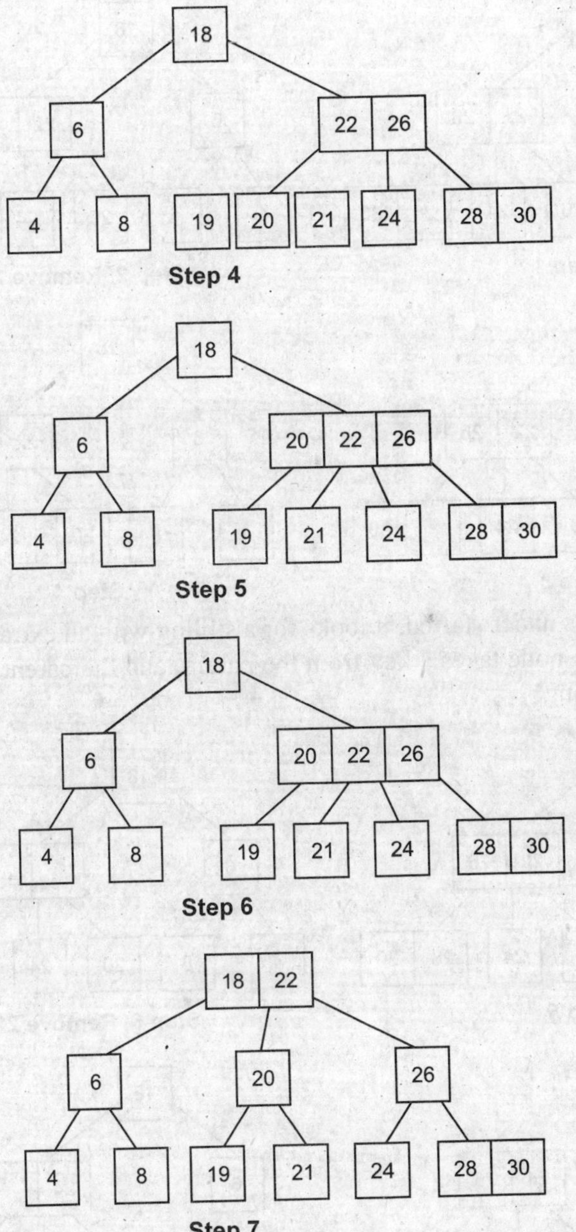

Step 4

Step 5

Step 6

Step 7

9.9.2 Deletions

Key that is to be removed from a node with non-empty subtrees is being replaced with the largest key of the left subtree or the smallest key in the right subtree. (The replacement is guaranteed to come from a leaf.)

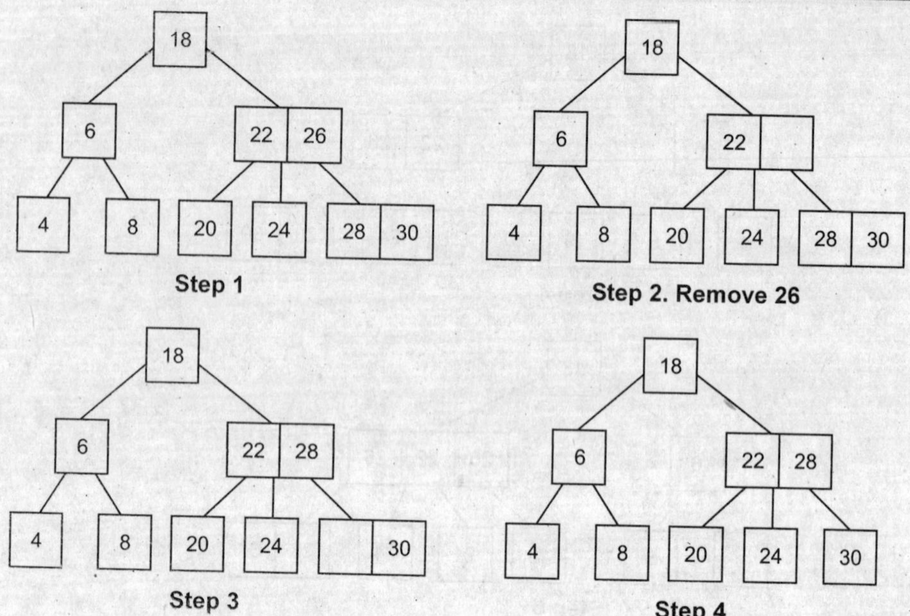

Step 1

Step 2. Remove 26

Step 3

Step 4

If a node becomes under staffed, it looks for a sibling with an extra key. If such a sibling exists, the node takes a key from the parent, and the parent gets the extra key from the sibling.

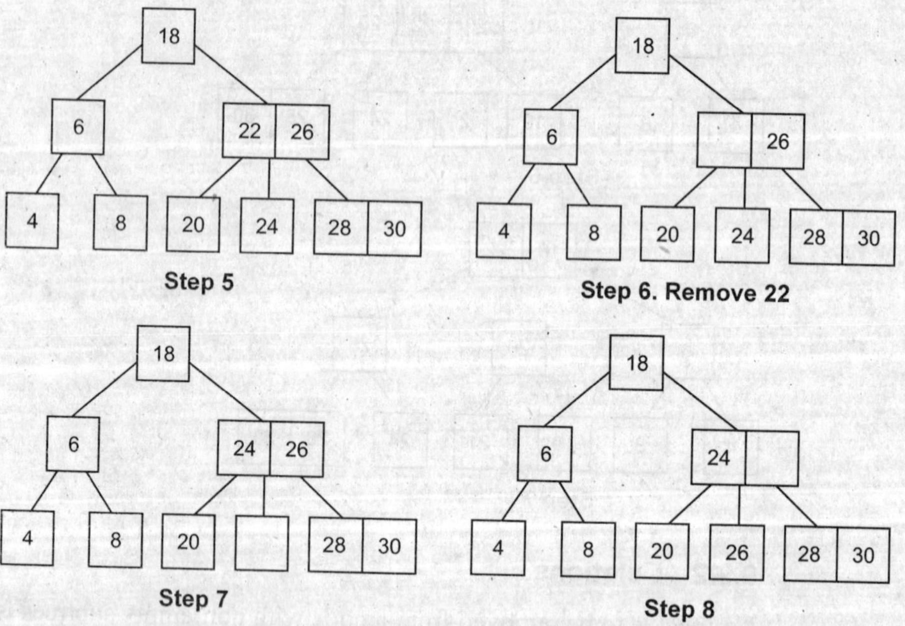

Step 5

Step 6. Remove 22

Step 7

Step 8

If a node becomes under staffed, and it can't receive a key from a sibling, the node is merged with a sibling and a key from the parent is moved down to the node.

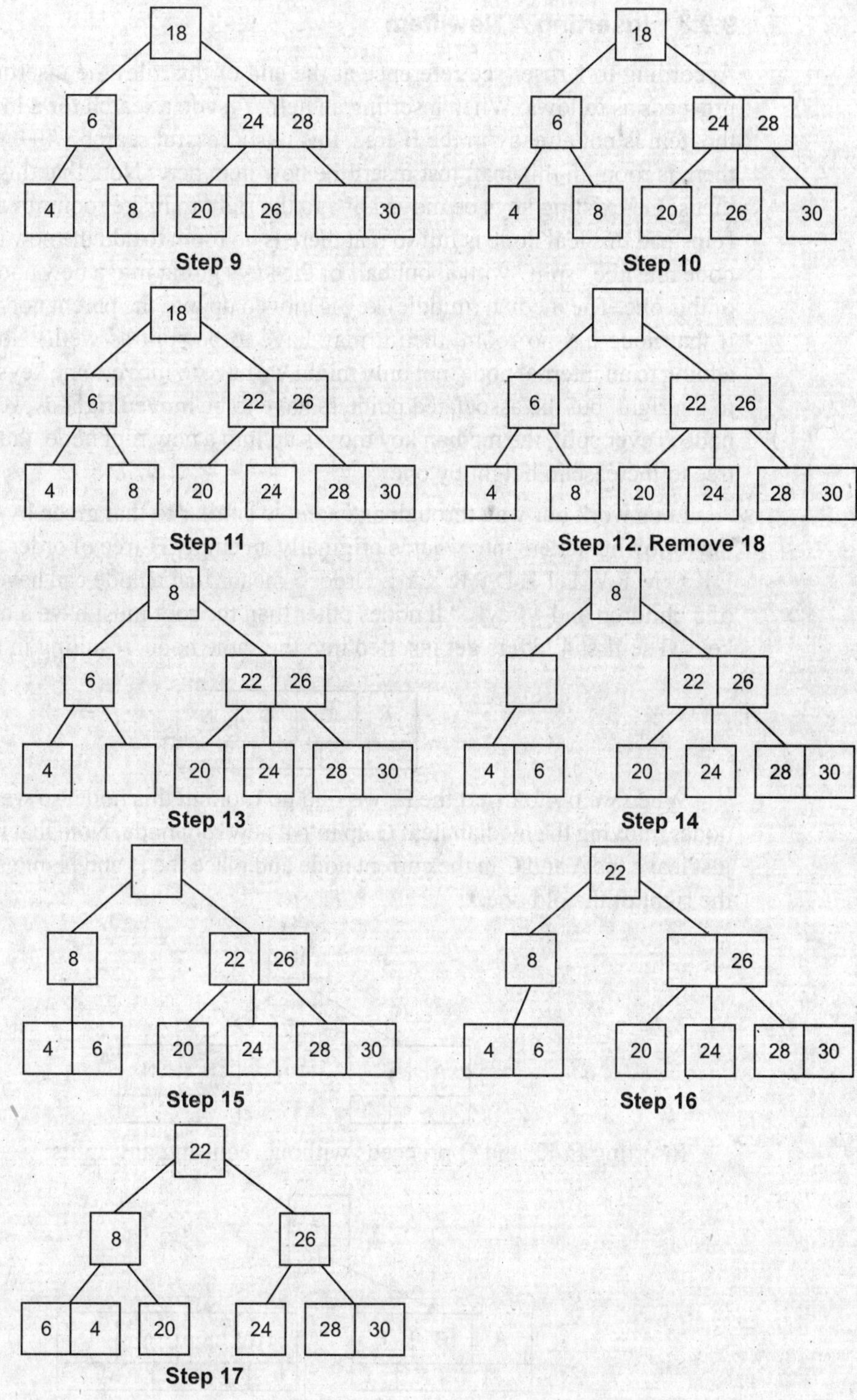
18
6
24 28
4
8
20
26
30
Step 9
18
6
24 28
4
8
20
26
30
Step 10
18
6
22 26
4
8
20
24
28 30
Step 11
6
22 26
4
8
20
24
28 30
Step 12. Remove 18
8
6
22 26
4
20
24
28 30
Step 13
8
22 26
4 6
20
24
28 30
Step 14
8
22 26
4 6
20
24
28 30
Step 15
22
8
26
4 6
20
24
28 30
Step 16
22
8
26
6 4
20
24
28 30
Step 17

9.9.3 Inserting A New Item

According to Kruse (see reference at the end of this file) the insertion algorithm proceeds as follows: When inserting an item, first do a search for it in the B-tree. If the item is not already in the B-tree, this unsuccessful search will end at a leaf. If there is room in this leaf, just insert the new item here. Note that this may require that some existing keys be moved one to the right to make room for the new item. If instead this leaf node is full so that there is no room to add the new item, then the node must be "split" with about half of the keys going into a new node to the right of this one. The median (middle) key is moved up into the parent node. (Of course, if that node has no room, then it may have to be split as well.) Note that when adding to an internal node, not only might we have to move some keys one position to the right, but the associated pointers have to be moved right as well. If the root node is ever split, the median key moves up into a new root node, thus causing the tree to increase in height by one.

Let's work our way through an example similar to that given by Kruse. Insert the following letters into what is originally an empty B-tree of order 5: C N G A H E K Q M F W L T Z D P R X Y S Order 5 means that a node can have a maximum of 5 children and 4 keys. All nodes other than the root must have a minimum of 2 keys. The first 4 letters get inserted into the same node, resulting in this picture:

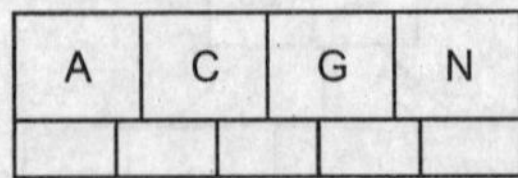

When we try to insert the H, we find no room in this node, so we split it into 2 nodes, moving the median item G up into a new root node. Note that in practice we just leave the A and C in the current node and place the H and N into a new node to the right of the old one.

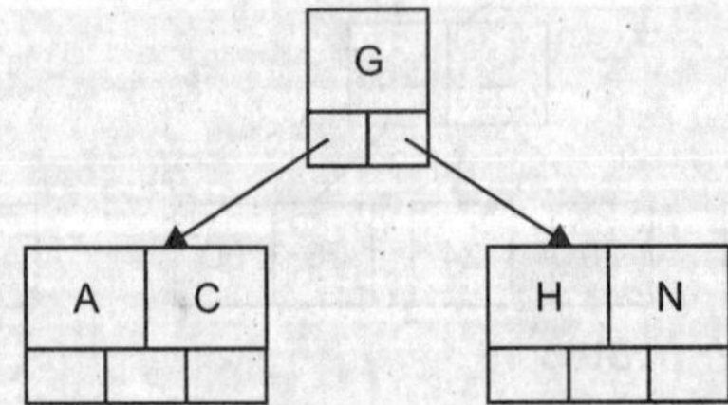

Inserting E, K, and Q proceeds without requiring any splits:

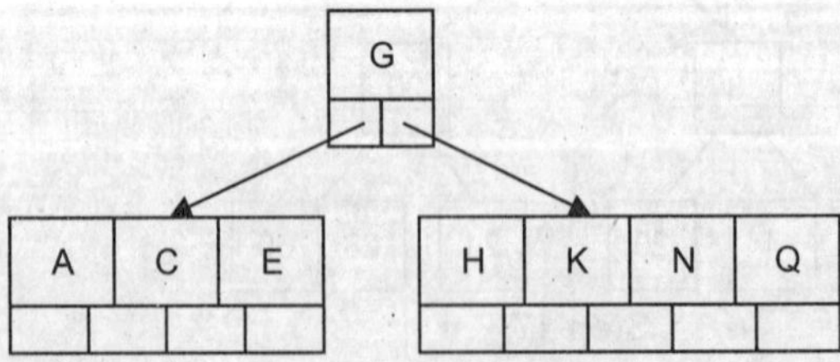

Inserting M requires a split. Note that M happens to be the median key and so is moved up into the parent node.

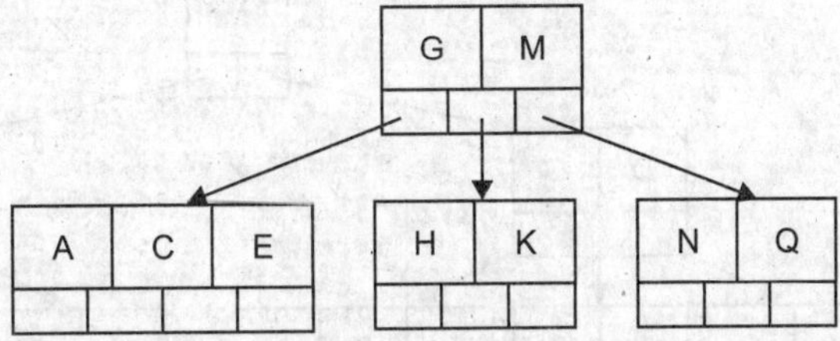

The letters F, W, L, and T are then added without needing any split.

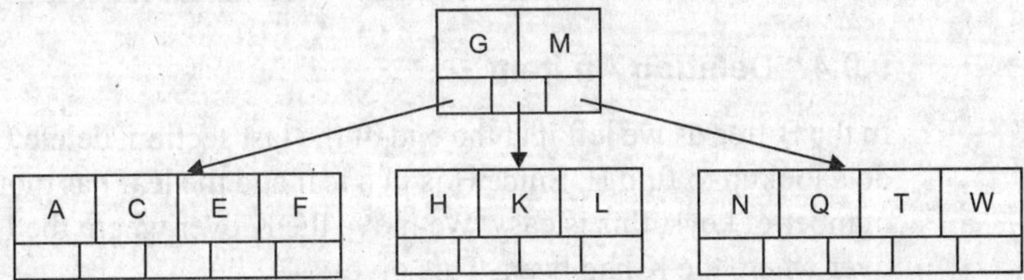

When Z is added, the rightmost leaf must be split. The median item T is moved up into the parent node. Note that by moving up the median key, the tree is kept fairly balanced, with 2 keys in each of the resulting nodes.

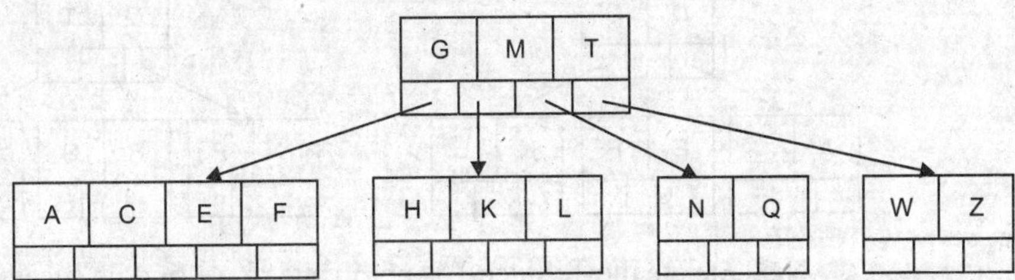

The insertion of D causes the leftmost leaf to be split. D happens to be the median key and so is the one moved up into the parent node. The letters P, R, X, and Y are then added without any need of splitting:

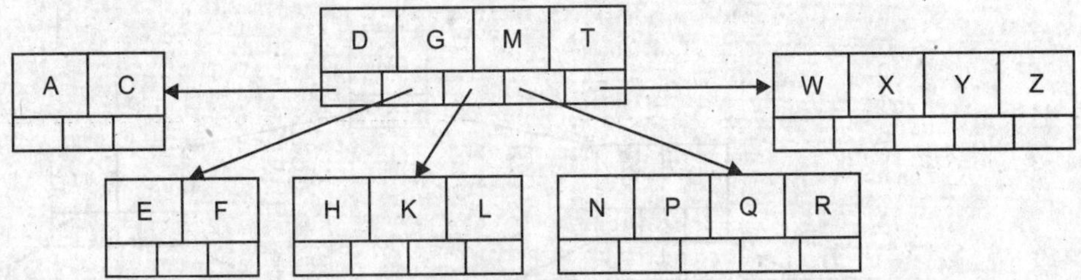

Finally, when S is added, the node with N, P, Q, and R splits, sending the median Q up to the parent. However, the parent node is full, so it splits, sending the median M up to form a new root node. Note how the 3 pointers from the old parent node stay in the revised node that contains D and G.

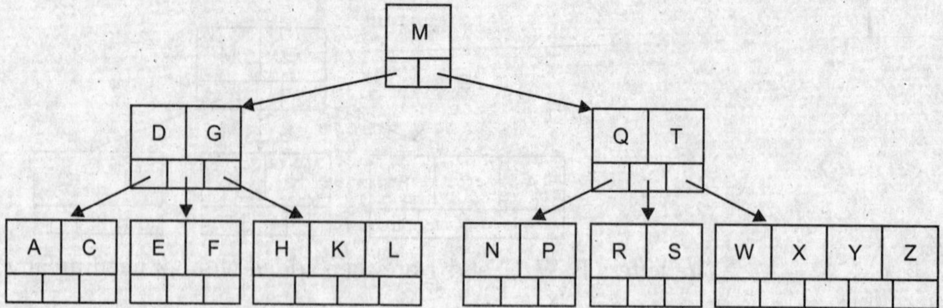

9.9.4 Deleting An Item

In the B-tree as we left it at the end of the last section, delete H. Of course, we first do a lookup to find H. Since H is in a leaf and the leaf has more than the minimum number of keys, this is easy. We move the K over where the H had been and the L over where the K had been. This gives:

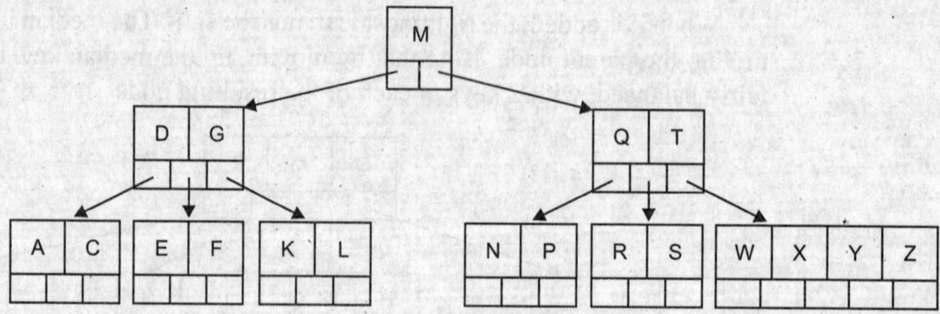

Next, delete the T. Since T is not in a leaf, we find its successor (the next item in ascending order), which happens to be W, and move W up to replace the T. That way, what we really have to do is to delete W from the leaf, which we already know how to do, since this leaf has extra keys. In ALL cases we reduce deletion to a deletion in a leaf, by using this method.

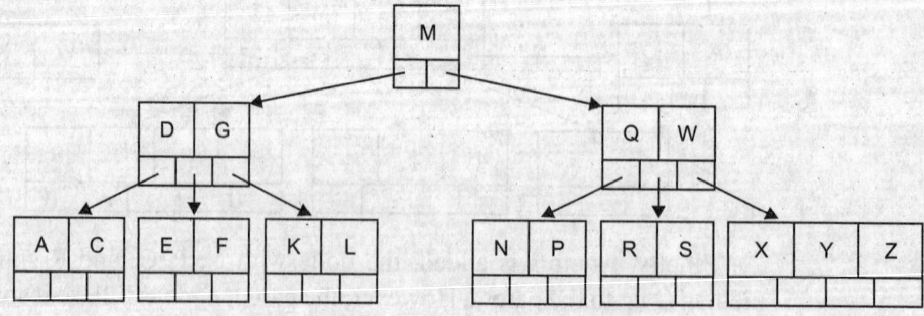

Next, delete R. Although R is in a leaf, this leaf does not have an extra key; the deletion results in a node with only one key, which is not acceptable for a B-tree of order 5. If the sibling node to the immediate left or right has an extra key, we can then borrow a key from the parent and move a key up from this sibling. In our specific case, the sibling to the right has an extra key. So, the successor W of S (the last key in the node where the deletion occurred), is moved down from the parent, and the X is moved up. (Of course, the S is moved over so that the W can be inserted in its proper place.)

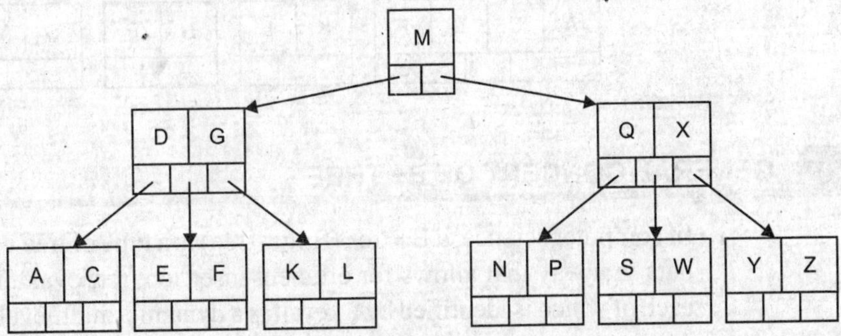

Finally, let's delete E. This one causes lots of problems. Although E is in a leaf, the leaf has no extra keys, nor do the siblings to the immediate right or left. In such a case the leaf has to be combined with one of these two siblings. This includes moving down the parent's key that was between those of these two leaves. In our example, let's combine the leaf containing F with the leaf containing A C. We also move down the D.

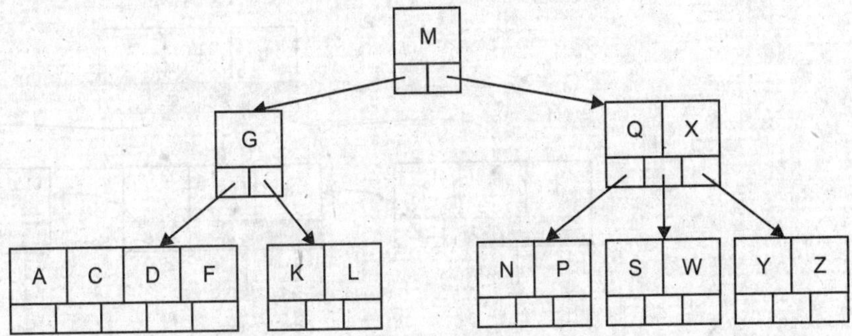

Of course, you immediately see that the parent node now contains only one key, G. This is not acceptable. If this problem node had a sibling to its immediate left or right that had a spare key, then we would again "borrow" a key. Suppose for the moment that the right sibling (the node with Q X) had one more key in it somewhere to the right of Q. We would then move M down to the node with too few keys and move the Q up where the M had been. However, the old left subtree of Q would then have to become the right subtree of M. In other words, the N P node would be attached via the pointer field to the right of M's new location. Since in our example we have no way to borrow a key from a sibling, we must again combine with the sibling, and move down the M from the parent. In this case, the tree shrinks in height by one.

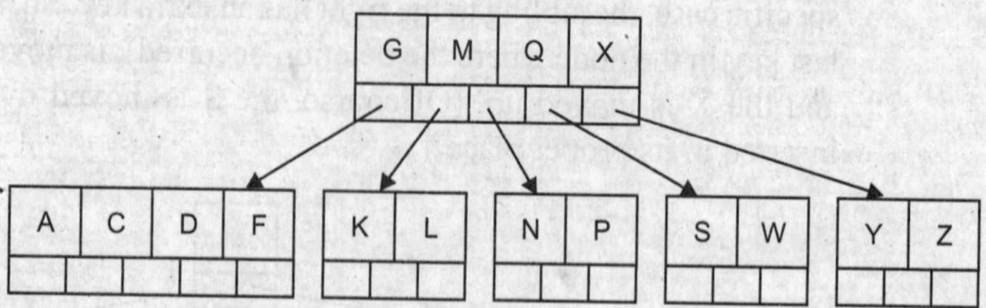

9.10 GENERAL CONCEPT OF B+ TREE

In computer science, a B+ tree (BplusTree) is a type of tree which represents sorted data in a way that allows for efficient insertion, retrieval and removal of records, each of which is identified by a key. It is a dynamic, multilevel index, with maximum and minimum bounds on the number of keys in each index segment (usually called a "block" or "node"). In a B+ tree, in contrast to a B-tree, all records are stored at the leaf level of the tree; only keys are stored in interior nodes.

The primary value of a B+ tree is in storing data for efficient retrieval in a block-oriented storage context. This is primarily because unlike binary search trees, B+ trees have very high fanout (typically on the order of 100 or more), which reduces the number of I/O operations required to find an element in the tree.

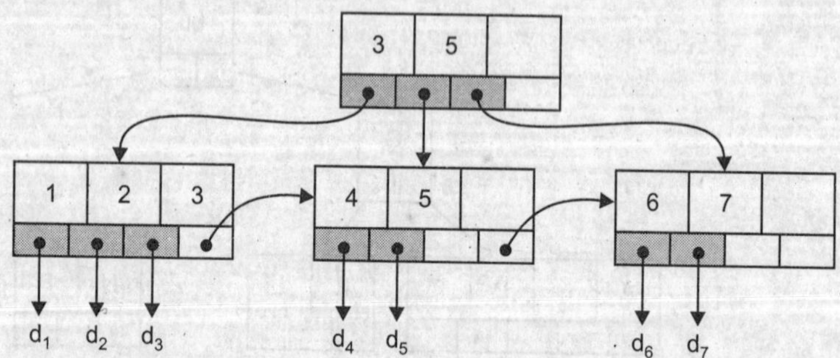

Figure 9.42: A simple B+ tree example linking the keys 1–7 to data values d1-d7. Note the linked list (red) allowing rapid in-order traversal.

The order (branching factor) of a B+ tree measures the capacity of nodes (i.e. the number of children nodes) in the tree. It is defined as a number d such that , where m is the number of children in each node. For example, if the order of a B+ tree is 7, each internal node (except for the root) may have between 4 and 7 children; the root may have between 2 and 7.

9.10.1 Characteristics of B+ Tree

1. For a b-order B+ tree with h levels of index.
2. The maximum number of records stored is n = bh
3. The minimum number of keys is 2(b / 2)h " 1
4. The space required to store the tree is O(n)
5. Inserting a record requires O(logbn) operations in the worst case
6. Finding a record requires O(logbn) operations in the worst case
7. Removing a (previously located) record requires O(logbn) operations in the worst case
8. Performing a range query with k elements occurring within the range requires O(logbn + k) operations in the worst case.

9.11 B+ TREES

B Trees: B Trees are multi-way trees. That is each node contains a set of keys and pointers. A B Tree with four keys and five pointers represents the minimum size of a B Tree node. A B Tree contains only data pages. B Trees are dynamic. That is, the height of the tree grows and contracts as records are added and deleted.

B+ Trees: A B+ Tree combines features of ISAM and B Trees. It contains index pages and data pages. The data pages always appear as leaf nodes in the tree. The root nodé and intermediate nodes are always index pages. These features are similar to ISAM. Unlike ISAM, overflow pages are not used in B+ trees. The index pages in a B+ tree are constructed through the process of inserting and deleting records. Thus, B+ trees grow and contract like their B Tree counterparts. The contents and the number of index pages reflects this growth and shrinkage.

B+ Trees and B Trees use a "fill factor" to control the growth and the shrinkage. A 50% fill factor would be the minimum for any B+ or B tree. As our example we use the smallest page structure. This means that our B+ tree conforms to the following guidelines.

Number of keys/page	4
Number of pointers/page	4
Fill factor	50%
Minimum keys in each page	2

As this table indicates each page must have a minimum of two keys. The root page may violate this rule. The following table shows a B+ tree. As the example illustrates this tree does not have a full index page. (We have room for one more key and pointer in the root page.) In addition, one of the data pages contains empty slots.

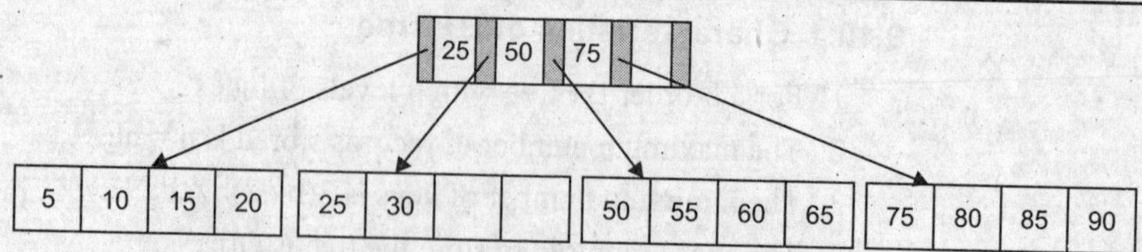

Figure 9.43: B+ tree with four keys.

9.11.1 Adding Records to A B+ Tree

The key value determines a record's placement in a B+ tree. The leaf pages are maintained in sequential order AND a doubly linked list (not shown) connects each leaf page with its sibling page(s). This doubly linked list speeds data movement as the pages grow and contract.

We must consider three scenarios when we add a record to a B+ tree. Each scenario causes a different action in the insert algorithm. The scenarios are:

The Insert Algorithm for B+ Trees

Leaf page full	Index page full	Action
No	No	Place the record in sorted position in the appropriate leaf page
Yes	No	1. Split the leaf page 2. Place middle key in the index page in sorted order 3. Left leaf page contains records with keys below the middle key. 4. Right leaf page contains records with keys equal to or greater than the middle key.
Yes	Yes	1. Split the leaf page 2. Records with keys < middle key go to the left leaf page 3. Recordes with keys >= middle key go to the right leaf page. 4. Split the index page. 5. Keys < middle key go to the left index page 6. Keys > middle key go to the right index page 7. The middle key goes to the next (higher lever) index If the next level index page is full, continue splitting the index pages.

Illustrations of the insert algorithm

The following examples illustrate each of the **insert** scenarios. We begin with the simplest scenario:

Inserting a record into a leaf page that is not full. Since only the leaf node containing 25 and 30 contains expansion room, we're going to insert a record with a key value of 28 into the B+ tree. The following figure shows the result of this addition.

Add record with key 28

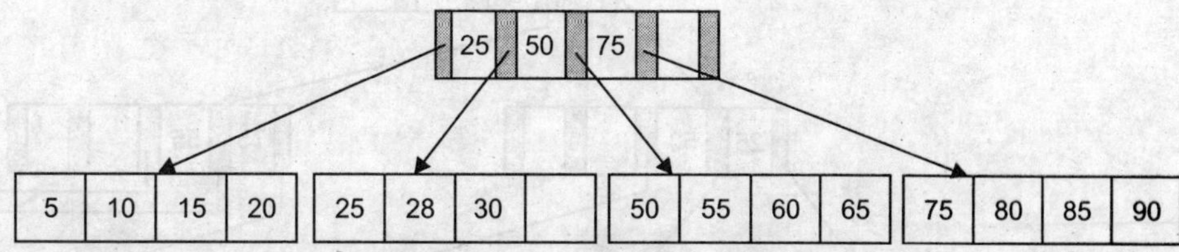

Adding a record when the leaf page is full but the index page is not

Next, we're going to insert a record with a key value of 70 into our B+ tree. This record should go in the leaf page containing 50, 55, 60, and 65. Unfortunately this page is full. This means that we must split the page as follows:

Left Leaf Page	**Right Leaf Page**
50 55	60 65 70

The middle key of 60 is placed in the index page between 50 and 75.

The following table shows the B+ tree after the addition of 70.

Add record with key 70

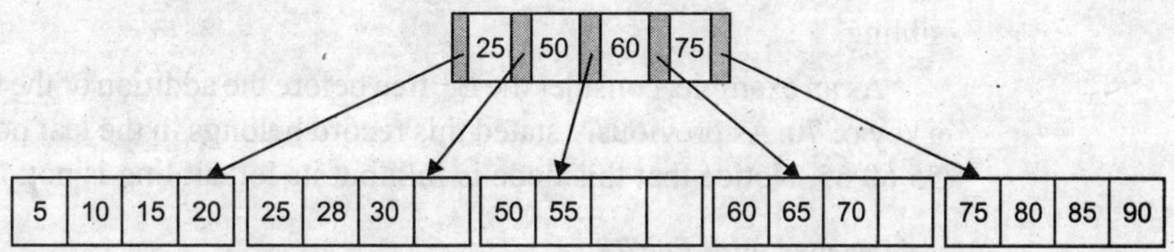

Adding a record when both the leaf page and the index page are full

As our last example, we're going to add a record containing a key value of 95 to our B+ tree. This record belongs in the page containing 75, 80, 85, and 90. Since this page is full we split it into two pages:

Left Leaf Page	**Right Leaf Page**
75 80	85 90 95

The middle key, 85, rises to the index page. Unfortunately, the index page is also full, so we split the index page:

Left Leaf Page	**Right Leaf Page**	**New Index Page**
25 50	75 85	60

The following table illustrates the addition of the record containing 95 to the B+ tree.

Add record with key 95

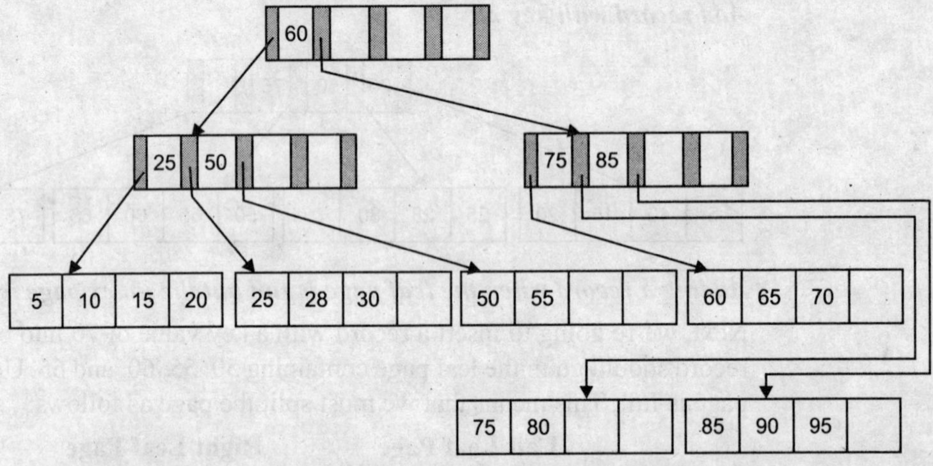

9.11.2 Rotation

B+ trees can incorporate rotation to reduce the number of page splits. A rotation occurs when a leaf page is full, but one of its sibling pages is not full. Rather than splitting the leaf page, we move a record to its sibling, adjusting the indices as necessary. Typically, the left sibling is checked first (if it exists) and then the right sibling.

As an example, consider the B+ tree before the addition of the record containing a key of 70. As previously stated this record belongs in the leaf node containing 50 55 60 65. Notice that this node is full, but its left sibling is not.

Add record with key 28

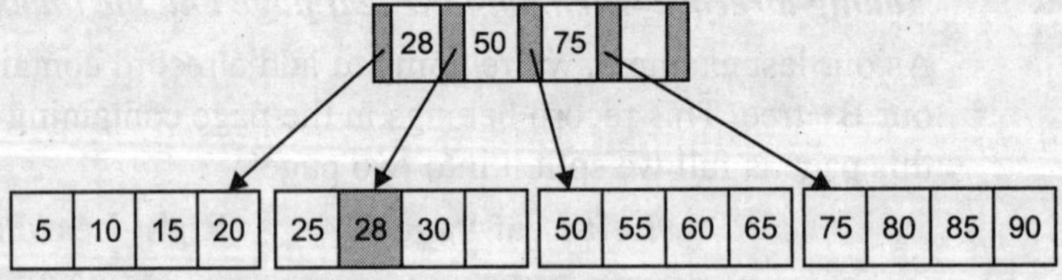

Using rotation we shift the record with the lowest key to its sibling. Since this key appeared in the index page we also modify the index page. The new B+ tree appears in the following table.

Illustration of rotation

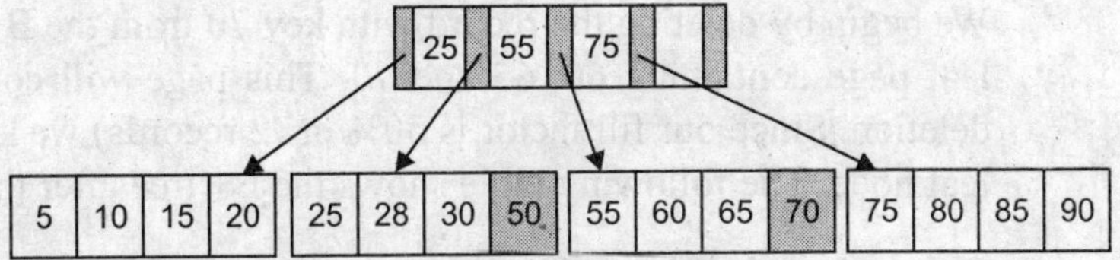

9.11.3 Deleting Keys from A B+ Tree

We must consider three scenarios when we delete a record from a B+ tree. Each scenario causes a different action in the delete algorithm. **The scenarios are:**

The delete algorithm for b+ trees

Leaf page below fill factor	Index page below fill factor	Action
No	No	Delete the record from the leaf page. Arrange keys in ascending order to fill void. If the key of the deleted record appears in the index page, use the next key to replace it.
Yes	No	Combine the leaf page and its sibling. Change the index page to reflect the change
Yes	Yes	1. Combine the leaf page and its sibling 2. Adjust the index page to reflect the change 3. Combine the index page with its sibling Continue combining index pages until you reach a page with the correct fill factor or you reach the root page

As our example, we consider the B+ tree after we added 95 as a key. As a refresher this tree is printed in the following table.

Add Record with Key 95

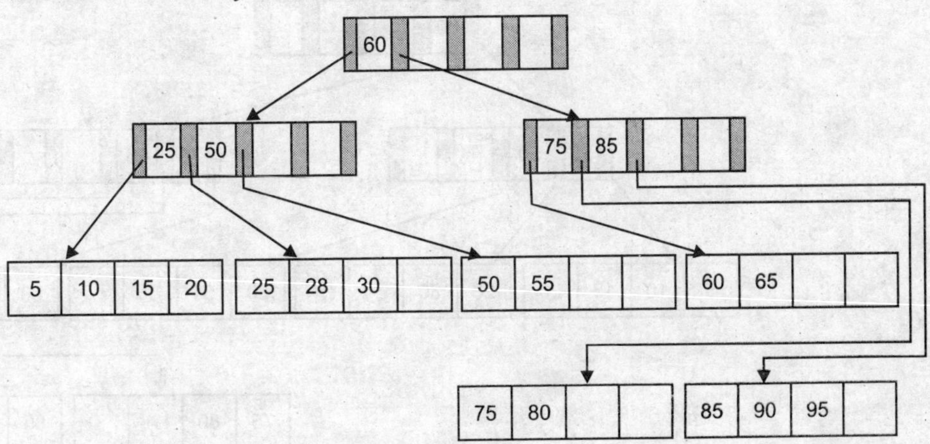

Delete 70 from the B+ tree

We begin by deleting the record with key 70 from the B+ tree. This record is in a leaf page containing 60, 65 and 70. This page will contain 2 records after the deletion. Since our fill factor is 50% or (2 records) we simply delete 70 from the leaf node. The following table shows the B+ tree after the deletion.

Delete record with key 70

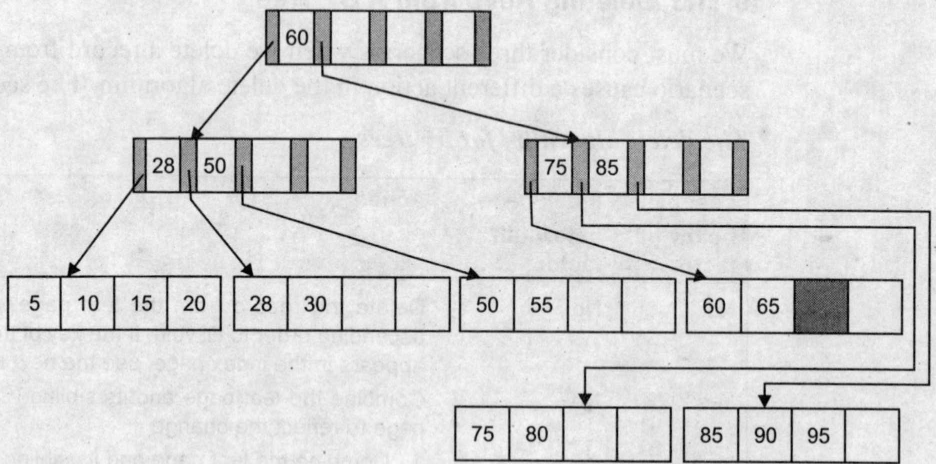

Delete 25 from the B+ tree

Next, we delete the record containing 25 from the B+ tree. This record is found in the leaf node containing 25, 28, and 30. The fill factor will be 50% after the deletion; however, 25 appears in the index page. Thus, when we delete 25 we must replace it with 28 in the index page. The following table shows the B+ tree after this deletion.

Delete record with key 25

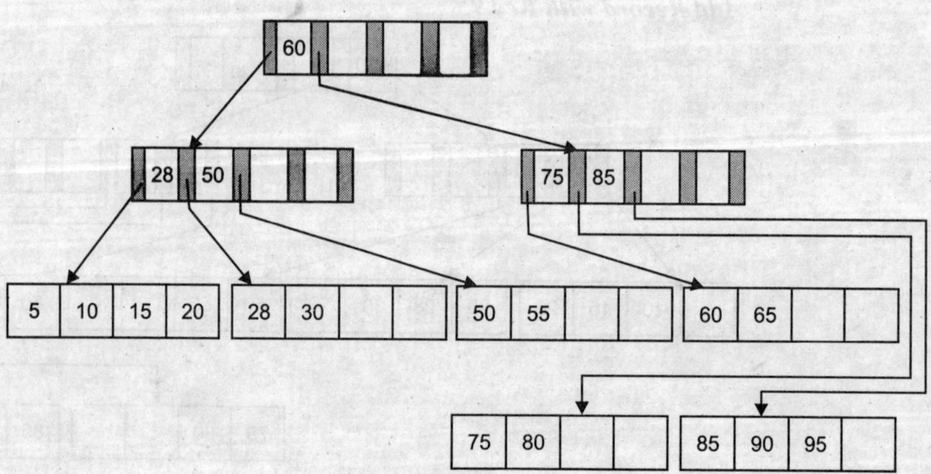

Delete 60 from the B+ tree

As our last example, we're going to delete 60 from the B+ tree. This deletion is interesting for several reasons:

1. The leaf page containing 60 (60 65) will be below the fill factor after the deletion. Thus, we must combine leaf pages.
2. With recombined pages, the index page will be reduced by one key. Hencc, it will also fall below the fill factor. Thus, we must combine index pages.
3. Sixty appears as the only key in the root index page. Obviously, it will be removed with the deletion. The following table shows the B+ tree after the deletion of 60. Notice that the tree contains a single index page.

Delete record with key 60

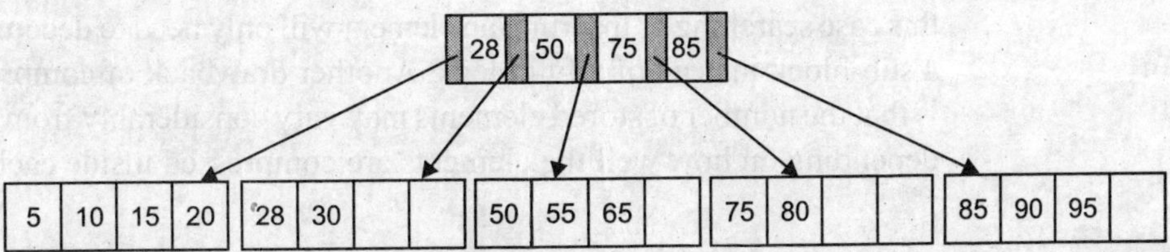

9.11.4 Implementation of the B+ Tree

The leaves (the bottom-most index blocks) of the B+ tree are often linked to one another in a linked list; this makes range queries simpler and more efficient (though the aforementioned upper bound can be achieved even without this addition). This does not substantially increase space consumption or maintenance on the tree.

If a storage system has a block size of B bytes, and the keys to be stored have a size of k, arguably the most efficient B+ tree is one where b = (B / k) " 1. Although theoretically the one-off is unnecessary, in practice there is often a little extra space taken up by the index blocks (for example, the linked list references in the leaf blocks). Having an index block which is slightly larger than the storage system's actual block represents a significant performance decrease; therefore erring on the side of caution is preferable.

If nodes of the B+ tree are organised as arrays of elements, then it may take a considerable time to insert or delete an element as half of the array will need to be shifted on average. To overcome this problem, elements inside a node can be organized in a binary tree or a B+ tree instead of an array.

B+ trees can also be used for data stored in RAM. In this case a reasonable choice for block size would be the size of processor's cache line. However some studies have proved that a block size few times larger than processor's cache line can deliver better performance if cache prefetching is used.

Space efficiency of B+ trees can be improved by using some compression techniques. One possibility is to use delta encoding to compress keys stored into each block. For internal blocks, space saving can be achieved by either compressing keys or pointers. For string keys, space can be saved by using the following technique: Normally the ith entry of an internal block contains the first key of block i+1. Instead of storing the full key, we could store the shortest prefix of the first key of block i+1 that is strictly greater (in lexicographic order) than last key of block i. There is also a simple way to compress pointers: if we suppose that some consecutive blocks i, i+1...i+k are stored contiguously, then it will suffice to store only a pointer to the first block and the count of consecutive blocks.

All the above compression techniques have some drawbacks. First, a full block must be decompressed to extract a single element. One technique to overcome this problem is to divide each block into sub-blocks and compress them separately. In this case searching or inserting an element will only need to decompress or compress a sub-block instead of a full block. Another drawback of compression techniques is that the number of stored elements may vary considerably from a block to another depending on how well the elements are compressed inside each block.

9.12 RED-BLACK TREES

A binary search tree in which

- The root is colored black
- All the paths from the root to the leaves agree on the number of black nodes
- No path from the root to a leaf may contain two consecutive nodes colored red

Empty subtrees of a node are treated as subtrees with roots of black color.

The relation $n \geq 2^{h/2} - 1$ implies the bound $h \leq 2 \log_2(n + 1)$.

9.12.1 Insertions

- Insert the new node the way it is done in binary search trees
- Color the node red
- If a discrepancy arises for the red-black tree, fix the tree according to the type of discrepancy.

A discrepancy can result from a parent and a child both having a red color. The type of discrepancy is determined by the location of the node with respect to its grand parent, and the color of the sibling of the parent.

Discrepancies in which the sibling is red, are fixed by changes in color. Discrepancies in which the siblings are black, are fixed through AVL-like rotations.

Changes in color may propagate the problem up toward the root. On the other hand, at most one rotation is sufficient for fixing a discrepancy.

Changes in color may propagate the problem up toward the root. On the other hand, at most one rotation is sufficient for fixing a discrepancy.

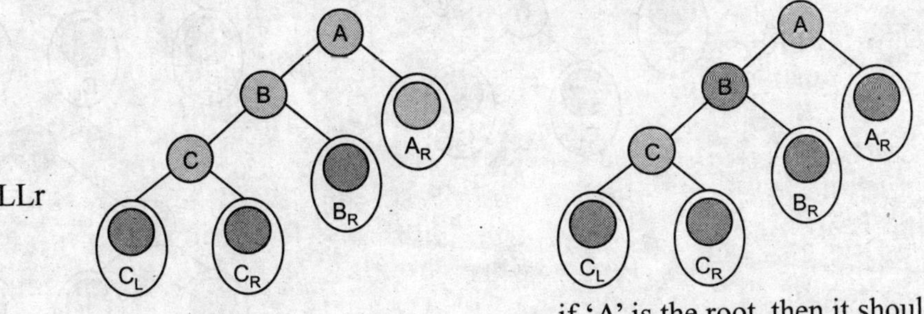

if 'A' is the root, then it should be repainted to black

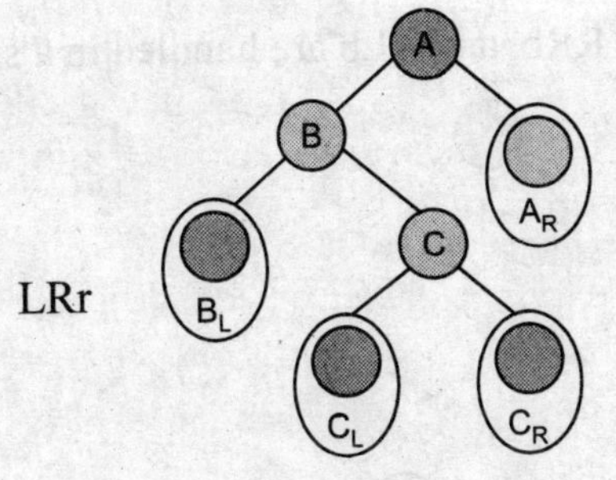

if 'A' is the root, then it should be repainted to black

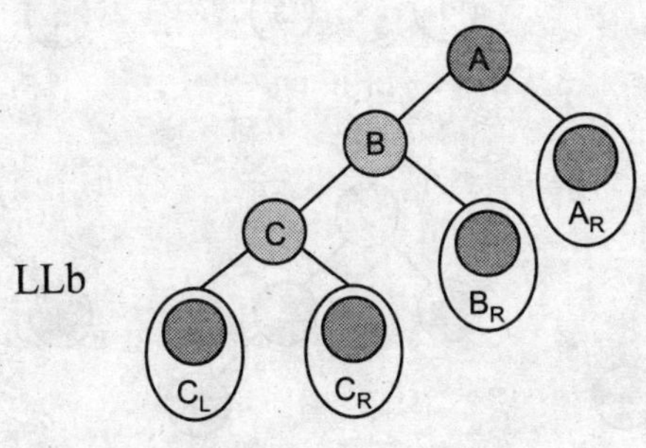

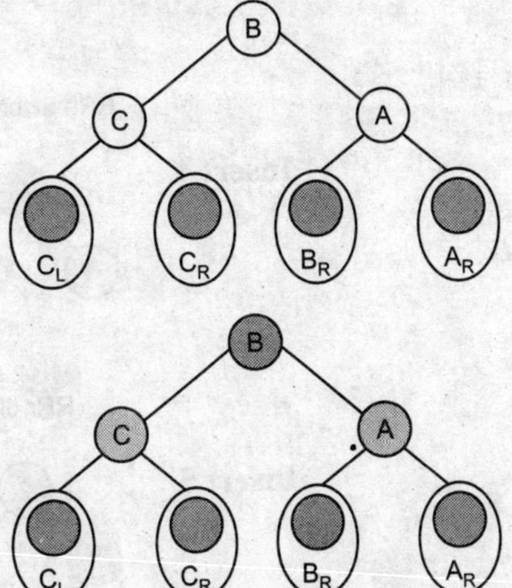

LRb

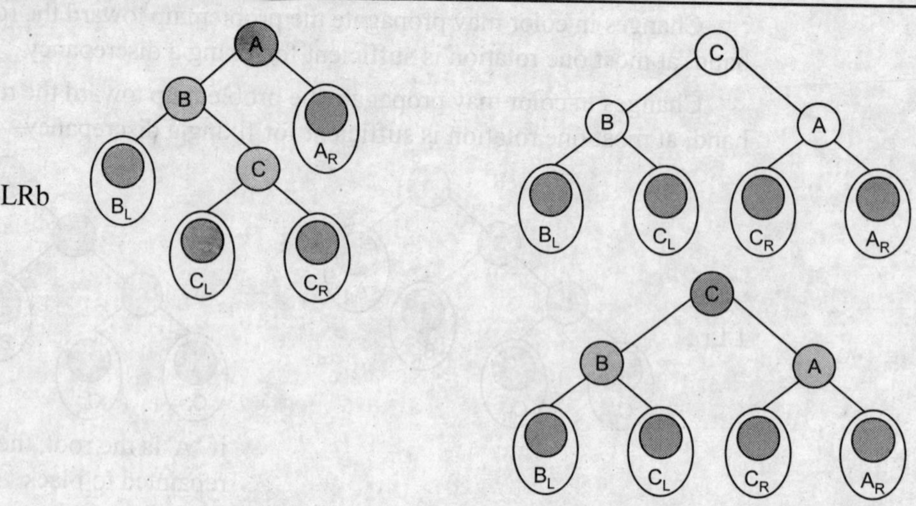

Discrepancies of type RRr, RLr, RRb, and RLb are handled in a similar manner.

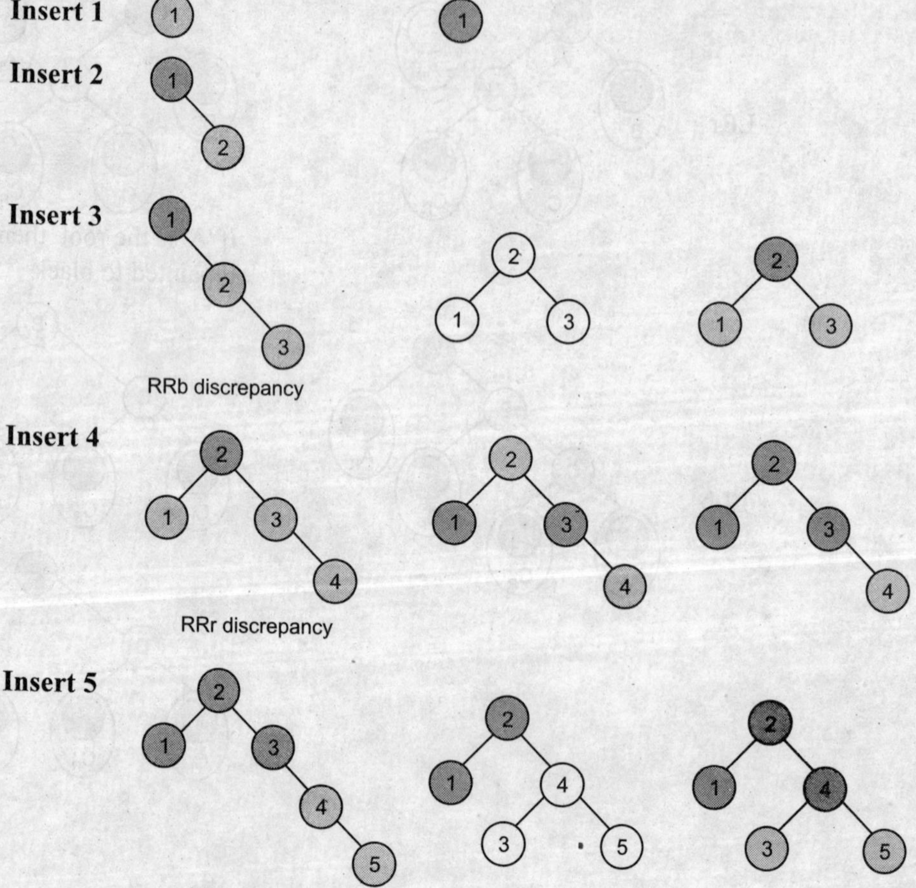

9.12.2 Deletions

- Delete a key, and a node, the way it is done in binary search trees.
- A node to be deleted will have at most one child. If the deleted node is red, the tree is still a red-black tree. If the deleted node has a red child, repaint the child to black.
- If a discrepancy arises for the red-black tree, fix the tree according to the type of discrepancy. A discrepancy can result only from a loss of a black node.

Let *A* denote the lowest node with unbalanced subtrees. The type of discrepancy is determined by the location of the deleted node (**R**ight or **L**eft), the color of the sibling (**b**lack or **r**ed), the number of red children in the case of the black siblings, and and the number of grand-children in the case of red siblings.

In the case of discrepancies which result from the addition of nodes, the correction mechanism may propagate the color problem (i.e., parent and child painted red) up toward the root, and stopped on the way by a single rotation. Here, in the case of discrepancies which result from the deletion of nodes, the discrepancy of a missing black node may propagate toward the root, and stopped on the way by an application of an appropriate rotation.

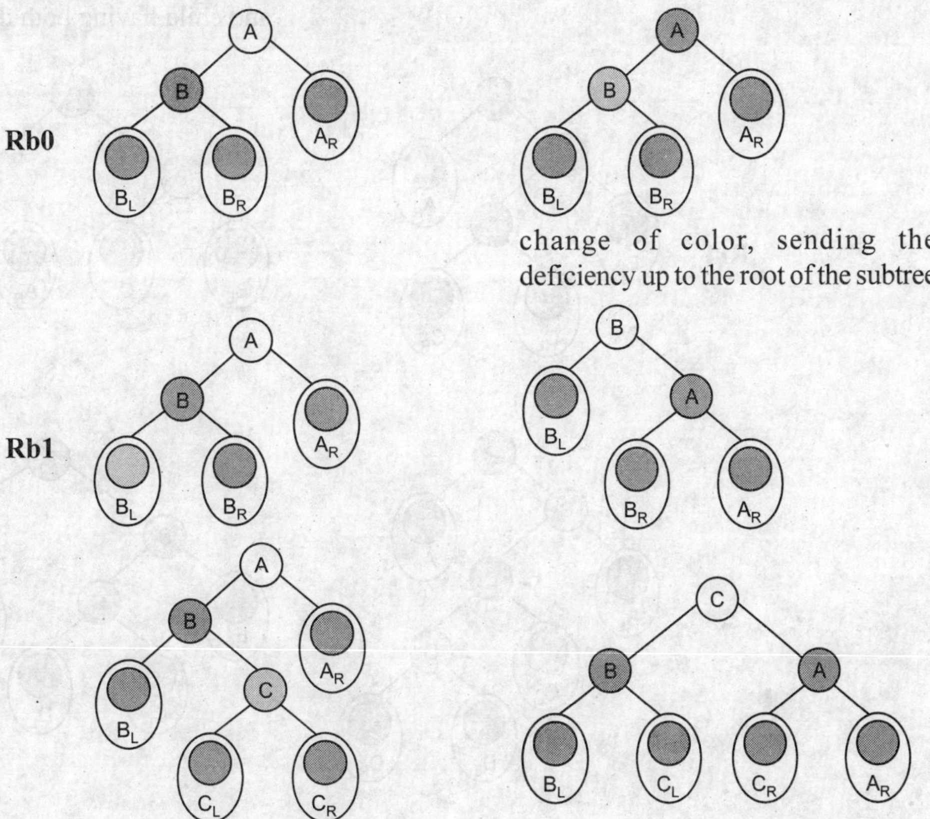

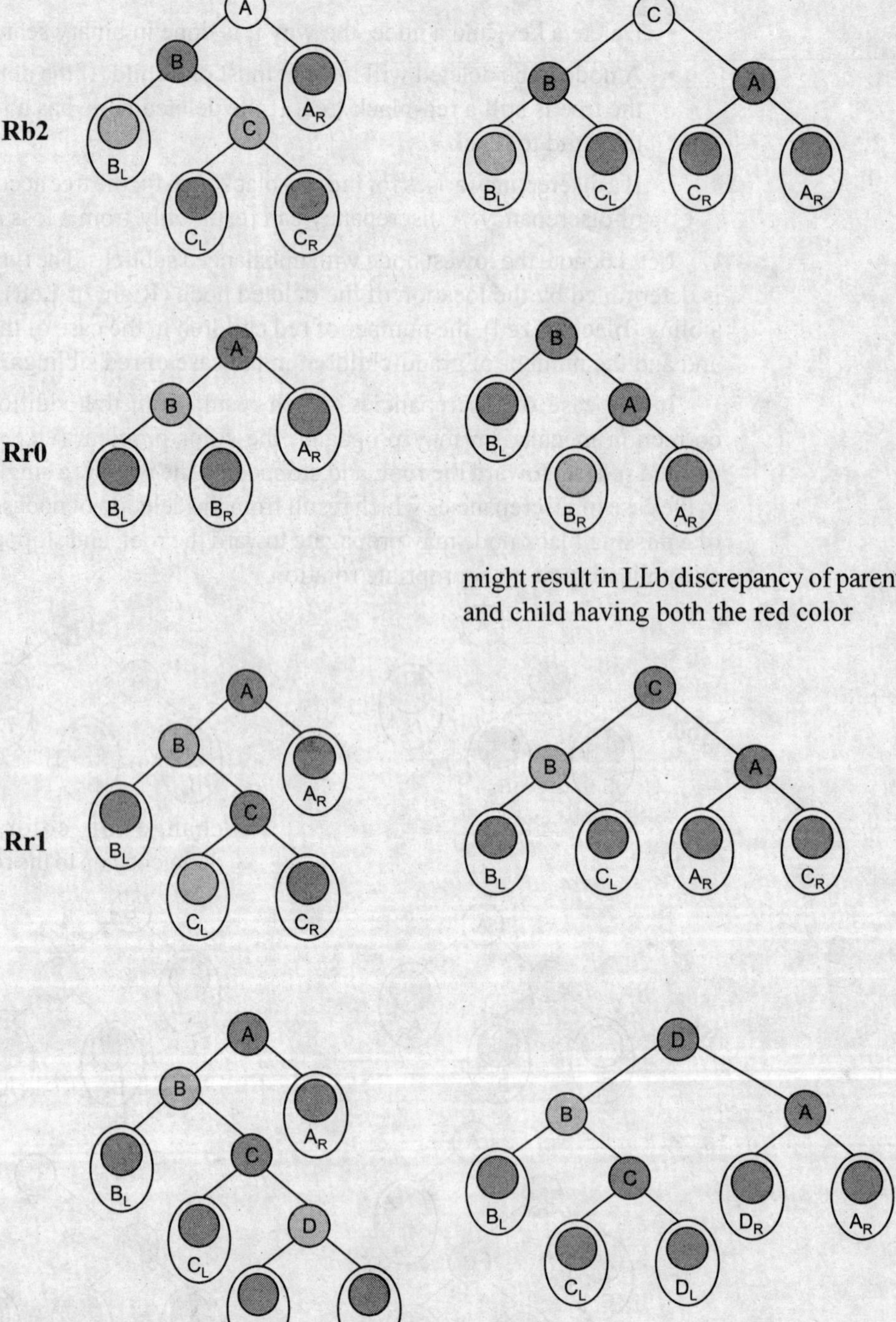
Rb2
A
B
C
A_R
B_L
C_L
C_R
Rr0
B_R
might result in LLb discrepancy of parent and child having both the red color
Rr1
D
D_L
D_R

Rr2

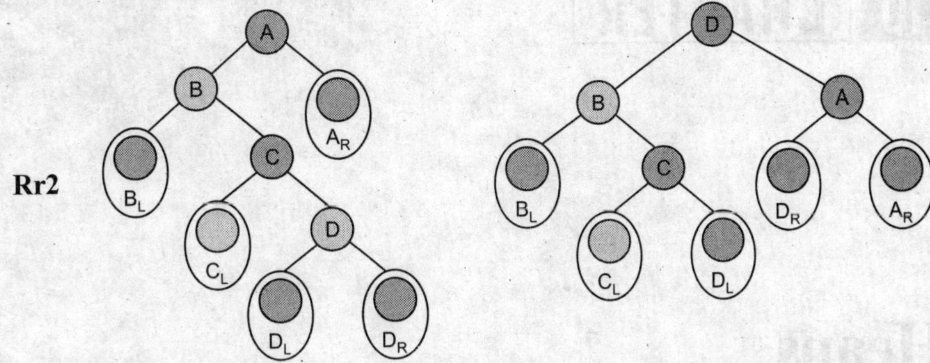

Similar transformations apply to Lb0, Lb1, Lb2, Lr0, Lr1, and Lr2.

EXERCISES

1. What do you understand by binary search trees?
2. Explain the basic terminology of binary search trees.
3. Explain the traversing of binary search trees.
4. Write an algorithm for operations given below:
   (i) Searching and inserting an item to a binary search tree
   (ii) Deleting an item from a binary search tree
   (iii) Computing the minimum and maximum values in a binary search tree
5. What do you understand by AVL trees.
6. Explain insertion, deletion and rotation operations performed on AVL search trees.
7. Explain the general concept of multi-way trees.
8. Explain searching operations in m-way search trees.
9. Explain insertion and deletion operation performed on m-way search trees.
10. Explain the general concept of b+-tree indexes.
11. What is B+-tree? Explain various operations performed on B+- trees.
12. What do you mean by B-trees? Explain various operations performed on B- trees.
13. What is B+ tree? Explain various operations performed on B+ trees.
14. What are red-black trees.
15. Explain Insertion and deletion operation in red-black trees.

Heaps

10.1 INTRODUCTION

A **binary heap** is a heap data structure created using a binary tree. It can be seen as a binary tree with two additional constraints:

- **The shape property:** the tree is an *almost complete binary tree*; that is, all levels of the tree, except possibly the last one (deepest) are fully filled, and, if the last level of the tree is not complete, the nodes of that level are filled from left to right.
- **The heap property:** each node is greater than or equal to each of its children according to some comparison predicate which is fixed for the entire data structure.

"Greater than" means according to whatever comparison function is chosen to sort the heap, not necessarily "greater than" in the mathematical sense (since the quantities are not always numerical). Heaps where the comparison function is mathematical "greater than" are called max-heaps; those where the comparison function is mathematical "less than" are called "min-heaps." Conventionally, min-heaps are used, since they are readily applicable for use in priority queues.

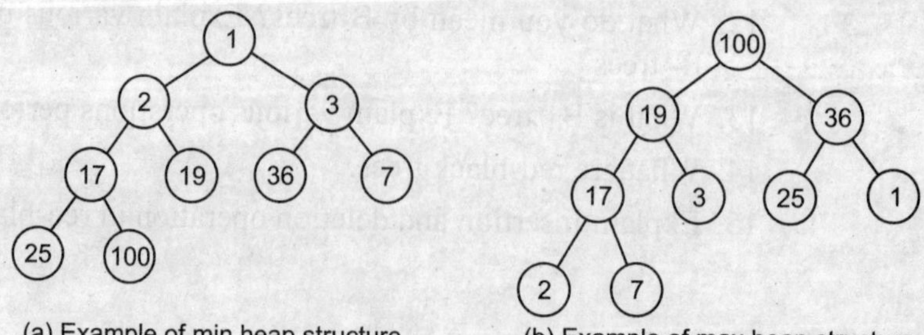

(a) Example of min heap structure (b) Example of max heap structure

Figure 10.1: Structure of Heaps.

Note that the ordering of siblings in a heap is not specified by the heap property, so the two children of a parent can be freely interchanged, as long as this does not violate the shape and heap properties (compare with treap).

The binary heap is a special case of the d-ary heap in which d = 2.

It is possible to modify the heap structure to allow extraction of both the smallest and largest element in $O(\log n)$ time. To do this the rows alternate between min heap and max heap. The algorithms are roughly the same, but in each step must consider the alternating rows with alternating comparisons. The performance is roughly the same as a normal single direction heap. This idea can be generalised to a min-max-median heap.

10.2 DESCRIPTION OF HEAP STRUCTURE

A Heap is a complete binary tree with the following properties:

- The value in the root is the smallest or largest value in the tree
- Every subtree is a heap

The (max)Heap property

The value of each node is less than or equal to the value of its parent, with the maximum-value element at the root. This is the heap ordering principle.

The (min)Heap property

The value of each node is greater than or equal to the value of its parent, with the maximum-value element at the root. This is the heap ordering principle.

10.2.1 Differences between the (min) Heap property and (max) Heap Property

The difference between the (min)HEAP property and the (max)HEAP property does not translate into differences in the overall characteristics of heaps, but merely defines the ordering principle. The ordering principle of the heap must be kept in mind when writing the code for heap operations. A heap only uses one of the ordering principles and because it affects the coding of the heap operations, one of the two ordering principles must be selected in advance, as is appropriate for the task.

For example, if low-value elements (say, job IDs) have a higher priority than high-value elements (job IDs), then the HEAP property is used. On the other hand, if high-values reflect greater importance/priority, then the (max)HEAP property is used. The HEAP property results in the *minimum* element being present at the root. The (max)HEAP property results in the *maximum* element being present at the root. We will be consistent with the lectures and use the **HEAP property** in this discussion.

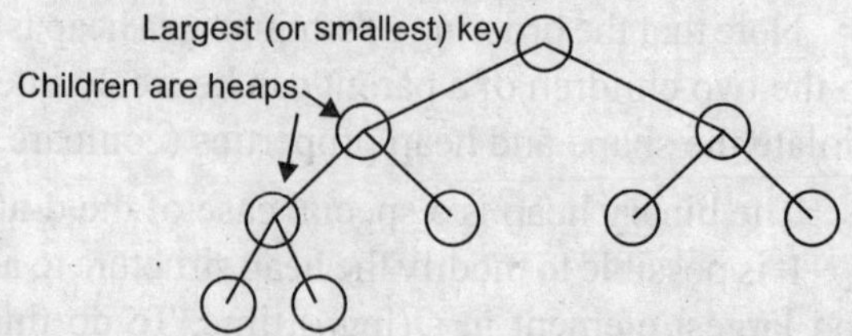

Figure 10.2: General heap structure with min HEAP and max HEAP property

10.3 THE HEAP APPROACH

A search tree organization is appealing because it yields such good insertion and retrieval results for an ordered collection, but unfortunately, it just doesn't seem appropriate for a queue. Can we take advantage of what we know about trees? The root is easy to locate; the leaves take the longest. Suppose we could create a tree in such a way that the highest-priority node was always at the root. Then accessing the highest-priority node would be easy (and would only require constant time). Unfortunately, removing the value would leave the root empty, but we already solved that problem (or one very much like it): deletion of an element from an ordered tree left a hole that had to be filled in logarithmic time. That's not as good as an ordered queue, but it is not bad. New items can be added to a tree in logarithmic time—and adding nodes is where our previous attempts broke down. Our previous attempts were unproductive because insertion was so expensive, but inserting in a binary tree was logarithmic, and that is encouraging.

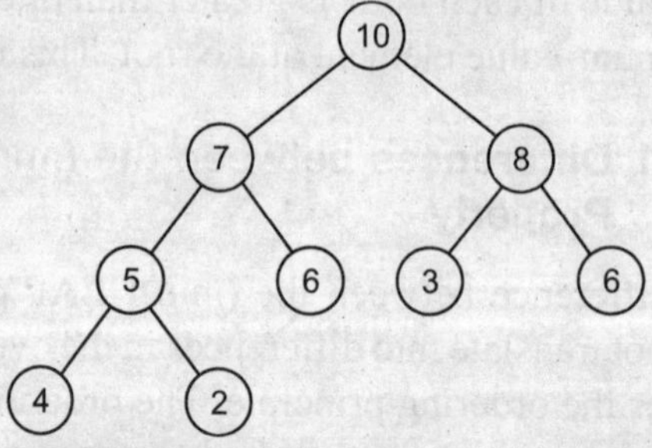

Figure 10.3: Structure of Max heap

A variant on the tree structure called a *heap* is ideal for this problem. We will define heap as a balanced tree in which both children of the root are also heaps and the roots of each have key values less than or equal to their parent, as illustrated by Figure 10.3. If the value used for organizing the heap is the priority of an element, a heap's definition guarantees that a highest-priority node is always at the root.

10.3.1 Deletion

It is actually easier to see how to remove an item, so let's look at that first. The only node to be deleted will be the one with the highest priority—the root.

The basic algorithm for removal, illustrated in Figure 10.4.

Algorithm 10.1: Delete Node From heap

Step 1: Remove the root.

Step 2: Raise an element from the bottom row to the root position.

Step 3: Focus on that new root

Step 4: While either child of current focus has a higher priority:

a. Switch the current node and that child.

b. Focus on the child.

Explanation

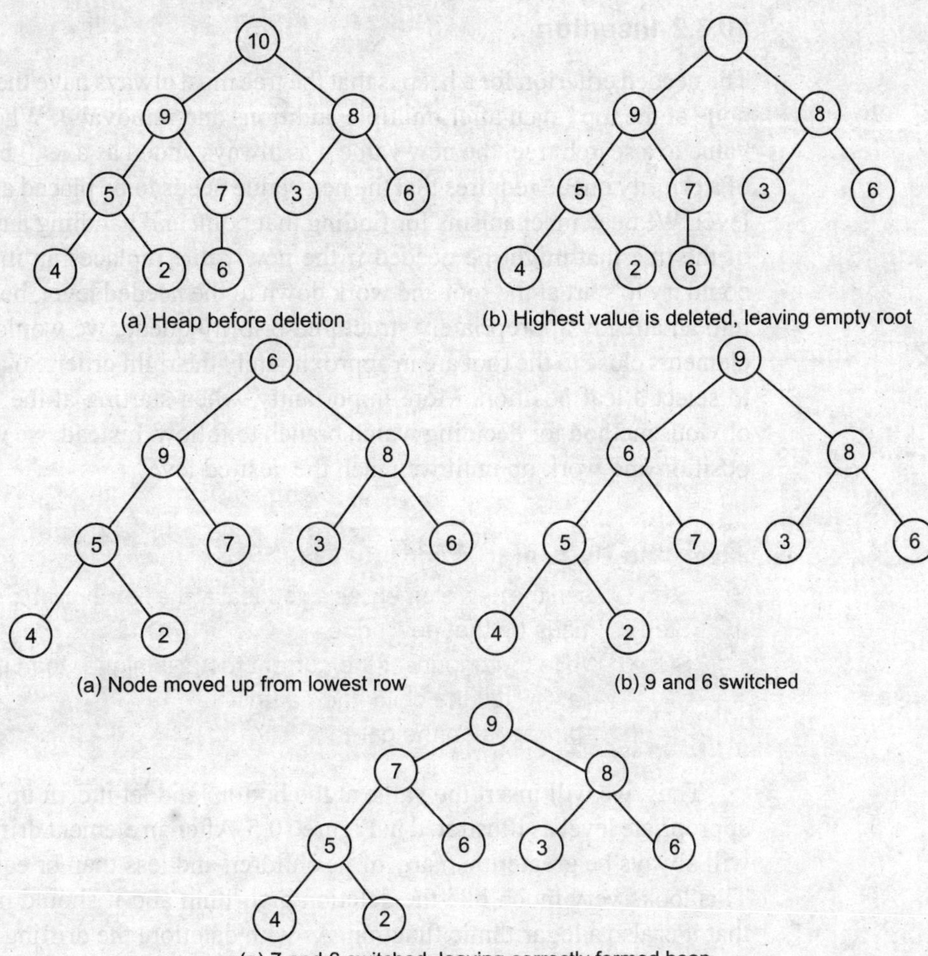

Figure 10.4: Removing a node from a heap.

Although the actual deletion takes just one step, filling in the missing value and letting it sink to its appropriate priority level takes more time. The bottom row of a balanced tree of n nodes must be at level:

$$h = \log \lceil n + 1 \rceil$$

After raising a node to the root, it will take at most h -1 iterations for the value to drift down. The total time for deletion is È(log n). Finally, notice two things about the shape of the tree. First, we have not yet specified exactly which node is raised, just that it is in the bottom row. Second, raising the selected node to the root is the only step that changes the shape of the tree. Since the drifting process is composed of swaps, it will not change the shape at all.

10.3.2 Insertion

The needed criterion for a heap is that the tree must always have the highest priority node at the top (even after multiple additions and removals). When adding a new value to a search tree, the new value was always added as a leaf, but the definition of a priority queue requires that the new value needs to be placed at the appropriate level. We need mechanisms for finding that point and handling any reorganization of the tree that might be needed if the new value replaces an internal node. We could try to start at the root and work down to the needed level, but when inserting into an already appropriately structured priority queue, we would expect that the elements close to the root are in approximately the right order. So it might be better to select a leaf position. More importantly, when starting at the root, there is no obvious method for deciding which branch to follow. Instead, we will start at a leaf position and work up until we reach the desired level:

Algorithm 10.2: Insert Node into heap.

Step 1: Insert the new element as a new leaf at the first available empty location.
Step 2: Focus on that new node.
Step 3: While the priority of the current focus is higher than its parent's:
  a. Switch the child and parent.
  b. Focus on the parent.

Thus, we will insert the value at the bottom and let it drift up until it finds the appropriate level as illustrated in Figure 10.5. After an element drifts up, its priority will always be greater than any of its children and less than or equal to its parent. This looks very much like the deletion algorithm and it should not be surprising that it is also a logarithmic function. As with deletion, the drifting process will not change the shape of the tree.

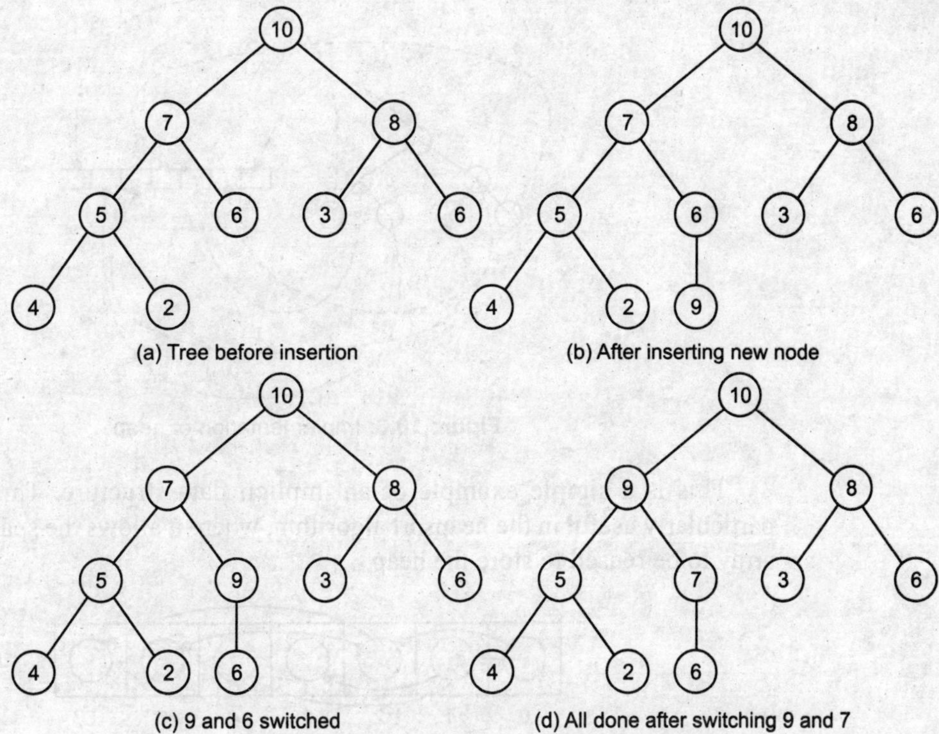

Figure 10.5: Inserting a new node into a heap.

Since both insertion and deletion traverse a single path from root partway to leaf or from leaf toward the root, both must work in logarithmic time, a result independent of the relative number of possible values compared to the total number of nodes. Construction of an entire tree should be no worse than $\Theta(n \log n)$.

10.4 IMPLEMENTATION OF HEAP USING ARRAYS

Because a heap is a complete binary tree, it can be implemented efficiently using an array instead of a linked data structure.

First element for storing a reference to the root data. Use next two elements for storing the two children of the root. Use elements with subscripts 3, 4, 5, and 6 for storing the four children of these two nodes and so on. See Figure 10.6.

Any binary tree can be stored in an array, but because a heap is always an almost complete binary tree, it can be stored compactly. No space is required for pointers; instead, for each index i, element $a[i]$ is the parent of two children $a[2i+1]$ and $a[2i+2]$, as shown in the figure 10.7. (Note that with an implementation starting at 0 for the root, the parent of $a[i]$ is $a[\text{floor}((i-1)/2)]$.

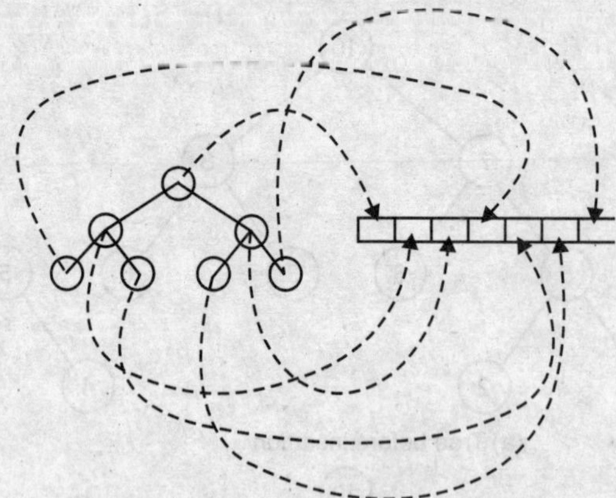

Figure 10.6: Implementation of heap

This is a simple example of an implicit data structure. This approach is particularly useful in the heapsort algorithm, where it allows the space in the input array to be reused to store the heap.

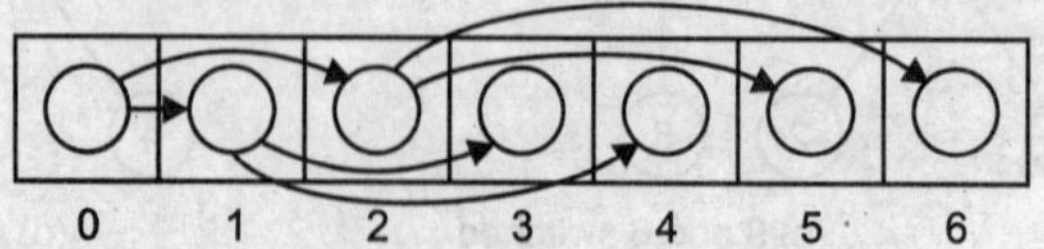

Figure 10.7: Array Implementation of Heap

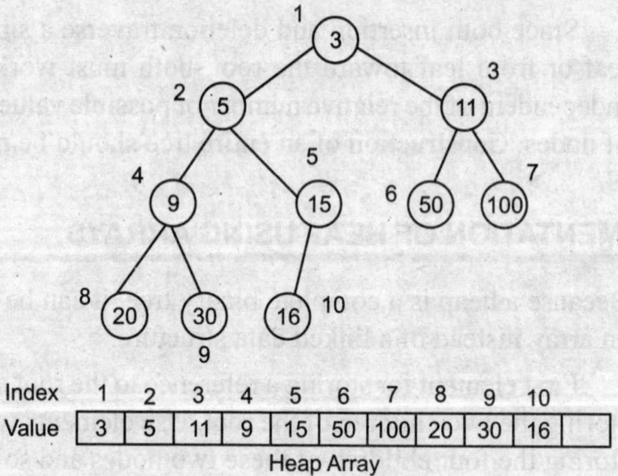

Figure 10.8: Heap stored as Array

Given an element at position i

Parent of **i**	**i/2**
Left child of **i**	**2i**
Right child of **i**	**2i+1**

Using this implementation, the minimum element of the HEAP (the root) is the first element in the array.

The index of the last member of HEAP gives the HEAP_SIZE and is equivalent to the number of elements in the heap.

10.5 VARIOUS OPERATIONS ON HEAP

The following are the various operations performed on Heap.

Consider HEAP_SIZE(A) a variable containing the array index of the last element of the Heap A. Elements in the array that are beyond this index are not part of the heap. Thus the last element of the heap is referenced by: A[HEAP_SIZE(A)]).

10.5.1 Traversal of Heap

Parent

This operation returns index of parent.

Let us assume that index i is given to us.

Algorithm 10.3: Parent operation

Step1: Start

Step2: Return i/2

Step3: End.

Left

This operation returns index of left child.Let us assume that index i is given to us.

Consider HEAP_SIZE(A) a variable containing the array index of the last element of the heap.

Algorithm 10.4: Left operation

Step1: Start

Step2: Compare Heap_Size(A) with 2i , if 2i>HEAP_SIZE(A) then goto step3 else goto step4

Step3: Return i i.e. leaf node

Step4: Return 2i

Step5: End.

Right

This operation returns index of right child of i. Let us assume that index i is given to us.

Algorithm 10.5: Right operation

Step1: Start

Step2: Compare HEAP_SIZE(A) with 2i+1,if 2i+1>HEAP_SIZE(A) then goto step3 else goto step4.

Step3: Return i i.e. leaf node

Step4: Return 2i+1

Step5: End.

10.5.2 Heapify

This operation makes element at index **i** and all its descendants a heap.

Let us assume that index i is given to us.

Algorithm 10.6: HEAPIFY operation

Step1: Start

Step2: Repeat the following steps for all levels of Heap

Step3: Compare the value of i with the children of i (left and right).If the value of i is the smallest of the three then goto step 5 else goto step 4.

Step4: Swap the position with the smaller child.

Step5: End.

HEAPIFY operates by comparing the value at **i** with the children of **i** and swapping positions with the smaller child. If the value at **i** is the smallest of the 3, then the procedure stops. This is sometimes called ***percolating down***. It is assumed that the subtrees rooted at the left and right children of **i** are already heaps. When coding this method, one pays special attention to whether there are an odd or even number of heap elements and maintains a pointer to the last element of the heap so that it can fill any violation of the complete binary tree structure after HEAPIFYhas run.

The percolating down effect of HEAPIFY turns the subtree rooted at index **i** into a heap.

Worse Case Comparisons

It takes 2 comparisons to move down 1 level, i.e. 1 iteration of the loop, comparing **i** to its left child and then the smaller of those to its right child. The maximum number times the procedure will make these comparisons is the height of the heap, $\log_2 n$. Therefore, the cost of HEAPIFY is approximately $2\log_2 n$ where **n** is the number of elements of the heap rooted at **i**. Thus, the worst case number of comparisons is $O(\log_2 n)$.

10.5.3 Build_Heap

This operation provide additional functionality for heaps, but isn't strictly necessary for the heap to implement a priority queue. Note that Build_Heap(**A**) is better than using Insert(**i**, **A**) repeatedly to build a heap.

Let us suppose that an array **A is given to us**, and is to be turned into a Heap. This operation uses HEAPIFY(**i**, **A**) to construct a heap from the array.

Algorithm 10.7: Build_Heap operation:

Step1: Start

Step2: Starting from i=n/4*2 repeat steps 3 and 4 until it reaches the first element of the array

Step3: Call the operation HEAPIFY(i,A)

Step4: i=i-1

Step5: End.

The n above should be the size of the heap if it were a full binary tree with the same number of levels.

Worse Case Comparisons (Build_Heap is better than Insert operation to build a Heap)

The elements in the last level of the heap are already single-element heaps and therefore Build_Heap(i, A) starts at the last element of the second last level and works its way back one element at a time until it reaches the first element of the array. HEAPIFY(i, A) uses two comparisons for each call.

Therefore, at the second last level, which contains elements, the cost will be n/4*2. For the third last level, which contains n/8 levels, the cost will be n/8*4, since each level is two comparisons. Summing the cost at each level gives the cost of Build_Heap(A) as: 2n = O(n)

This is much better than using Insert(k, A) n times, which would be O(n $\log_2$n).

10.5.4 Adding to the Heap

If we have a heap, and we add an element, we can perform an operation known as *up-heap*, *bubble-up*, *percolate-up*, *sift-up*, or *heapify-up* in order to restore the heap property. We can do this in O(log *n*) time, using a binary heap, by following this algorithm:

1. Add the element on the bottom level of the heap.
2. Compare the added element with its parent; if they are in the correct order, stop.
3. If not, swap the element with its parent and return to the previous step.

We do this at maximum for each level in the tree — the height of the tree, which is O(log *n*). However, since approximately 50% of the elements are leaves and 75% are in the bottom two levels, it is likely that the new element to be inserted will only move a few levels upwards to maintain the heap. Thus, binary heaps support insertion in *average* constant time, O(1).

Say we have a max-heap

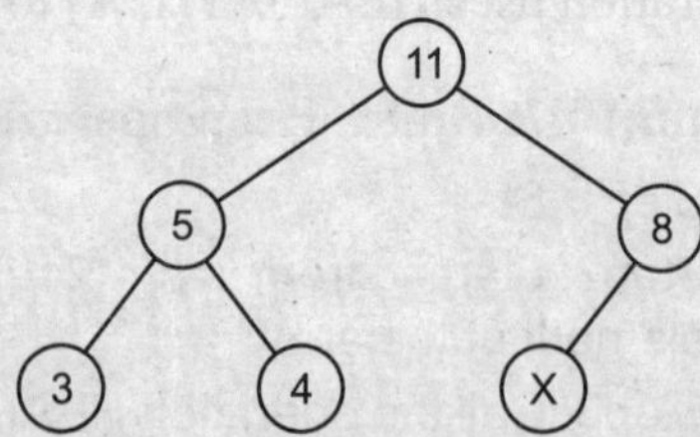

and we want to add the number 15 to the heap. We first place the 15 in the position marked by the X. However the heap property is violated since 15 is greater than 8, so we need to swap the 15 and the 8. So, we have the heap looking as follows after the first swap:

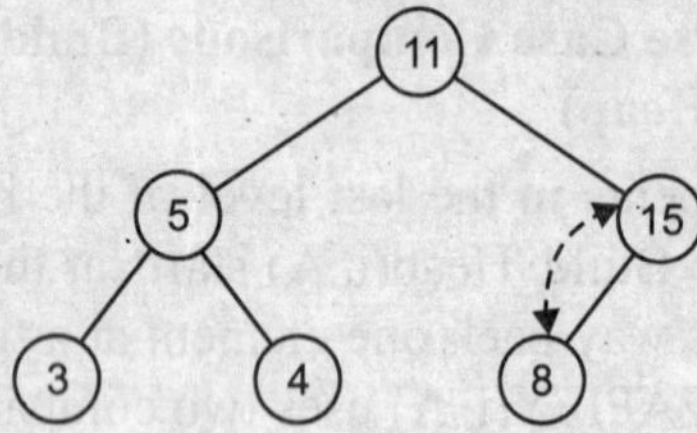

However the heap property is still violated since 15 is greater than 11, so we need to swap again:

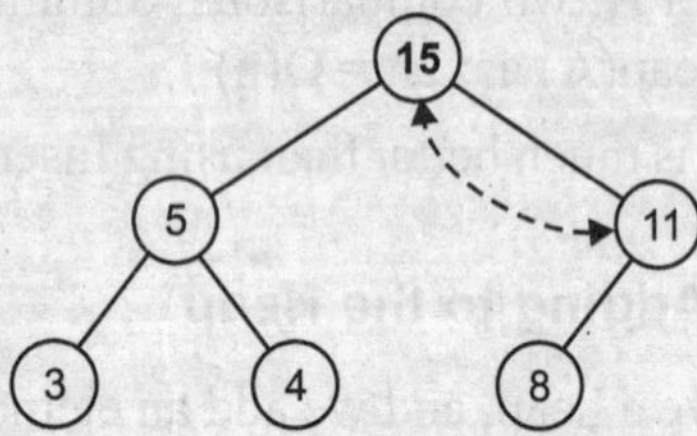

which is a valid max-heap.

Worse Case Comparisons

Since each iteration of the while loop has one comparison and the added element may have to be swapped upwards a maximum of $\log_2 n$ (height) times, the worst case time analysis is $O(\log_2 n)$ where n is the number of elements in the heap.

However, since approximately 50% of the elements in the heap are leaves and 75% of elements are in the bottom two levels, it is likely that new elements will not have to move more than 1 or 2 levels upwards to maintain the heap (the heap is *vertically* ordered). Therefore, $\log_2 n$ is pessimistic. The average time analysis for Insert operation is about O(1).

10.5.5 Deleting the Root from the Heap

The procedure for deleting the root from the heap — effectively extracting the maximum element in a max-heap or the minimum element in a min-heap — starts by replacing it with the last element on the last level. So, if we have the same max-heap as before, we remove the 11 and replace it with the 4.

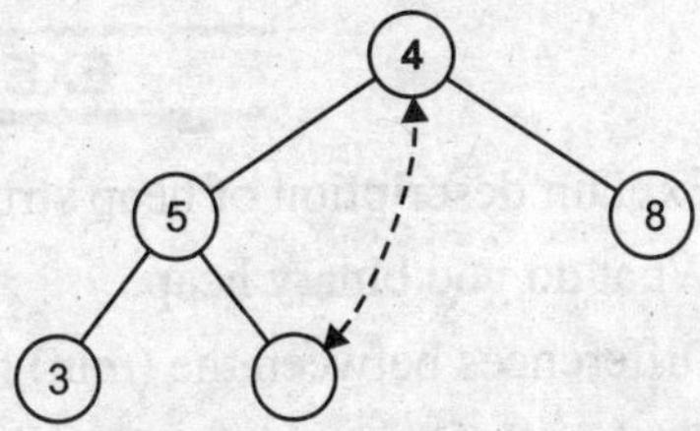

Now the heap property is violated since 8 is greater than 4. The operation that restores the property is called *down-heap, bubble-down, percolate-down, sift-down,* or *heapify-down*. In this case, swapping the two elements 4 and 8, is enough to restore the heap property and we need not swap elements further:

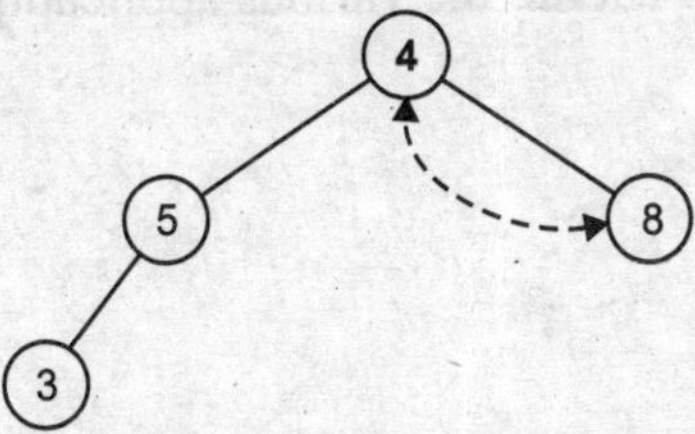

In general, the downward-moving node is swapped with its larger child in a max-heap (in a min-heap it would be swapped with its smaller child), until it satisfies the heap property in its new position. Note that the down-heap operation (without the preceding swap) can be used in general to modify the value of the root, even when an element is not being deleted.

Worse Case Comparisons

Since the assignments are all of O(1), HEAPIFY(1, A) is the main determinant of running time for this procedure. Therefore, the cost of Delete_Min(A) is: $O(\log_2 n)$ where n is the number of elements in the heap.

10.6 APPLICATIONS OF HEAP

A heap can be thought of as a priority queue; the most important node will always be at the top, and when removed, its replacement will be the most important. This can be useful when coding algorithms that require certain things to be processed in a complete order, but when you don't want to perform a full sort or need to know anything about the rest of the nodes. Heaps can also be used to sort data. A heap sort is O(n logn) efficiency, though it is not the fastest possible sorting algorithm. So, basically there are two applications of Heap:

(i) Implementation of Priority Queues: It is discussed in detail in chapter 7.

(ii) Heap Sort: It is discussed in detail in chapter 12.

EXERCISES

1. Explain description of heap structure.
2. What do you binary heap.
3. Differences between the (min) heap property and (max)heap property.
4. Explain the heap approach in detail.
5. Explain deletion and insertion operation in heap tree.
6. Explain implementation of heap using arrays.
7. Explain various operations performed on heap.
8. What are the various applications of heap tree?

11 CHAPTER

Graphs

11.1 INTRODUCTION

Graphs are natural models that are used to represent arbitrary relationships among data objects. We often need to represent such arbitrary relationships among the data objects while dealing with problems in computer science, engineering, and many other disciplines. Therefore, the study of graphs as one of the basic data structures is important.

Note that trees are just connected, acyclic graphs; therefore, there is exactly one path between any pair of vertices. Graphs that contain cycles, on the other hand, may have several different paths between a pair of vertices. Graphs and directed graphs are important to computer science for many real-world applications from building compilers to modeling physical communication networks.

A *graph* G=(V,E) is a finite nonempty set V of objects called *vertices* (the singular is *vertex*) together with a (possibly empty) set E of unordered pairs of distinct vertices of G called *edges*.

A graph is an abstract notion of a set of nodes (vertices or points) and connection relations (edges or arcs) between them. A graph G consists of nodes and edges. It is an important non-linear data structure.

11.2 GRAPHS

A graph G is a discrete structure consisting of nodes (called vertices) and lines joining the nodes (called edges). Two vertices are adjacent to each other if they are joint by an edge. The edge joining the two vertices is said to be an edge incident with them. We use V (G) and E(G) to denote the set of vertices and edges of G respectively.

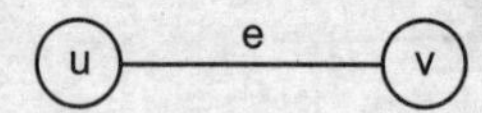

Figure 11.1: Simple Graph

u and v are adjacent vertices; e is an edge incident with u and v. e can also be denoted by uv or vu.

***Definition:** A set V of elements called nodes or points or vertices and a set E of edges such that edge e in E is identified with a unique pair [u,v] of unordered nodes in V. It is denoted by e=[u,v].*

11.2.1 Basic Definitions and Terminology

A graph is a structure made of two components: a set of vertices V, and a set of edges E. Therefore, a graph is G = (V,E), where G is a graph. The graph may be directed or undirected. In a ***directed graph***, every edge of the graph is an ordered pair of vertices connected by the edge, whereas in an ***undirected graph***, every edge is an unordered pair of vertices connected by the edge. Figure 11.2 shows an undirected and a directed graph.

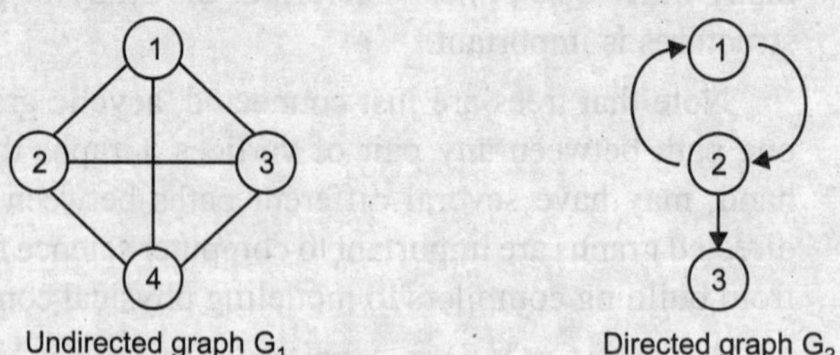

Figure 11.2: Graphs.

Incident edge: (v_i,v_j) is an edge, then edge(v_i,v_j) is said to be incident to vertices v_i and v_j. For example, in graph G_1 shown in Figure 22.1, the edges incident on vertex 1 are (1,2), (1,4), and (1,3), whereas in G_2, the edges incident on vertex 1 are (1,2).

Loops and Multiple Edges: An edge joining only one vertex is called a loop. If there are more than one edge joining u and v of G, then all edges joining u and v form a multiple edge of G.

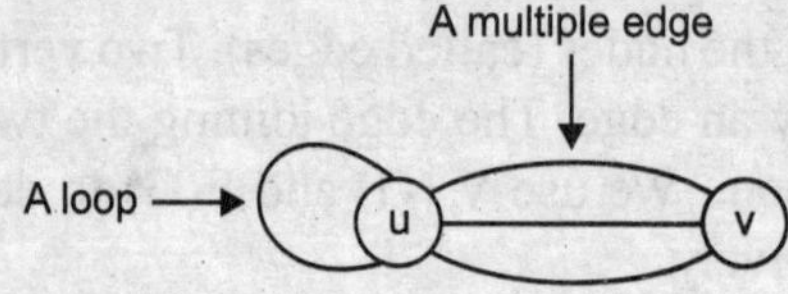

Figure 11.3: Loop and multiple edges.

Degree of vertex: The number of edges incident onto the vertex. For example, in graph G_1, the degree of vertex 1 is 3, because 3 edges are incident onto it. For a directed graph, we need to define indegree and outdegree. *Indegree* of a vertex vi is the number of edges incident onto vi, with vi as the head. *Outdegree* of vertex vi is the number of edges incident onto vi, with vi as the tail. For graph G_2, the indegree of vertex 2 is 1, whereas the outdegree of vertex 2 is 2.

Degrees of Vertices: The degree of a vertex is the number of edges incident with it, except that a loop at a vertex contributes twice to the degree of that vertex. The degree of the vertex v is denoted by deg(v) or d(v).

Example 11.1: d(u) = 5 , d(v) = 3 and d(w) = 2

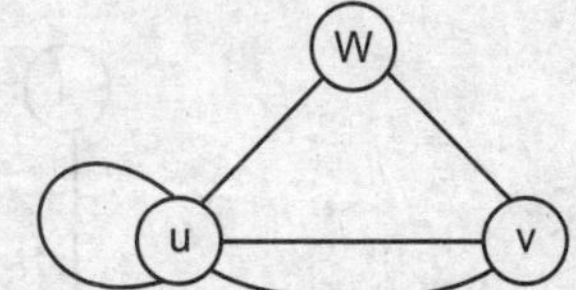

Figure 11.4: Degrees of vertices.

Directed edge: A directed edge between the vertices vi and vj is an ordered pair. It is denoted by <vi,vj>.

Undirected edge: An undirected edge between the vertices v_i and v_j is an unordered pair. It is denoted by (v_i,v_j).

Path: A path between vertices v_p and v_q is a sequence of vertices v_p, v_{i1}, v_{i2},…, v_{in},v_q such that there exists a sequence of edges (v_p, v_{i1}), (v_{i1}, v_{i2}), …, (v_{in}, v_q). In case of a directed graph, a path between the vertices v_p and v_q is a sequence of vertices v_p, v_{i1}, v_{i2},…, v_{in}, v_q such that there exists a sequence of edges $<v_p, v_{i1}>$, $< v_{i1}, v_{i2}>$, …, $<v_{in}, v_q>$. If there exists a path from vertex v_p to v_q in an undirected graph, then there always exists a path from v_q to v_p also. But, in the case of a directed graph, if there exists a path from vertex v_p to v_q, then it does not necessarily imply that there exists a path from v_q to v_p also.

Simple path: A simple path is a path given by a sequence of vertices in which all vertices are distinct except the first and the last vertices. If the first and the last vertices are same, the path will be a cycle.

Maximum number of edges: The maximum number of edges in an undirected graph with n vertices is $n(n–1)/2$. In a directed graph, it is $n(n–1)$.

Subgraph: A ***subgraph*** of a graph G = (V,E) is a graph G where V(G) is a subset of V(G). E(G) consists of edges (v1,v2) in E(G), such that both v1 and v2 are in V(G). [Note: If G = (V,E) is a graph, then V(G) is a set of vertices of G and E(G) is a set of edges of G.]

If E(G) consists of all edges (v1,v2) in E(G), such that both v1 and v2 are in V(G), then G is called an induced subgraph of G. For example, the graph shown in Figure 11.2 is a subgraph of the graph G2.

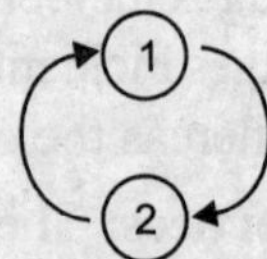

Figure 11.5: The subgraph of graph G2.

For the graph shown in Figure 11.6, one of the induced subgraphs is shown in Figure 11.7.

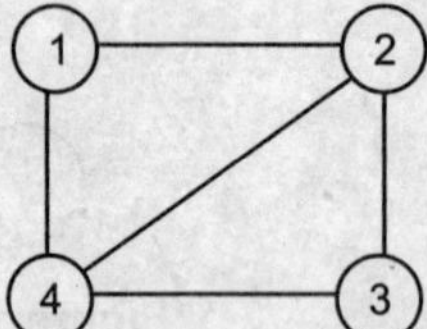

Figure 11.6: Graph G.

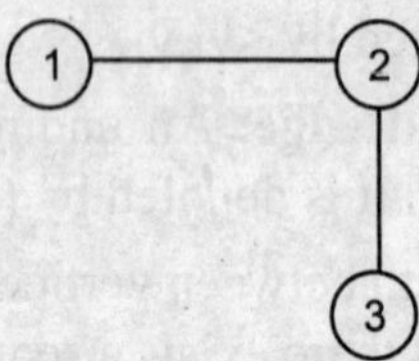

Figure 11.7: Induced subgraph of Graph G of Figure 22.3.

In the undirected graph G, the two vertices v_1 and v_2 are said to be connected if there exists a path in G from v_1 to v_2 (being an undirected graph, there exists a path from v_2 to v_1 also).

Connected graph: A graph G is said to be connected if for every pair of distinct vertices (v_i,v_j), there is a path from v_i to v_j. A connected graph is shown in Figure 11.8.

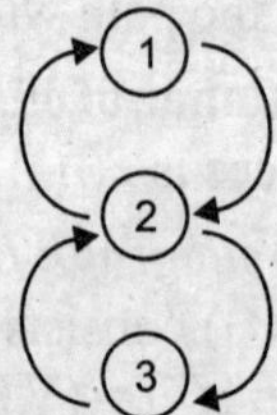

Figure 11.8: A connected graph.

Completely connected graph: A graph G is completely connected if, for every pair of distinct vertices (v_i,v_j), there exists an edge. A completely connected graph is shown in Figure 11.9.

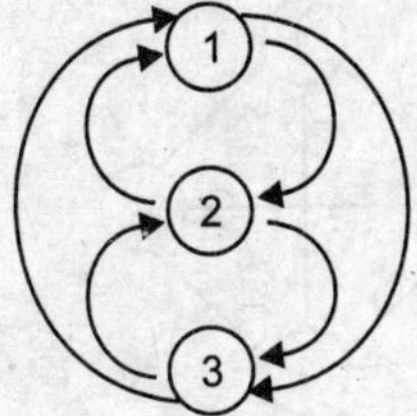

Figure 11.9: A completely connected graph.

Bipartite Graphs: A simple graph G is called bipartite if its vertex set V (G) can be partitioned into two disjoint sets of V_1 and V_2 such that every edge in the graph connects a vertex in V_1 and a vertex in V_2. In other words, any two vertices in the same set V_1 (and V_2) are not adjacent.

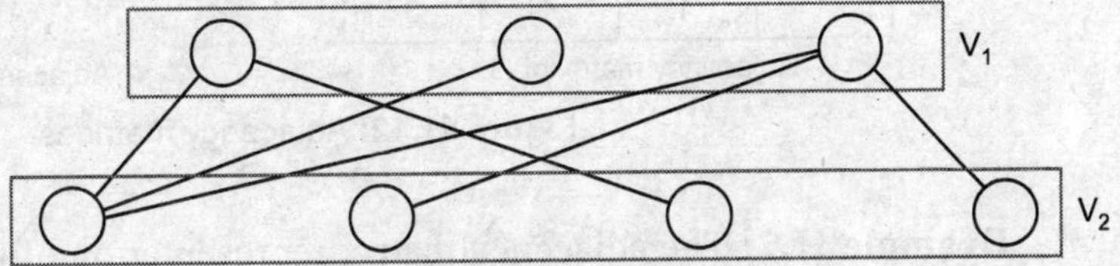

Figure 11.10: Bipartite Graphs

Complete Bipartite Graphs: A complete bipartite graph, denoted by K m, n, is the bipartite graph with |V1 |= m and |V2|= n , and vu–E(G) if and only if v–V1 and u–V2 .

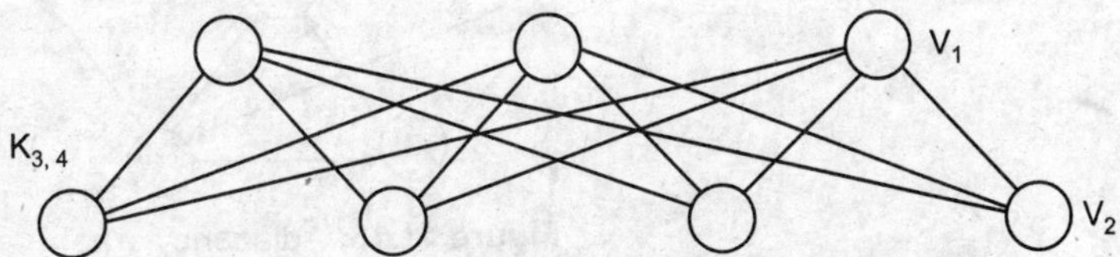

Figure 11.11: Complete Bipartite Graphs

11.3 ARRAY REPRESENTATION OR SEQUENTIAL REPRESENTATION

One way of representing a graph with n vertices is to use an n^2 matrix (that is, a matrix with *n* rows and *n* columns—that means there is a row as well as a column corresponding to every vertex of the graph). If there is an edge from v_i to v_j then the entry in the matrix with row index as v_i and column index as v_j is set to 1 (adj[v_i, v_j] = 1, if (v_i, v_j) is an edge of graph G). If e is the total number of edges in the graph, then there will 2e entries which will be set to 1, as long as G is an undirected graph.

Whereas if G were a directed graph, only e entries would have been set to 1 in the adjacency matrix. The adjacency matrix representation of an undirected as well as a directed graph is show in Figure 11.12.

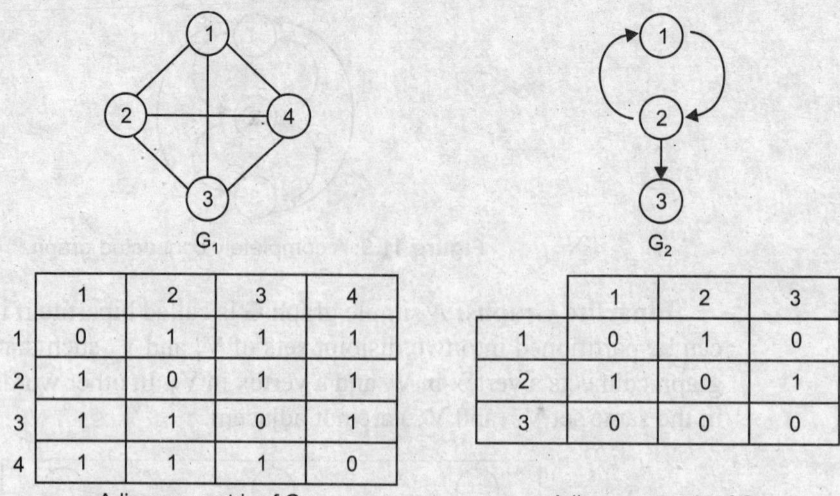

	1	2	3	4
1	0	1	1	1
2	1	0	1	1
3	1	1	0	1
4	1	1	1	0

Adjacency matrix of G_1

	1	2	3
1	0	1	0
2	1	0	1
3	0	0	0

Adjacency matrix of G_2

Figure 11.12: Adjacency matrices.

Example 11.2: The adjacency matrix representation of the following diagraph (directed graph), along with the indegree and outdegree of each node is shown here:

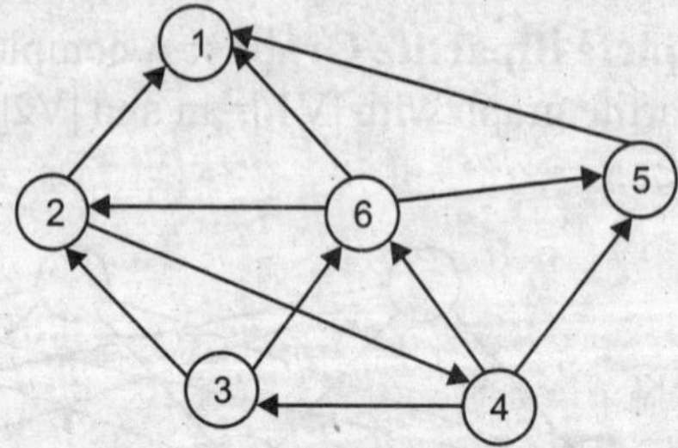

Figure 11.13: Adjacency graph.

The adjacency matrix representation of the above diagraph is shown here:

	1	2	3	4	5	6
1	0	0	0	0	0	0
2	1	0	0	1	0	0
3	0	1	0	0	0	1
4	0	0	1	0	1	1
5	1	0	0	0	0	0
6	1	1	0	0	1	0

The indegree and outdegree of each node is shown here:

	Indegree	Outdegree
1	3	0
2	2	2
3	1	2
4	1	3
5	2	1
6	2	3

11.3.1 Adjacency Matrices

Graphs $G = (V, E)$ can be represented by **adjacency matrices** $G[v_1..v_{|V|}, v_1..v_{|V|}]$, where the rows and columns are indexed by the nodes, and the entries $G[v_i, v_j]$ represent the edges. In the case of unlabeled graphs, the entries are just boolean values.

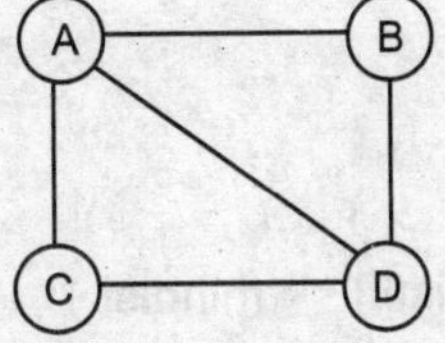

	A	B	C	D
A	0	1	1	1
B	1	0	0	1
C	1	0	0	1
D	1	1	1	0

In case of labelled graphs, the labels themselves may be introduced into the entries.

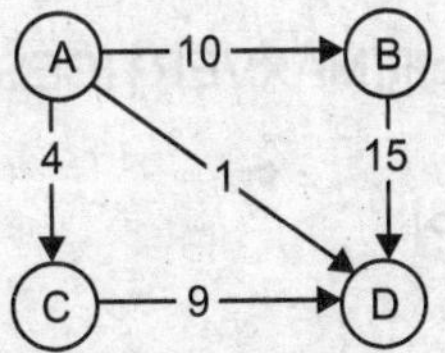

	A	B	C	D
A	∞	10	4	1
B	∞	∞	∞	15
C	∞	∞	∞	9
D	∞	∞	∞	∞

Adjacency matrices require $O(|V|^2)$ space, and so they are space-efficient only when they are dense (that is, when the graphs have many edges). Time-wise, the adjacency matrices allow easy addition and deletion of edges.

Finding the shortest path by using an adjacency matrix

Given a digraph represented as an adjacency matrix, find the shortest path from a vertex v to all the other vertices in the graph.

Program 1: Write a C++ program to find the shortest path by using an adjacency matrix.

```
#include <iostream.h>
#include<conio.h>
```

```
#define MAXINT 99999
#define MAXVERTICES 10
typedef enum {FALSE, TRUE} bool;
void print( int cost[][MAXVERTICES], int nvert )
{
int i, j;
for( i=0; i<nvert; ++i )
{
for( j=0; j<nvert; ++j )
cout<<cost[i][j];
cout<<"\n";
}
}
int choose( int dist[], bool s[], int nvert )
{
int i;
int u=-1;
int mindist = MAXINT;
for( i=0; i<nvert; ++i )
if( s[i] == FALSE && dist[i] <= mindist )
u=i, mindist=dist[i];
return u;
}
void sssp( int v, int cost[][MAXVERTICES], int dist[], int nvert )
{
bool s[MAXVERTICES];
int i, u, num, w;
for( i=0; i<nvert; ++i )
s[i] = FALSE, dist[i] = cost[v][i];
s[v] = TRUE;
dist[v] = 0;
num = 1;
while( num < nvert-1 )
{
u = choose( dist, s, nvert );
s[u] = TRUE;
num++;
for( w=0; w<nvert; ++w )
if( s[w] == FALSE && dist[u]+cost[u][w] < dist[w] )
```

```
dist[w] = dist[u] + cost[u][w];
}
}
void printDist( int v, int dist[], int nvert ) {
int i;
cout<<"min dist from vertex "<<v;
for( i=0; i<nvert; ++i )
cout<<"dist["<<<<i<<"]="<<dist[i];
}
void main()
{
int cost[][MAXVERTICES] = {{0,2,2,1},{3,0,4,1},{5,16,0,9},{1,1,2,0}};
int dist[MAXVERTICES];
int nvert = 4;          // no of vertices.
sssp( 2, cost, dist, nvert );
printDist( 2, dist, nvert );
getch();
}
```

Ouput:

1. The digraph is represented as an adjacency matrix. The size of the matrix is N×N where N is the number of vertices in the digraph. An entry matrix[i][j] specifies the cost of the directed edge from vertex i to vertex j. If such an edge does not exist, then the cost is set to MAXINT. All diagonal entries of the matrix matrix[i][i] are set to 0.
2. The function sssp(v, cost, dist, nvert) implements the single-source-shortest-path algorithm to find the shortest path from a vertex v in a digraph that is represented as an adjacency matrix cost. nvert is the number of vertices in the digraph and dist is the vector that will finally contain the output. Thus an entry dist[i] will be the minimum distance of vertex i from vertex v.
3. The function uses a vector s[] of Boolean to represent the status of each vertex: whether processed or not. It is initialized to FALSE. s[v] is marked, meaning it is processed. dist[v] is set to 0. Then the function chooses a vertex u that is yet to be processed and which is at a minimum distance from v. Vertex u is marked as processed. It then processes vector dist[], which may get updated because of the addition of u. The function checks whether dist[u]+cost[u][w] < dist[w] for each yet-to-be-processed node w in the digraph. If it is, then dist[w] is updated as dist[u]+cost[u][w]. When all the vertices are processed, dist[] contains the required result.

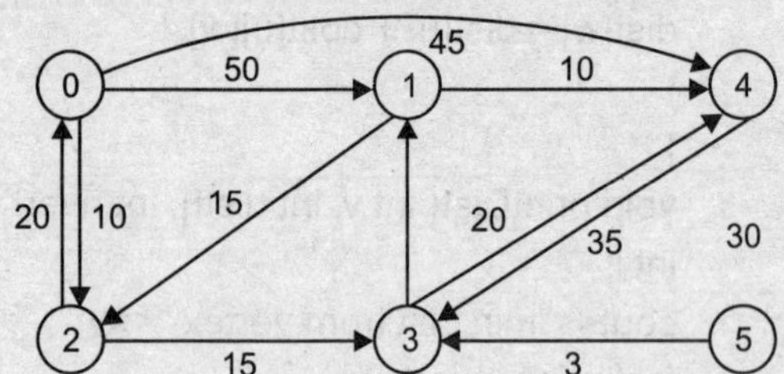

Let v=0. Then, different steps in the run of the algorithm are as follows:

M signifies MAXINT, which means that the vertex cannot be reached from v.

step	**u**	**dist**
0	nil	0 50 10 M 45 M
1	2	0 50 10 35 45 M
2	3	0 45 10 35 45 M
3	1	0 45 10 35 45 M
4	4	0 45 10 35 45 M
5	5	0 45 10 35 45 M

11.3.2 Adjacency Lists

A representation of the graph consisting of a list of nodes, with each node containing a list of its neighbouring nodes.

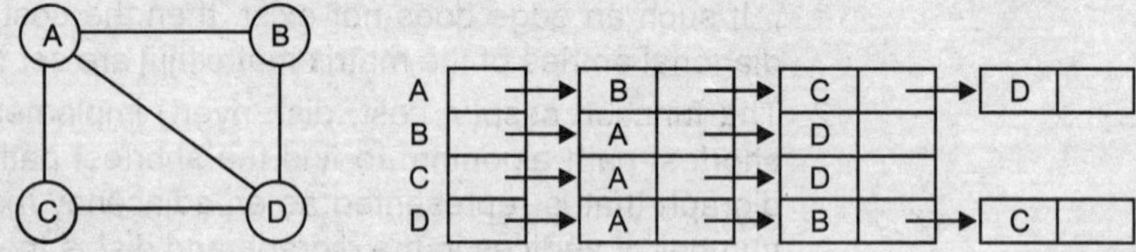

This representation takes $O(|V| + |E|)$ space.

Finding the shortest path by using an adjacency list

Rewrite the function sssp() for finding the shortest path, such that the digraph is represented by its adjacency lists instead of the adjacency matrix. Also, instead of maintaining set S of vertices to which the shortest paths have already been found, the set V(G)-S is represented by using a linked list where V(G) is the set of vertices in digraph G.

Program 2: Write a C++ program to finding the shortest path by using an adjacency list.

```
#include <iostream.h>
#include<conio.h>
#define MAXINT 99999
```

```
#define MAXVERTICES 10
typedef struct node node;
typedef struct setnode setnode;
typedef enum {FALSE, TRUE} bool;
struct node {
int dst;
int cost;
node *next;
};
struct setnode {
int v;
setnode *next;
};
void printGraph( node *cost[], int nvert ) {
int i, j;
for( i=0; i<nvert; ++i ) {
node *ptr;
for( ptr=cost[i]; ptr; ptr=ptr->next )
cout<<"["<<ptr->dst<<","<<ptr->cost<<"];
cout<<endl;
} }
void insertEdge( node **ptr, int dst, int cost ) {
node *newnode = (node *)malloc( sizeof(node) );
newnode->dst = dst;
newnode->cost = cost;
newnode->next = *ptr;
*ptr = newnode;
}
void buildGraph( node *cost[], int costnew[][3], int nedges ) {
int i;
for( i=0; i<nedges; ++i )
insertEdge( cost+costnew[i][0], costnew[i][1], costnew[i][2] );
}
int choose( int dist[], setnode *s ) {
int u=-1;
int mindist = MAXINT;
setnode *ptr;
for( ptr=s->next; ptr; ptr=ptr->next )
if( dist[ptr->v] <= mindist )
```

```
u=ptr->v, mindist=dist[ptr->v];
return u;
}
int getCost( node **cost, int src, int dst ) {
node *ptr;
for( ptr=cost[src]; ptr; ptr=ptr->next )
if( ptr->dst == dst )
return ptr->cost;
return MAXINT;
}
void removeFromSet( setnode *s, int v ) {
setnode *prev, *ptr;
for( prev=s, ptr=prev->next; ptr; prev=ptr, ptr=ptr->next )
if( ptr->v == v ) {
prev->next = ptr->next;
free(ptr);
return;
} }
void insertIntoSet( setnode *s, int v ) {
setnode *ptr = (setnode *)malloc( sizeof(setnode) );
ptr->v = v;
ptr->next = s->next;
s->next = ptr;
}
bool isInSet( setnode *s, int v ) {
setnode *ptr;
for( ptr=s->next; ptr; ptr=ptr->next )
if( ptr->v == v )
return TRUE;
return FALSE;
}
void sssp( int v, node **cost, int dist[], int nvert ) {
setnode s; // list of vertices yet to be considered.
int i, u, num, w;
node *ptr;
for( i=0; i<nvert; ++i ) {
insertIntoSet( &s, i );
dist[i] = MAXINT;
}
```

```
for( ptr=cost[v]; ptr; ptr=ptr->next )
dist[ptr->dst] = ptr->cost;
removeFromSet( &s, v );
dist[v] = 0;
num = 1;
while( num < nvert-1 ) {
u = choose( dist, &s );
removeFromSet( &s, u );
num++;
for( w=0; w<nvert; ++w ) {
int c = getCost( cost, u, w );
if( isInSet( &s, w ) && dist[u]+c < dist[w] )
dist[w] = dist[u] + c;
} } }
void printDist( int v, int dist[], int nvert ) {
int i;
cout<< "min dist from vertex" << v;
for( i=0; i<nvert; ++i )
cout<< "dist["<<i<<"]="<< dist[i] ;
}
void main() {
int costnew[][3] =    { {0,1,50},
                        {0,2,10},
                        {0,4,45},
                        {1,2,15},
                        {1,4,10},
                        {2,0,20},
                        {2,3,15},
                        {3,1,20},
                        {3,4,35},
                        {4,3,30},
                        {5,3,3}
                      };
int dist[MAXVERTICES];
int nvert = 6;        // no of vertices.
int nedges = 11;  // no of edges in costnew.
node **cost = (node **)calloc( nvert, sizeof(node *) );
buildGraph( cost, costnew, nedges );
printGraph( cost, nvert );
sssp( 4, cost, dist, nvert );
```

```
printDist( 4, dist, nvert );
getch();
}
```

Output:

1. Cost is maintained as an array containing adjacency lists for each vertex in the digraph. The function buildGraph() fills this array. An adjacency list for a vertex is a linked list where each node contains the vertex, the cost of the corresponding edge, and a pointer to the next node.

   For example, consider the following graph:

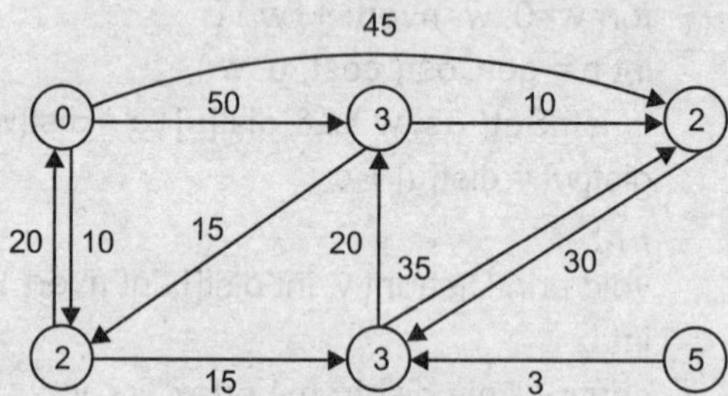

The adjacency lists are maintained as follows:

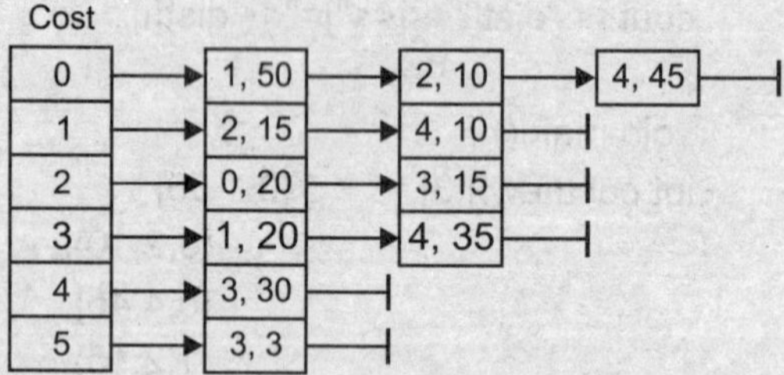

Note that each node contains a pair of integers, (vertex, cost).

2. The function sssp() remains nearly the same except getting the cost of an edge and accesses the set S. The cost of an edge can be retrieved using the function getCost(). It needs O(n) traversal of the adjacency list corresponding to the source vertex of the edge, where n is the number of nodes in the list. In the cost matrix-based algorithm, this was O(1). Removal of a vertex (removeFromSet()) from the list requires O(n) time. This time was also constant earlier as we flagged the vertex as FALSE. Furthermore, earlier we could check the status of a vertex to be TRUE or FALSE using s[i], but now the function isInSet() needs to traverse the list s to see whether the node has been processed or NOT. This makes it O(n). However, the function choose(), which was earlier O(n), now becomes O(1), as we need to remove only the first element from the list s.
3. The overall complexity of sssp() increases from O(n^2) to O(n^3) as getCost() and isInSet() become O(n), where n is the number of vertices in the digraph.

11.4 LINKED LIST REPRESENTATION

Let G be a directed graph in memory can be implemented or represented either by using the adjacency matrix or adjacency list. Mostly the representation of graph in memory by using the adjacency matrix is quite difficult and has many limitations to implement it in the memory.

As adjacency matrix is a sequential representation, so it is difficult to arrange graph nodes in particular sequence or order. Also it is difficult to insert, delete and modify the nodes in a particular graph. In the adjacency matrix, the size of the particular matrix changes and so the nodes in the graph need to be reordered again and again, which creates many changes and implementation becomes not even difficult, it becomes impossible also in many cases.

Implementation of graph in memory using the adjacency matrix also waste the space in memory because it creates the sparse matrix (a matrix with more zeros than numbers). Another difficulty with adjacency matrix is to add more information.

So to avoid all the above problems, it is easier to implement the graph in memory using the adjacency list. This can be done by the linked representation. Such types of operation are called adjacency list linked operation and the structure is called adjacency structure. An adjacency list is a listing for each node of all edges connecting it to adjacent nodes. Simplest representation of graph is by an edge list. This is also called storage representation of graph.

Consider the graph G in Figure 11.14(a). The table in Figure 11.14(b) shows each node in G followed by its adjacency list, which is its list of adjacent nodes, also called its successors or neighbors. Figure 11.15 shows a schematic diagram of a linked representation of G in memory. Specifically, the linked representation will contain two lists (or files), a node list NODE and an edge list EDGE as follows.

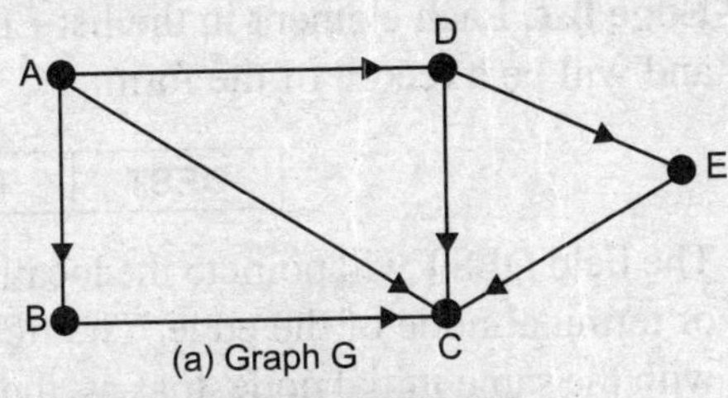

(a) Graph G

Node	Adjacency list
A	B, C, D
B	C
C	
D	C, E
E	C

(b) Adjacency list of G

Figure 11.14: Linked representation.

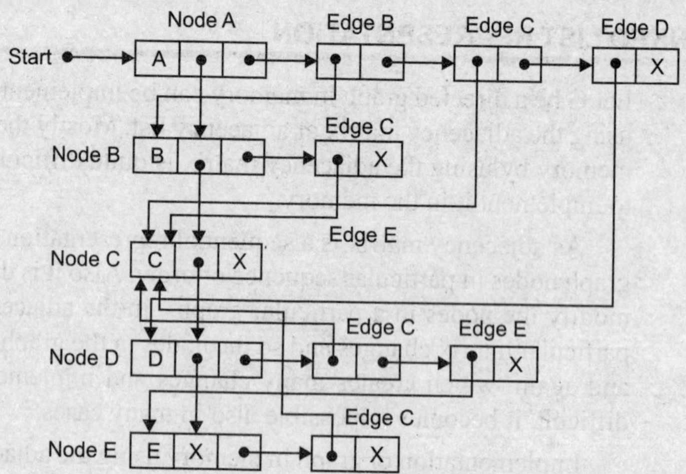

Figure 11.15: Schematic diagram of a linked representation of graph G.

(a) Node list. Each element in the list of NODE will correspond to a node in G, and it will be a record of the form:

NODE	NEXT	ADJ

Here NODE will be the name or key value of the node, NEXT will be a pointer to the next node in the list NODE and ADJ will be a pointer to the first element in the adjacency list of the node, which is maintained in the list EDGE. The nodes are pictured in Figure 11.14 will organized as a linked list in Figure 11.16 and hence will have a pointer variable START for the beginning of the list and a pointer variable AVAILN for the list of available space.

(b) Edge list. Each element in the list EDGE will correspond to an edge of G and will be a record of the form:

DEST	LINK

The field DEST will point to the location in the list NODE of the destination or terminal node of the edge. The field LINK will link together the edges with the same initial node, that is, the nodes in the same adjacency list. We also need a pointer variable AVAILE for the list of available space in the list EDGE.

Figure 11.16 shows how the graph G in Figure 11.14(a) may appear in memory. The choice of 10 locations for the list NODE and 12 locations for the list EDGE is arbitrary.

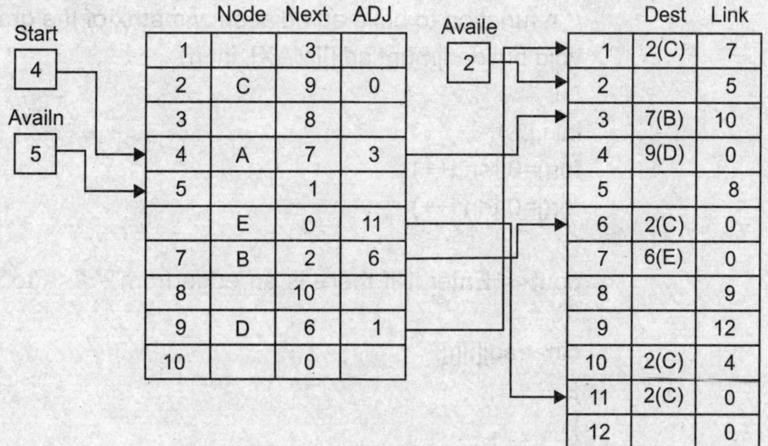

Figure 11.16: Graph G appears in memory.

Example 11.2: Another way of representing a graph G is to maintain a list for every vertex containing all vertices adjacent to that vertex, as shown in Figure 11.17.

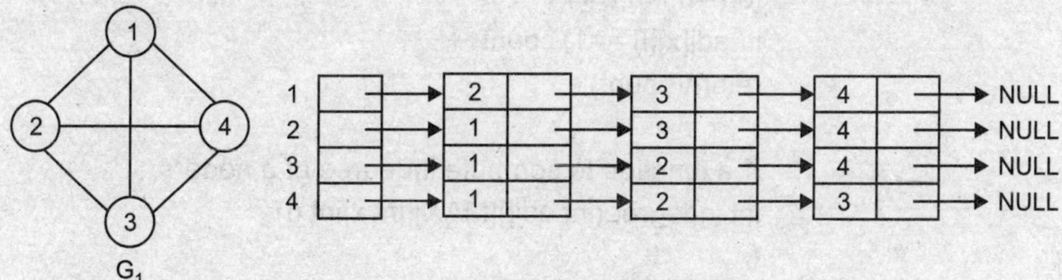

Figure 11.17: Adjacency list of G_1.

11.4.1 Computing Indegree and Outdegree of A Node of A Graph Using Adjacency Matrix Representation

To compute the indegree of a node n by using the adjacency matrix representation of a graph, use the node number n as a column index in the adjacency matrix and count the number of 1's in that column of the adjacency matrix. This count is the indegree of node n. Similarly, to compute the outdegree of a node n of a graph, use the node number n as the row index in the adjacency matrix and count the number of 1's in that row of the adjacency matrix. This is the outdegree of the node n. A complete C program to compute the indegree and outdegree of each node of a graph using the adjacency matrix representation of a graph follows.

Program 3: Write a C++ program for computing the indegree and outdegree.

```
#include <iostream.h>
#include<conio.h>
#define MAX 10
```

```
/* a function to build an adjacency matrix of the graph*/
void buildadjm(int adj[][MAX], int n)
{
int i,j;
for(i=0;i<n;i++)
for(j=0;j<n;j++)
{
cout<<"Enter 1 if there is an edge from"<<i<<"to"<<j<<",otherwise enter 0";
cin>>adj[i][j];
}
}
/* a function to compute outdegree of a node*/
int outdegree(int adj[][MAX],int x,int n)
{
int i, count =0;
for(i=0;i<n;i++)
if( adj[x][i] ==1) count++;
return(count);
}
/* a function to compute indegree of a node*/
int indegree(int adj[][MAX],int x,int n)
{
int i, count =0;
for(i=0;i<n;i++)
if( adj[i][x] ==1) count++;
return(count);
}
void main()
{
int adj[MAX][MAX],node,n,i;
cout<<"Enter the number of nodes in graph maximum = "<<MAX;
cin>>n;
buildadjm(adj,n);
for(i=0;i<n;i++)
{
cout<<"The indegree of the node"<<i<<"is "<<indegree(adj,i,n);
cout<<"The outdegree of the node "<<i<<" is"<<outdegree(adj,i,n);
}
}
```

Output:

1. This program uses the adjacency matrix representation of a directed graph to compute the indegree and outdegree of each node of the graph.
2. It first builds an adjacency matrix of the graph by calling a buildadjm function, then goes in a loop to compute the indegree and outdegree of each node by calling the indegree and outdegree functions, respectively.
3. The indegree function counts the number of 1's in a column of an adjacency matrix using the node number whose indegree is to be computed as a column index.
4. The outdegree function counts the number of 1's in a row of an adjacency matrix by using the node number whose outdegree is to be computed as a row index.

Input:

1. The number of nodes in a graph
2. Information about edges, in the form of values, to be stored in adjacency matrix 1, if there is an edge from node i to node j; 0 otherwise.

Output: The indegree and outdegree of each node.

Example 11.3

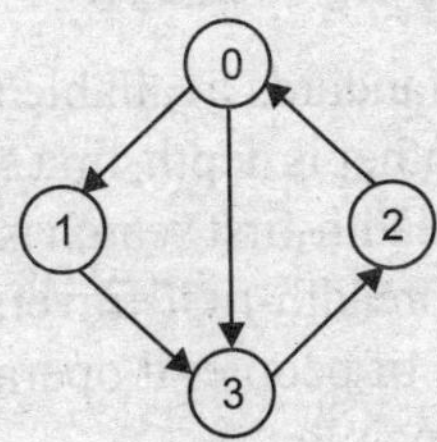

Graphs G_1

The adjacency matrix for graph G1 is:

	0	1	2	3
0	0	1	0	1
1	0	0	0	1
2	1	0	0	0
3	0	0	0	0

For this graph as the input, the output is:

- The indegree of node 0 is 1
- The outdgree of node 0 is 2
- The indegree of node 1 is 1
- The outdgree of node 1 is 1
- The indegree of node 2 is 1
- The outdgree of node 2 is 1

- The indegree of node 3 is 2
- The outdgree of node 3 is 1

11.5 OPERATIONS ON GRAPH

Graph can be used for handling different type of INFO (text and number). Every graph has number of operations, but all are not required for the graph operations. Mainly there are four operations can be applied with the graph.

These four different operations are discussed as below:

1. Traversing a graph
   (a) breadth-first search
   (b) depth-first search
2. Searching in a graph
3. Inserting in a graph
4. Deleting from a graph

11.5.1 Traversing A Graph

There are two standards available to perform traversing. One way is breadth-first search, and the other is depth-first search. Depth first traversal can be implemented recursively, a breadth-first search is not naturally recursive. Instead of using a stack data structure, breadth-first traversal usually makes use of a queue. A queue is much like a line of people; it operates on a FIFO (first in first out) or "first come, first served" principle.

Breadth First Search Algorithm

Breadth-first traversal algorithms visit each node in a connected graph. However, when a breadth-first traversal arrives at a certain node, *v*, it visits all neighbors of node *v* before continuing to process other, more distant, parts of the graph. Breadth-first traversal usually makes use of a queue. A queue is much like a line of people; it operates on a FIFO (first in first out) or "first come, first served" principle. The actual traversal procedure begins by enqueueing the starting node. Then the following process repeats:

- Dequeue a current node
- Enqueue all non-visited nodes adjacent to the current node
- Mark non-visited nodes adjacent to the current node visited

The above cycle repeats until the queue becomes empty.

A breadth first search traversal method, visits all the successors of a visited node before visiting any successor of any of its child nodes. This is a contradiction to depth first traversal method; which visits the successor of a visited node before visiting any of its brothers, i.e., children of the same parent. A depth first traversal method tends to create very long, narrow trees; whereas breadth first traversal method tends to create very wide, short trees.

Given an input graph G = (V, E) and source vertex s, from where to begin. BFS systematically explores the edges of G to discover every vertex that is reachable from s. It produces a breadth first tree with root s that contains all such vertices that are reachable from s. For every vertex v reachable from s, the path in the breadth first tree from s to v corresponds to a shortest path. During the execution of the algorithm, each node n of G will be one of the three states, called the status of n as follows:

- Status = 1 (ready state): the initial state of a node n.
- Status = 2 (waiting state): the node n is on the queue or stack waiting to be processed.
- Status = 3 (processed state): the node has been processed.

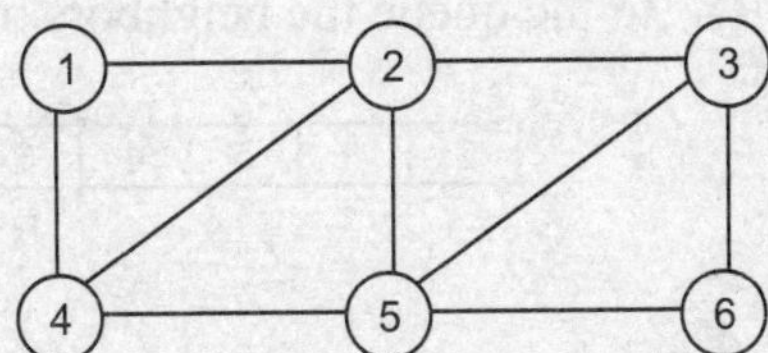

Figure 11.18: Undirected Graph

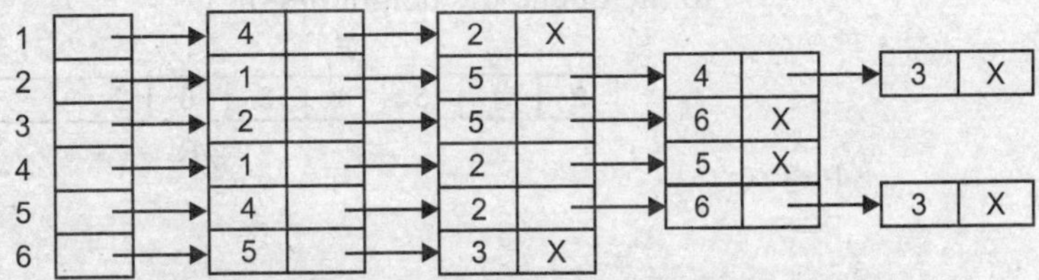

Figure 11.19: Adjacency list for above undirected graph.

Algorithm11.1: Traversing using Breadth first search.

Step 1: Initialize all nodes to ready state (status = 1)

Step 2: Put the starting node in queue and change its status to the waiting state (status = 2)

Step 3: Repeat step 4 and 5 until queue is empty

Step 4: Remove the front node n of queue. Process n and change the status of n to the processed state (status = 3)

Step 5: Add to the rear of the queue all the neighbors of n that are in ready state (status = 1), and change their status to the waiting state (status = 2). [End of the step 3 loop]

Step 6: Exit

Explanation

Step 1: Initially add 2 to the queue.

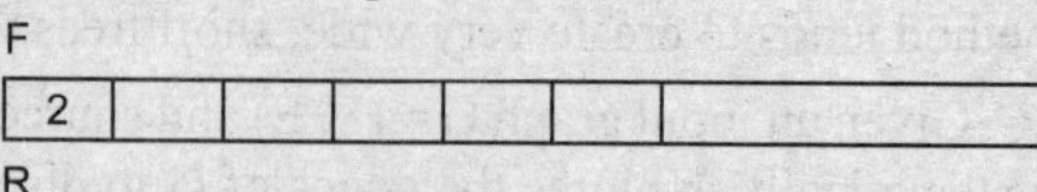

F = 0
R = 0

Step 2: Remove the front element 2 from queue by setting front = front +1 add to the queue the neighbors of 2.

F

2	1	5	4	3		

R

F = 0
R = 0

Step 3: Remove the front element 1 from queue by setting front = front +1 add to the queue the neighbors of 1.

F

2	1	5	4	3		

R

F = 2
R = 4

Step 4: Remove the front element 5 from queue by setting front = front +1 add to the queue the neighbors of 5.

F

2	1	5	4	3	6	

R

F=3
R=5

Step 5: Remove the front element 4 from queue by setting front = front +1 add to the queue the neighbors of 4.

F

2	1	5	4	3	6	

R

F=4
R=5

Step 6: Remove the front element 6 from queue by setting front = front +1 add to the queue the neighbors of 6

F

2	1	5	4	3	6	

R

F=5
R=5

Example 11.4: Consider the graph G in Figure 11.20(a). (The adjacency lists of the nodes appear in Figure 11.20(b). Suppose G represents the daily routes between cities of some airline, and suppose we want to go from city 1 to city 8 with the minimum number of stops. In other words, we want the minimum path P from 1 to 8 (where each edge has same length 1).

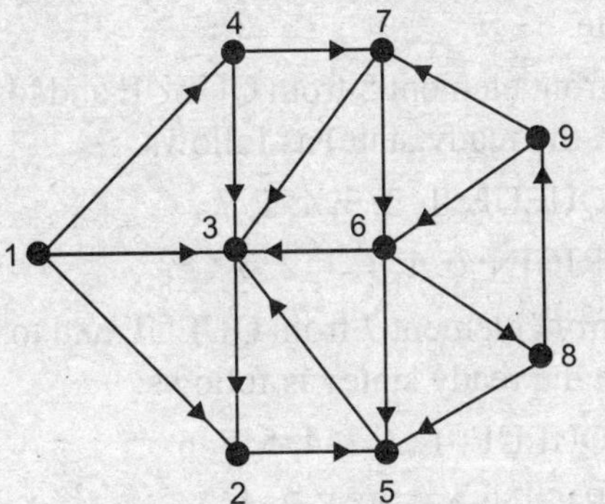

Adjacency lists
1: 2, 3, 4
2: 5
3: 2
4: 7, 3
5: 3
6: 5, 3, 8
7: .3, 6
8: 5, 9
9: 6, 7

Figure 11.20: Graph G having adjacency lists.

The minimum path P can be found by using a breadth-first search beginning at city 1 and ending when 8 is encountered. During the execution of the search, we will also keep track of the origin of each edge by using an array ORIGIN together with the array QUEUE. The steps of our search follow.

(a) Initially, add 1 to QUEUE and add NULL to ORIGIN as follows:

FRONT = 1 QUEUE: 1

REAR = 1 ORIGIN: ϕ

(b) Remove the front element 1 from QUEUE by setting FRONT := FRONT + 1, and add to QUEUE the neighbors of 1 as follows:

FRONT = 2 QUEUE: 1, 2, 3, 4

REAR = 4 ORIGIN: ϕ, 1, 1, 1

(c) Remove the front element 2 from QUEUE by setting FRONT := FRONT + 1, and add to QUEUE the neighbors of F as follows:

FRONT = 3 QUEUE: 1, 2, 3, 4, 5

REAR = 5 ORIGIN: ϕ, 1, 1, 1, 2

(d) Remove the front element 3 from QUEUE and to QUEUE the neighbors of 3 (which are in the ready state) as follows:

FRONT = 3 QUEUE: 1, 2, 3, 4, 5

REAR = 5 ORIGIN: ϕ, 1, 1, 1, 2

Note that the neighbor 2 of 3 is not added to QUEUE, since 2 is not in the ready state (because 2 has already been added to QUEUE).

(e) Remove the front element 4 from QUEUE and to QUEUE the neighbors of 4 (the ones in the ready state) as follows:

FRONT = 5 QUEUE: 1, 2, 3, 4, 5, 7

REAR = 6 ORIGIN: ϕ, 1, 1, 1, 2, 4

Note that only 7 is added to QUEUE, since the other neighbor, 3 is not in the ready state.

(f) Remove the front element 5 from QUEUE and to QUEUE the neighbors of 5 (the ones in the ready state) as follows:

FRONT = 6 QUEUE: 1, 2, 3, 4, 5, 7

REAR = 6 ORIGIN: ϕ, 1, 1, 1, 2, 4

(g) Remove the front element 7 from QUEUE and to QUEUE the neighbors of 7 (the ones in the ready state) as follows:

FRONT = 7 QUEUE: 1, 2, 3, 4, 5, 7, 6

REAR = 7 ORIGIN: ϕ, 1, 1, 1, 2, 4, 7

(h) Remove the front element 6 from QUEUE and to QUEUE the neighbors of 6 (the ones in the ready state) as follows:

FRONT = 8 QUEUE: 1, 2, 3, 4, 5, 7, 6, 8

REAR = 8 ORIGIN: ϕ, 1, 1, 1, 2, 4, 7, 6

We stop as soon as 8 is added to QUEUE, since 8 is our final destination. We now backtrack from 8, using the array ORIGIN to find the path P. Thus

$8 \leftarrow 6 \leftarrow 7 \leftarrow 4 \leftarrow 1$ is the required path P.

Breadth-first Traversal Implementation

When a graph is traversed by visiting all the adjacent nodes/vertices of a node/ vertex first, the traversal is called breadth-first traversal. For example, for a graph in which the breadth-first traversal starts at vertex v_1, visits to the nodes take place in the order shown in Figure 11.21.

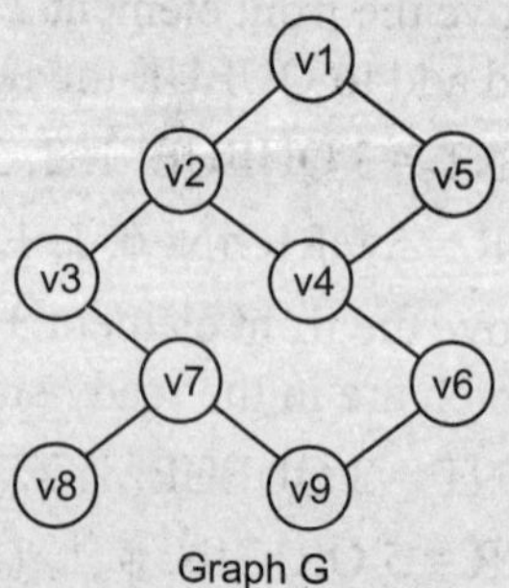

Figure 11.21: Breadth-first traversal of graph G starting at vertex v1.

Program 4: Write a C++ program to implement Breadth First search.

```
#include<iostream.h>
#include<conio.h>
class Queue
{
private:
int data;
Queue*next;
public:
void Enque(int);
int Deque();
}*head,*tail;
void Queue::Enque(int data)
{
Queue *temp;
temp=new Queue;
temp->data=data;
temp->next=NULL;
if(head==NULL)
head=temp;
else
tail->next=temp;
tail=temp;
}
int Queue::Deque()
{
Queue* temp;
temp=head;
head=head->next;
return temp->data;
}
int visit[100];
int bfs_span_tree[100][100];
class graph
{
private:
int a;
graph*next;
public:
void bfs();
```

```
graph* create(graph*);
void ftraverse(graph*);
};
graph* graph::create(graph*head)
{
int a;
graph*last;
head=last=NULL;
graph*temp;
cout<<"Enter  adjecent node ,-1 to stop:\n";
cin>>a;
while(a!=-1)
{
temp=new graph;
temp->a=a;
temp->next=NULL;
if(head==NULL)
head=temp;
else
last->next=temp;
last=temp;
cout<<"Enter  adjecent node ,-1 to stop:\n";
cin>>a;
}
return head;
}
void graph::ftraverse(graph*h)
{
while(h!=NULL)
{
cout<<h->a<<"->";
h=h->next;
}
cout<<"NULL\n";
}
void graph::bfs()
{
cout<<"*************************************************************\n";
cout<<"This program is to implement bfs for an unweighted graph \n";
cout<<"*************************************************************\n";
graph *ptr[100];
```

```
int n;
cout<<"Enter the no. of nodes in the grph:";
cin>>n;
for(int i=1;i<=n;i++)
{
cout<<"Enter the adjacent nodes to node no. "<<i<<endl;
cout<<"***************************************\n";
ptr[i]=create(ptr[i]);
}
cout<<"\n\nThe Entered Graph is ::\n";
for(i=1;i<=n;i++)
{
cout<<"< "<<i<<" > ::";
ftraverse(ptr[i]);
}
int x;
cout<<"\nEnter the start node <1,..."<<n<<">:";
cin>>x;
cout<<"\n\nThe Breadth first search traversal is:\n";
Queue object;
//Mark all the nodes as not viseted
for(i=1;i<=n;i++)
{
visit[i]=0;
}
for(i=1;i<=n;i++)
for(int j=1;j<=n;j++)
bfs_span_tree[i][j]=0;
//Enque the start node
object.Enque(x);
int p;
while(head!=NULL&&tail!=NULL)
{
//Deque a node
p=object.Deque();
int x=p;
//If it is not visited yet
while(ptr[p]!=NULL)
{
if(visit[ptr[p]->a]!=1)
{
```

```
cout<<"node "<<ptr[p]->a<<" is visited\n";
//Mark the node as visited
visit[ptr[p]->a]=1;
bfs_span_tree[ptr[p]->a][x]=1;
}
//Enque all its adjacent nodes
object.Enque(ptr[p]->a);
ptr[p]=ptr[p]->next;
}
}
cout<<"\n\nThe required bfs spanning tree is ::\n\n";
for(i=1;i<=n;i++)
{
for(int j=1;j<=n;j++)
cout<<bfs_span_tree[i][j]<<' ';
cout<<endl;
}
cout<<endl;
}
void main()
{
graph obj;
obj.bfs();
getch();
}
```

Depth First Search Algorithm

Depth-first searching, also sometimes known as backtracking, builds a path from emanating at the starting point and continuing as far as possible into the graph. Each new edge traversed must be one that has not already been covered by the algorithm. The path-building operation continues until it reaches a point at which there is no edge leading to a vertex that has not already been visited. At such a point we backtrack to the previous node, choose a new edge from that point, and build as long a path as possible from there. In backtracking, if all the edges from the previous node have been tried we backtrack again to the next-previous node and so on. Eventually this method will visit every node in a connected graph.

The actual traversal is often accomplished using a stack data structure. First, the starting node is pushed onto the stack. Then the following process repeats:

- Pop a node off the stack
- Traverse to this current node
- Push all nodes adjacent to the current node onto the stack

The process terminates when the stack is empty. The same process can be implemented as a recursive function which uses the system stack instead of a data segment structure.

Depth-first traversal of a graph is an $O(V + E)$ operation where V is the number of vertices in the graph and E is the number of edges.

A DFS algorithm, as the name implies, is used to search deeper in the graph, whenever possible. The edges are explored, out of the most recently discovered vertex **v** that still has unexplored edges leaving it. When all of **v**'s edges have been explored, the search backtracks to explore edges leaving the vertex from which **v** was discovered. This process continues until we have discovered all the vertices that are reachable from the source vertex. DFS uses stack structure to maintain the order in which the vertices are to be processed.

Algorithm 11.2: Traversing using depth first search.

Step 1: Initialize all nodes to ready state (status = 1)

Step 2: Push the starting node in stack and change its status to the waiting state (status = 2)

Step 3: Repeat step 4 and 5 until stack is empty

Step 4: pop the top node n of stack. Process n and change the status of n to the processed state (status = 3)

Step 5: Push on to the stack, all the neighbor of n that are in ready state (status = 1), and change their status to the waiting state (status = 2)

[End of the step 3 loop]

Step 6: exit

Example 11.5: Consider the graph G in Figure 11.22(a). Suppose we want to find and print all the nodes reachable from the node 8 (including 8 itself). One way to do this is to use a depth-first search of G starting at the node 8. The steps of our search follow.

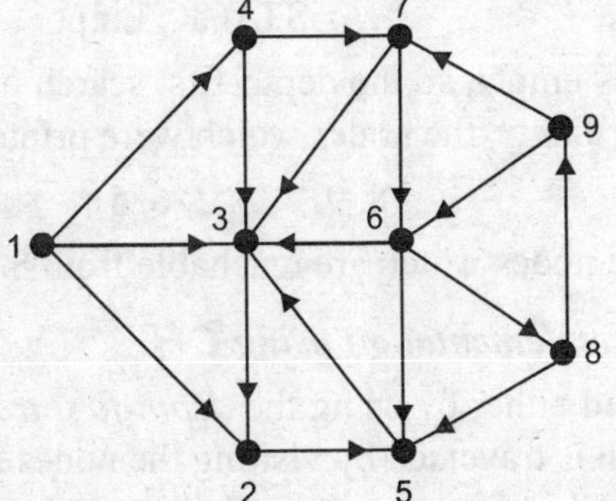

Adjacency lists
1: 2, 3, 4
2: 5
3: 2
4: 7, 3
5: 3
6: 5, 3, 8
7: 3, 6
8: 5, 9
9: 6, 7

Figure 11.22: Graph G having adjacency lists.

(a) Initially, push 8 onto the stack as follows: STACK: 8

(b) Pop and print the top element 8, and then push onto the stack all the neighbors of 8 (those that are in the ready state) as follows:

Print 8 STACK: 5, 9

(c) Pop and print the top element 9, and then push onto the stack all the neighbors of 9 (those that are in the ready state) as follows:

Print 9 STACK: 5, 6, 7

(d) Pop and print the top element 7, and then push onto the stack all the neighbors of 7 (those that are in the ready state) as follows:

Print 7 STACK: 5, 6, 3

Note that only 3 is pushed onto the stack, since the other neighbor, 6, is not in the ready state (because 6 has already been pushed onto the stack).

(e) Pop and print the top element 3, and then push onto the stack all the neighbors of 3 (those that are in the ready state) as follows:

Print 3 STACK: 5, 6, 2

(f) Pop and print the top element 2, and then push onto the stack all the neighbors of 2 (those that are in the ready state) as follows:

Print 2 STACK: 5, 6

Note that the only neighbor 5 of 2 is not pushed onto stack, since 5 is not in the ready state (because 5 has already been pushed onto the stack).

(g) Pop and print the top element 6, and then push onto the stack all the neighbors of 6 (those that are in the ready state) as follows:

Print 6 STACK: 5

(Note that none of the three neighbors of 6 is in the ready state.)

(h) Pop and print the top element 5, and then push onto the stack all the neighbors of 5 (those that are in the ready state) as follows:

Print 5 STACK: Empty

The stack is now empty, so the depth-first search of 7 starting at 8 is now complete. Accordingly, the nodes which were printed,

8, 9, 7, 3, 2, 6, 5

are precisely the nodes which are reachable from 8.

Depth-first Traversal Implementation using C++

A graph can be traversed either by using the *depth-first traversal* or *breadth-first traversal*. When a graph is traversed by visiting the nodes in the forward (deeper) direction as long as possible, the traversal is called depth-first traversal. For example, for the graph shown in Figure 11.23, the depth-first traversal starting at the vertex 0 visits the node in the orders:

(i) 0 1 2 6 7 8 5 3 4

(ii) 0 4 3 5 8 6 7 2 1

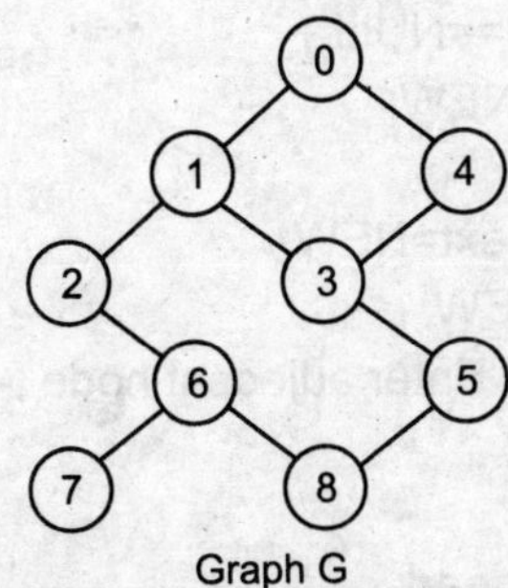

Figure 11.23: Graph G and its depth first traversals starting at vertex 0.

Program 5: Write a C++ program to implement Depth First search.

```
#include<iostream.h>
#include<conio.h>
int visit[100];
class graph
{
private:
int n;
graph*next;
public:
graph* read_graph(graph*);
void dfs(int); //dfs for a single node
void dfs(); //dfs of the entire graph
void ftraverse(graph*);
}*g[100];
int dfs_span_tree[100][100];
graph* graph::read_graph(graph*head)
{
int x;
graph*last;
head=last=NULL;
cout<<"Enter adjecent node ,-1 to stop:\n";
cin>>x;
while(x!=-1)
{
graph*NEW;
NEW=new graph;
```

```
NEW->n=x;
NEW->next=NULL;
if(head==NULL)
head=NEW;
else
last->next=NEW;
last=NEW;
cout<<"Enter adjecent node ,-1 to stop:\n";
cin>>x;
}
return head;
}
void graph::ftraverse(graph*h)
{
while(h!=NULL)
{
cout<<h->n<<"->";
h=h->next;
}
cout<<"NULL"<<endl;
}
void graph::dfs(int x)
{
cout<<"node "<<x<<" is visited\n";
visit[x]=1;
graph *p;
p=g[x];
while(p!=NULL)
{
int x1=p->n;
if(visit[x1]==0)
{
cout<<"from node "<<x<<' ';
//Add the edge to the dfs spanning tree
dfs_span_tree[x][x1]=1;
dfs(x1);
}
p=p->next;
}
}
void graph::dfs()
```

```
{
int i;
cout<<"************************************************************\n";
cout<<"This program is to implement dfs for an unweighted graph \n";
cout<<"************************************************************\n";
cout<<"Enter the no of nodes ::";
cin>>n;
for(i=1;i<=n;i++)
g[i]=NULL;
for(i=1;i<=n;i++)
{
cout<<"Enter the adjacent nodes to node no. "<<i<<endl;
cout<<"****************************************\n";
g[i]=read_graph(g[i]);
}
//display the graph
cout<<"\n\nThe entered graph is ::\n";
for(i=1;i<=n;i++)
{
cout<<" < "<<i<<" > ::";
ftraverse(g[i]);
}
for(i=1;i<=n;i++)
visit[i]=0; //mark all nodes as unvisited
cout<<"\nEnter the start vertex ::";
int start;
cin>>start;
for(i=1;i<=n;i++)
for(int j=1;j<=n;j++)
dfs_span_tree[i][j]=0;
cout<<"\nThe dfs for the above graph is ::\n";
dfs(start);
cout<<"\n\nThe required dfs spanning tree is ::\n";
for(i=1;i<=n;i++)
{
for(int j=1;j<=n;j++)
cout<<dfs_span_tree[i][j]<<' ';
cout<<endl;
}
}
void main()
```

```
{
graph obj;
obj.dfs();
getch();
}
```

Example 11.6

Input

	0	1	2	3	4	5
0	1	0	0	0	0	0
1	1	1	0	0	0	0
2	0	1	0	0	0	0
3	0	0	1	0	0	0
4	0	0	1	1	0	1
5	0	0	0	1	1	0
6	0	0	0	0	1	1

Output:

0, 1, 2, 6, 8, 5, 3, 4, 7

11.5.2 Searching In A Graph

Suppose we want to find the location LOC of a node N in a graph G.

Algorithm 11.3: FINDNOD(INFO, LINK START, ITEM, LOC)

Finds the location LOC of the first node containing ITEM, or sets LOC = NULL.

Step 1: Set P = START.

Step 2: Repeat while P ≠ NULL:

If ITEM = INFO[P], then: Set LOC := P, and Return.

Else: Set P = LINK[P]. [End of loop.]

Step 3: Set LOC = NULL, and Return.

Algorithm 11.4: FINDEDGE(NODE, NEXT, ADJNCY, START, DEST, LINK, A, B, LOC)

This algorithm finds the location LOC of an edge (A, B0 in the graph G, or sets LOC = NULL.

Step 1: Call FINDNOD(NODE, NEXT, START, A, LOCA).

Step 2: CALL FINDNOD(NODE, NEXT, START, B, LOCB).

Step 3: If LOCA = NULL or LOCB = NULL, then: Set LOC = NULL.

Else: Call FINDNOD(DEST, LINK, ADJNCY[LOCA], LOCB, LOC) and Return.

11.5.3 Inserting in A Graph

To insert a node into the graph, first of all create a graph. Let us take a node N and we want to insert this node in the graph G. For the insertion, first of all set the node to the first available node i.e. assign the node N to the first available node. As the node N is in an independent form, then we have to set its adjacency. For the insertion, below is the algorithm:

Algorithm 11.5: INSNODE(NODE, NEXT, ADJNCY, START, AVAILNOD, N, FLAG)

This algorithm inserts the node N is the graph G.

Step 1: [OVERFLOW?] If AVAILNOD = NULL, then: Set FLAG = FALSE, and Return.

Step 2: Set ADJNCY [AVAILNOD] = NULL.

Step 3: [Removes node from AVAILN list.]

Set NEW = AVAILNOD and AVAILNOD = NEXT [AVAILNOD].

Step 4: [Inserts node N in the NODE list.]

Set NODE = [NEW] = N, NEXT [NEW] = START and START = NEW.

Step 5: Set FLAG = TRUE, and Return.

Algorithm 11.6: INSEDGE(NODE, NEXT, ADJNCY, START, DEST, LINK, AVAILEDG, A, B, FLAG)

This algorithm inserts the edge (A, B) in the graph G.

Step 1: Call FINDNOD(NODE, NEXT, START, A, LOCA).

Step 2: Call FINDNOD(NODE, NEXT, START, B, LOCB).

Step 3: [OVERFLOW?] If AVAILEDG = NULL, then: Set FLAG = FALSE, and Return.

Step 4: [Remove node from AVAILEDG list.] Set NEW = AVAILEDG and AVAILEDG = LINK[AVAILEDG].

Step 5: [Insert LOCB in list of successors of A.] Set DEST[NEW] = LOCB, LINK[NEW] = ADJNCY[LOCA] and ADJNCY[LOCA] = NEW.

Step 6: Set FLAG = TRUE, and Return.

11.5.4 Deleting from A Graph

Let the node N is to be deleted from the graph G. Note that before deleting a node from the graph, edges linked with that node must be deleted first. Delete the beginning node in the list and ending of the node N. At end delete the node N and put it into the free available list of all the nodes.

Algorithm 11.7: DELFRSTNOD(INFO, LINK, START, AVAIL, ITEM, FLAG) .

Deletes the first node in the list containing ITEM, or sets FLAG = FALSE when ITEM does not appear in the list.

Step 1: [List empty?] If START = NULL, then: Set FLAG = FALSE, and Return.

Step 2: [ITEM in first node?] If INFO[START]. ITEM, then:

Set P = START, START = LINK[START],

LINK[P] := AVAIL, AVAIL := P,

FLAG = TRUE, and Return.

[End of If structure.]

Step 3: Set P = LINK[START] and SAVE := START. [Initializes pointers.]

Step 4: Repeat Steps 5 and 6 while PTR ≠ NULL.

Step 5: If INFO[P] =ITEM, then:

Set LINK[SAVE] = LINK[P], LINK[P] = AVAIL,

AVAIL := P, FLAG := TRUE, and Return.

[End of If structure.]

Step 6: Set SAVE = P and P = LINK[P]. [Updates pointers]

[End of Step 4 loop.]

Step 7: Set FLAG = FALSE and return.

Algorithm 11.8: DELGVNNODE(NODE, NEXT, ADI, START, AVAILN, DEST, LINK, AVAILE, N, FLAG)

This algorithm deletes the node N from the graph G.

Step 1: Call FINDNOD(NODE, NEXT, START, N, LOC). [Locates node N.]

Step 2: If LOC = NULL, then: Set FLAG = FALSE, and Return.

Step 3: [Deletes edges ending at N.]

(a) Set P= START.

(b) Repeat while P ≠ NULL.

(i) Call DELFRSTNOD(DEST, LINK, ADJNCY[P], AVAILEDG, LOC, FLAG).

(ii) Set P= NEXT[P].

[End of loop.]

Step 4: [Successor list empty?] If ADJNCY[LOC] = NULL, then: Go to Step 7.

Step 5: [Find the first and last successor of N.]

(a) Set BEG = ADJNCY[LOC], END := ADJNCY[LOC] and P= LINK[END]

(b) Repeat while P ≠ NULL:

Set END = P and P = LINK[P]. [End of loop.]

Step 6: [Add successor list of N to AVAILEDG list.]

Set LINK[END] := AVAILEDG and AVAILEDG = BEG.

Step 7: [Delete N using Procedure 8.4.]

Call DELFRSTNOD(NODE, NEXT, START, AVAILNOD, N, FLAG).

Step 8: Return.

Algorithm 11.9: DELEDGE(NODE, NEXT, ADJNCY, START, DEST, LINK, AVAILEDG, A, B, FLAG)

This algorithm deletes the edge (A, B) from the graph G.

Step 1: Call FINDNOD(NODE, NEXT, START, A, LOCA). [Locates node A.]

Step 2: Call FINDNOD(NODE, NEXT, START, B, LOCB). [Locates node B.]

Step 3: Call DELFRSTNOD(DEST, LINK, ADJNCY[LOCA], AVAILEDG, LOCB, FLAG).

Step 4: Return.

11.6 CONNECTED COMPONENT OF A GRAPH

The ***connected component*** of a graph is a maximal subgraph of a given graph, which is connected. For example, consider the graph that follows.

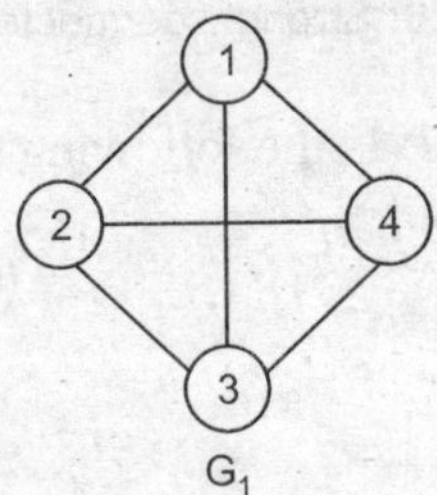

The connected component of the graph G1 is shown in Figure 11.24.

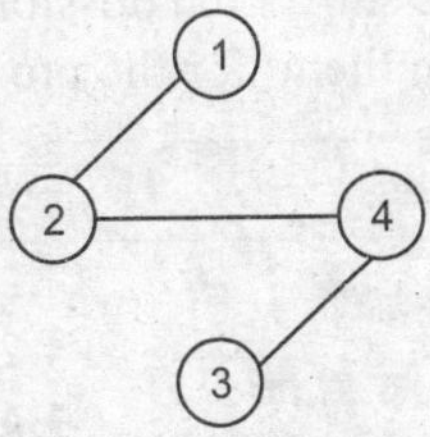

Figure 11.24: Connected component of G_1.

11.6.1 Strongly Connected Component

For a diagraph (directed graph), a ***strongly connected component*** is that component of the graph in which, for every pair of distinct vertices vi and vj, there is a directed path from vi to vj, and also a directed path from vj to vi. For example, consider the diagraph shown in Figure 11.25.

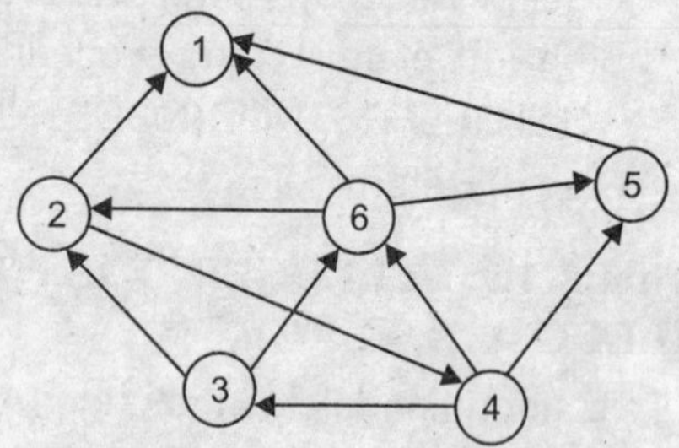

Figure 11.25: A diagraph.

The strongly connected components of the graph are shown in Figure 11.26.

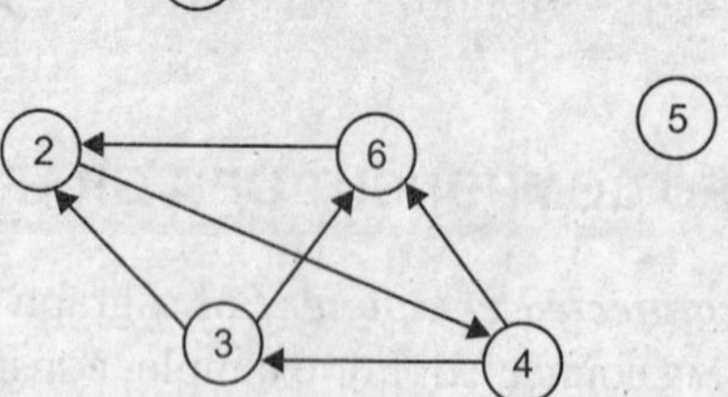

Figure 11.26: Strongly connected components of the graph shown in Figure 11.25.

Example 11.7: Is the following diagraph strongly connected?

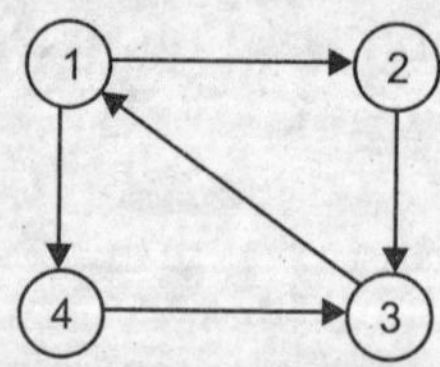

This table shows the possible pairs of vertices, and the forward and backward paths between them, for the previous graph:

Pair of vertices	Forward path	Backward path
<1, 2>	1-2	2-3-4
<1,3>	1-2-3	3-1
<1,4>	1-4	4-3-1
<2,3>	2-3	3-1-2
<2,4>	2-3-1-4	4-3-1-2
<3,4>	3-1-4	4-3

Therefore, we see that between every pair of distinct vertices of the given graph there exists a forward as well as a backward path, so it is strongly connected.

11.7 SPANNING TREES

A **spanning tree** in a graph is a **tree** that visits every node in the graph. Recall that a tree is a set of nodes and edges that has a single **root node** and no **circuits**.

In many graphs each edge has an associated weight or cost. Such graphs are called **weighted graphs**. Often in weighted graphs we want to find a spanning tree of minimal cost. In this section we explore several algorithms for finding minimal spanning trees in graphs.

11.7.1 Depth-first Spanning Tree and Breadth-first Spanning Tree

If graph G is connected, the edges of G can be partitioned into two disjointed sets. One is a set of tree edges, which we denote by set T, and the other is a set of back edges, which we denote by B. The tree edges are precisely those edges that are followed during the depth-first traversal or during the breadth-first traversal of graph G. If we consider only the tree edges, we get a subgraph of G containing all the vertices of G, and this subgraph is a tree called *spanning tree* of the graph G. For example, consider the graph shown in Figure 11.27.

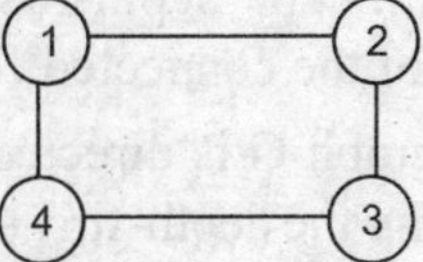

Figure 11.27: Graph G.

One of the depth-first traversal orders for this tree is 1-2-3-4, so the tree edges are (1,2), (2,3) and (3,4). Therefore, one of the spanning trees obtained by using depth-first traversal of the graph of Figure 11.27 is shown in Figure 11.28.

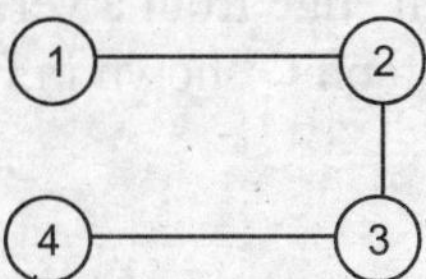

Figure 11.28: Depth first spanning tree of the graph of Figure 11.27.

Similarly, one of the breadth-first traversal orders for this tree is 1-2-4-3, so the tree edges are (1,2), (1,4) and (4,3). Therefore, one of the spanning trees obtained using breadth-first traversal of the graph of Figure 11.27 is shown in Figure 11.29.

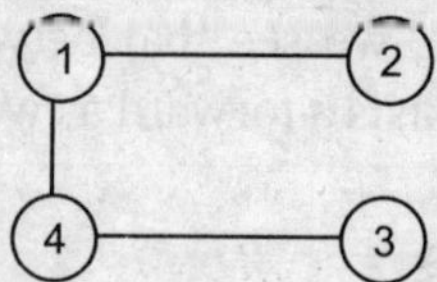

Figure 11.29: Breadth-first spanning tree of the graph of Figure 11.27.

The algorithm for obtaining the depth-first spanning tree (dfst) appears next.

```
T = f; {initially set of tree nodes is empty}
dfst( v : node);
{
if (visited[v] = false)
{
visited[v] = true;
for every adjacent i of v do
{
T = T È {(v,i)}
dfst(i);
}}}
```

If a graph G is not connected, the tree edges, which are precisely those edges followed during the depth-first, traversal of the graph G, constitute the depth-first *spanning forest*. The depth-first spanning forest will be made of trees, each of which is one of the connected components of graph G.

When a graph G is directed, the tree edges, which are precisely those edges followed during the depth-first traversal of the graph G, form a depth-first spanning forest for G. In addition to this, there are three other types of edges. These are called *back edges, forward edges*, and *cross edges*. An edge A $\rightarrow$ B is called a back edge, if B is an ancestor of A in the spanning forest. A non-tree edge that goes from a vertex to a proper descendant is called a forward edge. An edge which goes from a vertex to another vertex that is neither an ancestor nor a descendant is called a cross edge. An edge from a vertex to itself is a back edge. For example, consider the directed graph G shown in Figure 11.30.

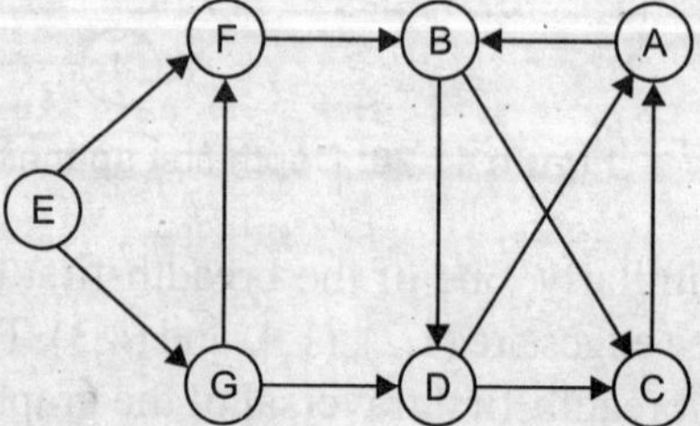

Figure 11.30: A directed graph G.

The depth-first spanning forest for graph G of Figure 11.30 is shown in Figure 11.31.

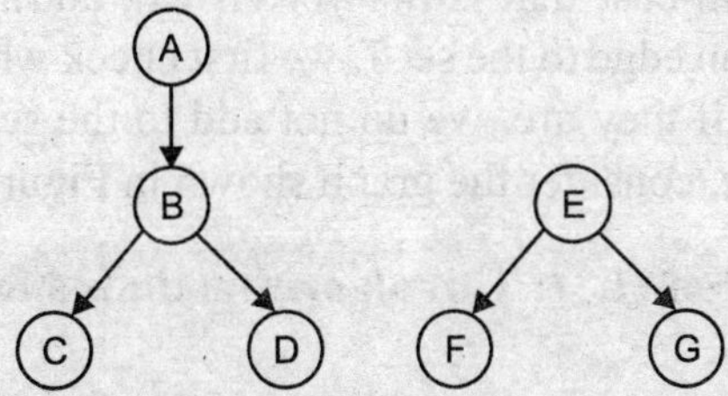

Figure 11.31: Depth-first spanning forest for the graph G of Figure 11.30.

In graph G of Figure 11.30, the edges such as C → A and D → A are the back edges, the edges such as D → C and G → D are cross edges.

Example 11.8: Consider the graph shown in Figure 11.32.

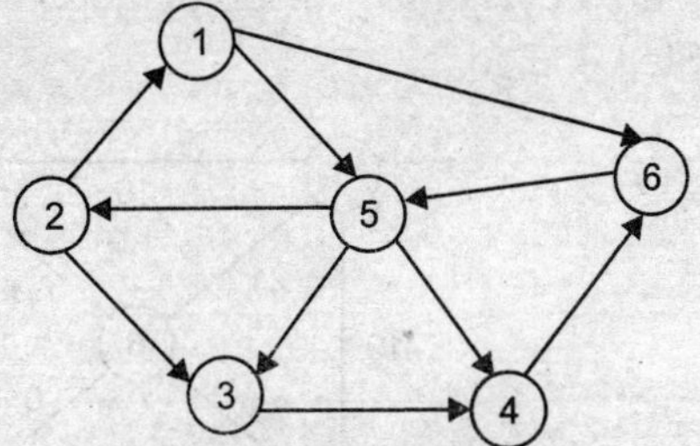

Figure 11.32: A graph G.

If we apply the procedure DFST to this graph, one of the depth-first spanning trees that we get by starting with vertex 1 is shown in Figure 11.33.

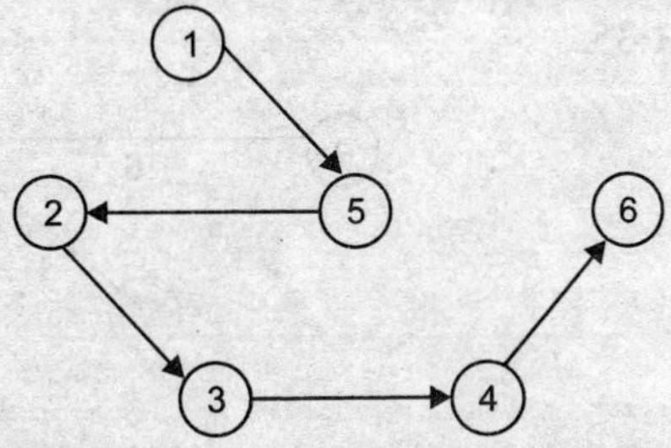

Figure 11.33: Depth-first spanning tree of the graph G of Figure 11.32.

11.8 MINIMUM-COST SPANNING TREE

When the edges of the graph have weights representing the cost in some suitable terms, we can obtain that spanning tree of a graph whose cost is minimum in terms of the weights of the edges. For this, we start with the edge with the minimum-cost/weight, add it to set T, and mark it as visited. We next consider the edge with minimum-cost that is not yet visited, add it to T, and mark it as visited. While adding an edge to the set T, we first check whether both the vertices of the edge are visited; if they are, we do not add to the set T, because it will form a cycle. For example, consider the graph shown in Figure 11.34.

Algorithm 11.11: This algorithm finds a minimum spanning T of a weighted graph G.

Step 1: Order all the edges of G according to increasing weights.

Step 2: Initialize T to be a graph consisting of the same nodes as G and no edges.

Step 3: Repeat the following M – 1 times, where M is the number of nodes in G:

Add to T an edge E of G with minimum weight such that E does not form a cycle in T. [End of loop.]

Step 4: End.

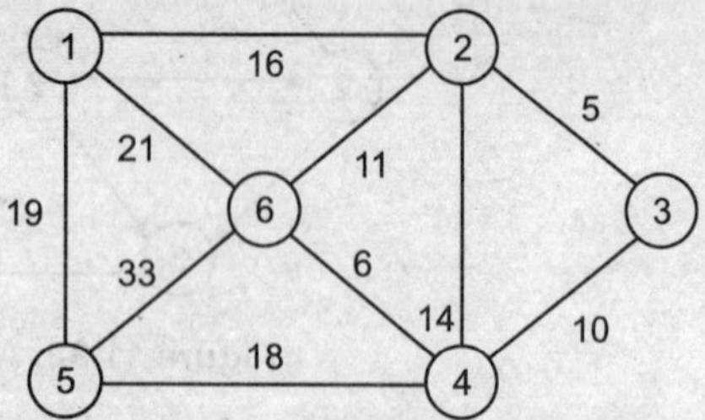

Figure 11.34: A graph G.

The ***minimum-cost spanning tree*** of the graph of Figure 22.21 is shown in Figure 11.35.

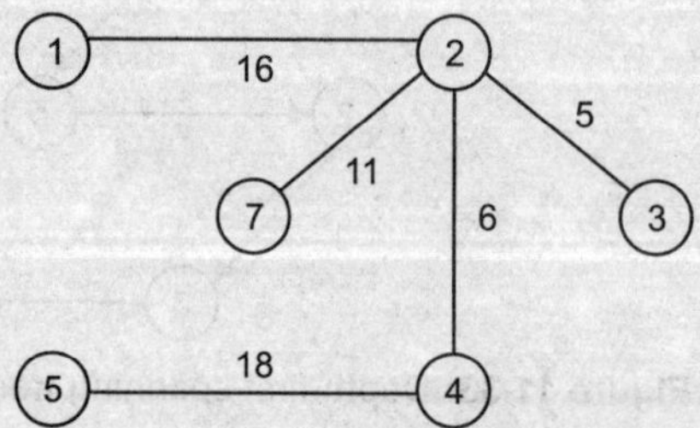

Figure 11.35: The minimum-cost spanning tree of graph G of Figure 11.34.

MST Property

Let G = (V,E) be a connected graph with a cost function defined on the edges. Let U be some proper subset of the set of vertices V. If (u,v) is an edge of lowest cost such that u is in U, and v is in V-U, there is a minimum-cost spanning tree that includes edge (u,v). Many of the methods of constructing a minimum-cost spanning tree use the following properties.

11.8.1 PRIM'S ALGORITHM

Prim's algorithm is an MST algorithm that works much like Dijkstra's algorithm does for shortest path trees. In fact, it's even simpler (though the correctness proof is a bit trickier).

1. Pick some arbitrary start node s. Initialize tree T = {s}.
2. Repeatedly add the shortest edge incident to T (the shortest edge having one vertex in T and one vertex not in T) until the tree spans all the nodes.

So the algorithm is the same as Dijsktra's algorithm, except you don't add distance(v) to the length of the edge when deciding which edge to put in next. For instance, what does Prim's algorithm do on the below graph?

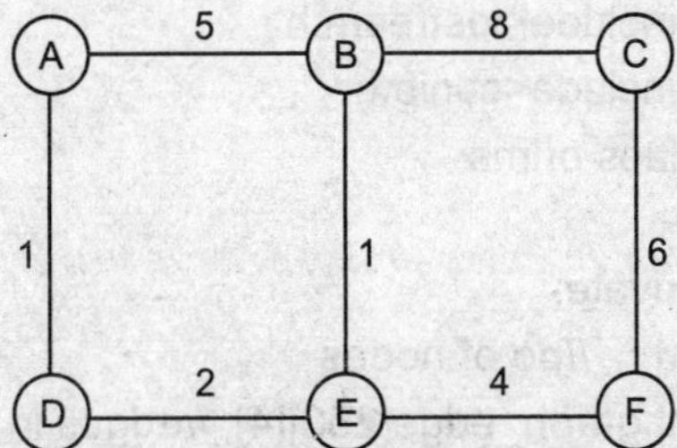

Before proving correctness for the algorithm, we first need a useful fact about spanning trees: if you take any spanning tree and add a new edge to it, this creates a cycle. The reason is that there already was one path between the endpoints (since it's a spanning tree), and now there are two. If you then remove any edge in the cycle, you get back a spanning tree (removing one edge from a cycle cannot disconnect a graph).

This algorithm for finding a minimal cost spanning tree in a connected graph is very easy to follow. It begins by adding the lowest cost edge and its two endpoints to the solution set. It then loops adding the lowest cost edge that connects a vertex in the solution set to one outside it. It also adds the endpoint of this edge that is not already in the solution set. The algorithm terminates when all vertices are in the solution set. The edges and vertices in the solution set at this point constitute a minimal cost spanning tree of the input graph.

Let G = (V,E) be a weighted graph, and suppose V = {1,2,…,n}. The Prim's algorithm begins with a set U initialized to {1}, and at each stage finds the shortest edge (u,v) that connects u in U and v in V-U, and then adds v to U. It repeats this step until U = V.

```
mcost(G is a graph; T is a set of edges)
U is a set of vertices
u,v are vertices;
{
T= ô
U = {1}
while U '" V
{
Find the lowest-cost edge (u,v) such that u is in U and v is in V-U
add (u,v) to T
add v to U
}
}
```

Program 6: Write a C++ program to implement Prims algorithm.

```
#include<iostream.h>
#include<conio.h>
class prims
{
private:
int n; //no of nodes
int graph_edge[250][4]; //edges in the graph
int g; //no of edges in the graph
int tree_edge[250][4]; //edges in the tree
int t; //no of edges in the tree
int s; //source node
//Partition the graph in to two sets
int T1[50],t1; // Set 1
int T2[50],t2; // Set 2
public:
void input();
int findset(int);
void algorithm();
void output();
};
void prims::input()
{
cout<<"*************************************************\n"
<<"This program implements the prims algorithm\n"
<<"*************************************************\n";
```

```
cout<<"Enter the no. of nodes in the undirected weighted graph ::";
cin>>n;
g=0;
cout<<"Enter the weights for the following edges ::\n";
for(int i=1;i<=n;i++)
{
for(int j=i+1;j<=n;j++)
{
cout<<" < "<<i<<" , "<<j<<" > ::";
int w;
cin>>w;
if(w!=0)
{
g++;
graph_edge[g][1]=i;
graph_edge[g][2]=j;
graph_edge[g][3]=w;
}
}
}
// print the graph edges
cout<<"\n\nThe edges in the given graph are::\n";
for(i=1;i<=g;i++)
cout<<" < "<<graph_edge[i][1]
<<" , "<<graph_edge[i][2]
<<" > ::"<<graph_edge[i][3]<<endl;
}
int prims::findset(int x)
{
for(int i=1;i<=t1;i++)
if(x==T1[i])
return 1;
for(i=1;i<=t2;i++)
if(x==T2[i])
return 2;
return -1;
}
void prims::algorithm()
{
```

```
t=0;
t1=1;
T1[1]=1; //The source node
t2=n-1;
int i;
for(i=1;i<=n-1;i++)
T2[i]=i+1; //The reamining nodes
cout<<"\n*****The algorithm starts*****\n\n";
while(g!=0 && t!=n-1)
{
// Find the least cost edge
int min=9999;
int p;
int u,v,w;
for(i=1;i<=g;i++)
{
bool flag1=false,flag2=false;
//if u and v are in different sets
if(findset(graph_edge[i][1])!=findset(graph_edge[i][2]))
{
if(min>graph_edge[i][3])
{
min=graph_edge[i][3];
u=graph_edge[i][1];
v=graph_edge[i][2];
w=graph_edge[i][3];
p=i;
}
}
}
//break if there is no such edge
cout<<"The edge included in the tree is ::";
cout<<" < "<<u<<" , "<<v<<" > "<<endl;
//delete the edge from graph edges
for(int l=p;l<g;l++)
{
graph_edge[l][1]=graph_edge[l+1][1];
graph_edge[l][2]=graph_edge[l+1][2];
graph_edge[l][3]=graph_edge[l+1][3];
```

```
}
g-;
//add the edge to the tree
t++;
tree_edge[t][1]=u;
tree_edge[t][2]=v;
tree_edge[t][3]=w;
//Alter the set partitions
t1++;
int m;
if(findset(v)==2)
{
T1[t1]=v;
m=v;
}
else if(findset(u)==2)
{
T1[t1]=u;
m=u;
}
int x;
for(x=1;T2[x]!=m;x++);
for(;x<t2;x++)
T2[x]=T2[x+1];
t2-;
// Print the sets
int k;
cout<<"NOW\nT1 :: ";
for(k=1;k<=t1;k++)
cout<<T1[k]<<' ';
cout<<endl;
cout<<"T2 :: ";
for(k=1;k<=t2;k++)
cout<<T2[k]<<' ';
cout<<endl;
cout<<"The graph edges are ::\n";
for(i=1;i<=g;i++)
cout<<" < "<<graph_edge[i][1]
<<" , "<<graph_edge[i][2]
```

```
<<" > ::"<<graph_edge[i][3]<<endl;
cout<<endl<<endl;
}
}
void prims::output()
{
cout<<"\nThe selected edges are ::\n";
for(int i=1;i<=t;i++)
cout<<" < "<<tree_edge[i][1] <<" , "<<tree_edge[i][2]
<<" > ::"<<tree_edge[i][3]<<endl;
}
void main()
{
prims obj;
obj.input();
obj.algorithm();
obj.output();
getch();
}
```

11.8.2 Kruskal's Algorithm

Kruskal's algorithm for finding a minimal spanning tree in a connected graph is a greedy algorithm; that is, given a choice, it always processes the edge with the least weight.

This algorithm operates by considering edges in the graph in order of weight from the least weighted edge up to the most while keeping track of which nodes in the graph have been added to the spanning tree. If an edge being considered joins either two nodes not in the spanning tree, or joins a node in the spanning tree to one not in the spanning tree, the edge and its endpoints are added to the spanning tree. After considering one edge the algorithm continues to consider the next higher weighted edge. In the event that a graph contains equally weighted edges the order in which these edges are considered does not matter. The algorithm stops when all nodes have been added to the spanning tree.

Sort edges by length and examine them from shortest to longest. Put each edge into the current forest (a forest is just a set of trees) if it doesn't form a cycle with the edges chosen so far.

E.g., let's look at how it behaves in the graph below:

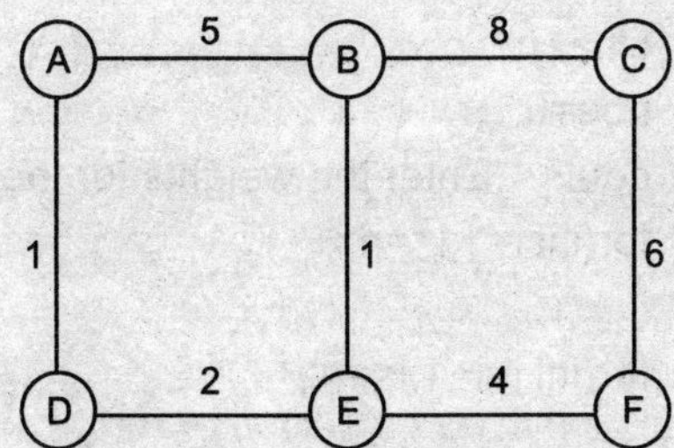

Kruskal's algorithm sorts the edges and then puts them in one at a time so long as they don't form a cycle. So, first the AD and BE edges will be added, then the DE edge, and then the EF edge. The AB edge will be skipped over because it forms a cycle, and finally the CF edge will be added (at that point you can either notice that you have included n – 1 edges and therefore are done, or else keep going, skipping over all the remaining edges one at a time).

Program 7: Write a C++ program to implement Kruskal algorithm.

```
#include<iostream.h>
#include<conio.h>
class kruskal
{
private:
int n; //no of nodes
int noe; //no edges in the graph
int graph_edge[100][4];
int tree[10][10];
int sets[100][10];
int top[100];
public:
void read_graph();
void initialize_span_t();
void sort_edges();
void algorithm();
int find_node(int );
void print_min_span_t();
};
void kruskal::read_graph()
{
cout<<"**************************************************\n"
<<"This program implements the kruskal algorithm\n"
<<"**************************************************\n";
cout<<"Enter the no. of nodes in the undirected weighted graph ::";
```

```
cin>>n;
noe=0;
cout<<"Enter the weights for the following edges ::\n";
for(int i=1;i<=n;i++)
{
for(int j=i+1;j<=n;j++)
{
cout<<" < "<<i<<" , "<<j<<" > ::";
int w;
cin>>w;
if(w!=0)
{
noe++;
graph_edge[noe][1]=i;
graph_edge[noe][2]=j;
graph_edge[noe][3]=w;
}
}
}
// print the graph edges
cout<<"\n\nThe edges in the given graph are::\n";
for(i=1;i<=noe;i++)
cout<<" < "<<graph_edge[i][1]
<<" , "<<graph_edge[i][2]
<<" > ::"<<graph_edge[i][3]<<endl;
}
void kruskal::sort_edges()
{
/**** Sort the edges using bubble sort in increasing order**************/
for(int i=1;i<=noe-1;i++)
{
for(int j=1;j<=noe-i;j++)
{
if(graph_edge[j][3]>graph_edge[j+1][3])
{
int t=graph_edge[j][1];
graph_edge[j][1]=graph_edge[j+1][1];
graph_edge[j+1][1]=t;
t=graph_edge[j][2];
```

```
graph_edge[j][2]=graph_edge[j+1][2];
graph_edge[j+1][2]=t;
t=graph_edge[j][3];
graph_edge[j][3]=graph_edge[j+1][3];
graph_edge[j+1][3]=t;
}
}
}
// print the graph edges
cout<<"\n\nAfter sorting the edges in the given graph are::\n";
for(i=1;i<=noe;i++)
cout<<" < "<<graph_edge[i][1]
<<" , "<<graph_edge[i][2]
<<" > ::"<<graph_edge[i][3]<<endl;
}
void kruskal::algorithm()
{
// ->make a set for each node
for(int i=1;i<=n;i++)
{
sets[i][1]=i;
top[i]=1;
}
cout<<"\nThe algorithm starts ::\n\n";
for(i=1;i<=noe;i++)
{
int p1=find_node(graph_edge[i][1]);
int p2=find_node(graph_edge[i][2]);
if(p1!=p2)
{
cout<<"The edge included in the tree is ::"
<<" < "<<graph_edge[i][1]<<" , "
<<graph_edge[i][2]<<" > "<<endl<<endl;
tree[graph_edge[i][1]][graph_edge[i][2]]=graph_edge[i][3];
tree[graph_edge[i][2]][graph_edge[i][1]]=graph_edge[i][3];
// Mix the two sets
for(int j=1;j<=top[p2];j++)
{
top[p1]++;
```

```
sets[p1][top[p1]]=sets[p2][j];
}
top[p2]=0;
}
else
{
cout<<"Inclusion of the edge "
<<" < "<<graph_edge[i][1]<<" , "
<<graph_edge[i][2]<<" > "<<"forms a cycle so it is removed\n\n";
}
}
}
int kruskal::find_node(int n)
{
for(int i=1;i<=noe;i++)
{
for(int j=1;j<=top[i];j++)
{
if(n==sets[i][j])
return i;
}
}
return -1;
}
void main()
{
kruskal obj;
obj.read_graph();
obj.sort_edges();
obj.algorithm();
getch();
}
```

11.9 APPLICATION OF MINIMUM-COST SPANNING TREE

A property of a spanning tree of a graph G is that a spanning tree is a minimal connected subgraph of G (by minimal, we mean the one with the fewest number of edges). Therefore, if nodes of G represent cities and the edges represent possible communication links connecting two cities, then the spanning trees of graph G represent all feasible choices of the communication network. If each edge has weight representing cost measured in some suitable terms (such as cost of construction or distance etc.), then the minimum-cost spanning tree of G is the selection of the required communication network.

11.9.1 Directed Acyclic Graph (DAG)

A *directed acyclic graph* (DAG) is a directed graph with no cycles. A DAG represents more general relationships than trees but less general than arbitrary directed graphs. An example of a DAG is given in Figure 11.36.

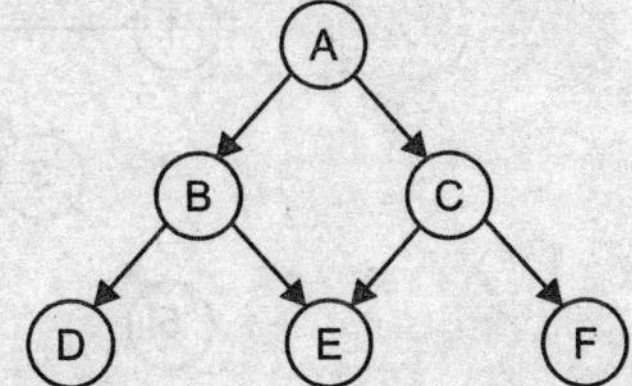

Figure 11.36: Directed acyclic graph.

DAGs are useful in representing the syntactic structure of arithmetic expressions with common sub-expressions. For example, consider the following expression:

$$(a+b)*c + ((a+b + e)$$

In this expression, the term $(a + b)$ is a common sub-expression, and therefore represented in the DAG by the vertices with more than one incoming edge, as shown in Figure 11.37

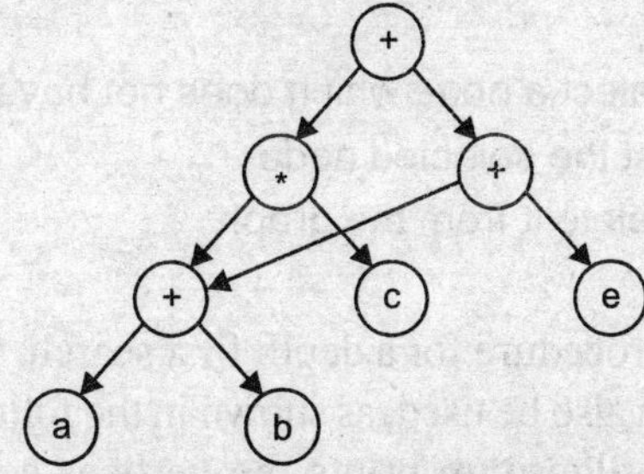

Figure 11.37: DAG representation of expression (a+b)*c +((a+b) + e).

11.10 TOPOLOGICAL SORT OF DIRECTED GRAPH

A ***topological sort*** is a method for ordering the nodes of the directed graph G in which the nodes represent tasks or activities, and the edges represent precedence relations between nodes, that is, when the edges of the graph represent dependency among the node/vertices of graph G. It lists the vertices/nodes in such an order that a vertex *vi* gets listed only after all the vertices on which *vi* depends have been listed. For a topological sort to be feasible, it is required that the directed graph G not have any directed cycles. In other words, the graph G should be a DAG. This also means that the precedence relation defined by the edges of G must be irreflexive. The precedence relation defined by the edges of G is certainly transitive and so is a partial order. It starts with a vertex that does not have any predecessor and lists it. After that it logically deletes it from the graph and once again searches for that vertex that does not have any predecessor, and repeats the procedure. It does not give a unique order. For example, consider the directed graph shown in Figure 11.38.

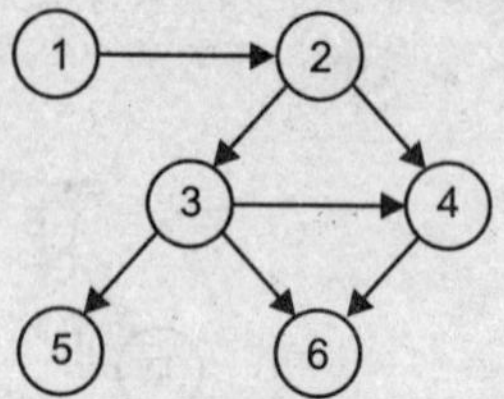

Figure 11.38: A graph G.

The topological sort of the graph in Figure 11.38 gives the following orders:

- 1-2-3-4-5-6
- 1-2-3-5-4-6
- 1-2-3-4-6-5

The algorithm for a topological sort is presented here:

```
while there exist a node
{
select a node which does not have any predecessor
list the selected node
delete it from the graph
}
```

The procedure for a depth first search, with a print statement added to print the nodes, can also be used, as shown in the following program, to perform a topological sort. This algorithm prints the vertices accessible from *x* in reverse topological sort.

Algorithm 11.11: This algorithm finds a topological sort t of a graph s without cycles.

Step 1: Find the indegree INDEG(N) of each node N of S. (This can be done by traversing each adjacency list as in Procedure below.)

Step 2: Put in a queue all the nodes with zero indegree.

Step 3: Repeat Steps 4 and 5 until the queue is empty.

Step 4: Remove the front node N of the queue (by setting FRONT := FRONT + 1).

Step 5: Repeat the following for each neighbor M of the node N:

(a) Set INDEG(M) := INDEG(M) – 1. [This deletes the edge from N to M.]

(b) If INDEG(M) = 0, then: Add M to the rear of the queue.

[End of loop.] [End of Step 3 loop.]

Step 6: End.

Algorithm 11.12: This algorithm finds the indegree INDEG and outdegree OUTDEG of each node in the graph G in memory.

DEGREE (NODE, NEXT, ADJNCY, START, DEST, LINK, INDEG, OUTDEG)

Step 1: [Intialize arrays INDEG and OUTDEG.]

a.Set P = START.

b.Repeat while P ≠ NULL: [Traverses node list.]

(i). Set INDEG[P]= 0 and OUTDEG[P] = 0.

(ii). Set P = NEXT[P].

Step 2: Set PA = START.

Step 3: Repeat STEPS 4 to 6 while PA ≠ NULL: [Traverses node list.]

Step 4: Set PB = ADJNCY[PA].

Step 5: Repeat while PB ≠ NULL: [Traverses node list.]

c. Set OUTDEG[PA]= OUTDEG[PA+1] and INDEG[DEST[PB]] = INDEG[DEST[PB]] + 1

[End of inner loop using pointer PB]

Step 6: Set PA = NEXT[PA]. [End of step3 outer loop using the pointer PA]

Step 7: Return.

Program 8: Write a C++ program to implement Topological sorting.

```
#include<iostream.h>
#include<conio.h>
class graph
{
private:
int n;
int data[20];
int gptr[20][20];
public:
void create();
void topological();
};
void graph::create()
```

```
{
cout<<"**************************************************************\n"
<<"This program sorts the given numbers in increasing order\n"
<<"\t\t using topological sorting\n"
<<"**************************************************************\n";
cout<<"Enter the no. of nodes in the directed unweighted graph ::";
cin>>n;
for(int i=1;i<=n;i++)
{
cout<<"enter data for the node "<<i<<" ::";
cin>>data[i];
}
cout<<"enter the adjacency matrix for the graph ::\n";
cout<<"( type 1 for graph[i][j] if there is an edge from i to j"
<<"else type 0 )\n\n";
int j;
for(i=1;i<=n;i++)
for(j=1;j<=n;j++)
cin>>gptr[i][j];
}
void graph::topological()
{
int flag;
int i,j;
int poset[20],included[20];
for(i=1;i<=n;i++)
{
poset[i]=0;
included[i]=false;
}
int k=1;
flag=true;
int zeroindegree;
int c=1;
while(flag==1)
{
for(i=1;i<=n;i++)
{
if(!included[i])
{
zeroindegree=true;
```

```
for(j=1;j<=n;j++)
{
if(gptr[j][i]>0)
{
zeroindegree=false;
break;
}
}
if(zeroindegree)
{
included[i]=true;
poset[k]=data[i];
k=k+1;
for(j=1;j<=n;j++)
{
gptr[i][j]=-1;
gptr[j][i]=-1;
}
break;
}
}
if(i==n+1)
{
if(zeroindegree==false)
{
cout<<"Graph is not acyclic\n";
return;
}
else
{
poset[k]=data[i-1];
k=k+1;
flag=false;
}
}
}
cout<<"After topological sorting the numbers are :\n";
for(i=1;i<=n;i++)
cout<<poset[i]<<"\t";
cout<<endl<<endl;
```

```
}
int main()
{
graph obj;
obj.create();
obj.topological();
getch();
}
```

11.11 FLOYD'S-WARSHALL'S ALGORITHM – SHORTEST PATHS

This algorithm is designed to find the least-expensive paths between all the vertices in a graph. It does this by operating on a matrix representing the costs of edges between vertices. Before we invoke Floyd's algorithm we must build a matrix, usually in a two-dimensional array. If there are n vertices in our graph, our matrix will be n x n. Each row in the matrix represents a "starting" vertex in the graph while each column in the matrix represents an "ending" point in the graph. If there is an edge between a starting point i and ending point j in the graph, the cost of this edge is placed in position (i,j) of the matrix. If we are dealing with an undirected graph in which all edges are bi-directional, an entry is also made in position (j,i) of the matrix. If there is no edge directly linking two vertices, an infinite (or, in practice, very large) value is placed in the (i,j) position of the matrix to specify that it is impossible to directly move from i to j.

For example, if we have a graph in which points 1 and 5 are connected by a bi-directional edge with a cost of 22 units, we would place the number 22 into positions (1,5) and (5,1) of our matrix.Once we have set this matrix up, we use Floyd's algorithm to compute the shortest distance between all points in the graph. Floyd's algorithm is given below in C:

```
int floyds(int *matrix) {
int k, i, j;
for (k = 1; k <= n; k++)
for (i = 1; i <= n; i++)
for (j = 1; j <= n; j++)
if (matrix[i][j] > (matrix[i][k] + matrix[k][j])) matrix[i,j] = matrix[i][k] + matrix[k][j];
}
```

When this routine finishes the entries in all positions of the matrix represent the lowest-cost traversal between the row-vertex and column-vertex.

Floyd's algorithm works by looking for all non-direct paths between two vertices that have a less-expensive total cost than the best way yet found to move between said vertices. If such a path is found, it becomes the value against which future indirect paths between these vertices are tested. In the end, each element of the matrix represents the lowest-cost traversal between the vertices it's row and column represent. Remember that if the graph is directed, so is the answer in (i,j) of the matrix; moreover, (i,j) may not be equal to (j,i) in a di-graph.

Algorithm 11.13: (warshall's algorithm) A directed graph g with m nodes is maintained in memory by its adjacency matrix a. This algorithm finds the path matrix p of the graph g.

```
Step 1: Repeat for I, J = 1, 2, ..., M: [Initializes P.]
            If A[I, J] = 0, then: Set P[I, J] := 0;
            Else: Set P[I, J] := 1.
        [End of loop.]
Step 2: Repeat Steps 3 and 4 for K = 1, 2, ..., M: [Updates P.]
Step 3: Repeat Step 4 for I = 1, 2, ..., M:
Step 4: Repeat for J = 1, 2, ...., M:
                    Set P[I, J] := P[I, J] v (P[I, K] ^ P[K, J]).
            [End of loop.]
        [End of Step 3 loop.]
    [End of Step 2 loop.]
Step 5: End.
```

It is clear that Floyd's algorithm takes n^3 time. In the next section we will discuss an alternative to Floyd's algorithm called Dijkstra's algorithm. It is important to note, however, that for dense graphs (i.e. graphs with many edges) Floyd's algorithm is as good as or better than Dijkstra's algorithm.

Example11.9

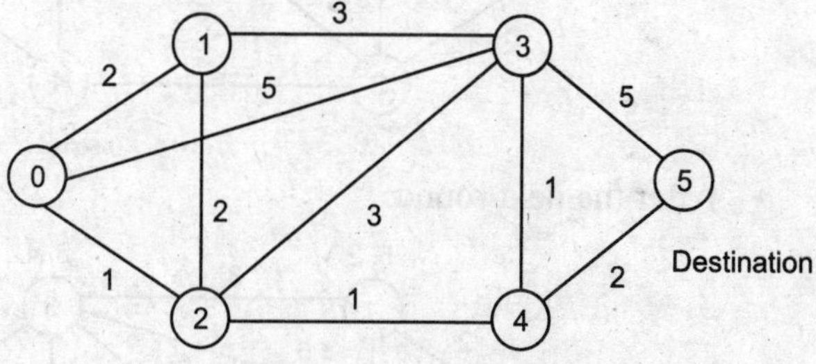

- We will show computations when node "5" is the destination.

  => in practice, the computation for all destinations occurs simultaneously.
- Each node maintains:
  - Its currently-known cost to get to "5",
  - Which neighbor is used in getting to "5"

Initially, nothing is known:

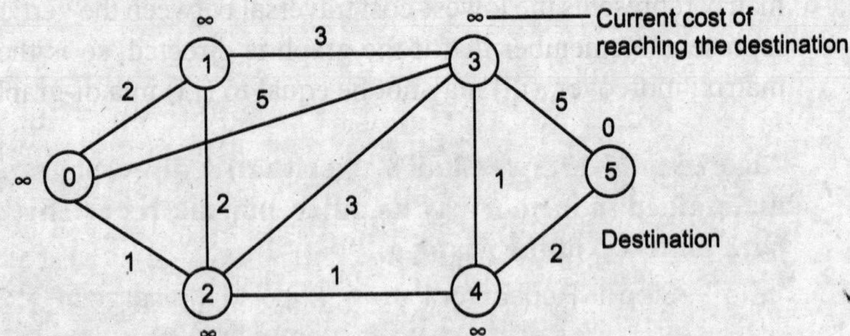

- After the first round of message-exchange between neighbors:

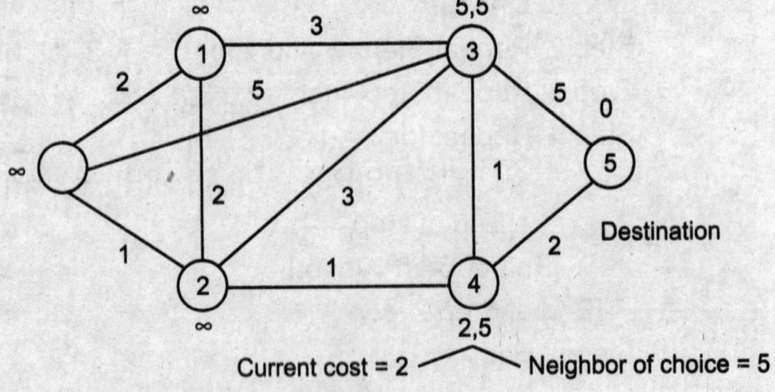

- After the next round:

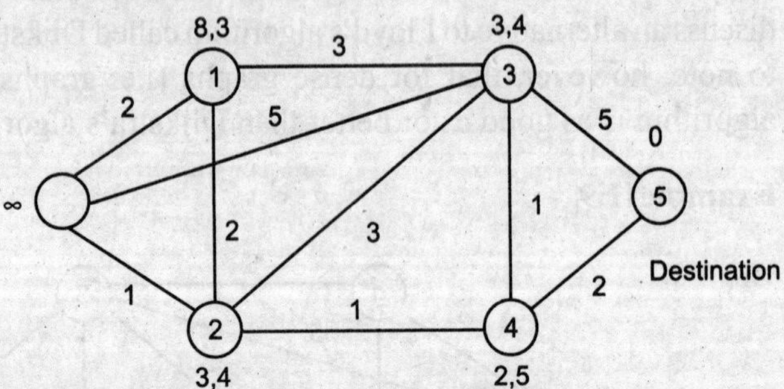

- After the next round:

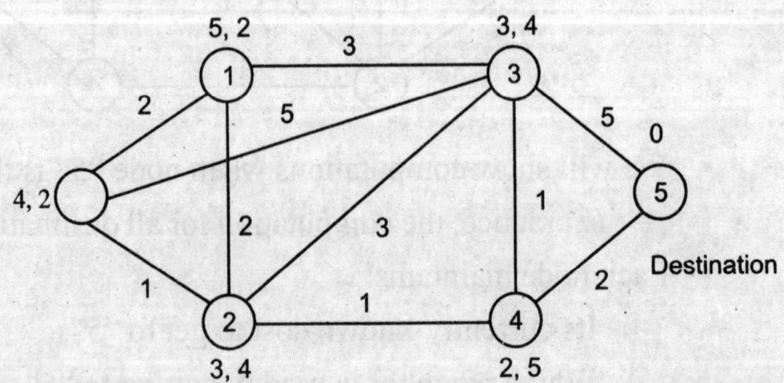

- The next round reveals no changes

  => algorithm halts (nodes stop exchanging information).

Example 11.11: **Consider the weighted graph G in Figure below. Then the weight matrix W of G is as follows:**

$$W = \begin{bmatrix} 0 & 8 & ? & 1 \\ ? & 0 & 1 & ? \\ 4 & ? & 0 & ? \\ ? & 2 & 9 & 0 \end{bmatrix}$$

Applying the warshall's algorithm, we obtain the following matrices $D^{(0)}$, $D^{(1)}$, $D^{(2)}$, $D^{(3)}$, $D^{(4)}$.

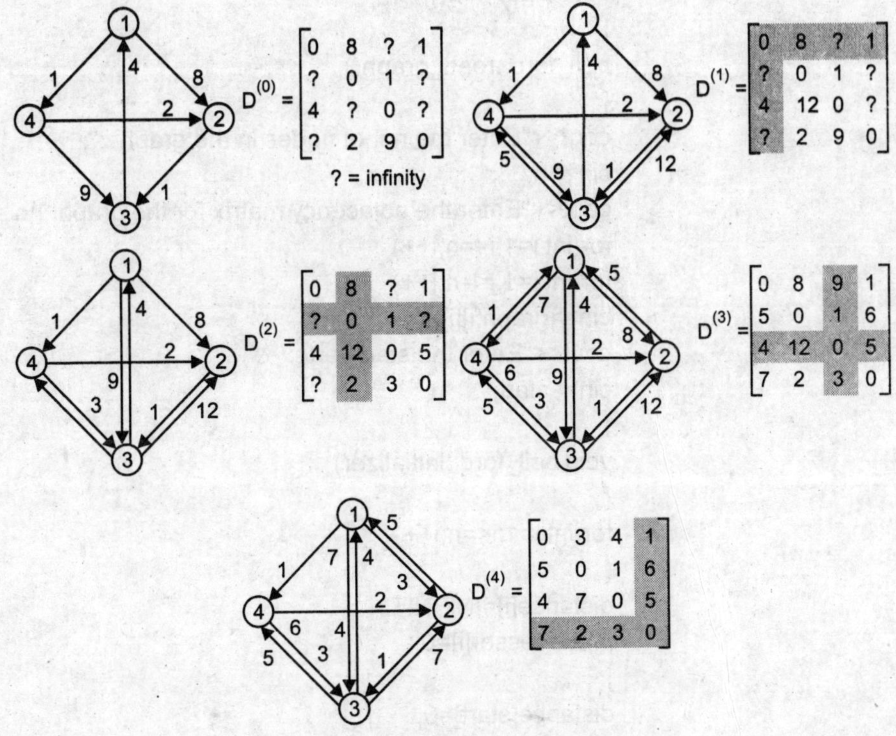

Floyd Warshall Example

Program 9: Write a C++ program is to implement Bellmen Ford algorithm.

```
#include<iostream.h>
#include<stdlib.h>
#define MAX 20
#define INFINITY 9999
class bell_ford
```

```
{
private:
int n;
int graph[MAX][MAX];
int start;
int distance[MAX];
int predecessor[MAX];
public:
void read_graph();
void initialize();
void update();
void check();
void algorithm();
};
bell_ford::read_graph()
{
cout<<"Enter the no. of nodes in the graph ::";
cin>>n;
cout<<"Enter the adjacency matrix for the graph ::\n";
for(int i=1;i<=n;i++)
for(int j=1;j<=n;j++)
cin>>graph[i][j];
cout<<"Enter the start vertex ::";
cin>>start;
}
void bell_ford::initialize()
{
for(int i=1;i<=n;i++)
{
distance[i]=INFINITY;
predecessor[i]=0;
}
distance[start]=0;
}
void bell_ford::update()
{
for(int i=1;i<=n-1;i++)
{
for(int u=1;u<=n;u++)
{
for(int v=1;v<=n;v++)
```

```
{
if(graph[u][v]!=0)
{
if(distance[v]>distance[u]+graph[u][v])
{
distance[v]=distance[u]+graph[u][v];
predecessor[v]=u;
}
}}
}}}
void bell_ford::check()
{
for(int u=1;u<=n;u++)
{
 for(int v=1;v<=n;v++)
{
if(graph[u][v]!=0)
{
if(distance[v]>distance[u]+graph[u][v])
{
cout<<"does not exist's ";
return;
}}}
}
cout<<"\n\nThere is no negative weight cycle and\n";
cout<<"****** The final paths and the distacnes are ******\n\n";
for(int i=1;i<=n;i++)
{
cout<<"path for node "<<i<<" is ::\n";
int arr[MAX],k=1;
int j=i;
while(predecessor[j]!=0)
{
arr[k]=predecessor[j];
k++;
j=predecessor[j];
}
for(-k;k>0;k-)
cout<<arr[k]<<"->";
cout<<i<<endl;
cout<<"distance is "<<distance[i]<<endl<<endl<<endl;
```

```
}
}
void bell_ford::algorithm()
{
read_graph();
initialize();
update();
check();
}
void main()
{
bell_ford obj;
obj.algorithm();
}
```

11.12 DIJKSTRA'S ALGORITHM – SHORTEST PATH

While Floyd's algorithm determines the lowest-cost path between all vertices in a graph, Dijkstra's was designed to find the lowest cost path between a single starting vertex and all of the other vertices in a graph. Dijkstra's can, clearly, be used to obtain the same information as Floyd's algorithm if it is called repeatedly for every vertex in a graph.

Dikjstra's algorithm is a **greedy algorithm** which means, if given a choice, it operates by choosing the biggest or most valuable alternative.

The first step of this algorithm is to "label" the starting vertex with an ordered pair, (–,0), and initialize a distance counter to one. Next, look at all edges between labeled vertices and unlabeled vertices. If the cost of a particular edge added to the second item in the ordered pair of the initial vertex is equal to the distance counter, label the terminal vertex of this edge and continue this process, incrementing the distance counter by one at each iteration and continuing until all vertices in the graph are labeled. The second member of the ordered pair at each vertex is the lowest cost walk from it to the starting vertex. The first member of the ordered pair of the ordered pair is the node immediately preceding the current node on the shortest path from source to destination.

The algorithm actually coded is implemented in a slightly different manner. Because it is inefficient to store the distance counter and look at every edge at every increment, I choose to begin at the starting vertex and traverse to all nodes reachable from it. Each node is labelled with a distance from the start and a previous vertex. Each node is also enqueued for later processing.

Once all nodes adjacent to the starting vertex are processed, labelled and enqueued, the algorithm dequeues the first node. All nodes adjacent to this vertex that have not been visited are labelled and enqueued. Additionally, any node that has been visited but can be reached more cheaply is re-labelled and enqueued.

This process continues until the queue is empty. The shortest path to a given vertex *n* is labelled on that vertex. The path can be determined by examining the prior steps recursively back to the starting node.

Algorithm 11.14: (Shortest-Path Algorithm) A weighted graph G with M nodes is maintained in memory by its weight matrix W. This algorithm finds a matrix Q such that Q[I, J] is the length of a shortest path from node V_I to node V_J. INFINITY is a very large number, and MIN is the minimum value function.

```
Step 1: Repeat of I, J = 1, 2, ..., M: [Initializes Q.]
        W[I, J] = 0, then: Set Q[I, J] := INFINITY;
        Else: Set Q[I, J] := W[I, J].
   [End of loop.]
Step 2: Repeat Steps 3 and 4 for K = 1, 2, ..., M: [Updates Q.]
Step 3: Repeat Step 4 for I = 1, 2, ..., M:
Step 4: Repeat for J = 1, 2, ..., M:
                        Set Q[I, J] := MIN(Q[I, J], Q[I, K] + Q[K, J]).
              [End of loop.]
        [End of Step 3 loop.]
    [End of Step 2 loop.]
Step 5: End.
```

Example 11.11

- We'll find the Shortest Path Tree (SPT) rooted at vertex 0 (the source).

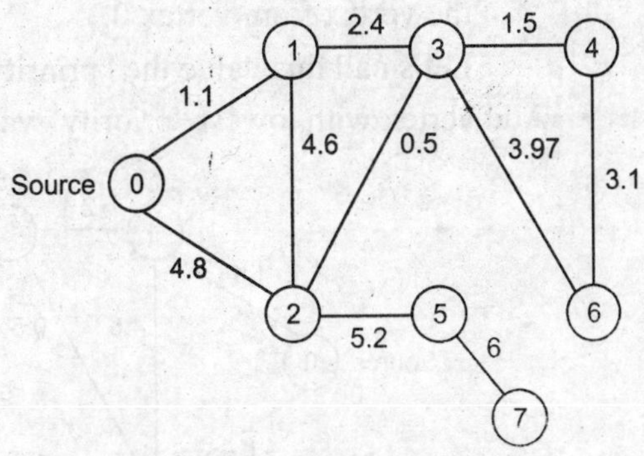

=> find shortest path from 0 to each vertex i.

- Current SPT contains vertex 0.
- Explore edges from most recently-added vertex (vertex 0):

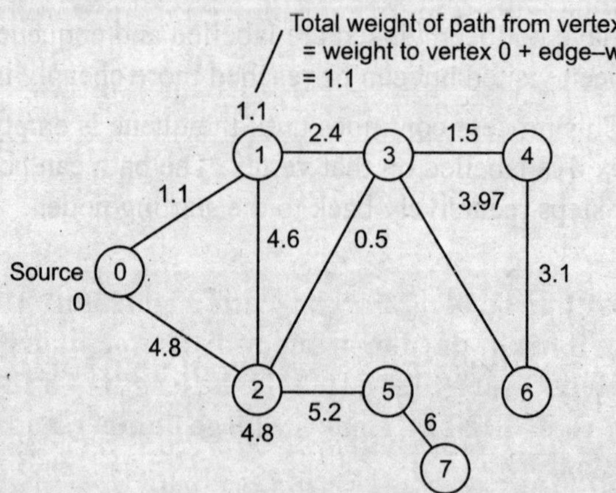

- Select vertex (outside SPT) with least weight (vertex 1), add it, and explore its edges:

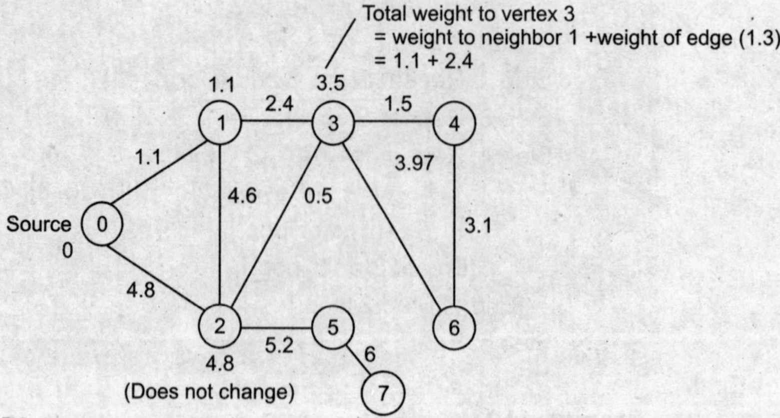

- **Note:**
  - We associate with each vertex the total (currently-known) weight to the vertex from vertex 0.
  - Let's call this value the "priority" of a vertex.
- Add vertex with lowest "priority" value (vertex 3) and explore its edges:

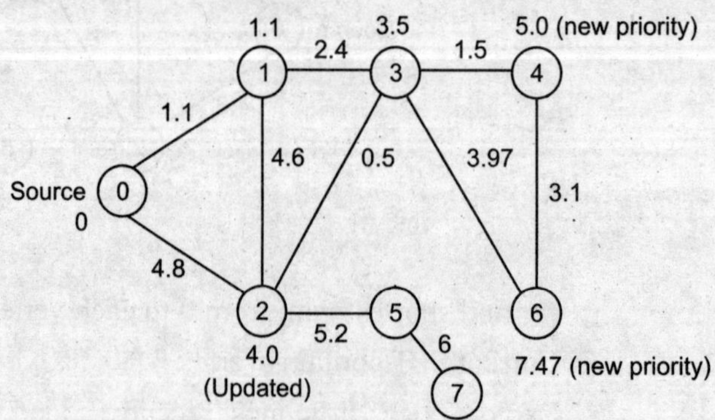

- Next vertex: 2

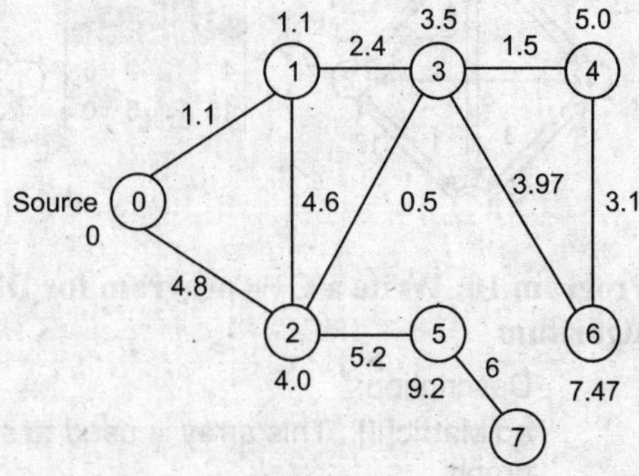

- Continuing, we add: 4, 6, 5 and 7:

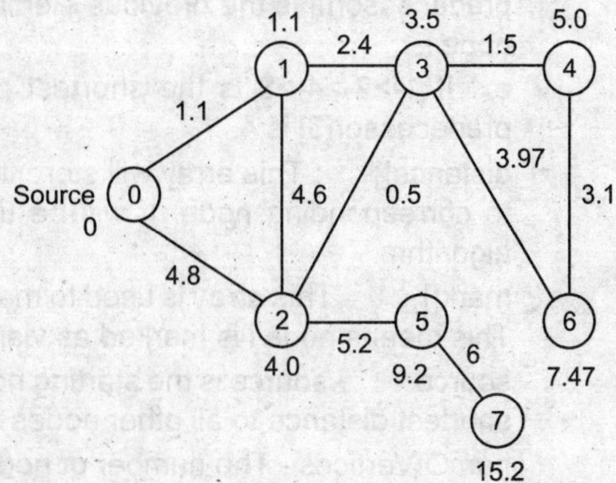

Example 11.12: Consider the weighted graph G in Figure below. Then the weight matrix W of G is as follows:

$$W = \begin{bmatrix} 0 & 8 & ? & 1 \\ ? & 0 & 1 & ? \\ 4 & ? & 0 & ? \\ ? & 2 & 9 & 0 \end{bmatrix}$$

? = Infinity

Applying the Dijkstra's algorithm, we obtain the following matrices $D^{(1)}$, $D^{(2)}$, $D^{(3)}$.

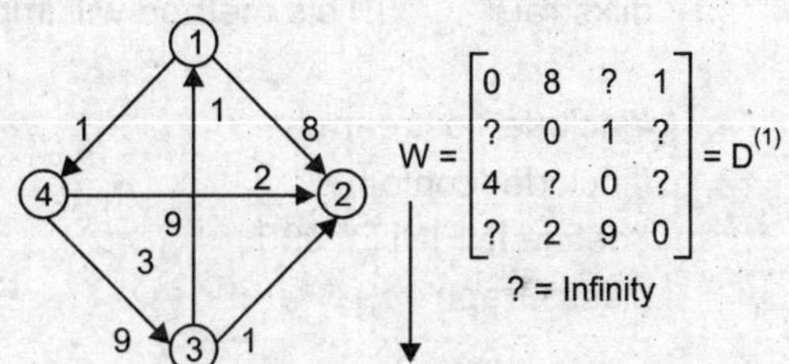

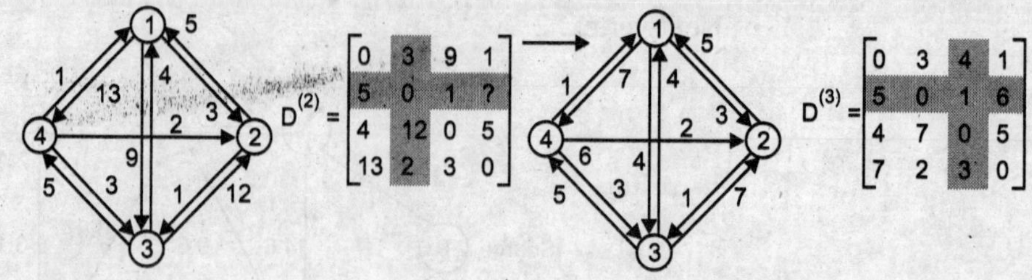

Program 10: Write a C++ program for Dijkstra's single source shortest path algorithm

Description:

adjMatric[][] : This array is used to store the adjacency matrix of the input graph

predecessor[] : This array is used to store the predecessor elements. predecessor[i] is the previous element in the path from source to current node i.

ex: If 1->2->4->3 is the shortest path from node1(source) to node 3. predecessor[3] is 4.

distance[] : This array will store the minimum distance from the source to corresponding node. It will be updated in each iteration in dijkstra's algorithm.

mark[] - This array is used to mark the nodes as visited. mark[i] = true, This means node i is marked as visited.

source - source is the starting node from which we have to find out the shortest distance to all other nodes in the graph.

numOfVertices - The number of nodes in the graph.

Note: Node ranges will be 0 to numOfVertices-1

getClosestUnmarkedNode() : This method will return the closest unmarked node from the current marked node.

printPath(i) : This will print the path from source node to i in recursive manner

output() : This method will print paths to all nodes from source and their shortest distance

read() : This method will read the graph values from input

initialize() : This method will set the initial values of predecessor[] to -1 and

dijkstra() : This method will implement the dijkstra's algorithm

```
#include<iostream.h>
#include<conio.h>
#define INFINITY 999
class Graph
{
```

```
private:
int adjMatrix[15][15];
int predecessor[15],distance[15];
bool mark[15];
int source;
int numOfVertices;
public:
void read();
void initialize();
int getClosestUnmarkedNode();
void dijkstra();
void output();
void printPath(int);
};
void Graph::read()
{
cout<<"Enter the number of vertices of the graph(should be > 0)\n";
cin>>numOfVertices;
//Number of vertices should always greater than zero
while(numOfVertices <= 0) {
cout<<"Enter the number of vertices of the graph(should be > 0)\n";
cin>>numOfVertices;
}
//Read the adjacency matrix for the graph with +ve weights
cout<<"Enter the adjacency matrix for the graph\n";
cout<<"To enter infinity enter "<<INFINITY<<endl;
for(int i=0;i<numOfVertices;i++)
{
cout<<"Enter the (+ve)weights for the row "<<i<<endl;
for(int j=0;j<numOfVertices;j++)
{
cin>>adjMatrix[i][j];
while(adjMatrix[i][j]<0)
{
cout<<"Weights should be +ve. Enter the weight again\n";
cin>>adjMatrix[i][j];
}
}
}
//read the source node from which the shortest paths to other nodes has to
be found
```

```
cout<<"Enter the source vertex\n";
cin>>source;
while((source<0) && (source>numOfVertices-1))
{
cout<<"Source vertex should be between 0 and "<<numOfVertices-1<<endl;
cout<<"Enter the source vertex again\n";
cin>>source;
}
}
void Graph::initialize()
{
for(int i=0;i<numOfVertices;i++) {
mark[i] = false;
predecessor[i] = -1;
distance[i] = INFINITY;
}
distance [source] = 0;
}
int Graph::getClosestUnmarkedNode()
{
int minDistance = INFINITY;
int closestUnmarkedNode;
for(int i=0;i<numOfVertices;i++) {
if((!mark[i]) && ( minDistance >= distance[i])) {
minDistance = distance[i];
closestUnmarkedNode = i;
}
}
return closestUnmarkedNode;
}
void Graph::dijkstra()
{
initialize();
int minDistance = INFINITY;
int closestUnmarkedNode;
int count = 0;
while(count < numOfVertices) {
closestUnmarkedNode = getClosestUnmarkedNode();
mark[closestUnmarkedNode] = true;
for(int i=0;i<numOfVertices;i++) {
if((!mark[i]) && (adjMatrix[closestUnmarkedNode][i]>0) ) {
```

```
if(distance[i] >
distance[closestUnmarkedNode]+adjMatrix[closestUnmarkedNode][i]) {
distance[i] =
distance[closestUnmarkedNode]+adjMatrix[closestUnmarkedNode][i];
predecessor[i] = closestUnmarkedNode;
}
}
}
count++;
}
}
void Graph::printPath(int node)
{
if(node == source)
cout<<node<<"..";
else if(predecessor[node] == -1)
cout<<"No path from "<<source<<"to "<<node<<endl;
else {
printPath(predecessor[node]);
cout<<node<<"..";
}
}
void Graph::output()
{
for(int i=0;i<numOfVertices;i++) {
if(i == source)
cout<<source<<".."<<source;
else
printPath(i);
cout<<"->"<<distance[i]<<endl;
}
}
int main()
{
Graph G;
G.read();
G.dijkstra();
G.output();
return 0;
}
```

Output:

```
Enter the number of vertices of the graph(should be > 0)
5
Enter the adjacency matrix for the graph
To enter infinity enter 999
Enter the (+ve)weights for the row 0
0
2
4
999
1
Enter the (+ve)weights for the row 1
2
0
7
3
999
Enter the (+ve)weights for the row 2
4
7
0
2
999
Enter the (+ve)weights for the row 3
999
3
2
0
6
Enter the (+ve)weights for the row 4
1
999
999
6
0
Enter the source vertex
0
0..0->0
0..1..->2
0..2..->4
0..1..3..->5
0..4..->1
```

OBJECTIVE TYPE QUESTIONS

1. The header is used to point
   (a) first node of the list
   (b) last node of the list
   (c) NULL value
   (d) None of the above
2. Traversing means
   (a) visiting all the nodes
   (b) shifting all the nodes at forward
   (c) randomly accessing the elements
   (d) None of the above
3. Graph is a
   (a) linear data structure
   (b) nonlinear data structure
   (c) None of the above
4. Graph contains
   (a) edges
   (b) arcs
   (c) edges and arcs
   (d) None of the above
5. The indegree of a node is
   (a) the total number of edges coming to that node.
   (b) the total number of edges leaving from that node
   (c) the total number of edges coming and leave to that node
   (d) None of the above
6. The directed graph is also called
   (a) trigraph
   (b) digraph
   (c) None of the above
7. Length of path is nothing but
   (a) total number of edges included in the path from source to destination node.
   (b) total number of edges included in the path from destination to source
   (c) none of the above.
8. When first and last nodes of the path are same such a path is known as
   (a) open path
   (b) closed path
   (c) None of the above
9. A directed acyclic graph is called
   (a) dag
   (b) acycle
   (c) none of the above

10. When a degree of node is zero then the node is called
    (a) group node (b) isolated node
    (c) None of the above
11. Traversal in graph is
    (a) to visit only few nodes of a graph
    (b) to visit all nodes of a graph
    (c) none of the above.

EXERCISES

1. What do you mean by graph.
2. Write basic definitions and terminology of graph.
3. Explain array representation of a graph.
4. What do you mean by adjacency matrices.
5. Explain representation of graph using adjacency lists
6. Explain linked list representation of a graph.
7. Explain and write an algorithm for these different operations are discussed as below:
    (a) Searching in a graph (b) Inserting in a graph
    (c) Deleting from a graph
8. Write an algorithm for traversing a graph using:
    (a) breadth-first search (b) depth-first search
9. What do you mean by connected component of a graph.
10. What is Spanning trees.
11. Explain minimum-cost spanning tree in detail.
12. Write an algorithm and C++ program for Prim's algorithm.
13. Write an algorithm and C++ program for Kruskal's algorithm
14. What is Directed acyclic graph.
15. Write an algorithm and C++ program for topological sort of directed graph.
16. Write an algorithm and C++ program for Floyd's-warshall's algorithm.
17. Write an algorithm and C++ program for Dijkstra's algorithm.

12 CHAPTER

Sorting and Searching Techniques

12.1 INTRODUCTION

In the computer science, Sorting is technique to arranging elements in some order. Typically this is an operation that applied to arrays or other index able data structures. In Standard English, "to sort" means to arrange by kind or to classify. The term "sort" came to be used in Computer Science because the earliest automated ordering procedures used punched card machines, which classified cards by their holes, to implement *radix sort*.

To arrange items in a predetermined order. There are dozens of algorithms, the choice of which depends on factors such as the number of items relative to working memory, knowledge of the orderliness of the items or the range of the *keys*, the cost of comparing keys vs. the cost of moving items, etc. Most algorithms can be implemented as an *in-place sort*, and many can be implemented so they are *stable*, too.

12.2 SORTING

The sort operation may be defined in terms of an initial array, S, of N items and a final array, S 2 , as follows:

1. $S_i' \leq S'_{i+1}$, $0 < i < N$
   (the items are in order) and
2. S′ is a *permutation* of S.

In terms of performance, sorting mostly comes in three flavors:

1. $O(n^2)$
2. O(n.log n) on average, but $O(n^2)$ at worst
3. O(n.log n)

The first class shouldn't be used for sorting really big arrays, say bigger than 2000 (there is no real limit; it depends on your time constraints). However they are usually very quick to code and debug, so always consider using them unless you are sure that they won't cut it. The algorithms in the second class are very seldom $O(n^2)$, so it is fine to use them in most applications, particularly in computer Olympiads where you only have 5 or 10 test cases and are highly unlikely to get a really slow case, and even if you do you only lose some of your points.

Sorting time may depend on:

- Initial order of data
- Data structure used to represent data
- Memory available
- Size of record
- Sort algorithm
- Location of list: internal storage, external storage, etc.
- And many more

12.3 CLASSIFICATION OF SORTING ALGORITHMS

Sorting algorithms used in computer science are often classified by:

- **Computational complexity (worst, average and best behaviour):** In terms of the size of the list (n). Typically, good behaviour is O(n log n) and bad behaviour is $O(n^2)$.

  Sort algorithms which only use an abstract key comparison operation always need at least O(n log n) comparisons on average; sort algorithms which exploit the structure of the key space cannot sort faster than O(n log k) where k is the size of the keyspace.

- **Memory usage (and use of other computer resources).**
- **Stability: Stable sorting algorithms** maintain the relative order of records with equal keys. That is, a sorting algorithm is *stable* if whenever there are two records *R* and *S* with the same key and with *R* appearing before *S* in the original list, *R* will appear before *S* in the sorted list.

  When equal elements are indistinguishable, such as with integers, stability is not an issue. However, say we were sorting these pairs of numbers by their first coordinate:

  (4, 3) (2, 1) (2, 7) (6, 6)

  In this case, two different results are possible, one which maintains the relative order records with equal keys, and one which doesn't:

  (2, 1) (2, 7) (4, 3) (6, 6) (order maintained)

  (2, 7) (2, 1) (4, 3) (6, 6) (order changed)

Unstable sorting algorithms may change the relative order of records with equal keys, stable sorting algorithms never so. Unstable sorting algorithms can be specially implemented to be stable. One way of doing this is to artificially extend the key comparison, so that comparisons between two objects with otherwise equal keys are decided using the order of the entries in the original data order as a tie-breaker. Remembering this order, however, often involves an additional space penalty.

There are different methods used for sorting the list or array. Some important methods are discusses in detail as below:

1. Bubble sort
2. Selection sort
3. Insertion sort
4. Quick sort
5. Heap sort
6. Merge sort
7. Radix sort
8. Bucket sort
9. Shell sort

12.4 BUBBLE SORT

Bubble sort is a simple sorting algorithm. It works by repeatedly stepping through the list to be sorted, comparing each pair of adjacent items and swapping them if they are in the wrong order. The pass through the list is repeated until no swaps are needed, which indicates that the list is sorted. Bubble sort belongs to O(n^2) sorting algorithms, which makes it quite inefficient for sorting large data volumes. Bubble sort is **stable** and **adaptive**.The algorithm gets its name from the way smaller elements "bubble" to the top of the list. Because it only uses comparisons to operate on elements, it is a comparison sort.

12.4.1 Analysis

1. Performance

Bubble sort has worst-case and average complexity both Î(n^2), where n is the number of items being sorted. There exist many sorting algorithms with substantially better worst-case or average complexity of O(n log n). Even other Î(n^2) sorting algorithms, such as Insertion sort, tend to have better performance than bubble sort. Therefore bubble sort is not a practical sorting algorithm when n is large.

However, one significant advantage that bubble sort has over most other implementations, even QuickSort, is that the ability to detect that the list is sorted is efficiently built into the algorithm. Performance of bubble sort over an already-sorted list (best-case) is O(n). By contrast, most other algorithms, even those with better average-case complexity, perform their entire sorting process on the set and thus are more complex. However, Insertion sort also has this mechanism, and also performs better on a list that is substantially sorted (having a small number of inversions).

2. Rabbits and Turtles

The positions of the elements in bubble sort will play a large part in determining its performance. Large elements at the beginning of the list do not pose a problem, as they are quickly swapped. Small elements towards the end, however, move to the beginning extremely slowly. This has led to these types of elements being named rabbits and turtles, respectively.

Various efforts have been made to eliminate turtles to improve upon the speed of bubble sort. Cocktail sort achieves this goal fairly well, but it retains $O(n^2)$ worst-case complexity. Comb sort compares elements large gaps apart and can move turtles extremely quickly, before proceeding to smaller and smaller gaps to smooth out the list. Its average speed is comparable to faster algorithms like Quicksort.

3. Step-by-step Example

A bubble sort makes use of an array and some sort of "swapping" mechanism. Most programming languages have a built-in function to swap elements of an array. Even if a swapping function does not exist, only a couple of extra lines of code are required to store one array element in a temporary field in order to swap a second element into its place. Then the first element is moved out of the temporary field and back into the array at the second element's position.

Example 12.1: How a bubble sort works: Suppose you have a row of children's toy blocks with letters on them. They are in random order and you wish to arrange them in alphabetical order from left to right.

Step 1: Begin with the first block. In this case, the letter **G.** (a)

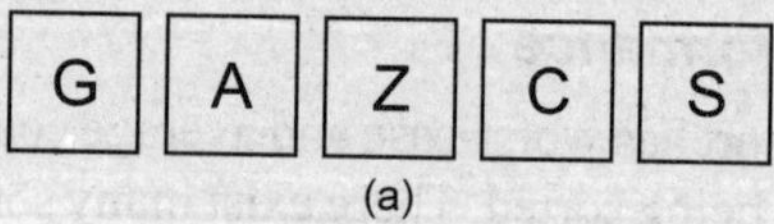

(a)

Step 2: Look at the block just to the right of it.

Step 3: If the block to the right should come before the block on the left, swap them so that they are in order (b)

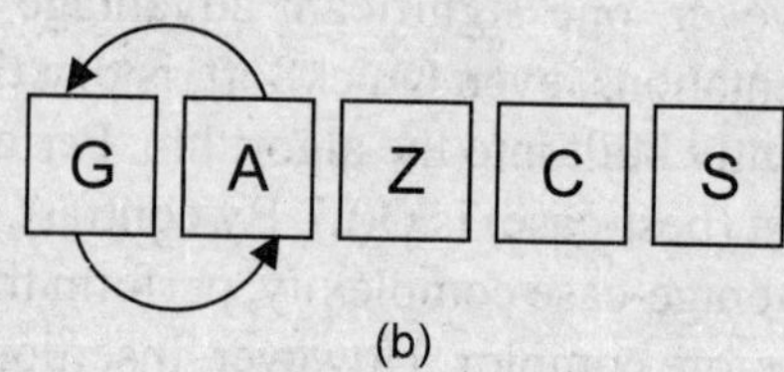

(b)

If you were doing this by hand, you might just pick the blocks to be moved with one in each hand and cross your arms to swap them. Or you might move the first one out of it's position temporarily, move the second one in its place, them move the first one to the now empty position (this is the difference between having a single function to do the swap, or writing some code to do it).

Step 4: Compare the next block in line with the first, and repeat step 3. Do this until you run out of blocks. Then begin step one again with the second block. (c,d,e)

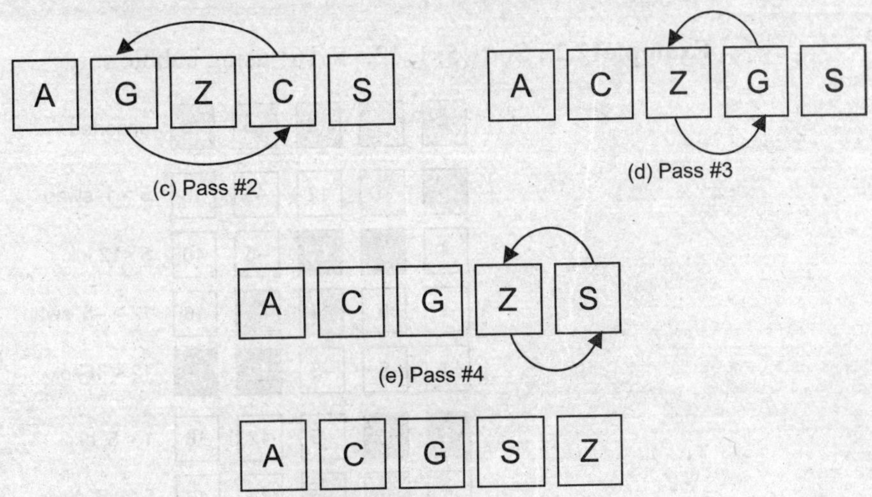

Figure 12.1: Bubble Sort.

12.4.2 Algorithm of Bubble Sort

1. Compare each pair of adjacent elements from the beginning of an array and, if they are in reversed order, swap them.
2. If at least one swap has been done, repeat step 1.
3. You can imagine that on every step big bubbles float to the surface and stay there. At the step, when no bubble moves, sorting stops.

Algorithm 12.1: BUBBLE(LA, N)

Here LA is an array with N elements. This algorithm sorts the elements in LA.

Step 1: START
Step 2: Repeat steps 3 and 4 For K=1 to N-1
Step 3: Set P =1 [Initializes pass pointer P]
Step 4: Repeat While P <=N-K [Execute Pass]

```
(a) if (LA[P] > LA [P+1]) then
Set TEMP=LA[P]
Set LA[P] = LA[P+1]
        Set LA[P+1] = TEMP
[End of if Structure]
(b) Set P = P+1
[End of inner loop (While loop)]
[End of Step 1 Outer Loop.]
Step 5: End.
```

Example12.2 : Sort {5, 1, 12, -5, 16} using bubble sort.

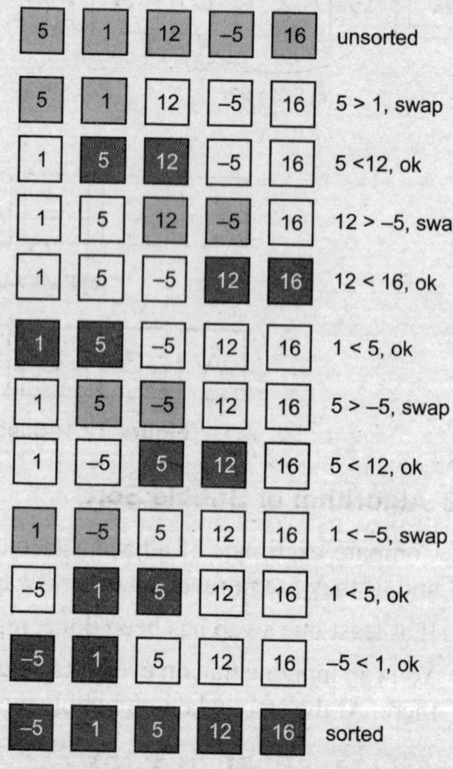

Figure 12.2: Example of bubble sort.

Program 1: Write a C++ program for Bubble sort(ascending order).

```
# include<iostream.h>
# include<conio.h>
# define size 20
class array
```

```
{
private:
int i;
float a[size];
public:
void read (int);
void display (int);
void bubble_sort (int);          // for sorting of elements
};
void array : : read (int n)
{
for (i=0;i<n;i++)
cin>>a[i];
}
void array : : display (int n)
{
for (i=0;i<n;i++)
cout<<a[i]<<" ";
}
void array : : bubble_sort (int n)
{
float temp;      // temp is used here for swapping
int last;        // last denotes the position of last unsorted element
int pass;        // pass denotes the position of last unsorted element and
denotes pass counter
int exchngs;     // exchngs denotes the no of exchanges during a pass
pass=0;
last=n-1;
do
{
pass++;
exchngs=0;
for (i=0;i<last;i++)
{
if (a[i]>a[i+1])
{
exchngs++;
```

```
temp=a[i];
a[i] =a [i+1];
a[i+1] = temp;
} // for loop ends here
last --;
}
while ((exchngs !=0) && (pass !=n-1));
cout<<"\n\nNo of pass used for sorting = '<<pass;
}

void main ( )
{
array obj;
int n;
clrscr ( );
cout<<"read no of elements<="<<size<<"\n";
cin>>n;
cout<<"\nread "<<n>>" elements\n";
obj.read (n);
cout<<"\ngiven array is \n\n";
obj.display (n);
obj.bubble_sort (n); // function call selection_sort
cout<<"\n\nSorted array is\n\n";
obj.display(n);
getch ( );
}
```

Output:

```
read no of elements<=20
7
read 7 elements
14    25    12    28    15    -2    35
given array is
14    25    12    28    15    -2    35
No of pass used for sorting = 6
Sorted array is
-2    12    14    15    25    28    35
```

Complexity analysis

Average and worst case complexity of bubble sort is $O(n^2)$. Also, it makes $O(n^2)$ swaps in the worst case. Bubble sort is adaptive. It means that for almost sorted array it gives O(n) estimation. Avoid implementations, which don't check if the array is already sorted on every step (any swaps made). This check is necessary, in order to preserve adaptive property.

Turtles and rabbits

One more problem of bubble sort is that its running time badly depends on the initial order of the elements. Big elements (rabbits) go up fast, while small ones (turtles) go down very slow. This problem is solved in the Cocktail sort.

Turtle example 12.3: Thought, array {2, 3, 4, 5, 1} is almost sorted, it takes $O(n^2)$ iterations to sort an array. Element {1} is a turtle.

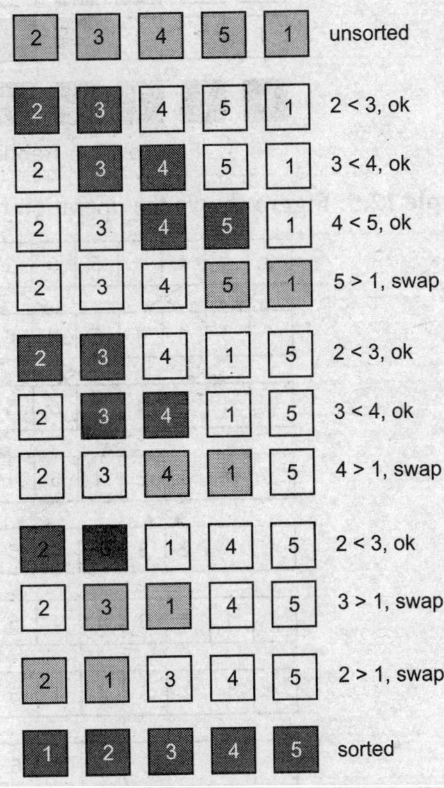

Figure 12.3: Turtle example.

Rabbit example12.4: Array {6, 1, 2, 3, 4, 5} is almost sorted too, but it takes O(n) iterations to sort it. Element {6} is a rabbit. This example demonstrates adaptive property of the bubble sort.

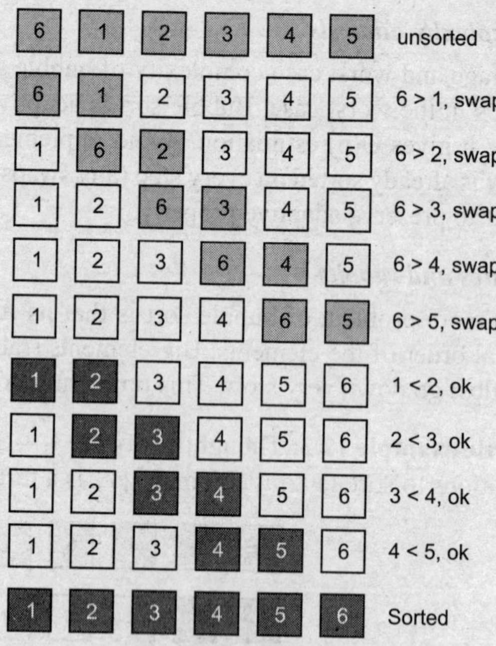

Figure 12.4: Rabbit example.

Example 12.5: Figure shows the operation of bubble sort.

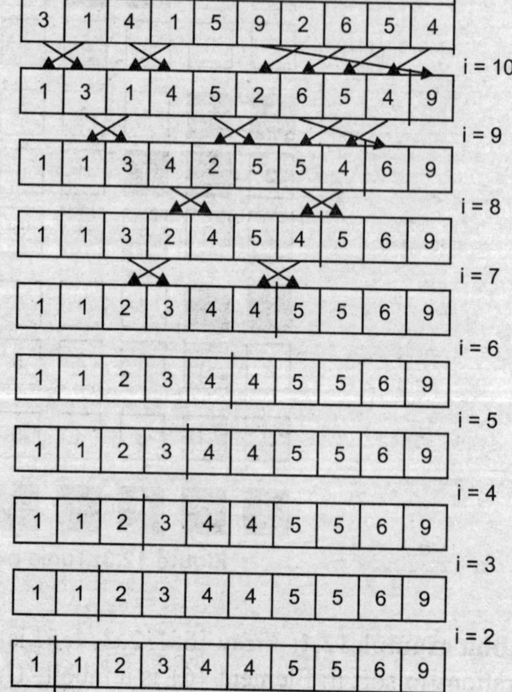

Figure 12.5: Bubble Sorting.

To sort the sequence $S = \{s_0, s_1, s_2, \ldots\ldots, s_{n-1}\}$, bubble sort makes n-1 passes through the data. In each pass, adjacent elements are compared and swapped if necessary. First, $s_0$and s_1 are compared; next, s_1 and s_2; and so on.

Notice that after the first pass through the data, the largest element in the sequence has *bubbled up* into the last array position. In general, after k passes through the data, the last k elements of the array are correct and need not be considered any longer. In this regard the bubble sort differs from the insertion sort algorithms—the sorted subsequence of k elements is never modified (by an insertion).

Figure also shows that while n-1 passes through the data are required to guarantee that the list is sorted in the end, it is possible for the list to become sorted much earlier! When no exchanges at all are made in a given pass, then the array is sorted and no additional passes are required. A minor algorithmic modification would be to count the exchanges made in a pass, and to terminate the sort when none are made.

The running time of bubble sort is $O(n^2)$.

12.4.3 Other Variations of Bubble Sort

1. Bubble Sort - Fixed Number of Passes

Bubble sort compares two values next to each other and exchanges them if necessary to put them in the correct order. There are many variations on bubble sort, but they all examine adjacent pairs.

This version of bubble sort makes a fixed number of passes (length of the array - 1). Each inner loop is one shorter than the previous one because the largest elements are being moved to the end of the array.

Algorithm 12.2: BubbleSort1 (x,n)

```
Where
x=Represents the list of elements
n=Represents the number of elements in the list
Step 1:  [Initialize] i=0
Step 2:  Repeat through step 7 while(i<n-1)
Step 3:  j=0
Step 4:  Repeat through step 6 while(j<n-i-1)
Step 5:  if(x[j]>x[j+1]
TEMP=x[j]; x[j]=x[j+1]; x[j+1]=TEMP
Step 6:  j++
Step 7:  i++
Step 8:  End.
```

Because this version of the bubble sort always makes n-1 passes over the array, it can't stop early if the array is already sorted.

2. Bubble Sort – stop when no exchanges

Algorithm 12.3: BubbleSort2(x,n)

```
Where
x=Represents the list of elements.
n=Represents the number of elements in the list.
Step 1:  [Assume no exchanges] exchanges=false
Step 2:  [Initialize] i=0
Step 3:  Repeat through step 5 while(i<n-1)
Step 4:  if(x[i]>x[i+1]
TEMP=x[i]; x[i]=x[i+1]; x[i+1]=TEMP
exchanges=true [after exchange, must look again]
Step 5:  i++
Step 6:  go back step 1 while(exchanges)
Step 7: End.
```

This version of bubble sort continues making passes over the array as long as there were any exchanges. If the array is already sorted, this sort will stop after only one pass.

Disadvantage: This algorithm doesn't shorten the range each time by 1 as it could.

3. Bubble Sort — stop when no exchanges, shorter range each time

This version of bubble sort combines ideas from the previous versions. It stops when there are no more exchanges, and it also sorts a smaller range each time.

Algorithm 12.4: BubbleSort3(x, n)

```
Where
x=Represents the list of elements.
n=Represents the number of elements in the list.
Step 1:  [Make loop smaller each time] n—
Step 2:  [Assume this is last pass over array] exchanges=false
Step 3:  [Initialize] i=0
Step 4:  Repeat through step 6 while(i<n)
Step 5:  if(x[i]>x[i+1])
TEMP=x[i]; x[i]=x[i+1] ;x[i+1]=TEMP
exchanges=true  [after exchange, must look again]
Step 6:  i++
Step 7:  go back step 1 while(exchanges)
Step 8:  End.
```

Disadvantage:

After the first pass it may not be necessary to examine the entire range of the array — only from where the lowest exchange occurred to where the highest exchange occurred. The parts above and below must already be sorted.

4. Bubble Sort — Sort only necessary range

Here's a version of bubble sort that, on each pass, looks only at the region of array where more exchanges might be necessary.

Algorithm 12.5: BubbleSortRange(x,n)

```
Where
x=Represents the list of elements.
n= Represents the number of elements in the list.
Step 1:  lowerbound=0      [First position to compare]
         upperbound=n     [First position NOT to compare]
         [Continue making passes while there is a potential exchange]
Step 2:  Repeat through step 11 while(lowerbound<=upperbound)
Step 3:  firstexchange=n    [Assume impossibly high index for low end]
         lastexchange=-1  [Assume impossibly low index for high end]
Step 4:  i=lowerbound             [Make a pass over the appropriate range]
Step 5:  Repeat through step 8 while(I<upperbound)
Step 6:  ifx[i]>x[i+1])
TEMP=x[i]; x[i]=x[i+1] ; x[i+1]=TEMP
 [Remember first and last exchange indexes]
Step 7:  if(i<firstexchange)  [true only for first]then firstexchange=i
Step 8:  lastexchange=i              [Prepare limits for next pass]
Step 9:  lowerbound=firstexchange-1
Step 10: if(lowerbound<0)  then lowerbound=0
Step 11: upperbound=lastexchange
Step 12:  End.
```

Disadvantage

Notice that the largest unsorted element will always be moved all the way to its correct position in the array, but small elements are shifted down by only one place on each pass.

Note that in all these sorts the part that is sorted grows at only one end of the array. The ability to quit early is not symmetrical. The extreme values move all the way to the end in one direction, but only one place in the other direction. The algorithm can be improved by alternately "bubbling" in opposite directions.

Efficiency: O(n²)

Pros

- Simple to implement and understand, but not much more so than several more efficient sorts
- Will be very quick on an already sorted list

Cons

- Probably the slowest sort ever invented

12.5 SELECTION SORT

Selection sort is one of the $O(n^2)$ sorting algorithms, which makes it quite inefficient for sorting large data volumes. Selection sort is notable for its programming simplicity and it can over perform other sorts in certain situations (see complexity analysis for more details).

Selection sort is a sorting algorithm, specifically an in-place comparison sort. It has $O(n^2)$ complexity, making it inefficient on large lists, and generally performs worse than the similar insertion sort. Selection sort is noted for its simplicity, and also has performance advantages over more complicated algorithms in certain situations.

Such algorithms construct the sorted sequence one element at a time by adding elements to the sorted sequence *in order*. At each step, the next element to be added to the sorted sequence is selected from the remaining elements.

Because the elements are added to the sorted sequence in order, they are always added at one end. This is what makes selection sorting different from insertion sorting. In insertion sorting elements are added to the sorted sequence in an arbitrary order. Therefore, the position in the sorted sequence at which each subsequent element is inserted is arbitrary.

Consequently, the sorts are implemented by exchanging array elements. Nevertheless, selection differs from exchange sorting because at each step we *select* the next element of the sorted sequence from the remaining elements and then we move it into its final position in the array by exchanging it with whatever happens to be occupying that position.

The simplest of the selection sorts is called *straight selection*. illustrates how straight selection works. In the version shown, the sorted list is constructed from the right (i.e., from the largest to the smallest element values).

At each step of the algorithm, a linear search of the unsorted elements is made in order to determine the position of the largest remaining element. That element is then moved into the correct position of the array by swapping it with the element which currently occupies that position.

Example 12.6: In the first step shown in Figure a linear search of the entire array reveals that 9 is the largest element. Since 9 is the largest element, it belongs in the last array position. To move it there, we swap it with the 4 that initially occupies that position. The second step of the algorithm identifies 6 as the largest remaining element an moves it next to the 9. Each subsequent step of the algorithm moves one element into its final position. Therefore, the algorithm is done after n-1 such steps.

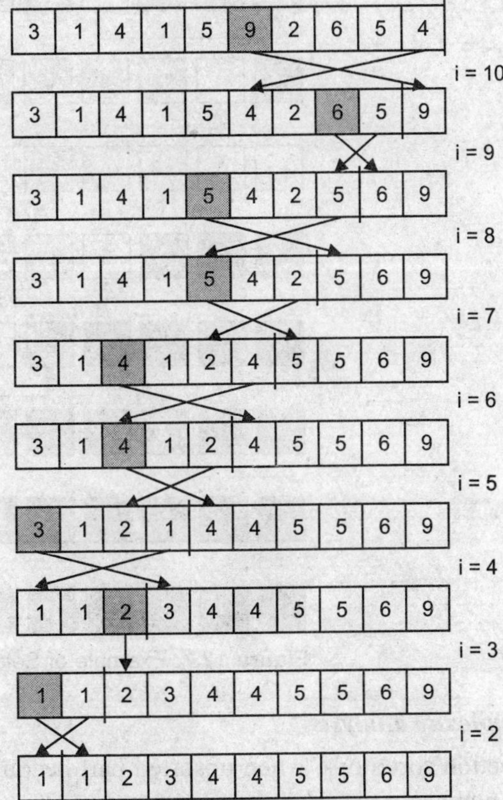

Figure 12.6: Straight Selection Sorting.

In all n-1 iterations of the outer loop are needed to sort the array. Notice that exactly one swap is done in each iteration of the outer loop. Therefore, n-1 data exchanges are needed to sort the list.

Furthermore, in the ith iteration of the outer loop, i-1 iterations of the inner loop are required and each iteration of the inner loop does one data comparison. Therefore, $O(n^2)$ data comparisons are needed to sort the list.

The total running time of the straight selection Do Sort routine is $O(n^2)$. Because the same number of comparisons and swaps are always done, this running time bound applies in all cases. I.e., the best-case, average-case and worst-case running times are all $O(n^2)$.

Let us see an example of sorting an array to make the idea of selection sort clearer.

Example 12.7: Sort {5, 1, 12, -5, 16, 2, 12, 14} using selection sort.

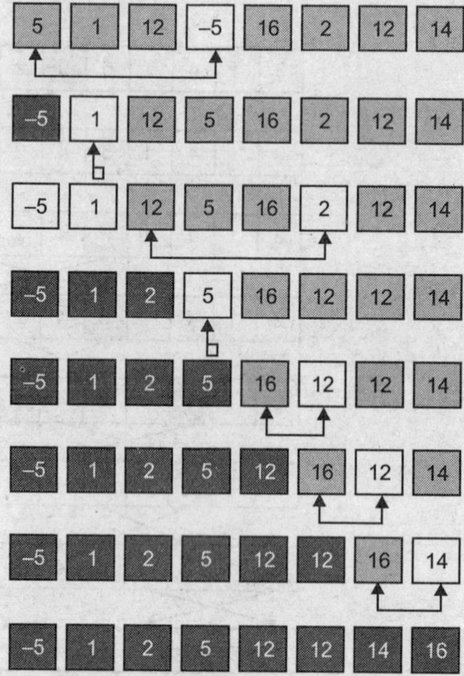

Figure 12.7: Example of Selection Sorting.

Complexity analysis

Selection sort stops, when unsorted part becomes empty. As we know, on every step number of unsorted elements decreased by one. Therefore, selection sort makes n steps (n is number of elements in array) of outer loop, before stop. Every step of outer loop requires finding minimum in unsorted part. Summing up, $n + (n - 1) + (n - 2) + ... + 1$, results in $O(n^2)$ number of comparisons. Number of swaps may vary from zero (in case of sorted array) to $n - 1$ (in case array was sorted in reversed order), which results in $O(n)$ number of swaps. Overall algorithm complexity is $O(n^2)$.

The idea behind selection sort is that to sort N items you make N passes through them.

1. On the first pass you find the largest value, and then swap it with the last item. Thus the largest item is now in position N.

2. On the second pass you scan through just the first N-1 entries. The largest of those items is swapped with the item in position N-1. Hence the largest item overall is now in the last position; the second largest item is now in the second last position.
3. This process is repeated, with one item being placed in its correct location each time.
4. After N passes, the entire collection of data is sorted.

A simple variation is to find the smallest item each time and put it at the front. To sort into descending order, the largest item is found each time and moved to the front (this is the algorithm that is used in the examples which follow).

12.5.1 Algorithm

The idea of algorithm is quite simple. Array is imaginary divided into two parts - sorted one and unsorted one. At the beginning, sorted part is **empty**, while unsorted one contains **whole array**. At every step, algorithm finds **minimal element** in the unsorted part and adds it to the end of the sorted one. When unsorted part becomes **empty**, algorithm stops.

When algorithm sorts an array, it swaps first element of unsorted part with minimal element and then it is included to the sorted part. This implementation of selection sort in **not stable**. In case of linked list is sorted, and, instead of swaps, minimal element is linked to the unsorted part, selection sort is **stable**.

The algorithm works as follows:

1. Find the minimum value in the list
2. Swap it with the value in the first position
3. Repeat the steps above for the remainder of the list (starting at the second position and advancing each time)

Effectively, the list is divided into two parts: the sublist of items already sorted, which is built up from left to right and is found at the beginning, and the sublist of items remaining to be sorted, occupying the remainder of the array.

Algorithm 12.6: SELECTIONSORT(A,N)

This algorithm sorts the array A with N elements.

Step 1: START

Step 2: Repeat Steps 3 and 4 For K=1,2,3,……,N-1

Step 3: Call MIN(A,K,LOC,N)

Step 4: [Interchange A[K] and A[LOC]]

Set TEMP=A[K]

Set A[K]=A[LOC]

Set A[LOC]=TEMP.

[End of Step 2 For loop]

Step 5: End.

Algorithm 12.7: MIN(A,K,N,LOC)

An array A is in memory. This algorithm finds the location LOC of the smallest elements among A[K], A[K+1], …………, A[N].

Step 1: Set MIN = A[K] and LOC = K [Initializes Pointers]

Step 2: Repeat For J = K+1, K+2,………, N.

If MIN>A[J] then

Set MIN = A[J] and LOC =A[J] and LOC =J.

[End of For loop of step 2]

Step 3: Return

Program 2: Write a C++ program for Selection sort.(ascending order)

```
# include<iostream.h>
# include<conio.h>
# define size 20
class array
{
private:
int i;
float a[size];
public:
void read (int);
void display (int);
void selection_sort (int); // for sorting of elements
};
void array : : read (int n)
{
for (i=0;i<n;i++)
cin>>a[i];
}
void array : : display (int n)
{
```

```
for (i=o;i<n;i++)
cout<<a[i]<<" ";
}
void array : : selection_sort (int n)
{
float  temp; // temp is used here for swapping
int min_index;
// min_index denotes the position of the least element during a pass
for (int pass=0; pass<n-1;pass++)
{
min_index=pass;
for (i=pass+1;i<n;i++)
{
if (a[i] <a[min_index])
min_index=i;
}
if (pass ! =min_index)
{
temp=a [pass];
a[pass]=a[min_index];
a[min_index]=temp;
}
}
}
void main ( )
{
array obj;
int n;
clrscr ( );
cout<<"read no of elements<="<<size<<"\n";
cin>>n;
cout<<"\nread "<<n>>" elements\n";
obj.read (n);
cout<<"\ngiven array is \n\n";
obj.display (n);
obj.selection_sort (n);
cout<<"\n\nSorted array is\n\n";
```

```
obj.display(n);
getch ( );
}
Output:
read no of elements<=20
7
read 7 elements
14    25    12    28    15    -2    35
given array is
14    25    12    28    15    -2    35
No of pass used for sorting = 6
Sorted array is
-2    12    14    15    25    28    35
```

12.6 INSERTION SORT

Insertion sort belongs to the O(n^2) sorting algorithms. Unlike many sorting algorithms with quadratic complexity, it is actually applied in practice for sorting small arrays of data. **For instance, it is used to improve quicksort routine.** Some sources notice, that people use same algorithm ordering items, for example, hand of cards.

Insertion sort algorithm somewhat resembles selection sort. Array is imaginary divided into two parts - sorted one and unsorted one. At the beginning, sorted part contains **first element** of the array and unsorted one contains the rest. At every step, algorithm takes **first element** in the unsorted part and **inserts** it to the right place of the sorted one. When unsorted part becomes **empty**, algorithm *stops*. Sketchy, insertion sort algorithm step looks like this:

Sorted partitial result		Unsorted data	
≤ x	> x	x	...

becomes

Sorted partitial result			Unsorted data
≤ x	x	> x	...

The idea of the sketch was originally posted here. Let us see an example of insertion sort routine to make the idea of algorithm clearer.

Example 12.8: Sort {7, -5, 2, 16, 4} using insertion sort.

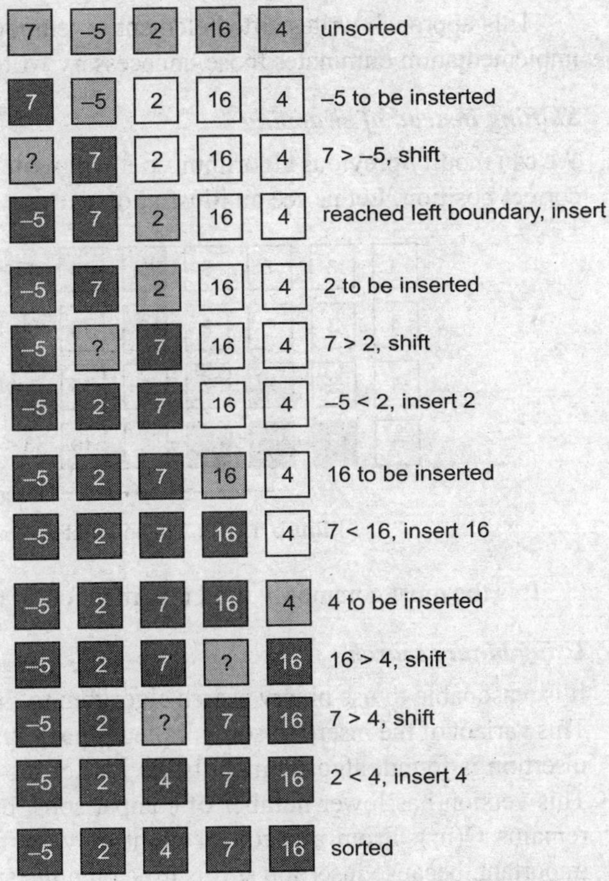

Figure 12.8: Example of Insertion Sort.

The ideas of insertion

The main operation of the algorithm is **insertion**. The task is to insert a value into the sorted part of the array. Let us see the variants of how we can do it.

"Shifting down" using swaps: The simplest way to insert next element into the sorted part is to sift it down, until it occupies correct position. Initially the element stays right after the sorted part. At each step algorithm compares the element with one before it and, if they stay in reversed order, swap them. Let us see an illustration.

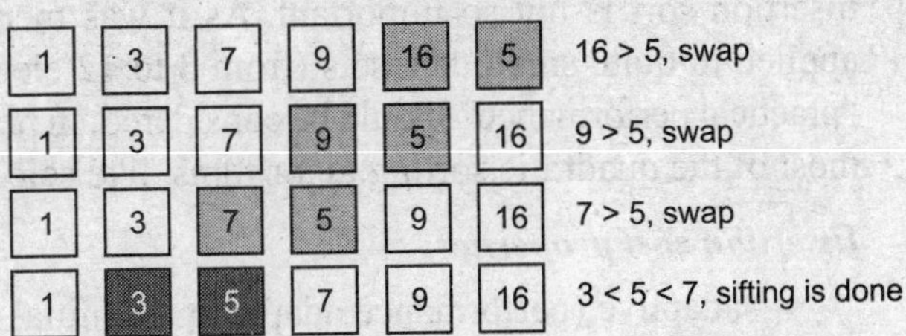

Figure 12.9: "Shifting down" using swaps.

This approach writes sifted element to temporary position many times. Next implementation eliminates those unnecessary writes.

Shifting instead of swapping

We can modify previous algorithm, so it will write sifted element only to the final correct position. Let us see an illustration.

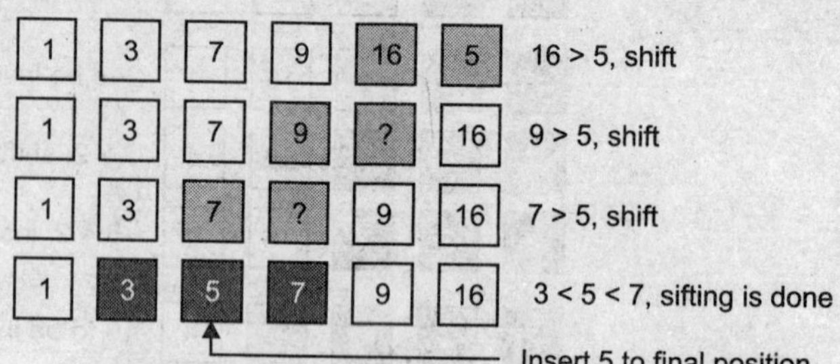

Figure 12.10: Shifting instead of swapping

It is the most commonly used modification of the insertion sort.

Using binary search

It is reasonable to use binary search algorithm to find a proper place for insertion. This variant of the insertion sort is called **binary insertion sort**. After position for insertion is found, algorithm shifts the part of the array and inserts the element. This version has lower number of comparisons, but overall average complexity remains $O(n^2)$. From a practical point of view this improvement is not very important, because insertion sort is used on quite small data sets.

Complexity analysis

Insertion sort's overall complexity is $O(n^2)$ on average, regardless of the method of insertion. On the almost sorted arrays insertion sort shows better performance, up to $O(n)$ in case of applying insertion sort to a sorted array. Number of writes is $O(n^2)$ on average, but number of comparisons may vary depending on the insertion algorithm. It is $O(n^2)$ when shifting or swapping methods are used and $O(n \log n)$ for binary insertion sort.

From the point of view of practical application, an average complexity of the insertion sort is not so important. As it was mentioned above, insertion sort is applied to quite small data sets (from 8 to 12 elements). Therefore, first of all, a "practical performance" should be considered. In practice insertion sort outperforms most of the quadratic sorting algorithms, like selection sort or bubble sort.

Insertion sort properties

- adaptive (performance adapts to the initial order of elements);
- stable (insertion sort retains relative order of the same elements);

- in-place (requires constant amount of additional space);
- online (new elements can be added during the sort).

Algorithm 12.8: INSERTION(A,N)

This algorithm sorts the array A with N elements. P is used as pointer.

Step 1: START

Step 2: Set A[0] = –∞ [Initializes sentinel element]

Step 3: Repeat steps 4 to 6 For K = 2, 3, 4,......, N.

Step 4: Set Temp = A[k] and P = K-1.

Step 5: Repeat While TEMP < A[P]

a. Set A[P+1] = A[P]. [Move Element Forward.]

b. Set P = P - 1.

[End of While Loop.]

Step 6: Set A[P+1] = TEMP. [Insert element in Proper Place.]

[End of for loop of Step 3]

Step 7: End.

Program 3: Write a C++ program for insertion sort.(ascending order)

```
# include<iostream.h>
# include<conio.h>
# define size 20
class array
{
private:
int i;
float a[size];
public:
void read (int);
void display (int);
void insertion_sort (int); // for sorting of elements
};
void array : : read (int n)
{
for (i=0;i<n;i++)
cin>>a[i];
}
void array : : display (int n)
{
```

```
for (i=o;i<n;i++)
cout<<a[i]<<" ";
}
void array : : insertion_sort (int n)
{
int current, pos;
for (i=1;i<n;i++)
{
current=a[i]; // current denotes the element to be arranged
pos=0;
while ((pos<i) && (a[pos]<=current))
pos++;
//pos increased till values in array are <= current
if (pos !=i)
{
for (int j=i-1;j>=pos;j--)
a[j+1]=a[j];
// insertion
a[pos]=current;
}
}
}
void main ( )
{
array obj;
int n;
clrscr ( );
cout<<"read no of elements<="<<size<<"\n";
cin>>n;
cout<<"\nread "<<n>>" elements\n";
obj.read (n);
cout<<"\ngiven array is \n\n";
obj.display (n);
obj.insertion_sort (n);
cout<<"\n\nSorted array is\n\n";
obj.display(n);
```

```
getch ( );
}
Output:
read no of elements<=20
7
read 7 elements
14    25    12    28    15    -2    35
given array is
14    25    12    28    15    -2    35
No of pass used for sorting = 6
Sorted array is
-2    12    14    15    25    28    35
```

Efficiency: O(n^2)

Pros

- Fairly easy to implement with a linear search
- If a backwards linear search is used, it is much faster on an partially sorted array

Cons

- On an array, insertion is slow because all the elements after it have to be moved up.

Note: *This sort isn't especially useful by itself (although it is a respectable O(n^2) sort), but forms the basis of Shell sort.*

12.7 QUICKSORT

One of the most popular sorting algorithms is Quick Sort. Quick Sort executes in O(n lg n) on average, and O(n^2) in the worst-case. However, with proper precautions, worst-case behavior is very unlikely. Quick Sort is a non-stable sort. It is not an in-place sort as stack space is required.

Quicksort is a *divide-and-conquer* style algorithm. A divide-and-conquer algorithm solves a given problem by splitting it into two or more smaller subproblems, recursively solving each of the subproblems, and then combining the solutions to the smaller problems to obtain a solution to the original one.

To sort the sequence $S = \{s_0, s_1, s_2, \ldots\ldots, s_n\}$, quicksort performs the following steps:

1. Select one of the elements of S. The selected element, p, is called the pivot .
2. Remove p from S and then partition the remaining elements of S into two distinct sequences, L and G, such that every element in L is less than or equal to the pivot and every element in G is greater than or equal to the pivot. In general, both L and G are unsorted.
3. Rearrange the elements of the sequence as follows:

$$S' = \underbrace{\{l_1, l_2, ..., l_{|L|}\}}_{L} : \underbrace{P}_{pivot} : \underbrace{\{g_1, g_2, ..., g_{|G|}\}}_{G}$$

   Notice that the pivot is now in the position in which it belongs in the sorted sequence, since all the elements to the left of the pivot are less than or equal to the pivot and all the elements to the right are greater than or equal to it.
4. Recursively quicksort the unsorted sequences L and G.

The first step of the algorithm is a crucial one. We have not specified how to select the pivot. Fortunately, the sorting algorithm works no matter which element is chosen to be the pivot. However, the pivot selection affects directly the running time of the algorithm. If we choose poorly the running time will be poor.

Illustrates the detailed operation of quicksort as it sorts the sequence {3, 1, 4, 1, 5, 9, 2, 6, 5, 4}. To begin the sort, we select a pivot. In this example, the value 4 in the last array position is chosen. Next, the remaining elements are partitioned into two sequences, one which contains values less than or equal to 4 (L={3, 1, 2, 1}) and one which contains values greater than or equal to 4 (G = {5, 9, 4, 6, 5). Notice that the partitioning is accomplished by exchanging elements. This is why quicksort is considered to be an **exchange sort.**

After the partitioning, the pivot is inserted between the two sequences. This is called *restoring* the pivot. To restore the pivot, we simply exchange it with the first element of G. Notice that the 4 is in its correct position in the sorted sequence and it is not considered any further.

Now the quicksort algorithm calls itself recursively, first to sort the sequence L = {3, 1, 2, 1}; second to sort the sequence G = {9, 4, 6, 5, 5}. The quicksort of L selects 1 as the pivot, and creates the two subsequences L' = {1} and G' = {2, 3}. Similarly, the quicksort of G uses 5 as the pivot and creates the two subsequences L" = {5, 4} and G" = {9, 6}.

At this point in the example the recursion has been stopped. It turns out that to keep the code simple, quicksort algorithms usually stop the recursion when the length of a subsequence falls below a critical value called the cut-off. In this example, the cut-off is two (i.e., a subsequence of two or fewer elements is not sorted).

Example 12.9

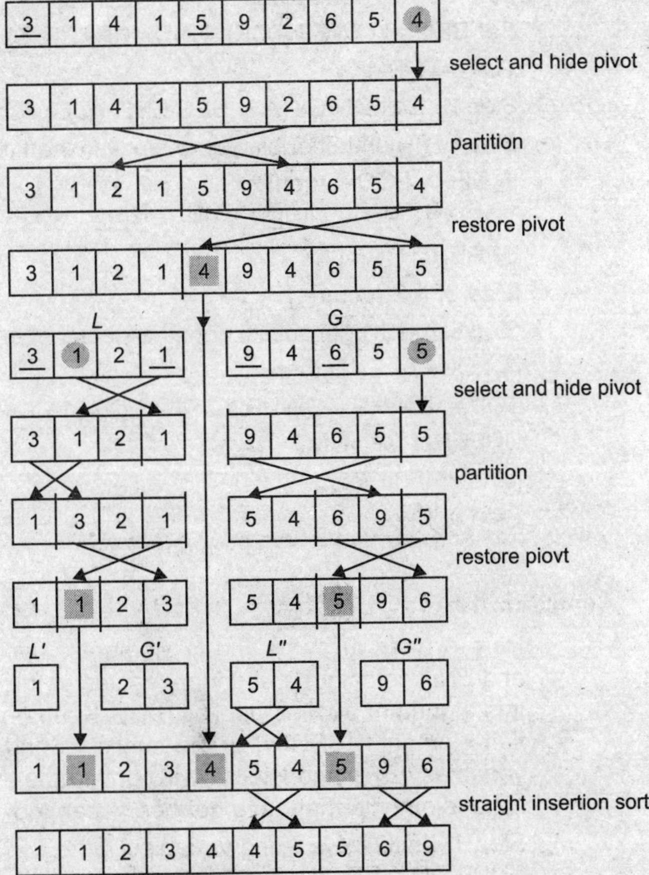

Figure 12.11: Quick Sorting

This means that when the algorithm terminates, the sequence is not yet sorted. However as Figure shows, the sequence is *almost* sorted. In fact, every element is guaranteed to be less than two positions away from its final resting place. In fact, if we know that every element of the sequence is at most d positions from its final resting place, the running time of straight insertion is O(dn) and since d=2 is a constant, the running time is O(n).

Algorithm 12.9: QUICKSORT

Step 1: START

Step 2: TOP=NULL [Initialize]

Step 3: [Push boundary values of a onto the stack when A has 2 or more elements]

If (N>1) then Set TOP = TOP+1, LOWER[1] = 1, UPPER[1]=N

Step 4: Repeat Steps 5 to 7 While TOP ≠ NULL
Step 5: [Pop sublist from Stacks]
Set BEG:=LOWER[TOP], END:=UPPER[TOP]
TOP:=TOP-1
Step 6: Call QUICK(A,N,BEG,END,LOC) Procedure
Step 7: [Push left sublist onto stacks when it has 2 or more elements]
If BEG <LOC-1 then:
TOP = TOP-1, LOWER[TOP] = BEG
UPPER[TOP]=LOC-1
[End of if Structure.]
Step 8: [push right sublist onto the stacks when it has 2 or more elements]
If LOC+1< END then:
TOP = TOP+1, LOWER[TOP] = LOC+1
UPPER[TOP]=END
[End of if Structure.]
Step 9: End.

Algorithm 12.10: QUICK(A, N, BEGIN, END, LOC)

Here A is an array having N elements. Two main parameters BEGIN and END contain the boundary values of the sublist of array A to which this algorithm applies applies. LOC Keeps track of the position of the first element A[BEGIN] of the sublist during the procedure. The local variables LEFT and RIGHT will contain the the boundary values of the list of elements that have not been scanned.

Step 1: [Initialize starting variables] Set LEFT = BEGIN, RIGHT = END AND LOC = BEGIN.
Step 2: [Scan elements from right to left.]
(a) Repeat Steps while A[LOC] ≤ A[RIGHT] and LOC ≠ RIGHT:
RIGHT = RIGHT – 1.
[End of while loop.]
(b) If LOC = RIGHT, then Return.
(c) If A[LOC]> A[RIGHT], then
(i) [Interchange elements A[LOC] and A[RIGHT].]
TEMP = A[LOC], A[LOC] = A[RIGHT].
A[RIGHT] = TEMP.
(ii) Set LOC = RIGHT.
(iii) GO to Step 3.
[End of If statement.]
Step 3: [Scan elements from left to right.]

(a) Repeat steps while A[LEFT] $\leq$ A[LOC] and LEFT $\neq$ LOC:
LEFT = LEFT + 1
[End of while loop.]
(b) If LOC = LEFT, then Return.
(c) if A[LEFT] > A[LOC], then
(i) [Interchange elements A[LEFT] and A[LOC].]
TEMP = A[LOC], A[LOC] = A[LEFT],
A[LEFT] = TEMP.
(ii) Set LOC = LEFT.
(iii) Go to step 2.
[End of If statement.]

Table12.1 : Running Times for Exchange Sorting

Algorithm	Best case	Running time Average case	Worst case
bubble sort	$O(n^2)$	$O(n^2)$	$O(n^2)$
quicksort (random pivot selection)	O(n log n)	O(n log n)	$O(n^2)$

Program 4: Write a C++ program for Quick sort.(ascending order)

```
# include<iostream.h>
# include<conio.h>
# define size 20
class array
{
private:
float a[size];
int i, low, high, pivot_value, temp;
public:
void read (float *,int);
void display (float *,int);
void quick_sort (float *,int beq, int end);
};
void array : : read (float a[], int n)
{
for (i=0;i<n;i++)
cin>>a[i];
}
void array : : display (float a[], int n)
{
```

```
for (i=0;i<n;i++)
cout<<a[i]<<" ";
}
void array : : quick_sort (float arr[], int beg, int end)
{
lot=beg;
high=end;
pivot_value=arr [(beg+end)/2];
do
{
while (arr[low]>pivot_value)
high--;
if (low<=high)
{
temp = arr[low]
arr [low++] = arr[high];
arr [high--] = temp;
}
}while (low<=high);
if (beg<high)
quick_sort [arr, beg, high); // recursive call to the function
if (low<end)
quick_sort (arr, low, end); // recursive call to the function
}
void main ( )
{
array obj;
float a[size];
int n;
clrscr ( );
cout<<"read no of elements<="<<size<<"\n";
cin>>n;
cout<<"\nread "<<n<<" elements \n\n;
obj.read (a, n);
cout<<"\ngiven array is \n\n";
obj.display (a, n);
obj.quick_sort(a,0,n-1);
cout<<"\n\n Sorted array is\n\n";
obj.display(a,n))
```

```
getch ( );
}
Output:
read no elements<=20
7
read 7 elements
14    25    12    28    15    -2    35
given array is
14    25    12    28    15    -2    35
No of pass used for sorting = 6
Sorted array is
-2    12    14    15    25    28    35
```

12.8 HEAP SORT

The Quick Sort on the average improves performance over linear sort algorithms. In this section we consider another important nonlinear sort, the **heap sort**, which performs as well as the quick sort on the average and performs better than the quick sort in the worst cases. The heap sort has better all-around performance than any other internal sort that we present; however it is rather complex to program. J. W. J. Williams developed the heap sort in 1964. The heap sort is based upon use of a special type of binary tree (called a heap) to structure the sorting process.

Heap is a complete binary tree in which each node satisfies the heap condition. Heap has been defined as: descending heap (also called a **max heap**) and ascending heap (also called a **min heap**). In descending heap, the root of the tree (or the first element of the array) contains the largest element in the heap. Also note that any path from the root to a leaf (or indeed, any path in the tree that includes no more than one node at any level) is an ordered list in descending order. In ascending heap, the root contains the smallest element of the heap, and any path from the root to a leaf is an ascending ordered list.

To define a descending heap of size n as an almost complete binary tree of n nodes such that the content of each node is less than or equal to the content of its father. To define an ascending heap as a complete binary tree such that the content of each node is greater than or equal to the content of its father.

The structure satisfies the condition of descending heap as root of the tree and sub trees have higher value than the children. The roots of the sub trees are also higher the value of their children as shown in the Figure 12.12:

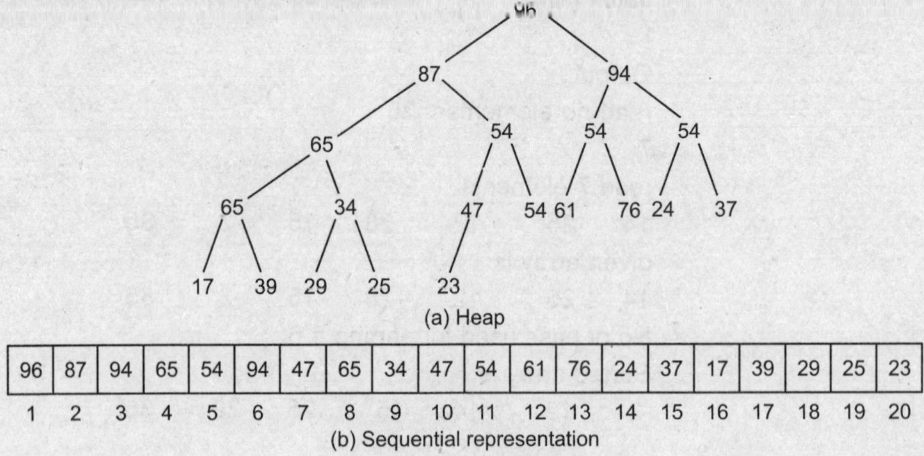

(a) Heap

96	87	94	65	54	94	47	65	34	47	54	61	76	24	37	17	39	29	25	23
1	2	3	4	5	6	7	8	9	10	11	12	13	14	15	16	17	18	19	20

(b) Sequential representation

Figure 12.12: Heap tree.

If the father is placed at say index 2, i.e., 87, its children will be placed at index 2*2 and (2*2)+1, i.e. 65 and 54.

12.8.1 Sorting Procedure

Heap sort involves three operations, insertion, deletion of nodes and building new heap tree in such a way so as to maintain the heap character of the tree. The sorting procedure of the Heap tree is very simple and the execution of this tree on computer is faster as compared to the other tree.

1. Inserting into a Heap

Suppose H is a heap with N elements, and suppose an ITEM of information is given. We insert ITEM into the heap H as follows:

1. First adjoin ITEM at the end of H so that H is still a complete tree, but not necessarily a heap.
2. Then let ITEM rise to its "appropriate place" in H so that H is finally a heap.

We illustrate the way this procedure works before stating the procedure formally.

Algorithm 12.11: INSHEAP(TREE, N, ITEM)

A heap H with N elements is stored in the array TREE, and an ITEM of information is given. This procedure inserts ITEM as a new element of H.

Pointer P gives the location of ITEM as it rises in the tree, and PARENT denotes the location of the PARENT of ITEM.

Step 1: [Add new node to H and initialize P.]

Set N = N + 1 and P = N.
Step 2: [Find location to insert ITEM.]
Repeat Steps 3 to 6 while P > 1.
Step 3: Set PARENT = [P/2]. [Location of PARENTent node.]
Step 4: If ITEM ≤ TREE[PARENT], then:
Set TREE[P] = ITEM, and Return.
[End of If statement.]
Step 5: Set TREE[P] = TREE[PARENT]. [Moves node down.]
Step 6: Set P = PARENT. [Updates P.]
[End of Step 2 loop.]
Step 7: [Assign ITEM as the ROOTNOD of H.]
Set TREE[1] = ITEM.
Step 8: Return.

Example 12.10: Consider the heap H in Figure 12.12. Suppose we want to add ITEM = 71 to H. First we adjoin 71 as the next element in the complete tree; that is, we set TREE[21] = 71. Then 71 is the right child of TREE [10] = 47. The path from 71 to the root of H is pictured in Figure 12.13(a). We know find the appropriate place of 71 in the heap as follows:

(a) Compare 71 with its parent, 47. Since 71 is greater than 47, interchange 71 and 47; the path will now look Figure 12.13(b).

(b) Compare 71 with its new parent, 54. Since 71 is greater than 54, interchange 71 and 54; the path will now look like Figure 12.13(c).

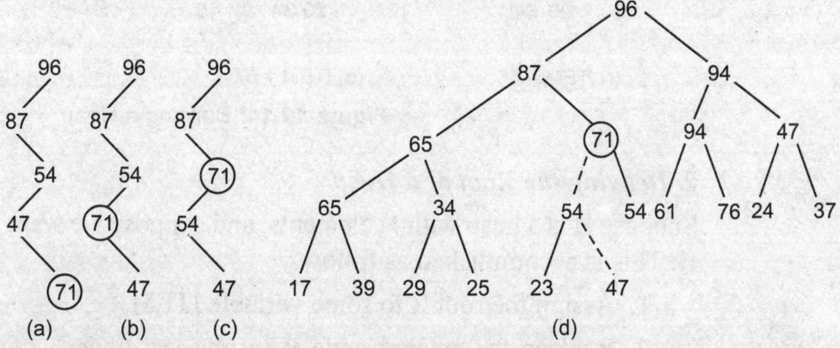

Figure 12.13: ITEM = 71 is Inserted

(c) Compare 71 with its new parent, 87. Since 71 does not exceed 87, ITEM = 71 has risen to its appropriate place in H.

Figure 12.13(d) shows the final tree. A dotted line indicate that an exchange has taken place.

Remark: One must verify that the above procedure does always yield a heap as a final tree, that is that nothing else has been disturbed. This is easy to see, and we leave this verification to the reader.

Example 12.11: Suppose we want to build a heap H from the following list of numbers:

34, 20, 40, 12, 50, 45, 67, 45

This can be accomplished by inserting the eight numbers one after the other into an empty heap H using the above procedure. Figure 12.14(a) through (h) shows the respective pictures of the heap after each of the eight elements has been inserted. Again, the dotted line indicated that an exchange has taken place during the insertion of the given ITEM of information.

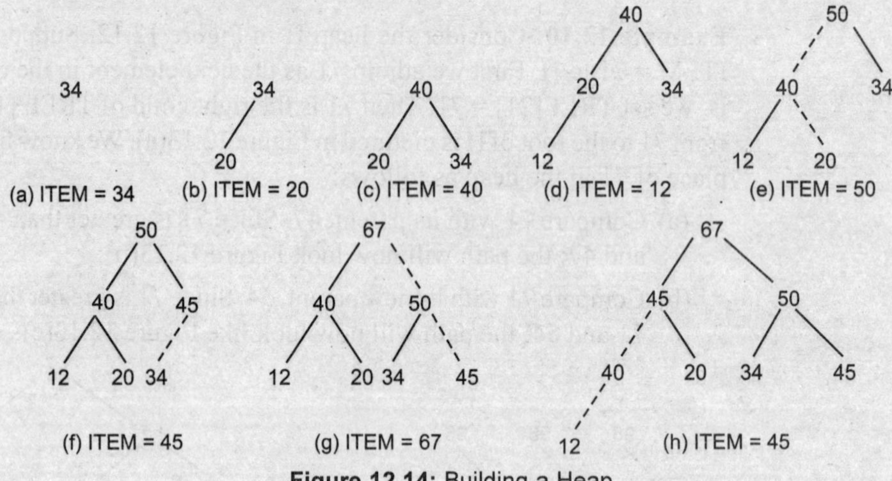

Figure 12.14: Building a Heap

2. Deleting the Root of a Heap

Suppose H is a heap with N elements, and suppose we want to delete the root R of H. This is accomplished as follows:

1. Assign the root R to some variable ITEM.
2. Replace the deleted node R by the last node L of H so that H is still a complete tree, but not necessarily a heap.
3. (Reheap) Let L sink to its appropriate place in H so that H is finally a heap.

Again we illustrate the way the procedure works before stating the procedure formally.

Algorithm 12.12: DELHEAP(TREE, N, ITEM)

A heap H with N elements is stored in the array TREE. This procedure assigns the ROOTNOD TREE[1] of H to the variable ITEM and then reheaps the remaining elements. The variable LAST saves the value of the original last node of H. The pointers P, LEFTNOD and RIGHTNOD give the locations of LAST and its LEFTNOD and RIGHTNOD children as LAST sinks in the tree.

Step 1: Set ITEM = TREE[1]. [Removes ROOTNOD of H.]

Step 2: Set LAST = TREE[N] and N = N – 1. [Removes last node of H.]

Step 3: Set P = 1, LEFTNOD = 2 and RIGHTNOD = 3. [Initializes pointers.]

Step 4: Repeat Steps 5 to 7 while RIGHTNOD ≤ N:

Step 5: If LAST ≥ TREE[LEFTNOD] and LAST ≥ TREE[RIGHTNOD], then:

Set TREE[P] = LAST and Return.

[End of If statement.]

Step 6: If TREE[RIGHTNOD] ≤ TREE[LEFTNOD], then:

Set TREE[P] = TREE[LEFTNOD] and P = LEFTNOD.

Else

Set TREE[P] = TREE[RIGHTNOD] and P = RIGHTNOD.

[End of If statement.]

Step 7: Set LEFTNOD = 2 * P and RIGHTNOD = LEFTNOD(2*P) + 1

[End of Step 4 loop.]

Step 8: If LEFTNOD = N and if LAST < TREE[LEFTNOD], then

Set TREE[P] = TREE[LEFTNOD] and P = LEFTNOD.

Step 9: Set TREE[P] = LAST.

Step 10: Return.

Example 12.12: Consider the heap H in Figure 12.15(a), where R = 93 is the root and L = 20 is the last node of the tree. Step 1 of the above procedure deletes R = 93, and Step 2 replaces R = 93 by L = 20. This gives the complete the tree in Figure 12.15(b), which is not a heap. Observe, however, that both the right and left subtrees of 20 are still heaps. Applying Step 3, we find the appropriate place of 20 in the heap as follows:

(a) Compare 20 with its two children, 83 and 68. Since 20 is less than the larger child, 83, interchange 20 and 83 so the tree now looks like Figure 12.15(c).

(b) Compare 20 with its two new children, 53 and 31. Since 20 is less than the larger child, 53, interchange 20 and 53 so the tree now looks like Figure 12.15(d).

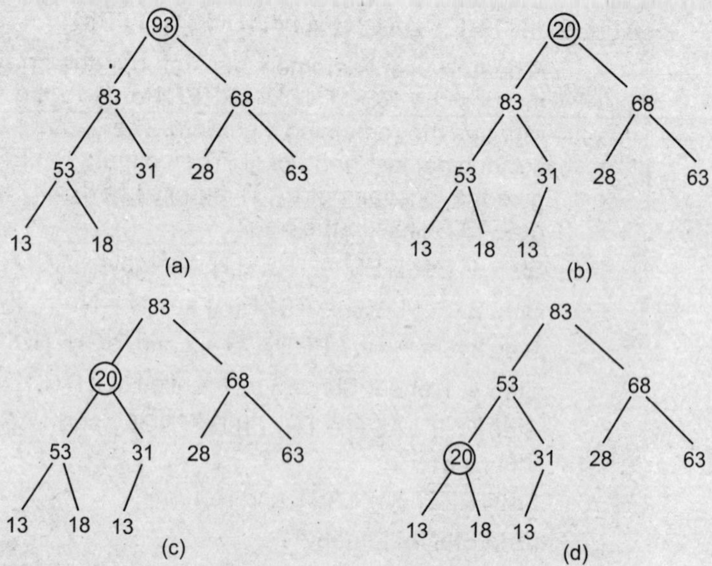

Figure 12.15: Reheaping.

(c) Compare 20 with its new children, 13 and 18. Since 20 is greater than both children, node 20 has dropped to its appropriate place in H.

Thus, Figure 12.15(d) is the required heap H without its original root R.

Remark: *As with inserting an element into a heap, one must verify that the above procedure does always yield a heap as a final tree. Again we leave this verification to the reader. We also note that Step 3 of the procedure may not end until the node L reaches the bottom of the tree, i.e., until L has no children.*

12.8.2 Application to Sorting

Suppose an array A and N elements is given. The heapsort algorithm to sort A consists of the two following phases:

Phase A: Build a heap H out of the elements of A.

Phase B: Repeatedly delete the root element of H.

Since the root of H always contains the largest node in H, Phase B deletes the elements of A in decreasing order. A formal statement of the algorithm, which uses Procedures 12.11 and 12.12, follows.

Algorithm 12.13: HEAPSORT(A, N)

An array A with N element is given. This algorithm sorts the elements of A.

Step 1: [Build a heap H, using Algorithm 12.11.]

```
    Repeat for I = 1 to N – 1
    Call INSHEAP(A, I, A[I + 1])
    [End of loop.]
Step 2: [Sort A by repeatedly deleting the ROOTNOD of H, using
algorithm 12.12.]
    Repeat while N> 1:
a. Call DELHEAP(A, N, ITEM).
b. Set A[N + 1] = ITEM.
    [End of loop.]
Step 3: End.
```

The purpose of step 2(b) is to save space makes the sorting technique more efficient. That is we can use another array B to hold the sorted elements of A and replace step 2(b) as

Set B[N + 1] = ITEM.

Note: *Step 2(b) not interfere with the algorithm, Since A[N + 1] does not belong to the heap H.*

12.8.3 Complexity of Heapsort

Suppose the heapsort algorithm is applied to an array A with n elements. The algorithm has tow phases, and we analyze the complexity of each phase separately.

Phase A: Suppose H is a heap. Observe that the number of comparisons to find the appropriate place of a new element ITEM in H cannot exceed the depth of H. Since H is a complete tree, its depth is bounded by $\log_2 m$ where m is the number of elements in H. Accordingly, the total number g(n) of comparison to insert the n elements of A into H is bounded as follows:

$$g(n) \leq n \log_2 n$$

Consequently, the running time of Phase A of heapsort is proportional to $n \log_2 n$.

Phase B: Suppose H is a complete tree with m elements, and suppose the left and right subtrees of H are heaps and L is the root of H. Observe that reheaping uses 4 comparisons to move the node L one step down the tree H. Since the depth of H does not exceed $\log_2 m$, reheaping uses at most $4 \log_2 m$ comparison to find the appropriate place of L in the tree H. This means that the total number h(n) of comparison to delete the n elements of A from H, which requires reheaping n times, is bounded as follows:

$$h(n) \leq n \log_2 n$$

Accordingly, the running time of Phase B of heapsort is also proportional to n $\log_2$ n.

Since each phase requires time proportional to n $\log_2$ n, the running time to sort the n-element array A using heapsort is proportional to n $\log_2$ n, that is, f(n) = O(n $\log_2$ n). Observe that this gives a worst-case complexity of the heapsort algorithm. This contrasts with the following two sorting algorithms already studied:

1. **Bubble sort:** The running time of bubble sort is $O(n^2)$.
2. **Quicksort:** The average running time of quicksort is O(n $\log_2$n), the same as heapsort, but the worst-case running time of quicksort is $O(n^2)$, the same as bubble sort.

Efficiency: O(nlog n)

Pros

- Guaranteed to be O(n.log n)
- One of the few non-recursive **O(nlog n) sorts.**
- Fairly easy to debug, because it is non-recursive and because it consists of two smaller and unrelated parts.

Cons

- Not as fast on average as Quick sort.
- Quite a lot of code to implement the heap operations.

Note: *This isn't an especially useful sort, but the running time is guaranteed O(n.log n) and it is very light on memory consumption. Also, if you have already implemented a heap for some other reason, then this sort comes almost for free.*

It is possible to get some extra speed by constructing the heap in one pass: put everything into the heap ignoring the heap condition, then work through the heap from bottom to top, bubbling elements down the heap where necessary. This makes the heap creation take linear time.

12.9 MERGE SORTING

Merging is the combination of two or more sorted sequences into a single sorted sequence. In a two-way merge, two sorted sequences are merged into one. Clearly, two sorted sequences each of length n can be merged into a sorted sequence of length 2n in O(2n)=O(n) steps. However in order to do this, we need space in which to store the result, i.e., it is not possible to merge the two sequences *in place* in O(n) steps.

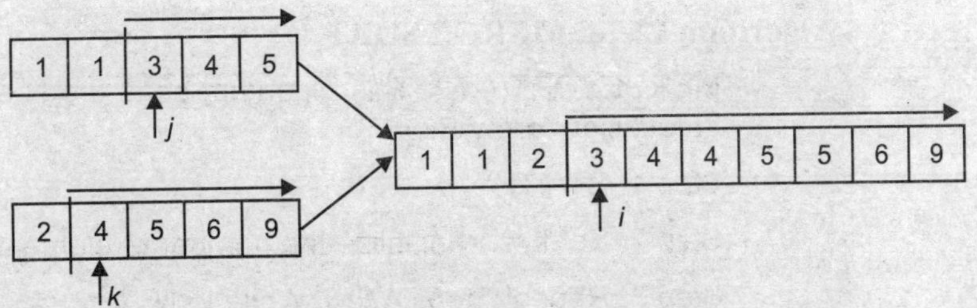

Figure 12.16: Two-Way Merging

Sorting by merging is a recursive, divide-and-conquer strategy. In the base case, we have a sequence with exactly one element in it. Since such a sequence is already sorted, there is nothing to be done. To sort a sequence of n>1 element:

1. Divide the sequence into two sequences of length[n/2] and[n/2];
2. Recursively sort each of the two subsequences; and then,
3. Merge the sorted subsequences to obtain the final result.

Example 12.13: Suppose the array a contain 14 elements as follows:

66,33,40,22,55,88,60,11,80,20,50,44,77,30

Each pass of the merge sort algorithm will start at the beginning of the array a and merge pairs of sorted subarray as follows:

Pass 1. Merge each pair of elements to obtain the following list of sorted pairs:

33, 66   22, 40   55, 88   11, 60   20, 80   44, 50   30, 70

Pass 2. Merge each pair of pairs to obtain the following list of sorted quadruplets:

22, 33, 40, 66   11, 55, 60, 88   20, 44, 50, 80   30, 70,

Pass 3. Merge each pair of sorted quardruplets to obtain the following two sorted subarrays:

11, 22, 33, 40, 55, 60, 66, 88   20, 30, 44, 50, 77, 80

Pass 4. Merge the two sorted subarrays to obtain the single sorted array

11 , 20 , 22 , 30 , 33 , 40 , 44 , 50 , 55 , 60 , 66 , 77 , 80 , 88

The original array A is now sorted.

Algorithm 12.14: MERGE SORT

MERGESORT(A,N): This algorithm sorts the N-element array A using an auxiliary array B.

Step 1: START

Step 2: Set L = 1 [Initialize the number of elements in the subarrays]

Step 3: Repeat Steps 4 to 7 While L<N

Step 4: Call MERGEPASS(A,N,L,B)

Step 5: Call MERGEPASS(B,N,2*L,A)

Step 6: Set L = 4*L

End of Step 3 of While loop

Step 7: End

Algorithm 12.15: MERGEPASS(A,N,L,B)

The N-element array A is composed of sorted subarrays where each subarray has L elements except possibly the last subarray, which may have fewer than L elements. The procedure merges the pairs of subarrays of A and assigns them to the array B.

Step 1: Set Q = INT(N/(2*L)), S = 2*L*Q and R = N-S

Step 2: [use procedure 2 to merge the Q pairs of subarrays]

Repeat For J=1, 2,………,Q:

a. Set LB =1+(2*J-2)*L. [Find lower bound of first array]

b. Call MERGE(A,L,LB,A,B,LB+L,B,LB) [End of for loop]

Step 3: [only one subarrays left]

If R ≤ L then

Repeat For J=1,2,…………., R

Set B(S+J) =A(S+J)

[End of the for loop]

Else

Call MERGE(A,L,S+1,A,R,L+S+1,B,S+1)

[End of if Structure]

Step 4: Return

Algorithm 12.16: MERGING(A,R,B,S,C)

Let A and B be sorted arrays with R and S elements, respectively. This algorithm merges A and B into an array C with N = R + S elements.

Step 1: Set NA = 1, NB = 1 and P = 1 [initialize]

Step 2: Repeat While NA ≤ R and NB ≤ S [Compare]

If (A[NA] < B[NB]) then

a. Set C[PTR] = A[NA] [Assign element from A to C]

b. Set P =P+1 and NA =NA+1 [Update Pointer P.]

Else

a. Set C[P] = B[NB] [Assign element from B to C]

b. Set P =P+1 and NB =NB+1 [Update Pointer]

End of if Structure

[End of While loop]

Step 3: [Assign remaining elements to C]

If (NA > R) then

Repeat For K=0,1,2,…………,S-NB

Set C[P+K] = B[NB+K]

[End of loop]

Else

Repeat For K=0, 1, 2,…………,R - NA:

Set C[P+K] = A[NA+K]

[End of loop]

[End of if Structure]

Step 4: End

Algorithm 12.17: MERGE(A, R, LBA, S, LBB, C, LBC)

This procedure merges the sorted arrays A and B into the arrays C.

Step 1: Set NA = LBA, NB = LBB, PTR = LBC, UBA = LBA + R – 1.

UBB = LBB + S – 1.

Step 2: Same as Algorithm 12.16 except R is replaced by UBA and S by UBB.

Step 3: Same as Algorithm 12.16 except R is replaced by UBA and S by UBB.

Step 4: Return.

Illustrates the operation of the two-way merge sort algorithm.

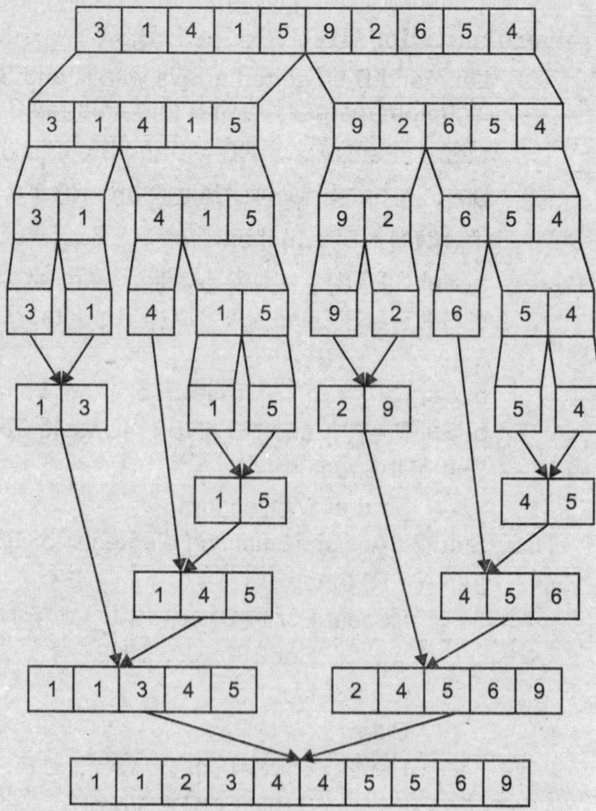

Figure 12.17: Two-Way Merge Sorting

Running Time Analysis

The running time of merge sort is determined by the running time of the recursive DoSort routine. (The main DoSort only adds a constant amount of overhead). The running time of the recursive DoSort routine is given by the following recurrence:

$$T(n) = \begin{cases} O(1) & n = 1, \\ T(\lfloor n/2 \rfloor) + T(\lceil n/2 \rceil) + O(n) & n > 1 \end{cases}$$

Where n = right – left + 1.

In order to simplify the solution of above Equation we shall assume that $n= 2^k$ for some integer k>=0. Dropping the O()s from the equation we get

$$T(n) = \begin{cases} 1 & n = 1, \\ 2T(n/2) + n & n > 1 \end{cases}$$

which is easily solved by repeated substitution:

$$
\begin{aligned}
T(n) &= 2T(n/2) + n \\
&= 4T(n/4) + 2n \\
&= 8T(n/8) + 3n \\
&\vdots \\
&= 8^kT(n/2^k) + kn \\
&\vdots \\
&= nT(1) + n\log_2 n \\
&= n + n\log_2 n
\end{aligned}
$$

Therefore, the running time of merge sort is O(n log n).

A Lower Bound on Sorting

The preceding sections present three O(n log n) sorting algorithms—quicksort, heapsort, and the two-way merge sort. But is O(n log n) the best we can do? In this section we answer the question by showing that any sorting algorithm that sorts using only binary comparisons must make O(n log n) such comparisons. If each binary comparison takes a constant amount of time, then running time for any such sorting algorithm is also O(n log n).

Consider the problem of sorting the sequence S = {a, b, c} comprised of three distinct items. i.e., $a \neq b \wedge a \neq c \wedge b \neq c$. illustrates a possible sorting algorithm in the form of a *decision tree* . Each node of the decision tree represents one binary comparison. I.e., in each node of the tree, exactly two elements of the sequence are compared. Since there are exactly two possible outcomes for each comparison, each non-leaf node of the binary tree has degree two.

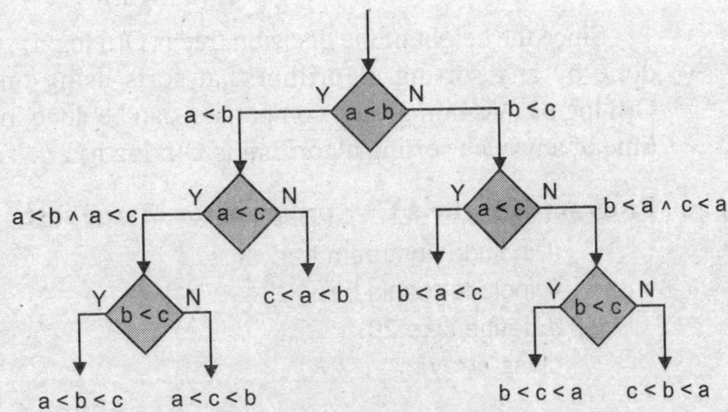

Figure 12.18: A Decision Tree for Comparison Sorting

For example, suppose that a<b<c. Consider how the algorithm shown in Figure ▒ discovers this. The first comparison compares a and b which reveals that a<b. The second comparison compares a and c to find that a<c. At this point it has

been determined that a<b and a<c the relative order of b and c is not yet known. Therefore, one more comparison is required to determine that b<c. Notice that the algorithm shown in Figure 12.18 works correctly in all cases because every possible permutation of the sequence S appears as a leaf node in the decision tree. Furthermore, the number of comparisons required in the worst case is equal to the height of the decision tree!

Any sorting algorithm that uses only binary comparisons can be represented by a binary decision tree. Furthermore, it is the height of the binary decision tree that determines the worst-case running time of the algorithm. In general, the size and shape of the decision tree is a function of the sorting algorithm and the number of items to be sorted.

Given an input sequence of n items to be sorted, every binary decision tree that correctly sorts the input sequence must have *at least* n! leaves—one for each permutation of the input. Therefore, it follows directly from Theorem that the height of the binary decision tree is *at least* $\log_2$ n!.

$$\lceil \log_2 n! \rceil \geq \log_2 n!$$

$$\geq \sum_{i=1}^{n} \log_2 i$$

$$\geq \sum_{i=1}^{n/2} \log_2 n/2$$

$$\geq n/2 \log_2 n/2$$

$$= \Omega(n \log n)$$

Since the height of the decision tree is O(n log n) , the number of comparisons done by any sorting algorithm that sorts using only binary comparisons is O(n log n). Assuming each comparison can be done in constant time, the running time of any such sorting algorithm is O(n log n).

Program 5: Write a C++ program for Merge sort.

```
# include<iostream.h>
# include<conio.h>
# define size 20
class array
{
private:
float a[size];
int i, low, high, pivot_value, temp;
public:
```

```
void read (float *,int);
void display (float *,int);
void merge_sort (float *,int, int, int);
void merge_pass(float *,int ,int);
};
void array : : read (float a[], int n)
{
for (i=0;i<n;i++)
cin>>a[i];
}
void array : : display (float a[], int n)
{
for (i=0;i<n;i++)
cout<<a[i]<<" ";
}
void array : : merge_sort (float arr[], int top, int s, int bot)
{
float temparr [size];
int first, second, third;
first=top;
second=s+1;
third=top;
while ((first<=s) && (second<=bot))
{
if (arr [first]<=arr[second])
{
temparr [third]=arr [first];
first++;
}
else
{
temparr [third]=arr[second];
second++;
}
third++;
}
if (first<=s)
{
for (first=first;first<s;first++)
{
tempar [third]=arr[first];
```

```
third++;
}
}
else
{
for (second=second;second<=bot;second++)
{
temparr[third]=arr[second];
third++;
}
}
// copy the elements from temparr[] to arr[]
for (int i=top;i<=bot;i++)
arr[i]=temparr[i];
}
void array ::merge_pass (float app[], int m, int n)
{
if (n !=m)
{
int middle=(m+n) / 2;
merge_pass (app, m, middle);
merge_pass(app, middle+1, n);
merge_sort (app, m,middle,n); // invoke function merge_sort( )
}
}
void main ( )
{
array obj;
float a[size];
int n;
clrscr ( );
cout<<"read no of elements<="<<size<<"\n";
cin>>n;
cout<<"\nread "<<n<<" elements \n\n;
obj.read (a, n);
cout<<"\ngiven array is \n\n";
obj.display (a, n);
obj.merge_pass(a,0,n-1);
cout<<"\n\n Sorted array is\n\n";
obj.display(a,n))
getch ( );
```

```
}
Output:
read no elements<=20
6
read 6 elements
13    5    7    10    26    19
given array is
13    5    7    10    26    19
Sorted array is
5    7    10    13    19    26
```

12.10 BUCKET SORT

Bucket sort is possibly the simplest distribution sorting algorithm. The essential requirement is that the size of the universe from which the elements to be sorted are drawn is a small, fixed constant, say m.

Example 12.14: Suppose that we are sorting elements drawn from {0, 1,…….., m-1}, i.e., the set of integers in the interval [0,m-1]. Bucket sort uses m counters. The ith counter keeps track of the number of occurrences of the ith element of the universe. Figure 12.19 illustrates how this is done.

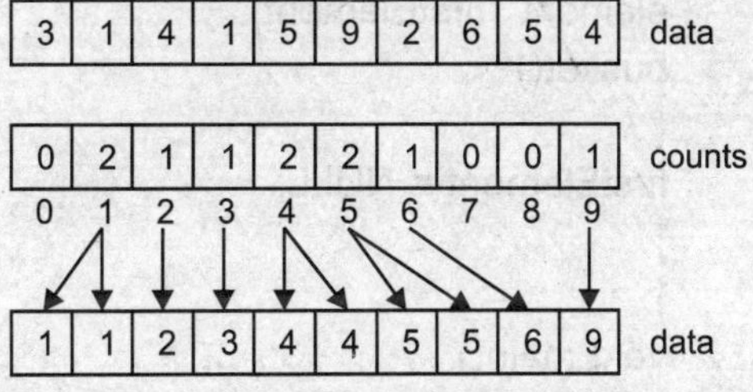

Figure 12.19: Bucket Sorting

In Figure 12.19, the universal set is assumed to be{0,1,……, 9}. Therefore, ten counters are required—one to keep track of the number of zeroes, one to keep track of the number of ones, and so on. A single pass through the data suffices to count all of the elements. Once the counts have been determined, the sorted sequence is easily obtained. E.g., the sorted sequence contains no zeroes, two ones, one two, and so on.

Thus, the running time of the bucket sort routine is O(m+n). Note that if m=O(n), the running time for bucket sort is O(n). i.e., the bucket sort algorithm is a *linear-time* sorting algorithm! Bucket sort breaks the O(n log n) bound associated with sorting algorithms that use binary comparisons because bucket sort does not do any binary comparisons. The cost associated with breaking the O(n log n) running time bound is the O(m) space required for the array of counters. Consequently, bucket sort is practical only for small m. E.g., to sort 16-bit integers using bucket sort requires the use of an array of $2^{16} = 65536$ counters.

Program 6: Write a C++ program for bucket sort.

```
#include <iostream.h>
#include<conio.h>
class element        //element
{
public:
int value;
element *next;
element()
{
value=NULL;
next=NULL;
}
};
class bucket         //bucket containing a perticular range of values
{
public:
element *firstElement;
bucket()
{
firstElement = NULL;
}
};
void main()
{
int lowend=0;        // minimum element
int highend=100;     //max element
int interval=10;     //number of intervals
const int noBuckets=(highend-lowend)/interval; //number of buckets
required
bucket *buckets=new bucket[noBuckets];
bucket *temp;
for(int a=0;a<noBuckets;a++)   //creation of required buckets
{
temp=new bucket;
buckets[a]=*temp;
}
```

```
cout<<"--------The Elements to be Sorted using Bucket sort are ------------
------\n";
int array[]={12,2,22,33,44,55,66,77,85,87,81,83,89,82,88,86,84,88,99};
for(int j=0;j<19;j++)   //sending elments into appropriate buckets
{
cout<<array[j]<<endl;
element *temp,*pre;
temp=buckets[array[j]/interval].firstElement;
if(temp==NULL)//if it is the first element of the bucket
{
temp=new element;
buckets[array[j]/interval].firstElement=temp;
temp->value=array[j];
}
else
{
pre=NULL;
while(temp!=NULL)     //move till the appropriate position in the bucket
{
if(temp->value>array[j])
break;
pre=temp;
temp=temp->next;
}
if(temp->value>array[j]) //if the new value is in betwen or at the begining
{
if(pre==NULL)  //insertion at first if the bucket has elements already
{
element *firstNode;
firstNode=new element();
firstNode->value=array[j];
firstNode->next=temp;
buckets[array[j]/interval].firstElement=firstNode;
}
else  //insertion at middle
{
element *firstNode;
firstNode=new element();
firstNode->value=array[j];
firstNode->next=temp;
pre->next=firstNode;
```

```
}
}
else// if the new value is to be created at last of bucket
{
temp=new element;
pre->next=temp;
temp->value=array[j];
}
}
}
cout<<"------------------------The Sorted Elements Are---------------\n";
for(int jk=0;jk<10;jk++)
{
element *temp;
temp= buckets[jk].firstElement;
while(temp!=NULL)
{
cout<<"*"<<temp->value<<endl;
temp=temp->next;
}
}
cout<<"--------------------------------END--------------------------------\n";
getch();
}
```

12.11 RADIX SORT

This section presents a sorting algorithm known as *least-significant-digit-first radix sorting*. Radix sorting is based on the bucket sorting algorithm discussed in the preceding section. However, radix sorting is practical for much larger universal sets than it is practical to handle with a bucket sort.

Radix sorting can be used when each element of the universal set can be viewed as a sequences of digits (or letters or any other symbols). For example, we can represent each integer between 0 and 99 as a sequence of two, decimal digits. (E.g., the number five is represented as “05”). To sort an array of two-digit numbers, the algorithm makes two sorting passes through the array. In the first pass, the elements of the array are sorted by the *least significant* decimal digit. In the second pass, the elements of the array are sorted by the *most significant* decimal digit. The key characteristic of the radix sort is that the second pass is done in such a way that it does not destroy the effect of the first pass. Consequently, after two passes through the array, the data is contained therein is sorted. Each pass of the radix sort is implemented as a bucket sort. In the example we base the sort on *decimal* digits. Therefore, this is called a *radix-10* sort and ten buckets are required to do each sorting pass.

Figure 12.20 illustrates the operation of the radix-10 sort. The first radix sorting pass considers the least significant digits. As in the bucket sort, a single pass is made through the unsorted data, counting the number of times each decimal digit appears as the least-significant digit. E.g., there are no elements that have a 0 as the least-significant digit; there are two elements that have a 1 as the least-significant digit; and so on.

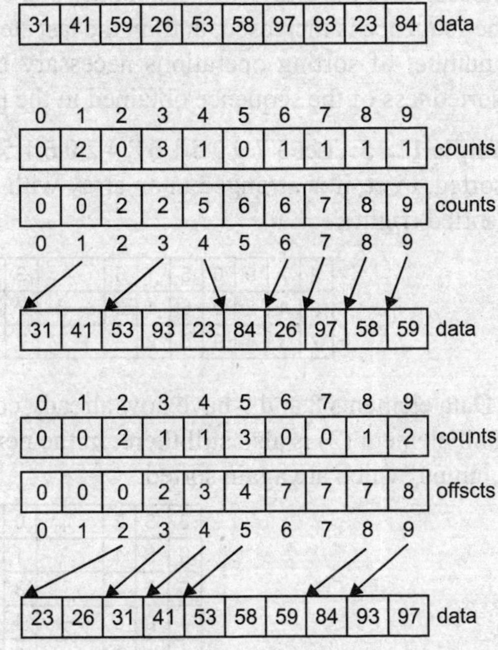

Figure 12.20: Radix Sorting

12.12 SHELL SORT

Shell sort developed by Donald L. Shell is a non-stable in-place sort. Shell sort improves on the efficiency of insertion sort by quickly shifting values to their destination. Average sort time is $O(n^{7/6})$ while worst-case time is $O(n^{4/3})$.

Shell sort is a sorting algorithm that is a generalization of insertion sort, with two observations:

- insertion sort is efficient if the input is "almost sorted", and
- insertion sort is typically inefficient because it moves values just one position at a time.

Shellsort is one of the oldest sorting algorithms, named after its inventor D.L. Shell (1959). It is fast, easy to understand and easy to implement. However, its complexity analysis is a little more sophisticated.

The idea of shellsort is the following:

(a) arrange the data sequence in a two-dimensional array

(b) sort the columns of the array

The effect is that the data sequence is partially sorted. The process above is repeated, but each time with a narrower array, i.e. with a smaller number of columns. In the last step, the array consists of only one column. In each step, the sortedness of the sequence is increased, until in the last step it is completely sorted. However, the number of sorting operations necessary in each step is limited, due to the presortedness of the sequence obtained in the preceding steps.

Example 12.15: Let 3 7 9 0 5 1 6 8 4 2 0 6 1 5 7 3 4 9 8 2 be the data sequence to be sorted. First, it is arranged in an array with 7 columns (left), then the columns are sorted (right):

3	7	9	0	5	1	6		3	3	4	0	5	1	5
8	4	2	0	6	1	6	→	7	4	4	0	5	1	5
7	3	4	9	8	2			7	7	9	9	8	2	

Data elements 8 and 9 have now already come to the end of the sequence, but a small element (2) is also still there. In the next step, the sequence is arranged in 3 columns, which are again sorted:

3	3	2		0	0	1
0	5	1		1	2	2
5	7	4		3	3	4
4	0	6	→	4	5	6
1	6	8		5	6	8
7	9	9		7	7	9
8	2			8	9	

Now the sequence is almost completely sorted. When arranging it in one column in the last step, it is only a 6, an 8 and a 9 that have to move a little bit to their correct position.

12.12.1 Implementation

Actually, the data sequence is not arranged in a two-dimensional array, but held in a one-dimensional array that is indexed appropriately. For instance, data elements at positions 0, 5, 10, 15 etc. would form the first column of an array with 5 columns. The "columns" obtained by indexing in this way are sorted with Insertion Sort, since this method has a good performance with presorted sequences.

The following program sorts an array *a* from index position 0 through *n*-1. The number of columns used for arranging data in each step is in array *cols*. Thus, data are arranged in 1391376 columns in the first step and in one column in the last step. (Note that essentially nothing is done if the number of columns *h* is larger than the number of data elements *n*.) Each column is sorted by Insertion Sort. First, data of the second row (beginning at $i = h$) are sorted to the correct position in their column, then data of the third row (when *i* reaches value 2*h*) etc.

Example 12.16: In Figure 12.21(a) we have an example of sorting by insertion. First we extract 1 shift 3 and 5 down one slot and then insert the 1 for a count of 2 shifts. In the next frame two shifts are required before we can insert the 2. The process continues until the last frame where a total of $2 + 2 + 1 = 5$ shifts have been made.

In Figure 12.21(b) an example of shell sort is illustrated. We begin by doing an insertion sort using a spacing of two. In the first frame we examine numbers 3-1. Extracting 1 we shift 3 down one slot for a shift count of 1. Next we examine numbers 5-2. We extract 2 shift 5 down and then insert 2. After sorting with a spacing of two a final pass is made with a spacing of one. This is simply the traditional insertion sort. The total shift count using shell sort is 1+1+1 = 3. By using an initial spacing larger than one we were able to quickly shift values to their proper destination.

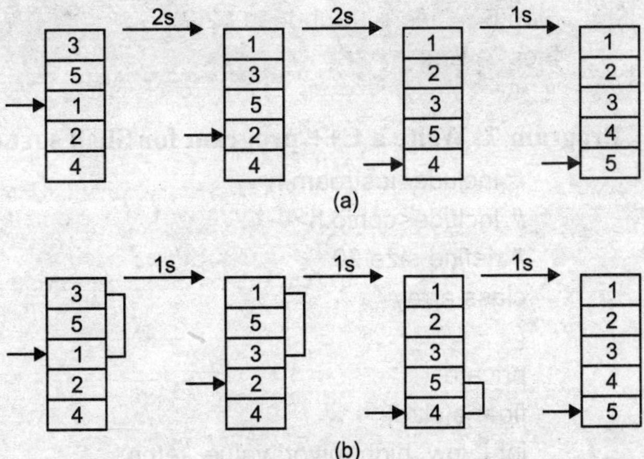

Figure 12.21: Shell Sort

Various spacings may be used to implement a shell sort. Typically the array is sorted with a large spacing the spacing reduced and the array sorted again. On the final sort spacing is one. Although the shell sort is easy to comprehend formal analysis is difficult. In particular optimal spacing values elude theoreticians. Knuth recommends a technique due to Sedgewick that determines spacing h based on the following formulas:

$h_s = 9 \cdot 2^s - 9 \cdot 2^{s/2} + 1$ if s is even

$h_s = 8 \cdot 2^s - 6 \cdot 2^{(s+1)/2} + 1$ if s is odd

These calculations result in values (h_0 h_1 h_2 ...) = (1 5 19 41 109 209 ...). Calculate h until $3h_t >= N$ the number of elements in the array. Then choose h_{t-1} for a starting value. For example to sort 150 items $h_t = 109$ ($3 \cdot 109 >= 150$) so the first spacing is h_{t-1} or 41. The second spacing is 19 then 5 and finally 1. The increment sequence used in this example code gives an $O(n^2)$ worst-case running time.

Algorithm 12.18: SHELL SORT

Step 1: input: an array a of length n with array elements numbered 0 to n – 1

Step 2: inc ← round(n/2)

Step 3: while inc > 0 do:

Step 4: for i = inc . n – 1 do:

TEMP ← a[i]

j ← i

Step 5. while j ≥ inc and a[j – inc] > TEMP do:

a[j] ← a[j – inc]

j ← j – inc

a[j] ← TEMP

Step 6: inc ← round(inc / 2.2)

Step 7: End.

Program 7: Write a C++ program for Shell sort.(ascending order)

```
# include<iostream.h>
# include<conio.h>
# define size 20
class array
{
private:
float a[size];
int i, low, high, pivot_value, temp;
public:
void read (float *,int);
void display (float *,int);
void shell_sort (float *,int beq, int end);
};
void array : : read (float a[], int n)
{
```

```
for (i=0;i<n;i++)
cin>>a[i];
}
void array : : display (float a[], int n)
{
for (i=0;i<n;i++)
cout<<a[i]<<" ";
}
void array : : shell_sort (float arr [], int n)
{
float temp;
int pass=0;
increment=1;
// choose sequence of increments
while (increment<=n)
increment = increment*3 + 1;
do
{
pass++;
increment /= 3;
cout<<"Iteration "<<pass<<" :\n;
do
{
exchngs=0;
for (i=0;i<n-increment;i++)
{
if(arr[i] >arr[i+increment] )
{
exchngs++; // increment no of exchanges
// swapping
temp = arr[i];
arr[i] = arr[i+increment);
arr[i+increment] = temp;
}
}
for (int j=0;j<n;j++)
cout<<arr[j]<<" ";
cout<<"exchngs= "<<exchngs<<"\n";
} while (exchngs);
```

```
} while (increment !=1);
}
void main ( )
{
array obj;
float a[size];
int n;
clrscr ( );
cout<<"read no of elements<="<<size<<"\n";
cin>>n;
cout<<"\nread "<<n<<" elements \n\n;
obj.read (a, n);
cout<<"\ngiven array is \n\n";
obj.display (a, n);
obj.shell_sort(a,n);
cout<<"\n\n Sorted array is\n\n";
obj.display(a,n))
getch ( );
}
```

Output:

```
read no elements<=20
6
read 6 elements
23    95    47    60    36    59
given array is
23    95    47    60    36    59
Trace of shell sort
Iteration 1:
23 59 47 60 36 95 exchngs=1
23 59 47 60 36 95 exchngs=0
Iteration 2:
23 47 59 36 60 95 exchngs=2
23 47 59 36 60 95 exchngs=1
23 36 47 59 60 95 exchngs=1
23 36 47 59 60 95 exchngs=0

Sorted array is
23    36    47    59    60    95
```

12.13 COMPARISON OF SORTING ALGORITHMS

The following chart compares sorting algorithms on the various criteria outlined above; the algorithms with higher constant terms appear first. Complexities below are in terms of n, the number of items to be sorted, k, the size of each key, and s, the chunk size used by the implementation. Many of them are based on the assumption that the key size is large enough that all entries have unique key values, and hence that $n << 2^k$, where << means "much less than."

Sort	Time Average	Best	Worst	Space	Stability	Remarks
Bubble Sort	$O(n^2)$	$O(n^2)$	$O(n^2)$	Constant	Stable	Always use a modified bubble sort
Selection Sort	$O(n^2)$	$O(n^2)$	$O(n^2)$	Constant	Stable	Even a perfectly sorted input requires scanning the entire array
Insertion Sort	$O(n^2)$	O(n)	$O(n^2)$	Constant	Stable	In the best case (already sorted), every insert requires constant time
Heap Sort	O(n*log(n))	O(n*log(n))	O(n*log(n))	Constant	Instable	By using input array as storage for the heap, it is possible to achieve constant space
Merge Sort	O(n*log(n))	O(n*log(n))	O(n*log(n))	Depends	Stable	On arrays, merge sort requires O(n) space; on linked lists, merge sort requires constant space
Quick Sort	O(n*log(n))	O(n*log(n))	$O(n^2)$	Constant	Stable	Randomly picking a pivot value (or shuffling the array prior to sorting) can help avoid worst case scenarios such as a perfectly sorted array.

Sort	Time Average	Best	Worst	Space	Stability	Remarks
Radix sort	O(n. k/s)	—	O(n. k/s)	O(n)	Stable	Assumes uniform distribution of elements from the domain in the array.
Bucket sort	O(n.k)	$O(n^2 .k)$	—	O(n.k)	Stable	Assumes uniform distribution of elements from the domain in the array.
Shell sort	—	$O(n \log^2 n)$	—	Constant	Instable	This sorting is generalization of insertion sort.

12.14 SEARCHING

Searching is a process of finding a given element in an array. Suppose LIST is collection of data maintained in memory by a table using some type of data structure. Searching is the operation which finds the location in memory of some given element of information or sends some message that element does not belong to LIST.

The search is said to be successful or unsuccessful according to whether the given element does or does not belong to LIST .The searching algorithm that is used depends mainly on the type of data structure that is used to maintain LIST in memory.

There are two frequently used methods of searching:

1. LINEAR SEARCH
2. BINARY SEARCH

12.14.1 Linear Search

If the elements in the array are unordered then linear search is performed comparing the given element against each element in the array in turn until match is found or the array comes to end and given element is not found.

Suppose LA is a linear array with n elements. In this searching method to search for a given ITEM in LA is to compare ITEM with each element of LA one by one. That is, first we test whether LA[1]= ITEM, and then we test whether LA[2]= ITEM, and so on. This method, which traverses LIST sequentially to locate ITEM, is called linear search.

In this searching algorithm, we first assign ITEM to LA[N+1], the position following the last element of LA. Then the outcome LOC = N+1

Where LOC denotes the position where ITEM first occurs in LA, signifies the search is unsuccessful. The purpose of this initial assignment is to avoid repeatedly testing whether or not we have reached the end of the array LA.

Algorithm 12.19: Linear Search

```
LINEAR (LA, N, ITEM, LOC)
Taking LA is a linear array with N elements, and ITEM is a given item of
information. This algorithm find the location LOC of ITEM in LA, or set
LOC = 0 if the search is unsuccessful.
Step 1: [Insert ITEM at the end of LA.] Set LA [N + 1] = ITEM.
Step 2: [Initialize the value of LOC.] Set LOC = 1.
Step 3: [Search for ITEM.]
   Repeat steps while LA [LOC] ≠ ITEM
      Set LOC = LOC + 1
   [End of while loop.]
Step 4: [Successful or Unsuccessful?] if LOC = N + 1, then Set LOC = 0.
Step 5: End.
```

Evaluation of Linear Search

The linear search is quite handy and efficient for short lists. It will be time consuming for a long lists.

If the given element is the first in the array, the number of comparisons will be 1. If the given element is last in the array, the number of comparisons will be n. This will cover best-case performance and worst-case performance.

Therefore, the average number of comparisons in linear search is:

$$\frac{1+2+3+...+n}{n} = \frac{n(n+1)}{2*n} = \frac{(n+1)}{2}$$

Thus the number of comparisons in the linear search will be O(n).

In case of sorted data, search will come to end as soon as value of the sorted data exceeds the value of element being searches.

In case of sorted data, assuming that values of data is uniformly distributed over the entire range of data, the number of comparisons will come down to n/2 on an average. In certain cases it may be preferable to sort the data before searching. The number of comparisons can also be reduced if most frequently accessed elements are placed in the beginning of the list.

Program 8: Write a C++ program for Linear Search.

```
# include<iostream.h>
# include<conio.h>
#define size 20
```

```
class array
{
private:
int i;
float a[size];
public:
void read (int);
void display (int);
int linear_search (int, float); // for searching of element
};
void array :: read (int n)
{
for (i=0;i<n;i++)
cin>>a[i];
}
void array : : display(int n)
{
for (i=0;i<n;i++)
cout<<a[i]<<" ";
}
int array : : linear_search (int n, float data)
{
// searching
i=0;
while (i<n)
{
if (a[i]= =data)
{
return (i);
}
else
i++;
}
return (-1);
}
void main ( )
{
array obj;
int n, position;
float data;
```

```
clrscr ( );
cout<<"read no of elements<="<<size<<"\n";
cin>>n;
cout<<"\nRead the element to be searched: ";
cin>>data;
cout<<"\ngiven array is \n\n";
obj.display (n);
cout<<"\n\nElement to be searched is "<<data;
// searching
position=obj.linear_search(n, data);
if (position= = -1)
cout<<"\n\nSearch is unsuccessful";
else
{
cout<<"\n\nSearch is successful \n\n";
cout<<data<<" found at position "<<position+1;
}
getch ( );
}
Output:
read no of elements<=20
8
read 8 elements
12    5    13    15    17    43    61    24
Read the element to be searched: 15
Given array is
12    5    13    15    17    43    61    24
Element to be searched is 15
Search is successful
15 found at position 4

read no of elements<=20
5
read 5 elements
14    17    14    13    38
Read the element to be searched: 15
Given array is
14    17    14    13    38
Element to be searched is 15
Search is unsuccessful
```

12.14.2 Binary Search

Binary search is a method by using which searching is fast in comparison to linear search but the main drawback of binary search is before binary search sorting is necessary.

In binary search the array list is divided into two equal parts (approximately). Suppose the elements of array list are in ascending order then if desired element is less than the middle element of array list, it will never be present in the second half of the array. Similarly if the desired element is greater than the middle element of array, it will never be present in the first half of the array list.

Thus we can focus our attention on one half of the array list. The process is repeated and in the next stage we have to search for the element only is one quarter of the array list. This process reduces the search length and search time.

There is an extremely efficient searching algorithm, called binary search, which can be used to find the location LOC of a given ITEM of information in LA.

The binary search algorithm applied to our array LA woks as follows. During each stage of algorithm, our search for ITEM is reduced to a segment of elements of LA:

LA[BEG], LA[BEG + 1], LA[BEG+2] , ...,LA[END].

Note that the variables BEG and END denote beginning and end locations of the segment. The algorithm compares ITEM with the middle element LA[MIDLOC] of the segment, where MIDLOC by

MIDLOC = INT ((BEGIN + END)/2)

If LA[MIDLOC] = ITEM, then the search is successful and set LOC = MIDLOC. Otherwise a new segment of LA is as follows:

(a) If ITEM < LA [MID], then ITEM is in left half of the segment:

LA[BEG], LA[BEG + 1], LA[BEG+2] , ...,LA[MID - 1].

Set END = MIDLOC – 1 and begin searching again.

(b) If ITEM > LA [MID], then ITEM is in right half of the segment:

LA[MID + 1], LA[MID +2], LA[BEG+3] , ...,LA[END].

Set BEGIN = MIDLOC + 1 and begin searching again.

We start with the entire array LA i.e. BEG =1 and END = n, or, more generally, with BEG = LB and END =UB.

If ITEM is not present in LA, then WE obtain

END < BEG

This condition signals that the search is unsuccessful and such a case we assign LOC = NULL. Here NULL means that item is not present in array LA.

Algorithm 12.20: Binary Search

BINARYSEARCH (LA, LB, UB, ITEM, LOC)

Taking LA is a sorted array with lower bound LB and upper bound UB, and ITEM is a given item of information. The variables BEGIN, END and MIDLOC denote as beginning, ending and middle locations of elements of LA. This algorithm find the location LOC of ITEM in LA or if LOC not found set LOC = NULL.

Step 1: [Initialize starting variables.]

Set BEGIN = LB, END = UB and MIDLOC = INT ((BEGIN + END)/2).

Step 2: Repeat steps 3 and 4 while BEGIN ≤ END and LA [MIDLOC] ≠ ITEM.

Step 3: If ITEM < LA [MID], then

    Set END = MIDLOC – 1.

    Else

    Set BEGIN = MIDLOC + 1.

    [End of If statement.]

Step 4: Set MIDLOC = INT ((BEGIN + END)/2).

  [End of Step 2 loop.]

Step 5: If LA [MIDLOC] = ITEM, then:

Set LOC = MIDLOC.

else

    Set LOC = NULL.

  [End of If statement.]

Step 6: End. Explanation

Example 12.17

3	6	8	9	12
0	1	2	3	4

Suppose we want to search 9, then in first pass: MIDLOC = INT ((BEGIN + END)/2).

MIDLOC = (0+4)/2 = 2

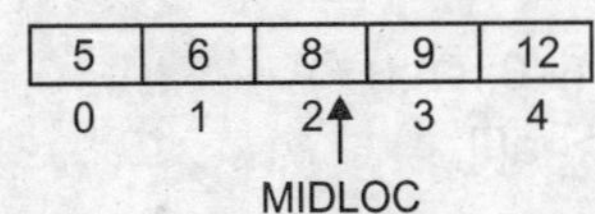

9 is greater than the middle element, then BEGIN = MIDLOC + 1. process is repeated in second half

MIDLOC = (3+4)/2 = 3

5	6	8	9	12
0	1	2	3	4

MIDLOC (↑ at 3)

If LA [MIDLOC] = ITEM means LA[3] = 9

LOC = MIDLOC LOC = 3

Now the position is found that is LOC = 3.

Evaluation Of Binary Search

Binary search takes maximum ($\log_2$ n)+1 comparisons as compared to (n+1)/2 taken for a linear search. Even in the worst case binary search will take $\log_2 n$ running time. For a million items, it will take only 20 comparisons. Binary search is definitely an improvement over the linear search. It takes far less time as compared to the linear search. On the negative side data has to be sorted and access to middle of the time has to be maintained. Sorting becomes more costly in cases of large number of insertions and deletions.

Program 9: Write a C++ program for Binary Search.

```
# include<iostream.h>
# include<conio.h>
#define size 20
class array
{
private:
int i;
float a[size];
public:
void read (int);
void display (int);
int linear_search (int, float); // for searching of element
};
void array :: read (int n)
{
for (i=0;i<n;i++)
cin>>a[i];
}
void array : : display(int n)
{
for (i=o;i<n;i++)
cout<<a[i]<<"\t ";
```

```
}
int array : : binary_search (int n, float data)
{
int low, high, mid;
// searching
low=0;
high=n-1;
while(low<=high)
{
mid= (low+high) /2;
if (a[mid]= = data) // when element has been found
return (mid+1);
else
{
if (data>a [mid])
low= mid+1;
else high= mid-1;
}
}// while loop ends here
return (-1); // when element is not in array
}
void main ( )
{
array obj; //object created
int n, position;
float data;
clrscr ( );
cout<<"read no of elements<="<<size<<"\n";
cin>>n;
cout<<"\nRead the element to be searched: ";
cin>>data;
cout<<"\ngiven array is \n\n";
obj.display (n);
cout<<"\n\nElement to be searched is "<<data;
position=obj.binary_search(n, data);
if (position= = -1)
cout<<"\n\nSearch is unsuccessful";
else
{
```

```
cout<<"\n\nSearch is successful \n\n";
cout<<data<<" found at position "<<position;
}
getch ( );
}
```

Output:

```
read no of elements<=20
8
read 8 elements
12      5       13      15      17      43      61      24
Read the element to be searched: 15
Given array is
12      5       13      15      17      43      61      24
Element to be searched is 15
Search is successful
15 found at position 4

read no of elements<=20
5
read 5 elements
14      17      14      13      38
Read the element to be searched: 15
Given array is
14      17      14      13      38
Element to be searched is 15
Search is unsuccessful
```

12.15 IS BINARY SEARCH EFFICIENT THAN LINEAR SEARCH?

12.15.1 Efficiency of Linear Search

Having implemented the linear search algorithm, how would you measure its efficiency? A useful measure (or *metric*) would be general, applicable to any (search) algorithm. Since a more efficient algorithm would take less time to execute, one approach would be to write a program for each of the algorithms to be compared, and execute them, measuring the time each takes to finish. However, a better metric would allow algorithms to be evaluated before implementing them.

One such metric is the number of main steps the algorithm will require to finish. Of course, the exact number of steps depends on the input data. For the linear search algorithm, the number of steps depends on whether the target is in the list, and if so, where in the list, as well as on the length of the list. For search algorithms, the main steps are the comparisons of list values with the target value. Counting these for data models representing the **best case**, the **worst case**, and the **average case** produces the following table. For each case, the number of steps is expressed in terms of n, the number of items in the list.

Model	Number of Comparisons (for n = 100000)	Comparisons as a function of n
Best Case (fewest comparisons)	1 (target is first item)	1
Worst Case (most comparisons)	100000 (target is last item)	n
Average Case (average number of comparisons)	50000 (target is middle item)	n/2

The best case analysis doesn't tell us much. If the first element checked happens to be the target, *any* algorithm will take only one comparison. The worst and average case analyses give a better indication of algorithm efficiency.

Notice that if the list grows in size, the number of comparisons required to find a target item in both worst and average cases grows *linearly*. In general, for a list of length n, the worst case is n comparisons. The algorithm is called **linear search** because its complexity/efficiency can be expressed as a linear function: the number of comparisons to find a target increases linearly as the size of the list.

12.15.2 Efficiency of Binary Search

Is binary search more efficient than linear search? If so, how much more efficient is it? To evaluate binary search, count the number of comparisons in the best case and worst case. This analysis omits the average case, which is a bit more difficult, and ignores any differences between algorithms in the amount of computation corresponding to each comparison.

The best case occurs if the middle item happens to be the target. Then only one comparison is needed to find it. As before, the best case analysis does not reveal much.

When does the worst case occur? If the target is not in the array then the process of dividing the list in half continues until there is only one item left to check. Here is the pattern of the number of comparisons after each division, given the simplifying assumptions of an initial array length that's an even power of 2 (1024) and exact division in half on each iteration:

Items Left to Search	Comparisons So Far
1024	0
512	1
256	2
128	3
64	4
32	5
16	6
8	7
4	8
2	9
1	10

For a list size of 1024, there are 10 comparisons to reach a list of size one, given that there is one comparison for each division, and each division splits the list size in half. In general, if n is the size of the list to be searched and C is the number of comparisons to do so in the worst case, $\mathbf{C = \log_2 n}$. Thus, the efficiency of binary search can be expressed as a logarithmic function, in which the number of comparisons required to find a target increases only logarithmically with the size of the list. The following table summarizes the analysis for binary search.

Model	Number of Comparisons (for n = 100000)	Comparisons as a function of n
Best Case (fewest comparisons)	1(target is middle item)	1
Worst Case (most comparisons)	16(target not in array)	$\log_2 n$

12.15.3 Efficiency Comparison

Note that the worst-case number of comparisons is just 16 with 100,000 items, versus 100,000 for linear search! Furthermore, if the array were doubled in size to 200,000, the maximum number of comparisons for binary search would only increase by 1 to 17, whereas for linear search it would double from 100,000 to 200,000.

The following table shows how the maximum number of comparisons increases for binary search and linear search.

Array Size	Worst Case Comparisons	
	Linear Search	Binary Search
100,000	100,000	16
200,000	200,000	17
400,000	400,000	18
800,000	800,000	19
1,600,000	1,600,000	20

Remember following in case of Searching Algorithms

1. A common operation on arrays of records is to search the list to retrieve a particular record.
2. There are alternative algorithms for searching an array. The number of comparisons required is a useful metric for their efficiency.
3. Linear search examines each list item in turn until the target is located or the end of the list is reached.
4. Linear search efficiency for the worst case data model is a linear function of the number of items in the list.
5. If the list is sorted, a binary search strategy may be used.
6. Binary search uses the result of each comparison to eliminate half of the list from further searching.
7. Binary search efficiency for the worst case is a logarithmic function of list size.

OBJECTIVE TYPE QUESTIONS

1. Sorting is a
   (a) Linear data structure (b) Non-linear data structure
   (c) Data structure operation (d) None
2. Which of the following is the sorting method?
   (a) Bubble (b) Heap
   (c) Insertion (d) All of the above
3. Which of the following is not the sorting method?
   (a) Bubble (b) Heap
   (c) Deletion (d) All of the above
4. Sorting operation can be implemented by using
   (a) Array (b) Stack
   (c) Pointer (d) Linked list
   (e) None
5. Which of the following is the type of Sorting?
   (a) City names (b) Heap of books
   (c) Marks list (d) All of the above
6. Which of the following is the operation of Fastest?
   (a) Bubble (b) Heap
   (c) Insertion (d) Selection

7. Which of the following is the operation of Slowest?
   (a) Bubble (b) Heap
   (c) Insertion (d) Selection
8. Which of the following is not the operation of has more phase of sorting?
   (a) Bubble (b) Heap
   (c) Insertion (d) Selection
9. Which of the following is the utility of Sorting?
   (a) Arrangement of flower(b) Arrangement of data
   (c) Concatenation of data (d) All of the above
   (e) None of the above
10. Which sorting method starts with minimum value?
    (a) Bubble (b) Heap
    (c) Insertion (d) Selection
11. The process of arranging records in ordered manner is called
    (a) sorting (b) searching
    (c) indexing (d) None of the above
12. In insertion sort, the shifting of numbers are:
    (a) shift greater number at end and smaller at beginning of the array
    (b) shift greater number at the middle and smaller at right
    (c) shift smaller at the center and greater at beginning
    (d) None of the above
13. In this type of sort list is divided in two sub-lists:
    (a) quick sort (b) exchange sort
    (c) merge sort (d) None of the above
14. The exchange sort is also called:
    (a) bubble sort (b) merge sort
    (c) shell sort (d) None of the above
15. In the bubble sort the sorting is done with comparing
    (a) successive elements (b) first and last elements
    (c) last and middle elements (d) None of the above
16. In tree sort the elements are sorted with
    (a) inorder traversing (b) preorder traversing
    (c) post order traversing (d) None of the above

17. Radix sort method is based on
    (a) the positions of the digits (b) the squares of digits
    (c) the squares of digits (d) None of the above
18. For sorting the elements with partition exchange sort which method is used?
    (a) bubble sort (b) quick sort
    (c) heap sort (d) None of the above
19. In heap sort the numbers are initially arranged in
    (a) ascending order (b) descending order
    (c) binary tree (d) None of the above
20. With merge sort number of list that can be sorted are
    (a) one list (b) more than one lists
    (c) none of the above.
21. The process of finding a particular record is called
    (a) sorting (b) searching
    (c) indexing (d) None of the above
22. In this type of searching the records must be sorted
    (a) linear search (b) binary search
    (c) selection search (d) None of the above
23. Using bubble sort, the number of comparison for the letter PEOPLE is:
    (a) 20 (b) 10
    (c) 15 (d) 14
    (e) None

EXERCISES

1. What do you mean by sorting?
2. Explain the concept of bubble sort with the help of example.
3. Write an algorithm and C++ program for Bubble sort.
4. Explain the concept of selection sort with the help of example.
5. Write an algorithm and C++ program for Selection sort.
6. Explain the concept of insertion sort with the help of example.
7. Write an algorithm and C++ program for Insertion sort.
8. Explain the concept of quick sort with the help of example.
9. Write an algorithm and C++ program for Quick sort.

10. Explain the concept of heapsort with the help of example.
11. Write an algorithm and C++ program for Heap sort.
12. Explain the concept of merge sort with the help of example.
13. Write an algorithm and C++ program for Merge sort.
14. Explain the concept of radix sort with the help of example.
15. Write an algorithm and C++ program for Radix sort.
16. Explain the concept of bucket sort with the help of example.
17. Write an algorithm and C++ program for Bucket sort.
18. Explain the concept of shell sort with the help of example.
19. Write an algorithm and C++ program for Shell sort.
20. Write comparison of various sorting algorithms.
21. What do you mean by searching?
22. Write an algorithm and C++ program for linear search.
23. Write an algorithm and C++ program for binary search.
24. Difference between linear search and binary search.

13 CHAPTER

Hashing

13.1 HASHING

Hashing is mainly a searching technique. This is also called hash addressing. Also the implementation of hash table is called hashing. Hashing is a method to store data in an array so that storing, searching, inserting and deleting data is fast. For this every record needs an unique key. The basic idea is not to search for the correct position of a record with comparisons but to compute the position within the array. The function that returns the position is called the 'hash function' and the array is called a 'hash table'. Producing hash values for accessing data or for security. A hash value (or simply hash), also called a message digest, is a number generated from a string of text. The hash is substantially smaller than the text itself, and is generated by a formula in such a way that it is extremely unlikely that some other text will produce the same hash value.

Hashing involves computing the address of a data item by computing a function on the search key value. A **hash function h** is a function from the set of all search key values K to the set of all bucket addresses B.

- We choose a number of buckets to correspond to the number of search key values we will have stored in the database.
- To perform a lookup on a search key value K_i, we compute $h(K_i)$, and search the bucket with that address.
- If two search keys i and j map to the same address, because $h(K_i) = h(K_j)$, then the bucket at the address obtained will contain records with both search key values.
- In this case we will have to check the search key value of every record in the bucket to get the ones we want.
- Insertion and deletion are simple.

- When referring to databases, hashing is a method of sorting and indexing data. The idea behind hashing is to allow large amounts of data to be indexed using keywords or keys commonly created by complex formulas. Hashing allows for large amounts of information to be quickly searched and listed. When referring to security, hashing is a method of taking data, encrypting it, and creating unpredictable, irreversible output. There are many different types of hashing algorithms. Trivial hash function, Perfect hashing Minimal perfect hashing, Hashing uniformly distributed data are examples of hashing algorithms.

Hashing is the transformation of a string of **characters** into a usually shorter fixed-length value or key that represents the original string. Hashing is used to index and retrieve items in a **database** because it is faster to find the item using the shorter hashed key than to find it using the original value. It is also used in many **encryption** algorithms. As a simple example of the using of hashing in databases, a group of people could be arranged in a database like this:

Abhi, Sonam
Daman, Robin
Monika, Willy
Smith, David
(and many more sorted into alphabetical order)

Each of these names would be the key in the database for that person's data. A database search mechanism would first have to start looking character-by-character across the name for matches until it found the match (or ruled the other entries out). But if each of the names were hashed, it might be possible (depending on the number of names in the database) to generate a unique four-digit key for each name. For example:

4765 Abhi, Sonam
6802 Daman, Robin
1560 Monika, Willy
8342 Smith, David
(and so forth)

13.2 WHY WE USE HASH TABLES

Having now looked at arrays, linked lists, stack, queues and trees we will conclude the concept of **hash tables**. The efficiency of storage, retrieval and sorting has been discussed elsewhere and not dealt with in detail when discussing the earlier data structures. Now, however, it becomes one of the main reasons for introducing this final data structure.

We finished discussion of each of our earlier structures by moving for array-based to linked list-based implementations; amongst other benefits, these eliminated the wastage of unoccupied storage while providing an ability to order data. Hash tables, on the other hand, make a virtue of wasted storage and non-ordered storage, and trading these off against large efficiency gains for data access.

13.2.1 Dictionaries and Skip Lists

The term **dictionary** can be used to describe a collection of pairs (**k**,**e**) where:

k = a key (used for looking up data, as in a database); and

e = the data which is to be operated on (eg, with a **get**, **put** or **remove**).

Data of this type **can** be stored in, eg, linked lists or trees. A linked list can be slow for a **get** and a tree can be awkward to 'balance' (eg, an AVL or red-black tree). Some improvements can be made with the compromise of a **skip list**. In brief, this uses intermediate pointers to allow a search to 'skip' to the middle of a list if the element being looked for is in the upper half of that list; commonly, several such pointers can be used to further speed up searches. This is, however, simply a way of enhancing data structures which we have already discussed.

Let us start by going all the way back to storing data in an array, say information about students. If we have a single, small class and the students each have an enrolment number (eg, in the range 1 to 40) then we can store the data in an array and use the enrolment number as an index (assuming for now that the elements have indices in the range 1 .. 40, not the actual 0 .. 39). It could be that there are 7 such classes and our students have enrolment numbers in the range 241 .. 280. We could declare a 280-element array and only use 40 of its elements for our class but a better method would be to stay with a 40-element array and calculate the index (or dictionary key) using the mapping: index = enrolment number - 240.

13.2.2 Collisions, Buckets and Slots

If no two values are able to map into the one table position then we have what is called **ideal hashing**. For hash function f, each key, k, maps into position f(k). In searching for an element, we compute its expected position: if there is an element present then we operate on it; if not then the element was not present in the table.

Each of our earlier examples suffers from a major problem, however: students with, say, the same last three matric number digits (or the first three characters in their name) will generate the same hash code (ie, array index). If we try to use the same position to store data for both of them, we have a **collision**.

We will now describe each position in the table as a **bucket** with position f(k) being the **home bucket** (the number of buckets in a table equals the table length).

Since several keys can map into the same bucket, it is possible to design buckets with several **slots** (this is common for disk-stored hash trees), each slot holding a different value. We will generally have just one slot per bucket, although the linked list approach is different again.

People solve the 'collision' problem on a regular basis when visiting the cinema or sporting event! If you are allocated seat number 47 in a half- full stadium and, on arrival, you discover someone sitting there (but the next seat is free), what would you do? You could ask the usurper to move … or you could (calmly!) take the next available seat. But what if a complete stranger was looking for you and only knew your ticket number? If they had been told that you were a placid, reasonable person and discovered seat 47 was otherwise occupied then they might keep walking by the higher-numbered seats asking the occupants their ticket numbers until they found you (or discovered that you weren't in the stadium, after also checking seats 1 .. 46).

13.3 DIRECT ADDRESSING

Direct addressing is one of the simpler and quicker methods of look up used. Is it possible to design a search of O(1)– that is, one that has a constant search time, no matter where the element is located in the list? In theory, this goal is not an impossible dream. Let's look at an example. We have a list of employees of a fairly small company. Each of 100 employees has an ID number in the range 0 – 99. If we store the elements (employee records) in the array, then each employee's ID number will be an index to the array element where this employee's record will be stored.

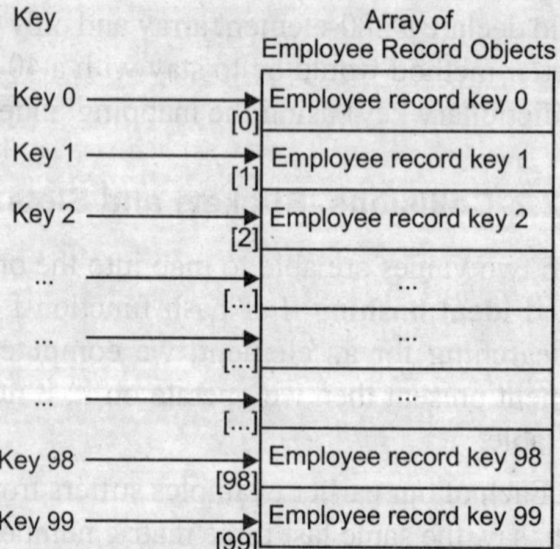

Figure 13.1: Direct Addressing.

In this case once we know the ID number of the employee, we can directly access his record through the array index. There is a one-to-one correspondence between the element's key and the array index. However, in practice, this perfect relationship is not easy to establish or maintain.

Example 13.1: The same company might use employee's five-digit ID number as the primary key. In this case, key values run from 00000 to 99999. If we want to use the same technique as above, we need to set up an array of size 100,000, of which only 100 elements will be used:

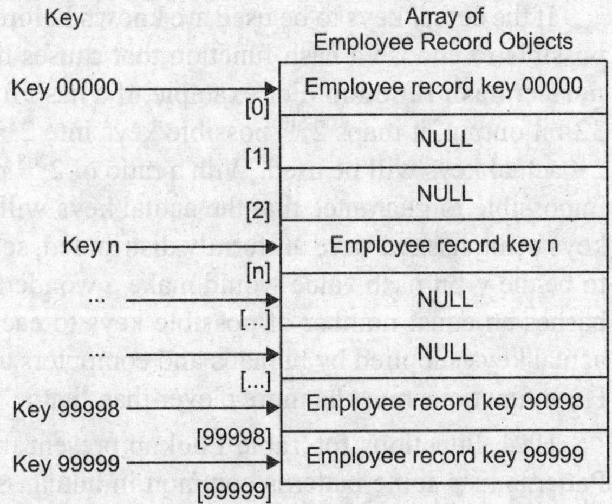

Figure 13.2: Example of employee's ID number.

Obviously it is very impractical to waste that much storage in order to make sure that each employee' record in a unique and predictable location.

But what if we keep the array size down to the size that we will actually be using (100 elements) and use just the last two digits of key to identify each employee? For example, the employee with the key number 54876 will be stored in the element of the array with index 76. And the employee with the key 98759 will be stored in the element of the array with index 59. Note that the elements are not stored according to the value of the key as they were in the previous example. In fact, the record of the employee with the key number 54876 precedes the record of the employee with key number 98759, even though the value of its key is larger. Moreover, we need a way to convert a five-digit key number to two-digit array index. We need some function that will do the transformation. Using this technique we call the array a **Hash Table** and a function is called a **Hash Function**.

13.4 HASH TABLE

Hash tables are a common data structure. They consist of an array (the **hash table**) and a mapping (the **hash function**). The hash function maps **keys** into **hash values**. Items stored in a hash table must have keys. The hash function maps the key of an item to a hash value, and that hash value is used as an index into the hash table for that item. This allows items to be inserted and located quickly. It is the best search method introduced for the binary search. Note that binary search has a search time which is proportional to $\log_2 n$ for a table of n entries. What if an item hashes to a value that some other item has already hashed to? This is a **collision**. There are several strategies for dealing with collisions, but the strategies all make the hash tables slower than if no collisions occurred.

If the actual keys to be used are known before the hash function is chosen, it is possible to choose a hash function that causes no collisions. This is known as a **perfect hash function**. For example, if a hash function maps 30-byte keys into a 32-bit output, it maps 2^{240} possible keys into 2^{32} possible hash values. Less than 2^{32} actual keys will be used. With a ratio of 2^{208} possible keys per hash value, it is impossible to guarantee that the actual keys will have no collisions. If the actual keys being hashed were uniformly distributed, selecting the first v bits of the input to be the v-bit hash value would make a wonderful hash function. It is fast and it hashes an equal number of possible keys to each hash value. Unfortunately, the actual keys supplied by humans and computers are seldom uniformly distributed. Hash functions must be more clever than that.

Hash Functions for Table Lookup present the new 32-bit and 64-bit hashes. Patterns lists some patterns common in human-selected and computer-generated keys. A Hash Model names common pieces of hash functions.

The specification of our table abstract data type is this:

1. A table can be used to store objects.
2. The objects can be quite complicated. However, for our purposes, the only relevant detail is that each object has a unique key, and that keys can be compared for equality. The keys are used in order to identify objects.
3. We assume that there are methods for
   - (i) determining whether the table is empty or full;
   - (ii) inserting of a new object into the table, provided the table is not full already;
   - (iii) given a key, retrieving the object with that key;
   - (iv) given a key, updating the item with that key (usually by replacing the item with a new one with the same key, which is what we will assume here, or by overwriting some of the items variables);
   - (v) given a key, deleting the object with that key, provided such object is stored into the table;
   - (vi) listing all the items in the table (if there is an order on the keys then we would expect this to occur in increasing order).

Notice that we are assuming that each object is uniquely identified by its key.

Symbols are stored in a hash table, indexed by a hash function applied to the key value (e.g., multiply a symbol by itself and take some bits from the middle of the product). The hash function always produces the same value for a given symbol, but is otherwise "random". If there is a collision (two different symbols hash to the same value), it is necessary to rehash (e.g., try the next place in the table).

Insert:	O(1)	Depends on table fullness
Search:	O(1)	Depends on table fullness

The expected time is only 5 comparisons for a table that is 90% full; time depends on fullness but not on table size.

Advantages

- Fast
- Works for symbols without a natural sort order

Disadvantages

- More complex code
- Have to find a good hashing function
- Must dedicate a large table (can't expand).

Practical Approach: Hash Table

Hash Table is a data structure in which keys are mapped to array positions by a hash function. This table can be searched for an item in O(1) time using a hash function to form an address from the key. The easiest way to conceptualize a hash table is to think of it as an array. When a program stores an element in the array, the elements key is transformed by a **hash function** that produces array indexes for that array.

Hash Function is a function which, when applied to the key, produces an integer which can be used as an address in a hash table. The intent is that elements will be relatively randomly and uniformly distributed. In the example above the code for the hash function would look like this (assuming TABLE_SIZE was defined 100):

```
int Hashtable::hash_function(int id_num)
{       return (id_num % TABLE_SIZE);     }
```

Then, for example, to find an element in the table, a program applies hash function to the element's key, producing the array index at which the element is stored.

```
Type* Hashtable::find (char* key)
{ int index;    index = hash_function(key); }
```

Unfortunately, this is not quite simple. For example, we have already stored several employees' records, and our table looks something like this:

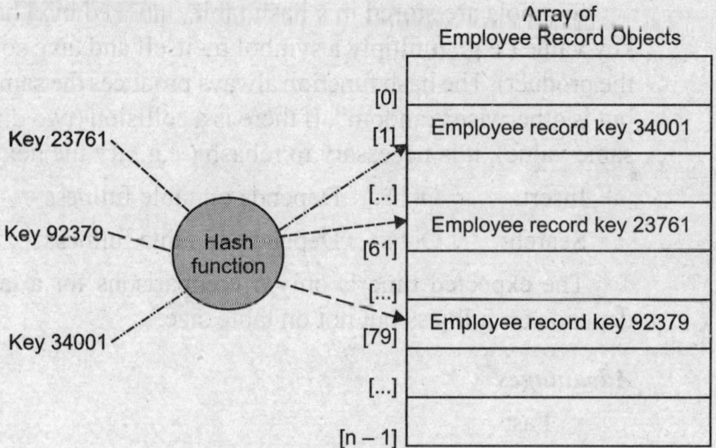

Figure 13.3: Hash Table.

Suppose, our next employee's key is 57879. Then our hash function will produce array index 79. But the array element with index 79 already has a value. As the array begins to fill, keys will inevitably produce the same array index when transformed by the hash function. When more than one element tries to occupy the same array position, we have a collision.

Collision is a condition resulting when two or more keys produce the same hash location. Now, another question arises: can't we generate the hash function that never produces a collision? The answer is that in some cases it is possible to generate such a function. This is known as a perfect hash function.

Perfect Hash Function is a function which, when applied to all the members of the set of items to be stored in a hash table, produces a unique set of integers within some suitable range. Such function produces no collisions.

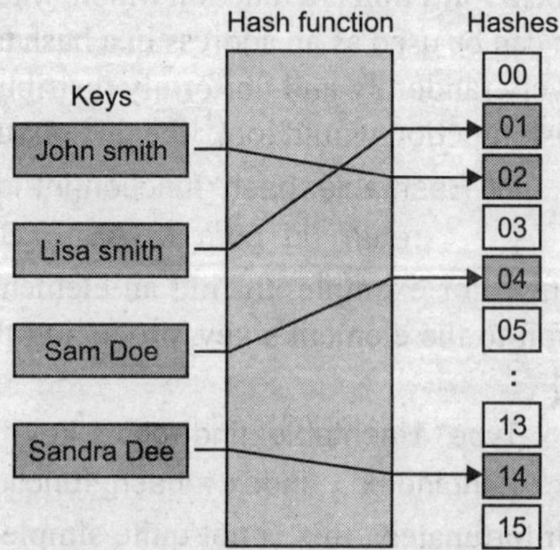

Figure 13.4: A perfect hash function for the four names shown.

A hash function that is injective — that is, maps each valid input to a different hash value — is said to be **perfect**. With such a function one can directly locate the desired entry in a hash table, without any additional searching.

Unfortunately, perfect hash functions are effective only in situations where the inputs are fixed and entirely known in advance, such as mapping month names to the integers 0 to 11, or words to the entries of a dictionary. A perfect function for a given set of *n* keys, suitable for use in a hash table, can be found in time proportional to *n*, can be represented in less than 3**n* bits, and can be evaluated in a constant number of operations. There are generators that produce optimized executable code to evaluate a perfect hash for a given input set.

Minimal Perfect Hashing

A perfect hash function for *n* keys is said to be **minimal** if its range consists of *n* *consecutive* integers, usually from 0 to *n*"1. Besides providing single-step lookup, a minimal perfect hash function also yields a compact hash table, without any vacant slots. Minimal perfect hash functions are much harder to find than perfect ones with a wider range.

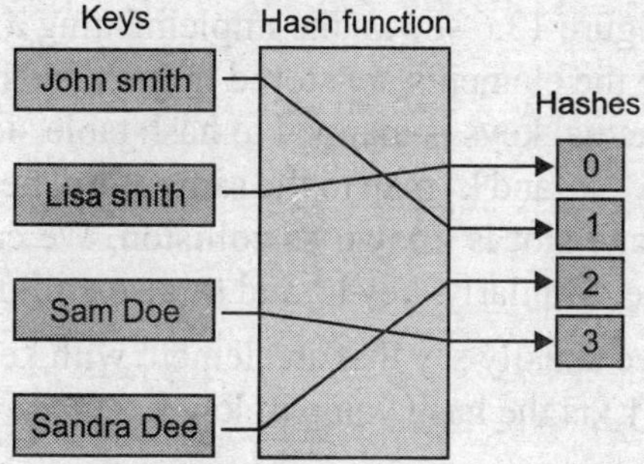

Figure 13.5: A minimal perfect hash function for the four names shown.

Good Hash Function minimizes collisions by spreading the elements uniformly throughout the array.

There is no magic formula for the creation of the hash function. It can be any mathematical transformation that produces a relatively random and unique distribution of values within the address space of the storage. Although the development of a hash function is trial and error, here are some hints that may make process easier:

- Set the size of the storage space to a prime number. This will help generate a more uniform distribution of addresses.
- Use modulo arithmetic (%). Transform a key in such a way that you can perform X % TABLE_SIZE to generate the addresses
- To transform a numeric key, try something like adding the digits together or picking every other digit.

- To transtorm a strlng key, try to add up the ASCII codes of the characters in the string and then perform modulo division.

However, finding a perfect hash function that works for a given data set can be extremely time consuming and very often it is just impossible. Therefore we must live with collisions and learn how to handle them.

Example 13.2: When the set of K of keys stored is much smaller than the universe U of all possible keys, a hash table requires much less storage space than a direct-address table. In fact, the storage requirements can be reduced to Q(|k|), while maintaining the search operation an O(1) operation. The difference here is that this bound is for average-case time, whereas for direct addressing it holds for the worst-case time.

While in a direct-address table, an element with key k is stored in slot k, whereas this element is stored in slot h(k); that is, a hash function h is used to compute the slot from the key k. Here, the hash function h maps the universe U of keys into the slots of a hash table T[0..m-1). This process of mapping keys to appropriate slots in a hash table is known as hashing.

Figure 13.6 shows the implementing a dynamic set by a hash table T[0..m-1], where the elements are stored in the table itself. Here each key in the dynamic set K of actual keys is mapped to hash table slots using hash function h. Note that the keys k_2, k_4 and k_7 map to the same slot. The mapping of more than one key maps to the same slot is known as collision. We can also say that the keys k_2, k_4 and k_7 collide. Similarly, key k_3 and k_5 also collide.

We usually say that an element with key k hashes to slot h(k). We can also say that j(k) is the hash value of key k.

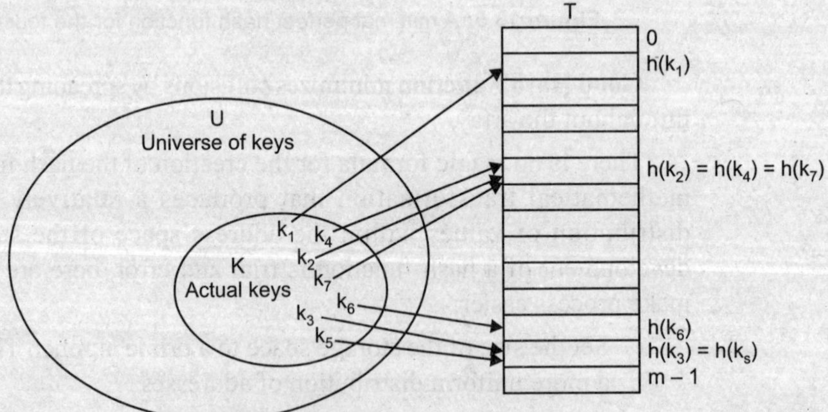

Figure 13.6: Implementing a dynamic set by a hash table T[0..m-1], where the elements are stored in the table itself.

The purpose of the hash function is to reduce the range of array indices that need to be handled. Therefore, instead of |U| values, we need to handle only m values which led to the reduction in the storage requirements.

The main flaw of this beautiful idea is that two or more keys (unequal keys) may hash to the same slot, which lead to the condition called collision. Ideally, it would have been nice if the collision could be avoided by carefully choosing a hash function. But in practice, it is not possible to avoid collision irrespective of the nature of the hash function. Therefore, in these circumstances, the best solution is to minimize the number of collisions and device a scheme to resolve these collisions if they occur.

The following schemes for resolving collisions will be discussed in this chapter.

1. Collision resolution by separating chaining.
2. Collision resolution by open addressing.

Before describing these collision resolution schemes, let us first discuss more about hash functions.

13.5 HASH FUNCTION

A hash function h is simply a mathematical formula that manipulates the key in some from to compute the indeed for this key in the hash table. For example, a hash function can divide the key by some number, usually the size of the hash table, and return remainder as the index for the key.

In general, we say that a hash function h maps the universe U of keys into the slots of a hash table T[0..m-1]. This process of mapping keys to appropriate slots in a hash table is known as hashing. The hash function is used to index the original value or key and then used later each time the data associated with the value or key is to be retrieved. Thus, hashing is always a one-way operation. There's no need to "reverse engineer" the hash function by analyzing the hashed values. In fact, the ideal hash function can't be derived by such analysis. A good hash function also should not produce the same hash value from two different inputs. If it does, this is known as a collision. A hash function that offers an extremely low risk of collision may be considered acceptable.

There is variety of hash functions. But before we discuss them, lets what are main considerations while choosing a particular hash function.

The main considerations while choosing a particular hash function h are

1. It should be possible to compute it efficiently.
2. It should distribute the keys uniformly across the hash-table i.e. it should keep the number of collisions as minimum as possible.

Some popular hash functions are described below.

13.5.1 Division Method

It is the first hash function and is mostly used in all the searching and sorting operations in the data structure.

In division method, key k to be mapped into one of the m slots in the hash-table is divided by m and the remainder of this division is taken as index into the hash-table.

That is, the hash function is

$$h(k) = k \bmod m$$

where mod is the modulus operator. In C, its equivalent operator is % character.

The above has function will map the keys in the range 0 to m-1 and is acceptable in C. But if some language supports the index from 1 onwards, then the hash function becomes

$$h(k) = k \bmod m + 1$$

Example 13.3: Consider a hash table with 10 slots i.e. m = 10, then the hash function

$$h(k) = k \bmod m$$

will map the key 17 mod 10 = 7

$$h(17) = 17 \bmod 10 = 7$$

Since it requires only a single division operation, hashing is quite fast.

When using the division method, certain values of m should be avoided. It has been proved in literature that good values for m are prime values not too close to exact powers of 2.

13.5.2 Multiplication Method

The multiplication method operates in two steps:

1. The key value k is multiplied by a constant A in the range $0 < A < 1$ and extract the fractional part of value kA.
2. The fractional value obtained above is multiplied by m and the floor of the result is taken as the hash value. That is, the hash function is

$$h(k) = \lfloor m\,(k\,A \bmod 1)\rfloor$$

where "k A mod 1" means the fractional part of k A i.e. $k\,A - \lfloor k\,A\rfloor$. Note that $\lfloor x\rfloor$ read as floor of x and represents the largest integer less than or equal to x.

Although this method works with any value of A, it works better with some values than others. The best choice depends on the characteristics of the key values.

Knuth has suggested in his study that the following value of A is likely to work reasonably well.

$$A = (\sqrt{5} - 1) / 2 = 0.6180339887 \ldots..$$

EXAMPLE 13.4: Consider a hash table with 10000 slots i.e. m = 10000, then the hash function

$$h(k) = \lfloor m\ (k\ A \bmod 1) \rfloor$$

will map the key 123456 to slot 41 since

$$\begin{aligned} h(123456) &= \lfloor 10000 \times (123456 \times 0.61803 \ldots \bmod 1) \rfloor \\ &= \lfloor 10000 \times (76300.0041151 \ldots \bmod 1) \rfloor \\ &= \lfloor 10000 \times .0041151 \ldots \rfloor \\ &= \lfloor 41.151 \ldots \rfloor \\ &= 41 \end{aligned}$$

13.5.3 Midsquare Method

This function is also widely used in many applications. In this key is squared. In other words in this method a key is multiplied by itself and the address is obtained by selecting an appropriate number of bits or digits from the middle of the square.

The midsquare method also operates in two steps:

1. The square of they key value **k** is taken.
2. The hash value is obtained by deleting digits from ends of the squared value i.e. k^2. It is important to note that same position of k^2 must be used for all keys. Thus, the hash function is

$$h(k) = s$$

where s is obtained by deleting digits from both sides of k^2.

EXAMPLE 13.5: Consider a hash table with 100 **slots** i.e. m = 100, and key values k = 3202, 7144, 2471

Solution: The calculations are shown below:

k:	3202	7144	2471
k^2:	10252804	51036736	6105841
h(k):	52	36	58

The hash values are obtained by taking fourth and fifth digits counting from right.

13.5.4 Folding Method

This method divides the original value (digits in this case) into **several** parts, adds the parts together, and then uses the last four digits (or some other arbitrary number of digits that will work) as the hashed value or key.

The folding method also operates in two steps:

1. The key value k is divided into number of parts, $k_1, k_2, k_3, \ldots, k_r$ where each part has the same number of digits except the last part, which can have lesser digits.
2. These parts are added together and the hash value is obtained by ignoring the last carry, if any. For example, if the hash table has 1000 slots, each part will have three digits, and the sum of these parts after ignoring the last carry will also be three-digit number in the range 0 to 999.

EXAMPLE 13.6: Consider a hash table with 100 slots i.e. m = 100, and key values k = 8235, 824, 72558

Solution: The calculations are shown below:

k:	8235	824	72558
parts:	82, 35	82, 4	72, 55, 8
sum of parts:	117	86	135
h(k):	17	86	35

In above examples, we have assumed that keys are numeric. However, if the keys are alphanumeric, then the ASCII codes of fixed number of characters can be added together to transfer the character key to its equivalent numeric key, and then any of the above hash function can be applied.

13.5.5 Characteristics of Good Hash Functions

Following are the some basic characteristics of Hash function:

1. A good hash function gives an average-case lookup that is a small constant, independent of the number of search keys.
2. We hope records are distributed uniformly among the buckets.
3. The worst hash function maps all keys to the same bucket.
4. The best hash function maps all keys to distinct addresses.
5. Ideally, distribution of keys to addresses is uniform and random.
6. Suppose we have 26 buckets, and map names beginning with ith letter of the alphabet to the ith bucket.
   - **Problem:** this does not give uniform distribution.
   - Many more names will be mapped to "A" than to "X".
   - Typical hash functions perform some operation on the internal binary machine representations of characters in a key.

- For example, compute the sum, modulo # of buckets, of the binary representations of characters of the search key.
- See Figure 11.18, using this method for 10 buckets (assuming the ith character in the alphabet is represented by integer i).

13.6 COLLISION RESOLUTION BY CHAINING HASH FUNCTIONS

A collision is when two keys get mapped to the same position in the Hash Table. The following table contains the probabilities that at least two people in group have the same birthday. This is equivalent to considering the probability that there is at least one collision in a table of size 365, given a number of entries in the table.

Number of People	Probability
10	0.11694818
20	0.41143838
30	0.70631624
40	0.89123181
50	0.97037358
60	0.99412266
70	0.99915958
80	0.99991433
90	0.99999385
100	0.99999969

In order to address the problem of collisions, we switch to a new hashing method called chained hashing or bucket hashing. A chained hash table is a table of linked lists (as opposed to a table of individual elements). As before, we use a hash algorithm to derive an index value for each key. We then add the record to the linked list pointed to by the given index value.

The ith entry in the array points to a list of items whose hash code is i. These lists are called chains or buckets.

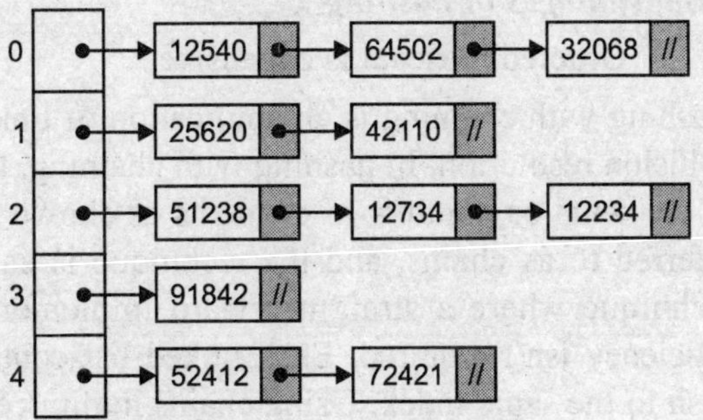

For example, the hash function for the following diagram uses only the first 3 digits of the key, and takes these 3 digits mod 5 as the hash index. The table is implemented as a chained hash table.

When we search for a record, we begin by hashing its key to get an index value. We then search the linked list pointed to by the index value. If our record is not in the linked list, then it is not stored in our hash table. Note that we no longer have to check to see if our table is full. We handle collisions by adding our new record to a linked list which has all the synonyms. In fact, we can store many more elements than the size of the table. Although chained hashing solves our collision problems, we have to stress that the overall performance of the hash table still depends on the hash function. If we have a perfect hash function, each bucket should only be one item in length. If we have a poor hash function, then we have to resort to doing linear searches through some long chains.

Advantages of chained hashing

- Each cluster is maintained as a separate list.
- Clusters never merge (no secondary clustering).
- Size of the table is not required to be much greater than the number of items.
- Table of pointers saves space if the item record is large.
- No degeneration as table fills up.
- If the hash function is good and the size of the table is right, the average number of items per list is small.
- Deletion is simple.
- Simple efficient collision handling.
- Best hashing technique (fastest).

Disadvantages of chained hashing

- Uses more space if the item record is very small (i.e. only the key).

Disadvantages of hashing

- Ordered retrieval is expensive.

Hashing with chaining is an application of linked lists and gives an approach to collision resolution. In hashing with chaining, the hash table contains linked lists of elements or pointers to elements as shown in the figure below. The lists are referred to as chains, and the technique is called chaining. This is a common technique where a straightforward implementation is desired and maximum efficiency isn't required. Each linked list contains all the elements whose keys hash to the same index. Using chains minimizes search by dividing the set to be searched into lots of smaller pieces. There's nothing inherently wrong with linear search with small sequences; it's just that it gets slower as the sequences to be searched get longer. In this approach to resolving collisions, each sequence of elements whose keys hash to the same value will stay relatively short, so linear search is adequate.

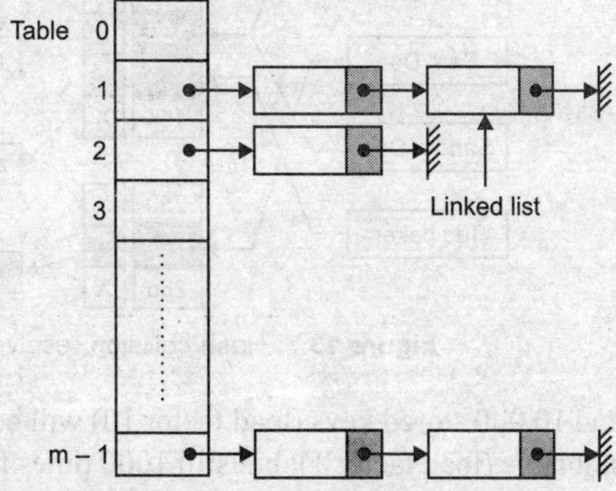

This Hash Table is an array [0 ... m-1] of linked_list.

The table entries are called buckets or slots, and the linked lists are called chains. **x** is placed in linked_list #h[**x**] (number of hash function).

13.7 COLLISION RESOLUTION BY SEPARATE CHAINING

In the strategy known as separate chaining, direct chaining, or simply chaining, each slot of the bucket array is a pointer to a linked list that contains the key-value pairs that hashed to the same location. Lookup requires scanning the list for an entry with the given key. Insertion requires appending a new entry record to either end of the list in the hashed slot. Deletion requires searching the list and removing the element. (The technique is also called open hashing or closed addressing, which should not be confused with 'open addressing' or 'closed hashing'.)

Chained hash tables with linked lists are popular because they require only basic data structures with simple algorithms, and can use simple hash functions that would be unsuitable for other methods.

The cost of a table operation is that of scanning the entries of the selected bucket for the desired key. If the distribution of keys is sufficiently uniform, the *average* cost of a lookup depends only on the average number of keys per bucket — that is, on the load factor.

Chained hash tables remain effective even when the number of entries *n* is much higher than the number of slots. Their performance degrades more gracefully (linearly) with the load factor. For example, a chained hash table with 1000 slots

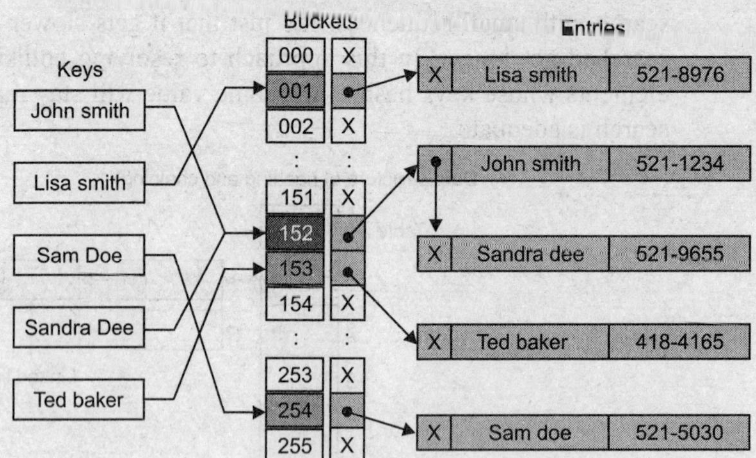

Figure 13.7: Hash collision resolved by separate chaining.

and 10,000 stored keys (load factor 10) will be 5 to 10 times slower than a 10,000-slot table (load factor 1); but still 1000 times faster than a plain sequential list, and possibly even faster than a balanced search tree.

For separate-chaining, the worst-case scenario is when all entries were inserted into the same bucket, in which case the hash table is ineffective and the cost is that of searching the bucket data structure. If the latter is a linear list, the lookup procedure may have to scan all its entries; so the worst-case cost is proportional to the number n of entries in the table.

The bucket chains are often implemented as ordered lists, sorted by the key field; this choice approximately halves the average cost of unsuccessful lookups, compared to an unordered list. However, if it is expected that some keys will be much more likely to come up than others, an unordered list with move-to-front heuristic may be more effective. More sophisticated data structures, such as balanced search trees, are worth considering only if the load factor is large (about 10 or more), or if the hash distribution is likely to be very non-uniform, or if one must guarantee good performance even in the worst-case. However, using a larger table and/or a better hash function may be even more effective in those cases.

Chained hash tables also inherit the disadvantages of linked lists. When storing small keys and values, the space overhead of the next pointer in each entry record can be significant. An additional disadvantage is that traversing a linked list has poor cache performance, making the processor cache ineffective.

13.8 COLLISION RESOLUTION BY OVERFLOW CHAINING

Overflow chaining is a method of implementing a hash table in which the collisions are handled automatically. In this method, we use two tables: a symbol table to accommodate identifiers and their attributes, and a **hash table**, which is an array of pointers pointing to symbol table entries. Each symbol table entry is made of three fields: the first for holding the identifier, the second for holding the attributes, and the third for holding the link or pointer that can be made to point to any symbol table entry.

The insertions into the symbol table are done as follows:

If x is the symbol to be inserted, it will be added to the next available entry of the symbol table. The hash value of x is then computed. If h(x) = i, then the ith hash table pointer is made to point to the symbol table entry in which x is stored, if the ith hash table pointer does not point to any symbol table entry. If the ith hash table pointer is already pointing to some symbol table entry, then the link field of the symbol table entry containing x is made to point to that symbol table entry to which the ith hash table pointer is pointing to, and the ith hash table pointer is made to point to the symbol entry containing x. This is equivalent to building a linked list on the ith index of the hash table.

The retrieval of attributes is done as follows:

If x is a symbol, then we obtain h(x), use this value as the index of the hash table, and traverse the list built on this index to get that entry which contains x. A typical hash table implemented using this technique is shown here.

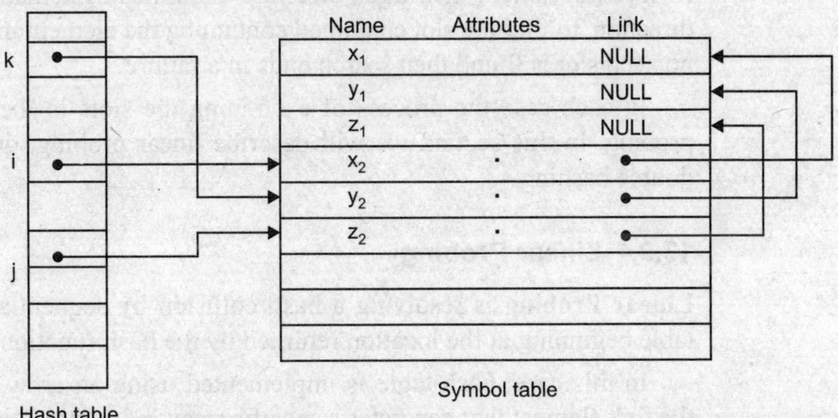

Figure 13.8: Hash table implementation using overflow chaining for collision handling.

The symbols to b stored are $x_1, y_1, z_1, x_2, y_2, z_2$. The hash function that we use is h(symbol) = (value of first letter of the symbol) mod n, where n is the size of table.

if $h(x_1) = i$

$h(y_1) = j$

$h(z_1) = k$

then

$h(x_2) = i$

$h(y_2) = j$

$h(z_2) = k$

Therefore, the contents of the symbol table will be the one shown in Figure 13.8.

13.9 COLLISION RESOLUTION BY OPEN ADDRESSING

In the open addressing scheme all the elements of the dynamic set are stored in the hash-table itself. That is, each entry of the hash table either contains the element of the dynamic set or some sentinel value to indicate that slot is free. In case if it is known that no key can be negative, value -1, can be taken as sentinel value.

In order to insert a key in a hash table under this scheme, if the slot to which key is hashed is free then the element is stored at that slot. In case the slot is filled, then other slots are examined systematically, in the forward direction, to find the free slot. If no such slot is found then overflow condition occurs.

In case of searching, the element stored in the slot to which key is hashed is compared with element to be searched and if it matches search operations succeeds. If does not match, then other slots are examined systematically, in the forward direction, to find the slot contained containing the element under consideration. If no such slot is found then search ends in a failure.

In each case the process of examining the slots in the hash table is called probing. In this section we will describe linear probing, quadratic probing and double hashing.

13.9.1 Linear Probing

Linear Probing is resolving a hash collision by sequentially searching a hash table beginning at the location returned by the hash function.

In this case, hash table is implemented using an array. The program stores the first element that generates a specific array index at that index. For example, if the hash function generates 79, then you use array index 79 to store the element. When the hash function generates the key 79 again, the program begins a sequential search starting at location 79, looking for the next available spot. The second element whose key was transformed by hash function into 79 will be stored at the location 80, the third at 81 and so on. Of course, if 80 and 81 are already occupied, the elements will be stored farther away from the location generated by hash function.

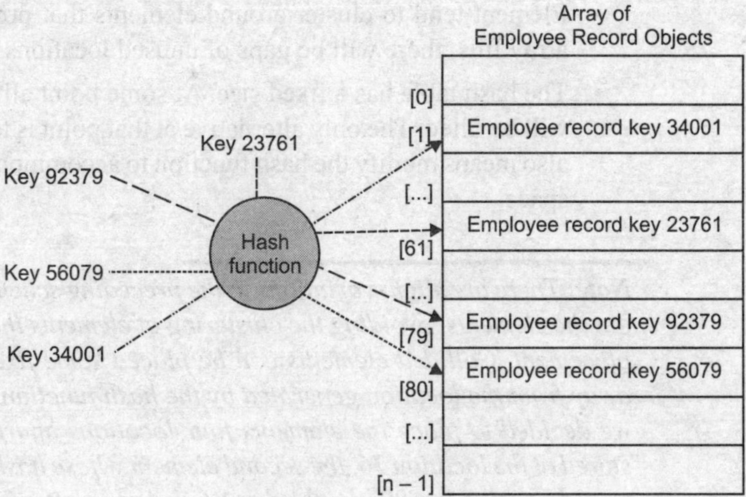

Figure 13.9: Linear probing.

Retrieving A Value

When it comes to retrieving a value, the program recomputes the array index and checks the key of the element stored at that location. If the desired key value matches the key value at that location, then the element is found. The search time is on the order of 1, O(1) (1 comparison per data item). If the key doesn't match, then the search function begins a sequential search of the array that continues until:

- the desired element is found
- the search encounters an unused position in the array, indicating that the element is not present
- the search encounters the index which was produced by the hash function, indicating that the table is full and the element is not present

In worst case, the search takes (n-1) comparison, which is on the order of n, O(n). "Worst case" is if the table is full and the search function goes through the whole array, (n-1) elements, every time comparing the desired key value with the key at the array location. In the worst case element is either found at the last position before the one that was produced by the hash function or not found at all.

Advantages to this approach

- All the elements (or pointer to the elements) are placed in contiguous storage. This will speed up the sequential searches when collisions do occur.

Disadvantages to this approach

- As the number of collisions increases, the distance from the array index computed by the hash function and the actual location of the element increases, increasing search time.

- Element tend to cluster around elements that produce collisions*. As the array fills, there will be gaps of unused locations.
- The hash table has a fixed size. At some point all the elements in the array will be filled. The only alternative at that point is to expand the table, which also means modify the hash function to accommodate the increased address space.

Note: *There are slight variations to the preceding scheme that attempt to space out the elements, avoiding the clustering of elements that occurs with adjacent placement. Collided elements can be placed some fixed number of locations away from the location generated by the hash function. For example, suppose we decided to place the elements four locations apart. If the first element is stored at the location 76, the second element whose hashed key generated is 76, would be stored at 80, the third at 84 and so on. If a location is occupied, the program adds four and checks again, until it finds an unused location.*

Practical Approach: Linear Probing

The linear probing uses the following hash function

$$h(k, i) = [h'(k) + i] \bmod m \qquad \text{for } i = 0, 1, 2, \ldots, m-1$$

where m is the size of the hash table and h'(k) = k mod m the basic hash function (division method), and i is the probe number.

Therefore, for a given key k, the first slot probed is T[h'(k)]. The next slots are T[h'(k) + 1], T[h'(k)+2], T[h'(k)+3), and so on up to slot T[m-1]. Then we wrap around to slots T[0], T[1], T[2], and so on until we finally probe slot T[h'(k) -1]. Since the initial probe position determines the entire sequence, only m distinct probe sequences are used with linear probing.

EXAMPLE 13.7: Consider inserting the keys 76, 26, 37, 59, 21, 65, 88 into a hash table of size m = 11 using linear probing. Further consider that the primary hash function is h'(k) = k mod m.

Solution:

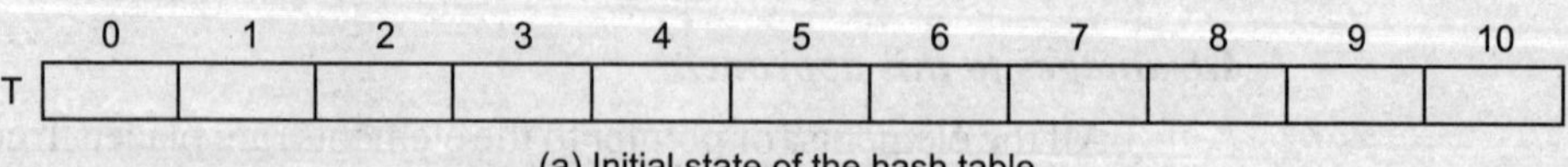

(a) Initial state of the hash table

Step 1: Consider first key k = 76

$$\begin{aligned} h(76, 0) &= (76 \bmod 11 + 0) \bmod 11 \\ &= (10 + 0) \bmod 11 = 10 \bmod 11 = 10 \end{aligned}$$

Since slot T[10] is free, insert key 76 at this place.

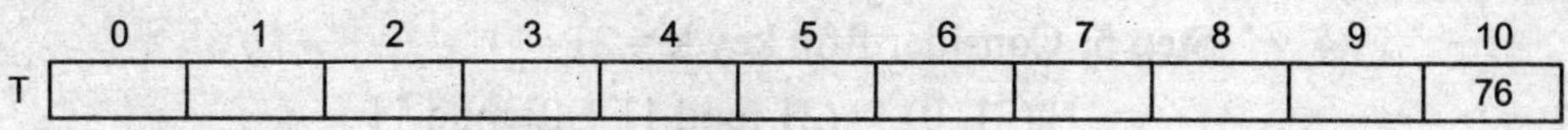

	0	1	2	3	4	5	6	7	8	9	10
T											76

(b) Hash table after inserting key 76

Step 2: Consider second key k = 26

h(26, 0) = (66 mod 11 + 0) mod 11

= (4 + 0) mod 11 = 4 mod 11 = 4

Since slot T[4] is free, insert key 26 at this place.

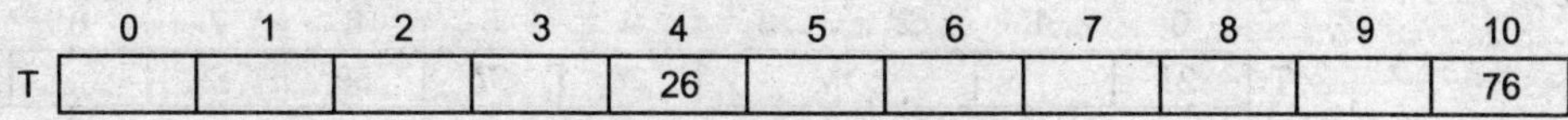

	0	1	2	3	4	5	6	7	8	9	10
T					26						76

(c) Hash table after inserting key 26

Step 3: Consider third key k = 37

h(37, 0) = (37 mod 11 + 0) mod 11

= (4 + 0) mod 11 = 4 mod 11 = 4

Since slot T[4] is occupied, the next probe sequence is computed as

h(37, 1) = (37 mod 11 + 1) mod 11

= (4 + 1) mod 11 = 5 mod 11 = 5

Since slot T[5] is free. Insert key 37 at this place.

	0	1	2	3	4	5	6	7	8	9	10
T					26	37					76

(d) Hash table after inserting key 37

Step 4: Consider fourth key k = 59

h(59, 0) = (59 mod 11 + 0) mod 11

= (4 + 0) mod 11 = 4 mod 11 = 4

Since slot T[4] is occupied, the next probe sequence is computed as

h(59, 1) = (57 mod 11 + 1) mod 11

= (4 + 1) mod 11 = 5 mod 11 = 5

Since slot T[5] is also occupied, the next probe sequence is computed as

h(59, 2) = (57 mod 11 + 1) mod 11

= (4 + 2) mode 11 = 6 mod 11 = 6

Since slot T[6] is free. Insert key 59 this place.

	0	1	2	3	4	5	6	7	8	9	10
T					26	37	59				76

(e) Hash table after inserting key 59

Step 5: Consider fifth key k = 21

$h(21, 0) = (21 \bmod 11 + 0) \bmod 11$

$= 10 + 0) \bmod 11 = 10 \bmod 11 = 10$

Since slot T[4] is occupied, the next probe sequence is computed as

$h(21, 1) = (21 \bmod 11 + 1) \bmod 11$

$= (10 + 1) \bmod 11 = 11 \bmod 11 = 0$

Since slot T[5] is free. Insert key 21 at this place.

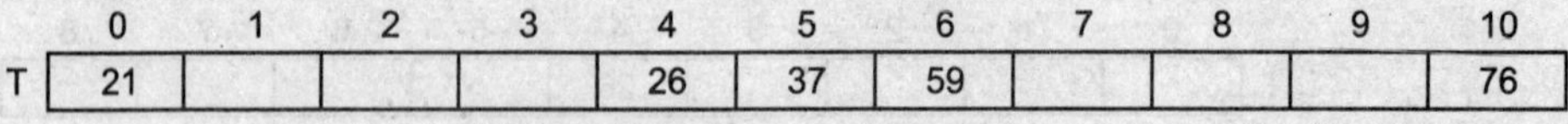

	0	1	2	3	4	5	6	7	8	9	10
T	21				26	37	59				76

(f) Hash table after inserting key 21

Step 6: Consider sixth key k = 65

$h(65, 0) = (65 \bmod 11 + 0) \bmod 11$

$= (10 + 0) \bmod 11 = 10 \bmod 11 = 10$

Since slot T[10] is occupied, the next probe sequence is computed as

$h(65, 1) = (65 \bmod 11 + 1) \bmod 11$

$= (10 + 1) \bmod 11 = 11 \bmod 11 = 0$

Since slot T[0] is also occupied, the next probe sequence is computed as

$h(65, 2) = (65 \bmod 11 + 1) \bmod 11$

$= (10 + 2) \text{ mode } 11 = 12 \bmod 11 = 1$

Since slot T[1] is free. Insert key 59 this place.

	0	1	2	3	4	5	6	7	8	9	10
T	21	65			26	37	59				76

(g) Hash table after inserting key 65

Step 7: Consider seventh key k = 88

$h(88, 0) = (88 \bmod 11 + 0) \bmod 11$

$= (0 + 0) \bmod 11 = 0 \bmod 11 = 0$

Since slot T[0] is occupied, the next probe sequence is computed as

$h(88, 1) = (88 \bmod 11 + 1) \bmod 11$

$= (0 + 1) \bmod 11 = 1 \bmod 11 = 1$

Since slot T[1] is also occupied, the next probe sequence is computed as

$h(88, 2) = (88 \bmod 11 + 1) \bmod 11$

$= (0 + 2) \text{ mode } 11 = 2 \bmod 11 = 2$

Since slot T[2] is free. Insert key 88 this place.

	0	1	2	3	4	5	6	7	8	9	10
T	21	65	88		26	37	59				76

(h) Hash table after inserting key 88

Figure 13.10: (a)-(h) Illustrates the insertion of keys 76, 26, 37, 59, 21, 65, 88 in open address hash table with linear probing.

The above process is called **linear probing**. Taking the cinema/stadium analogy a bit further, what if you sold 1000 tickets (numbered 0 .. 999) and then discovered that no more than 400 people were going to attend, causing you to move the event to, say, a 500-seat capacity venue? If you take the ticket number (t) and find its value mod 400 (t % 400) then you will have a new ticket number (n) in the range 0 ..399. Up to three people (eg, tickets 73, 473 and 873) may be given the same value of n but they will still find a seat somewhere using linear probing. A simple numerical example would be where we wished to insert data with keys 28, 19, 59, 68, 89 into a table of size 10.

These entries are made in the table with the following decisions, as shown in Figure 2:

(i) Enter 28 = 28 % 10 = 8; position is free, 28 placed in element 8;

(ii) Enter 19 = 19 % 10 = 9; position is free, 19 placed in element 9;

(iii) Enter 59 = 59 % 10 = 9; position is occupied; try next place in table (using wraparound), ie 0; 59 placed in element 0;

(iv) Enter 68 = 68 % 10 = 8; position is occupied; try next place in table (0) - occupied; try next (1); 68 placed in element 1;

(v) Enter 89 = 89 % 10 = 9; position is occupied; next two places in table are occupied; try next (2); 89 placed in element 2.

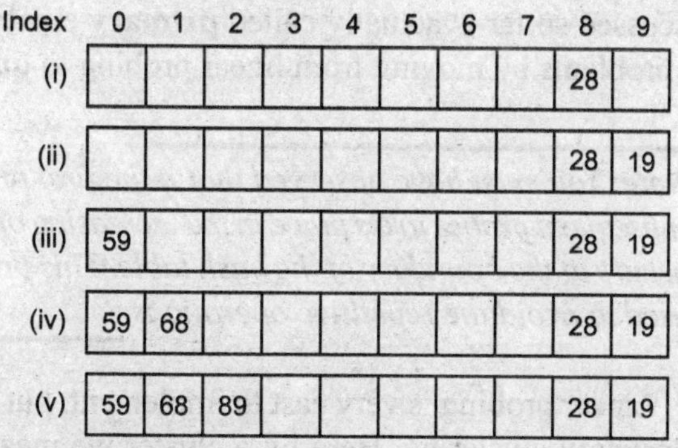

Figure 13.11: Example of linear probing.

Analysis of linear probing

Let us assume for now that we are using a large hash table and that each probe (**search, get** or **put**) is independent of the previous one [we shall see that this is a false assumption but read on …].

The proportion of the table that is full is called a **load factor**, usually represented by the symbol **l** (lambda). So, a 40 element table holding only 10 elements has a **l** of 0.25 - which is also the probability of finding an occupied cell. Therefore the probability of finding an empty cell during a probe is **(1 - l)**. And the expected number of probes needed to find an empty element is **1/(1 - l)**.

[Think of rolling dice - if the probability of throwing a three is 1/6 then the average number of rolls needed to get a three result is 6 rolls. Also, each roll is independent of the last - with four consecutive twos, the chances of a two next time are still only 1/6.]

For example, if our table is a fifth full then you would expect an average of 1.25 probes (= 1/(1 - 0.20)) to find an empty element. If it is nine-tenths full, ten probes would be expected on average.

Unfortunately, this is not true! Clustering means that one failed insertion in a bucket (causing an insertion further up the table) has a knock-on effect on other attempted insertions. Knuth2 has demonstrated that the actual number of probes needed is:

$$\mathbf{(1 + 1/(1 - l)^2)/2}$$

Recalculating our examples above, we now have that

- For a fifth- full table, we expect an average of 1.28 probes (not 1.25, but close)
- For a half- full table, we expect an average of 2.5 probes (not 2.0, but close-ish)
- For a nine-tenths full table, we expect an average of 50.5 probes (nothing like the 10.0 probes predicted earlier).

Most of these problems are caused by clustering. The type which we have discussed so far is actually called **primary clustering**. We can alleviate many of its problems by moving from linear probing to **quadratic probing.**

Note: *You must have observed that if the first probe finds an occupied slot, the subsequent probes takes place in the increasing order of slots except wrap around occurs at the boundary of the hash table. This property of linear probing can be used to avoid the repetitive operations.*

Linear probing is very east to implement, but it suffers from a problem known as primary clustering. Here by a cluster we mean a block of occupied slots and primary clustering refers to many such blocks separated by free slots. Therefore, once clusters are formed there are more chances that subsequent insertions will also end up in one of the cluster and thereby increasing the size of cluster. Thus, increasing the number of probes required to find a free slot, and hence worsening the performance further.

To avoid problem of primary clustering, some remedies are suggested in literature. Two of them are quadratic probing and double hashing.

13.9.2 Quadratic Probing

The quadratic probing uses the following hash function

$$h(k, i) = [h'(k) + c_1 i + c_2 i^2] \text{ mode } m \qquad \text{for } i = 0, 1, 2, \ldots, m-1$$

where m is the size of the hash table, h'(k) = k mod m the basic hash function (division method), c_1 and c_2 ¹ 0 are auxiliary constants), and i is the probe number.

The initial slot probed is T[h'(k)] and the other slots probed are offset by factors that depend in a quadratic manner on the probe number i. This method works much better than linear probing, but to make full use of the hash table, the values of c_1, c_2 and m are constrained. Also, if the two keys have the same initial probe slot, the their probe sequences are same, since $h(k_1, 0) = h(k_2, 0)$ implies $h(k_1, i) = h(k_2, i)$. This leads to a milder form of clustering called secondary clustering. As in linear probing, the initial probe determines the entire sequence, so only m distinct sequences are used.

EXAMPLE 13.8: Consider inserting the keys 76, 26, 37, 59, 21, 65, 88 into a hash table of size m = 11 using linear probing with $c_1 = 1$ and $c_2 = 3$. Further consider that the primary hash function is h'(k) = k mod m.

Solution:

We have $h(k, i) = [k \text{ mod } m + c_1 i + c_2 i^2] \text{ mod } m$

$= [K \text{ mod } m + i + 3xi^2] \text{ mod } m$

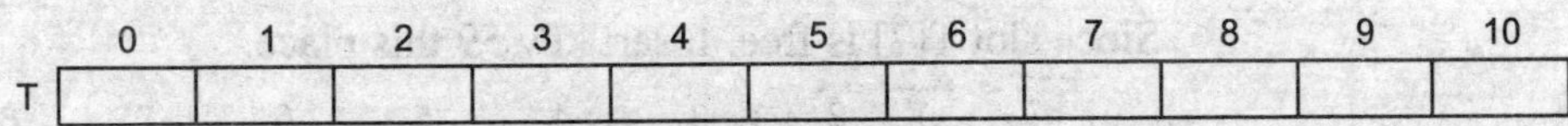

	0	1	2	3	4	5	6	7	8	9	10
T											

(a) Initial state of the hash table

Step 1: Consider first key k = 76

$h(76, 0) = (76 \text{ mod } 11 + 0 + 3 \text{ x } 0) \text{ mod } 11$

$= (10 + 0 + 0) \text{ mod } 11 = 10$

The initial probe is T[10], since T[10] is free, insert the key 76 at this place.

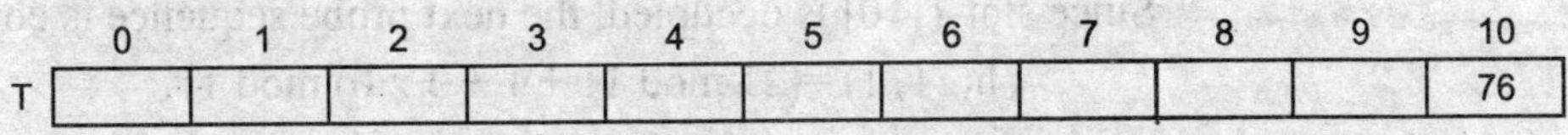

	0	1	2	3	4	5	6	7	8	9	10
T											76

(b) Hash table after inserting key 76

Step 2: Consider first key k = 26

$h(26, 0) = (26 \text{ mod } 11 + 0 + 3 \text{ x } 0) \text{ mod } 11$

$= (4 + 0 + 0) \text{ mod } 11 = 4 \text{ mod } 11 = 4$

Since slot T[4], since T[4] is free, insert the key 26 at this place.

	0	1	2	3	4	5	6	7	8	9	10
T					26						76

(c) Hash table after inserting key 26

Step 3: Consider first key k = 37

h(37, 0) = (37 mod 11 + 0 + 3 x 0) mod 11

= (4 + 0 + 0) mod 11 = 4 mod 11 = 4

Since slot T[4] is occupied, the next probe sequence is computed as

h(37, 1) = (37 mod 11 + 1 + 3 x 1^2) mod 11

= (4 + 1 + 3) mod 11 = 8 mod 11 = 8

Since slot T[8] is free. Insert key 37 at this place.

	0	1	2	3	4	5	6	7	8	9	10
T					26				37		76

(d) Hash table after inserting key 37

Step 4: Consider first key k = 59

h(59, 0) = (59 mod 11 + 0 + 3 x 0) mod 11

= (4 + 0 + 0) mod 11 = 4 mod 11 = 4

Since slot T[4] is occupied, the next probe sequence is computed as

h(59, 1) = (57 mod 11 + 1 + 3 x 2^2) mod 11

= (4 + 1 + 3) mod 11 = 8 mod 11 = 8

Since slot T[8] is also occupied, the next probe sequence is computed as

h(59, 2) = (59 mod 11 + 2 + 3 x 2^2) mod 11

= (4 + 2 + 12) mode 11 = 18 mod 11 = 7

Since slot T[7] is free. Insert key 59 this place.

	0	1	2	3	4	5	6	7	8	9	10
T					26			59	37		76

(e) Hash table after inserting key 59

Step 5: Consider first key k = 21

h(21, 0) = (21 mod 11 + 0 + 3 x 0) mod 11

= (10 + 0 + 0) mod 11 = 10 mod 11 = 10

Since slot T[10] is occupied, the next probe sequence is computed as

h(21, 1) =(21 mod 11 + 1 + 3 x 0) mod 11

= (10 + 1 + 3) mod 11 = 14 mod 11 = 3

Since slot T[3] is free. Insert key 21 at this place.

	0	1	2	3	4	5	6	7	8	9	10
T				21	26			59	37		76

(f) Hash table after inserting key 21

Step 6: Consider first key k = 65

h(65, 0) = (65 mod 11 + 0 + 3 x 0) mod 11

= (10 + 0 + 0) mod 11 = 10 mod 11 = 10

Since slot T[10] is occupied, the next probe sequence is computed as

h(65, 1) =(65 mod 11 + 1 + 3 x 1^2) mod 11

= (10 + 1 + 3) mod 11 = 14 mod 11 = 3

Since slot T[3] is also occupied, the next probe sequence is computed as

h(65, 2) = (65 mod 11 + 2 + 3 x 2^2) mod 11

= (10 + 2 + 12) mode 11 = 24 mod 11 = 2

Since slot T[2] is free. Insert key 65 this place.

	0	1	2	3	4	5	6	7	8	9	10
T			65	21	26			59	37		76

(g) Hash table after inserting key 65

Step 7: Consider first key k = 88

h(88, 0) = (88 mod 11 + 0 + 3 x 0) mod 11

= (0 + 0 + 0) mod 11 = 0 mod 11 = 0

Since slot T[0] is free, insert the key 88 at this place.

	0	1	2	3	4	5	6	7	8	9	10
T	88		65	21	26			59	37		76

(h) Hash table after inserting key 88

Figure 13.12: (a)-(h) Illustrate the insertion of keys 76, 26, 37, 59, 21, 65, 88 is open address hash table with quadratic probing.

EXAMPLE 13.9: Let us try a numerical example similar to that of Figure 13.13, this time using quadratic probing. Fig. 4 shows where the values end up with quadratic probing and the decisions involved are:

(i) Enter 28 = 28 % 10 = 8; position is free, 28 placed in element 8 (result is **same as before**);

(ii) Enter 19 = 19 % 10 = 9; position is free, 19 placed in element 9 (result is **same as before**);

(iii) Enter 59 = 59 % 10 = 9; position is occupied; try 1 (=12) places along in table (using wraparound), ie 0; 59 placed in element 0 (result is **same as before**);

(iv) Enter 68 = 68 % 10 = 8; position is occupied; try next place in table (0) - occupied; try next (1); 68 placed in element 1 (result is **same as before** for same reasons as iii);

(v) Enter 89 = 89 % 10 = 9; position is occupied; **previously we tried positions 0 and 1 then put data in 2.** This time, we try 0 then **go directly to 3, jumping over the existing cluster**.

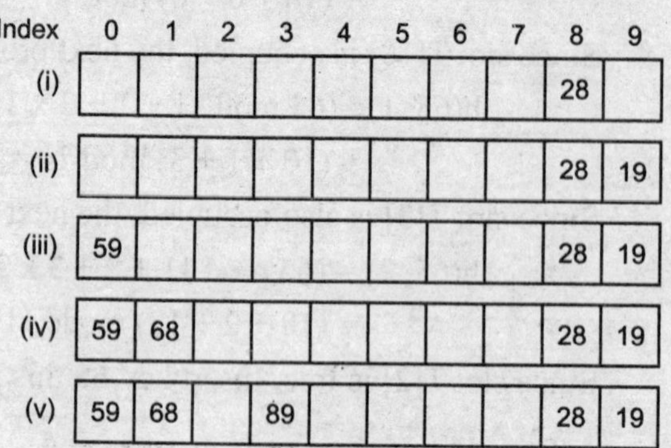

Index	0	1	2	3	4	5	6	7	8	9
(i)									28	
(ii)									28	19
(iii)	59								28	19
(iv)	59	68							28	19
(v)	59	68		89					28	19

Figure 13.13: Example of quadratic probing.

Effectiveness of quadratic probing

This brief example—which only saves one collision - might not seem proof of effectiveness but a full statistical analysis of quadratic probing shows its benefits over linear probing. It can be shown that, if the table is less than half full and its size is prime, then quadratic probing guarantees that a new element can always be inserted into the table and no cell is probed twice in the process. The fact that we are adding squares to location numbers instead of just incrementing them might suggest that there is a much larger computational cost from squaring. This is not so, as simpler processes can be used.

In a table of size **S**, if our home bucket is called **P0** then the our **i**-th probe after that will be:

$$Pi = P0 + i^2 \text{ (MOD S)}$$

and the one prior to that will be:

$$Pi\text{-}1 = P0 + (i-1)^2 \text{ (MOD S)}$$

Subtracting the second equation from the first gives:

$$Pi - Pi\text{-}1 = i^2 - (i-1)^2 = (2i-1) \text{ (MOD S)}$$

Therefore

$$Pi = Pi\text{-}1 + (2i-1) \text{ (MOD S)}$$

Now we are dealing with a multiplication by 2 and adding 1. Multiplication by 2 is simply a shift- left of a binary number and an increment is a very fast operation for a microprocessor. The **(MOD S)** is still needed to deal with wraparound, but it is simply dealt with by subtracting **S** as and when the element index overshoots the table's last element.

13.9.3 Double Hashing

Double hashing is one of the best methods available for open addressing because the permutations produced have many of the characteristics of randomly chosen permutations. Double hashing uses a hash function of the form

$$h(k, i) = [h_1(k) + i\, h_2(k)] \bmod m \qquad \text{for } i = 0, 1, 2, \ldots, m-1$$

where m is the size of the hash table; h_1 (k) [= k mod m] and h_2(k) [= k mod m') are two auxiliary hash function. Here m's is chosen to be slightly less than m (say, m–1 or m–2).

Therefore, for a given key k, the first slot probed is $T[h_1(k)]$ and the successive probes are offset from previous positions by the amount $h_2(k)$ modulo m. Thus, unlike the case of linear or quadratic probing, the probe sequence depends in two ways on the key value k, since the initial probe position and/or the offset may vary.

Double hashing represents an improvement over linear or quadratic probing as $O(m^2)$ probe sequence are used rather than O(m), since each possible pair $<h_1(k), h_2(k)>$ yields a distinct probe sequence, and as we vary the key value, the initial probe position $h_1(k)$, and the offset $h_2(k)$ may vary independently. As a result, the performance of double hashing appears to be very close to the performance of the ideal scheme of uniform hashing.

EXAMPLE 13.10: Consider inserting the keys 76, 26, 37, 59, 21, 65, 88 into a hash table of size m = 11 using double hashing. Further, consider that the auxiliary hash functions are $h_1(k) = k \bmod 11$ and $h_2(k) = k \bmod 9$.

Solution:

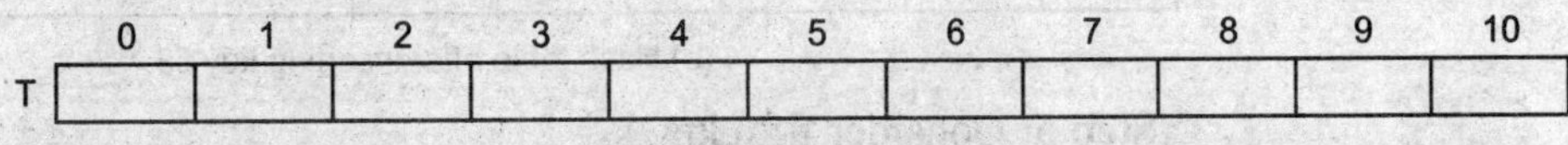

(a) Initial state of the hash table

Step 1: Consider first key k = 76

$h_1(76) = 76 \bmod 11 = 10 \qquad h_2(76) = 76 \bmod 9 = 4$

$h(76, 0) = (10 + 0 \times 4) \bmod 11 = 10 \bmod 11 = 10$

Since slot T[10] is free, insert key 76 at this place.

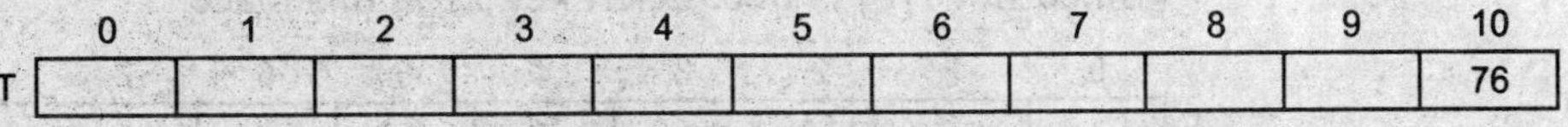

(b) Hash table after inserting key 76

Step 2: Consider second key k = 26

$h_1(26) = 26 \bmod 11 = 4 \qquad h_2(26) = 26 \bmod 9 = 8$

$h(26, 0) = (4 + 0 \times 8) \bmod 11 = 4 \bmod 11 = 4$

Since slot T[4] is free, insert key 26 at this place.

	0	1	2	3	4	5	6	7	8	9	10
T					26						76

(c) Hash table after inserting key 26

Step 3: Consider third key k = 37

$h_1(37) = 37 \text{ mod } 11 = 4 \qquad h_2(37) = 37 \text{ mod } 9 = 1$

$h(37, 0) = (4 + 0 \text{ x } 1) \text{ mod } 11 = 4 \text{ mod } 11 = 4$

Since slot T[4] is occupied, the next probe sequence is computed as

$h(37, 1) = (4 + 1 \text{ x } 1) \text{ mod } 22 = 5 \text{ mod } 11 = 5$

Since slot T[5] is free. Insert key 37 at this place.

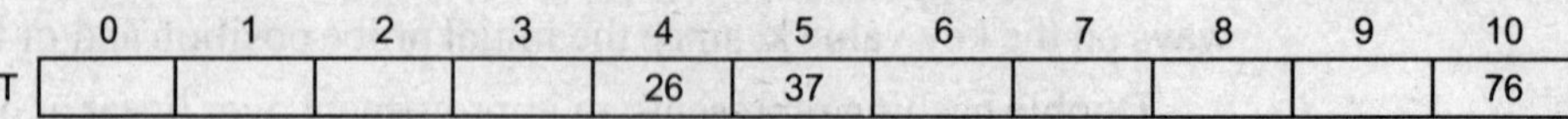

	0	1	2	3	4	5	6	7	8	9	10
T					26	37					76

(d) Hash table after inserting key 37

Step 4: Consider fourth key k = 59

$h_1(59) = 59 \text{ mod } 11 = 4 \qquad h_2(59) = 59 \text{ mod } 9 = 5$

$h(59, 0) = (4 + 0 \text{ x } 5) \text{ mod } 11 = 4 \text{ mod } 11 = 4$

Since slot T[4] is occupied, the next probe sequence is computed as

$h(59, 1) = (4 + 1 \text{ x } 5) \text{ mod } 11 = 9 \text{ mod } 11 = 9$

Since slot T[9] is free. Insert key 59 at this place.

	0	1	2	3	4	5	6	7	8	9	10
T					26	37				59	76

(e) Hash table after inserting key 59

Step 5: Consider fifth key k = 21

$h_1(21) = 21 \text{ mod } 11 = 10 \qquad h_2(21) = 21 \text{ mod } 9 = 3$

$h(21, 0 = (10 + 0 \text{ x } 3) \text{ mod } 11 = 10 \text{ mod } 11 = 10$

Since slot T[10] is occupied, the next probe sequence is computed as

$h(21, 1) = (10 + 1 \text{ x } 3) \text{ mod } 11 = 13 \text{ mod } 11 = 2$

Since slot T[2] is free. Insert key 21 at this place.

	0	1	2	3	4	5	6	7	8	9	10
T			21		26	37				59	76

(f) Hash table after inserting key 21

Step 6: Consider sixth key k = 65

$h_1(65) = 65 \text{ mod } 11 = 10 \qquad h_2(65) = 65 \text{ mod } 9 = 2$

$h(65, 0) = (10 + 0 \text{ x } 2) \text{ mod } 11 = 10 \text{ mod } 11 = 10$

Since slot T[10] is occupied, the next probe sequence is computed as

$h(65, 1) = (10 + 1 \text{ x } 2) \text{ mod } 11 = 12 \text{ mod } 11 = 1$

Since slot T[1] is free. Insert key 65 at this place.

	0	1	2	3	4	5	6	7	8	9	10
T		65	21		26	37				59	76

(g) Hash table after inserting key 65

Step 7: Consider seventh key k = 88

$h_1(88) = 88 \bmod 11 = 10 \qquad h_2(88) = 88 \bmod 9 = 7$

$h(88, 0) = (0 + 0 \times 7) \bmod 11 = 0 \bmod 11 = 0$

Since slot T[0] is free. Insert key 88 at this place.

	0	1	2	3	4	5	6	7	8	9	10
T	88	65	21		26	37				59	76

(h) Hash table after inserting key 88

Figure 13.14: (a)-(h) Illustrate the insertion of keys 76, 26, 37, 59, 21, 65, 88 is open address hash table with double hashing.

13.10 COLLISION RESOLUTION USING LINKED LIST

The major alternative to using adjacent storage is to use linked list. In this case table is implemented as an array of linked lists. Every element of the table is a pointer to a list. The list will contain all the elements with the same index produced by the hash function.

Example 13.11: When the hash function produces key 79, the new node is created and the array element with index 79 now points to this node. When another element's key produces index 79, the new node will be created and attached to the first one and so on. The same set of data as in the previous example will be organized as follows when we use linked list for handling collisions:

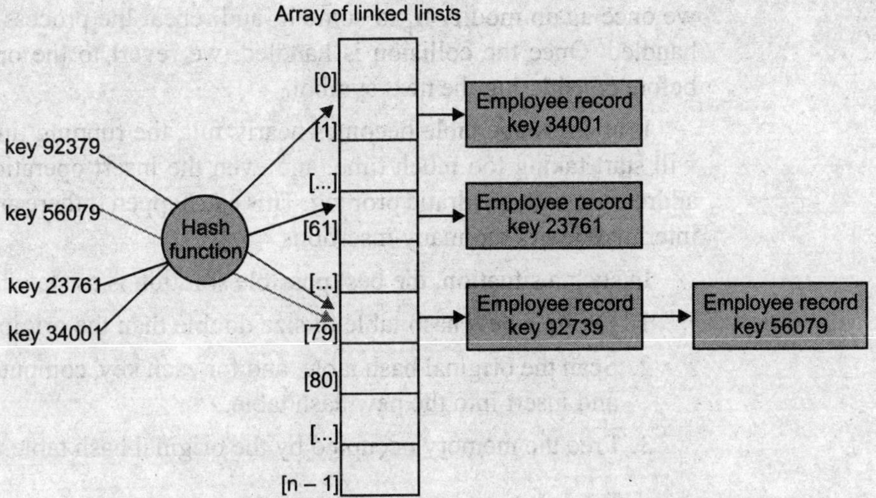

Figure 13.15: Collision Resolution Using Linked List.

Retrieving A Value

When it comes to retrieve a value, the hash function is applied to the desired key and the array index is produced. Then the search function accesses the list to which this array element points to. It compares the desired key to the key in the first node. If it matches, then the element is found. In this case the search of the element is on the order of 1, O(1). If not, then the function goes through the list comparing the keys. Search continues until the element is found or the end of the list is detected. In this case the search time depends on the length of the list.

Advantages to this approach

- The hash table size is unlimited (or limited only by available storage space). In this case you don't need to expand the table and recreate a hash function.
- Collision handling is simple: just insert colliding records into a list.

Disadvantages to this approach

- As the list of collided elements (collision chains) become long, search them for a desired element begin to take longer and longer.
- Using pointers slows the algorithm: time required is to allocate new nodes.

13.11 REHASHING

In rehashing we find an alternative empty location by modifying the hash function and applying the modified hash function to the colliding symbol.

For example, if x is the symbol and h(x) = i, and if the ith location is already occupied, then we modify the hash function h to h_1, and find out $h_1(x)$, if $h_1(x) = j$. If the jth location is empty, then we accommodate x in the jth location. Otherwise, we once again modify h_1 to some h_2 and repeat the process until the collision is handled. Once the collision is handled, we revert to the original hash function before considering the next symbol.

If at any stage table becomes nearly full, the running time for the operations will start taking too much time, and even the insert operation may fail for open addressing with quadratic probing. This can happen if there are too many deletions intermixed with too many insertions.

In such a situation, the best possible solution is as stated below:

1. Create a new hash table of size double than the original hash table.
2. Scan the original hash table, and for each key, compute the new hash value and insert into the new hash table.
3. Free the memory occupied by the original hash table.

13.12 COMPLEXITY CONSIDERATIONS FOR HASH TABLES

This table gives the average number of locations that have to be checked to conduct successful and unsuccessful searches in hash tables with different collision handling strategies, depending on the load factor given in the top column.

	0.10	0.25	0.50	0.75	0.90	0.99
Successful Search						
Direct chaining	1.05	1.12	1.25	1.37	1.45	1.48
Linear probing	1.06	1.17	1.50	2.50	5.50	50.5
Double hashing	1.05	1.15	1.39	1.85	2.56	4.65
Unsuccessful search						
Direct chaining	0.10	0.25	0.50	0.75	0.90	0.99
Linear probing	1.12	1.39	2.50	8.50	50.5	5000
Double hashing	1.11	1.33	2.00	4.00	10.0	100

This shows the considerable advantage double hashing has over linear probing. Whether or not the former is preferable to direct chaining is dependent on the circumstances.

The following table shows a comparison for different implementation of the table interface. Hash tables perform rather well. In practice, when deciding what to use, it will have to depend on the mix of operations typically performed. Lots of insertions and in particular deletions don't sit very well with hash tables, as explained above. The complexity of updating and retrieving is the same as that of searching.

	Search	Insert	Delete	Traverse
Sorted array	O(log n)	O(n)	O(n)	O(n)
Balanced bst	O(log n)	O(n log n)	O(log n)	O(n)
Hash table	O(1)	O(1)	O(1)	O(n log n)

Just to give an example, if there are 4096 entries in a balanced binary search tree, it takes on average 13.25 comparisons to complete a successful search. On the other hand, we can get as few as 1.39 comparisons by using a hash table, provided that we keep its load factor below 50 percent.

13.13 SOME USES OF HASHING

1. CD Databases

For CD's, what we would like to do, is have a world-wide CD database so that when users put there disk in the CD player, they get a full table of contents on there own computers. These tables are not on the disks themselves. No information about the songs is stored on the cd. It must be downloaded from the database. The problem is that CD's have no ID numbers stored on them. So how can the computer know which CD is in the player? Well, it can use the only information on the CD, the track length, and every cd is different. Basically, a big number is cooked up from the track lengths, a "signature" that identifies our CD. This signature is a value obtained by hashing. For example, a number of length of 8 or 10 hex. digits is cooked up; the number is then sent to the data base, and that data base just looks for the closest match. The reason being, that track length may not be measured exactly.

For example: a 35 0b ff 35 → looks in the library for a match Signature

an 35 0b ff 35	→	Searches database for a matching signature
signature		

The principle in hashing, is that x is put in a table in position h[x]. For the cd, you have a big table, some entries possibly nill. And then placed x in the table.

2. Drivers Licences/Insurance Cards

Exactly the same as the cd example. If you look at drivers license numbers or insurance card numbers, they are cooked up also from things that never change: date of birth, name, etc. Again, some digits are taken and placed in a certain place. The numbers are the way they are, so that inside the computers they can be put into a table.

3. Sparse Arrays

A sparse array is an array which is mostly 0, and in which a few are non-zero entries. Of course one could store the array, but that would not make a lot of sense The storage would be proportional to n squared. Another possibility is to cut it up into huge blocks, so that we would have 1 element per block on the average. The number of blocks is about equal to the number of non-zero elements. Then you

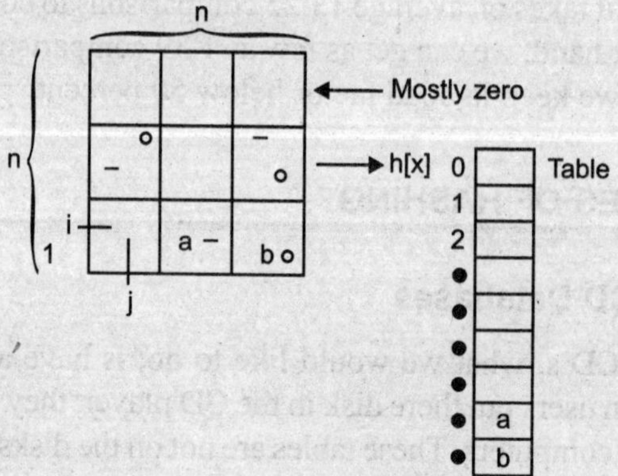

store the elements in a table. We store a two dimensional array in a one dimensional array. There is a one to one correspondence between the elements in the array and the elements in the table.

# of blocks ~= # non-zero elements

Let the array be n x n, and let there be N nonzero entries. From the coordinates (i,j) of an array element, we determine an index k in an array by a simple calculation. Thus, we have k=h(i,j) for some function h, called a hash function. All elements with the same hashed value k are put in the k-th slot of a simple table. The storage is proportional to N. Had we stored the array, we would have required storage proportional to n x n.

4. File Signatures

File signatures provide a compact means of identifying files. The files may be large, such as audio files, picture files, or text files. We extract a function, h[x], the file signature, which is a property of the file.

As an example, if we have a binary file, the signature could consist of bits# {17, 21, 1003, 905, 904, and 3}, a six bit signature. This signature is very compact. Another possibility for a file signature is the name. Storing files by name is customary, but you can also store by signature, because the signature identifies the file.

If changes are made to the file, then the signature will generally change. In this way, the signature of a file can be used as a quick verification to see if anyone has altered the file, or if it has lost a bit during transmission. A frequently used application is for files storing student's marks.

5. Game Boards

Consider a game board for tic-tac-toe or chess. A position in a game may be stored using a hash function. A tic-tac-toe board consists of nine cells, each of which may contain an 'X', an 'O', or nothing. The standard notation for "nine digits, each chosen from the set {0, 1, 2}" is "{0,1,2}^9". We adopt this notation with (0,1,2) corresponding to (X,O,empty). Reading left to right and top to bottom yields (010021000) in base three, or 1*3^4 +2*3^5 +1*3^8. That is the numerical index for this game position, a hash function: From our object, we are cooking up a number.

Game Board Hashing Example 13.12

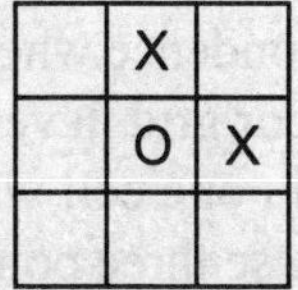

$h[x] \rightarrow \{0,1,2\}^9$

$(010021000)_3 = 1*3^8 + 2*3^5 + 1*3^4 = h[x]$

The nine squares in a TIC-TAC-TOE board can be mapped to digits in a ternary number. In this example, blank space is mapped to 0, X to 1 and O to 2.

6. A.D.T. Dictionary (Searching, Sorting)

The main application of hashing is for the ADT dictionary (insert, search, sort). It is a serious competitor for binary search trees. However, to appreciate the difference with binary search trees, it helps to understand the difference between various models of computation.

The model which we will use in this example is the RAM model. Recall that the RAM model allows us to perform any operation on a real number in one time unit, regardless of its length.

You are given n different integers from{0, 1, 2, ... n^17}. Using the RAM model, these numbers can be sorted in linear time. (If you discover the answer, you will have rediscovered a famous method of sorting.)

This may appear surprising, because we all have, stored at the back of our minds, that n*log(n) is about the best that you can do for sorting. The trick is that we are talking about a different model. When someone says that n*log(n) is the best that can be done for sorting in the worst case, they are talking about a model which only allows comparisons between two elements at a time. (In that model, one comparison requires one time unit, while all other operations take zero time units.) That is very restrictive. As an analogy, imagine that you are given a scale. You are asked to sort everything using this balance alone. With a RAM model, you have more tricks at your disposal. You can take a number and look at the bits and bytes. The RAM model is more powerful. You can do more, and you can do it faster. The teaser above is a demonstration of the fact that the two models are very different. Comparing estimates of algorithms obtained from different computational is not meaningful.

7. Graphics

In graphics, a central problem is the storage of objects in a scene or view. We have already seen a structure for separating objects in a scene. For the Binary search trees, the strategy was to partition everything by light. You may also organize your data by hashing. The hashing approach to this is to make a grid of appropriate size, an ordinary vertical-horizontal grid. A grid is basically a double array, and there is a one to one correspondence when you go from a double array to a single array. As such, we will store our grid in very much the same way as we did the sparse array. All points that fall in one cell will be stored in the same place. If a cell contains three points, then these three points will be stored in the same entry. The mapping from the grid cell to the memory location is our hash function. An advantage of this method of storage is that certain operations are very fast, such as the nearest neighbour search. If you store your data like this, and you are asked to find the nearest neighbour of a point, the first place to look is in the surrounding cell, then two layers out, then three layers out, and so on, until another point is found.

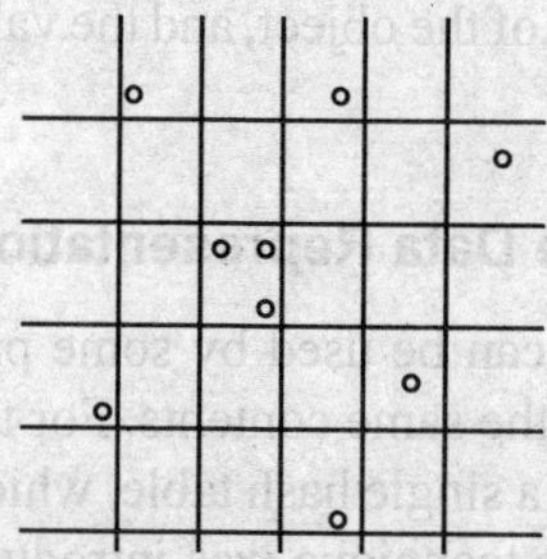

One method for organizing objects that lie in the plain is to create a grid of appropriate size, and to store the objects that lie in the same grid square together. One advantage to this is that it facilitates "Nearest Neighbor" Searches.

8. Associative Arrays

Hash tables are commonly used to implement many types of in-memory tables. They are used to implement associative arrays (arrays whose indices are arbitrary strings or other complicated objects), especially in interpreted programming languages like AWK, Perl, and PHP.

9. Database Indexing

Hash tables may also be used for disk-based persistent data structures and database indices (such as dbm) although balanced trees are more popular in these applications.

10. Caches

Hash tables can be used to implement caches, auxiliary data tables that are used to speed up the access to data that is primarily stored in slower media. In this application, hash collisions can be handled by discarding one of the two colliding entries — usually the one that is currently stored in the table.

11. Sets

Besides recovering the entry which has a given key, many hash table implementations can also tell whether such an entry exists or not.

Those structures can therefore be used to implement a set data structure, which merely records whether a given key belongs to a specified set of keys. In this case, the structure can be simplified by eliminating all parts which have to do with the entry values. Hashing can be used to implement both static and dynamic sets.

13. Object Representation

Several dynamic languages, such as Python, JavaScript, and Ruby, use hash tables to implement objects. In this representation, the keys are the names of the members and methods of the object, and the values are pointers to the corresponding member or method.

13. Unique Data Representation

Hash tables can be used by some programs to avoid creating multiple character strings with the same contents. For that purpose, all strings in use by the program are stored in a single hash table, which is checked whenever a new string has to be created. This technique was introduced in Lisp interpreters under the name hash consigns, and can be used with many other kinds of data (expression trees in a symbolic algebra system, records in a database, files in a file system, binary decision diagrams, etc.)

EXERCISES

1. Why we use hash tables.
2. What do you mean by direct addressing?
3. What do you mean by hash table?
4. What is hash function? Explain various hashing functions.
5. Explain concept of collision resolution by chaining hash functions.
6. Explain concept of collision resolution by separate chaining.
7. Explain concept of collision resolution by overflow chaining.
8. Explain concept of collision resolution by open addressing.
9. Explain the techniques given below:
   (a) Linear probing
   (b) Quadratic probing
   (c) Double hashing
   (d) Rehashing
10. Explain the concept of collision resolution using linked list.
11. Explain complexity considerations for hash tables.
12. Explain various uses of hashing.

14 CHAPTER

File and Storage Management

14.1 INTRODUCTION

As in our daily life, huge amount of data collected and processed, so it is very difficult to handle it. But this can be handled fast and easily by using files. Files are the mega data structure used in information processing. Actually a file itself is a bunch of bytes stored on some storage devices like magnetic disk, magnetic drum and magnetic tape etc.

In a modern computer system files play an important role. One of the main requirements for the user to participate meaningfully in the designing of a system is to have a basic understanding of computer files .the first constraint that we generally encounter in developing information systems is the files. Sometimes the amount of data to be stored is too great for the capacity of the file storage device to permit the desired response time .In other, instances complex information retrieval requirement for the accessing the files make the program too difficult to write or too large for the computer systems.

A file is a collection of records. Each record is made up of fields. The various fields consists of groups of character, say the decimal digits 0 through 9and alphabet A through Z. groups of fields are combined to form a logical record. This logical record contains all the data of interest about some entity. These files are generally stored on secondary storage devices like magnetic tapes, magnetic disks, etc. The records on these devices are called the physical records. These devices are much cheaper than the primary in the computer and have greater capacity. It is not advisable to hold all the data in the primary memory. Since this may not be used all the time .The files are to be used only when necessary and, so it is preferable to use the secondary storage for storing files.

Different application requires a variety of record types and file structure; one basic distinction is between fixed and variable length records. A fixed length record has all the field sizes and a number of fields fixed or known in advance whereas in the variable length record type the number of fields is not specified in advance .the variable length record makes programming and file design a complex one. The only way out will be to break this variable –length record in to several fixed length records and identify them as a header and trailer records (which may be a variable).

There are various kinds of file structures. The simplest kind of file is one in which all the records are in sequence. Many computer applications rely on sequential files .Another kind of file organization is indexed sequential organization. Though the basic organization is sequential, the correspondence is provided by an index. Though in the sequential file the records are located by scanning records one by one in sequence in index sequential file organization, the records are located through directory wherein the correspondence between record key and record location is established.

The files can also be stored on the direct access storage. There is yet another type of file organization called random organization file organization .In this case the records are stored without regard to the sequence of record keys. The location of a record is determined by transforming record key in to a physical address. The address is generated by either (a) Record key for transformation organization (b) Direct addressing

The file as input and output medium has the following advantages from different point of view:

1. Files are used to save time for data entry and reduce its processing time also.
2. These are used for storage and subsequent retrieval of data.
3. Files are also used to correcting the incorrect data and also update the correct form data.
4. Files are used in testing and debugging of programs.
5. Files are used for processing the voluminous data.
6. Data validation for the accuracy of data can be measured by using files.
7. Using files data can be stored on many devices like floppy disks, hard disks, magnetic tapes, magnetic drum etc, which helps for the permanent storage and distributed data processing.

1. Field

A field is a meaningful collection of related characters. It is the smallest logical data entity that is treated as a single unit in data processing .For example, if we are processing employees data of a company, we may have an employee code field, employee name, an hourly pay field, a tax deduction field etc.

2. Record

Fields are generally grouped together to form a **record**. A record is a collection of related fields that are treated as a single unit. An employee record would be a collection of fields of one employee which include the employee's code, name, pay rate, tax etc.

A record can be classified as:

- Logical record
- Physical record

A logical record is a group of related information uniquely identifiable and treated as a unit. The data record is usually considered to be a group item comprising of several related items. For example, in a employees master file, an employee's record is a logical record.

A physical record is a physical unit of information whose size and record mode is convenient to a particular input or output device for the storage of data .The physical and the logical records are related to each other in many possible ways. A physical record may consist of several logical records. A physical record may consist of a portion of the logical record and may consist of the mixture of several complete and partial logical records. The following figure shows various types of physical record.

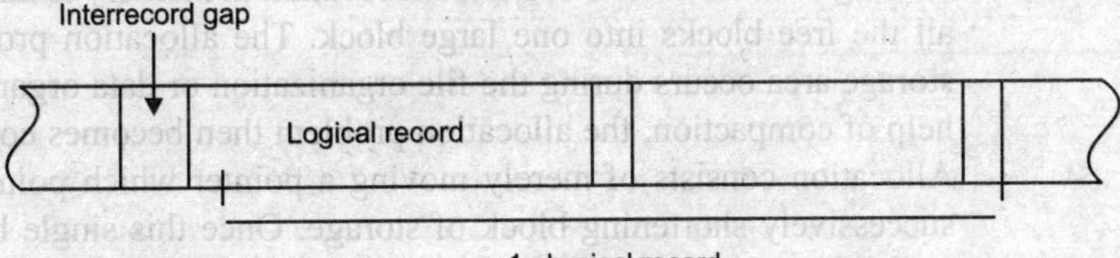

3. Label Records

Label records are normally used for files that are stored on magnetic tape or direct access devices. The record usually contain the information relative to the file .Card files do not contain any label records. Generally label records are written at the beginning and end of the file.

4. File

A file is a collection of number of related records that may have the same or varying length. For example collection of all employee records for one company would be an employee file. Similarly collection of all inventory records for a company forms an inventory file. It is customary to set up a *master file* of permanent data and to use *transaction file* containing data of temporary nature.

A file is a collection of related data stored in a particular area on the disk. There are two types of access on the files (two ways to access the files). These are sequential access files and random access file. In the sequential access files, the data or text can be store or read back sequentially. In the random access files, data can be accessed and processed randomly. Also files can be divided into two types. One is data file and second one is program file. There are two types of operations can be done on data i.e. data can be transferred between the console and the program and further can be transferred between program and a disk file.

5. Blocking

A block is referred to as a physical record containing a series of logical records .A physical record is a group of characters or records which are treated as an entity when move into and out of the main storage.

When data is stored in the magnetic tape or direct access devices, the logical records are grouped into blocks. Each read or writes operation may transfer the entire block of the data to or from main storage at one time and to or from an input/output device. Each logical record within the block is then processed separately .Once the relationship between logical and physical record is established, only logical records are made available to the program.

6. Compaction

Compaction is technique for reclaiming the storage. Compaction works by actually moving blocks of data etc. from one location in memory to another so as to collect all the free blocks into one large block. The allocation problem of data in the storage area occurs during the file organization or data organization. So with the help of compaction, the allocation problem then becomes completely simplified. Allocation consists of merely moving a pointer which points to the top of this successively shortening block of storage. Once this single block gets too small again, the compaction mechanism is again invoked to reclaim what unused storage may now exists among allocated blocks. There is generally no storage release mechanism. For this purpose, a marking technique or algorithm is used to mark all those blocks which are still in use. Then instead of freeing each unmarked block by calling a release mechanism to put it on to the free list. The compactor simply collects all the unmarked blocks into one large blocks at one end of the memory segment. So this is the concept of Compaction.

14.2 CLASSIFICATION OF FILES

Files are classified into different categories. User can decide what type of file it required for its data processing. Some files can be classified as:

14.2.1 Master Files

Master files are the files of a fairly permanent nature e.g, Customer ledger, purchase ledger, inventory, payroll etc. They include some information, which is of a permanent nature and also data, which is updated by recent transactions. For example a sales ledger might contain the customer's names and address as well as their current position which is updated periodically.

The normal means of updating a master file is by adding, deleting organization amending records in the file

Static master files: The business entities that these files describe are of a permanent organization semi permanent nature (e.g., products, suppliers, customers, employers etc.)

Dynamic master files: The business entities that these files describe are of a transitory importance to the business (e.g, customers orders, Works orders, projects, price lists etc).

14.2.2 Transaction Files

Transaction files are the files in which the data relating to the business events is recorded, prior to a further stage of processing and are created from source documents used for recording events organization transactions .This further processing may be the use of the transaction data to update master files .

After the master file is processed, it is usually re initialized, and further transactions are then recorded in it.

Examples of transaction files are:

1. Customer's orders for products (to update an order file)
2. Details of price changes for products (to update a product file)
3. Purchase orders, job cards, invoice, dispatch notes etc.
4. Details of cash postings in customers account.

14.2.3 Work File

A work file is a temporary file. This type of file is created temporarily by an application of some purpose and the removed automatically when it is no more required.

14.4.4 Backup Files

These files are taken in order to provide back copies, in case of loss organization damage to current versions, and are copies of currently used master files kept in the computer library as a measure of security.

14.3 VARIOUS OPERATIONS ON FILES

- Create: Essential if a system is to add files. Need not be a separate system call (can be merged with open).

- Delete: Essential if a system is to delete files.
- Open: Not essential. An optimization in which the translation from file name to disk locations is perform only once per file rather than once per access.
- Close: Not essential. Free resources.
- Read: Essential. Must specify filename, file location, number of bytes, and a buffer into which the data is to be placed. Several of these parameters can be set by other system calls and in many OS's they are.
- Write: Essential if updates are to be supported. See read for parameters.
- Seek: Not essential (could be in read/write). Specify the offset of the next (read or write) access to this file.
- Get attributes: Essential if attributes are to be used.
- Set attributes: Essential if attributes are to be user settable.
- Rename: Tanenbaum has strange words. Copy and delete is not acceptable for big files. Moreover copy-delete is not atomic. Indeed link-delete is not atomic so even if link is provided, renaming a file adds functionality.

14.3.1 File Updation

The active lifetime of a file is usually short. Very soon the information stored on a file becomes old and it becomes necessary to modify the file with current information. This process of modifying an old file with current information is known as file updation. The problem of file updation can be defined as follows: given an old master file and a transaction file, the problem is to create an updated new master file.

The process of updating may include:

(i) Insertion of new records.

(ii) Modification of some existing records

(iii) Deletion of obsolete records and

(iv) Copy of those records which are neither obsolete nor require any modification.

Consider an example in which the list of subscribers of a magazine to computerized. The master file contains the following information: subscriber number, name, address, age, sex, etc. The transaction file contains records having the following fields: subscriber number, transaction code, name and address, age, sex.

The transaction code indicates the type of transaction. If the code is 1, it is assumed to be the record of a new subscriber. Code 2 indicates that the subscriber has not renewed his subscription and the record is to be deleted. Code 3 indicates that there has been a change of address for the subscriber and the record is to be modified.

Both the files are stored in the ascending order of their key which is the subscriber number. The logic of the file updation is as follows:

In the beginning, one record from each file is read.

(i) If the key of transaction record is lower than the master record a new record will be created in the new master file for this new subscriber. Subsequently next transaction is read and the procedure is repeated.

(ii) If the key of the master record is less than the transaction record, the record will be simply copied onto the new master file without any charges. After this, next master is read and same procedure is repeated.

(iii) In case keys of transaction and master records are equal then the master record will be deleted or updated depending on whether the transaction code is 2 or 3. In either case, next master record and transaction record will be read and procedure is repeated.

The above logic will work until either of the file is exhausted. Note that either of these files can be exhausted earlier. In that case, the remaining records of the other ifle will be copied on to the New Master file.

14.3.2 File Referencing

When access is made to a particular record to ascertain what is contained therein, e.g., reference is made to a 'process' file during an invoicing run. Note that this does not involve any alteration to the record itself.

14.3.3 File Maintenance

This is the process of adding, amending or deleting standing data on a reference or master file. Examples include adding the price of a new product to a prices file and deleting the details of an employee who has left, from the payroll file:

Transaction data File maintenance Master file / Reference file.

(update)

File maintenance of reference file will be a separate procedure, whereas file maintenance of master files may be combined with the updating.

14.3.4 File Enquiry

It is the examination of both reference and master files to obtain information contained therein. This does not involve any alternation to the file contains.

***Remark:** Header and trailer label of a magnetic tape. In any file maintenance procedure, care must be taken to see that the correct files are being processed. To ensure that the correct file is used and the entire file is processed, file labels are used for magnetic tape.*

The label at the beginning of the file is the header label while the trailer label appears at the end of each file. The header label identifies the file for a programmer so that he does not, by mischance, process some wrong file. The header label, typically, contains information regarding file name, file number, real no, date file written, retention period, identify no, etc. This would also ensure that the programmer updates the file at the right date.

14.3.5 File Design Considerations

Business data processing systems are oriented toward file processing. This orientation means that storage files are a critical component of any data processing system. File structure and file access determines which input, processing and output devices may be employed most effectively.

Much of the structure of the files for the computer system depends on the individual application and the designer will have to make a number of decisions from the information developed during the system analysis steps proceeding file design.

The first file design decisions involve the data to be stored on the files. As the design for a new information system is developed, the requirements for information to be stored for subsequent retrieval will be specified. Related information is grouped also records and there may be several types of records in a single physical file. Record types and key fields for retrieval purposes must be defined.

Information in a file is updated in two ways. First, routine transaction occur which change fields very often in the file. Second, the updations in the master information fields occur less frequently and can be termed as file maintenance transactions. In principle it would be possible to change any field in the file with proper authorization because errors can occur anywhere and provisions must be made to correct them.

The next task is defining the record format. Fixed length records are the earliest and simplest to use from a processing and programming point of view. It is better always to use fixed-length records. However, if the lengths of record vary, then variable-length records are necessary.

14.4 FILE ORGANIZATION TECHNIQUES

The basic technology of the data organization is based on a hierarchy. Data must be approached on an organized basis, if it is to be use full, in data processing; the hierarchy of data is described below.

1. A character is any single number, alphabetic letter organization special symbol.

2. A data records consists of a group of related data fields (e.g, employee'sequential record, customer record, organization inventory record)
3. A data field is an area that can hold one organization more characters that, together represents a specific data element (e.g., the name field, the quantity field).
4. A data file is a compilation of related data records maintained in some prearranged order.
5. A database usually consists of several related organization integrated data files.

A file consists of a number of records. Each record is made up of a number of fields and each field consists of a number of characters.

Clock number	Employees name	Date of birth	Sex	Grade	Hourly rate
1301	Sukhwant	24-041977	M	5	Rs 20000
↑	Field	Note 1. Clock number is the key field			
Characters		2. Grade is coded			

In order to produce useful information by means of computerized data processing. It is necessary to organize data in a systematic way. Methods of organizing data are referred to as data structures. The most important structure is a vertical hierarchy of data consisting of files, records, data items (or fields) and characters with characters encoded in terms of bits.

It will be seen that at the top of the hierarchy is a file. When all records of the same record content are gathered as a single collection of information, the collection is referred to as a file (or data set).

The records in a file, in turn, are groupings of related data items (or fields) and then specific data values.

For ease of access or reference, each record is allocated a key field- that is a field by which it is identified. The files are, normally, organized in key field sequences. A record may contain two or more keys. For example, an invoice may also be required by customer number. Here, the customer number will be referred to as the primary key and the invoice number, the secondary key.

Data organization may culminate in a data bank. A data bank is a collection of librates of files. To clarify further: one line of an invoice may form a data-item, a complete invoice may form a record, a complete set of such records may form a file, the collection of files (say, for inventory control) may form a library. In turn, librates are referred to as data bank.

Fixed-length Records

A file is said to consist of fixed-length records when each record is the some length.

This can be achieved in two ways, either all the records are identical in layout or where the layout is different each record is padded so that the total length is equal to that of the longest. The first is common on most master files while the second approach is often found in transaction files where the data required for different transactions varies.

Fixed length records are usually easier to design and write programs for but can be more wasteful in backing storage than variable-length records.

Variable-length Records

There are several types of variable-length record situations for example:

- a group of different types of record, each of fixed but differing lengths;
- records with a fixed minimum length and a variable number of fixed-length items following the fixed portion :
- records with a fixed minimum length and a fixed number of variable-length items following the fixed portion :
- records with fixed minimum length and variable number of variable-length items following the fixed portion :
- complete and random variability of length.

Often, it is possible to break down a variable-length record into a group of fixed-length records, so that with careful design, the advantages of both fixed and variable working can be achieved.

Given that a file consists, generally speaking, of a collection of records, a key element in file management is the way in which the records themselves are organized inside the file, since this heavily affects system performances ad far as record finding and access. Note carefully that by "organization" we refer here to the *logical* arrangement of the records in the file (their ordering or, more generally, the presence of "closeness" relations between them based on their content), and not instead to the physical layout of the file as stored on a storage media.

Choosing a file organization is a design decision, hence it must be done having in mind the achievement of good performance with respect to the most likely usage of the file. The criteria usually considered important are:

1. Fast access to single record or collection of related records.
2. Easy record adding/update/removal, without disrupting.
3. Storage efficiency.
4. Redundancy as a warranty against data corruption.

Needless to say, these requirements are in contrast with each other for all but the most trivial situations, and it's the designer job to find a good compromise among them, yielding and adequate solution to the problem at hand. For example, easiness of adding/etc. is not an issue when defining the data organization of a CD-ROM product, whereas fast access is, given the huge amount of data that this media can store. However, as it will become apparent shortly, fast access techniques are based on the use of additional information about the records, which in turn competes with the high volumes of data to be stored.

Logical data organization is indeed the subject of whole shelves of books, in the "Database" section of your library. Here we'll briefly address some of the simpler used techniques, mainly because of their relevance to data management from the lower-level (with respect to a database's) point of view of an OS. Six organization models will be considered:

- Pile.
- Sequential.
- Indexed-sequential.
- Indexed.
- Hashed.
- Direct

The term file organization refers to the relationship of the key of the record to the physical location of that record in the computer file.

Distinction may be made at the outset between physical and logical files and records. A physical file is a physical unit, such as magnetic tape or a disk. A logical file, on the other hand, is a complete set of records for a specific application or purpose. It may occupy only part of a physical file or may extend over more than one physical file, e.g., an inventory master file, which is a logical file, containing a record for each item in inventory, may require one or more reels of magnetic tape.

There are two objectives of computer based file organization: ease of file creation and maintenance, and, providing an efficient means of storing and retrieving information.

The Four file organization methods that are commonly used in business data processing application are:

- Sequential
- Indexed
- Indexed-sequential
- Direct or random access

The selection of a particular file organization depends upon:

(a) The type of application

(b) The method of processing for updating files,

(c) Size of the file,

(d) File inquiry capabilities,

(e) File volatility, and

(f) The response time.

14.4.1 Sequential File Organization

This is the most common structure for large files that are typically processed in their entirety, and it's at the heart of the more complex schemes. In this scheme, all the records have the same size and the same field format, with the fields having fixed size as well. The records are sorted in the file according to the content of a field of a scalar type, called "key". The key must identify uniquely a records, hence different record have different keys. This organization is well suited for batch processing of the entire file, without adding or deleting items: this kind of operation can take advantage of the fixed size of records and file; moreover, this organization is easily stored both on disk and tape. The key ordering, along with the fixed record size, makes this organization amenable to dichotomy search.

However, adding and deleting records to this kind of file is a tricky process: the logical sequence of records typically matches their physical layout on the media storage, so to ease file navigation, hence adding a record and maintaining the key order requires a reorganization of the whole file. The usual solution is to make use of a "log file" (also called "transaction file"), structured as a pile, to perform this kind of modification, and periodically perform a batch update on the master file.

In a sequential file, records are arranged in the ascending or descending order of chronological order of a key field which may be numeric (such as customer's name), or both (a file of vehicle license including both letters of alphabet and numerals). Since the records are ordered by the key field, there is no storage location identification. Sequential file organization is particularly suited to such applications are payroll in which the file is to be processed in entirely, i.e, each and every record is processed in the same setup.

For locating a record in the file. It is necessary to start at a given reference point (which in after the beginning of the file) and example each record in sequence until the desired record is located. There are often gaps in the numbering of the records, for example, record number 23 may be followed by record number 31.

Transactions affecting the sequential files are accumulated in batches, which are then used to update the sequential file at periodic intervals.

Sequential files are normally created and maintained on magnetic tape. (An exception is a card file). The vast majority are updated vita batch processing, which is the most efficient method to use with a sequential file). All updated data is sorted prior to its use. (During batch processing, the updated data and the sequential file data are alternately read and processed.) After scanning each incoming record, the computer determines which records require updating. After all the changes are made, the update is complete.

Sequential files can also be constructed on magnetic disk. However, when this is done, the direct access capabilities of disk are not taken advantages of.

With most tape units, it is impractical to write a new record back to the same position as the old one occupied and as a result the master file is updated in the CPU and then written on to a new tape.

Advantages

1. Sample to understand approach.
2. Easy to organize, maintain and understand.
3. Loading a record requires only the record key.
4. Efficient and economical if the activity rate, i.e., the proportion of file records to be processed is high.
5. Relatively inexpensive I/O media and devices may be used.
6. Errors in files remain localized.
7. Files may be relatively easy to reconstruct since a good measure of built-in backup is usually available.

Disadvantages

1. Entire file must be processed even when the activity rate is very low.
2. Transactions must be sorted and placed to sequence prior to processing.
3. Timeliness of data in file deteriorates while batches are being accumulated.
4. Data redundancy is typically high since the same data may be stored in several files sequenced in different keys.
5. Random enquiries are virtually impossible to handle.
6. Applications. Payroll A/C financial K/C etc.

14.4.2 Indexed File Organization

Why using a single index for a certain key field of a data record? Indexes can be obviously built for each field that uniquely identifies a record (or set of records within the file), and whose type is amenable to ordering. Multiple indexes hence provide a high degree of flexibility for accessing the data via search on various attributes; this organization also allows the use of variable length records (containing different fields).

It should be noted that when multiple indexes are used the concept of sequentially of the records within the file is useless: each attribute (field) used to construct an index typically imposes an ordering of its own. For this very reason is typically not possible to use the "sparse" (or "spaced") type of indexing previously described.

Two types of indexes are usually found in the applications: the exhaustive type, which contains an entry for each record in the main file, in the order given by the indexed key, and the partial type, which contain an entry for all those records that contain the chosen key field (for variable records only).

14.4.3 Indexed Sequential Access Organization

An index file can be used to effectively overcome the above mentioned problem, and to speed up the key search as well. The simplest indexing structure is the single-level one: a file whose records are pairs key-pointer, where the pointer is the position in the data file of the record with the given key. Only a subset of data records, evenly spaced along the data file, are indexed, so to mark intervals of data records.

A key search then proceeds as follows: the search key is compared with the index ones to find the highest index key preceding the search one, and a linear search is performed from the record the index key points onward, until the search key is matched or until the record pointed by the next index entry is reached. In spite of the double file access (index + data) needed by this kind of search, the decrease in access time with respect to a sequential file is significant.

Consider, for example, the case of simple linear search on a file with 1,000 records. With the sequential organization, averages of 500 key comparisons are necessary (assuming uniformly distributed search key among the data ones). However, using and evenly spaced index with 100 entries, the number of comparisons is reduced to 50 in the index file plus 50 in the data file: a 5:1 reduction in the number of operations.

This scheme can obviously be hierarchically extended: an index is a sequential file in itself, amenable to be indexed in turn by a second-level index, and so on, thus exploiting more and more the hierarchical decomposition of the searches to decrease the access time. Obviously, if the layering of indexes is pushed too far, a point is reached when the advantages of indexing are hampered by the increased storage costs and by the index access times as well.

The sequential and the direct access files are considered the opposites of each other. The indexed sequential file is a synthesis of these files types. The organization of an indexed sequential file combines the positive aspects of both the sequential and the direct access files. In an indexed sequential file, records are stored sequentially on a direct access device (i.e., magnetic disk) and data is accessible either randomly or sequentially. The sequential access of data occurs one record at a time until the desired item of data found.

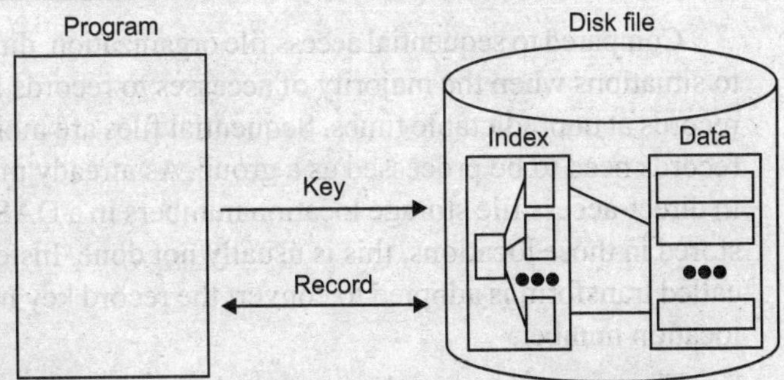

This type of file organization is best suited for situations where both batch and on-line processing are to be supported. The records in these files are organized in sequence for the efficient processing of large batch jobs but an index is also used to speed up access to the records. This type of file organization combines advantages of both the sequential and direct approaches.

Records are stored sequentially by a key record in a DASD. At the time of periodic updating during a batch run, the direct access capability is not in use, only the first record may be directly accessed, while all others records are read in sequence in the same manner as records stored on a magnetic tape. However, indexes permit access to selected records without searching the entire file. This technique is known as indexed sequential access method (ISAM).

Indexed sequential file organization is best suited for situations where it is not known in advance whether a particular record exists. The index is scanned for the requisite data-item by employing a technique known as binary search.

This is a way of narrowing the scope of the search by looking at the middle of the index and half of the index. Each subsequent search is begun at the remaining records until the desired record is found. If the desired entry is not found in the index, no further search need be made and time wasted.

14.4.4 Direct Or Random or Relative File Organization

Files in this type of organization are stored in a direct access storage device (DASD) like, magnetic disk, using an identifying key. This identifying key relates a record to its actual storage position in the file. The computer can directly locate the key to find the desired record without having to search through any other records first. For example, employee records could be accessed by using the employee number assigned to them. Usually, record (employees', customers' etc.) are assigned numbers in a chronological order as new number are added to the file. When inactive numbers are removed from a file, these numbers become available to be assigned to new employees, customers, etc. Consequently, records stored to such systems appear to be in a random order: hence the name random file for the direct access type of file. The processing in this case is referred to as random processing. It is used in online system where rapid response and fast updating are important.

Compared to sequential access file organization, direct-access file is more useful to situations when the majority of accesses to records in that file are for individual records at unpredictable times. Sequential files are more useful when most or all of records need to be processed as a group. As already mentioned, records are stored in direct-access file storage location numbers in a DASD as the key for the records stored in those locations, this is usually not done. Instead, an arithmetic procedure called transform is adopted to convert the record key number into a DASD storage location number.

The transactions can be processed in any order and written at many locations through the stored file. To access a record, prior records need not be examined first. The CPU can go directly to the desired record without searching all the others in the file. In other words, this schemes permits immediate access to records for inquiring and updating purposes. Direct access is used where file activity is low.

Advantages

1. Immediate access to records for updating purposes is possible.
2. Immediate updating of several files as a result of a single transaction is possible.
3. Transactions need not be sorted.
4. Different discs or disc units are not required for updating records as existing records may be amended by overwriting.
5. Random inquiries which are too frequent in business situations can be easily handled.
6. It is also possible to process direct file records sequentially in a record key sequence.
7. A direct file organization is most suitable for interactive online applications such as airline or railway reservations systems, teller facility in banking applications, etc.

Disadvantages

1. Data may be accidentally erased or over-written unless special precautions are taken.
2. Records in the online file may be exposed to the risks of loss of accuracy and a breach of security special backup and reconstruction procedures must be established.
3. May be less efficient in the use of storage space than sequentially organized file.
4. Expensive hardware and software resources are required.
5. Relative completely of programming.

6. System design around it is complex and costly.
7. File updation (addition and deletion of records) is more difficult as compared to sequential files.
8. Special security measures are necessary for online direct files that are accessible from several stations.

14.5 STORAGE MANAGEMENT

In the earlier chapters we made use of data structures that required some form or rnemory management in order to handle requests for allocation and release of memory. When the lists and tree structures were discussed, we saw that nodes were simply created but it was out considered how these nodes will be released when they were no longer needed.

14.5.1 Dynamic Storage Management

In many cases we assumed that storage is allocated and freed one node at a time. There are two characteristics of nodes that make the above methods suitable. The first is that each node of a given type is of fixed size and the second is that the size clench node is fairly small. But in some cases a program might require a 'large amount of contiguous storage: which would be difficult to obtain uric block at a time, or a program may require storage blocks in a large variety of sizes. In such cases, memory management system must be able to process requests for variable length blocks. Thus processing certain types of data structures efficiently requires dynamic storage management capability.

Consider a small memory of 1024 bytes. Suppose a request is made for three blocks of storage of 348, 100 and 2 l2 bytes. Let us assume that these blocks arc allocated sequentially.

0 Block-1 348	Block-2 458	Block-3 670	1023
348 bytes	110 bytes	212 bytes	Free space 354 bytes

Now let us suppose that the second block of 110 bytes is set free. Although there are now 464 bytes of free space, a request of 400 bytes could not be satisfied since the free space is divided into non-contiguous blocks.

If block three is set to be free, it is not desirable to retain three free blocks of 110, 212 and 354 bytes. Rather the block can be combined into a single large block of 676 bytes so that large memory requests can be further satisfied. After combination they appear in two fragments of that of size 348 bytes and 676 bytes respectively.

14.6 GARBAGE COLLECTION

Garbage collection is a form of automatic memory management. It is a special case of resource management, in which the limited resource being managed is memory. The garbage collector, or just collector, attempts to reclaim garbage, or memory occupied by objects that are no longer in use by the program. Garbage collection was invented by John McCarthy around 1959 to solve problems in Lisp.

Garbage collection is often portrayed as the opposite of manual memory management, which requires the programmer to specify which objects to deallocate and return to the memory system. However, many systems use a combination of the two approaches, and other techniques such as stack allocation and region inference can carve off parts of the problem.

Garbage collection does not traditionally manage limited resources other than memory that typical programs use, such as network sockets, database handles, user interaction windows, and file and device descriptors. Methods used to manage such resources, particularly destructors, may suffice as well to manage memory, leaving no need for GC. Some GC systems allow such other resources to be associated with a region of memory that, when collected, causes the other resource to be reclaimed; this is called finalization. Finalization may introduce complications limiting its usability, such as intolerable latency between disuse and reclaim of especially limited resources.

14.6.1 Description

The basic principles of garbage collection are:

1. Find data objects in a program that cannot be accessed in the future
2. Reclaim the resources used by those objects

By making manual memory deallocation unnecessary (and often forbidding it), garbage collection frees the programmer from having to worry about releasing objects that are no longer needed, which can otherwise consume a significant amount of design effort. It also aids programmers in their efforts to make programs more stable, because it prevents several classes of runtime errors. For example, it prevents dangling pointer errors, where a reference to a deallocated object is used. (The pointer still points to the location in memory where the object or data was, even though the object or data has since been deleted and the memory may now be used for other purposes, creating a dangling pointer. This can, and often does, lead to storage violation errors that are extremely difficult to resolve.)

Many computer languages require garbage collection, either as part of the language specification (e.g., Java, C#, and most scripting languages) or effectively for practical implementation (e.g., formal languages like lambda calculus); these are said to be **garbage collected languages**. Other languages were designed for use with manual memory management, but have garbage collected implementations available (e.g., C, C++). Some languages, like Ada, Modula-3, and C++/CLI allow both garbage collection and manual memory management to co-exist in the same application by using separate heaps for collected and manually managed objects; others, like D, are garbage collected but allow the user to manually delete objects and also entirely disable garbage collection when speed is required. In any case, it is far easier to implement garbage collection as part of the language's compiler and runtime system, but *post hoc* GC systems exist, including ones that do not require recompilation. The garbage collector will almost always be closely integrated with the memory allocator.

14.6.2 Benefits

Garbage collection frees the programmer from manually dealing with memory allocation and deallocation. As a result, certain categories of bugs are eliminated or substantially reduced:

- **Dangling pointer bugs**, which occur when a piece of memory is freed while there are still pointers to it, and one of those pointers is then used.
- **Double free bugs**, which occur when the program attempts to free a region of memory that is already free.
- Certain kinds of **memory leaks**, in which a program fails to free memory occupied by objects that will not be used again, leading, over time, to memory exhaustion.

Researchers draw a distinction between "physical" and "logical" memory leaks. In a physical memory leak, the last pointer to a region of allocated memory is removed, but the memory is not freed. In a logical memory leak, a region of memory is still referenced by a pointer, but is never actually used. Garbage collectors generally can do nothing about logical memory leaks. Novice programmers sometimes believe that garbage collection makes memory leaks impossible, not realizing that *logical* leaks are still possible.

14.6.3 Advantages of Garbage Collection

1. Development Effort

Garbage collected applications often require significantly less development time than their counterparts with explicit memory management. It is hard to measure this, but commonly proposed estimates are that 30% or 40% of **development** time devoted to storage management for programs that manipulate **complex linked** data structures.

2. Reusability

In the case of the linked list, memory allocated to some node when we free that memory then it can be reuse by the new node. Reusability is the technique to reuse the memory to make the technique of efficient programming.

3. Functionality

In general, it is considerably easier to implement and use sophisticated data structures in the presence of a garbage collector. As a result, it is easier to avoid imposing arbitrary limits on program parameters (*e.g.* string lengths), and to ensure that performance scales reasonably for large inputs

4. Safety

Conservative garbage collectors require mild restrictions on both the source code and the compiler.

5. Space Performance

The presence of garbage collection typically allows the user to allocate fewer, and smaller, data structures.

6. Cpu-time Performance

The overall processor time used by the collector for small objects allocation and collection is comparable to a good malloc/free implementations.

14.6.4 Disadvantages

Typically, garbage collection has four main disadvantages.

1. Garbage collection is a process that consumes computing resources in deciding what memory is to be freed and when, reconstructing facts that may have been known to the programmer. The penalty for the convenience of not annotating memory usage manually in the code is overhead leading, potentially, to decreased performance.
2. The point when the garbage is actually collected can be unpredictable, resulting in delays scattered throughout a session. Unpredictable delays can be unacceptable in real-time environments such as device drivers, or in transaction processing.
3. Recursive algorithms that take advantage of automatic storage management often delay automatic release of stack objects until after the final call has completed, causing increased memory requirements.
4. Memory may leak despite the presence of a garbage collector if references to unused objects are not themselves manually disposed of.

5. Perhaps the most significant problem is that garbage collectors often exhibit poor *locality* (interacting badly with cache and virtual memory systems), occupying more address space than the program actually uses at any one time, and touching otherwise idle pages. These may combine in a phenomenon called *thrashing*, in which a program spends more time copying data between various grades of storage than performing useful work. They may make it impossible for a programmer to reason about the performance effects of design choices, making performance tuning difficult. They can lead garbage-collecting programs to interfere with other programs competing for resources.

14.7 ALGORITHM FOR GARBAGE COLLECTION

Tracing collectors are so called because they trace through the working set of memory. These garbage collectors perform collection in cycles. A cycle is started when the collector decides (or is notified) that it needs to reclaim memory, which happens most often when the system is low on memory. The original method involves a naïve **mark-and-sweep** in which the entire memory set is touched several times.

14.7.1 Naive Mark-and-sweep

In the naïve mark-and-sweep method, each object in memory has a flag (typically a single bit) reserved for garbage collection use only. This flag is always *cleared* (counter-intuitively), except during the collection cycle. The first stage of collection sweeps the entire 'root set', marking each accessible object as being 'in-use'. All objects transitively accessible from the root set are marked, as well. Finally, each object in memory is again examined; those with the in-use flag still cleared are not reachable by any program or data, and their memory is freed. (For objects which are marked in-use, the in-use flag is cleared again, preparing for the next cycle.)

This method has several disadvantages, the most notable being that the entire system must be suspended during collection; no mutation of the working set can be allowed. This will cause programs to 'freeze' periodically (and generally unpredictably), making real-time and time-critical applications impossible. In addition, the entire working memory must be examined, much of it twice, potentially causing problems in paged memory systems.

14.7.2 Tri-colour Marking

Because of these pitfalls, most modern tracing garbage collectors implement some variant of the *tri-colour marking* abstraction, but simple collectors (such as the *mark-and-sweep* collector) often do not make this abstraction explicit. Tri-colour marking works as follows:

1. Create initial white, grey, and black sets; these sets will be used to maintain progress during the cycle.
    - Initially the white set or *condemned set* is the set of objects that are candidates for having their memory recycled.
    - The black set is the set of objects that cheaply can be proven to have no references to objects in the white set; in many implementations the black set starts off empty.
    - The grey set is all the objects that are reachable from root references but the objects referenced by grey objects haven't been scanned yet. Grey objects are known to be reachable from the root, so cannot be garbage collected - grey objects will eventually end up in the black set. The grey state means we still need to check any objects that the object references.
    - The grey set is initialised to objects which are referenced directly at root level; typically all other objects are initially placed in the white set.
    - Objects can move from white to grey to black, never in the other direction.
2. Pick an object from the grey set. *Blacken* this object (move it to the black set), by *greying* all the white objects it references directly. This confirms that this object cannot be garbage collected, and also that any objects it references cannot be garbage collected.
3. Repeat the previous step until the grey set is empty.
4. When there are no more objects in the grey set, then all the objects remaining in the white set have been demonstrated not to be reachable, and the storage occupied by them can be reclaimed.

The 3 sets partition memory; every object in the system, including the root set, is in precisely one set.

The tri-colour marking algorithm preserves an important invariant:

No black object points directly to a white object.

This ensures that the white objects can be safely destroyed once the grey set is empty. (Some variations on the algorithm do not preserve the tricolour invariant but they use a modified form for which all the important properties hold.)

The tri-colour method has an important advantage: it can be performed 'on-the-fly', without halting the system for significant time periods. This is accomplished by marking objects as they are allocated and during mutation, maintaining the various sets. By monitoring the size of the sets, the system can perform garbage collection periodically, rather than as-needed. Also, the need to touch the entire working set each cycle is avoided.

14.8 MARKING PHASE

14.8.1 Determining Garbage

In the garbage collection process, a basic presupposition is that it can be determined what is garbage and what is not.

- Memory locations are not garbage (i.e., they are active) if they are parts of nodes directly accessible (through a spe-cific pointer variable) or indirectly accessible (by being ac-cessible from another non-garbage node). Memory loca-tions are also not garbage if they are scalar variables or arrays.
- All memory locations not accessible are considered "garbage".

14.8.2 Marking Algorithm

Some way of marking a cell is needed, and usually this is achieved by using one bit (of a word) as a flag. Sometimes a pointer can be negated, especially if a program is simulating dynamic storage in an array.

The marking algorithm is summarized in the following three steps:

1. Mark all scalar and array variables;
2. Mark all pointer variables;
3. For every pointer variable, traverse all nodes it leads to (us-ing a version of depth-first search), and mark each of them.

Step 3 can cause problems and requires careful program-ming, Traversing a tree or a list is most easily done recursively. But recursive code, when executed, uses an internal stack that dynamically uses memory space. Unfortunately, the marking algorithm is done as part of garbage collection, and thus is performed only when there is very little space left in memory.

Thus, marking algorithms are written so that they run with very little additional space needed for variables, if any. As a result, the algorithm can be rather slow. A common algorithm includes double traversal of linked structures, including a tem-porary reversal of links.

14.9 COLLECTION AND COMPACTION

After the marking phase, the next step of garbage collection goes through memory and collects all unmarked (i,e., unused) cells, and then links them together to be able to be used again. This can be done by a simple sweep of memory, linking all unmarked cells to each other, while ignoring all marked cells.

Especially when a program has run awhile and has allo-cated and de-allocated numerous blocks of memory, the avail-able sections of memory may be scattered throughout memory. Taken together, there may be a lot of memory available, but each individual section may be quite small. In this case, even a moderately sized array (if one needs to be allocated when a procedure is called) may not be able to be stored, since arrays need to be stored sequentially in one contiguous section of memory. This situation is called memory fragmentation. To remedy this, a process called compaction is sometimes used after the collection phase, which moves all "in use" memory locations to one contiguous section of memory, resulting in all the unused memory being together.

However, since pointers contain specific memory ad-dresses, moving information in memory cells means having to re-address all pointers. Typically this is done by determining the new address of a node and then leaving a "forwarding" address in the old location. Then, the pointers are all updated by looking at the old location (still pointed to) and copying the new address left there. The exact order of each of these compo-nents may vary from algorithm to algorithm.

Typically, the compaction phase involves three passes:

1. Scan memory, computing and assigning new addresses to nodes in use;
2. Update all pointers;
3. Relocate all active nodes.

EXAMPLE: The following example depicts 10 blocks of memory. The various configurations can be described as follows;

(a) Initial Configuration of Memory: It is unknown which blocks are not in use. It is known that block A is in use, though.

Name	Starting Location	Size	Links to:
A	100	50	E
B	150	275	H
C	425	25	G
D	450	282	F
E	732	18	C
F	750	61	—
G	811	39	I
H	850	100	D
I	950	50	—
J	1000	....	—

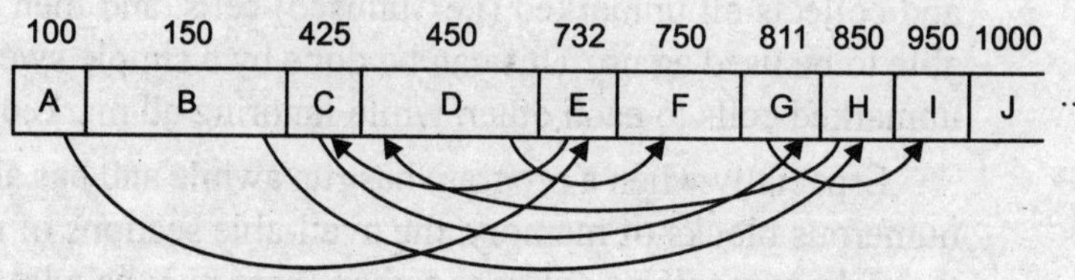

(b) After the Marking Phase: It has been determined that the shaded blocks (B, D, F, H, and J) are not in use.

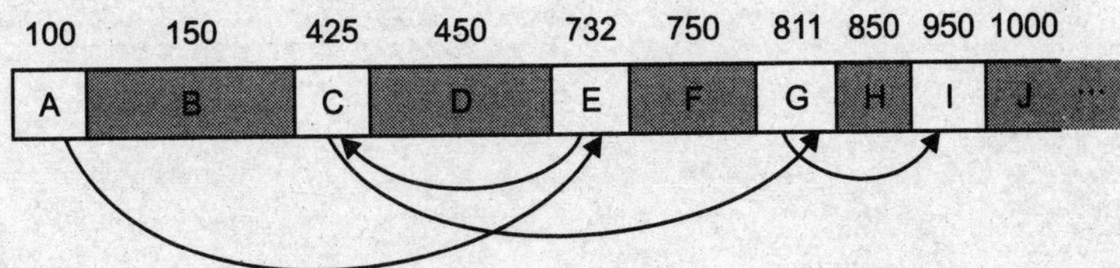

(c) After Collection and Compaction: blocks A, C, E, G, and I have been moved to *be* contiguous. However, the final links from these blocks and other internal links all have to be re-addressed.

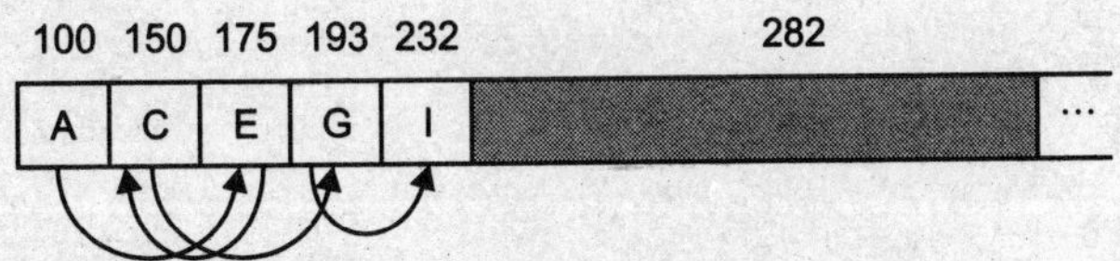

EXERCISES

1. What are files? Explain basic terminology of files.
2. Explain classification of files.
3. Explain various operations performed on files.
4. Explain various file organization techniques.
5. What do you mean by Storage management?
6. What is garbage collection? Explain various benefits of garbage collection.
7. What are the various advantages and disadvantages of garbage collection.
8. Write an algorithm for garbage collection
9. Explain concept of collection and compaction.
10. Why we can perform compaction?

Glossary

abstract data type (ADT): a data declaration packaged together with the operations that are meaningful on the data type.

adjacency list: a method of representing a graph that uses a linked list to store the vertices and a two-dimensional, linked list array to store the lines.

adjacency matrix: a method of representing a graph that uses a vector for the vertices and a matrix (square two-dimensional array) to store the lines.

adjacent vertices: two vertices in a graph that are connected by a line.

ADT: see abstract data type.

algorithm: the logical steps necessary to solve a problem; a module or a part of a module.

algorithmic: the term created by Brassard and Bartley that refers to the study of techniques used to create efficient algorithms.

ancestor: any node in the path from the current mode to the root of a tree.

arc: a directed line in a graph; contrast edge.

array: a fixed-size, sequenced collection of elements of the same data type.

AVL tree: a height-balanced binary search tree that uses a balance factor to control the balance.

backtracking: an algorithmic process, usually implemented with t attack or through recursion, that remembers the path through a data structure and can retrace the path in reverse order.

balance: a tree node attribute representing the difference in height between the node's subtrees.

balance factor: in an AVL tree, metadata used to maintain the tree's balance.

balanced binary tree: a binary tree in which the height of the subtrees differs by no more than one and the subtrees are balanced.

big-() notation: a measure of the efficiency of an algorithm in which only the dominant factor is considered.

binary search: a search algorithm in which a target is located by repeatedly dividing the list in half.

binary search tree (BST): a binary tree in which: (1) the keys of the left subtree are all less than the root key, (2) the keys of the right subtree are greater than or equal to the root key, and (3) the subtrees are binary search trees.

binary tree: a tree in which no node can have more than two children; a tree with a maximum outdegree of 2.

binary tree search: a binary tree with the following properties: (1) All items in the left subtree are less than the root. (2) All items in the right subtree are greater than or equal to the root. and (3) each subtree is itself a binary search tree.

binary tree traversal: a binary tree processing sequence that processes each node of the tree once and only once in a predetermined sequence.

breadth-first traversal: a graph traversal in which nodes adjacent to the current (siblings) node are processed before their descendents.

BST: see binary search tree.

B* tree: a B-tree in which each node is at least two-thirds full.

B+tree: a B-tree in which all data are represented at the leaf level, and each leaf node has a pointer to the next sequential leaf node in the tree.

B-tree: an m-way tree in which all nodes except the root have an minimum number of entries, and except for leaves each node entry has a nonnull subtree.

B-tree order: the maximum number of subtrees from a B-tree node.

bubble sort: a sort algorithm in which each pass through the data moves (bubbles) the lowest element to the beginning of the unsorted portion of the list.

bucket: in a hashing algorithm, a node that can accommodate multiple data occurrences.

child: a node in a tree or a graph that has a predecessor.

circularly linked list: a linked list in which the last node's link points to the first node in the list.

collision: an event that occurs when the hashing algorithm produces an address for an insertion and that address is already occupied.

complete tree: a tree with a restricted outdegree that has the maximum number of nodes for its height.

complete binary tree: a complete tree with a outdegree of 2.

connected graph: a graph is connected if, when direction is suppressed, there is a path from any vertex to any other vertex.

cycle: a graph path whose length is greater than 1 and that starts and ends at the same vertex.

data node: in a data structure, a node that contains application data or a pointer to application data; contrast header node.

data structure: an aggregation of atomic and composite data types into a set with defined relationships.

degree: the number of lines incident to a node in a graph.

deletion: in a list, any process that removes data.

depth of tree: see height.

depth first traversal: a traversal in which all of node's descendents are processed before any adjacent nodes (siblings).

dequeue: delete an element from a queue.

diagraph: a directed graph.

direct hashing: a hashing method in which the key is used without modification.

disjoint graph: a graph that is not connected.

double hashing: a hashing collision resolution method in which the collision address is hashed to determine the next address.

double linked list: a linked list structure in which each node has a pointer to both its successor and its predecessor; contrast singly linked list.

dynamic memory: memory whose use can change during the execution of the program (often referred to as heap).

edge: a line in an undirected graph.

empty list: a list that has been defined but that contains no data. Also known as a null list.

enqueue: insert an element into a queue.

exchange sort: the sort algorithm that exchanges elements that are out of order until the entire list is sorted.

expression tree: a binary tree representation of an expression.

external sort: a sort that uses primary memory for the data currently being sorted and secondary storage for any data that does not fit in primary memory.

factorial: an arithmetic function whose value is the product of the integral values from 1 to the number.

factorial efficiency: a measure of the efficiency of a module in which the run time is proportional to the number of elements factorial, as in O(n) = n!.

Fibonacci numbers: a number series discovered by Leonardo Fibonacci in which each number is the sum of the previous two numbers.

FIFO: see first in-first out.

FIFO insertion: an insertion method that places data in a list such that a subsequent traversal processes data in first in-first out sequence.

first-in-first-out (FIFO): a data structure processing sequence in which data are processed in the order that they are retrieved. A queue.

front: in a list, a reference that identifies the first element. In a queue, the next element to be removed.

general list: a list in which data can be inserted and deleted anywhere in the list.

general tree: a tree with an unlimited outdegree.

graph: a non-linear list in which each element can have zero, one, or more predecessors and zero, one, or more successors.

greatest common devisor (GCD): in mathematics, the largest integral divisor of two numbers.

hashed list: a list in which the location of the data is determined by a hashing algorithm.

hashed search: any of the methods used to locate data in a hashed list.

hashing: a key-to-address transformation in which the key, through an algorithmic transformation, directly determines the location of the data.

heap: a binary tree in which the root is the largest node in the tree and the subtrees are also heaps; See also minimum heap.

heap memory: a pool of memory that can be used to dynamically allocate space for data while the program is running; see also dynamic memory.

heap sort: a selection sort algorithm that uses a heap to determine the largest element in the unsorted area of an array.

heapify: the heap-processing algorithm that bubbles the largest element to the top of the heap.

height: a tree attribute indicating the length of the path from the root to the last level; the level of the leaf in the longest path from the root plus 1.

height-balanced tree: a balanced tree in which the balance if controlled through the height of its subtrees. An AVL tree is a height-balanced tree.

Huffman Code: a compression algorithm that assign shorter codes to characters that occur more frequently and longer codes to those that occur less frequently.

indegree: in a tree or graph, the number of lines inserting a node.

index: the address of an element within an array.

infix: a binary arithmetic notation in which the operator is placed between two operands.

infix traversal: in an expression tree, the transversal that results in the operator being placed between two operands. See inorder.

inorder: a binary tree traversal in which the root is processed after the left subtree and before the right subtree; an LNR traversal.

insert: the addition of an element in a data structure or a file.

insertion: in a list, any process that adds data.

insertion sort: a sort algorithm in which the first element from the unsorted portion of the list is inserted into its proper position relative to the data in the sorted portion of the list.

internal node: any tree node except the root and the leaves; a node in the middle of a tree.

internal sort: a sort in which all of the data are held in primary storage during the sorting process.

key: one or more fields in a data structure that are used to identify the data or otherwise control its use.

key offset: a hashed list collision resolution method in which the next address is a function of the current address and the key.

key-sequenced insertion: in a general tree, the insertion method that places the new node in key sequence among the sibling nodes.

last in-first out (LIFO): a data structure processing sequence in which data are processed in the reverse order that they are retrieved; a stack.

leaf: a graph or tree node with an outdegree of 0.

leaf subtree: in a binary tree, the subtree on the left branch from a node.

left high: in a AVL tree, a tree or subtree whose left subtree has a height greater than its right subtree.

left to left: a temporary state of an unbalance AVL tree in which a left high node has a left high subtree.

left to right: a temporary state of an unbalance AVL tree in which a right high node has a left high subtree.

level: in a tree or graph, an attribute of a node, indicating its distance from the root.

LIFO: see last in-first out.

LIFO insertion: an insertion method that places data in a list such that a subsequent traversal processes data in last in-first out sequence.

linear list: a list structure in which each element, except the last, has a unique successor.

linear loop: a loop whose execution is a function of the number of elements being processed; see also linear efficiency.

linear probe: the collision resolution algorithm that determines the next candidate address by adding or subtracting 1.

linear search: any search algorithm used to locate data in a linear list.

link: in a list structure, the field that identifies the next element in the list.

linked list: a structure in which the ordering of the elements is determined by link fields.

list: an ordered set of data contained in main memory.

list traversal: the list-processing algorithm that processes each element in a list in sequence.

LRN: left, right, node; see postorder.

m-way: the order in an m-way tree.

m-way tree: a search tree structure with multiple data entries and subtrees per node; the maximum number of subtrees is known as the order of the m-way tree.

max-heap: see heap.

merge: to combine two or more sequential files into one sequential file based on a common key and structure format.

merge phase: in an external sort, a pass through the data that combines the data from two or more files.

merge sort: any sort technique that orders data by the repetitive merging of files.

midsquare hashing: a hashing method in which the key is squared and the address is selected from the middle of the squared number.

minimum heap: a binary tree in which the root is the smallest node in the tree and the subtrees are also min-heaps; contrast heap and max-heap.

minimum spanning tree: a spanning tree in which the sum of the weights is the minimum of all possible trees contained in the graph.

module-division: a hashing method that divides the key by the array size and uses the remained for the address.

NLR: node, left, right; see preorder.

node: in a data structure, an element that contains both data structural elements used to process the list.

open addressing: a collision resolution method in which the new address is in the home area.

order: in an m-way tree, the maximum number of subtrees allowed for a node.

ordered list: a list in which the elements are arranged so that the key values are placed in ascending or descending sequence.

outdegree: the number of lines leaving a node in a tree or a graph.

overflow: the condition that results when an attempt is made to insert data into a full list.

parent: a tree or graph node with an outdegree greater than 0; that is, with successors.

path: in a tree or graph, a sequence of nodes in which each node is adjacent to the next one.

pivot: in quicksort, the key value used to arrange the data such that all of the data with keys less than the pivot are on the left of the pivot in the array, and all of the data with keys greater than or equal to the pivot are on the right of the pivot.

pointer: a constant or variable that contains the address of a location in memory.

pointer to function: a pointer that identifies the entry points to a function. It is used to pass a function's address as a parameter.

pointer to void: a generic pointer type that can store a pointer to any type.

pop: the stack delete operation.

postfix: a binary arithmetic notation in which the operator is placed after its operands.

postfix traversal: in an expression tree, the traversal that results in the operator being placed after its two operands. See postroder.

postorder: a binary tree traversal in which the left subtree is processed before the right subtree and both are processed before the root; an LRN traversal.

postroder traversal: see postorder.

prefix: a binary arithmetic notation in which the operator is placed before the operands.

preorder traversal: see preorder.

probe: in a hashing algorithm, the calculation of an address and a test for success; in a search algorithm, one iteration of the loop that includes the test for the search argument.

pseudocode: English-like statements that follow a loosely defined syntax and are used to convey the design of an algorithm or a function.

push: the stack insert operation.

quadratic efficiency: a measure of the efficiency of a module in which the run time is proportional to the number of elements squared. Quadratic efficiency is one of the polynomic factors, as in $O(n) = n^2$.

queue: a linear list in which data can be inserted only at one end, called the rear, and deleted from the other end, called the front.

queue data node: a node that contains the user data and a link field pointing to the next node.

quick sort: the exchange sort developed by C.A.R. Hoare that sorts by repetitively dividing the list into three groups: a partition of elements whose keys are less than the pivot's key, the pivot element that is placed in its ultimately correct location in the list, and a partition of elements greater than or equal to the pivot's key.

rear: in a linked list, a pointer that identifies the last element; in a queue, the most recent element inserted into the structure.

rear pointer: in a list, a pointer that points to the last entry in the list.

recursion: a repetitive process in which an algorithm calls itself.

retrieval: the location and return of an element in a list.

right high: in an AVL tree, a tree or subtree whose right subtree has a height greater than its left subtree.

right of left: a temporary state of an unbalanced AVL tree in which a left high node has a right high subtree.

right of right: a temporary state of an unbalanced AVL tree n which a right high node has a right high subtree.

right subtree: in a binary tree, the subtree on the right branch from a node.

rotation: a hashing method in which the end portion of a key is copied to the front of the key.

search: the process that examines a list to locate one or more elements containing a designated value known as a search argument.

selection sort: the sort algorithm in which the smallest value in the unsorted portion of a list is selected and placed at the end of sorted portion of the list.

selection statement: a statement that evaluates a condition and executed zero or more alternatives.

sequential file: a file structure in which data must be processed serially from the first entry in the file.

shell sort: an insertion sort that uses a list divided into partitions. Each sort pass orders the data in their respective partitions. After each pass, the partition size is reduced and the sort repeated until the list is completely sorted.

sort: the process that orders a list or a file.

sort efficiency: a measure of sort performance.

sort order: the arrangement of data in a list or a file, either ascending or descending.

stability: see sort stability.

strongly connected graph: a graph in which there is a path from every node to every other node; contrast weakly connected graph.

subtree: any connected structure below the root of the tree.

threaded tree: a tree structure in which null (leaf) pointers are replaced with pointers to their successor nodes.

top: in a stack, the next element to be removed.

traversal: an algorithmic process in which each element in a structure is processed once and only once.

tree: a non-linear list in which each node has only one predecessor.

underflow: an event that occurs when an attempt is made to delete data from a data structure and it is empty.

undirected graph: a graph in which there is no indication of direction on the lines.

vertex: a node in a graph.

vertex list: in a graph, a list of vertices.

weakly connected graph: a graph in which there is at least one node with no path to any other node; contrast strongly connected graph.

weighted graph: a graph whose lines are weighted.

Index

N

O

P

Q

R